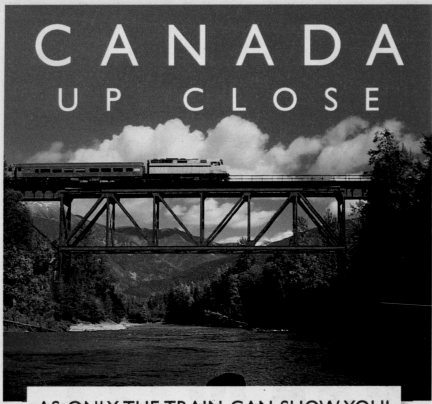

Western Canada and Alaska

Published by:
AAA Publishing
1000 AAA Drive
Heathrow, FL 32746-5063
Copyright AAA 2000

Send Written Comments to:
AAA Member Comments
1000 AAA Drive, Box 61
Heathrow, FL 32746-5063

**Advertising Rate and Circulation
Information**
Call: (407) 444-8280

Printed in the USA by Quebecor
Printing, Buffalo, NY

Western Canada and Alaska

TourBook Navigator

■ Manitoba

■ Alaska

■ Northwest Territories and Nunavut

■ Saskatchewan

■ Yukon Territory

Featured Information

4

The One That Does It All

*F*or years, people have turned to AAA/CAA for their emergency road service needs. But AAA/CAA is more than just towing. Access to AAA/CAA's travel services can give you the world. Its financial services can help you pay for it. And AAA/CAA insurance can give you the peace of mind to enjoy the ride. Plus, AAA/CAA gives you exclusive Show Your Card & Save® offers, bail bond benefits, and much more.

Discover the ways AAA/CAA can simplify your life. Call or stop by your nearest AAA/CAA office today. And make AAA/CAA the one for you.

When it comes to personal trip planning, nobody beats trained AAA/CAA travel counselors.

*O*nly AAA/CAA offers an integrated travel information system that is tailored to your individual needs.

*O*ur highly trained counselors can assist you with all facets of planning your trip, from designing the route to making reservations. In addition, only AAA/CAA travel counselors can provide our exclusive collection of travel materials selected especially for you.

TourBook® guides are comprehensive travel guides listing AAA/CAA Approved attractions, lodgings and restaurants. In addition to the coveted Diamond Ratings, you'll find descriptions of towns and cities and information on discounts available only to AAA /CAA members. TourBooks are updated annually and cover every state and province in the United States and Canada.

TripTik® routings trace your route mile-by-mile and are clearly marked with the vital information you need while on the road, such as highway exits and rest stops. These handy maps are custom-configured by your AAA/CAA travel counselor and can highlight the quickest, shortest or most scenic routes, as well as highway construction projects along the way.

Sheet maps are updated annually and cover every state and province, plus regional areas throughout North America. An extensive network of road reporters and club staff works with AAA cartographers to ensure that AAA/CAA maps are the most detailed and accurate maps available.

CampBook® guides list AAA/CAA Approved camping and RV facilities, both public and private, throughout the United States and Canada.

So the next time you're planning a trip, remember to visit your local AAA/CAA travel counselor.

Travel With Someone You Trust®

Trust the AAA TourBook for objective travel information.

Follow the pages of TourBook Navigator to thoroughly understand this unique member benefit.

Making Your Way Through the AAA Listings

Attractions, lodgings and restaurants are listed on the basis of merit alone after careful evaluation, approval and rating by one of our full-time inspectors or, in rare cases, a designated representative. Annual lodging inspections are unannounced and conducted on site by random room sample.

Those lodgings and restaurants listed with an [fyi] icon have not gone through the same inspection process as other rated properties. Individual listings will denote the reason why this icon appears. Bulleted attraction listings are not inspected but are included for member information.

An establishment's decision to advertise in the TourBooks has no bearing on its inspection, evaluation or rating. Advertising for services or products does not imply AAA endorsement.

All information in this TourBook was reviewed for accuracy before publication. However, since changes inevitably occur between annual editions, we suggest you contact establishments directly to confirm prices and schedules.

How the TourBook is
Organized

Geographic listing is used for accuracy and consistency. This means attractions, lodgings and restaurants are listed under the city in which they physically are located—or in some cases under the nearest recognized city. A comprehensive TourBook City Index located in the back of the book contains an A-to-Z list of cities. Most listings are alphabetically organized by state or province, city, and establishment name. A color is assigned to each state so that you can match the color bars at the top of the page to switch from Points of Interest to Lodgings and Restaurants.

Destination Cities and Destination Areas

The TourBook also groups information by destination city and destination area. If a city is grouped in a destination vicinity section, the city name will appear at its alphabetical location in the book, and a handy cross reference will give the exact page on which listings for that city begin. Maps are placed at the beginning of these sections to orient you to the destinations.

Destination cities, established based on government models and local expertise, are comprised of metropolitan areas plus nearby vicinity cities.

Destination areas are regions with broad tourist appeal. Several cities will comprise the area.

Points of Interest Section

Orientation maps

near the start of each Attractions section show only those places we call points of interest. Coordinates included with the city listings depict the locations of those cities on the map. Stars accent towns with "must see" attractions. And the black ovals with white numerals locate items listed in the nearby Recreation Areas chart.

Destination area maps

illustrate key travel areas defined by local travel experts. Communities shown have listings for AAA approved attractions.

National park maps

represent the area in and around the park. Some campground sites and lodges spotted on the maps do not meet AAA/CAA criteria, but are shown for members who nevertheless wish to stay close to the park area.

Walking or self-guiding tour maps

correspond to specific routes described in TourBook text.

City maps

show areas where numerous points of interest are concentrated and indicate their location in relation to major roads, parks, airports and other landmarks.

Featured Information Section

Driving distance maps

are intended to be used only for trip-distance and driving-time planning.

Lodgings & Restaurants Section

State or province orientation maps appear before the property listings in the Lodgings & Restaurants section of selected TourBooks and show the relative positions of major metropolitan areas and the vicinity towns in those areas.

Area maps denote large geographical areas in which there are many towns containing lodgings and/or restaurants. Due to these maps' small scale, lodgings and restaurants are not shown; towns with lodgings and/or restaurants are printed in magenta type.

Destination area maps illustrate key travel areas defined by local travel experts. Communities shown have listings for AAA-RATED® lodgings and/or restaurants.

Spotting maps show the location of lodgings and restaurants. Lodgings are spotted with a black-background (22 for example); restaurants are spotted with a white-background (23 for example). Spotting map indexes have been placed after the main city heading to provide the user with a convenient method to identify what an area has to offer at a glance. The index references the map page number where the property is spotted, indicates if a property is an Official Appointment and contains an advertising reference if applicable. It also lists the property's diamond rating, high season rate range and listing page number.

Downtown/city spotting maps are provided when spotted facilities are very concentrated. Starred points of interest also appear on these maps.

Vicinity spotting maps spot those properties that are outside the downtown or city area. Major roads, landmarks, airports and starred points of interest are shown on vicinity spotting maps as well. The names of suburban communities that have AAA-RATED® accommodations are shown in magenta type.

Sample Attraction Listing

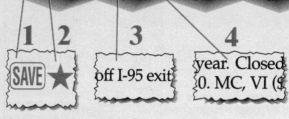

[SAVE] ★ **RED OAK** is off I-95 exit 4A, then 2 mi. e. to 610 Magnolia St. The restored 1812 house has eight 60-foot columns and is furnished in period. Allow 1 hour minimum. Daily 9-5, Apr. 1-Labor Day; Thurs.-Sun. 9-5, mid-Feb. through Mar. 31 and day after Labor Day-Nov. 30; by appointment rest of year. Closed holidays. Admission $4; over 65 and ages 6-12, $3; ages 2-5, $2; family rate $10. MC, VI ($10). Phone (601) 222-2222 or (800) 222-3333.

1   2   3   4

[SAVE] ★   off I-95 exit   year. Closed
                                     0. MC, VI ($

                                         5

gh Mar. 31 and day after Labor Day-Nov. 30;
Admission $4; over 65 and ages 6-12, $3; a

1 [SAVE] Participating attractions offer AAA/CAA cardholders or holders of a AAA MasterCard or AAA Visa Card and up to six family members at least 10% off admission for the validity period of the TourBook. Present your card at the admissions desk. A list of participating attractions appears in the Indexes section of the book. The SAVE discount may not be used in conjunction with other discounts. Attractions that already provide a reduced senior rate may not honor the SAVE discount for this age group. Discounts may not apply during special events or particular days or seasons.

2 ★ Attraction is of exceptional interest and quality.

3 Unless otherwise specified, directions are given from the center of town, using the following highway designations: I (interstate highway), US (federal highway), Hwy. (Canadian highway), SR (state route), CR (county road), FM (farm to market road), FR (forest road), MM (mile marker)

4 AE=American Express   JC=Japanese Credit Bureau
CB=Carte Blanche   MC=MasterCard
DI=Diners Club   VI=VISA
DS=Discover

Minimum amounts that may be charged appear in parentheses when applicable.

5 Admission prices are quoted without sales tax. Children under the lowest age specified are admitted free when accompanied by an adult. Days, months and age groups written with a hyphen are inclusive. Prices pertaining to attractions in the United States are quoted in U.S. dollars; Canadian province and territory attraction prices are quoted in Canadian dollars.

Bulleted Listings: Casino gambling establishments not contained within hotels are visited by club personnel to ensure safety. Recreational activities of a participatory nature (requiring physical exertion or special skills) are not inspected. Both are presented in a bulleted format for informational purposes.

Attraction Partners

These Show Your Card & Save® attraction partners provide the listed member benefits. Admission tickets that offer greater discounts may be available for purchase at the local AAA club. A maximum of six tickets is available at the discount price.

Universal Studios Escape
Universal Studios Hollywood

SAVE Save $3 on 1-day admission, $4 on 2-day admission, and $5 on 3-day admission at the gate (Universal Studios Florida and Hollywood)

SAVE Save 10% on selected souvenirs and dining

SeaWorld/Busch Gardens

Save at SeaWorld, Busch Gardens, Sesame Place, Water Country USA and Adventure Island.

SAVE Save 10% on general admission

Six Flags Adventure Parks

SAVE Save $4 on admission at the gate

SAVE Save $12 on admission at the gate each Wednesday

SAVE Save 10% on selected souvenirs and dining

Citizens or permanent residents of the United States who are 62 and older can obtain Golden Age Passports for a one-time $10 fee. Golden Access Passports are free to citizens or permanent residents of the United States (regardless of age) who are medically blind or permanently disabled. Both cover entrance fees for the holder and accompanying private party to all national parks, historic sites, monuments and battlefields within the U.S. national park system, plus half off camping and other fees. Apply in person at most federally operated areas.

The Golden Eagle Passport is available to everyone, despite country of origin. It costs $50 annually and covers entrance fees for the holder and accompanying private party to all federally operated areas. Obtain the pass in person at any national park or regional office of the U.S. park service or forest service.

Golden Passports

Sample Lodging Listing

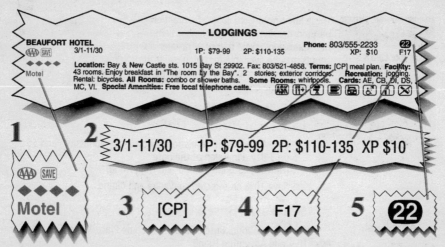

1 ⓐⓐⓐ or ⓒⓐ indicates our Official Appointment (OA) lodgings. The OA Program permits properties to display and advertise the ⓐⓐⓐ or ⓒⓐ emblem. We highlight these properties with red diamonds and classification. Some OA listings include special amenities such as free breakfast; early check-in/late check-out; free room upgrade or preferred room, such as ocean view or poolside (subject to availability); free local phone calls; and free daily newspaper. This does not imply that only these properties offer these amenities. The ⓐⓐⓐ or ⓒⓐ sign helps traveling members find accommodations that want member business.

◆◆◆ or ◆◆◆ The number of diamonds—not the color—informs you of the overall level of quality in a lodging's amenities and service. More diamond details appear on page 14.

Motel or Motel: Diamond ratings are applied in the context of lodging type, or classification. See pages 20-21 for our Lodging Classifications.

Discounts

SAVE Official Appointment properties guarantee members a minimum 10% discount off the published TourBook rates.

SAVE AAA's Show Your Card & Save® chain partners provide special values to our members: Select Choice Hotels, Days Inn, Hilton, Hyatt, and La Quinta . Individual properties in these chains appearing in the TourBook have been inspected and approved by AAA. Be sure to read How to Get the Best Room Rates on page 19.

Discounts normally offered at some lodgings may not apply during special events or holiday periods. Special rates and discounts may not apply to all room types.

S6 Establishments offer a minimum senior discount of 10% off the listed rates. This discount is available to members 60 or older.

ASK Many TourBook properties offer discounts to members even though the lodgings do not participate in a formal discount program. The ASK is another reminder to inquire about available discounts when making your reservations or at check-in.

To obtain published rates or discounts, you must identify yourself as a AAA or CAA member and request AAA rates when making reservations. The SAVE or senior discount may not be used in conjunction with other discounts. Be sure to show your card at registration and verify the room rate.

The rates listed for approved properties are provided to AAA by each lodging and represent the regular (rack) rate for a standard room. Printed rates, based on rack rates and last room availability, are rounded to the nearest dollar. Rates do not include taxes and discounts. U.S. rates are in U.S. dollars; rates for Canadian lodgings are in Canadian dollars.

2 Rate Lines

Shown from left to right: dates the rates are effective; rates for 1 person or 2 persons; extra person charge (XP); and any applicable family plan indicator.

Rates Guaranteed

AAA members are guaranteed that they will not be charged more than the maximum regular rate printed in each rate range for a standard room. Rates may vary within the range depending on season and room type. Listed rates are based on last standard room availability.

Exceptions

Lodgings may temporarily increase room rates, not recognize discounts or modify pricing policies during special events. Examples of special events range from Mardi Gras and Kentucky Derby (including pre-Derby events) to college football games, holidays, holiday periods and state fairs. Although some special events are listed in AAA TourBook guides, it is always wise to check, in advance, with AAA travel counselors for specific dates.

Discounts

Member discounts will apply to rates quoted, within the rate range, applicable at the time of booking. Special rates used in advertising, and special short-term, promotional rates lower than the lowest listed rate in the range, are not subject to additional member discounts.

3 Meal Plan Indicators

The following types of meal plans may be available in the listed room rate:

AP = American Plan of three meals daily
BP = Breakfast Plan of full hot breakfast
CP = Continental Plan of pastry, juice and another beverage
ECP = Expanded Continental Plan, which offers a wider variety of breakfast items
EP = European Plan, where rate includes only room
MAP = Modified American Plan of two meals daily

> Check-in times are shown in the listing only if they are after 3 p.m.; check-out times are shown only if they are before 10 a.m. Parking is on the premises and free unless otherwise noted.

4 Family Plan Indicators

F17 = Children 17 and under stay free (age displayed will reflect property's policy)
D17 = Discount for children 17 and under
F = Children stay free
D = Discounts for children

5 Lodging Locators

Numerals are used to locate, or "spot," lodgings on maps we provide for larger cities.

The few lodgings with **fyi** in place of diamonds are included as an "informational only" service for members. The icon indicates that a property has not been rated for one or more of the following reasons: too new to rate; under construction; under major renovation; not inspected; or may not meet all AAA requirements. Listing prose will give insight as to why the **fyi** rating was assigned.

The Lodging Diamond Ratings

AAA field inspectors evaluate and rate each lodging based on the overall quality and services offered at a property. The size, age and overall appeal of an establishment are considered as well as regional decorating and architectural differences.

While guest services are an important part of all diamond ratings, they are particularly critical at the four and five diamond levels. A property must provide a high level of service, on a consistent basis, to obtain and support the four and five diamond rating.

Properties are world-class by definition, exhibiting an exceptionally high degree of service as well as striking, luxurious facilities and many extra amenities. Guest services are executed and presented in a flawless manner. The guest is pampered by a professional, attentive staff. The properties' facilities and operation help set industry standards in hospitality and service.

Properties are excellent and display a high level of service and hospitality. They offer a wide variety of amenities and upscale facilities in the guest rooms, on the grounds and in the public areas.

Properties offer a degree of sophistication. Additional amenities, services and facilities may be offered. There is a noticeable upgrade in physical attributes, services and comfort.

Properties maintain the attributes offered at the one diamond level, while showing marked enhancements in decor and furnishings. They may be recently constructed or older properties, both targeting the needs of a budget-oriented traveler.

Properties offer good but modest accommodations. Establishments are functional, emphasizing clean and comfortable rooms. They must meet the basic needs of comfort and cleanliness.

Guest Safety

Room Security

In order to be approved for listing in AAA/CAA TourBook® guides for the United States and Canada, all lodgings must comply with AAA's guest room security requirements.

In response to AAA/CAA members' concern about their safety at properties, AAA-RATED® accommodations must have deadbolt locks on all guest room entry doors and connecting room doors.

If the area outside the guest room door is not visible from inside the room through a window or door panel, viewports must be installed on all guest room entry doors. Bed and breakfast properties and country inns are not required to have viewports. Ground floor and easily accessible sliding doors must be equipped with some other type of secondary security locks.

Field inspectors view a percentage of rooms at each property since it is not feasible to evaluate every room in every lodging establishment. Therefore, AAA cannot guarantee that there are working locks on all doors and windows in all guest rooms.

Fire Safety

Because of the highly specialized skills needed to conduct professional fire safety inspections, AAA/CAA inspectors cannot assess fire safety.

All U.S. and Canadian lodging properties must be equipped with an operational, single-station smoke detector, and all public areas must have operational smoke detectors or an automatic sprinkler system. A AAA/CAA inspector has evaluated a sampling of the rooms to verify this equipment is in place.

For additional fire safety information read the page posted on the back of your guest room door, or write:

**National Fire Protection Association
1 Batterymarch Park, P.O. Box 9101
Quincy, MA 02269-9101**

Access for Travelers with Disabilities

Qualified properties listed in this book have symbols indicating they are fully accessible, semi-accessible or meet the needs of the hearing-impaired. This two-tiered mobility standard was developed to meet members' varying degrees of accessibility needs.

(&) Fully accessible properties meet the needs of those that are significantly disabled and utilize a wheelchair or scooter. A fully accessible lodging will provide at least one guest room meeting the designated criteria. A traveler with these disabilities will be able to park and access public areas, including restrooms, check-in facilities and at least one food and beverage outlet. A fully accessible restaurant indicates that parking, dining rooms and restrooms are accessible.

(f) Semi-accessible properties meet the needs of those that are disabled but do have some mobility. Such travelers would include people using a cane or walker, or a disabled individual with good mobility but a limited arm or hand range of motion. A Semi-accessible lodging will provide at least one guest room meeting the designated criteria. A traveler with these disabilities will be able to park and access public areas, including restrooms, check-in facilities and at least one food and beverage outlet. A semi-accessible restaurant indicates that parking, dining rooms and restrooms are accessible.

(𝄞) This symbol indicates a property with the following equipment available for hearing impaired travelers: TDD at front desk or switchboard; visual notification of fire alarm, incoming telephone calls, door knock or bell; closed caption decoder available; text telephone or TDD available for guest room use; telephone amplification device available, with shelf and electric outlet next to guest room telephone.

The criteria used by AAA/CAA do not represent the full scope of the Americans With Disabilities Act of 1990 Accessibility Guidelines (ADAAG); they are, however, consistent with the ADAAG. Members can obtain from their local AAA/CAA club the AAA brochure, "AAA Accessibility Criteria for Travelers with Disabilities", which describes the specific criteria pertaining to the fully accessible, semi-accessible and hearing-impaired standards.

The Americans With Disabilities Act (ADA) prohibits businesses that serve the public from discriminating against persons with disabilities who are aided by service animals. Some businesses have mistakenly denied access to their properties to persons with disabilities who use service animals. ADA has priority over all state and local laws, as well as a business owner's standard of business, that might bar animals from the premises. Businesses must permit guests and their service animal entry, as well as allow service animals to accompany guests to all public areas of a property. A property is permitted to ask whether the animal is a service animal or a pet, or whether a guest has a disability. The property may not, however, ask questions about the nature of a disability or require proof of one.

No fees or deposits (even those normally charged for pets) may be charged for the service animal.

AAA/CAA urges members with disabilities to always phone ahead to fully understand the accommodation's offerings. Some properties do not fully comply with AAA/CAA's exacting accessibility standards but may offer some property design standards that meet the needs of some guests with disabilities.

AAA/CAA does not evaluate recreational facilities, banquet rooms or convention and meeting facilities for accessibility. Call a property directly to inquire about your needs for these areas.

What The Icons Mean

Member Values

- Ⓐ or Ⓐ Official Appointment
- SAVE Offers minimum 10% discount
- SAVE SYC&S chain partners
- ASK May offer discount
- S Offers senior discount
- fyi Informational listing only

Member Services

- ✈ Airport transportation
- 🐾 Pets allowed
- 🍴 Restaurant on premises
- 🍴→ Restaurant off premises (walking distance)
- 24hr 24-hour room service
- 🍸 Cocktail lounge

Special Features

- 🖥 Business services
- VALET Valet parking
- 👔 Laundry service
- 👶 Child care
- ♿ Fully accessible
- 🚶 Semi-accessible
- 🚿 Roll-in showers
- 👂 Hearing impaired

In-Room Amenities

- ⊠ Non-smoking rooms
- AC No air conditioning
- ☎ No telephones
- CTV No cable TV
- 🎥 Movies
- VCR VCR
- 📻 Radio
- ☕ Coffee maker
- 🍽 Microwave
- 🍴 Refrigerator
- DATA PORT Data port/modem line

Sports/Recreation

- 🏊 Outdoor pool
- 🏊 Indoor pool
- 🏊 Indoor/outdoor pool
- 💪 Fitness center
- ⊠ Recreational facilities

Please see listing prose for specific details regarding any item represented by an icon.

Additional Fees

Fees may be charged for some of the services represented by the icons listed here; please refer to the listing text and inquire when making reservations.

If a pet icon is not present, assume that the property does not accept pets; although deposits and fees are stated in the listing, check policies and restrictions when making reservations.

Preferred Lodging Partners

**Call the member-only toll-free numbers below
or your club to get these member benefits.
Have your membership card on hand when calling.**

Show Your Card & Save

GUARANTEED RATES - Lowest public rate available for dates of stay when booked in advance
via the toll-free numbers listed below.
SATISFACTION GUARANTEE - If you're not satisfied with your stay, it's free. *Member must provide
opportunity for lodging to correct any problem.*

Save 10%.   Save 10%.   Save 10%.   Save 20%.*   Save 10%.   Save 10%.
Satisfaction Guarantee. Children under 18 stay free.   *(most Clarion & Carriage House Inns)
(800) 228-1222

Guaranteed Rates. Satisfaction Guarantee. Children under 12 stay free.
(800) 432-9755

Guaranteed Rates. Satisfaction Guarantee. Children under 18 and spouse stay free.
(800) 221-4731

Guaranteed Rates. Satisfaction Guarantee. Children under 18 stay free.
Receive second entree at half price when staying in hotel.
(800) 532-1496

Hilton

Guaranteed Rates. Satisfaction Guarantee. Children under 18 stay free. Save up to 25%
(800) 916-2221

Lowest Public Rate. Satisfaction Guarantee. Children 18 and under stay free.
(800) 456-7793

Making Reservations

Give Proper Identification

When making reservations, you must identify yourself as a AAA/CAA member. Give all pertinent information about your planned stay. Request written confirmation to guarantee: type of room, rate, dates of stay, and cancellation and refund policies. Note: Age restrictions may apply.

Confirm Deposit, Refund and Cancellation Policies

Most establishments give full deposit refunds if they have been notified at least 48 hours before the normal check-in time. Listing prose will note if more than 48 hours notice is required for cancellation. However, when making reservations, confirm the property's deposit, cancellation and refund policies. Some properties may charge a cancellation or handling fee.

When this applies, "cancellation fee imposed" will appear in the listing. If you cancel too late, you have little recourse if a refund is denied.

When an establishment requires a full or partial payment in advance, and your trip is cut short, a refund may not be given.

When canceling reservations, call the lodging immediately. Make a note of the date and time you called, the cancellation number if there is one, and the name of the person who handled the cancellation. If your AAA/CAA club made your reservation, allow them to make the cancellation for you as well so you will have proof of cancellation.

Review Charges for Appropriate Rates

When you are charged more than the maximum rate listed in the TourBook, question the additional charge. If management refuses to adhere to the published rate, pay for the room and submit your receipt and membership number to AAA/CAA within 30 days. Include all pertinent information: dates of stay, rate paid, itemized paid receipts, number of persons in your party, the room number you occupied, and list any extra room equipment used. A refund of the amount paid in excess of the stated maximum will be made if our investigation indicates that unjustified charging has occurred.

Get the Room You Reserved

When you find your room is not as specified, and you have written confirmation of reservations for a certain type of accommodation, you should be given the option of choosing a different room or finding one elsewhere. Should you choose to go elsewhere and a refund is refused or resisted, submit the matter to AAA/CAA within 30 days along with complete documentation, including your reasons for refusing the room and copies of your written confirmation and any receipts or canceled checks associated with this problem.

How to Get the Best Room Rates

You'll find the best room rate if you book your reservation in advance with the help of a travel counselor or agent at your local AAA/CAA office.

If you're not yet ready to make firm vacation plans or if you prefer a more spontaneous trip, take advantage of the partnerships that preferred hotel chains have arranged with AAA. Call the toll-free numbers on the previous page that have been set up exclusively for members for the purpose of reserving with these Show Your Card & Save® chain partners.

Even if you were unable to make a reservation, be sure to show your membership card at the desk and ask if you're being offered the lowest rate available for that time. Many lodgings offer reduced rates to members.

Lodging Classifications

AAA inspectors evaluate lodgings based on classification, since all lodging types by definition do not provide the same level of service and facilities. Thus, hotels are rated in comparison to other hotels, resorts to other resorts—and so on. A lodging's classification appears beneath its diamond rating in the listing.

Hotel — *full service*
Usually high-rise establishments, offering a wide range of services and on-premise food/beverage outlets, shops, conference facilities and recreational activities.

Motel — *limited service*
Low-rise or multi-story establishment offering limited public and recreational facilities.

Country Inn — *moderate service*
Similar in definition to a bed and breakfast, but usually larger in size, with a dining facility that serves at least breakfast and dinner.

Resort — *full service*
Offers a variety of food/beverage outlets, and an extensive range of recreational and entertainment programs - geared to vacation travelers.

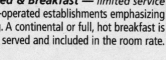

Bed & Breakfast — *limited service*
Usually smaller, owner-operated establishments emphasizing an "at home" feeling. A continental or full, hot breakfast is served and included in the room rate.

Condominium — *limited service*
Apartment-style units or homes primarily owned by individuals and available for rent. A variety of room styles and décor treatments, as well as limited housekeeping service, is typical.

Motor Inn — *moderate service*
Single or multi-story establishment offering on-premise food/ beverage service, meeting and banquet facilities and some recreational facilities.

Complex — *service varies*
A combination of two or more types of lodging classifications.

Lodge — *moderate service*
Typically two or more stories with all facilities in one building. Rustic décor is common. Usually has food/beverage service.

Apartment — *limited service*
Primarily offers temporary guest accommodations with one or more bedrooms, a living room, a full kitchen and an eating area. Studio apartments may combine the sleeping and living areas into one room.

Cottage — *limited service*
Primarily individual housing units that may offer one or more separate sleeping areas, a living room and cooking facilities.

Ranch — *moderate service*
Often offers rustic décor treatments and food/beverage facilities. Entertainment and recreational activities are geared to a Western theme.

Subclassifications

The following are subclassifications that may appear along with the classifications listed above to provide a more specific description of the lodging.

Suite
One or more bedrooms and a living room/sitting area, closed off by a full wall. Note: May not have a partition bedroom door.

Extended Stay
Properties catering to longer-term guest stays. Will have kitchens or efficiencies and may have a separate living room area, evening office closure and limited housekeeping services.

Historic
Accommodations in restored structures built prior to 1920, with décor reflecting the ambiance of yesteryear. Rooms may lack some modern amenities and may have shared bathrooms.

Classic
Renowned and landmark properties, older than 50 years, known for their unique style and ambiance.

Sample Restaurant Listing

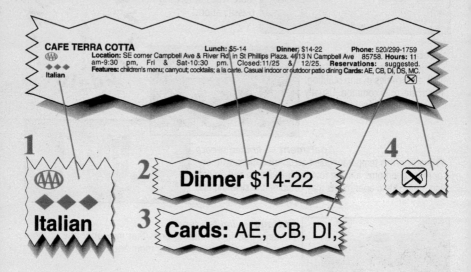

CAFE TERRA COTTA   Lunch: $5-14   Dinner: $14-22   Phone: 520/299-1759
Location: SE corner Campbell Ave & River Rd in St Phillips Plaza. 4613 N Campbell Ave 85758. **Hours:** 11 am-9:30 pm, Fri & Sat-10:30 pm. Closed:11/25 & 12/25. **Reservations:** suggested. **Features:** children's menu; carryout; cocktails; a la carte. Casual indoor or outdoor patio dining **Cards:** AE, CB, DI, DS, MC.
Italian

1 Italian

2 Dinner $14-22

3 Cards: AE, CB, DI,

4

1   ⓐ or ⓐ indicates our Official Appointment (OA) restaurants. The OA Program permits properties to display and advertise the ⓐ or ⓐ emblem. We highlight these properties with red diamonds and cuisine type. The ⓐ or ⓐ sign helps traveling members find restaurants that want member business.

◆◆◆ or ◆◆◆ The number of diamonds—not the color—informs you of the overall level of quality for food and presentation, service and ambiance. Restaurants also are classified by cuisine type.

2   The dinner price range is approximate and includes a salad or appetizer, an entrée, a vegetable and a non-alcoholic beverage for one person. Taxes and tip are not included. Some listings include additional information such as the availability of a senior citizen menu, children's menu or "early bird specials," if offered at least 5 days a week.

3
AE=American Express	JC=Japanese Credit Bureau
CB=Carte Blanche	MC=MasterCard
DI=Diners Club	VI=VISA
DS=Discover	

Minimum amounts that may be charged appear in parentheses when applicable.

4   This icon indicates that the restaurant has a designated non-smoking section or is entirely smoke-free.

fyi   The restaurants with **fyi** in place of diamonds are included as an "informational only" service for members. This designation indicates that the restaurant has not been inspected.

The Restaurant Diamond Ratings

AAA field inspectors evaluate and rate each restaurant on the overall quality of food, service, décor and ambiance—with extra emphasis given to food and service.

The ratings represent a range of member dining needs and expectations. A one diamond rating indicates simple, family or specialty meals, while a five diamond rating indicates an ultimate dining experience that is truly a memorable occasion.

A memorable occasion—the ultimate in adult dining. Food shows the highest culinary skills, evident in all areas of preparation and presentation. An extensive wine list is available. A professional staff—often in formal attire—provides flawless and pampering service. The decor has classic details, often formal, and reflects comfort and luxury.

A high degree of sophistication, thus creating an adult dining experience. Complex food is creatively presented. An extensive wine list is offered. The service staff, often formally attired, is professionally trained. The decor is distinctive, stylish and elegant; some establishments are casual while still offering refinement or formality.

An upscale or special family dining experience. Food is cooked to order and creatively prepared with quality ingredients. A wine list is available. A skilled, often uniformed staff provides service. The usually professional and inviting decor projects a trendy, upbeat, casual or formal atmosphere.

More extensive menus for family or adult dining. Food is prepared with standard ingredients. Service is attentive but may be informal, casual, limited or self-serve. The decor presents a unified theme that is comfortable but also may be trendy, casual or upbeat.

Provides a simple, family or specialty meal in clean, pleasant surroundings. Food is basic and wholesome. Service is casual, limited or self-serve. Decor is informal.

Note: Major restaurant chains are not listed due to their widespread recognition.

Savings... you'll flip over!

You'll be head over heels in savings when you Show Your Card & Save®. With discounts on everything from food to car rental to attractions to lodgings, your AAA membership delivers more value than ever before.

Make the most of your membership.
Show Your Card & Save®!

aaa.com

If You Like This Book ...
You'll Love Our Others

Special People Get Special Treatment

Want to be sure you'll be treated right on your next travel adventure?

*L*ook for establishments that advertise in the AAA/CAA TourBook® guides. These are the businesses that cater to AAA/CAA members. They value the business they receive from AAA/CAA members, and are willing to go the extra mile to get it. And in turn, they pass value on to you.

So, when you're using the TourBook to make your travel plans, be sure to look at the advertisements first.

Travel With Someone You Trust®

*A*lberta

Camping
Doesn't get better than in Alberta

Shop 'til You Drop
In a mall so large it has a hotel and a waterpark

The Old West is Alive and Well
For 10 days in the Canadian Rockies during the Calgary Stampede

Variety Unsurpassed
Placid lakes, prairies, red rock canyons, lush forests, and soaring mountains

Lake Louise
Ski it in winter, hike it in summer, admire it all year

seasons in the sun

Alberta is a happening place. In any season you're bound to find Albertans commemorating some aspect of their multifaceted province. And with the Canadian Rockies blocking eastbound Pacific moisture, odds are great that whatever the event, it will take place in sunshine.

Winter festivals in Jasper and Banff showcase snowy weather sports like skiing, sledding and ice skating against a backdrop of postcard-beautiful alpine scenery.

As spring and summer heat things up, Edmonton earns its reputation as "Canada's Festival City," with events celebrating local ethnic diversity. First Nations films, singing and dancing are highlights of The Dreamspeakers Festival, while food lovers can take a gastronomic trip

around the world as they sample from a spectrum of cuisines during Edmonton's Heritage Festival.

The bronc-buckin' Calgary Stampede all but steals the spotlight. Much more than a big-time rodeo, this Wild West exhibition turns into a huge outdoor party with parades and a carnival midway.

In autumn, the Calgary Zoo—distinguished by its painting elephant and an array of artificial dinosaurs— gets into the Halloween spirit with Boo at the Zoo, when ghosts and witches haunt the grounds.

Of course, you don't have to trick or treat or rope a steer if you travel to Alberta. Just visiting Canada's sunniest province is a special event.

Mirror images of mountain peaks reflected in calm, clear lakes. The twinkling, shimmering dance of lights known as "aurora borealis." Blankets of golden wheat and vivid canola pulled up snugly over the rolling countryside.

Typical visions of the Wild West? Hardly.

But Alberta urges you to stretch the definition of what the Canadian West is all about.

Plenty in the province fits neatly into the Western mold. Take Calgary, for instance. The former cow town's very roots are in ranching and meatpacking. Thousands of folks in denim and 10-gallon hats gather to watch the rough-and-tumble rodeo and chuckwagon races of the 10-day Calgary Stampede. Even the roof of the Saddledome, home of the National Hockey League's Calgary Flames, is in the shape of—you guessed it—a saddle.

But although Calgary is decidedly Western in many ways, it prides itself on having cultured a personality that's much more well-rounded.

A Multifaceted Identity

In 1988 the world's best athletes united in the city for the Olympic Winter Games. The renowned Calgary Zoo is home not only to such residents as the Siberian tiger and whooping crane but also to more than 10,000 plants and 20 life-size replicas of dinosaurs in a simulated Mesozoic landscape. Futuristic elevated "pedways" link nearly half of the buildings downtown.

And so it goes with the rest of the province, where such dichotomies are commonplace.

The faintly sweet aroma of 16 varieties of orchids in Cypress Hills Provincial Park lends to an air of tranquility and peace. But just a scant hop and skip to the northwest, volatile Medicine Hat harnesses an extensive reserve of natural gas that prompted Rudyard Kipling to describe the city as having "all hell for a basement."

Rafters steel themselves against the raging rapids of the Elbow, Highwood and Kananaskis rivers in Kananaskis Country. Turbulent rushes of water sweeping over rock at Athabasca and Sunwapta falls become imposing towers of irresistible ice to climbers who chink away at them in winter.

The Hudson's Bay Co. gets fur-trading rights in the territory.
1670

Anthony Henday is the first European to visit the area.
1754

Robert Rundle, the first missionary, arrives.
1840

1795
Edmonton is founded as a Hudson's Bay trading fort.

Alberta Historical Timeline

1875
Calgary is established as a North West Mounted Police fort.

Amid the chaos, however, canoeists ply the placid, emerald waters of Banff National Park's Moraine Lake and gaze upon the 10 glaciated summits that rise around it to provide a serene habitat for elk, deer and bighorn sheep.

The ground in Fort McMurray holds a significant reserve of lucrative oil sands deposits, but most people visit the town for its treasure in the sky: a spectacular view of the northern lights.

A Canadian Melting Pot

Alberta's diversity also stems from the many ethnic currents that run through it.

A strong Ukrainian heritage marks the area east of Edmonton. At a restored village near Elk Island National Park, costumed interpreters demonstrate what life was like for settlers from the late 1800s to the 1930s. The design of Vegreville's famed bronze, gold and silver pysanka, or Ukrainian Easter egg, depicts the people's faith and commemorates the protection provided to them by the Royal Canadian Mounted Police. In nearby Mundare a museum holds a collection of cultural items.

West of Edmonton, English-, French- and German-speaking emigrants from central Europe established villages. A living-history museum in Stony Plain tells their story.

The history of native cultures is evident at the well-preserved buffalo jump near Fort Macleod and in the petroglyphs and pictographs at Writing-on-Stone Provincial Park, near Milk River. A park in Lethbridge details the site of a significant battle between the Cree and Blackfoot Indians.

Traditions of the aboriginal people are remembered in Edmonton's Provincial Museum of Alberta. The territory around Elkwater's Cypress Hills Provincial Park—now home to ruminants, beavers and coyotes—nurtured a community of aborigines more than 7,000 years ago.

Prehistoric denizens of the Red Deer Valley, the dinosaurs, left their mark on the region by way of the fossils left behind in walls of sediment. Drumheller best captures the age through displays in its museums and along the Dinosaur Trail. To the southeast, a fertile fossil bed in Brooks contains the remains of 35 species of dinosaurs.

Alberta weaves a rich, vibrant tapestry of cultures, geography and a wealth of experiences. Westward ho.

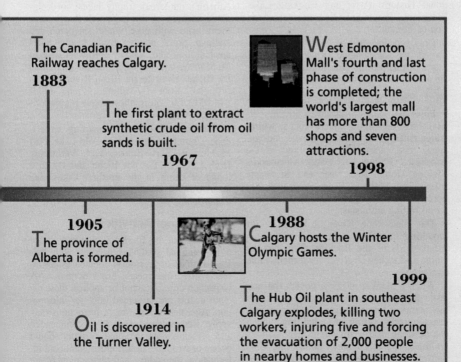

The Canadian Pacific Railway reaches Calgary.
1883

The first plant to extract synthetic crude oil from oil sands is built.
1967

West Edmonton Mall's fourth and last phase of construction is completed; the world's largest mall has more than 800 shops and seven attractions.
1998

1905
The province of Alberta is formed.

1988
Calgary hosts the Winter Olympic Games.

1914
Oil is discovered in the Turner Valley.

1999
The Hub Oil plant in southeast Calgary explodes, killing two workers, injuring five and forcing the evacuation of 2,000 people in nearby homes and businesses.

Recreation

Alberta is a nature lover's paradise. A place where unspoiled landscapes lend themselves to exploration in any season. A place where midnight summer sunsets in the north cap off long days of rest and relaxation. A place where towering mountains in the west beckon to all who appreciate unrestrained beauty.

Outdoor enthusiasts often look to Alberta's five national parks. Hikers, golfers, boaters, bicyclists, horseback riders, anglers and skiers are among the people who trek to them: Banff, Canada's first national park; Elk Island, an oasis for rare and endangered species; Jasper, a land of glaciers; Waterton Lakes, where the Rockies and prairie meet; and Wood Buffalo, which reaches north into Northwest Territories.

And although the national parks are arguably the most popular spots for recreational escape, sites throughout the grand expanse of untamed Alberta are equally as irresistible.

Experienced guides lead half-day to multiweek **trail riding** expeditions through the Elbow and Sheep valleys in the Kananaskis high country, west of Calgary; Ram Falls, southwest of Rocky Mountain House National Historic Park; and Cooking Lake-Blackfoot Provincial Recreational Area, east of Edmonton.

Only your imagination limits what you can do in the challenging Rockies. **Hiking, mountain climbing** and **mountain biking** are among the ways to get to know the peaks.

High-Octane Excitement

Pulse-pounding thrills await adventurists who take on raging rivers for a **whitewater rafting** diversion. Beginners and veterans alike appreciate the draw of the Athabasca, Elbow, Highwood, Kananaskis, Kicking Horse, Red Deer and Sunwapta rivers. The Maligne River in Jasper National Park challenges even the most seasoned rafting enthusiast.

The Blackstone River, a hot spot for **kayaking** in inflatable boats, cuts through the foothills of the Rockies. Slip into the North Saskatchewan River for a memorable **canoeing** experience.

When a blanket of snow covers the majestic Rockies, bundle up and head for the mountains. **Snowshoeing, tobogganing, cross-country skiing** and **sledding,** which can be done nearly anywhere there's snow, are mainstays of Canadian family fun.

To up the exhilaration factor, take advantage of one of North America's longest ski seasons, which can range from early November to late May in places. Some of the best **downhill skiing** and **snowboarding** the province has to offer is at Ski Marmot Basin, 19 kilometres (12 miles) south of Jasper; Lake Louise, 57 kilometres (35 miles) northwest of Banff; Sunshine Village and Banff Mount Norquay, both within 15 minutes of Banff; Fortress Mountain, in Kananaskis Country; and Nakiska, at 90 kilometres (55 miles) west the closest mountain ski area to Calgary. The boldest of the bold tackle waterfall **ice climbing** or **heli-skiing,** in which a helicopter takes skiers to untouched powder.

Leaving a Wake of Powder

Wide, open expanses of windswept grasslands, rolling hills and heavily dusted valleys make for lots of good **snowmobiling,** too. For cheek-reddening mirth, zip through the region around Grande Prairie.

One of Alberta's most popular winter adventures is a trip to Fort McMurray to catch the best view of the awe-inspiring aurora borealis, or "northern lights."

Nearly anywhere you go in the province, you'll find opportunities galore for **fishing.** Alberta's numerous trophy lakes, so designated because of the huge fish that inhabit them, brim with pike, whitefish, perch and walleye. Some notable fly-in trophy lakes are Gardiner and Namur, northwest of Fort McMurray, and Winefred, northeast of Lac La Biche. Head to the Bow River for exceptional trout fly-fishing. Phone (403) 944-0313 for information about regulations and licensing.

For an unforgettable **camping** experience, charter a plane out of Cold Lake, Fort McMurray, Fort Smith, Fort Vermilion, High Level or Lac La Biche and fly to a lodge or camp in the northern lakes. *See the AAA/CAA Western Canada and Alaska CampBook.*

Recreational Activities

Throughout the TourBook, you may notice a Recreational Activities heading with bulleted listings of recreation-oriented establishments listed underneath. Since normal AAA inspection criteria cannot be applied, these establishments are presented only for information. Age, height and weight restrictions may apply. Reservations often are recommended and sometimes are required. Visitors should phone or write the attraction for additional information; the address and phone number are provided for this purpose.

Fast Facts

POPULATION: 2,747,000.

AREA: 661,185 sq km (255,284 sq mi).

CAPITAL: Edmonton.

HIGHEST POINT: 3,747 m/12,293 ft., Mount Columbia.

LOWEST POINT: 183 m /600 ft., Salt River at border with the Northwest Territories.

TIME ZONE: Mountain. DST.

MINIMUM AGE FOR DRIVERS: 16.

MINIMUM AGE FOR GAMBLING: 18.

SEAT BELT/CHILD RESTRAINT LAWS: Seat belts required for drivers; child restraints required for under 6 or under 18 kilograms (40 lbs.).

HELMETS FOR MOTORCYCLISTS: Required for driver and passenger.

RADAR DETECTORS: Permitted.

FIREARMS LAWS: Vary by province. Contact Revenue Canada Customs, 10242 105th St., Room 800, Edmonton, AB, Canada T5J 4H8; phone (780) 495-3400.

HOLIDAYS: Jan. 1; Good Friday; Easter Monday; Victoria Day, May 24 or the closest prior Mon.; Canada Day, July 1; Heritage Day, Aug. (1st Mon.); Labour Day, Sept. (1st Mon.); Thanksgiving, Oct. (2nd Mon.); Remembrance Day, Nov. 11; Dec. 25 and 26.

TAXES: Alberta has no provincial sales tax. However, there is a 5 percent provincial rooms tax in addition to the 7 percent national GST.

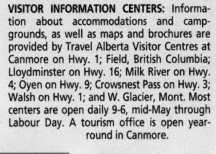

VISITOR INFORMATION CENTERS: Information about accommodations and campgrounds, as well as maps and brochures are provided by Travel Alberta Visitor Centres at Canmore on Hwy. 1; Field, British Columbia; Lloydminster on Hwy. 16; Milk River on Hwy. 4; Oyen on Hwy. 9; Crowsnest Pass on Hwy. 3; Walsh on Hwy. 1; and W. Glacier, Mont. Most centers are open daily 9-6, mid-May through Labour Day. A tourism office is open year-round in Canmore.

FURTHER INFORMATION FOR VISITORS:
Travel Alberta
10155 102nd St., 3rd Floor
Edmonton, AB, Canada
T5J 4G8
(780) 427-4321 or
(800) 661-8888

RECREATION INFORMATION:
Alberta Environment
Natural
Resources Service
Oxbridge Place
9820 106th St., 2nd Floor
Edmonton, AB, Canada
T5K 2J6
(780) 427-7009

FISHING AND HUNTING REGULATIONS:
Alberta Environmental
Protection Fish and Wildlife
Services
9920 108th St.
Edmonton, AB, Canada T5K 2M4
(780) 944-0313

ALCOHOL CONSUMPTION:
Legal age 18.

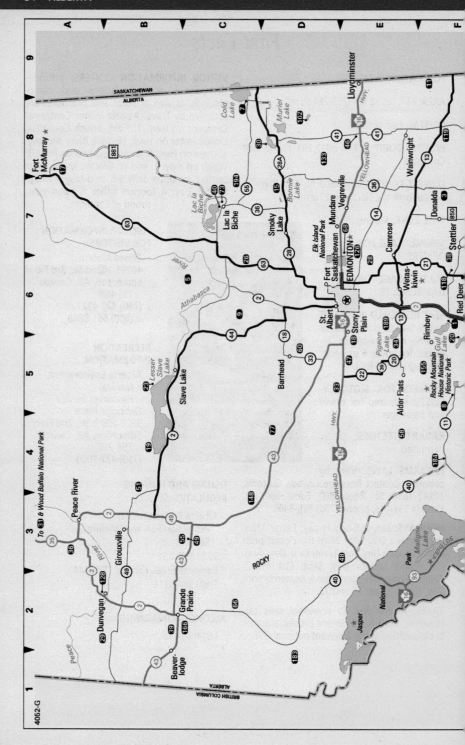

4052-G

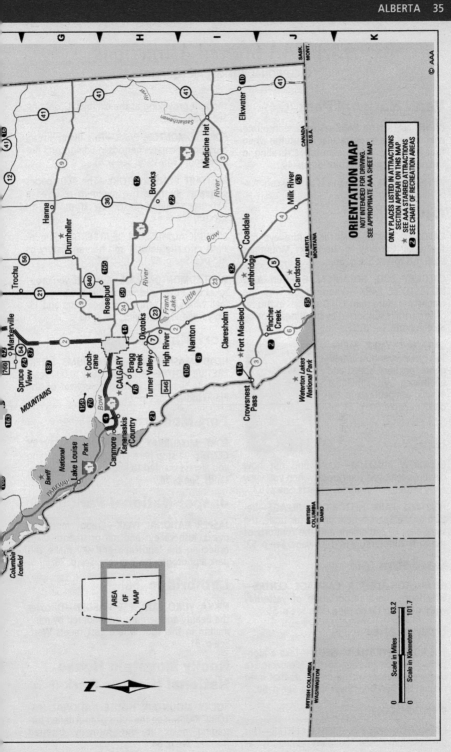

G   H   I   J   K

SASK.
MONT.

41

41

Elkwater 11

Saskatchewan River

41

106

41

12

9

Hanna

Medicine Hat 1

36

Brooks 12

22

Drumheller ★

56

Bow River

153

840

Rosebud

9

155

Trochu

21

24

59

Frank Lake

23

Coaldale

Milk River 53

4

CANADA
U.S.A.

Markerville ○

1760

23

54

87

2

14

Okotoks

23

7

Little Bow River

23

82

Lethbridge

Cardston 15 ★

ALBERTA
MONTANA

Spruce View ★

137

Cochrane ★

High River

Nanton

6

Claresholm

Fort Macleod ★ 11

Pincher Creek 2 ★

6

3

69

MOUNTAINS

153

CALGARY ★

76 ○

Bragg Creek

Turner Valley ○

546

105

11

Crowsnest Pass

3

Waterton Lakes National Park

69

Bow

Canmore ○

Kananaskis Country

22

21

11

BRITISH COLUMBIA
IDAHO

National Park

Banff ★

Lake Louise ★

PARKWAY

Columbia Icefield

106

N

BRITISH COLUMBIA
WASHINGTON

AREA OF MAP

0   Scale in Miles   63.2

0   Scale in Kilometers   101.7

AAA/CAA Starred Attractions
EXCEPTIONAL INTEREST AND QUALITY

Banff National Park (G-4)

BANFF NATIONAL PARK—This awe-inspiring wildlife refuge is spectacular in autumn when four-footed residents seem to be reveling in the riotous display of color. See p. 40.

ICEFIELDS PARKWAY—This is a really cool scenic drive. See p. 44.

Calgary (H-5)

CALGARY TOWER—"As far as the eye can see" is all the way to the Rocky Mountains atop this tower. See p. 50.

CALGARY ZOO, BOTANICAL GARDEN AND PREHISTORIC PARK—Whoop it up with the cranes and more than 1,100 animals in this facility partially supported by paintings done by an elephant. See p. 51.

CANADA OLYMPIC PARK—Test your strength, intelligence, accuracy, speed and endurance in simulated athletic competitions in the park's museum. See p. 51.

GLENBOW MUSEUM—You'll find out how cowboys removed their boots when you view early settlement everyday objects. See p. 52.

HERITAGE PARK HISTORICAL VILLAGE—Return to the Spartan days of the fur trade, the stark days of settlement and the comforts of the early 20th century at this village. See p. 52.

Cardston (J-6)

REMINGTON-ALBERTA CARRIAGE CENTRE—Experience the transportation of yesterday without being taken for a ride. See p. 58.

Drumheller (G-7)

THE ROYAL TYRRELL MUSEUM—Take a high-tech, hands-on journey to the Mesozoic Era and see skeletons of the dinosaurs that lived here in the Red Deer River Valley. See p. 60.

Edmonton (E-6)

EDMONTON SPACE & SCIENCE CENTRE—This ultra-modern 1984 building is nearly as thought provoking as the exhibits it contains. See p. 66.

FORT EDMONTON PARK—This living-history museum re-creates periods in Edmonton's history from 1846-1920. See p. 67.

MUTTART CONSERVATORY—The 700 species of plants in these five pyramids received a two-green-thumbs-up review from our inspector. See p. 67.

PROVINCIAL MUSEUM OF ALBERTA—Gain insight into the natural and human history of Alberta. See p. 67.

WEST EDMONTON MALL—"Shop 'til you drop" takes on a new meaning in this 800-plus store mall which also offers a bungee jump and 13-story free-fall experience. See p. 68.

Fort Macleod (I-6)

HEAD-SMASHED-IN BUFFALO JUMP INTERPRETIVE CENTRE—For more than 10,000 years this site was crucial to the survival of the Plains Indians. See p. 74.

Fort McMurray (A-8)

FORT McMURRAY OIL SANDS DISCOVERY CENTRE—A stop here will tell you everything you always wanted to know about mining oil sands. See p. 74.

Jasper National Park (E-2,3)

JASPER NATIONAL PARK—Craggy mountain peaks, lush valleys and mirror smooth lakes reflecting the landscape and sky make this park a photographer's dream. See p. 76.

Lethbridge (I-6)

NIKKA YUKO JAPANESE GARDEN—Discover the beauty and serenity engendered by minimalism in this spot where East meets West. See p. 81.

Rocky Mountain House National Historic Park (F-5)

ROCKY MOUNTAIN HOUSE NATIONAL HISTORIC PARK—See the ruins of four failed fur-trading posts at this formerly forested frontier. See p. 84.

Waterton Lakes National Park (J-5)

WATERTON LAKES NATIONAL PARK—The prairies meet the mountains in this popular summer vacation site. See p. 86.

Wetaskiwin (E-6)

REYNOLDS-ALBERTA MUSEUM—In the summer you can ride in a vintage automobile or airplane at this museum which presents the history of agriculture, industry and transportation in the province. See p. 87.

RECREATION AREAS

	MAP LOCATION	CAMPING	PICNICKING	HIKING TRAILS	BOATING	BOAT RAMP	BOAT RENTAL	FISHING	SWIMMING	PETS ON LEASH	BICYCLE TRAILS	WINTER SPORTS	VISITOR CENTER	LODGE/CABINS	FOOD SERVICE
NATIONAL PARKS *(See place listings)*															
Banff (G-4) 6,641 square kilometres. Horse rental.		•	•	•	•	•	•	•	•			•	•	•	•
Elk Island (D-7) 195 square kilometres.		•	•	•	•				•				•	•	•
Jasper (E-2,3) 10,878 square kilometres. Horse rental.		•	•	•	•	•	•	•	•			•	•	•	•
Waterton Lakes (J-5) 525 square kilometres. Golf; horse rental.		•	•	•	•	•	•	•	•			•	•	•	•
PROVINCIAL															
Aspen Beach (F-6) 214 hectares 17 km w. of Lacombe on Hwy. 12. *(See Red Deer p. 84.)*	❶	•	•	•	•	•		•	•	•			•		
Beauvais Lake (J-5) 769 hectares 11 km w. and 8 km s. of Pincher Creek off Hwy. 507.	❷	•	•	•	•	•		•	•	•					
Big Knife (F-7) 295 hectares 8 km w. and 13 km s. of Forestburg on Hwy. 855.	❸	•	•	•	•	•		•	•	•					
Blue Rock (I-5) 46 km w. of Turner Valley.	105	•	•	•				•		•					
Brazeau Reservoir (E-4) 46 hectares 25 km s.w. of Lodgepole along CR 620.	58	•		•	•	•		•		•					
Carson-Pegasus (D-4) 1,209 hectares 6 km w. of Whitecourt on Hwy. 43, 11 km n. on Hwy. 32, then 5 km e. on access road.	77	•	•	•	•	•	•	•	•	•			•		
Chain Lakes (I-5) 409 hectares 38 km s.w. of Nanton off Hwy. 2.	❻	•	•		•	•		•	•	•					
Chinook (I-5) 48 hectares 12 km n.w. of Coleman. Canoeing.	116	•	•					•	•	•					
Cold Lake (C-8) 5,855 hectares 3 km n.e. of Cold Lake off Hwy. 28.	❼	•	•	•	•	•		•	•	•					
Cooking Lake-Blackfoot (E-7) 9,700 hectares 24 km e. of Sherwood Park on Hwy. 16. Canoeing.	68		•	•				•		•					
Crimson Lake (F-5) 3,208 hectares 12 km w. and 8 km n. of Rocky Mountain House on Hwy. 756. Interpretive programs.	❽	•	•	•	•	•		•	•	•	•		•		•
Cross Lake (C-6) 2,075 hectares 8 km n. and 19 km n.e. of Jarvie off Hwy. 663.	❾	•	•	•	•	•		•	•	•					•
Cypress Hills (I-9) 20,450 hectares 70 km s.e. of Medicine Hat on Hwy. 41. Interpretive programs. *(See Elkwater p. 73.)*	❿	•	•	•	•	•	•	•	•	•		•	•	•	•
Dillberry Lake (F-9) 988 hectares 15 km s. of Chauvin on Hwy. 17.	⓫	•	•	•	•	•		•	•	•					
Dinosaur (H-8) 7,332 hectares 48 km n.e. of Brooks off Hwy. 1. Interpretive programs. Historic. *(See Brooks p. 45.)*	⓬	•	•	•				•		•			•		•
Dunvegan (B-2) 9 hectares 21 km s.w. of Fairview on Hwy. 2. Interpretive programs.	128	•	•												
Fish Creek (H-6) 1,189 hectares in Calgary off Bow Bottom Trail. Interpretive program. Horse rental.	⓮		•	•				•	•	•	•		•		•
Ghost Reservoir (G-5) 24 hectares 22 km w. of Cochrane on Hwy. 1A on Ghost Lake.	70	•	•		•	•		•	•	•					
Gooseberry Lake (F-8) 52 hectares 12 km n. of Consort, 2 km e. of Hwy. 41.	⓰	•	•					•	•	•					
Gregoire Lake (A-8) 696 hectares 19 km s. and 10 km e. of Fort McMurray off Hwy. 881.	⓱	•	•	•	•	•		•	•	•			•		•
Hilliard's Bay (B-4) 2,323 hectares 8 km s.e. of Grouard off Hwy. 750. Interpretive programs.	⓳	•	•	•	•	•		•	•	•			•		
Iosegun Lake (C-3) 11 km n. of Fox Creek off Hwy. 43.	148	•	•		•	•		•	•	•			•		

RECREATION AREAS

	MAP LOCATION	CAMPING	PICNICKING	HIKING TRAILS	BOATING	BOAT RAMP	BOAT RENTAL	FISHING	SWIMMING	PETS ON LEASH	BICYCLE TRAILS	WINTER SPORTS	VISITOR CENTER	LODGE/CABINS	FOOD SERVICE
Kananaskis Country *(See place listing.)*															
Bow Valley (H-5) 1,281 hectares 28 km e. of Canmore on Hwy. 1 and .5 km n. on Hwy. 1X. Interpretive programs.	4	•	•	•				•		•	•	•	•		
Bragg Creek (H-5) 128 hectares 2 km s. of Bragg Creek on Hwy. 758.	76		•	•				•		•		•			
Peter Lougheed (H-5) 50,142 hectares 50 km s. of Kananaskis off Hwy. 40. Interpretive programs.	21	•	•	•	•	•		•		•		•	•		•
Kinbrook Island (H-7) 540 hectares 13 km s. of Brooks, then 2 km w. on Hwy. 873.	22	•	•	•	•	•		•	•	•					•
Lakeland (C-8) 59,030 hectares 40 km s.e. of Lac La Biche off Hwy. 36. *(See Lac La Biche p. 80.)*	194	•	•	•	•			•	•	•		•			
Lesser Slave Lake (B-5) 7,566 hectares 32 km n. of Slave Lake off Hwy. 88. Water sports. Interpretive programs. *(See Slave Lake p. 85.)*	23	•	•	•	•	•		•	•	•			•		
Long Lake (C-6) 769 hectares 20 km s. of Boyle off Hwy. 831.	26	•	•	•	•	•	•	•	•	•		•			•
Medicine Lake (F-5) 24 hectares 37 km n.w. of Rimbey off Hwy. 22.	155	•	•		•	•		•	•	•					
Miquelon Lake (E-6) 835 hectares 3 km s. of New Sarepta then 20 km e. on Hwy. 623. Interpretive program.	28	•	•	•				•	•	•		•	•		
Moonshine Lake (B-2) 1,103 hectares 27 km w. of Spirit River on Hwy. 49, then 7 km n. on Hwy. 725.	29	•	•	•	•			•	•	•					•
North Ghost (G-5) 140 hectares 55 km n.w. of Cochrane on Forestry Trunk Rd.	159	•	•	•				•		•					
Notikewin (A-3) 9,697 hectares 37 km n. of Manning via Hwy. 35, then 30 km e. on Hwy. 692.	31	•	•	•				•		•					
Park Lake (I-6) 224 hectares 17 km n.w. of Lethbridge on Hwy. 25, then n. on Hwy. 101.	32	•	•	•	•	•	•	•	•	•			•		•
Pembina River (D-5) 167 hectares 3 km n.e. of Evansburg on Hwy. 16A.	33	•	•	•				•	•	•					
Peppers Lake (F-4) 18 hectares 84 km s.w. of Rocky Mountain House on Forestry Trunk Rd.	163	•	•	•				•	•						
Pigeon Lake (E-5) 443 hectares 5 km w. and 10 km n. of Westerose off Hwy. 771.	34	•	•	•	•	•		•	•	•			•		•
Police Outpost (J-6) 223 hectares 10 km s. and 23 km w. of Cardston on Hwy. 2.	35	•	•	•	•			•		•		•	•		
Prairie Creek (F-5) 42 hectares 41 km s.w. of Rocky Mountain House on Hwy. 752.	167	•	•	•				•		•		•			
Queen Elizabeth (A-3) 86 hectares 3 km n. and 5 km w. of Grimshaw off Hwy. 35.	36	•	•	•					•	•		•			
Ram Falls (F-4) 16 hectares 64 km s. of Nordegg on Sec. Rd. 940.	168	•	•	•				•		•		•			•
Red Lodge (G-5) 129 hectares 15 km w. of Bowden off Hwy. 587. Canoeing.	37	•	•						•	•		•			
Rochon Sands (F-6) 119 hectares 14.5 km n. of Erskine off Hwy. 835.	38	•	•		•	•		•	•	•					
Saskatoon Island (B-2) 101 hectares 19 km w. and 3 km n. of Grande Prairie off Hwy. 2. Water sports.	39	•	•	•					•	•			•		•
Sir Winston Churchill (C-7) 239 hectares 13 km n.e. of Lac La Biche off Hwy. 881. Interpretive program. *(See Lac La Biche p. 80.)*	40	•	•	•	•	•		•	•	•			•		
Sylvan Lake (F-5) 85 hectares 18 km n.w. of Red Deer on Hwy. 11. *(See Red Deer p. 83.)*	42		•					•	•	•		•			
Two Lakes (D-1) 47 hectares 114 km s.w. of Grande Prairie.	183	•	•	•	•	•		•		•					
Upper Shunda Creek (F-4) 47 hectares 3 km n.w. of Nordegg off Hwy. 11.	184	•	•					•		•		•			
Vermilion (E-8) 759 hectares 2 km n. of Vermilion via Hwy. 41.	46	•	•	•				•	•	•			•		
Wabamun Lake (E-5) 231 hectares 3 km e. and 1 km s. of Wabamun off Hwy. 16. Interpretive programs.	47	•	•	•	•	•	•	•	•	•		•			
Whitney Lakes (D-8) 1,489 hectares 24 km e. of Elk Point off Hwy. 646. Interpretive programs.	102	•	•	•	•	•		•	•	•	•	•			
William A. Switzer (E-3) 2,686 hectares 3 km w. and 19 km n. of Hinton off Hwy. 40. Interpretive programs.	48	•	•	•	•	•		•	•	•		•		•	

RECREATION AREAS

Name	MAP LOCATION	CAMPING	PICNICKING	HIKING TRAILS	BOATING	BOAT RAMP	BOAT RENTAL	FISHING	SWIMMING	PETS ON LEASH	BICYCLE TRAILS	WINTER SPORTS	VISITOR CENTER	LODGE/CABINS	FOOD SERVICE
Williamson (C-3) 17 hectares 17 km w. and 2 km n. of Valleyview on Hwy. 43. Water sports.	49	●	●		●	●		●	●	●					●
Winagami Lake (B-4) 1,211 hectares 4 km s. and 10 km e. of Kathleen of Hwy. 679.	51	●	●	●	●	●		●		●			●		
Writing-on-Stone (J-8) 1,718 hectares 32 km e. and 10 km s. of Milk River on Sec. Hwy. 501. Interpretive program. Historic. (See Milk River p. 82.)	53	●	●	●				●	●						
Young's Point (B-3) 3,072 hectares 26 km w. and 9 km n.e. of Valleyview off Hwy. 43. Water sports.	55	●	●	●	●	●		●	●	●					
OTHER															
Beaver Lake (C-7) 15 hectares 4 km e. of Lac La Biche on Hwy. 663.	73	●	●		●	●		●							
Calling Lake (C-6) 738 hectares 65 km n. of town of Athabasca on Hwy. 813.	5	●	●		●	●		●							
Content Bridge (F-6) 12 hectares 6 km. s. of Nevis off Hwy. 21.	118	●	●		●			●							
Dickson Dam (G-5) 5 km s. of Spruce View off Hwy. 54. (See Spruce View p. 85.)	24	●	●		●	●		●	●	●					
Eagle Lake Park (H-6) 8 km e. and 6 km s. of Strathmore via Hwy. 1.	59				●	●		●							
Elks Beach (D-5) 14 km s. of Barrhead, e. off Hwy. 33.	60	●	●	●	●			●	●						●
Garner Lake (D-7) 74 hectares 4 km n. of Spedden off Hwy. 28.	15	●	●	●	●	●		●	●	●					
Half Moon Lake (E-7) 4 hectares 3 km e. of Sherwood Park on Hwy. 630. Horse rental.	126	●	●		●	●		●	●	●					
Hasse Lake (E-5) 81 hectares 5 km w. and 10 km s. of Stony Plain on Hwy. 16.	18		●	●				●	●	●					
Jarvis Bay (F-5) 86 hectares 4 km n. of Sylvan Lake townsite off Hwy. 20.	20	●						●		●		●			
Moose Lake (D-8) 736 hectares 5 km n. and 10 km w. of Bonnyville off Hwy. 660.	30	●	●	●	●	●		●	●	●		●			
Musreau Lake (C-2) 80 km s. of Grande Prairie via Hwy. 40.	66	●	●					●	●	●				●	
Pioneer Park (H-6) 13 km n.e. of Standard.	165	●	●		●	●		●							
Pipestone Creek (C-2) 15 km s. of Wembley.	166	●	●	●	●			●							
Shorncliff Lake (F-8) 2 hectares 3 km w. of Czar.	119	●	●	●	●				●						
Stony (D-8) 158 hectares on Siler Lake, 16 km s.w. of Elk Point off Hwy. 646.	133	●	●			●		●							
Westward Ho Park (G-5) 8 km e. of Sundre off Hwy. 27.	187	●	●	●				●	●						
Wizard Lake (E-6) 20 km s.w. of Calmar.	189		●		●	●		●	●						
Wyndham-Carseland (H-6) 178 hectares 2 km s. of Carseland on Hwy. 24.	54	●	●	●				●				●	●		

Alberta Temperature Averages
Maximum/Minimum (Celsius)
From the records of the National Weather Service

	JAN	FEB	MAR	APR	MAY	JUN	JUL	AUG	SEP	OCT	NOV	DEC
Banff	-6 / -16	-2 / -14	3 / -10	10 / -4	15 / 1	18 / 4	23 / 6	22 / 5	16 / 5	10 / -2	1 / -8	-4 / -13
Calgary	-3 / -15	-2 / -14	3 / -9	11 / -3	17 / 3	20 / 7	25 / 10	24 / 8	18 / 4	12 / -1	3 / -8	-2 / -13
Edmonton	-8 / -18	-6 / -17	1 / -10	11 / -2	18 / 4	21 / 8	24 / 11	22 / 8	17 / 4	11 / -1	1 / -9	-7 / -16
Jasper	-6 / -16	-1 / -13	4 / -8	11 / -3	16 / 1	20 / 5	24 / 7	22 / 6	17 / 3	11 / -1	2 / -8	-4 / -13

Points of Interest

ALDER FLATS (E-5)
pop. 100, elev. 953 m/3,125'

EM-TE TOWN, 3 km (1.9 mi.) s. jct. Hwys. 13 and 22, then 10 km (6.2 mi.) w. on gravel road following signs, is a replica of a Western ghost town. Highlights include a saloon, gazebo, church, blacksmith shop, school, emporium, jail and swinging bridge. Trail rides are offered. Food is available June through September. Allow 1 hour minimum. Daily 9-6, May-Oct. Admission $5.35; over 64, $4.30; ages 6-17, $3.75. MC, VI. Phone (780) 388-2166.

★ BANFF NATIONAL PARK (G-4)

Elevations in the park range from 1,326 metres (4,350 ft.) around the Bow River to 3,625 metres (11,900 ft.) at Mount Forbes. Refer to CAA/AAA maps for additional elevation information.

The majestic beauty of Banff National Park can be approached from the southeast via the Trans-Canada Highway (Hwy. 1) west of Canmore, from the northeast via Hwy. 11 southwest of Abraham Lake, or from the north via Hwy. 93 from Jasper. These routes lead to a region where mountains and the forces of nature inspire awe and command respect.

Canada's oldest national park, Banff is 138 kilometres (86 mi.) west of Calgary. Evidence suggests that prehistoric habitation dates back 11,000 years; remnants of the more recent Assiniboine, Blackfoot, Cree, Kootenay and Stoney settlements also have been found in the park. European explorers did not arrive until the early 1800s, and when they did, they argued over the land's resources, prompting the government to establish the park in 1885.

In this 6,641-square-kilometre (2,564-sq.-mi.) section of the Canadian Rockies there are only two main centers of activity: Banff and Lake Louise. The glacial-green Bow River flows through the mountain-ringed valley that is the setting for Banff. The dry, bracing climate, alpine grandeur and mineral hot spring pools enhance Banff's attractiveness.

The town of Banff, granted autonomy from federal jurisdiction Jan. 1, 1990, is within the park. Development within the town is strictly controlled; residents do not own their land but lease it from the park.

Situated 58 kilometres (36 mi.) west of Banff at an elevation of 1,731 metres (5,680 ft.) is icy, blue-green Lake Louise. About 2 kilometres (1.2 mi.) long, .6 kilometres (.4 mi.) wide and 69 metres (225 ft.) deep, it was discovered in 1882. Lake Louise springs from Victoria Glacier, whose meltwater carries the silt and rock flour that gives the lake the opaque turquoise color common to most of the area's waters. The upper portion of the glacier is 61 to 91 metres (200 to 300 ft.) thick; the lower part ranges from 122 to 152 metres (400 to 500 ft.).

The park's well-known peaks include Rundle, Cascade, Victoria, Lefroy, Temple, Castle, Forbes, Chephren, Hector and the Ten Peaks, all ranging from 2,752 to 3,618 metres (9,030 to 11,870 ft.) above sea level. The upper slopes of the ranges are either bare and rugged or glacier crowned, while the lower slopes are forested. Many mountains are mirrored in Moraine, Peyto and other lakes.

Banff National Park is a wildlife refuge. Animals are especially visible in the fall; elk, deer and bighorn sheep are most common, while

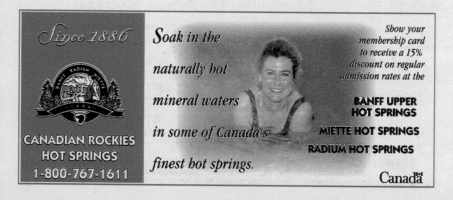

sightings of mountain goats and moose often require binoculars. Bears, wolves, coyotes, lynxes and other predators are seen occasionally. Black magpies and other members of the crow family, including the gray jay, Clark's nutcracker and the raven, dart through the trees.

Although most of the park's lakes and rivers—particularly Bow River—sustain healthy fish populations, some lakes cannot due to the "winter kill." This phenomenon occurs when a lake freezes to such a great depth that oxygen is depleted at the bottom of the lake, thereby killing all fish.

Note: Night travelers should be alert for animals on the highways. It is not only dangerous but also contrary to park regulations to feed, molest, touch or tease the animals.

General Information and Activities

The park, which is open all year, has about 354 kilometres (219 mi.) of scenic roads. Hwy. 1 to Vancouver and Hwy. 93 (Banff-Windermere Highway) are open year-round, as is the northern end of Hwy. 93 (Icefields Parkway) from Lake Louise to Jasper; check locally for road conditions. One- or multi-day bus tours of the park's major points of interest also are available.

More than 1,300 kilometres (800 mi.) of trails traverse the park. All activities involving an overnight stay in the back country require a park use permit obtainable at information centers and park warden offices in the Banff and Lake Louise townsites. The many public campgrounds in the park are available on a first-come-first-served basis; no reservations are accepted.

If such potentially risky activities as mountain climbing or hiking away from designated trails are planned, visitors should register their trips in person at a park warden office or information center. Upon return, notify the warden office or information center in person or by phone. Phone (403) 762-1550 for back-country travel information, including weather and avalanche bulletins.

Lake Louise's waters, about 6 degrees Celsius (43 degrees Fahrenheit), are too cold for swimming but are ideal for boating. Motors are not permitted; motorboats may be used only on Lake Minnewanka. Cruises on Lake Minnewanka are offered during the summer. Skating, skiing, curling and hockey are available in the park in winter.

Park naturalists conduct interpretive evening film and slide programs at major campgrounds. Bankhead, a once-booming mining town 4.8 kilometres (3 mi.) northeast of Banff, has a self-guiding trail with explanatory signs and a mining exhibit. The trail is open daily 24 hours.

Summer events include art classes at Banff Centre and Banff Festival of the Arts. Held in July and August, the festival highlights the work of professional artists from all corners of the globe. Dance, drama, opera, music and visual arts are showcased. Throughout the summer guides and outfitters offer fishing, hiking and float trips. Helicopters and saddle horses are available for trips through the mountains to glacier-fed lakes.

Information, interpretive program schedules and back-country trail tips are available at Banff Information Centre, (403) 762-1550, 224 Banff Ave., and Lake Louise Information Centre, (403) 522-3833, on Village Rd.; topographical maps and trail guides are sold at both locations. Both centers are open daily 8-8, late June-early Sept.; 9-5, rest of year.

Fishing is permitted; national park fishing permits are sold at park information, administration and warden offices as well as at some boat concessionaires and tackle shops (see Recreation in the Introduction p. 32). Check at the information centers in Banff or Lake Louise for a summary of park fishing regulations.

Hunting is strictly prohibited; visitors entering the area must have firearms dismantled. See Recreation Chart and the AAA/CAA Western Canada and Alaska CampBook.

ADMISSION to the park for one day is $5; over 64, $4; ages 6-16, $2.50. An annual pass is $70; over 64, $53. MC, VI.

PETS are allowed in the park but must be leashed, crated or physically restrained.

ADDRESS inquiries to the Superintendent, Banff National Park, Box 900, Banff, AB, Canada T0L 0C0; phone (403) 762-1550.

BANFF SULPHUR MOUNTAIN GONDOLA LIFT, 3.2 km (2 mi.) s. of Banff on Mountain Ave. (lower terminal next to the Upper Hot Springs), rises 701 metres (2,300 ft.) from the 1,585-metre (5,200-ft.) level to the 2,451-metre (8,040-ft.) peak in 8 minutes. The open-air observation deck affords spectacular views of Banff and the surrounding mountains. Food is available.

Daily 7:30 a.m.-9 p.m., June 17-Aug. 25; otherwise varies. Closed Nov. 29-Dec. 25. Fare $16; ages 5-11, $8. AE, MC, VI. Phone (403) 762-5438 for recorded information or (403) 762-2523 for additional information.

CCINC. AUTO TAPE TOURS combine the enrichment of a guided tour with the convenience of traveling at your own pace. Two tapes are offered: The first covers Banff north to the Icefields, the second from the Icefields to Jasper. Each 90-minute tour highlights park history, geology and biology with narration, music and sound effects. The tapes, which come with a map, can be bought at the Banff Information Centre or ordered from CCInc., P.O. Box 227, Allendale, NJ 07401. Cost by mail, in U.S. currency, $12.95 plus $2 shipping and handling per tape. Phone (201) 236-1666.

LAKE LOUISE SIGHTSEEING LIFT AND GONDOLA, just n. of Hwy. 1 interchange, offers an impressive aerial view of Lake Louise and the mountains of the Continental Divide. Food is available. Daily 8-6, June 1-Sept. 26. Fare $10.65; over 65 and students age 16-21 with ID $9.95; ages 6-15, $7.95. AE, MC, VI. Phone (403) 522-3555.

MINNEWANKA TOURS LTD. is on Lake Minnewanka, 8 km (5 mi.) n.e. of Banff on Hwy. 1, then n. on the Minnewanka Loop. The interpretive sightseeing cruises last 1 hour, 40 minutes. Motorboats can be rented. Cruises depart daily at 10:30, 12:30, 3 and 5 (weather permitting), mid-May through first weekend in Oct. (also at 7, mid-May through Aug. 31). Fare $26; ages 5-11, $11. MC, VI. Phone (403) 762-3473.

ROCKY MOUNTAIN RAFT TOURS offers scenic 1-hour float trips on the Bow River. Tickets are available at Brewster Transport Co., at Banff Springs Hotel and at the canoe rental dock at jct. Wolf and Bow sts.; bus transportation to the launching area departs from Banff Springs Hotel, the bus depot and the Christmas Store on Banff Ave. Canoe rentals also are available. One-hour raft trips depart daily at 9, 11, 1 and 3, mid-May through Labour Day (weather permitting). Fare $24; under 12, $12. AE, VI. Phone (403) 762-3632.

RECREATIONAL ACTIVITIES
Horseback Riding

- **Trail Riders of the Canadian Rockies**, depart from Banff. Write Box 6742, Station D, Calgary, AB T2P 2E6. Six-day trips depart Sun. July-Aug. Phone (403) 264-8656.

White-water Rafting

- **Wild Water Adventures** departs from the lobby of Chateau Lake Louise Hotel. Write

Box 25, Lake Louise, AB, Canada T0L 1E0. Departures twice daily mid-May to mid-Sept. (weather permitting). Phone (403) 522-2211 or (888) 647-6444.

Points of Interest

Natural points of interest within the park include hoodoos—mushroom-shaped pillars of glacial silt and clay—east of Banff; Vermilion Lake and Johnston Canyon to the west; Bow Falls to the south; Mount Norquay, Lake Louise, Moraine Lake and Valley of the Ten Peaks to the northwest via the Trans-Canada Highway; and Hector, Bow and Peyto lakes and Bow Summit to the northwest on the Icefields Parkway.

BANFF PARK MUSEUM, 91 Banff Ave., was established in 1895 and moved to its present building in 1903. The museum depicts the way natural history exhibits were presented and interpreted at the beginning of the 20th century. Exhibits include mounted animals and mineral specimens. Allow 30 minutes minimum. Daily 10-6, June 12-Sept. 12; 1-5, rest of year. Guided tours are given daily at 3. Closed Jan. 1 and Dec. 25-26. Admission $2.50; over 64, $2; ages 6-16, $1.50; family rate $5. Phone (403) 762-1558.

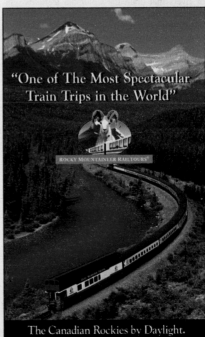

THE CASCADE ROCK GARDENS, encircling the park's administration building, are built in a series of rock terraces connected by small cascades that highlight flowers, plants and shrubs, rustic bridges, pavilions and flagged walks. Allow 30 minutes minimum. Free.

THE CAVE AND BASIN NATIONAL HISTORIC SITE, 311 Cave Ave., is a complex centered on the cave and hot springs discovered in 1883 by three Canadian Pacific Railway workers. Their mutual claim and subsequent dispute over the springs prompted government intervention in 1885, which led to the establishment of the park. Exhibits, interpretive trails and a slide show explain the history of the springs.

Allow 1 hour minimum. Daily 9-6, June 12-Sept. 12; 9:30-5, Apr. 1-June 11 and Sept. 13-Oct. 31; 11-4, rest of year. Hours may vary; phone ahead. Guided tours are given daily at 11, July-Aug. Closed Jan. 1 and Dec. 25. Admission $2.50; over 64, $2; ages 6-18, $1.50; family rate $5. Phone (403) 762-1566.

★ **ICEFIELDS PARKWAY** (Hwy. 93) was named for the obvious features of the area it traverses. Completed in 1940, it connects the towns of Lake Louise and Jasper as it crosses Banff and Jasper national parks. In the shadow of the Great Divide, the 230-kilometre (143-mi.) route offers spectacular vistas of snowcapped mountains interspersed with waterfalls, lakes and a succession of rivers that drain the Columbia Icefields' glacial meltwater into the Arctic, Pacific and Atlantic oceans.

Although the terrain is rugged, the road is well-engineered and provides a relatively easy drive without excessive grades or hairpin turns. Those who wish to pause and experience the area more intimately will not be disappointed—in addition to several campgrounds along the route, numerous turnouts at viewpoints provide opportunities to relax and enjoy more of the scenery.

Roadside signs explain the terrain, and many trails beckon the hiker. Long treks through the wilderness are available, as are shorter trails leading to such scenic spots as Sunwapta Falls and Athabasca Falls, 55 kilometres (34 mi.) and 32 kilometres (20 mi.) south from Jasper, respectively. About 76 kilometres (47 mi.) north of Lake Louise at the Saskatchewan River crossing, David Thompson Highway (Hwy. 11) meets the Icefields Parkway.

Fifty kilometres (31 mi.) farther north, just inside the entrance to Jasper National Park, is the Athabasca Glacier. A tongue of the Columbia Icefield *(see Jasper National Park p. 78)*, it comes to within 1.5 kilometres (.9 mi.) of the parkway. Just across the road, snowcoach trips onto the glacier are available May 1 to mid-October, weather permitting. Columbia Icefield Centre offers information and interpretive displays. Maps and schedules for events along the

parkway also are available. Although there is no toll for using the Icefields Parkway, drivers must pay the national park entrance fee regardless of whether they plan to stop inside the park.

Note: Drivers should be alert for slow or stopped vehicles as well as for animals on or near the highway. Snow tires and/or chains are recommended in winter; check locally for weather and road conditions. Phone (403) 762-2088 for weather information, or phone 762-1450 for road condition information.

NATURAL HISTORY MUSEUM is at 112 Banff Ave. Exhibits explain area geology, archeology and botany. Native art also is displayed. Daily 10-6, July-Sept.; 1-5, rest of year. Closed Dec. 25. Free. Phone (403) 762-4652.

UPPER HOT SPRINGS is 4 km (2.5 mi.) s. of Banff via Mountain Ave. Natural hot springs feed this bathing pool with temperatures ranging between 34 and 42 degrees Celsius (93 and 108 degrees Fahrenheit). Allow 1 hour minimum. Pool open daily 9 a.m.-11 p.m., May 16 to mid-Sept.; Sun.-Thurs. 10-10, Fri.-Sat. 10-11, rest of year. May 16 to mid-Sept. admission $7; over 64 and under 17, $6; family rate (2 adults and 2 children) $20, $2 each additional child. Admission rest of year $5; over 64 and under 17, $4; family rate $14, $2 each additional child. Swimsuit, towel and locker rentals are available. MC, VI. Phone (403) 762-1515. *See color ad p. 40.*

WALTER PHILLIPS GALLERY, in Glyde Hall at The Banff Centre at jct. Mountain Dr. and St. Julien Rd., exhibits international and Canadian contemporary art. Media include painting, sculpture, printmaking, textiles, ceramics, photography, videotape and performance art. Works by both established and emerging artists are featured. Tues.-Sun. noon-5; closed national holidays. Free. Phone (403) 762-6281.

WHYTE MUSEUM OF THE CANADIAN ROCKIES, 111 Bear St., features the works of regional and national artists as well as displays that detail the story of Banff and the national park. Heritage homes are open in the summer; phone for schedule. Allow 30 minutes minimum. Daily 10-5; closed Jan. 1 and Dec. 25. Admission $4; over 64 and students with ID $2; under 6 free. Phone (403) 762-2291.

BARRHEAD (D-5)

pop. 4,200, elev. 648 m/2,125'

BARRHEAD CENTENNIAL MUSEUM, 5629 49th St., offers displays depicting early area history. Exhibits include farm equipment, pioneer furniture, tools, woodcrafts and Indian artifacts. The museum also serves as a visitor information center. Allow 1 hour minimum. Mon.-Sat. and holidays 10-4, Sun. noon-5, May 1-Labour Day. Donations. Phone (780) 674-5203.

BEAVERLODGE (B-1) pop. 2,000

First settled in 1908, Beaverlodge derives its name from the Beaver Indians who made their temporary home, or lodge, in the area. With the arrival of the railway in 1928, a new townsite was created about 1.6 kilometres (1 mi.) northwest of the original hamlet; many original buildings were moved. In the Beaverlodge Valley, the town serves as a gateway to Monkman Pass and is a large agricultural center.

Beaverlodge & District Chamber of Commerce: P.O. Box 303, Beaverlodge, AB, Canada T0H 0C0; phone (780) 354-8785.

SOUTH PEACE CENTENNIAL MUSEUM, 3 km (1.9 mi.) n.w. on Hwy. 2, displays pioneer items, equipment and furnishings used in the early 1900s. A 1928 pioneer house is furnished in period. Other exhibits include a trading post, general store, flour mill, schoolhouse, railway caboose, Anglican church and vintage cars and trucks. Daily 10-6, early May-early Sept. Admission $2, under 12 free. Phone (780) 354-8869.

BRAGG CREEK—*see Calgary p. 56.*

BROOKS (H-7) pop. 10,100

Brooks is surrounded by 105,222 hectares (260,000 acres) of irrigated farmland and more than 404,700 hectares (1 million acres) of rangeland used for cattle grazing. An aqueduct that was operational until 1977 has been preserved as a monument to the engineers and agriculturalists who developed the region. This semiarid shortgrass section of the province is the setting for wildlife and horticultural research centers.

Brooks Chamber of Commerce Tourist Information Centre: 208 2nd Ave. W., P.O. Box 400, Brooks, AB, Canada T1R 1B4; phone (403) 362-7641.

BROOKS AND DISTRICT MUSEUM, .4 km (.2 mi.) s. of Trans-Canada Hwy., traces local history from the late 19th and early 20th centuries through exhibits about Indian culture, ranchers, homesteaders, the Royal Canadian Mounted Police, railroading and irrigation. Several restored buildings, including a log cabin and a church, are on the grounds. Allow 1 hour, 30 minutes minimum. Tues.-Fri. 10-6, Sat.-Sun. noon-5, May-Aug. Donations. Phone (403) 362-5073 or 362-6782.

DINOSAUR PROVINCIAL PARK, 48 km (30 mi.) n.e. via Hwys. 873 and 544 following signs, covers 7,332 hectares (18,116 acres) of badlands and prairie along the Red Deer River. One of the richest fossil beds in the world, the park contains the remains of 35 species of dinosaurs from 75 million years ago. The United Nations declared the park a World Heritage Site in 1979. Self-guiding trails, which explore three habitats, offer opportunities for bird-watching and other nature observation. Interpretive programs are available Victoria Day through the second Monday in October.

Camping and picnicking are permitted. Food is available. Daily 24 hours. Park admission free. Interpretive program $4.50; ages 6-15, $2.25. Reservations recommended for campsites and interpretive programs. Phone (403) 378-4344 for information and interpretive program, or (403) 378-3700, May-Aug., for camping reservations. *See Recreation Chart and the AAA/CAA Western Canada and Alaska CampBook.*

The Royal Tyrrell Museum Field Station is an interpretive center and research facility. The station contains dinosaur skeletons, interpretive displays depicting the park's geological and paleontological resources, a preparation lab and the park administration office. Daily 8:30 a.m.-9 p.m., Victoria Day-Aug. 31; daily 8:30-4:30, Sept. 1-second Mon. in Oct.; Mon.-Fri. 9-4, rest of year. Closed national winter holidays. Admission $2; over 64 and ages 7-17, $1.50. Phone (403) 378-4342.

Calgary

Calgary, once considered a cow town, now is a city of skyscrapers, light-rail transit, shopping complexes and contemporary houses. The city's economy began with—and still includes—ranching and the subsequent meatpacking industry, but the discovery of oil just south of the city in 1914 and just north in 1947 fueled a spurt of growth that turned an agricultural community into a metropolis.

Calgary today boasts a high concentration of head offices and supports such high-technology industries as software and telecommunications development.

The region's history of human habitation began almost 10,000 years before the first 19th-century fur and whiskey traders arrived. Indian tribes chose the confluence of the Bow and Elbow rivers as a campsite; emerging as the dominant tribe was the Blackfoot. Their acquisition of horses allowed them to hunt buffalo and fight almost every other prairie tribe with great success. As European settlement increased, so did the friction between the natives and the newcomers.

An 1877 treaty calmed the rough waters, and relative peace among all factions has existed since. Several reservations, including the Tsuu T'ina Reserve south of the city, are near Calgary. Native North Americans have sought to assimilate themselves into Canadian culture while retaining their native heritage.

Chinese were recruited abroad in the early 1900s to build the railroads; once the trains were running, however, Chinese immigration was restricted severely. The scent of oil and money lured many American entrepreneurs who brought the technology and investment funds needed to get Calgary's petroleum industry started. But many of those who came for the money stayed to enjoy the area and became Canadian citizens.

Calgary's modern sophistication is offset by a romantic perception of the past—a past in which the city was established as a North West Mounted Police fort in 1875. The Calgary Stampede, a 10-day Western wingding, is attended by thousands who relive the days of chuckwagons and lassos. Those days existed more than a century ago, after the North West Mounted Police—the forerunner of today's Royal Canadian Mounted Police—and the railroad brought law, order and homesteaders to a region previously settled by trappers, buffalo hunters and whiskey traders.

Although Calgary's growth has been rapid, it has been practical. The bustling downtown district was designed to accommodate a large amount of activity, even during winter when below-freezing temperatures normally would inhibit commerce. Enclosed walkways called "plus-15s" (they are 15 feet above street level) connect almost half the downtown buildings, making it

possible to eat, work, shop or visit neighbors without donning so much as a mitten.

The Stephen Avenue pedestrian mall, lined with trees, benches and fountains, in the city center is an urban refuge from traffic as well as a nice place to enjoy lunch or a stroll in warm weather.

All is not business in Calgary. Music, ballet, theater and plenty of outdoor recreation are readily available. In addition Calgary distinguished itself as host city of the 1988 Winter Olympic Games. Such educational institutions as Mount Royal College, Southern Alberta Institute of Technology and the University of Calgary prepare Canadians for the future. Natural resources and man-made technology will continue to drive Calgary in the 21st century.

Approaches
By Car

Two major highways pass through Calgary. Hwy. 2 runs north and south through the city; Trans-Canada Hwy. provides access from the east and west. Hwy. 1A, which connects Calgary and Cochrane, also serves as an alternate route between Calgary and the towns of Canmore and Banff. Hwy. 8 connects Calgary with Bragg Creek.

Getting Around
Street System

Calgary is divided into quadrants, with Centre Street separating the east and west sectors and the Bow River and Memorial Drive delineating north and south. Streets run north and south, avenues east and west. All are numbered from the intersection of Centre Street and Centre Avenue, just north of downtown. Roads in suburban areas are numbered where they form grids and named where they do not.

The speed limit is 50 kilometres per hour (30 mph) or as posted. A right turn on red after stopping is permitted unless otherwise posted; U-turns are not. Other restrictions apply during rush hours in certain areas; be aware of signs, especially in school and playground zones. Pedestrian crosswalks are designated by "X" signs, and motorists must yield to pedestrians.

Parking

Parking is not permitted on major roads between 7 and 9 a.m. and 4:30 and 6 p.m. Downtown street parking usually is limited to 2 hours at a cost of $1 per hour. Pay parking for extended periods of time is available at numerous locations; rates start at $1-$1.25 per hour or portion thereof, to a maximum of $10 per day.

What To See

THE AERO SPACE MUSEUM OF CALGARY, 4629 McCall Way N.E., contains exhibits about western

(continued on p. 50)

The Informed Traveler

City Population: 768,100

Elevation: 1,200 m/3,937 ft.

Sales Tax: The federal Goods and Services Tax is 7 percent and applies to most goods, food/beverages and services, including hotels. Alberta does not have a Provincial Sales Tax but does impose a 5 percent tax on accommodations.

WHOM TO CALL

Emergency: 911

Police (non-emergency): (403) 266-1234

Fire: (403) 287-4299

Time: (403) 263-3333

Weather: (403) 299-7878

Road Conditions: (403) 246-5853

Hospitals: Foothills Provincial General, (403) 670-1110; Peter Lougheed General Hospital, (403) 291-8555; Rockyview General Hospital, (403) 541-3000.

WHERE TO LOOK

Newspapers

Calgary's daily newspapers are the *Calgary Herald* and the *Calgary Sun*; the national newspaper is *The Globe and Mail*.

Radio and TV

Calgary radio station CBC (1010 AM) is a member of Canadian Broadcasting Corporation. The major TV channels are 2/7 (Calgary 7), 3 (CFCN), 6/9 (CB6) and 8 (A-Channel).

Visitor Information

For tourist information contact the Calgary Convention & Visitors Bureau, 237 Eighth Ave. S.E., Room 200, Calgary, AB, Canada T2G 0K8; phone (800) 661-1678. Visitor service centers are at Calgary International Airport on the arrivals level, and at the base of Calgary Tower, downtown at Centre Street and Ninth Avenue S.E.

TRANSPORTATION

Air Travel

Calgary International Airport is northeast of downtown. Cardinal Coach Lines provides transportation between the airport and downtown. Buses run between the airport and eight major hotels daily every half-hour 6:30 a.m.-11:30 p.m. Rates are $8.50 one-way, $15 round-trip; phone (403) 531-3909.

Rental Cars

Hertz—(403) 221-1300 downtown, (403) 221-1676 at the airport, (800) 263-0600 in Canada, or (800) 654-3001 out of Canada—offers discounts to AAA and CAA members. Check the telephone directory for other companies.

Rail Service

The nearest VIA Rail stations are in Jasper and Edmonton; phone (506) 857-9830 or (800) 561-8630 in western Canada.

Buses

Greyhound Lines Inc. operates from the depot at 877 16th St. S.W.; phone (403) 265-9111. Red Arrow Express operates luxury motorcoaches between Calgary, Red Deer, Edmonton and Fort McMurray; phone (403) 531-0350.

Taxis

Taxi companies include Checker Cab, (403) 299-9999; Mayfair Taxi, (403) 255-6555; Prestige Limousine, (403) 730-6666; Red Top Taxi, (403) 974-4444; and Yellow Cab, (403) 974-1111. Rates begin at $2.20, plus 20c for each additional 220 metres (over 1/5 km) or 721 ft. (about 1/2 mi.). Cabs can be hailed on the street, but phoning ahead is recommended.

Public Transport

Calgary has both bus and light-rail rapid transit ("C-train") service; the latter is free in the downtown core. Calgary Transit's office, 240 7th Ave. S.W., has schedules and maps and sells transit passes. Fares are $1.60 for adults and $1 for ages 6-14. Day passes are $5 for adults and $3 for children; phone (403) 262-1000. Handi-Bus provides transportation for the physically and mentally impaired (visitors and residents alike) within the city limits. A day's notice is requested. The fare is $1.60; phone (403) 276-8028.

Destination Calgary

*A*lthough a thriving ranching industry and the discovery of oil helped put Calgary on the map, it was the 1988 Olympic Games that turned all eyes on the former cow town.

*T*oday visitors can travel to an observation terrace in the sky, peruse museums and historic sites, and ski in the same park where the games once were held.

Calgary Tower.
The 191-metre (626-ft.) tower has an observation terrace and a revolving restaurant on top.
(See listing page 50)

Devonian Gardens, Calgary.
With waterfalls, a reflecting pool and about 15,000 subtropical plants and trees, you may never want to "leaf" here!
(See listing page 52)

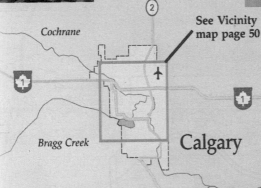
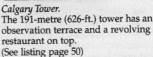

Cochrane

See Vicinity map page 50

Bragg Creek

Calgary

Okotoks

Canada Olympic Park, Calgary.
This public ski area was the site of the ski jumping and bobsledding events at the 1988 Winter Olympic Games. Visitors can try the Bobsleigh Bullet, open late October through March.
(See listing page 51)

Calgary Science Centre/Discovery Dome. Get bitten by the science bug at hands-on exhibits, but watch out for sharp teeth.
(See listing page 50)

*P*laces included in this AAA Destination City:

Canada's aviation history. Aircraft are displayed, including an F86 Sabre jet, a Bell 476 helicopter and one of Calgary's first airplanes, the West Winds. Also featured are piston and jet aircraft engines, aviation artwork and a Martin Baker ejection seat.

Allow 30 minutes minimum. Daily 10-5; closed Jan. 1 and Dec. 24-26. Admission $6; over 59 and ages 12-17, $3.50; ages 6-11, $2; family rate $15. AE, MC, VI. Phone (403) 250-3752.

CALAWAY PARK, 10 km (6 mi.) w. on Hwy. 1 at the Springbank Rd. exit, is a 28-hectare (69-acre) entertainment and amusement park. Among the 26 rides are a roller coaster, log ride, Ferris wheel and bumper boats. Live musical shows are presented daily. The Amazement Park is an outdoor science playground open in spring and summer. The landscaped grounds include waterfalls, a miniature golf course, a fishing pond and picnic areas. Small kennels for pets are available.

Allow 4 hours minimum. Daily 10-8, mid-June through Aug. 31; Fri. 5-10, Sat.-Sun. 10-8, Victoria Day to mid-June; Sat.-Sun. 11-6, Sept. 1-second Mon. in Oct. All-inclusive admission $18.50; ages 3-6, $12.50; over 50, $10. AE, MC, VI. Phone (403) 240-3822.

CALGARY SCIENCE CENTRE/DISCOVERY DOME, 11th St. and 7th Ave. S.W., presents multimedia productions and large-format 70 mm films in the Discovery Dome. Science is at the core of hands-on exhibits, demonstrations and live theater. Daily 9:30-5:30, July 1-Sept. 1; Tues.-Thurs. 10-4, Fri.-Sun. 10-5, rest of year. Closed Dec. 25. Admission $9; over 64 and ages 13-17, $7; ages 3-12, $6. MC, VI. Phone (403) 221-3700.

[SAVE] ★ **CALGARY TOWER,** in Tower Centre at 101 9th Ave. S.W. at Centre St. S., rises 191 metres (626 ft.) above the city. An observation terrace and revolving restaurant provide a panorama of the city and the nearby Rocky Mountains. The reception lobby offers a display from the World Federation of Great Towers, photographs and historical perspectives of the Calgary skyline.

A torch atop the tower burned nonstop during the 1988 Olympic Games; it is illuminated on special occasions. Daily 8 a.m.-10 p.m. Admission $6.15; ages 13-18, $4.30; over 64, $4; ages 3-12, $2.95. AE, DI, MC, VI. Phone (403) 266-7171. *See color ad p. 51.*

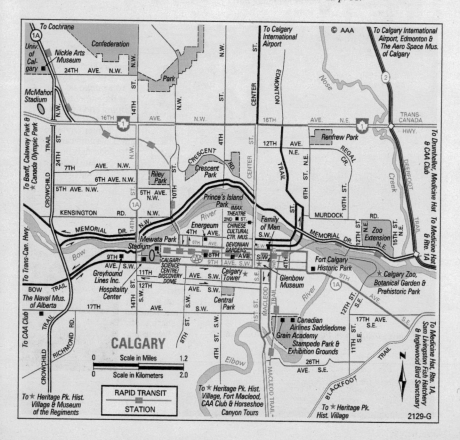

CALGARY ZOO, BOTANICAL GARDEN AND PREHISTORIC PARK, 1300 Zoo Rd. S.E. at Memorial Dr. and 12th St. E., is dedicated to conservation, education, recreation and scientific study. Such rare and endangered species as the Siberian tiger and the whooping crane are among the more than 1,100 animals in the zoo. Varied habitats simulate such ecosystems as the boreal forest. An Asian elephant is noteworthy for her ability to paint; profits from the sale of her works benefit the environmental enrichment fund.

A tropical aviary and conservatory contains more than 10,000 plants. The prehistoric park contains more than 20 life-size replicas of dinosaurs in 2.6 hectares (6.5 acres) of re-created Mesozoic landscape. Zoo events include Bloom-Fest in late May and Wildlights, a holiday light display from late November to early January.

Allow 3 hours minimum. Open daily at 9; closing time varies depending on the season. Admission (May-Sept.) $10; over 64, $5 Tues.-Thurs.; ages 2-17, $5. Admission (rest of year) $8; over 64, $4 Tues.-Thurs.; ages 2-17, $4. AE, MC, VI. Phone (403) 232-9300. *See color ad.*

CANADA OLYMPIC PARK, off Trans-Canada Hwy. at the Bowfort Rd. exit, was the host area for ski jumping, free-style skiing, bobsled and luge events at the 1988 Winter Olympic Games. The area now serves as a seasonal public ski area and a year-round training and visitor center. Bus tours stop at the bobsleigh run and the 90-metre (295 ft.) ski jump. Visitors can test the bobsleigh/luge track via Bobsleigh Bullet, which runs late October through March. Also on the premises is a mountain-bike park with a dual-slalom course and an 18-hole miniature golf course. Food is available.

Allow 2 hours minimum. Mon.-Fri. 9-9, Sat.-Sun. and holidays 9-5, mid-May to mid-Nov.; Mon.-Fri. 9 a.m.-10 p.m., Sat.-Sun. and holidays 9-5, mid-Nov. to mid-Mar.; daily 9-5, rest of year. Self-guiding tour $7; family rate (two adults and their children) $24. Guided tour $10; family rate $35. Both tours include free access to the 90-metre ski-jump tower, the bobsleigh start house and the Olympic Hall of Fame and Museum, as well as the chairlift ride (in the summer and weather permitting). Bobsleigh Bullet $45. AE, CB, MC, VI. Phone (403) 247-5452. *See color ad p. 52.*

Olympic Hall of Fame and Museum, a tribute to the achievements of Canada's Winter Olympians, presents the highlights of the Winter Olympic Games since 1924. An Olympic timeline, photographs, medals, relics and interactive videotapes present the highlights and prominent athletes of past games. A bobsled simulator re-creates the twists and curves of a mile-long track. A ski jump simulator re-creates the tower.

The Olympic Challenge Gallery has five interactive exhibits that test a would-be athlete's

strength, intelligence, accuracy, speed and endurance. Admission included in Canada Olympic Park admission. Phone (403) 247-5452. *See color ad.*

CHINESE CULTURAL CENTRE MUSEUM, 197 1st St. S.W., has exhibits representing Chinese culture and history. Permanently displayed is a replica of the army of terra-cotta soldiers found during a 1974 excavation at Mount Li. The clay archers, bowmen, cavalry, chariots and saddled cavalry horses were found in battle-ready formation guarding the Tomb of Qin Shihuang; each figure is unique. Daily 11-5. Admission $2; over 64, students with ID and ages 6-12, $1. Phone (403) 262-5071.

DEVONIAN GARDENS is at 8th Ave. between 2nd and 3rd sts. W. These 1-hectare (2.5-acre) glassed-in gardens contain 15,700 subtropical trees and plants as well as waterfalls and an ice-skating rink/reflecting pool. Monthly exhibits display works by local artists. A 200-seat amphitheater hosts occasional shows at noon. Daily 9-9. Free. Phone (403) 268-5207.

ENERGEUM, in the Energy Resources Building at 640 5th Ave. S.W., features interactive and informative displays exploring the history of Alberta's energy resources. Highlights include computer games, videotapes, working models, a restored Limited Edition Buick and memorabilia

from Alberta's oil boom from the 1950s to the '70s. A wildcat drilling game and a fiber-optics map detail Alberta's energy resources. Allow 1 hour minimum. Mon.-Sat. and holidays 10:30-4:30, May-Aug.; Mon.-Fri. 10:30-4:30, rest of year. Free. Phone (403) 297-4293.

FAMILY OF MAN, outside the Calgary Board of Education Building at 515 Macleod Tr. S.E., is a grouping of sculpted metal figures 6.5 metres (21 ft.) tall. Originally commissioned as part of Great Britain's exhibit for Expo 67, the statues were created by Mario Armengol. Nude and lacking a discernible race, the figures extend their arms and hands in gestures of goodwill and friendship. Daily 24 hours. Free.

FORT CALGARY HISTORIC PARK, 750 9th Ave. S.E., uses interactive interpretation, exhibits and hands-on discovery areas to tell the story of the site, the settlement and the people of Calgary. Visitors can watch the "building" of the fort in 1875, send a telegram from an 1888 railway station or experience a 1920s picnic. Exhibits include a carpentry and blacksmith shop and a turn-of-the-20th-century boarding house. Food is available.

Daily 9-5, May 1-second Mon. in Oct. Admission $6.50; over 64, $5.50; ages 7-17, $3.50. AE, MC, VI. Phone (403) 290-1875.

★ **GLENBOW MUSEUM,** 130 9th Ave. S.E. across from the Calgary Tower, is a museum, art gallery, library and archives. Colorful displays trace the history of the settlement of western Canada. From a Blackfoot tepee and the elegant quillwork of the Plains Cree, to the hard-won comforts of a settler's cabin, the museum celebrates pioneer heritage. Interactive exhibits about warriors, gemstones and West Africa are available. The art galleries showcase historical, modern and contemporary art from extensive collections. Food is available.

Allow 2 hours minimum. Daily 9-5 Also Thurs.-Fri. 9-9); closed Jan. 1 and Dec. 25-26. Admission $8; over 65 and students with ID $6; ages 7-12, $4. AE, MC, VI. Phone (403) 268-4100.

GRAIN ACADEMY, at Stampede Park off 4th St. S.E. on the second floor of Round Up Centre, traces the process of bringing grain from the field to the table. Highlights include a miniature grain elevator and a working model train which depicts the transportation of grain from the prairie to the Pacific coast. A movie theater and displays describing the history of grain also are featured. Allow 1 hour minimum. Mon.-Fri. 10-4, Sat. noon-4, Apr.-Sept.; Mon.-Fri. 10-4, rest of year. Closed holidays and holiday weekends. Free. Parking $5. Phone (403) 263-4594.

[SAVE] ★ **HERITAGE PARK HISTORICAL VILLAGE,** 2.5 km (1.5 mi.) w. off Hwy. 2, then s. to 1900 Heritage Dr. S.W., is a re-created pre-1914 village on a 25-hectare (60-acre) site. The village reflects the fur trade of the 1860s, the pre-railway settlements of the 1880s and businesses and residences of 1900-14.

Among the park's more than 150 exhibits are a general store, an antique midway, pioneer farm machinery, a smithy and a Hudson's Bay Co. trading post. Most of the buildings are originals that have been moved to the park. An antique steam train circles the park, and a 200-passenger stern-wheeler boat cruises Glenmore Reservoir.

Daily 9-5, May 13-Sept. 3; Sat.-Sun. 9-5, Sept. 4 to mid-Oct. Admission with rides $18; ages 3-17, $14. Village only $11; ages 3-17, $7. MC, VI. Phone 259-1900 to verify prices. *See color ad.*

HORSESHOE CANYON TOURS, 17 mi. s. on Hwy. 9, has a visitor information center with exhibits about the geology and history of Horseshoe Canyon. Self-guiding audiotape tours into the canyon in all-terrain vehicles are available; vehicles hold six to eight passengers. Daily 9:30-5, May 21-Sept. 5. Visitor center free. Tour fare $20 plus $1 per person for 20 minutes, $25 plus $1 per person for 30 minutes. MC, VI. Phone (403) 823-2200.

IMAX® THEATRE AT EAU CLAIRE MARKET, jct. 2nd Ave. and 2nd. St. S.W., presents movies on a screen more than five and a half stories tall. Allow 1 hour minimum. Films shown daily at noon, 1, 2, 3, 7 and 9 (also Sat. at 4); closed after 5 Dec. 24 and all day Dec. 25. Phone for current features. Single show $8.50; over 60, $7.50; under 12, $6.50. Double feature $12; over 60, $11; under 12, $10. AE, MC, VI. Phone (403) 974-4629.

INGLEWOOD BIRD SANCTUARY, 2425 9th Ave. S.E., is on the Bow River. Self-guiding trails wind throughout the forest where some 250 species of birds and various mammals have been sighted. Natural history programs and guided nature walks also are offered. Allow 1 hour minimum. Sanctuary trails open dawn-dusk. Visitor

center open daily 10-5, May-Sept; Tues.-Sun. 10-4, rest of year. Closed Nov. 11 and Dec. 24-26. Free. Phone (403) 269-6688.

MUSEUM OF THE REGIMENTS is at 4520 Crowchild Tr. S.W., off Flanders Ave. exit. This museum depicts the history of Southern Alberta and the Calgary Regiments: Lord Strathcona's Horse (Royal Canadians), Princess Patricia's Canadian Light Infantry, The King's Own Calgary Regiment and The Calgary Highlanders. Changing exhibits include uniforms, weapons, medals, high-tech battle dioramas, photographs and videotape presentations. Allow 1 hour minimum. Thurs.-Tues. 10-4; closed Jan. 1 and Dec. 24-25. Donations. Phone (403) 974-2853 or 974-2869 for guided tours.

THE NAVAL MUSEUM OF ALBERTA, 1820 24th St. S.W., presents the history of the Royal Canadian Navy and the Royal Canadian Naval Reserve, which existed 1910-68, together with Canada's the Merchant Marine. The display commemorates the men and women of Canada who served in World Wars I and II and the Korean War. Housed in the building are the only three fighter aircraft flown by the Canadian Navy as well as exhibits and photographs documenting the history and heritage of the service.

Guided tours can be arranged during or after regular museum hours. Allow 30 minutes minimum. Daily 10-4, July-Aug.; Thurs.-Fri. 1-5, Sat.-Sun. and holidays 10-6, rest of year. Closed Jan. 1 and Dec. 25. Admission $5; over 64 and students with ID $3; under 12, $2; family of five or more $12. Phone (403) 242-0002.

THE NICKLE ARTS MUSEUM is on the University of Calgary campus at 434 Collegiate Blvd. N.W. Three galleries present changing exhibits of contemporary and historical arts and numismatic

collections. Lectures, gallery talks and other events are offered throughout the year. Allow 1 hour minimum. Tues.-Fri. 10-5, Sat. 1-5; closed holidays. Admission $2; over 59 and ages 13-18, $1; college students with ID and under 13, free; free to all Tues. Phone (403) 220-7234.

SAM LIVINGSTON FISH HATCHERY, 1440-17A St. S.E. in Pearce Estate City Park, houses exhibits about fisheries management and fish culture programs in Alberta. Aquariums of trout and a film are featured. Allow 30 minutes minimum. Mon.-Fri. 10-4, Sat.-Sun. and holidays 1-5, Apr.-Sept.; Mon.-Fri. 10-4, rest of year. Donations. Phone (403) 297-6561.

CASINOS

- **Cash Casino Place**, 4040 Blackfoot Tr. S.E. Daily 10 a.m.-3 a.m.; closed Dec. 25. Phone (403) 287-1635.

- **Casino Calgary**, 1420 Meridian Rd. N.E. Daily 10 a.m.-3 a.m. Phone (403) 248-9467.

- **Frank Sisson's Silver Dollar Casino**, 1010 42nd Ave. S.E. Slots Mon.-Sat. 10 a.m.-3 a.m., Sun. 11 a.m.-3 a.m.; game tables Mon.-Thurs. noon-1 a.m., Fri.-Sat. noon-2 a.m. Closed Dec. 25. Phone (403) 287-1183.

- **Stampede Casino**, 1801 Big Four Tr. S.E. Daily 10 a.m.-3 a.m.; Closed Dec. 25. Phone (403) 261-0422.

What To Do

Sightseeing

Bus, Train and Van Tours

Brewster Transportation and Tours *(see color ad p. 42)* offers a 4-hour bus tour of Calgary's attractions as well as trips to Banff, Lake Louise, Jasper and the Columbia Icefield; phone (403) 221-8242 for schedules and fares. Van tours of both the Calgary and Banff/Lake Louise areas are offered by White Stetson Tours Ltd.; phone (403) 274-2281.

Exclusive Mountain Tours specializes in tours of Drumheller, the Rockies and Calgary; phone (403) 282-3980.

Rocky Mountaineer Railtours *(see color ad p. 43)* offers scenic, 2-day rail tours between western Alberta and Vancouver, British Columbia, May through October. Trains depart from Jasper and Calgary and travel west over the Canadian Rockies. The one-way trip is made during daylight hours with an overnight stay in Kamloops, British Columbia. Longer trips are available. On-board meals, hotel, transfers and narration are included; phone (604) 606-7200, 606-7245 or (800) 665-7245.

Walking Tours

The City of Calgary Planning Department, 800 Macleod Tr. S.E., 4th Floor, offers free pamphlets about a self-guiding tour of Stephen Avenue Mall. This pedestrian mall, which extends from Macleod Trail west along 8th Avenue to 3rd Street S.W., is a showcase for historic buildings, many of which are restored. Other walking-tour and historical pamphlets also are available.

Sports and Recreation

Calgary was an appropriate choice as host of the 1988 Winter Olympic Games—opportunities for indoor and outdoor recreation abound. In winter public **skiing** facilities at Canada Olympic Park and in numerous areas nearby are available. At Lindsay Park Sports Centre, 2225 Macleod Tr. S., **swimming, track** events, **weight lifting** and **squash** are among the popular activities; phone (403) 233-8393.

Similar facilities are offered at the following leisure centers: Eau Claire YMCA, 101 Third St. S.W.; YWCA, 320 Fifth Ave. S.E.; Southland, 19th St. and Southland Dr. S.W.; and Village Square, 2623 56th St. N.E. The latter two offer wave pools. **Ice skating** is featured at Olympic Plaza as well as at more than two dozen other locations.

Several parks dot the city, particularly along the Bow River. Fish Creek Provincial Park *(see Recreation Chart)* has a visitor center and a small lake providing swimming in summer and ice skating in winter. Joggers and bicyclists use the park's extensive trail system. Other recreation sites include Bowness, Edworthy and Riley parks in northwest Calgary; and Prince's Island Park in the city center.

The 145-hectare (360-acre) Glenmore Reservoir provides ample space for **sailing** and **canoeing**; the Dragon Boat races are held in August.

With spectacular natural areas nearby, many visitors to Calgary will be lured to the wilds to enjoy canoeing, **camping, rafting, hiking** and other outdoor pursuits. **Walking** and **bicycling** trails meander through these regions, as do **cross-country skiing** routes. **Bowling, tennis** and swimming enthusiasts will find public lanes, courts and pools throughout Calgary; for details phone the parks and recreation office at (403) 268-3888.

Golf lovers can play 18 holes at McCall Lake, 1600 32nd Ave. N.E.; and Shagnappi, 2900 Bow Tr. S.W. Nine-hole courses are at Confederation, 19th Street and Collingwood Drive N.W.; Lakeview, 5840 19th St. S.W.; Mapleridge, 1240 Mapleglade Dr. S.E.; and Richmond Green, 2539 33rd Ave. S.W. Some private courses accept visiting golfers; check locally for greens fees and restrictions.

With names like Flames, Stampeders and Cannons, Calgary's major sports teams cannot help but be exciting. The Flames play **ice hockey** at Canadian Airlines Saddledome in Stampede Park; their popularity is such that getting tickets for individual games is nearly impossible; phone (403) 777-0000.

The local Canadian **Football** League team, the Stampeders, pounds the turf at McMahon Stadium on Crowchild Trail N.W., off 16th Avenue. Tickets are $25-$45 and can be obtained by phoning the box office at (403) 289-0258.

The Calgary Cannons, a farm team of the American League's Seattle Mariners, play **baseball** at Foothills Stadium, Crowchild Trail and 24th Ave. N.W. Tickets, $6.50-$10, over 60 and ages 4-12 are $4.50-$8, are available at the gate or by phoning (403) 284-1111.

Kart Gardens International, 9555 Barlow Tr. N.E. and 5202 1st S.W., offers **kart racing,** a popular spectator sport. For those wishing to get behind the wheel, karts can be rented. A driver's license is required; helmets, clothing and instructions are provided. Tamer tracks for children also are available. For details phone the gardens at (403) 250-9555 or 250-9556.

Horse racing, including Thoroughbred and harness varieties, is featured at Stampede Park. The park's entrances are at the intersection of 4th Street and 14th Avenue S.E., and on 25th Avenue off Macleod Trail. Phone (403) 261-0214 for race dates and (403) 261-0120 for clubhouse reservations. Legalized **gambling** casinos and "bingo barns" are available if you care to try your luck.

Note: Policies concerning admittance of children to pari-mutuel betting facilities vary. Phone for information.

Spruce Meadows, an outdoor equestrian center and show jumping venue 3 kilometres (2 mi.) west on Hwy. 22 from Hwy. 25, has world-class programs, including dressage and international show jumping events. On days when no shows are scheduled, the grounds are open daily 9-5 free to the public. Visitors are invited to wander the grounds, picnic and view horses in the stables. Phone (403) 974-4200 for a schedule of Spruce Meadows events.

Shopping

Stephen Avenue Mall, a downtown pedestrian walkway, extends from Bankers Hall to the city municipal buildings. This popular spot for people-watching features shops, galleries and restaurants housed within historic buildings. Also downtown, a five-block shopping complex linked by an indoor walkway includes the more than 200 boutiques, department stores and retail chains of Calgary Eaton Centre/TD Square, Bankers Hall, Scotia Centre and Penny Lane Mall.

Unique specialty shops, kiosks and restaurants are the draw at Eau Claire Market *(see color ad)*, adjacent to the Bow River and Prince's Island Park at 2nd Ave. and 2nd St. S.W.

The trendy Uptown 17th Avenue, a scenic neighborhood and upscale shopping district, features stylish fashion shops, antiques stores and eclectic craft boutiques. The avenue also is home to one of the city's most exclusive malls, Mount Royal Village. The Kensington district features smaller stores in new and old buildings. Originally Atlantic Avenue, Ninth Avenue S.E. now is

lined with antiques and home-furnishings stores, bookstores and cappuccino bars.

Major department stores and a wide variety of chain and specialty stores occupy the city's shopping centers: Chinook Centre at the corner of Macleod Trail and Glenmore Trail S.W., Deerfoot Mall at 901 64th Ave. N.E., Market Mall at 3625 Shaganappi Trail N.W., Northland Village Mall at Crowchild Trail and Northland Drive N.W., South Centre Mall at Macleod Trail and Anderson Rd. S.E. and Sunridge Mall at 2525 36th St. N.E.

Theater and Concerts

Four of Calgary's most illustrious theater and music companies perform in the Calgary Centre for the Performing Arts at 205 8th Ave. S.E. Called simply The Centre, it is shared by Alberta Theater Projects, Theatre Calgary, One Yellow Rabbit Theatre Company and Calgary Philharmonic Orchestra. In addition to four theaters and a concert hall, it contains shops, a restaurant and a coffee bar. For information about performance schedules and ticket sales phone Ticketmaster at (403) 777-0000 or 299-8888.

Southern Alberta Jubilee Auditorium, just south of 14th Avenue and 14th Street N.W., stages a variety of performing arts, including the touring companies of Broadway musicals such as "Showboat" and "Cats" and presentations by The Calgary Opera; for details phone the opera company at (403) 262-7286 or the auditorium at (403) 297-8000.

Loose Moose Theatre Company performs adult comedy and drama as well as children's theater. For information contact the office at 2003 McKnight Blvd. N.E.; phone (403) 265-5682. Pumphouse Theatre, 2140 Pumphouse Ave. S.W., gets its name from the 1913 former pumphouse that the city converted into two theaters; phone (403) 263-0079 for schedule and ticket information. Midday performances take place in the aptly named Lunchbox Theatre on the second level in Bow Valley Square, 205 Fifth Ave. S.W.; phone (403) 265-4292.

A popular dinner theater that often showcases well-known performers in its productions is Stage West, 727 42nd Ave. S.E.; phone (403)

243-6642. Other theater, dance and music companies operate locally; check newspapers for performance schedules.

Special Events

The lifestyle of the cowboy is celebrated for 10 days at the beginning of February during the Cowboy Festival. Western art and gear exhibits complement cowboy concerts, Old West films, poetry readings and demonstrations of cowboy skills; phone (403) 261-8500. Also in February, Calgary Winter Festival features dog sledding, snowboarding and the Winter Village; phone (403) 543-5480.

Calgary International Children's Festival, which begins the third Wednesday in May and continues for 5 days, draws performers from such locales as Peru, Germany, Russia and Zimbabwe. The festival's many offerings include music, puppetry, dance and storytelling. Phone (403) 294-7414

Musicians from all corners of the world gather in mid-June at Calgary International Jazz Festival to celebrate jazz as well as world music, blues and gospel. Cabarets, dance parties and other outdoor festivities also are characteristic of the celebration. Phone (403) 249-1119

Despite a focus on the modern oil and gas industry, Calgary citizens recall their past starting the first Friday after Canada Day with The Calgary Stampede. This 10-day Wild West exhibition features a rodeo, chuckwagon races, livestock shows, a turn-of-the-20th-century western village, a Las Vegas-style revue, a midway with amusements, and informative displays. The event also features parades, fireworks, street dancing, pancake breakfasts and other activities that create a carnival-like atmosphere. Tickets for the rodeo and chuckwagon races are $19-$50; phone (800) 661-1260.

Calgary Folk Festival is held for 4 days in late July and early August. In mid-September the Spruce Meadows outdoor equestrian center, off Hwy. 22 and Macleod Trail, plays host to the International Horse Show. Other racing and dressage events are held at the center throughout the year. Phone (403) 974-4200 for a schedule of Spruce Meadows events.

The Calgary Vicinity

BRAGG CREEK (H-5) pop. 700

Bragg Creek, 40 kilometres (25 mi.) southwest of Calgary on Hwy. 22, was named after Albert Bragg, a rancher who settled in the area in 1894. The town has been a popular weekend getaway and year-round recreation area since the 1920s. Known as the "Gateway to the Kananaskis" for its proximity to the Northern Rockies, the area

has evolved as an artist's community with sculptors, potters, weavers, painters and other artisans practicing their crafts.

Bragg Creek offers picnic areas, hiking trails, cross-country skiing, campgrounds and scenic Elbow Falls.

Bragg Creek Chamber of Commerce: 23 White Ave., Bragg Creek, AB T0L 0K0; phone (403) 949-0004.

COCHRANE (G-5) pop. 7,400

Cochrane—named for Sen. Matthew Henry Cochrane, who initiated the first large-scale cattle ranch in the area in the 1880s—is known locally for its homemade ice cream, hang gliding, horseback riding and canoe trips down the Bow River. Stoney Indian Reserve, 16 kilometres (10 mi.) west on Hwy. 1A, was the site of several movies, including Arthur Penn's "Legends of the Fall" and "Little Big Man," and of the television series "Lonesome Dove." The downtown's Western-style architecture provides a backdrop for local arts and crafts and specialty shops. Of particular interest is a foundry and art gallery where visitors can view the 3,000-year-old sculpting technique known as the "lost wax" process.

Cochrane & District Chamber of Commerce: #5, 205 First St. E., Cochrane, AB, Canada T0L 0W1; phone (403) 932-6810.

COCHRANE RANCHE, a 60-hectare (150-acre) provincial historic site and park near jct. Hwys. 1A and 22, is where Sen. Matthew Cochrane began his large-scale cattle operation in 1881. A visitor center, interpretive programs, walking trails and picnic grounds are available. The "Men of Vision" bronze statue overlooks the grounds. Allow 30 minutes minimum. Daily 10-6, mid-May through Labour Day. Donations. Phone (403) 932-1193 or 932-2902.

★ **THE WESTERN HERITAGE CENTRE,** .8 km (.5 mi.) n. of Hwy. 1A on Hwy. 22, focuses on the past, present and future of western life and its great ranches, farmers and cowboys. Touch-screen technology lets visitors explore such realities of pioneer ranching as veterinary surgery. Among other activities in which visitors can participate are calf-roping, branding and sheep-shearing.

Features include interactive ranching exhibits; a theater that shows an orientation presentation as well as films about rodeo, farming and the cattle industry; a shop in which craftsmen make saddles and harnesses; a Western library and the Canadian Rodeo Hall of Fame. A 3,000-square-foot art gallery houses rotating exhibits. Food is available.

Allow 1 hour, 30 minutes minimum. Daily 9-5, Victoria Day-Thanksgiving; Thurs.-Sun. 9-5, rest of year. Admission $7.50; over 59 and ages 12-17, $5.50; ages 7-11, $3.50; family rate (two adults and two children ages 7-17) $20. AE, MC, VI. Phone (403) 932-3514.

OKOTOKS (H-6)
pop. 8,500, elev. 3,400'

Incorporated in 1904, Okotoks thrived on brickmaking, lumber and oil distribution in its early days. Today Okotoks is a commuter community of Calgary. The town gets its name from the Blackfoot name "okatoks," meaning "rocks." Big Rock, 7 kilometers (4 miles) west, is the continent's largest known glacial boulder, having been carried here during an ice age.

A popular recreational retreat, Okotoks offers such leisure pursuits as fishing and hiking. Events include a parade and Youth Festival in mid-June, and the Coors Pro Rodeo and Western Art Show in late August.

Okotoks Chamber of Commerce: The Station Cultural Centre, 53 N. Railway St., Okotoks, AB, Canada T0L 1T0; phone (403) 938-3204.

Self-guiding tours: Heritage Walking Tour brochures are available from the information desk at the Station Cultural Centre.

This ends listings for the Calgary Vicinity.
The following page resumes the alphabetical listings of cities in Alberta.

CAMROSE (E-7) pop. 13,700

Camrose, first settled around 1900 as a trading post, has a strong sense of its Norwegian heritage. Known originally as the Hamlet of Sparling, its name was changed to Camrose in 1906.

Camrose salutes country music during Big Valley Jamboree, the first week in August.

Camrose Chamber of Commerce: 5402 48 Ave., Camrose, AB, Canada T4V 0J7; phone (780) 672-4217.

CAMROSE AND DISTRICT CENTENNIAL MUSEUM, 2 blks. s. of Hwy. 13 at jct. 53rd St. and 46th Ave., houses items from Camrose's pioneer days. Buildings include a country school, a fire hall and a restored log pioneer house and church, both furnished in period. A steam engine, a replica of the first newspaper building and a working model of an early threshing machine are displayed. Tues.-Sun. 10-5, Victoria Day-Labour Day; by appointment rest of year. Donations. Phone (780) 672-3298 or 672-5373 for off-season appointments.

CANMORE (H-4)

pop. 8,400, elev. 1,341 m/4,400′

Established in 1883 as a coal-mining center, Canmore was the first Canadian Pacific Railroad divisional point west of Calgary. Recreational activities are abundant; the town was the site of the biathlon and cross-country ski events of the 1988 Winter Olympics. Hiking, mountain biking and cross-country skiing are popular along the area's numerous trails.

For more than 10,000 persons, music is the focal point during the Folk Festival, held the first weekend in August. A trace of the town's Scottish heritage can be found during Canmore Highland Games in early September. Activities include a highland dance competition, a soccer game, children's games, traditional Scottish foods and a Scottish Ceilidh with Celtic music.

Canmore/Kananaskis Chamber of Commerce: 12-801 8th St., P.O. Box 1178, Canmore, AB, Canada T0L 0M0; phone (403) 678-4094.

CANMORE CENTENNIAL MUSEUM, 907 7th Ave., details Canmore's past through photographs, coal-mining artifacts and items used during the cross-country skiing competition of the 1988 Winter Olympics. The museum also houses a geology exhibit. Allow 30 minutes minimum. Daily 9-5, June 1-Labour Day; daily noon-4, rest of year. Donations. Phone (403) 678-2462.

HELICOPTER SIGHTSEEING TOURS, Hwy. 1 Canmore exit, following signs to Canmore Municipal Heliport, offers scenic flights over the Canadian Rockies. Passengers can view alpine valleys, glaciers, ice fields, the Continental Divide, Banff National Park and towering Mount Assiniboine—the "Matterhorn of the Canadian

Rockies." Operators include [SAVE] Alpine Helicopters, (403) 678-4802. Flights are offered daily (weather permitting) 8:30-5; closed Jan. 1 and Dec. 25-26. Prices start at $120 per passenger for a 25-minute tour; helicopters carry 4-6 passengers. Reservations are required.

RECREATIONAL ACTIVITIES
White-water Rafting
- **Mirage Adventure Tours Ltd.,** 999 Bow Valley Tr., Suite 3, Canmore, AB, Canada T1W 1N4. Daily at 9:45 and 1:15, May-Sept.; by request (four person minimum) rest of year. Phone (403) 678-4919 or (888) 312-7238.

CARDSTON (J-6)

pop. 3,400, elev. 1,185 m/3,888′

A son-in-law of Brigham Young, Charles Ora Card, led 10 Mormon families from Utah into Canada in 1887, hoping to find freedom from American anti-polygamy laws. Settling in Cardston, the immigrants founded the country's first Mormon settlement and named the town after their leader, who became its first mayor. Alberta Temple of the Church of Jesus Christ of Latter-day Saints, 348 3rd St. W., is built on land donated by Card in 1887. It was completed and dedicated in 1923.

The Temple serves a large area of western Canada and Montana, including the 80 percent of Cardston residents who are Mormon. People who are not Mormon are not permitted to enter the structure, but can tour the grounds, where a visitor center offers information; phone (403) 653-1696.

Cardston & District Chamber of Commerce: P.O. Box 1212, Cardston, AB, Canada T0K 0K0; phone (403) 653-2798.

C. ORA CARD HOME, 337 Main St., is the log cabin of the Mormon leader and has been restored and refurnished with hand-carved furniture. Allow 30 minutes minimum. Mon.-Sat. 10-5, June-Aug. Donations. Phone (403) 653-4322.

COURT HOUSE MUSEUM, 89 2nd Ave. W., displays local pioneer memorabilia in a stone courthouse dating from 1907. Allow 1 hour minimum. Mon.-Sat. 10-5, June-Aug. Donations. Phone (403) 653-4322.

★ **REMINGTON-ALBERTA CARRIAGE CENTRE,** 623 Main St., lets visitors appreciate more than 250 19th- and early 20th-century horse-drawn vehicles. Interactive displays and exhibit galleries provide the feeling of riding in the horse-drawn transportation of that era.

The exhibit galleries, which include a smithy and livery stable, carriage factory, carriage dealership, frontier settlement and racetrack, depict 19th-century society and its dependence on this mode of transportation. A working stable shows horses being groomed and harnessed. In summer visitors may schedule rides on vintage and reproduction vehicles for a fee. Guided 75-minute tours and food are available. Picnicking is permitted.

Allow 1 hour, 30 minutes minimum. Daily 9-8, May 15-Labour Day; 9-5, rest of year. Closed Jan. 1, Easter and Dec. 25. Admission $6.50; over 64, $5.50; ages 7-17, $3; family rate $15. Fifteen-minute carriage ride $3; ages 4-17, $1.50; family rate $9. MC, VI. Phone (403) 653-5139.

CLARESHOLM (I-5) pop. 3,400

CLARESHOLM MUSEUM, 5126 1st St. W., is housed in an historic sandstone Canadian Pacific Railway station and features early 20th-century items relating to pioneer life. Town history is highlighted in railway, medical and educational displays. On the grounds is a one-room schoolhouse. Daily 9:30-5:30, Victoria Day-Labour Day; by appointment rest of year. Donations. Phone (403) 625-3131.

COALDALE (I-7) pop. 5,700

THE ALBERTA BIRDS OF PREY CENTRE, 3 blks. n. of jct. Hwys. 3/845, then w. on 16th Ave., rehabilitates injured and orphaned birds of prey and prepares them for release back to the wild. A captive breeding program returns threatened and endangered species to their native habitats. A self-guiding nature walk provides a close-up view of caged or tethered hawks, falcons, owls, eagles and vultures. Birds fly freely during daily demonstrations. Picnicking is permitted. Guided 90-minute tours are available.

Allow 1 hour, 30 minutes minimum. Daily 10-5, May-Sept. Admission $4.75; over 64 and ages 6-18, $4; family rate $13. MC, VI. Phone (403) 345-4262.

COCHRANE—*see Calgary p. 57.*

COLUMBIA ICEFIELD—
see Jasper National Park p. 78.

CROWSNEST PASS (I-5)
pop. 6,400

An area of wild beauty and haunting legends, the municipality of Crowsnest Pass is an amalgamation of the former coal-mining towns of Bellevue, Blairmore, Coleman, Frank and Hillcrest. Scenic Hwy. 3 through Crowsnest Pass connects Burmis to Fernie, British Columbia, via the Rocky Mountain Range and the Continental Divide.

The area provides visitors with recreational opportunities and stimulates the imagination with such stories as the curse of the Lost Lemon Gold Mine, rum-running and the shootout at Bellevue Cafe.

The town of Frank made national headlines April 29, 1903, when more than 60 residents were killed in the spectacular slide of Turtle Mountain on the east side of the pass. Ninety million tons of limestone swept over 1.5 kilometres (.9 mi.) of the valley before dawn, destroying part of the town and burying a mine plant and railway. The old town was at the western edge of the slide; many cellars still are visible.

FRANK SLIDE INTERPRETIVE CENTRE, 1.5 km (.9 mi.) n. off Hwy. 3 at w. edge of Frank Slide, overlooks the site of the 1903 rockslide. Displays and a 20-minute audiovisual program, "In the Mountain's Shadow," describe area history from early settlement to the decline and fall of the mining industry and the events surrounding the Frank Slide. A 1.5-kilometre (.9-mi.) self-guiding trail is available. Interpretive programs are offered in summer.

Allow 1 hour, 30 minutes minimum. Daily 9-8, May 15-Labour Day; 10-4, rest of year. Closed Jan. 1, Easter and Dec. 25. Admission $4; over 64, $3; ages 7-17, $2; family rate $10. Phone (403) 562-7388.

LEITCH COLLIERIES, 3 km (1.9 mi.) e. of Bellevue on Hwy. 3, was founded in 1907 and was the first wholly Canadian-owned mine. The area was the site of a sophisticated early colliery—a coal mine and the buildings and equipment connected with it. The remains of the power house, washery, mine manager's residence and coke ovens still stand. Interpretive signs explain the mining and processing methods. Self-guided tours daily 9-5. Tours are given daily 10-4, May 15-Labour Day. Admission $2; over 64 and ages 7-17, $1.50; family rate (two adults and two children) $5. Phone (403) 562-7388.

DONALDA (F-7) pop. 200

DONALDA AND DISTRICT MUSEUM, Main St. and Railway Ave., houses more than 850 lamps ranging from the antique bicycle variety to colorful living room types. More than 40 tiny courting lamps, which hold only an hour's worth of fuel and were used in the 1800s to signal the end of a suitor's visit, are displayed. Allow 30 minutes minimum. Mon.-Fri. 9-5, Sat.-Sun. 11-5, Victoria Day-Thanksgiving; Mon.-Fri. 9-5, rest of year. Donations. Phone (403) 883-2100.

DRUMHELLER (G-7) pop. 6,600

About 65 million years before Sam Drumheller began promoting the 1910 townsite later named for him, the surrounding Red Deer Valley was the home of immense dinosaurs. Plant-eating hadrosaurs, flesh-eating tyrannosaurs and their formidable cousins stomped through the swampy lowlands and forests bordering the Mowry Sea, which once covered the North American plains.

Fossils of prehistoric creatures often are discovered in the multilayered sedimentary walls of the valley; several life-size dinosaur replicas can be seen in town. Although the local coal industry founded in 1911 by American Jesse Gouge has declined, remnants of old mines still exist.

In Midland Provincial Park off North Dinosaur Trail (Hwy. 838), a self-guiding walking trail leads to the former site of Midland Mine. Gas and oil wells sporadically dot the nearby rolling prairies, but the shortgrass country is occupied mostly by geese and antelopes. Hoodoos—mushroom-shaped rock pillars carved by thousands of years of wind and rain—can be seen 18 km (11 mi.) southeast on Hwy. 10. Because of their fragile nature, climbing these formations is not permitted.

Stretching over the Red Deer River, the Rosedale Suspension Bridge on Hwy. 10 originally was used to carry miners across the river to the now-abandoned Star Mine. In 1931 the swinging bridge replaced the original cable car system and was used until the mine closed in 1957. A park with picnic facilities is available.

Drumheller Regional Chamber of Development and Tourism: 60 First Ave. W., P.O. Box 999, Drumheller, AB, Canada T0J 0Y0; phone (403) 823-8100.

DINOSAUR TRAIL (Hwy. 838) is a 50-km (30-mi.) circle tour which winds w. from Drumheller through the Red Deer Valley, part of Alberta's Badlands; the trail is marked by signs. The arid terrain is marked with hoodoos—mushroom-shaped rock pillars carved by thousands of years of wind and rain. A short distance along the north trail is The Little Church, a meditation chapel which attracts 150,000 visitors a year—six at a time. Another feature of the trail is the Bleriot Ferry, a cable ferry that crosses the Red Deer River on demand from early May through October. A natural amphitheater is the yearly site of six performances of a passion play.

Drumheller Valley Interpretive Centre, 335 1st St. E., exhibits bones and fossils collected by Drumheller's early fossil hunters. Of interest is a bison skeleton dating from the ice age. A rounded stone embedded in the bison's skull is possibly the earliest evidence of man in Alberta. A lapidary collection contains gems, minerals, petrified wood and other natural treasures. Also displayed is an aboriginal tepee.

Daily 10-6, May-Oct. Admission $3; over 64, $2.50; ages 6-17, $2; family rate $10. Phone (403) 823-2593.

SAVE **HOMESTEAD ANTIQUE MUSEUM,** .7 km (.5 mi.) n.w. via Hwy. 9 to 901 N. Dinosaur Tr., displays pioneer and Indian items as well as clocks, gramophones, radios, early cars, clothing, fine china, jewelry, tractors and farm implements. There also are collections of military badges and medals as well as early 20th-century clothing. Allow 1 hour, 30 minutes minimum. Daily 9-8, mid-June through Labour Day; 9-6, mid-May to mid-June and day after Labour Day-Thanksgiving; by appointment rest of year. Admission $3; over 64 and ages 6-17, $2; family rate $10. Phone (403) 823-2600.

REPTILE WORLD, 1222A Hwy. 9W, is home to more than 85 species of reptiles and amphibians including snakes, frogs and turtles. The facility features "Fred," a 600-pound alligator. Allow 1 hour minimum. Daily 9 a.m.-10 p.m., July-Aug.; Thurs.-Tues. 10-6, rest of year. Closed Jan. 1 and Dec. 25. Admission $4.50; over 64 and ages 5-17, $3.50. VI. Phone (403) 823-8623.

★ **THE ROYAL TYRRELL MUSEUM,** 6 km (4 mi.) n.w. on N. Dinosaur Tr. (Hwy. 838), is in the badlands of the Red Deer River Valley, surrounded by one of the richest fossil deposits in the world. Dinosaurs that once roamed Alberta are now showcased in the museum's Dinosaur Hall, where more than 35 complete skeletons and lifelike models are displayed.

Fossils, models, computers, videotapes, a preparation laboratory, hands-on exhibits and an indoor garden illustrate millions of years of geological and biological development. The museum also houses a research center and operates a field station near Brooks (see place listing p. 45). Allow 3 hours minimum. Daily 9-9, Victoria Day weekend-Labour Day; daily 10-5, day after Labour Day-second Mon. in Oct.; Tues.- Sun. 10-5, rest of year. Closed Dec. 25. Admission $6.50; over 64, $5.50; ages 7-17, $3; family rate $15. MC, VI. Phone (403) 823-7707.

DUNVEGAN (A-2)

HISTORIC DUNVEGAN, off Hwy. 2 on the n. side of the Peace River beside Dunvegan Suspension Bridge, was a fur-trading post and the site of one of the first Roman Catholic missions in Alberta. It contains three original buildings: the 1877-78 Factor's House, part of the Hudson's Bay Co.'s trading fort; the church of St. Charles Mission, built in 1885; and the mission's rectory, built in 1889. Guided walks and educational programs explain the site's history. The visitor center offers a video disc presentation of the history of Dunvegan.

Allow 1 hour minimum. Daily 10-6, May 15-Labour Day. Admission $3; over 64, $2; ages 7-17, $1.50; family rate $8. Phone (780) 835-7150.

Well Read

*W*hen you pick up a AAA/CAA TourBook® guide, look for the establishments that display a bright red CAA logo beside their listings. These establishments place a high value on the patronage they receive from AAA/CAA members. They are telling you they're willing to go the extra mile to get your business.

So, when you turn to the AAA/CAA TourBook to make your travel plans, be on the lookout for the establishments that will give you the special treatment you deserve.

And don't forget to look for the establishments that display the familiar SAVE *icon to receive discounts.*

Travel With Someone You Trust®

Edmonton

Few first-time visitors to Edmonton are prepared for what they discover when they arrive. From trading post to metropolis within some 200 years, this capital city continues to surprise visitors by its size, quality of life, sophistication and its beautiful river valley location.

Edmonton owes its existence to an abundant and varied supply of natural resources which prompted each of its three major booms. In 1795 the Hudson's Bay Co. founded Fort Edmonton on the banks of the North Saskatchewan River. Traders bartered with Cree and Blackfoot Indians for luxuriant and sought-after pelts of otters, beavers, muskrats, minks and foxes. A trading settlement developed and became the main stopping point on routes to the north and to the Pacific.

This stopping point became a starting point for prospectors rushing to the Klondike for gold; they stocked up on supplies in Edmonton for the harsh trip northward. When gold failed to materialize and many prospectors realized they were not going to get rich, let alone get rich quick, they headed back to Edmonton to settle for a slower but surer way of life.

A bust for prospectors was a boom for Edmonton. The city grew to six times its previous size, making it a prime choice for the provincial capital when Alberta was formed in 1905.

In the years that followed, the capital city earned its nickname, "Gateway to the North," because of its status as a transportation hub and gateway to the regions beyond. In 1915 Edmonton became a major link in the Canadian Pacific Transcontinental Railroad, emerging as an important crossroads stop between east and west as well as north and south.

The city's reputation as a transportation center was reinforced during the 1930s as bush pilots transported vital medical supplies, food and mail to northern communities. And when construction began on the Alaska Highway in 1942, Edmonton found itself again in the role of a major distribution and supply center. Edmonton also is an important air travel link.

When the last big boom was fading from memory, the Leduc Number One Well gushed forth black crude oil only 40 kilometres (25 mi.) southwest of Edmonton. This discovery in February 1947 was just the beginning. Since then more than 2,250 wells within a 40-kilometre (25-mi.) radius of Edmonton have coaxed the precious natural resource to the surface. Enormous industrial growth resulted; the city's population quadrupled in the 25 years following the Leduc gusher.

"Canada's Festival City" is a city growing in both prosperity and beauty. With about 900,000 residents in the greater metropolitan area, Edmonton has been careful not to sacrifice the natural resource that makes

it liveable—its green space. Edmonton's river valley parkland is reputed to be the largest stretch of urban parkland in North America, encompassing 7,340 hectares (18, 348 acres). The city contains more than 11,000 hectares (27,181 acres) of parkland, playgrounds and open areas.

Stretches of parks along the North Saskatchewan river valley let residents spend long summer days enjoying the outdoors. The city park system provides a winter playground for such activities as cross-country skiing, ice skating, dog sledding and snowshoeing. For visitors who prefer the indoors, an extensive system of underground and overhead "pedways" in the downtown area makes it possible to travel in climate-controlled comfort regardless of the weather; Edmonton Tourism provides pedway maps.

Approaches

By Car

Two major highways run through Edmonton. The Trans-Canada Yellowhead Hwy. (Hwy. 16) provides access from the east and west; Hwy. 2 runs north and south.

Getting Around

Street System

Edmonton's street system is a grid with streets running north and south and avenues running east and west. Most streets and avenues are numbered starting from the southeast corner of the city; a few are named.

Edmonton's street plan includes several traffic circles. When approaching a traffic circle, make sure you are in the correct lane. Use the right lane if you plan to exit, the left lane if you are traveling around the circle. When in the circle, the vehicle on the outside must yield to the vehicle on the inside.

The city speed limit is 50 kilometres per hour (30 mph) or as posted. A right turn on red after stopping is permitted; U-turns are not. A sign that reads "Bus and Taxi Lane Only" means it is illegal to drive, park or stop any vehicle other than the above in that lane.

Parking

Street parking restrictions vary throughout the city; watch for and heed the signs. Parking is not permitted in the residential areas surrounding Northlands Park, Telus Field and Commonwealth Stadium during major events; cars parked there will be towed.

Rates for city-operated parking meters are $1.25 per hour. Most meters are free after 6 p.m. and on Sundays and holidays; however, there are some 24-hour meters.

Rates for downtown parking lots range $1-$3 per hour during the day. At lots participating in the city's Park in the Heart program, parking costs $2 from 6

(continued on p. 66)

The Informed Traveler

City Population: 616,300

Elevation: 670 m/2,198 ft.

Sales Tax: The federal Goods and Services Tax is 7 percent and applies to most goods, food/beverages and services, including hotel and motel accommodations. Alberta does not have a Provincial Sales Tax but does impose a 5 percent tax on hotel and motel accommodations.

WHOM TO CALL

Emergency: 911

Police (non-emergency): (780) 423-4567

Fire: (780) 496-3900

Ambulance: 911

Distress Line: (780) 482-4357

Time: (780) 449-4444

Weather: (780) 468-4940

Road Reports: (780) 471-6056

Hospitals: Grey Nuns, (780) 450-7000; Misericordia, (780) 930-5611; Royal Alexandria, (780) 477-4111; University of Alberta, (780) 407-8822.

WHERE TO LOOK

Newspapers

Edmonton has two daily newspapers, the *Edmonton Journal* and the *Edmonton Sun.* Canada's national newspaper, The Globe and Mail, also is available at newsstands.

Radio and TV

Radio station CBC (740 AM) is a member of Canadian Broadcasting Corp.

The major TV channels are 3 (CTV), 5 (CBC) and 13 (ITV Edmonton).

Visitor Information

Write Edmonton Tourism, 9797 Jasper Ave., Edmonton, AB, Canada T5J 1N9. Visitor information centers are at Shaw Conference Centre, 9797 Jasper Ave.; on Hwy. 2 at the south entrance to the city at Gateway Park; and at Edmonton International Airport. During the summer a center operates on Hwy. 16 (The Yellowhead) at Spruce Grove. Phone (780) 496-8400 or (800) 463-4667. *See ad p. 54 & color ad p. 69.*

TRANSPORTATION

Air Travel

Edmonton International Airport is 29 kilometres (18 mi.) south of the city. The Sky Shuttle service to downtown costs $11 one way and $18 round trip; phone (780) 465-8515 or (888) 438-2342. A $35 rate applies to taxi service between the airport and downtown.

Rental Cars

Hertz, downtown or at the airport, offers discounts to CAA and AAA members. Phone (780) 423-3431 downtown, (780) 890-4435 at the airport, (800) 263-0600 in Canada or (800) 654-3001 out of Canada.

Rail Service

The VIA Rail station is at 12360 121st St.; phone (780) 448-8822 or (800) 835-3037.

Buses

Greyhound Lines Inc.'s downtown depot is at 10324 103rd St.; phone (780) 413-8747. Red Arrow Express offers luxury motorcoach service between Edmonton, Calgary, Fort McMurray and Red Deer; phone (780) 424-3339.

Taxis

Taxi companies include Alberta Co-Op Taxi, (780) 425-8310; Checker Cabs, (780) 484-8888; Skyline Cabs Ltd., (780) 468-4646; and Yellow Cab, (780) 462-3456. Taxi rates are $2.20 for the first 95 metres (.1 km/.065 mi.) and 10c for each additional 105 metres. Taxis can be hailed, but phoning is recommended.

Public Transport

Edmonton Transit Downtown Information Centre, 100A Street and Jasper Avenue, is open Mon.-Fri. 9-5; phone (780) 496-1611. Buses operate 6 a.m.-1 a.m., Mon.-Sat., and 6:30 a.m.-12:30 a.m., Sun. and holidays. The Light-Rail Transit (LRT) operates from 5:30 a.m. to 1 a.m. Fare is $1.60; over 64 and ages 6-16,$1.

Disabled Adult Transportation System (DATS) serves those who can't use other transit facilities. Visitors may request a temporary registration number by phoning (780) 496-4567. Rides must be booked 1 day in advance.

Destination Edmonton

*O*nce a tiny settlement where traders sought to swap for furs with Cree and Blackfoot Indians, today's bustling Edmonton holds its heritage in high regard.

*R*eminders of the city's past can be found at museums, living-history demonstrations, historic sites and archives. But don't forget to step into the present for a visit to what may be the world's largest mall.

Edmonton Space & Science Centre.
See IMAX films and take a mock Challenger mission at a museum that's out of this world. (See listing page 66)

World Waterpark, West Edmonton Mall.
Shop 'til you drop at the more than 800 stores, then take a dip in the refreshing pool. (See listing page 68)

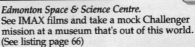

Edmonton

2

Fort Saskatchewan

St. Albert

16   16

Stony Plain

14

See Vicinity map page 66

2   21

Fort Edmonton Park.
Take a tour through the city's early days at this living-history museum, said to be Canada's largest. Authentically garbed interpreters depict four noteworthy years in Edmonton's history: 1846, 1885, 1905 and 1920. (See listing page 67)

Ukrainian Cultural Heritage Village, Edmonton.
Demonstrations detail the lives of the area's Ukrainian immigrants in the early 1900s. (See listing page 68)

*P*laces included in this AAA Destination City:

p.m. to midnight Monday through Friday and for the first 3 hours on Saturdays and Sundays.

What To See

ALBERTA AVIATION MUSEUM is at 11410 Kingsway Ave., 4 km (2.5 mi.) n.w. opposite Tower Rd. at the s. end of City Centre Airport. This double-long, double-wide hangar was a training facility for air crews during World War II. The museum displays 27 aircraft including a carefully restored Fairchild 71, a fighter-bomber version of the De Havilland Mosquito and a replica of a Hawker Hurricane. Other displays detail the history of aviation in Edmonton and Alberta.

Allow 1 hour minimum. Mon.-Sat. 10-4:30, Sun. 11-4:30; closed Jan. 1 and Dec. 25-26. Hours may vary; phone ahead. Admission $6; over 64, $5; ages 13-17, $4; ages 6-12, $3; family rate $14. AE, MC, VI. Phone (780) 453-1078.

ALBERTA LEGISLATURE BUILDING, 10800 97th Ave., was completed in 1912. Public-use parkland, monuments, pools and fountains surround the building, which was built with imported sandstone and marble. Displays outline Alberta's history and parliamentary tradition. Guided 40-minute tours begin in the Legislature Interpretive Center.

Allow 1 hour minimum. Tours are given daily at 9, 10 and 11 and every half-hour noon-4, Victoria Day weekend-Labour Day; tour schedule varies Mon.-Fri. 9-4:30, Sat.-Sun. noon-5, rest of year. Closed Jan. 1, Good Friday and Dec. 25. Free. Phone (780) 427-7362 for tour times and reservations.

EDMONTON ART GALLERY, 2 Sir Winston Churchill Sq., exhibits fine and applied arts, with emphasis on Canadian historical art and Western Canadian contemporary art. Allow 1 hour minimum. Mon.-Wed. 10:30-5, Thurs.-Fri. 10:30-8, Sat.-Sun. and holidays 11-5; closed Jan. 1 and Dec. 25. Admission $3, over 64 and students with ID $1.50, under 12 free; free to all Thurs. 4-8. MC, VI. Phone (780) 422-6223.

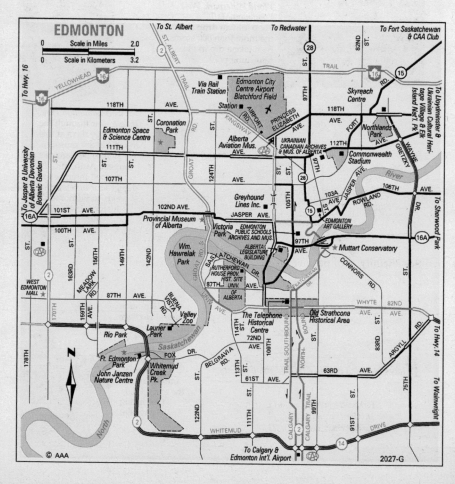

EDMONTON PUBLIC SCHOOLS ARCHIVES AND MUSEUM, 10425 99th Ave., is housed the historic McKay Avenue School, site of first convocation of the Alberta Legislature. This 1905 brick school has been carefully restored and features the 1906 legislative chamber, period classrooms and displays which trace the history of Edmonton public schools. Also on the grounds is the restored Edmonton 1881 Schoolhouse, the first public school in Alberta. Allow 1 hour minimum. Tues.-Fri. 12:30-4 (also Wed. 4-9), Sun. 1-4, Apr.-Oct.; Tues.-Fri. 12:30-4, rest of year. Closed holidays. Free. Phone (780) 422-1970.

SAVE ★ **EDMONTON SPACE & SCIENCE CENTRE**, 142nd St. and 112th Ave., examines the world and beyond through sight and sound experiences. Exhibits, games, models and galleries explain and explore unique phenomena. Films in IMAX® Theatre give visitors a "larger-than-life" sensation. Margaret Zeidler Star Theatre presents planetarium and laser shows on its 23 m (75 ft.) domed ceiling.

Weekend visitors can take mock *Challenger* missions into outer space or can explore the world of computers in the Dow Computer Lab. Food is available. Center open daily 10-9:30, mid-June through Labour Day; Tues.-Sun. and holidays 10-10, rest of year. Observatory open daily 1-5 and 8-midnight, mid-June through Labour Day; Fri.-Sun. 8-midnight, Sat.-Sun. 1-5, rest of year.

Exhibit galleries and planetarium show $6.95; over 64 and ages 13-17, $5.95; ages 3-12, $4.95; family rate $27.95. Exhibit galleries and planetarium theater *and* IMAX® show $11.95; over 64 and ages 13-17, $10.95; ages 3-12, $7.95; family rate $44.95. MC, VI. Phone (780) 451-3344.

★ **FORT EDMONTON PARK** is at the jct. of Fox and Whitemud drs. This park, reputed to be Canada's largest living-history museum, depicts Edmonton in four eras: as an 1846 Hudson's Bay Co. fur-trading fort, as an 1885 settlement, as a developing capital in 1905 and as a 1920 business community.

Costumed interpreters give demonstrations and encourage visitor participation in various period activities such as playing pool and horseshoes, driving in antique cars, firing a round in the shooting gallery and tasting bannock. The park also includes an interpretive children's gallery. Food is available.

Allow 3 hours minimum. Daily 10-6, late June-late Aug.; Mon.-Fri. 10-4, Sat.-Sun. 10-6, Victoria Day weekend-late June; open for special events rest of year. Admission $7; over 64 and ages 13-17, $5.25; ages 2-12, $3.50; family rate $21. Admission includes steam-driven train and streetcar rides. Pets are not permitted. MC, VI. Phone (780) 496-8787. *See color ad p. 69.*

JOHN JANZEN NATURE CENTRE, jct. Fox Dr. and Whitemud Dr. adjacent to Fort Edmonton Park, has exhibits, trails, small animals, interpretive programs and events designed to promote awareness and appreciation of wildlife and the environment. Allow 1 hour minimum. Mon.-Fri. 9-6, Sat.-Sun. and holidays 11-6, July 1-Labour Day; Mon.-Fri.

9-4, Sat.-Sun. and holidays 1-4, rest of year. Closed Dec. 25-Jan. 1. Admission $1; seniors 75c; children 50c; family rate $3. Phone (780) 496-2939.

SAVE ★ **MUTTART CONSERVATORY**, 9626 96A St. at the east end of the James MacDonald Bridge, consists of five pyramid-shaped greenhouses. Plants from varied climates thrive in the Tropical Pavilion, the Arid Pavilion and the Temperate Pavilion. The Show Pavilion features seasonal exhibits of colorful floral displays. An Orchid Show is held each February; African violet, bonsai and other shows are held throughout the year. Food is available.

Allow 1 hour minimum. Mon.-Fri. 9-6; Sat.-Sun. 11-6; closed Dec. 25. Admission $4.50; over 64, students with ID and ages 13-18, $3.50; ages 2-12, $2; family rate $12.50. Phone to confirm prices. MC, VI. Phone (780) 496-8755. *See color ad p. 69.*

★ **PROVINCIAL MUSEUM OF ALBERTA**, 12845 102nd Ave., is Alberta's natural and human history museum. The facility, a 1967 Canadian centennial project, is surrounded by a sculpture park overlooking the river valley.

Within the museum, four galleries reflect Alberta's heritage. The Habitat Gallery presents birds and animals in natural settings that replicate the various regions of Alberta. The Natural History Gallery offers specimens of plants and animals from the past and present. The Syncrude Gallery of Aboriginal Culture tells the story of 500 generations of aboriginal peoples. The Human History Gallery depicts European settlement in Alberta. Changing exhibits and events are scheduled throughout the year. Food is available.

Allow 2 hours minimum. Daily 9-5; closed Dec. 24-25. Hours may vary during special exhibits. Admission $6.50; over 64, $5.50; ages 7-17, $3; family rate $15. Additional fee may be charged during special exhibits. MC, VI. Phone (780) 453-9100.

RUTHERFORD HOUSE PROVINCIAL HISTORIC SITE, 11153 Saskatchewan Dr., was the home of A.C. Rutherford, Alberta's first premier and a founder of the University of Alberta. Completed in 1911, the substantial Jacobethan (a blend of Jacobean and Elizabethan styles) Revival house established a new standard in domestic architecture and marked the end of the pioneer style in Alberta. Guides in period dress conduct 45-minute house tours upon request. Events are scheduled throughout the year. Food is available.

Allow 1 hour minimum. Daily 10-6, May 15-Labour Day; Tues.-Sun. noon-5, rest of year. Closed Jan. 1, Good Friday and Dec. 25. Admission $2; over 64 and ages 7-17, $1.50; family rate $5. Phone (780) 427-3995.

SAVE **THE TELEPHONE HISTORICAL CENTRE**, 10437 83rd Ave., presents the history of telecommunications in Edmonton dating from the introduction of telephone service in 1885. The facility features numerous interactive displays and a 30-minute theater presentation with Xeldon the Robot. Allow 1 hour minimum. Tues.-Fri. 10-4, Sat. noon-4; phone to confirm holiday hours. Admission

$3; over 64 and ages 6-18, $2; family rate $5. Phone (780) 441-2077.

UKRAINIAN CANADIAN ARCHIVES & MUSEUM OF ALBERTA, 9543 110th Ave., contains exhibits tracing the history of Alberta's Ukrainian pioneers. Displays include traditional apparel and musical instruments, costumes, Ukrainian currency, photographs, church artifacts and folk art. Allow 1 hour minimum. Tues.-Fri. 10-5, Sat. noon-5; closed national holidays. Donations. Phone (780) 424-7580.

SAVE **UKRAINIAN CULTURAL HERITAGE VILLAGE** is 35 km (21 mi.) e. along Hwy. 16. The pre-1930 lifestyle of the region's Ukrainian immigrant population is portrayed via living-history demonstrations around 34 restored historic buildings, including houses, farm buildings, churches and stores. The site comprises four areas: a town, a farmstead, a rural community and an overview area. Costumed interpreters depicting a wide variety of characters from the turn of the 20th century demonstrate the settlers' daily routines. Events are held year-round.

Allow 2 hours minimum. Daily 10-6, May 15-Labour Day; 10-4, day after Labour Day-Thanksgiving. Admission $6.50; over 64, $5.50; ages 7-17, $3; family rate $15. Admission after Labour Day is half-price. MC, VI. Phone (780) 662-3640.

UNIVERSITY OF ALBERTA DEVONIAN BOTANIC GARDEN, 14 km (9 mi.) s. on Hwy. 60 from jct. Hwy. 16W and the Devon Hwy. overpass, comprises 32 hectares (80 acres) of cultivated gardens and 44.5 hectares (110 acres) of natural area. Features include Kurimoto Japanese Garden, a tropical butterfly house, ecological reserves and collections of native and alpine plants. Food and picnic facilities are available. Allow 2 hours minimum. Daily 10-7, May-Oct. Admission $5.50; over 64, $4.50; students and ages 4-12, $3.25. MC, VI. Phone (780) 987-3054 or 987-3055.

VALLEY ZOO, Buena Vista Rd. (87th Ave.) and 134th St., features more than 350 domestic and exotic animals from around the world. Pony and camel rides, a miniature train, a merry-go-round, paddleboats and a petting zoo are available during summer. Food is available. Allow 1 hour, 30 minutes minimum. Daily 9:30-8, July-Aug.; Mon.-Fri. 9:30-4, Sat.-Sun. 9:30-6, day after Labour Day-second Mon. in Oct.; 9:30-4, rest of year. Closed Dec. 25.

Admission $5.25; over 64 and ages 13-17, $3.75; ages 2-12, $2.75; family rate $16. Admission is reduced in winter. MC, VI. Phone (780) 496-6911. *See color ad p. 69.*

★ **WEST EDMONTON MALL**, jct. of 87th Ave. and 170th St., is a huge, two-level shopping and entertainment complex. With more than 800 stores and services, 26 movie theaters, more than 110 eateries and seven major attractions, it claims the distinction of being the world's largest mall. Virtually a self-contained city, the mall attractions are the foundation for a comprehensive indoor recreation complex.

Galaxyland amusement park features 25 rides and attractions, including a triple-loop roller coaster, a 13-story free-fall experience and a motion-simulator theater. The Deep Sea Adventure features submarine rides, live dolphin presentations and a life-size replica of Christopher Columbus' *Santa Maria*. The Sea Life Caverns contains more than 100 species of marine life, including sharks and penguins. With more than 2 hectares (5 acres) under one roof, World Waterpark houses what is purported to be the world's largest indoor wave pool, with 20 water activities and miles of water slides and a bungee jump.

The Ice Palace is an NHL-size ice rink in the center of the complex. The Professor WEM'S Adventure Golf offers a challenging 18-hole miniature golf course. Aquariums also are in the mall. Allow a full day. Shops open Mon.-Fri. 10-9, Sat. 10-6, Sun. and most holidays noon-6. Attractions, theaters and restaurants are open later. Call for hours.

Galaxyland unlimited one-day pass $29.95, under 48 inches tall and senior citizens $21.95, family rate (up to four members) $69.95. Individual ride ticket $1.20. World Waterpark $29.95; senior citizens and ages 3-10, $21.95; family rate (up to four members) $49.95. Ice Palace $5.50; senior citizens and ages 3-10, $3. Deep Sea Adventure $13; senior citizens and ages 3-10, $6.50; family rate (up to four members) $16.95. Miniature golf $9; ages 3-10, $6. Dolphin Presentation $2. Sea Life Caverns $3. AE, MC, VI. Phone (780) 444-5300 or (800) 661-8890 for attraction hours of operation. *See color ad p. 69.*

CASINOS

- **Baccarat Casino**, 10128 104th Ave. N.W. Slots daily 10 a.m.-3 a.m., table games daily noon-2 a.m., poker daily noon-4 a.m.; closed Dec. 25. Phone (780) 413-3178.

- **Casino ABS**, 10549 102nd St. N.W. Daily 10 a.m.-3 a.m.; closed Dec. 25. Phone (780) 424-9467.

- **Casino Edmonton**, 7055 Argyll Rd. Daily 10 a.m.-3 a.m.; closed Dec. 25. Phone (780) 465-5377.

- **Palace Casino**, 2710 West Edmonton Mall, 8770 170th St. N.W. Daily 10 a.m.-3 a.m.; closed Dec. 25. Phone (780) 444-2112.

What To Do
Sightseeing
Bus Tours

Nite Tours offers pub, club and comedy bus crawls; phone (780) 453-2134.

Driving Tours

The most scenic areas in Edmonton are along the North Saskatchewan River valley. On the south side, the drive north along Saskatchewan Drive from 76th Avenue and 120th Street to 99th Street offers a picturesque trip around the University of Alberta campus. The views from Provincial Museum, 102nd Avenue and 128th Street, and the residential district of Glenora are impressive.

Walking Tours

Heritage Trail leads from the conference center to the Legislature Building, a route that links government and industry by way of Edmonton's past. Old Strathcona, south of the North Saskatchewan River, offers a view of many original buildings and street scenes characteristic of an early 20th-century prairie town. Edmonton Gallery Walk joins eight private art galleries around Jasper Avenue and 124th Street.

Guided walking tours of the 30,000-student University of Alberta are available during the summer; phone (780) 492-4236, or (780) 492-4413 for the "Tour of Trees." For information about walking tours, phone Edmonton Tourism Visitor Information Centre at (780) 496-8400.

Sports and Recreation

Whatever the season, there are opportunities for both indoor and outdoor recreation. The North Saskatchewan River valley is an oasis of parkland, with more than 100 kilometres (62 miles) of trails, four lake systems and 22 parks. Depending on the time of year, you can **golf, hike, jog, cycle, ride horseback, fish, ski (cross-country** and **downhill), skate** or even pan for gold in a park.

The largest park is Capital City Recreation Park, composed of many smaller areas in the center and on the east side of the city. Within the park are 30 kilometres (19 mi.) of paths for **bicycling** and **jogging.** For information about activities and facilities phone River Valley Centre at (780) 496-7275.

Playing host to two major sporting events—the Commonwealth Games in 1978 and the World University Games in 1983—has provided Edmonton with a legacy of world-class sporting facilities. Several multiple-purpose centers—including Commonwealth Stadium Recreation Centre, Stadium Road and 91st Street, (780) 496-6999; Kinsmen Sports Centre, 9100 Walterdale Rd., (780) 496-7300; and Mill Woods Recreation Centre, 7207 28th Ave., (780) 496-2900—offer such activities as **swimming, diving, racquetball, squash** and **track** events.

Spectator sports also can be enjoyed throughout the year. Labatt Raceway, 2 kilometres (1.2 mi.) west of Hwy. 2 on Hwy. 19, offers motorsport racing May through August; phone (780) 461-5801. Northlands Park *(see color ad p. 69),* 7300 116th Ave., offers a chance to watch **harness racing** from early March to mid-June and from October to mid-December. **Thoroughbred racing** takes place from June to October; phone (780) 471-7379.

Note: Policies concerning admittance of children to pari-mutuel betting facilities vary. Phone for information.

Home to four professional sports teams, Edmonton is referred to fondly as the City of Champions. The Edmonton Oilers, several-time Stanley Cup Champions of the National **Hockey** League, play from September to April in Skyreach Centre at 118th Avenue and 74th Street; phone (780) 414-4400. The Edmonton Eskimos **football** team, many times the Grey Cup Champions of the Canadian Football League, play at Commonwealth Stadium, 111th Avenue and Stadium Road, from June to November; phone (780) 448-3757.

Baseball is the game of the Edmonton Trappers, members of the Pacific Coast League. They play from April to September at Telus Field, south of downtown at 96th Avenue and 102nd Street; phone (780) 429-2934. The Edmonton Drillers of the National Professional Soccer League play at Skyreach Centre from November through March; phone (780) 425-5425.

Shopping

For the intrepid shopper, there is nothing like West Edmonton Mall *(see attraction listing p. 68),* which occupies a 44-hectare (110-acre) site at 87th Avenue and 170th Street. Inside are more than 800 stores, including a Planet Hollywood, where movie buffs can find merchandise from key chains to trendy T-shirts to leather jackets.

For those who want shopping on a less imposing scale, other popular malls include Heritage Mall, 23rd Avenue and 111th Street; Kingsway Garden Mall, 109th Street and Princess Elizabeth Avenue; Londonderry Mall, 137th Avenue and 66th Street; and Southgate Centre, 111th Street and 51st Avenue.

Downtown offers boutiques and restaurants as well as covered shopping areas joined by enclosed walkways. The four-level Edmonton Centre contains Hudson's Bay Co. and 100 other shops. A pedway links it to Eaton Centre and ManuLife Place, 101st Street and 102nd Avenue.

Eaton Centre comprises four glittering floors decorated with mirrored glass and brass. It features Eaton's and more than 120 other shops and services, including a nine-hole miniature golf course and a nine-screen theater. ManuLife Place contains designer boutiques and Holt Renfrew, an elegant retail store with a quaint in-store cafe. Connected to ManuLife Place is Commerce Place, which features several shops with signature fashions.

Rice Howard Way, an attractive outdoor pedestrian area lined with sidewalk seating and eateries, is downtown at 100th Street and 101A Avenue. It is particularly popular in summer.

Old Strathcona at Whyte Avenue (82nd Avenue), the main outdoor shopping street on the south side of the city, has the look of historic Edmonton and offers boutiques, specialty shops, restaurants, bistros and coffee bars.

Don't forget that the major museums have interesting shops with items sometimes impossible to find elsewhere. Of particular interest are the six period shops in Fort Edmonton Park.

Theater and Concerts

Theater season runs from September through May. For live theater visit the Citadel Theatre complex, 99th Street and 101A Avenue, which consists of four theaters, an amphitheater and a beautiful atrium. Phone (780) 425-1820.

Family entertainment is the specialty at Stage Polaris, whose productions are given at the Kaasa Theatre at the Jubilee Auditorium at 87th Ave. and 114th St.; phone (780) 432-9483. Prominent Canadian and American performers take to the stage at Mayfield Dinner Theatre at Mayfield Inn & Suites, 166th Street and 109th Avenue; phone (780) 483-4051. Celebrations Dinner Theatre, 13103 Fort Rd., provides an entertainment experience for all ages; phone (780) 448-9339. Jubilations Dinner Theatre, in the West Edmonton Mall at the intersection of 87th Ave. and 170th St., features musical comedy; phone (780) 484-2424.

The Alberta Ballet Company, (780) 447-6812, and the Edmonton Opera, (780) 429-1000, perform in Jubilee Auditorium on the University of Alberta campus at 87th Avenue and 114th Street; phone (780) 427-9622 for auditorium information. Edmonton Symphony Orchestra, (780) 428-1414, performs at Francis Winspear Centre, 4 Sir Winston Churchill Sq.; phone (780) 428-1414 for concert information. Shaw Conference Centre, Francis Winspear Centre, Jubilee Auditorium and Skyreach Centre play host to a variety of concerts ranging from classical music to rock.

Billy's Guide, See Magazine and *Where Edmonton* give detailed, up-to-date information about arts and entertainment in Edmonton, and local newspapers provide current performance information. Ticketmaster outlets handle ticket sales for most sports, recreation, theater and concert events; phone (780) 451-8000.

Special Events

Edmonton offers a smorgasbord of events.

Independent short and feature-length movies are celebrated in March at the week-long Local Heroes International Screen Festival. In late May performers in varied arts are offered a showcase for their theater, music, dance, storytelling and puppetry at the Northern Alberta International Children's Festival.

Concerts, workshops, club dates and outdoor events characterize the Jazz City International Music Festival, held from mid- to late June; phone (780) 432-7166. Also in June, The Works: A Visual Arts Celebration brings together artists and artisans; phone (780) 426-2122.

Edmonton Celebrate Canada is a 10-day celebration, beginning June 21 with National Aboriginal Day. On June 24 are Francophone festivities honoring St. Jean Baptiste. The last Sunday of June is the Italian-Canadian Festival for Giovanni Caboto, the discoverer of Canada. The celebration concludes on Canada Day, July 1, with a full day of events and the Fireworks Finale.

Edmonton International Street Performers Festival in mid-July offers 10 days of free performances by street acts including magicians, clowns, jugglers, mime artists, musicians and comics. Also during July, the River City Shakespeare Festival presents two shows on alternating nights in William Hawrelak Park.

The city's biggest event is Klondike Days (*see color ad p. 69*). Every July Edmontonians don their finest Gay '90s apparel for the event that commemorates Edmonton's early days as a frontier community and gateway to the Yukon during the gold rush. Parades, casinos, gold panning and various other forms of entertainment keep the city alive with activity for 10 days. The World Championship Sourdough Raft Race, the Sunday Promenade and A Taste of Edmonton are highlights.

Colored lights illuminate Great Divide Waterfall on Sunday evenings of summer holiday weekends; the best view is from the High Level Bridge at 109th Street and 97th Avenue.

August brings the world to Edmonton during the 3-day Heritage Festival, which offers more than 50 outdoor ethnic pavilions showcasing international music, dance, art and cuisine. Also in August are the Edmonton Folk Music Festival, Edmonton Sports Festival and Marathon and Edmonton's International Fringe Theatre Festival, a 9-day extravaganza of plays, dance, music, mime and street entertainment. In September is the Edmonton Symphony Orchestra's five-day Symphony Under the Sky Festival at Hawrelak Park.

Post-summer events include the Canadian Finals Rodeo (*see color ad p. 69*) in mid-November and First Night Festival on New Year's Eve.

The Edmonton Vicinity

FORT SASKATCHEWAN (D-6)

pop. 12,400

FORT SASKATCHEWAN MUSEUM AND HISTORIC SITE, downtown at 10104 101st St., includes an early 20th-century pioneer house, schoolhouse, church and smithy. Displays include a vintage firetruck, antique automobiles, carriages and farm equipment. A 1909 courthouse contains clothing and documents pertaining to area history, exhibits about the North West Mounted Police, and the original courtroom. Allow 1 hour minimum. Daily 10-6, July-Aug.; daily 11-3, May-June and Sept. 1-Dec. 24; Mon.-Fri. 11-3, rest of year.

Closed holidays and Dec. 26-31. Admission $2, under 10 free. Phone (780) 998-1750.

ST. ALBERT (D-6) pop. 46,900

Said to be Alberta's oldest nonfortified community, St. Albert is the site of the first cathedral west of Winnipeg, Manitoba. Its builder—Father Albert Lacombe—devoted 62 years to acting as a peacemaker between the Crees and the Blackfoot, a negotiator between the Blood Indians and the Canadian Pacific Railway, and was a savior in the smallpox epidemic of 1870. The city is named in his honor.

Events include Northern Alberta International Children's Festival and Kinsmen Rainmaker Rodeo, both in late May.

St. Albert Economic Development and Tourism: 71 St. Albert Rd., St. Albert, AB, Canada T8N 6L5; phone (780) 459-1724.

FATHER LACOMBE CHAPEL, just w. of Hwy. 2 at 7 St. Vital Ave., was built under Lacombe's direction in 1861. The log chapel is typical of western Canada's early churches. Guided tours explain the importance of Lacombe to the French/Métis community and the priest's role as spiritual leader, peacemaker and negotiator in the 1860s. Tours are conducted in both English and French. Allow 30 minutes minimum. Tours upon request daily 10-6, May 15-Labour Day. Admission $2; over 64 and ages 7-17, $1.50; family rate $5. Phone (780) 459-7663.

MUSÉE HERITAGE MUSEUM, w. of Hwy. 2 at 5 St. Anne St. in St. Albert Place, presents exhibits dedicated to the heritage of St. Albert. Changing displays are featured. Allow 1 hour minimum. Mon.-Sat. 10-5, Sun. noon-4; closed legal holidays. Donations. Phone (780) 459-1528.

VITAL GRANDIN CENTRE, just w. of Hwy. 2 at 5 St. Vital Ave., is the former residence of Alberta's first Catholic bishop. Completed in 1887, the structure still houses several Oblate priests; a museum wing on the main floor contains the restored living quarters and private chapel of Bishop Vital Grandin. Allow 30 minutes minimum. Guided tours in English and French are given daily upon request 10-6, May 15-Labour Day; by appointment rest of year. Free. Phone (780) 459-2116.

STONY PLAIN (E-6) pop. 8,300

Plentiful water and abundant fish and game attracted the first settlers to the region in 1881. By 1892 the name of the community itself was changed from Dogrump Creek or Dog Creek to Stony Plain. The Stony Plain of today is an agricultural community.

Murals depicting historical remembrances, events and pioneers prominent in the early settlement of Stony Plain have been painted by local artists on 18 buildings in town. Memories of an early 1900s Christmas from a child's point of view are the basis for one mural, while another shows the multiculturalism of the area's early residents. The Heritage Walk Murals can be seen on a walking tour.

Stony Plain & District Chamber of Commerce: Rotary Park, 4815-44 Ave., P.O. Box 2300, Stony Plain, AB, Canada T7Z 1X7; phone (780) 963-4545.

MULTICULTURAL HERITAGE CENTRE AND OPPERTSHAUSER HOUSE, 5411 51 St., are restored buildings featuring local history and art exhibits, programs and events. The center, built as the area's first high school in 1925, offers regional archives as well as a living-history museum and an art gallery. The 1910 Oppertshauser House is home to museum exhibits. Food is available. Allow 30 minutes minimum. Mon.-Sat. 10-4, Sun. 10-6; closed Dec. 24-Jan. 3. Donations. Phone (780) 963-2777.

WINERIES

• **Andrew Wolf Wine Cellars,** 2 km (1.2 mi.) e. on Hwy. 16. Mon.-Sat. 10-6; closed holidays. Phone (780) 963-7717.

This ends listings for the Edmonton Vicinity. The following page resumes the alphabetical listings of cities in Alberta.

ELK ISLAND NATIONAL PARK (D-7)

Elevations in the park range from 709 metres (2,326 ft.) at Goose Lake to 754 metres (2,475 ft.) at Lake Tawayik. Refer to CAA/AAA maps for additional elevation information.

About 45 kilometres (28 mi.) east of Edmonton, Elk Island National Park is reached by Hwy. 15 from the north and Hwy. 16 from the south. The park is small—only 195 square kilometres (75 sq. mi.)—but its lakes, ponds, forests and meadows provide a haven for many species of animals and plants.

The park occupies the Beaver Hills region, which first was settled by Sarcee and Plains Cree Indians. They trapped beavers and hunted bison and elk, as did the European fur traders who arrived between the late 18th and the mid-19th centuries. Soon the animals became nearly extinct, and the natives were forced to seek sustenance elsewhere.

In 1906 five local men asked that the government establish a wildlife refuge to preserve the remaining elk. A year later the refuge contained 400 bison, while another preserve near Wainwright was being established. Most of these animals later were transferred, but about 50 uncatchables stayed and produced the plains bison herd of more than 600 that remains today north of Hwy. 16. A herd of several hundred wood bison, a threatened subspecies, is kept separate from this herd south of Hwy. 16.

As the wildlife populations grew, so did the park's area; more land was added to the refuge in 1922, 1947, 1957 and 1978. Many small lakes dot the landscape, but the major bodies are Tawayik and Astotin, the latter being the larger. The lakes and marshes support the more than 230 bird species, including ducks, gulls, terns, grebes and loons.

Marsh marigolds and several types of lilies are among several plants rarely seen outside the park. Song birds occupy the many poplar, spruce and birch forests, but few fish inhabit the waters due to low oxygen levels. The herd of elk for which the park was established flourish nicely among the meadows and forests, as do reintroduced colonies of beavers. Deer, minks, moose and coyotes also roam the park.

General Information and Activities

The park is open daily all year. Most recreation facilities center on Astotin Lake, which offers boating (no motors), wildlife observations, picnic facilities, a nine-hole golf course and camping and walking trails. A campground is on the east side of the lake; interpretive talks, events and displays explain the park's history and features.

A visitor information center is .8 kilometres (.5 mi.) north of Hwy. 16 before the park's south gate entrance. Staff members and displays describe Elk Island and other national parks. The center is open Mon.-Fri. 10:30-6, Sat.-Sun. 9-8. Phone (780) 922-5790.

Camping and picnicking are popular in summer. The park's approximately 100 kilometres (60 mi.) of trails are popular with hikers and cross-country skiers. Hunting and fishing are prohibited. *See Recreation Chart and the AAA/CAA Western Canada and Alaska CampBook.*

ADMISSION to the park is $4; over 64, $3; ages 6-16, $2. Admission for two to seven persons in a private vehicle is $8; over 64, $6. Camping fee $5-$14.

PETS must be kept on a leash at all times. Dogs are discouraged from using trails to prevent potential conflicts with free-ranging bison.

ADDRESS inquiries for additional information to the Superintendent, Elk Island National Park, Site 4, RR 1, Fort Saskatchewan, AB, Canada T8L 2N7; phone (780) 992-2950.

ELKWATER (I-9) pop. 100

Before Europeans came to the Elkwater region, Assiniboine, Blackfoot, Cree and Sioux shared the land with grizzly bears, wolves, bison and a large number of elk. After settlers and trappers arrived, the wolves and elk were hunted to extinction; the elk population since has been reintroduced. An 1873 massacre of Assiniboine Indians by wolf hunters and whiskey traders prompted the formation of the North West Mounted Police and the establishment of Fort Walsh.

CYPRESS HILLS PROVINCIAL PARK, on Hwy. 41 70 km (43 mi.) n. of the U.S. border, straddles the boundary between Alberta and Saskatchewan. Dating back 40 million years, fossils of early mammals have been found in the hills. An aboriginal culture flourished in the area more than 7,000 years ago. Ruminants, beavers, coyotes and varied birds and plants now live in the park. Park interpreters schedule programs year-round. Camping is permitted. The visitor center offers information, displays and audiovisual presentations.

Park open daily 24 hours. Visitor center open daily 10-6, Victoria day weekend-June 30; 9-9, July 1-Labour Day. Free. Phone (403) 893-3833 or 893-3782, or (403) 893-3782 for camp reservations, May 1-Labour Day. *See Recreation Chart and Medicine Hat in the AAA/CAA Western Canada and Alaska CampBook.*

FORT MACLEOD (I-6)
pop. 3,000, elev. 955 m/3,133'

At the end of their 1,126-kilometre (700-mi.) march through the prairie wilderness to rid western Canada of whiskey traders, in 1874 the North

West Mounted Police, now the Royal Canadian Mounted Police, chose the site of what is now Fort Macleod as their first headquarters.

A commanding view of the countryside and the natural protection afforded by the Oldman River made Fort Macleod an important outpost; a cairn at 2nd Avenue and 25th Street commemorates its founding. Guided walking tours, ranging from 20 minutes to 2 hours, of the historic district can be arranged in advance during the summer by contacting the Main Street Office; phone (403) 553-2500.

The highland physical geography that made the Fort Macleod outpost successful also helped the Plains Indians survive long before the first traders appeared in the area. In order to kill the buffalo for food, the Plains hunters stampeded them over the high cliffs.

Fort Macleod & District Chamber of Commerce: 7th Ave., P.O. Box 178, Fort Macleod, AB, Canada T0L 0Z0; phone (403) 553-4955 Victoria day weekend-Labour Day.

[SAVE] **FORT MACLEOD MUSEUM,** 25th St. and 3rd Ave., is a representation of the original Fort Macleod. Exhibits set among historic structures focus on pioneer settlers, southern Alberta Indians and the history of the fort and its mounted police. Of particular interest are the Mounted Patrol Musical Rides, 8 persons in replicas of 1878 RCMP uniforms whose mounts perform precision movements to music. Picnic facilities are available.

Allow 1 hour minimum. Daily 9-8, July 1-Labour Day; 9-5, rest of year. Mounted Patrol Musical Rides are given daily at 10, 11:30, 2 and 3:30, July-Aug. Admission $4.50; over 64, $4; ages 12-17, $2.50; ages 6-11, $1.50. Phone (403) 553-4703.

★ **HEAD-SMASHED-IN BUFFALO JUMP INTERPRETIVE CENTRE,** 18 km (11 mi.) n.w. on Hwy. 785, documents the buffalo-hunting culture of the Plains Indians. For more than 10,000 years the Plains Indians stampeded herds of buffalo over sandstone cliffs to their deaths. The hunters then butchered and processed the kill at their campsite below the cliffs. Head-Smashed-In is one of the oldest and best-preserved of these buffalo jump sites. A 12-minute film re-enacts these hunts.

The site's graphic name is derived from a young brave who stood under a ledge of the cliff to watch the buffalo as they fell past him. As the number of carcasses multiplied, his skull was crushed as he became trapped between the animals and the cliff.

Built into that cliff today is a seven-story interpretive center presenting displays about the ecology, history and culture of the Plains Indians. Exhibits focus on the geographical and climatic factors affecting these tribes as well as their lifestyle and history. A re-created archeological dig

provides additional insights into this way of life. The entire hunting site is preserved; short trails lead to the main areas. Food is available.

Allow 2 hours minimum. Daily 9-7, May 15-Labour Day; 9-5, rest of year. Closed Jan. 1, Easter and Dec. 25. Admission $6.50; over 64, $5.50; ages 7-17, $3; family rate $15. MC, VI. Phone (403) 553-2731.

FORT McMURRAY (A-8)

At the confluence of the Clearwater and Athabasca rivers in the fur country of northern Alberta, Fort McMurray began as the home of the Woodland Cree and Chipewyan Indians. In 1778 explorers and fur traders led by Peter Pond opened the vast fur trade region of the Mackenzie River basin. In 1870 Henry John Moberly built a post and named it Fort McMurray after his chief factor, William McMurray of Hudson's Bay Co.

Soon after a steamboat terminus was established near Fort McMurray in 1884, the region's vast resources began to attract attention. Oil sands containing some 500 billion barrels of oil were found around Lake Athabasca. The first commercially successful extractions, however, did not take place until the late 1960s. Since then Fort McMurray has boomed, serving oil recovery plants that now extract from the sands about 350,000 barrels of synthetic crude oil per day.

The city is the southern terminus of the vast water transportation system that navigates Great Slave Lake and the Mackenzie River en route to the Arctic. Logging and tourism further bolster the economy. Fort McMurray is a service center for surrounding areas and the Oil Sands plants.

Re-creating the city's past is Heritage Park, on the banks of the Hangingstone River just off King Street on Tolen Drive. A museum highlights the history of boat building, aviation, river travel, lumbering, fishing, salt production and fur trading. Phone (780) 791-7575.

Fort McMurray Visitors Bureau: 400 Sakitawaw Tr., Fort McMurray, AB, Canada T9H 4Z3; phone (780) 791-4336 or (800) 565-3947.

★ **FORT McMURRAY OIL SANDS DISCOVERY CENTRE,** jct. Hwy. 63 and MacKenzie Blvd., relates the science and history of the Athabasca Oil Sands, one of the world's largest single oil deposits. Oil sands mining and technology is explained through colorful exhibits, interpretive presentations and a videotape, "Quest for Energy." Outside in the Industrial Garden are a seven-story bucket-wheel excavator and other pieces of massive mining equipment.

From the vantage point of Oil Sands Viewpoint, 45 kilometres (30 mi.) north of Fort McMurray, visitors can view the vast production facilities of Syncrude Canada Ltd., including draglines the length of a football field and miles of conveyor belts.

Allow 1 hour, 30 minutes minimum for the center. Daily 10-6, May 15-Labour Day; 10-4, rest of year. Bus tours of the plants last 3.5 hours and are given daily July-Aug.; Sat.-Sun. rest of year. Closed Jan. 1, Good Friday and Dec. 25. Admission $3; over 64, $2; ages 7-17, $1.50; family rate $8. Bus tour $12. Reservations are required for tours. VI. Phone (780) 743-7167, or 791-4336 or (800) 565-3947 for tour reservations.

FORT SASKATCHEWAN—

see Edmonton p. 71.

GIROUXVILLE (B-3) pop. 300

GIROUXVILLE MUSEUM, on Main St. (Hwy. 49), uses more than 5,000 artifacts to tell the story of the indigenous people, devout missionaries and rugged pioneers who lived and settled here. Nature admirers will enjoy the display of more than 200 mounted birds and fur-bearing animals. The Transportation Means of Yesterday includes sleighs, an antique snowmobile and a 1927 Chevrolet truck.

This quaint museum also displays the works of local artists Leon Tremblay and Alfred Gaboury. Allow 1 hour minimum. Mon.-Fri. 10-5, May 1-Sept. 15; by appointment rest of year. Admission $3; ages 6-17, $1.50. Phone (780) 323-4252.

GRANDE PRAIRIE (C-2)
pop. 31,100

Surrounded by a colorful checkerboard of rich farmland along the gateway to the Alaska Highway, Grande Prairie serves as the business and transportation center of Alberta's Peace River country.

Glimpses into the Peace River region's past are evident in the Kleskun Hills, just east via Hwy. 43. Erosion of the glacial drift of clay, sand, gravel and boulders has uncovered dinosaur tracks and aquatic fossils embedded in a prehistoric river delta formed more than 70 million years ago.

Local culture and artistry are displayed at Prairie Gallery, 10209 99th St.; phone (780) 532-8111. Muskoseepi Park has hiking and bicycling trails, picnicking areas and recreation facilities. Other area recreational pursuits include swimming, boating, birdwatching and fishing. A pioneer-oriented event is the Grande Prairie Stompede, the first weekend in June.

Grande Prairie Chamber of Commerce: 10011 103 Ave., Grande Prairie, AB, Canada T8V 1B9; phone (780) 532-5340.

Shopping areas: Prairie Mall, 11801 100th St., features Sears, Shopper's and Zeller's.

GRANDE PRAIRIE MUSEUM, 102nd St. and 102nd Ave. in Muskoseepi Park, is a 10-building village featuring a one-room schoolhouse, country store, church and a log homesteader's cabin.

The main exhibit building houses artifacts depicting the life of Peace River area pioneers 1908-16. The gallery also features natural history items, dinosaur bones and aboriginal artifacts. Daily 10-6, May-Sept.; 10-4, rest of year. Admission $2; ages 6-12, $1. Phone (780) 532-5482.

HANNA (G-7) pop. 3,000

A 1912 roundhouse, a throwback to the town's beginning as a Canadian National Railway terminal, still graces Hanna's skyline.

HANNA PIONEER MUSEUM, at Pioneer Tr. and 4th Ave. E., re-creates the past through restored 19th-century buildings. Arranged in a pioneer village setting, the buildings include a general store, school, four-room hospital, church, power windmill, Canadian National Railway Station, telephone office, ranch house and smithy, and the Hanna archives. Among displays are antique automobiles and farm machinery. Guided 2.5-hour tours around the village and inside the buildings are offered. Allow 1 hour, 30 minutes minimum. Daily 10-5, May 24-Labour Day; by appointment rest of year. Last tour begins at 4:30. Admission $3, under 12 free with adult. Phone (403) 854-4244.

HIGH RIVER (H-6) pop. 7,400

A ranching and farming town, High River counts among its events Little Britches Rodeo and Parade, on Victoria Day weekend in late May; and the North American Chuckwagon Championship and the Guy Weadick Memorial Rodeo, both held in June.

High River Chamber of Commerce: 406 1st St., P.O. Box 5244, High River, AB, Canada T1V 1M4; phone (403) 652-3336.

HIGH RIVER HISTORICAL MURALS are viewed via guided or self-guiding tours that begin at Museum of the Highwood (*see attraction listing*). Area history unfolds on 18 colorful paintings that decorate exteriors of many commercial buildings. The murals illustrate varied subjects, ranging from farming, chuckwagons and polo to famous High Riverites W.O. Mitchell and former Prime Minister Joe Clark. Viewable daily. Guided tours can be booked through the chamber of commerce from May through August. Brochures of a self-guiding tour are available year-round. Free. Phone (403) 652-3336.

MUSEUM OF THE HIGHWOOD, jct. 4th Ave. and 1st St. S.W. at 129 3rd Ave. S.W., is in a 1911 sandstone building once used as a train station. Rotating exhibits detail local history, primarily from the mid-19th century to the present. Included is a post World War II train exhibit. The museum takes its name from the nearby Highwood River. Food is available. Allow 30 minutes minimum. Mon.-Sat. 10-5, Sun. 1-5, Victoria Day-Labour Day; Tues.-Sun. noon-4, rest of year. Closed Jan. 1 and Dec. 25. Admission $2.50; over 64 and ages 13-19, $2. Phone (403) 652-7156.

★ JASPER NATIONAL PARK (E-2,3)

Elevations in the park range from 1,000 metres (3,300 ft.) in the town of Jasper to 3,747 metres (12,293 ft.) at Mount Columbia. Refer to CAA/AAA maps for additional elevation information.

Jasper National Park, Banff National Park's northern neighbor, is reached from the east and west via the Yellowhead Highway (Hwy. 16) and from the south by the Icefields Parkway (Hwy. 93). Established in 1907, the park was named after Jasper Hawes, who was in charge of a Hudson's Bay Co. trading post in the early 1800s.

Less developed and less crowded than Banff National Park, its 10,878 square kilometres (4,200 sq. mi.) of majestic mountains, valleys and lakes offer equally spectacular views of the Rocky Mountain wilderness. The variety and beauty of its numerous lakes, of which Maligne Lake is the largest, is perhaps the area's chief attraction.

Nature's scenic sculpting process at work can be seen at Athabasca Falls and Sunwapta Falls, both just west of Icefields Parkway south of Jasper. To the east off Hwy. 16 is Miette Hot Springs, where mineral pools are open for bathing Victoria Day weekend through the second Monday in October, weather permitting. Northeast of Jasper, 51-metre-deep (170-ft.) Maligne Canyon surrounds the river that carved it over the years.

Park wildlife is as diverse as its peaks and valleys. Mountain goats and bighorn sheep inhabit the crags and highlands, although the sheep frequently wander down within good viewing distance.

The lower slopes and meadows are home to deer, elk, moose and bears, which never should be fed or approached. More elusive are coyotes, wolves, lynxes and other predators that usually avoid humans. Lodgepole pines, spruces, poplars and firs forest the area, and eagles, jays, magpies and other birds dot the skies.

Note: Since hunting is illegal, some animals may have lost their fear of human activity; be alert for animals on the highways both day and night, and never feed them.

General Information and Activities

The park is open all year, though weather conditions in winter make some portions inaccessible except to cross-country skiers. Some business concessions operate only from May to September or October. Park headquarters is in the townsite of Jasper. Many hiking trails, including the 11.2-kilometre (7-mi.) trip to Valley of Five Lakes and the loop to Lac Beauvert, depart from Old Fort Point, 1.6 kilometres (1 mi.) east of Jasper on Hwy. 93.

Hikers and skiers staying overnight in the back country must have a valid back-country use permit. These permits are available at the Jasper townsite information center, at Icefield Centre from early June to mid-October and at the Sunwapta (Poboktan) warden station during the winter. Campgrounds are open varying durations: Whistler early May through the second Mon. in October; Snaring River mid-May through the last Saturday in September; Wapiti mid-June through mid-Sept.; Wabasso late June through Labour Day. Limited camping facilities are available in winter.

There are many ways to explore the park's features, either alone or with a guide. One- or multiple-day bus tours to attractions within the park depart from Jasper. Several stables in the Jasper area offer 1-hour and half- and full-day trail rides from mid-May to mid-September and sleigh rides in winter.

Winter sports include curling, skating, tobogganing, ice climbing and hockey. Cross-country skiing tours operate out of Jasper. Downhill skiing is available at Marmot Basin; cross-country trails also traverse the Maligne and Pyramid lake areas. Evening fireside gatherings and slide talks are held in campground theaters; the park's interpretive program features special winter activities.

Fishing permits can be obtained at information centers, campgrounds and local sport fishing shops (see Recreation in the Introduction p. 32). Gas-powered boats are permitted only on Pyramid Lake; boats with electric motors are allowed on other lakes unless signs indicate otherwise. See Recreation Chart and the AAA/CAA Western Canada and Alaska CampBook.

ADMISSION to the park for 1 day is $10 per private vehicle; over 65, $8 per private vehicle; annual pass, $70. MC, VI.

PETS are allowed in the park but must be leashed, crated or physically restrained at all times.

ADDRESS inquiries to the Superintendent, Jasper National Park, P.O. Box 10, Jasper, AB, Canada T0E 1E0; phone (780) 852-6161. For other area information contact Jasper Park Chamber of Commerce, P.O. Box 98, Jasper, AB, Canada T0E 1E0; phone (780) 852-3858.

CCINC. AUTO TAPE TOURS provide hour-long highlights of the park's history, geology and biology with narration, music and sound effects. The tapes, which come with a map, can be purchased at Dianne's Gifts at Chateau Jasper, 98 Geikie St., Jasper Tree House at Lobstick Hotel, 96 Geikie St. or by contacting CCInc., P.O. Box 227, Allendale, NJ 07401. Two tapes (full trip) $27.71, when purchased locally; $25.90 plus $4

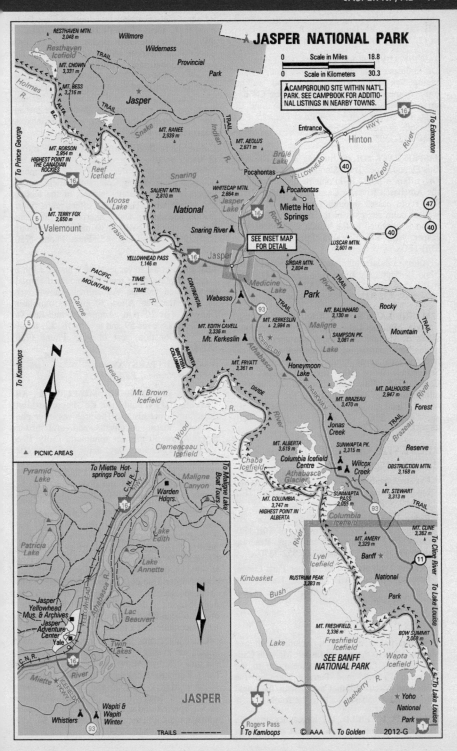

JASPER NATIONAL PARK

Scale in Miles   0 — 18.8
Scale in Kilometers   0 — 30.3

△ CAMPGROUND SITE WITHIN NAT'L. PARK. SEE CAMPBOOK FOR ADDITIONAL LISTINGS IN NEARBY TOWNS.

shipping and handling (U.S. currency) by mail. AE, DS, MC, VI. Phone (780) 852-3810 locally, or (202) 236-1666 to order by mail.

JASPER ADVENTURE CENTRE, on Connaught Dr. in Jasper National Park, offers guided sightseeing van tours, wildlife tours and walking tours. Some tours include a 57 kilometre (34 mi.) drive to Miette Hot Springs. Daily 8-8, June 15-Sept. 15; 8-6, rest of year. Closed Dec. 25. Fare $35-$60; ages 6-15, $17.50-$30. MC, VI. Phone (780) 852-5595.

JASPER RAFT TOURS, meeting in the Brewster Bus Depot/Jasper Train Station at 607 Connaught Dr., offers 3-hour, 14-kilometre (9-mi.) trips on the Athabasca River, a Canadian Heritage River. The route passes through short, easy rapids as well as calm stretches of the river. Bus transportation is provided to the launch site and back to Jasper. Write P.O. Box 398, Jasper, AB, Canada T0E 1E0.

Allow 3 hours minimum. Trips depart daily, May 15-Sept. 30; times vary. Fare $41; ages 6-15, $16.05. AE, MC, VI. Phone (780) 852-2665, 852-3332 or (888) 553-5628.

MALIGNE LAKE BOAT TOURS, 48 km (30 mi.) s.e. via Maligne Lake Rd., affords exceptional views of Maligne Narrows. White-water rafting, hiking and trout-fishing trips as well as boat, canoe and sea kayak rentals are available June-September. Write P.O. Box 280, Jasper, AB, Canada T0E 1E0. Allow 1 hour, 30 minutes minimum. Trips depart daily on the hour 10-5, May 1-Thanksgiving. Fare $32; over 64, $27.50; ages 6-12, $16. AE, MC, VI. Phone (780) 852-3370.

RECREATIONAL ACTIVITIES
Horseback Riding

- **Pyramid Stables**, 4 km (2.5 mi) n on Pyramid Lake Rd., Box 1200, Jasper, AB T0E 1E0. Daily 9-5. Phone (780) 852-3562.

- **Ridge Line Riders**, 626 Connaught Dr., c/o Maligne Tours, Box 280, Jasper, AB T0E 1E0. Daily 10-2, mid-June to mid-Sept. Reservations are required. Phone (780) 852-3370.

- **Skyline Trail Rides Ltd.**, Jasper Park Lodge, Box 207, Jasper, AB T0E 1E0. Daily 9:30-6:30, mid-Apr. to mid-Oct. Phone (780) 852-3301, ext. 6189.

Points of Interest

Natural points of interest include Edith and Annette lakes to the east of Jasper; Maligne Canyon, Maligne Lake and Medicine Lake to the northeast; and Pyramid and Patricia lakes to the north; and Mount Edith Cavell, with its Angel Glacier, and Athabasca Falls to the south.

COLUMBIA ICEFIELD, the largest ice mass in the Rocky Mountains, is a remnant of the great ice sheet that once blanketed most of Canada. Its main bulk, about 16 by 24 kilometres (10 by 15 mi.), straddles the Great Divide, part of the British Columbia border and portions of Banff and Jasper national parks. The ice covers about 325 square kilometres (130 sq. mi.) to an estimated depth of 350 metres (1,148 ft.). Three glaciers—Stutfield, Athabasca and Dome—can be seen from Icefields Parkway. The glaciers are just inside the Jasper National Park boundary next to Banff National Park.

Columbia Icefield Centre, 108 km (67 mi.) s. of Jasper on Hwy. 93N, overlooks Athabasca and Dome glaciers and offers views of major mountain peaks surrounding Columbia Icefield. An interpretive center contains models of the icefield and an ice cave. The center offers maps, information and details about interpretive programs. Food is available. Allow 30 minutes minimum. Daily 9-6, May 1-Oct. 15. Free. Phone (780) 852-6550.

THE DEN, in the lower level of Whistler's Inn in Jasper, displays more than 150 mounted animals in simulated habitats. All animals shown were native to the area. Allow 30 minutes minimum. Daily 9 a.m.-10 p.m. Admission mid-June to mid-Sept. $3; over 59 and ages 6-16, $2; family rate $6. Donations rest of year. Phone (780) 852-3361.

★ **ICEFIELDS PARKWAY—**
see Banff National Park p. 44.

JASPER YELLOWHEAD MUSEUM & ARCHIVES, 400 Pyramid Lake Rd., houses exhibits depicting Jasper history. The archives offer photographs, maps, documents and oral history tapes. Allow 30 minutes minimum. Daily 10-9, Victoria Day-Labour Day; daily 10-5, day after Labour Day-second Mon. in Oct.; Thurs.-Sun. 10-5, rest of year. Closed Jan. 1 and Dec. 25-26. Admission $3; over 64 and students with ID $2; family rate $8. Phone (780) 852-3013.

MIETTE HOTSPRINGS POOL is 61 km (37 mi.) n.e. of Jasper on Miette Rd., then 17 km (11 mi.) e. from the jct. with Hwy. 16. Two man-made pools are fed primarily by Sulphur Hot Spring. Comfortable water temperatures are maintained to 39 C (103 F) by the addition of artificially cooled water. One pool is about 1.5 metres (5 ft.) deep; the second pool averages .5 metres (2 ft.) deep. Staying in the pool for longer than 20 minutes at a time can cause dizziness because of water temperature and altitude.

Changing rooms and bathing suit and towel rentals are available. Hiking trails and picnic areas are nearby. Allow 30 minutes minimum. Daily 8:30 a.m.-10:30 p.m., June 26-Labour Day; 10:30-9, May 15-June 25 and day after Labour Day-second Mon. in Oct. Summer admission $5.50; over 64 and ages 3-17, $4.50. Off-season admission $4.50; over 64 and ages 3-17, $4. MC, VI. Phone (780) 866-3939. See color ad p. 40.

SNOCOACH TOURS ON THE ATHABASCA GLA-CIER, 125 km (78 mi.) n. of Lake Louise on Hwy. 93N or 108 km (67 mi.) s. of Jasper on Hwy. 93N, provides the opportunity to see and walk on a glaciated ice field formed by snow falling as long ago as 400 years. The bus driver provides anecdotes and information during this 80-minute excursion. Allow 1 hour, 30 minutes minimum. Tours depart daily from Columbia Ice-field Centre every 15 minutes (weather permitting) 9-5, May-Sept.; 10-5, Oct. 1-15. Fare $24.95; ages 6-15, $10; under 6 in lap free. MC, VI. Phone (877) 423-7433.

KANANASKIS COUNTRY (H-4)

Kananaskis Country is a four-season, multiuse recreation area that encompasses more than 4,000 square kilometres (1,544 sq. mi.) of land. West of Calgary, the area contains Bow Valley, Elbow-Sheep Wildland and Peter Lougheed provincial parks; Bragg Creek Provincial Park is outside Kananaskis Country boundaries but is managed by Kananaskis Country *(see Recreation Chart).*

The resort area offers year-round recreational activities, including hiking, horseback riding, snowmobiling and downhill and cross-country skiing. The area begins just south of Hwy. 1 and extends south on Hwy. 40 to the intersection of Hwys. 532 and 940. Animals, including elk, deer, bighorn sheep, lynxes, moose, mountain goats, bears and porcupines, are best observed in the parks, where they are protected.

Visitor information centers throughout Kananaskis Country offer brochures, displays and information. Campground amphitheaters offer interpretive presentations. The area is open daily. Hwy. 40 from Peter Lougheed Provincial Park to Hwy. 541 is closed from December 1 to June 15.

Kananaskis Country General Inquiries: Suite 201, Provincial Building, 800 Railway Ave., Canmore, AB, Canada T1W 1P1; phone (403) 678-5508 or 673-3985.

PASSING OF THE LEGENDS MUSEUM is at Rafter 6 Ranch, 2 km (1.2 mi.) s. of Hwy. 1 overpass after the Seebe exit. Exhibits include Indian, Northwest Mounted Police and pioneer memorabilia; antique carriages, including a Budweiser carriage; and artworks. Movies and television commercials have been filmed on the property.

Adventure programs, including trail riding, white-water rafting and hiking tours, can be organized at the museum. Daily 9-5, Victoria day-Labour Day. Donations. Phone (403) 673-3622 or 264-1251.

RECREATIONAL ACTIVITIES
White-water Rafting
- **Mirage Adventure Tours Ltd.,** Kananaskis Resort Village, Box 233, Kananaskis Village,

AB, Canada T0L 2H0. Other activities are offered. Trips depart daily at 9:45 and 1:15, May-Sept. Phone (403) 591-7773 or (888) 312-7238.

LAC LA BICHE (C-7) pop. 2,600

South of town, Portage La Biche was discovered in 1798 by renowned geographer and explorer David Thompson of the North West Co. This area encompasses the land between the Churchill and Athabasca-Mackenzie basins. Soon after its discovery, the portage became a key link in Canada's main fur trade routes and a passageway to the Pacific Ocean.

The 1853 founding of Lac La Biche Mission played a vital role in the settlement of the area, which quickly developed into a major transportation center of the north.

Lakeland Provincial Park provides such recreational opportunities as camping, canoeing, cross-country skiing, biking, birdwatching, nature photography, fishing and swimming. Sir Winston Churchill Provincial Park, 10 km (6 mi.) n.e. on Hwy. 881, is the largest of 12 islands in Lac La Biche. In 1920 Lac La Biche and its islands were designated as a migratory bird sanctuary; today visitors can view more than 200 species. *See Recreation Chart and the AAA/CAA Western Canada and Alaska CampBook.*

LAKE LOUISE—

see Banff National Park p. 40.

LETHBRIDGE (I-6)
pop. 63,100, elev. 930 m/3,051′

Founded in the 1870s, abundant agricultural resources helped Lethbridge to become one of Alberta's major meatpacking and grain distribution centers. The region reportedly receives more hours of sunshine annually than any other spot in Canada and therefore requires irrigation to counterbalance the semiarid climate; more than 400,000 hectares (988,000 acres) produce crops of grain and sugar beets. Livestock, oil and gas also support the economic base.

Numerous parks and green spaces complement the city's commercial enterprises. Two popular areas are Lethbridge Nature Preserve in Indian Battle Park at 3rd Avenue South and Scenic Drive, and Henderson Lake Park at South Parkside Drive and Mayor Magrath. Henderson Lake Park has a golf course, a 60-acre lake with boat rentals, tennis courts, a picnic area and a campground. Rose and Japanese gardens and a bowling green are in Henderson Lake Park.

Lethbridge holds Whoop-Up Days in July and International Airshow in mid-August.

Lethbridge Chamber of Commerce: 529 6th St. S., Lethbridge, AB, Canada T1J 2E1; phone (403) 327-1586. *See color ad.*

Shopping areas: Park Place Mall, 1st Ave. S. on Scenic Drive, has more than 100 stores and features Eaton's and Sears. Hudson's Bay Co. anchors Lethbridge Centre, off Hwy. 3 at 200 4th Ave. S.

BREWERY GARDENS is just w. off 1st Ave. S. at Brewery Hill on Scenic Dr. The gardens present eight floral displays May through the first frost, as well as displays on Easter, Halloween, Remembrance Day and Christmas. The gardens are not walk-through gardens, but are a 1 hectare (2.5 acre) plot on the side of a coulee. Visitors view them across the coulee. Daily dawn-dusk. Free. Phone (403) 320-4097.

INDIAN BATTLE PARK, 1 km (.6 mi.) w. of the jct. of Scenic Dr. and 3rd Ave. S. under the High Level Bridge, is the site of the last intertribal battle in North America, between the Cree and Blackfoot Indians. Within the park are attractions, self-guiding trails and picnic and playground facilities. Daily 7 a.m.-10:30 p.m., May-Sept.; 7 a.m.-8:30 p.m., rest of year. Free.

Coal Banks Interpretive Sites are scattered throughout the city. These five informational signs explain the origin of coal mining in the area and its significance to Lethbridge's development. Three of the signs are in or near the park at Helen Schuler Coulee Centre (*see attraction listing p. 81*), by the Elks Recreation Centre and

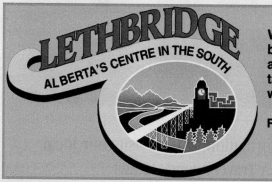

between the Lodge and the Sir Alexander Galt Museum *(see attraction listing p. 81)*. The other two are at Brewery Gardens *(see attraction listing p. 80)*, and on Hwy. 2 near Kipp. Daily 24 hours. For more information phone the museum at (403) 320-3898.

Fort Whoop-Up, on the river in Indian Battle Park, is a replica of a fort built in 1869 by American traders in Canadian territory. Trade in guns and illegal alcohol, in addition to reports of an American flag flying in Canada, led to both the formation of the North West Mounted Police and their march west in 1874. An interpretive center offers videotaped presentations, exhibits and dioramas as well as replicas of period shops and housing. Guided tours are available upon request. Pony rides are available in the summer. A wagon offers 10- and 35-minute rides through the park all year.

Allow 30 minutes minimum. Mon.-Sat. 10-6, Sun. noon-5, May-Sept.; Tues.-Fri. 10-4, Sun. 1-4, rest of year. Closed major holidays. Admission $2.50, over 54 and students with ID $1.50, family rate $6. Wagon ride $5; over 54 and age 4 through college, $4. Ten-minute wagon ride $2. Pony ride $2. Phone (403) 329-0444.

Helen Schuler Coulee Centre and Nature Reserve provides a sanctuary for plants and animals. Desertlike flora and fauna are found on the coulee slopes and in cottonwood forests along the Oldman River. The 79-hectare (196-acre) reserve boasts such residents as the great horned owl, porcupines and white-tailed deer. Most of the park is accessible via three self-guiding trails which take about 30 minutes each to walk; pets, bicycles, inline skates and skateboards are not permitted on the trails. The center houses exhibits which change seasonally; interpretive programs also are offered.

Allow 30 minutes minimum. Reserve open daily 7 a.m.-11 p.m. Center open Sun.-Thurs. 10-8, Fri.-Sat. 10-6, June 1-Labour Day; Tues.-Sun. 1-4, rest of year. Closed Dec. 25. Free. Phone (403) 320-3064.

The High Level Bridge, spanning the Oldman River, is one of the highest and longest steel viaduct railroad bridges in the world. Daily 24 hours. Free.

★ **NIKKA YUKO JAPANESE GARDEN,** 7th Ave. and Mayor Magrath Dr. in Henderson Park, is one of the most authentic of its kind in North America. Five basic types of traditional Japanese gardens are incorporated into the overall design. A pavilion, bridges, a bell tower imported from Japan and cypress wood from Taiwan are featured; paths punctuated by footbridges over ponds and streams weave through the gardens.

Hostesses in traditional kimonos conduct half-hour tours as needed. Allow 30 minutes minimum. Daily 9-9, June 13-Aug. 29; daily 9-5, June 1-12 and Aug. 30-Sept. 6; Thurs.-Sun. noon-5, May 9-31 and Sept. 7-Oct. 17. Admis-

sion $4; over 54, $3; ages 6-17, $2. Phone (403) 328-3511.

ST. MARY'S RIVER DAM, 78 km (47 mi.) s., is one of the largest earth-filled dams in Canada. Water sports and a campground are available. **Note:** At press time the campground was only partially open; phone to determine availability. Phone (403) 381-5745.

SIR ALEXANDER GALT MUSEUM AND ARCHIVES, at the w. end of 5th Ave. S., is named after the founder of North Western Coal and Navigation Co. Exhibits deal primarily with the growth of Lethbridge following the rise and fall of the coal industry in the 1870s and the development of dry farming and variation techniques suited to the area's semiarid climate. Allow 30 minutes minimum. Daily 10-5; closed winter holidays. Free. Phone (403) 320-3898.

SOUTHERN ALBERTA ART GALLERY, 601 3rd Ave. S., exhibits works of Canadian and international artists with an emphasis on contemporary art. Allow 30 minutes minimum. Tues.-Sat. 10-5, Sun. 1-5; closed holidays except July 1. Free. Phone (403) 327-8770.

CASINOS

- **Casino Lethbridge,** 1251 3rd Ave. S. Daily 10 a.m.-3 a.m.; closed Dec. 25. Phone (403) 381-9467.

LLOYDMINSTER—

see Saskatchewan p. 240.

MARKERVILLE (F-6) pop. 100

On June 27, 1888, 50 Icelanders from the drought-plagued Dakota Territory crossed the Red Deer River to settle in Markerville, where they hoped to maintain their language and customs. For a time they produced woolen outerwear, pastries, sweets and smoked mutton in the traditional Icelandic manner.

During the 1920s, however, an increase in intermarriage with other ethnic groups and improved transportation diluted their cultural isolation. Less than 10 percent of the population is now of purely Icelandic descent, but many traditional customs are celebrated during heritage days.

MARKERVILLE HISTORIC CREAMERY MUSEUM is off Hwys. 781 and 592 on Creamery Way. Begun by 34 Icelandic farmers as a cooperative in 1899 and in operation until 1972, the creamery has been restored to depict the operation as it was in the 1930s. Costumed guides offer tours. Picnicking is permitted. Food is available. Allow 30 minutes minimum. Daily 10-5:30, May 15-Labour Day; Sat.-Sun. 10-5:30, day after Labour Day-Sept. 30. Admission $2; over 64 and ages 7-17, $1.50; family rate (two adults and two children) $5. MC, VI. Phone (403) 728-3006 or 728-3495.

STEPHANSSON HOUSE HISTORIC SITE, 7 km (4 mi.) n.w. on either Hwy. 592 or Hwy. 781, following signs, highlights the history of the Icelanders who founded Markerville, especially Stephan G. Stephansson, a prominent poet and farmer. His restored home contains original furnishings from the early 1900s. Costumed guides give 15- to 30-minute tours. Allow 30 minutes minimum. Daily 10-6, May 15-Labour Day. Last tour begins 30 minutes before closing. Admission $2; over 64 and ages 7-17, $1.50; family rate $5. Phone (403) 728-3929 or 427-3995 in the off season.

MEDICINE HAT (I-8)
pop. 46,800, elev. 715 m/2,346′

According to popular legend, the name Medicine Hat originated because of a battle between Cree and Blackfoot Indians on the banks of a southern Alberta river. The Cree fought bravely until their medicine man deserted them, losing his headdress in midstream. Believing this to be a bad omen, the Cree put down their weapons and were killed by the Blackfoot. This site became known as "Saamis," which translates as "medicine man's hat."

A buried prehistoric river, or aquifer, serves as a source of unlimited cool water. More than 20 billion cubic metres (26 billion cubic yards) of natural gas reserves inspired Rudyard Kipling in 1907 to describe Medicine Hat as possessing "all hell for a basement."

Outdoor opportunities include swimming, boating and fishing at Echo Dale Park; phone (403) 527-2202. Riverside Amusement offers waterslides, miniature golf and karts. Circuit cowboys and spectators gather July 26-29 for Medicine Hat's Exhibition and Stampede 2000.

Medicine Hat & District Chamber of Commerce: 413 6th Ave. S.E., Medicine Hat, AB, Canada T1A 2S7; phone (403) 527-5214.

Shopping areas: Medicine Hat Mall, 3292 Dunmore Rd. S.E., features The Bay, Sears and Zellers among its more than 100 stores.

MEDICINE HAT MUSEUM AND ART GALLERY, 1302 Bomford Crescent, presents the region's cultural heritage through Indian artifacts, pioneer items and art exhibits. Allow 1 hour minimum. Mon.-Fri. 9-5, Sat.-Sun. and holidays 1-5. Closed Jan. 1, Good Friday and Dec. 25. Donations. Phone (403) 527-6266.

WORLD'S TALLEST TEPEE, jct. Hwy. 1 and South Ridge Dr., is made of steel and stands approximately 22 stories high. Storyboards incorporated in the tepee stand 3.6 metres (12 ft.) high and depict Indian history. Used during the 1988 Olympics in Calgary, the tepee was moved to Medicine Hat where it now stands on Saamis Archaeological Site—the location of a 16th-century buffalo camp. Allow 1 hour minimum. Daily 8-8, Victoria Day weekend-Sept. 30. Donations. Phone (403) 527-6773.

CASINOS

• **Casino by Van Shaw,** 1051 Ross Glenn St. S.E. Slots daily 10 a.m.-2 a.m., table games daily 4-midnight; closed Dec. 25. Phone (403) 529-2222.

MILK RIVER (J-7) pop. 900

Milk River lies on the east side of Milk River Ridge, an area more than 1,200 metres (3,900 ft.) high, 39 kilometres (24 mi.) long and 29 kilometres (18 mi.) wide. Quartzite, granite and gneiss rock formations indicate prehistoric glacial action; meltwater carved the Milk River Valley 10,000 years ago.

Throughout the area and predominantly in Writing-on-Stone Provincial Park *(see attraction listing)* are mushroom-shaped sandstone hoodoos, odd rock formations that once led Indians to believe spirits inhabited the valley.

The Alberta Tourism Information and Interpretive Centre: General Delivery, Milk River, AB, Canada T0K 1M0; phone (800) 661-8888.

WRITING-ON-STONE PROVINCIAL PARK, 32 km (20 mi.) e. and 10 km (6 mi.) s. on secondary Hwy. 501 to the jct. with Hwy. 500, following signs, is an archeological preserve overlooking the Milk River. Massive sandstone outcrops display pictographs and petroglyphs created by nomadic Shoshoni and Blackfoot Indians. Fire-burned stones, broken bones and horn tools as well as other implements have been found at their former campsites. Members of the Blackfoot tribe also used local caves for burial sites. Access to the preserve is permitted only by 90-minute guided tours, which depart from the preserve entrance, 2 kilometres (1.2 mi.) west of the campground. Interpretive programs are mid-May through early September.

Park open daily 24 hours. Tours are given Mon.-Fri. at 10 and 2, Sat. at 2 and 4, Sun. at 10, 1 and 3, July-Aug. Times may vary; phone ahead. Park admission free. Free tour tickets, available from the interpreter's office an hour before departure, are required for tours. Phone (403) 647-2364. *See Recreation Chart and the AAA/CAA Western Canada and Alaska CampBook.*

MUNDARE (D-7) pop. 600

BASILIAN FATHERS MUSEUM, 3 km (1.9 mi.) n. of Hwy. 16 on Hwy. 855, is operated by the Basilian Fathers and houses ancient manuscripts, church artifacts and items of Ukrainian and Canadian culture. An adjacent grotto depicts the life of Christ through pictures and statues. Guided tours are available. Mon.-Fri. 10-4 (also Sat.-Sun. 1-5, July-Aug.); closed legal holidays. Donations. Phone (780) 764-3887.

NANTON (I-6) pop. 1,700

NANTON LANCASTER SOCIETY AIR MUSEUM, s. on Hwy. 2 following signs, honors Royal Canadian Air Force and Royal Air Force members who waged bombing operations during World War II. Among displays are a Canadian-built Lancaster bomber and other training planes, simulators, gun turrets and instrumentation and photographs of Lancaster training aircraft in action. Allow 1 hour minimum. Daily 9-5, May-Oct.; Sat.-Sun. 10-4, rest of year. Closed Jan. 1, Good Friday and Dec. 25. Donations. Phone (403) 646-2270.

OKOTOKS—*see Calgary p. 57.*

PEACE RIVER (A-3) pop. 6,500

Formed by the confluence of the Smoky and Heart rivers, the Peace River flows north and east of the town of the same name to Lake Athabasca and to the west into British Columbia. The area was known as "The Forks" by trappers and traders in the 1700s and "Sagitawa" (meeting of the waters) by the Cree Indians. On his historic trek across the northern continent, Alexander Mackenzie explored the region and built a fort and wintered here 1792-93.

A wooden statue honors prospector and local legend Henry Fuller "Twelve-Foot" Davis. The Vermont native, known for his generosity and hospitality, achieved great social stature when he mined $15,000 worth of gold from a 3.5-metre (12-ft.) plot between two gold claims. Davis said on his deathbed that he was not afraid to die because "I never kilt nobody, I never stole from nobody and I kept open house for travelers all my life." His grave overlooks the confluence of the Peace, Heart and Smoky rivers.

Land of the Mighty Peace: 9309 100th St., P.O. Box 6599, Peace River, AB, Canada T8S 1S4; phone (780) 624-4166.

PINCHER CREEK (J-6) pop. 3,700

Pincher Creek was established in 1878 by the North West Mounted Police as a horse farm to provide remounts for Fort Macleod *(see place listing p. 73).* The town was named for a pair of pincers that presumably were left behind by prospectors. After hearing that the area had ample grassland, other settlers soon arrived.

Pincher Creek & District Chamber of Commerce and Information Centre: 782 Main St., P.O. Box 2287, Pincher Creek, AB, Canada T0K 1W0; phone (403) 627-5199 or 627-5855.

KOOTENAI BROWN HISTORICAL PARK AND MUSEUM, 1069 James Ave., displays more than 14,000 local relics—including military uniforms, agricultural equipment, jewelry, clothing and books about local history—in 12 historical buildings. On the grounds is the restored log cabin of George "Kootenai" Brown, an Irish adventurer and one of the region's first settlers. Other period buildings are on the grounds. Allow 2 hours minimum. Daily 10-8, mid-May to mid-Sept.; Sun. and Wed. 1-5 or by appointment, rest of year. Admission $4; over 64, $3; ages 10-17, $2. Phone (403) 627-3684.

RED DEER (F-6)
pop. 60,100, elev. 905 m/2,969′

Red Deer's name comes from the Cree Indian word *was-ka-soo,* meaning "elk." Early Scottish settlers mistook the native elk for the red deer of their homeland and the name stuck. A creek running through Red Deer still bears the name Waskasoo.

The original settlement was several kilometres upstream on the Red Deer River where the water was shallow and easy to cross. Dr. Leonard Gaetz, a Methodist minister who arrived in 1884, persuaded the Calgary and Edmonton Railway to cross the river on his property by donating half of his land for use as a townsite. The trains came through, and the town took root at its current site. Agriculture and petroleum products are the major local industries.

City Hall Park, 48th Avenue and Ross Street, is a landscaped oasis known for its Christmas displays. West in wooded countryside is Sylvan Lake, which accommodates Jarvis Bay and Sylvan Lake parks *(see Recreation Chart and Sylvan Lake in the AAA/CAA Western Canada and Alaska CampBook).* A noteworthy lake resort

DID YOU KNOW

Alberta was named for Louise Alberta, daughter of Queen Victoria and Prince Albert.

north at Gull Lake is Aspen Beach Provincial Park *(see Recreation Chart and Lacombe in the AAA/ CAA Western Canada and Alaska CampBook)*.

Lacombe, also north of the city, is the site of the Canadian Agriculture Department's experimental farm; visitors can walk or drive through the gardens.

Events include Silver Buckle Rodeo in April; the Highland Games in June; International Folk Festival on July 1; Westerner Days in mid-July; and Heritage Day and the International Air Show, both in August.

Red Deer Visitors and Convention: 30 Riverview Park, P.O. Box 5008, Red Deer, AB, Canada T4N 3T4; phone (403) 346-0180 or (800) 215-8946.

Self-guiding tours: A brochure outlining a walking tour of historic downtown is available from The Red Deer and District Museum and from the visitor information center at Heritage Ranch in Waskasoo Park *(see attraction listings)*.

Shopping areas: Bower Place, Hwy. 2A and 28th Street, features Eaton's and The Bay. Parkland Mall, 67th St. and Gaetz Ave., has Sears and Wal-Mart as well as 120 smaller shops.

THE RED DEER AND DISTRICT MUSEUM, 4525 47A Ave., displays items relating to the development of Red Deer as well as exhibits about natural history. Mon.-Sat. 10-5 (also Wed.-Thurs. 5-9), Sun. and holidays 1-5, June-Aug.; Mon.-Fri. 10-5 (also Wed.-Thurs. 5-9), Sat.-Sun. and holidays 1-5, rest of year. Closed Jan. 1 and Dec. 25. Donations. Phone (403) 309-8405.

ST. MARY'S CHURCH is at 3715 39th St. E.; enter through the s. entrance only. This ultramodern 1968 structure of unusual design is the work of architect Doug Cardinal. Local architect Graham Leadbeater designed the parish center addition. Alois Peter Marx of Germany created the sculpture displays. Mon.-Fri. 10-4; closed legal holidays. Free. Phone (403) 347-3114.

WASKASOO PARK, bordering the Red Deer River and running throughout the city, offers more than 70 kilometres (43 mi.) of trails. The park encompasses Bower Ponds, popular for canoeing, bicycling, fishing and cross-country skiing; Cronquist House Multicultural Centre, a restored 1911 Victorian-style farmhouse; Fort Normandeau, with its interpretive center, canoe launch and picnic area; Heritage Ranch, which provides horseback riding, hiking and fishing; Kerry Wood Nature Centre, which houses nature displays; and Gaetz Lake Sanctuary, a wildlife preserve.

CASINOS

- **Jackpot Casino Ltd.,** 4705 50th St.. Mon.-Thurs. 10 a.m.-2 a.m., Fri.-Sat. 10 a.m.-3 a.m., Sun. 10 a.m.-midnight. Phone (403) 342-5825.

RIMBEY (F-6) pop. 2,100

PAS-KA-POO HISTORICAL PARK, 1 km (.6 mi.) n. at Hwy. 20 and 56th Ave., includes a truck museum and a restored village. The truck museum features 19 Smithson's International half-ton trucks dating 1934-74. The village comprises a log schoolhouse, town office, homesteader's cabin, general store, church, sawmill, barber shop and blacksmith shop; exhibited relics range from old uniforms to household items and farm machinery. Guided tours are available. Truck museum open daily 10-6. Village open daily 10-6, May-Oct. Truck museum $2.50. Village $2.50. Phone (403) 843-2004 or 843-2084.

★ROCKY MOUNTAIN HOUSE NATIONAL HISTORIC PARK (F-5)

Rocky Mountain House National Historic Park is in west central Alberta, about 80 kilometres (50 mi.) west of Red Deer on Hwy. 11 and 7 kilometres (4.3 mi.) from the town of Rocky Mountain House via Hwy. 11A, following signs.

The park contains the sites of four fur-trading posts, the first of which was founded by North West Co. in 1799 near the confluence of the North Saskatchewan and Clearwater rivers. The post was designed to stimulate trade with the Kootenay, to be used as a base for exploration through the surrounding mountains and to serve as a Pacific link to North West Co.'s Montréal headquarters.

The efforts of the Blackfoot Indians to prevent other tribes from trading prevented the four forts, which spanned 76 years of operation, from being lucrative. An alternate route through the mountains farther north also diminished the posts' importance.

The first post experienced a brief boom in the late 1820s after Hudson's Bay Co. merged with North West Co. The influx of illegal whiskey traders into southern Alberta in 1869 disrupted trade with the Indians, and in 1875 the last of the four posts was abandoned. By then the North West Mounted Police virtually had stopped the whiskey trade and its attendant violence and lawlessness, and the trading post was moved farther south near Calgary on the Bow River.

The remnants of the old trading post lie just east of the rugged wilderness areas of the Rocky Mountains Forest Reserve and Banff and Jasper national parks. Elk, deer, bears, bighorn sheep and mountain goats are among the region's native animals. The North Saskatchewan River is the major waterway; smaller creeks and rivers branch off from it at Rocky Mountain House.

A trail system along the North Saskatchewan River and through a scenic wooded area connects the four post sites of the 1799-1834 and 1835-75 periods. A short 30-minute walk leads past the two later forts; a longer 90-minute walk travels to the first two forts built at Rocky Mountain House. Solar-powered audio guides with illustrated panels are stationed at eight sites along the trails.

Signs along the trails describe native plants. Hikers taking the longer trail may see buffaloes in their natural habitat. At a demonstration site along the longer trail, park interpreters in period costume make pemmican—dried meat and fat pounded into a paste and preserved—and tea, tan hides, perform handicraft work and demonstrate other period activities during July and August. Visitors are encouraged to participate and to sample various teas.

Subjects of visitor center exhibits include the fur industry; David Thompson, who discovered the northern gateway through the Rockies; and Plains Indians. Relics displayed include surveying equipment, ethnographic material and items from archeological excavations. A theater presents films and interpretive programs on a regular basis.

The park and visitor center are open daily 10-6, first Sat. in May-Labour Day weekend; Mon.-Fri. 8:30-5, Sat.-Sun. and holidays 10-6, day after Labour Day weekend-last Sun. in Sept. Admission $2.50; over 64, $2; ages 6-16, $1.50. MC, VI. Phone (403) 845-2412.

ROSEBUD (H-6)

A pioneer ranching settlement founded in the 1880s, Rosebud has become a thriving cultural center with a population of 90. The community participates in the activities of Rosebud School of The Arts. Rosebud Theatre offers matinees, evening performances, dinner theater and concerts from March through December; phone (403) 677-2001 or (800) 267-7553.

Among historic buildings is an early 20th-century Chinese laundry which now is home to Centennial Museum. The museum displays local memorabilia and an array of western Canadiana. Local and regional arts and crafts are exhibited in Akokiniskway Art Gallery and other shops along the town's self-guiding historic walking tour.

ST. ALBERT—see Edmonton p. 72.

SLAVE LAKE (C-5) pop. 6,600

Slave Lake is on the southeast shore of Lesser Slave Lake, Alberta's largest lake. Lesser Slave Lake Provincial Park (see Recreation Chart and the AAA/CAA Western Canada and Alaska CampBook), which surrounds a golf course and hugs the lake's east shore, provides snowshoeing and cross-country skiing opportunities in winter.

The Provincial Sandcastle Championship and Riverboat Daze both are held in late July.

SMOKY LAKE (D-7) pop. 1,100

VICTORIA SETTLEMENT PROVINCIAL HISTORIC SITE, 10 km (6 mi.) s. on Hwy. 855 and 6 km (3.6 mi) e. on Victoria Trail, began in 1862 as a Methodist mission. A Hudson's Bay Co. fur-trading post soon followed, and by the beginning of the 20th century the area was settled. Guided tours of the clerk's quarters, furnished with pioneer articles, are offered. A videotape presentation describes local history. Allow 1 hour minimum. Daily 10-6, May 15-Labour Day. Admission $2; over 64 and ages 7-17, $1.50; family rate $5. Phone (780) 645-6256 or 656-2333.

SPRUCE VIEW (F-5) pop. 100

Founded at the turn of the 20th century, Spruce View was named for the its omnipresent spruce trees. Such recreational opportunities as boating, camping, fishing and picnicking are available at Dickson Dam (see Recreation Chart and Innisfail in the AAA/CAA Western Canada and Alaska CampBook).

DICKSON DAM VISITOR CENTRE is 6 km (4 mi.) e. on Hwy. 54, following signs. Perched on a hillside, the center offers a bird's-eye view of Dickson Dam. Exhibits and a short video focus on the dam's history and topography. Mon.-Fri. 8-4:30, Sat.-Sun. 9-5, May-Sept.; Mon.-Fri. 8-4:30, rest of year. Donations. Phone (403) 227-1106.

DICKSON STORE MUSEUM is 3.2 km (2 mi.) s., following signs from Hwy. 54. This restored, family-owned general store, dating from the early 1900s, also served as the town post office and local gathering place. Renovated to a style typical of the 1930s, the museum features exhibits of dry goods, hardware and groceries common to that time. The second floor contains the family living quarters, furnished in period.

Allow 30 minutes minimum. Mon.-Sat. 10-5:30, Sun. 12:30-5:30, mid-May through Labour Day weekend; Sat. 10-5:30, Sun. 12:30-5:30, day after Labour Day-second Sun. in Oct. Donations. Phone (403) 728-3355.

STETTLER (F-7) pop. 5,200

SAVE ALBERTA PRAIRIE RAILWAY EXCURSIONS, at the train station at 47th Ave. and 47th St., provides steam-powered rail excursions through the Alberta countryside in vintage passenger coaches. Trips last 4.5 to 9 hours; all include a buffet-style meal at the destination. Theme trips also are scheduled. Trains operate Thurs.-Sun., July-Aug.; Sat.-Sun., May-June and Sept.-Oct. Departure times vary. Fare $59-$100; over 59, $50-$90; ages 11-17, $42-$90; ages 4-10, $29.50-$90. Reservations are required. AE, MC, VI. Phone (403) 742-2811.

STONY PLAIN—see Edmonton p. 72.

TROCHU (G-6) pop. 1,000

ST. ANN RANCH TRADING CO. PROVINCIAL HISTORIC SITE, .5 km (.3 mi.) s. on King George Ave., is a reconstructed 1905 French settlement comprising restored historic houses and reproductions of period buildings. The site includes a small school, post office, hospital and chapel. An interpretive center contains displays recounting the history of the settlement, which was founded by aristocratic officers from the French cavalry. Allow 30 minutes minimum. Daily 9-9. Admission $2. Phone (403) 442-3924 or (888) 442-3924.

TURNER VALLEY (H-5)

pop. 1,500, elev. 4,000'

TURNER VALLEY GAS PLANT HISTORIC SITE, 1 km (.6 mi.) s.e. at 223 Main St. N.W. (Hwy. 22), features artifacts related to the natural gas industry. A 20-minute videotape documents the discovery of gas in the area. Guided 1-hour tours, offered on request, educate visitors about the impact of the industry on the provincial economy. Allow 1 hour minimum. Daily 10-6, May 15-Aug. 31. Plant visitation is only by guided tour. Last tour departs 1 hour before closing. Free. Phone (403) 933-7738.

VEGREVILLE (E-7) pop. 5,300

The center of eastern Alberta's Ukrainian culture, Vegreville has the distinction of possessing the largest known Easter egg, or *pysanka*, in the world. The 9-metre-high (30-ft.) egg, decorated to reflect Ukrainian folk art, was built in 1975 for the centennial of the formation of the Royal Canadian Mounted Police in Alberta.

The egg's bronze, gold and silver design, made from more than 3,500 pieces of aluminum, illustrates the local settlers' struggles and the protection the mounted police provided them. Queen Elizabeth and Prince Phillip unveiled the plaque next to the giant egg in Heritage Park during their visit in 1978. The Ukrainian Festival is held the first weekend in July.

Vegreville & District Chamber of Commerce: P.O. Box 877, Vegreville, AB, Canada T9C 1R9; phone (780) 632-2771 Victoria Day-Labour Day.

WAINWRIGHT (E-8) pop. 5,100

WAINWRIGHT & DISTRICT MUSEUM, 101 Main St. at 1st Ave., displays items and memorabilia relating to family life in the town since its founding in 1908. The museum is housed in a restored Canadian National Railway station built in the early 1930s. Allow 30 minutes minimum. Daily 9-5; closed Jan. 1, Good Friday and Dec. 25. Donations. Phone (780) 842-3115.

★ WATERTON LAKES NATIONAL PARK (J-5)

Elevations in the park range from 1,279 metres (4,200 ft.) in the town of Waterton Park to 2,920 metres (9,580 ft.) at Mount Blakiston. Refer to CAA/AAA maps for additional elevation information.

Covering 525 square kilometres (203 sq. mi.), Waterton Lakes National Park adjoins Glacier National Park in Montana; together they form Waterton-Glacier International Peace Park. The most direct approach into Waterton Lakes National Park from the south is over Chief Mountain International Highway (SR 17/Hwy. 6) from Glacier National Park. The park also is accessible via Hwy. 5 from Cardston or Hwy. 6 from Pincher Creek. The customs office is open daily 7 a.m.-10 p.m., June 1 to mid-Sept.; 9-6, Victoria Day weekend through May 31.

For thousands of years this was Aboriginal territory, where the Kootenai and Blackfoot were the primary Aboriginal tribes. In 1858 Lt. Thomas Blakiston became the first European on record to explore the area; he named the lakes for Charles Waterton, an 18th-century English naturalist.

Local rancher Fred Godsal, American journalist and naturalist George Bird Grinnell and others lobbied their respective governments in the late 19th century to set aside parts of this wilderness area for future generations. They succeeded, and Waterton Lakes and Glacier national parks were established in 1895 and 1910, respectively.

Waterton Lake is divided into three parts: Upper, Middle and Lower Waterton lakes. The townsite, the location of park headquarters, is on the west shore of Upper Waterton Lake, which juts 4.7 kilometres (3 mi.) into Glacier National Park. The mountains on either side tower 900 to 1,200 metres (3,000 to 4,000 ft.) above the lake. Mount Crandell rises to the north; Sofa Mountain and Vimy Peak are east across the lake.

Wildlife ranging from squirrels and marmots to deer and bears inhabit the park. A small herd of plains bison is in the buffalo paddocks on the northern boundary, 1.6 kilometres (1 mi.) north of the Waterton River Bridge on Hwy. 6. Thousands of waterfowl visit the lakes during spring and fall migrations. Hunting is prohibited.

Among the many rare wildflowers that grace prairie and mountain landscapes are beargrass, pygmy poppy and mountain lady-slipper. Evergreens blanket the slopes and peaks below mountain goat country at an altitude of about 2,286 metres (7,500 ft.).

General Information and Activities

The park is open all year, though most concessions operate only from Victoria Day weekend through the second Monday in October. Red Rock Canyon, 15 kilometres (11 mi.) northwest of Waterton, offers a .7-kilometre (.4-mi.) loop trail along the canyon and a 1-kilometre (.6-mi.) trail to Blakiston Falls. Riding stables are 2.5 kilometres (1.5 mi.) north of town near the main entrance road; horses can be rented.

Just north of the national park is an 18-hole public golf course that is open daily, Victoria Day weekend through the second Monday in October. A free four-court tennis facility is on Cameron Falls Drive.

The park visitor center, at the junction of the entrance road and Prince of Wales Road, is open daily 8-8, mid-June through Labour Day (weather permitting); 8-6, day after Labour Day to mid-September. Interpretive display centers at Cameron Lake and Waterton townsite describe the park's subalpine forest and the history of the International Peace Park. A display at Red Rock Canyon features the area's history and ecology. All are open daily 24 hours.

Illustrated talks are given every evening at 8:30 at the park's indoor theaters. There also are guided walks and other interpretive programs; phone (403) 859-5133.

Those wishing to camp in Waterton's back-country campsites must obtain a park use permit at the visitor center. You also can register your outing with the Park Warden Service. Registrations must be returned upon completion of the trip.

Hunting is prohibited. Anglers need a fishing license, which can be obtained along with fishing regulations at the park offices, information center, campgrounds, from park wardens and at service stations in the townsite (*see Recreation in the Introduction p. 32*). Motorboats and water skiing are permitted only on the Middle Waterton lakes. *See Recreation Chart and the AAA/CAA Western Canada and Alaska CampBook.*

ADMISSION to the park is $4; over 64, $3; ages 6-16, $2. Admission for two to seven people in a private vehicle is $8.

PETS must be leashed at all times while in the park.

ADDRESS inquiries to the Superintendent, Waterton Lakes National Park, Waterton Park, AB, Canada T0K 2M0; phone (403) 859-5133.

WATERTON SHORELINE SIGHTSEEING CRUISES departs from Waterton Marina. Narrated trips cross Waterton Lake, with stops at the 49th parallel; at Goat Haunt in Montana, where passengers may stay and return on a later boat; and at Crypt Landing, where hikers are picked up or dropped off. Trips depart daily at 9, 10, 1, 4 and 7, late June-Labour Day; at 10 and 2:30, early May to mid-June; at 10, 1 and 4, mid- to late June and day after Labour Day to mid-Sept. Fare $20; ages 13-17, $12; ages 4-12, $8. Phone (403) 859-2362, or 859-2180 in winter.

WETASKIWIN (E-6) pop. 11,000

Wetaskiwin is a Cree name meaning "the hills where peace was made." The Red Deer River was the dividing line between the Blackfoot in the south and the Cree in the north, but the Blackfoot often crossed the river to hunt buffalo in Cree territory, causing dissension between the tribes. It is believed that a peace agreement was made in the area during the 1860s to end the conflicts.

Wetaskiwin Economic Development: 4910 55A St., Wetaskiwin, AB, Canada T9A 2R7; phone (780) 352-4636 or (800) 989-6899.

SAVE ★ **REYNOLDS-ALBERTA MUSEUM,** 1 km (.6 mi.) w. on Hwy. 13, interprets the history of ground and air transportation, agriculture and industry in Alberta. Audiovisual presentations, displays and demonstrations supplement the actual operation of vintage automobiles, bicycles, and farm and industrial machinery. One area features

a reproduction of a small drive-in theater, complete with old films, metal speakers and seats shaped like the back end of 1950-era automobiles. Food is available.

The museum also is home to Canada's Aviation Hall of Fame in a nearby hangar. Vintage aircraft are displayed, and Canadians who have contributed significantly to aviation history are recognized.

Allow 2 hours minimum. Daily 9-7, June 30-Labour Day; Tues.-Sun. 9-5, rest of year. Closed Jan. 1, Good Friday and Dec. 24-25. Admission $6.50; over 64, $5.50; ages 7-17, $3; family rate $15. MC, VI. Phone (780) 361-1351 or (800) 661-4726. *See ad p. 87.*

REYNOLDS MUSEUM, 4110 57th St., contains antique automobiles, trucks, aircraft, tractors, military vehicles and steam engines as well as vintage household appliances, musical instruments, Indian relics and weapons. Allow 1 hour minimum. Daily 10-5, May 15-Labour Day; by

appointment rest of year. Admission $3.50; over 64 and under 13, $2.50. Phone (780) 352-6201 or 352-5201.

WETASKIWIN & DISTRICT MUSEUM, 5010 53rd Ave., is housed in the 1908 Electric Light Building. Displays depict local history and include a pioneer schoolroom, an 1891 railway exhibit, a pioneer kitchen and a pioneer street. Allow 30 minutes minimum. Tues.-Sat. 10-5, Sun. 1-5, June-Aug.; Tues. and Fri. 1-4, rest of year. Closed Good Friday and Dec. 25-26. Admission $2; ages 6-12, $1; family rate $5. Phone (780) 352-0227.

WOOD BUFFALO NATIONAL PARK

Wood Buffalo National Park straddles the Alberta and Northwest Territories border. *See Northwest Territories and Nunavut p. 225.*

British Columbia

Tea Rooms & Totem Poles

British and Indian influences profile a cultural potpourri

Beautiful Victoria

English gardens and turreted buildings reflect a distinctive British essence

Splendid by Nature

The Canadian Rockies create a mountain playground amid glacial lakes and parks

Relaxing Hot Springs

Soak your stresses away and get an invigorating rush in warm mineral baths

A Land of Plenty

Orchards, vineyards and farms produce bountiful harvests

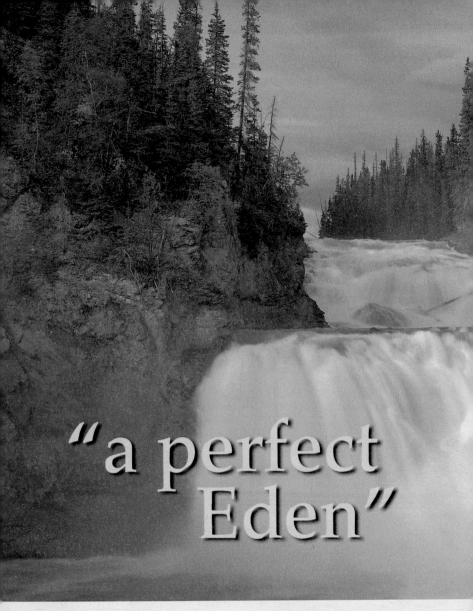

"a perfect Eden"

Sailing along Vancouver Island's untamed coast in 1842, James Douglas visited the site of present-day Victoria and reported: "The place itself appears a perfect Eden... one might be pardoned for supposing it had been dropped from the clouds...."

Prophetic words considering that Douglas, who later became colonial governor of British Columbia, was describing the "Garden City" many years before its first flower beds were planted.

Today, Edenic gardens are the province's forte: From Victoria's renowned, blossom-loaded Butchart Gardens to lush Queen Elizabeth Park atop the city of Vancouver's tallest hill, horticultural delights are everywhere.

And if a single apple was enough to tempt Adam and Eve, then they would

no doubt have found BC's fertile Okanagan Valley irresistible. Not only do orchards here produce more than a third of Canada's apples, the valley also lures vacationers with sunny weather, sandy lakefront beaches and picturesque rolling hills striped by orderly rows of grapevines. According to legend, Okanagan Lake even harbors a serpentlike monster called Ogopogo, although unlike the biblical serpent, this elusive beast seems quite shy.

If you were searching for the Garden of Eden on Earth, British Columbia wouldn't be a bad place to start.

"Once upon a time...."

For generations, parents have used these four words to introduce children to the fantastic, magic-filled realms of fairy tales. Say them, and a spell is cast, transforming restless young ones into an attentive audience eagerly awaiting a story. Maybe you remember feeling such anticipation yourself.

If not, then a trip to British Columbia might just help recapture that youthful expectation of adventure. Though far removed from the Old World settings popularized in the works of Hans Christian Andersen and the Brothers Grimm, this far western province—with its daunting, snowcapped mountains and mist-filled rain forests—seems to have sprung from the pages of a storybook.

Into the Woods

Walk among centuries-old Douglas firs in MacMillan Provincial Park's Cathedral Grove and it's easy to imagine bumping into Little Red Riding Hood on her way to grandmother's house. Not only will these giants make you feel child-size by comparison; the perpetual twilight created by their lofty, intertwining branches can play tricks on your eyes, too. Look up at the high, dim ceiling of needle-heavy boughs arching

overhead, and you'll understand how this grove got its name. Logging may have taken its toll on British Columbia's old-growth forests, but many stands continue to thrive in such havens as Pacific Rim National Park and Strathcona Provincial Park, both on Vancouver Island.

Another of these sylvan sanctuaries is in the city of Vancouver's Stanley Park. This urban wilderness embraces an evergreen woodland so extensive that while wandering its paths you might forget you're in the heart of Canada's third largest city. A miniature railway, children's zoo and the Vancouver Aquarium make this park a great Sunday getaway for families—and a perfect backdrop for storytelling.

Some of the most interesting tales told in Stanley Park are silently portrayed by stylized figures carved into totem poles. A thicket of these cedar columns loom at the park's eastern edge, and each one communicates its own story, whether it be a family history, a notable event or an age-old myth. Travel along the mainland coast or among British Columbia's offshore islands and you'll find more outstanding examples

The Queen Charlotte Islands are occupied by Haida Indians.
1750

George Vancouver, an English explorer, surveys the British Columbian coast.
1792

Spanish explorers first sight the coast of Vancouver Island.
1774

Vancouver Island becomes a crown colony.
1849

1786
The British establish profitable fur trade with local Indians.

British Columbia Historical Timeline

1820
The powerful Hudson's Bay Co. controls fur trading in the Pacific Northwest.

carved by the Bella Coola, Haida, Kwak-iutl, Nootka, Salish, Tlingit and Tsimshian peoples.

Symbolizing strength and authority, the bears glaring down from totem poles may not be the only ones you see in British Columbia: Grizzlies are common within Mount Revelstoke and Glacier national parks. Part of the Columbia Mountains, the terrain here consists of narrow, steep-walled valleys that fill with snow in winter to create icebound Shangri-Las. And like the heart of Andersen's title character in "The Snow Queen," the glaciers here never thaw.

Not far away, in the Canadian Rockies, Kootenay National Park preserves land that seems equally imbued with magic. At the park's southern end are the Radium Hot Springs, which bubble forth hot, mineral-tinged water no matter what time of year it is.

Enchanted Gardens

On the other hand, changing seasons mean a world of difference at Victoria's flower-crowded Butchart Gardens. As some plants bloom, others fade, producing a dramatic shift in hues seemingly conjured by a wizard's wand. Meandering paths thread among blossoming trees and shrubs, past softly splashing fountains and around countless flower beds in this rainbow-saturated wonderland. Rhododendrons and azaleas enjoy the limelight in spring and early summer; roses steal the show in late June.

Across the Straits of Georgia, Vancouver's VanDusen Botanical Gardens is similarly endowed with floral color. Careful tending has transfigured this former golf course into a city showplace of lakes, streams, hedge mazes and whimsical topiary figures.

And what childhood fantasy would be complete without a castle? Victoria boasts two. Turrets, columns and rough sandstone walls lend 19th-century Craigdarroch Castle a medieval air that greatly pleased its builder, Robert Dunsmuir, a wealthy Scottish immigrant and industrialist. Hatley Castle, on the Royal Roads University campus, looks even more like a genuine fortress from the Middle Ages. Topped by battlements, this imposing mansion would be at home in a European fable.

To anyone who has ever been mesmerized by fanciful storybook illustrations, British Columbia should seem delightfully familiar.

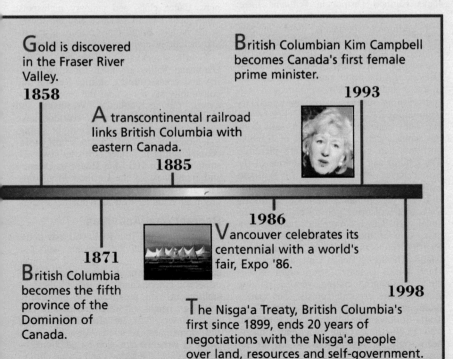

Gold is discovered in the Fraser River Valley.
1858

British Columbian Kim Campbell becomes Canada's first female prime minister.
1993

A transcontinental railroad links British Columbia with eastern Canada.
1885

1986
Vancouver celebrates its centennial with a world's fair, Expo '86.

1871
British Columbia becomes the fifth province of the Dominion of Canada.

1998
The Nisga'a Treaty, British Columbia's first since 1899, ends 20 years of negotiations with the Nisga'a people over land, resources and self-government.

Recreation

The Rocky Mountain and Cascade ranges, a lush valley, and a system of rivers, lakes and protected ocean waterways are the hallmarks of British Columbia's natural beauty and the sources of unlimited recreational possibilities.

Summer Sojourns

Extended **canoeing** trips await you on the Outside Trail, a chain of lakes in the Kootenay region's Champion Lakes Provincial Park. The coastal area's 57-kilometre (35-mi.) Powell Forest Canoe Route, eight lakes connected by portage routes, begins on Lois Lake and ends at the marina on Powell Lake.

The 116-kilometre (72-mi.) canoeing and **kayaking** circuit (plus portage routes) in Bowron Lake Provincial Park is so popular that reservations are required and daily access is limited to 25 boats. Paddling through this unspoiled wildlife sanctuary could take up to 7 days, depending on the weather or how much time you spend gawking at bears, deer, moose, mountain goats or the beautiful Cariboo Mountains. Approach the park from Wells, which is just north of Barkerville Historic Town. For more information contact BC Parks Cariboo District in Williams Lake; phone (250) 398-4414.

In addition to spectacular mountain scenery, canoers will find calm, turquoise-colored glacial lakes nestled in the snowcapped Rockies; two of these—O'Hara and the aptly named Emerald—are in Yoho National Park.

If rushing water is more your speed, try negotiating the Thompson and Fraser rivers. They converge near Lytton, said to be the white-water rafting capital of Canada; outfitters and guide services are plentiful. The Chilko and Chilcotin tributaries of the Fraser River, which lie west of Williams Lake, also have a reputation for adventure.

Every region has a network of **hiking** trails that will bring you up close and personal with British Columbia's natural wonders. One of the best coastal hikes is in Pacific Rim National Park, on Vancouver Island. The Long Beach Unit, accessed off Hwy. 4 near Ucluelet, offers eight moderately challenging hiking venues ranging from beaches to rain forests. The park's pride and joy—the rugged West Coast Trail—follows the shoreline from Port Renfrew to Bamfield. Only experienced hikers need apply for reservations, which are restricted to 50 per day during the season, May through September.

But that's just the tip of the iceberg when it comes to trekking around the province. Five national and nearly 650 provincial parks and recreation areas are your gateways to discovery.

Take the family **swimming**, **water skiing** or **windsurfing** inland at one of seven provincial beach parks on Okanagan Lake, or to Osoyoos Lake, the warmest in the province; both are in the desertlike Okanagan Valley.

The valley's climate and terrain invite other types of activities. The Kettle Valley Railway bed, west of Penticton, provides easy **mountain biking**, while tougher trails cross nearby Campbell Mountain and Ellis Ridge.

World-class Wintering

The **skiing** amenities at Whistler and Blackcomb mountains, north of Vancouver, are world renowned. Some 32 high-speed lifts, 200 trails and 12 alpine bowls—all on more than 2,800 hectares (7,000 acres)—make up one of the largest ski resorts in North America. **Snowboarding** and skiing lessons keep the children happy. Off the slopes, adults have unlimited après ski options in Whistler Village's eclectic mix of pubs, dance clubs and culinary nightspots; shops, spas and art galleries also are tucked in the hamlet. Bonus conveniences at the resort include several ski-in/ski-out lodgings.

Gentle slopes and rolling hills in the Okanagan Valley are ideal for snowboarding and **cross-country skiing**. Resorts and community ski areas near the towns of Osoyoos, Oliver, Penticton, Westbank and Kelowna, along the Hwy. 97 corridor, have quite a following; most offer night skiing, too. Some of western Canada's best cross-country skiing is farther north on Hwy. 97, stretching from 100 Mile House to Quesnel and lying west of the Cariboo Mountains. The area is laced with dozens of marked, groomed trails as well as wilderness paths.

Recreational Activities

Throughout the TourBook, you may notice a Recreational Activities heading with bulleted listings of recreation-oriented establishments listed underneath. Since normal AAA inspection criteria cannot be applied, these establishments are presented for information only. Age, height and weight restrictions may apply. Reservations are often recommended and sometimes required. Visitors should phone or write the attraction for additional information, and the address and phone number are provided for this purpose.

Fast Facts

POPULATION: 3,766,100.

AREA: 948,600 sq km (366,254 sq. mi.).

CAPITAL: Victoria.

HIGHEST POINT: 4,663 m/15,295 ft., Mount Fairweather.

LOWEST POINT: Sea level, Pacific Ocean.

TIME ZONES: Mountain/ Pacific. DST in portions of the province.

MINIMUM AGE FOR DRIVERS: 16.

SEAT BELT/CHILD RESTRAINT LAWS: Seat belts required for driver and passengers; child restraints required for under 6.

HELMETS FOR MOTORCY-CLISTS: Required.

RADAR DETECTORS: Permitted.

PROVINCIAL INFORMATION CENTERS: British Columbia has more than 120 travel information centers throughout the province. Of these more than 80 are open all year and can be found in all major cities including Victoria and Vancouver. The smaller community travel information centers are open June through August. For further information phone Discover BC at (800) 663-6000.

FURTHER INFORMATION FOR VISITORS:
Tourism BC Information/ Reservation Service
P.O. Box 9830
Stn. Prov. Gov.
Victoria, BC, Canada V8W 9W5
(800) 663-6000

RECREATION INFORMATION:
BC Parks
800 Johnson St.
Victoria, BC, Canada V8V 1X4
(250) 387-4550
(800) 689-9025
(camping reservations)

FIREARMS LAWS: Vary by province or county. Contact Ministry of Attorney General, Security Programs Division, 2881 Nanaimo St., Second Floor, Victoria, BC, Canada V8V 1X4; phone (250) 387-6981, or (604) 660-2421 in Vancouver.

HOLIDAYS: Jan. 1; Easter Monday; Victoria Day, May 24 (if a Mon.) or closest prior Mon.; Canada Day, July 1; British Columbia Day, Aug. (1st Mon.); Labour Day, Sept. (1st Mon.); Thanksgiving, Oct. (2nd Mon.); Remembrance Day, Nov. 11; Dec. 25 and 26.

TAXES: British Columbia's provincial sales tax is 7 percent. There also is a provincial room tax of 8 percent or 10 percent on lodgings. A 7 percent Goods and Services Tax (GST) also is levied.

FISHING AND HUNTING REGULATIONS:
Ministry of Environment, Lands and Parks
Fisheries & Wildlife Branch
780 Blanshard St.
Victoria, BC, Canada V8V 1X4
(250) 387-9717
(wildlife inquiries)
(250) 356-7285
(freshwater fishing inquiries)

Saltwater/Tidal Fishing
Department of Fisheries and Oceans
555 W. Hastings St.
Vancouver, BC, Canada V6B 5G3
(604) 666-2828 or 666-6331.

ALCOHOL CONSUMPTION:
Legal age 19.

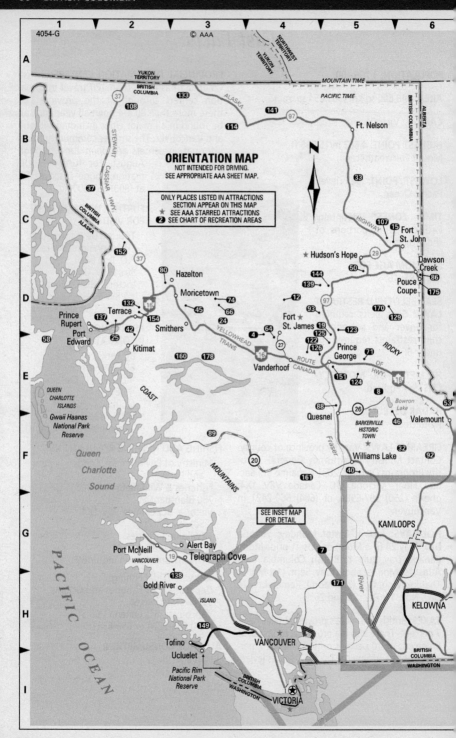

4054-G

© AAA

ORIENTATION MAP
NOT INTENDED FOR DRIVING.
SEE APPROPRIATE AAA SHEET MAP.

ONLY PLACES LISTED IN ATTRACTIONS
SECTION APPEAR ON THIS MAP
★ SEE AAA STARRED ATTRACTIONS
❷ SEE CHART OF RECREATION AREAS

YUKON TERRITORY
BRITISH COLUMBIA
NORTHWEST TERRITORY
YUKON TERRITORY
MOUNTAIN TIME
PACIFIC TIME
BRITISH COLUMBIA
ALBERTA

37
108
133
ALASKA
141
97
114
Ft. Nelson

STEWART
CASSIAR HWY.
37
33

BRITISH COLUMBIA
ALASKA
152
37
107 15 Fort St. John
HIGHWAY
Hudson's Hope ★ 29 Dawson Creek
80 Hazelton 144 50 86 Pouce Coupe
Moricetown 139 175
132 74 12 93 97 170
Terrace 16 45 66 Fort ★ 125 129 123
137 154 24 St. James 19
Prince Rupert 42 Smithers YELLOWHEAD 4 64 122 126 Prince George 71 ROCKY
Port Edward 25 TRANS 27 16 ROUTE 151 124 OF HWY. 16
58 Kitimat 160 178 Vanderhoof CANADA 8
QUEEN CHARLOTTE ISLANDS 88 26 Bowron Lake 53
Gwaii Haanas National Park Reserve 89 Quesnel BARKERVILLE HISTORIC TOWN 46 Valemount
Queen Charlotte Sound 20 161 40 Williams Lake 32 92

SEE INSET MAP FOR DETAIL
KAMLOOPS
Port McNeill Alert Bay 7
Telegraph Cove
19 VANCOUVER ISLAND
138 171
Gold River KELOWNA
149
Tofino VANCOUVER
Ucluelet BRITISH COLUMBIA WASHINGTON
Pacific Rim National Park Reserve BRITISH COLUMBIA WASHINGTON
VICTORIA

PACIFIC OCEAN
COAST MOUNTAINS
Fraser River

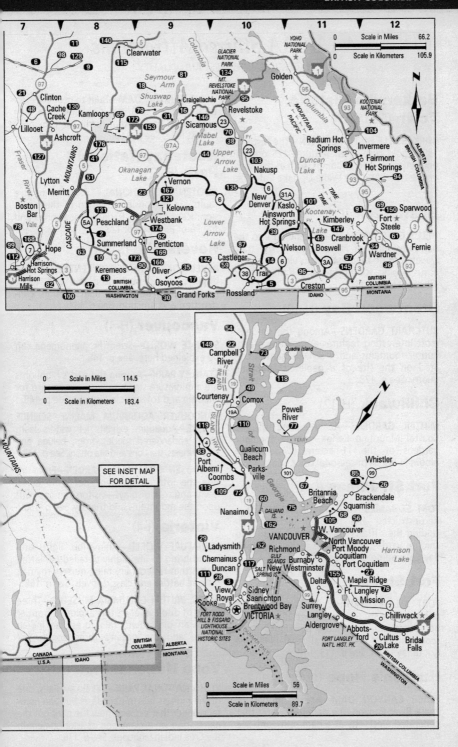

7   8   9   10   11   12

Scale in Miles   66.2
Scale in Kilometers   105.9

11 140 5 Clearwater
98 128
6   115
9

YOHO NATIONAL PARK

Columbia R.

GLACIER NATIONAL PARK
81 Seymour Arm
18 Shuswap Lake
MT. REVELSTOKE NATIONAL PARK 134
95 Golden
95

KOOTENAY NATIONAL PARK
104

21 97 Clinton
48 Cache 130
Creek Kamloops
Ashcroft 65 172
153 Craigellachie
16 146 Sicamous
79 31 Revelstoke
23 70
38
MOUNTAIN PACIFIC
Radium Hot Springs
Invermere
Fairmont Hot Springs
97
94

Lillooet
127 97
Lytton Merritt
176
41
51
97A
97
Okanagan Lake
Vernon 167 121
Kelowna
97C
131 Peachland
5A Westbank 174
2 Summerland 62
63 Penticton 169
173
10 90 Oliver
Keremeos 166
13 35 17
47 Osoyoos
100
WASHINGTON 30 Grand Forks Rossland

Upper Arrow Lake 44
23 103 Nakusp
135
New Denver 31A
Ainsworth Hot Springs 101
39
Castlegar 87 142
59
38 Trail 14 6
5 96
Creston 3A

Lower Arrow Lake
6
Kaslo 147
Kimberley
43 Cranbrook
Boswell 57
34 Wardner
145 36
Nelson

TIME TIME
69 150 Sparwood
91 Fort Steele
61 Fernie
3
WELL
BRITISH COLUMBIA
IDAHO 95 MONTANA

Boston Bar
78 Yale
168
99 7
112
Harrison Hot Springs
Harrison Mills 82
CASCADE MOUNTAINS
FRASER River

MOUNTAINS

Scale in Miles   114.5
Scale in Kilometers   183.4

SEE INSET MAP
FOR DETAIL

MOUNTAINS

CANADA   ALBERTA
U.S.A. IDAHO BRITISH COLUMBIA MONTANA

54
148 22
Campbell River 73
Quadra Island
84 118
Courtenay 49
19A Comox
Powell River 77
INLAND HWY
Strait of Georgia
119 110
83 4
Port Alberni Qualicum Beach
Parksville
113 109 72
Coombs
19 60
Nanaimo GALIANO IS. 75
29 Ladysmith 52
Chemainus Richmond
111 Duncan 117 SALT SPRING IS. 162
28 View Sidney
Royal Saanichton
Sooke Brentwood Bay
FORT RODD HILL & FISGARD LIGHTHOUSE NATIONAL HISTORIC SITES
VICTORIA

FERRY
101 67
85
1
26
Whistler
99
Britannia Beach
Brackendale
Squamish
68 56
105 162
VANCOUVER
W. Vancouver
North Vancouver
Port Moody
Coquitlam
Port Coquitlam
Burnaby 27
New Westminster 155 Maple Ridge 76
Delta Ft. Langley
99 Mission
Surrey 7
Langley Chilliwack
Aldergrove
Abbots- Cultus Bridal
ford 20 Lake Falls
FORT LANGLEY NAT'L HIST. PK.
Harrison Lake
BRITISH COLUMBIA
WASHINGTON

Scale in Miles   56
Scale in Kilometers   89.7

AAA/CAA Starred Attractions

EXCEPTIONAL INTEREST AND QUALITY

Barkerville Historic Town (F-5)

BARKERVILLE HISTORIC TOWN—The restored 1870s gold rush town features 125 original and reconstructed buildings, such as the Barkerville Hotel and the Wake Up Jake Cafe. See p. 106.

Boston Bar (C-7)

HELL'S GATE AIRTRAM—Descending into the narrowest part of Fraser Canyon, the tram travels a route that lets visitors view fishways, a suspension footbridge and a film about salmon. See p. 106.

Brentwood Bay (H-10)

BUTCHART GARDENS—Among the gardens' most interesting features are a show greenhouse, fountains and a sunken garden created on the site of a depleted limestone quarry. See p. 173.

Chilliwack (H-12)

MINTER GARDENS—At the base of the Coastal Mountain Range, the 11 thematic gardens of the 11-hectare (27-acre) site bloom in bursts of seasonal color. See p. 155.

Fort St. James (D-4)

FORT ST. JAMES NATIONAL HISTORIC SITE—Reconstructed and restored buildings—including the officers' dwelling, fish cache and chicken yard—comprise the former Hudson's Bay Co. trading post. See p. 113.

Fort Steele (C-12)

FORT STEELE HERITAGE TOWN—A bakery, photography studio, restaurant and newspaper office are among the buildings in this representation of a typical 1890-1905 East Kootenay town. See p. 113.

Hudson's Hope (C-4)

PEACE CANYON DAM—At the outlet of Peace River Canyon, the dam uses water that generated electricity at a dam upstream. See p. 118.

W.A.C. BENNETT DAM—Built to produce electrical power for British Columbia, the dam produces a backup that forms the province's largest lake. See p. 119.

Kootenay National Park (B-12)

KOOTENAY NATIONAL PARK—Extensive faults are responsible for two of the park's significant features: Radium Hot Springs and the Paint Pots. See p. 123.

Revelstoke (B-10)

REVELSTOKE DAM VISITOR CENTRE—Lighted displays, audiovisual programs and topographic maps detail the dam's design, construction and function. See p. 134.

Vancouver (H-4)

SCIENCE WORLD—Scientific phenomena can be explained here. See p. 148.

STANLEY PARK—Among the park's highlights are a miniature steam railway, a farmyard for children and totem pole displays. See p. 148.

VANCOUVER AQUARIUM MARINE SCIENCE CENTRE—Aquarium exhibits let visitors learn about endangered species, frogs, beluga and killer whales, sea lions and sea otters. See p. 148.

VANDUSEN BOTANICAL GARDEN—From inside the intricate gardens—set amid lakes, lawns and rock displays—visitors can gaze out upon the mountains and the city. See p. 150.

Victoria (I-4)

MINIATURE WORLD—Animation, lights and sound bring to life highly detailed miniature scenes that reflect fairy tales, nursery rhymes, historic battles and classic novels. See p. 168.

ROYAL BRITISH COLUMBIA MUSEUM—Three floors of displays let visitors explore a frontier town, an old-growth rain forest, an Indian village and the ocean's three zones. See p. 169.

Yoho National Park (A-11)

YOHO NATIONAL PARK—Takakkaw Falls, one of the highest falls in Canada, is but one natural wonder that explains how the park got the name yoho, an exclamation of astonishment in the Cree Indian language. See p. 176.

RECREATION AREAS

	MAP LOCATION	CAMPING	PICNICKING	HIKING TRAILS	BOATING	BOAT RAMP	BOAT RENTAL	FISHING	SWIMMING	PETS ON LEASH	BICYCLE TRAILS	WINTER SPORTS	VISITOR CENTER	LODGE/CABINS	FOOD SERVICE
NATIONAL PARKS *(See place listings)*															
Glacier (A-10) 1,350 square kilometres.		•	•	•				•		•		•	•	•	•
Gwaii Haanas (F-11) 1,470 square kilometres.		•						•					•		
Kootenay (B-12) 1,406 square kilometres.		•	•	•	•			•	•	•	•	•	•	•	•
Mount Revelstoke (A-10) 260 square kilometres.			•	•				•		•			•		
Pacific Rim (I-3) 510 square kilometres.		•	•	•	•			•	•	•					
Yoho (A-11) 1,313 square kilometres. Horse rental.		•	•	•	•			•	•	•	•	•	•	•	•
PROVINCIAL															
Adams Lake (A-9) 56 hectares 15 km n. of Chase off Hwy. 1.	18	•						•	•	•					
Alice Lake (G-12) 396 hectares 13 km n. of Squamish on Hwy. 99. Nature programs. Cross-country skiing.	1	•	•	•				•	•	•		•			
Allison Lake (C-8) 23 hectares 28 km n. of Princeton on Hwy. 5A.	2	•	•		•	•		•	•	•					
Andrews Bay (E-3) 45 hectares 60 km w. of Hwy. 35, s. of Burns Lake on Ootsa Lake.	160	•	•		•	•		•			•				
Andy Bailey (C-5) 174 hectares 11 km s.e. of Hwy. 97 near Fort Nelson.	33		•		•	•		•	•	•					
Arrow Lakes (Shelter Bay) (B-10) 93 hectares on Hwy. 23 at Shelter Bay.	38	•	•		•	•		•		•					
Bamberton (H-10) 28 hectares 32 km n. of Victoria off Hwy. 1.	3	•	•					•	•	•					
Barkerville (F-6) 55 hectares 8 km e. of Wells on Hwy. 26. *(See Barkerville Historic Town p. 106)*	46	•	•	•						•			•		
Bear Creek (C-9) 178 hectares 8 km n. of Hwy. 97 near Kelowna.	121	•	•	•				•	•	•	•				
Beatton (C-5) 312 hectares 13 km n. of Hwy. 97 near Fort St. John. Cross-country skiing.	107	•	•	•	•	•		•	•	•	•	•			
Beaumont (E-4) 191 hectares on Fraser Lake, 129 km w. of Prince George off Hwy. 16.	4	•	•		•	•		•	•	•					
Beaver Creek (D-10) 44 hectares 12.9 km e. of Trail on Hwy. 22A.	5		•					•		•					
Big Bar Lake (A-7) 332 hectares 40 km n. of Clinton off Hwy. 97.	6	•	•		•			•	•	•					
Birkenhead Lake (G-5) 3,642 hectares 55 km n.e. of Pemberton off Hwy. 99.	7	•	•	•	•	•		•	•	•	•				
Blanket Creek (B-10) 316 hectares 30 km s. of Revelstoke on Hwy. 23.	70	•	•					•	•	•					
Bowron Lake (E-5) 123,117 hectares 112.5 km e. of Quesnel via a gravel access road off Hwy. 26. Nature programs. Water circuit of connecting lakes.	8	•	•	•	•	•	•	•	•				•	•	•
Boya Lake (B-2) 4,597 hectares 40 km n.e. of Cassiar off Hwy. 37.	108				•	•		•	•	•					
Brandywine Falls (F-11) 143 hectares 25 km s. of Whistler on Hwy. 99.	85	•	•	•						•		•			
Bridge Lake (A-7) 6 hectares 51 km e. of 93 Mile House off Hwy. 24.	9	•			•	•		•	•	•					
Bromley Rock (D-8) 149 hectares 19 km e. of Princeton off Hwy. 3.	10	•	•		•	•		•	•	•					
Bull Canyon (F-4) 369 hectares 10 km w. of Alexis Creek on Hwy. 20.	161	•	•					•							
Canim Beach (A-8) 6 hectares on Canim Lake, 43 km e. of 100 Mile House off Hwy. 97.	11	•	•		•			•	•	•					
Carp Lake (D-4) 19,344 hectares 32 km s.w. of McLeod Lake off Hwy. 97. Canoeing.	12	•	•	•	•	•		•	•	•					
Cathedral (D-8) 33,272 hectares 24 km s.w. of Keremeos off Hwy. 3.	13	•	•	•				•		•				•	•
Champion Lakes (D-10) 1,426 hectares 10 km s. of Castlegar off Hwy. 3B. Nature programs. Cross-country skiing.	14	•	•	•	•			•	•	•		•	•		
Charlie Lake (C-5) 92 hectares 13 km n.w. of Fort St. John off Hwy. 97.	15	•	•	•	•	•		•		•					
Chilliwack Lake (D-8) 162 hectares 84 km s.e. of Chilliwack via an access road off Hwy. 1.	100	•	•	•	•	•		•	•	•					

RECREATION AREAS

	MAP LOCATION	CAMPING	PICNICKING	HIKING TRAILS	BOATING	BOAT RAMP	BOAT RENTAL	FISHING	SWIMMING	PETS ON LEASH	BICYCLE TRAILS	WINTER SPORTS	VISITOR CENTER	LODGE/CABINS	FOOD SERVICE
Cinnemousun Narrows (B-9) 533 hectares 22.5 km n. of Sicamous. No road access.	16		•	•	•			•	•	•					
Conkle Lake (D-9) 587 hectares 28 km n.e. of Osoyoos via Hwy. 3, then 26 km to entrance. Hunting.	17	•	•	•	•	•		•	•	•					
Crooked River (D-5) 873 hectares 72 km n. of Prince George on Hwy. 97. Cross-country skiing, ice fishing.	19	•	•	•				•	•	•		•	•		
Cultus Lake (H-12) 656 hectares 11 km s.w. of Chilliwack off Hwy. 1.	20	•	•	•	•	•		•	•	•					
Dionisio Point (G-10) 142 hectares 64 km n. of Victoria on Galiano Island via car ferry.	162	•	•					•	•	•					
Downing (A-7) 100 hectares 16 km s.e. of Clinton off Hwy. 97.	21	•	•		•	•		•	•	•					
Elk Falls (E-10) 1,087 hectares 10 km n.w. of Campbell River off Hwy. 28.	22	•	•	•				•	•	•					
Ellison (C-9) 219 hectares on Okanagan Lake, 16 km s.w. of Vernon off Hwy. 97.	23	•	•	•	•	•		•	•	•			•		
Englishman River Falls (G-10) 97 hectares 13 km s.w. of Parksville off Hwy. 4.	109	•	•	•				•	•	•					
Ethel F. Wilson Memorial (D-3) 29 hectares 24 km n. of Hwy. 16 at Burns Lake.	24	•			•	•		•	•						
Exchamsiks River (E-2) 18 hectares 57.9 km w. of Terrace off Hwy. 16.	25	•	•		•	•		•	•						
Fillongley (F-10) 23 hectares on Denman Island via ferry from Buckley Bay.	110	•	•					•	•	•					
French Beach (H-9) 59 hectares 5 km e. of Jordan River off Hwy. 14.	111	•	•					•	•						
Garibaldi (G-12) 194,650 hectares accessible by trail from Hwy. 99 or the British Columbia Railway. Cross-country skiing. Pets prohibited in Black Tusk area. *(See Squamish p. 136)*	26	•	•	•	•			•				•	•		•
Gladstone (D-9) 39,322 hectares 5 km e. of Christina Lake on Hwy. 3.	142	•	•	•	•	•		•	•	•					
Golden Ears (H-12) 55,590 hectares 11 km n.w. of Maple Ridge off Hwy. 7. Horse rental.	27	•	•	•	•	•	•	•	•	•					
Goldpan (B-7) 5 hectares 10 km s. of Spences Bridge on Hwy. 1.	127	•	•					•		•			•		
Goldstream (H-10) 388 hectares 19.3 km n.w. of Victoria via Hwy. 1. Salmon spawning in fall.	28	•	•					•	•	•			•		
Gordon Bay (G-9) 51 hectares 14 km w. of Lake Cowichan off Hwy. 18.	29	•	•	•	•	•		•	•	•					
Green Lake (A-8) 347 hectares 16 km e. of Hwy. 97 at 70 Mile House.	128	•	•		•	•		•	•	•					
Gwillim Lake (D-5) 9,200 hectares 40 km. n.w. of Tumbler Ridge on Hwy. 29.	129	•	•		•	•		•							
Haynes Point (D-9) 38 hectares 2 km s. of Osoyoos on Hwy. 97.	30	•	•		•	•		•	•	•					
Herald (B-9) 79 hectares 12.8 km n.e. of Tappen off Hwy. 1.	31	•	•	•	•	•		•	•	•					
Horsefly Lake (F-6) 148 hectares 68 km e. of 150 Mile House off Hwy. 97.	32	•	•		•	•		•	•	•					
Inkaneep (D-9) 21 hectares 5 km n. of Oliver on Hwy. 97.	166	•						•	•						
Jimsmith Lake (C-12) 12 hectares 2 km s.w. of Cranbrook off Hwy. 3.	34	•	•		•	•		•	•	•			•		
Juniper Beach (B-8) 260 hectares 20 km e. of Cache Creek on Hwy. 1.	130	•	•					•	•	•					
Kawkawa Lake (C-7) 7 hectares 10 km e. of Hope off Hwy. 5.	168		•		•	•		•							
Kalamalka Lake (C-9) 978 hectares 10 km s.e. of Vernon off Hwy. 6.	167		•	•				•	•						
Kentucky-Alleyne (C-8) 144 hectares 30 km s. of Merritt on Hwy. 5A.	131	•	•	•				•	•	•					
Kettle River (D-9) 179 hectares 5 km n. of Rock Creek on Hwy. 33.	35	•	•	•	•			•	•	•			•		
Kickininee (C-9) 49 hectares 8 km n. of Penticton on Hwy. 97.	169		•		•	•		•	•						

RECREATION AREAS

	MAP LOCATION	CAMPING	PICNICKING	HIKING TRAILS	BOATING	BOAT RAMP	BOAT RENTAL	FISHING	SWIMMING	PETS ON LEASH	BICYCLE TRAILS	WINTER SPORTS	VISITOR CENTER	LODGE/CABINS	FOOD SERVICE
Kikomun Creek (D-12) 682 hectares 64 km e. of Cranbrook via Hwy. 3, then 11 km s. to entrance.	36	•	•		•	•		•	•	•	•				
Kilby (D-7) 3 hectares 2 km e. of Harrison Mills on Hwy. 7. Historic.	112	•	•		•	•		•	•				•		
Kinaskan Lake (C-1) 1,800 hectares on Hwy. 37 at Kinaskan Lake.	37	•	•	•	•	•		•		•					
Kleanza Creek (D-2) 269 hectares 20 km e. of Terrace on Hwy. 16.	132	•	•	•				•		•					
Kokanee Creek (C-10) 260 hectares 19 km n.e. of Nelson on Hwy. 3A. Cross-country skiing.	39	•	•	•				•	•				•	•	
Kootenay Lake (C-11) 343 hectares near Kaslo on Hwy. 31.	147	•						•	•	•					
Lac la Hache (F-5) 24 hectares 13 km n. of Lac la Hache on Hwy. 97. Cross-country skiing.	40	•	•		•	•		•	•				•		
Lac Le Jeune (B-8) 47 hectares 28 km s.w. of Kamloops off Hwy. 5.	41	•	•	•	•	•	•	•	•				•		
Lakelse Lake (D-2) 362 hectares 26 km s.w. of Terrace on Hwy. 37.	42	•	•	•	•	•		•	•						
Liard River Hotsprings (A-3) 976 hectares at Liard River on Hwy. 97.	133	•	•					•	•				•		
Little Qualicum Falls (F-10) 440 hectares 13 km s.w. of Parksville off Hwy. 4.	113	•	•	•				•	•	•					
Lockhart Beach (C-11) 3 hectares 53 km n. of Creston on Hwy. 3A.	43	•	•					•	•	•					
Loveland Bay (E-9) 30 hectares 18 km w. of Campbell River off Hwy. 28.	148	•	•		•	•		•	•						
Mabel Lake (B-9) 187 hectares 76 km n.e. of Vernon via an access road off Hwy. 6.	44	•	•		•	•		•	•	•			•		
Manning (D-8) 66,884 hectares on Hwy. 3 between Hope and Princeton. Nature programs. Scenic. Horse rental. *(See Hope p. 118)*	47	•	•	•	•	•	•	•	•	•	•	•	•	•	•
Marble Canyon (B-7) 335 hectares 40 km n.w. of Cache Creek off Hwy. 12.	48	•	•					•	•	•					
Martha Creek (A-10) 71 hectares 20 km n. of Revelstoke on Hwy. 23.	134	•	•	•	•	•		•	•						
McConnell Lakes (B-8) 189 hectares 23 km s.w. of Kamloops off Hwy. 5.	176	•	•	•				•	•						
McDonald Creek (C-10) 468 hectares 10 km s. of Nakusp on Hwy. 6.	135	•	•		•	•		•	•	•					
Meziadin Lake (C-2) 335 hectares 50 km e. of Stewart off Hwy. 37.	152	•	•		•	•		•	•						
Miracle Beach (E-10) 137 hectares 22.5 km n. of Courtenay off Hwy. 19.	49	•	•	•				•	•	•			•		
Moberly Lake (D-5) 98 hectares 24 km n.w. of Chetwynd on Hwy. 29.	50	•	•	•	•	•		•	•	•					
Monck (B-8) 87 hectares 22 km n.e. of Merritt off Hwy. 5A.	51	•	•	•	•	•		•	•	•					
Monkman (D-5) 32,000 hectares 60 km s. of Tumbler Ridge off Hwy. 29.	170	•	•	•				•							
Montague Harbour Marine (G-10) 97 hectares 48 km n. of Victoria on Galiano Island via car ferry.	52	•	•	•	•	•		•	•						
Morton Lake (E-10) 67 hectares 32 km n.w. of Campbell River on Hwy. 19.	54	•	•		•	•		•	•	•					
Mount Robson (E-6) 219,534 hectares bordering Jasper National Park on Hwy. 16. Horse rental. *(See Valemount p. 138)*	55	•	•	•	•	•		•	•	•	•	•	•	•	
Mount Seymour (G-11) 3,508 hectares 24 km n.e. of Vancouver off Hwy. 1. Cross-country skiing. *(See Vancouver p. 159)*	56		•	•						•				•	•
Moyie Lake (D-11) 91 hectares 19 km s. of Cranbrook on Hwy. 3.	57	•	•		•	•		•	•	•					
Muncho Lake (B-3) 88,420 hectares on Hwy. 97 at Muncho Lake.	114	•	•	•	•	•		•		•				•	•
Naikoon (E-1) 73,325 hectares on n. tip of Graham Island in the Queen Charlotte Islands.	58	•	•	•				•		•			•	•	
Nairn Falls (H-5) 171 hectares 4 km s. of Pemberton on Hwy. 99.	171	•	•	•				•							

RECREATION AREAS

	MAP LOCATION	CAMPING	PICNICKING	HIKING TRAILS	BOATING	BOAT RAMP	BOAT RENTAL	FISHING	SWIMMING	PETS ON LEASH	BICYCLE TRAILS	WINTER SPORTS	VISITOR CENTER	LODGE/CABINS	FOOD SERVICE
Nancy Greene (D-10) 5,140 hectares 26 km n.w. of Rossland via Hwy. 3B. Cross-country skiing, snowshoeing.	59	•	•	•	•	•		•	•	•		•		•	
Newcastle Island Marine (G-10) 336 hectares on an island e. of Nanaimo via passenger ferry.	60	•	•	•	•			•	•	•			•		•
Niskonlith Lake (B-8) 238 hectares 8 km n.w. of Chase off Hwy. 1.	172	•						•	•						
Norbury Lake (C-12) 97 hectares s.e. of jct. hwys. 93 and 95 at Fort Steele.	61	•	•		•	•		•	•	•					
North Thompson River (A-8) 126 hectares 5 km s. of Clearwater off Hwy. 5.	115	•	•	•				•	•				•		
Okanagan Falls (D-8) 2 hectares at Okanagan Falls on Hwy. 97.	173	•						•							
Okanagan Lake (C-9) 99 hectares 28 km n.w. of Penticton off Hwy. 97.	62	•	•	•	•	•		•	•	•				•	•
Okanagan Mountain (C-9) 10,562 hectares 40 km n. of Penticton off Hwy. 97.	174	•	•	•				•	•						
One Island Lake (D-6) 61 hectares 30 km s. of Tupper off Hwy. 2.	175	•	•		•	•		•	•						
Otter Lake (C-8) 51 hectares on Otter Lake, 25 km w. of Princeton off Hwy. 5A.	63	•	•		•	•		•	•						
Paarens Beach (D-4) 43 hectares 10 km s.w. of Fort St. James off Hwy. 27.	64	•	•		•	•		•	•						
Paul Lake (B-8) 402 hectares 25 km n.e. of Kamloops off Hwy. 5.	65	•	•	•	•	•		•	•	•			•		
Pendleton Bay (D-3) 8 hectares 35 km n. of Burns Lake off Hwy. 16.	66	•	•		•	•		•	•						
Porpoise Bay (F-11) 61 hectares 4 km n.e. of Sechelt on East Porpoise Bay Rd.	67	•	•	•				•	•	•					
Porteau Cove (G-11) 50 hectares 30 km n. of Vancouver on Hwy. 99. Scuba diving.	68	•	•					•	•	•					
Premier Lake (C-12) 662 hectares 16 km e. of Skookumchuck via Hwy. 95.	69	•	•		•	•		•	•	•			•		
Prudhomme Lake (D-2) 7 hectares 20 km e. of Prince Rupert on Hwy. 16.	137	•		•				•	•						
Purden Lake (E-5) 321 hectares 64 km e. of Prince George off Hwy. 16. Cross-country skiing, ice fishing.	71	•	•		•			•	•	•					
Rathtrevor Beach (G-10) 347 hectares 3 km s. of Parksville on Hwy. 19.	72	•	•	•					•	•			•		
Rearguard Falls (E-6) 49 hectares 4.5 km e. of Tete Jaun Cache on Hwy. 16.	53		•	•				•							
Rebecca Spit Marine (E-10) 177 hectares on Quadra Island via ferry from Campbell River, then 5 km e. on Heriot Bay Rd.	73		•	•	•	•		•	•	•					
Red Bluff (D-3) 148 hectares 48 km n. of Topley via an access road.	74	•	•	•	•	•		•	•	•					
Roberts Creek (G-11) 40 hectares 10 km w. of Gibsons Landing on Hwy. 101.	75	•	•		•			•	•	•					
Roderick Haig-Brown (B-9) 988 hectares 5 km n. of Hwy. 1 at Squilax.	153		•					•		•	•	•	•		
Rolley Lake (H-11) 115 hectares 13 km n.w. of Mission off Hwy. 7.	76	•	•	•	•			•	•	•					
Ruckle (G-10) 486 hectares at Beaver Point on Saltspring Island via ferry from Swartz Bay.	117	•	•	•				•		•			•		
Saltery Bay (F-11) 69 hectares at Saltery Bay w. of ferry landing on Hwy. 101.	77	•	•	•	•			•	•	•					
Sasquatch (C-7) 1,217 hectares 6.4 km n. of Harrison Hot Springs via an access road off Hwy. 7.	78	•	•	•	•			•	•	•					
Schoen Lake (H-3) 8,430 hectares 20 km n. of Sayward, 12 km s. of Hwy. 19.	138	•	•	•	•			•	•						
Seeley Lake (D-2) 24 hectares 6 km w. of Hazelton on Hwy. 16.	80	•	•		•			•	•	•					
Shuswap Lake (B-9) 149 hectares 19.25 km n. of Squilax. Nature programs.	79	•	•	•	•	•		•	•	•			•	•	

RECREATION AREAS

	MAP LOCATION	CAMPING	PICNICKING	HIKING TRAILS	BOATING	BOAT RAMP	BOAT RENTAL	FISHING	SWIMMING	PETS ON LEASH	BICYCLE TRAILS	WINTER SPORTS	VISITOR CENTER	LODGE/CABINS	FOOD SERVICE
Silver Beach (A-9) 130 hectares at n. end of Shuswap Lake at Seymour Arm.	81	•		•				•	•	•					
Skagit Valley (D-7) 27,948 hectares 8 km w. of Hope via Hwy. 1, then 43 km s. on Second Rd.	82	•	•	•	•	•		•	•	•			•		
Smelt Bay (E-10) 16 hectares on Cortes Island via ferry from Campbell River.	118	•	•					•	•	•					
Sowchea Bay (D-4) 13 hectares on Stuart Lake, 13 km w. of Fort St. James off Hwy. 27.	139	•			•	•		•	•	•					
Spahats Creek (A-8) 270 hectares 15 km n. of Hwy. 5 at Clearwater.	140	•	•	•						•					
Sproat Lake (F-9) 39 hectares 13 km n.w. of Port Alberni on Sproat Lake Rd.	83	•	•		•	•		•		•					
Stamp Falls (F-9) 234 hectares 14 km w. of Port Alberni on Stamp River Rd.	119	•	•	•				•		•					
Stone Mountain (B-4) 25,691 hectares 125 km n. of Fort Nelson on Hwy. 97.	141	•	•	•				•		•		•	•		
Strathcona (E-10) 253,773 hectares 48.25 km w. of Campbell River via Hwy. 28. Cross-country and downhill skiing.	84	•	•	•	•	•		•	•	•		•			
Swan Lake (D-6) 67 hectares at Tupper, 38 km s. of Dawson Creek via Hwy. 2.	86	•	•	•	•	•		•	•	•					
Syringa Creek (C-10) 4,417 hectares 17 km n. of Robson off Hwy. 3.	87	•	•	•	•	•		•	•	•					
Taylor Arm (H-3) 71 hectares 15 km w. of Port Alberni on Hwy. 4.	149	•	•	•				•	•	•	•				
Ten Mile Lake (E-4) 260 hectares 10 km n. of Quesnel on Hwy. 97. Cross-country skiing.	88	•	•	•	•	•		•	•	•					
Top of the World (C-12) 8,791 hectares 95 km e. of Kimberley off Hwy. 93, then 54 km e. on a gravel access road.	150	•	•	•				•		•					
Tudyah Lake (D-4) 56 hectares on Hwy. 97 at Mackenzie.	144	•	•		•	•		•	•	•					
Tweedsmuir (F-3) 994,246 hectares 349 km n.w. of Williams Lake on Hwy. 20. Horse rental.	89	•	•	•	•	•	•	•	•	•			•	•	•
Tyhee Lake (D-3) 33 hectares 8 km w. of Telkwa on Hwy. 16. Cross-country skiing.	45	•	•	•				•	•	•		•			
Vaseux Lake (D-9) 12 hectares at Vaseux Lake on Hwy. 97.	90	•			•			•		•					
Wasa Lake (C-11) 144 hectares 21 km n. of Fort Steele off Hwy. 93/95. Nature programs. Cross-country skiing.	91	•	•		•	•		•	•	•			•		
Wells Gray (F-6) 529,748 hectares 30 km n. of Clearwater via an access road off Hwy. 5. Cross-country skiing; horse rental.	92	•	•	•	•	•	•	•	•	•	•	•	•	•	•
West Lake (E-5) 258 hectares 29 km s.w. of Prince George off Hwy. 16.	151		•		•	•		•	•	•			•		
Whiskers Point (D-4) 50 hectares 127 km n. of Prince George off Hwy. 97.	93	•	•		•	•		•	•	•					
Whiteswan Lake (C-12) 1,994 hectares 25 km s. of Canal Flats off Hwy. 93/95. Cross-country skiing.	94	•	•	•	•	•		•		•		•			
Wistaria (E-3) 40 hectares 40 km w. of Hwy. 35, s. of Burns Lake on Ootsa Lake.	178	•	•		•	•		•							
Yahk (D-11) 9 hectares on Hwy. 3/93 at Yahk.	145	•	•					•		•					
Yard Creek (B-9) 61 hectares 20 km n. of Sicamous on Hwy. 1.	146	•	•	•				•		•			•		
OTHER															
Berman Lake Park (E-4) 38 hectares 45 km w. of Prince George. Canoeing.	122		•	•					•	•					
Canyon Hot Springs (B-10) Hot mineral springs 35.5 km e. of Revelstoke. *(See Revelstoke p. 134)*	95	•	•	•				•	•						•
Creston Valley (D-11) 7,000 hectares 9.5 km w. of Creston on Hwy. 3. Birdwatching, canoeing, hunting. *(See Creston p. 110)*	96	•	•	•				•				•	•		•
Fairmont Hot Springs (B-11) Hot mineral springs on Hwy. 95 in Fairmont Hot Springs. Horse rental. *(See place listing p. 111)*	97	•	•	•					•			•	•	•	•

RECREATION AREAS

	MAP LOCATION	CAMPING	PICNICKING	HIKING TRAILS	BOATING	BOAT RAMP	BOAT RENTAL	FISHING	SWIMMING	PETS ON LEASH	BICYCLE TRAILS	WINTER SPORTS	VISITOR CENTER	LODGE/CABINS	FOOD SERVICE
Ferry Island (D-2) 61 hectares 1 km e. of Terrace off Hwy. 16. Cross-country skiing. *(See Terrace p. 137)*	154	•	•	•				•		•		•			
Giscome Portage Park (D-5) 22 hectares 50 km n. of Prince George. Historic. Cross-country skiing.	123		•	•						•		•			
Green Lake Area (A-7) 347 hectares 10 km e. of 70 Mile House on Green Lake Rd. Hunting, snowmobiling, water skiing; horse rental.	98	•	•		•	•	•	•	•	•				•	•
Harold Mann Park (E-5) 13 hectares 50 km n.e. of Prince George. Canoeing; nature trail.	124	•						•	•	•					
Harrison Hot Springs (C-7) Hot mineral springs on Harrison Lake, 5 km n. of Hwy. 7 on Hwy. 9. Canoeing, golf, hunting, rock hunting; horse rental. *(See place listing p. 117)*	99	•	•	•	•	•	•	•	•	•	•	•	•	•	•
Kanaka Creek Regional Park (H-11) 400 hectares 2 km e. of Haney. Canoeing; fish hatchery, horse trails. *(See Maple Ridge in Vancouver p. 156)*	155		•	•				•		•					
Kootenay Lake (C-11) e. of Balfour.	101	•	•		•	•		•						•	
Nakusp Hot Springs (B-10) Hot mineral springs 3 km n. of Nakusp on Hwy. 23, then e. on Hot Springs Rd. Cross-country skiing. *(See Nakusp p. 125)*	103	•	•	•				•	•				•	•	
Ness Lake Park (E-5) 14 hectares 32 km n.w. of Prince George. Canoeing, cross-country skiing.	125	•	•					•	•	•		•			
Radium Hot Springs (B-12) Hot mineral springs near the w. entrance of Kootenay National Park. Horse rental. *(See place listing and Kootenay National Park p. 123)*	104	•	•	•	•	•	•	•		•	•	•	•	•	•
Whytecliff Park (G-11) 40 acres 22.5 km n.e. of Vancouver on the North Shore. Scuba diving.	105		•	•				•	•						•
Wilkins Park (E-4) 57 hectares 14 km w. of Prince George. Cross-country skiing; nature trail.	126		•	•	•					•		•			

British Columbia Temperature Averages Maximum/Minimum (Celsius)

From the records of the National Weather Service

	JAN	FEB	MAR	APR	MAY	JUN	JUL	AUG	SEP	OCT	NOV	DEC
Fort St. John	-11 / -19	-7 / -17	-1 / -10	8 / -2	17 / 4	20 / 8	22 / 11	20 / 10	16 / 5	9 / 0	-2 / -10	-9 / -17
Kamloops	-2 / -10	4 / -5	10 / -1	16 / 3	22 / 7	26 / 11	29 / 13	28 / 12	23 / 8	14 / 3	6 / -1	1 / -6
Prince George	-7 / -17	-1 / -12	3 / -8	10 / -2	17 / 2	20 / 6	22 / 8	21 / 7	17 / 3	10 / 0	1 / -7	-4 / -12
Prince Rupert	4 / -1	5 / -1	7 / 1	10 / 3	13 / 6	16 / 9	17 / 10	17 / 11	16 / 9	12 / 6	8 / 3	5 / 1
Vancouver	6 / 1	8 / 1	11 / 3	15 / 6	18 / 8	21 / 11	24 / 13	24 / 12	20 / 10	15 / 7	10 / 4	7 / 2
Victoria	6 / 2	8 / 3	10 / 4	13 / 6	16 / 7	18 / 10	20 / 11	20 / 11	18 / 10	14 / 8	10 / 5	7 / 3

Points of Interest

ABBOTSFORD (H-11)
pop. 105,400, elev. 58 m/190'

Abbotsford is the regional shopping center as well as the center of trade and industry for the fruit, livestock, poultry and dairy farms of the surrounding Fraser Valley. Several area industries and farms offer tours, including Clayburn Industries Ltd., at Railway and Pine streets. Castle Park Golf and Games Amusement Park, 36165 N. Parallel Rd., provides a range of family entertainment.

Abbotsford Chamber of Commerce: 2462 Mc-Callum Rd., Abbotsford, BC, Canada V2S 3P9; phone (604) 859-9651.

FRASER VALLEY TROUT HATCHERY, about 3 km (1.9 mi.) s. of the Trans-Canada Hwy. at 34345 Vye Rd., offers self-guiding tours tracing the growth of rainbow, cutthroat and steelhead trout. Free slide shows and aquarium exhibits are available. Allow 30 minutes minimum. Daily 10-5, July-Aug.; Sun.-Thurs. 10-3, Sept.-Nov. and Feb.-June. Donations. Phone (604) 852-5388.

TRETHEWEY HOUSE ON MILL LAKE HERI-TAGE SITE is off Hwy. 1 exit 90, n. on McCallum Rd., w. on Marshall Rd., then n. to 2313 Ware St. Furnishings reflect the 1920s. The MSA Museum, which includes an archives library, is housed inside. Allow 30 minutes minimum. Museum open Thurs.-Sun. 11-5, Mon.-Wed. 1-5, July-Aug.; Mon.-Fri. 1-5, rest of year. Closed Jan. 1 and Dec. 25-31. Library open Tues.-Fri. 9-noon and 1-5; closed Jan. 1 and Dec. 25-31. Donations. Phone (604) 853-0313.

AINSWORTH HOT SPRINGS
(C-11) elev. 538 m/1766'

AINSWORTH HOT SPRINGS is 62 km (39 mi.) n. of Nelson on Hwy. 31. The natural cave steam baths and heated mineral pools were discovered by Indians about 1800. The springs, which have an average temperature of 45 C (113 F), border Kootenay Lake. Towels can be rented. Food is available. Daily 10-9:30. Admission $6.50; ages 13-15, $6; over 65, $5.50; ages 3-12, $4.50. Day passes $10; ages 13-15, $9; over 65, $8.50; ages 3-12, $6.50. AE, DI, MC, VI. Phone (250) 229-4212 or (800) 668-1171.

ALDERGROVE—see Vancouver p. 155.

ALERT BAY (G-3)
pop. 600, elev. 15 m/49'

On crescent-shaped Cormorant Island off Vancouver Island's northeast coast, Alert Bay is a fishing village reached by ferry from Port Mc-Neill (see place listing p. 130). The influence of native cultures is evident in the many totem poles, including a memorial pole for totem carver Chief Mungo Martin.

Travel InfoCentre: 118 Fir St., Alert Bay, BC, Canada V0N 1A0; phone (250) 974-5024.

ALERT BAY LIBRARY/MUSEUM, 118 Fir St., is a small museum with Kwakiutl artifacts and items depicting local history. Allow 30 minutes minimum. Mon.-Sat. 1-4, July-Aug.; Mon. and Wed. 7-9 p.m., Fri.-Sat. 1-4, rest of year. Closed holidays. Donations. Phone (250) 974-5024.

ANGLICAN CHURCH, on Front St., is an 1881 cedar church with stained-glass windows that reflect the blending of Indian and European cultures. Allow 30 minutes minimum. Mon.-Sat. 8-5, June 15-Sept. 15. Donations. For information contact the Travel InfoCentre; phone (250) 974-5024.

TOTEM POLE can be seen near the Big House, a Kwakiutl community center not open to the public. The 53-metre (173-ft.) pole was erected in 1973 and is considered to be the world's tallest. It features 22 figures, including a sun at the top. Binoculars are recommended. Allow 30 minutes minimum. Daily dawn-dusk. Free.

U'MISTA CULTURAL CENTRE, 2 km (1.2 mi.) from the ferry on Front St., displays a collection of masks, cedar baskets, copper items and other artifacts from Indian potlatches, the gift-giving ceremonies that mark such important occasions as birth, marriage and death. There also are films and small galleries with short-term exhibits. Guided tours are available.

Daily 9-6, Victoria Day-Labour Day; Mon.-Fri. 9-5, rest of year. Closed holidays. Admission $5; over 59, $4; under 13, $1. Guided tour $2. MC, VI. Phone (250) 974-5403.

ASHCROFT (B-7)
pop. 1,900, elev. 305 m/1,000'

Ashcroft Manor, a roadside house on Cariboo Wagon Road, was named for the English home of its settlers, Clement and Henry Cornwall. The Cornwalls established themselves as cattlemen in 1862 and lived the pioneer life in the style of gentlemen, practicing such rituals as afternoon tea and riding to hounds through sagebrush and scrub in pursuit of coyotes. The manor is south of town on Hwy. 1.

ASHCROFT MUSEUM, 404 Brink St., has exhibits about the history of the southern Cariboo, the

Indian tribes that first settled Ashcroft. Artifacts and photographs are displayed in the windows of old shops, churches and houses along a board sidewalk, depicting life as it was in Ashcroft's glory days between the first settlement in 1884 and the great fire in 1916. A re-creation of the Hat Creek Mine also is on display. A slide show is presented. Daily 10-6, July-Aug.; Tues.-Sat. 10-6, Sept.-Oct.; Wed.-Sun. 9-5, Apr.-June; otherwise varies. Closed holidays. Donations. Phone (250) 453-9232.

★ BARKERVILLE HISTORIC TOWN (F-5)

Barkerville, approximately 96.5 kilometres (60 mi.) east of Quesnel via Hwy. 26, is a restored 1870s gold rush town that once had the largest population north of San Francisco and west of Chicago. In those days when more than $50 million of gold—at $16 per ounce—had been mined from the area, soap cost $1 a bar and a dance with a hurdy-gurdy girl cost $1 a whirl.

The town was named for Billy Barker, a Cornish miner who first found gold in large quantities in the early 1860s. Barkerville became a virtual ghost town a few years later when the gold ran out.

The town contains 125 original and reconstructed buildings, including the Barkerville Hotel, St. Saviours Church, the Mason and Daly General Store and the Wake Up Jake Cafe; many are manned by attendants in period dress. Board sidewalks and dirt streets help preserve the essence of the original site.

Theatre Royale presents period melodrama, dance and music Victoria Day-Labour Day. Treasure seekers can pan for gold at Eldorado Mine. A visitor center presents videos and exhibits about the history of Barkerville. Guided tours, cemetery tours and living-history programs are offered.

The townsite is open daily 8-dusk. Programs and concessions operate daily, mid-May-Labour Day. Limited programs are offered daily Labour Day to mid-Sept.; hours may vary. Visitor center open daily 8:30-5, mid-May to mid-Sept. Entrance fee mid-May through Sept. 30 (good for 2 days) $5.50; over 65 and ages 13-18, $3.25; ages 6-12, $1; family rate $10.75. Free rest of year. Pets are not permitted. Phone (250) 994-3332.

Barkerville Provincial Park offers camping, picnicking and hiking trails. The park is open daily 8-dusk, May-Oct. *See Recreation Chart and the AAA/CAA Western Canada and Alaska CampBook.*

BOSTON BAR (C-7)
pop. 500, elev. 309 m/1,013′

Boston Bar, which began as a gold mining town, was named for a Dutchman who came from Boston to prospect in the 1860s. Because the home port of many of the ships bringing prospectors was Boston, local Indians called the newcomers Boston men. Boston Bar is a logging and trade center, with the Canadian National Railway passing through town. The Canadian Pacific Railway parallels the National on the other side of Fraser River Canyon.

Boston Bar is the access point for the Nahatlach Valley, which features the Nahatlach River and a chain of lakes. Recreation includes camping, fishing and white-water rafting.

SAVE ★ **HELL'S GATE AIRTRAM** is 11.25 km (7 mi.) s. on Hwy. 1 to 43111 Trans-Canada Hwy. in Fraser River Canyon. The tram descends 153 metres (502 ft.) across the river to the narrowest part of Fraser Canyon and across Hell's Gate Fishways, where 2 million salmon annually swim upstream to their spawning grounds. Visitors can see eight fishways from observation decks or a suspension bridge. A film about the life cycle of the salmon is shown at the education center. Food is available.

Allow 1 hour minimum. Daily 9-6, May 19-22 and June 16-Sept. 4; 9-5, Apr. 28- June 15 and Sept. 5-24; 10-4, Mar. 30-Apr. 27 and Sept. 25-Oct. 28. Fare $10; over 64, $8.50; ages 6-18, $6.50; family rate $26.50. MC, VI. Phone (604) 867-9277.

RECREATIONAL ACTIVITIES
White-water Rafting
• **REO Rafting Adventure Resort** is 16 km (10 mi.) n.w. on Nahatlatch River FR. Write 535 Thurlow St., Vancouver, BC, Canada V6E 3L2. Trips operate Apr.-Sept. Phone (604) 684-4438 or (800) 736-7238.

BOSWELL (C-11)
pop. 100, elev. 533 m/1,748′

THE GLASS HOUSE, on Hwy. 3A (Southern Trans-Canada Hwy.) 40 km (25 mi.) n. of Creston, is a six-room, castlelike house built of empty 16-ounce embalming fluid bottles. A funeral director built the house, archway and several terraces on the landscaped lakefront grounds. Allow 30 minutes minimum. Daily 8-8, July-Aug.; 9-5, May-June and Sept. 1 to mid-Oct. Admission $6; ages 13-19, $5; ages 6-12, $4. VI. Phone (250) 223-8372.

BRACKENDALE (G-11)
RECREATIONAL ACTIVITIES
White-water Rafting
• **Bald Eagle Rafting** is at 70002 Government Rd. Write P.O. Box 244, Brackendale, BC, Canada V0N 1H0. Daily 9-5, June-Sept. and Nov.-Feb. Phone (604) 898-1537.

BRENTWOOD BAY—
see Victoria p. 173.

BRIDAL FALLS (H-12)
elev. 61 m/200'

DINOTOWN, off Hwy. 1 exit 135 following signs, is an amusement park geared for ages 2-12. The 12-acre park features a dinosaur exhibit, shows, a train, paddleboats, bumper cars, games, a parade and a water park. Picnicking is permitted. Food is available. Allow 3 hours minimum. Daily 10-7, July-Aug.; daily 10-5, day after Father's Day-June 30; Sat.-Sun. 10-5, Mother's Day weekend-Father's Day and in Sept. Admission $9.50, under 3 free. MC, VI. Phone (604) 794-7410 or (800) 491-7627.

TRANS-CANADA WATERSLIDES, at jct. hwys. 1 and 9 on Bridal Falls Rd., features 10 waterslides, a giant hot pool, miniature golf course, river ride, video arcade and picnic and barbecue facilities. Food is available. Allow 2 hours minimum. Daily 10-8, mid-June through Labour Day; Sat.-Sun. opens at 10, closing time varies, Victoria Day weekend to mid-June. Admission $15; ages 4-12, $12. MC, VI. Phone (604) 794-7455.

BRITANNIA BEACH (G-11)
pop. 300, elev. 6 m/20'

From 1930 to 1935 the Britannia Mine at Britannia Beach was the largest producer of copper in the British Empire. No longer in operation, the mine is now part of the British Columbia Museum of Mining.

BRITISH COLUMBIA MUSEUM OF MINING, on Hwy. 99, presents the history of this industry. Among the above-ground displays are an audiovisual presentation and a museum of mining equipment and models as well as photographs, maps and artifacts. A mine train carries visitors through a restored tunnel, where mining equipment and techniques are demonstrated (hard hats are provided). Gold panning is available. Casual clothes are recommended.

Daily 10-4:30, July-Aug.; Wed.-Sun. 10-4:30, May 9-June 30 and Sept. 1-second Mon. in Oct. Admission $10, over 65 and students with ID $8, family rate $36. Gold panning $3.50. MC, VI. Phone (604) 688-8735 or 896-2233.

BURNABY—see Vancouver p. 155.

CACHE CREEK (B-8)
pop. 1,100, elev. 450 m/1,500'

[SAVE] HISTORIC HAT CREEK RANCH is 11 km (7 mi.) n. on Hwy. 97 at jct. hwys. 97 and 99. The 130-hectare (320-acre) ranch, on one of the few sections of the Cariboo Wagon Road still accessible to the public, consists of more than 20 historic buildings constructed 1863-1915 when the ranch served as a roadhouse for the horse-drawn stagecoaches and freight wagons of the B.C. Express line (known as the B.X.).

Guided tours of the house include the ranch kitchen, saloon and passenger waiting room. Self-guiding tours of the remainder of the complex cover the horse barns; a blacksmith shop; a native interpretation center; the mower shed, with an original Concord stagecoach; a collection of agricultural machinery; a pig barn; a chicken coop; a garden; and an apple orchard. Food is available. Daily 10-6, mid-May to mid-Oct. Admission $5; senior citizens $4; ages 13-18, $3; ages 6-12, $2; family rate $10. MC, VI. Phone (250) 457-9722 or (800) 782-0922.

CAMPBELL RIVER (E-10)
pop. 28,900, elev. 18 m/59'

An important lumber, mining and commercial fishing center, Campbell River is near a noted Vancouver Island timber stand. The Elk Falls Pulp and Paper Mill offers tours in the summer. Campbell River is headquarters of the Tyee Club, whose members must catch a salmon of 30 pounds or more while fishing from a rowboat in the raging waters of Discovery Passage.

Provincial parks preserve the area's natural beauty, typified by waterfalls and mountainous wilderness. At Elk Falls Provincial Park the Campbell River drops 27 metres (90 ft.) into a deep canyon. Strathcona Provincial Park contains Mount Golden Hinde, at 2,200 metres (7,218 ft.) the highest mountain on Vancouver Island, and 440-metre (1,445-ft.) Della Falls, the highest waterfall in Canada. Scuba diving is popular during the winter when the waters are particularly clear. *See Recreation Chart and the AAA/CAA Western Canada and Alaska CampBook.*

The 183-metre-long (600-ft.) Campbell River Fishing Pier, 655 Island Hwy., is available for fishing, strolling or watching the cruise ships pass through the Strait of Georgia.

Campbell River Visitor InfoCentre: 1235 Shoppers Row, P.O. Box 400, Campbell River, BC, Canada V9W 5B6; phone (250) 287-4636.

MUSEUM AT CAMPBELL RIVER, 470 Island Hwy. with an entrance off 5th Ave., displays artifacts crafted by First Nations people of northern Vancouver Island, principally Kwakwaka'wakw, Nuu-cha-nulth and Coast Salish. Exhibits also follow the pioneer and industrial history of the island's northern section. Audiovisual footage of the Ripple Rock explosion is shown in the theater. During the summer, ecology tours and a puppet theatre also are offered.

Allow 1 hour minimum. Mon.-Sat. 10-5, Sun. noon-5, mid-May through Sept. 30; Tues.-Sun. noon-5, rest of year. Closed Easter, Thanksgiving, Nov. 11, and Dec. 25 and 31. Admission $2.50, senior citizens and students with ID $2, under 6 free, family rate $7.50. Phone (250) 287-3103.

QUINSAM RIVER HATCHERY, .5 km (.3 mi.) w. on Hwy. 28, then 2.4 km (1.5 mi.) on Quinsam

Rd. to 4217 Argonaut Rd., is a salmon enhancement project that produces pink, coho and chinook salmon and steelhead trout. A display room chronicles the life cycle of a salmon. Facilities range from an incubation unit to adult holding ponds. Adult salmon viewing is best from mid-September to mid-November. Daily 8-4. Free. Phone (250) 287-9564.

CASTLEGAR (D-10)
pop. 7,000, elev. 494 m/1,620′

At the junction of hwys. 3 and 3A, Castlegar is considered the crossroads of the Kootenays. Just north is the 51-metre-high (167-ft.) Hugh Keenleyside Dam, which is open daily for guided tours May through August; phone (250) 365-5299. Behind the dam is Arrow Lake, a popular summer recreation spot featuring Syringa Creek Provincial Park *(see Recreation Chart and the AAA/CAA Western Canada and Alaska CampBook)*.

Castlegar Chamber of Commerce: 1995 Sixth Ave., Castlegar, BC, Canada V1N 4B7; phone (250) 365-6313.

DOUKHOBOR VILLAGE MUSEUM, opposite the airport just off Hwy. 3A to 125 Heritage Way, is a replica of the communal settlement of the Doukhobors, a pacifist group of Russian immigrants who lived in the area from 1908 until the 1930s. There were about 60 such villages. Highlights include a collection of artifacts with farm tools and an art gallery depicting Doukhobor life. Spinning and weaving demonstrations occur July through August. Food is available.

Allow 30 minutes minimum. Daily 9-5, May-Sept. Admission $3, students with ID $2. Phone (250) 365-6622.

KOOTENAY GALLERY OF ART, HISTORY AND SCIENCE, opposite the airport just off Hwy. 3A at 120 Heritage Way, next to Doukhobor Historic Village, has historical, scientific and artistic permanent displays and changing exhibits of local, national and international origin. Allow 30 minutes minimum. Mon.-Fri. 10:30-4:30, Sat.-Sun. noon-4:30, July-Aug.; Tues.-Fri. 10:30-4:30, Sat.-Sun. noon-4:30, rest of year. Donations. Phone (250) 365-3337.

ZUCKERBERG ISLAND HERITAGE PARK, Seventh Ave. and Ninth St., is at the confluence of the Columbia and Kootenay rivers. A suspension bridge leads to the island, where a walking tour offers such sights as an Indian Kekuli or pit house, a cemetery, a log house, a sculpture of a seated woman carved from a tree stump and the Chapel House with its Russian Orthodox onion dome. Picnicking is permitted.

Allow 30 minutes minimum. Park open daily dawn-dusk. Chapel House open 11-6, May-Aug. Donations. Phone (250) 365-6440.

CHEMAINUS (G-10)
pop. 3,500, elev. 6 m/20′

A lumber and manufacturing town, Chemainus added tourism to its economy with the creation of murals. More than 30 professional paintings on the walls of buildings portray the history of the Chemainus Valley. Subjects range from North American Indians to dramatic depictions of the logging industry.

Begun by local artists, the series of murals has attracted artists from around the world. Walking tour maps can be bought at the kiosk in the central parking area. Prearranged guided tours and horse-drawn carriage tours also are available for a fee; phone (250) 246-4701.

Chemainus Theatre offers dramas, comedies and musical productions; phone (250) 246-9820 or (800) 565-7738.

Chemainus Chamber of Commerce: 9758 Chemainus Rd., P.O. Box 575, Chemainus, BC, Canada V0R 1K0; phone (250) 246-3944.

CHILLIWACK—*see Vancouver p. 155.*

CLEARWATER (A-8) pop. 3,500

Clearwater gets its name from the clear waters of the nearby Clearwater River. Opportunities for riding, hiking, canoeing, skiing and fishing abound in the surrounding North Thompson Valley.

Wells Gray Provincial Park, north off Hwy. 5, offers a variety of scenery, particularly with regard to water. Scattered throughout its boundaries are five large lakes, two river systems, many streams and waterways and a multitude of waterfalls. Extinct volcanoes and lava beds recall the region's fiery past. Spahats Creek Provincial Park is a short distance away. *See Recreation Chart and the AAA/CAA Western Canada and Alaska CampBook.*

Clearwater Chamber of Commerce: 425 E. Yellowhead Hwy., P.O. Box 1988, Clearwater, BC, Canada V0E 1N0; phone (250) 674-2646.

RECREATIONAL ACTIVITIES
White-water Rafting

- **Interior Whitewater Expeditions** is on Hwy. 5. Write P.O. Box 383, Clearwater, BC, Canada V0E 1N0. Rafting season is mid-May to mid-Sept. Daily 8-8, mid-May to mid-Sept., depending on water level Phone (250) 674-3727 or (800) 661-7238.

CLINTON (A-7)
pop. 700, elev. 274 m/898′

During the gold rush of the late 1850s and early 1860s Clinton was the junction of several wagon roads leading to northern goldfields. In

1863 Queen Victoria changed the town's name from Junction to Clinton. Retaining much of its frontier look, Clinton is a supply center for surrounding resorts, fishing camps and ranches. Summer activities include boating, fishing and camping at area lakes, which also attract various wildlife.

Clinton Chamber of Commerce: P.O. Box 256, Clinton, BC, Canada V0K 1K0; phone (250) 459-2640.

SOUTH CARIBOO HISTORICAL MUSEUM is at 1419 Cariboo Hwy. Built in 1892, this building has served as the town's schoolhouse and courthouse. Displays include photographs and pioneer artifacts. Allow 30 minutes minimum. Daily 11-7, late June-Aug. 31. Admission $2, under 12 free. Phone (250) 459-2442.

COMOX (E-10) pop. 11,100

COMOX AIR FORCE MUSEUM is e. on Ryan Rd. following signs to Canadian Forces Base Comox main entrance. Museum displays outline the history of the base and West Coast aviation. Three squadrons continue to fly Labrador helicopters and Aurora, T-33 and Buffalo aircraft. A heritage aircraft park displays vintage aircraft. Canada's flight pioneers are recognized in a videotape presentation. Allow 30 minutes minimum. Daily 10-4, June-Aug.; Sat.-Sun. and holidays 10-4, rest of year. Closed Dec. 25-26. Donations. Phone (250) 339-8162.

FILBERG HERITAGE LODGE AND PARK, 61 Filberg Rd., consists of the 1929 Filberg Lodge and 4 hectares (9 acres) of landscaped grounds. The lodge is restored and furnished in period. Magnolia and cedar trees are among the many varieties of plants found in the park. Food is available.

Allow 1 hour minimum. Park open daily 8 a.m.-dusk. Lodge open daily 11-5, June 1-Labour Day; Sat.-Sun. 11-5, Easter weekend-May 31 and day after Labour Day-Thanksgiving. Lodge admission $1; ages 6-12, 50c. Animal farm $1; ages 6-12, 50c. Phone (250) 339-2715.

COOMBS (F-10)

Coombs retains the atmosphere of a quaint village settled around 1910. The Coombs General Store, which has operated continuously since the settlement days, and the Old Country Market, unusual for the goats that are kept on the roof in summer, are two landmarks.

The town is midway between Little Qualicum River Falls Provincial Park *(see Recreation Chart)* and Englishman River Falls Provincial Park *(see Recreation Chart)*, where there are many recreational opportunities.

SAVE **BUTTERFLY WORLD,** 1 km (.6 mi.) w. on Hwy. 4A at 1080 Winchester Rd., has a tropical garden containing more than 80 species of butterflies. The insect's life cycle is portrayed through displays. Other exhibits include birds in an outdoor aviary and a Japanese water garden with exotic fish. Allow 30 minutes minimum. Daily 10-5, May-Sept.; 10-4, Mar.-Apr. and in Oct. Admission $6; over 64, $5; students with ID $4.50; ages 3-12, $3.50. MC, VI. Phone (250) 248-7026.

COQUITLAM—*see Vancouver p. 155.*

COURTENAY (E-10)
pop. 17,300, elev. 25 m/82′

Courtenay was established in the late 1860s when settlers began a major farming community near the Comox Valley. Known for a garden called the Mile of Flowers, the town is now a year-round recreation area with good skiing and sailing nearby.

The 1989 Puntledge River discovery of the fossilized intact skull of a 14-metre-long (46-ft.) elasmosaur, a long-necked Cretaceous marine reptile 80 million years old, brought Courtenay to the attention of the world of paleontology.

Courtenay is the terminus of the Powell River Ferry, which makes round-trip excursions to the mainland.

Comox Valley Travel Infocentre: 2040 Cliffe Ave., Courtenay, BC, Canada V9N 2L3; phone (250) 334-3234.

COURTENAY AND DISTRICT MUSEUM AND ARCHIVES, 360 Cliffe Ave., is in the Native Sons Hall, an expanse of vertical cedar logs built in 1928. Permanent exhibits, enhanced by audiovisuals, focus on native history, exploration, agriculture, logging and pioneer life. A reconstruction of an elasmosaur is displayed. The museum has archival material pertaining to the nearby Comox Valley. Allow 1 hour minimum. Daily 10-4:30, May-Sept.; Tues.-Sat. 10-4:30, rest of year. Donations. Phone (250) 334-3611.

PUNTLEDGE HATCHERY is 3 km (1.9 mi.) w. on Lake Trail Rd., then 2 km (1.2 mi.) n. on Powerhouse Rd. following signs. The hatchery nurtures and releases several varieties of salmon and steelhead trout into the Puntledge River. Photographic displays outline the species' various stages of development. Daily 8-4. Free. Phone (250) 338-7444.

RECREATIONAL ACTIVITIES
Skiing

- **Mount Washington Ski Resort**, 30 km (19 mi.) w. on the Strathcona Pkwy., P.O. Box 3069, Courtenay, BC, Canada V9N 5N3. Daily 9:30-3:30, early Dec. to mid-Apr. Phone (250) 338-1386.

CRAIGELLACHIE (B-9) pop. 100

SAVE **BEARDALE CASTLE MINIATURELAND,** 5549 Hwy. 1, displays such miniature reproductions as a 1950s prairie town, a Swiss mountain village, a medieval German town, an English Tudor village and presents a Canadian railroad heritage exhibit. Life-size animated fairy tale characters are featured along with an area devoted to Mother Goose nursery rhymes. Allow 30 minutes minimum. Daily 9-6, May-Sept. (also 6-8 p.m. July-Aug.) Admission $5; ages 3-14, $2.75. MC, VI. Phone (250) 836-2268.

CRANBROOK (C-11)

pop. 18,100, elev. 940 m/3,083′

Cranbrook is the key city of the eastern Kootenays and the center of many circle tours. Nearby lakes, rivers and mountains provide such recreational opportunities as swimming, fishing, hiking, hunting and skiing. A scenic portion of Hwy. 93 runs north from Cranbrook into Alberta to the junction with Hwy. 16 in Jasper.

Cranbrook Chamber of Commerce: 2279 Cranbrook St. (Hwy. 3/95), P.O. Box 84, Cranbrook, BC, Canada V1C 4H6; phone (250) 426-5914 or (800) 222-6174.

Self-guiding tours: Information about driving and walking tours is available from the chamber of commerce.

CANADIAN MUSEUM OF RAIL TRAVEL, on Hwy. 3/95, has restored and preserved a set of cars from the Trans-Canada Limited, a luxury train built in 1929. The restored dining, sleeping and lounge cars contain inlaid black walnut and mahogany paneling, carpets, brass light fixtures and original upholstered furniture.

The dining car contains displays of original Canadian Pacific Railway china, glassware and silver and offers tea and light refreshments. A business car, the "British Columbia," also is displayed with its original 1928 sitting room, dining room and bedrooms. The combination baggage and sleeping car contains the interpretation area, which has exhibits and a slide show of the restoration work. A night car, built for Canadian Pacific's board of directors, and cars from the Soo Spokane train deluxe also are featured.

The rail station contains archives. A model railway display depicts the 1900s era of train travel. Daily 8-8, July 1-Labour Day; daily 10-6, Easter-June 30 and day after Labour Day-Thanksgiving; Tues.-Sat. noon-5, rest of year. Hours may vary; phone ahead. Closed Jan. 1 and Dec. 25-26. Admission $6.31; over 64, $4.67; students with ID $2.80; family rate $15.42. Phone (250) 489-3918 to verify schedule and rates.

CRESTON (D-11)

pop. 4,800, elev. 636 m/2,086′

The unusual Kutenai canoe, which has a bow and stern that both meet the waterline, was used by Indians in the area around Creston in pre-pioneer days. The only other place such a canoe has been found is the Amur River region in southeastern Russia. The canoe's use in this area supports the theory that Asians migrated to North America over a frozen Bering Strait.

In the 1930s about 8,100 hectares (20,000 acres) of land were reclaimed from the Kootenay Delta for agriculture. The Creston Valley floor is now quilted with a variety of seed and root crops, grains and fruit orchards. Other Creston industries include forestry, dairying and brewing.

The Columbia Brewing Co., 6 blocks south on 16th Avenue, offers free narrated tours of its facilities mid-June through mid-September. Complimentary beer is available at the end of the tour.

Summit Creek Park, 9 kilometres (6 mi.) west, offers camping, natural history programs and hiking along the old Dewdney Trail, which carried gold seekers from Hope to the Wild Horse goldfields in the 1860s. Mountain Stream Trout Farm and Recreation Area, 7 kilometres (4 mi.) north, features nature trails and ponds stocked with fish for catching and barbecuing on the premises.

Creston Chamber of Commerce: 1711 Canyon St., P.O. Box 268, Creston, BC, Canada V0B 1G0; phone (250) 428-4342.

[SAVE] **CRESTON AND DISTRICT MUSEUM,** 219 Devon St. via Hwy. 3A N, is in the Stone House, which has walls more than one-third metre (1 ft.) thick as well as four stone fireplaces. Built in 1957, the museum houses more than 5,000 pioneer and Indian artifacts, including a replica of a Kutenai Indian canoe and early agricultural tools. A schoolroom exhibit can be seen in the restored Kingsgate Schoolhouse on the museum grounds. Allow 1 hour minimum. Daily 10-3:30, May-Oct.; by appointment rest of year. Admission $2; ages 6-16, $1; family rate $5. Phone (250) 428-9262.

CRESTON VALLEY WILDLIFE MANAGEMENT AREA (INTERPRETATION CENTRE) is 9.5 km (6 mi.) w. on Hwy. 3. The 7,000-hectare (17,297-acre) area permits hiking, seasonal camping, bicycling, hunting, canoeing and picnicking in a managed waterfowl habitat. A variety of programs and canoe trips originate at the Interpretation Centre, which houses natural history displays and a theater. Center open daily 8-6, last weekend of Apr.-Labour Day; Wed.-Sun. 9-4, day after Labour Day-Thanksgiving. Admission $3; ages 2-18, $2; family rate $9. Phone (250) 428-3259. *See Recreation Chart.*

KOOTENAY CANDLES, just n. on Hwy. 3 at 1511 Northwest Blvd., offers guided tours of the candlemaking factory Mon.-Fri. at 10:30 and 1:30, mid-May to mid-Sept. Free. Phone (250) 428-9785.

CULTUS LAKE (H-12)

pop. 500, elev. 45 m/150'

Cultus Lake is a popular recreational area and offers camping, boating, fishing, horseback riding and hiking. Cultus Lake Waterpark, Hwy. 1 exit 119A, has giant waterslides, twisting tunnels, pools and inner tube rides; phone (604) 858-7241 for more information.

DAWSON CREEK (D-6)

pop. 11,100, elev. 655 m/2,148'

Named for George Mercer Dawson of the Geological Survey of Canada, Dawson Creek was settled in 1912. Growth accelerated during World War II, as this was the southern terminus of the Alaska Highway. The highway was then called the Alcan Military Highway, and it served as a supply road to bases in Alaska. The Mile Zero Cairn, which marks the start of the Alaska Highway, and the Zero Milepost are in the center of town. Alpine skiing, camping, hiking and fishing are popular recreational activities.

Dawson Creek Chamber of Commerce: 906 102 Ave., Dawson Creek, BC, Canada V1G 3W2; phone (250) 782-4868.

DAWSON CREEK STATION MUSEUM AND VISITORS' INFORMATION CENTRE, 900 Alaska Ave., has artifacts, fossils and mounted animals and birds from the Peace River region. Highlights include an early 1900s railway caboose and a 1930s grain elevator as well as an art gallery and a video presentation about construction of the Alaska Highway. Daily 8-7, May 15-Labour Day; Tues.-Sat. 9-5, rest of year. Donations. Phone (250) 782-9595.

WALTER WRIGHT PIONEER VILLAGE, just w. of jct. 97N (Alaska Hwy.) and 97S (Hart Hwy.), is a complex of pioneer buildings, including a log schoolhouse, log cabin, general store, smithy and two churches. All contain period furnishings. An extensive collection of farm machinery and implements also is featured as well as nine flower gardens, a memorial rose garden and a lake for swimming. Food is available. Allow 1 hour minimum. Daily 9-7, mid-May to late Aug. Donations. Phone (250) 782-7144.

DELTA—*see Vancouver p. 156.*

DUNCAN (G-10)

pop. 4,600, elev. 15 m/49'

Founded in 1887 as Alderlea, Duncan was renamed in 1912 in honor of farmer William Duncan, who gave his land for the original townsite. Settlers were attracted by the promise of copper and coal on nearby Mount Sicker, where abandoned mines and original homesteads still can be seen. The growth of the logging and farming industries brought increasing numbers to Duncan and the Cowichan Valley.

The area around Duncan is known for the hand-spun woolen sweaters produced by the Cowichan Indians. West on Hwy. 18 is the Cowichan Valley Demonstration Forest with scenic viewpoints and signs describing forest management practices and ecology.

Duncan-Cowichan Chamber of Commerce: 381 Trans-Canada Hwy., Duncan, BC, Canada V9L 3R5; phone (250) 746-4636.

Shopping areas: Whippletree Junction, a group of shops and boutiques with late 1800s storefronts, is 5 kilometres (3 mi.) south on the Trans-Canada Highway.

BRITISH COLUMBIA FOREST DISCOVERY CENTRE, 1.5 km (1 mi.) n. off Hwy. 1 to 2892 Drinkwater Rd., has more than 40 hectares (99 acres) of forest and interactive displays and videotapes depicting British Columbia's forestry heritage, management practices and renewal efforts. In addition to a logging museum there are Douglas fir trees, a smithy, a sawmill, and an old-time logging camp. A nature trail and a ride in a steam-powered logging train are available. Daily 10-6, May 1-Labour Day. Admission $8; over 65 and ages 13-18, $7; ages 5-12, $4.50. VI, MC. Phone (250) 715-1113.

COWICHAN NATIVE VILLAGE, 1 blk. w. of Hwy. 1 at 200 Cowichan Way, is a living-history museum and gallery dedicated to the preservation and dissemination of the culture of the Northwest Coast Indians. In addition to a gallery there are demonstrations of carving and basket weaving. Food is available. Allow 1 hour minimum. Daily 9-5. Guided tours are offered on the hour; multimedia presentations begin on the half-hour. Admission $6; over 60 and students with ID $5; under 13, $3. Phone (250) 746-8119.

FAIRMONT HOT SPRINGS

(B-12) pop. 400, elev. 810 m/2,657'

At the north end of Columbia Lake, Fairmont Hot Springs were discovered about 1840. This popular resort area offers four hot mineral springs with temperatures averaging 35 to 45 C (95 to 113 F). Water sports and alpine and cross-country skiing also are available. *See Recreation Chart and the AAA/CAA Western Canada and Alaska CampBook.*

RECREATIONAL ACTIVITIES

Skiing

• **Fairmont Hot Springs Resort**, on Hwy. 93/95, P.O. Box 10, Fairmont Hot Springs, BC, Canada V0B 1L0. Daily 9:30-4, mid-Dec. to early Apr. Phone (250) 345-6311.

FERNIE (C-12)

pop. 4,900, elev. 1,005 m/3,297'

At the foot of Trinity Mountain in the British Columbia Rockies, Fernie is a year-round recreation center. The many surrounding lakes and mountains provide opportunities for boating, fishing, hiking, camping and skiing. Mount Fernie Provincial Campground is 4.8 kilometres (3 mi.) east *(see the AAA/CAA Western Canada and Alaska CampBook)*. Prentice and Rotary parks are downtown.

Fernie Chamber of Commerce: Hwy. 3 and Dicken Rd., Fernie, BC, Canada V0B 1M0; phone (250) 423-6868.

RECREATIONAL ACTIVITIES

Skiing

- **Fernie Alpine Resort**, 5 km (3 mi.) s.w. off Hwy. 3. Write Ski Area Rd., Fernie, BC, Canada V0B 1M1. Other activities offered. Daily 9-4, late Nov. to mid-Apr. Lifts operate daily 10-5, July-Aug. Phone (250) 423-4655.

FORT LANGLEY (H-11)

pop. 2,300, elev. 12 m/39'

SAVE **BRITISH COLUMBIA FARM MACHINERY AND AGRICULTURAL MUSEUM**, 9131 King St., is a complex of buildings with artifacts and exhibits devoted to the development of farm machinery in British Columbia. Included are a handwrought plow, a threshing machine, carriages and buckboards, and a Tiger-Moth airplane used for crop dusting. Allow 30 minutes minimum. Daily 10-4:30, Apr. 1-Thanksgiving. Admission $4; over 60 and ages 13-18, $2; ages 6-12, $1. Phone (604) 888-2273.

LANGLEY CENTENNIAL MUSEUM AND NATIONAL EXHIBITION CENTRE, 9135 King St., displays regional artifacts reflecting the lifestyle of early settlers as well as early Indian artifacts. Re-created period rooms include a parlor, a kitchen and a general store. Displays also feature wood carvings, stone artifacts and baskets from the Coast Salish culture. Changing exhibits focus on art, science and Canadian and world history. Mon.-Sat. 10-4:45, Sun. 1-4:45, Victoria Day weekend-Labour Day; Tues.-Sat. 10-4:45, Sun. 1-4:45, rest of year. Donations. Phone (604) 888-3922.

FORT LANGLEY NATIONAL HISTORIC SITE (H-11)

Fort Langley National Historic Site is 6.5 kilometres (4 mi.) north of Langley off Hwy. 1 at 23433 Mavis Ave. The park occupies the Fraser River site of the 19th-century Hudson's Bay Co. depot that provided supplies for fur-trading operations in the area. The fort also was the site of

the reading of the proclamation that established the Crown Colony of British Columbia in 1858.

Reconstructed buildings include the Big House, bastions and servant's quarters as well as an artisan shop and smithy, which feature daily demonstrations. An original storehouse, built in 1840, contains furs, clothing and goods representative of those sold or traded in the 1850s. Interpreters in period costumes perform tasks that were part of routine life in the 19th century. A visitor center displays native tools and artifacts found in the area. Special events are presented in the off season.

Allow 1 hour minimum. Daily 10-5, Mar.-Oct.; closed Good Friday. Admission $4; over 65, $3; ages 6-16, $2; family rate $10. Phone (604) 513-4777.

FORT NELSON (B-5)

pop. 4,400, elev. 405 m/1,350'

Originally a fur-trading post, Fort Nelson thrived with the building of the Alaska Highway during World War II. Nearby mountains, lakes, parks, forests and diverse wildlife populations make Fort Nelson a destination for adventurous tourists, anglers and hunters.

Fort Nelson-Liard Regional District: 5500 Simpson Tr., Bag Service 399, Fort Nelson, BC, Canada V0C 1R0; phone (250) 774-6400.

FORT NELSON HERITAGE MUSEUM, w. on Hwy. 97, houses artifacts relating to the history of Fort Nelson. Among the items on display are vintage cars; stuffed animals, including an albino moose; photographs of the construction of the Alaska Highway; and, behind the main building, a trapper's log cabin. Allow 30 minutes minimum. Daily 8:30-7:30, May 1 to mid-Sept. Admission $2.50; senior citizens and ages 5-15, $1.25; family rate $5.50. VI. Phone (250) 774-3536.

FORT RODD HILL AND FISGARD LIGHTHOUSE NATIONAL HISTORIC SITES—*see Victoria p. 173.*

FORT ST. JAMES (D-4)

pop. 2,000, elev. 680 m/2,230'

Established in 1806 by Simon Fraser and John Stuart, the fur-trading post of Fort St. James became the capital of New Caledonia in 1821. Furs from outlying New Caledonia posts were brought overland to Fort St. James by dog sled and then shipped south during the spring thaw to the coast by canoe and horse.

During this time George Simpson, governor of the Hudson's Bay Co.'s vast empire, visited the fort. Determined to impress the Carrier Indians,

Simpson organized a flamboyant procession complete with flute, bugle and bagpipe players in Highland dress, accompanied by a dog with a music box around its neck. Thereafter, the awestruck Indians reverently referred to Simpson as the "great chief whose dog sings."

A Roman Catholic mission was founded at the fort in 1843. Services continue to be held in Our Lady of Good Hope Church, which was built in 1873 and is one of the oldest churches in British Columbia.

Mining activity supplemented the capital's trapping enterprises after the discovery of gold in the Omineca region in 1869. Interest in mining rekindled during World War II when the Pinchi Mine a few kilometres north yielded more mercury than any other mine in the British Commonwealth.

A lack of highways and railways prompted Fort St. James to pioneer bush flying as a means of transportation; it has served as an air base since the earliest days of charter flight.

The north shore of Stuart Lake, 16 kilometres (10 mi.) west, features some of the earliest signs of habitation in the form of prehistoric rock paintings just above the high-water mark. Although Fort St. James has emerged from relative wilderness, its surrounding evergreen forests continue to be among the best big-game hunting areas in the province. Alpine skiing is available nearby.

Fort St. James Chamber of Commerce: 115 Douglas Ave., P.O. Box 1164, Fort St. James, BC, Canada V0J 1P0; phone (250) 996-7023.

★**FORT ST. JAMES NATIONAL HISTORIC SITE,** 2 blks. w. of Hwy. 27, is a former Hudson's Bay Co. trading post. The 19th-century post on the shore of Stuart Lake features reconstructed and restored buildings, including the officers' dwelling, trade store and general warehouse, fish cache and chicken yard. Buildings display original and reproduced furnishings and artifacts that capture the atmosphere of daily life in this isolated outpost.

The visitor reception center provides pictorial displays, artifacts and an audiovisual presentation. Interpreters in period costume are on hand to answer questions. Food and self-guiding audiotape tours are available. Allow 2 hours minimum. Daily 9-5, May-Sept. Admission $4; over 65, $3; ages 6-18, $2; family rate $12. Audiotape tour $2. Phone (250) 996-7191.

FORT ST. JOHN (C-6)
pop. 15,000, elev. 695 m/2,280'

One of the oldest European settlements in the province, Fort St. John was established in 1793 as a fur-trading outpost called Rocky Mountain Fort. Residents engage in gas and oil exploration as well as the lumber industry and cattle ranching. There are coalfields to the south and west.

Recreational activities include fishing for Arctic grayling and gray trout in nearby Charlie Lake (see Recreation Chart and the AAA/CAA Western Canada and Alaska CampBook), canoeing the rapids of the Peace River, skiing, and hunting for mountain caribous, mountain goats and black bears in the Rocky Mountain foothills. Floatplanes operating out of Charlie Lake provide access to the wilderness surrounding Fort St. John, and Hwy. 29 provides scenic driving to Chetwynd.

Fort St. John Chamber of Commerce: 9923 96th Ave., Fort St. John, BC, Canada V1J 1K9; phone (250) 785-3033.

FORT STEELE (C-12)
pop. 600, elev. 771 m/2,529'

Founded during the 1864 Kootenay gold rush, Fort Steele, then known as Galbraith's Ferry, became the site of the first North West Mounted Police west of the Rockies. In 1888 the settlement's name was changed to honor police superintendent Samuel Steele, who peacefully settled tensions between European settlers and the Ktunaxa people.

As a result of the mining boom of the 1890s the town became a thriving center of trade, transportation, communication and social activity, with a population of more than 2,000. In 1898 the British Columbia Southern Railroad bypassed Fort Steele in favor of Cranbrook, 16 kilometres (10 mi.) southwest, and the town began its decline. At the end of World War II Fort Steele had fewer than 50 residents.

★**FORT STEELE HERITAGE TOWN,** 3 km (1.9 mi.) s.w. on Hwy. 93/95, preserves an 1890s boomtown. On the 11 hectares (27 acres) are more than 60 restored, reconstructed or original buildings, including an operating bakery and a

DID YOU KNOW

British Columbia has thousands of tea rooms and coffeehouses.

general store, restaurant, tinsmith shop, blacksmith shop and newspaper office. Street dramas and demonstrations such as quilting, horse farming and ice cream making help re-create life in the era.

Fort Steele's Clydesdales give wagon rides daily and perform a six-horse hitch show on special occasions, mid-June through Labour Day. Live entertainment is presented in the Wild Horse Theatre, late June through Labour Day. Steam train rides are available during this time. A visitor reception center contains exhibits about the town's history.

Programs, including street skits depicting daily life of the late 1800s, are presented daily 9:30-5:30, late June to mid-Sept. The Wild Horse Theatre and other attractions have evening hours, late June to mid-Sept.; phone for schedule. Grounds open daily dawn-dusk. Admission May 1-Thanksgiving, $7.50; over 64 and ages 13-17, $4.50; ages 6-12, $2; family rate $17; reduced rates after 5:30 late June-Labour Day. Admission free rest of year. Phone (250) 417-6000 or (250) 426-7352.

GALIANO ISLAND—
see Gulf Islands p. 116.

GLACIER NATIONAL PARK (A-10)

Elevations in the park range from 500 metres (1,640 ft.) at Revelstoke to 3,390 metres (11,121 ft.) at Mount Dawson. Refer to CAA/AAA maps for additional elevation information.

The 1,350 square kilometres (521 sq. mi.) of Glacier National Park and its smaller counterpart Mount Revelstoke National Park *(see place listing p. 125)* encompass portions of the rugged Columbia Mountains, which lie west of the Rockies. The hard rock presents a jagged profile of angular mountains with narrow steep-walled valleys. The steep mountain slopes and enormous snowfall make this region susceptible to avalanches.

Rogers Pass in the heart of the park became the scene of a pitched 19th-century battle between the railroad engineers and these mountains. Sheer walls, numerous slide areas and severe weather proved almost insurmountable obstacles to the completion of Canada's first transcontinental railroad. Some of the largest railroad trestles then known were built to carry the line across raging streams to the summit of this pass across the Selkirks.

From there the tracks crossed to the southern wall of the valley on several loops to avoid the numerous avalanche slopes and the steep downgrade. Despite the ingenuity of its engineers, the new railroad had to be abandoned to the devastating winter forces that closed the pass the first year of construction. Avalanches attaining speeds of up to 325 kilometres (202 mi.) per hour tore up sections of the new track and left other sections buried under tons of snow.

Thirty-one snowsheds were built to shield the track, but even this was not enough. In 1910, 58 men were killed by an avalanche as they were clearing snow from an earlier slide. This incident, mounting costs and the dangerous grades of this section convinced the railroad to tunnel under Mount Macdonald.

The Trans-Canada Highway met similar obstacles as it crossed the pass, but the use of mobile howitzers to dislodge potential slides and other methods of controlling avalanches have held the road's position in the pass. Evidence of the struggle to build the railroad is visible from the road and the park's various campgrounds.

Several short trails follow the railroad's progress, winding past the ruins of Glacier House, a 19th-century resort hotel, remains of former snow sheds and the stone pillars that once supported the railroad trestles.

History is only part of the park's attractions. Twelve percent of the park is covered perpetually by snow and ice; more than 400 glaciers are scattered throughout the park. The contrast of the deep green forests and meadows with the glacial whites of these crags makes the park especially scenic.

Towering above the richly wooded valleys, the 3,297-metre (10,817-ft.) Mount Sir Donald rises to the east of the campgrounds, with Eagle and Uto peaks to the north. Day-hiking trails lead toward the Illecillewaet and Asulkan glaciers.

General Information and Activities

The park is open all year, but winter conditions are rigorous. Illecillewaet campground, the center of the park's best ski touring area, and Beaver River picnic area offer limited winter skiing. During the summer some of the popular activities are camping, hiking and mountaineering.

From Illecillewaet campground interpreters lead evening strolls and campfire talks as well as summer hikes that pass through the different life zones of the park's flora and fauna.

In addition, an extensive network of challenging day-hiking trails leads to such attractions as the Illecillewaet and Asulkan glaciers; Mount Abbott, with several fine viewpoints; Mount Tupper; and the Rogers group of peaks.

Grizzly and black bears are common in Glacier National Park; be cautious and make noise frequently as you hike. Climbers and overnight hikers may register at Rogers Pass Centre before and after every trip. Topographical maps and a hiker's guide also are available. Park use permits can be purchased at the welcome stations and the Rogers Pass Centre. *See Recreation Chart and the AAA/CAA Western Canada and Alaska CampBook.*

ADMISSION to the park is $4; over 65, $3; ages 6-16, $2; all occupants of a private vehicle $10. Annual passes are available.

PETS are permitted in the park provided they are on a leash at all times.

ADDRESS inquiries to the Superintendent, Glacier and Mount Revelstoke National Parks, P.O. Box 350, Revelstoke, BC, Canada V0E 2S0; phone (250) 837-7500.

ROGERS PASS CENTRE, 1.3 km (.8 mi.) e. of the Rogers Pass summit, was modeled after the snowsheds that once protected the railroad from avalanches. It includes a theater, an exhibit hall with railway models and displays about natural history. Allow 30 minutes minimum. Daily 8 a.m.-8:30 p.m., mid-June to mid-Sept.; otherwise varies. Phone (250) 814-5232.

GOLDEN (A-10)
pop. 4,000, elev. 785 m/2,575′

On the Trans-Canada Highway at the confluence of the Columbia and Kicking Horse rivers, Golden is near Glacier *(see place listing p. 114)* and Yoho national parks *(see place listing p. 176)* as well as Banff National Park *(see place listing in Alberta p. 40).* The community also is an outfitting point for sports enthusiasts.

The Golden and District Museum is at 11th Avenue and 13th Street. The museum is housed in a restored one-room schoolhouse and contains local historical items.

Golden & District Chamber of Commerce: 500 10th Ave. N., P.O. Box 1320, Golden, BC, Canada V0A 1H0; phone (250) 344-7125.

RECREATIONAL ACTIVITIES
White-water Rafting
- SAVE **Alpine Rafting Co.,** 1020 N. Hwy. 1, P.O. Box 1272, Golden, BC, Canada V0A 1H0. Trips depart daily at 9, 11:30, mid-May to mid-Sept. Phone (250) 344-6778 or (888) 599-5299.
- **Glacier Raft Co.,** on Hwy. 1, P.O. Box 428, Golden, BC, Canada V0A 1H0. Daily at 10 and 1, mid-May to mid-Sept. Phone (250) 344-6521.
- **Whitewater Voyageurs Ltd.** provides shuttle transportation to river departure points. Write P.O. Box 1983, Golden, BC, Canada V0A 1H0. Other activities are offered. Trips depart daily mid-May to mid-Sept. Phone (250) 344-7335 or (800) 667-7238.

GOLD RIVER (H-2)
pop. 2,000, elev. 122 m/400′

At the joining of the Gold and Heber rivers, the town of Gold River was built in 6 months in 1965 for employees of a pulp mill. The town, with its beautiful untamed countryside, has become popular with fishermen, photographers, hikers and campers.

Full-day and overnight cruises aboard the MV *Uchuck III* depart from the dock on Hwy. 28. The trips explore Tahsis, Nootka Sound and Friendly Cove, where Capt. James Cook met Chief Maquinna and the Nootka Indians when he landed on Vancouver Island in 1778; phone (250) 283-2325.

GRAND FORKS (D-10) pop. 4,000

Settlement at the confluence of the Kettle and Granby rivers began in the late 1800s when copper, gold and silver were discovered in the area. After 20 years of prosperity, Grand Forks suffered reverses when the local copper smelter, said to be the largest in the British Empire, closed due to faltering copper prices. The logging industry and seed growing operations later restored stability to the community.

The downtown Boundary District contains preserved historic homes, stores and civic buildings from the settlement period. It is flanked on the south and east by rivers, on the west by 5th Avenue and on the north by 75th Avenue. A walking tour map is available at the Boundary Museum *(see attraction listing).*

Chamber of Commerce of the City of Grand Forks: P.O. Box 1086, Grand Forks, BC, Canada V0H 1H0; phone (604) 442-2833.

BOUNDARY MUSEUM, 7370 Fifth St., chronologically depicts the area's history since the late 1800s. Artifacts, maps and photographs show the lifestyles of the Doukhobor and First Nations cultures. An art gallery adjacent to the museum displays art by local, Canadian and international artists. Changing thematic exhibits also are featured. Daily 9-4, July-Aug.; Mon.-Fri. 9-4, rest of year. Admission $2; senior citizens and ages 12-18, $1; under 12 free with paying adult. Phone (250) 442-3737.

GULF ISLANDS (H-10)

Separated from the San Juan Islands in Washington only by an international boundary, the almost 200 islands of various shapes and sizes that make up the Gulf Islands nestle against the southeast coast of Vancouver Island. Formed by a series of moving land masses beginning about 100 million years ago, today's Gulf Islands are the result of a mass collision of land that produced the long ridges of sandstone, conglomerate and shale that constitute the islands' geology.

The area was discovered by Capt. George Vancouver while on a quest to find a northwest passage to the Orient in 1792. Erroneously named Gulf of Georgia by Vancouver, the water separating Vancouver Island from the southwestern portion of British Columbia was later correctly termed the Strait of Georgia. The islands, however, retained the designation Gulf Islands.

The area features a climate that is sunnier and milder than that found on the nearby mainland. The quiet waters promote a much quieter lifestyle as well, and the islands are a haven from the frantic pace of nearby cities. Each island, though similar in many respects, has its own distinct identity. Easily reached from the mainland, they have become popular weekend retreats offering varying degrees of amenities and activities. Artists and professionals have joined the population of local fishermen who relish the peaceful lifestyle created by the sparkling waters, cliffs, winding roads and parks.

The main components of the southern Gulf Islands are Galiano, Mayne, North and South Pender, Salt Spring and Saturna islands. Although they can be explored by automobile, the best way to experience the islands is by bicycle or foot. The Islands Trust, a governmental agency, is charged with preserving and protecting the islands and waters in the Strait of Georgia.

BC Ferries provides year-round service to the main islands from Tsawwassen, south of Vancouver, and Swartz Bay, near Victoria. Vehicle reservations are recommended for travel between the mainland and the islands, but are not available for travel between Vancouver Island and the Gulf Islands or for inter-island travel. It is advisable to make reservations as far in advance as possible for summer and holiday travel. For schedule information and reservations phone (250) 386-3431 from the Victoria area and outside British Columbia or (888) 223-3779 from elsewhere in the province. Air service also is available.

Galiano Island (G-10) pop. 1,000

Named after Spanish explorer Dionisio Alcala Galiano, Galiano Island is a long, narrow island that is a haven for bird watchers and naturalists. Bicycling, horseback riding, kayaking, fishing, sailing, diving, swimming and hiking are popular recreational activities. The efforts of hikers and cyclists are rewarded with grand vistas and viewpoints.

Montague Harbour Provincial Park has 3,000-year-old Indian middens; camping facilities are available at the park as well as at Dionisio Point Provincial Park (see Recreation Chart and the AAA/CAA Western Canada and Alaska CampBook).

Galiano Island Chamber of Commerce: P.O. Box 73, Galiano Island, BC, Canada V0N 1P0; phone (250) 539-2233.

Mayne Island (H-11)

Although visited by the Spanish in the 1790s, it was not until the 1850s that British Capt. George Richards surveyed and mapped the area. Capt. Richards named Mayne Island after his lieutenant, Richard Charles Mayne. During the

gold rush of the mid-1800s the island, halfway between Victoria and the mouth of the Fraser River, was a stopping point for miners heading for the riches to be found at the gold fields along the river.

The island is known as a haven for artists and artisans. Small and sparsely settled, Mayne offers quiet beaches and hiking trails; wildflowers; a landscape heavy with trees; seals, sea lions, salmon and sole offshore; and a large variety of birds, from tiny hummingbirds to soaring bald eagles.

Mayne Island Community Chamber of Commerce: 302-45 Bastion Square, Victoria, BC, Canada V8W 1J1; phone (250) 382-3551.

Pender Islands (H-11)

The Penders, consisting of North and South Pender islands, are connected by a one-lane wooden bridge that spans the canal linking Bedwell and Browning harbors. An archeological dig conducted at the time the bridge was built found evidence of island occupation dating back 4,000 years.

The island's 20 public ocean access points and many coves allow ample opportunities for swimming and picnicking. Hiking, boating, fishing, golfing, bicycling, kayaking and scuba diving are other available recreational activities. Roadside stands offer locally grown produce. The view from the summit of Mount Norman is worth the climb.

Tourism Association of Vancouver Island: 302-45 Bastion Square, Victoria, BC, Canada V8W 1J1; phone (250) 382-3551.

Quadra Island (E-11) pop. 2,000

Old totem poles are found within the Indian reservation on Quadra Island, which is reached by a 15-minute ferry ride from Campbell River (see place listing p. 107).

KWAGIULTH MUSEUM AND CULTURAL CENTRE, 3.6 km (2.2 mi.) s. of the ferry terminal at 34 Green Rd. in Cape Mudge, displays items used in potlatches, ceremonial feasts of the Indians of the Northwest. The collection includes masks, rattles, whistles, head and neck rings and various other headgear. Photographs of traditional Kwakiutl villages at the turn of the 20th century are displayed.

A videotape station contains cultural and natural history presentations, and a demonstration about items made from cedar trees is offered. Puppet theater productions are scheduled July through August. Guided tours are available. Allow 30 minutes minimum. Mon.-Sat. 10-4:30, Sun. noon-4:30, June-Sept.; Tues.-Sat. 10-4:30, rest of year. Admission $3; over 64, $2; ages 6-12, $1. Phone (250) 285-3733.

Salt Spring Island (H-10)

Originally called Chuan Island, then Admiral Island, Salt Spring Island is the largest of the

Gulf Island group and a popular spot for yachting, cycling, fishing and golfing. Bicycle and kayak rentals are available.

Although it is one of the most developed of the islands, it retains a rural feel. Mount Maxwell Park has a scenic drive leading to 610-metre (2,001-ft.) Baynes Peak. The island also features popular Saturday farmers markets, arts and crafts, and is home to many fine artists such as Robert Bateman and Carol Evans. Ganges is the island's commercial hub.

Ferries operate daily from the island's three ferry terminals—between Swartz Bay and Fulford Harbour, between Crofton and Vesuvius Bay and between Long Harbour and Tsawwassen; for schedules and information phone BC Ferries, (250) 537-9921 or (888) 223-3779. Long Harbour is the largest of the terminals.

Salt Spring Island Travel InfoCentre: 121 Lower Ganges Rd., Salt Spring Island, BC, Canada V8K 2T1; phone (250) 537-5252.

Saturna Island (H-11) pop. 9,200

Saturna Island—remote, rugged and sparsely populated—is probably the least visited of the Gulf Islands. Mountain bicycling is one of the best ways to see the island. Its bays, beaches and tidal pools offer glimpses of many varieties of marine life. The southernmost of the Gulf Islands, Saturna offers hiking, bicycling and boating opportunities. There is no camping available and lodging is limited.

Tourism Association of Vancouver Island: 302-45 Bastion Square, Victoria, BC, Canada V8W 1J1; phone (250) 382-3551.

GWAII HAANAS NATIONAL PARK RESERVE/HAIDA HERITAGE SITE (F-1)

Elevations in the park range from sea level along Kunghit and Moresby islands to 1,123 metres (696 ft.) at Mount de la Touche. Refer to CAA/AAA maps for additional elevation information.

The 1,470 square kilometres (912 sq. mi.) of Gwaii Haanas National Park Reserve/Haida Heritage Site offer a rich and fascinating diversity of flora, sea creatures and wildlife. Remnants of native village sites capture the history of the Haida.

The reserve is in the southern part of the Queen Charlotte/Haida Gwaii Islands (see place listing p. 133), a remote island chain off the British Columbia coast west of Prince Rupert. This protected area is jointly managed by the Government of Canada and the Council of the Haida Nation. Access to the reserve is challenging: The only way to and around Gwaii Haanas is by air

or sea. Solo travel is recommended only for the experienced outdoor traveler. Licensed tour operators provide a variety of excursions.

Sea kayaking, sailboat and powerboat charters are the most popular ways to tour Gwaii Haanas. There are no maintained trails or designated campsites, and only limited visitor facilities are provided within the reserve. Haida Gwaii Watchmen basecamps have been established at major sites of cultural and natural significance. Watchmen provide site security and protection of the cultural features.

The Queen Charlotte Islands can be reached by air from Vancouver and Prince Rupert. BC Ferries also provides year-round service between the islands and Prince Rupert. Arrangements for ferry transportation should be made well in advance; phone (250) 669-1211.

Reservations are required to visit the reserve, and a fee is charged. Regulations allow for no more than 12 people on shore in one place at one time. All visitors must participate in an orientation session, held daily at visitor centers in Sandspit and Queen Charlotte. For more information write to Gwaii Haanas National Park Reserve/ Haida Heritage Site, P.O. Box 37, Queen Charlotte, BC, Canada V0T 1S0; or contact Tourism BC; phone (800) 663-6000.

HARRISON HOT SPRINGS
(D-7) pop. 900, elev. 11 m/36'

At the foot of Harrison Lake, Harrison Hot Springs (see Recreation Chart) is a well-known health and vacation resort with two mineral springs and a sandy beach on the lakeshore. Strong area winds make this a favorite spot for windsurfing. The surrounding mountains are known as Sasquatch country, where sightings of the legendary apelike creature twice the size of a man have been reported dozens of times.

More likely to be found in the mountains are mutton-fat jades, garnets, agates, fossils and gold; the area is renowned among rockhounds.

Harrison Hot Springs Chamber of Commerce: 499 Hot Springs Rd., P.O. Box 255, Harrison Hot Springs, BC, Canada V0M 1K0; phone (604) 796-3425.

HARRISON MILLS (D-7)
pop. 100, elev. 11 m/36'

KILBY STORE AND FARM is 1.6 km. (.9 mi.) s. of Hwy. 7 at 215 Kilby Rd. A 5-acre 1920s living-history site that includes costumed interpreters, it once was the heart of a thriving community of lumber mills. The store has items reminiscent of the early 20th century—forgotten foodstuffs, a wood stove and the traditional checkerboard. The Waterloo Farm features animals. Food is available. Open Thurs.-Mon. 10-5, May-Dec. Admission $5; over 59, $4; ages 6-14, $2; family rate $12. Phone (604) 796-9576.

HAZELTON (D-3)

pop. 300, elev. 306 m/1,004'

A showplace of Indian culture, Hazelton originally was called Git-an-maks, meaning "where people fish by torchlight." European settlers arriving in 1872 renamed the area Hazelton, after the profusion of hazelnut trees covering the fertile farmland.

Considered holy by the Gitksan Indian community, the forest land within a 64.4-kilometre (40-mi.) radius of Hazelton has the province's greatest concentration of standing totem poles, many portrayed in paintings by British Columbia artist Emily Carr.

'KSAN INDIAN VILLAGE, 5 km (3 mi.) s. on Hwy. 62, is a Gitksan Indian village consisting of seven tribal houses. The 'Ksan Museum, the Frog House of the Stone Age, the Wolf House or Feast House, the Fireweed House, the studio, the 'Ksan Shop, and the carving shed and workshop are decorated with paintings, carved interior poles and painted scenes in classic West Coast Indian style. Guided tours are available.

Daily 9-6, June-Sept.; 9-5, rest of year. Admission $2. Tour $7, students with ID $6. MC, VI. Phone (250) 842-5544.

HOPE (C-7) pop. 6,200, elev. 39 m/127'

At the entrance to the Fraser River Valley, Hope dates from 1848 when the Hudson's Bay Co. established a fort. The town developed rapidly, especially during the gold rush of 1858. The 1859 Anglican Christ Church is one of the province's oldest churches. Visitors also may walk through the Othello Quintette tunnels that once were used by the Kettle Valley Railway; the tunnels are in the Coquihalla Canyon Recreation Area.

From Hope the Trans-Canada Highway leads north to Fraser Canyon (*see Boston Bar p. 106*). Kawkawa Lake (*see Recreation Chart*), Lake of the Woods, Mount Hope, Mount Ogilvie and Skagit Valley (*see Recreation Chart*) are just some of the nearby places that offer year-round recreational opportunities.

The result of the 1965 Hope Slide is evident about 16 kilometres (10 mi.) east beside Hwy. 3. A plaque at the edge of the present roadway explains the collapse of the side of Johnson Peak, which buried the highway under 45 metres (148 ft.) of rubble.

Hope & District Chamber of Commerce: 919 Water Ave., P.O. Box 370, Hope, BC, Canada V0X 1L0; phone (604) 869-2021.

★ **HELL'S GATE AIRTRAM—**
see Boston Bar p. 106.

MANNING PROVINCIAL PARK, e. on Hwy. 3, is a 66,884-hectare (165,270-acre) mountain area. The Hope-Princeton Highway (Hwy. 3), a 134-kilometre (83-mi.) ride, climbs from near sea level at Hope to the 1,346-metre (4,416-ft.) summit of Allison Pass. In summer the alpine meadows along the highway are graced with blue lupine, yellow arnica and red Indian paintbrush.

Points of interest along the highway include remnants of the Dewdney Trail and Rhododendron Flats, a marked spot off the highway where a footpath leads through the mauve flowers and into Sumallo Grove, a collection of large first-growth cedar and Douglas fir trees. Black Wall Road, west of Allison Pass off Hwy. 3, leads to Cascade Lookout and offers access to a subalpine meadow. Recreational activities include hiking, camping, cross-country skiing, mountain bicycling and horseback riding. A visitor center on the highway displays exhibits about the park's natural features.

The park is open daily 24 hours. The visitor center is open daily 8:30-4:30, mid-June to mid-Sept.; Mon.-Fri. 8:30-4, rest of year. Campgrounds are open Apr.-Oct. Park free. Camping $12-$18.50 per night. Phone (250) 840-8836. *See Recreation Chart and the AAA/CAA Western Canada and Alaska CampBook.*

HUDSON'S HOPE (C-4)

pop. 1,100, elev. 520 m/1,706'

Hudson's Hope is one of the oldest settlements in the province: Only two communities on Vancouver Island have been continuously occupied from earlier dates. First discovered in 1793 by Alexander Mackenzie, the area was the site of a small fur-trading post built in 1805. In 1900 the post was moved to the present site of Hudson's Hope on the north side of the Peace River, where it flourished as a center of trade for the Hudson's Bay Co.

Hudson's Hope is an important supplier of hydroelectricity; its dams generate about 38 percent of the hydropower used in British Columbia. The dams also are major recreation centers for the area.

Hudson's Hope Travel InfoCentre: Hwy. 29, Hudson's Hope, BC, Canada V0C 1V0; phone (250) 783-9154 mid-May through Aug. 31, or (250) 783-9901 rest of year.

HUDSON'S HOPE MUSEUM, 10508 105th Ave., is housed in a 1942 Hudson's Bay Co. store. It contains local historical artifacts and a collection of prehistoric items including ichthyosaur fossils. Outbuildings include an old log church, a trapper's cabin, a fur cache and a pioneer house. A steamboiler and other antique machines are displayed on the grounds. Daily 9:30-5:30, mid-May to mid-Sept.; by appointment rest of year. Donations. Phone (250) 783-5735.

★ **PEACE CANYON DAM,** 4 km (2.5 mi.) s. on Hwy. 29, is a run-of-the-river installation 50 metres (164 ft.) high and 533 metres (1,749 ft.) long. At the outlet of Peace River Canyon, 23 kilometres (14 mi.) downstream from W.A.C. Bennett Dam, Peace Canyon Dam uses water that has generated electricity at the Bennett Dam station. Recreational facilities .8 kilometres (.5 mi.) upstream from the dam include a campground, picnic facilities and a boat launch.

The Visitor Centre, next to the powerhouse, has exhibits about the area's natural history, its exploration, pioneer history and the Peace Canyon Project. Dominating the prehistory display are two life-size models of duckbill dinosaurs, which lived in the area about 100 million years ago. Casts of dinosaur tracks and 11,600-year-old mammoth tusks found during excavations are displayed.

Among the exhibits is a replica of the SS *Peace River,* one of the early stern-wheelers that helped open the Peace River region to exploration. A large model of one of the project's generating units and similar displays explain the damming of the Peace River. Visitors also can view the project's central control system, the powerhouse and the switchgear station. An open-air observation deck is one level above the main exhibit floor. Daily 8-4, Victoria Day-Labour Day; Mon.-Fri. 8-4, rest of year. Closed Jan. 1, Easter, Thanksgiving, Nov. 11 and Dec. 25-26. Free. Phone (250) 783-9943.

★ **W.A.C. BENNETT DAM,** on Canyon Dr. 21 km (13 mi.) w. following signs, is a major hydroelectric project on the Peace River. The dam, built to produce electrical power for British Columbia, is 183 metres (600 ft.) high, 2 kilometres (1.2 mi.) long and .8 kilometre (.5 mi.) thick at the base. Backup water from the dam forms 164,600-hectare (406,727-acre) Williston Lake, British Columbia's largest lake. Its 1,770-kilometre (1,100-mi.) shoreline offers many recreational opportunities.

The Visitor Centre, about 1 km (.6 mi.) s.e. of the dam, has a participatory exhibit about the generation of electricity and magnetism. Photographs and artifacts chronicle the history and geology of the region and the construction of the dam and powerhouse. Underground bus tours into the powerhouse and manifold chambers are available. Center daily 9-6, Victoria Day-Labour Day; bus tours are available 9:30-4:30. Free. Reservations are required for the tour. Phone (250) 783-5048 or (888) 333-6667.

INVERMERE (B-12) pop. 2,700

In the summer Invermere offers recreational opportunities that include hiking and camping, and fishing, boating and sailboarding on Lake Windermere. Hang gliders often are seen launching off nearby Mount Swansea. Birds can be seen at Wilmer National Wildlife Area, about 5 kilometres (3 mi.) north.

Travel InfoCentre: 651 Hwy. 93/95, P.O. Box 2605, Invermere, BC, Canada V0A 1K0; phone (250) 342-6316 or 342-2844.

WINDERMERE VALLEY MUSEUM, 622 Third St., displays pioneer artifacts and local archives in a complex in a small park. The six log outbuildings have thematic displays. Allow 1 hour minimum. Tues.-Sat. 10-4, July 1-early Sept.; 1-4 in June. Admission $2, under 17 free. Phone (250) 342-9769.

KAMLOOPS (B-8)
pop. 76,400, elev. 345 m/1,131'

Founded in 1812 as a North West Co. depot, Kamloops later was a Hudson's Bay Co. post. Developed where the north and south branches of the Thompson River converge to form Kamloops Lake, Kamloops was named after an Indian word, *cumcloups,* or "the meeting of the waters." During the gold rush of the 1860s the Overlanders reached the city by rafting down the North Thompson.

Since the Cariboo's gold supply disappeared in the 1860s, Kamloops has developed as a center of cattle and sheep ranching.

Lumber is an important natural resource in the area. Weyerhaeuser Canada Ltd., a pulp mill on Mission Flats Road, offers guided tours of its facility in July and August. Under 12 are not permitted; long pants and flat, closed shoes are required. For information or reservations phone (250) 828-7363.

Area lakes offer good fishing; Kamloops trout are known to jump a few feet in the air after being hooked.

Visitor InfoCentre: 1290 W. Trans-Canada Hwy., Kamloops, BC, Canada V2C 6R3; phone (250) 374-3377 or (800) 662-1994.

Self-guiding tours: Kamloops is the site of several historical attractions, including the provincial courthouse and several old houses and churches. Self-guiding tour brochures are available from Kamloops Museum and Archives.

KAMLOOPS ART GALLERY, 101-465 Victoria St., presents works by contemporary artists. Exhibits change monthly and include paintings, sculpture, prints, drawings, photographs and video art. Allow 30 minutes minimum. Tues-Sat. 10-5 (also Thurs. 5-9), Sun. noon-4, Sept.-May; Tues.-Sat. 10-5 (also Tues. and Thurs. 5-9), Sun. 1-8, June-Aug. Closed holidays. Admission $3, senior citizens and students with ID $2, family rate $5. MC, VI. Phone (250) 828-3543.

KAMLOOPS MUSEUM AND ARCHIVES, 207 Seymour St., portrays the area's history. Featured are displays of Indian culture, fly-fishing, a reconstructed Hudson's Bay Co. fur-trading cabin, pioneer and Victorian artifacts and tableaux, transportation items and natural history specimens. The archives has collections of photographs and manuscripts. Guided tours are available.

Allow 1 hour minimum. Mon.-Fri. 9-8, Sat. 10-5, Sun. 1-5, July-Aug.; Tues.-Sat. 9:30-4:30, rest of year. Closed holidays. Guided walking tours are available Mon.-Fri., July-Aug. Donations. Phone (250) 828-3576.

KAMLOOPS WATERSLIDE, e. on Hwy. 1 to 9225 Hwy. 1E, has slides, miniature golf, hot tubs and a picnic area. Daily 10-7, July-Aug.; 10-5, June 13-30. Admission $12; over 65 and ages 4-6, $8.50; nonslider $4.50; over 65, $2.50. MC, VI. Phone (250) 573-3789.

SAVE **KAMLOOPS WILDLIFE PARK,** 17 km (10.2 mi.) e. on Hwy. 1, features more than 70 species of local and endangered wildlife, including grizzly bears and Siberian tigers, in natural habitats. Other highlights include a children's zoo, gardens, and a visitor center showing educational exhibits. The park is decorated for the winter holidays. A miniature railway runs in summer and mid-Dec. to early Jan. Daily 8-6, late June-late Aug.; 8-4:30, rest of year. Train rides daily 10-3:45, July-Aug.; daily 5-9, mid-Dec. to early Jan. Admission $6.54; ages 13-16, $4.67; ages 3-12, $3.74. Train $1; under 12, 50c. MC, VI. Phone (250) 573-3242.

ST. JOSEPH'S CHURCH is n. on Mount Paul Way, then w. to end of Chilcotin St. Constructed by Roman Catholic missionaries and the Kamloops Indian Band in the late 19th century, the church has been meticulously renovated. The

building's elaborate gilded altar and its many period religious artifacts also have been restored. Allow 30 minutes minimum. Wed.-Sun. 12:30-7:30, July 1-Labour Day. Donations. Phone (250) 374-7323.

SECWEPEMC MUSEUM AND NATIVE HERITAGE PARK, 355 Yellowhead Hwy., is designed to interpret the history and culture of the Secwepemc, or Shuswap, nation. A full-scale reconstruction of a traditional Shuswap winter village and a 2,400-year-old archeological site are within the park. Visitors can experience native song, dance and theater presentations. The park also features a museum with exhibits and a videotape describing the Shuswap nation.

Allow 1 hour minimum. Mon.-Fri. 8:30-8, Sat.-Sun. 10-6, June 1-early Sept.; Mon.-Fri. 8:30-4:30, rest of year. Closed Jan. 1 and Dec. 25. Admission $6; over 59 and ages 7-12, $4. MC, VI. Phone (250) 828-9801.

SAVE *WANDA SUE*, 1140 River St., at the end of 10th Ave., is a 26-metre (85-ft.) stern-wheeler that offers 2-hour narrated cruises on the Thompson River. Food is available. Cruises depart Mon.-Fri. at 1:30 and 6:30, Sat. at 1:30, Sun. at 1:30, 3:30 and 6:30, July-Aug.; Mon.-Fri. at 6:30, Sat. at 1:30, Sun. 1:30, 3:30 and 6, Mother's Day-June 30; Mon.-Fri. at 6, Sat. at 1:30, Sun. at 2 and 6, in Sept. Fare $12.50; over 59, $11.50; ages 6-12, $7. Phone (250) 374-7447.

RECREATIONAL ACTIVITIES
Skiing

• **Sun Peaks Resort at Tod Mountain** is 54 km (32.4 mi.) n. on Hwy. 5. Write Suite 50, 3150 Creekside Way, Sun Peaks, BC, Canada V0S 1Z1. Daily 9-3:30, mid-Nov. to Mid-Apr. Phone (250) 578-7842.

KASLO (C-11)
pop. 1,100, elev. 588 m/1,929′

Kaslo began as a mill site in 1888. Following large silver strikes in 1893 the town quickly expanded to city proportions. A village once again, Kaslo is a distribution center for the Lardeau Valley.

Duncan Dam, 42 kilometres (26 mi.) north, was the first of the three dams constructed by B.C. Hydro in accordance with the Columbia River Treaty, ratified by British Columbia and the United States in 1964. Southwest of the dam is the Kokanee Spawning Channel, built to compensate for the loss of natural spawning areas resulting from the dam's construction. The 3.2-kilometre (2-mi.) channel, one of the longest in the world, is said to be the first constructed for freshwater fish.

Kaslo & District Chamber of Commerce: P.O. Box 329, Kaslo, BC, Canada V0G 1M0; phone (250) 352-3433.

SS *MOYIE* NATIONAL HISTORIC SITE, 1 blk. n. off Hwy. 31 on Front St., following signs, is considered to be the world's oldest passenger sternwheeler. It operated on Kootenay Lake 1898-1957, hauling passengers and freight from Nelson to several northern destinations along the lake. The last active commercial stern-wheeler in the province, it now contains artifacts, antiques, an agricultural display, a model railway display and photographs relating to the vessel's history.

Allow 30 minutes minimum. Daily 9:30-5, mid-May to mid-Oct. Admission $5; over 64 and students with ID $4; ages 6-12, $2; family rate $15. MC, VI. Phone (250) 353-2525.

KELOWNA (C-9)
pop. 89,400, elev. 420 m/1,387'

Kelowna is the center of a fruit, vegetable and vineyard region around Okanagan Lake, from which one-third of all apples harvested in Canada are shipped. The lake also is known for its legendary monster, the Ogopogo, a Loch Ness type beast reportedly 9 to 21 metres (30-69 ft.) long with a head resembling that of a horse, goat or sheep.

The Kelowna Community Theatre stages productions during fall and winter; phone (604) 860-1470. The Okanagan Symphony Orchestra is another prominent cultural feature; phone (604) 763-7544.

Recreation in the area includes water sports, fishing and golf. City Park on Lake Okanagan is the city's largest park, with a beach, tennis courts and a children's water park. Kettle Valley Railway, an abandoned rail line, is popular with cyclists and hikers. Passing through Myra Canyon, the trackless trail comprises 18 trestles in a 5-mile loop.

Kelowna Chamber of Commerce: 544 Harvey Ave., Kelowna, BC, Canada V1Y 6C9; phone (250) 861-1515. *See color ad.*

B.C. ORCHARD INDUSTRY MUSEUM, 1304 Ellis St., traces the development of the orchard industry in the province. Displays also explain fruit production from planting to processing and preserving. Allow 30 minutes minimum. Tues.-Sat. 10-5. Closed Dec. 25. Donations. Phone (250) 763-0433.

The Wine Museum, 1304 Ellis St., is housed in a converted packing house built 1917-18. Displays include machines used for pressing and bottling as well as exhibits featuring the history of wine production in the area. Wine tastings are offered. Guided tours are available by appointment. Open Mon.-Sat. 10-5, Sun. noon-5; closed Dec. 25. Donations. Phone (250) 868-0441.

GEERT MAAS SCULPTURE GARDENS, GALLERY AND STUDIO is 10 km (6.2 mi.) n. on Hwy. 97, then w. on Sexsmith Rd. to 250 Reynolds Rd. Maas' semi-abstract sculptures of

bronze, aluminum, stainless steel, stoneware and mixed media are exhibited in the gallery and in the .4-hectare (1-acre) sculpture garden. The complex contains one of the largest collections of bronze sculptures in Canada. Medallions, paintings and etchings also can be seen in the permanent collection; changing exhibits also are offered. Allow 1 hour minimum. Mon.-Sat. 10-5, May 1-Oct. 1; by appointment rest of year. Donations. Phone (250) 860-7012.

KELOWNA CENTENNIAL MUSEUM, 470 Queensway Ave., displays Indian arts and crafts, a Chinese store and fossils and other collections about natural history. Also exhibited are materials relating to the Okanagan First Nation as well as the cultures of Africa, Asia, the Americas and the Pacific Islands. Mon.-Sat. 10-5, July-Aug.; Tues.-Sat. 10-5, rest of year. Donations. Phone (250) 763-2417.

KELOWNA LAND & ORCHARD CO. is 3 km (1.9 mi.) s. on Gordon Rd., 4 km (2.5 mi.) e. on K.L.O. Rd., then 1 km (.6 mi.) n. on E. Kelowna Rd. to 2930 Dunster Rd. The family-owned, working orchard offers visitors a chance to see techniques of the past as well as farm animals and current technologies used in growing apples. Self-guiding walking tours and guided wagon tours of the orchard are available. Juice and fruit samples are included.

Allow 30 minutes minimum for the walking tour, 1 hour minimum for the wagon tour. Daily 9-5, May-Oct. Guided wagon tours depart daily at 11, 1 and 3, July-Aug.; at 11 and 1, May-June and Sept.-Oct. Tours $5.25; ages 12-16, $2; under 12 free if accompanied by a parent. MC, VI. Phone (250) 763-1091.

MV *FINTRY QUEEN*, foot of Bernard Ave., offers cruises on Okanagan Lake. Food is available. Evening cruises sail Mon.-Sat. 7-9, Sun. 5:30-8. Afternoon cruises are available Mon.-Sat. noon-2. Cruises are available late spring to late fall (weather permitting). Fares for afternoon and Mon.-Fri. and Sun. evening cruises $8; over 64, $7; ages 7-13, $6; under 7, $3. Lunch and dinner cruises also are available; phone for information. MC. Phone (250) 763-2780.

RECREATIONAL ACTIVITIES
Skiing

• **Big White Ski Resort**, 55 km (34 mi.) e. on Hwy. 97C, P.O. Box 2039, Station R, Kelowna, BC, Canada V1X 4K5. Tues.-Sat. 8:30 a.m.-9 p.m., Sun.-Mon. 8-3:30, mid-Nov. to mid.-Apr. Phone (250) 765-3101.

WINERIES

• **Calona Vineyards**, 1125 Richter St. Tours begin at 11, 1, 3, and 5, May-Sept.; tours are at 2, rest of year. Phone (250) 762-9144.

• **Cedar Creek Estate Winery**, 12 km (7 mi.) s. on Lakeshore Rd. following signs. Tours and tastings are available on the hour daily 11-4, Apr.-Oct. Phone (250) 764-8866.

• **Gray Monk Cellars** is 22.5 km (14 mi.) n. via Hwy. 97, w. on Berry Rd., n. on Okanagan Centre Rd., then w. on Camp Rd. Tours on the hour daily 11-4.; closed Nov. 11. Phone (250) 766-3168.

KEREMEOS (D-8)
pop. 900, elev. 1,356′

THE GRIST MILL OF KEREMEOS, 1.5 km (.9 mi.) n.e. on Hwy. 3A, then .8 km (.5 mi.) e. on Upper Bench Rd., features demonstrations of the principles of milling and restoration. An exhibit building, apple orchard, wheat fields, circle gardens and visitor center also are on the grounds. Food is available. Allow 30 minutes minimum. Daily 9:30-5, Mother's Day-Thanksgiving. Admission $5; over 59, $4; ages 5-18, $3; family rate $12. Phone (250) 499-2888.

KIMBERLEY (C-11)
pop. 6,700, elev. 1,113 m/3,651′

Kimberley is a winter sports center with a Bavarian theme and a pedestrian mall—the Platzl—complete with wandering minstrels and a huge cuckoo clock. The Kimberley Community Gardens present colorful views June through October.

Built on the slopes of Sullivan and North Star hills, Kimberley is one of Canada's highest cities. It is perhaps best known as the site of the Sullivan Mine, one of the world's largest underground silver, lead and zinc mines.

Kimberley Bavarian Society Chamber of Commerce: 350 Ross St., Kimberley, BC, Canada V1A 2Z9; phone (250) 427-3666.

BAVARIAN CITY MINING RAILWAY, Gerry Sorenson Way, offers narrated 1-hour train rides on a narrow-gauge mine track. Miniature golf also is available. Daily 10-9, July 1-Labour Day. Admission $6; over 60 and ages 13-18, $5; ages 6-12, $3. Miniature golf additional. MC, VI. Phone (250) 427-3666.

KIMBERLEY HERITAGE MUSEUM, in the Platzl at 105 Spokane St., features artifacts and exhibits as well as displays about the history of mining in the area. Archives are available for research. Mon.-Sat. 9-4:30, July-Aug.; Mon.-Sat. 1-4, Sept.-Dec. and Mar.-June; Mon.-Fri. 1-4, rest of year. Closed July 1. Donations. Phone (250) 427-7510.

RECREATIONAL ACTIVITIES
Skiing

• **Kimberley Alpine Resort** is above town via Gerry Sorenson Way following signs. Write

P.O. Box 40, Kimberley, BC, Canada V1A 2Y5. Other activities are offered. Daily Dec.-Apr. Phone (250) 427-4881 or (800) 258-7669.

KITIMAT (E-2)
pop. 11,100, elev. 130 m/426'

Kitimat is a planned city built in the early 1950s by Alcan Smelters and Chemicals Ltd. The company chose the wilderness site for a new plant because of the area's deepwater harbor, flat land and hydroelectric plant.

Kitimat Chamber of Commerce: 2109 Forest Ave., P.O. Box 214, Kitimat, BC, Canada V8C 2G7; phone (250) 632-6294 or (800) 664-6554.

ALCAN SMELTERS AND CHEMICALS LTD., n. on Hwy. 37, offers lectures, films and bus tours of its aluminum smelter, one of the world's largest. Guided tours depart Mon.-Fri. at 10:30 and 1:30, June-Aug.; Tues. and Thurs. at 1:15, rest of year. Free. Reservations are recommended June-Aug. and are required during the rest of the year. Phone (250) 639-8259.

★ KOOTENAY NATIONAL PARK (B-12)

Elevations in the park range from 918 metres (3,011 ft.) at the park entrance to 3,424 metres (11,235 ft.) at Deltaform Mountain. Refer to CAA/AAA maps for additional elevation information.

The 1,406 square kilometres (543 sq. mi.) of Kootenay National Park straddle the Banff-Windermere Highway (Hwy. 93) as it travels down the western slope of the Rocky Mountains. Following the Vermilion and Kootenay river valleys, this slender 94-kilometre-long (63-mi.) park embraces several significant geologic features; Kootenay National Park, a World Heritage Site, is representative of the Rocky Mountain landscape.

Extensive faults created two of the park's significant and different features. Radium Hot Springs at the park's southern end resulted from rainwater and runoff being vaporized deep underground. The steam then returned to the surface via the earth's fissures and condensed in these springs, which were popularized by health buffs at the turn of the 20th century.

At the other end of the park are the Paint Pots, cold springs with a spiritual significance rather than physical. The exit holes, formed by the deposits of the iron-laden water, resemble earthen pots; Blackfoot, Stoney and Kootenay Indians once used the bright bronze mud to stain their bodies, decorate their tepees and draw rock paintings once visible near Sinclair Canyon.

Less dramatic are the topographic differences in the park. The Brisco and Stanford ranges intercept much of the coastal moisture bound for the park's southern region, but to the north, beyond Kootenay Crossing, the climate becomes much damper .

The dry southern climate offers winter shelter for animals migrating from the north and provides good grazing conditions for herds of bighorn sheep. Bears, moose, mountain goats and elk are common. Trails ranging from short hikes to overnight treks explore the park's wealth of evergreen forests, alpine meadows, glaciers and lakes.

General Information and Activities

Although the park is open all year, its three campgrounds are open only from early May to late September. Information about self-guiding walks, trails, features and facilities can be obtained from information centers at the Radium Hot Springs Pool and in the Kootenay Park Lodge at Vermilion Crossing from Victoria Day weekend through Labour Day and at the gateway or park headquarters during the rest of the year.

Nonmotorized watercraft are permitted on all lakes and rivers in the park. Climbers can register at the information centers, and back-country campers must obtain a wilderness pass. *See Recreation Chart and the AAA/CAA Western Canada and Alaska CampBook.*

ADMISSION to the park is $5; senior citizens $4; ages 6-16, $2.50. MC, VI.

PETS must be leashed at all times. Pets are permitted in the back-country overnight.

ADDRESS inquiries to the Superintendent, Kootenay National Park, Box 220, Radium Hot Springs, BC, Canada V0A 1M0; phone (250) 347-9615 or (800) 748-7275.

Points of Interest

MARBLE CANYON is north of McLeod Meadows along the Vermilion River and 90 m (295 ft.) from the road. The walls of gray limestone and quartzite laced with a stratum of white and gray dolomite make this one of the most beautiful canyons in the park. Tokumm Creek has cut a sheer, narrow cleft to the depth of about 39 metres (128 ft.).

A self-guiding trail follows the top edge of the canyon and leads to a waterfall. Interpretive signs describe the power of water in shaping the canyon's features. Allow 30 minutes minimum.

RADIUM HOT SPRINGS, just n. of the w. entrance to Kootenay National Park, range from 35 to 47 C (95 to 117 F). There is a hot pool as well as a cool pool. Iron oxide also colors the towering sandstone cliffs, giving a perpetual sunset quality. Pools open daily 9 a.m.-11 p.m., mid-May to mid-Oct.; noon-9, rest of year. Admission

May-Sept. $5.50; over 64 and ages 3-17, $5; family rate $16.50. Admission rest of year $5; over 64 and ages 3-17, $4.50; family rate $15. MC, VI. Phone (250) 347-9485 or (800) 767-1611. *See place listing p. 133 and Recreation Chart. See color ad p. 40.*

LADYSMITH (G-10)
pop. 6,500, elev. 40 m/131′

On the 49th parallel, Ladysmith is noted for its scenic position between mountain and sea. Founded during the Boer War, Ladysmith was named for a sister city in South Africa. Transfer Beach Park offers a playground, picnic tables and a swimming area watched by lifeguards.

Ladysmith & District Chamber of Commerce: P.O. Box 598, Ladysmith, BC, Canada V0R 2E0; phone (250) 245-2112.

BLACK NUGGET MUSEUM, 12 Gatacre St., is a former hotel that now houses a collection of antiques and memorabilia from the late 19th and early 20th centuries. The highlight is a restored barroom with the original bar. Allow 30 minutes minimum. Daily noon-4, late June-early Sept. Admission $2; over 65 and students with ID $1; ages 6-15, 75c. Phone (250) 245-4846.

LANGLEY—*see Vancouver p. 156.*

LILLOOET (B-7)
pop. 2,000, elev. 290 m/951′

Lillooet, on the Fraser River, marked the end of the first leg of the water route from the Pacific coast to the Cariboo gold mines. The Cariboo Trail traveled north to such destinations as 100 Mile House and 150 Mile House, named for their distances from the start of the trail. The surrounding area is of particular interest to rockhounds.

Lillooet Chamber of Commerce: 930 Main St., P.O. Box 650, Lillooet, BC, Canada V0K 1V0; phone (250) 256-4364.

LILLOOET MUSEUM, 790 Main St., is in a former Anglican church. Displays include local

pioneer relics, farm equipment, Indian artifacts, Chinese utensils and late 19th-century rooms. Daily 9-5, July-Aug. Donations. Phone (250) 256-4308.

LYTTON (C-7)
pop. 300, elev. 199 m/650′

At the junction of the Thompson and Fraser rivers, Lytton derives its livelihood from its location. Indians harvested tons of salmon from this river junction. Their trail along the Fraser became a major route to the gold fields, with Lytton as a base of supplies. This community calls itself the Rafting Capital of Canada and claims some of the warmest weather in the country.

Lytton & District Chamber of Commerce: 400 Fraser St., P.O. Box 460, Lytton, BC, Canada V0K 1Z0; phone (250) 455-2523.

RECREATIONAL ACTIVITIES
White-water Rafting

• **Kumsheen Rafting Adventures,** 6 km (4 mi.) n.e. on Trans-Canada Hwy., P.O. Box 30, Lytton, BC, Canada V0K 1Z0. Other activities are offered. Trips operate May-Oct. Phone (250) 455-2296, or (800) 663-6667 in British Columbia. *See color ad.*

MAPLE RIDGE—
see Vancouver p. 156.

MAYNE ISLAND—
see Gulf Islands p. 116.

MERRITT (C-8)
pop. 7,600, elev. 858 m/2,814′

Merritt is known for its many lakes. Of particular interest is Nicola Lake, a large warm-water lake 10 kilometres (6 mi.) north of town. Recreational activities include swimming, fishing, sailing, water skiing and windsurfing.

Monck Park, on the west side of the lake, offers camping and picnic facilities.

Merritt Chamber of Commerce: Jct. Hwys. 5 and 97C, P.O. Box 189, Merritt, BC, Canada V0K 2B0; phone (250) 378-2281.

NICOLA VALLEY MUSEUM ARCHIVES, 2202 Jackson Ave., chronicles the history of the region with exhibits about mining, logging and ranching. Indian and pioneer artifacts are displayed, along with photographs depicting the lives of early settlers. Allow 30 minutes minimum. Mon.-Fri. 9-4:30, July-Aug.; Mon.-Fri. 10-3, rest of year. Closed holidays and Dec. 20-Jan. 3. Donations. Phone (250) 378-4145.

MISSION—*see Vancouver p. 156.*

MORICETOWN (D-3)
pop. 700, elev. 411 m/1,348'

MORICETOWN CANYON, on Hwy. 16, once was the site of the largest village of the Bulkley Valley Indians, whose diet depended on salmon. During the summer Indians still can be seen gaffing the salmon as the fish fight their way upstream to spawn. Allow 1 hour minimum.

MOUNT REVELSTOKE NATIONAL PARK (A-10)

Elevations in the park range from 760 metres (2,493 ft.) at the bottom of Mount Revelstoke to 1,920 metres (6,300 ft.) at the Mount Revelstoke summit at Balsam Lake. Refer to CAA/AAA maps for additional elevation information.

Mount Revelstoke National Park is 260 square kilometres (100 sq. mi.) of sharp peaks, heavily timbered slopes and flowering meadows on the west edge of the Selkirk Range in southeastern British Columbia. Flanked on the east by the Purcell Range and on the west by the Monashee Range, the Selkirk Mountains are distinguished by their height and geologic complexity.

Erosion by glaciers and the heavy rainfall of the region have carved the rock of the Selkirks into jagged forms. Complementing the park's dense green forests and lush wildflower meadows are glacier-fed streams and lakes as well as the deep snows that blanket the slopes until late June.

Deer inhabit the lower slopes; black and grizzly bears and mountain caribou also may be seen in the park. Most mountain species of birds are represented, including fox sparrows, hermit thrushes and northern hawk owls.

The Trans-Canada Highway passes through the southeastern portion of the park for 13 kilo-

metres (8 mi.) and parallels its southern boundary for 18 kilometres (11 mi.).

General Information and Activities

The park is open all year. Visitor facilities and accommodations are available in Revelstoke at the western entrance. A park pass must be purchased at the park gates.

From Hwy. 1, a 26-kilometre (16-mi.) hard surface road that is open only in summer leads to the summit of Mount Revelstoke, which provides an excellent panoramic view. Along its length are several viewpoints; many wildflowers bloom in August. Picnic areas are available at Monashee, the 8-kilometre (5-mi.) viewpoint on this road, and at Balsam Lake, 1 kilometre (.6 mi.) from the summit. Other picnic areas and nature trails are along the Trans-Canada Highway.

Recreation includes subalpine hiking, mountain climbing and fishing. More than 44 kilometres (27 mi.) of hiking trails lead to such sites as Miller and Jade lakes. Climbers and hikers traveling off park trails may register with a park warden before and after each trip. Fishing is by permit, available at the park administrative office in Revelstoke. *See Recreation Chart.*

ADMISSION to the park is $4; over 65, $3; ages 6-16, $2; all occupants of vehicle $10. Four-day and annual passes are available.

PETS are permitted in the park provided they are on leashes or otherwise restricted at all times.

ADDRESS inquiries to the Superintendent, Mount Revelstoke and Glacier National Parks, P.O. Box 350, Revelstoke, BC, Canada V0E 2S0; phone (250) 837-7500.

NAKUSP (B-10)
pop. 1,700, elev. 914 m/2,998'

Nakusp, on the shore of Upper Arrow Lake, is named for an Indian word meaning "safe, closed in harbor." Winter skiing is available.

Nakusp Chamber of Commerce: 92 W. Sixth Ave., P.O. Box 387, Nakusp, BC, Canada V0G 1R0; phone (250) 265-4234, or (800) 909-8819 in British Columbia and Alberta.

NAKUSP HOT SPRINGS, 1.5 km (.9 mi.) n. on Hwy. 23, then 12 km (7 mi.) e. on Hot Springs Rd., offers several mineral baths in an outdoor cedar structure. The temperature of the pools varies from 38 to 42 C (102-111 F). Picnicking is permitted. Food is available. Daily 9:30 a.m.-10 p.m., June-Sept.; 11-9:30, rest of year. Admission $5.50; over 64 and ages 6-18, $4.50. Day pass $8; over 64 and ages 6-18, $7. MC, VI. Phone (250) 265-4528. *See Recreation Chart.*

NANAIMO (G-10)
pop. 70,100, elev. 30 m/98'

Some 120 kilometres (75 mi.) north of Victoria, Nanaimo began as a Hudson's Bay Co. outpost called Colvilletown, established for miners brought from England and Scotland to mine coal.

A thriving forest products industry and important deep-sea fishing port have replaced coal's economic influence. Nanaimo has made tourism and recreation a part of the economy.

Offshore islands and nearby mountains and lakes provide a variety of recreational opportunities including hiking, swimming, camping and picnicking. During winter and early spring charter companies offer marine wildlife tours to view the bald eagles and sea lions that winter in the area.

Exotic trees provide a setting for picnicking at Harmac Arboretum, 11 kilometres (7 mi.) south at Harmac Pulp Mill and Duke Point roads. Newcastle Island *(see Recreation Chart and the AAA/CAA Western Canada and Alaska CampBook)* is a provincial marine park accessible by a 10-minute ferry ride from Maffeo-Sutton Park, behind the Civic Arena. Automobiles are not permitted; the ferry operates daily on the hour, May 1 through Thanksgiving.

Salmon sport fishing, scuba diving, wind surfing and sailing are available from Nanaimo's natural harbor, regularly visited by the ferry from Vancouver. An intertidal lagoon park with three lighted water curtains and a 4-km (2.5-mi.) walkway along the seawall graces Nanaimo's waterfront. St. Jean's Custom Cannery is one of three factories where fishing enthusiasts can have their catch canned or smoked.

On a landscaped hillside, Malaspina College offers a view of the city and harbor below and is also the site of Nanaimo Art Gallery and Exhibition Centre. Visitors interested in prehistoric art can see Indian sandstone carvings at Petroglyph Park, 3.25 kilometres (2 mi.) south on scenic Hwy. 1.

Nanaimo is accessible from the mainland by BC Ferries, which sail from Horseshoe Bay to Departure Bay and from Tsawwassen to Duke Point, 8 km (5 mi.) south. For more information, phone (888) 223-3779.

Tourism Nanaimo: 2290 Bowen Rd., Nanaimo, BC, Canada V9T 3K7; phone (250) 756-0106 or (800) 663-7337.

NANAIMO ART GALLERY, on the Malaspina University-College campus at 900 Fifth St., displays local, regional and national exhibits in two galleries. New exhibits are installed frequently. Allow 1 hour minimum. Mon.-Sat. 10-5; closed holidays. Admission $2, under 12 free. MC, VI. Phone (250) 755-8790.

[SAVE] **NANAIMO DISTRICT MUSEUM,** 100 Cameron St., has exhibits about local history, including the arrival of the Spaniards, the discovery of coal and the beginning of mining. Displays include a Coast Salish diorama, Vancouver Island Indian artifacts and a restored miner's cottage. Daily 9-5, Victoria Day weekend-Labour Day; Tues.-Sat. 9-5, rest of year. Closed winter holidays. Admission $2; over 60 and students with ID $1.75; under 12, 75c. MC, VI. Phone (250) 753-1821.

The Bastion, on Front St. across from Coast Bastion Hotel, was built in 1853 to protect the early settlers. A display shows how the small fort was used in the 1860s. A noon ceremonial cannon firing is conducted by staff dressed in period costumes. Wed.-Mon. 9-5, July-Aug. Admission $1, under 12 free.

RECREATIONAL ACTIVITIES

Bungee Jumping

- [SAVE] **Bungy Zone,** 35 River Rd., Nanaimo, BC, Canada V9R 5K2. Daily Feb.-Nov. Hours vary; phone ahead. Phone (250) 753-5867 or (800) 668-7771.

NELSON (C-11)
pop. 9,600, elev. 535 m/1,755'

An old iron and silver mining town, Nelson was settled by prospectors in the late 1880s. With the depletion of its mines, the town turned to logging, sawmilling and area trade. However, the legacy of the bonanza days lives on in the more than 350 heritage sites. Most of Nelson's historic commercial buildings are open to the public, but homes are private and closed to visitors. Free guided tours of Nelson's heritage attractions are available from the chamber of commerce early July through Labour Day.

Nearby parks, lakes, streams and mountains offer all types of summer and winter recreation. At Kokanee Creek Park *(see Recreation Chart and the AAA/CAA Western Canada and Alaska CampBook)*, 19 kilometres (12 mi.) northeast on Hwy. 3A, a visitor center has displays about regional natural life and human history, and park naturalists conduct walks and lectures and show films.

Nelson Chamber of Commerce: 225 Hall St., Nelson, BC, Canada V1L 5X4; phone (250) 352-3433.

Self-guiding tours: Maps detailing walking and driving tours are available from the chamber of commerce.

NELSON MOUNTAIN AIR, departing from the Nelson Airport at 91 Lakeside Dr., offers half-hour sightseeing tours of Kokanee Glacier Park and the surrounding mountain wilderness. Floatplane, hiking and fishing excursions also are available. Sightseeing departures require a minimum of 2 people. Daily 9-5:30, Apr.-Oct.; 9-4, rest of year; holidays by appointment. Fare $37.50 per person for half-hour sightseeing tour. MC, VI. Phone (250) 354-1456.

THE NELSON MUSEUM, 402 Anderson St. and Nelson Ave., displays Indian flint, Doukhobor historical items and Kootenay Lake boating displays, along with nature and art exhibits. Tours are available on request. Mon.-Sat. 1-6, July-Aug.; Mon.-Sat. 1-4, rest of year. Closed holidays. Admission $2; over 60 and ages 5-12, $1. Phone (250) 352-9813.

RECREATIONAL ACTIVITIES

Skiing

- **Whitewater Ski Resort**, 20 km (12 mi.) s. off Hwy. 6, P.O. Box 60, Nelson, BC, Canada V1L 5P7. Daily 9-3:30, mid-Dec. to early Apr. Phone (250) 354-4944 or (800) 666-9420.

NEW DENVER (C-10)

pop. 600, elev. 555 m/1,850'

NIKKEI INTERNMENT MEMORIAL CENTRE, 306 Josephine St., is said to be the only museum in Canada dedicated to remembering the Japanese internment experience during World War II. The center commemorates the 22,000 Nikkei (people of Japanese descent) removed from their British Columbia homes and relocated to such camps.

A visitor center, a typical shack that housed two families as well as an outhouse and a peace garden are among the exhibits. Tribute also is paid to the first generation of Japanese who arrived in Canada in 1877. Allow 30 minutes minimum. Daily 9:30-5, May 15-Sept. 15. Admission $4; over 60 and ages 13-17, $3; ages 5-12, $2; family rate $10. Phone (250) 358-7288.

NEW WESTMINSTER—

see Vancouver p. 157.

NORTH VANCOUVER—

see Vancouver p. 157.

OLIVER (D-9)

pop. 4,300, elev. 307 m/1,007'

The northern tip of the American Great Basin Desert, which extends to Mexico, begins at Oliver. Irrigation begun in the 1920s converted the once desertlike valley floor and arid hillsides surrounding the town into productive orchards and vineyards. Abundant sunshine and little rain provide ideal conditions for growing wine grapes.

The area's climate also promotes numerous recreational activities. An 18-kilometre (11-mi.) paved bicycle trail travels through Oliver's rolling hills and along the Similkameen River. The valley lakes and streams offer boating and fishing. Vaseux Lake and Inkaneep provincial parks (*see Recreation Chart*) are nearby, as are Bear and Madden lakes, known for excellent trout fishing.

The Fairview Townsite, 3 kilometres (1.9 mi.) west on Fairview Road, formerly was the site of an 1880s boomtown. The town disappeared along with the gold in 1906; plaques at the site provide historical information.

Oliver & District Chamber of Commerce: 36205-93 St., P.O. Box 460, Oliver, BC, Canada V0H 1T0; phone (250) 498-6321.

WINERIES

- **Inniskillin Okanagan Vineyards**, 5 km (3 mi.) s. on Hwy. 97 to Rd. 11. Daily 9-5, June-Sept.; Mon.-Fri. 9-4, rest of year. Tours at 10 and 2, June-Sept. Phone (250) 498-6663 or 498-6411.
- **Vincor International Inc.**, 1.5 km (1 mi.) n. on Hwy. 97. Tours are given at 10 and 2, May-Oct.; by appointment rest of year. Phone (250) 498-4981.

OSOYOOS (D-9)

pop. 4,000, elev. 335 m/1,099'

From Osoyoos on the east side of Osoyoos Lake, an area of desert sand extends 48 kilometres (30 mi.) north to Skaha Lake and 24 kilometres (15 mi.) west along the Similkameen River. The area's similarity to Spain in climate and terrain inspired the citizens to adopt an Iberian style in their buildings. Despite its arid surroundings, Osoyoos has 19 kilometres (12 mi.) of sandy beach lining one of Canada's warmest freshwater lakes.

Man-made recreational facilities include the Wild Rapids on East Lakeshore Drive, with three large waterslides, five giant hot tubs and two minislides. Skiing is available nearby.

A heavy concentration of minerals, including evaporated copper, silver, gold and sulfate and Epsom salts, can be found at Spotted Lake, west on Crowsnest Hwy. 3, which provides 446 kilometres (277 mi.) of scenic driving all the way to Hope.

Osoyoos & District Chamber of Commerce: Jct. Hwys. 3 and 97, P.O. Box 227, Osoyoos, BC, Canada V0H 1V0; phone (250) 495-7142.

OSOYOOS MUSEUM, in Community Park, has a provincial police exhibit and a log building that depicts the interior of a late 19th-century pioneer cabin. The museum also has mining displays, Indian artifacts, a butterfly collection and a moonshine still. Allow 1 hour minimum. Daily 10-3, May 15-Sept. 15. Last admission 30 minutes before closing. Admission $3; ages 6-14, $1. Phone (250) 495-2582.

PACIFIC RIM NATIONAL PARK RESERVE (I-3)

Elevations in the park range from sea level along the Long Beach area to 140 metres (459 ft.) at Radar Hill. Refer to CAA/AAA maps for additional elevation information.

Pacific Rim National Park Reserve is in three sections with different entry points on the west coast of Vancouver Island: the Long Beach area between Ucluelet and Tofino; the Broken Island Group, a cluster of islands in Barkley Sound; and the 75-kilometre-long (47-mi.) West Coast Trail between Bamfield and Port Renfrew.

Numerous contrasts exist in the 510-square-kilometre (197-sq.-mi.) reserve, which has sandy beaches, tranquil estuaries and lakes, rugged headlands, dense rain forests and rocky islands. Wildflowers nurtured by the area's moist and temperate climate thrive in an immense old-growth rain forest.

A stopping place for geese and ducks during their yearly migrations, the shoreline zone also accommodates colonies of sea birds and wildlife. Each spring, some 20,000 gray whales migrate through the reserve's waters.

General Information and Activities

The reserve is open all year, although many facilities are seasonal. The Long Beach area, about 16 kilometres (10 mi.) west of the junction of Hwy. 4 and the Ucluelet highway, has 19 kilometres (12 mi.) of sandy beach and shoreline which are popular year-round with surfers and beachcombers. Long Beach Information Centre, open mid-June to mid-September, is on Hwy. 4 inside the park boundary. There are self-guiding nature trails in the surrounding rain forest and other interpretive programs. The Wickaninnish Interpretive Centre features displays and films chronicling marine life of the Pacific.

The Broken Group Islands, accessible only by boat, offers pristine wilderness spread over a 100-island chain in the center of Barkley Sound. Eagles and sea lions are abundant, while varied sea life and sunken ships create a diver's paradise. Camping is available in designated areas on eight islands.

The West Coast Trail, which had its beginnings as an avenue of rescue for shipwrecked sailors, follows the reserve's rugged coastline between Port Renfrew and Bamfield. The trail is open to experienced hikers only and offers spectacular coastal scenery along its challenging path. Remnants of former settlements and shipwrecks can be seen along the shoreline.

The West Coast Trail Registration Centre, at Pachena Bay near Bamfield, and an information center at the Port Renfrew trail head offer details about the weather, trail conditions and facilities and collects the fares for use of the ferry. The trail and centers are open May through September. Reservations are recommended to hike the trail; phone (800) 663-6000. *See Recreation Chart and the AAA/CAA Western Canada and Alaska CampBook.*

ADMISSION to the Long Beach area of the reserve for private motor vehicles is $8 per day, Mar.-Oct., or $42 for an annual permit. Camping fee at Long Beach $12-$20 per person per night.

Camping fee at other designated sites is $5 per person per night. Trail use permit is $70; reservation fee $25 (non-refundable); ferry fee $12.50.

ADDRESS inquiries to the Superintendent, Pacific Rim National Park Reserve, 2185 Ocean Terrace Rd., P.O. Box 280, Ucluelet, BC, Canada V0R 3A0; phone (250) 726-7721 or 726-4212 mid-Mar. to mid-Oct.

PARKSVILLE (F-10)
pop. 9,500, elev. 80 m/262'

With its 1.6-kilometre-long (1-mi.) sandy beach on the Strait of Georgia, Parksville is a popular summer resort. Nearby Englishman and Little Qualicum rivers and parks, with scenic waterfalls, provide many opportunities for recreation, as do other area lakes, streams, mountains and parks. Rathtrevor Beach Provincial Park offers a beach, camping and picnicking. *See Recreation Chart and the AAA/CAA Western Canada and Alaska CampBook.*

Parksville & District Chamber of Commerce: 1275 E. Island Hwy., P.O. Box 99, Parksville, BC, Canada V9P 2G3; phone (250) 248-3613.

CRAIG HERITAGE PARK AND MUSEUM, 14 km (9 mi.) s. at 1245 E. Island Hwy., is a collection of historic buildings, including a church, a log house, a fire station, a turn-of-the-20th-century schoolhouse and two 19th-century post offices. Exhibits inside the buildings depict local history. Guided tours are available. Allow 30 minutes minimum. Daily 9-5, June 1-Sept. 7; by appointment rest of year. Admission $2; ages 8-18, $1; family rate $4. Phone (250) 248-6966.

PEACHLAND (C-8)
pop. 4,500, elev. 366 m/1,200'

Peachland's rolling green countryside is a prosperous fruit growing, farming, lumber producing and mining area. The mining of molybdenum and copper from the Brenda Mines complex in the hills above Hwy. 97 drastically increased Peachland's population during the 1970s.

Nearby mountains, rivers and lakes, including Okanagan Lake *(see Recreation Chart)*, offer abundant opportunities for skiing, hiking, fishing and water sports.

WINERIES
• **First Estate Cellars Ltd.** is just n. on Trepanier Bench Rd., which then becomes Cousins Rd., to 5031 Cousins Rd. Tours and tastings offered daily 11-5, Victoria Day weekend-Oct. 31. Phone (250) 767-9526.

PENDER ISLANDS—
see Gulf Islands p. 116.

PENTICTON (C-9)
pop. 31,000, elev. 345 m/1,131'

The first orchard in Okanagan Valley was planted in 1874 by Thomas Ellis, and the fruits, especially peaches, became a staple of the area. Penticton's fruit industry combines with tourism and lumber industries to keep the community strong.

Okanagan and Skaha lakes, at opposite ends of the city, offer ample expanses of shoreline for recreational pursuits. A popular summer activity is floating down the 8-kilometre (5-mi.) river channel from the mouth of Okanagan Lake *(see Recreation Chart and the AAA/CAA Western Canada and Alaska CampBook)* to Skaha Lake. The channel has rest and picnic areas and is paralleled by a bicycle path and a jogging trail.

Tourism Penticton 888 Westminster Ave. W., Penticton, BC, Canada V2A 8R2; phone (250) 490-2464 or (800) 663-5052.

ART GALLERY OF THE SOUTH OKANAGAN, 11 Ellis St., features works produced by local, provincial and internationally-known artists. On Okanagan Lake, the facility includes three exhibition halls and an art exchange showroom. Allow 30 minutes minimum. Tues.-Fri. 10-5, Sat.-Sun. 1-5; closed most holidays. Admission $2. MC, VI. Phone (250) 493-2928.

DOMINION RADIO ASTROPHYSICAL OBSERVATORY, 16 km (10 mi.) s.w. on Hwy. 97, then 7 km (4 mi.) s. on White Lake Rd., features radio telescopes used to study the universe. A self-guiding tour of the site includes a 26-metre (85-ft.) parabolic antenna and an array of more sophisticated, computer-linked, 9-metre (30-ft.) antennae.

Since automobile ignitions cause radio interference, visitors are asked to leave their vehicles at the road and walk the 600 metres (.4 mi.) to the facility. Allow 30 minutes minimum. Visitor center daily 10-5, Mar. 15-Oct. 15; Mon.-Fri. 10-5, rest of year. Guided tours are given Sun. 2-5, July-Aug. Free. Phone (250) 493-2277.

PENTICTON (R.N. ATKINSON) MUSEUM, 785 Main St., contains displays describing the natural and social histories of the southern Okanagan Valley. A historic transportation exhibit about the Kettle Valley Railway is available along with an exhibit about the Canadian military. Allow 1 hour minimum. Tues.-Sat. 10-5; closed holidays. Donations. Phone (250) 490-2451.

SS *SICAMOUS*, on Okanagan Lake Beach at 1099 Lakeshore Dr., is the last stern-wheeler to operate on Okanagan Lake. Visitors can experience what once was a major means of transportation in the area. Kettle Valley Model Railway is displayed on board. Allow 30 minutes minimum. Daily 9-9, July-Aug.; daily 9-7 in June; Mon.-Fri. 9-7, Apr.-May and in Sept.; Mon.-Fri. 9-5, Oct. 1 to mid-Dec. Closed Easter. Admission $3; ages 8-12, $1. MC, VI. Phone (250) 492-0403.

WONDERFUL WATERWORLD, 225 Yorkton Ave. at Skaha Lake Rd., has seven large slides, five small slides, a hot pool, picnic area and minia-

ture golf. Mon.-Sat. 10-8, Sun. 11-7, July 1-Labour Day. Admission Mon.-Sat. $13; ages 4-6, $11; Sun. $12, ages 4-6, $10. Half-day admission (4-8 p.m.) Mon.-Sat. $9; ages 4-6, $8; Sun. (3-7 p.m.) $8. Observer rates are available. MC, VI. Phone (250) 493-8121.

RECREATIONAL ACTIVITIES

Skiing

- **Apex Mountain Resort**, 32 km (20 mi.) w. on Green Mountain Rd., P.O. Box 1060, Penticton, BC, Canada V2A 7N7. Daily 9-3:30, mid-Nov. to late Apr. Other activities are available. Phone (877) 777-2739.

PORT ALBERNI (F-9)
pop. 18,500, elev. 60 m/197'

A deepwater port and important fishing and lumber shipping center, Port Alberni was discovered in 1791 by Don Pedro Alberni, a Spanish sea captain. Industry began in 1860 when nine workmen arriving on the schooner *Meg Merrilees* built a sawmill on the harbor's edge.

Port Alberni's harbor remains the city's focal point, enhanced by the Alberni Harbour Quay at the foot of Argyle Street. The $2 million facility includes shops, an arts and crafts outlet and the MV *Lady Rose* office. "Two Spot," an original logging railroad steam locomotive, takes visitors on a 25-minute journey along the waterfront.

Surrounded by mountains, lakes and forests, the city is a good base for naturalists and outdoors enthusiasts. Alpine and cross-country skiing is available nearby. Sproat Lake Provincial Park *(see Recreation Chart and the AAA/CAA Western Canada and Alaska CampBook)* features Indian carvings of mythological beasts. There are hundreds of giant Douglas firs, many that date from the late 12th century, at Cathedral Grove in MacMillan Provincial Park, 16 kilometres (10 mi.) east.

The region's natural wonders are protected by the Martin Mars Water Bombers based at Sproat Lake. Designed to combat forest fires, these huge aircraft carry 6,000 imperial gallons (7,206 U.S. gallons) of water.

During summer Pacifica Paper offers free forestry and mill tours of its facilities in Port Alberni. The Alberni Pulp and Paper Division, 4000 Stamp Ave., Somass Division, 3500 Harbor Rd., and the Alberni Pacific Sawmill, 2500 First Ave., offer 2-hour tours. Proper footwear and long pants are advised at the mills. Tours must be booked in advance; phone (250) 724-7890.

Alberni Valley Chamber of Commerce: 2533 Redford St., R.R. #2, Site 215, C-1O, Port Alberni, BC, Canada V9Y 7L6; phone (250) 724-6535.

ALBERNI VALLEY MUSEUM, in Echo Recreation Centre at 4255 Wallace St., displays Vancouver Island First Nations and pioneer artifacts and a basket collection. The commercial fishing and industrial exhibit has a working model of the Pelton Power Generator. Hands-on exhibits include a sawyer's mill and the West Coast Life Saving Trail Telegraph. Tues.-Sat. 10-5 (also Thurs. 5-8). Free. Phone (250) 723-2181.

SAVE **MV** *LADY ROSE*, docked at the Argyle Pier in the Alberni Harbour Quay at the foot of Argyle St., takes visitors on an all-day cruise. This packet freighter, and the MV *Frances Barkley*, deliver mail and cargo to isolated villages, fishing resorts and camps. The freighters sail down the Alberni Inlet to Bamfield, Ucluelet and the Broken Group Islands. Sensible shoes and a sweater or light jacket are advisable. Food is available.

Departures to Bamfield Tues. and Thurs.-Sun. at 8 a.m., July-Aug.; Tues., Thurs. and Sat. at 8 a.m., rest of year. Sailings from Port Alberni to Ucluelet and Broken Group Islands Mon., Wed. and Fri. at 8 a.m., early June-late Sept. Full-day, round-trip fares $40-$46; ages 7-15, $20-$23; under 7 free when accompanied by an adult. Reservations are recommended in summer. AE, MC, VI. Phone (250) 723-8313, or (800) 663-7192, Apr.-Sept.

ROBERTSON CREEK FISH HATCHERY, 5 km (3 mi.) w. on Hwy. 4, then 7 km (4 mi.) n.w. on Great Central Lake Rd., has an annual output of 9 million chinook and 1.5 million coho salmon and 250,000 steelhead trout. Displays explain the fish breeding process from incubation through release. Facilities include outdoor raising ponds and raceways. Daily 8:30-4. Free. Phone (250) 724-6521.

PORT COQUITLAM—

see Vancouver p. 159.

PORT EDWARD (E-1) pop. 700

The river of mists, as the Indians called the Skeena River, bursts through the Coast Range and empties into the Pacific Ocean near Port Edward. The river provides the community's major commodity, fish, which is processed by local canneries. Salmon and steelhead trout, besides being economic staples, also offer a recreational challenge to anglers.

NORTH PACIFIC CANNERY VILLAGE AND MUSEUM is 10 km (6 mi.) s. of Hwy. 16 at 1889 Skeena Dr. The restored 1889 cannery village includes the main cannery, reduction plant, staff housing and mess house. Artifacts of the fishing industry are displayed throughout the complex. Food is available. Daily 9-6, May-Sept.; otherwise varies rest of year. Admission $6; over 64 and students with ID $5; ages 7-12, $3. MC, VI. Phone (250) 628-3538.

PORT McNEILL (G-2)

pop. 2,900, elev. 15 m/49'

In the scenic, untamed wilderness of northern Vancouver Island, Port McNeill occupies a rich

lumber and fishing region popular with adventurous hikers, campers, spelunkers, fishermen and other sports enthusiasts.

Of interest to rock collectors and geologists are several nearby natural phenomena, including the Vanishing River, which plunges underground into a maze of caves and tunnels; the Devil's Bath, a huge rock bowl continuously filled by an underground spring; and the Eternal Fountain, which gushes from a rock crevice and then disappears underground again. All are reached by logging roads that are accessible only in summer.

An inter-island ferry operates a shuttle service between Port McNeill, Sointula and Alert Bay (*see place listing p. 105*).

Port McNeil & District Chamber of Commerce: Beach Dr., P.O. Box 129, Port McNeill, BC, Canada V0N 2R0; phone (250) 956-3131.

PORT MOODY—

see Vancouver p. 159.

POUCE COUPE (D-6)

pop. 900, elev. 652 m/2,139'

The village of Pouce Coupe is referred to as the gateway to Peace country because it is one of the first communities travelers will see when entering British Columbia from Alberta.

POUCE COUPE MUSEUM, 5006 49th Ave., displays pioneer artifacts in the former Northern Alberta Railway station. Daily 8-5, May 15-Sept. 15. Donations. Phone (250) 786-5555.

POWELL RIVER (E-11)

pop. 13,100, elev. 55 m/180'

The first roll of newsprint manufactured in western Canada was produced at Powell River in 1912 by what is now Pacifica Paper Ltd. In addition to forest products, the major industries are tourism, fishing and mining.

The area offers year-round freshwater and saltwater fishing and scuba diving; several local charter boats and marinas offer scuba gear rentals. Visitors must obtain a license for oyster harvesting and clam digging. A canoe portage connects eight lakes around Powell River; camping areas are within a day of each other along this scenic circuit and along the coast. Other activities available include hiking, kayaking, cycling and camping.

A panorama of the Strait of Malaspina unfolds from the Mount Valentine viewpoint, reached by a rock stairway. Bald eagles can be observed at any time of year, especially in late fall when they are attracted by salmon spawning in channels and small streams. Also of interest are Sliammon Fish Hatchery and Powell River Salmon Society Hatchery.

Powell River Visitor Information Centre: 4690 Marine Ave., Powell River, BC, Canada V8A 2L1; phone (604) 485-4701.

INLAND LAKE SITE AND TRAIL SYSTEM, 12 km (7 mi.) n. on Inland Lake Rd., offers wheelchair accessible facilities for outdoor activities including camping, fishing and hiking. The site is along a 5.5-kilometre-long (3-mi.) lake in a semiremote area with abundant and varied wildlife.

The 13-kilometre-long (8-mi.) wheelchair accessible circuit of crushed limestone with minimal grades has eight picnic and rest areas, four overnight camping areas and six fishing wharves. Amenities include small rustic cabins exclusively for use by the disabled in addition to wheelchair accessible outhouses. A caretaker is at the main site 24 hours a day (except on Tuesdays) to offer assistance when requested.

For camping reservations or information contact . For further information contact BC Parks. Site open for day use daily 7 a.m.-10 p.m., Apr. 15-Oct. 15. Hours may vary; phone ahead. Donations. Phone (604) 485-0775.

PACIFICA PAPER INC., 6270 Yew St., offers tours of one of the area's largest pulp and paper mills. Part of the tour is outside; appropriate dress and low-heeled, closed footwear are advised. Allow 2 hours minimum. Tours Mon.-Fri. 8-4:30, June-Aug. Visitors should arrive at the main gate 10 minutes before the tour begins. Free. Under 12 are not permitted. Phone (604) 485-4701.

POWELL RIVER MUSEUM, on Marine Ave. across from Willingdon Beach, houses artifacts, archival material and displays about the area's history. A children's treasure hunt is featured. An art gallery displays art by local artisans. Allow 30 minutes minimum. Daily 9-5, June-Aug.; Mon.-Fri. 9-5, rest of year. Closed holidays. Admission $2; ages 5-12, $1; family rate $5. Phone (604) 485-2222.

PRINCE GEORGE (E-5)
pop. 75,100, elev. 691 m/2,267′

At the confluence of the Nechako and Fraser rivers, the area was visited in 1793 by Alexander Mackenzie in his trek down the Fraser to the Pacific. In 1807 it became the site for Simon Fraser's North West Co. fort. Fraser's canoe brigades soon gave way to paddlewheelers and then railroads, which converged on this important northern crossroads. Prince George remains a major transportation and trade center, a role enhanced by a thriving forest industry.

Despite its urban transformation, the city has retained much of its natural heritage in its 116 parks. Of interest are Fort George Park, which contains a replica of Fraser's trading post; Connaught Park's manicured gardens and scenic views; and Cottonwood Island Park, which includes the Prince George Railway Museum and its collection of railroad artifacts and cars.

Prince George blends its pastoral features with such cultural centers as Studio 2880 and Vanier Hall. Studio 2880, home to six craft guilds, is the site of craft markets and special events throughout the year. Concerts by the Prince George Symphony and by visiting performers are held in Vanier Hall.

These cultural amenities coexist with the more rugged recreational opportunities available in the wilderness that surrounds the city. Nearby lakes, rivers and mountains present an array of activities ranging from rugged back-country hikes and fishing to skiing and ice skating.

Tourism Prince George: 1198 Victoria St., Prince George, BC, Canada V2L 2L2; phone (250) 562-3700 or (800) 668-7646.

FRASER-FORT GEORGE REGIONAL MUSEUM, at the end of 20th Ave. at 333 Gorse St. in Fort George Park, has displays about Fort George's early history and development. Topics include transportation, lumber and First Nations peoples history; traveling exhibits periodically are scheduled. The Northwood Explorations Hands-on Science Gallery features live animals as well as interactive computer terminals covering topics such as dinosaurs, forestry and the environment. A small interactive theater also is featured in the history hall. An .8-kilometre (.5-mi.) ride on a steam locomotive train is available on weekends and holidays.

Allow 30 minutes minimum. Daily 10-5, Victoria Day weekend-Thanksgiving; Wed.-Sun. noon-5, rest of year. Closed Labour Day and Dec. 25. Admission $6.50; senior citizens $5.50; under 13, $4.50; family rate $10. Train rides $1. AE, MC, VI. Phone (250) 562-1612.

PRINCE RUPERT (D-1)
pop. 16,700, elev. 50 m/164′

At the turn of the 20th century Prince Rupert existed only in the imagination of Charles Hays, manager of the Grand Trunk Pacific Railway. Hays died with the sinking of the SS *Titanic*, but the Grand Trunk Pacific Railway carried out his intention to build a port to rival Vancouver on this rugged, uninhabited island bordered by a natural harbor. The new site was expected to be successful because it was closer to the Far East than Vancouver and would provide an outlet for the untapped resources of Canada's far north.

Prince Rupert has fulfilled that potential and is now one of Canada's major seaports. It is the southernmost port of the Alaska Ferry System, the northern terminus of the British Columbia Ferry Corp. and the western terminus of the Canadian National Railway. Cruise ships en route to coastal glaciers and fjords also stop at Prince Rupert's harbor, said to be the world's third largest natural ice-free deep-sea harbor.

Before the coming of the railroad the northern coast was home to the Tsimpsean and Haida, cultures whose ancestors inhabited the area for almost 5,000 years. Both are renowned for their stylized artworks, the most familiar of which are totem poles. Many of these graceful monuments are shown in such city parks as Service Park, the colorful terraced Sunken Gardens, and Roosevelt Park with its sweeping views of the Pacific.

On the waterfront, Kwinitsa Railway Station is a relic of the modern era. Restored and moved from its original location, Kwinitsa is one of the last of the Grand Trunk Pacific Railway stations; inside are exhibits about the railroad's history.

Just beyond the city, climate and soil have stunted and twisted lodgepole pines into a natural bonsai garden at Oliver Lake Provincial Park. Another interesting phenomenon is Butze Rapids, a series of reversing rapids between Wainwright and Morse basins that rival the reversing falls at Saint John, New Brunswick. A dramatic view of the rapids occurs during a falling tide and can be seen from a viewing point on Hwy. 16, which offers scenic driving east to Terrace *(see place listing p. 137).*

Just off Hwy. 16 on Wantage Road, a gondola lift takes visitors to Mount Hays Recreation Area in July and August. Sweeping views of the surrounding region unfold and on a clear day extend as far as Alaska and the Queen Charlotte Islands.

Guided tours are offered during the summer by Farwest Bus Lines Ltd., 225 Second Ave. W. Trans-Provincial Airlines and Northcoast Air Services offer flight tours of the region. For information about harbor tours and charters contact Prince Rupert Charter Operators, 100 First Ave. W., Prince Rupert, BC, Canada V8J 3S1; phone (250) 624-3207. Guided walking tours are available mid-May to mid-September from the visitor information center.

Prince Rupert Visitor Information Centre: 100 First Ave. W., P.O. Box 69, Prince Rupert, BC, Canada V8J 3S1; phone (250) 624-3207 or (800) 667-1994.

DID YOU KNOW

British Columbia is truly immense—seven times the size of the state of New York.

Self-guiding tours: A walking tour that includes sunken gardens, the harbor, sections of the downtown area and various attractions is detailed on maps and brochures available from the visitor bureau at the Museum of Northern British Columbia *(see attraction listing).*

MUSEUM OF NORTHERN BRITISH COLUMBIA, 100 First Ave. W. and McBride St., contains objects from the Northwest Coast First Nations culture. Reconstructed models, maps, graphic displays and an ethnological collection explain pioneer history and the lifestyles of the coastal First Nations groups from prehistoric times through their contacts with Europeans. Changing exhibits are displayed in the art gallery.

Also of interest are an early Skeena River cannery boat, an early 20th-century steamroller and a modern First Nations carving shed with local artists on site. Visitor information is available. Mon.-Sat. 9-8, Sun. 9-5, May 25-Sept. 3; Mon.-Sat. 9-5, Sept. 4-Apr. 30; daily 9-5, rest of year. Closed Jan. 1, Nov. 11 and Dec. 25-26. Admission $5; students with ID $2; ages 6-11, $1. MC, VI. Phone (250) 624-3207.

QUADRA ISLAND—
see Gulf Islands p. 116.

QUALICUM BEACH (F-10)
pop. 6,700, elev. 9 m/30′

A popular resort and arts community, Qualicum Beach is known for its white sand beaches. Nearby Little Qualicum Falls, Englishman River Falls and Horne Lake Provincial Park also present abundant recreational opportunities *(see Recreation Chart).* Salmon and trout are raised at fish hatcheries on the Big and Little Qualicum rivers.

Qualicum Beach Visitor Information Centre: 2711 W. Island Hwy., Qualicum Beach, BC, Canada V9K 2C4; phone (250) 752-9532.

BIG QUALICUM RIVER HATCHERY is 12 km (7 mi.) n. on Hwy. 19, then 1 blk. w. to 215 Fisheries Rd. Millions of chum, coho and chinook salmon are hatched here each year as part of the country's efforts to restore its salmon population. Steelhead and cutthroat trout also are raised. Visitors can see holding ponds, rearing channels and incubation units. Allow 30 minutes minimum. Daily dawn-dusk. Free. Phone (250) 757-8412.

GOOD EARTH FARM is 5 km (3 mi.) n. on Hwy. 19A, w. on Texada Rd. to Ganske Rd., then 2 blks. s. This garden includes seasonal floral displays, lily ponds and a permanent bonsai collection. A pottery workshop and showroom features handmade stoneware, porcelain and raku, a Japanese style of pottery. Allow 30 minutes minimum. Mon.-Sat. 9-6, Sun. 10-5. Free. Phone (250) 752-9332.

QUEEN CHARLOTTE ISLANDS (E-1)

The Queen Charlotte Islands were occupied by Haida Indians when Spanish sea captain Juan Pérez sighted the archipelago in 1774. A seafaring and artistic people, the Haida traded sea otter pelts with European traders during the early 1800s. By the late 19th century, however, the Haida had to vacate many of their ancestral villages to escape a devastating smallpox epidemic.

Only a fraction of their original number still inhabit the island—at Haida, near Masset, and Skidegate, near Queen Charlotte City. Continuing their cultural traditions, they carve elaborate works of art from argillite, a black slatelike stone found only in mountain deposits off the coast.

A group of about 150 islands forming an elongated triangle, the Queen Charlotte Islands stretch 250 kilometres (157 mi.) from north to south, 90 kilometres (56 mi.) off the coast of British Columbia. Characterized by fog and low clouds, these islands also are known as the Misty Islands. The towns are small and decidedly rural; the entire population of the Queen Charlotte Islands is about 5,000.

The largest of the islands is Graham. In the north on its broad and flat eastern side are most of the archipelago's communities—Masset, Old Masset, Port Clements, Skidegate, Tlell and Queen Charlotte City—which are linked by a paved road. An airport is at Masset as well as at Sandspit, on the northeastern tip of Moresby Island.

A temperate marine climate supports dense coniferous forests, which, as the basis of the islands' economy, have been logged extensively. The fish and shellfish in the coastal waters supply the islands' important commercial fishing industry.

Visitors are attracted by the pristine wilderness, the hunting and fishing prospects, kayaking and hiking opportunities, and the handicrafts and art of the Haida. Wildlife is abundant; tiny Sitka deer and bald eagles frequent the shores, and seals, porpoises and whales often appear in the inlets. Bird watching is a popular activity.

Points of interest include Naikoon Provincial Park (see Recreation Chart) on Graham Island, the remote Haida village sites, the Delkatla Wildlife Sanctuary in Masset, the Queen Charlotte Islands Museum in Skidegate and the various carving sheds in Skidegate and Old Massett.

Permission to visit Haida unoccupied village sites must be obtained from Band Council offices, (250) 559-4496 in Skidegate or (250) 626-3337 in Old Massett.

The Queen Charlotte Islands can be reached by air from Prince Rupert and Vancouver and by ferry from Prince Rupert. Kayak rentals, fishing charters and various guided boat and land tours are available.

Queen Charlotte Visitor Information Centre: 3220 Wharf St., P.O. Box 819, Queen Charlotte, BC, Canada V0T 1S0; phone (250) 559-8316.

QUESNEL (F-4)
pop. 8,500, elev. 545 m/1,788′

Discovery of gold in the surrounding area in the 1860s contributed to Quesnel's growth. The city is the center of a popular hunting and fishing region at the junction of the Fraser and Quesnel rivers. Lumber, pulp and plywood manufacturing, tourism, cattle ranching and mining are the city's primary sources of income.

East of the city on Hwy. 26 is a historic remnant of the gold rush days, Barkerville Historic Town (see place listing p. 106), a restored boomtown of that era. Just beyond Barkerville is Bowron Lake Provincial Park (see Recreation Chart and the AAA/CAA Western Canada and Alaska CampBook), which has a 116-kilometre (72-mi.) canoe circuit of interconnecting lakes. Alpine skiing is available nearby.

Quesnel Visitor Information Centre: 703 Carson Ave., Quesnel, BC, Canada V2J 2B6; phone (250) 992-8716 or (800) 992-4922 in British Columbia.

COTTONWOOD HOUSE, 28 km (17 mi.) e. on Hwy. 26, with its hewn log walks and dovetail corners, was built 1864-65 as a roadhouse to accommodate travelers using the Cariboo Wagon Road en route to the gold fields. A reconstructed farm includes a double barn, stable, guesthouse and other old buildings and farm equipment.

Costumed interpreters conduct tours and give farming demonstrations. Stagecoach rides, gold panning and picnic facilities are offered. Food is available. Daily 8-5, May-Sept. Admission $2; over 54 and ages 5-17, $1; family rate $4. Stagecoach rides $4; over 54 and ages 5-17, $3; family pass including admission and stagecoach rides, $13. Gold panning $4, over 54 and ages 5-17, $3.50; family pass including admission, stagecoach rides and gold panning, $26. MC, VI. Phone (800) 992-4922.

QUESNEL & DISTRICT MUSEUM AND ARCHIVES, .75 km (.5 mi.) s. on Hwy. 97 at 705 Carson Ave., marks the area's history from the days of Alexander Mackenzie's explorations and the 1862 gold rush. The museum also contains exhibits about pioneer life, a hands-on area for children and an archives.

Allow 1 hour minimum. Daily 8-6, Victoria Day weekend-Labour Day; Tues.-Sat. 8:30-4:30, rest of year. Admission $2, under 13 free. Phone (250) 992-9580.

RADIUM HOT SPRINGS (B-11)
pop. 500, elev. 805 m/2,641′

Renowned for its mineral hot springs (see Kootenay National Park p. 123 and Recreation

Chart), Radium Hot Springs also is a popular departure point for scenic and white-water river excursions. More than 10 golf courses are in the vicinity

RECREATIONAL ACTIVITIES
Skiing

- **Panorama Mountain Village** is 12 km (7.5 mi.) w. on Hwy. 95. Write Panorama, BC, Canada V0A 1T0. Other activities are offered. Daily 9-4, Dec.-Apr. Phone (800) 3663-2929.

White-water Rafting

- **Kootenay River Runners** is at 4987 Hwy. 93. Write P.O. Box 81, Edgewater, BC, Canada V0A 1E0. Daily at 9, early June to mid-Sept.; afternoon trips also are available. Phone (250) 347-9210 or (800) 599-4399.

REVELSTOKE (B-10)
pop. 8,000, elev. 440 m/1,433′

Revelstoke is at the western end of Rogers Pass, the section of the Trans-Canada Highway that traverses Glacier National Park *(see place listing p. 114)*. Rogers Pass is one of the world's most scenic mountain roads. Downhill skiing is available nearby.

Revelstoke Chamber of Commerce: 204 Campbell Ave., P.O. Box 490, Revelstoke, BC, Canada V0E 2S0; phone (250) 837-5345 or (800) 487-1493.

CANYON HOT SPRINGS, 35.5 km (22 mi.) e., offers a dip in a pool of 40 C (104 F) mineral waters or a swim in a pool that is 30 C (86 F). Camping is permitted. Food is available. Daily 9 a.m.-10 p.m., July-Aug.; 9-9, May-June and in Sept. Day passes $7.50; over 59, $6; family pass $20. Single swim $5; over 59, $4.50; ages 5-14, $4; family rate $15. Phone (250) 837-2420. *See Recreation Chart.*

ENCHANTED FOREST, 32 km (20 mi.) w. on Hwy. 1, has 300 handmade figurines that include castles, dragons and dungeons in a natural forest setting with giant cedars, a stump house and a fish pond. Swamp boat rides and boardwalks also are offered. Daily 8 a.m.-30 minutes before dusk, May 15-Sept. 15. Admission $5; ages 3-15, $3.50. MC, VI. Phone (250) 837-9477.

★ **REVELSTOKE DAM VISITOR CENTRE,** off Hwy. 23 following signs, contains lighted displays, topographic maps and audiovisual programs about the dam's design, construction and function. A large window overlooks the plant's generating units; an elevator provides access to an outdoor observation point at the top of the dam. Allow 1 hour minimum. Daily 8-8, mid-June to mid-Sept.; 9-5, early May to mid-June and mid-Sept. to mid-Oct. Free. Phone (250) 837-6515.

[SAVE] **REVELSTOKE RAILWAY MUSEUM,** 719 Track St. W. off Victoria Rd., traces the building of the Canadian Pacific Railway with artifacts, photographs and original equipment. One of the railway company's largest steam locomotives is displayed beside a restored 1929 solarium car inside the museum, while the yard features such rolling stock as a caboose, a snow plow and a flange car. A diesel cabin simulator allows visitors to experience the feeling of driving a train.

Allow 30 minutes minimum. Daily 9-8, July-Aug.; daily 9-5, Apr.-June and Sept.-Nov.; Mon.-Fri. 1-5, rest of year. Admission $5; over 60, $3; ages 7-16, $2; family rate $10. MC, VI. Phone (250) 837-6060 or (877) 837-6060.

THREE VALLEY GAP GHOST TOWN is 19 km (12 mi.) w. on Hwy. 1, near the site of the original lumber and mining town of Three Valley. The more than 25 relocated historic buildings include a church, a hotel, a general store, two schoolhouses and an 1862 roadhouse and saloon. A fully furnished private railway coach and an antique car museum also are on the grounds. Live performances of a musical stage show take place nightly May through September.

Guided tours daily 8-5, May-Sept. Admission $6.50; over 65 and ages 12-17, $5; ages 3-11, $3; family rate $19. Show tickets $12; over 65 and ages 12-17, $10; ages 4-11, $6. AE, MC, VI. Phone (250) 837-2109 or (888) 667-2109.

RECREATIONAL ACTIVITIES
Bicycling

- **Summit Cycle Tours,** n. of Hwy. 1 on Victoria Rd., P.O. Box 2647, Revelstoke, BC, Canada V0E 2S0. Daily 8:30-8:30, mid-June to mid-Sept. Phone (250) 837-3734.

RICHMOND—*see Vancouver p. 159.*

ROSSLAND (D-10)
pop. 3,600, elev. 1,039 m/3,408′

The 1890 gold rush on Red Mountain spurred the growth of Rossland from a prospectors' camp to a bustling town with 42 saloons, 17 law firms, four breweries and two distilleries. The area's vast mineral wealth, which supported a booming mining industry for 40 years, produced more than 6 million tons of ore valued at about $125 million.

Camping and picnicking are offered at King George VI Provincial Park, 9.6 kilometres (6 mi.) south near the U.S. border *(see the AAA/CAA Western Canada and Alaska CampBook);* fishing, swimming and canoeing are available at Nancy Greene Park, 26 kilometres (16 mi.) northwest at hwys. 3 and 3B *(see Recreation Chart and the AAA/CAA Western Canada and Alaska CampBook).*

Rossland Chamber of Commerce: 2185 Columbia Ave., P.O. Box 1385, Rossland, BC, Canada V0G 1Y0; phone (250) 362-5666.

ROSSLAND HISTORICAL MUSEUM AND LE ROI MINE, at jct. hwys. 3B and 22, offers 45-minute tours into a section of a hard-rock mine tunnel. The museum has mining artifacts and rock and mineral samples. There also are outdoor exhibits. Gold panning is offered. Allow 2 hours minimum. Daily 9-5, mid-May to mid-Sept. Last mine tour departs 90 minutes before closing. Museum $4; over 59 and students with ID $3; ages 6-13, $1.50. Mine tours (museum included) $8; over 59 and students with ID $5; ages 6-13, $3; family rate $25. MC, VI. Phone (250) 362-7722.

RECREATIONAL ACTIVITIES

Skiing

- **Red Mountain Ski Area,** 3 km (1.5 mi.) n. on Hwy. 3B, P.O. Box 670, Rossland, BC, Canada V0G 1Y0. Mon.-Fri. 9-3, Sat.-Sun. 8:30-3, early Dec.-early Apr. Phone (250) 362-7384 or (800) 663-0105 in British Columbia.

SAANICHTON—*see Victoria p. 173.*

SALT SPRING ISLAND—
see Gulf Islands p. 116.

SATURNA ISLAND—
see Gulf Islands p. 117.

SICAMOUS (B-9)
pop. 2,800, elev. 352 m/1,155′

Flanked by Mara and Shuswap lakes, Sicamous has abundant recreational opportunities, including swimming, fishing, boating and other water sports. Full- and half-day cruises on Shuswap Lake *(see Recreation Chart)* and 2- and 3-hour evening excursions on Mara Lake depart from the public wharf at the foot of Finlayson Street. Houseboats, which can be rented, are a popular way of touring the arms of Shuswap Lake.

At nearby Adams River almost 10 million scarlet sockeye salmon bury their eggs each October; it is one of the largest spawning grounds in the country. Several spawning grounds can be seen at Roderick Haig-Brown Provincial Park *(see Recreation Chart).*

Sicamous & District Chamber of Commerce: 110 Finlayson Rd., P.O. Box 346, Sicamous, BC, Canada V0E 2V0; phone (250) 836-3313.

SIDNEY—*see Victoria p. 173.*

SMITHERS (D-2)
pop. 5,600, elev. 520 m/1,706′

Smithers, at the base of 2,621-metre (8,599-ft.) Hudson Bay Mountain, is a year-round skiing center. Its location also makes it convenient for fossil hunting, fishing, mountain climbing and trail riding.

Smithers & District Chamber of Commerce: 1411 Court St., P.O. Box 2379, Smithers, BC, Canada V0J 2N0; phone (250) 847-5072 or (800) 542-6673.

ADAMS IGLOO, 10 km (6 mi.) w. on Hwy. 16, has mounted animals and birds native to British Columbia displayed inside an igloo. Allow 30 minutes minimum. Daily 9-9, Apr. 1.-Nov. 1. Admission $4; over 55 and ages 13-19, $3; ages 5-12, $2. MC, VI. Phone (250) 847-3188.

SOOKE—*see Victoria p. 174.*

SPARWOOD (C-12)
pop. 4,000, elev. 1,143 m/3,750′

Once known as a mining town, Sparwood offers guided tours of the Elkview Coal Mine during summer. Popular area recreational activities include fly fishing, whitewater rafting, hiking and mountain biking.

Sparwood Chamber of Commerce: Hwy. 3 and Aspen Dr., Sparwood, BC, Canada V0B 2G0; phone (250) 425-2423.

SQUAMISH (G-11)
pop. 14,000, elev. 5 m/16′

Overshadowed by Stawamus Chief Mountain and other snowcapped peaks, Squamish was named for the Indian word meaning "mother of the wind." It is a popular stopover for tourists and recreation seekers. Rock climbing and windsurfing are popular activities.

Picnic facilities are available 3 kilometres (1.9 mi.) south at Shannon Falls, and camping facilities are available at Alice Lake Park *(see Recreation Chart and the AAA/CAA Western Canada and Alaska CampBook)* 13 kilometres (8 mi.) to the north.

Squamish & Howe Sound Chamber of Commerce: 37950 Cleveland Ave., P.O. Box 1009, Squamish, BC, Canada V0N 3G0; phone (604) 892-9244.

GARIBALDI PROVINCIAL PARK is accessible by trail from Hwy. 99 or the British Columbia Railway. Covering 194,650 hectares (480,980 acres), Garibaldi Provincial Park is a pristine wilderness of magnificent peaks, glaciers, meadows, lakes and streams. There are many interesting geologic features near Garibaldi Lake.

Black Tusk, Diamond Head and Cheakamus Lake have been developed for various recreational activities. Access to the Garibaldi Lake/Black Tusk Area is by a 7.25-kilometre (5-mi.) trail from the Rubble Creek parking lot off Hwy. 99, about 37 kilometres (23 mi.) north of Squamish.

The Diamond Head Area is near Squamish and the south side of Mount Garibaldi. Just north of Squamish off Hwy. 99 a gravel road leads 16 kilometres (10 mi.) to the base camp parking lot, where a trail follows Paul Ridge 11.25 kilometres (7 mi.) to the Diamond Head Area. Glacier-fed Cheakamus Lake lies at an elevation of less than 914 metres (2,999 ft.). The park is open all year and free. *See Recreation Chart.* For more information, phone (604) 898-3678.

GLACIER AIR TOURS, at Squamish Municipal Airport, offers helicopter and airplane sightseeing flights and glacier-landing flights. The latter may include dining on a glacier. Bus and train tours also are available. Daily 9-8 (departure times vary), May 15-Oct. 15; on demand, rest of year. Fares for sightseeing flights start at $79. Reservations are recommended. AE, MC, VI. Phone (604) 898-9016 or (800) 265-0088.

[SAVE] **WEST COAST RAILWAY HERITAGE PARK,** 1 km (.6 mi.) w. off Hwy. 99 Industrial Way, n. on Queensway Rd. (which becomes Government Rd.) to 39645 Government Rd., is an outdoor museum of railway equipment dating to the early 1900s. Visitors can ride a miniature train on a 7.5 gauge track around the property. Displays include steam and diesel locomotives, a sleeping car, caboose, bunk cars and a business car; the collection of more than 60 railway heritage pieces depicts a typical railway environment of the mid-20th century. A restoration exhibit demonstrates the process of restoring old railway cars. Food is available.

Allow 30 minutes minimum. Daily 10-5. Miniature train operates daily 11-4. Admission $4.50; over 59 and ages 5-16, $3.50; family rate $12. Miniature railway rides, $1. AE, MC, VI. Phone (604) 898-9336.

SUMMERLAND (C-8)
pop. 10,600, elev. 454 m/1,489′

Surrounded by lush orchards and vineyards, Summerland depends on fruit cultivation as its main industry. Overlooking Okanagan Lake *(see Recreation Chart and the AAA/CAA Western Canada and Alaska CampBook),* the first commercial orchard in the Okanagan Valley was planted in 1890.

Summerland also was the first town on the lake to employ electricity as an energy source; it was generated by a small hydroelectric plant built on the lakeshore in 1905. These and other historical landmarks are the focus of Summerland Museum on Wharton Street.

Fruit stands are the best way to sample the region's bountiful produce. The public can visit a fruit packing facility at B.C. Fruit Packers Co-op on Jubilee Road, depending on availability of fruit in season (usually June through October).

Giants Head Park on 910-metre (2,986-ft.) Giants Head Mountain offers picnic facilities and views of Summerland, the valley below, and Okanagan Lake.

Many beaches, including Sunoka, Peach Orchard *(see the AAA/CAA Western Canada and Alaska CampBook),* Powell and Rotary, line the shores of Okanagan Lake. Also of interest is the Summerland Trout Hatchery, Lakeshore Drive S., where rainbow, brook and Kokanee trout are raised.

Summerland Chamber of Commerce: 15600 Hwy. 97, P.O. Box 1075, Summerland, BC, Canada V0H 1Z0; phone (250) 494-2686.

[SAVE] **KETTLE VALLEY STEAM RAILWAY**, 5 km (3 mi.) w. on Prairie Valley Rd., then s. on Bathville Rd. following signs, offers 1-hour, 30-minute narrated tours of the Okanagan Valley. The train departs from Prairie Valley Station Thurs.-Mon. at 10:30 and 1:30, mid-May to mid-Oct. Fare $9.75; senior citizens and ages 13-18, $8.75; ages 4-12, $6.50; family rate $35. MC, VI. Phone (250) 494-8422.

SUMMERLAND ORNAMENTAL GARDENS, s. on Hwy. 97 to 4200 Hwy. 97, comprises 300 hectares (741 acres) and includes xeriscape gardens, which contain plants that don't require a lot of water. Picnic facilities are available. Allow 1 hour minimum. Mon.-Fri. 8-8, Sat.-Sun. and holidays 9-8, Apr.-Oct.; daily 9-5, rest of year. Donations. Phone (250) 494-7711 or 494-6385.

SUMMERLAND SWEETS, 6206 Canyon View Dr., offers tours of its factory, where fruit syrups, jams and candy are made from fresh and frozen fruits. Allow 30 minutes minimum. Tours are given Mon.-Fri. 10-4, June-Sept., 9-5, Jan.-Apr. Free. Phone (250) 494-0377 or (800) 577-1277.

WINERIES

- **Scherzinger Vineyards Winery**, 7311 Fiske St. Daily 10-6, Apr.-Oct. Phone (250) 494-8815.

- **Sumac Ridge Estate Winery**, 1 km (.6 mi.) n. on Hwy. 97 following signs. Tours are given daily on the hour 10-4, May 1-Thanksgiving. Phone (250) 494-0451.

SURREY—see Vancouver p. 159.

TELEGRAPH COVE (G-3)
pop. 1,600

The bay community served as the northern terminus of the telegraph line along the coast of Vancouver Island and later became a logging and salmon fishing area. Whale watching, fishing and camping are popular during the summer.

STUBBS ISLAND WHALE WATCHING, 24 Boardwalk St., offers excursions on the Johnstone Strait. Vessels are equipped with underwater microphones for listening to whale vocalizations. Warm clothing is recommended. Allow 4 hours minimum. Daily departures June 1 to mid-Oct. Hours vary; phone ahead. Fare $65; over 64 and under 13, $58.50. Reservations are required. Parking $5. MC, VI. Phone (250) 928-3185 or (800) 665-3066.

TERRACE (D-2)
pop. 12,800, elev. 215 m/705'

On the banks of the Skeena River, Terrace is a major producer of forest products. The area provides excellent recreational opportunities ranging from hiking on a variety of trails to fishing in nearby rivers and creeks. Among the region's wildlife is a rare species of black bear, the white Kermodei. Native to the area, it is the city's symbol.

Among the most popular recreation areas are Lakelse Lake (see Recreation Chart and the AAA/CAA Western Canada and Alaska CampBook); Lakelse River, a tributary of the Skeena River that harbors record-size salmon; and Williams Creek, which teems with spawning sockeye each August.

Several places of natural interest are near. At the eastern entrance to the city is Ferry Island, a park with hiking trails, swimming and camping (see Recreation Chart). About 20 kilometres (12 mi.) south of Terrace is Mount Layton Hot Springs Resort, which has waterslides and a pool filled with natural hot spring mineral water. Hwy. 16 offers a scenic drive west along the Skeena River to Prince Rupert.

Travel InfoCentre: 4511 Keith Ave., Terrace, BC, Canada V8G 1K1; phone (250) 635-2063.

HERITAGE PARK MUSEUM, Kalum St. at Kerby Rd., contains original log buildings depicting the history of pioneers in the region, including a number of cabins, a hotel, a barn and a dance hall. The structures contain items relevant to the original use of each building. Guided tours are available. Allow 1 hour minimum. Park open Tues.-Sat. 10-6, Apr. 1-Labour Day. Tours are given 10:30-4:30. Admission $3, over 65 and students with ID $2, family rate $7. Phone (250) 635-4546.

NISGA'A MEMORIAL LAVA BED PROVINCIAL PARK is 4 km (2.5 mi.) w. on Hwy. 16, then 80 km (50 mi.) n. on Kalum Lake Dr. Kalum Lake Drive is paved for the first 51 kilometres (32 mi.) and then joins Nass Road, a gravel route. On each of these roads logging trucks have the right-of-way and drivers must pull over to let them pass.

The many miles of lava beds resulted from a volcanic eruption approximately 250 years ago that destroyed two Nisga'a tribal villages, causing 2,000 deaths. The eruption formed a valley with a floor that resembles the moon's surface. Interpretive trails provide easy access through the park. Camping is available. The New Aiyansh Indian Village, 16 kilometres (10 mi.) north of Lava Lake outside the park, features totem poles and a tribal council hall. Daily 9-6, June 1-Oct. 30. Free. Phone (250) 638-9589.

TOFINO (H-3) pop. 1,200

A fishing and resort village with sandy beaches, Tofino is on the western side of Vancouver Island at the end of Hwy. 4. The area was the site of Fort Defiance, where Boston fur trader Robert Gray and his men spent the winter of 1791. The fort was stripped and abandoned the next spring, and all that remains are scattered bricks and ruins.

Near Clayoquot Sound and the northern end of Pacific Rim National Park, the town's shoreline and waters are popular with scuba divers and beachcombers. In the spring whales often can be seen migrating along the coast. The Whale Centre at 411 Campbell St. exhibits scientific and artistic displays, photographs and artifacts depicting past and present whale encounters.

Several companies, including Adventures Pacific, (250) 725-2811; Jamie's Whaling Station, (250) 725-3919; [SAVE] Remote Passages, (250) 725-3330, and Sea Trek Tours and Expeditions, (250) 725-4412, offer whale-watching excursions on Clayoquot Sound. Tours lasting up to 2.5 hours may afford sightings of sea lions, porpoises and eagles. Combination whale-watching and hot springs cruises that last approximately 6.5 hours also are available.

Tofino-Long Beach Chamber of Commerce: 380 Campbell St., P.O. Box 249, Tofino, BC, Canada V0R 2Z0; phone (250) 725-3414.

TRAIL (D-10)
pop. 7,700, elev. 430 m/1,410′

At City Hall a sculptured screen titled "City of Lead and Zinc" illustrates Trail's mineral and industrial strength, steadily developed since the discovery of gold and copper in the area about 1890. Hydroelectric dams along the Kootenay River power extensive mining and smelting operations, dominated by Cominco Ltd.

The Seven-Mile Dam Project on Pend O'Reille River has a visitor center and viewpoint that can be reached by the project access road, 22 kilometres (14 mi.) southeast off Hwy. 22A. Free guided walking tours are offered in summer. Visitors should note that the tour includes a considerable amount of walking and stairs; low-heeled shoes are advised. Children under 12 must be accompanied by an adult. Phone (250) 367-7521 for more information.

Trail Chamber of Commerce: 1199 Bay Ave., Trail, BC, Canada V1R 4A4; phone (250) 368-3144.

Self-guiding tours: Brochures for walking tours are available at the chamber of commerce.

COMINCO LTD., 1 km (.6 mi.) n. on Hwy. 22, is one of the largest lead-zinc smelters in the world. Guided tours of its metallurgical operations begin at the Interpretive Centre downtown on Bay Avenue. Long pants and closed shoes are required. Cameras and video equipment are prohibited. Allow 2 hours minimum. Center daily 9-5, July-Aug.; Mon.-Fri. 9-5, rest of year. Tours Mon.-Fri. at 10, June-Aug.; by appointment rest of year. Closed holidays. Free. Under 12 are not permitted on tours. Phone (250) 368-3144.

UCLUELET (I-3) pop. 1,700

On Barkley Sound, Ucluelet was named for an Indian word meaning "safe harbor." Charter boats for salmon fishing, whale watching, skin diving and nature excursions are available; phone (250) 726-7289. The MV *Lady Rose* makes round trips between Port Alberni *(see place listing p. 129)* and Ucluelet June through September. He Tim Kis Park allows visitors to experience a Canadian rain forest and follow a boardwalk trail that leads to the ocean.

Ucluelet Chamber of Commerce: P.O. Box 428, Ucluelet, BC, Canada V0R 3A0; phone (250) 726-4641.

VALEMOUNT (F-6)
pop. 1,300, elev. 792 m/2,600′

Valemount, the valley in the mountains, offers many activities for outdoor enthusiasts. The village, where the Rocky, Cariboo and Monashee mountain ranges meet, is popular for both summer and winter pursuits, including hiking, rafting, skiing and snowmobiling. The area is rich with birds and other wildlife. Off Hwy. 16 is Mount Terry Fox Provincial Park. A viewing area affords vistas of the peak named for the late athlete.

Village of Valemount Visitor Information Centre: 98 Gorse St., P.O. Box 168, Valemount, BC, Canada V0E 2Z0; phone (250) 566-4846.

GEORGE HICKS REGIONAL PARK, off Hwy. 5, offers a bird's-eye view of Chinook salmon as they near the end of a 1,280-kilometre (768-mi.) upstream trip from Aug. 15-Sept. 15. Daily 24 hours. Free. Phone (250) 566-4846.

MOUNT ROBSON PROVINCIAL PARK, on Hwy. 16, has as its major feature Mount Robson, at 3,954 metres (12,972 ft.) the highest peak in the Canadian Rockies. Other park highlights include glacier-fed lakes, valleys, canyons, waterfalls, rivers and streams. Scenic views abound on the many walking and hiking trails. A visitor center is at the Mount Robson viewpoint. Park open daily 24 hours. Visitor center open May-Sept. Free. Phone (250) 566-4325. *See Recreation Chart and the AAA/CAA Western Canada and Alaska CampBook.*

R.W. STARRATT WILDLIFE SANCTUARY, 1 (.6 mi.) s. on Hwy. 5, is home to a variety of waterfowls, songbirds and other animals. Informational signs line a trail to two viewing platforms. Allow 30 minutes minimum. Daily 24 hours. Free. Phone (250) 566-4846.

RECREATIONAL ACTIVITIES
Summer Activities
- **Mount Robson Adventure Holidays Ltd.,** 30 km (18 mi.) n.e. on Hwy. 16 at Mount Robson Viewpoint, P.O. Box 687, Valemount, BC, Canada V0E 2Z0. Trips daily June 1-Sept. 26. Phone (250) 566-4386 or (800) 882-9921.

Winter Activities
- **Robson Helimagic,** 5 km (3 mi.) n. on Hwy. 16, P.O. Box 18, Valemount, BC, Canada V0E 2Z0. Daily 8-dusk. Phone (250) 566-4700.

Vancouver

A great port, cultural center and tourist area, Vancouver is the crown jewel of western Canada. The city is dotted lavishly with greenery, posed against the rugged peaks of the perpetually blue Coast Range and ringed with sparkling Pacific waters. Although many think Vancouver occupies Vancouver Island, the city is on the mainland; Vancouver Island lies across the Strait of Georgia and on the island is the provincial capital of Victoria.

The first recorded exploration of the Strait of Georgia and English Bay was made by Don José Narváez in 1791. The second was by Capt. George Vancouver, who sailed into Burrard Inlet in 1792 while searching for the legendary Northwest Passage. At the time of his arrival, the area was a seasonal home for First Nations peoples. Fur traders followed Vancouver; in 1858 came the prospectors in the wake of a gold strike.

A wild community sprang up on the peninsula between the Fraser River and Burrard Inlet. Later that year Royal Engineers sent to keep law and order named the settlement Queensborough. Queensborough became New Westminster, now part of the Vancouver metropolitan area.

Settlers gradually drifted in to populate other parts of the peninsula, and in April 1886, Vancouver, with a population of 2,000, formally became a city. Two months later a fire destroyed the community and caused an estimated $1.3 million in damage. Undaunted by the disaster, residents began rebuilding, and by the year's end the reconstructed community housed approximately 2,500 people.

Two milestones marked Vancouver's rapid progress. On May 23, 1887, the first passenger train to cross the vast Canadian expanses from the East chugged into the city and belched soot and cinders onto an exuberant crowd. In 1891 the great white ships of the Canadian Pacific fleet sailed into Burrard Inlet to inaugurate transpacific shipping and to mark Vancouver as a major world port. The population mushroomed to 100,000 by 1900.

Vancouver has expanded to cover most of the peninsula between Fraser River and Burrard Inlet. Bordered by the Coastal Mountain Range, the downtown area occupies a tiny peninsula jutting into the inlet, with the magnificent harbor to the east and beautiful English Bay to the west. Broad beaches along English Bay enable office workers to join the bathers during lunch hours.

Behind the beaches rise pastel apartment buildings and fine old houses, some with a Tudor influence. Within walking distance is the busy waterfront, where ships of many nations discharge passengers, unload

cargo or fill up for the return voyage. Vancouver also is the main terminal for cruise ships traveling to Alaska. Towering bridges link the downtown area with the city and suburbs.

Atop suburban Burnaby Mountain is Simon Fraser University, British Columbia's instant university. Constructed in only 18 months, it is a bold concept of integrated design, with buildings executed in natural materials for a classic effect. One of the most beautifully located universities in North America is the University of British Columbia; from a forested campus its Gothic buildings overlook the Strait of Georgia while the North Shore Mountains form a distant backdrop.

Vancouver's character is West Coast with a liberal Oriental essence. The city's Chinatown is second only to San Francisco's in size in North America. Visitors to Vancouver can watch an engaging cricket match, celebrate Chinese New Year or enjoy a colorful Japanese summer festival—all without leaving town.

Vancouver is a big city—the financial, industrial, shipping and cultural center of Canada's west coast. Rapid growth has been tempered by the gentler influences of the arts and sciences. The city has much that is reminiscent of other parts of Canada and much of Europe as well as the Orient and the United States. The resulting blend is happy, carefree and relaxed.

Approaches
By Car

Hwy. 1 and hwys. 1A and 7 are the major east-west routes to Vancouver. To reach downtown on the Trans-Canada Highway, use the First Avenue exit or continue to Hastings Street.

Hwy. 99, Vancouver's southern entrance, becomes the major downtown artery, Granville Street. Before becoming a city street, Hwy. 99 begins its journey as I-5 at the Mexican border and crosses through California and the Pacific Northwest.

Aqua Bus Ltd., (604) 689-5858, provides ferry service between Granville Island, Hornby Street, Yaletown, Stamps Landing and Science World daily 7 a.m.-10:30 p.m. Times vary according to destination. Fare ranges $1.75-$4. The Aqua Bus from Granville Island to Hornby Street is equipped to carry bicycles for an extra 50c.

Getting Around
Street System

All streets and avenues in Vancouver are named; many are one-way. Outside the business section, east-west avenues are numbered beginning with First Avenue, and north-south streets are named. Addresses begin at Ontario-Carrall streets for all east-west numbering and at Powell-Dundas streets for all north-south numbering.

(continued on p. 146)

The Informed Traveler

City Population: 514,000

Elevation: 3 m/10 ft.

Sales Tax: British Columbia's provincial sales tax is 7 percent. A Room Tax of 10 percent on lodgings also is levied in the Vancouver area.

WHOM TO CALL

Emergency: 911

Police (nonemergency): (604) 665-3535

Time and Temperature: (604) 664-9010

Hospitals: St. Paul's Hospital, (604) 682-2344; St. Vincent's Hospital-Heather Site, (604) 876-7171; Vancouver Hospital and Health Sciences Centre, (604) 875-4111; Vancouver Hospital and Health Sciences Centre-UBC, (604) 822-7121.

WHERE TO LOOK

Newspapers

The two major daily newspapers, both published in the morning, are the *Province* and the *Vancouver Sun*.

Radio and TV

Vancouver radio station CBU-AM (93.1) and CBU-FM (107.1) have news and weather reports and are programmed by the Canadian Broadcasting Corp.

The major TV networks are BCTV, CBC, Global and UTV; channels vary by district. For a complete list of radio and television programs, consult the daily newspapers.

Visitor Information

Maps, lodging reservations and literature about attractions as well as tickets for tours are available at Vancouver Travel InfoCentre, 200 Burrard St., Plaza Level, Vancouver, BC, Canada V6C 3L6; phone (604) 683-2000. It is open daily 8-6, Victoria Day weekend-Labour Day; Mon.-Fri. 8:30-5, Sat. 9-5, rest of year.

TRANSPORTATION

Air Travel

Vancouver International Airport is reached via Hwy. 99, then Sea Island Way, which leads into Grant McConachie Way. Vancouver Airporter buses run every 15 minutes 6 a.m.-midnight. One-way bus service departs most major downtown hotels every 30 minutes; fare $10, round trip $17; phone (604) 946-8866 or (800) 668-3141. Taxis average $22 one-way.

Rental Cars

Hertz, at 1128 Seymour St., offers discounts to AAA and CAA members; phone (604) 688-2411, (800) 263-0600 in Canada, or (800) 654-3001 out of Canada. Additional agencies are listed in the telephone directory.

Rail Service

The Via Rail passenger train terminal is at 1150 Station St.; phone (800) 561-8630 or (800) 835-3037. The BC Rail passenger train station is at 1131 W. First Ave. in North Vancouver; phone (604) 631-3500 or 984-5246.

Buses

The bus terminal is at 1150 Station St.; phone (604) 482-8747.

Taxis

Fares start at $2.10, plus $1.21 per kilometre (.6 mi.). Companies include Black Top, (604) 731-1111; MacLure's, (604) 731-9211; and Yellow Cab, (604) 681-1111 or 876-5555.

Public Transport

The BC Transit offers bus service as well as SeaBus and SkyTrain service. *See Public Transportation for details.*

Boats

BC Ferries *(see color ad p. 152)* links Vancouver Island with the rest of the province. Nanaimo and Sunshine Coast ferries leave from Horseshoe Bay, 21 kilometres (13 mi.) west of the city in West Vancouver. From Tsawwassen south of Vancouver automobile/passenger ferries make frequent trips to the Southern Gulf Islands, Nanaimo and Swartz Bay, north of Victoria; Vancouver-Victoria bus service is available on most sailings.

For schedules phone the British Columbia Automobile Association, (604) 268-5555, British Columbia Ferries Information Centre, (888) 273-3779, or Tourism Vancouver, (604) 683-2000.

Destination Vancouver

*T*he nuances of cosmopolitan Vancouver's multiple cultures are revealed through the arts, in neighborhood preservation and by observing the lifestyle enjoyed by residents.

*Y*ou'll find ambience in green spaces and historic places; at galleries and gardens; and on beaches, bays and gap-spanning bridges.

Stanley Park.
With more than 400 hectares of lawn, forest and waterfront, Vancouver's versatile urban park can be a place for sweet serenity or sheer serendipity. (See listing page 148)

Vancouver Art Gallery.
Built in 1907, Vancouver's former courthouse now houses works by renowned artists, including Canada's Emily Carr.
(See listing page 149)

See Vicinity map page 144

Queen Elizabeth Park, Vancouver.
From one of the city's highest points, let your eyes wander over a collection of flowers, plants and trees to the magnificent views on the horizon. (See listing page 148)

West Vancouver

North Vancouver

Port Moody

Vancouver

Burnaby

Coquitlam

New Westminster

Port Coquitlam

Richmond

Delta

Surrey

Maple Ridge

Mission

Chilliwack

Langley

Aldergrove

UNITED STATES

CANADA

BRITISH COLUMBIA

WASHINGTON

*P*laces included in this AAA Destination City:

Vancouver Aquarium Marine Science Centre.
Beluga and killer whales are among the permanent residents here.
(See listing page 148)

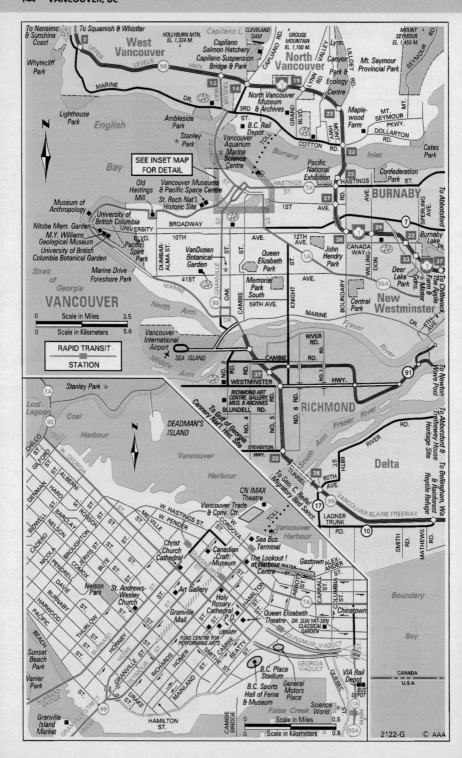

To Nanaimo & Sunshine Coast
To Squamish & Whistler
HOLLYBURN MTN. EL. 1,324 M.
Capilano L.
CLEVELAND DAM
GROUSE MOUNTAIN EL. 1,100 M.
MOUNT SEYMOUR EL. 1,450 M.

West Vancouver
UPPER LEVELS HWY.
MARINE DR.
99

Capilano Salmon Hatchery
Capilano Suspension Bridge & Park
North Vancouver
Lynn Valley
Lynn Canyon Park & Ecology Centre
Mt. Seymour Provincial Park

Whytecliff Park

13
14
TAYLOR WAY
North Vancouver Museum & Archives
3RD ST.
1
19
GRAND BLVD.
LYNN VALLEY RD.
22
MONT. HWY.
Maplewood Farm
MT. SEYMOUR PKWY.
DOLLARTON RD.

Lighthouse Park
English
Ambleside Park
Stanley Park
B.C. Rail Depot
TOLL
Vancouver Aquarium Marine Science Centre
Burrard
COT-TON RD.
23
Burrard Inlet
Cates Park

SEE INSET MAP FOR DETAIL

Museum of Anthropology
Old Hastings Mill
Vancouver Museums & Pacific Space Centre
St. Roch Nat'l. Historic Site
HASTINGS ST.
7A
Pacific National Exhibition
25
HASTINGS
Confederation Park ST.
BURNABY
SPERLING AVE.
To Abbotsford

University of British Columbia
UNIVERSITY
1ST AVE.
27

Nitobe Mem. Garden
M.Y. Williams Geological Museum
University of British Columbia Botanical Garden
BLVD.
Pacific Spirit Park
BROADWAY
10TH
AVE.
12TH AVE.
28
CANADA WAY
WILLINGDON
29
7
1
32
Burnaby Lake Pk.
33
1
37

Strait of Georgia
DUNBAR-ALMA ST.
VanDusen Botanical Garden
GRANVILLE ST.
OAK ST.
41ST
Queen Elizabeth Park
John Hendry Park
DON
Deer Lake Gdns.
Lake Park
To Chilliwack
The Apple Farm & Miner

VANCOUVER
MARINE DR.
99
Memorial Park South
59TH AVE.
KNIGHT ST.
1A
AVE.
MARINE
BOUNDARY RD.
Central Park
New Westminster
DR.
6TH AVE.

Scale in Miles 0   3.5
Scale in Kilometers 0   5.6

North Arm
Vancouver International Airport
SEA ISLAND
Middle Arm
CAMBIE RD.
RIVER RD.
NO. 7 RD.
Fraser River
91
To Newton Wave Pool

RAPID TRANSIT
STATION

Stanley Park
1A
Lost Lagoon
Coal Harbour
DEADMAN'S ISLAND
Vancouver
Harbour
NO. 3 RD.
37
WESTMINSTER HWY.
NO. 4 RD.
RICHMOND ART CENTRE, GALLERY, MUS. & ARCHIVES
BLUNDELL RD.
NO. 5 RD.
NO. 6 RD.
RICHMOND
Fraser River
RIVER RD.
To Abbotsford & Bellingham, Wa
Trethewey House Heritage Site
Rainforest Reptile Refuge

CHILCO ST.
GILFORD ST.
W. GEORGIA
ALBERNI ST.
DENMAN ST.
HARO ST.
BIDWELL ST.
NELSON ST.
ROBSON ST.
MELVILLE ST.
W. HASTINGS ST.
W. PENDER ST.
CORDOVA ST.
Cannery Nat'l. Hist. Site
STEVESTON HWY.
32
TUNNEL
To Gulf of Georgia
To Geo. C. Reifel Migratory Bird Sanct.
28
60TH AVE.
Delta
189
SMITH RD.
MATHEWS RD.

CADERO ST.
NICOLA ST.
BROUGHTON ST.
JERVIS ST.
BUTE ST.
COMOX ST.
PENDRELL ST.
DAVIE ST.
BURNABY ST.
HARWOOD ST.
PACIFIC
BEACH
Sunset Beach Park
Vanier Park
Nelson Park
St. Andrews-Wesley Church
Christ Church Cathedral
Canadian Craft Museum
CN IMAX Theatre
Vancouver Trade & Conv. Ctr.
Sea Bus Terminal
The Lookout! at Harbour Centre
WATER
Gastown
7A
ALEXANDER
CARRALL ST.
COLUMBIA ST.
Chinatown
17
99
LADNER TRUNK RD.
Vancouver Harbour
Vancouver-Blaine Freeway
10

THURLOW ST.
BURRARD STREET
HORNBY ST.
HOWE ST.
SEYMOUR ST.
GRANVILLE STREET
RICHARDS ST.
HOMER ST.
MAINLAND ST.
SMITHE ST.
CAMBIE ST.
BEATTY ST.
Art Gallery
Granville Mall
Holy Rosary Cathedral
P.O.
LIBRARY
FORD CENTRE FOR PERFORMING ARTS
Queen Elizabeth Theatre
DR. SUN YAT-SEN CLASSICAL GARDEN
DUNSMUIR VIADUCT
Boundary Bay

BURRARD BRIDGE
GRANVILLE ST. BRIDGE
DRAKE ST.
HAMILTON ST.
CAMBIE BRIDGE
B.C. Place Stadium
B.C. Sports Hall of Fame & Museum
General Motors Place
Science World
GEORGIA VIADUCT
QUEBEC ST.
MAIN ST.
VIA Rail Depot
BUS DEPOT
CANADA
U.S.A.
False Creek
99A

Granville Island Market

Scale in Miles 0   0.5
Scale in Kilometers 0   0.8

2122-G   © AAA

The downtown peninsula is connected to western Vancouver by the Burrard and Granville bridges and to North Vancouver and West Vancouver by the Lions Gate and the Iron Workers Memorial (Second Narrows) bridges.

Rush hours are 6-9:30 a.m. and 3-6:30 p.m. Right turns on red are permitted after a stop, unless otherwise posted; drivers must yield to pedestrians and vehicles in the intersection and to city buses pulling into traffic.

Parking

On-street parking, controlled by meter, is restricted on many thoroughfares during rush hours; violators' cars will be towed. Off-street parking is available in lots and garages at rates ranging from $1.25 per half-hour to $11 or more per day. Parking in a school zone between 8 and 5 on any school day is strictly prohibited unless otherwise posted.

Public Transportation

The Translink (see color ad) offers bus service to points throughout Vancouver and to all suburban areas; it also offers SeaBus and SkyTrain service as well as the West Coast Express commuter rail. Fare within the city is $1.50, students with ID $1. Exact change is required. Rush hour fares are higher.

All-day passes, available from SkyTrain ticket machines, Vancouver ticket agencies, branches of the Bank of Nova Scotia, Safeway food stores and 7-11 stores, cost $6, senior citizens $4.

SeaBus service conveys commuters between North Vancouver and the city of Vancouver, connecting with the bus system at the foot of Granville Street; phone (604) 521-0400 between 6:30 a.m.-11:30 p.m. for more information.

SkyTrain, Vancouver's rapid transit system, runs from Waterfront Station through downtown Vancouver to the suburb of New Westminster and across the Fraser River to the suburb of Surrey. Trains operate every 5 minutes 5:30 a.m.-1 a.m. A one-zone fare (within Vancouver) is $1.50, two-zone fare is $2.25 and three-zone fare is $3. Fares are subject to change. Every SkyTrain station has information panels; phone (604) 521-0400.

What To See

SAVE **THE B.C. SPORTS HALL OF FAME AND MUSEUM**, at 777 Pacific Blvd., Gate A in the B.C. Place Stadium, shows the history of sports in British Columbia. Galleries include the Hall of Champions, which has computers, photographs and videotapes; Builders Hall, which gives tribute to the referees and coaches; the Joseph H. Cohen Theatre; Discovery Gallery; Terry Fox

and Rick Hansen galleries; the Participation Gallery, which provides opportunities for running, climbing, throwing, riding and rowing; and the History galleries.

Rotating exhibits, a sports library and a stadium tour also are featured. Daily 10-5. Admission $6, senior citizens and students $4, under 5 free, family rate $15. Phone (604) 687-5520 or 687-5523.

BLOEDEL CONSERVATORY—
see Queen Elizabeth Park p. 148.

SAVE **CANADIAN CRAFT MUSEUM,** 639 Hornby St. in Cathedral Place Courtyard, exhibits and preserves crafts while demonstrating their social relevance. Allow 30 minutes minimum. Mon.-Sat. 10-5 (also Thurs. 5-9), Sun. and holidays noon-5, June-Aug.; Mon. and Wed.-Sat. 10-5 (also Thurs. 5-9), Sun. noon-5, rest of year. Closed Jan. 1 and Dec. 25-26. Admission $5, over 59 and students with ID $3, under 13 free. AE, MC, VI. Phone (604) 687-8266.

CHINATOWN—*see Shopping p. 153.*

CHRIST CHURCH CATHEDRAL, 690 Burrard St., is one of Vancouver's oldest stone churches and has English and Canadian stained-glass windows. Mon.-Fri. 10-4. Donations. Phone (604) 682-3848.

SAVE **CN IMAX THEATRE,** 201-999 Canada Pl., presents various films on a screen five stories tall. Three-dimensional movies are shown periodically. Food is available. Allow 1 hour minimum. Daily every hour 11-10, July-Aug.; noon-10, rest of year. Closed Dec. 25. Admission $8; over 64, $7; ages 3-12, $6. AE, MC, VI. Phone (604) 682-4629 or (800) 582-4629.

SAVE **DR. SUN YAT-SEN CLASSICAL CHINESE GARDEN,** 578 Carrall St. in the heart of Chinatown, is modeled after private classical gardens developed in the city of Suzhou during the 1368-1644 Ming Dynasty. Most of the garden's elements—from hand-fired roof tiles, carved woodwork and lattice windows to courtyard pebbles—are from China.

The garden has four main components: buildings, rocks, plantings and water. Its design reflects the Taoist philosophy of yin and yang, with light balanced by dark, small by large, and rugged and hard by soft and flowing. Food and garden tours are available. Allow 30 minutes minimum. Daily 9:30-7, June 15-Sept. 15; 10-6, May 1-June 14; 10-4:30, rest of year. Admission $7.50; over 64, $6.50; ages 5-17, $5; family rate $15. Admission price includes a tour and tea. Phone (604) 662-3207 or 689-7133.

HOLY ROSARY CATHEDRAL, 646 Richards St., has stained-glass windows and eight bells hung in the rare English ringing style. Bell ringing takes place Tuesday at 7:30 p.m. and Sunday at 10:30 a.m. Open Mon.-Sat. 6:15-6, Sun. 7 a.m.-9:30 p.m. Phone (604) 682-6774.

SAVE **THE LOOKOUT! AT HARBOUR CENTRE TOWER,** 555 W. Hastings St., has an observation deck offering a spectacular panoramic view of the city and outlying districts. Two glass elevators ascend the outside of the tower. A large-screen video theatre introduces visitors to Vancouver and British Columbia. The complex includes a revolving restaurant at the top of the tower and a shopping mall. Food is available.

Skylift elevator runs daily 8:30 a.m.-10:30 p.m. (also Fri.-Sat. 10:30-11:30 p.m.), Apr.-Oct.; 9-9, rest of year. Admission $8.41; over 59, $6.54; students with ID $4.67, family rate $20.56. Phone (604) 689-0421. *See color ad.*

OLD HASTINGS MILL STORE MUSEUM is at 1575 Alma Rd. in Hastings Mill Park. The mill was the first industrial facility on the south shore of what is now Vancouver. One of the few buildings to withstand the ravages of the 1886 fire, it contains relics of early Vancouver. Allow 30 minutes minimum. Tues.-Sun. 11-4, mid-June to mid-Sept.; Sat.-Sun. 1-4, rest of year. Closed holidays. Donations. Phone (604) 734-1212.

PACIFIC NATIONAL EXHIBITION occupies 69 hectares (170 acres) bounded by E. Hastings, Renfrew, Cassiar and Wall sts. It is home to Pacific Coliseum. The Pacific National Exhibition Fair is held in late August. Various trade and hobby shows, rock concerts and sporting events

are scheduled throughout the year. Fair admission $6; over 60 and ages 6-18, $4. Phone (604) 255-5161.

Playland Amusement Park, at Renfrew, E. Hastings and Cassiar sts., has rides, games, miniature golf and a large roller coaster.

Daily 11 a.m.-midnight, Aug. 22-Labour Day; daily 11-9, mid-June through Aug. 21; Sat.-Sun. and holidays 11-7, mid-Apr. to mid-June (weather permitting). Park admission $17.95, under 122 centimetres (48 in.) tall $14.95, over 60 and under 3 free. Parents $8 when accompanied by a paying child. AE, MC, VI. Phone (604) 255-5161.

PACIFIC SPACE CENTRE, 1100 Chestnut St. in Vanier Park, offers interactive exhibits about Canada's role in space as well as a space flight simulator. The Star Theatre presents laser light shows and programs dealing with astronomy, solar history and space explorations.

Allow 1 hour, 30 minutes minimum. Daily 10-5, July-Aug.; Tues.-Sun. 10-5, rest of year. Laser shows daily at 9:30 p.m. (also Thurs.-Sat. at 10:45 p.m.), July 1-Labour Day; Thurs.-Sun. at 9 p.m. (also Fri.-Sat. at 10:30 p.m.), rest of year. Closed Dec. 25. Show times may vary; phone ahead. Admission $12.50; over 64 and ages 11-18, $9.50; ages 5-10, $8.50; family rate $38. Laser light show $7.75. MC, VI. Phone (604) 738-7827.

QUEEN ELIZABETH PARK, off Cambie St. and W. 33rd Ave., is on 150-metre (492-ft.) Little Mountain, the highest point in Vancouver. The park offers magnificent views of the city, harbor and North Shore mountains. Other highlights include an arboretum; rose, sunken and quarry gardens; tennis courts; and pitch and putt greens. Open daily 24 hours. Free.

SAVE **Bloedel Conservatory,** 33rd Ave. and Cambie St., provides a controlled atmosphere for growing climatically varied species of plants under an illuminated triodetic dome 43 metres (141 ft.) in diameter and 21 metres (70 ft.) high. Tropical birds and a fish pond are other highlights. Allow 30 minutes minimum. Mon.-Fri. 9-8, Sat.-Sun. 10-9, Apr.-Sept.; daily 10-5, rest of year. Closed Dec. 25. Admission $3.50; over 65, $2; ages 6-17, $1.65; family rate $7. MC, VI. Phone (604) 257-8570.

ST. ANDREW'S-WESLEY CHURCH, 1012 Nelson St., is a Gothic structure with many stained-glass windows. Tues.-Sat. 10-4, July-Aug. Phone (604) 683-4574.

SAVE ★ **SCIENCE WORLD,** 1455 Quebec St., has hands-on exhibits and demonstrations to explain scientific phenomena. The origins of the universe and the nature of matter and energy are explored in Matter and Forces. Mine Games centers on the mining industry; natural history and optical illusions are the subjects of additional galleries. Also

of interest is a 3-D laser theater and an OMNIMAX theater that presents nature and science films. Food is available.

Allow 2 hours minimum. Daily 10-6, July 1-Labour Day; Mon.-Fri. 10-5, Sat.-Sun. and holidays 10-6, rest of year. Exhibits and laser theater $11.75, over 54 and students with ID $7.75, under 4 free. OMNIMAX $10, under 4 free. Exhibits, laser theater and OMNIMAX admission $14.75; over 54 and ages 4-18, $10.50. Parking $2-$4. MC, VI. Phone (604) 268-6363. *See color ad p. 145.*

★ **STANLEY PARK,** on the peninsula near the business district, is one of the finest natural parks on the continent. Visitors can lawn bowl, watch a cricket match, swim, golf, play tennis or checkers, jog, learn archery or go bicycling over some of the 80 kilometres (50 mi.) of roads and trails. Also featured are a children's farmyard, rose garden, miniature steam railway and totem pole displays. Shows are presented at the open-air theater at Malkin Bowl in July and August.

An information booth is in the lower farmyard parking lot on Park Dr. just off the Georgia St. entrance. Park open daily 24 hours. Information booth open 10-5, June 15-Sept. 15; 10-4, May 1-June 14 and Sept. 16-Oct. 15. Children's farmyard daily 11-4. Railway daily 11-5, May-Sept (weather permitting). Shuttle runs daily 9:30-6, July 1-Labour Day.

Park admission and shuttle service are free. Farmyard and railway each $2.60; over 64 and under 12, $1.30; family rate $5.25. Combination farmyard/railway family rate $8.90. A fee is charged for parking. Phone (604) 257-8531.

SAVE **Stanley Park Horse-drawn Tours Ltd.** depart from beside the information booth on Park Dr. The narrated, 1-hour horse-drawn vehicle tours highlight the park's points of interest. Tours depart daily every 20-30 minutes 9:40-5:20, July 1-Sept. 4; 10-5, Apr.-June and Sept. 8-30; 10-4, Mar. 15-31 and in Oct. Fare $14.95; over 65 and students with ID, $13.95; ages 3-12, $9.95; family rate (two adults and two children) $46.69. MC, VI. Phone (604) 681-5115.

★ **Vancouver Aquarium Marine Science Centre** exhibits more than 8,000 marine animals with emphasis on such diverse habitats as Arctic Canada and the Amazon Rain Forest. Visitors can study endangered species and the illegal trade of animals in the Wildlife Crimebusters exhibit. Also shown is an exhibit about frogs. A wetlands center provides the opportunity to wade through a freshwater pond or enter a swamp environment. A radio broadcast features sounds of live whales.

The ocean floor and its inhabitants can be viewed through the simulated porthole of a submarine in the North Pacific Gallery. Other highlights include beluga whales, killer whales, sea lions and a sea otter colony as well as an exhibit about giant fishes of the Amazon. Whale shows, sea otter feedings and shark dives also are offered. Food is available.

Allow 2 hours minimum. Daily 9:30-7, June 27-Sept. 5; 10-5:30, rest of year. Admission $13.95; over 64 and ages 13-18, $11.85; ages 4-12, $9.25; family rate (two adults and three children) $41.25. AE, MC, VI. Phone (604) 659-3474 or (800) 931-1186. *See color ad p. 145.*

UNIVERSITY OF BRITISH COLUMBIA, on Point Grey, encompasses 2,470 hectares (6,103 acres) overlooking the Strait of Georgia, making it the largest university in the province.

Botanical Garden, 6804 S.W. Marine Dr., is made up of more than 70 acres of plants from around the world. The main garden at the south end of the campus includes the E.H. Lohbrunner Alpine Garden, an Asian garden with blue Himalayan poppies, a winter garden, a 16th-century Physick garden, a food garden with espalier fruit trees, medicinal plants and plants native to British Columbia.

Off N.W. Marine Drive is Nitobe Memorial Garden, one of the most accurately represented Japanese gardens in North America. It combines a tea garden and a landscape garden, with seasonal displays of irises, Japanese maples and flowering cherries.

Allow 1 hour minimum. Main garden open daily 10-6. Nitobe Garden open daily 10-6, Mar. 6 to mid-Oct.; Mon.-Fri. 10-2:30, rest of year. Main garden $4.50; senior citizens and grades 8-12, $2.25; grades 1-7, $1.75; under 6 free. Nitobe Garden $2.50; senior citizens and grades 8-12, $1.75; grades 1-7, $1.50; under 6 free. Phone (604) 822-9666.

Museum of Anthropology, 6393 N.W. Marine Dr. on the Point Grey Cliffs, houses a major collection of Northwest Coast First Nations artwork. Displays include totem poles, feast dishes and canoes as well as artifacts from around the world. European ceramics also are displayed.

Allow 1 hour minimum. Daily 10-5 (also Tues. 5-9), Victoria Day-Labour Day; Tues.-Sun. 11-5 (also Tues. 5-9), rest of year. Closed Dec. 25-26. Admission $6, over 59 and students with ID $3.50, under 6 free, family rate $15; free to all Tues. 5-9. MC, VI. Phone (604) 822-3825.

M.Y. Williams Geological Museum, just off the West Mall of the university at 6339 Stories Rd., displays minerals and fossils. A highlight of the collection is an 80-million-year-old Lambeosaurus dinosaur. Allow 30 minutes minimum. Mon.-Fri. 8:30-5. Free. Phone (604) 822-2449.

★ **VANCOUVER AQUARIUM MARINE SCIENCE CENTRE**—*see Stanley Park p. 148.*

VANCOUVER ART GALLERY, 750 Hornby St., houses major paintings by Canadian artist Emily Carr and American, British, Dutch and French works from the 17th century to the present. Changing art, photography and video exhibits also are featured.

Allow 1 hour minimum. Daily 10-5:30 (also Thurs. 5:30-9), holidays noon-5, Easter-second Mon. in Oct.; Tues.-Sun. 10-5:30 (also Thurs. 5:30-9), rest of year. Admission mid-June through Sept. 30, $10; over 65, $8; students with ID, $6; under 13 free. Admission rest of year $8; over 65, $6; students with ID $4; under 13 free. Admission $5 Thurs. 5-9. AE, MC, VI. Phone (604) 662-4700. *See color ad p. 149.*

VANCOUVER MARITIME MUSEUM, 1905 Ogden Ave. at n. foot of Chestnut and Cypress sts., has model ships, naval uniforms and other artifacts relating to man's interaction with the sea. Historic vessels are displayed outside in the harbor. The Children's Maritime Discovery Centre features hands-on activities to introduce youngsters to ships and pirates of the sea. Allow 1 hour minimum. Daily 10-5, Victoria Day-Labour Day; Tues.-Sun. 10-5, rest of year. Museum admission (including the *St. Roch*) $6; senior citizens and under 19, $3; family rate $14. AE, MC, VI. Phone (604) 257-8300.

St. Roch National Historic Site is next to the museum. The *St. Roch* was built in 1928 for the Royal Canadian Mounted Police Arctic supply and patrol. During World War II it became the first vessel to travel from the Pacific to the Atlantic via the treacherous Northwest Passage in the Arctic. In 1944 the *St. Roch* completed the return trip from Halifax, Nova Scotia, to Vancouver, marking the first round-trip voyage through the Northwest Passage.

Assigned to Halifax after the war, the schooner reached its destination by going through the Panama Canal, thus becoming the first vessel to circumnavigate the North American continent. The ship was retired in 1954. Preserved in dry dock, the vessel is displayed as it appeared in 1944.

Allow 1 hour minimum. Guided tours daily every hour 10-4. Admission is included in the museum charge. Phone (604) 666-3201.

SAVE **VANCOUVER MUSEUM,** s.w. end of Burrard St. in Vanier Park at 1100 Chestnut St., is devoted to the art, natural history, anthropology and history of the lower mainland. Collections include regional artifacts, including pieces from First Nations peoples, as well as ancient and contemporary objects from around the world. Daily 10-5, July-Aug.; Tues.-Sun. 10-5, rest of year. Closed Dec. 25. Admission $8; over 64, students with ID and ages 4-19, $5.50. MC, VI. Phone (604) 736-4431 or 736-7736.

★ **VANDUSEN BOTANICAL GARDEN** is at 5251 Oak St. at 37th Ave. The 55-acre area has an outstanding plant collection arranged to show geographical origin and botanical relationships. Gardens are set amid lawns, lakes and rock displays with vistas of the mountains and city. A hedge maze provides entertainment for children. Food is available.

Allow 1 hour minimum. Daily 10-9, June 1 to mid-Aug.; 10-8, mid-Aug. through Labour Day and in May; 10-6, day after Labour Day-Sept. 30 and in April; 10-4 (also 5-9:30 in Dec. during Festival of Lights), rest of year. Closed Dec. 25. Admission $5.50; over 65 and ages 6-18, $2.75; family rate $11. Half-price admission Oct.-Mar. MC, VI. Phone (604) 878-9274.

Industrial Tours

Tours are available of the Alberta Wheat Pool, (604) 684-5161, at the foot of Cassiar Street, and the Post Office, (604) 662-1388, 349 W. Georgia St. Reservations are required.

What To Do

Sightseeing

Opportunities to watch bustling port activities are available at several vantage points in Vancouver. Seaplanes, barges, tugboats, cargo ships, ferries and the SeaBus can be observed from Granville Square at the foot of Granville Street; from Lynnterm at 1300 Stewart St.; from Stanley Park; and from the observation deck at Vanterm at the north foot of Clarke Drive. Fine views of the city, sea and mountains are available at CypressBowl, Simon Fraser University atop Burnaby Mountain and Queen Elizabeth Park.

Boat Tours

HARBOUR CRUISES offers tours departing from n. end of Denman St., next to Stanley Park, aboard the stern-wheeler MPV *Constitution* and the MV *Britannia*. *Constitution* 1.25-hour harbor tours depart daily at 11:30, 1 and 2:30, May-Sept. *Britannia* 6.5-hour round-trip cruises to Squamish depart Wed.-Sun. at 9:30, June-Sept. An optional 6.5-hour return trip by train also is available. *Constitution* fare $18; over 59 and ages 12-17, $15; ages 5-11, $6. *Britannia* fare $46.50; over 59 and ages 12-17, $41.50; ages 5-11, $15. Fare for combination boat/train tour $72.50; over 59 and ages 12-17, $61.25; ages 5-11, $20. Phone (604) 688-7246 or (800) 663-1500. *See color ad.*

Bus Tours

SAVE Gray Line *(see color ad)* offers daily tours, including many from double-decker buses, departing from the Plaza of Nations at 700 Pacific Blvd.; phone (604) 879-3363. West Coast City and Nature Sightseeing Ltd. *(see color ad p. 150)*, 3955 Myrtle St. in Burnaby, features sightseeing trips of the city and its surrounding natural areas in 20-31 passenger minibuses. Full-day trips to Victoria and the Whistler resort area also are available; phone (604) 451-1600 or 451-1777.

Plane Tours

Another way to see Vancouver and its surroundings is by air. Flights, lasting from 35 minutes to 1.25 hours, depart from the Vancouver International Airport South Terminal, following signs to the ESSO Avitat Building. Fares vary and reservations are required; phone (604) 278-1608 or (800) 228-6608.

Train Tours

Rocky Mountaineer Railtours *(see color ad p. 43)* offers scenic, deluxe 2-day, all daylight rail tours between Vancouver and the Canadian Rockies late April to mid-October. Destinations include Jasper, Banff, Lake Louise and Calgary, Alberta. The entire trip is made during daylight hours with an overnight stay in historic Kamloops. Longer trips also are available. Onboard meals, hotel, transfers and commentary are included; phone (604) 606-7200, 606-7245, or (800) 665-7245 for reservations.

The steam locomotive "Royal Hudson" makes a 6-hour round trip through magnificent scenery between North Vancouver and Squamish; phone (604) 631-3500 or 984-5246. The train departs from the BC Rail Station at Pemberton and First avenues in North Vancouver.

Trolley Tours

Trolley tours provide visitors a look at the city at a relaxed pace. The Downtown Historic Railway, comprised of two electric interurban railcars, skirts False Creek between Ontario and Granville streets; phone (604) 325-9990.

THE VANCOUVER TROLLEY CO., which has 16 stops citywide, offers a narrated city highlights tour of Vancouver's major attractions. Passengers may board, depart or reboard at any stop on the route; trolleys stop at each point on the route every 30 minutes. Allow 2 hours minimum. Daily 9-6, Apr.-Oct.; 9-5, rest of year. A sunset tour leaves Gastown at 7, July-Aug. Highlights pass, valid for one full circuit, $22; ages 4-12, $10. Sunset tour $28; ages 4-12, $18. Phone (604) 801-5515 or (888) 451-5581. *See color ad.*

Sports and Recreation

Vancouver offers such a diversity of recreational opportunities that anyone with a yen for variety can ski on Grouse Mountain in the morning, golf on the banks of the Fraser River in the afternoon, fish for salmon in Horseshoe Bay at dusk and top off the day with a dip in English Bay.

Vancouver's park system has tennis courts, swimming pools, putting greens, golf courses, lawn bowling greens, hiking paths and a comprehensive bike route. For park information phone the Vancouver Park Board at (604) 257-8400.

Swimming is available along English Bay, which is bordered by beaches from West Point Grey to Stanley Park. Beaches are easily accessible from Northwest Marine Drive in West Point Grey, Point Grey Road in Vancouver West and from Beach Avenue downtown.

White-water rafting is available April through September on the nearby Chilliwack River and a little farther afield on the Lillooet, Fraser and Thompson rivers. Vancouver rafting companies offering day trips as well as multiday trips include REO Rafting Adventure Resort; phone (604) 684-4438 or (800) 736-7238 and Kumsheen Raft Adventures; phone (250) 455-2296 or (800) 663-6667. Vancouver Wilderness Paddle offers **sea kayaking** trips on Indian Arm; phone (604) 684-4922 or (800) 528-3531.

Winter visitors with a penchant for **skiing** can tackle the challenging slopes of Grouse Mountain or Mount Seymour Park in North Vancouver. East of Vancouver are Hemlock Valley and Manning Park ski resorts, offering both downhill and cross-country treks. Cypress Provincial Park in North Vancouver also has cross-country and downhill skiing. Summit Leisure Adventures, (604) 921-1660, offers ski packages for the Okanagan Valley which include Apex, Big White, Silver Star and Sun Peaks ski areas. Reservations are required.

When the waters sparkle from the summer sun, Vancouver becomes a **boating** paradise. For visitors without a boat, several companies have craft for hourly or daily rental. For charter yachts phone Harbour Cruises, (604) 687-9558, or Westin Bayshore Yacht Charters, (604) 682-3377 or 691-6936.

For **fishing** charters and boat rentals phone Sewell's Ltd., (604) 921-3474, at Horseshoe Bay. COHO Sports also provides charters and guided fishing trips departing from Secret Cove; phone (604) 435-7333.

Vancouver residents love spectator sports, especially **football, hockey** and **soccer.** The B.C. Lions of the Canadian Football League play before capacity crowds in B.C. Place Stadium. The Canucks of the National Hockey League and the Grizzlies, an NBA **basketball** team, compete in General Motors Place. For football, hockey, and basketball ticket information phone Ticketmaster, (604) 280-4444. **Baseball** is played by the Vancouver Canadians at Nat Bailey Stadium; phone (604) 872-5232 for schedule and ticket information. Indoor **lacrosse** can be enjoyed at Bill Copeland Sports Complex in Burnaby and at Kerrisdale Arena and Queens Park in New Westminster.

Thoroughbred racing with pari-mutuel betting is held at Hastings Park Race Course; phone (604) 254-1631.

Note: Policies concerning admittance of children to pari-mutuel betting facilities vary. Phone for information.

Shopping

Befitting an international port, Vancouver has a wealth of marketplaces. These emporiums give definition to a metropolis that can be broken easily into a series of villages. From the cosmopolitan heart of the West End to historic Gastown to exotic Chinatown, Vancouver is a shopper's paradise.

Streets of fashionable boutiques are the signature of the West End. Representative of this area is Robson Street and its high-fashion boutiques. Enhancing the shops are the gardens, pools and waterfalls of Robson Square, a three-block area that stretches from the Vancouver Art Gallery to the glass-tiered pyramid of the Law Courts. Among the interesting shopping options on Robson Street is Planet Hollywood.

When the pleasure of the outdoors fades with the weather, there are nearby underground malls. The largest of these is Granville Mall, which includes Pacific Centre, anchored by the aboveground department stores The Bay and Eatons, and the adjoining Vancouver Centre. Beneath the Hyatt Regency Hotel is Royal Centre with its fashion boutiques and a 10-theater cineplex.

In Burnaby, MetroTown contains MetroTown Centre, Eaton Centre, Metropolis and Station Square. The area features more than 550 shops, restaurants and theaters as well as a virtual reality entertainment center.

Expo '86 created a world village and left a legacy of buildings and the light rail system known as SkyTrain. SkyTrain and its water counterpart, SeaBus, link two of the city's several marketplaces. Lonsdale Quay and Westminster Quay (in North Vancouver and New Westminster respectively) both offer shops, eateries and promenades along the waterfront.

Near the SeaBus terminal is the former Canadian Pavilion, now Canada Place. The distinctive white sails of this complex embrace the trade and convention center, cruise terminal, a hotel and the Promenade Shops, featuring the Made in BC shop and an IMAX theater.

East of the SeaBus terminal are the restored 19th-century buildings and cobblestone streets of Gastown. Carrall, Powell, Walter and Alexander streets meet at Maple Tree Square, defining this historic area and embracing specialty and antique shops, art galleries and restaurants. Most shops are open Sundays. Street vendors add to the area's charm, as does the 2-ton Gastown Steam Clock at the corner of Cambie and Water streets.

The warehouses of the reclaimed industrial area of Granville Island have become a refuge for artists and casual shoppers. The centerpiece of this community is Granville Island Market, off W. Fourth Street by False Creek, an open market that offers fresh fruits, vegetables, seafood, meats, gourmet foods, baked goods, many fine restaurants (reservations are recommended), handicrafts and live theater.

Another cluster of abandoned warehouses has been rejuvenated into one of the trendiest areas of Vancouver—Yaletown. Bordered by Nelson and Homer streets and Pacific Boulevard, the community is filled with stores featuring everything from imported designer clothing to home furnishings and giftware by Canadian craftsmen. Old warehouse loading bays have been converted into cafes and restaurants, which use the wide sidewalks for patio dining.

South Vancouver features Oakridge Shopping Centre, 49th Avenue and Oak Street; its vaulted glass ceilings shelter a collection of shops as well as giant fig trees. Across Burrard Inlet in West Vancouver are the twin malls of Park Royal. This complex has more than 190 shops offering everything from furnishings to groceries; the largest stores are The Bay and Eatons.

CHINATOWN, centering on E. Pender St. between Carrall and Gore sts., is the second largest area of its kind in North America. Elaborately carved and gilded shops display jade and ivory, bamboo and rattan, brassware, silk and brocade. Sidewalk markets feature Oriental produce. Even the phone booths are topped with pagoda roofs. During Chinese New Year the streets resound with the din of drums and fireworks.

Theater and Concerts

The Queen Elizabeth Theatre at 649 Cambie St. is home to Ballet British Columbia, (604) 732-5003, and the Vancouver Opera Association, (604) 683-0222. The adjacent Vancouver Playhouse presents professional theater, recitals and chamber music; phone (604) 873-3311. The Vancouver Symphony Orchestra performs at the Orpheum Theatre, Smithe and Seymour streets; phone (604) 876-3434 for ticket information.

Other prominent metropolitan theaters presenting dramatic productions include the Arts Club Theatre, with two stages on Johnston Street on Granville Island and one stage at 1181 Seymour St.; the Back Alley Theatre, 751 Thurlow St.; the Metro Theatre, 1370 S.W. Marine Dr.; the Playhouse Theatre, 575 Beatty St.; Studio 58, 100 W. 49th Ave.; and the Vancouver East Cultural Centre, 1895 Venables St.

During the summer concerts and musicals are presented in Stanley Park's Malkin Bowl. Kitsilano Showboat at Kitsilano Beach presents an outdoor variety show Monday, Wednesday and Friday at 8 p.m. during July and August (weather permitting).

The daily papers carry listings of cultural events, as do weekly and monthly magazines. For free information about cultural events, phone (604) 299-9000. Ticket outlets include Concert Box Office, 501 W. Georgia St.; Eaton's Ticket Centre, 701 Granville St.; and Vancouver Ticket Centre, 830 Hamilton St.

Special Events

Life in a city where your office is only 25 minutes from a ski slope is worth celebrating,

and the residents of Vancouver celebrate their setting throughout the year. New Year's Day sees the Polar Bear Swim at English Bay; the event draws many swimmers and hundreds of spectators.

The Vancouver Children's Festival in May ushers in summer, while cultural entertainment sails in with the Canadian International Dragon Boat Festival in mid-June. The Vancouver Folk Music Festival draws fans from as far away as Los Angeles for concerts during mid-July. The Symphony of Fire International Fireworks Competition is held at English Bay the last week of July and the first week in August.

Virtually all facets of life and work in British Columbia are celebrated in the Pacific National Exhibition, held at the Exhibition Grounds from late August through Labour Day. In late September and early October the Oktoberfest is held at the Exhibition Grounds, where the revelry continues into the wee hours.

The Christmas season begins with the Christmas Carol Ships, which lead a flotilla of private watercraft decorated with Christmas lights around the harbor in mid-December. More information about events is available from your CAA or AAA club.

The Vancouver Vicinity

ALDERGROVE (H-11)
pop. 9,500, elev. 61 m/200'

A small town on the Lower Fraser Valley's southern side, Aldergrove is near the Fraser River and the Canada-United States border. Dairy, chicken, strawberry and raspberry farms dot the surrounding area. Just northeast of Aldergrove, Bradner grows about 400 varieties of daffodils.

Langley Chamber of Commerce: 5761 Glover Rd., Suite 1, Langley, BC, Canada V3A 8M8; phone (604) 530-6656.

SAVE **GREATER VANCOUVER ZOOLOGICAL CENTRE,** 48 hectares (120 acres) at 5048 264th St., is devoted to the preservation and breeding of endangered species. The resident 165 species from around the world, including monkeys, giraffes, llamas and tigers, live in large paddocks. A petting zoo as well as bus and train rides also are available. Picnicking is permitted. Food is available. Allow 2 hours minimum. Daily 9-dusk. Admission $10.50; over 64 and ages 3-15, $7.50. Bus or train ride $2-$3. MC, VI. Phone (604) 857-9005.

BURNABY (G-11)
pop. 179,200, elev. 40 m/130'

DEER LAKE PARK, 14.5 km (9 mi.) s.e. at 6450 Deer Lake Ave. at Canada Way, contains the Century Gardens, with its distinctive rhododendron display and rose gardens. The Shadbolt Centre for the Arts offers community arts programs as well as theater and dance performances in its James Cowan Theatre. Several walking trails provide scenic views throughout the park. Daily 24 hours. Free. Phone (604) 291-0922 or 420-1778.

SAVE **Burnaby Village Museum,** off Hwy. 1 Kensington S. exit to 6501 Deer Lake Ave., re-creates the sights and sounds of an 1890-1925 village in lower mainland British Columbia. Townsfolk in period costumes welcome visitors to their shops and homes with demonstrations, displays and hands-on activities, including printing, blacksmithing, early education and use of herbs. A restored 1912 Parker carousel is on the site. Food is available.

Allow 1 hour minimum. Daily 11-4:30, May. 1-Sept. 19 and Nov. 27-Dec. 23 (also Thurs. 4:30-8, July-Aug. and Dec. 1-23). Admission $6.45; ages 13-18, $4.45; over 65 or physically impaired $4.35; ages 6-12, $3.85; family rate $3.80 per person. carousel ride $1. MC, VI. Phone (604) 293-6501.

CHILLIWACK (H-12)
pop. 60,200, elev. 10 m/33'

In the heart of the upper Fraser River Valley, Chilliwack is the center of a prosperous farming and dairy region. The surrounding lakes, rivers, mountains and nearby provincial parks offer such varied recreation as skiing, hiking, fishing, rock hunting and white-water rafting. Scenic views and picnicking are available at Bridal Falls Provincial Park, 17 kilometres (11 mi.) east on Hwy. 1, and Chilliwack Lake Provincial Park, 84 kilometres (54 mi.) southeast off Hwy. 1 *(see Recreation Chart).*

Chilliwack Chamber of Commerce: 44150 Luckakuck Ave., Chilliwack, BC, Canada V2R 4A7; phone (604) 858-8121.

SAVE **THE APPLE FARM** is off Trans-Canada Hwy. exit 104, then 4 km (2.5 mi.) e., following signs. Dwarf trees yield 25 varieties of apples, including Tokyo Rose, Belle de Boskoop and Jonagold. Visitors can wander the orchards and watch the work area where fruit is sorted, washed and polished. Food is available. Guided tours and tastings are available by reservation. Daily 9-5, Aug.-Dec. Free. Guided tours $4.50-$6. MC, VI. Phone (604) 823-4311.

SAVE ★ **MINTER GARDENS** is 19 km (12 mi.) e. on Hwy. 1 at Hwy. 9 jct. Covering nearly 11 hectares (27 acres) at the base of the Coastal Mountain Range, 11 thematic gardens display seasonal colors and the changing moods of spring, summer and autumn. Highlights include a maze, topiary sculptures, a fragrance garden, three aviaries and a Chinese garden as well as a children's play area. Food is available.

Allow 1 hour minimum. Daily 9-6, June-Aug.; 9-5, Apr.-May and Sept.- Oct. Admission May-Sept., $11; over 64, $10; ages 6-18, $5; family rate available. Admission in Apr. and Oct. $10; over 64, $9; ages 6-18, $4.50; family rate available. AE, MC, VI. Phone (604) 794-7191 or (888) 646-8377.

COQUITLAM (G-11)
pop. 101,800, elev. 137 m/449'

Named for a type of landlocked salmon, Coquitlam borders Pitt Lake and encompasses Burke Mountain. Recreational opportunities, including swimming, canoeing, hiking and fishing, are available throughout the area.

Nearby parks and lakes include Mundy Park, 4 kilometres (2.5 mi.) south off Mariner Way; Belcarra Park, 15 kilometres (9 mi.) northwest off Ioco and Bedwell Bay roads; Buntzen Lake, 12 kilometres (7 mi.) northwest off East and Sunnyside roads; Minnekhada Regional Park, 13 kilometres (8 mi.) northeast off Victoria Drive and Quarry Road; Town Centre Park and Lafarge Lake, on Pinetree Way just north of Lougheed Hwy. and Burke Mountain, 11 kilometres (7 mi.) northeast off Coast Meridian and Harper roads.

Coquitlam Chamber of Commerce: 1180 Pinetree Way #3, Coquitlam, BC, Canada V3B 7L2; phone (604) 464-2716.

DELTA (H-11)
pop. 95,400, elev. 10 m/33'

Delta, composed of the three distinct communities of Ladner, Tsawwassen and North Delta, is an amalgam of commerce, fisheries, industry, farmland, beaches and suburban residences. The warm-water beaches on Boundary Bay and Tsawwassen are popular spots for swimming and sunbathing. Other recreational opportunities in the area include fishing for salmon and boating on the Fraser River and the Strait of Georgia.

Delta Chamber of Commerce: 6201 60th Ave., Delta, BC, Canada V4K 4E2; phone (604) 946-4232.

DELTA MUSEUM AND ARCHIVES, 4858 Delta St., houses marine, fishing and farming exhibits, pioneer and First Nations displays, reconstructed rooms of a late Victorian household and an early 1900s Delta street scene. Allow 1 hour minimum. Museum open Tues.-Sat. 10-3:30, Sun. 2-4. Archives open Tues.-Sat. 10-3; closed Dec. 25-Jan. 1. Donations. Phone (604) 946-9322.

GEORGE C. REIFEL MIGRATORY BIRD SANCTUARY, 5191 Robertson Rd. on Westham Island, comprises 344 hectares (850 acres) with 4 kilometres (2.5 mi.) of trails. More than 268 species of fowl have been observed. Allow 1 hour minimum. Daily 9-4. Admission $3.25; over 59 and ages 2-14, $1. Bird seed 50c per bag. Phone (604) 946-6980.

LANGLEY (H-11)
pop. 80,200, elev. 10 m/33'

Langley, the site of a Hudson's Bay Co. fort built in 1840 *(see Fort Langley National Historic Site p. 112),* is in an important farming region. Orchards, strawberry and raspberry farms, horse ranches and dairy, chicken and mink farms make a patchwork of the countryside.

Langley Chamber of Commerce: Unit One, 5761 Glover Rd., Langley, BC, Canada V3A 8M8; phone (604) 530-6656.

SAVE **CANADIAN MUSEUM OF FLIGHT** is at Hangar 3, Unit 200, 5333 216th St., at the Langley Airport. The museum features aircraft, some restored, in an outdoors setting as well as in a hangar. The aircraft and aircraft artifacts also displayed represent Canada's aviation history. A collection of other aviation items is available.

Allow 30 minutes minimum. Daily 10-4; closed Jan. 1 and Dec. 25-26. Admission $5, over 59 and students with ID $4, under 6 free, family rate (includes two adults and up to four children) $12. MC, VI. Phone (604) 532-0035.

MAPLE RIDGE (H-11)
pop. 56,200, elev. 30 m/98'

Maple Ridge lies on the north shore of the Fraser River, with the Coast Mountains to the north and the Stave and Pitt Rivers forming its east and west boundaries. Snow-capped peaks overlook this Fraser Valley community.

The Fraser River Heritage Walk, which starts at Port Haney Wharf, passes many of the town's notable spots. The Haney House at 11612 224th St. was built in 1878 and contains many furnishings and artifacts owned by three generations of the Haney family. Displays at Maple Ridge Museum, 22520 116th Ave., reflect the history and geography of the area.

Kanaka Creek Regional Park offers hiking and horseback riding trails as well as picnicking, canoeing, kayaking and fishing. A fish hatchery is on the grounds. Phone (604) 530-4983. *See Recreation Chart.* Maple Ridge also has a large per capita horse population and an extensive riding trail system.

Maple Ridge Chamber of Commerce: 22238 Lougheed Hwy., Maple Ridge, BC, Canada V2X 2T2; phone (604) 463-3366.

THE UNIVERSITY OF BRITISH COLUMBIA RESEARCH FOREST, n. on Silver Valley Rd., offers self-guiding tours. Trails of various lengths lead visitors through the forest. Bicycles and pets are not permitted. Daily dawn-dusk. Guide booklet $1. Phone (604) 463-8148.

MISSION (H-12)
pop. 30,500, elev. 55 m/180'

Mission developed from a Roman Catholic mission built in 1861 to serve the Indian tribes. The site became a popular stopping place for trappers, settlers and other river travelers.

The Fraser River provides opportunities for swimming, fishing, boating and water sports; its sandbars are good for rockhounds in search of agates, jades and garnets. Motocross and boat races are held at Mission Raceway from March through October.

Mission Regional Chamber of Commerce: 34033 Lougheed Hwy., Mission, BC, Canada V2V 5X8; phone (604) 826-6914.

MISSION MUSEUM is at 33201 Second Ave. Housed in a historic 1907 building, the museum displays exhibits of pioneer and Indian artifacts, farming and logging equipment, fossils, minerals and photographs. Allow 30 minutes minimum. Tues.-Thurs. and Sat. 1-4, May-Aug.; Tues.-Thurs. 1-4, rest of year. Closed Dec. 25-Jan. 1. Donations. Phone (604) 826-1011.

WESTMINSTER ABBEY is 1.5 km (.9 mi.) e., .75 km (.5 mi.) n. of Hwy. 7 to 34224 Dewdney Trunk Rd. The Seminary of Christ the King is managed by Benedictine monks. Of interest are the view and architecture. Modest dress is required. Allow 30 minutes minimum. Mon.-Sat. 1:30-4:30, Sun. 2-4. Free. Phone (604) 826-8975.

NEW WESTMINSTER (G-11)
pop. 49,400, elev. 75 m/246'

The oldest incorporated city in British Columbia, New Westminster—also known as the Royal City—was named by Queen Victoria. Transformed into a boomtown by the lure of gold in 1857, it plunged into a depression when the gold rush subsided in the late 1860s. The city was the provincial capital until 1868.

New Westminster also is known for its architecture. Parts of the city were built by the Royal Engineers, sent in 1855 to keep order in the new crown colony. Former members of this organization later formed the New Westminster Regiment, whose history is recounted in the Museum of the Royal Westminster Regiment at Sixth and Queens streets.

Other places of interest include old houses, many of which survived a devastating fire in 1898. The houses can be toured in May. Tickets must be purchased in advance; for information phone the New Westminster Hyack Festival Association at (604) 522-6894.

Westminster Quay, on the waterfront, maintains a tradition started in 1892 when farmers, hunters and settlers came to barter for goods. Fresh meat, baked goods, produce and local crafts can be purchased daily.

Also of interest is *Sampson V* Maritime Museum aboard the stern-wheeler berthed on the Fraser River at the foot of Tenth Street. The stern-wheeler, the last to operate on the Fraser, can be toured. The Canadian Lacrosse Hall of Fame is at Sixth Avenue and McBride Boulevard.

New Westminster Chamber of Commerce: 601 Queens Ave., New Westminster, BC, Canada V3L 3E7; phone (604) 521-7781 or 526-1905.

IRVING HOUSE AND NEW WESTMINSTER MUSEUM is at 302 Royal Ave. It is a well-preserved 1864 Victorian mansion. Built in the popular San Francisco Gothic Revival style for Capt. William Irving, who pioneered the riverboat trade of the lower Fraser River, the 14-room residence is furnished to represent the period 1864-90. The house is bedecked in Victorian Christmas decor during December.

The museum, behind the Irving House, has artifacts and displays about local history. Of note is the coach that was built in 1876 to carry the governor general of Canada and the Marchioness of Dufferin to the Cariboo goldfields. Allow 1 hour minimum. Tues.-Sun. 11-5, May 1-Labour Day; Sat.-Sun. 1-5, rest of year. Closed holidays. Donations. Phone (604) 527-4640.

JAPANESE FRIENDSHIP GARDEN, on Queens Ave. adjacent to the city hall at 511 Royal Ave.,

has beautiful pathways, flowers and 100 Yoshino cherry trees. The trees were a gift from the city of Moriguchi, Japan. Allow 1 hour, 30 minutes minimum. Daily dawn-dusk. Free. Phone (604) 527-4567.

PADDLEWHEELER RIVER ADVENTURES, departing from the boardwalk of the Westminster Quay Public Market at 810 Quayside Dr., takes passengers along the Fraser River on a replica of a late 19th-century paddlewheeler. The narrated excursions, which include lunch, provide insights into the area's history and wildlife. The 7-hour trip includes a stopover at Fort Langley. Thematic, dance and dinner cruises, including an English high tea, also are available.

Seven-hour cruises depart Thurs., Sat. and Sun. at 10, June-Sept. Three-hour cruises depart Wed. at 11, June-Sept. Fare for 7-hour cruise $53.95; senior citizens and students with ID $48.95; ages 6-12, $21.95. Fare for 3-hour cruise $37.95; senior citizens and students with ID $33.95; ages 6-12, $11.95. Reservations are required. AE, MC, VI. Phone (604) 525-4465.

QUEENS PARK, in the center of town, has a Salish totem pole, a stadium, an arena, a picnic area, tennis courts, botanical gardens, an art gallery and a band shell in which concerts are presented in July and August. A spray pool, children's playland and petting zoo are open in summer. Allow 1 hour, 30 minutes minimum. Daily dawn-dusk. Free.

[SAVE] **STARLINE TOURS** depart from the Westminster Quay Public Market boardwalk. The narrated cruises along the Fraser River highlight the area's wildlife, natural history and development. A 6-hour excursion to the wilderness of Pitt Lake includes lunch, while a 5.5-hour trip to the fishing village of Steveston allows time for exploring ashore. Sunset cruises also are available. A combination boat and bus tour to Harrison Hot Springs also is offered. Cruises departing from Steveston in nearby Richmond offer opportunities to view two breeds of sea lions.

Cruises depart at 10, Apr.-Oct.; phone for exact schedule. Sea lion cruises available Apr.-May. Fare for 6-hour cruise $52.95; over 64 and students 13-18 with ID $48.95; under 13, $31.95. Fare for 5.5-hour cruise $41.95; over 64 and students 13-18 with ID $36.95; under 13, $25.95. Fee for parking. Reservations are recommended. MC, VI. Phone (604) 522-3506 or 272-9187.

NORTH VANCOUVER (G-11)
pop. 80,400, elev. 99 m/325'

CAPILANO SALMON HATCHERY, 4500 Capilano Park Rd., allows self-guiding tours of its architecturally acclaimed facility. Displays trace the development of coho, chinook and steelhead salmon. Visitors may see live adult salmon in the fish ladder July through November. Scenic picnic areas are available. Allow 30 minutes minimum. Daily 8-8, June-Aug.; 8-7, in May and Sept.; 8-6, in Apr. and Oct.; 8-4, rest of year. Free. Phone (604) 666-1790.

SAVE **CAPILANO SUSPENSION BRIDGE AND PARK** is off Hwy. 1 exit 14, then 2 km (1.2 mi.) n. to 3735 Capilano Rd. The swinging 137-metre-long (449-ft.) footbridge spans the spectacular 70-metre-deep (230-ft.), densely wooded gorge. The park has gardens and shrubs as well as an outdoor forestry exhibit and story center that displays artifacts of the bridge. Totem poles, masks and life-size carvings of Indians are sculpted on site. First Nations dancers perform and costumed guides offer tours of the park and nature trails during the summer. Food is available.

Allow 1 hour minimum. Daily 8:30-dusk, mid-May through Sept. 30; 9-5, rest of year. Closed Dec. 25. Admission $10.75; over 65, $8.75; students with ID $6.75; ages 6-12, $3.25. AE, MC, VI. Phone (604) 985-7474. *See color ad p. 145.*

SAVE **GROUSE MOUNTAIN**, at 6400 Nancy Greene Way, offers a panorama of the city from a height of 1,100 metres (3,609 ft.). On clear nights floodlit buildings and twinkling lights are reflected in the still harbor. Skiing and sleigh rides are available in the winter while helicopter and mountain bicycle tours are popular in the summer. Sports events and shows take place year-round. An aerial tramway operates all year to the chalet, a striking winglike building at the 1,128-metre (3,701-ft.) level. Daily bus service to the tramway is available.

At the foot of the mountain, Cleveland Dam and Capilano Lake offer picnic facilities and walking trails. Theatre in the Sky shows a videotape hourly about Vancouver's history. Allow 1 hour minimum. Grouse Mountain open daily 9 a.m.-10 p.m. Tram $16.95; over 65, $14.95; ages 13-18, $10.95; ages 7-12, $5.95; family rate $43.95. AE, DI, MC, VI. Phone (604) 984-0661.

LYNN CANYON PARK AND ECOLOGY CENTRE, off Lynn Valley Rd. following signs, is a municipal park with paths, natural streams and rivers and a 50-metre-high (166-ft.) suspension bridge spanning a waterfall and the canyon. The ecology center offers films, displays and guided nature walks. Food is available. Park open daily dawn-dusk; closed Jan. 1 and Dec. 25-26. Ecology center open daily 10-5, Mar.-Sept.; noon-4, rest of year. Guided nature walks Sat.-Sun. and holidays at 2, July-August. Donations. Phone (604) 981-3103.

MAPLEWOOD FARM, 405 Seymour River Pl., is a zoo geared toward small children, who may pet the domestic animals. Pony rides are available on Sunday, weather permitting. Cow milking demonstrations are given daily at 1:15. Allow 1 hour

minimum. Tues.-Sun. and Mon. holidays 10-4; closed Dec. 25. Admission $2.25; over 54 and ages 19 months-16 years, $1.75. Pony rides $2.50. Phone (604) 929-5610.

MOUNT SEYMOUR PROVINCIAL PARK, 24 km (15 mi.) n.e., is a scenic area of 3,508 hectares (8,668 acres) on the slopes of 1,433-metre (4,701-ft.) Mount Seymour. A good highway goes to the 1,006-metre (3,330-ft.) level. Hiking trails and downhill skiing are available in season. Picnicking is permitted. Daily 7 a.m.-11 p.m. Free. Phone (604) 924-2200. *See Recreation Chart.*

NORTH VANCOUVER MUSEUM AND ARCHIVES is in Presentation House at 209 W. Fourth St. The museum's artifacts document the community's growth from pioneer days. Documentary and photographic collections are housed in the archives. Allow 1 hour minimum. Museum open Tues.-Sun. noon-5. Archives open Tues.-Fri. 9:30-4:30. Complex closed Jan. 1 and Dec. 25. Free. Phone (604) 987-5618.

PORT COQUITLAM (G-11)
pop. 46,700 elev. 10 m/33′

The 29-kilometre (18-mi.) Poco Trail passes through wooded areas and runs alongside the Pitt River; the Pitt Dikes can be seen from the trail.

PORT MOODY (G-11)
pop. 20,800, elev. 10 m/33′

Port Moody once was the terminus of the Canadian Pacific Railway—the first train from Montréal to the Pacific arrived July 4, 1886. A year later the line was extended 20 kilometres (12 mi.) west to Vancouver. Rocky Point Park on Burrard Inlet offers picnicking, swimming, boating and nature trails.

STATION MUSEUM, 2734 Murray St., displays railroad artifacts and historical information about Port Moody in a former train depot with working and living areas restored to their early 1900s appearance. A restored railroad car sits on tracks outside the museum. Daily 10-7, May-Aug.; Sat.-Sun. and holidays 10-4, rest of year. Closed winter holidays. Donations. Phone (604) 939-1648.

RICHMOND (G-10)
pop. 148,900, elev. 5 m/16′

On an island at the mouth of the Fraser River, Richmond first was settled in 1879. The town grew and prospered with its farming, fishing and waterborne trade industries.

Steveston, an early fishing village now part of the southwest corner of Richmond, has been restored and is an area of shops, restaurants and businesses. Hundreds of boats line the docks as fishermen dry their nets and unload their catches for sale.

The Richmond Nature Park, 44 hectares (109 acres) at 1181 Westminster Hwy., has a bird pond, beehive displays, mounted birds, a quaking bog and plants identified by markers. A naturalist conducts hourlong tours of the park on Sunday.

Tourism Richmond: 11980 Deas Thruway, Richmond, BC, Canada V6W 1L1; phone (604) 271-8280 or (877) 247-0777.

GULF OF GEORGIA CANNERY NATIONAL HISTORIC SITE is at 12138 Fourth Ave. in Steveston Village. The 1894 salmon cannery has been restored to serve as an interpretive center for Canada's West Coast fishing industry. Interactive video presentations, guided tours of the plant and replicated 1930s canning line, and equipment demonstrations are offered. The Boiler House Theatre presents a film about the West Coast fishing industry every 30 minutes.

Daily 10-5, June 1-Labour Day; Thurs.-Mon. 10-5, Apr.-May and day after Labour Day-Oct. 31. Admission $5; over 64 and students with ID $3.75; ages 6-16, $2.50. VI. Phone (604) 664-9009.

RICHMOND ART CENTRE, GALLERY, MUSEUM AND ARCHIVES, off Granville St. at 7700 Minoru Gate, provides programs and events in art, music, drama and dance. The gallery exhibits art in various media by local artists and works from traveling exhibits. The museum depicts Richmond's history through early household items, personal effects and articles relating to the area's agriculture, dairying, fishing and transportation. Exhibits change regularly.

The archives preserve public and community records, which are available for research. Allow 1 hour minimum. Museum open Mon.-Fri. 9 a.m.-9:30 p.m.; Sat.-Sun. 10-5. Archives open Mon.-Thurs. 9:30-4:45. Complex closed holidays. Free. Phone (604) 231-6440.

STARLINE TOURS—*see New Westminster p. 157.*

SURREY (H-11)
pop. 304,500, elev. 80 m/262′

Surrey's sights are popular with nature buffs. Bear Creek Park features a garden area that includes rhododendrons, azaleas, ornamental grasses and bulb displays. A shoreline walk extends from Crescent Beach to Peace Arch Park. Walkers can observe tide pools, dig for clams or watch the myriad native birds.

Surrey Regional Chamber of Commerce: 14439 104 Ave., Suite 101, Surrey, BC, Canada V3R 1M1; phone (604) 581-7130.

NEWTON WAVE POOL is at 13730 72nd Ave. at the corner of King George Hwy. The indoor aquatic center houses, in addition to the wave pool, two water slides, a wading pool and a lagoon. The complex also includes exercise and steam rooms and a whirlpool. Pool accessories can be rented. Food is available. Thurs.-Sun and

Tues. 12:30-9; Mon. and Wed. 1:15-9. Pool admission $5.05; over 59, $3.85; ages 2-18, $2.90. MC, VI. Phone (604) 501-5540.

[SAVE] **RAINFOREST REPTILE REFUGE,** 2 km (1.2 mi.) n. of the Pacific Border Crossing to 1395 176th St., is a haven for unwanted and abused reptiles and amphibians that once were pets and cannot be returned to their wilderness environments. Allow 1 hour minimum. Tues.-Sun. 10:30-4:30. Admission $4.50; over 59 and students with ID $3.95; ages 3-12, $2.95. AE, MC, VI. Phone (604) 538-1711.

SURREY MUSEUM AND ARCHIVES, 6022 176th St., has period room displays of pioneer history, Northwest Coast Indian basketry and archeological material. Extensive document and photograph archives also are featured. Located at 13723

Crescent Rd., the Historic Stewart Farmhouse is open for viewing. Allow 1 hour minimum. Museum open Tues.-Sat. 9-4. Archives open Tues.-Sat. 10-4. Farmhouse open Tues.-Fri. 10-4, Sat.-Sun. noon-4. Donations. Phone (604) 502-6456.

WEST VANCOUVER (G-11)

pop. 40,900

ROCKWOOD ADVENTURES RAINFOREST WALKS departs from downtown hotels and takes visitors to area ecological systems for half-day and full-day guided nature walks. Destinations include Lynn Canyon, a rain forest in Capilano River Canyon, a coastal forest at Burrard Inlet and Mount Gardner on Bowen Island. Trips daily Mar.-Oct. Fee $45-$190. Reservations are required. MC, VI. Phone (604) 926-7705 or (888) 236-6606.

This ends listings for the Vancouver Vicinity.
The following page resumes the alphabetical listings of
cities in British Columbia.

VANDERHOOF (E-4)
pop. 4,400, elev. 915 m/2,050'

When the last spike of the railroad was driven in 1914, the Grand Trunk Pacific Development Company offered land for sale. The decision of where to put the new settlement in the wilderness was decided by Herbert Vanderhoof, a railroad employee, and a town was built in just a few weeks. The site, unfortunately, was a poor choice, as the land flooded every spring. In 1919 the townspeople moved to higher ground on the opposite side of the tracks.

Mr. Vanderhoof's legacy to the town is its name, Dutch for "of the farm." The name is fitting, as farming has always been an economic mainstay in the area.

Vanderhoof & District Chamber of Commerce: 2353 Burrard Ave., P.O. Box 126, Vanderhoof, BC, Canada V0J 3A0; phone (250) 567-2124.

VANDERHOOF HERITAGE VILLAGE MUSEUM COMPLEX, w. on Hwy. 16 to 478 W. First St., is a collection of reconstructed buildings depicting rural agriculture in the 1920s. Among the buildings restored and open are the 1914 Board of Trade Building, a cafe, an ice-cream parlor, a police office, a 1914 jail cell and a home typical of those built in the area by early Mennonite settlers. In the town square are examples of farm machines and equipment. Food is available. Allow 30 minutes minimum. Daily 9-7, Victoria Day weekend-Labour Day. Donations. Phone (250) 567-2991.

VERNON (C-9)
pop. 31,800, elev. 383 m/1,256'

At the confluence of five valleys and bounded by three lakes, Vernon is an important shipping and trading center for the surrounding area. On Hwy. 97 at 25th Avenue, Polson Park encompasses a Japanese garden, a Chinese tea house and a floral clock made of 3,500 plants.

Several recreational opportunities are available at nearby Ellison Provincial Park *(see Recreation Chart and the AAA/CAA Western Canada and Alaska CampBook)* and Kalamalka Lake Provincial Park *(see Recreation Chart).*

Silver Star Provincial Park *(see Recreation Chart)* offers mountain bicycle tours from late June to mid-September. A chairlift to the top of Silver Star Mountain operates daily, July 1 to mid-Sept.

For relaxation, the Kalamalka Lake viewpoint, 5 kilometres (3 mi.) south of 25th Avenue on Hwy. 97, provides an excellent view of the lake.

Vernon Travel InfoCentre: 6326 Hwy. 97N, Box 520, Vernon, BC, Canada V1T 6M4; phone (250) 542-1415.

[SAVE] **ATLANTIS WATERSLIDES AND RECREATIONS LTD.,** 8 km (5 mi.) n. on Hwy. 97A at Pleasant Valley Rd., has a waterslide with 10 flumes of varying lengths and slopes, a giant hot tub, miniature golf and a picnic area. Food is available. Allow 2 hours, 30 minutes minimum. Daily 10-8, late June-Labour Day. Admission $15.50; ages 4-9, $9.25; over 65, $5.50; family rate (two adults and two children) $45. MC, VI. Phone (250) 549-4121.

[SAVE] **HISTORIC O'KEEFE RANCH,** 12 km (7 mi.) n. on Hwy. 97, is the site of one of the earliest cattle empires in the Okanagan Valley. The 1867 O'Keefe homestead has several original buildings furnished in period, including a mansion, a church and a general store. Guides are available. Allow 1 hour, 30 minutes minimum. Daily 9-5, May 1-Thanksgiving. Admission $6; over 64, $5; ages 6-18, $4; family rate $18. MC, VI. Phone (250) 542-7868.

INTERIOR SPACE AND SCIENCE CENTRE, 2704 Hwy. 6, in Polson Park, offers hands-on exhibits that focus on such topics as rocks, fossils, illusions, recycling and the environment. Allow 1 hour minimum. Tues.-Sun. 10-5; closed holidays. Admission $5; over 54 and ages 7-17, $4. Phone (250) 545-3644.

VERNON ART GALLERY, 3228 31st Ave. on the ground level of the Parkade Bldg., has two exhibition rooms featuring works of local, regional and nationally known artists. Allow 30 minutes minimum. Mon.-Fri. 10-5, Sat. 11-4. Donations. Parking 75c per hour. Phone (250) 545-3173.

VERNON MUSEUM AND ARCHIVES, 3009 32nd Ave., displays local and natural history items, Indian artifacts and period costumes and furniture. Archives and a research facility also are on the premises. Allow 1 hour minimum. Mon.-Sat. 10-5; closed holidays. Donations. Phone (250) 542-3142.

RECREATIONAL ACTIVITIES
Skiing

- **Silver Star Mountain Resort**, 22 km (15 mi.) e. on Silver Star Rd., Box 3002, Silver Star Mountain, BC, Canada V1B 3M1. Daily 8:30-3:30, mid-Nov. to mid-Apr.; 11-6, July-Sept. Phone (250) 542-0224 for information, or (800) 663-4431 for reservations.

Victoria

"To realize Victoria," Rudyard Kipling wrote, "you must take all that the eye admires in Bournemouth, Torquay, the Isle of Wight, the Happy Valley at Hong Kong, the Doon, Sorrento, Camp's Bay, add reminiscences of the Thousand Islands and arrange the whole around the Bay of Naples with some Himalayas for the background."

Yet the capital of British Columbia remains quintessentially British. Along with its tearooms, double-decker buses, horse-drawn tallyho carriages and shops that sell china and woolens, Victoria proudly claims another, much older culture. Totem poles can be seen throughout local parks, reflecting the city's dual heritage.

Regarded as Canada's gentlest city, Victoria has uncluttered streets, gardens that bloom year-round and hotels that have been serving high tea for decades. Sharing a passion for gardening, Victoria residents tend their prim English gardens. The city's innumerable flower beds and hanging baskets, nurtured by the mild climate brought by the California Current, bloom in bright displays while the rest of Canada shivers.

The heart of the city curves around the stone-walled Inner Harbour, alive with bobbing pleasure craft, fishing boats and coastal shipping vessels. Facing the harbor are the Parliament Buildings and the blocklong, ivy-covered Empress Hotel.

Emily Carr, a native of Victoria, devoted her artistic career to capturing on canvas the brilliant totem poles carved by the vanishing Indian civilizations of the Pacific coast. Like those she found in deserted Indian villages, the fanciful totems in Thunderbird Park evoke the highly developed ancient culture that dominated the area long before Victoria was settled in the mid-19th century.

Fort Victoria was built by Hudson's Bay Co. in 1843. Six years later Vancouver Island became a crown colony, and as British Columbia's only port, it became a passage to the Cariboo goldfields on the mainland in 1858. Violence around Bastion Square was so commonplace during this rowdy boomtown period that the *Victoria Gazette* reported no deaths "from natural causes in the city during the last 30 days." Local politicians supposedly settled their debates with fist fights on Government Street.

After the gold fever broke, Victoria began to assume its characteristic cool reserve. Lured by modest land prices, English settlers developed their queen's namesake city into a thriving government and commercial center. In 1868 Victoria became the capital of the newly joined crown colonies of Vancouver Island and British Columbia.

Since commercial supremacy passed to Vancouver after the completion of the Canadian Pacific Railway, Victoria has adopted a slower pace with few heavy industries. Victoria's harbor is a center for commercial trade. Lumber and fishing also contribute to the bustle of this port. The dry dock at the Canadian Forces Base-Pacific Command is one of the world's largest.

The city's strong tourism industry is buoyed by the continuous stream of travelers who come by ferry from Washington and throughout British Columbia.

Whether or not Victoria is more British than Britain remains an ongoing debate among Victoria's residents. Few would contest, however, that nature's blessings have endowed the city with ample charm in its own right. No one understood this better than its native Indians, whose awesome totems continue to speak the land's wonder.

Approaches
By Car

Victoria is the western terminus of the 7,760-kilometre (4,850-mi.) Trans-Canada Highway. The highway traverses the mainland to Horseshoe Bay in West Vancouver and resumes at the Nanaimo ferry terminal. It then proceeds south along the island's eastern shore to Victoria. Hwy. 17, the other major artery into the city, connects Victoria with the ferry terminals at Swartz Bay and Sidney on the Saanich Peninsula.

By Boat

Several ferry systems connect Vancouver Island and Victoria with mainland Canada and the United States. The most direct route is the Tsawwassen-Swartz Bay automobile/passenger ferry service used by the intercity buses between Vancouver and Victoria. British Columbia Ferries *(see color ad p. 170)* also connects Nanaimo, 111 kilometres (69 mi.) north of Victoria, to Horseshoe Bay in West Vancouver. Phone (250) 386-3431 for ferry information.

Ferries linking the southern end of the island and Victoria with the United States include Black Ball Transport Inc., (250) 386-2202, from Port Angeles, Wash.; and Washington State Ferries, (250) 381-1551, from Anacortes, Wash., to Sidney. Reservations are available for the Anacortes, Wash., to Sydney route; phone 1 day in advance to determine estimated waiting time.

Connecting Seattle and Victoria is the high-speed passenger ferry, the *Victoria Clipper (see color ad p. 171)*; phone (250) 382-8100.

Departing from the north end of the island at Port Hardy, British Columbia Ferries' vessels voyage through the Inside Passage to Prince Rupert, where they connect with the Alaska State Ferry system.

(continued on p. 166)

The Informed Traveler

City Population: 73,500

Elevation: 17m/56 ft.

Sales Tax: British Columbia's provincial sales tax is 7 percent. A Room Tax of 10 percent on lodgings also is levied in the Victoria area.

WHOM TO CALL

Emergency: 911

Police (nonemergency): (250) 995-7654

Time and Temperature: (250) 656-3978

Hospitals: Royal Jubilee Hospital, (250) 370-8000; Victoria General Hospital, (250) 727-4212.

WHERE TO LOOK

Newspapers

Victoria's daily paper is the *Times-Colonist,* which is distributed in the morning.

Radio and TV

Victoria radio stations CKKQ (100.3 FM), CFAX (1070 AM) and CKXM (1200 AM) have news and weather reports.

The major TV stations are BCTV, CBC, CHEK and UTV; channels vary by district. For a complete list of television programs consult the Friday newspaper.

Visitor Information

The Victoria Travel InfoCentre provides maps and brochures outlining various self-guiding walking and driving tours. The center is open daily 9-9, late May to mid-Oct.; 9-5, rest of year. Contact 812 Wharf St., Victoria, BC, Canada V8W 1T3; phone (250) 953-2033.

Victoria Today is a monthly publication with information to orient visitors.

TRANSPORTATION

Air Travel

Victoria International Airport is 20 kilometres (12 mi.) north on Hwy. 17 (Patricia Bay Highway). Air Canada makes frequent flights to Victoria from Vancouver and Seattle. International air connections are made in Vancouver.

Airport Bus Service runs between the airport and downtown hotels; phone (250) 386-2525. Fare $13, under 6 free.

Rental Cars

Auto rental agencies include Hertz, 9429 Canora Rd. and 655 Douglas St., which offers discounts to AAA and CAA members; phone (250) 656-2312 or 360-2822, or (800) 263-0600 in Canada, or (800) 654-3080 out of Canada. Additional agencies are listed in the telephone directory.

Rail Service

From its depot at 450 Pandora Ave., Via Rail has weekday passenger service between Victoria and Courtenay; phone (250) 383-4324 or (800) 561-8630.

Buses

Pacific Coach Lines, 700 Douglas St., provides daily bus service between Vancouver and Victoria via British Columbia Ferry. The vessels transport buses and personal vehicles; phone (250) 385-4411.

Taxis

Taxis charge $2.15 minimum plus $1.30 per kilometre (.6 mi.). Companies include Blue Bird Cabs, (250) 382-4235; Empress Taxi, (250) 381-2222; and Victoria Taxi, (250) 383-7111.

Public Transport

BC Transit provides bus service for Greater Victoria. Buses serve the downtown area 6:30 a.m.-midnight. Fare $1.75; senior citizens, students and children $1.10. Buses run frequently between downtown and the ferry terminal. For route information phone (250) 382-6161.

Island Coach Lines provides bus transportation between Victoria and Campbell River; Nanaimo; Port Alberni; Port Hardy, with connections to the *Queen of the North* ferry; and Port McNeill. For information phone (250) 385-4411.

Boats

Several ferry systems make connections with mainland Canada and the United States. *See Approaches By Boat for details.*

Destination Victoria

*T*he British legacy is indelibly stamped on the city. Here you will find massive stone castles, palatial government buildings, quaint cottages and gardens that bloom almost all year.

*B*ut look closer–another culture has left its mark: Native Indian icons are displayed with equal prominence throughout Victoria.

Butchart Gardens, Brentwood Bay. One of the Victoria vicinity's "must see" gardens dates to 1904. (See listing page 173)

Miniature World, Victoria. Elaborately detailed dollhouses and other diminutives are among the delightful displays here. (See listing page 168)

BRITISH COLUMBIA
WASHINGTON

Sidney

Saanichton
Brentwood Bay

Victoria 17

Sooke

View
Royal

CANADA
UNITED STATES

Parliament Buildings and totem poles. Symbols of a dual heritage share the spotlight in Victoria. (See listing page 169)

See Vicinity map page 166

Royal Roads University. Although it is not the only castle in Victoria, this one has the distinction of housing academia. (See listing page 169)

*P*laces included in this AAA Destination City:

Information can be obtained from the British Columbia Ferries office, (250) 386-3431, 1112 Fort St., Victoria, BC, Canada V8V 4V2; or from the Ministry of Tourism, (250) 474-2152, 812 Wharf St., Victoria, BC, Canada V8W 1T3.

Getting Around

Street System

Most traffic activity is on Wharf, Government and Belleville streets, which embrace the Inner Harbour. Ferries arrive from Port Angeles, Wash., all year and from Seattle in summer. The main east-west streets are Yates, Fort and Johnson. Pandora Avenue, renamed Oak Bay Avenue in midtown, crosses the city from the Inner Harbour to Oak Bay.

Major north-south thoroughfares are Blanshard Street (Hwy. 17) and Douglas Street (Hwy. 1), which begins at Victoria's southern coast along the Juan de Fuca Strait. Dallas Road borders the shore and continues as Beach Drive along Victoria's eastern coast. Many Victoria streets are one-way.

Parking

On-street parking is controlled by meters and posted restrictions Mon.-Sat. 9-6. Vehicles parked on specially posted blocks are subject to towing during rush hours. Downtown off-street parking is available in civic parkades and shopping center lots.

What To See

ANNE HATHAWAY'S COTTAGE, 429 Lampson St. at Olde England Inn, includes replicas of William Shakespeare's birthplace, the Harvard House and The Olde Curiosity Shoppe in an English village. Armor, crossbows, flintlocks and 16th- and 17th-century furniture are displayed. Guided tours are given daily 9-7, May-Sept.; 10-4, rest of year. Hours may vary; phone ahead. Closed Dec. 25. Admission $8; over 59, $7; ages 14-18, $6.25; ages 7-13, $5; family rate $23. AE, DI, DS, MC, VI. Phone (250) 388-4353.

SAVE **ART GALLERY OF GREATER VICTORIA,** 1040 Moss St., mounts contemporary, traditional and Asian exhibitions, including many paintings by Emily Carr. Mon.-Sat. 10-5 (also Thurs. 5-9), Sun. 1-5; closed Jan. 1, Nov. 11 and Dec. 25. Admission $5, over 64 and students with ID $3, under 12 free. Admission by donation Mon. MC, VI. Phone (250) 384-4101.

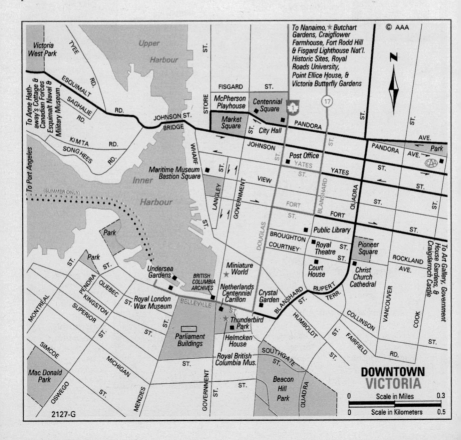

DOWNTOWN VICTORIA

2127-G

© AAA

BASTION SQUARE, overlooking the harbor, is the site where James Douglas established Fort Victoria in 1843. Restored and preserved buildings from the 19th-century boom days surround a courtyard plaza.

BEACON HILL PARK, 74 hectares (183 acres) at Douglas and Dallas sts., comprises attractive flowerbeds, small lakes, playing fields and lawns that slope to the sea, and a totem pole carved by Chief Mungo Martin. Daily dawn-dusk. Free.

BRITISH COLUMBIA ARCHIVES, in Heritage Court at 655 Belleville St., has extensive public records available to those conducting historical, genealogical or other research. The archives are open to the public Mon.-Fri. 9:30-4:45. A photo identification card is required. Free. Phone (250) 387-5885.

★ **BUTCHART GARDENS—**
see Brentwood Bay p. 173.

CANADIAN FORCES BASE ESQUIMALT NAVAL & MILITARY MUSEUM, 6 km. (4 mi.) w. on Esquimalt Rd., then n. on Admirals Rd. to the main gate of Naden, preserves and displays historic artifacts, documents and photographs relating to the naval and military heritage of the area. Allow 2 hours minimum. Mon.-Fri. 10-3:30; closed holidays. Free. Phone (250) 363-4312.

Esquimalt Navy Base Summer Bus Tour, departing from 1234 Wharf St. downtown, is a 2-hour tour of the base. The bus also passes the harbor, where navy warships can be seen. Departures are daily at 10, June-Aug. Free. Phone (250) 363-7060.

CHRIST CHURCH CATHEDRAL (Anglican-Episcopal), Quadra and Rockland sts., is reminis-

cent of the great Gothic churches of the Middle Ages. Originally founded in 1856, the present cathedral is the third church built on this site. Started in the late 1920s and completed in 1986, it is one of Canada's largest cathedrals. The bells are replicas of those at Westminster Abbey in London. Daily 8:30-6. Free. Phone (250) 383-2714.

CRAIGDARROCH CASTLE, 1050 Joan Crescent St., is a sandstone castle built in the late 1880s for Robert Dunsmuir, a Scottish immigrant who attained wealth and fame through politics and industry on Vancouver Island. Dunsmuir died before the castle was completed, but his widow and three of their 10 children moved in.

Since Mrs. Dunsmuir's death in 1908, the castle has served diverse functions. It was a convalescent home for soldiers following World War I, Victoria College 1921-46, the Victoria School Board office until 1968 and the Victoria Conservatory of Music until 1979.

Visitors can appreciate the castle's stained-glass windows, intricate woodwork and Victorian furnishings representing late 19th-century lifestyles. There are numerous staircases throughout, but no elevators. Allow 1 hour minimum. Daily 9-7, June 15-Labour Day; 10-4:30, rest of year. Closed Jan. 1 and Dec. 25-26. Admission $8; students with ID $5; ages 6-12, $2. MC, VI. Phone (250) 592-5323.

CRYSTAL GARDEN, 713 Douglas St., is a tropical conservatory with exotic plants and trees. The garden is embellished by winding walkways, a stream and a waterfall. Some of the world's smallest monkeys are displayed in addition to tropical butterflies. An aviary features many rare and colorful birds. Allow 30 minutes minimum. Daily 8:30-8, July-Aug.; 9-6, Apr.-June and

Sept.-Oct.; 10-4:30, rest of year. Closed Dec. 25. Admission $7.50; over 65, $6.50; ages 5-16, $4. MC, VI. Phone (250) 381-1213.

EMILY CARR HOUSE, 207 Government St., was built in 1864 a few blocks from the harbor. Birthplace of artist and writer Emily Carr, the Victorian house is restored to the ambiance the Carr family experienced in the 1870s. Family possessions, including some of Emily's early pottery and sculpture are displayed. Daily 10-5, mid-May to mid-Oct. Admission $5; over 54 and students with ID $4; under 18, $3; family rate $12. MC, VI. Phone (250) 383-5843.

GOVERNMENT HOUSE GARDENS, 1401 Rockland Ave., is 14 hectares (35 acres) of formal lawn, perennial flowerbeds, blossoming shrubs, ivy, heather, azaleas and rhododendrons. Of particular note are a sunken rose garden and lily pond. The lieutenant governor's residence is closed to the public. The gardens are most resplendent in summer. Daily dawn-dusk. Free.

HELMCKEN HOUSE is next to the Royal British Columbia Museum, behind Thunderbird Park. Built in 1852, it is considered to be the oldest house in British Columbia. The house was the residence of John Sebastian Helmcken, a doctor and clerk for Hudson's Bay Co. at Fort Victoria and one of the country's Fathers of the Confederation. The house is refurbished and displays many original furnishings as well as a fine collection of period medical instruments.

Actors portraying Helmcken family members and friends are on hand during the Christmas season to provide a glimpse of the doctor's life. An audiotape tour is available. Allow 30 minutes minimum. Daily 10-5, Victoria Day-late Oct.; noon-4, rest of year. Closed mid-Nov. through

Dec. 21. Admission $5; senior citizens and students with ID $4; ages 6-12, $3; family rate $12. Phone (250) 361-0021.

SAVE **MARITIME MUSEUM OF BRITISH COLUMBIA,** 28 Bastion Sq., explores the Pacific Northwest's maritime heritage through ship models, figureheads, ships' tools and naval uniforms. Also featured is the 1860 *Tilikum*, an 11-metre (36-ft.) dugout canoe converted to a schooner, which sailed from Victoria to England 1901-04. Exhibits are housed in an 1889 building, which features one of the oldest operating birdcage elevators in North America.

Allow 1 hour minimum. Daily 9:30-4:30; closed Dec. 25. Admission $5; over 64, $4; ages 12-18. $3; ages 6-11, $2; family rate $13. MC, VI. Phone (250) 385-4222.

SAVE ★ **MINIATURE WORLD,** in the Empress Hotel at 649 Humboldt St., uses animation, lighting and sound effects to bring more than 80 highly detailed miniature scenes to life. Displays include a circus, two of the world's largest dollhouses and a futuristic space diorama. Visitors also can view scenes illustrating historic battles, fairy tales, nursery rhymes, "Gulliver's Travels" and novels by Charles Dickens. The Great Canadian Railway exhibit re-creates rail transportation in late-19th-century Canada.

Allow 1 hour minimum. Daily 8:30 a.m.-9 p.m., July-Sept.; 9-5, rest of year. Closed Dec. 25. Admission $8; ages 12-17, $7; ages 5-11, $6. AE, MC, VI. Phone (250) 385-9731. *See color ad p. 167.*

THE NETHERLANDS CENTENNIAL CARILLON, corner of Government and Belleville sts., houses 62 bells donated by British Columbians of Dutch

origin as a tribute to the 1967 Canadian Confederation Centennial. Recitals are held periodically April through December. It is the largest carillon in Canada. Free. Phone (250) 387-1616.

PARLIAMENT BUILDINGS overlook the Inner Harbour and yacht basin. The seat of British Columbia's Legislative Assembly, the buildings have elaborately carved facades and are surrounded by 5 hectares (12 acres) of lawns, gardens, fountains and statues of dignitaries. The rooms have mosaic tile floors, rotundas, stained-glass windows, woodcarvings and murals. Guided tours, conducted in several languages, are given daily, June 1-Labour Day; Mon.-Fri., rest of year. Contact the Tour Coordinator office for tour times. Closed winter holidays. Phone (250) 387-3046.

POINT ELLICE HOUSE, 2616 Pleasant St., was built in 1861 and contains many of its original furnishings. The rambling Italianate house is surrounded by lawns and a restored 19th-century garden. Self-guiding audiotapes are available. Tea is served in the garden by servers dressed in period costumes noon-4.

Allow 30 minutes minimum. Daily 10-5, mid-May to mid.-Sept.; closed Dec. 25. Admission $5; over 64 and students with ID $4; ages 6-12, $3. MC, VI. Phone (250) 380-6506.

★ **ROYAL BRITISH COLUMBIA MUSEUM,** next to the Parliament Buildings at 675 Belleville St., has three floors of displays about the human and natural history of British Columbia. A turn-of-the-20th-century frontier town has a theater with silent movies, a steam train pulling into its station and the aroma of apple pie wafting from a kitchen. An old-growth rain forest is highlighted by live plants and ocean animals. Other features include a simulated journey into the ocean's three zones as well as an Indian village.

A National Geographic IMAX Theater is on site. Opportunities to experience British Columbia first-hand are offered by the museum April through October. Ecologically sensitive tours are offered; for additional information phone (250) 387-5745.

Museum open daily 9-5. Theater open daily 10-9. Closed Jan. 1 and Dec. 25. Museum $9.65; over 64, $6.65; ages 6-18, $4; family rate $23.35. Theater $9; over 64, $8; ages 6-18, $6. Combination passes for museum and theater are available. MC, VI. Phone (250) 387-3701 or (888) 447-7977.

Thunderbird Park, at the corner of Douglas and Belleville sts., is known for its collection of Indian totem poles. Many of the poles are crested with carvings of the mythical thunderbird, thought by some to be a representation of the California condor. According to tribal legend, the Indians were inspired by this creature and believed that thunder issued from the movement of its wings and lightning from its eyes. Carvers can be seen at work in summer. Park open daily dawn-dusk. Free.

SAVE **ROYAL LONDON WAX MUSEUM,** 470 Belleville in the Inner Harbour opposite the Parliament Buildings, presents some 300 wax figures in more than 51 scenes. A featured exhibit highlights events of the 20th century. Daily 9-7:30, July-Aug.; 9:30-5, rest of year. Admission $8; over 54, $7; students with ID $6.50; ages 6-12, $3; family rate (four persons) $22. AE, DI, MC, VI. Phone (250) 388-4461.

ROYAL ROADS UNIVERSITY, at 2005 Sooke Rd., was one of Canada's three military colleges devoted to the training of officer cadets. Hatley Castle, built around 1900 as the private estate for British Columbia's former lieutenant governor James Dunsmuir, now houses university offices. A museum chronicles the history of the Dunsmuir family and Royal Roads Military College.

The 262-hectare (647-acre) grounds have a formal lawn and Japanese and Italian gardens. Grounds open daily 24 hours. Museum Mon.-Fri. 1-4. Free. Phone (250) 391-2511.

UNDERSEA GARDENS, 490 Belleville St., is an observation room on the sea bottom, where visitors can view native marine life through large underwater windows. Daily 10-7, June-Aug.; 9-5, rest of year. Admission $7; over 64, $6.25; ages

12-17, $5; ages 5-11, $3.50. MC, VI. Phone (250) 382-5717.

UNIVERSITY OF VICTORIA, on McKenzie Ave. at Gordon Head Rd., has a 160-hectare (395-acre) campus that includes the Mystic Vale Ecological Protection Area, several totems carved by local artists and Finnerty Gardens, known for its collection of more than 200 rhododendron species. A self-guiding walking tour brochure is available. Grounds open daily 24 hours. Tours are given Mon.-Fri. 8-4:30 by appointment. Free. Parking $5. Reservations are required for tours. Phone (250) 721-7645.

What To Do

Sightseeing

Boat Tours

Sightseers using Victoria as a base for their travels can explore the Gulf Islands and Vancouver by ferry from Swartz Bay, north of Victoria via Hwy. 17; for schedule and toll phone the British Columbia Ferry Service *(see color ad)* at (250) 386-3431.

Opportunities for whale watching are offered by several boating companies, the oldest of which is Seacoast Expeditions, 1655 Ash Rd.; phone (250) 383-2254.

Bus and Carriage Tours

Guided tours of the city in red double-decker buses from London enhance Victoria's British atmosphere. Many of these tour operators are found along Belleville and Menzies streets by the harbor. ⟨SAVE⟩ Gray Line, 710 Douglas, (250) 388-5248, conducts bus tours.

Enchanted Tours of Victoria conducts narrated sightseeing tours daily in motorcoaches; guests are picked up at their hotels. Different versions of city tours and excursions to Butchart Gardens are offered lasting 2 to 5 hours. Phone (250) 475-3396.

The Tallyho offers horse-drawn narrated tours of the city from late March through September (weather permitting); phone (250) 383-5067. Black Beauty Victorian Carriage Tours offers horse-drawn carriage rides through downtown and Beacon Hill Park; phone (250) 361-1220. Both tours leave from the corner of Belleville and Menzies streets.

Driving Tours

The Greater Victoria Visitors Information Centre has information about such scenic drives as Marine Drive along the shoreline, a trip to Sooke Harbour on the west coast and the Malahat Drive, which runs along the east coast and reaches an elevation of 381 metres (1,250 ft.). The trip to Butchart Gardens is one of the most popular drives, following Hwy. 17 and Hwy. 17A through the rural communities and pastoral valleys of the Saanich Peninsula.

Walking Tours

Victoria is the perfect size for visitors keen on walking. A favorite thoroughfare of strollers and shoppers is Government Street, graced by banners and five-globe Victorian lampposts supporting baskets of geraniums and petunias.

Sports and Recreation

The English spirit still is manifest in such games as **lawn bowling** behind the Crystal Garden and **cricket** at Beacon Hill Park. Any notion, however, that Victoria's sports are too staid is dispelled quickly by a **box lacrosse** game. This offspring of the Indian game of *baggataway* is a rough-and-tumble version of field lacrosse confined to a smaller, enclosed area. Canada's Parliament designated boxla, as it also is called, the national sport in 1867. The game is played from April to August at Memorial Arena, 1925 Blanshard.

All-star **wrestling** and **ice hockey,** two other spectator sports that hardly could be considered sedate, also are held at the arena.

Water sports have obvious appeal in this island city. The wide variety of game fish around southern Vancouver Island includes rockfish, lingcod, sole and flounder; fishing licenses are required. Surf **fishing** often yields rewarding catches of salmon and black sea bass. Clamming and oyster harvesting are popular activities on any of the

Gulf Islands, which are accessible by ferry from Swartz Bay.

Oak Bay Marina, 1327 Beach Dr., offers fishing charters at an hourly rate in the protective waters off Discovery Island. Fishing equipment, rental boats, a tackle shop and marine store are available; phone (250) 598-3369. Other nearby marinas include Angler's Anchorage Marina, 933 Marchant, Brentwood Bay; North Saanich Marina, 1949 Marina Way, Sidney; and the West Bay Marina, 453 Head St.

Sailing is enjoyed in the Strait of Georgia and the Saanich Inlet. Sailing excursions, including day trips and cruising vacations, are offered by Alberta Yachts; phone (403) 228-4641. Uplands Park on Oak Bay is equipped with boat ramps. Fine beaches border Dallas Road and Beach Drive.

With its scenic coastal location and balmy climate, Victoria offers excellent playing conditions for **golf**. On a peninsula jutting into the Juan de Fuca Strait, Victoria Golf Club is open to members of other clubs.

Other golf clubs include Ardmore (nine holes), 930 Ardmore Dr., Central Saanich; Cedar Hill (18 holes), 1400 Derby Rd.; Cordova Bay (18 holes), 5333 Cordova Bay Rd.; Glen Meadows (18 holes), near Sidney; Gorge Vale (18 holes), 1005 Craigflower Rd.; Olympic View Golf Course (18 holes), 643 Latoria Rd.; Prospect Lake (18 holes), 4633 Prospect Lake Rd.; Royal Colwood (18 holes), 629 Goldstream Ave.; Royal Oak Golf Club (nine holes), 540 Marsett Pl.; and Uplands (18 holes), 3300 Cadboro Bay Rd.

Many parks are scattered throughout Victoria and its surrounding municipalities of Oak Bay, Saanich and Esquimalt. Some offer **swimming**, such as Thetis Lake Park, Mount Work Park, Elk/Beaver Lake Park, Willows Beach Park and Island View Beach Park. Swimmers also might wish to try the Crystal Pool in Central Park.

Hiking, nature and horse trails are found at several parks administered by the Capital Regional Park Division; phone (250) 478-3344. Bamberton Provincial Park (see *Recreation Chart and the AAA/CAA Western Canada and Alaska CampBook*) offers developed recreational facilities, including **camping**.

Hiking trails and floating walkways weave through the Swan Lake-Christmas Hill Nature Sanctuary, 6.5 kilometres (4 mi.) north via the Patricia Bay Highway. Excellent views of Victoria and the sea are at Mount Douglas, Mount Tolmie and Beacon Hill Park.

Shopping

Lined with shops carrying English tweeds and fine china, Government Street maintains Victoria's heritage as a trading post of the British Empire. Such shops as E.A. Morris Tobacconist have distinguished Government Street since the 19th century. Established in 1833, Rogers' Chocolate Shop is a Victoria institution that counts British royalty in its clientele. The Rogers' factory, behind the store at 913 Government St., still produces its renowned bittersweet chocolate according to a guarded recipe.

Shoppers determined to bring home something other than a few extra pounds might want to explore the craft and specialty shops in the renovated squares and malls off Government Street. More than 30 quaint stores and restaurants in revitalized old buildings highlight Market Square, bounded by Johnson, Pandora and Store streets.

Trounce Alley, in the downtown core, is a hideaway of eclectic shops. Shops of mid-19th-century architecture display modern items in Bastion Square, once a hangout for prospectors and drifters. An attractive shopping arcade is in Centennial Square off Douglas Street. Nootka Court between Courtney and Humboldt streets contains small arts and crafts shops.

Popular items available in Victoria include handwoven woolens from Ireland and England, hand-knit Cowichan Indian sweaters, Eskimo jade sculpture and Northwest Indian masks and prints. The Bay department stores, 1701 and 3125 Douglas St., sell authentic Cowichan sweaters. Other major department stores in Victoria are Eaton's, 1150 Douglas St., and Simpsons-Sears, 3190 Shelbourne St.

In keeping with its Victorian image, Victoria has more than 50 antique shops. Many are found

along Government and Fort streets and Oak Bay Avenue.

Theater and Concerts

McPherson Playhouse in Centennial Square is the center of Vancouver Island's regional and professional theater. The restored old theater regularly presents noontime concerts and musical comedy productions in the evening; phone (250) 386-6121. The Pacific Opera Society, (250) 385-0222, performs at the McPherson as well.

The Royal Theatre on Broughton Street is the home of the Victoria Symphony Orchestra, (250) 386-6121, which offers a pop and masterworks series September through April. The Victoria Conservatory of Music sometimes offers performances; phone (250) 386-5311. Free outdoor concerts and events are presented at Beacon Hill Park and Centennial Square from May to September; phone (250) 381-2341.

Comedy revues and music hall shows also are staged frequently at the Belfry, (250) 385-6815, 1291 Gladstone, and the Royal Theatre, (250) 386-6121, 805 Broughton. The University of Victoria Auditorium on Finnerty Road also presents various cultural events; phone (250) 721-8480. Butchart Gardens mounts musical stage shows during the summer. Kaleidoscope Theatre, an open-air theater at the Inner Harbour, also offers summer productions.

Top-name entertainers, rock groups and other performers draw large audiences to Memorial Arena, 1925 Blanshard. A carillon at the Parliament Buildings can be heard daily at 3 during the summer.

Special Events

As a city of traditions, Victoria celebrates many events and festivals year after year. Victoria Day, a Canadian national holiday, launches a week of festivities highlighted by a parade. The weekend following Victoria Day features the classic Swiftsure Race, which has drawn an armada of more than 450 sailboats from all over the world since 1930. The Highlander Games take place in mid-May. The performing arts provide a theme for the Victoria Harbour Festival the last week in May.

Victoria Folkfest, held the last week in June, shows the costumes, dances and music of Victoria's cultural mélange. The Inner Harbour is the site of the Classic Boat Festival from late August to early September.

Autumn shows off its best colors along the rural Saanich Peninsula, where the Saanich Fair has been held in early September for more than a century. Fall's lower temperatures provide an energy boost for several major sports events, including the Victoria Open PGA Tournament Players Series and the Royal Victoria Marathon.

The Victoria Vicinity

BRENTWOOD BAY (H-10)

★ **BUTCHART GARDENS**, 20 hectares (50 acres) 2 km (1.2 mi.) s. on W. Saanich Rd., then w. to 800 Benvenuto Ave., contains the Rose Garden, Japanese Garden, Italian Garden, Star Pond, Concert Lawn, Show Greenhouse and Ross Fountains. The Sunken Garden was created by the Butcharts on the site of their depleted limestone quarry.

The spring season brings azaleas, tulips, daffodils and other delicate blossoms; breathtaking roses, annuals and perennials bloom in summer; bursts of colorful foliage appear in autumn; and winter's starkness invites crisp strolls. Subtle colored lighting illuminates the gardens June 15 through September 15; from December 1 to January 6 they sparkle with festive lights and decor.

Musical entertainment is offered nightly June through September with fireworks displays Saturday nights in July and August. Food is available.

Allow 2 hours minimum. Gardens open daily at 9; closing times vary depending on the season. Admission $16.50; ages 13-17, $8.25; ages 5-12, $2. Reduced admission Nov.-Mar. AE, MC, VI. Phone (250) 652-4422. *See color ad p. 168.*

[SAVE] **VICTORIA BUTTERFLY GARDENS**, 2 km (1.2 mi.) s. on W. Saanich Rd. and Keating Cross, is an indoor tropical garden containing an array of free-flying birds and butterflies. Displays and guides explain the transformations the butterflies undergo during their life cycle. Food is available. Allow 30 minutes minimum. Daily 9:30-5:30, Mar.-Oct.; otherwise varies. Admission $8; senior citizens and students with ID $7; ages 3-12, $5; family rate $25. MC, VI. Phone (250) 652-3822. *See color ad p. 169.*

FORT RODD HILL AND FISGARD LIGHTHOUSE NATIONAL HISTORIC SITES (H-9)

Fort Rodd Hill, 14.5 kilometres (9 mi.) west of Victoria via Hwy. 1A, was a coastal artillery fort 1895-1956. Of interest are the loophole walls, underground magazines, artillery stores, command posts, barracks and gun and searchlight emplacements. Audiotape and videotape presentations, along with period rooms, depict life at the fort. The 1860 Fisgard Lighthouse, restored to its 1873 appearance, was the first built on this part of the coast. Still operational, the lighthouse has two floors of historical exhibits. A nature trail follows the paths formerly used by soldiers. Historical exhibits also are featured. Picnic facilities are available.

Allow 1 hour, 30 minutes minimum. Park open daily 10-5:30, Mar.-Oct.; 9-4:30, rest of year. Lighthouse and fort exhibits daily 10-5, Mar.-Oct.; 9-4, rest of year. Closed Jan. 1 and Dec. 25-26. Limited services Nov.-Feb. Admission (includes fort and lighthouse) $3; over 64, $2.25; ages 6-16, $1.50; family rate $7.50. MC, VI. Phone (250) 478-5849.

SAANICHTON (H-10)
elev. 58 m/194'

HERITAGE ACRES (SAANICH HISTORICAL ARTIFACTS SOCIETY) is off Hwy. 17, e. on Island View Dr., then n. to 7321 Lochside Dr. The society is dedicated to maintaining artifacts from the area's rural past on 12 hectares (29 acres) of parkland. A museum exhibits historic household items, furnishings and farm equipment. Also part of the complex are a blacksmith's shop, a sawmill, nature trails and a one-room log cabin. Picnicking is permitted.

Allow 30 minutes minimum. Daily 9-4, June-Aug.; 9-noon, rest of year. Closed Dec. 25. Donations. Admission is charged during events held Father's Day weekend and the third weekend in Sept. Phone (250) 652-5522.

SIDNEY (H-10)
pop. 10,700, elev. 9 m/30'

Salish Indians were the earliest known inhabitants of the area now called Sidney. Incorporated into a town in 1967, Sidney is known for its fishing and waterfront activity. Picnicking, beachcombing and camping are popular at Sidney Spit Marine Park. Narrated tours of the town are available June-September from Celebration Carriage Services Ltd.; reservations are recommended. Phone (250) 655-3672.

Saanich Peninsula Chamber of Commerce: 10382 Pat Bay Hwy., P.O. Box 2014, Sidney, BC, Canada V8L 3S3. Phone (250) 656-0525.

BRITISH COLUMBIA AVIATION MUSEUM, Victoria Airport at 1910 Norseman Rd., houses a variety of aircraft and memorabilia. World War II planes and bush planes are on display as well as a model plane exhibit, photographs and aircraft engines. Guided tours are available. Allow 1 hour minimum. Daily 10-4, Apr. 15-Oct. 15; 11-3, rest of year. Closed Jan. 1 and Dec. 25. Admission $4; over 65, $3; under 13 free with adult. VI. Phone (250) 655-3300.

SIDNEY WHALE MUSEUM, 9801 Seaport Pl., traces the evolution of the whale through models, skeletons, murals and audiotape displays in the Marine Mammal Gallery. The Historical Gallery features photographs of and artifacts used by early Sidney inhabitants, including North Saanich Coast Salish natives and settlers from Europe and Asia. Birds and seashore ecology are the subjects of other displays. Allow 1 hour minimum. Daily 10-5, May-Sept.; 10-4, rest of year. Closed Jan. 1 and Dec. 25-26. Admission $4.50; over 64 , college students with ID and under 18, $3. Phone (250) 656-2140.

SOOKE (H-10)
pop. 7,600, elev. 38 m/125'

A natural harbor off the Juan de Fuca Strait, Sooke was discovered and claimed by the Spanish in 1790. The area, soon traded to the British by treaty, was named after a local Indian tribe, T'Soke. It is a popular fishing site and the center of a large forest industry. A scenic portion of Hwy. 14 runs 43 kilometres (27 mi.) east from Sooke to Victoria.

Sooke Travel InfoCentre: 2070 Phillips Rd., Box 774, Sooke, BC, Canada V0S 1N0; phone (250) 642-6351.

SOOKE REGION MUSEUM, 1 km (.6 mi.) e. on Hwy. 14 at 2070 Phillips Rd., illustrates the history and economy of the west coast region. The 1870 Moss Cottage depicts late 19th-century family life. Documentary films are shown and tours are available. In the summer salmon barbecues are scheduled. Allow 30 minutes minimum. Daily 9-6, July-Aug.; Tues.-Sun. 9-5, rest of year. Closed Dec. 25-26. Donations. Phone (250) 642-6351.

VIEW ROYAL (H-10)
pop. 6,400, elev. 22 m/72'

CRAIGFLOWER FARMHOUSE is at the corner of Craigflower and Admirals rds. Built in 1856 on an original homestead, the farmhouse is a fine example of early Georgian architecture. The heavy oak door reinforced with iron studs is a reminder of the British class system. Farm animals, on view in the summer, and a kitchen garden complement the atmosphere.

Allow 30 minutes minimum. Daily noon-4, Victoria Day-Sept. 30. Admission $5; senior citizens and ages 6-18, $3. MC. Phone (250) 383-4627.

This ends listings for the Victoria Vicinity. The following page resumes the alphabetical listings of cities in British Columbia.

VIEW ROYAL—*see Victoria p. 174.*

WARDNER (D-12) pop. 100

KOOTENAY TROUT HATCHERY, 8 km (5 mi.) n. on the e. side of the Kootenay River, annually raises 3 million trout. An aquarium contains native fish, and displays explain fish raising. Allow 30 minutes minimum. Daily 8-4. Free. Phone (250) 429-3214.

WESTBANK (C-9)
pop. 1,300, elev. 411 m/1,348′

Westbank was a link on the fur-trading route from the north-central part of the province, called New Caledonia, to the Columbia River. In the early 1860s fortune seekers en route to the Cariboo gold mines followed the old trail through the Okanagan Valley.

Ideal climatic conditions in the Okanagan Valley nurture Westbank's many orchards and vineyards. Vacationers also are drawn by the favorable weather in the valley. Downhill and cross-country skiing in the surrounding countryside are popular in winter.

Westbank Chamber of Commerce: 2375 Pamela St., Suite 4, Westbank, BC, Canada V4T 2H9; phone (250) 768-3378.

MARINER REEF WATER SLIDES, 5 km (3 mi.) n. on Hwy. 97, offers quad and twisting slides, a tube ride, picnic facilities and two hot tubs which can accommodate 100 people each. Daily 11-8, July 1-Labour Day; Sat.-Sun. 10-6, Victoria Day weekend-June 30. Admission $12.95; ages 7-13, $9.95; ages 4-6, $7.95; spectators $3.95. Rates decrease after 4 p.m.; phone ahead to verify rates. MC, VI. Phone (250) 768-5141 or 768-7600.

OLD MACDONALD'S FARM, 2 km (1.2 mi.) n. on Hwy. 97, features farm animals, many of which can be petted. The 3.5-hectare (9-acre) farm, oriented to children, offers pony rides. Facilities include a miniature golf course, waterslide, trout fishing pond, toy shooting gallery and a picnic area. Allow 3 hours minimum. Daily 9-6, Apr.-Sept. Admission $7.95; over 64 and ages 2-12, $6.95. AE, MC, VI. Phone (250) 768-5167.

WINERIES
• **Mission Hill Vineyards Winery,** 4.5 km (3 mi.) e. off Hwy. 97 via Boucherie Rd., following signs. Tours on the hour daily 10-5, July-Aug. Times vary, rest of year; phone ahead. Phone (250) 768-7611.

WEST VANCOUVER—
see Vancouver p. 160.

WHISTLER (F-12)
pop. 7,200, elev. 640 m/2,009′

Whistler, a popular year-round resort village and skiing destination, is cradled by Whistler and Blackcomb mountains.

Walking trails start at Whistler Village for such destinations as Alta and Lost lakes, nearby alpine meadows and glacier regions. The Valley Trail is available for roller skating, cycling and walking. Day excursions to the southern Cariboo region are available aboard the British Columbia Railway. This railway also makes daily runs to Whistler from North Vancouver; phone (604) 984-5246.

Several golf courses as well as tennis facilities and riding stables provide additional opportunities to enjoy the area in summer. The Whistler River is known for white-water rafting.

For information about the many private sightseeing companies, including float plane services, contact Whistler Resort Association, 4010 Whistler Way, Whistler, BC, Canada V0N 1B0; phone (604) 664-5625 or (800) 944-7853.

BLACKCOMB HORSEDRAWN SLEIGH RIDES, departing from Base II on Blackcomb Mountain, at the end of Glacier Dr., offers tours of the wooded countryside including a stop at a warming cabin, where musical entertainment is provided. Dinner sleigh rides also are available. Trips daily on the hour 5-8, Dec.-Mar. Fare $45; ages 2-11, $25. Phone (604) 932-7631.

Whistler Chamber of Commerce: Hwy. 99 and Lake Placid Rd., P.O. Box 181, Whistler, BC, Canada V0N 2B0; phone (604) 932-5528.

Shopping areas: Whistler Village features more than 150 specialty shops in a pedestrian enclave.

RECREATIONAL ACTIVITIES
Skiing
• **Whistler/Blackcomb Mountain,** Hwy. 99. Write P.O. Box 67, Whistler, BC, Canada V0N 1B0. Other activities are offered. Whistler daily mid-Nov. to early June. Blackcomb mid-Nov. to early Apr. Phone (604) 932-3434 or (800) 766-0449.

Snowmobiling
• **Whistler Snowmobile Tours,** 4314 Main St., Suite 36, Whistler, BC, Canada V0N 1B4. Daily 9-9, Nov.-Apr. Phone (604) 932-4086.

White-water Rafting
• SAVE **Whistler River Adventures,** departing from the base of the Whistler Mountain gondola in Whistler Village. Write P.O. Box 202, Whistler, BC, Canada V0N 1B0. Other activities are offered. Two-hour and full-day trips depart daily May 1 to mid-Sept. (weather permitting). Phone (604) 932-3532 or (888) 932-3532.

WILLIAMS LAKE (F-5) pop. 10,500

The rush for gold brought prospectors to the heart of the Cariboo in the 1860s, but it was the 1920s Canadian Railway push that put Williams Lake on the map. Cattle ranching and timber production now are the economic mainstays.

Williams Lake and District Chamber of Commerce: 1148 South Broadway, Williams Lake, BC, Canada V2G 1A2; phone (250) 392-5025.

[SAVE] **MUSEUM OF THE CARIBOO CHILCOTIN,** 113 N. Fourth Ave., features displays about ranching and rodeo history of the Cariboo Chilcotin. Artifacts and photographs depict the lifestyles of cowboys and ranchers as well as First Nations people. Allow 30 minutes minimum. Mon.-Sat. 10-4, June-Aug.; Tues.-Sat. 11-4, rest of year. Closed Easter, Thanksgiving and Dec. 25. Admission $2, under 13 free. Phone (250) 392-7404.

YALE (C-7)

Settled at the southern entrance to Fraser Canyon, Yale was a major steamship port during the gold rush. Several buildings from the mid-1800s still stand. A hiking trail in the area offer access to views of the canyon.

[SAVE] **YALE MUSEUM AND HISTORIC CHURCH** is at 7 Douglas St. The museum displays artifacts about mining and the lifestyles of the early settlers. The Church of St. John the Divine has served the area since 1860. Guided tours of the old townsite and a cemetery are offered in the summer; phone for schedule. Gold panning instructions and trips also are available. Daily 10-5, June-Sept.; Wed.-Sun. 11-4, rest of year. Admission $4.50; over 54 and students with ID $3.50; ages 6-12, $2.50; family rate $11. MC, VI. Phone (604) 863-2324.

RECREATIONAL ACTIVITIES

White-water Rafting

• **Fraser River Raft Expeditions,** 1 km (.6 mi.) w. on Hwy. 1. Write P.O. Box 10, Yale, BC, Canada V0K 2S0. The season is mid-Apr. to mid-Oct.; departure times vary with trip. Phone (604) 863-2336 or (800) 363-7238.

★YOHO NATIONAL PARK (A-11)

Elevations in the park range from 1,098 metres (3,600 ft.) at the West Gate of the park to 3,562 metres (11,686 ft.) on Mount Goodsir at the South Tower. Refer to CAA/AAA maps for additional elevation information.

Yoho National Park, reached by hwys. 1 and 93, covers 1,310 square kilometres (507 sq. mi.) just west of the Great Divide and Banff National Park. The word *yoho* is an exclamation of wonder or astonishment in the language of the Cree Indians.

In 1884 the Canadian Pacific Railway laid tracks through Kicking Horse Pass, discovered by Sir James Hector during his search for the best transportation route through the Rockies. The Trans-Canada Highway later was built along this same route.

Yoho Valley, a narrow valley between high, wooded mountain slopes, is 13 kilometres (7.8 mi.) long. Takakkaw Falls ("magnificent" in the Cree language) drops 380 metres (1,265 ft.) in all, its highest sheer fall being 254 metres (833 ft.), making it one of the highest falls in Canada.

Other sights in the park include Lake O'Hara, Natural Bridge, Emerald Lake, Wapta Falls and the Spiral Tunnels of the Canadian Pacific Railway. The lower Spiral Tunnel can be viewed from the Trans-Canada Highway, 7 kilometres (4 mi.) east of Field. The upper Spiral Tunnel can be viewed from the Yoho Valley Road.

The park also contains the Burgess Shale fossil beds, which have more than 120 species of preserved fossils, including rare soft-bodied creatures dating back 515 million years to the Cambrian period. Specimens from the beds are displayed at the park's visitor information center. Access to the fossil beds is limited to guided tours; phone (800) 343-3006.

General Information and Activities

Although the park is open all year, most facilities and interpretive programs operate only during July and August. A park information center on Hwy. 1 at Field is open all year. The Trans-Canada Highway traverses the park and provides access to most of its roads and trails.

There are several campgrounds in the park. Prices range $13-$18 for sites and $4 for firewood. A wilderness pass is required to stay overnight in the backcountry. Passes are $6 per person each night and are available from the visitor information center.

Hiking trails range from nature walks to extended back-country trips; mountain climbers and travelers in the back country may register at the visitor information center or with any park warden. Fishing, particularly rewarding to those in search of char and many other varieties of trout, is by a $13 annual permit, or a $6 weeklong permit.

Horses, canoes and rowboats are available for rent at Emerald Lake. Winter activities include cross-country skiing, snowshoeing, ice climbing and winter camping. *See the Recreation Chart and the AAA/CAA Western Canada and Alaska CampBook.*

ADMISSION to the park is $5; senior citizens $4; ages 6-16, $2.50. The maximum per vehicle charge is $10.

ADDRESS inquiries to the Superintendent, Yoho National Park, P.O. Box 99, Field, BC, Canada V0A 1G0; phone (250) 343-6783.

Manitoba

Location is Everything
Winnipeg's position at the junction of two rivers led to its prominence as a trading post

Nature Made
Lakes, forests, rolling prairies and subarctic tundra are part of Manitoba's landscape

Polar Bears and Beluga Whales
Churchill is the place for viewing these magnificent creatures of the wild

The Water's Fine
Myriad lakes and rivers are popular with anglers, canoeists and boaters

Interpretive Sites
Manitoba's history is remembered at restored forts and trading posts

voice
of the
spirit

aves pound a rock-strewn shore at the narrows of Lake Manitoba, producing a noise oddly like a beating drum. To the Cree Indians, this sound was the great spirit Manitou, whose name was given to the lake, and in 1870, the entire province.

From clear water lapping in giant lakes—Winnipeg, Winnipegosis and Manitoba—to the rustling sigh of wind across golden seas of wheat, the great spirit of this province speaks with many voices and conveys many moods.

It echoes in the plaintive cry of migrating geese winging south and the hoarse chuffing of a protective mother polar bear herding her cubs along Hudson Bay's icy shore.

The spirit sings within a chorus of steel wheels as trains carry freight across

the prairies from west to east and back again. It proclaims itself in the bustling streets of Winnipeg, where sundry languages—French, English, Russian, Chinese and others—blend into a rich, evocative murmur, and laughs amid the joyous din of the city's various celebrations.

Even the silence deep within Manitoba's immense evergreen forests seems heavy with something left unsaid.

A province this vast has a lot to say; make the journey and let it speak to you.

Look north into the night sky. There. See it? A faint glow high above the horizon....

Watch as an arc of yellow light gradually forms. As it drifts upward, shimmering yellow-green streamers rise from it, rippling like a breeze-blown curtain. New arcs appear lined with bright amber streaks that curl like wisps of smoke. Eventually the swirls of color fade and darkness returns, ending your encounter with the aurora borealis.

In Manitoba you won't have to wait long for a repeat performance. This far north you can count on basking in the aurora's eerie luminescence nearly 90 nights a year. Even citizens of Winnipeg, the capital, are often treated to this celestial light show, despite living in the province's extreme south.

Gem of the Prairies

Sky-obscuring pollution may be the bane of many cities, but Winnipeg's clean air isn't likely to spoil your auroral view. And while multihued lights dance overhead, visitors to the "Gem of the Prairies" can enjoy an equally colorful cultural spectrum spread out before them. Home to more than half of all Manitobans, Winnipeg is a city of surprising diversity; the Ellice-Sargent neighborhood alone boasts 43 resident nationalities. Here it's not unusual to find a German butcher shop sandwiched between an Italian clothing store and a Vietnamese restaurant, all within a few steps of a Portuguese cafe.

Finding the cuisine you crave is a snap in this polyglot town. For Italian, follow your nose to the source of the garlic-tinged scents wafting from Corydon Avenue, Winnipeg's Little Italy. Here you'll find delicious pastas galore—from agnolotti to tufoli—and a table at a sidewalk bistro is perfect for people-watching while you nibble on a biscotti.

Those desiring a bit of Gallic flavor should saunter over to St. Boniface, home to Canada's largest French community west of the province of Québec. Restaurants serving French dishes are easy to find here, especially along Provencher Boulevard. And in the dead of winter St. Boniface comes alive during Le Festival du Voyageur, when Winnipegers turn out to celebrate the *joie de vivre* of the French fur traders who explored the area.

Red northern lights were once regarded as omens of war. If so, the skies must have

Manitoba Historical Timeline

Capt. Thomas Button winters at Port Nelson on Hudson Bay and claims the land for England.
1612

Henry Kelsey of the Hudson's Bay Co. spends 2 years exploring the province to find new sources of fur.
1690-92

1738
French fur-trader Pierre Gaultier de la Vérendrye arrives at the site now known as Winnipeg.

The Red River Colony, Manitoba's first permanent settlement, is established with a land grant from the Hudson's Bay Co.
1812

1869-70
The Métis, native people of mixed European and Indian ancestry, are led by Louis Riel in the Red River Rebellion to protect their language and property rights.

shone red fairly often during the 18th century as conflicts escalated between French *voyageurs* and their English rivals. During this strife-ridden period, Fort Rouge—site of modern Winnipeg—was established where the Red and Assiniboine rivers meet.

Now known as the Forks, this riverfront area is a park where you can take a tree-shaded stroll past splashing fountains and vibrantly hued flower beds. During warm weather, people flock to the numerous festivals held here, including Winnipeg's International Children's Festival in early June.

Nearby, the Manitoba Museum of Man and Nature invites visitors to take a whirlwind tour of the entire province by way of seven main galleries. And to learn more about auroras, stop by the museum's planetarium.

The Great White North

Follow your compass farther north and the chances of seeing Mother Nature's silent fireworks multiply. The northern lights not only occur more frequently in Manitoba's subarctic areas, but are brighter, too. In towns like Churchill, the lights are a major attraction.

But the real stars in this small community are its big, furry neighbors: polar bears. Sightings of the great white animals are common in October, when they migrate onto rapidly freezing Hudson Bay to fish, and late June, when thawing ice forces a return to shore.

The best way to meet these deceptively cuddly looking carnivores is safely ensconced in a specially designed, balloon-tired tundra vehicle. Climb aboard one for an unforgettable in-the-wild encounter. And when you're ready to thaw out, visit Churchill's Eskimo Museum, which is filled with ancient Inuit tools and other artifacts, as well as the recent, burnished wildlife sculptures carved in serpentine that are prized by international collectors.

Well-acquainted with the aurora's haunting glow, the Inuits crafted stories as elaborate as their carvings to explain what they saw. According to one tale, the lights are torches lit by spirits to guide those who will follow across the narrow bridge to heaven.

But you don't have to study Inuit mythology to appreciate the northern lights' otherworldly beauty, nor must you understand the scientific principles behind the phenomenon. All you really need to know is that the skies in Manitoba are perfect for admiring them.

Manitoba becomes the fifth Canadian province.
1870

Manitoba's boundary is extended north to Hudson Bay.
1912

Manitoba's French speakers win an important victory when the Supreme Court rules that all provincial laws passed since 1870 are invalid because they were written only in English.
1986

1878
The first railroad in the province reaches Winnipeg.

1997
More than 25,000 residents between the U.S. border and Winnipeg are forced to evacuate as Red River flood waters surge north.

1900-13
Manitoba's grain production increases dramatically, and Winnipeg becomes the trade center for the prairie region.

1999
The Pan Am Games are held in Winnipeg.

Recreation

The overwhelming bulk of Manitoba's populace resides in a thin strip just above the U.S. border, which leaves a vast region of unspoiled territory farther north that's prime for exploration.

Much of the province's outdoor fun involves its 100,000 lakes and the many rivers that link them.

Colorful sails glide across the surface of Lake Winnipeg as **windsurfing** enthusiasts take advantage of breezy days. Put in at Grand Beach Provincial Park, at the far southeast end of the lake. **Canoeing** down the Grass River, near the junction of hwys. 10 and 39, gives you the opportunity to see the beauty of the northern frontier.

Manitoba's lakes are home to dozens of species of fish, including walleye, northern pike, smallmouth bass, trout, arctic grayling, sturgeon, channel catfish and arctic char. Fly-in fishing—at such isolated spots as Aikens and Dogskin lakes, northeast of Pinawa in Atikaki Provincial Park; Island Lake, Gods Lake and Gods River, all in east central Manitoba; and Sickle Lake, south of Hwy. 391 near Granville Lake—attracts anglers of all skill levels. Contact Manitoba Natural Resources for information about licensing and regulations; phone (204) 945-6784.

Chilling Out

When the lakes freeze over, **ice fishing** and **ice skating** warm up as favored pursuits. Smooth blankets of snow—at such places as Assiniboine Park in Winnipeg—are irresistible for **snowshoeing** and **cross-country skiing.**

Many adventurers, too, have a hard time resisting the many **snowmobiling** trails that criss-cross the province. Kick up some powder in Duck Mountain and Turtle Mountain provincial parks.

Although **downhill skiing** is hard to come by in a province that's known mostly for its lowlands, skiers can take on 15 runs at Agassiz Ski Hill, in the southeast corner of Riding Mountain National Park. **Snowboarders** can practice their skills in the snowboard park.

For **tobogganing** fun, head for the slides at Kildonan Park in Winnipeg.

Riding Mountain National Park rises from the flat prairie to provide a wealth of opportunity for activity. Self-guiding **hiking** trails range from the easy Beach Ridges Trail to the difficult Bald Hill Trail, named for the barren hill towering over scores of lush, green trees. Most memorable is the grueling but beautiful Ochre River Trail, which entices both trekkers and cross-country skiers.

The park's Clear Lake Trail is a challenging **cycling** route that traverses part of an unmaintained Indian reserve. Before tackling the entire 25-kilometre (16-mile) trail, obtain permission from the reserve; phone (204) 625-2004. **Mountain bikers** favor the exhilarating J.E.T. Trail, which rewards risk-takers with great views from the ridge. The multiuse Central Trail, the longest at 73 kilometres (45 miles), is especially popular for **horseback riding.**

Taking A Dive

Even **scuba divers** can indulge their passion in the crystal waters of Clear Lake. Register with the park before heading to facilities at Glen Beag day-use area. Divers also frequent West Hawk Lake, Manitoba's deepest. Formed by a meteorite, the lake is near the eastern entrance to Whiteshell Provincial Park.

Cree for "white bear," Wapusk National Park fittingly lives up to its name as a hot spot for polar bear viewing.

Black bears, whitetail deer, caribou and moose are among the big game species that contribute to the province's excellent rifle and bow **hunting** reputation. Contact Travel Manitoba for licensing information *(see Fast Facts box).*

An abundance of specimens draws **rockhounders** to Flin Flon, Souris, Thompson and Bissett, a former gold-mining town northwest of Nopiming Provincial Park. Contact the Marketing Branch Information Center of Manitoba Energy and Mines for maps and information about rocks and minerals; phone (204) 945-6541 or 945-4154.

Recreational Activities

Throughout the TourBook, you may notice a Recreational Activities heading with bulleted listings of recreation-oriented establishments listed underneath. Since normal AAA inspection criteria cannot be applied, these establishments are presented for information only. Age, height and weight restrictions may apply. Reservations are often recommended and sometimes required. Visitors should phone or write the attraction for additional information, and the address and phone number are provided for this purpose.

Fast Facts

POPULATION: 1,137,500.

AREA: 649,947 sq km (250,946 sq mi).

CAPITAL: Winnipeg.

HIGHEST POINT: 831 m/2,727 ft., Baldy Mountain.

LOWEST POINT: Sea level, Churchill.

TIME ZONE: Central. DST.

MINIMUM AGE FOR DRIVERS: 16.

MINIMUM AGE FOR GAMBLING: 18.

SEAT BELT/CHILD RESTRAINT LAWS: Seat belts required for driver and all passengers in vehicles built after 1970; child restraints required for under age 5 and under 50 pounds.

HELMETS FOR MOTORCYCLISTS: Required.

RADAR DETECTORS: Use not permitted; will be confiscated. Visitors traveling in or passing through Manitoba should detach their units and store them inside their luggage.

FIREARMS LAWS: Vary by province. Contact the Firearms Control Section, 405 Broadway, 5th Floor, Winnipeg, MB, Canada R3C 3L6; phone (204) 945-4379.

HOLIDAYS: Jan. 1; Good Friday; Easter; Victoria Day, May 24 (if a Mon.) or the closest prior Mon.; Canada Day, July 1; Civic Holiday, Aug. (1st Mon.); Labour Day, Sept. (1st Mon.); Thanksgiving, Oct. (2nd Mon.); Remembrance Day, Nov. 11; Dec. 25-26.

TAXES: Manitoba's provincial sales tax is 7 percent.

PROVINCIAL INFORMATION CENTERS: Free travel literature and information are available at the following locations: Canada/United States border, Hwy. 75 (daily 8 a.m.-9 p.m., Victoria Day-Labour Day; Thurs.-Mon. 9-5, rest of year); Canada/United States border, Hwy. 10; Manitoba/Ontario boundary, Hwy. 1; Manitoba/Saskatchewan boundaries on Hwys. 1 and 16 (daily 8 a.m.-9 p.m., mid-May through Labour Day); the Explore Manitoba Centre at The Forks in Winnipeg; and Tourism Winnipeg Information Centre at Winnipeg International Airport (daily 8 a.m.-9:45 p.m.).

FURTHER INFORMATION FOR VISITORS:

Explore Manitoba Centre
The Forks
21 Forks Market Rd.
Winnipeg, MB, Canada R3C 4T7
(204) 945-3777
(800) 665-0040, ext. RM0

Travel Manitoba
Dept. RM0
7th Floor, 155 Carlton St.
Winnipeg, MB, Canada R3C 3H8
(204) 945-3777
(800) 665-0040, ext. RM0

SPECIAL REGULATIONS:

Dogs and cats transported from the United States must have proof of rabies vaccination.

ALCOHOL CONSUMPTION: Legal age 18.

Manitoba Temperature Averages
Maximum/Minimum (Celsius)
From the records of the National Weather Service

	JAN	FEB	MAR	APR	MAY	JUN	JUL	AUG	SEP	OCT	NOV	DEC
The Pas	-16	-12	-4	7	16	21	25	23	16	8	-4	-13
	-27	-25	-17	-6	2	8	12	10	4	-2	-13	-22
Winnipeg	-13	-10	-2	9	18	23	27	26	19	11	-1	-10
	-22	-21	-13	-2	5	11	14	12	7	1	-9	-17

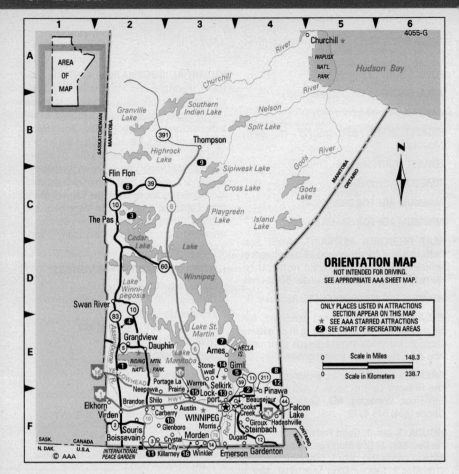

AAA/CAA *Starred Attractions*

EXCEPTIONAL INTEREST AND QUALITY

Churchill (A-5)

ESKIMO MUSEUM—The museum's collections of Inuit artifacts are among the finest in the world. See p. 190.

Riding Mountain National Park (E-2)

RIDING MOUNTAIN NATIONAL PARK—The park's grasslands, forests and lakes are home to a diverse population that includes elk, bears and moose as well as pike and several varieties of trout. See p. 196.

Selkirk (E-3)

LOWER FORT GARRY NATIONAL HISTORIC SITE—Costumed interpreters re-create daily life during the 1850s at this restored stone fur-trading outpost. See p. 197.

Winnipeg (F-3)

DALNAVERT MUSEUM—The 1895 home of a prominent lawyer and politician is furnished with Victorian antiques. See p. 206.

THE FORKS—People meet today at The Forks just as they have for over 6,000 years; a national historic site, a marketplace, a sports hall of fame and a children's museum currently occupy the area at the confluence of the Red and Assiniboine rivers. See p. 207.

MANITOBA MUSEUM OF MAN AND NATURE—The museum's exhibits, audiovisual presentations and dioramas all center on a common theme—the historical relationship of Manitoba's citizens and the environment of the province. See p. 208.

ROYAL CANADIAN MINT—A production facility for Canadian and foreign coins, the facility is considered one of the world's most modern; a viewing gallery provides an observation point. See p. 209.

RECREATION AREAS

	MAP LOCATION	CAMPING	PICNICKING	HIKING TRAILS	BOATING	BOAT RAMP	BOAT RENTAL	FISHING	SWIMMING	PETS ON LEASH	BICYCLE TRAILS	WINTER SPORTS	VISITOR CENTER	LODGE/CABINS	FOOD SERVICE
NATIONAL PARKS *(See place listings)*															
Riding Mountain (E-2) 2,978 square kilometres. Backpacking, cross-country skiing, downhill skiing, golfing, hiking, horseback riding, paddle boats, scuba diving, tennis, water skiing, wind surfing.		•	•	•	•	•	•	•	•	•	•	•	•	•	•
Wapusk (A-5) 11,475 square kilometres. Polar bear viewing.										•					
PROVINCIAL															
Asessippi (E-2) 2,460 hectares 13 km from Shellmouth Dam on Hwy. 83. Snowmobiling; nature trail.	❶	•	•	•	•	•		•	•			•		•	•
Birds Hill (F-4) 3,350 hectares 24 km n.e. of Winnipeg on Hwy. 59. Cross-country skiing, horseback riding, snowmobiling; interpretive programs.	❷	•	•	•					•	•	•	•			•
Clearwater (C-2) 59,616 hectares 19 km n. of The Pas on Hwy. 10. Cross-country skiing, snowmobiling; interpretive trail.	❸	•	•	•	•	•		•	•			•		•	•
Duck Mountain (E-2) 127,567 hectares 56 km n. of Roblin off Hwy. 83. Canoeing, cross-country skiing, snowmobiling.	❹	•	•	•	•	•	•	•	•			•		•	•
Grand Beach (E-4) 24,601 hectares 92 km n.e. of Winnipeg on Hwy. 59. Cross-country skiing, sailing, sand beaches, snowmobiling, tennis, windsurfing; interpretive programs.	❺	•	•	•	•	•		•	•	•		•		•	•
Grass River (C-2) 229,133 hectares at Cranberry Portage off Hwy. 10. Canoeing; interpretive trail.	❻	•	•	•	•	•		•	•	•		•		•	•
Hecla/Grindstone (E-3) 83,376 hectares 175 km n. of Winnipeg via Hwy. 8. Cross-country skiing, golfing, sailing, snowmobiling, tennis, windsurfing; interpretive programs. *(See Hecla Island p. 193)*	❼	•	•	•	•	•		•	•	•	•	•	•	•	•
Nopiming (E-4) 143,856 hectares 70 km n.e. of Lac du Bonnet. Canoeing; interpretive trail.	❽	•	•	•	•	•	•	•	•	•		•		•	•
Paint Lake (B-3) 22,380 hectares 32 km s. of Thompson on Hwy. 6. Canoeing, cross-country skiing, ice skating, snowmobiling, tobogganing, windsurfing.	❾	•	•	•	•	•	•	•	•	•		•		•	•
St. Ambroise (E-3) 17 hectares 13.8 km w. on Hwy. 1 from Winnipeg, 42 km n.w. on Hwy. 26, then 27 km n. on Hwy. 430. Windsurfing; interpretive trail.	⓯	•		•	•		•	•		•					
Spruce Woods (F-3) 24,848 hectares 27 km s.e. of Hwy. 1 on Hwy. 5 near Carberry. Canoeing, cross-country skiing, ice skating, snowmobiling, tobogganing; horse rental, interpretive programs, riding trails. *(See Carberry p. 188)*	❿	•	•	•		•		•	•			•	•	•	•
Turtle Mountain (F-2) 18,922 hectares 23 km s. of Boissevain off Hwy. 10. Cross-country skiing, ice skating, snowmobiling, tobogganing; interpretive trail, riding trails. *(See Boissevain p. 187)*	⓫	•	•	•	•	•		•	•	•	•	•	•	•	
Whiteshell (E-4) 273,715 hectares 126 km from Winnipeg via Hwy. 1E near the Ontario border. Cross-country skiing, downhill skiing, golfing, horseback riding, sailing, snowmobiling, tennis, tobogganing, windsurfing; interpretive programs, museum. *(See Falcon Lake p. 192)*	⓬	•	•	•	•	•	•	•	•	•	•	•	•	•	•

RECREATION AREAS

	MAP LOCATION	CAMPING	PICNICKING	HIKING TRAILS	BOATING	BOAT RAMP	BOAT RENTAL	FISHING	SWIMMING	PETS ON LEASH	BICYCLE TRAILS	WINTER SPORTS	VISITOR CENTER	LODGE/CABINS	FOOD SERVICE
OTHER															
Assiniboine (F-3) 153 hectares at jct. Park Blvd. and Wellington Crescent in Winnipeg. Cross-country skiing, ice skating, tobogganing. *(See Winnipeg p. 206)*			•	•						•	•	•			•
Harbour View (F-3) 162 hectares at 1867 Springfield Rd. in Winnipeg. Cross-country skiing, golfing, horse-shoes, ice skating, lawn bowling, shuffleboard, tennis, tobogganing, pedal boats.								•		•	•	•			•
Kildonan (F-3) 40 hectares at 2021 Main St. in Winnipeg. Cross-country skiing, ice skating, tobogganing, pool. *(See Winnipeg p. 208)*			•	•						•	•	•			•
La Barriere (F-3) 21 hectares 6 km s. of jct. Waverley St. and Perimeter Hwy. in Winnipeg. Canoeing, cross-country skiing, naturalist-guided hikes, snowshoeing.			•	•				•		•		•			
Lake Minnewasta (F-3) 125 hectares 2 km w. of Morden on Hwy. 3, then 1 km s. on Hwy. 434. Boating, fishing, hiking, swimming.	16	•	•	•	•	•		•	•	•		•			•
Little Mountain (F-3) 65 hectares 2 km e. of Sturgeon Rd. off Oak Point Hwy. in Winnipeg. Cross-country skiing; interpretive center.			•	•								•	•	•	
Selkirk Park (F-3) On the banks of the Red River at Eveline St. in Selkirk. Cross-country skiing, ice fishing; bird sanctuary.	13	•	•		•	•		•	•			•			•
Stonewall Quarry (E-3) 341 hectares 4 blks. n. on Main St. in Stonewall. Cross-country skiing, ice skating, tobogganing; nature programs. *(See Stonewall p. 198)*	14	•	•	•					•			•	•		•

Points of Interest

ARNES (E-3) elev. 225 m/739'

An old fishing village, Arnes today offers sandy beaches, a marina and a nine-hole golf course. A monument to writer and explorer Vilhjalmur Stefansson is inscribed "I know what I have experienced, and I know what it has meant to me," a statement from his autobiography. Born in 1879, Stefansson traveled by boat and dog sled across the Arctic, mapping large areas of the archipelago and collecting ethnological data from the central Arctic coast. He proved through his explorations that it was possible to live off the land in this forbidding area.

Gimli and District Chamber of Commerce: 3rd St., P.O. Box 1246, Gimli, MB, Canada R0C 1B0; phone (204) 642-8593.

AUSTIN (F-3)
pop. 400, elev. 262 m/860'

MANITOBA AGRICULTURAL MUSEUM, 2.5 km (1.6 mi.) s. of Hwy. 1 on Hwy. 34, displays a large collection of steam engines, gasoline tractors, farm equipment and artifacts of pioneer farmers. The location also is home of the Manitoba Amateur Radio Museum. Daily 9-5, mid-May through Sept. 30. Admission $5, under 12 free. MC, VI. Phone (204) 637-2354.

Homesteaders' Village depicts pioneer life in the late 19th century through furnished buildings of the period. Included are log cabins, an 1883 schoolhouse, two churches, a printing office, blacksmith's shop, grain elevator, pioneer-style store and gristmill.

BEAUSEJOUR (F-4)
pop. 2,700, elev. 247 m/810'

Beausejour and District Chamber of Commerce: P.O. Box 224, Beausejour, MB, Canada R0E 0C0; phone (204) 268-4811.

BROKEN BEAU HISTORICAL SOCIETY PIONEER VILLAGE MUSEUM, 1 blk. n. of Park Ave. and Seventh St. N., features a reassembled pioneer village with a restored railroad station, blacksmith shop, school, an old church, a community hall, general store, tailor's shop, harness shop and house, as well as pioneer artifacts and farm implements. Allow 1 hour minimum. Mon.-Fri. 8:30-4:30, Sat.-Sun. and holidays 1-5, July-Aug.; by appointment rest of year. Admission $2, under 15 free. Phone (204) 268-3048.

BOISSEVAIN (F-2) pop. 1,500

Nearby Turtle Mountain Provincial Park *(see Recreation Chart)* is named for the Western painted turtle, which lives in the park's many shallow lakes. The park is the year-round home of a large number of waterfowls and of migratory birds in spring and fall. Summer activities in the park include windsurfing, fishing, mountain bicycling and camping; hiking and fitness trails also are available. In the winter there are snowmobile trails and such activities as cross-country skiing, skating and hockey. A wildlife center also is available.

An outdoor art gallery throughout the town depicts the area's history through wall-sized murals. Scenic Hwy. 10 leads south to the North Dakota border and the International Peace Garden *(see place listing p. 194).*

Community Development Board: P.O. Box 368, Boissevain, MB, Canada R0K 0E0; phone (204) 534-6303 or (800) 497-2393.

BECKONING HILLS MUSEUM is at 425 Mill Rd. S. The museum exhibits pioneer artifacts, mementos from World War I and World War II, farming equipment, early photographs and items relating to culture, education and literature. Allow 1 hour minimum. Daily 1-5, June-Sept.; by appointment rest of year. Donations. Phone (204) 534-6544 or 534-6718.

MONCUR GALLERY, in the Civic Centre/Library Complex at 420 S. Railway St., contains 10,000 years of archeological history of early southwestern Manitoba. Included in the collection are projectile points, scrapers, ceremonial items and food preparation utensils. Allow 30 minutes minimum. Tues.-Sat. 9-5. Donations. Phone (204) 534-6478.

BRANDON (F-2)
pop. 39,200, elev. 409 m/1,300'

An agricultural and industrial center, Brandon is the second largest city in the province after Winnipeg and is known for its small-town warmth and its big-city amenities. The Keystone Centre, with more than 3.5 hectares (9 acres) under one roof, plays host to some of Manitoba's larger events, concerts and sports competitions; phone (204) 726-3500. The Canada Games Sportsplex offers both winter and summer recreational activities. Built for the 1979 Canada Winter Games, the structure houses racquetball courts, an ice arena, Olympic-size swimming pool, indoor water slide and an outdoor running track; phone (204) 729-2475.

The Brandon Hills Wildlife Management Area, just a short drive south of the city on Hwy. 10 and east along Beresford Road, provides a setting for a variety of recreational pursuits such as hiking, mountain bicycling and cross-country skiing.

Brandon is host to many world-class events; it hosted the 1997 Canada Summer Games and the Canadian Olympic Curling Trials.

Regional Tourism Centre/Riverbank Discovery Centre: #1-545 Conservation Dr., Brandon, MB, Canada R7A 7L8; phone (204) 729-2141.

Self-guiding tours: A historical walking tour of the residential area between 10th and 18th streets offers interesting architecture and turn-of-the-20th-century homes; a booklet describing the tour is available for $3 from the tourism and convention services office.

AGRICULTURE AND AGRI-FOOD CANADA RESEARCH CENTRE, at 18th St. and Grand Valley Rd., is a national center of expertise for land resource management in western Canada. For more than a century, its activities have been involved with the growth and development of the agriculture and food industry in the Prairie provinces. Visitors can view many of the research facilities, including a library, laboratories, greenhouses, field plots, an arboretum and cattle barns.

Open Mon.-Fri. 8-4:30. Guided tours are given Tues. and Thurs. at 1:30 and 3:30; reservations required 24 hours in advance. Free. Phone (204) 726-7650.

ART GALLERY OF SOUTHWESTERN MANITOBA, 638 Princess Ave. in the Centennial Library Arts Centre, features changing exhibits with an emphasis on contemporary Manitoba artists; displays change every 6 weeks. Workshops and art classes are offered for a fee. Mon.-Sat. 10-5 (also Mon. and Thurs. 5-9), Sept.-June; Mon.-Fri. 10-5 (also Mon. and Thurs. 5-9), rest of year. Closed major holidays. Donations. Phone (204) 727-1036.

COMMONWEALTH AIR TRAINING PLAN MUSEUM is in Hangar 1 at Brandon Airport. Dedicated to the preservation of the history of the British Commonwealth Air Training Plan of 1939-45, the museum contains many of the aircraft used to train airmen, along with a collection of photographs, artifacts and memorabilia of the period.

Of the 11 aircraft displayed, four are in flying condition. A chapel contains a book with the names of more than 18,000 Canadian Air Force personnel who died during World War II. Guided tours are available by appointment. Daily 10-4, May-Sept.; 1-4, rest of year. Closed Dec. 25. Admission $3.50, students with ID $2, under 6 free. MC, VI. Phone (204) 727-2444.

DALY HOUSE MUSEUM, 122 18th St., was built in 1882 and was the home of Brandon's first mayor. It is furnished with late 19th-century upper middle-class pieces and houses photographs and artifacts that relate to the city's history. Also featured are a general store and Brandon's old

city hall council chambers. A research center on the third floor is available by appointment. Guided tours are available. Allow 1 hour minimum. Mon.-Sat. 10-noon and 1-5, Sun. noon-5; closed major holidays in winter. Admission $2; over 65 and under 18, $1; family rate $5. Phone (204) 727-1722.

THUNDER MOUNTAIN WATERSLIDE, 8 km (5 mi.) s. off Hwy. 1 on Hwy. 459, offers a speed slide, twister slides, a tube slide, a two- and three-person river raft ride and three children's slides, all in a 21-hectare (52-acre) setting. Picnic facilities and changing rooms are available. Daily 11-7:30, June 1-Labour Day (weather permitting). Admission $12; ages 4-7, $8; over 65, $3.50. DS, MC, VI. Phone (204) 727-1056.

CARBERRY (F-3)
pop. 1,500, elev. 369 m/1,210'

The forests and sand dunes of nearby Spruce Woods Provincial Heritage Park inspired many of the works of artist, naturalist and writer Ernest Thompson Seton, including his stories "The Trail of the Sandhill Stag" and "Wild Animals I Have Known." He was appointed naturalist to the Manitoba government in 1892. A small highway park 15 kilometres (9 mi.) east of Carberry on Hwy. 1 has been dedicated to Seton.

Carberry Tourism: P.O. Box 130, Carberry, MB, Canada R0K 0H0; phone (204) 834-2195.

CARBERRY PLAINS MUSEUM, at 520 4th Ave., contains pioneer artifacts relating to the area, including period clothing, pictures and furniture as well as displays of original 19th-century art, a schoolroom, church, store, bedroom and kitchen. Military memorabilia from World War II also are displayed. Allow 30 minutes minimum. Daily 1-6, July-Aug.; by appointment in June and Sept. Donations. Phone (204) 834-2284 or 834-2797.

THE SETON CENTRE, 116 Main St., features artwork and photographs depicting the life and philosophies of writer, artist, naturalist and early conservationist Ernest Thompson Seton. Allow 30 minutes minimum. Tues.-Sat. 1-5, June-Sept. (other times by appointment); by appointment rest of year. Donations. Phone (204) 834-2509.

SPRUCE WOODS PROVINCIAL PARK is 27 kilometres (17 mi.) s.e. on Hwy. 5. The 24,848-hectare (61,400-acre) park is a mosaic of geographic features, including deciduous forests, creeping sand dunes, white spruce-covered sand hills, pots of quicksand and mixed grass prairie. The Assiniboine River meanders throughout the park.

Spruce Woods is home to the western plains hognose snake; the northern prairie skink, Manitoba's only lizard; wapiti (elk); white-tailed deer; coyotes; and pin cushion and prickly pear cactuses.

The Spirit Sands are remnants of an ancient river delta. Rainwater trapped beneath the sandy surface emerges to create springs and quicksand. This desertlike area is a 5-kilometre (3-mi.) tract of open sand dunes that tower 30 metres (98 ft.) above the surrounding prairie.

The Devil's Punch Bowl, near the Spirit Sands, is a bowl-shaped depression caused by the currents of an underground stream. The eerie blue-green pond color can be observed from several viewpoints.

An 8.2-kilometre (5-mi.) self-guiding trail leads through the dunes to the Punch Bowl, and a 4-kilometre (2.5-mi.) trail meanders through the Spirit Sands. Both trail entrances are located just north of the Assiniboine River off Hwy. 5. Interpretive signs along the trails provide insight into the cultural and natural surroundings. Comfortable walking shoes, a hat and drinking water are recommended. Allow 2 hours minimum.

Interpretive programs about park resources and natural and cultural history are offered. Every weekend May through September, family events, camp fire and amphitheater programs and guided hikes are offered. For information contact the Department of Natural Resources, Spruce Woods Provincial Park, P.O. Box 900, Carberry, MB, Canada R0K 0H0.

Park open daily 24 hours. Entrance fee $5 per vehicle for a 3-day pass, or $20 for an annual provincial park pass. Phone the visitor center at (204) 827-2543 May-Sept., or (204) 834-3223 rest of year. *See Recreation Chart and Glenboro in the AAA/CAA Western Canada and Alaska CampBook.*

Spirit Sands Wagon Outfitters offers 90-minute covered wagon rides through the Spirit Sands and Devil's Punch Bowl, providing views of sand dunes, cactuses, rare snakes and lizards, rolling grasslands and marshes. Trips depart daily mid-May through Labour Day. Fare $8; ages 3-16, $5; ages 2 and under on lap free. Phone (204) 827-2800 for wagon office, or (204) 379-2007 off season.

CHURCHILL (A-5)
pop. 1,100, elev. 29 m/100'

Churchill, on the shore of Hudson Bay, is Canada's northernmost subarctic sea port. It also is the site of the Hudson's Bay Co.'s Prince of Wales Fort, a partially restored ruin across from Churchill and Cape Merry Battery at the mouth of the Churchill River. Built over a period of 40 years during the 1700s to hold as many as 400 soldiers, the impressive stone fortress housed only 39 untrained men when three French warships mounted a surprise attack in 1782. The fort's governor wisely surrendered without engaging in battle.

After spending 3 unsuccessful days trying to demolish the 12-metre-thick (40-ft.) outer walls, the French abandoned the fort; it was never occupied again. The site is accessible by boat July through August (weather and tides permitting).

The area around Churchill holds an attraction for two giant mammals: the polar bear and the beluga whale. In fact the Churchill region is said to have the greatest concentration of accessible polar bears in the world. Having spent the winter hunting on the frozen bay, the bears come to shore south of Churchill as the ice melts, scatter along the coast and up to 50 km (31 mi.) inland, and then return to the ice in autumn when the bay refreezes. Beluga whales are often sighted off the coast of Cape Merry during July and August.

SAVE Churchill Wilderness Encounter and Frontiers North Inc. are among the companies that offer boat tours to view the whales and seals after the ice melts. Tours last approximately 2.5 hours and usually include a stop at Prince of Wales Fort National Historic Site *(see attraction listing)*. Specially designed tundra vehicles provide half- and full-day tours to view the polar bears October through November. Regular bus tours of the area also are available. Reservations are advisable for all tours.

Other natural features include flowers, arctic plant life, various wildlife and some 200 species of birds, which nest or pass through Churchill on their yearly migrations. An excellent spot for birdwatching is Bird Cove, on the coast 16 kilometres (9 mi.) east of Churchill. The aurora borealis (northern lights) seen from Churchill during the fall and winter months, are among the most brilliant in the world.

Via Rail Canada runs trains from Winnipeg and Thompson to Churchill; phone (800) 561-8630 in Canada or (800) 561-3949 out of Canada. Calm Air offers flights from Winnipeg to Churchill; phone (800) 665-1177, or (800) 426-7000 in the United States.

The Parks Canada Visitor Reception Center in the Bayport Plaza offers information, interpretive

DID YOU KNOW

The region around Churchill is said to be the most accessible in the world for viewing polar bears.

displays and programs, historical exhibits and videotaped presentations (fee charged) daily 1-5 and 6-9 p.m., June-Nov.; by appointment rest of year. Phone (204) 675-8863.

Churchill Chamber of Commerce: P.O. Box 176, Churchill, MB, Canada R0B 0E0; phone (204) 675-2022 or (888) 389-2327.

CAPE MERRY NATIONAL HISTORIC SITE, accessible via the Cape Merry Centennial Pkwy., 3 km (1.9 mi.) w. to the e. shore of the Churchill River, is marked by a stone cannon battery built in 1746 to compliment the defenses of Prince of Wales Fort. An original cannon and powder magazine remain. A cairn commemorating Capt. Jens Munk, the first European to enter the Churchill River in 1619, is displayed. The cape offers views of harbor activity as well as whales, waterfowls and Prince of Wales Fort.

Allow 30 minutes minimum. Daily 24 hours. Guided tours are offered daily, June-Aug.; phone Parks Canada for tour times. Donations. Phone (204) 675-8863.

★ **ESKIMO MUSEUM,** 242 La Verendrye St., contains exhibits that depict the history and culture of the northern region of Canada. Highlights of the museum are items relating to the Inuits. Inuit carvings in bone, ivory, stone and antler as well as wildlife specimens and artifacts and tools dating from 1700 B.C. are displayed. Tues.-Sat. 9-noon and 1-5, Mon. 1-5, June-Oct.; Tues.-Fri. 10:30-noon and 1-4:30, Mon. and Sat. 1-4:30, rest of year. Closed holidays. Donations. Phone (204) 675-2030.

NORTH STAR TOURS, 204 La Verendrye St., conducts historical and cultural tours of the Churchill area by bus as well as wildlife tours, including beluga whale-watching tours, by boat. Allow 2 hours, 30 minutes minimum. Tues., Thurs, and Sat. 8-1, July-Oct. Fare $50-$162; ages 13-21, $25-$162; ages 3-12, free-$118. AE, MC, VI. Phone (204) 675-2629 or (800) 665-0690.

PRINCE OF WALES FORT NATIONAL HISTORIC SITE, accessible by boat only, is at the mouth of the Churchill River. A huge stone fortress built 1731-71 by the Hudson's Bay Co., the fort fell to the French without incident in 1782. Whale-watching boat tours usually include the fort on their itineraries. Allow 2 hours minimum. Access is possible on the changing tides for 6 hours daily, July-Aug. (weather permitting); by appointment in Sept. Boat fare $45 (site admission included). Contact Parks Canada for more information; phone (204) 675-8863.

SEA NORTH TOURS LTD., at 39 Franklin St., offers boat tours in craft ranging in size up to the 32-passenger *Sea North II.* This vessel is equipped with stereo hydrophones, a system that enables passengers to listen to the sounds made by the beluga whales that swim within feet of the boat. Tours also offer chances of sighting polar bears, ice formations and indigenous birds. Allow 3 hours minimum. Daily dawn-dusk, mid-June to late Aug. Fare $68; ages 3-12, $34. VI. Phone (204) 675-2195.

TUNDRA BUGGY TOURS LTD. is at 124 Kelsey Blvd. Specially designed vehicles carry passengers across the tundra to view the polar bears in the Cape Churchill Wildlife Management Area. Birdwatching and ecological tours are offered in summer.

Half-day tours Tues., Thurs. and Sat. 1-5, July-Sept. Full-day tours daily 8-5, Oct. 1-early Nov. Half-day tours $74; under 13, $47. Full-day tours, including lunch and snacks, $162; under 13, $118. Fares include transportation to and from area hotels. Reservations made at least 2 weeks in advance are recommended. MC, VI. Phone (204) 675-2121, or (800) 544-5049 mid-Nov. through June 30. *See color ad.*

YORK FACTORY NATIONAL HISTORIC SITE 250 kilometres (150 mi.) s.e. of Churchill near the mouth of the Hayes River, was established by the Hudson's Bay Co. as part of a series of fur trading posts. The 1832 depot is the oldest wooden structure still standing on permafrost. Interpretive tours of the site feature reconstructed buildings containing area artifacts as well as a videotaped presentation.

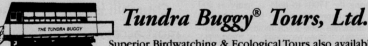

Access to the site is limited to charter plane or boat. Visitors should contact Parks Canada for transportation and safety information. Facilities at the site are limited; camping is not permitted. Allow 4 hours minimum. Daily 8-5, June 1-Sept. 15. Site free. Guided tour $5, under 5 free. Phone (204) 675-8863.

COOKS CREEK (F-4)
elev. 238 m/780'

COOKS CREEK HERITAGE MUSEUM, jct. Hwy. 212 and Sapton Rd., houses objects pertaining to the life of the early settlers from Poland and Ukraine. Highlights include religious artifacts, a carpenter shop, blacksmith, pioneer houses furnished in period and farm machines. Allow 1 hour minimum. Mon.-Fri. 9-5 (also Thurs. 5-7), Sat. noon-4, Sun. noon-7, June 1-last Sun. in Aug. Admission $3; over 65 and ages 5-17, $1. Phone (204) 444-4448.

IMMACULATE CONCEPTION CHURCH AND THE GROTTO OF OUR LADY OF LOURDES (Ukrainian Catholic), is 3 km (1.9 mi.) n. on Hwy. 212 from jct. Hwy. 213 (Garvin Rd.). Built by Father Philip Ruh 1930-52, features of the church include onion domes and the Icon of Our Lady of Perpetual Help, a replica of the Miraculous Icon in Rome. The grotto adjacent to the church is a replica of the original Grotto of Lourdes in France. Guided tours are available.

Allow 1 hour minimum. Daily noon-8, July 1-Labour Day; Sat.-Sun. noon-8, in June and day after Labour Day-Sept. 30. Admission $1. Phone (204) 444-2478 or 224-1430.

CRYSTAL CITY (F-3)
pop. 400, elev. 459 m/1,507'

CRYSTAL CITY COMMUNITY PRINTING MUSEUM INC., at 218 Broadway St. S., is said to be the oldest operating printing shop in Western Canada. The museum features a collection of antique printing equipment still in operation. Guided tours are available. Allow 30 minutes minimum. Mon.-Fri. 9-5:30. Admission $2, students $1.50, under 5 free. Phone (204) 873-2293.

DAUPHIN (E-2)
pop. 8,300, elev. 293 m/960'

Dauphin (DOE-feen) lies in a fertile farming valley between Duck Mountain Provincial Park (see Recreation Chart) and Riding Mountain National Park (see place listing p. 196). Lake Dauphin, 15 kilometres (9 mi.) east of Dauphin, offers fishing.

Dauphin District Chamber of Commerce: Unit C, #21 3rd Ave. N.E., Dauphin, MB, Canada R7N 0Y5; phone (204) 638-4838.

FORT DAUPHIN MUSEUM, 140 Jackson St., is surrounded by a wooden palisade suggestive of a fur trading fort of the North West Co. A trapper's cabin, schoolhouse, church, blacksmith shop, trading post and pioneer house inside the fort are furnished in the style of the early settlers. Archeological, fur-trade and pioneer artifacts also are featured.

Allow 1 hour minimum. Daily 9-5, mid-June through Aug. 31; Mon.-Fri. 9-5, May 1 to mid-June and Sept. 1 to mid-Oct. Admission $3, students with ID $2, under 12 free if accompanied by an adult, family rate $5. Phone (204) 638-6630.

DUGALD (F-4)
pop. 400, elev. 242 m/795'

Dugald is a hamlet east of Winnipeg's perimeter highway. Although many residents now commute to jobs in the city, farming is still important to the area.

DUGALD COSTUME MUSEUM, just n. of jct. Hwys. 206 and 15, features a 35,000-piece collection of clothing and accessories dating from 1565. The Costume Museum of Canada displays selected items depicting a different theme each year. The museum's exhibitions are presented in a *tableau vivant*, or living-picture style. A visual storage room offers a close-up view of accessories.

Allow 1 hour, 30 minutes minimum. Mon.-Fri. 10-5, Sat.-Sun. noon-5, Victoria Day weekend-Labour Day weekend; by appointment Apr. 1-day before Victoria Day weekend and day after Labour Day weekend-Nov. 30. Admission $4, students with ID $3, family rate $12. MC, VI. Phone (204) 853-2166.

Pioneer Home was built in 1886 about 8 km (5 mi.) from its present site on the Dugald property. The restored house has been decorated to resemble its appearance in the late 1800s. Guided tours explain the purpose of each room and its furnishings. Mon.-Fri. 10-5, Sat.-Sun. noon-5, Victoria Day weekend-Labour Day weekend; by appointment Apr. 1-day before Victoria Day weekend and day after Labour Day weekend-Nov. 30 (weather permitting). Admission $1.

ELKHORN (F-2)
pop. 500, elev. 526 m/1,700'

[SAVE] ELKHORN AUTOMOBILE MUSEUM is on Hwy. 1W. The museum displays some 90 vintage automobiles dating from 1908 to the mid-1960s; several are in operating condition. Also exhibited are steam engines, gas tractors and other farm machinery as well as aboriginal, household and pioneer artifacts. Allow 1 hour minimum. Daily 9-9, May 1-late Sept. Admission $5; ages 5-16, $2. Phone (204) 845-2604, or 845-2356 late Sept.-Apr. 30.

EMERSON (F-3) pop. 700

Emerson was named after American poet Ralph Waldo Emerson. When Manitoba became a province in 1870, this town on the border of the United States and Canada was the site of the province's first customs house. The original log buildings still stand just north of the Customs Port of Entry.

In 1874 the North West Mounted Police, later renamed the Royal Canadian Mounted Police, organized at Fort Dufferin, thus beginning their career of maintaining law and order in the untamed western areas of Canada. A 15-foot bronze statue of a North West Mounted Police Officer and his horse is located next to the Tourist Information Centre on Hwy. 75. The statue is a tribute to the members of the force who made the historic "Trek West" from Emerson to Fort McLeod, Alberta.

The Boundary Commission Trail provides 3 kilometres (1.9 mi.) of hiking along the Red River north to the Historic Fort Dufferin Site. At the fort are the remains of old buildings, grave sites and a memorial to the North West Mounted Police.

Town of Emerson: P.O. Box 340, Emerson, MB, Canada R0A 0L0; phone (204) 373-2002.

FALCON LAKE (F-4)
elev. 305 m/1,001′

WHITESHELL PROVINCIAL PARK is accessible via an especially scenic stretch of Hwy. 1E. The park is composed of four districts: Falcon Lake, Rennie, Seven Sisters and West Hawk Lake. Both wilderness and developed resort areas surround more than 200 lakes and 12 rivers, which include the Winnipeg River with numerous falls and rapids. West Hawk Lake, near the Ontario border, is one of the deepest lakes in Manitoba. It is thought that the lake was formed by a meteor more than 100 million years ago.

Alfred Hole Goose Sanctuary, east of Rennie on Hwy. 44, is a nesting ground for giant Canada geese which were believed extinct 1930-1960. The birds can be seen at close range from an interpretive center's observation deck. The center contains exhibits and informative videotapes.

The rocks found throughout the park are part of the Precambrian Shield, the oldest geological formation in the world. Near Betula Lake are the Bannock Point Petroforms—ceremonial Anishinabe boulder mosaics of snakes, turtles and geometric shapes.

Along with its beauty and tranquility, the park is popular during the summer for interpretive programs, swimming, scuba diving, canoeing, lawn bowling, tennis, miniature golf, horseshoes, horseback riding, sailing and hiking; in winter it provides ample opportunities for cross-country and downhill skiing, snowmobiling and snowshoeing.

Park open daily 24 hours. Interpretive center open daily 8:30-5, late May to mid-Oct. Entrance fee $5 per private vehicle for a 3-day pass or $20 for an annual provincial park pass. Phone the

Falcon Lake District at (204) 349-2201, West Hawk District at (204) 349-2245, Rennie District at (204) 369-5246 and Seven Sisters District at (204) 348-2203. *See Recreation Chart and the AAA/CAA Western Canada and Alaska CampBook.*

RECREATIONAL ACTIVITIES
Horseback Riding

- **Falcon Beach Riding Stables and Guest Ranch,** off Hwy. 1 exit Falcon Lake. Write Falcon Beach P.O., Falcon Lake, MB, Canada R0E 0N0. Daily 9-9, July-Aug.; by appointment rest of year. Phone (204) 349-2410.

FLIN FLON (C-2)
pop. 6,600, elev. 304 m/1,000′

Flin Flon was founded in 1915 when Tom Creighton, one of six prospectors, discovered an ore body which led to the development of Flin Flon as a mining town. The community owes its name to Josiah Flintabbatey Flonatin, the major character of "The Sunless City," a dime novel found in the area by the discoverers of the mineral deposits. Off Hwy. 10 is a humorous 7.5-metre (25-ft.) statue of Flintabbatey Flonatin designed by the American cartoonist Al Capp, of L'il Abner fame. Bordering Saskatchewan, Flin Flon is the northern terminus of the Manitoba stretch of scenic Hwy. 10.

The Flin Flon Station Museum, north on Hwy. 10A, displays artifacts collected from mining, transportation and cultural sources; phone (204) 687-2946. The Hudson Bay Mining and Smelting Co. offers tours of its surface operation; under 16 are not permitted. Reservations are required; phone (204) 687-2050.

Flin Flon and District Chamber of Commerce: P.O. Box 806, Flin Flon, MB, Canada R8A 1N6; phone (204) 687-4518.

GARDENTON (F-4) elev. 298 m/979′

Some of the earliest Ukrainian settlers in Manitoba came to Gardenton in 1896. Built 1897-99, St. Michael's Ukrainian Orthodox Historical Church, 4 kilometres (2.5 mi.) west, is purportedly North America's first Ukrainian Orthodox church. Lithographed icons from St. Petersburg, Moscow and Kiev ornament the sanctuary. A pilgrimage is held the third Sunday in August. Phone (204) 425-3595 for an appointment to tour the church.

The Ukrainian Museum contains articles of clothing and hand tools depicting life in the late 1800s and early 1900s, a one-room schoolhouse and a thatched roof house. Also in the area is a tall grass prairie. For further information about the festival or the museum phone (204) 425-3072 in summer, or (204) 425-3501 rest of year.

GIMLI (E-3)
pop. 3,100, elev. 220 m/723'

Established in 1875, Gimli was the site of Canada's first permanent Icelandic settlement, the largest outside Iceland. The town's name, derived from Norse mythology, means "home of the gods." A Viking statue designed by Gissur Eliasson and the oldest Icelandic cemetery in Canada testify to Gimli's Nordic heritage. Gimli is located on the western shore of Lake Winnipeg, one of the largest freshwater lakes in the world.

Gimli and District Chamber of Commerce: P.O. Box 254, Gimli, MB, Canada R0C 1B0; phone (204) 642-7974.

GIROUX (F-4)
pop. 100, elev. 271 m/888'

PHILIP'S MAGICAL PARADISE, 39 Municipal Rd. at the corner of Hwy. 311, houses a variety of items donated by magicians from around the world. Allow 30 minutes minimum. Mon.-Fri. 7 p.m.-9 p.m., Sat.-Sun. 1-8, mid-May to late Sept. Donations. Phone (204) 326-1219 or 326-5575.

GLENBORO (F-3)
pop. 700, elev. 375 m/1,230'

Glenboro is known as the gateway to Spruce Woods Provincial Heritage Park *(see Carberry p. 188)* and the Manitoba Desert. At the junction of Hwys. 2 and 5 in Camel Park stands Sara the Camel, a 7-metre-high (24-ft.) symbol of the Spirit Sands. A portion of the SS *Alpha*, a steamship that ran aground on the Assiniboine River in 1885, also is displayed in the park.

Slightly northwest of Glenboro on Hwy. 2 is what is purported to be the last cable river ferry in southern Manitoba. Phone (204) 827-2250.

Community Development Corporation: P.O. Box 296, Glenboro, MB, Canada R0K 0X0; phone (204) 827-2083.

GRANDVIEW (E-2)
pop. 900 elev. 434 m/1,425'

WATSON CROSSLEY COMMUNITY MUSEUM is on the w. side of town at the sports grounds on Railway Ave. The museum displays regional pioneer items including automobiles, horsedrawn equipment, tractors, farm machinery and other artifacts. A restored 1896 homesteader's cabin, a pioneer church with a free-standing bell tower, a rural schoolhouse and a three-story 1918 pioneer house are furnished in their respective periods.

Allow 2 hours minimum. Daily 10-6, late June-early Sept.; by appointment rest of year. Admission $1, under 16 free. Phone (204) 546-2040 in summer, (204) 546-2661 or 546-2764 rest of year.

HADASHVILLE (F-4)
pop. 100, elev. 297 m/975'

SANDILANDS FOREST CENTRE, about 2 km (1.2 mi.) s. of jct. Hwys. 1 and 11, educates visitors about forest conservation, fire prevention and reforestation processes. Displayed is a railroad car used by forestry officials 1919-74 to promote the nationwide planting of trees. An electronic display of bark, leaves and seeds tests visitors' knowledge of tree species. A museum displays plants and animals found in the area.

The Old Beaver Dam Trail, reached by a suspension bridge over the Whitemouth River, penetrates aspen parkland and a boreal forest. Guided tours of the center are available. Allow 1 hour minimum. Thurs.-Mon. noon-5, mid-May to mid-Oct. Hours may vary; phone ahead. Donations. Guided tours $3. Reservations are required for guided tours. Phone (204) 453-3182.

HECLA ISLAND (E-4)
elev. 210 m/690'

HECLA/GRINDSTONE PROVINCIAL PARK, 175 km (109 mi.) n. of Winnipeg, or 54 km (34 mi.) n. of Riverton, on Hwy. 8, is comprised of several islands in Lake Winnipeg, the largest of which is Hecla Island. The original settlers were Icelanders displaced from their homeland in 1876, fleeing poverty and Danish rule.

Guided walks through Hecla Village—which consists of a restored church, school, community hall, period house, dockside fish station, a tool display and a partially completed boarding house—also are offered. Interpretive programs are offered. Camping facilities, cabins, hiking trails, picnic areas, bicycling, fishing and swimming also are available. For further information contact the Department of Natural Resources, P.O. Box 70, Riverton, MB, Canada R0C 2R0.

DID YOU KNOW

Flin Flon, in western Manitoba, was named after a character in a dime novel, Josiah Flintabbatey Flonatin.

Park open daily 24 hours. Entrance fee $5 per private vehicle for a 3-day pass, or $20 for an annual provincial park pass. Phone (204) 279-2056 May-Sept., or (204) 378-2945 rest of year. *See Recreation Chart.*

Grassy Narrows Marsh and Wildlife Viewing Tower offers opportunities for wildlife viewing from trails and boardwalks along the marsh as well as from towers along the trails. Some trails are designated bicycling trails. The marsh, a nesting area for Canada geese and other waterfowls, is named after the Narrows, a channel between Hecla Island and the mainland. The tower was built for viewing moose as they feed in the marsh. Visitors should bring drinking water and wear comfortable walking shoes.

Hecla Fish Station, in an old ice house, or "fish station," provides a look at the commercial fishing industry of Lake Winnipeg through artifacts and wall plaques and a small museum. Visitors also can view fishermen bringing in the day's catch. Daily June 30-Aug. 30. Schedule may vary; phone ahead. Free.

Hecla Island Heritage Home Museum depicts the lifestyle of an Icelandic family from the 1920s to the 1940s. The restored 1928 house is furnished in period with items donated by descendants of the original owners and by other islanders. Thurs.-Mon. and holidays 10-4, June 15-Labour Day. Schedule may vary; phone ahead. Donations.

INTERNATIONAL PEACE GARDEN (F-2)

Consisting of 586 hectares (1,451 acres) in Canada and an adjoining 360 hectares (888 acres) in the United States, the International Peace Garden is on US 281 and scenic Hwy. 10. The botanical garden and park commemorates the friendship between these two countries on the longest unfortified border in the world.

Centers of attraction are an interpretive center depicting the history and development of the park; the Peace Chapel, which includes quotations etched in limestone walls; more than 150,000 annual flowers in the formal gardens that line the boundary; and a floral clock.

Other facilities include campgrounds, hiking and bicycling trails, and picnic areas. Walking tours of the garden, nature hikes and arts and crafts classes are offered daily. Horse-drawn carriage rides also are available. The International Music Camp Summer School of Fine Arts is held June through July; the Canadian Legion Sports Camp takes place July through August. Self-guiding walking and driving tours are available. Flowers are in full bloom mid-July to early September (weather permitting).

The garden is open daily 24 hours. Vehicle permits (required mid-May to mid-Sept.) $20 per private vehicle for a season pass, $7 per private vehicle for day-use, $3 for a pedestrian pass. Phone (204) 534-2510 in Canada, or (701) 263-4390 in the U.S.

KILLARNEY (F-2)
pop. 2,200, elev. 495 m/1,625'

The area's resemblance to Ireland's Killarney Lakes prompted John Sidney O'Brien to change the name of the town of Oak Lake to Killarney. Green fire engines and a replica of the Blarney Stone are further evidence of the town's Irish heritage. A fountain statue of a leprechaun riding a turtle is in Erin Park.

Killarney and District Chamber of Commerce: P.O. Box 809, Killarney, MB, Canada R0K 1G0; phone (204) 523-4202.

J.A.V. DAVID MUSEUM, 414 Williams Ave., displays Indian and pioneer artifacts, local memorabilia, quilts and collections of birds, butterflies and animals. Also featured are an early 1900s schoolroom, a Ninette Sanitorium display, a post office display and a country store. Allow 1 hour minimum. Tues.-Sat. 10-noon and 1-5, June-Aug.; by appointment rest of year. Closed holidays. Donations. Phone (204) 523-7325.

LOCKPORT (F-3) elev. 313 m/1,000'

At Lockport Heritage Park, on PTH 44 just east of the Lockport bridge, is St. Andrews Lock and Dam. This rare structure on Canada's flat prairies was completed in 1910 to allow access and permit navigation on the Red River from Lake Winnipeg to Winnipeg; it is purportedly the only lock and dam of its kind still standing in North America. Picnic sites and footpaths overlook the dam.

The Manitoba Fun Belt: 356 Main St., 2nd Floor, Selkirk, MB, Canada R1A 1T6; phone (204) 482-2022 or (800) 894-2621.

SKINNER'S WET N WILD WATERSLIDE PARK, on Hwy. 44 just w. of Lockport bridge, includes four adult and two children's water slides, bumper boats, miniature golf, a hot tub, a wading pool, a video arcade, volleyball courts and horseshoe pits. Picnic areas and food are available. Open daily (weather permitting) 10-8, July-Aug.; 10-6 in June. Admission $10; ages 4-12, $8; spectator pass $3.50; family rate $40. Miniature golf $2.25 extra. Bumper boats $2.25. VI. Phone (204) 757-2623.

MORDEN (F-3)
pop. 5,700, elev. 302 m/990'

Named after the area's first settler, Alvey Morden, the town grew almost overnight when the Canadian Pacific Railroad arrived in 1882. Located near the Boundary Commission-NWMP Trail in the Boundary Trail Heritage Region,

Morden has a progressive industrial and business sector. Abundant recreational activities at Lake Minnewasta and Colert Beach *(see Recreation Chart)* include camping, swimming, fishing, water skiing, canoeing, sailing, bicycling and hiking in the summer. Winter activities include cross-country skiing, snowmobiling and ice fishing.

The Agriculture and Agri-Food Canada Research Station, at Hwy. 3 and Hwy. 100, develops field crops, fruits and ornamentals on 254 hectares (627 acres). Tours of the Morden area and the research station are offered May through September. For further information phone (204) 822-4471.

A mural on the corner of Stephen and Nelson streets is a re-creation of one of the earliest known photographs taken in the area. The scene depicts the supply train for Her Majesty's British North American Boundary Commission at Dead Horse Creek in June 1873. Another mural, at the corner of Stephen and 7th streets, was dedicated in 1997 and remembers the visit of Canada's first prime minister Sir John A. MacDonald to the town on July 15, 1886. The depiction features Sir John speaking from the rear of his railcar and Philip Locke presenting him with a bouquet of prairie flowers; a version of an Indian war dance also is depicted.

Morden and District Chamber of Commerce: 102-195 Stephen St., Morden, MB, Canada R6M 1V3; phone (204) 822-5630.

Self-guiding tours: A walking tour guide describing a self-guiding architectural/historical tour of Morden's turn-of-the-20th-century homes and buildings is available for $2 from the chamber of commerce.

MORDEN AND DISTRICT MUSEUM is in the lower level of the recreation center at 2nd St. and Gilmour Ave. Fossil displays chronicle regional archeology and paleontology. Marine reptile fossils, such as mosasaurs and plesiosaurs, date from 80 million years ago when the Colorado Sea covered much of North America. The process of finding, excavating and displaying the fossils also is depicted. Other exhibits deal with First Nations and pioneer life.

Allow 1 hour minimum. Daily 1-5, June-Aug.; Wed.-Sun. 1-5, rest of year. Closed Dec. 25. Admission $2; ages 6-17, $1. Phone (204) 822-3406.

MORRIS (F-3)
pop. 1,600, elev. 236 m/775'

Two rival fur-trading companies—the North West Co. and the Hudson's Bay Co.—set up shop on the Morris River in 1801. Not until 1874 did a permanent settlement take hold; incorporation took place in 1883. Both the town and the river on which it grew were named for Alexander Morris, the second lieutenant governor of Manitoba during the 1870s.

Town of Morris: P.O. Box 28, Morris, MB, Canada R0G 1K0; phone (204) 746-2531.

MORRIS & DISTRICT CENTENNIAL MUSEUM, on Main St. at jct. Hwys. 75 and 23, consists of two buildings. The original building is an old school which contains pioneer era displays of farm tools and a laundry and dairy section. The second building contains five rooms furnished with furniture and artifacts from the turn of the 20th century. Daily 2-5 and 6-8 p.m., June-Aug. Donations. Phone (204) 746-2169.

NEEPAWA (E-3)
pop. 3,300, elev. 400 m/1,300'

Neepawa, whose name derives from a native word for plenty, is a service center for the surrounding grain and livestock farms on the fertile plains northwest of Winnipeg and is known as the lily capital of the world. This community of tree-lined streets is known around the world as the birthplace of author Margaret Laurence. Riverbend Park offers many pleasant diversions for residents and travelers alike, including a fitness trail and camping area.

Neepawa and District Chamber of Commerce: P.O. Box 726, Neepawa, MB, Canada R0J 1H0; phone (204) 476-5292 or (877) 633-7292.

BEAUTIFUL PLAINS MUSEUM, 80 Hamilton St. W., is housed in a former CNR station. The museum features several rooms filled with historical items. A children's room contains antique toys and books, and a military room has uniforms and pictures of local residents who were involved in World Wars I and II. Other rooms include those dedicated to nature, stores, Masonic lodges, sports and vintage clothing. An extensive doll collection also is on display. Allow 30 minutes minimum. Mon.-Fri. 9-5, Sat.-Sun. 1-5, July 1-early Sept.; Mon.-Fri. 9-5, late May-June 30. Donations. Phone (204) 476-3896.

MARGARET LAURENCE HOME, 312 First Ave., contains photographs, memorabilia, autographed books and research materials of the award-winning Canadian author, born here in 1926. The house also features writers workshops and educational programs. Daily 10-6, July-Aug.; Mon.-Fri. 10-6, Sat.-Sun. noon-6, May-June; daily noon-5, Sept. 1 to mid-Oct. Admission $2, students $1, family rate $5. Phone (204) 476-3612.

PINAWA (F-4)
pop. 1,700, elev. 282 m/925'

Named "Pinnawak," meaning calm waters, by the aboriginal people, Pinawa was first settled by families who operated one of the earliest hydroelectric power dams built between Sault Ste. Marie, Ontario, and the Rockies. The townsite was abandoned in 1951, and now the historic site is a provincial heritage park. The new Pinawa was built in 1963 when the Federal Crown Corp., Atomic Energy of Canada Limited (AECL) built its research center near the old townsite.

Whiteshell Laboratories of AECL, on the banks of the Winnipeg River, is 4 km (2.5 mi.) north of Hwy. 211 on a marked access road. This facility conducts research into nuclear fuel waste management, reactor safety and advanced materials. Nearby is the underground research laboratory built to investigate the underground disposal of used nuclear fuel. Phone (204) 753-2311, ext. 2270 or (800) 665-0436 in Canada.

PORTAGE LA PRAIRIE (E-3)
pop. 13,100, elev. 332 m/1,100'

The city's name is derived from the prairie portage between the Red and Assiniboine rivers and Lake Manitoba. In the heart of the city at Crescent Road and Royal Road S. is Island Park. Surrounded by horseshoe-shaped Crescent Lake, this scenic park has a deer sanctuary, a large captive flock of Canada geese and offers opportunities for other birdwatching. Park features include exhibition grounds, seasonal harness racing, a golf course, an arboretum, tennis courts, picnic areas and bicycling and hiking trails.

The Portage la Prairie City Hall, built in 1898, was designed by one of Canada's foremost architects, Thomas Fuller. Historic walking tours of Portage la Prairie are available by appointment July through August; phone (204) 857-7778.

Portage and District Chamber of Commerce: 11 Second St. N.E., Portage la Prairie, MB, Canada, R1N 1R8; phone (204) 857-7778.

FORT LA REINE MUSEUM, PIONEER VILLAGE AND TOURIST BUREAU is at jct. Hwys. 26 and 1A E. The central museum includes pioneer household articles and implements, a log fort, school, doctor's office, trading post, furnished homestead and church as well as railway, farming and military displays. Canadian railway official Sir William Van Horne's business car also is displayed. A tourist bureau and picnic facilities are available.

Allow 1 hour minimum. Daily 9-6, mid-May to mid-Sept. Admission $3.50; senior citizens $3; ages 6-12, $1.50. Phone (204) 857-3259.

★ RIDING MOUNTAIN NATIONAL PARK (E-2)

Elevations in the park range from 230 metres (755 ft.) at Henderson Creek in the northeastern area to 756 metres (2,480 ft.) at Bald Hill in the eastern side of the park. Refer to CAA/AAA maps for additional elevation information.

Accessible from the north and south via scenic Hwy. 10, or from the east via Hwy. 19, Riding Mountain National Park lies on the plateau of the Manitoba escarpment, 197 kilometres (123 mi.) north of the U.S. border and 259 kilometres (162 mi.) northwest of Winnipeg. This 2,978-square-kilometre (1,150-sq.-mi.) area is blanketed with forests, lakes and meadows. The park is home to elk, moose, deer, bears and a wide variety of birds and vegetation. Waterfowls and beavers populate the waterways, and a herd of bison grazes in a large enclosure near Lake Audy.

General Information and Activities

Although the park is open year-round, complete facilities are available only from mid-May to mid-October. The park also encompasses the historic resort town of Wasagaming on Clear Lake, which offers the amenities of a resort destination.

Recreational activities available within the park include tennis, golfing, lawn bowling, swimming, hiking, fishing, canoeing, sailing, cross-country and downhill skiing, horseback riding, bicycling, camping and snowshoeing. More than 400 kilometres (250 mi.) of hiking, bicycling and horseback trails lead to lakes, meadows and evergreen forests. Bicycle and boat rentals are available.

Several forms of recreation can be pursued nearby. Guides and outfitters offer horseback riding and wagon excursions along with other wilderness activities. Located at Lake Katherine, the Native Cultural Anishinabe Village, or "Shawenequanape Kipichewin," offers tours, interpretation programs and powwows. There are boat launching facilities at Clear Lake and downhill skiing is available at the Mount Agassiz ski area from late November through March. Cross-country skiing, snowshoeing and dog sledding are other popular activities. *See Recreation Chart and the AAA/CAA Western Canada and Alaska CampBook.*

ADMISSION is $3.25; over 64, $2.50; ages 6-16, $1.75; family rate $7.50. Four-day pass $7.50; over 64, $5.50; ages 6-16, $3.75; family rate $16. Annual family rate $43; over 64, $16. MC, VI.

PETS are allowed in the park. Dogs must be leashed at all times.

ADDRESS inquiries to Visitor Information, Riding Mountain National Park, Wasagaming, MB, Canada R0J 2H0; phone (204) 848-7275 or (800) 707-8480.

VISITOR INFORMATION CENTRE OF WASAGAMING is on the s. shore of Clear Lake. The center maintains exhibits and displays about the natural and human history of the area. Interpretive programs include nature walks, campfires and guided hikes. Clear Lake is so named because it is so clear that the bottom of the lake can often be seen at the deepest location.

Daily 10-8, July 1-Labour Day weekend; 10-6, Victoria Day weekend-June 30 and day after Labour Day weekend-Thanksgiving weekend. Phone (800) 707-8480 for campground reservations and general park information.

SELKIRK (E-3)
pop. 9,900, elev. 231 m/800′

Selkirk's name honors Lord Selkirk, the Scottish philanthropist whose 1803 settlement in the Red River Valley to the south laid the foundation for Winnipeg. During the late 19th and early 20th centuries, Selkirk's position on the Red River made it a base for trade and communication with the more isolated settlements around Lake Winnipeg.

Chuck the Channel Catfish, a 9-metre (30-ft.) fiberglass statue, greets visitors on Main Street. The over-sized catfish is an apt representation of the live version: Catfish weighing more than 9 kilograms (20 lbs.) abound in the Red River between Selkirk and Lockport.

St. Peter's Dynevor Church, 6.5 kilometres (4 mi.) northeast off Hwy. 59, was built in 1853. The original church, erected in 1836, was the center for Anglican missionary work among the Saulteaux Indians.

Manitoba Fun Belt: 356 Main St., Selkirk, MB, Canada R1A 1T6; phone (204) 482-2022 or (800) 894-2621.

★ **LOWER FORT GARRY NATIONAL HISTORIC SITE,** 5 km (3 mi.) s. on Hwy. 9, is purportedly the oldest intact stone fur-trading post in North America. The 19th-century buildings are restored and furnished as they might have been in their early days. Costumed staff members perform tasks and re-enact events that re-create the early 1850s atmosphere of the fort in its heyday. The Visitor Reception Centre offers exhibits and a slide presentation about the fort's history. Picnic facilities and food are available.

Allow 2 hours minimum. Daily 10-6, mid-May through Labour Day. Admission $5.50; over 65, $4; ages 6-16, $2.75; family rate $14. MC, VI. Phone (877) 534-3678.

MARINE MUSEUM OF MANITOBA, at the entrance to Selkirk Park at Eveline and Queen sts., reflects Selkirk's nautical past through displays of outboard motors, tools used in shipbuilding in the early 1900s, two lighthouses and seven restored ships. The SS *Keenora*, built in 1897 and brought to Lake Winnipeg in 1923, is one of Manitoba's oldest passenger steamships. The ship houses nautical artifacts and photographs.

Also displayed are the 1942 *Chickama II;* the 1944 MS *Northland Lady Canadian;* the CGS *Bradbury,* an ice-breaker steam vessel built in 1915; the MS *Peguis II,* a lake and river tug built in 1955; the *Joe Simpson,* a freighter built in 1963; and the 1952 *Jackie S.,* the last all wood, white fish (gas boat) to sail Lake Winnipeg.

Other displays include an exhibit about underwater diving in the early 1900s and a graphite exhibit representing all the species of fish caught in Lake Winnipeg and the Red River. A written documentary

Bison

The Europeans who explored Canada in the 18th century were awed by the throngs of huge furry cattle that swarmed across the plains. Then, as many as 60 million North American bison, or plains buffalo, roamed the Canadian flatlands. They were the main food source for the Plains Indians, who had mastered the art of harvesting bison for food and clothing: Scaring the animals into a stampede, the Indians then ran them into corrals, where the bison could be killed as they were needed.

Later, the Métis, people of French

and Indian heritage, became expert bison hunters as well. Hides were transformed into heavy robes that became the fashion in Europe; tongues were cooked and prized as delicacies; and bison meat, dried and pounded and mixed with fat and sometimes berries, was used to make pemmican, a Canadian aboriginal food which was packed in bags and stored.

As the Europeans fought the Indians and each other, the bison fell victim to reckless slaughter, the repeating rifle and politics. Carcasses of animals killed solely for their tongues or hides littered the plains. When the white settlers realized they could starve the natives by killing the bison, they set fire to the plains, killing thousands of the animals and driving others into what is now the United States. By 1885 the bison faced extinction in Canada.

Around 1900 a handful of conservation-minded cattlemen convinced the Canadian government to protect the bison, and the killing stopped. Manitoba acknowledges its debt to the bison by placing its image on the province's crest.

chronicles the history of water skiing. Allow 1 hour minimum. Mon.-Fri. 9-5, Sat.-Sun. and holidays 10-6, May 1-last week in Sept. Admission $3.50; over 65, $3; ages 6-17, $2. Phone (204) 482-7761.

SHILO (F-2)

THE ROYAL REGIMENT OF CANADIAN ARTILLERY MUSEUM is on the Canadian Forces Base via Hwy. 340. This indoor-outdoor museum exhibits more than 10,000 articles of dress, technical instruments, ammunition, small arms, guns and World War II vehicles. Among the more than 150 pieces of major military equipment dating to 1796 are German, Russian and French guns.

Allow 1 hour minimum. Mon.-Fri. 8-4, Sat.-Sun. 1-4, Victoria Day-Thanksgiving; Tues.-Fri. 8-4, rest of year. Donations. Phone (204) 765-3000, ext. 3534.

SOURIS (F-2)
pop. 1,600, elev. 396 m/1,300′

The free-swinging 177-metre (581-ft.) footbridge built in 1904 over the Souris (SIR-iss) River is considered the longest free-suspension foot bridge in Canada. The bridge was reconstructed after being destroyed by a flood in 1976. Victoria Park has more than 6 kilometres (4 mi.) of walking trails, a viewing tower and a bird sanctuary containing geese, peacocks and swans (*see the AAA/CAA Western Canada and Alaska CampBook*).

Rockhounding in nearby agate pits yields agate, dendrite, jasper, petrified wood and epidote; the area offers one of the largest varieties of semi-precious stones found in North America. Permits are required and cost $10 per private vehicle. Contact the Rock Shop, 8 First St. S., Souris, MB, Canada R0K 2C0; phone (204) 483-2561.

HILLCREST MUSEUM, Crescent Ave. and Sowden St. next to the swinging bridge, is a restored late 19th-century residence furnished with settler artifacts and antiques. Highlights include an agricultural display with a covered wagon, tractor and farm tools as well as a printing press and caboose. Allow 30 minutes minimum. Daily 10-6, July 1-Labour Day. Admission $2; ages 6-15, 50c. Phone (204) 483-2008.

STEINBACH (F-4)
pop. 8,500, elev. 261 m/900′

SAVE **MENNONITE HERITAGE VILLAGE,** 3 km (1.9 mi.) n. on Hwy. 12, centers on a replica of a Mennonite village with more than 20 completely furnished buildings that were moved to the site. On the 16-hectare (40-acre) grounds are a fruit garden, stock pens, a steam engine, gas tractors and other machinery. The village windmill is said to be the only one of its kind in Canada. A museum displays antiques and manuscripts.

Allow 1 hour minimum. Mon.-Sat. 10-7, Sun. noon-7, June-Aug.; Mon.-Sat. 10-5, Sun. noon-5, in May and Sept.; Mon.-Fri. 10-4, rest of year. Admission $5; over 65, $4; grades 1-12, $3. Admission may be increased during special events. MC, VI. Phone (204) 326-9661.

STONEWALL (E-3) pop. 3,700

Nobody knows for sure if Stonewall was named after founding father S.J. "Stonewall" Jackson or the limestone ridge on which the town is built. The name fits well, though, since limestone quarrying sustained the area's economy from the early 1880s until 1967. Stonewall's past is captured through the old stone buildings dotting its streets.

Stonewall and District Chamber of Commerce: P.O. Box 762, Stonewall, MB, Canada R0C 2Z0; phone (204) 467-8377.

OAK HAMMOCK MARSH INTERPRETIVE CENTRE, 13 km (8 mi.) e. on Hwy. 67, then 4 km (2.5 mi.) n. on Hwy. 220, is a 3,600-hectare (8,900-acre) restored prairie wetland that is home to more than 295 species of birds, 25 species of mammals and thousands of other plant and animal species. Hundreds of thousands of ducks, geese, shorebirds and songbirds migrate through the marsh in the spring and fall. The area is a remnant of the historic St. Andrews Bog that once covered much of southern Manitoba's Interlake area.

Hikers can explore 32 kilometres (17 mi.) of trails over a system of boardwalks and dikes. There are daily marsh canoe excursions spring through fall and snowshoe walkabouts in the winter. The interpretive center features displays, films and tours and interpretive programs designed to educate visitors about the important role wetland environments play in the Earth's ecology. Picnicking is permitted. Food is available.

Allow 2 hours minimum. Area open daily 24 hours. Interpretive center open daily 10-8, May-Oct.; 10-4:30, rest of year. Interpretive center (includes guided tours) $3.75; over 55 and ages 3-17, $2.75; family rate $13. AE, MC, VI. Phone (204) 467-3300 or (800) 665-3825.

STONEWALL QUARRY PARK, on the n. end of Main St., commemorates the important role limestone played in the town's development. An interpretive center offers videotape presentations and exhibits, and an observation tower affords a panorama of the area. Visitors can take a self-guiding tour around the grounds for a closer look at kilns, fossil deposits in rock and wildlife.

Kinsmen Lake offers a sandy beach and swimming in summer and ice skating on the pond in winter. Snowfall launches the park's tobogganing season. Guided tours are offered. Picnicking is permitted. Food and camping facilities are available.

Allow 1 hour minimum. Interpretive center daily 11-5, May 1-Labour Day. Hours vary rest of year; phone ahead. Interpretive trail open daily 8 a.m.-10 p.m. Admission to park and observation tower is free. Museum admission $1. Admission to the lake area for swimming $3.75; over 65 and ages 6-17, $2.75. Prices may vary; phone ahead. Reservations are required for guided tours. Phone (204) 467-5354. *See Recreation Chart.*

SWAN RIVER (D-2)
pop. 4,000, elev. 340 m/1,116′

During the last 13 years of the 18th century, control of the Swan River Valley was sought by both the North West Co. and the Hudson's Bay Co. Each company built fur-trading posts in the area, but by 1800 the concentrated trapping generated by the rivalry had depleted the number of fur-bearing animals. The Hudson's Bay Co. abandoned the area until the two companies joined in 1821. Scenic Hwy. 10 passes just east of town.

Swan River Valley, nestled between the Duck and Porcupine mountains, offers fishing, hunting, boating, camping, swimming and picnicking.

Swan River Chamber of Commerce: P.O. Box 1540, Swan River, MB, Canada R0L 1Z0; phone (204) 734-3102.

SWAN VALLEY MUSEUM, 1.5 km (1 mi.) n. on Hwy. 10, reflects life in Manitoba's pioneer era through artifacts and restored buildings. Highlights include two machine sheds, two log cabins, a CN railroad, a local library and telephone stations, a blacksmith shop, pioneer store, two churches and a 1900s one-room schoolhouse.

Allow 1 hour minimum. Mon.-Fri. 9-5, Sat.-Sun. and holidays 1-5, May-Sept.; by appointment rest of year. Admission $2; under 12 free. Phone (204) 734-3585 or 238-4935 May-Sept., or (204) 734-3382.

THE PAS (C-2)
pop. 5,900, elev. 274 m/900′

A cairn in Devon Park at The Pas (pronounced "the paw") honors Henry Kelsey, the first known European to see the northern prairies in 1690. It is rumored that the first wheat on the prairies was planted in the area in 1734. Natural history exhibits, local historical materials and Indian and fur-trading artifacts are displayed in the Sam Waller Museum at 306 Fischer Ave. The museum also offers historic walking tours of the downtown and riverfront areas; phone (204) 623-3802.

Christ Church (Anglican), on Edwards Avenue, was founded in 1840 by Henry Budd, the first native Indian ordained to the Anglican ministry. The church contains hand-hewn furnishings made by ships' carpenters in 1847. Tours are offered by appointment; phone (204) 623-2119 or 624-5433.

Tolko Manitoba Inc., 7.5 kilometres (5 mi.) north on scenic Hwy. 10, then 7 kilometres (4 mi.) east on Hwy. 610, operates a large pulp, paper and saw mill. Tours of the facilities are available by appointment June through August. Children under 12 and cameras are not permitted. Closed-toe shoes must be worn; safety equipment is provided. Phone (204) 623-7411.

The Pas and District Chamber of Commerce: P.O. Box 996, The Pas, MB, Canada R9A 1L1; phone (204) 623-7256.

THOMPSON (B-3)
pop. 14,400, elev. 206 m/675′

Thompson sprang up after the discovery of one of the world's largest nickel deposits and is a major mining, communications, transportation, medical and retailing center.

Lakes and rivers abound in this rugged, picturesque area. Paint Lake Provincial Recreation Park *(see Recreation Chart and the AAA/CAA Western Canada and Alaska CampBook)* is 32 kilometres (20 mi.) south on Hwy. 6.

South of Thompson on Hwy. 6 is the starting point for a 10 kilometre (6-mi.) hiking trail that will take you over a bridge to Kwasitchewan Falls, the highest waterfall in the province. In between Wabowden and Thompson is Pisew Falls, the second highest waterfall in Manitoba accessible by road. A 1.3-kilometre (.8-mi.) trail leads from the highway through the dense foliage to a platform overlooking the 12.8-metre (42-ft.) falls. Twelve site plaques describe the flora and fauna of this boreal forest. Picnic facilities are available.

Thompson Chamber of Commerce: 4 Nelson Rd., Thompson, MB, Canada R8N 0B4; phone (204) 677-4155 or (888) 307-0103.

HERITAGE NORTH MUSEUM, in a log cabin at the corner of Princeton Dr. and Mystery Lake Rd., also serves as the tourist information center. Displayed are an assortment of stuffed and mounted animals native to the area, minerals, fossilized rocks, a mining exhibit, a woolly mammoth tusk found near Thompson, a boreal forest exhibit which includes a Cree tepee, and occasional changing exhibits. A second building houses a mining exhibit. An audiovisual reference library is available.

Daily 10-6, in summer; otherwise varies. Admission $3; over 59 and ages 12-18, $1.50; under 12, 75c. Phone (204) 677-2216.

INCO LIMITED (MANITOBA DIVISION), 2 km (1.2 mi.) s.e. on a paved plant rd., is one of the world's largest nickel operations and is recognized as the world's first fully integrated nickel mining and processing complex. The company offers 90-minute walking tours of its surface facility, tracing the refining process from the natural ore to the finished product. Arrive 15 minutes early and wear sturdy shoes and durable clothing; shorts, tank tops and open-toed shoes are not permitted.

Tours depart Tues.-Sat. at 10 and 1:30, in June and Aug.; Thurs. at 1:30, Jan.-May and Sept.-Dec. Free. Under 14 are not permitted. Phone (204) 778-2454.

VIRDEN (F-2)
pop. 3,000, elev. 439 m/1,440′

About 1,200 oil wells dot the landscape in and around Virden—the richest source of petroleum in Manitoba. The first oil-producing well was sunk in the 1950s in the Rosalee field northwest of Virden. Many original fieldstone buildings, such as the 1892 St. Mary's Anglican Church at the corner of Queen Street and 9th Avenue, are still in use today.

The site of Fort Montagne á la Bosse, built by the North West Co. in 1790, is northeast of Virden on the old Trans Canada Highway. To help cool things off in the summer, the fair grounds has a public pool and waterslides.

Virden and District Chamber of Commerce: P.O. Box 899, Virden, MB, Canada R0M 2C0; phone (204) 748-3955.

VIRDEN PIONEER HOME MUSEUM INC. is at 390 King St. W. The museum, in a large brick house, is a living memorial to the pioneers who came to the region by ox cart. Built in 1888, it is furnished with family pieces donated by descendants of the pioneers. Allow 30 minutes minimum. Daily 9-6, June-Aug.; by appointment rest of year. Donations. Phone (204) 748-1659, 748-1897, or 748-2740.

WAPUSK NATIONAL PARK (A-5)

Elevations in the park range from sea level along the Hudson Bay coastal areas to 94 metres (308 ft.) at Silcox Creek. Refer to CAA/AAA maps for additional elevation information.

Established in 1996, Wapusk (pronounced to rhyme with tusk) is Canada's newest national park. Its 11,475 square kilometres (7,119 sq. mi.) south and east of Churchill are on the shore of Hudson Bay. Translated from the Cree language, Wapusk means "white bear," a fitting name for a park created to preserve the area chosen by female polar bears for their dens and birthing spot.

Much of the national park, part of the Hudson Bay lowlands, is a flat plain covered by an extensive layer of peat; a layer of permafrost lies underneath. The treeless tundra consists mainly of wetlands—lakes, streams, bogs and rivers.

Polar bears congregate in the northern part of the park near Churchill around October, as they wait for freezing weather and the time when they can return to the ice in search of seals, their main food. The females dig their dens, and their young are born in late November and in December. The area around Churchill (*see place listing p. 189*) is one of the world's best places for viewing polar bears in their native habitat. Tundra vehicles take visitors for close-up encounters.

The park, along a migratory flyway, also is a popular spring and fall feeding spot for waterfowls and shorebirds, including such rare species as the king eider, Ross' gull and gyrfalcon. Many build their nests here on the coast of Hudson Bay during the summer.

Churchill, in a somewhat remote location in northern Manitoba, can be reached by air and rail from Winnipeg. Since Wapusk is a wilderness park, it has no roads or trails. Several commercial operators provide tours into the park by plane, helicopter or tundra vehicle. The park office can provide a list. Park admission is free. For additional information contact Wapusk National Park, P.O. Box 127, Churchill, MB, Canada R0B 0E0; phone (204) 675-8863.

WARREN (E-3)
pop. 600, elev. 248 m/815′

V. GROSS' DOLL DISPLAY, on Golf Course Rd., 3 km (1.9 mi.) n. of jct. Hwys. 6 and 67, displays some 900 dolls, ranging from those of the late 1890s to the present. Allow 30 minutes minimum. Sun.-Fri. 10-5 (also Sat. and evenings by appointment), May-Dec.; by appointment rest of year. Admission $2, under 6 free. Phone (204) 322-5346.

WINKLER (F-3)
pop. 7,200, elev. 271 m/890′

SAVE **PEMBINA THRESHERMAN'S MUSEUM,** 6 km (4 mi.) w. on Hwy. 3, features guided tours through displays of agricultural machinery, tools and household items as well as a steam threshing unit and a working saw mill. Allow 1 hour minimum. Mon.-Fri. 9-5, Sat.-Sun. and holidays 1-5, May-Sept. Admission $3, under 13 free. Phone (204) 325-7497.

LOOK FOR
THE RED

*N*ext time you pore over a AAA/CAA TourBook® guide in search of a lodging or restaurant, take note of the vibrant red CAA logo just under the property's name! These properties place a high value on the business they receive from dedicated AAA/CAA travelers.

As a member, you already turn to TourBooks for quality travel information. Now look for lodging and dining establishments that display the red CAA logo beside their listing for experiences you'll long remember!

Travel With Someone You Trust®

Winnipeg

The real estate agent's cry of "Location!" could have been invented in Winnipeg; the position of Manitoba's capital has determined both the city's past and present. Archeological evidence shows that Winnipeg has been an important place of settlement for more than 6,000 years.

The confluence of the Red River, which flows from south to north, and the Assiniboine River, whose eastward flowing waters were a main route of Western exploration, led to the founding of fur-trading posts in the early 18th century near the present site of Winnipeg. The fertile lands created by the rivers later drew farmers and other settlers.

Still later, the area's position south of the peaks of the Canadian Shield meant that roads and railroads were forced to converge at Winnipeg, making it the point through which the eastbound raw materials of the West and the westbound manufactured goods of the East passed. Profiting by the hydroelectric power generated from its rivers, the city emerged in the 20th century as a manufacturing center in its own right.

The French Canadian explorer and trader Pierre Gaultier de la Vérendrye founded Fort Rouge at the confluence of the rivers in 1738. This fur-trading post was succeeded by Fort Gibraltar, built by the North West Co. in 1804, and Fort Garry, founded by the Hudson's Bay Co. in 1821. In the same year, Lord Selkirk brought a party of Scottish settlers to these fertile lands, a move that greatly disturbed the trappers and voyageurs who feared their livelihoods would be destroyed.

The small settlement managed to survive, and the shift from trapping and hunting to agriculture began. Because of aggressive Canadian advertising campaigns in Europe and a homestead policy similar to that being used to settle the plains of the United States, large numbers of immigrants began to flow into the area in the 1860s.

In 1873 the village that had grown about a half mile north of Fort Garry was incorporated and named for the Cree Indian words *win* (muddy) and *nipee* (water). The railroad aided Winnipeg's growth still further: In 1876 the city began to ship wheat east, and when the Canadian Pacific Railway connected the coasts in 1885, freight and passengers began to flow through the city in both directions.

The diversity of today's Winnipeg mirrors the many nationalities who settled it, some drawn by agriculture, some by the railroad, some by industry. From countries throughout Great Britain and Europe they came, creating a cultural mix that is reflected in the city's skyline, which includes the neoclassical splendor of

the Legislative Building *(see attraction listing p. 208)*, the century-old buildings of Old Market Square and the rounded spires of the Ukrainian Greek Orthodox Cathedral.

The Golden Boy, sculpted by Charles Gardet of Paris, the 4-metre-tall (13.5-ft.), 4.5-metric-ton (5-ton) gilt statue atop the dome of the Legislative Building, in many ways symbolizes both the past and the future of the residents of Winnipeg. The statue was diverted on its journey from a French foundry during World War I, while the vessel that was carrying it served as a troop transport for 2 years.

After crossing the Atlantic many times, the golden immigrant was finally placed where he stands today, one hand holding aloft the torch of progress, the other cradling a symbolic sheaf of wheat. High above the city, he strides toward the increasingly important natural resources of the north, his color echoing the golden hue of the rolling fields of grain that brought the city below both population and prosperity.

Evidence has been uncovered through archeological digs that the current site of The Forks *(see attraction listing p. 207)* was a seasonal meeting place for aboriginal peoples more than 6,000 years ago. Tools, bones, footprints and pottery have been unearthed at the site located at the confluence of the Red and Assiniboine rivers.

Approaches
By Car

Forming a circle around Winnipeg is a perimeter highway. To the north of the Trans Canada Highway, the major approach from the east and west, this perimeter road is designated Hwy. 101. To the south of the Trans Canada Highway it is numbered Hwy. 100.

There are three major approaches to the perimeter highway: the Trans Canada Highway, which approaches from both the east and west, and Hwy. 75, which approaches from the south. To the west of the city the Trans Canada Highway is posted Hwy. 1W; from the east, Hwy. 1E.

Within the perimeter highway all three major approaches change designation: Hwy. 1W becomes Metro Rte. 85, Hwy. 1E becomes Metro Rte. 135, and Hwy. 75 becomes Metro Rte. 42.

Getting Around

Generally, rush hour in Winnipeg is from 7 to 9 a.m. and 3:30 to 5:30 p.m. As in most cities, stress can be alleviated if driving during rush hour is avoided. If driving during these times, be careful and be patient; the city's speed limit is 50 kilometres per hour (30 mph) unless otherwise posted.

Note the pedestrian crosswalks marked by pavement stripes and illuminated overhead signs. All vehicles

(continued on p. 205)

The Informed Traveler

City Population: 618,500

Elevation: 229 m/763 ft.

Sales Tax: Manitoba's provincial sales tax is 7 percent. A 7 percent Goods and Services Tax (GST) also is levied in Canada on most sales and services. There is no additional local sales tax or tax on hotel/motel rooms or car rentals.

WHOM TO CALL

Emergency: 911

Police (non-emergency): (204) 986-6222

Time and Temperature: (204) 783-2119

Weather: (204) 983-2050

Hospitals: Misericordia General, (204) 788-8364; St. Boniface General Hospital, (204) 233-8563; Salvation Army Grace General Hospital, (204) 837-8311; Victoria General Hospital, (204) 269-3570.

WHERE TO LOOK

Newspapers

Winnipeg has two daily newspapers, the *Free Press* and the *Sun.*

Radio and TV

The Canadian Broadcasting Corporation (CBC) has both AM (990) and FM (98.3) stations in Winnipeg as well as an AM (1050) station broadcasting in French.

CBC television stations are CBWT, channel 6 (cable channel 2) and CBWFT, channel 10 (cable channel 3). The Canadian Television Network operates CKY on channel 7 (cable channel 5). Craig Broadcast Systems operates MTN (Manitoba Television Network) cable channel 8W/13E.

Visitor Information

Tourism Winnipeg, open Mon.-Fri. 8:30-4:30, is at 279 Portage Ave., Winnipeg, MB, Canada R3B 2B4; phone (204) 943-1970 or (800) 665-0204. A second branch, at Winnipeg International Airport, is open daily 8 a.m.-9:45 p.m.; phone (204) 774-0031.

Travel Manitoba's Explore Manitoba Centre, at The Forks, is staffed with travel counselors. To obtain information about area attractions, visitors can write Travel Manitoba, 155 Carlton St., 7th Floor, Dept. RM9, Winnipeg, MB, Canada R3C 3H8; phone (204) 945-3777 or (800) 665-0040, ext. RM9. A 24-hour Forks Hot Line also provides information; phone (204) 957-7618. For recorded information about local attractions phone (204) 942-2535.

TRANSPORTATION

Air Travel

Winnipeg International Airport is about 8 kilometres (5 mi.) northwest of downtown off Metro Route 90. Daily bus service between the airport and downtown is provided by Winnipeg Transit between 5:58 a.m. and 12:17 a.m. The one-way fare is $1.50; passengers must have exact change. Major hotels offer limousine service to and from the airport.

Rental Cars

Hertz, (204) 925-6600, (800) 263-0600 in Canada, or (800) 654-3001 out of Canada, offers discounts to AAA and CAA members and has offices at Winnipeg International Airport, Winnipeg Square and 1577 Erin St. For listings of other agencies check the telephone directory.

Rail Service

The Via Rail Canada depot is downtown at 123 Main St.; phone (800) 561-8630 in Canada, or (800) 561-3949 out of Canada.

Taxis

Cab companies include Blueline, (204) 925-8887; Blueline Premium, (204) 925-8888; Duffy's, (204) 775-0101; and Unicity, (204) 925-3131. Base fare is $2.55 ($4.10 for Blueline Premium), plus a charge of 10c for each additional 93 metres (305 ft.) or 15 seconds of metered waiting time.

Public Transport

Winnipeg Transit, the public bus system, serves downtown Winnipeg and its suburbs. Route maps and route information are available by phoning (204) 986-5700. The average bus fare is $1.55; riders must have exact change.

must stop if the crosswalk is occupied by a pedestrian or if a pedestrian on the curb indicates an intention to cross. No vehicle may pass another that is stopped or slowing to yield to a pedestrian. Right turns on red are permitted after a stop, unless otherwise posted.

Street System

Winnipeg's streets are laid out in a number of grids, but each is oriented to a different compass direction. Visitors will find it easiest to orient themselves to the major thoroughfares, which have signs carrying the word "Route" and a number. Routes ending in even numbers designate north-south thoroughfares, and those ending in odd numbers designate major east-west arteries.

The primary north-south routes that cross the downtown area are 42, 52 and 62. The major east-west highways include 105, 115, 57 and 85.

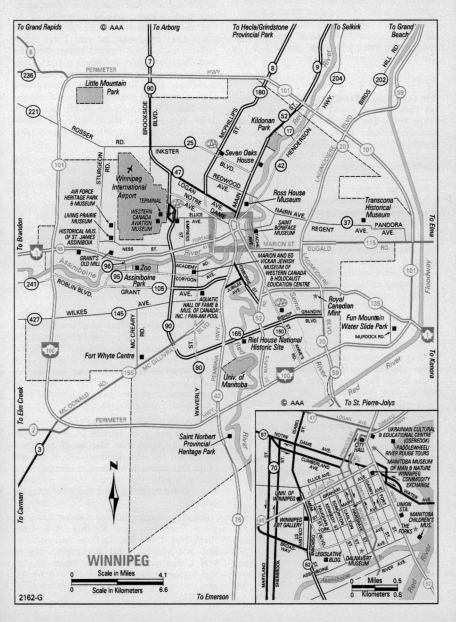

WINNIPEG

Scale in Miles 4.1
Scale in Kilometers 6.6

2162-G

A good street map will enable drivers to see how the various grids of named streets connect with the main numbered routes.

Parking

Visitors will do best to park in a commercial lot, where rates average about $1.10 to $1.35 for the first hour and $1.10 to $1.60 for subsequent hours. Daily rates are about $4 to $7. Parking meters downtown cost $1 an hour, but most carry a 1- or 2-hour limit. Some parking in downtown is free in designated metered areas.

Parking is strictly controlled along major downtown streets. Cars parked between signs reading "No Parking Between" from 7 to 9 a.m. and 3:30 to 5:30 p.m. will be towed.

What To See

AIR FORCE HERITAGE PARK AND MUSEUM is off Ness Ave. at n. end of Sharpe Blvd. (Air Force Way). The museum, in Air Force headquarters, includes three Victoria Crosses, the highest medal awarded to British Commonwealth service personnel. Historical Canadian Air Force aircraft and memorabilia are displayed in an outdoors setting; included are military fighters, helicopters and transport aircraft. Allow 1 hour minimum. Museum open Mon.-Fri. 8-5. Air park open daily 24 hours. Donations. Phone (204) 833-2500, ext. 5993. *See color ad p. 207.*

AQUATIC HALL OF FAME AND MUSEUM OF CANADA INC./PAN-AM POOL is in the Pan-Am Building off Grant Ave. at 25 Poseidon Bay. Museum displays include aquatic memorabilia, a sports-stamp collection and The Cutty Sark Collection of models of well-known sailing ships. A library of aquatic literature is available. Mon.-Fri. 6 a.m.-9:30 p.m., Sat.-Sun. 9-5; closed Jan. 1 and Dec. 25-26. Free. Phone (204) 986-5890.

ASSINIBOINE PARK, jct. of Park Blvd. and Wellington Crescent at 2355 Corydon Ave., comprises 153 hectares (378 acres) on the Assiniboine River. The park features a zoo, miniature railway, duck pond, walking and biking paths, a conservatory, the Leo Mol Sculpture Garden, a Tudor-style pavilion, Citizens Hall of Fame, a French formal garden and an English garden. Facilities for tobogganing, cross-country skiing and ice skating are available in the winter. Winnipeg's only cricket tournaments are played in the park. The park may be accessed from Portage Ave. via a footbridge over the Assiniboine River.

Assiniboine Forest is a 283-hectare (700-acre) forest of aspen and oak off Grant Avenue and is one of the largest urban nature parks in Canada. The forest is home to more than 39 species of mammals, including deer and foxes and more than 80 species of birds. The 1.5 km (.9 mi.) Saginay Trail leads hikers to Eve Werier Pond, where a variety of waterfowls can be seen. Daily dawn-dusk. Free. Phone (204) 986-7233. *See Recreation Chart.*

Assiniboine Park Conservatory features indoor gardens, changing floral and plant displays and art work by local artists. A tropical palm house contains orchids, ferns and banana plants. Food is available. Daily 9-8, Apr.-Sept.; 9-4:30, rest of year. Free. Phone (204) 986-5537.

Assiniboine Park Zoo has a collection of more than 1,200 different animals housed in naturalistic settings. The zoo specializes in animals found in cooler climates from around the world, as well as native North American species. Siberian tigers, snow leopards, polar bears, lynxes, elk, bison, and many other hardy species can be seen out-of-doors throughout the year. Large indoor facilities such as the Tropical House, the Kinsmen Discovery Centre and others provide warm-weather viewing of many tropical animals. Food is available. Daily 10-dusk; closed Remembrance Day morning and morning of Dec. 25. Admission Mar.-Oct. $3; over 65, $2.75; ages 13-17, $1.50; ages 2-12, $1; family rate $7.50. Admission $1 rest of year. MC, VI. Phone (204) 986-6921.

Leo Mol Sculpture Garden, in Assiniboine Park at 2355 Corydon Ave., is said to be the first sculpture garden in North American dedicated to the works of a single artist. The garden and gallery feature bronze sculptures, porcelains, paintings and sketches of the Winnipeg artist. The gardens also are home to the Leo Mol Schoolhouse Studio. A reflecting pool and fountain are located in front of the gallery. Audiotape tours are available. Grounds open daily at 7 a.m. Gallery and studio open Tues.-Sun. 10-8, May 31-Sept. 1; Sat.-Sun. 11-5, rest of year. Free. Phone (204) 986-3050.

Pavilion Gallery Museum is in Assiniboine Park at the corner of Park Blvd. and Wellington Crescent. Housed in a restored 1929 pavilion, the museum contains a permanent collection featuring the work of three prominent artists: Ivan Eyre, Walter Phillips and Clarence Tillenius. Allow 1 hour minimum. Tues.-Sun. 10-8, Victoria Day-Labour Day; Tues.-Sun. 11-5, rest of year. Free. Phone (204) 888-5466.

SAVE ★**DALNAVERT MUSEUM,** .5-blk. s. of Broadway Ave. at 61 Carlton St., is the former home of Sir Hugh John MacDonald, prominent lawyer and politician. Built in 1895, it was one of the first houses in Winnipeg to have hot-water heating, electric lighting and indoor plumbing. The restored house is furnished with Victorian antiques.

Allow 1 hour minimum. Guided tours are given Tues.-Thurs. and Sat.-Sun. 10-6, June-Aug.; Tues.-Thurs. and Sat.-Sun. noon-5, Sept.-Dec. and Mar.-May; Sat.-Sun. noon-5, rest of year. Closed holidays. Last tour begins 30 minutes before closing. Admission $4; over 65, $3; ages 5-17, $2; family rate $8. Phone (204) 943-2835.

DUGALD COSTUME MUSEUM—
see Dugald p. 191.

★ **THE FORKS**, at the confluence of the Red and Assiniboine rivers, was a meeting place for aboriginal peoples more than 6,000 years ago. By virtue of location the 23-hectare (56-acre) site evolved into the center of the European fur trade in the 1730s. Métis, natives and eventually European settlers created a community along the rivers. More than a century later, the area became a transportation center as the early railways laid tracks of steel across the prairie.

The Riverwalk follows the water's edge from the Manitoba Legislature to The Forks through downtown Winnipeg. Through outdoor interpretive panels and drawings, The Wall Through Time chronicles the area's history from glacial Lake Agassiz, 10,000 years ago, to the present.

The Splash Dash Water Bus Service operates daily Victoria Day through Thanksgiving (weather permitting). The water bus transports visitors to five downtown docks, including one at the legislative buildings. Phone (204) 783-6633.

A variety of water activities is possible at The Forks Historic Port. Canoes and "sea cycles" can be rented Victoria Day through Labour Day (weather permitting).

Special events and festivals take place at The Forks throughout the year *(see Special Events p. 212)*. Travel Manitoba's Explore Manitoba Centre, located at The Forks, provides year-round information about events and attractions throughout Manitoba and The Forks; phone (204) 945-3777, 957-7618 for 24-hour event information, or (800) 665-0040, ext. 766.

The Forks Market, housed in refurbished stable buildings, contains shops that offer jewelry and crafts; fresh, specialty and ethnic foods; produce; and baked goods. A six-story glass tower affords a view of the rivers and the downtown area. Daily 9:30-6:30 (also Fri. 6:30-9 p.m.); extended hours during summer. Free. Phone (204) 942-6309.

The Forks National Historic Site is a 3.5-hectare (9-acre) park that offers an outdoor playground and a riverside amphitheater with a view of historic St. Boniface. Interpretive programs and festivals are held Victoria Day through Labour Day. Daily 24 hours. Free. Phone (204) 983-2007.

The Johnston Terminal, in the heart of The Forks, features several shops, boutiques and eateries. Allow 1 hour minimum. Daily 10-6:30 (also Fri.-Sat. 6:30-9 p.m.). Free. Phone (204) 947-1200.

Manitoba Children's Museum, in the Kinsmen Building at The Forks, houses six galleries offering a wide variety of hands-on activities. Children can explore a 1952 diesel locomotive and vintage passenger coaches, take a behind-the-scenes look at a television studio, explore the Internet and play inside a beaver lodge. An infrastructure gallery allows children to build bridges, open water aqueducts and design their own community.

Allow 1 hour minimum. Mon.-Fri. 9:30-5 (also Thurs.-Fri. 5-8), Sat. 10-8, Sun. 10-5; Mon.-Fri. 9:30-5 (also Fri. 5-8), Sat. 11-8, Sun. and holidays 11-5, rest of year. Admission $4, senior citizens $3.50, under 2 free. MC, VI. Phone (204) 924-4000 or 956-1888.

FORT WHYTE CENTRE, 1961 McCreary Rd., is home to white-tailed deer, red foxes, rabbits, minks, muskrats, 23 species of waterfowls and numerous species of songbirds and other small animals. Facilities and activities include self-guiding trails, floating marsh boardwalks, waterfowl gardens, year-round fishing, summer boat and canoe rentals, snowshoeing, skating and tobogganing. Picnic facilities are available.

The interpretive center features a theater, the Aquarium of the Prairies, an energy exhibit, the Honeybee Observation Hive, and the Touch Museum. Allow 1 hour minimum. Mon.-Fri. 9-5, Sat.-Sun. and holidays 10-5; closed Dec. 25. Special evening hours in summer and fall; phone for hours. Admission $4; over 65 and ages 3-17, $3. MC, VI. Phone (204) 989-8355.

FUN MOUNTAIN WATER SLIDE PARK, off Hwy. 1, 6 km (3.6 mi.) e. of Lagimodière Blvd., then 1

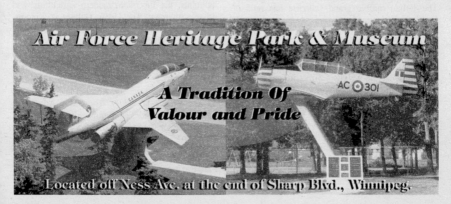

km (.6 mi.) s. on Murdock Rd., offers 10 water-slides, a swimming area, a hot tub, bumper boats, miniature golf, picnic areas and locker and changing facilities. Food is available. Daily 10-8, June-Aug. (weather permitting). Admission $12; ages 4-12, $9.50; over 55, $6. Twilight rate, $7.25. AE, MC, VI. Phone (204) 255-4542.

GRANT'S OLD MILL is at Portage Ave. and Booth Dr. This operational, reconstructed log mill—the original was built in 1829—marks the first use of water power in the Western provinces. Guided tours are available. Allow 30 minutes minimum. Daily 10-6, mid-May through Labour Day. Donations. Phone (204) 986-5613.

HISTORICAL MUSEUM OF ST. JAMES-ASSINIBOIA, 3180 Portage Ave., is in Assiniboia's old municipal hall. The museum houses a collection of artifacts relating to the history of the St. James-Assiniboia area and a display building of pioneer activities. Guided tours through the mid-19th-century William Brown Log House offer a glimpse of the pioneer lifestyle. Allow 1 hour minimum. Daily 10-5, mid-May to late Aug.; Mon.-Fri. 10-5, rest of year. Donations. Phone (204) 888-8706.

KILDONAN PARK, 2021 Main St., comprises 40 hectares (99 acres) bordering the Red River. The park's giant trees are considered some of the oldest and largest in the province. In the park are flower gardens, a rock garden and a model of the witch's hut from the Hansel and Gretel fairytale.

During the summer the park is home to Rainbow Stage, Winnipeg's outdoor theater. Summer activities in the park center around the Olympic-size swimming pool, public boat dock and areas for bicycling, walking and in-line skating. In winter, tobogganing, ice skating and cross-country skiing are the chief sports. Food is available. Daily 8 a.m.-10 p.m. Free. Phone (204) 986-3753, or 780-7328 for theater information. *See Recreation Chart.*

LEGISLATIVE BUILDING, on 12 hectares (30 acres) bordered by Broadway Ave., Kennedy and Osborne sts. and the Assiniboine River, reflects neo-classical design in native Tyndall limestone. The Italian marble grand staircase has rails of fossil-marked limestone and is guarded at its base by the two life-size bronze bison that are the emblems of Manitoba.

Atop the dome is the Golden Boy, the work of Parisian sculptor Charles Gardet. This 4.9-metre-tall (16-ft.) statue weighs 4.5 metric tons (5 tons) and is sheathed in 23.5 carat goldleaf. The torch in the figure's right hand points to economic development and progress in the north; the sheaf of wheat in the left arm represents agriculture.

Plots containing several hundred varieties of flowers, foliage and ornamental plants are on the property. Guided tours are conducted every hour daily 9-6, July 1-Labour Day; by appointment rest of year. Free. Phone (204) 945-5813 for reservations.

LIVING PRAIRIE MUSEUM is at 2795 Ness Ave. This 12-hectare (30-acre) unplowed tract supports more than 160 native plant species and is a remnant of the prairie that once covered much of North America. An interpretive center features displays of plants and animals of the tall grass prairie. Nature talks and hikes are offered, and a self-guiding trail brochure is available.

Allow 1 hour minimum. Interpretive center open daily 10-5, July-Aug.; Sun. 10-5, May-June; by appointment rest of year. Free. Phone (204) 832-0167.

SAVE ★ **MANITOBA MUSEUM OF MAN AND NATURE**, Main St. and Rupert Ave., is part of the Manitoba Centennial Centre complex. The extensive exhibits—including collections, audiovisual presentations and dioramas—elaborate on the museum's major theme: the relationship of people and their environment throughout the history of Manitoba. The purpose of the museum is introduced in the Orientation Gallery.

The Earth History Gallery depicts the geologic and organic evolution of Manitoba, while the Arctic/Sub-Arctic Gallery explores facets of the Inuit culture and supplies information about the wildlife and vegetation of the Arctic zone. The Boreal Forest Gallery deals with the relationship of people and their environment in the province's northern coniferous forests. The core of the gallery is a walk-through diorama of a granite cliff with a waterfall, a small marsh, a Cree family and wandering moose.

The *Nonsuch* is a replica of a ship that sailed from England to the Hudson Bay in 1668, establishing a direct sea route to the valuable furs of the great northern forests. The voyage led to the founding of the Hudson's Bay Co. in 1670. The 15.3-metre (50-ft.) ketch is anchored in a reconstruction of a 17th-century Thames River wharf with surrounding buildings.

The Grasslands Gallery deals with southern Manitoba, focusing on the province's early inhabitants, the fur trade, modern agriculture and urban settlement. The Urban Gallery is a reconstruction of Winnipeg in the boom town era of the 1920s.

Allow 1 hour minimum. Museum galleries open daily 10-6, Victoria Day-Labour Day; Tues.-Fri. 10-4, Sat.-Sun. and holidays 10-5, rest of year. Closed Dec. 25. Admission $4.99; over 65 and ages 3-17, $3.99. The 3-day Adventure Value Pass includes museum, planetarium and science center for $10.99; over 65 and ages 3-17, $7.99. AE, MC, VI. Phone (204) 956-2830 or 943-3139.

Planetarium Theatre, on the lower level of the Manitoba Museum of Man and Nature, presents multimedia shows about our universe.

Allow 1 hour minimum. Shows are presented on the hour daily 11-6, Victoria Day-Labour Day; Tues.-Fri. at 3, Sat.-Sun. and holidays at noon, 2 and 4, rest of year. Family shows are presented Sat.-Sun. and holidays at 11, 1 and 3. Admission $3.99; over 65 and ages 3-17, $2.99. The 3-day Adventure Value Pass includes museum, planetarium and science center for $10.99; over 65 and ages 3-17, $7.99. AE, MC, VI. Phone (204) 956-2830, or 943-3139 for show times.

Science Centre is a hands-on learning center that depicts the ways in which the human senses perceive the universe. Allow 1 hour minimum. Daily 10-6, Victoria Day-Labour Day; Tues.-Fri. 10-4, Sat.-Sun. and holidays 10-5, rest of year. Admission $3.99; over 65 and ages 3-17, $2.99. The 3-day Adventure Value Pass includes museum, planetarium and science center for $10.99; over 65 and ages 3-17, $7.99. AE, MC, VI. Phone (204) 956-2830 or 943-3139.

MARION AND ED VICKAR JEWISH MUSEUM OF WESTERN CANADA AND HOLOCAUST EDUCATION CENTRE, 123 Doncaster St., shares the history, experiences, achievements and culture of the Jewish people in Western Canada. The museum's permanent exhibit depicts the settlement of Jews in Western Canada through mementoes, photographs and archival material. The education center features items from the Holocaust. Changing exhibits and a library also are available. Allow 30 minutes minimum. Sun.-Fri. noon-4. Free. Phone (204) 477-7464.

RIEL HOUSE NATIONAL HISTORIC SITE, 330 River Rd., was the home of the mother of Louis Riel. Although this leader of the Métis and founder of the provisional government of Manitoba never lived in the house, his body lay in state for several days after his execution in 1885. The small log building with board siding is furnished in period.

The walkway to the house has signs explaining the history of the Métis and of the Riel family. Allow 30 minutes minimum. Guided tours daily 10-6, mid-May through Labour Day. Donations. Phone (204) 257-1783.

ROSS HOUSE MUSEUM, 140 Meade St. N. in Joe Zuken Heritage Park, was originally founded as the first post office in western Canada in 1855. Displays reflect the life of the Ross family when their home served as the post office. Allow 30 minutes minimum. Wed.-Sun. 11-6, June-Aug. Free. Phone (204) 943-3958.

★ **ROYAL CANADIAN MINT,** 520 Lagimodière Blvd. at jct. Trans Canada Hwy. and Hwy. 59, is considered one of the world's most modern mints. The Winnipeg Plant produces all of the circulation coinage for Canada and coinage for many foreign countries. The building includes a landscaped interior courtyard, a glass tower and a horseshoe-shaped tour route. A coin display

provides historical information. Guided tours are available.

Mon.-Fri. 9-5, May-Aug.; 10-2, rest of year. Closed holidays. Last tour begins 1 hour before closing. Admission $2, under 6 free, family rate $8. Phone (204) 257-3359.

SAINT BONIFACE MUSEUM, s.e. on Main St. (Hwy. 1), then n. to 494 Taché Ave., was built 1846-51 as the first convent and hospital in western Canada. Displays depict the Red River Settlement and early French and Métis Manitoba. Visitors also can view the nearby ruins of the cathedral as well as the cemetery where Louis Riel, leader of the Red River Resistance, is buried.

Allow 30 minutes minimum. Mon.-Fri. 9-5, Sat. 10-4, Sun. 10-8, May-Sept.; Mon.-Fri. 9-5, Sat.-Sun. 10-4, in Oct.; Mon.-Fri. 9-5, rest of year. Closed Dec. 24-25 and 31. Admission $2, senior citizens, physically impaired and students with ID $1.50, under 5 free, family rate $6. Phone (204) 237-4500.

SAINT NORBERT PROVINCIAL HERITAGE PARK, 40 Turnbull Dr., is a 7-hectare (17-acre) park at the forks of the Red and La Salle rivers. The park is near the former village of St. Norbert, which is rich in historical sites and linked to Manitoba's entry into the Confederation. Maison Bohémier, a 19th-century French Canadian farmhouse, and Maison Turenne, a 19th-century French Canadian village house, have been restored and decorated with period furnishings.

A self-guiding walking trail offers interpretations of native inhabitants and the history of Manitoba. A Red River frame log house belonging to Pierre Delorme, a member of the Louis Riel Provisional Government, also is displayed. Guided tours are available. Picnicking and fishing are permitted. Allow 1 hour minimum. Thurs.-Mon. 10:30-5:30, mid-May through Labour Day. Free. Phone (204) 269-5377, or 945-4375 in the off-season.

SEVEN OAKS HOUSE, 1.5 blks. e. of Main St. on Rupertsland Blvd. in W. Kildonan, is said to be the oldest habitable house in Manitoba. This sturdy building, with its stone foundation, handhewn oak timbers, hand-split shingles and buffalo hair-bound plaster, was built 1851-53. The house displays belongings of the original occupants. Guided tours are available. Allow 30 minutes minimum. Daily 10-5, last weekend in May-Labour Day. Admission $1; under 12, 25c. Phone (204) 339-7429.

TRANSCONA HISTORICAL MUSEUM, 141 Regent Ave. W., is housed in a 1927 bank building and contains items pertaining to the history of Transcona, a railroad town that was amalgamated into greater Winnipeg. The museum contains railroad memorabilia, a butterfly collection, firearms, pioneer articles, native artifacts and more than 25,000 photographs. Highlights include the ship's wheel from the World War II HMCS

Transcona, a 1913 hand-carved grandfather clock from the Fort Garry Hotel and a Royal Canadian Mounted Police tunic. Allow 30 minutes minimum. Mon.-Sat. 10-5, Sun. 1-5, June-Aug.; Tues.-Fri. noon-5, Sat. 10-5, Feb.-May and Sept.-Dec. Free. Phone (204) 222-0423.

UKRAINIAN CULTURAL AND EDUCATIONAL CENTRE (OSEREDOK), 184 Alexander Ave. E., at Main St. and Disraeli Frwy., is dedicated to the preservation of the Canadian-Ukrainian experience. Highlights include a museum, an art gallery, a library and archives. Interpretive exhibits relate to the Ukrainian heritage around the world, and include a wide range of artifacts, from fine art to farm implements to rare 16th-century maps. Guided tours are available by appointment. Allow 30 minutes minimum. Mon.-Fri. 9:30-4:30, Sat. 10:30-3, Sun. 2-5. Donations. Phone (204) 942-0218.

[SAVE] **WESTERN CANADA AVIATION MUSEUM** in an Aircraft Hangar off Ellice Ave. at 958 Ferry Rd., displays a large collection of vintage aircraft. Artifacts and exhibits portray all aspects of aviation, from bush planes to commercial airliners, from combat planes to homemade aircraft. Children can explore the interactive Skyways exhibit and Spaceways, a simulated trip through space to Mars. Videotape presentations about historical aircraft are offered. Guided tours and a research library and archives are available by appointment.

Allow 1 hour minimum. Mon.-Sat. 10-4, Sun. 1-4; closed Jan. 1, Good Friday and Dec. 25-26. Admission $3; ages 3-17, $2; family rate $7.50. MC, VI. Phone (204) 786-5503.

WINNIPEG ART GALLERY is at 300 Memorial Blvd. Eight galleries contain contemporary and historical works by Manitoban, Canadian and international artists. The Inuit art collection is reputed to be one of the most significant collections of contemporary Inuit art in the world. Guided tours and lectures are offered. Food is available.

Allow 1 hour minimum. Daily 10-5 (also Wed. 5-9), June-Sept.; Tues.-Sun. 11-5 (also Wed. 5-9), rest of year. Admission $4, over 59 and students with ID $3, under 12 free, family rate $6; free to all Wed. AE, MC, VI. Phone (204) 786-6641.

WINNIPEG COMMODITY EXCHANGE is at 500-360 Main St. The exchange, established in 1887, is Canada's oldest and largest agricultural futures and options exchange. Guided tours are available by reservation. A visitor gallery in room 500 is open Mon.-Fri. 9:30-1:30; closed holidays. Free. Phone (204) 925-5000.

CASINOS

- **Club Regent**, 1425 Regent Ave. Daily noon-2 a.m.; closed major holidays. Phone (204) 957-2700.

- **Crystal Casino**, 222 Broadway Ave., 7th floor. Mon.-Sat. noon-2 a.m., Sun. 2 p.m.-2 a.m.; closed major holidays. Phone (204) 957-2600.

- **McPhillips Street Station**, 484 McPhillips St. Daily noon-2 a.m.; closed major holidays. Phone (204) 957-3900.

What To Do

Sightseeing

The intersection of Portage Avenue and Main Street, a few blocks from the juncture of Winnipeg's two rivers, has been the major crossroads since the city's earliest days and is a good place to start a sightseeing foray.

Although now part of Winnipeg, the early settlement of St. Boniface has retained its French Canadian identity. A monument honoring the explorer Pierre Gaultier de la Vérendrye is on Taché Avenue opposite St. Boniface Hospital. Also in St. Boniface is the grave of Louis Riel, leader of the Métis and of the provisional government 1869-70. The grave is at Taché and Cathedral avenues in the churchyard of the St. Boniface Basilica.

Boat and Bus Tours

PADDLEWHEEL/RIVER ROUGE TOURS offer boat and bus tours of Winnipeg. The river boats are docked downtown on the banks of the Red River near the Forks. The MS *Paddlewheel Queen*, MS *Paddlewheel Princess* and the MS *River Rouge* offer daytime and evening cruises on the Assiniboine and Red rivers. Paddlewheel double-decker buses offers pick-up at and return service to downtown hotels and motels. Food is available.

Two-hour sightseeing cruise departs daily at 1, May-Oct. Three-hour dinner/dance cruise departs daily at 7, May-Oct. Three-hour moonlight dance cruise departs Fri.-Sat. at 10 p.m., May-Oct. Historic cruise departs Wed.-Fri. at 9 and returns at 4, July-Aug. Bus tour departs daily 9-noon, June-Sept. Combination cruise and bus tour departs at 9 and returns at 4, June-Sept. Fares range $11.75-$28.75; over 65, $10.25-$25.70; under 12, $6.50-$16.50. Reservations are recommended. MC, VI. Phone (204) 942-4500.

Plane Tours

The Winnipeg Flying Club, (204) 338-7927, 16 kilometres (10 mi.) north of the perimeter on Hwy. 9 at St. Andrews Airport, offers scenic flights over Winnipeg, the Red River and the Lake Winnipeg area. Tours are offered daily with 2 days' advance notice.

Walking Tours

Guided walking tours in the Exchange District of the 20-block Historic Winnipeg area near Portage Avenue and Main Street are available during

July and August. Departing from the entrance of the Pantages Playhouse Theatre at 180 Market Ave. E., these tours visit many of Manitoba's finest historical buildings. For schedule information phone (204) 986-4718.

One of the original ethnic neighborhoods of the city, Selkirk Avenue is a mini-city that grew with the development of the railway in the 1880s. One-hour walking tours of the area depart from the Amphitheater on Selkirk Avenue, 4 blocks west of Main Street, from June to August. For information phone (204) 586-3445.

Walking tours of the old Saint Boniface area also are available. Phone (204) 235-1406 for information and reservations.

Sports and Recreation

Devotees of organized sports will find many opportunities to indulge themselves in Winnipeg. Canadians love **hockey,** and those who fancy flying sticks and flashing skates will find the International Hockey League's Manitoba Moose locking horns with their opponents at the Winnipeg Arena in the city's sports complex at 1430 Maroons Rd. Fans of **wrestling** will also find their sport at the arena.

Football fans can watch the Canadian Football League's Blue Bombers playing at the sports complex from June to November. The Northern **Baseball** League's Winnipeg Goldeyes play at The Forks from June to September.

To obtain additional information and tickets for sports and recreation events listed above, phone (204) 780-8080 for recorded information, or 780-7328, or (800) 465-7328 in Canada, N.D., Minn., S.D. and Wis.

Sports car racing enthusiasts converge at the Victory Lanes Speedway, (204) 582-0527, Hwy. 75, 5 kilometres (3 mi.) south of St. Norbert, on Tuesday at 7:30 p.m. from May through September (weather permitting).

Assiniboia Downs, 3975 Portage Ave. at the Perimeter Highway, offers **Thoroughbred racing** early May through early October. Simulcast races are offered year-round; phone (204) 885-3330.

Note: Policies concerning admittance of children to pari-mutuel betting facilities vary. Phone for information.

Other spectator sports include minor league hockey, **curling** and **ringette** games, held at municipal skating rinks, and **cricket** played in Assiniboine Park.

There are 23 **golf** courses in Winnipeg. Public courses include Crescent Drive, (204) 453-4875; Harbour View, (204) 222-2751; John Blumberg, (204) 888-8860; Kildonan Park, (204) 334-0452; Tuxedo, (204) 888-2867; and Windsor Park, (204) 257-1264 or 257-1265.

Winnipeg has more than 280 **tennis** courts, some lighted for night matches. Many courts are at community centers. Championship matches are held during the summer at various locations throughout the city. **Squash, handball** and **racquetball** players can avail themselves of courts at a number of athletic clubs and local universities. For information contact the Manitoba Sports Federation; phone (204) 985-4000.

Fans of **bicycling** and **in-line skating** take to the marked paths in Winnipeg's city parks. Bicycle trails along less-traveled side streets in and around Winnipeg also have been established. **Cross-country skiing, tobogganing** and **ice skating** facilities are available at Assiniboine, Kildonan and St. Vital parks; facilities for ice skating also are found at numerous schools and community clubs.

Downhill skiing is available at Spring Hill Winter Park Ski Area, (204) 224-3051, near Birds Hill Provincial Park, at the junction of Hwy. 59N at the Floodway; and Stony Mountain Winter Park, (204) 344-5977, 10 kilometres (6 mi.) north of the perimeter of Hwy. 7. Birds Hill Provincial Park, (204) 222-9151, also is a site for **snowmobiling** and cross-country skiing.

Swimming can be pursued all year in Winnipeg, where numerous indoor pools include those at four YM-YWCAs; phone (204) 989-4100. The Pan-Am Swimming Pool, 25 Poseidon Bay, is one of the largest indoor bodies of water in Canada and is open all year; phone (204) 986-5894.

Many recreational activities are available at the Harbour View Recreation Complex in the northeastern section of Winnipeg in Kil-Cona Park, 1867 Springfield Road (*see Recreation Chart*). At this 162-hectare (400-acre) park are facilities for **miniature golf, lawn bowling, shuffleboard** and **horseshoes** as well as tennis courts, a golf course, a driving range and pedal boats during the summer. Golf and tennis lessons are available April to October. Ice skating, tobogganing, cross-country skiing and skiing lessons are available during the winter. Phone (204) 222-2751.

Shopping

The intersection of Portage Avenue and Main Street is a good starting point for a shopping excursion. Winnipeg Square and the underground Lombard Concourse offer shops ranging from boutiques to bookstores. Portage Avenue also is the site of the city's largest department stores. Portage Place connects Eatons to The Bay (the Hudson's Bay Co.) with an extensive system of skywalks.

Winnipeg has an historic area where shoppers can browse through merchandise of today amid structures of the past. The Forks Market is behind Union Station, off Main Street (near Portage and Main). The shops and restaurants are located in an indoor market with more than 80 vendors selling everything from fresh fish and baked goods to arts and crafts items. The Johnston Terminal, across from the market, offers specialty boutiques and eateries

Shopping for Western wear and accessories is possible at such factory outlet stores as Canada West Boots, Boulet Boots or MWG Apparel. More than 50 shops and restaurants can be found at Osborne Street Village, between River and Stradbrook avenues 2 blocks south of the Legislative Building. Travelers in search of a truly representative souvenir may want to examine the native arts and crafts and western wear available at the Winnipeg Fur Exchange at 250 McPhillips.

Finally, visitors who like their shopping climate controlled and under one roof can visit the malls at Eaton Place, 234 Donald St.; Garden City, 843 Leila Ave.; Grant Park, 1120 Grant Ave.; Kildonan Place, 1555 Regent Ave.; Polo Park, 1485 Portage Ave.; Portage Place, 393 Portage Ave.; St. Vital Centre, 1225 St. Mary's; or Unicity Mall, 3605 Portage Ave.

Theater and Concerts

Canada's Royal Winnipeg Ballet, Winnipeg Symphony Orchestra and Manitoba Opera perform in Centennial Concert Hall, 555 Main St., opposite City Hall. The oldest company in Canada and the second oldest in North America, Canada's Royal Winnipeg Ballet is known for its versatile style and performs an eclectic mix of classical and contemporary ballets. At home performances are in October, December, March and May. For ticket information phone (204) 956-2792 or (800) 667-4792.

The Winnipeg Symphony Orchestra performs September to May and offers classical, contemporary and popular orchestral music. For concert information phone (204) 949-3999. The Manitoba Opera performs three productions November through April; phone (204) 942-7479, 780-7328 or (888) 780-7328.

Modern dance is presented by Winnipeg's Contemporary Dancers from September through May at the Gas Station Theatre, 445 River Ave. For information phone (204) 452-0229.

Theater lovers can enjoy performances of the classics, comedies and modern dramas at the Manitoba Theatre Centre Mainstage, 174 Market St., from October to April. For general information or tickets phone (204) 942-6537. The MTC Warehouse Theatre, 140 Rupert Ave., (204) 942-6537, features alternative theater performances from October to February. The Lyric Theatre, just east of the Pavilion in Assiniboine Park, (204) 888-5466, ext. 5, is an outdoor theater showcasing drama festivals as well as performances by the Royal Winnipeg Ballet and the Winnipeg Symphony Orchestra.

For both adults and young people, the Prairie Theatre Exchange, at Portage Place, 393 Portage Ave., (204) 942-7291, presents a season of modern Canadian plays from September to March.

Rainbow Stage in Kildonan Park offers musicals in a covered outdoor theater during July and August; phone (204) 784-1288, or 780-7328 for tickets. Celebrations Dinner Theatre, 1824 Pembina Hwy., combines an original, three-act musical comedy with a four-course dinner for a one-stop evening out; phone (204) 982-8282.

The IMAX Theater, Portage Place, 393 Portage Ave. in downtown Winnipeg, features a five-and-one-half-story-high by 22-metre-wide (72-ft.) screen. Phone (204) 956-4629 for information or (204) 780-7328 to reserve tickets.

The French Canadian heritage of St. Boniface, in the heart of the French district, is remembered through the support of the Centre Culturel Franco-Manitobain at 340 Provencher Blvd. The center is the home of such cultural groups as Le Cercle Molière theater company (Canada's oldest active theater group), the dance group L'Ensemble Folklorique de la Rivière Rouge, and the choral groups L'Alliance Chorale Manitoba, La Chorale des Intrépides and Les Blés au Vent. Phone (204) 233-8053 for more information.

Special Events

Winnipeg's calendar of events, with more than 130 days of festivals, reflects more than 43 nationalities that have made the city home. The spirit of the French pioneers is revived each February during the Festival du Voyageur, a weeklong celebration including winter sports, ice-sculpting contests, music and food.

The city plays host to the 4-day Winnipeg International Children's Festival at The Forks in early June. Music, theater, dance and comedy performances are offered as well as hands-on workshops and evening shows; for tickets and information phone (204) 958-4730.

The week-long Jazz Winnipeg Festival in late June features jazz performers on an outdoor stage. The Red River Exhibition, known locally as the "The Ex" is held during late June. The Ex's many rides, midway activities and games of chance as well as nightly concerts take place at Red River Exhibition Park off Perimeter Highway behind Assiniboia Downs.

In early July is the 10-day Winnipeg Fringe Festival, with various theater performances in the Exchange District. Mid-July brings the 4-day Winnipeg Folk Festival to nearby Birds Hill Provincial Park, where more than 200 concerts, children's activities, music workshops and food are highlighted. In late July A Taste of Manitoba features some 30 restaurants offering samples of their food along with entertainment.

Early August brings the 8-day Folklorama multicultural celebration, Winnipeg's largest event and reputedly the largest multicultural festival of its kind. The following month, those of German extraction host Oktoberfest, a celebration in mid-September with lively music and plenty of beer, wurst and Bavarian delicacies.

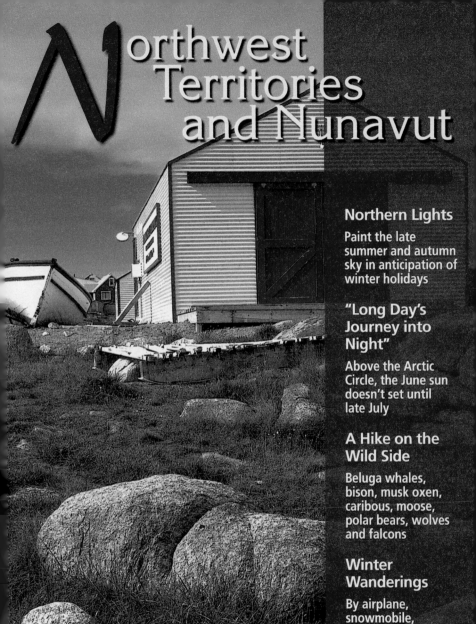

Northwest Territories and Nunavut

Northern Lights

Paint the late summer and autumn sky in anticipation of winter holidays

"Long Day's Journey into Night"

Above the Arctic Circle, the June sun doesn't set until late July

A Hike on the Wild Side

Beluga whales, bison, musk oxen, caribous, moose, polar bears, wolves and falcons

Winter Wanderings

By airplane, snowmobile, dog sled or on a highway of ice

Sundry Scenery

Tundras, alpine plains, mountains, spruce forests, pristine lakes and rivers

head north

Take a journey into northern Canada and you may be surprised at your options for enjoyment.

Residents joke that the four seasons in the Northwest Territories and Nunavut—June, July, August and winter—are a bit unlike seasons in the rest of the world. The absence of a "real" spring or fall leaves busy summers and extra-long winters.

Arrive in June, July or August and you can dip your toes in the Arctic Ocean and marvel at the wildflower-dotted tundra under a midnight sun.

Or visit during the 8 months of winter and you can choose from myriad activities that involve snow and ice: snowmobiling, building an igloo, ice fishing, riding on a paw-powered sled or simply driving on an "ice highway," made of hard-packed

snow piled on frozen lakes.

Celebrate the end of a long, dark winter by living it up at Inuvik's Sunrise Festival—held in honor of the sun's appearance after months of hiding.

Other diversions do not depend on snow or sun: Try a moose burger or dine on arctic char. Shop for such treasures as whalebone or soapstone carvings. Learn about the traditions of the Inuit and Dene cultures. Set your sights on beluga whales or polar bears. See a shaggy musk-ox up close or listen to the roar of hooves from a migrating herd of caribous.

Whatever the season, the Northwest Territories and Nunavut invite you to refresh your senses in the north.

On April Fools' Day, 1999, in the eastern Northwest Territories, very few Inuit people were worried about such practical jokes as sugar in the salt shaker.

Instead, the focus was on celebrating the birth of Nunavut, Canada's newest province. On this night, Inuit eyes were toward the heavens, watching as a grand display of colorful explosions lit up the black sky. Matching the glow of the fireworks were the sparks in the hearts of the Inuit, whose hopes are high for a bright future.

Twenty-four years after a separation was proposed, Nunavut (meaning *our land* in the Inuktitut language) officially seceded from the expansive Northwest Territories to form its own province. A new line on the Canadian map allows its approximately 25,000 residents—85 percent of whom are Inuit—the chance to reclaim and govern what they have always believed to be their own.

Where the Streets Have No Name

Nunavut, a giant chunk of arctic earth stretching so far northeast it almost tickles the shores of Greenland, contains only one road within its 2 million square kilometres. Above the tree line, it's a place where animals outnumber humans; where brightly colored rhododendron, lupines, yellow buttercups and mountain avens sprinkle treeless tundra; and where it may be easier to hook a 30-pound trout for dinner than pick up a cheeseburger at a drive-thru.

The tiny capital city of Iqaluit rests at the southern tip of mountainous Baffin Island, from which steep cliffs drop about 610 metres to the sea. Here it's no surprise to see caribou wander along unnamed streets, passing St. Jude's Anglican church—which, by the way, is shaped like an igloo. But don't worry; there are plenty of folks who can show you around, and during summer the midnight sun shines bright to light your way.

Even farther north is Ellesmere Island National Park Reserve, which extends above the 80th parallel, just a snowball's throw from Santa's workshop. In this globe-top world of snowcapped peaks and glaciers, ice simply does not melt.

Despite the recent division of Nunavut and Northwest Territories, the two still share identical features. Take light, for example. During summer above the Arctic Circle, days have no end. A shining sun never dips below the horizon, and the sky

Sir Martin Frobisher, searching for the Northwest Passage to the Orient, arrives.
1576

The Treaty of Paris grants Canada to the British.
1763

Alexander Mackenzie establishes a trading post for the North West Co.
1789

1771
Hudson's Bay Co. explorer-trader Samuel Hearne arrives at Great Slave Lake.

NW Territories Historical Timeline

1845
Capt. Robert Le Mesurier McClure discovers the Northwest Passage.

is illuminated 24 hours a day. In winter, the opposite occurs as days and nights melt together under a cold, dark sky.

Sound dismal and depressing? Well, picture the sight of a black sky pin-pricked with stars surrounding a full, glowing moon, its light sprawling across wide, snow-covered tundra and frozen lakes. On such a clear winter night the flat, stark-white landscape glistens and appears endless.

Bright Lights, Small Cities

The Northern Lights, or "aurora borealis," painting the winter sky are no less impressive. A faint glow slightly above the horizon serves as the show's opening act. When the lights rise, they resemble curtains in shades of red, lavender and green. Feather-shaped and stretching across the night sky, the lights ripple and curl, forming watercolored waves.

In the Northwest Territories, you'll have a good chance to catch this dazzling display from October through February. A spot void of city lights is best; try giant Great Slave Lake, the sixth largest freshwater lake in North America (near Yellowknife). Frozen in winter, it provides a fine view of the vivid night sky.

Then visit Yellowknife, on the lake's north arm. Once glittering with gold, this former 1930s mining camp now flaunts its colorful past in Old Town, where shops and quaint neighborhoods nestle against the shore.

West of the city is Nahanni National Park, where 90-metre-high Virginia Falls plummets into South Nahanni River. The falls, arguably more spectacular than Niagara, form a pool of eddies and perilous rapids surrounded by cliffs taller than Toronto's CN Tower.

Roads are in short supply here, but sparkling falls and rivers await you on scenic drives. Mackenzie Highway, the territories' only paved highway, crosses the Mackenzie River near Fort Providence. Continue east along the "Waterfall Route" to Sambaa Deh Falls Park, where trails lead to two cascades.

Many motorists also choose to navigate the Dempster Highway, which dead-ends at Inuvik, the continent's farthest point north accessible by road.

In fact, visiting the lands north of the 60th parallel may be the brightest idea you've ever had.

Hudson's Bay Co. cedes the region to Canada.
1870

A Soviet nuclear-powered satellite crashes into the Great Slave Lake area; debris is spread over 124,000 square kilometres.
1978

1911
Oil is discovered at Norman Wells.

1934
Gold is discovered at Yellowknife on Great Slave Lake.

Discovery of diamond-bearing rock in the Lac de Gras area sets off a diamond rush at Yellowknife.
1991

1992
The Nunavut Land Claim Agreement, under which the Inuit give up any future aboriginal rights to their traditional land in return for the power to govern their own territory, is passed.

1999
Northwest Territories divides into two territories; the eastern, Inuit-governed territory becomes Nunavut.

Recreation

Welcome to the top of the world. The vast Northwest Territories and Nunavut boast an area filled with wild rivers, icy seas, lofty mountains and Arctic tundra. Recreational diversions for both the adventure seeker and casual traveler are numerous.

Summer days, typically June through August, are long and surprisingly mild. With an average temperature of 21 C (70 F), visitors can enjoy the outdoors without the gear that winter demands. **Hikers** can check out a wide variety of topography, from steep mountain trails to Arctic tundra. The Canol Heritage Trail, en route to the Yukon, offers some challenging terrain.

Snowmobiling, snowshoeing and **cross-country skiing** are a way of life that has been known to extend into June—the warmer air and long days make this the perfect time for such outdoor pursuits. Recreational activities also can be combined with viewing the spectacular Northern Lights. Many outfitters offer snowmobile tours or flights to remote areas to observe this brilliant display. Hint: The best time for viewing these dancing lights is September through January.

Getting There is Half the Fun

Travel anywhere in the territories can include aircraft, boat, automobile, snowmobile, Inuit qomatiq (sled) and even dog sled. Of the Northwest Territories' four national parks, only Wood Buffalo can be reached by road. Nahanni is accessible solely by air; its rugged beauty is best explored by the experienced canoer. Only the hardy recreationalist should fly to the extremely remote Aulavik, where craggy badlands include thousands of archeological sites. The newest park, Tuktut Nogait, is a hiker's paradise where float planes begin landing on the Homaday River in mid-June.

High in Canada's eastern Arctic is Nunavut's Baffin Island and its two national parks. Auyuittug, reached by dog sled in winter and boat in summer, draws **climbers** to its lofty peaks. The sheer cliffs and arctic fiords of Ellesmere Island, North America's northernmost national park, can be explored by guided tour; outfitters are available in Grise Fiord, Iqaluit and Resoloute.

Land of Adventure

Water challenges come in varying degrees of difficulty. **Canoeing** and **kayaking** conditions depend on the weather. Arctic rivers, while dangerous, can offer the ultimate thrill if explored cautiously. Sea kayakers can flow beside towering icebergs, while the many rivers stemming off the meandering Mackenzie are a canoeist's dream. Paddlers will be dazzled by the breathtaking scenery on the Nahanni. Hoist your sails on Great Slave Lake, where the wind is just right for **sailing**, or if you are brave enough, **scuba dive** in the frigid waters. Slave River rapids await **white-water rafting** enthusiasts.

Cold northern waters yield excellent **fishing**. Plenty of lakes, streams and rivers are full of prize catches, from the feisty arctic char to the fierce northern pike. Some of the territories' waters are ranked the best in the world for angling, including Great Slave and Murky lakes and the Stark and Snowdrift rivers. **Ice fishing** is another way to reel in the big one. Don't forget your fishing license.

The land's beauty, combined with unspoiled wilderness and vast game selections, makes **hunting** quite a rewarding experience. For the ultimate hunt, sports enthusiasts can track down one of the world's largest predators—the polar bear—by dog sled. Musk ox hunting is another option. Other prized trophies include caribou, moose, wolverines, and grizzly and black bears. Hunts are strictly controlled; licensed guides and permits are required.

For those who like to shoot with a camera, **wildlife viewing** is rewarding. An outfitter will increase your chances of spotting the Arctic's resident polar bear. **Birdwatchers** flock to the Mackenzie River delta, one of the world's biggest nesting grounds.

Whether you are seeking adventure for a few hours or several days, an outfitter will help. NWT Arctic Tourism, (867) 873-7200, or Nunavut Tourism, (867) 979-6551, can offer information about tour companies and outfitters. For information about camping see the AAA/CAA Western Canada and Alaska CampBook.

Recreational Activities

Throughout the TourBook, you may notice a Recreational Activities heading with bulleted listings of recreation-oriented establishments listed underneath. Since normal AAA inspection criteria cannot be applied, these establishments are presented for information only. Age, height and weight restrictions may apply. Reservations are often recommended and sometimes required. Visitors should phone or write the attraction for additional information, and the address and phone number are provided for this purpose.

Fast Facts

POPULATION: 64,400.

AREA: 3,376,698 sq km (1,303,743 sq mi).

CAPITAL: Yellowknife, Northwest Territories; Iqaluit, Nunavut.

HIGHEST POINT: 2,762 m/9,062 ft., Cirque of the Unclimbables Mountain northwest of Nahanni National Park Reserve.

LOWEST POINT: Sea level, Beaufort Sea.

TIME ZONES: Mountain/Central/Eastern/ Atlantic. DST.

MINIMUM AGE FOR DRIVERS: 16.

SEAT BELT/CHILD RESTRAINT LAWS: Seat belts required for driver and all passengers; child restraints required for children weighing less than 18 kilograms (40 pounds).

HELMETS FOR MOTORCYCLISTS: Required for driver and passenger.

RADAR DETECTORS: Not permitted; visitors traveling in or passing through the Northwest Territories and Nunavut should detach their units and store them inside their luggage.

FIREARMS LAWS: Vary by province and territory. Contact Renewable Resources, Box 2668, Yellowknife, NT, Canada X1A 2P9; phone (867) 873-7184.

HOLIDAYS: Jan. 1; Good Friday; Easter Monday; Victoria Day, May 24 (if a Mon.) or the closest prior Mon.; Canada Day, July 1; Civic Holiday, Aug. (1st Mon.); Labour Day, Sept. (1st Mon.); Thanksgiving, Oct. (2nd Mon.); Remembrance Day, Nov. 11; Dec. 25-26.

TAXES: The Northwest Territories and Nunavut have no territorial sales tax.

TERRITORIAL INFORMATION CENTERS: An office at the Alberta border on the 60th parallel is open 8 a.m.-10 p.m., late May to mid-September. A center at Km-post 77 on Hwy. 8 near Fort McPherson is open 10-10, early June to mid-September. The Northern Frontier Visitor's Centre in Yellowknife is open Mon.-Fri. 8:30-6:30, Sat.-Sun. 9-6, June-Sept.; Mon.-Fri. 8:30-5, Sat.-Sun. noon-4, rest of year. Phone (867) 873-4262.

FURTHER INFORMATION FOR VISITORS:

NWT Arctic Tourism
Box 610
Yellowknife, NT, Canada X1A 2N5
(867) 873-7200
(800) 661-0788

Nunavut Tourism
Box 1450
Iqaluit, NT, Canada X0A 0H0
(867) 979-6551
(800) 491-7910

FISHING AND HUNTING INFORMATION:

NWT Wildlife & Parks
Box 1320
Yellowknife, NT, Canada XIA 2L9
(867) 873-7184

FERRY AND ROAD INFORMATION: For information about the condition of hwys. 1 (Mackenzie), 3 (Yellowknife) and 7 (Fort Liard), phone (800) 661-0750. For Hwy. 8 (Dempster) information phone (800) 661-0752. For information about ferries serving hwys. 1 and 7, phone (800) 661-0751; for ferries serving Hwy. 8, phone (800) 661-0752.

ALCOHOL CONSUMPTION: Legal age 19.

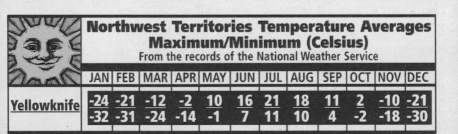

Northwest Territories Temperature Averages
Maximum/Minimum (Celsius)
From the records of the National Weather Service

	JAN	FEB	MAR	APR	MAY	JUN	JUL	AUG	SEP	OCT	NOV	DEC
Yellowknife	-24	-21	-12	-2	10	16	21	18	11	2	-10	-21
	-32	-31	-24	-14	-1	7	11	10	4	-2	-18	-30

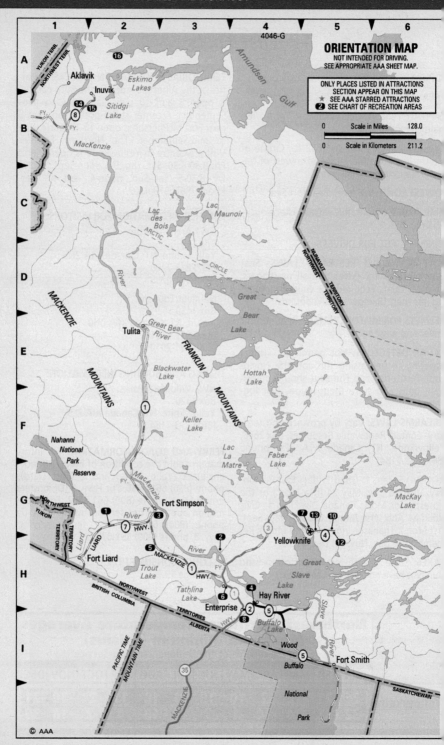

ORIENTATION MAP
NOT INTENDED FOR DRIVING.
SEE APPROPRIATE AAA SHEET MAP.

ONLY PLACES LISTED IN ATTRACTIONS
SECTION APPEAR ON THIS MAP
★ SEE AAA STARRED ATTRACTIONS
❷ SEE CHART OF RECREATION AREAS

Scale in Miles 128.0
Scale in Kilometers 211.2

© AAA

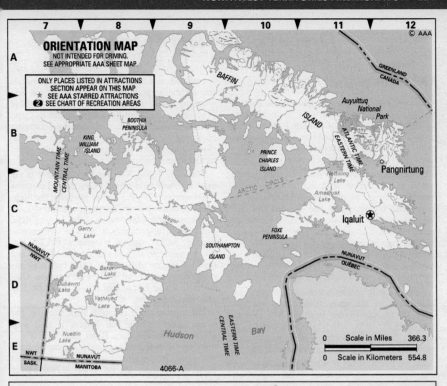

ORIENTATION MAP
NOT INTENDED FOR DRIVING.
SEE APPROPRIATE AAA SHEET MAP.

ONLY PLACES LISTED IN ATTRACTIONS
SECTION APPEAR ON THIS MAP
★ SEE AAA STARRED ATTRACTIONS
2 SEE CHART OF RECREATION AREAS

RECREATION AREAS

	MAP LOCATION	CAMPING	PICNICKING	HIKING TRAILS	BOATING	BOAT RAMP	BOAT RENTAL	FISHING	SWIMMING	PETS ON LEASH	BICYCLE TRAILS	WINTER SPORTS	VISITOR CENTER	LODGE/CABINS	FOOD SERVICE
NATIONAL PARKS *(See place listings)*															
Nahanni (G-1) 4,784 square kilometres 145 km w. of Fort Simpson. The park is not accessible by road; no motor boats allowed.		●	●	●	●	●		●	●	●			●		
Wood Buffalo (I-4) 44,980 square kilometres on Hwy. 5.		●	●	●	●			●	●	●			●	●	
TERRITORIAL															
Blackstone (G-2) on Hwy. 7, 161 km s. of Fort Simpson.	1	●	●	●	●	●		●					●		
Chuk (B-2) s. of Inuvik on Hwy. 8.	15	●	●	●				●		●			●		
Fort Providence (H-3) at Fort Providence on Hwy. 3.	2	●	●	●	●								●		
Fort Simpson (G-3) in Fort Simpson on Hwy. 1.	3	●	●	●									●		
Fred Henne (G-5) on Hwy. 3 across from Yellowknife airport. *(See Yellowknife p. 226.)*	7	●	●	●	●	●		●	●	●			●		●
Gwich'in Reserve (B-1) s. of Inuvik on Hwy 8.	14	●	●		●			●		●	●				
Hay River (H-4) in Hay River.	4	●	●	●	●			●	●	●					
Lady Evelyn Falls (H-3) 6.5 km off Hwy. 1 near Kakisa.	6	●	●	●	●			●	●	●			●		
Paniksak (A-2) w. of Tuktoyaktuk.	16	●	●							●			●	●	●
Prelude Lake (G-5) 29 km w. of Yellowknife on Hwy. 4.	10	●	●	●	●	●	●	●	●	●				●	●
Reid Lake (G-5) 61 km n.w. of Yellowknife on Hwy. 4.	12	●	●	●	●	●		●	●	●					
Sambaa Deh Falls (H-2) s. of Fort Simpson on Hwy. 1.	5	●	●	●				●	●	●			●		
Twin Falls Gorge (I-4) at Km-post 75 on Hwy 1.	8	●	●	●				●							
Yellowknife River (G-5) 8 km n.w. of Yellowknife on Hwy. 4.	13		●			●	●	●	●						

Points of Interest

AKLAVIK (A-1) pop. 700

Aklavik, which means "the place of the Barren-land grizzly," was founded in 1912 as the Mackenzie River delta outpost of Hudson's Bay Co. A thriving company base in addition to a trading and trapping center, the town became the administrative center of the Western Arctic region.

However, since the community rested in the middle of the largest delta in Canada, it faced constant change as the powerful Mackenzie River built up new land and flooded the old. These conditions prevented the construction of major roads and airstrips. As a result, the newer town of Inuvik (see place listing p. 224) absorbed Aklavik's administrative role. There are no roads into Aklavik; it is accessible by air from Inuvik or by ice roads during winter.

Many Aklavik residents refuse to move. The descendants of the early traders and trappers work on oil rigs in the Beaufort Sea or trap muskrat in the delta, which is rich in wildlife. A museum, the original company store and restored log cabins serve as reminders of the past.

Just off Main Street is a tree stump in which Albert Johnson, the suspected "Mad Trapper of Rat River," carved his initials. The town also contains his grave. Johnson, who allegedly killed prospectors and trappers for the gold in their teeth, was shot in 1932 after one of the most intensive manhunts in Canadian history. Whether he actually was the "mad trapper" has been a subject explored in both books and film.

BAFFIN ISLAND pop. 7,500

High in Nunavut's Eastern Arctic lies Baffin Island, the homeland of the Inuit, Aboriginal Canadians. It is a land of majestic fiords, icebergs, bountiful wildlife and the midnight sun, which shines until 3 a.m. from March to June. Although Baffin Island is not accessible by car, Iqaluit (see place listing p. 224), Nunavut's capital city, is served by two airlines.

Quammaarviit Historic Park, 12 kilometres (7 mi.) west of Iqaluit, can be reached by boat in summer or by dog sled and snowmobile in spring. An easy-to-follow trail links the island's ruins with signs depicting aspects of prehistoric life and culture.

Auyuittuq National Park, 32 kilometres (20 mi.) from Pangnirtung, is accessible by dog sled, snowmobile or boat. The park is notable for its fiords and glaciated valleys and mountains and for being the first national park established above the Arctic Circle. Polar bears, arctic foxes, caribous, seals, walruses, whales and narwhals inhabit the region.

Included in the approximately 40 bird species spotted in the park are the rare gyrfalcon and whistling swan. Remains of the 1,000-year-old Thule Eskimo culture have been found in Cumberland Sound. Hikers and mountain campers traversing Auyuittuq's Pangnirtung Pass will find challenging trails, abundant wildlife and spectacular scenery.

Ellesmere Island National Park Reserve is the most northerly land mass in Canada and contains 2,604-metre (8,544-ft.) Mount Barbeau, the highest mountain in eastern North America, and Lake Hazen, the largest lake north of the Arctic Circle. The reserve is primarily a polar desert encompassing 39,500 square kilometres (15,250 sq. mi.) of mountain ranges, glaciers, ice shelves and fiords. Remains of buildings from European expeditions can be found on the rocky terrain. Outfitters in Grise Fiord, Iqaluit and Resolute Bay can arrange trips into the park.

The uninhabited Katannilik Park Reserve, between Lake Harbour and Iqaluit, is rich with wildlife and unique flora. River tours, hiking and northern survival challenge even the hardiest adventurers. Information can be obtained from Nunavut Tourism; phone (867) 979-6551 or (800) 491-7910.

In spring and summer licensed guides from Angmarlik Visitors Centre lead expeditions into Kekerten Historic Park, 50 kilometres (32 mi.) south of Pangnirtung; phone (867) 473-8737 or (800) 491-7910. Visitors can see remains of whale lookouts, blubber vats, whalers' houses and Inuit homes. A self-guiding trail connects dozens of ruins.

ENTERPRISE (H-4) pop. 100

Enterprise is the first Northwest Territories community encountered by travelers heading north on Mackenzie Highway. A major service center for commercial traffic, the town is best known for its spectacular view of Hay River Gorge near the local Esso station.

Scenic 33-metre (108-ft.) Alexandra Falls and 15-metre (50-ft.) Louise Falls in Twin Falls Gorge Territorial Park (see Recreation Chart and the AAA/CAA Western Canada and Alaska CampBook) are about 9 kilometres (6 mi.) south on Mackenzie Highway. Camping and picnicking are permitted.

FORT LIARD (H-1) pop. 500

Fort Liard is in the Territories' southwest corner. Nearby archeological digs have revealed strata showing 9,000 years of human occupancy. Prior to 1807 Northwest Co. founded a post that was taken over by Hudson's Bay Co. in 1821 when both companies merged. An earnest fur trade continues.

The opening of Liard Highway in the early 1980s put the quiet village on the map. The community is characterized by lush growth and a relatively mild climate, despite its northern location. Birdwatchers will find many songbirds during spring and summer. A small lakefront campground is nearby.

Boat launching is possible on the Petitot and Liard rivers, where visitors can see interesting rock formations and fish for pickerel at the rivers' mouth. Fort Liard is a good jumping-off point for exploring the surrounding mountains or Nahanni National Park Reserve *(see place listing p. 224)*. Chartered flights and a forestry office are available in town.

FORT SIMPSON (G-2) pop. 1,300

Established in 1804 at the fork of the Mackenzie and Liard rivers, Fort Simpson is the oldest continuously occupied trading post in the Mackenzie River Valley. Once a district headquarters for Hudson's Bay Co., the town developed into a center of river trade. Originally Fort of the Forks, the town was renamed to honor Thomas Simpson, first governor of the merged Northwest and Hudson's Bay companies.

Today, Fort Simpson is a gathering place for people and a center for territorial government administration, logging, oil and mining exploration. It also serves as a departure point for air, raft and canoe trips into Nahanni National Park Reserve *(see place listing p. 224)*.

A visitor center offers interpretive films, historical walking tours and a native crafts display; the center also can arrange riverboat tours. Phone (867) 695-3307.

Fort Simpson Visitor Information Centre: P.O. Box 177, Fort Simpson, NT, Canada X0E 0N0; phone (867) 695-3182.

FORT SMITH (I-5) pop. 2,400

Initially a link in a strategic chain of 19th-century trading posts along the Mackenzie portage route to the Arctic, Fort Smith became an autonomous town in 1966. It is regional headquarters for the government of the Northwest Territories and contains several governmental offices. The town also is the site of the Aurora Campus of Arctic College.

Nearby Wood Buffalo National Park *(see place listing p. 225)* is home to one of the largest buffalo herds in the world.

Fort Smith Tourist Information Bureau: 56 Portage Ave., P.O. Box 121, Fort Smith, NT, Canada X0E 0P0; phone (867) 872-2515.

NORTHERN LIFE MUSEUM, 110 King St., examines area history through collections of Indian artifacts, Inuit and pioneer tools, crafts, dinosaur bones, mammoth tusks, manuscripts and paintings. Also displayed are photographs of traders, explorers and missionaries. The museum features revolving exhibits from Canadian museums. Daily 1-5 (also Tues. and Thurs. 7-9 p.m.),

Permafrost

Permafrost, or permanently frozen ground, is a fact of life in most of the Northwest Territories. In his "Observations on Hudson's Bay 1743," James Isham wrote "the shortness of the summers is not sufficient to thaw the ice...therefore it gathers more and more every year." The permafrost layer is estimated to be as deep as 500 metres (1,640 ft.) in some areas.

Settlers found that attempts to build on the ice-filled ground were thwarted when heat from their structures melted the permafrost's top

layer, causing foundations to crack and buildings to sink. Nearby Yukon Territory gold miners had to thaw and remove permafrost before they could extract the gold that lay beneath it.

In the 20th century Canadians began to work with permafrost. They found they could maintain its frozen state by insulating or preserving the top layer, making a surface strong enough to support any construction. Gravel pads 3 to 4 feet thick were used beneath smaller structures; pilings driven into the permafrost elevated larger buildings, preventing heat from penetrating the ground beneath them. In some instances, permafrost was excavated and replaced with various forms of fill.

In 1954 the Canadian government spent $34 million to build the new town of Inuvik on stilts. Pilings support buildings and connecting "utilidors," insulated corridors that house heating, water and sewage pipes.

Although the number of successful settlements built on top of permafrost is growing, mining is still a problem. To prevent shaft collapses resulting from a permafrost thaw, miners must shore open their holes with timbers or concrete.

June 1-Labour Day; Tues.-Fri. and Sun. 1-5, rest of year. Donations. Phone (867) 872-2859.

HAY RIVER (H-4) pop. 3,600

Recent archeological finds show that the Slavey Dene have used the area around Hay River for thousands of years, but the first buildings did not appear until 1868 when Hudson's Bay Co. established a trading post. The town's strategic location prompts its occasional reference as the "Hub of the North."

Hay River is the southernmost port of the Mackenzie River system. During the 5-month shipping season barges, fishing boats and Coast Guard craft clog the protected river channels. The town serves as headquarters of the Great Slave Lake commercial fishing industry, which supplies the demand for Great Slave Lake whitefish. Dene Cultural Institute, on the Hay River Dene Reserve, is open for tours mid-May to mid-September. A visitor center on Mackenzie Highway is open mid-May to mid-September; phone (867) 874-3180.

Hay River Chamber of Commerce: 10 K. Gaginier St., Hay River, NT, Canada X0E 1G1; phone (867) 874-2565.

INUVIK (B-2) pop. 3,300

Inuvik, meaning "place of man," was erected in 1958 to replace nearby Aklavik (see place listing p. 222), which appeared to be sinking into the Mackenzie River delta. The town boomed in the 1970s as the center of the Beaufort Sea oil exploration, which since has shifted to other areas. As well as being the communications, commerce and government center for the Western Arctic, the town was the site of a Canadian Forces station until 1986.

Accessible via Dempster Highway, Inuvik is one of the northernmost points on the North American continent that can be reached by public road; during June and most of July there are 24 hours of daylight. The town also serves as a departure point for plane trips to the Arctic Ocean and the Mackenzie River delta system.

IQALUIT (C-12) pop. 4,200

In 1576 British explorer Martin Frobisher arrived at Iqaluit's bay in present-day Nunavut and assumed that he had discovered the Northwest Passage. A discovery he had believed to be gold proved to be iron pyrite, or "fools gold." The Baffin Island town honored his memory in its name—Frobisher Bay—until 1987, when its name officially was changed back to the traditional Inuit name, Iqaluit (ih-KA-loo-it), which means "more than two fish."

Iqaluit, now the capital of Nunavut, began as a small trading post. During the 19th century European and American whalers frequented the bay

waters hoping to supply their home ports with whalebone for women's corsets and blubber for lamp oil. Hiking opportunities are plentiful on the outskirts of town or through the nearby mountains. Unaccessible by car, Iqaluit can be reached by air from Yellowknife, Montréal and Ottawa.

With the construction of the Distant Early Warning (DEW) Line in 1954, the town became an important defense site and a major refueling station for both commercial and military aircraft. Iqaluit is one of the largest communities in Nunavut and the educational, administrative, transportation and economic center for the Baffin region. A focal point for Inuit art, the town boasts numerous galleries.

In 1971 Astro Hill Complex, which includes retail stores, a hotel, high-rise apartments, offices and a swimming pool, was completed using modular precast concrete units. Of architectural interest at the time, the complex was designed to withstand northern climatic extremes.

Nunavut Tourism: P.O. Box 1450, Iqaluit, NT, Canada X0A 0H0; phone (867) 979-6551 or (800) 491-7910.

NUNATTA SUNAKKUTAANGIT (Things of the Land Museum) is on the beach in building 212, a renovated Hudson's Bay Co. warehouse. Exhibits include Inuit sculpture and local artifacts. Visitors may access the beach, where local residents prepare for and return from their hunts. Tues.-Sun. 1-5; closed Good Friday, July 1, Nov. 11 and Dec. 25. Donations. Phone (867) 979-5537.

NAHANNI NATIONAL PARK RESERVE (G-1)

Elevations in the park range from 1,853 metres (6,079 ft.) at the South Nahanni River to 2,652 metres (8,700 ft.) on the north end of the park near Hole-in-the-Wall Lake. Refer to CAA/AAA maps for additional elevation information.

Steeped in myth, mystery and adventure, Nahanni National Park Reserve covers 4,784 square kilometres (1,847 sq. mi.) of wilderness in the South Nahanni country about 145 kilometres (90 mi.) west of Fort Simpson (see place listing p. 223). Accessible only by air, the park uses Fort Liard and Fort Simpson in the Territories, Muncho Lake in British Columbia, and Watson Lake in the Yukon Territory as its major supply and jumping-off points.

Liard Highway, linking Fort Nelson and Fort Simpson, passes within 30 kilometres (19 mi.) of Nahanni Butte, providing access to the Liard River at Blackstone Territorial Park, east of Nahanni reserve.

A land of rivers, ragged peaks, more than 30 species of mammals and a waterfall twice the height of Niagara Falls, Nahanni National Park Reserve was created in 1974. It was placed on the UNESCO (United Nations Educational, Scientific and Cultural Organization) World Heritage list 4 years later and cited as an "exceptional natural site forming part of the heritage of mankind."

In the early 1900s the area received a reputation for myth and adventure. Gold prospectors, drawn by rumors of placer deposits, began to arrive. When the decapitated bodies of the two MacLeod brothers were found, stories of huge mountain men and fierce natives proliferated.

Although no real mountain men ever were seen, the park remains a place of rugged beauty with little development, including accommodations for visitors. Those who come to raft and canoe on the rivers and hike the forests, alpine tundra and canyons of Nahanni will find it a bracing experience. Travel by water is an excellent way to enjoy the park; however, it can be dangerous and should be attempted only by those experienced in canoeing and rafting.

Less hardy individuals should hire a licensed outfitter for guided tours down the South Nahanni River. Tours pass Virginia Falls, where the South Nahanni River plunges more than 90 metres (295 ft.); the Gate, a 90-degree river bend below 213-metre (700-ft.) vertical cliffs; and hot springs such as those at First Canyon and Rabbitkettle. Visitors to Rabbitkettle **must** register at the warden's cabin and have a warden accompany them to the springs. Daytime air trips to Virginia Falls should be prearranged through an air charter company in Fort Simpson or Fort Liard.

Fishing for arctic grayling, lake and bull trout and northern pike is permitted with a national park fishing license (annual pass $13), which can be obtained at the Fort Simpson Administration Office or at the warden's office at Rabbitkettle Lake. All national park regulations apply. Firearms are not permitted.

Wildlife species include moose, beavers, woodland caribou, Dall's sheep, grizzly and black bears, white-tailed deer and mountain goats. Visitors should take particular care when traveling in areas where they are likely to encounter bears.

The park is open year-round. The park administration office at Fort Simpson is open daily 8:30-5, mid-June to mid-Sept.; Mon.-Fri., rest of year. Overnight visitors must register before entering the park and upon leaving.

One-day admission to the park is $10 per person. For route information, permit regulations, weather conditions and park activities write to the Superintendent, Nahanni National Park Reserve, P.O. Box 348, Fort Simpson, NT, Canada X0E 0N0; phone (867) 695-3151. *See Recreation Chart.*

TULITA (E-2) pop. 400

Because of the lack of roads on the frontier, most towns were founded along rivers. Originally called Fort Norman, Tulita was established in 1810 when Northwest Co. built a trading post at the confluence of the Great Bear and Mackenzie rivers. The town's name means "where two rivers meet."

Later years brought additional industries. In 1920 pitchblende—the chief ore-mineral source of uranium—was discovered, and in the early 1980s the Wells-Zama oil pipeline was built.

Tulita is accessible via air service from Norman Wells. No all-weather roads lead into the community, but a winter road—open from late January to mid-March—connects Tulita to surrounding communities. Nearby is one of the Northwest Territories' oldest Anglican churches, built of squared logs in the 1860s. The restored church can be visited.

About 20 kilometres (12 mi.) away is a bed of low-grade coal that has been burning for centuries. Although the fire likely was ignited by lightning, Dene legend attributes it to a giant's campfire. During the summer the surface of the bed sometimes rises and the coals are exposed. Firefighters' attempts to extinguish the smoldering coals have failed.

Hamlet Office at General Delivery: Box 91, Tulita, NT, Canada X0E 0K0; phone (867) 588-4471.

WOOD BUFFALO NATIONAL PARK (I-4)

Elevations in the park range from 183 metres (600 ft.) at the Little Buffalo River to 945 metres (3,100 ft.) in the Caribou Mountains. Refer to CAA/AAA maps for additional elevation information.

Accessible by Hwy. 5, which connects with Mackenzie Highway at Hay River, Wood Buffalo National Park is the second largest park in the world. Covering about the same area as the states of Maryland and New Jersey combined, the national park straddles the border between the Northwest Territories and Alberta.

This vast subarctic wilderness contains such remarkable geological features as the Salt Plains, Alberta Plateau, the deltas and lowlands of the Peace and Athabasca rivers, and extensive gypsum karst formations. The park was established in 1922 to protect the world's largest free-roaming herd of wood bison; more than 2,500 of these animals now live within. Moose, caribous, muskrats, beavers and black bears are among other park residents.

The Peace Athabasca Delta is the staging ground for North America's four major waterfowl flyways. Varied birds, including hawks, eagles and pelicans, are present for part of the year. The northeastern corner of the park is one of the last nesting grounds in the world for the endangered whooping crane. The park's lakes and rivers are sources of pike, pickerel, trout and whitefish. Wildflowers and berries abound in the rolling meadows.

Boating, picnicking and camping are permitted on a limited basis at Pine Lake. The park has snowshoeing and cross-country skiing trails. Guided nature hikes, slide and lecture presentations and birdwatching and canoeing programs are held during July and August.

The 400-kilometre (250-mi.) Fort Chipewyan Winter Road is open December 15 to March 15 (weather permitting). The road runs from Fort McMurray, Alberta, to Fort Smith; part of the road is formed by ice. Phone the park office to check road conditions.

Visitors can see such magnificent snow-covered scenery as boreal forest, sand dunes, lakes and wide-open meadows. Before departure travelers should contact the park office for a list of driving regulations and recommended travel supplies.

The park's gravel roads are open May through October. The park office at McDougal Road and Portage Avenue in Fort Smith is open Mon.-Fri. 8:30-5, Sat.-Sun. 10-5, July-Aug.; Mon.-Fri. 8:30-5, rest of year.

Admission to the park is free. For route information, road conditions or details about park activities contact the Superintendent, Box 750, Fort Smith, NT, Canada X0E 0P0; phone (867) 872-2349. *See Recreation Chart and the AAA/CAA Western Canada and Alaska CampBook.*

YELLOWKNIFE (G-5) pop. 17,300

Although the Dene hunted the Yellowknife region for thousands of years and Europeans explored it in 1771, a permanent settlement was not established until the discovery of gold in 1934. Taking the name of the copper knives carried by the Chipewyan Indians, the town is now the capital of the Northwest Territories and the site of two gold mines and a booming diamond industry.

In 1967 Yellowknife replaced Ottawa as the seat of government for the Northwest Territories. Tours of the Legislative Assembly are available daily when the House is in session; phone (867) 669-2200. On the northern shore of Great Slave Lake, this "metropolis" of the north lies less than 500 kilometres (311 mi.) from the Arctic Circle. A transportation and service center, Yellowknife serves as a base for exploring the Territories; float plane trips into the surrounding countryside depart from the city's Old Town.

Best viewed from December to March, the *aurora borealis,* or northern lights, are produced when atomic particles from outside the atmosphere strike and excite atoms within the upper atmosphere. The lights sweep mysteriously across the clear night sky as luminescent curtains of red, green, pink and purple light in patterns called rayed bands. Guided viewing trips are available.

The scenic 71-kilometre (44-mi.) Ingraham Trail (Hwy. 4) to Tibbett Lake allows year-round access to several chains of lakes and streams. Seven boat launches and two campgrounds lie along the road. Prelude Wildlife Trail runs from Prelude Lake Campground *(see Recreation Chart and the AAA/CAA Western Canada and Alaska CampBook)* through the wilderness to several lookout points.

Prospector's Trail is in Fred Henne Park *(see Recreation Chart and the AAA/CAA Western Canada and Alaska CampBook),* west near Long Lake. The 4-kilometre (2.5-mi.) loop points out the region's varied geological features and is of interest to rock hounds; sturdy footwear and insect repellent are necessary. Walsh Lake has good trout fishing. Other hiking trails lead from Ingraham Trail; information and brochures are available in town.

The scenic portion of Hwy. 3 runs north from Mackenzie Bison Sanctuary to Edzo, then parallels the northern shore of Great Slave Lake. Driving anywhere in the area, or throughout the Northwest Territories, demands that a vehicle be in top mechanical condition.

Northern Frontier Regional Visitor Center: 4807 49th St., Yellowknife, NT, Canada X1A 3T5; phone (867) 873-4262.

Self-guiding tours: The visitor center provides brochures for a walking tour of the Old Town district.

THE PRINCE OF WALES NORTHERN HERITAGE CENTRE preserves area history through exhibits depicting aspects of Dene and Inuit cultures. Displays pertain to geology, archeology, exploration, fur trading, transportation, natural history, artwork and handicrafts. Daily 10:30-5, June-Aug.; Tues.-Fri. 10:30-5, Sat.-Sun. noon-5, rest of year. Closed Jan. 1 and Dec. 25. Donations. Phone (867) 873-7551.

Saskatchewan

The Last Frontier

Rolling grasslands and evergreen forests create an unspoiled paradise

Big Muddy Badlands

Trace Butch Cassidy's Outlaw Trail through this colorfully rugged terrain

Call of the Wild

Whistling swans and white-tail deer are among the many wilderness residents

Qu' Appelle Valley

The sun seems a little brighter as it shines upon this region's golden farmland

The Mounties

Explore the history of those who brought law and order to the Canadian West

a pastoral
portrait

A visit to Saskatchewan is a perfect escape from the hustle and bustle.

Named after the Plains Indian term *ksiskatchewan,* meaning "the river that flows swiftly," Saskatchewan boasts more than just a great river with an unusual name.

Along country roads, you'll encounter prairies, mountains, grasslands and even sand dunes. While approximately half the province is covered in pine, white spruce and other trees, a good portion is blanketed with fields of wheat.

Look for signs marked with a barn symbol; they designate bed and breakfast inns and vacation farms, where you can take part in milking cows and—if you're lucky—enjoy homemade berry preserves or baked goods.

Take a dip into one of more than 100,000 fresh-water lakes, some of which can be found in the Qu'Appelle Valley. Nestled among the water holes in this region are resorts and golf courses with rolling fairways.

For history, head to towns that preserve the origin of the Mounted Police, the heritage of Metis culture or the rough-and-tumble cowboy lifestyle.

Or visit the Beaver Lodge Cabin on Ajawaan Lake in Prince Albert National Park, residence of naturalist author Grey Owl, who coined the now-popular belief that "you belong to nature, not it to you."

The hues of Saskatchewan's palette were determined both with and without man's help. Painted by nature and the history of the plains, vibrant gold, green and red are the prominent colors in the province's scheme.

Sheaves of Golden Wheat

Shimmering fields of grain, glinting gold in the sunlight, are probably the image most associated with Saskatchewan. Captured on innumerable postcards and snapshots, the plains seem to stretch to the horizon in a never-ending symphony of undulating waves, interrupted only by an occasional silo. And the fields are certainly productive—more than 50 percent of Canada's wheat crop comes from this land.

Proof of the grain's economic importance to the province are the three golden wheat sheaves on its coat of arms. Saskatchewan's flag provides further evidence; its lower half, a solid band of gold, represents the grainfields dominating the province's southern portion.

You can experience early 20th-century pioneer prairie life at Motherwell Homestead National Historic Site, near Abernethy. Costumed interpreters busily carry out typical daily tasks of the period at the 1912 farmstead of William Richard Motherwell, farmer, politician and agricultural innovator. Motherwell developed techniques enabling early settlers to overcome the region's dry soil and short growing season.

If a more modern approach to rural life appeals to you, spend a few days at one of Saskatchewan's vacation farms. Helping with chores can offset the pounds you might gain from the hearty meals provided by your hosts. More than 70 Saskatchewan families offer visitors a chance to experience what living on a farm is all about.

Landscapes of Green

Color Regina green—the city is known for having more than 350,000 trees. A particularly verdant section of town is Wascana Centre, a 930-hectare urban park that is truly the heart of Saskatchewan's capital.

The center, lining the rambling shoreline of Wascana Lake, is home to cultural and educational institutions as well as the architecturally impressive Legislative Building, the seat of provincial government. Works by Canadian artists grace the building's walls. Galleries at the nearby Royal Saskatchewan Museum are devoted to earth and life sciences and the First Nations

Henry Kelsey of the Hudson's Bay Co. is the first European to explore Saskatchewan.
1690

Fur-trading posts are established along the North Saskatchewan River.
1750

The North West Mounted Police is created in response to a clash between a party of Montana wolf hunters and a band of Assiniboine Indians at Cypress Hills.

1873

1870
Canada acquires the Northwestern Territory, which includes present-day Saskatchewan, from the Hudson's Bay Co.; the area is renamed Northwest Territories.

Saskatchewan Historical Timeline

1885
Louis Riel leads the Métis and other Indian tribes in the Northwest Rebellion, an uprising against the Canadian government.

People. Young guests will have fun visiting a robotic dinosaur and digging into the hands-on exhibits in the Paleo Pit.

Initially known as Pile-O-Bones (the translation of the Cree word *Oscana*), Regina's early name is a reference to the buffalo remains left behind when the site served as a hunters' camp. Its present name was adopted in honor of Queen Victoria—Regina being Latin for queen. And the good monarch's husband was not forgotten when provincial town names were assigned—the city of Prince Albert was named for Victoria's consort in 1886.

The nearly 1 million acres of nearby Prince Albert National Park encompass other shades of green, primarily those of aspens and evergreens. Its woodlands, boreal landscapes and grasslands are just a small portion of the forests covering half the province.

Within the park is the simple lakeside cabin of Grey Owl, the Indian name assumed by Englishman Archibald Belaney. This early environmentalist, writer and lecturer, accepted into the Ojibwa tribe in the 1930s, was dedicated to the preservation of the Canadian wilderness and its wildlife. His gravesite is close by on a wooded hill.

Red Coats of the Canadian West

The Royal Canadian Mounted Police are immediately recognizable by their scarlet tunics. In fact, the route they took across the prairie in 1874 to establish law and order in western Canada is retraced along Hwy. 13, the Red Coat Trail. Many of their early posts are now national historic sites, including Fort Battleford, off Hwy. 4 near Battleford, and Fort Walsh, southwest of Maple Creek.

Regina is home to the RCMP's only training academy. Visitors are welcome to tour the facility, known as the Royal Canadian Mounted Police Depot, as well as a museum recounting the force's history. If your timing is right, you can watch the cadets drill at the Sergeant Major's Parade, usually held Monday through Friday at 12:45.

If you're in town in July or August and truly want to be inspired by the colors of the province, try to catch the Sunset Retreat Ceremony. Culminating in the lowering of the Canadian flag at dusk, the golden glow cast by the fading sun seems a fitting background as the cadets, in traditional red jackets, proudly march against the backdrop of lush greenery bordering the parade grounds.

Saskatchewan becomes a province.
1905

A lack of rainfall and low wheat prices affect Saskatchewan's economy.
1988

The University of Saskatchewan is established in Saskatoon by the provincial government.
1907

Saskatchewan establishes the first medical care program in North America.
1962

1974
The first female Royal Canadian Mounted Police recruits begin training in Regina.

1931-41
A prolonged drought, grasshoppers and drifting topsoil cause agricultural and economic turmoil; immigration ceases and the province's population declines.

1994
An almost complete tyrannosaurus rex skeleton is discovered in the Frenchman River Valley.

Recreation

Contrary to popular belief, Saskatchewan is not all prairie. Even in the southern half, where farming is predominant, lakes and parks abound with recreational options.

Angling Heaven

With more than 100,000 lakes, rivers and streams to choose from, you're never really far from a good freshwater **fishing** spot. While northern pike, rainbow trout and walleye will take your bait at fishin' holes throughout the province, you'll have to head for northern waters to land trophy-size lake trout, Arctic grayling and other sport fish.

Lake Diefenbaker, south of Outlook, is a favorite fishing destination with both locals and visitors; this is the place to go if you're after walleye or northern pike. The Precambrian Shield, in the northern third of the province, is just about as good as it gets for anglers, with almost 40 percent of its area consisting of H20. Try Lac la Ronge if you're a trout fishing devotee. Outfitters will be happy to fly you to some of the more remote northern fishing lakes.

Tumbling east to west across the province north of the 55th parallel, the Churchill River provides some of North America's best white-water **canoeing.** Should you choose to experience white water by **rafting,** check out the Clearwater River. Both of these bodies of water flow in northern Saskatchewan.

If the rush of white-water action is too intense, consider paddling your boat along calmer waters. The Bagwa Canoe Route, in Prince Albert National Park, will take you through several pristine lakes. Late May through September, when the lakes are at their warmest, is the best time to dip your oars. A bonus is the chance to sight bald eagles, ospreys and loons.

For the ultimate in calm, head to Little Manitou Lake, near the resort community of Manitou Beach. Indians knew about the lake's curative powers long before the arrival of European settlers. And there's no danger of sinking in these waters—the high concentration of minerals makes this impossible, so float to your heart's content.

Fun in the Snow

When the weather turns cold, bundle up and try **cross-country skiing.** Groomed and marked trails are easily accessible throughout the province—even in cities. Prince Albert National Park, almost in the middle of Saskatchewan, has more than 100 kilo-metres (60 mi.) of trails. Moose Mountain Provincial Park, north of Carlyle, adds another 50 kilometres (30 mi.) to explore, while the forests, lakes and valleys of Duck Mountain Provincial Park, east of Kamsack, provide a picturesque backdrop for cross-country excursions.

If you prefer to stay within city limits, the Meewasin Valley Trail follows the Saskatchewan River through the middle of Saskatoon, the province's largest city.

Snowmobiling enthusiasts love the thousands of kilometres of interconnected, groomed trails linking towns and parks along Canada's version of Route 66, in this case a cross-country snowmobile route. Popular put-in points include Hudson Bay, Nipawin, North Battleford and Yorkton. Trail permits are mandatory; phone Tourism Saskatchewan, (800) 667-7191, for a provincial snowmobile trail map.

Warm Weather Choices

When the weather turns warm, everyone flocks to Prince Albert National Park. You don't even need **hiking** boots on a few of the park's short trails. Boundary Bog, Mud Creek and Treebeard, all loop trails, traverse fairly level terrain and take no longer than an hour each. They will, however, put you in touch with a variety of Mother Nature's handiworks—a black spruce and tamarack bog; sightings of beavers, otters and great blue herons; and forests of aspens and balsam firs.

An abundance of lakes and trails also makes **boating, bicycling, horseback riding** and fishing popular choices.

Another popular summer playground is the Qu'Appelle Valley, a broad swath of land in southern Saskatchewan bordered by rolling hills. A chain of lakes and three provincial parks are the setting for resort villages where guests enjoy boating, **water skiing** and **swimming.**

Recreational Activities

Throughout the TourBook, you may notice a Recreational Activities heading with bulleted listings of recreation-oriented establishments listed underneath. Since normal AAA inspection criteria cannot be applied, these establishments are presented for information only. Age, height and weight restrictions may apply. Reservations are often recommended and sometimes required. Visitors should phone or write the attraction for additional information, and the address and phone number are provided for this purpose.

Fast Facts

POPULATION: 1,015,600.

AREA: 651,903 sq km (251,700 sq mi).

CAPITAL: Regina.

HIGHEST POINT: 1,392 m/4,566 ft., Cypress Hills.

LOWEST POINT: 65 m/213 ft., Lake Athabasca.

TIME ZONES: Central and Mountain.

MINIMUM AGE FOR DRIVERS: 16.

MINIMUM AGE FOR GAMBLING: 19.

SEAT BELT/CHILD RESTRAINT LAWS: Seat belts required for driver and all passengers; child restraints or seat belts required for children.

HELMETS FOR MOTORCYCLISTS: Required.

RADAR DETECTORS: Permitted.

FIREARMS LAWS: Vary by province. Contact the Federal Chief Firearms Officer, Services-Saskatchewan, 1405 Albert St., Regina, SK, Canada S4R 2R8; phone (800) 731-4000.

HOLIDAYS: Jan. 1; Good Friday; Victoria Day, May 24 (if a Mon.) or the closest prior Mon.; Canada Day, July 1; Saskatchewan Day, Aug. (1st Mon.); Labour Day, Sept. (1st Mon.); Thanksgiving, Oct. (2nd Mon.); Remembrance Day, Nov. 11; Dec. 25; Boxing Day, Dec. 26.

TAXES: Saskatchewan's provincial sales tax is 6 percent.

PROVINCIAL INFORMATION CENTERS: Free information and literature is distributed at travel planning centers along Hwy. 1 east of Fleming; at 500-1900 Albert St. in Regina; near Maple Creek on Hwy. 1; Hwy. 16 at Langenburg and Lloydminster; and Hwy. 39 at North Portal. All information centers are open daily mid-May to early September except the center in Regina, which is open Mon.-Fri. 8-5.

FURTHER INFORMATION FOR VISITORS:

Tourism Saskatchewan
500-1900 Albert St.
Regina, SK, Canada S4P 4L9
(306) 787-2300 or (800) 667-7191

FISHING AND HUNTING REGULATIONS:

Saskatchewan Environment and Resource Management
3211 Albert St.
Regina, SK, Canada S4S 5W6
(306) 787-2700

ALCOHOL CONSUMPTION:
Legal age 19.

Saskatchewan Temperature Averages Maximum/Minimum (Celsius)
From the records of the National Weather Service

	JAN	FEB	MAR	APR	MAY	JUN	JUL	AUG	SEP	OCT	NOV	DEC
Prince Albert	-13	-10	-2	9	18	22	25	24	17	10	-2	-10
	-24	-22	-15	-3	3	8	12	10	4	-1	-11	-21
Regina	-11	-9	-2	10	19	23	27	26	20	12	-1	-8
	-22	-21	-13	-3	3	8	11	10	4	-2	-11	-18

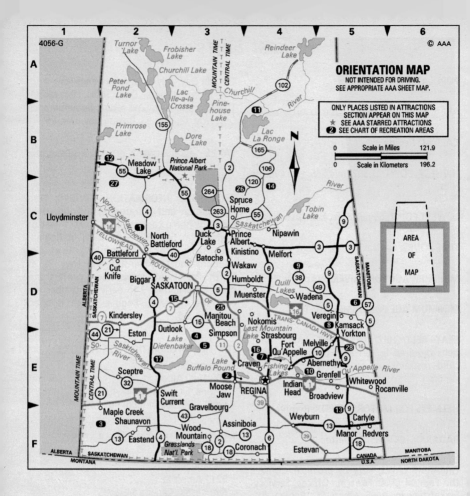

AAA/CAA Starred Attractions

EXCEPTIONAL INTEREST AND QUALITY

Prince Albert National Park (B-3)

PRINCE ALBERT NATIONAL PARK—This wilderness area is a beautiful example of Saskatchewan's transition from poplar bluffs and prairie lands to the evergreen forests and spruce bogs of the north. See p. 245.

Saskatoon (D-3)

WANUSKEWIN HERITAGE PARK—The Cree word for "seeking peace of mind," Wanuskewin is a fitting name for this park, once a center of spiritual renewal used by the Northern Plains Indians. See p. 250.

RECREATION AREAS

	MAP LOCATION	CAMPING	PICNICKING	HIKING TRAILS	BOATING	BOAT RAMP	BOAT RENTAL	FISHING	SWIMMING	PETS ON LEASH	BICYCLE TRAILS	WINTER SPORTS	VISITOR CENTER	LODGE/CABINS	FOOD SERVICE
NATIONAL PARK *(See place listings)*															
Grasslands 906 square kilometres.		•	•	•						•			•		
Prince Albert 3,875 square kilometres. Horse rental.		•	•	•	•	•	•	•	•	•	•	•	•	•	•
PROVINCIAL															
The Battlefords (C-2) 600 hectares 4.75 km n. of Cochin off Hwy. 4. Cross-country skiing, golf; horse rental.	❶	•	•	•	•	•	•	•	•	•		•	•	•	•
Blackstrap (D-3) 530 hectares 8 km e. of Dundurn via Hwy. 211. Cross-country and downhill skiing; sailboard rental.	25	•	•		•	•	•	•	•	•		•			•
Buffalo Pound (E-3) 1,930 hectares 19 km n. of Moose Jaw on Hwy. 2, then 13 km e. on Hwy. 202. Cross-country and downhill skiing, tennis; pool.	❷	•	•	•	•	•		•	•	•		•	•		•
Candle Lake (C-3) 1,270 hectares 60 km n.e. of Prince Albert on hwys. 55 and 120. Cross-country skiing.	26	•	•	•	•	•	•	•	•	•		•		•	•
Clearwater River 224,040 hectares 50 km n.e. of La Loche on Hwy. 955 *(north of area shown on map).* Canoeing.		•	•	•				•							
Crooked Lake (E-5) 190 hectares 30 km n. of Broadview on Hwy. 605. Golf.	28	•	•		•	•	•	•	•	•				•	•
Cypress Hills (F-1) 18,410 hectares 30 km s. of Maple Creek on Hwy. 21. Cross-country skiing, golf, tennis; horse rental, pool. Five horsepower limit for boats.	❸	•	•	•	•	•	•	•	•	•		•	•	•	•
Danielson (E-3) 2,910 hectares on n. end of Lake Diefenbaker via hwys. 44, 45 or 219.	❹	•	•		•	•		•	•	•			•		•
Douglas (E-3) 4,430 hectares 11 km s.e. of Elbow on Hwy. 19. Houseboat rental.	❺	•	•	•	•	•		•	•	•			•		•
Duck Mountain (D-5) 26,160 hectares 25 km e. of Kamsack on Hwy. 57. Cross-country and downhill skiing, golf, tennis; horse rental.	❻	•	•	•	•	•	•	•	•	•		•		•	•
Echo Valley (E-4) 640 hectares 8 km w. of Fort Qu'Appelle off Hwy. 10. Cross-country skiing; horse rental.	❼	•	•	•	•	•		•	•	•		•	•		•
Good Spirit Lake (E-5) 1,900 hectares 24 km n.e. of Springside via Hwy. 47. Cross-country skiing, tennis.	❽	•	•	•	•	•		•	•	•		•			•
Greenwater Lake (D-4) 20,720 hectares 38 km n. of Kelvington on Hwy. 38. Cross-country skiing, golf, tennis.	❾	•	•	•	•	•	•	•	•	•		•	•	•	•
Katepwa Point (E-4) 8 hectares 10 km s.e. of Lebret on Hwy. 56.	❿		•		•	•		•	•	•					•
Lac la Ronge (B-4) 344,470 hectares 48.25 km n. of La Ronge on Hwy. 102. Cross-country skiing; houseboat rental.	⓫	•	•	•	•	•	•	•	•	•		•	•	•	
Makwa Lake (C-2) 2,560 hectares n.w. of Loon Lake off Hwy. 26. Cross-country skiing; horse rental.	27	•	•	•	•	•	•	•	•	•		•		•	•
Meadow Lake (B-2) 156,970 hectares 5 km n. of Goodsoil via Hwy. 26. Cross-country skiing, tennis; horse rental, sailboat rental.	⓬	•	•	•	•	•	•	•	•	•		•		•	•
Moose Mountain (F-5) 40,060 hectares 22.5 km n. of Carlyle on Hwy. 9. Cross-country skiing, golf (18 holes), tennis; horse rental.	⓭	•	•	•	•	•	•	•	•	•	•	•	•	•	•
Narrow Hills (C-4) 53,610 hectares 64.25 km n. of Smeaton on Hwy. 106. Cross-country skiing.	⓮	•	•	•	•	•	•	•	•	•		•		•	•
Pike Lake (D-3) 500 hectares 30.5 km s. of Saskatoon on Hwy. 60. Golf, tennis; pool. Ten horsepower limit for boats.	⓯	•	•		•			•	•	•			•		•
Rowan's Ravine (E-4) 270 hectares 22.5 km w. of Bulyea on Hwy. 220.	⓰	•	•	•	•	•	•	•	•	•			•		•
Saskatchewan Landing (E-2) 5,600 hectares 45 km n. of Swift Current via Hwy. 4. Horse rental, windsurfer rental.	⓱	•	•	•	•	•	•	•	•	•			•	•	•

Points of Interest

ABERNETHY (E-5) pop. 200

In 1882, about 2 decades before he began his distinguished career in Canadian politics, William Richard Motherwell arrived in southeastern Saskatchewan from his Ontario birthplace and acquired a 64-hectare (160-acre) homestead grant near Abernethy. He farmed the land using several techniques of scientific agriculture then considered revolutionary.

Motherwell was later instrumental in launching the Territorial Grain Growers Association. His knowledge of the land groomed him for later roles as Saskatchewan's minister of agriculture 1905-18 and federal minister of agriculture during the 1920s.

MOTHERWELL HOMESTEAD NATIONAL HISTORIC SITE, 8 km (5 mi.) s. on Hwy. 22, commemorates William Richard Motherwell and his contributions to agriculture in Canada. Motherwell's farmstead, including 8 acres of landscaped grounds, Ontarian-style barn and six-bedroom fieldstone house have been restored by Parks Canada to the pre-World War I era.

Allow 1 hour minimum. Daily 9-5, May-June; 10-6, July 1-Sept. 1. Admission $4; senior citizens $3; ages 6-16, $2; family rate $10. MC. Phone (306) 333-2116.

ASSINIBOIA (F-3) pop. 2,700

Assiniboia is an Ojibwa Indian word meaning "one who cooks with stones." Southeast of town off Hwy. 2 is St. Victor Petroglyphs Provincial Historic Park, the site of a sandstone cliff etched with prehistoric Indian carvings. The carvings at the top of the cliff depict human faces, footprints and animal tracks. Since they have faded with time, the designs are best seen late in the afternoon or on a cloudy day. There is a picnic site near the base of the cliff. Phone (306) 694-3659 for more information.

The Assiniboia and District Museum on 3rd Ave. W. has displays depicting early 20th-century life as well as a tourist information center; phone (306) 642-5353.

BATOCHE (D-3)

Having had their lands in Manitoba's Red River Valley divided and bought out from under them by the swelling numbers of homesteaders, the Métis, a people of mixed Indian and French heritage, migrated to Batoche in the valley of the South Saskatchewan River about 1870. After farming and hunting buffalo for almost 15 years, they petitioned the Canadian government for rights to the land, but their requests were ignored.

Finally, in March 1885, their leader Louis Riel declared a provisional Métis government with Batoche as capital. With the fall of Batoche after a 4-day siege in early May, the group's dream of independence ended.

BATOCHE NATIONAL HISTORIC PARK, w. on Hwy. 225, covers 914 hectares (2,258 acres) on the South Saskatchewan River. The decisive battle of the Northwest Rebellion of 1885 was fought at this site. Features include the ruins of a Batoche village, the St. Antoine de Padoue church and a Visitor Reception Centre, where an audiovisual presentation is given. Interpretive signs and costumed interpreters are found in key locations throughout the park. Marked paths connect points of interest.

Daily 9-5, Victoria Day weekend-Thanksgiving weekend. Admission $4; senior citizens $3; ages 6-16, $2; family rate $10. Phone (306) 423-6227 or 423-6228.

BATTLEFORD (D-2) pop. 3,900

Once capital of the Northwest Territories, Battleford is one of Saskatchewan's oldest communities. As soon as the Canadian Pacific Railway began construction, citizens made plans for their town to become a western metropolis. But the railroad took a more southerly route, and in 1883 the capital was moved to Regina.

Battleford's hopes revived in 1905 when the Canadian Northern Railway proposed a westward route, but the line was built north of town on the other side of the Saskatchewan River, spawning the new town of North Battleford (*see place listing p. 244*). Battleford and its sister city have continued to grow as the province's vast northwest region has become more developed.

FORT BATTLEFORD NATIONAL HISTORIC SITE, 2 km (1.2 mi.) off Hwy. 4, preserves the old North West Mounted Police district headquarters established in 1876 to enforce law and order in the Northwest Territories. The commanding officer's residence, officers' quarters, sick horse stable and guardhouse are within a reconstructed stockade and furnished in the 1885 era. Barracks No. 5 houses exhibits that illustrate the history of the post and the role of the Mounted Police in the growth of Western Canada. Staff in period costumes provide interpretive information. Guided tours are available.

Allow 1 hour, 30 minutes minimum. Daily 9-5, Victoria Day-Labour Day. Admission $4; over 65, $3; ages 6-16, $2; family rate $10. Phone (306) 937-2621.

BIGGAR (D-2) pop. 2,400

BIGGAR MUSEUM AND GALLERY, 105 3rd Ave. W., highlights the story of settlement in Biggar. Featured are two outdoor murals, a plesiosaurus diorama, First Peoples display and replicas of a CN railway station and a silent film theater. Also included is a small art gallery exhibiting on a monthly basis works by different artists. Allow 30 minutes minimum. Mon.-Sat. 9-5, May-Aug.; 1-5, rest of year. Closed holidays. Free. Phone (306) 948-3451.

HOMESTEAD MUSEUM, 1.8 km (1 mi.) w. on Hwy. 51, houses an early 20th-century wooden home, a replica of a sod house, a store with a barbershop, a school, a restored 1923 homestead with a collection of character dolls, a church, a barn and a general display building. Allow 2 hours minimum. Mon.-Sat. 9-9, Sun. noon-9, Victoria Day weekend-Thanksgiving. Free. Phone (306) 948-3427.

BROADVIEW (E-5) pop. 800

Broadview began as a division point on the Canadian Pacific Railway. A marker in a park on the west side of town marks the location of the original tracks laid in 1882. Also in town is a sanctuary for Canada geese.

Broadview Chamber of Commerce: P.O. Box 556, Broadview, SK, Canada S0G 0K0; phone (306) 696-2443.

BROADVIEW MUSEUM, 1 blk. s. of Hwy. 1 on N. Front St., consists of an Indian log house, an 1897 rural school and a Canadian Pacific Railroad station and caboose. Displays include Indian and pioneer artifacts and old photographs and maps of early homesteads and trails. Daily 10-6, June 1-Sept. 1. Donations. Phone (306) 696-2286, 696-3244 or 696-2612.

CARLYLE (F-5) pop. 1,300

CARLYLE RUSTY RELIC MUSEUM AND TOURIST INFORMATION CENTRE, Railway Ave. and 3rd St. W., is housed in the former Canadian National Railway Station and features historical items from the area. Thirteen rooms contain such exhibits as a dentistry collection, farm equipment, World War II military uniforms, medical equipment, a restored kitchen and photographs. A restored one-room schoolhouse and a tourist information center also are on the grounds.

Allow 1 hour minimum. Mon.-Sat. 9-5, Sun. 1-5, mid-June through Labour Day. Admission $2; ages 6-18, $1. Phone (306) 453-2266.

CORONACH (F-4) pop. 900

POPLAR RIVER POWER STATION AND STRIP MINE is 10 km (6 mi.) s.e. Buses depart from the information center at the junction of Centre St. and Railway Ave. (Hwy. 18). Guides provide interpretive explanations of the power plant during the walking tour and of the strip-mining site during the bus tour. Durable clothing and flat-heeled shoes are recommended. Allow 2 hours minimum. Tours are given daily at 9:30 and 1, May-Sept. Free. Phone (306) 267-2078, or 267-2157 Sat.-Sun.

CRAVEN (E-4) pop. 300

Last Mountain Provincial Historic Park, 8 kilometres (5 mi.) north of town on Hwy. 20, preserves the site of a fur-trade outpost that operated 1869-71. Park interpreters offer guided tours of the site's three reconstructed buildings Thurs.-Sun. 10-5, July 1-Sept. 1; phone (306) 787-9573.

CUT KNIFE (D-2) pop. 600

In 1885 Cut Knife was the site of several Indian uprisings that were inspired by the Métis rebellion *(see Batoche p. 236).* The Battle of Cut Knife Hill, between the Cree tribe led by Chief Poundmaker and the North West Mounted Police under Col. W.D. Otter, ended in the retreat of the Mounties to Battleford.

Poundmaker, who stopped his warriors from pursuing and ambushing Otter's troops, later surrendered to the authorities to help restore peace between the Indians and settlers. A national historic plaque and a framework of tepee poles mark the chief's grave at the Poundmaker Reserve.

Dominating Cut Knife's horizon is the massive tomahawk in Tomahawk Park. The handle, carved from a British Columbian fir tree, is 16.4 metres (54 ft.) long and weighs 5.5 metric tons (6 tons); the fiberglass blade weighs 1,250 kilograms (2,750 lbs.).

Cut Knife Chamber of Commerce: P.O. Box 195, Cut Knife, SK, Canada S0M 0N0; phone (306) 398-2504.

CLAYTON McLAIN MEMORIAL MUSEUM, 3 blks. w. on Hill St. in Tomahawk Park, contains Indian artifacts, local historical records and articles used by early settlers. The museum also has several old buildings depicting an early pioneer settlement. A trout pond is next to the museum. Allow 1 hour minimum. Mon.-Sat. 9-7, Sun. 1-7, July-Aug.; Mon.-Fri. 2-5, in June. Admission $1; under 12, 50c; family rate $3. Phone (306) 398-2345.

DUCK LAKE (C-3) pop. 700

The town of Duck Lake lies between the North Saskatchewan and South Saskatchewan rivers. The actual lake is a few kilometres west of town. A nearby cairn marks the site of the Battle of Duck Lake, in which the Métis Indians defeated the North West Mounted Police on March 26, 1885.

DUCK LAKE REGIONAL INTERPRETIVE CENTRE is at the jct. of Hwys. 11 and 212. The center focuses on the historical contributions made by Indian, Métis and pioneer populations in the area's development. A museum features collections of traditional clothing, early school records and books, tools used in buffalo hunts, pioneer implements and contemporary paintings by local artists. The history and cultures of the area are presented in a 15-minute video, and a tower provides panoramic views.

Allow 30 minutes minimum. Daily 10-5:30, Victoria Day weekend-Labour Day weekend. Admission $4, senior citizens $3, students $2, under 5 free, family rate $10. MC, VI. Phone (306) 467-2057.

FORT CARLTON PROVINCIAL HISTORIC PARK, 26 km (16 mi.) w. on Hwy. 212, contains a reconstruction of the fort that played a part in the settlement of north-central Saskatchewan. The park also features three tepees depicting the Plains Cree culture as it existed 1860-70.

A replica of the Hudson's Bay Store is a museum of fur-trading history. The visitor center, next to the parking lot, is a reconstruction of the 1879 home of the factor (overseer) of the trading post. Allow 30 minutes minimum. Daily 10-6, Victoria Day-Labour Day. Admission $2.50; ages 6-17, $1; family rate $6. MC, VI. Phone (306) 467-5205.

EASTEND (F-2) pop. 600

EASTEND MUSEUM-CULTURAL CENTRE, on Hwy. 13 at Elm Ave., displays items of local interest, which include early settler, business and Indian artifacts and a collection of dinosaur bones found in the area. Adjoining the museum is a rancher's restored log house dating from around 1911. Allow 30 minutes minimum. Daily 10-8, May 24-Labour Day; by appointment rest of year. Admission $2, under 12 free. Phone (306) 295-3375.

ESTEVAN (F-5)
pop. 10,800, elev. 570 m/1,870'

Estevan, founded in 1892 just north of the Souris River, is one of Saskatchewan's major centers for coal and oil. The sun shines an average of 2,536 hours annually, making the town among the sunniest spots in Canada.

Southeast of town off Hwy. 39 is Roche Percée, a group of strangely eroded rock formations that were once venerated by local Indians. Although most of the animals and initials carved on the rocks can no longer be seen, the site is still supposedly visited by spirits whose murmurs can be heard when the wind blows.

On Hwy. 39 at 118 4th St. is the Estevan National Exhibition Centre. The center provides information about local events and also presents changing exhibitions and occasional interpretive programs or tours. It is open Mon.-Fri. 9-5, Sat.-Sun. and holidays 1-3:30; phone (306) 634-7644.

The Wood End Building, next to the center, was the 1893 barracks for the North West Mounted Police and contains artifacts that relate to the organization's early days. Also nearby is Eli Mandel Heritage Park, which contains an oil field display.

Tours to Boundary Dam Power Station, Shand Power Station and Luscar Boundary Mine can be arranged June through September through the Estevan Tourism Booth; phone (306) 634-6044.

Estevan Chamber of Commerce: 1102 4th St., Estevan, SK, Canada S4A 0W7; phone (306) 634-2828.

BOUNDARY DAM POWER STATION is 5 km (3 mi.) s. on Hwy. 47. The power station contains one of the largest lignite-burning plants in Canada. The dam depends on southeast Saskatchewan's vast coal reserves to produce more kilowatts than any other dam in the province. Boundary Dam Lake extends to the U.S. border; swimming and boating are permitted. Guided tours of the power station can be arranged. Daily 1:30-5. Free. Phone (306) 634-1300.

RECREATIONAL ACTIVITIES
Recreational Complex

• **Souris Valley Aquatic and Leisure Center**, 701 Souris Ave., Estevan, SK, Canada S4A 2T1. Mon.-Sat. 6 a.m.-10 p.m., Sun. noon-10. Phone (306) 634-1888.

ESTON (E-2)
pop. 1,100, elev. 682 m/2,240'

Founded in 1916, Eston has developed into a major grain source. More than one million bushels of grain are produced annually.

PRAIRIE WEST HISTORICAL CENTRE, 946 2nd St. S.E., consists of the restored 1910 Evans house and the Lovedale school. The museum contains more than 3,000 artifacts that include period furnishings and photographs as well as a pioneer schoolroom, agricultural displays and the Heritage Art Gallery. Allow 30 minutes minimum. Mon.-Sat. 9-noon and 1-5, Sun. 1-5, July-Aug.; Mon.-Sat. 1:30-4:30, Sun. 1-5, in June and Sept. Free. Phone (306) 962-3772.

FORT QU'APPELLE (E-4)
pop. 2,000

With the 1874 signing of Treaty Number IV, representatives of the Cree and Saulteaux Indians gave away their legal right to vast tracts of southern Saskatchewan; near the center of Fort Qu'Appelle (kwah-PELL) a cairn marks the site of the signing. The fort for which the town is named was built in 1864 mainly for use as a trading post.

Fort Qu'Appelle is on the Qu'Appelle River in a broad valley of lush farmland. The area is known for the wide variety of berries growing on the moist, north-facing slopes. The dry, south-facing slopes are carpeted with wildflowers. Several kinds of hawks soar above this peaceful valley, and pelicans, herons, ducks and geese nest in the marshes. Near Fort Qu'Appelle the river widens into a chain of lakes.

The river's unusual name is the French translation of the Cree word *ca-ta-buy-se-pu,* or "the river that calls." According to Indian legend, the river was haunted by a spirit that could be heard crying as it moved up and down the water.

Also taking its name from this Cree expression is nearby Katepwa Point Provincial Park, a lakeside recreation area offering day-use facilities. Another provincial park, Echo Valley, is west of town. *See Recreation Chart and the AAA/CAA Western Canada and Alaska CampBook.*

Fort Qu'Appelle Chamber of Commerce: P.O. Box 1273, Fort Qu'Appelle, SK, Canada S0G 1S0; phone (306) 332-6688.

FISH CULTURE STATION is 6 km (4 mi.) w. on Hwy. 210. The station raises such fish as northern pike, arctic grayling, whitefish, walleye, and rainbow, brown, lake and brook trout through their life cycle from the egg stage to adult and distributes them to various lakes and rivers to bolster fish population. Allow 30 minutes minimum. Mon.-Fri. 9-noon and 1-4, May-Sept. Guided tours are given on the hour. Free. Phone (306) 332-3200.

FORT QU'APPELLE MUSEUM is at Bay Ave. and 3rd St. A small log building remaining from the original 1864 Hudson's Bay Co. trading post adjoins a modern structure displaying relics of the past, Indian crafts and a model of Fort Qu'Appelle. Daily 10-noon and 1-5, June 1-Labour Day; other times by appointment. Admission $2, children 50c, family rate $5. Phone (306) 332-6443 or 332-4319.

GRASSLANDS NATIONAL PARK (F-2)

Elevations in the park range from 747 metres (2,450 ft.) at the Frenchman River to 998 metres (3,275 ft.) at Horse Creek. Refer to CAA/AAA maps for additional elevation information.

Grasslands National Park encompasses the grasslands in two separate blocks between Val Marie and Killdeer in the southern part of the province. When completed, it will preserve 900 square kilometres (350 sq. mi.) of Saskatchewan's original mixed-grass prairie, including such topographic features as buttes and coulees. Among the wildlife species found in the park are prairie dogs, golden eagles, rattlesnakes, pronghorn antelopes and mule deer.

The Grasslands also claim a rich history. The first recorded discovery of dinosaur remains in Canada was made in the Killdeer Badlands in 1875. Proof of early Indian habitation includes remnants of tepee rings left by the Plains Indians.

Ranching operations exist in the area, and some of the proposed parkland is still under private ownership. Visitors are asked not to venture off public roads before contacting the park office in Val Marie. Interpretive programs, maps and information are available at the visitor center. Write Grasslands National Park, P.O. Box 150, Val Marie, SK, Canada S0N 2T0; phone (306) 298-2257. *See Recreation Chart.*

GRAVELBOURG (F-3) pop. 1,200

CATHEDRALE NOTRE-DAME DE L'ASSOMPTION, Main St., is noted for the beauty of the interior murals painted over a 10-year period by the founding pastor Monsignor Charles Maillard. Guided tours are available. The 1918 cathedral is open daily 9-5, July-Aug.; by appointment rest of year. Free. Phone (306) 648-3322, 648-3269, or 648-3105 to schedule a guided tour.

GRENFELL (E-5) pop. 1,100

Grenfell lies at the western terminus of scenic Hwy. 247, which arcs northeast past Crooked and Round lakes and then heads south to end at Hwy. 1, about 49 kilometres (30 mi.) east of the town.

GRENFELL MUSEUM, Wolseley Ave. and Stella St., is housed in Adare, the former home of the

---

DID YOU KNOW

Estevan is the province's sunshine capital, averaging 2,540 hours of sunshine each year.

editor/publisher of Grenfell's first newspaper. The 1904 house, furnished in period, contains a brass bed, a wood-burning kitchen range, an icebox, a hand-operated vacuum cleaner and a dining table set with china. A separate building displays antiques, pioneer artifacts and military uniforms and weapons. Allow 2 hours minimum. Fri.-Sun. 2-8, late June-late Aug.; other times by appointment. Donations. Phone (306) 697-2930.

HUMBOLDT (D-4) pop. 5,100

Named after German author, explorer and scientist Baron Friedrich Heinrich Alexander von Humboldt, the town's heritage is evident in its architecture, parks, streets and festivals.

Town of Humboldt: 601 Main St., P.O. Box 1598, Humboldt, SK, Canada S0K 2A0; phone (306) 682-3444.

HUMBOLDT AND DISTRICT MUSEUM AND GALLERY, Main St. and Sixth Ave., is in a restored, early 20th-century post office. The gallery contains exhibits about local wildlife, art and history. Allow 30 minutes minimum. Tues.-Sat. 10-5, Sun. 1-5, July-Aug.; Tues.-Sun. 1-5 or by appointment, rest of year. Donations. Phone (306) 682-5226.

INDIAN HEAD (E-4) pop. 1,800

PFRA SHELTERBELT CENTRE, 1.6 km (1 mi.) s. of Indian Head exit off Hwy. 1, has a short, self-guiding nature trail, picnic areas and an interpretive center, which is part of the Prairie Farm Rehabilitation Administration (PFRA). Outdoor areas open daily dawn-dusk. Interpretive center open Mon.-Fri. 9-4. Free. Phone (306) 695-2284.

KAMSACK (E-5) pop. 2,300

KAMSACK AND DISTRICT MUSEUM, 1.5 km (1 mi.) w. of Hwy. 5 to the Riverside Golf Course, following signs, is housed in a 1914 power plant. The museum features a 1914 generator, old farm equipment, household artifacts, a printing press, vintage clothing and replicas of an early 1900s doctor's office, hospital room and barber shop. Daily 1-5, Victoria Day-Labour Day; by appointment rest of year. Admission $1, under 18 free. Phone (306) 542-4415 or 542-4381.

KINDERSLEY (D-2) pop. 4,700

Kindersley is a popular stop for bird-watchers. Its surrounding marshy terrain annually attracts thousands of migrating geese, more than 10 species of ducks and a few whistling swans and whooping cranes.

Kindersley Chamber of Commerce: 305 Main St., Box 1537, Kindersley, SK, Canada S0L 1S0; phone (306) 463-2320.

KINDERSLEY PLAINS MUSEUM, 1 km (.6 mi.) e. on Hwy. 7, contains geological displays, Indian artifacts and farming and military items. Guided tours are available. Allow 30 minutes minimum. Daily 9-5, May 1-Labour Day. Donations. Phone (306) 463-6620.

KINISTINO (D-4) pop. 700

One of the oldest purely agricultural settlements in the province, Kinistino takes its name from *kinistineaux,* meaning "they who were the first to arrive." The allusion refers to the Cree Indians, who lived in the area before the arrival of homesteaders.

KINISTINO DISTRICT PIONEER MUSEUM, on Main St., displays pioneer and Indian artifacts. Allow 30 minutes minimum. Daily 2-7, June 1-Oct. 15. Donations. Phone (306) 864-2838 or 864-3106.

LLOYDMINSTER (C-1) pop. 7,600

A group of settlers led by Rev. Isaac Barr founded what is now Lloydminster in 1903. Named for Rev. G.E. Lloyd, who later took charge of the settlement, this busy community astride the Alberta-Saskatchewan border holds city status in both provinces. In fact, Lloydminster is Canada's only border city. Border markers—100-foot orange towers shaped like the survey stakes used by the land surveyors—are aligned along the border, which is the 4th meridian. The 4th meridian is said to be one of the longest, straightest surveyed lines in North America.

Lloydminster has a central location within the province's heavy oil country. Of interest is the Char-Mil Rig, a scale model of an oil derrick located at 4721 46th St. The Oil Technical Society Heavy Oil Science Centre, at the Barr Colony Heritage Cultural Centre *(see attraction listing),* offers interpretive, educational displays as well as an account of heavy oil history.

Bud Miller All Seasons Park, 2902 59th Ave., consists of 81 hectares (200 acres) and features fishing, paddleboating, walking and bicycling trails, bird and wildlife watching, picnicking, tennis, baseball diamonds, playgrounds, gardens and a water park.

Lloydminster Tourism: 5011 49th Ave., Lloydminster, SK, Canada S9V 0T8; phone (306) 825-6180 or (800) 825-6180.

WEAVER PARK, on Hwy. 16E at 44th St. and 45th Ave., is where the Barr colonists built their first settlement in 1903; restored buildings mark the spot. Also on the park grounds are the Barr Colony Heritage Cultural Centre with museums and art galleries, a miniature golf course, camping and picnic areas. Allow 2 hours minimum. Park open daily 7 a.m.-9 p.m. Park free. Phone (306) 825-5655 for the museums or 825-3726 for the campground. *See the AAA/CAA Western Canada and Alaska CampBook.*

Barr Colony Heritage Cultural Centre consists of The Richard Larsen Museum, The Fuchs Wildlife Exhibit, The Imhoff Art Collection and The Oil Technical Society Heavy Oil Science Centre.

The Richard Larsen Museum depicts the history of the Barr colonists, the European settlers of the region, through such artifacts as old machinery, cars, furniture and household items. In addition to the museum displays are Lloydminster's first church, a 1906 schoolhouse, a log cabin furnished in early 20th-century style, an old-time filling station and an oil refinery display.

The Fuchs Wildlife Exhibit features mounted birds and wildlife in natural settings. The Imhoff Collection displays some 250 religious and historical paintings. The gallery features a comprehensive collection of paintings by Berthold Imhoff, an artist renowned for his murals in North American churches and public buildings.

The Oil Technical Society Heavy Oil Science Centre provides interactive opportunities to learn about the geology, drilling, refining and uses of the region's heavy oil reserves. Center open daily 10-8, Victoria Day weekend-Labour Day; Wed.-Fri. noon-5, Sat.-Sun. 1-5, rest of year. Admission $3; senior citizens and students with ID $2.50; ages 6-12, $2; ages 2-5, $1. Phone (306) 825-5655.

MANITOU BEACH (D-3) pop. 100

The resort community of Manitou Beach is on the shore of Little Manitou Lake. The mineral waters of this lake were believed by the Indians to possess curative powers, and the sick of the tribe were brought for treatment long before Europeans knew of the land. The 19-kilometre-long (12-mi.) lake is three times saltier than the ocean. The resort has a nine-hole golf course, hotel, convention center, mini-mall, tennis courts, cross-country ski trails and an indoor heated mineral pool.

Along the lake lies Camp Easter Seal, which provides summer recreation for the physically impaired; visitors are welcome.

MANOR (F-5) pop. 300

Northwest of Manor is Moose Mountain Provincial Park *(see Recreation Chart)*, which began as a resort beach on Lake Kenosee in 1906. The park is home to herds of moose and elk and is a nesting place for geese and other birds. There also are more than 450 beaver lodges.

Recreational facilities include an 18-hole golf course, hiking and equestrian trails, a clubhouse, riding stables and a swimming beach. Across from the park entrance is Kenosee Superslide, a water park.

CANNINGTON MANOR PROVINCIAL HISTORIC PARK is 13 km (8 mi.) n., then 2 km (1.2 mi.) e. and 2 km (1.2 mi.) n. on gravel roads. The village of Cannington Manor, founded in 1882, was an attempt to duplicate the upper-middle-class English way of life, including cricket matches and fox hunts. The museum and seven buildings—three originals and the rest reconstructions—contain antiques, artifacts and farming implements used by the settlers.

Guides in period costumes demonstrate activities typical of the settlement in the last 2 decades of the 19th century. Picnicking is permitted. Wed.-Mon. 10-5, Victoria Day-Labour Day. Admission $2, students with ID $1, under 6 free, family rate $5. Phone (306) 577-2600 or 739-2617.

MAPLE CREEK (F-2) pop. 2,300

The town of Maple Creek was named by the Canadian Pacific Railway workers who spent the winter of 1882 on the banks of Maple Creek. Livestock, grain, tourism, natural gas and oil development provide the area with a stable economy.

South of town on Hwy. 21 is Cypress Hills Inter-Provincial Park *(see Recreation Chart and the AAA/CAA Western Canada and Alaska CampBook)*. The lofty hills are characterized by forest-covered buttes, plateaus and ridges interspersed with large areas of ranchland. Maple Creek also features a golf course, campgrounds, stores and museums.

Cypress Hills Regional Economic Development Authority: 205 Jasper St., P.O. Box 428, Maple Creek, SK, Canada S0N 1N0; phone (306) 662-4299.

FORT WALSH NATIONAL HISTORIC SITE, 55 km (34 mi.) s.w. off Hwy. 271, was an early North West Mounted Police fort. Reconstructed period buildings house exhibits of original post artifacts. Tours include trips to a reconstructed whiskey trading post and the fort. A bus trip around the park includes an interpretive commentary. Allow 2 hours minimum. Daily 9-5:30, Victoria Day weekend-Thanksgiving. Admission (includes bus tour) $6; over 65, $4.50; ages 6-16, $3; family rate $15. MC, VI. Phone (306) 662-3590.

THE JASPER CULTURAL AND HISTORICAL CENTRE, 311 Jasper St., features several rooms of historical displays housed in a two-story brick school building built in 1913. Exhibits include ranching, railroad, rodeo and school memorabilia. An art gallery displays Western-themed paintings. Allow 30 minutes minimum. Daily 10-4, May-Sept.; Mon.-Fri. 10-4, rest of year. Admission $4; students with ID $2; ages 6-12, $1. Phone (306) 662-2434.

OLDTIMER'S MUSEUM, 218 Jasper St., contains collections of photographs, artifacts and archival material relating to the First Nations people, the North West Mounted Police, ranching and early settlement. Tues.-Sat. 9-5:30, Sun.-Mon. 1-5,

Victoria Day weekend-Labour Day; Tues.-Wed. 9-5:30, rest of year. Admission $3, students $1. Phone (306) 662-2474.

MEADOW LAKE (B-2) pop. 4,800

Meadow Lake is an outfitting point for recreation in the northwestern Saskatchewan lakes area. Pastimes include fishing for lake trout, pike, pickerel and arctic grayling and hunting for big game, ducks, geese and sharp-tailed grouse. In Meadow Lake Provincial Park *(see Recreation Chart and the AAA/CAA Western Canada and Alaska CampBook)*, a 179-kilometre (111-mi.) canoe route stretches along the Waterhen and Beaver rivers. Canoes and kayaks as well as lessons are available in the park.

Of historical interest is Steele Narrows Provincial Historic Park, 72 kilometres (45 mi.) southwest via hwys. 304 and 26. The last armed conflict on Canadian soil occurred between Big Bear and his band of Cree Indians and Maj. Sam Steele of the North West Mounted Police. The defeat of Big Bear on June 3, 1885, was the end of the Métis and Indian rebellion that began in March 1885 *(see Batoche p. 236)*.

Meadow Lake & District Chamber of Commerce: P.O. Box 1168, Meadow Lake, SK, Canada S0M 1V0; phone (306) 236-4447.

MEADOW LAKE MUSEUM, 9th Ave. and Hwy. 4, displays local pioneer artifacts and antiques. Mon.-Sun. 9-8 (also Fri. 8-9 p.m.), Victoria Day weekend-Labour Day. Admission $2, under 10 free. Phone (306) 236-4447.

MELFORT (D-4)
pop. 5,800, elev. 457 m/1,500'

Known as the City of Northern Lights due to the visibility of the aurora borealis in the night sky for much of the year, Melfort is in the Carrot River Valley, an area known for its fertile black loam. Agriculture has been the major industry in the area since early settlement days in the late 19th century. Melfort was incorporated as a village in 1903, as a town in 1907 and as the province's twelfth city on September 2, 1980.

Melfort & District Chamber of Commerce: Box 2002, Melfort, SK, Canada S0E 1A0; phone (306) 752-4636.

MELFORT & DISTRICT MUSEUM, 401 Melfort St. W., encompasses several buildings including a 1912 power house, reconstructed log farmhouse, general store and post office, barber shop, one-room schoolhouse, blacksmith shop and real estate office. The museum also features an extensive collection of farm machinery, equipment and tools that were used in the development of the local agricultural industry. Guided tours are available.

Allow 1 hour minimum. Mon.-Sat. 9-5, mid-May to early Sept.; closed holidays. Admission

$2; ages 6-10, $1; family rate $6. Phone (306) 752-5870.

MELVILLE (E-5)
pop. 4,600, elev. 555 m/1,820'

Situated on the east-west main line of the Canadian National Railway and also on an important north-south line of that company, Melville is known as "The Rail Centre." It came to provincial prominence when it was selected as a major railway service center early in the 20th century. The railway is still the city's largest employer, and its facilities are essential in marketing agricultural products as well as potash from nearby Esterhazy.

Melville & District Chamber of Commerce: P.O. Box 429, Melville, SK, Canada S0A 2P0; phone (306) 728-4177.

MOOSE JAW (E-3)
pop. 33,000, elev. 542 m/1,778'

Moose Jaw's unusual name is probably derived from the big bend in Moose Jaw Creek. The Indians called this creek *moosichappishannissippi,* or "the creek that bends like a moose's jaw." Another popular theory is that an early traveler through the area fixed his cart wheel with a moose's jawbone found in the vicinity.

During Prohibition in the United States Moose Jaw was the home of an industrious band of bootleggers and American gangsters, earning the town the nickname "Little Chicago of the Prairies." Moose Jaw is now an important industrial city in western Canada; hard spring wheat is grown in the area. The Canadian Forces base just south of Moose Jaw is home to one of Canada's busiest airports and headquarters of the Snowbirds, the Canadian armed forces aerobatic team.

The Murals of Moose Jaw, painted on several downtown buildings, are a collection of more than 20 murals depicting the town's history. Also of historic significance is Hwy. 2, south of town, which was once part of the Powder River Trail used by freighters and ranchers to reach Denver before the advent of the railroad.

Forty-two kilometres (25 miles) north of town off Hwy. 2 is Buffalo Pound Provincial Park *(see Recreation Chart and the AAA/CAA Western Canada and Alaska CampBook),* where 350 hectares (865 acres) are set aside as grazing land for a herd of buffaloes.

Wildlife of a different type can be found along Hwy. 1 north of Moose Jaw. It's hard to miss Mac; at more than 30-feet tall the statue is said to be the world's largest moose. Adjacent to the statue, at 99 Diefenbaker Dr., is the Tourist Information Centre. The center can arrange tours of the murals and heritage buildings in the downtown Moose Jaw area; phone (306) 693-8097.

Wakamow Valley, in Moose Jaw, is a recreational development that includes Plaxton's

Lake, North River Park, Kiwanis River Park, Kinsmen Wellesley Park, Connor Park and the Devonian Trail, a pedestrian and bicycle trail system. Visitors can enjoy picnicking, camping, bird-watching, hiking, jogging and bicycling.

Moose Jaw Chamber of Commerce: 88 Saskatchewan St. E., Box 1359, Moose Jaw, SK, Canada S6H 4R3; phone (306) 692-6414.

Self-guiding tours: Brochures outlining a self-guiding tour of some of downtown Moose Jaw's most significant historic sites are available at the Moose Jaw Art Museum and National Exhibits in Crescent Park *(see attraction listing).*

CRESCENT PARK, at Fairford and Athabasca sts., has an outdoor swimming pool, war memorial gardens and recreational facilities on its 11 hectares (27 acres). Free entertainment is presented Wednesday evenings July through August. The Moose Jaw Art Museum and National Exhibits, next to the public library, displays historical items of local, regional and national interest.

Museum open Tues.-Sun. noon-5 (also Tues.-Wed. 7-9 p.m.); closed Good Friday, Easter and Dec. 25. Outdoor pool open daily 1-4 and 7-8:30, June 1-Labour Day. Museum free. Admission to pool $3; ages 13-17, $2; ages 3-12, $1.75; family rate $7. Phone (306) 692-4471, or 694-4500 for the pool.

SUKANEN SHIP, PIONEER VILLAGE AND MUSEUM, 13 km (8 mi.) s. on Hwy. 2, preserves an old post office, blacksmith shop, school, church, railroad station and general store as well as a collection of antique tractors, trucks and cars. The large, unfinished ship was built by Tom Sukanen, a Finnish settler who had planned to sail the boat home to his native country by way of the South Saskatchewan River, Hudson Bay, Greenland and Iceland.

Mon.-Sat. 9-5, Sun. noon-8, June 1 to mid-Sept. Admission $4; over 65 and students with ID $3; ages 8-12, $2. Phone (306) 693-7315.

TUNNELS OF LITTLE CHICAGO, 108 Main St. N. Lower Level, were originally built by Chinese railroad workers trying to avoid paying a "head tax." Once connecting several businesses downtown, the tunnels were used by bootleggers during Saskatchewan's Prohibition era 1916-24. American gangster Al Capone supposedly used the tunnels to hide from American authorities.

Allow 1 hour minimum. Daily 10-8, May-Nov.; Sun.-Thurs. 1-3, Fri. 11-3, Sat. 10-4, rest of year. Closed Jan. 1 and Dec. 25. Admission $7; over 64 and ages 13-16, $6; ages 6-12, $4. MC. Phone (306) 693-5261.

WESTERN DEVELOPMENT MUSEUM'S HISTORY OF TRANSPORTATION is at 50 Diefenbaker Dr. Displays illustrate air, water, rail and land transportation. The museum also houses an observatory and Cinema 180. The Snowbird Gallery contains aircraft and memorabilia from the Canadian armed forces aerobatic team. Trips aboard the Short Line, a miniature steam locomotive, are available on weekends; phone for schedule. Picnicking is permitted.

Allow 2 hours minimum. Museum open daily 9-6, Apr.-Dec. Cinema 180 open daily 10-5, July-Aug.; Sat.-Sun. and holidays 10-7, rest of year. Museum $5; over 64, $4; ages 5-12, $1.75. Theater $1.50. Train rides $1. AE, MC, VI. Phone (306) 693-5989.

CASINOS

- **Golden Nugget Casino,** 250 Thatcher Dr. Thurs.-Sun. noon-midnight. Phone (306) 692-5858.

RECREATIONAL ACTIVITIES

Recreational Complex

- **Kinsmen Sportsplex,** 855 McDonald St. W., Moose Jaw, SK, Canada S6H 2W3. Daily 1-4 and 7-9, mid-Mar. to mid-Oct.; Sat. 2-3 and Sun. 7-8, rest of year. Closed Jan. 1, Good Friday and Dec. 25. Phone (306) 694-4483.

MUENSTER (D-4) pop. 400

ST. PETER'S ABBEY is 1 km (.6 mi.) e. off Muenster access rd. on Hwy. 5. A self-guiding walking tour of the abbey complex enables visitors to learn about monastic life. Brochures are available at Severin Hall. Sts. Peter and Paul Church, recreational facilities, a farm, gardens, an orchard, trails, print shop, workshops, cemetery and greenhouse are points of interest. Allow 1 hour minimum. Daily 8-dusk. Free. Phone (306) 682-1777.

ST. PETER'S CATHEDRAL, 1 km (.6 mi.) n. of Hwy. 5 on the Muenster access rd., is a church as well as a virtual gallery of Berthold Imhoff paintings. The cathedral's walls and ceiling are lined with the artist's work, which incorporates 80 life-size figures executed as a gift to the abbot of St. Peter's monastery. Allow 30 minutes minimum. Daily 9-9, Mar.-Dec. Free. Phone (306) 682-1777 or 682-5484.

NIPAWIN (C-4) pop. 4,300

The Nipawin Hydroelectric Station, northwest of town, uses water impounded in Codette Lake by the Francois-Finlay Dam to generate 1.1 billion kilowatt hours of electricity annually. Guided tours of the facility are conducted by the chamber of commerce on Thursdays, June through July; phone ahead to confirm tour availability. SaskPower also conducts tours, but requires 2 weeks advance notice; phone (306) 882-3148.

Nipawin & District Chamber of Commerce: Box 177, Nipawin, SK, Canada S0E 1E0; phone (306) 862-5252.

LIVING FORESTRY MUSEUM is just w. on Hwy. 35N. The museum contains rotating exhibits which describe the history of the area. Several historic buildings have been relocated to the vicinity, including a sawmill, schoolhouse, shingle mill, church and the 1924 Hornseth House. Demonstrations of the saw and shingle mills and a steam engine are provided during the summer months. Allow 1 hour minimum. Daily 1-5:30, May-Aug. Admission $2, under 14 free. Phone (306) 862-9299.

NOKOMIS (E-4) pop. 500

First named Blakemore and then Blaikie by railroad officials, Nokomis began as the junction of the Old Grand Trunk Railway and the Canadian Provincial Railway. Arriving from England, Mrs. Thomas Halstead, the town's postmistress, was intrigued by the West and the romantic domain of the Indians and chose the name Nokomis, from Henry Wadsworth Longfellow's poem "Hiawatha," for the young town.

NOKOMIS AND DISTRICT MUSEUM, 3rd Ave. and Queen St., is housed in the former railway station and features re-creations of a post office, schoolhouse, dentist's office, hospital room and equipment, hardware store, a garage with a 1930 Chevrolet and a church. Photographs, vintage clothing and antiques are displayed. Junction City 1907, behind the museum, is a replica of a small town. Allow 1 hour minimum. Daily 10-5, June 1-Labour Day weekend. Admission $2, family rate $5. Phone (306) 528-2979.

NORTH BATTLEFORD (C-2)
pop. 14,100

On the bank of the North Saskatchewan River, North Battleford is a gateway to the province's northwest parkland area. Agriculture is the backbone of the area's economy, with farms producing cereal grains, oil seeds and hay crops as well as cattle, hogs, poultry and bison. Forestry, manufacturing and heavy crude oil development also are important industries.

The Battlefords Provincial Park *(see Recreation Chart and Cochin in the AAA/CAA Western Canada and Alaska CampBook)* is approximately 42 kilometres (26 mi.) north off Hwy. 4 and offers fishing, water skiing, boating and hiking trails. Cross-country skiing and ice fishing are popular winter activities at the park.

Battlefords Chamber of Commerce: Junction Hwys. 40 & 16E, P.O. Box 1000, North Battleford, SK, Canada S9A 3E6; phone (306) 445-6226.

ALLEN SAPP GALLERY, 1 Railway Ave., features the paintings of this nationally known Cree artist from the Red Pheasant Reserve, 48 kilometres (30 mi.) south of North Battleford. Allen Sapp, recipient of the Order of Canada, depicts in his works the culture of his people and the day-to-day events of life on the reserve during the 1930s and '40s. The gallery occupies the main floor of a restored Andrew Carnegie library.

The permanent collection consists of more than 400 paintings contributed by Allan Gonor, Sapp's North Battleford mentor and patron. Changing exhibits also are presented every 6 months. Daily 1-5 (also Wed.-Sun. 5-8), May-Sept.; Wed.-Sun. 1-5, rest of year. Donations. Phone (306) 445-1760.

WESTERN DEVELOPMENT MUSEUM'S HERITAGE FARM AND VILLAGE, jct. hwys. 16 and 40, focuses on the story of agriculture and pioneer life. It preserves a 1920s pioneer village, including a working farm with demonstrations of early agricultural equipment and techniques. Picnicking is permitted.

Allow 2 hours minimum. Daily 8:30-6:30, Victoria Day weekend-Labour Day weekend; Wed.-Sun. 1-5, rest of year. Admission (good for 2 consecutive days) $5; over 65 and students with ID $4; ages 5-12, $1.75; family rate $12. MC, VI. Phone (306) 445-8033.

CASINOS

• **Gold Eagle Casino,** 11902 Railway Ave. Mon.-Sat. 10 a.m.-2 a.m., Sun. noon-midnight; closed Dec. 25. Phone (306) 446-3833.

OUTLOOK (E-2) pop. 2,100

Outlook, on the South Saskatchewan River, is known for the old elm trees that are in the regional park.

Town of Outlook: 400 Saskatchewan St., Box 518, Outlook, SK, Canada S0L 2N0; phone (306) 867-8663.

SOUTH SASKATCHEWAN RIVER PROJECT consists of two dams on the South Saskatchewan and Qu'Appelle rivers. Gardiner Dam, midway between Elbow and Outlook, is 6 kilometres (4 mi.) long, 64 metres (210 ft.) high and 1,615 metres (5,300 ft.) wide at its base—one of the largest rolled-earth dams in Canada. The impounded water forms Lake Diefenbaker, about 225 kilometres (140 mi.) long, up to 5 kilometres (3 mi.) wide and 56 metres (184 ft.) deep. The second, smaller structure is Qu'Appelle Dam.

A visitor center near Gardiner Dam presents a photographic history of the project. Food is available. Allow 30 minutes minimum. Self-guiding tours of the power station are offered Mon.-Fri. 10-3. Visitor center open daily 9-5, Victoria Day weekend-Labour Day weekend. Free. Phone (306) 857-2123.

PRINCE ALBERT (C-4) pop. 34,800

The gateway to Saskatchewan's north country, Prince Albert is one of the province's oldest communities. Trapper Peter Pond built a trading post on the north side of the North Saskatchewan River in 1776. Credited with founding the town, the Rev. James Nisbet settled on the south shore in 1866.

The log Presbyterian church that Nisbet built that year is now in Kinsmen Park. A blockhouse next to the church dates from the Riel Rebellion of 1885. The Prince Albert Historical Museum *(see attraction listing)* occupies the site of the church built by Nisbet.

Ski slopes and jumps and toboggan runs just outside Prince Albert offer recreational opportunities throughout the winter.

Prince Albert Chamber of Commerce: 3700 2nd Ave. W., Prince Albert, SK, Canada S6W 1A2; phone (306) 953-4386 or 953-4385.

DIEFENBAKER HOUSE MUSEUM, 246 19th St. W., was the home of the Right Honourable John G. Diefenbaker 1947-75. The museum contains furniture and other possessions of the prime minister of Canada 1957-63. Allow 30 minutes minimum. Daily 10-6 (also Sun. 6-9 p.m.), May 12-Aug. 31. Donations. Phone (306) 953-4863.

EVOLUTION OF EDUCATION MUSEUM is at the corner of Marquis Rd. and Hwy. 2 at 3700 2nd Ave. W. The one-room, 1920 schoolhouse was designed to provide maximum warmth and light, with all large windows on the building's east side and desks facing south so that daylight would shine over the students' left shoulders. Exhibits relate to area education and include pencil boxes, Dick and Jane readers and chalk clamps once used to draw lines on a blackboard.

An interpreter is on site to answer questions; a visitor information center also is in the building. Allow 30 minutes minimum. Daily 10-8, Victoria Day weekend-Labour Day weekend; by appointment rest of year. Free. Phone (306) 763-3506 Victoria Day weekend-Labour Day weekend, or 764-2999 rest of year.

LITTLE RED RIVER PARK is at the confluence of the North Saskatchewan and Little Red rivers on Hwy. 55, the scenic drive that follows the north bank of the North Saskatchewan River. Picnic facilities and winter sports are available. Swimming in the river is not recommended. Free.

PRINCE ALBERT HISTORICAL MUSEUM, 10 River St. E. at Central Ave., is in the old fire hall that overlooks the North Saskatchewan River. Featured is the first fire engine pumper used in the territory. Other displays include Indian, fur trade and pioneer artifacts as well as a table and benches carved by the Rev. James Nisbet. A tearoom provides a view of the river. Allow 1 hour minimum. Mon.-Sat. 10-6, Sun. 10-9, May 15-Labour Day. Admission $1; ages 6-12, 50c. Phone (306) 764-2992.

ROTARY MUSEUM OF POLICE AND CORRECTIONS is at the corner of Marquis Rd. and Hwy. 2 at 3700 2nd Ave. W. The museum is in a landscaped park that contains a garden as well as RV facilities. Displays pertain to the Royal Canadian Mounted Police, local police, provincial police and corrections services. Exhibits include corporal punishment items, police uniforms and weapons.

An interpreter is on site to answer questions; a visitor information center also is on the premises. Allow 30 minutes minimum. Daily 10-6, Victoria Day weekend-Labour Day weekend; by appointment rest of year. Free. Phone (306) 922-3313.

★ PRINCE ALBERT NATIONAL PARK (B-3)

Elevations in the park range from 488 metres (1,600 ft.) on the western side of the park to 724 metres (2,375 ft.) on the southern side of the park. Refer to CAA/AAA maps for additional elevation information.

Prince Albert National Park covers 3,875 square kilometres (1,496 sq. mi.) of wilderness in central Saskatchewan. The park's main entrance is 81 kilometres (50 mi.) north of the city of Prince Albert via hwys. 2 and 264.

The area's lakes, ponds, streams, bogs and rolling hills are a legacy of the glacial epoch. Notable are Sandy, Waskesiu, Kingsmere, Namekus, Crean and the Hanging Heart lakes. There also are several hundred smaller lakes and ponds and many sand beaches.

Heavy growths of conifers and several species of hardwoods surround the lakes, along with numerous shrubs and wildflowers. Fall foliage is especially colorful. Such wild animals as elk, deer, moose and bears are plentiful. A herd of free-roaming bison wander throughout the park, and a fenced paddock near the south entrance contains a smaller herd of the woolly mammals.

Early morning and evening provide the best chances of seeing wildlife along park roads, especially the Narrows and Kingsmere roads along Waskesiu Lake. Although some animals may seem tame, they are wild and should be observed only from a safe distance.

The park also preserves the legacy of Grey Owl. Born as Archibald Stansfeld Belaney, this controversial Englishman arrived in Canada in 1905. Adopted by the Ojibwa Indians and later married into the tribe, Grey Owl turned his love of nature to the re-establishment of the region's beaver population, which had been decimated by hunters and trappers. For 7 years he lived at Beaver Lodge on Ajawaan Lake, where he continued his restoration and conservation efforts.

General Information and Activities

Although the park is open throughout the year, complete facilities are provided Victoria Day-Labour Day only. Information is available from the information bureau in the Waskesiu Lake Visitor Services Centre, 8 kilometres (5 mi.) from the park's main gate on Hwy. 264.

Roads traverse the park and lead to Waskesiu, Namekus, Sandy and the Hanging Heart lakes and to the Kingsmere River. Although no roads lead directly to Kingsmere and Crean lakes, access is possible by boat. A light railway with handcars assists in portaging around the unnavigable stretch of the Kingsmere River.

There are more than 100 kilometres (60 mi.) of hiking trails traversing the park, with some suitable for day walks and others requiring overnight hikes. Pamphlets of self-guiding tours are available for the Mud Creek and Boundary Bog nature trails. From the boat dock on the north shore of Kingsmere Lake a 3-kilometre (1.9-mi.) trail leads to the home and grave of Grey Owl.

Park facilities include boat launching and berthing areas at the Hanging Heart Lakes, the Narrows and the main marina on Waskesiu Lake. Boats, canoes and outboard motors can be rented at all three marinas; paddle-wheeler tours are offered daily in summer. There are bicycle rentals, tennis and volleyball courts and bowling greens at the Waskesiu Lake Visitor Services Centre. Horse rental and trail rides also are available.

Waskesiu Lake's 18-hole golf course ranks among the finest in Canada. A 150-kilometre (93-mi.) network of groomed cross-country ski trails is open in winter. Snowshoeing and ice fishing also are permitted. Fishing licenses are required and can be obtained at the park information center, park entrances and campground offices.

Park naturalists offer a free summer interpretive program that includes car caravans on park roadways and special daily events. Interpretive programs are regularly presented at the outdoor theaters at the Narrows and Beaver Glen campgrounds.

At the Waskesiu Lake Visitor Services Centre is the Park Nature Centre, which has natural history exhibits, a bookstore and a theater; the nature center is open in July and August. *See Recreation Chart and the AAA/CAA Western Canada and Alaska CampBook.*

ADMISSION to the park is $4 per day; over 65, $3; ages 6-15, $2. Admission any 3 consecutive days $18 per family. A 7-day pass is $26 per family.

PETS (dogs and cats) are permitted in the park as long as they are on leashes.

ADDRESS inquiries to the Superintendent, Prince Albert National Park, P.O. Box 100, Waskesiu Lake, SK, Canada S0J 2Y0; phone (306) 663-5322.

REDVERS (F-5)
pop. 1,000, elev. 1,000'

The rich soil of the gently rolling countryside near Redvers has been extensively cultivated for agriculture. Wheat is the major crop, followed by canola and barley. The Redvers Tourist Information Centre, 1 kilometre (.6 mi.) west on Hwy. 13, offers visitors a booklet describing a self-guiding, 90-kilometre (56 mi.) driving tour of the area.

The tour, on gravel roads, allows visitors an opportunity to experience the local lifestyle by visiting nearby farms for a closer look; stopping at a historic church; seeing oil wells and a crude oil gathering system; and walking through land set aside for habitat protection. The center is open daily 9-8, July-Aug.; 10-6, May 21-June 30. Phone (306) 452-3276, or 452-3854 day after Labour Day-day before Victoria Day.

REGINA (E-4)
pop. 180,400, elev. 578 m/1,896'

Indians once used the banks of Wascana Creek for drying buffalo meat and cleaning and stretching the hides. Thus the area became known as *Oscana,* a Cree word meaning "pile of bones." In 1882 the Canadian Pacific Railway completed its track across the plains, and the settlement of Pile-O-Bones sprang up at the rail terminal on Wascana Creek.

The seat of government of the Northwest Territories and the headquarters of the North West Mounted Police were established the same year. A few years later Princess Louise, the wife of Canada's governor-general, renamed the city Regina (Latin for queen) to honor her mother, Queen Victoria. In 1905 Saskatchewan became a province, with Regina as its capital.

In the heart of downtown is the City Centre, the site of such buildings as the municipal government offices and the public library. The library has the Prairie History Room, which documents local history, and the Dunlop Art Gallery, which displays works by regional artists. The Gallery on the Roof, in the Saskatchewan Power Building, contains changing art exhibits.

The Globe Theatre in the old City Hall is the home of Regina's professional acting company. A glockenspiel chimes at the corner of 12th Avenue and Scarth Street in tribute to the city's ethnic vitality. Sports activities in Regina include harness racing at Exhibition Park and summer football played by the Saskatchewan Roughriders at Taylor Field.

Following Wascana Creek for 11 kilometres (7 mi.) is the Devonian Pathway, a paved bicycle trail that passes through six city parks; in winter it is groomed and lighted for cross-country skiing. The Condie Nature Refuge, just north of the city on Hwy. 11, offers nature trails that afford views of the refuge's grassland and marsh animals.

Further information is available from Tourism Saskatchewan, 500-1900 Albert St., Regina, SK, Canada S4P 4L9; phone (306) 787-2300 or (800) 667-7191.

Regina Convention and Visitors Bureau: Victoria Ave. E., P.O. Box 3355, Regina, SK, Canada S4P 3H1; phone (306) 789-5099 or (800) 661-5099.

Shopping areas: Regina's major shopping malls include Cornwall Centre, 2101 11th Ave., with 102 stores, including Eatons and Sears. Northgate Mall, 489 Albert St. N., has more than 70 stores. Another shopping area of note is the Scarth Street Mall, between 11th and 12th avenues. The mall's specialty shops line a street closed to traffic.

GOVERNMENT HOUSE HISTORIC PROPERTY, 4607 Dewdney Ave., was the home of the lieutenant governors of the Northwest Territories 1891-1905 and the lieutenant governors of Saskatchewan 1905-45. It is now the office of the provincial lieutenant governor. Surrounded by 2.5 hectares (6 acres) of landscaped grounds, the spacious mansion has been restored to its early 20th-century elegance. Guided tours of the house are available. Allow 30 minutes minimum. Tues.-Sun. 1-4. Free. Phone (306) 787-5773.

LEGISLATIVE BUILDING (Capitol), in Wascana Centre off Albert St., is an impressive building surrounded by 67 hectares (165 acres) of landscaped grounds. This is the seat of provincial government and houses ministers' offices in addition to the legislative assembly. On the east side of the building is Trafalgar Fountain, which was in London's Trafalgar Square 1845-1939.

On the building's first and ground floors are changing displays of artwork. The Native Heritage Gallery contains a permanent collection of artwork by noted Canadian artists. Each of the exhibit areas is named for one of the six major river systems in the province. Guided tours are available.

Allow 30 minutes minimum. Legislative building open daily 8 a.m.-9 p.m., Victoria Day-Labour Day; 8-5, rest of year. Free. Phone (306) 787-5358.

REGINA PLAINS MUSEUM, at 1801 Scarth St., contains exhibits about the Plains Indian culture. A gallery features First Nations and Métis exhibits as well as displays about the lives of Saskatchewan's early settlers. The museum also houses the Regina Gallery, Community of Cultures Building Community and Regina's Market Square.

Daily 10-4, Apr.-Sept.; Mon.-Fri. 8-5, rest of year. Admission $2, senior citizens and students with ID $1, under 6 free. Phone (306) 780-9435.

ROYAL CANADIAN MOUNTED POLICE DEPOT AND MUSEUM, Dewdney Ave. W., is the training center for cadets. The regimental museum of the Royal Canadian Mounted Police recounts its history of more than a century of service. Photographs, weapons, personal items, uniforms and related artifacts on display reflect the tragedies, successes, history and human side of this well-known Canadian institution.

A colorful Sergeant Major's parade is usually held Monday through Friday at 12:45 p.m., except for Fridays that precede a holiday weekend. Sunset ceremonies are held Tuesday at 6:45, July 1 to mid-August. Depot and chapel tours are available and begin at the museum. Allow 2 hours minimum. Museum open daily 8-6:45, June 1-Sept. 15 (also Tues. 6:45-8:45 p.m., July 1 to mid-Aug.); 10-4:45, rest of year. Depot and chapel tours Mon.-Fri. at 9, 10, 11, 1:30, 2:30 and 3:30. Free. Phone (306) 780-5838.

SASKATCHEWAN SCIENCE CENTRE, Winnipeg St. at Wascana Dr. in Wascana Centre, consists of two sections. The Powerhouse of Discovery houses more than 80 permanent hands-on science exhibits, features live stage shows and demonstrations, and hosts a variety of changing exhibits. The 165-seat Kramer IMAX Theatre utilizes a five-story screen and four-way sound system to present science and nature films in a giant format.

Allow 2 hours minimum. Daily 9-6, Victoria Day-Labour Day weekend; 9-5, rest of year. Admission $5.50; senior citizens and ages 5-13, $3.75; under 5, $2. MC, VI. Phone (306) 791-7900, (800) 667-6300 in Saskatchewan, or (306) 522-4629 for IMAX information.

SASKATCHEWAN SPORTS HALL OF FAME, 2205 Victoria Ave., houses photographs, trophies, records and other memorabilia of noted athletes

---

DID YOU KNOW

Regina was originally known as "Pile O' Bones" because of the large number of buffalo bones found in the area.

---

and teams from Saskatchewan. Mon.-Fri. 9-5, Sat.-Sun. and holidays 1-5, May-Sept.; Mon.-Fri. 9-5, rest of year. Free. Phone (306) 780-9232.

WASCANA CENTRE, a 930-hectare (2,300-acre) park built around Wascana Lake, is the center of recreational and cultural activity in Regina. It encompasses the Legislative Building, Diefenbaker Homestead, Joe Moran Gallery, MacKenzie Art Gallery, Royal Saskatchewan Museum, University of Regina College Avenue campus, Saskatchewan Centre of the Arts—home of the Regina Symphony—and the Saskatchewan Science Centre.

Wascana Place, the information center, has films and exhibits about the history and future of Wascana Centre and is both a departure point for sightseeing tours and a reservation office for special events. Ferry boat rides to the Willow Island picnic area in Wascana Lake must be booked in advance at Wascana Place; phone (306) 347-1810.

Next to the lakeshore near the arts center, the Wascana Waterfowl Park harbors a large number of Canada geese and other waterfowls that choose not to fly south for the winter. Speakers' Corner, a monument to freedom of speech on the north shore of Wascana Lake, features gas lamps from London and birch trees from Runnymede Meadow, where King John signed the Magna Carta in 1215. Ferry boat rides Mon.-Fri. noon-4, Sun. 1-4:30. Ferry boat fare $2.

Diefenbaker Homestead, in Wascana Centre, was the boyhood home of John G. Diefenbaker, prime minister of Canada 1957-63. The dwelling contains many of his family's original furnishings. Guided tours are available. Allow 30 minutes minimum. Daily 9-6, Victoria Day-Labour Day. Free. Phone (306) 522-3661.

MacKenzie Art Gallery is in the T.C. Douglas Building in the s.w. corner of Wascana Park at Albert St. and 23rd Ave. A major exhibition center for Saskatchewan, it contains permanent and changing exhibits of Canadian and international art. Allow 30 minutes minimum. Daily 11-6 (also Wed.-Thurs. 6-10 p.m.). Guided tours are available Sun. 2-4. Donations. Phone (306) 522-4242.

Royal Saskatchewan Museum, College Ave. and Albert St. in Wascana Centre, has a variety of exhibits related to Saskatchewan. The Earth Sciences Gallery focuses on the geological and paleontological evolution of the province and includes Canada's only resident robotic dinosaur. An extension of this gallery, the Paleo Pit, features hands-on exhibits.

The First Nations Gallery portrays the culture and heritage of the province's Indian population through artwork and artifacts. Allow 1 hour minimum. Daily 9-5:30, May 1-Labour Day; 9-4:30, rest of year. Closed Dec. 25. Free. Phone (306) 787-2815.

CASINOS

- **Casino Regina**, 1880 Saskatchewan Dr. Daily 9 a.m.-4 a.m.; closed Dec. 25. Phone (306) 565-3000 or (800) 555-3189.

ROCANVILLE (E-5) pop. 900

ROCANVILLE AND DISTRICT MUSEUM, Qu'Appelle Ave. and Saint Albert St., contains a variety of local artifacts that include working steam tractors. Some steam equipment may be in operation every Sunday during the season (weather permitting). Allow 2 hours minimum. Daily 1-4, May 1 to mid-Sept. Admission $2; over 65, $1; under 12 free. Phone (306) 645-2113 or 645-2605.

SASKATOON (D-3)
pop. 193,600, elev. 487 m/1,598'

Saskatoon was founded in 1882 as a temperance colony under leader John Lake. According to legend a Cree Indian brought Lake a handful of the purple berries that grew in abundance alongside the river. Lake was so taken with the fruit he named his settlement Saskatoon, after "misaskwatomin," the Indian name for the wild berries. Today a slice of Saskatoon pie is a traditional treat recalling the city's past.

Straddling the South Saskatchewan River, Saskatoon is known as "The City of Bridges" because of the seven spans connecting its banks. It also is home to the University of Saskatchewan, which is building a reputation for research and development in science, medicine and agriculture. The John Diefenbaker Centre on campus showcases memorabilia of Canada's 13th prime minister.

The Saskatchewan Railway Museum, 6 km (4 mi.) west on Hwy. 7, then 2 km (1.2 mi.) south on Hwy. 60, is operated by the Saskatchewan Railroad Historical Association and displays old railroad buildings and artifacts, including a 1912 flatcar and a 1923 boxcar; phone (306) 382-9855.

The Centennial Auditorium, 35 22nd St. E., is a convention center as well as a cultural and civic center. The auditorium is home to the Saskatoon Symphony and the site of traveling shows throughout the year. The Meewasin Valley Centre, 402 3rd Ave. S., features interpretive displays pertaining to the area's history. Saskatchewan Place features rock concerts; trade shows; hockey, basketball and baseball games; and other sporting events. The facility is on the north side of the city next to hwys. 16 and 2.

For a different perspective of the city, Shearwater Properties Boat Cruise offers sightseeing tours on the South Saskatchewan River. The Meewasin Valley Trail, following the Saskatchewan River through the heart of the city, has bicycle and jogging trails, picnic areas and playgrounds and provides opportunities for cross-country skiing and ice skating. Recreational activities are available at nearby Pike Lake and Blackstrap provincial parks *(see Recreation Chart and the AAA/CAA Western Canada and Alaska CampBook).*

Racing fans can enjoy horse racing at Marquis Downs from early May to mid-October, drag racing at the Saskatchewan International Raceway from early May to mid-September and stock car racing at the Bridge City Speedway from May through September.

Note: Policies concerning admittance of children to pari-mutuel betting facilities vary. Phone for information.

Tourism Saskatoon: 6-305 Idylwyld Dr. N., Saskatoon, SK, Canada S7K 0Z1; phone (306) 242-1206 or (800) 567-2444.

BEAVER CREEK CONSERVATION AREA, 13 km (8 mi.) s. on Hwy. 219 (Lorne Ave.), features self-guiding nature trails and interpretive displays. Allow 2 hours minimum. Daily 9-9, May 1-Labour Day; Sat.-Sun. and holidays 9-5, day after Labour Day-Oct. 31 and Jan. 1-Apr. 30. Free. Phone (306) 374-2474 or 665-6887.

DIEFENBAKER CENTRE, 101 Diefenbaker Pl. on the University of Saskatchewan campus, contains the archives and personal belongings of prime minister John Diefenbaker; his grave site is on the grounds. The museum also offers changing exhibits about Canadian history, art, politics, science, culture and current affairs.

Mon.-Fri. 9:30-4:30 (also Tues.-Thurs. 4:30-8), Sat.-Sun. and holidays 12:30-5; closed Jan. 1, Good Friday, Nov. 11 and Dec. 25-26. Admission $2; ages 4-15, $1; family rate $5 (parents and dependent children). Phone (306) 966-8384. *See ad.*

FORESTRY FARM PARK AND SASKATOON ZOO is n.e. off Attridge Dr. following signs. Displayed in settings resembling their natural habitats are 300 species of birds and animals native to Saskatchewan and western Canada, including wolves, bears, eagles, bison and hawks. The park offers a children's petting zoo, a reptile and tropical fish display, nature walkways, a stocked fishing pond and cross-country skiing trails. The Kinsmen Express train provides a tour around the park and zoo.

Allow 1 hour minimum. Park and zoo open daily 9-9, May 1-Labour Day; 10-4, rest of year. Admission $4; ages 6-18, $2.50; family rate $8. An additional $2 fee per vehicle is charged May 1-Labour Day. Train 50c. Fishing pond $2; ages 6-18, $1. Phone (306) 975-3382.

GLADYS' DOLL HOUSE, 4 km (2.5 mi.) n. on Hwy. 12 from 71st St., then 1.6 km (1 mi.) e. and 1 km (.6 mi.) n., features more than 800 new and antique dolls and furnishings dating from the 1860s. Allow 1 hour minimum. Daily 1-7, May 27-Sept 11; by appointment rest of year. Admis-

sion $3; students with ID $2.50; ages 6-12, $1. Phone (306) 933-2638.

MENDEL ART GALLERY AND CIVIC CONSERVATORY, 950 Spadina Crescent E. in a park between Queen and 25th sts., is an attractive complex overlooking the South Saskatchewan River. In the art gallery are exhibitions of international, national and regional works.

Floral displays in the conservatory change frequently, and lectures and films are regularly presented in the auditorium. Allow 30 minutes minimum. Daily 9-9; closed Dec. 25. Donations. Phone (306) 975-7610.

MUSÉE UKRAINA MUSEUM, 202 Ave. M S., is next to St. George's Ukrainian Greek Catholic Cathedral. Ethnographic collections represent the spiritual, material and folkloric cultural heritage of Ukraine. Interpretive tours portray Ukrainian civilization from prehistory to the commencement of emigration. Ukrainian Eastern Byzantine Rite architecture, art and iconography of the adjacent cathedral may be viewed upon request.

Allow 1 hour, 30 minutes minimum. Mon.-Sat. 11-5, Sun. 1-5. Admission $2, family rate (two adults and two children) $5. Phone (306) 244-4212.

UKRAINIAN MUSEUM OF CANADA, 910 Spadina Crescent E., exhibits folk and fiber art, domestic and agricultural tools, and documents and

photographs of Ukrainian immigrants. Guided tours are available. Allow 30 minutes minimum. Mon.-Sat. 10-5, Sun. 1-5, day after Victoria Day-day before Labour Day; Tues.-Sun. 1-5, rest of year. Closed Jan. 1 and 7, Good Friday, Ukrainian Good Friday, Victoria Day, Labour Day and Dec. 25. Admission $2; over 64, $1; ages 6-16, 50c. Phone (306) 244-3800.

★ **WANUSKEWIN HERITAGE PARK** is 5 km (3.1 mi.) n. on Hwy. 11, 3 km (1.9 mi.) s. on Warman Rd., then 2 km (1.2 mi.) e. on Penner Rd. following signs. Cree for "seeking peace of mind," Wanuskewin is a 116-hectare (290-acre) heritage park that traces more than 6,000 years of area history. The park showcases 19 archeological sites where such artifacts as a medicine wheel and tipi rings have been unearthed. An interpretive center overlooks a ledge where stampeding bison plunged over a cliff to their death. Hands-on exhibits, computer-activated displays and two audiovisual presentations portray the Northern Plains Indian culture.

An outdoor activity area allows visitors to help build a tipi, tan a hide or bake a bannock—a thick, flat cake made of flour. Native performers present Indian dances, songs and storytelling in a 500-seat amphitheater. Self-guiding trails meander through the park and feature interpretive signs explaining the past uses of the land. Food is available.

Allow 2 hours minimum. Daily 9-9, Victoria Day weekend-Labour Day weekend; 9-5, rest of year. Closed Good Friday and Dec. 25. Admission $6.50; over 65, $4.50; students with ID $4; ages 5-12, $2.50; family rate $15. MC, VI. Phone (306) 931-6767.

WESTERN DEVELOPMENT MUSEUM'S 1910 BOOMTOWN, 2610 Lorne Ave., is an indoor representation of a typical prairie town complete with more than 30 buildings. Displays include transportation artifacts and vintage agricultural equipment. Food is available. Allow 2 hours minimum. Daily 9-5, Apr.-Dec.; Tues.-Sun. 9-5, rest of year. Admission $4.50; over 65 and students with ID $3.50; ages 5-12, $1.50; family rate $12. Phone (306) 931-1910.

CASINOS

• **Prairieland Exhibition Emerald Casino**, at Ruth St. W. and Lorne Ave. S. Mon.-Sat. 11 a.m.-1 a.m., Sun. noon-10 p.m.; closed Good Friday and Dec. 25. Phone (306) 683-8848.

SCEPTRE (E-2)
pop. 200, elev. 671 m/2,200′

GREAT SANDHILLS MUSEUM, off Hwy. 32, features rooms representing a historic building in the community including a boarding house, library, hospital, blacksmith shop, dentist office, schoolhouse, barn and church. An interpretive center provides information about the great sand-

hills. Allow 30 minutes minimum. Mon.-Sat. 10-noon and 1-4, Sun. 1-5, July-Aug.; by appointment rest of year. Admission $2; ages 7-18, $1. Phone (306) 623-4345.

SHAUNAVON (F-2) pop. 1,900
GRAND COTEAU HERITAGE AND CULTURAL CENTRE, 2 blks. n. of Third Ave. in the town center, features natural history exhibits of fossils, birds, mammals, fish and rocks. Human history exhibits display pioneer artifacts. An art gallery hosts local, regional and provincial exhibitions. Also located at the museum is the Shaunavon Tourist Information Centre. Picnicking is permitted. Allow 30 minutes minimum. Mon.-Sat. 9-5, May 1-Sept. 1; Tues.-Sat. 1:30-5, rest of year. Free. Phone (306) 297-3882.

SIMPSON (E-3) pop. 200
LAST MOUNTAIN LAKE SANCTUARY, 14 km (9 mi.) e. on Hwy. 748, then 3 km (1.9 mi.) s. via a gravel road, is said to be the oldest bird sanctuary in North America. Covering 1,012 hectares (2,500 acres), the wildlife area's favorable habitats and location in the heart of the central flyway of North America make it a haven for more than 150 species of birds. Each year during May and between mid-August and mid-September more than 20,000 sandhill cranes stop at the sanctuary in the course of their seasonal migration.

There are two self-guiding nature trails as well as a self-guiding driving tour. Picnicking is permitted. Allow 1 hour minimum. Daily dawn-dusk. Free. Phone (306) 836-2022.

SPRUCE HOME (C-3) pop. 3,400
THE BUCKLAND HERITAGE MUSEUM AND THE NATURAL RESOURCES MUSEUM, on Hwy. 2, feature items donated by area residents and the local Conservation Officers of Saskatchewan. Exhibits include the wreckage of a Vickers Vedette airplane, a Bombardier snow bus and a Ford Model T car. Agricultural equipment and early 20th-century household items also are on display. A large mural depicts rural life in the region. Allow 30 minutes minimum. Mon.-Fri. 10-6, Sat.-Sun. 10-8, late June-Aug. 31. Admission $1, under 12 free. Phone (306) 764-8470 or 764-8394.

STRASBOURG (E-4) pop. 800
STRASBOURG AND DISTRICT MUSEUM, Mountain St. and Railway Ave., houses nature displays, handicrafts and pioneer artifacts. Fri.-Tues. 2-8, July-Aug.; Sat.-Mon. 2-5, rest of year. Donations. Phone (306) 725-4487.

SWIFT CURRENT (E-2)
pop. 14,900

Once the site of transient Indian and fur trader camps, Swift Current began as a North West

Mounted Police encampment on Swift Current Creek in 1874. Soon after, the Canadian Pacific Railway built a depot, and the settlement became the freight terminus for western Canada. From this point goods were hauled by wagon on overland trails; deep ruts can still be seen on the old North Battleford Trail north of Swift Current.

With the turn of the 20th century came the farmers and ranchers whose trades formed the backbone of the city's economy. Since the discovery of oil in the area in 1952, Swift Current has developed rapidly as a base for oil exploration; agriculture, however, remains the most important industry.

Swift Current Creek runs through town, and two nearby lakes offer recreational facilities. At Saskatchewan Landing Provincial Park (see Recreation Chart), a plaque marks the spot where pioneers once forded the South Saskatchewan River on their way into the wilds of the northern province. In the park's hills are several Indian grave sites and tepee rings.

Swift Current Chamber of Commerce: Rte. 35, Mobile Delivery, Swift Current, SK, Canada S9H 3X6; phone (306) 773-7268.

ART GALLERY OF SWIFT CURRENT, 411 Herbert St. E., is a public art gallery offering exhibitions of local, provincial and national artwork. Guided tours are available. Daily 2-5 (also Mon.-Thurs. 7-9 p.m.), Sept.-June; Mon.-Sat. 2-5 (also Mon.-Thurs. 7-9 p.m.), rest of year. Closed major holidays and during exhibition changes. Free. Phone (306) 778-2736.

SWIFT CURRENT MUSEUM, 105 Chaplin St. E., presents exhibits of natural and human history. Mon.-Fri. 1:30-4:30 and 7-9, Sat.-Sun. 1:30-4:30, Victoria Day-Labour Day; Mon.-Fri. 1:30-4:30, rest of year. Closed major holidays. Free. Phone (306) 778-2775.

VEREGIN (D-5) pop. 100

Emigrating from Russia in 1899 due to persecution, the Doukhobours named their village after their theocratic leader, Peter Vasilovich Veregin. The Doukhobour way of life centers around communal living and renounces violence and war. Its followers do not eat meat or use alcohol or tobacco. The community flourished for 2 decades before a majority of the sect relocated to British Columbia. A prayer house built by Veregin and a machine shed are all that remain of the original Doukhobour colony.

NATIONAL DOUKHOBOUR HERITAGE VILLAGE, across the tracks s. of Hwy. 5, is composed of the original Doukhobour prayer home and several reconstructed buildings typical of Veregin's Doukhobour village dwellings at the turn of the 20th century. A museum displays Doukhobour handicrafts, clothing, hand tools, a collection of Leo Tolstoy's works and other artifacts.

Allow 30 minutes minimum. Daily 10-6, mid-May to mid-Sept.; Mon.-Fri. 10-4, rest of year. Admission $3; students with ID $1.50; ages 5-15, 50c. Phone (306) 542-4441.

WADENA (D-4)
pop. 1,500, elev. 488 m/1,600′

WADENA & DISTRICT MUSEUM, 302 Main St. S., preserves items relating to the history of the pioneers who settled the area in the early 20th century. Housed in a 1904 train station, the museum features antique farm equipment, a country school house and a blacksmith shop. A caboose is adjacent to the building. Allow 30 minutes minimum. Tues.-Fri. 9-5, Sat.-Sun. 2-5, June 1-Sept. 1; closed holidays. Donations. Phone (306) 338-3454.

WAKAW (D-3) pop. 900

WAKAW HERITAGE MUSEUM is in the center of town at 300 1st St. S. Exhibits include Ukrainian artworks and implements, mementos from both world wars, homestead displays and a wide assortment of items dating from the early to late 1900s. Allow 1 hour minimum. Daily 10-6; otherwise by appointment. Admission $2; ages 10-18, $1. Phone (306) 233-4223.

John Diefenbaker's Law Office, off 1st St. S. at 3rd Ave. S., is a replica of the original office where the 13th prime minister of Canada practiced law 1919-25. Guides are available at the Wakaw Heritage Museum. Daily 10-6, July-Aug. Phone (306) 233-4223.

WEYBURN (F-4) pop. 9,700

Weyburn's name was coined in 1893 by Scottish railroad workers, who called this marshy area at the headwaters of the Souris River "wee burn." From these humble beginnings the town has grown into a major marketing center for the surrounding agricultural area. Weyburn is the southeastern terminus of scenic Hwy. 39, which continues to Moose Jaw.

The town was immortalized as "Crocus, Saskatchewan" in the works of W.O. Mitchell, who was born and reared in Weyburn and penned the book "Who Has Seen the Wind." A summary of Weyburn's history since its earliest days is depicted on the "Wheel of Progress" at City Hall. Between the spokes of the brass-rimmed mahogany wheel, which weighs 909 kilograms (2,000 lbs.) and has a diameter of 3.9 metres (13 ft.), are 10 mosaic panels showing highlights of the city's past.

Weyburn Chamber of Commerce: 409 Coteau Ave., Box 1300, Weyburn, SK, Canada S4H 3J9; phone (306) 842-4738.

Shopping areas: A major outlet mall in the Weyburn area is Weyburn Square Mall, off Hwy.

39 at 110 Souris Ave. The mall contains 28 stores, including Best Value.

SOO LINE HISTORICAL MUSEUM is e. on Hwy. 39 at 411 Industrial Ln. A restored 1902 house and an old powerhouse display local Indian and pioneer artifacts tracing the area's early history. Allow 30 minutes minimum. Mon.-Sat. 9-8, Sun. noon-8, July-Aug.; Mon.-Fri. 9-5, rest of year. Admission $2; under 12, $1; family rate $5. Phone (306) 842-2922.

WHITEWOOD (E-5) pop. 1,000

OLD GEORGE AUTHENTIC COLLECTABLES, on Hwy. 1 just w. of town, is a 30-room, brick dwelling that houses such collectibles as oil lamps, clocks, crocks and jugs, Indian artifacts, antique bottles and spinning wheels. Food is available. Allow 1 hour minimum. Daily 10-7, May 31-Oct. 31; by appointment rest of year. Admission $5; under 12, $1. Phone (306) 735-2255.

WOOD MOUNTAIN (F-3) pop. 100

RODEO RANCH MUSEUM is 6 km (4 mi.) s. on Hwy. 18 at Wood Mountain Post Historic Site. The museum features exhibits about local ranching, Indians and saddle making. An adjacent adobe and log building houses blacksmithing tools. A rodeo is held on the grounds during the second weekend in July. Camping and picnicking are available. Allow 1 hour minimum. Daily 10-noon and 1-5, mid-May through Labour Day. Admission $2, students with ID $1, under 10 free with adult. Phone (306) 266-4953.

WOOD MOUNTAIN POST HISTORIC SITE is 8 km (5 mi.) s. on Hwy. 18. Two buildings are on the site of the North West Mounted Police post that stood 1874-1918; small stumps outline the rest of the post. Inside the buildings are displays on the Mounted Police, Sioux Indians and local history. An interpretive staff is on duty to answer questions. Allow 1 hour minimum. Thurs.-Mon. 9-5, June 1 to mid-Aug. Donations. Phone (306) 787-2700.

YORKTON (E-5) pop. 15,200

In 1882 some 200 settlers from Ontario bought land in the Northwest Territories in what is now southeastern Saskatchewan. They called the community around their trading post York City. In 1890 the railroad arrived in the area 5 kilometres (3 mi.) to the south. The York City colonists relocated to be near the railroad and named the new settlement Yorkton. A plaque marks the site of York City; nearby are millstones from the original colony's gristmill.

Recreation is available at nearby Good Spirit Lake Provincial Park *(see Recreation Chart and the AAA/CAA Western Canada and Alaska CampBook)*. The park, originally a Hudson's Bay Co. post in the 1880s, is noted for its miles of sandy beaches and fine dunes.

Tourism Yorkton Visitor Information Centre: Box 460, Yorkton, SK, Canada S3N 2W4; phone (306) 783-8707.

WESTERN DEVELOPMENT MUSEUM'S STORY OF PEOPLE, .4 km (.25 mi.) w. on Hwy. 16A, focuses on the cultural roots of the settlers of western Canada. Picnicking is permitted. Allow 1 hour minimum. Daily 9-6, May 1 to mid-Sept. Admission $5; over 65, $4; ages 5-12, $1.75. Phone (306) 783-8361.

YORKTON ARTS COUNCIL GALLERY operates the gallery at the Godfrey Dean Centre, 49 Smith St. E. Assorted art forms are displayed; local and regional works are featured. Exhibits change monthly. Tues.-Fri. 1-5, Sat.-Sun. 2-5; closed holidays. Donations. Phone (306) 783-8722.

CASINOS
- **Painted Hand Casino**, 30 3rd Ave. N. Mon.-Sat. 10 a.m.-2 a.m., Sun. noon-2 a.m.; closed Dec. 25. Phone (306) 786-6777.

Yukon Territory

A Panful of Nuggets

Miners still find gold a century after the great Klondike gold rush

Spirit of Adventure

Wild waterways, rugged mountains and unexplored wilderness await

All That Glitters

Black diamond jade, amber, topaz, malachite, obsidian and gold bejewel the territory

Lofty Mount Logan

Canada's highest peak rises from the icy St. Elias Mountains

The Northern Lights

Aurora borealis offers nature's nightly light show

unspoiled majesty

To find gleaming gifts of topaz in outcroppings of rock. To wander trails once trodden by miners and trappers. To cry "Mush!" behind a stalwart team of sturdy Alaskan huskies.

To do any of these is to begin to understand the majestic allure of the endless Yukon.

The roughly triangular territory is a land of adventure, a lonely wilderness, a rugged and pristine land of splendor and beauty.

Turbulent rivers of splashing white water weave through soaring mountain ranges. Soft blankets of white pull up snugly over a serene countryside.

The very essence of the sprawling territory is aptly captured in one moving

stanza from poet Robert Service's
homage, "The Spell of the Yukon":

There's gold, and
it's haunting and haunting;

It's luring me on as of old;

Yet it isn't the gold that I'm wanting
so much as just finding the gold.

It's the great, big, broad land
'way up yonder,

It's the forests
where silence has lease;

It's the beauty
that thrills me with wonder,

It's the stillness
that fills me with peace.

"Thick between the flaky slabs, like cheese sandwiches"—this was how prospector George Washington Carmack described the gold he saw glimmering between rocks in Bonanza Creek near Dawson City in August 1896.

On July 14, 1897, the steamship *Excelsior* arrived in San Francisco carrying a treasure worth more than $500,000; a few days later the *Portland* docked in Seattle with one ton of gold piled on its deck. News of these recently discovered riches spread like wildfire, and thousands of get-rich-quick hopefuls began to head for the wealth that lay in Yukon Territory.

Klondike or Bust

That following winter, some 40,000 prospectors began a long, arduous journey to the Yukon to seek their fortunes. While the rush only lasted about 5 years, history was left in its trampled tracks. Following the Yukon River from British Columbia's border to Dawson City, you can explore the past on a course pursued by gold diggers more than 100 years ago.

If stampeders survived the trek through Chilkoot Pass in British Columbia—a climb over frozen mountains with heavy packs full of supplies strapped to their backs—they crossed the border into Yukon Territory at Bennett Lake.

The lake, surrounded by mighty peaks and woodlands, links to the Yukon River. Most fortune seekers waited out the harsh winter at the southern shore, which quickly transformed into a crowed tent city. Transients built boats, temporary shelter and a little log church out of timber hewn from the forest. In late May of 1898, the lake's ice broke and 7,000 handmade vessels headed across its waters, leaving memories of a bitter season behind.

Today, original miners' cabins still line Bennett Lake's northern shore at Carcross, a town chock full of gold rush history. The Caribou Hotel, built in 1898 to welcome gold rushers, is downtown, and graves of such early pioneers as Kate Carmack, Skookum Jim Mason and Tagish Charlie dot the city's cemetery.

From Carcross the gold route followed the Yukon River to Miles Canyon, just south of Whitehorse. Currents here were so dangerous that hundreds of boats capsized, and licensed guides were a must for piloting would-be

---

The Hudson's Bay Co. sets up trading posts in the Yukon.
1800

Yukon Territory becomes a provisional district of the Northwest Territories.
1895

Gold rush veteran Martha Black is elected to the House of Commons.
1935

1898-1904
More than $100 million in gold is mined in the region.

1942
The Alaska Highway is constructed, creating a new overland transportation route.

Yukon Territory Historical Timeline

miners with smaller vessels through the rocks and whirlpools.

Cheechakos, or newcomers, relied upon their own floating devices until stern-wheelers became a popular means of travel; by the early 1950s, more than 250 steamboats plied the Yukon. Boats were specifically designed for the river, employing flat bottoms that allowed for docking on sandbars. Nevertheless, many ran aground or were smashed by rapids or rocks on the Yukon's perilous waters.

Modern-day visitors can encounter reminders of this turbulent time. SS *Tutshi*, a stern-wheeler launched in 1917, sits beached on the narrows near Carcross. Several steamers also reside in Whitehorse, such as the restored SS *Klondike II*.

The River to Riches

After stopping to relax and dry out in Whitehorse, miners pressed on, traversing Lake Laberge to enter a stretch of the Yukon called Thirty Mile. Due to swift currents and rocks, it was perhaps the most dangerous portion of the entire route. Historical sites along Thirty Mile—which is designated a Historic River—include abandoned Northwest Mounted Police posts,

simple grave markers, woodcutters' cabins, telegraph stations, old log buildings and remains of beached paddlewheelers. They all bring yesteryear into focus.

More dangerous eddies had to be negotiated at Five Finger Rapids, just outside Carmacks, before exhausted voyagers passed Fort Selkirk and reached Dawson City—the golden ticket.

Downtown Dawson City remains much as it was when prospectors arrived, thanks to codes requiring new buildings to sport fronts reminiscent of the gold rush era. And old buildings have been restored: Cancan dancing takes place at Diamond Tooth Gertie's Gambling Hall; the Palace Grand Theatre presents vaudeville shows; and the log cabins once inhabited by author Jack London and poet Robert Service remain as examples of gold rush housing. Remnants of dredges can be seen along the Klondike River, and placer mining still occurs at nearby Eldorado Creek.

And don't forget to stop by where it all began—a brass plaque on Bonanza Creek Road marks the spot that caused a great many to risk life and limb for a golden nugget that promised a change of fate.

Yukon's capital is moved from Dawson City to Whitehorse.
1953

Kluane National Park is declared a Natural World Heritage Property.

1979

The Council for Yukon Indians and the Canadian and Yukon Territory governments sign an agreement stating the terms for final land claim settlements in the territory.
1993

1959
At a cost of $1 million, a large fish ladder is built at the Whitehorse Rapids for migrating chinook salmon.

1997
Yukon spends $37 million on mining exploration.

1999
Yukon signs an accord with the Vuntut Gwitchin people, thereby recognizing a First Nation tribe as a legitimate government for the first time in the territory's history.

1975
Yukon's first senator is appointed.

Recreation

Through its pristine waterways, rugged mountains and unexplored wilderness, the Yukon evokes a spirit of adventure in visitors.

Highways to Adventure

There is no better place than the Chilkoot Trail to understand the challenges faced by early pilgrims—the gold-rush stampeders—coming into Yukon Territory. The Yukon's original inroad, with its trail head in Dyea, Alaska, affords today's experienced **hiking** enthusiasts a 53-kilometre (33-mi.), one-way walk through history that can take 3 to 5 days to complete.

Preparation—proper gear, provisions, permits—is key to enjoying this demanding trip through boreal forests and over alpine tundra and snow-patched mountains. You must reserve a campsite for each night you plan to spend on the trail. The Trail Centre in Skagway, Alaska, is the official registration point and offers maps, safety tips and a few words about bears during the Chilkoot hiking season, May through early September. For information phone Parks Canada year-round at (800) 661-0486.

At trail's end in Bennett, British Columbia, reward yourself with a railroad ride back to Skagway aboard the White Pass & Yukon Route, which shuttles returning Chilkoot hikers regularly. Reservations are a must; phone (907) 983-2217 or (800) 343-7373. Another return option is to hop a bus at Log Cabin, British Columbia, or Carcross, on the Klondike Highway.

Roadside **camping** in summer, June through mid-September, truly is a wilderness experience. While you won't have to chop firewood (it's there and it's free), you will have to pump your own water. Most of the public campgrounds are in the southern part of the territory beside lakes, rivers or streams, where you might hook a few Arctic graylings for dinner. Of the 10 campgrounds along the Alaska Highway (Hwy. 1), Watson Lake is one of the first you'll find as you enter the Yukon from British Columbia; it has 55 campsites. Farther west near the Alaska border is Congdon Creek; with 78 campsites, it's one of the largest in the province. Both areas offer **fishing**, **swimming** and hiking.

Take scenic Dempster Highway (Hwy. 5) from Dawson City to Rock River Campground, the northernmost public facility at Km-post 447. Congratulate yourself upon arriving: You've crossed the Continental Divide—twice—*and* the Arctic Circle! There is no well water for the 14 sites at Rock River, so be sure to stock up on supplies in Dawson City or when you get to Eagle Plains—your last chance—at Km-post 371.

The Klondike Highway (Hwy. 2), open all year, is dotted with roadside respites for camping and **picnicking**. You also can camp just off the Robert Campbell and Haines highways (hwys. 4 and 3, respectively). Travelers can access daily road condition reports by dialing the Department of Community and Transportation Services' toll-free hotline; phone (877) 456-7623. Wherever the road leads, watch for wildlife, especially around viewing areas identified with a sign picturing binoculars.

The Other Extremes

With almost 8 months of winter (October through May), **snow skiing** is a way of life in the Yukon. Near Whitehorse, a chalet and night lighting attract cross-country skiers to Mount McIntyre's world-class trails, while Mount Sima, one of the largest ski areas in the Yukon, appeals to downhill skiers with its nine runs and one chairlift. **Snowboarding**, too, is a favorite at Mount Sima's snowpark. Power up a snowmobile and glide on groomed trails around Whitehorse, or venture over more rugged terrain out of Dawson City, said to be the **snowmobiling** capital of the Yukon.

The territory's rich "veins"—its wild rivers—yield excitement other than gold finds. Outfitters are available in Whitehorse to take you **kayaking** or **white-water rafting** on the Tatshenshini's class three and four rapids, or through Kluane National Park on the Alsek, a designated heritage river. Many sections of the Yukon River, which once ushered fortune seekers north to the Klondike goldfields, are easily navigated by canoe. And there are tons more nuggets of adventure to be discovered in the Yukon Territory.

Recreational Activities

Throughout the TourBook, you may notice a Recreational Activities heading with bulleted listings of recreation-oriented establishments listed underneath. Since normal AAA inspection criteria cannot be applied, these establishments are presented for information only. Age, height and weight restrictions may apply. Reservations are often recommended and sometimes required. Visitors should phone or write the attraction for additional information, and the address and phone number are provided for this purpose.

Fast Facts

POPULATION: 30,800.

AREA: 483,450 sq km (186,660 sq mi).

CAPITAL: Whitehorse.

HIGHEST POINT: 5,959 m/19,545 ft., Mount Logan.

LOWEST POINT: Sea level, Beaufort Sea.

TIME ZONE: Pacific.

MINIMUM AGE FOR DRIVERS: 16.

MINIMUM AGE FOR GAMBLING: 19.

SEAT BELT/CHILD RESTRAINT LAWS: Seat belts required for driver and all passengers; restraints required for children under age 7 or 40 pounds.

HELMETS FOR MOTORCYCLISTS: Required.

RADAR DETECTORS: Prohibited.

FIREARMS LAWS: Vary by province. Contact Canada Customs, P.O. Box 4520, Whitehorse, YT, Canada Y1A 2R8; phone (867) 667-3964.

HOLIDAYS: Jan. 1; Heritage Day, Feb. 25; Good Friday; Easter Monday; Victoria Day, May 24 or the closest prior Mon.; Canada Day, July 1; Discovery Day, Aug. (3rd Mon.); Labour Day, Sept. (1st Mon.); Thanksgiving, Oct. (2nd Mon.); Remembrance Day, Nov. 11; Dec. 25 and 26.

TAXES: The Yukon Territory has no territorial sales tax.

TRAVEL INFORMATION CENTERS: Yukon government information centers in Beaver Creek, Carcross, Dawson City, Haines Junction, Watson Lake and Whitehorse are open 12 hours a day, mid-May to mid-September.

FERRY SCHEDULES AND INFORMATION:
The Department of Highways runs ferries along Dempster Highway. Phone (867) 667-3710.

ROAD CONDITION REPORTS:
Through its Yukon Network the Canadian Broadcasting Corporation reports road conditions on the Alaska Highway and all other Yukon highways. Major participating stations, with their frequencies in kilohertz (kHz), are listed from south to north: Watson Lake, 990; Swift River, 970; Teslin, 940; Whitehorse, 570; Haines Junction, 860; Destruction Bay, 940; Beaver Creek, 690; Carmacks, 990; Mayo, 1230; Elsa, 560; Dawson City, 560; Faro, 105.1 FM; and Ross River, 990.

FURTHER INFORMATION FOR VISITORS:
Tourism Yukon
P.O. Box 2703
Whitehorse, YT, Canada Y1A 2C6
(867) 667-5340

FISHING AND HUNTING REGULATIONS:
Yukon Government Fish and Wildlife Branch
P.O. Box 2703
Whitehorse, YT, Canada Y1A 2C6
(867) 667-5221

ALCOHOL CONSUMPTION:
Legal age 19.

	JAN	FEB	MAR	APR	MAY	JUN	JUL	AUG	SEP	OCT	NOV	DEC
Watson Lake	-11	-12	-2	6	15	7	21	20	13	5	-9	-18
	-30	-25	-18	-7	1	3	8	6	2	-3	-17	-27
Whitehorse	-14	-9	-2	5	14	20	20	18	13	5	-5	-11
	-22	-19	-13	-6	1	6	7	6	3	-2	-12	-19

Yukon Territory Temperature Averages Maximum/Minimum (Celsius)
From the records of the National Weather Service

AAA/CAA Starred Attractions

EXCEPTIONAL INTEREST AND QUALITY

Whitehorse (F-10)

YUKON RIVER CRUISE—Narrated trips on the Yukon River travel through Miles Canyon and pass the remains of a wooden tramway, the site of Canyon City and the ruins of the Camp McCrae laundry. See listing p. 266 and map p. 274.

AAA Accessibility Criteria for Travelers With Disabilities

*A*ccessibility is an important issue for travelers with disabilities. In an effort to provide this imperative information to our members with disabilities, AAA/CAA has created ***AAA Accessibility Criteria for Travelers With Disabilities***, a brochure that outlines the criteria used by our inspectors to determine if a AAA/CAA Rated® property is considered accessible.

Once all applicable criteria have been met, the appropriate icons indicating a property's level of accessibility can be found in the lodging listings of the TourBook® guides.

For more information or to receive a copy of this brochure, call or stop by your local AAA/CAA Club.

Points of Interest

Map coordinates relate to the map on
page 274.

BURWASH LANDING (F-9)
pop. 100

In 1904, a year after gold was discovered in
Fourth of July Creek, Morley Bones staked a discovery claim on Burwash Creek. Soon after the
small community of Burwash sprang up around a
trading post. Burwash Landing, with an airstrip
and a resort, lies between the Kluane Lake and
Kluane Game Sanctuary.

KLUANE MUSEUM OF NATURAL HISTORY,
Km-post 1093 on the Alaska Hwy., contains a
nature and taxidermy display, handmade First
Nations crafts and costumes, a mineral and fossil
collection and a large topographical map of the
surrounding area. Allow 1 hour minimum. Daily
9-9, mid-May through Labour Day. Admission
$3, children $1.50, family rate $7.50. Phone
(867) 841-5561.

CARCROSS (F-10) pop. 200

Carcross, 53 kilometres (33 mi.) off the Alaska
Highway at Km-post 904.5, originally was called
Caribou Crossing. The town's current name is a
combination of the first syllable of each word.
From this settlement George Carmack's party set
out on the prospecting trip that began the gold
rush of 1898. Three years later a golden spike
was driven, marking the completion of the White
Pass and Yukon Route, which linked Alaska and
the Yukon Territory by rail.

Recalling the feverish gold rush days is the
Caribou Hotel, regarded as the Yukon's oldest
operating hotel, which opened in 1898 to accommodate gold seekers heading north.

Near the town's train depot is the "Duchess," a
tiny locomotive that ran the 6.4 kilometre (4-mile)
line from Taku Arm on Tagish Lake to Atlin Lake
in the early 1900s. It supposedly was the shortest
and most expensive rail trip in the world—one-way
fare was $2—and passengers had to sit on their
baggage in the cramped compartment.

The Carcross Visitor Reception Centre on the
Klondike Highway at Km-post 106 is in the old
White Pass and Yukon Route train depot. The
center contains displays about the role of stern-
wheelers in the development of the Yukon;
phone (867) 821-4431.

Just north of town along the Klondike Highway lies the Carcross Desert, considered the
smallest desert in the world. The 260-hectare
(650-acre) area was created by retreating glaciers
that left a sandy lake bottom; today winds from

Lake Bennett constantly shift the sand, limiting
vegetation to such plants as kinnikinnick and
lodgepole pine.

**MUSEUM OF YUKON NATURAL HISTORY AND
FRONTIERLAND,** 3.2 km (2 mi.) n. on S. Klondike Hwy., is a 12-hectare (30-acre) museum
where visitors can view mounted animals in dioramas representing their natural habitats; hike a
nature trail past indigenous flora and fauna; and
climb to a lookout that provides a view of Lake
Bennett, historic Carcross and the mountains that
surround the museum. A miniature golf course
also is in the park.

Allow 30 minutes minimum. Daily 8:30-6,
mid-May to mid-Sept. Admission $4; under 13,
$3. Combination admission with Frontierland
$6.50; under 13, $4. Miniature golf tickets $4;
under 13, $2.50. Phone (867) 821-4055.

Frontierland, in the museum complex, is 2.5
hectares (6 acres) shaped like a map of the
Yukon Territory. Gold panning is available. Allow 1 hour minimum. Daily 8:30-6, mid-May to
mid-Sept. Admission $4; under 13, $3. Combination admission with Museum of Yukon Natural
History $6.50; ages 3-12, $4.

CARMACKS (E-9) pop. 500

Carmacks, named for George Washington Carmack, one of the discoverers of gold in the
Klondike, was an important stopover point on
the Overland Trail that linked Whitehorse and
Dawson City before the Klondike Highway was
built. Items from early travelers still can be
found along the trail near town.

About 22 kilometres (14 mi.) north of Carmacks are the Five Fingers Rapids, which
claimed the lives of many prospectors trying to
reach Dawson City by way of the Yukon River.

DAWSON CITY (E-9) pop. 1,300

Dawson City was the center of the excitement
caused by one of the world's most fabulous gold
strikes. On Aug. 17, 1896, George Washington
Carmack and his companions Skookum Jim and
Dawson Charlie made the first strike on Bonanza
Creek, a tributary of the Klondike River.

In the summer of 1897 miners from Dawson
City arrived in Seattle and San Francisco with
nearly $2 million as they carried word of the dis-
covery to the United States, then in the midst of
a depression. By the next spring more than
60,000 men and women had passed through Seattle and Alaska's Chilkoot and White passes on
their way to the Klondike.

The Dawson settlement, which sprang up at
the confluence of the Yukon and Klondike rivers,

became a thriving city with some 30,000 inhabitants by the summer of 1898, making it the largest city west of Winnipeg and north of San Francisco.

All the creeks in the area had been staked by the spring of 1899. Hillside and bench claims were made, some yielding rich gold finds in the White Channel gravels. Between 1896 and 1904 Klondike creeks brought in more than $100 million in gold.

This period of Dawson City's history has been preserved by Rex Beach, Jack London, Robert W. Service and others who wrote colorful tales of personal experiences.

It was in Dawson City that London became acquainted with a large dog that he named Buck, a cross between a St. Bernard and a German shepherd that became the prototype for the dog in "Call of the Wild." Daily readings from the works of Jack London are given 10-6, May 18 through September 20 at his cabin on Eighth Avenue.

Many historic buildings, some still in use, survive from the days when Dawson City was the gold capital of the world. The Midnight Sun and Eldorado conjure memories of a lively past.

Harrington's Store, Princess Street and Third Avenue, has a free photographic exhibit titled "Dawson as They Saw It." The 1901 Post Office, King Street and Third Avenue, offers a visitor information exhibit; phone (867) 993-7200. Both are open June through September.

The SS Keno, in drydock on First Avenue between King and Queen streets, is typical of the stern-wheelers of the gold rush era. Built in 1922, it was one of the last riverboats to run between Dawson City and Whitehorse. Tours are not available.

The summit of Midnight Dome, 7 kilometres (4 mi.) southeast via Front Street, offers a panorama of Dawson City, the Yukon and Klondike rivers and the gold fields. Many Dawson City pioneers are buried in cemeteries on the hillsides flanking the dome.

South on Bonanza Creek Road is the Discovery Claim, which started the great rush. Panning for gold is possible at several locations along the Klondike Highway: Claim 33, Guggieville RV Park, Dawson City RV Park, Early Day Adventure and Tourgold.

Yukon Queen River Cruises has one-way and round-trip cruises to Eagle, Alaska; for schedule and information phone (867) 993-5599.

Visitor Reception Center: Front and King Streets, Dawson City, YT, Canada Y0B 1G0; phone (867) 993-5566.

Self-guiding tours: The visitor reception center has maps detailing walking tours. Parks Canada offers summer guided walking tours of historic sites, departing from the visitor center.

SAVE **BONANZA CREEK DISCOVERY CLAIM** is 14.8 km (9.3 mi.) s. on Bonanza Creek Rd. Signs

portray the story of gold mining along this famous creek. Discovery Claim #1 is the spot where gold first was discovered. A historical marker at Km-post 17.71 identifies the town of Grand Forks, which had a population of 5,000 during its prime. Dredge #4 at Km-post 12.3 was used to recover gold from creekbeds.

A trailer with exhibits about the dredge is open daily 9-5, mid-June to late Aug. Admission $5, under 13 free. Phone (867) 993-5462.

DAWSON CITY MUSEUM, Fifth Ave., displays gold rush items and contains a smithy, a general store, an old miner's cabin, a saloon and Chilkoot Hall. First Nations artifacts and an outdoor transportation exhibit with locomotives from the Klondike Mines railway also are featured. Daily 10-6, June 1-Labour Day; limited hours in May and day after Labour Day-Sept. 30. Admission $4, over 60 and students with ID $3, family rate $10. Phone (867) 993-5291.

GOLD CITY TOURS depart from Front St., across from the SS Keno. Tours of Dawson and local gold fields include panning for gold. The 3.5-hour bus tours depart daily at 1, May 15-Sept. 15. The 1-hour Midnight Dome Tour departs the Palace Grand Theatre after the evening show. Fare $10-$34. AE, CB, DI, MC, VI. Phone (867) 993-5175.

SAVE **THE PALACE GRAND THEATRE,** Third Ave. and King St., presents the "Gaslight Follies" variety show with entertainment that was popular during the gold rush. The Commissioners' Ball, with guests dressed in period costumes, takes place in June. Follies presented Wed.-Mon. at 8 p.m., May 20-Sept. 10. Balcony $18; main floor $15; under 12, $8. Reservations are advised. Phone (867) 993-5575.

ROBERT SERVICE CABIN, 1 blk. s. of Church St. on Eighth Ave., is the restored log cabin of the Bard of the Yukon. The cabin, built in 1898, is furnished as it was 1909-12 when Service was resident and wrote many of his ballads and poems. Allow 30 minutes minimum. Daily 9-5, mid-May to mid-Sept. Readings are given daily at 10 and 3. Admission $6. Phone (867) 993-5462.

CASINOS

- **Diamond Tooth Gertie's Gambling Hall,** Queen and Fifth Ave. Daily 7 p.m.-2 a.m., May 15-Sept. 20. Phone (867) 993-5575.

IVVAVIK NATIONAL PARK (B-9)

Ivvavik National Park, in the extreme northwestern corner of the Yukon, is an Arctic wilderness virtually untouched by humans. Of great geologic interest, it is one of the few regions in Canada that contains areas never covered by glaciers.

Every spring it becomes the calving grounds of Porcupine caribous that arrive after a long, difficult migration from the south and east. The park provides an important nesting area for North American waterfowls and a home to grizzly, black and polar bears. The only access to the park is by air.

KLUANE NATIONAL PARK (F-9)

Elevations in the park range from 400 metres (1,300 ft.) in the Alsek River to 5,959 metres (19,545 ft.) at Mount Logan. Refer to CAA/AAA maps for additional elevation information.

Kluane (kloo-AH-nee) National Park covers 22,015 square kilometres (8,500 sq. mi.) of wilderness. The Haines (Hwy. 3) and Alaska (Hwy. 1) highways run along the park's northeastern border.

Near its southeastern boundary was the Dalton Trail, a route used during the Klondike Rush of 1898. In 1904 a North West Mounted Police post was established on the south shore of Kluane Lake, and in 1942 the lake became a meeting place for crews building the Alaska Highway.

During the building of the highway the wilderness area was preserved as the Kluane Game Sanctuary. In 1979 Kluane was declared a World Heritage Site for its impressive topographical features and its massive nonpolar ice fields.

The park is dominated by the Saint Elias Mountains, which run through the park in a southeasterly direction. Mount Logan, Canada's highest peak at 5,959 metres (19,545 ft.), and Mount St. Elias at 5,489 metres (18,008 ft.) dominate the range. The Saint Elias Mountains hold extensive ice fields that date from the last ice age and constitute the largest nonpolar glacier systems in the world.

An extensive network of glaciers, together with the ice fields, covers more than half the park's area throughout the year. Notable are the Steele Glacier, which moves sporadically at a relatively rapid rate, and the Kaskawulsh and Lowell glaciers, which are flanked by moraines—accumulations of earth and stones carried and deposited by the glaciers. The movement and debris of the glaciers contribute to such park features as sand dunes and dust storms.

The park has a variety of flora. Such coniferous species as white spruce characterize the boreal forest of the river valleys. Lichens, dwarf birch trees and low shrubs distinguish the tundra uplands in the northern section, and colorful Arctic flowers cling to the crevices and ledges of the mountains. In the southeastern section where the Pacific Ocean's moderating influence is felt in the climate, the vegetation is more luxuriant.

Arctic grayling, lake trout, northern pike and kokanee salmon are found in lakes and streams. Other park species include golden eagles, ptarmigans, Dall

Sourdoughs And Cheechakos

To distinguish between the fortune seekers who entered the Yukon Territory during the 1897-98 Klondike Gold Rush, veterans of the '49 California Rush labeled the seasoned arrivals "Sourdoughs" and the greenhorns "Cheechakos" (CHE-chakos). Named after the staple bread of the frontier, Sourdoughs were prospectors who had survived a Yukon winter. The term Cheechako came from the Chinook Indian word for "new to come."

Once off the steamer at Skagway, Alaska, these newcomers had to transport thousands of pounds of survival gear—the Northwest Mounted Police wisely required each prospector to bring a year's supply of food—over the precipitous Chilkoot Pass. After that they had to float their unwieldy cargo over the treacherous rapids of the Yukon River.

More obstacles awaited the greenhorns at the gold sites. By the time the Cheechakos arrived, much of the gold field already was depleted or staked. To make things worse, Cheechakos were often directed to the hills by unscrupulous Sourdoughs who knew the gold nuggets tended to settle in creek beds. Nonetheless, some did tap into a channel of an ancient gold-bearing stream on Cheechako Hill.

Those who had survived to see the ice melt were dubbed Sourdoughs; the graveyards of those who had not succeeded dotted the route all the way back to Skagway. As one cynical Sourdough put it: "We were SOUR on the Yukon and didn't have enough DOUGH to get out."

sheep, mountain goats, caribou, moose and wolves. Kluane has one of the largest populations of grizzly bears and subspecies of moose in the world.

General Information and Activities

The park is open all year, but access may be limited in the winter, depending on weather conditions. The Kluane National Park Reserve Headquarters, at Km-post 1635 in Haines Junction, is open year round. The Sheep Mountain Visitor Centre at Km-post 1707 is open mid-May to early September.

The park primarily is a wilderness area, so there are no roads except on the eastern and northern perimeters, traversed by Hwy. 3 and Hwy. 1, respectively. Hiking is the most popular activity in the park, with approximately 250 kilometres (155 mi.) of hiking trails. Hiking is possible along a few old mining roads, creekside paths and marked trails. Some trails are self-guiding. All overnight hikers must register at one of the information centers or with a park warden before and after hikes.

Mountain climbing should be done only by well-trained climbers, who must obtain a climbing permit and register with the Warden Service before and after climbs.

Other recreational pursuits include fishing, backpacking, boating, cross-country skiing and ice fishing. All anglers within the park must obtain a national park fishing license, available at the park visitor centers and from area stores and lodges. Camping, fishing and picnic facilities are available at Kathleen Lake, 27 kilometres (17 mi.) south of Haines Junction.

During the summer the Kluane National Park Reserve Headquarters sponsors interpretive activities including campfire talks and guided walks. A relief map and an interactive computer touch screen are available. Information about recreational opportunities, sightseeing by small aircraft and other guided tours is available.

ADMISSION to the park is free.

PETS are permitted in the park if kept on a leash, but visitors are advised not to bring them.

ADDRESS inquiries about the park to Kluane National Park Reserve Headquarters, P.O. Box 5495 Haines Junction, YT, Canada Y0B 1L0; phone (867) 634-2251.

MAYO (D-10) pop. 400

Mayo lies 53 kilometres (33 mi.) northeast of the Klondike Highway at the confluence of the Stewart and Mayo rivers. Both the town and the river were named for the pioneer prospector and trader Alfred Mayo. In the early 1900s Mayo Landing became a shipping point for the gold and silver that was mined farther north in Elsa.

Mayo Lake to the northeast provides excellent fishing. The summit of nearby 1,890-metre (6,200-ft.) Keno Mountain provides a scenic view of the mining village of Keno. This once bustling community has a mining museum.

Further details about the silver mining towns of Mayo, Elsa and Keno, known collectively as the Silver Trail, are available at the unmanned information booth at Stewart Crossing.

TESLIN (F-11) pop. 200

The Nisutlin Bay Bridge, the longest water span on the Alaska Highway, crosses an arm of Teslin Lake at Teslin. The highway parallels the 116-kilometre (72-mi.) lake for about 55 kilometres (34 mi.), providing a scenic drive bordered on both sides by mountains. The area is noted for abundant game, and the fjordlike lake provides excellent fishing. The economy of the community depends heavily on hunting, fishing and trapping.

Teslin has one of the largest First Nations populations in the Yukon, with many of its residents descended from the coastal Tlingit tribe. The original First Nations settlement is reached by a loop road. In the old village are Catholic and Anglican missions as well as a Royal Canadian Mounted Police Station.

GEORGE JOHNSTON MUSEUM is 1 km (.5 mi.) w. of the Alaska Hwy. George Johnston, a Tlingit Indian, recorded his culture through his camera. A selection of Johnston's work, displays of the Tlingit tribe's rich and colorful history, Tlingit dancing costumes and pioneer items are exhibited. Daily 9-7, Victoria Day-Labour Day; closed holidays. Admission $3; senior citizens $2.50; ages 6-12, $1; family rate $7. Phone (867) 390-2550.

WATSON LAKE (F-12) pop. 1,000

At Km-post 1016.8 on the Alaska Highway, Watson Lake is an important transportation, distribution and communication center for the southern Yukon. The town was named for Frank Watson, a trapper from England who settled there in 1898.

Watson Lake is known for the signpost collection that was begun by a homesick soldier during construction of the Alaska Highway in 1942. Over the years, tourists have continued adding signs showing the names of their hometowns, and now the collection includes more than 30,000 signs.

From Watson Lake the historic Robert Campbell Highway loops north and west through the wilderness of southeastern Yukon.

WATSON LAKE VISITOR RECEPTION CENTRE, jct. Alaska and Robert Campbell hwys., features photograph murals and an audiovisual program explaining the construction of the Alaska Highway in

1942. Visitor information also is available. Allow 30 minutes minimum. Daily 8-8, mid-May to mid-Sept. Free. Phone (867) 536-7469.

WHITEHORSE (F-10)
pop. 19,200, elev. 689 m/2,260′

Whitehorse began during the Klondike gold rush when thousands of prospectors journeyed by ship to Skagway, Alaska, then climbed the rugged mountain passes to the headwaters of the Yukon River. They constructed nearly anything floatable for the more than 900-kilometre (559-mi.) trip to Dawson City via Whitehorse. Above Whitehorse many prospectors died in the dangerous Whitehorse Rapids.

When stern-wheeler service to Dawson became available, the trip from Whitehorse took 2.5 days; the return trip against the current took 5 days. The first rails of the White Pass and Yukon Route railway were laid at Skagway in May 1898, and the line to Whitehorse opened in July 1900.

During World War II Canadian and United States Army personnel building the Alaska Highway moved to Whitehorse, which became the capital of the Yukon Territory in 1953.

Evolving into the transportation, communication and distribution center of the Yukon, Whitehorse also became the territorial headquarters of the Royal Canadian Mounted Police as well as the heart of the territorial government and federal departments.

Attractions on a much larger scale include Lake Laberge, the setting for Robert W. Service's "The Cremation of Sam McGee," and the Robert Lowe Suspension Bridge across Miles Canyon.

The Whitehorse power dam features one of the world's longest wooden fish ladders; the salmon run in late July or early August can be seen from viewing windows. Lake Schwatka, impounded by the power dam, was named after the first European to navigate the entire length of the Yukon River.

Visible from the Alaska Highway, 24 kilometres (15 mi.) south of Whitehorse, is Marsh Lake Lock, the northernmost lock in the Western Hemisphere. It is used by small craft navigating the upper Yukon River.

Several guided tours of the town and surrounding area are available. SAVE Gray Line/Yukon offers guided bus tours of Whitehorse and Miles Canyon as well as cruises from Lake Schwatka through Miles Canyon. Several companies provide Yukon River cruises, guided hikes, and canoe, boat and raft trips on area rivers. The Yukon Conservation Society gives guided nature walks in the summer.

Tourism Yukon: P.O. Box 2703, Whitehorse, YT, Canada Y1A 2C6; phone (867) 667-5340.

Self-guiding tours: Maps detailing walking tours are available from the Yukon Historical and Mu-

seums Association, 3126 Third Ave., P.O. Box 4357, Whitehorse, YT, Canada Y1A 3T5; phone (867) 667-4704.

"FRANTIC FOLLIES" is presented in the Village Square room of the Westmark Whitehorse Hotel at Wood St. and Second Ave. The Gay '90s vaudeville revue has cast of professional actors, dancers and musicians and recaptures the spirit and enthusiasm of the Klondike gold rush. The 1.7-hour family-style show includes music, comedy, magic, dancing and the poetry of Robert W. Service, Bard of the Yukon. For reservations write P.O. Box 4609, Whitehorse, YT, Canada Y1A 2R8.

Performances are given nightly at at 7 and 9:15, June 14-July 22, at 8:30, May 17-June 13 and July 23-Sept. 12. Admission $18; under 12, $9. Phone (867) 668-2042.

SAVE **THE GRAY LINE WHITEHORSE CITY TOUR,** leaving from the Westmark Hotel, provides an overview of the area. The narrated tour passes historical points of interest, stops at the stern-wheeler Klondike II and concludes at the Yukon Wildlife Preserve. Bus tours depart daily at 9, May 10-Sept. 15. Fare $27; ages 1-12, $13.50. Phone (867) 668-3225.

MACBRIDE MUSEUM, First Ave. and Wood St., offers an in-depth look at the Yukon heritage with exhibits ranging from prehistoric mammals to the 1898 gold rush. Displays include Sam McGee's 1899 cabin, First Nations relics and sample minerals of the territory. On the grounds are an old steam locomotive, a sleigh wagon and a giant nugget of copper weighing about 1,170 kilograms (2,580 lbs.).

Daily 10-6, June 1-Labour Day; otherwise varies. Admission $4; over 49, $3.50; ages 6-12, $2. Phone (867) 667-2709.

OLD LOG CHURCH MUSEUM, Third Ave. and Elliott St., was built in 1900 and features many missionary, First Nation and Inuit items as well as an audiovisual presentation about the history of the Anglican church in the Yukon. Guided tours are available. Allow 30 minutes minimum. Mon.-Sat. 9-5, Sun. noon-4, late May-Labour Day. Admission $2.50; over 55 and students with ID $2; ages 6-12, $1; family rate $6. Phone (867) 668-2555.

THE SS KLONDIKE II, next to the river at Second Ave. and Robert Campbell Bridge, was one of the largest stern-wheelers on the Yukon River. Typical of the many boats of this kind that operated on the river, the Klondike II ran 1937-55. The original Klondike struck a reef in 1936; a replacement was built the same year.

Tours are available. A videotape, "In the Days of the Riverboat," is presented prior to each tour. Allow 30 minutes minimum. Daily 9-7, mid-June to mid-Sept. Last tour begins 30 minutes before closing. Admission $3.50; under 18, $2; family rate (2 adults and 6 children under 18), $8. Phone (867) 667-4511.

TAKHINI HOT SPRINGS, 10 km (6 mi.) w. off Klondike Hwy. at Km-post 5, has natural mineral hot spring pools that are maintained at 36 degrees C (96.8 degrees F) for year-round swimming. Other activities include horseback riding, hiking, camping and cross-country skiing. Pool open Mon.-Fri. 10-10, Sat.-Sun. 8 a.m.-10 p.m. Admission $4; over 59 and students with ID $3.50; ages 4-12, $3. Phone (867) 633-2706.

WHITEHORSE FISHWAY, at the end of Nisutlin Dr. via Lewes Blvd., enables chinook salmon and other fish to bypass the Whitehorse Rapids Dam during their 3000-km (1,860-mi.) migration between the Bering Sea and their freshwater spawning grounds in southern Yukon. Said to be the longest wooden fish ladder in the world, the Whitehorse Fishway includes underwater windows providing a close view of the migrating fish.

Allow 30 minutes minimum. Daily 8:30-8:30, late June-early Sept. Donations. Phone (867) 633-5965.

YUKON ARTS CENTRE, 80 Range Rd., features an art gallery with contemporary revolving exhibits. A theater presents concerts, dramas and musicals throughout the year; phone for schedules and show information. Allow 1 hour minimum. Mon.-Fri. 11-5 (also Thurs. 5-9), Sat.-Sun. noon-5; closed major holidays. Donations. Phone (867) 667-8575.

★ **YUKON RIVER CRUISE** offers transportation to the departure site from downtown hotels to the MV Schwatka. The Schwatka, docked 3.2 kilometres (2 mi.) s.e. just beyond the power plant and dam, makes 2-hour narrated excursions on the Yukon River through Miles Canyon. The boat passes the remains of a wooden tramway built to carry freight around the rapids, the site of Canyon City and the ruins of the Camp McCrae laundry, which served 30,000 troops stationed nearby during the construction of the Alaska Highway. Write MV *Schwatka,* Yukon River Cruises, P.O. Box 4001, Whitehorse, YT, Canada Y1A 3S9.

Cruises depart daily at 2 and 7, June 15-Aug. 15; at 2, June 1-14 and Aug. 16-Sept. 7. Transportation departs hotels about 30 minutes before cruise time. Cruise fare $18. For reservations phone (867) 668-4716.

YUKON TRANSPORTATION MUSEUM, off Alaska Hwy. at Km-post 1475.7 by Whitehorse Airport, exhibits various modes of transportation, including snowshoes, dog sleds, stage coaches, boats, aircraft and military vehicles used during the construction of the Alaska Hwy. The *Queen of the Yukon,* the sister plane of Charles A. Lindbergh's *Spirit of St. Louis,* also is displayed.

Allow 30 minutes minimum. Daily 10-6, Victoria Day to mid-Sept. Admission $4.25; over 60, $3.25; ages 6-18, $2; family rate $9. Phone (867) 668-4792.

RECREATIONAL ACTIVITIES
White-water Rafting

- **Tatshenshini Expeditions,** 1602 Alder St., Whitehorse, YT, Canada Y1A 3W8. Daily mid-June to early Sept. Phone (867) 633-2742.

Alaska

Batter-up at Midnight

Fairbanks hosts late-night baseball as the Arctic Circle is blanketed with continuous sunshine

Dancing Northern Lights

Brilliant bands of yellow, green and red quietly jump across night skies

"The Mountain"

Mount McKinley, North America's tallest mountain, towers over Denali National Park

Seward's Folly

Bought at just 2 cents per acre, Alaska surprised the world with its wealth of natural resources

Pacific Fire Ring

Volcanoes are common in the Valley of Ten Thousand Smokes

sounds of The Great Land

W hile the sights of The Last Frontier can be described as splendid, its sounds are no less spectacular.

A breathy blow accompanied by a geyserlike spray of sea water alerts you to the presence of a humpback whale. It's hard to ignore the loud, slapping sound associated with tail lobbing or breaching— when a whale will throw itself completely out of the water and smack the sea upon return—and it's usually followed by hoots and hollers from observers.

Sea lions make music all their own. Their squawky barking can be heard as you approach a rock packed with the huge creatures.

Drop anchor in ice-filled waters to experience the most spectacular sounds: A popping noise similar to a firecracker

signals a calving, when ice separates from a glacier. As chunks detach and fall, a thunderous roar echoes against the mountains, followed by a crash as they hit the sea. The show ends with the soft hiss of settling water.

Alaskan sounds identify the state's history and culture: Drumbeats, clapping, rattle-shaking, foot-tapping and rhythmic chanting resonate from native performances. A sharp a cry of "Mush!" or "All right!" from a musher gets a team of sled dogs moving; a command of "Come gee!" alerts the huskies to a right turn.

And just when a hush falls over The Great Land, the low hum of a float plane is heard from the clouds, ready to take you to another adventure.

Totem poles—slender cedar logs with intricately carved and brightly painted bears, eagles, fish, whales, ravens or frogs—are true artistic works representing the history and customs of native Alaskans. Features of these poles give insight to the blessings of the 49th state.

When visiting Alaska, a stop at a totem pole park should be high on your list of things to do. To get the full effect, choose a tall, colorful totem and stand about 2 feet from it. After admiring the details, look up. Your first impression? Massive. At 85 feet tall and too big to hug, you may have to step back just to be able to catch a glimpse of the figure at the top of the pole. A glance at an Alaska state map also may elicit amazement—it's *huge,* and there's much to see and do.

Natives didn't call this state *Alyeska*—"the Great Land"—for nothing. It looms larger than life. There are approximately 3 million lakes, 3,000 rivers, 1,800 islands and 100,000 glaciers in Alaska's 586,000 square miles of untamed wilderness. And if that isn't enough, nine national parks and preserves and two expansive national forests total about 66 million acres of undisturbed land. Don't be upset when you find that little of this grandiose scenery fits nicely into your camera lens.

Tales from The Last Frontier

When examined in sequence, the array of symbolic figures on totem poles describe native tales. Likewise, Alaska's diversity is illustrated through its distinct natural features, which leave most anyone speechless. The state is home to towering Mount McKinley—so high that it's cloaked in clouds most of the time. Long, bright days are typical during the summer solstice, when the sun accompanies your every move and never completely disappears.

Options for excitement in The Land of the Midnight Sun seem endless. You can walk on an ice field and feel the crunch of ice under your boots; explore muted, willow-covered desert tundra; peer over chunky glaciers and sweeping mountain ranges from the seat of a helicopter; gaze at a sky painted with watercolored northern lights; enjoy a ride on a boat navigating through blue-green waters packed with bobbing icebergs; marvel at 25-foot-tall sand dunes; or board a bush plane to catch a glimpse of steam from an active volcano.

U.S. Secretary of State William H. Seward purchases Alaska from Russia for less than 2 cents per acre; the unpopular deal becomes known as "Seward's Folly."

1867

Russian explorer Vitus Bering, sent by Peter the Great to explore the North Pacific, is the first European to set foot on Alaskan soil.

1725

A submarine cable links Seattle to Sitka and Sitka to Valdez, increasing communication between Alaska and the rest of the world.

1903

1880

"Seward's Folly" becomes a gold mine as vast deposits of precious metals are discovered in Juneau, followed by discoveries in Skagway in 1897, Nome in 1898 and Fairbanks in 1903.

Alaska Historical Timeline

1942

Japan attacks Dutch Harbour and consequently occupies the Aleutian Islands for nearly a year during World War II.

Tribe members, ingenious at adapting to their variable and sometimes hostile surroundings, made the most of the state's natural offerings, which included the creatures portrayed in their art.

Salmon and orcas are just a couple of animals that appear on totems. Used for sustenance, they were often depicted in oral tales; today animals remain the focus of many pictures and the subjects of travelogues. Visitors relish the opportunity to snap a photograph of a moose cow nibbling grass alongside her twins or grizzly cubs wrestling under the protective watch of mama bear.

Affluent Alaska

For many residents Alaska's riches are liquid: The creation of the Trans-Alaska Pipeline made it possible to transport crude oil almost 800 miles from Prudhoe Bay south to Valdez. The pipeline, an amazing engineering feat crossing three mountain ranges and three fault lines, is able to withstand an earthquake measuring up to 8.5 on the Richter scale as well as temperatures as low as minus 80 F.

Oil isn't Alaska's only rich resource. Discoveries of gold in Fairbanks, Fort Yukon, Juneau, Nome, Skagway and Wrangell lured prospectors from the "Lower 48" to seek their fortune. Visit abandoned gold dredges, camps and mines scattered throughout the state and imagine the fervor that once pervaded these sites, many of which now serve as attractions.

And there was more money to be made. Russian trappers came in search of valuable sea otter pelts, placing the term "fur trade" in Alaskan history books. The first capital of Russian America, Kodiak's early culture is represented in the form of domes that grace downtown's Russian Orthodox church.

But Alaska's native tribes have left the most enduring impact. Traditions of the Aleut, Alutiiq, Athabascan, Cup'ik, Haida, Inupiaq, Tlingit, Tsimpshian and Yup'ik tribes can be appreciated through the acts of proud dancers and storytellers who keep family legacies alive. And artisans create soapstone and whalebone carvings, clothing adorned with intricate beading and baskets made from white birch bark—all coveted by visitors.

And totem poles, Alaska's silent, symbolic sentries, are just one reminder of what makes this land truly great.

A Good Friday earthquake destroys Anchorage, the Northwest Panhandle and Cook Inlet and sends a tsunami that wipes out the town of Valdez.

1964

One of the most devastating fires in state history destroys homes and property in the south central area near Big Lake.

1996

International efforts to rescue two whales trapped in ice off the Barrow coast captures world-wide attention.

1988

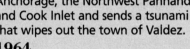

1968

"Black Gold" is discovered on Prudhoe Bay, spurring the construction of an 800-mile pipeline to transport the oil to an ice-free port at Valdez.

1989

The worst oil spill in U.S. history occurs when the Exxon *Valdez* spills some 11 million gallons of crude oil into Prince William Sound.

1977

Construction of the Trans-Alaska Pipeline is complete.

Recreation

In the Land of the Midnight Sun, it's a far better idea to set your itinerary by "sight" rather than time. While there's lots of activities to keep your blood pumping, most people visit Alaska for what there is to *see:* Chances for **wildlife viewing** are as plentiful as snowflakes during winter.

Oh, *Another* Bald Eagle?

This phrase, overheard on a small boat weaving through the watery inlets of the Tongass National Forest, testifies to the fact that Alaska has one of the largest bald eagle populations in the world. If you know what to look for—white dots on dark spruce tree branches—you may lose count of all these stately birds. They aren't difficult to spot at the Chilkat Bald Eagle Preserve near Haines; more than 3,500 visit the area to feed.

Many **wildlife cruises** headed for the Inside Passage depart from Juneau. Arm yourself with some good binoculars, a camera and a journal to record your sightings. Entries might include descriptions of huge, barking Steller sea lions lounging on top of each other; Dall porpoises frolicking in a boat's wake; Sitka black- or white-tailed deer sipping from a stream; soaring peregrine falcons; or furry otters doing the backstroke.

Black bears fish for salmon in Anan Creek near Wrangell Island, and the west coast of Prince of Wales Island (near Ketchikan) is a great spot for watching tufted puffins. It's no "fluke" to see a whale tail—humpbacks often make appearances in Prince William Sound, and wherever there's an iceberg, you can be sure to find harbor seals resting upon floating ice chunks.

Day cruises depart from Seward and Whittier to explore Prince William Sound and Kenai Fjords National Park, home to sea mammals galore. Along the Kenai Peninsula, both humpback and beluga whales perform aquatic acrobatics near the Turnagain Arm. Nearby, Dall sheep can be seen grazing atop steep cliffs that grace Cook Inlet.

Looking for bears? The Kodiak National Wildlife Refuge is home to some 3,000 Kodiak bears, and Brooks Camp in Katmai National Park and Preserve safeguards one of the world's largest brown bear populations.

Grizzlies as well as caribou and moose roam the desertlike tundra of Denali National Park; take a narrated bus tour into the interior to catch a glimpse. Near the park entrance, forest rangers give a demonstration of sled dogs at work, which is a howling good show. Even better, hang on tight for a **sled ride** pulled by Iditarod huskies in Seward.

And a View, Too

Seward Highway, connecting Seward and Anchorage, is Alaska's most traveled scenic byway, and it's easy to see why. Snaking along the coast of Turnagain Arm, scenes from the road include the lush Kenai Mountains, saltwater bays, jagged ridges and green alpine meadows. **Rock climbers** dangle from cliffs between Potters Marsh and Bird Creek.

As a matter of fact, any activity in Alaska includes a magnificent view: Try **rafting** in Denali on the Nenana River Gorge or **canoeing** near Admiralty Island National Monument. **Kayakers** also enjoy the Sarkar Lake Canoe Route in Tongass National Forest. Winter options include **cross-country skiing, dog sledding** or **snowmobiling** on the Twin Ridge or Upper Twin ski trails in Tongass National Forest, or **downhill skiing** at Mount Aleyska in Girdwood.

Want to stand on a glacier? **Hikers** in Kenai Fjords National Park follow rangers on **nature walks** to a nearby ice field. For a bit of history, try **bicycling** or **walking** the first mile of the original Iditarod Trail, now a paved beach path in Seward. Horseshoe Lake Trail provides a leisurely walk through the woods of Denali National Park.

Floatplane or **helicopter sightseeing** is an excellent way to see glaciers, ice fields, mountain ranges, waterfalls, lakes or stark tundra. Nearly every city has **flightseeing** tour operators.

A **fishing** charter from one of various harbors is a good way to hook steelhead, grayling or rainbow trout. **Sport fishing** yields red snapper or cod—and Resurrection Bay (near Seward), Sitka and Wrangell are home to world-class halibut and salmon.

Recreational Activities

Throughout the TourBook, you may notice a Recreational Activities heading with bulleted listings of recreation-oriented establishments listed underneath. Since normal AAA inspection criteria cannot be applied, these establishments are presented for information only. Age, height and weight restrictions may apply. Reservations are often recommended and sometimes required. Visitors should phone or write the attraction for additional information, and the address and phone number are provided for this purpose.

Fast Facts

POPULATION: 609,300.

AREA: 586,412 square miles, ranks 1st.

CAPITAL: Juneau.

HIGHEST POINT: 20,320 ft., Mount McKinley.

LOWEST POINT: Sea level, Pacific Ocean.

TIME ZONES: Alaska for most of the state; Hawaii-Aleutian for the extreme western portion of the Aleutian Islands. DST.

MINIMUM AGE FOR DRIV-ERS: 16; learner's permit at 14 with parental consent.

SEAT BELT/CHILD RESTRAINT LAWS: Seat belts required; child restraints required for under 7.

HELMETS FOR MOTORCY-CLISTS: Required for driver under 19 and passenger.

RADAR DETECTORS: Permitted.

FIREARMS LAWS: Vary by state and/or county. Contact the Division of State Troopers, Headquarters, 5700 E. Tudor Rd., Dept. P, Anchorage, AK 99507; phone (907) 269-5511.

HOLIDAYS: Jan. 1; Lincoln's Birthday, Feb. 12; Washington's Birthday, Feb. (3rd Mon.); Seward's Day, Mar. (last Mon.); Memorial Day, May (last Mon.); July 4; Labor Day, Sept. (1st Mon.); Alaska Day, Oct. 18; Veterans Day, Nov. 11; Thanksgiving and Dec. 25.

TAXES: Alaska does not have a statewide sales tax, but cities and boroughs may levy a sales tax of up to 6 percent, plus special taxes on goods and services.

STATE INFORMATION CENTER: Tok Information Center, jct. SR 2 (Alaska Hwy.) and SR 1, provides general tourist literature, as well as reports on highway and weather conditions.

FURTHER INFORMATION FOR VISITORS:
Alaska State Division of Tourism
Dept. VP
P.O. Box 110801
Juneau, AK 99811-0801
(907) 465-2010

FISHING AND HUNTING REGULATIONS:
Alaska Department of
  Fish and Game
P.O. Box 25526
Juneau, AK 99802-5526
(907) 465-4180 for fishing
(907) 465-4190 for
  wildlife

ALASKA FERRY INFORMATION:
Department of
  Transportation and
  Public Facilities
Division of Marine
  Highways
P.O. Box 25535
Juneau, AK 99802-5535
(800) 642-0066 in the U.S.
(800) 665-6414 in Canada

NATIONAL FOREST INFORMATION:
U.S. Forest Service
101 Egan Dr.
Juneau, AK 99801
(907) 586-8751
(800) 444-6777 (reservations)

NATIONAL PARK INFORMATION:
Alaska Public Lands
250 Cushman St.
Fairbanks, AK 99701
(907) 456-0527

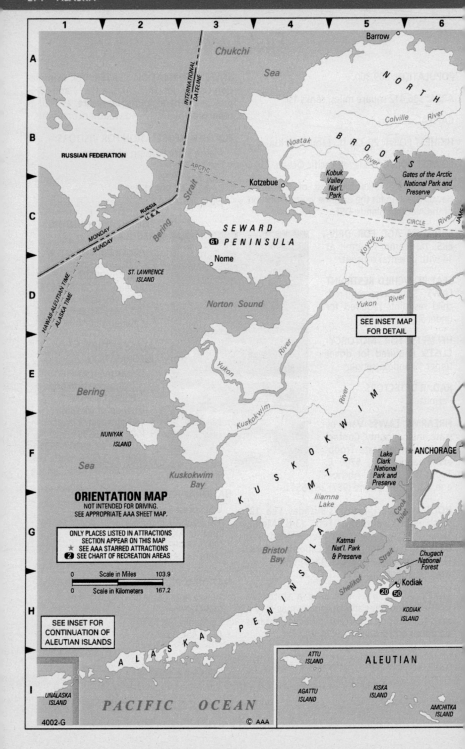

ORIENTATION MAP
NOT INTENDED FOR DRIVING.
SEE APPROPRIATE AAA SHEET MAP.

ONLY PLACES LISTED IN ATTRACTIONS
SECTION APPEAR ON THIS MAP
★ SEE AAA STARRED ATTRACTIONS
❷ SEE CHART OF RECREATION AREAS

0   Scale in Miles   103.9
0   Scale in Kilometers   167.2

SEE INSET FOR
CONTINUATION OF
ALEUTIAN ISLANDS

SEE INSET MAP
FOR DETAIL

4002-G   © AAA

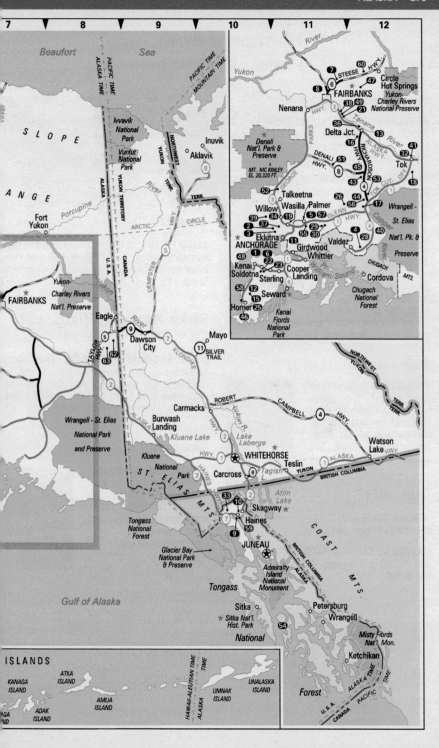

AAA Starred Attractions

EXCEPTIONAL INTEREST AND QUALITY

Anchorage (C-10, F-6)

ALASKA NATIVE HERITAGE CENTER—Why did Tlingit tribe members carve totem poles? Learn about this and other traditions of native Alaskans. See p. 284.

ANCHORAGE MUSEUM OF HISTORY AND ART—The art, history and culture of the 49th state are presented in various exhibits. See p. 284.

Denali National Park & Preserve (B-10)

DENALI NATIONAL PARK & PRESERVE—Home of Mount McKinley, North America's highest peak, the park covers 9,375 square miles of native wildlife, active glaciers, snowcapped peaks and arctic tundra. See p. 291.

Fairbanks (B-11, D-7)

RIVERBOAT DISCOVERY—A trip aboard the sternwheeler *Discovery III* offers views of the Alaskan wilderness and an old Athabascan Indian village. See p. 295.

Juneau (G-10)

ALASKA STATE MUSEUM—Displays chronicle the state's history. See p. 300.

GASTINEAU SALMON HATCHERY—More than 160 million salmon eggs hatch here annually. See p. 301.

MENDENHALL GLACIER—Trails on both sides of the 12-mile-long glacier offer spectacular views of the river of blue ice. See p. 301.

Seward (D-11)

KENAI FJORDS TOURS—Cruises into the waters surrounding Kenai Fjords National Park offer views of marine life and active glaciers. See p. 311.

Sitka National Historical Park (H-10)

SITKA NATIONAL HISTORICAL PARK—This 107-acre park, commemorating the Tlingit Indian heritage, contains a fort that was the site of the 1804 Battle of Sitka as well as the 1853 Russian Bishop's House. See p. 312.

Skagway (G-10)

WHITE PASS & YUKON ROUTE—A 3-hour narrated ride on this narrow-gauge railroad chugs across mountain rivers and chasms. See p. 313.

RECREATION AREAS

RECREATION AREAS	MAP LOCATION	CAMPING	PICNICKING	HIKING TRAILS	BOATING	BOAT RAMP	BOAT RENTAL	FISHING	SWIMMING	PETS ON LEASH	BICYCLE TRAILS	WINTER SPORTS	VISITOR CENTER	LODGE/CABINS	FOOD SERVICE
NATIONAL PARKS AND PRESERVES															
Denali (B-10) 6,000,000 acres. *(See place listing p. 291)*		•	•	•				•		•			•	•	•
Gates of the Arctic (C-6) 8,500,000 acres. *(See place listing p. 296)*		•		•				•					•	•	
Glacier Bay (G-9) 3,283,168 acres. *(See place listing p. 296)*		•		•	•		•	•		•			•	•	•
Katmai (G-5) 4,159,097 acres. *(See place listing p. 302)*		•	•	•	•	•	•	•					•	•	•
Kenai Fjords (D-11) 600,000 acres. *(See place listing p. 303)*		•		•				•		•			•	•	
Kobuk Valley (C-5) 1,710,000 acres. *(See place listing p. 305)*		•		•	•			•							
Lake Clark (F-5) 4,000,000 acres. *(See place listing p. 307)*		•						•		•			•	•	•
Wrangell-St. Elias (C-12, F-8) 13,000,000 acres. *(See place listing p. 319)*		•						•		•			•	•	•
Yukon-Charley Rivers (B-12, D-8) 2,500,000 acres. *(See place listing p. 319)*		•						•							
NATIONAL FORESTS															
Chugach (D-12) 5,400,000 acres in southcentral Alaska. *(See place listing p. 288)*		•	•	•	•	•		•					•	•	•
Tongass (G-9) 17,000,000 acres in southeastern Alaska. *(See place listing p. 315)*		•	•	•				•					•	•	•
STATE															
Anchor River (D-10) 264 acres near Anchor Point on Sterling Hwy., Milepost 157.	46	•	•	•				•		•					
Bernice Lake (D-10) 152 acres 10 mi. n. of Kenai on N. Kenai Rd.	1	•			•	•		•	•	•					
Big Lake (North) (C-10) 19 acres 10 mi. w. of Wasilla on Parks Hwy., then 6 mi. s.w. on Big Lake Rd.	2	•			•	•		•	•	•		•			
Big Lake (South) (C-10) 16 acres 10 mi. w. of Wasilla on Parks Hwy., then 4 mi. s.w. on Big Lake Rd. and 2 mi. s.	3	•			•	•		•	•	•		•			
Bings Landing (D-10) 126 acres e. of Soldotna on Sterling Hwy., Milepost 79.	48	•	•	•	•	•		•		•					
Birch Lake (B-12) 191 acres n.e. of Delta Junction on Richardson Hwy., Milepost 305.5.	49	•			•	•		•	•						
Blueberry Lake (C-12) 192 acres e. of Valdez on Richardson Hwy., Milepost 23.	4	•	•	•				•		•					
Bonnie Lake (C-11) 129 acres e. of Palmer on Glenn Hwy., Milepost 83. Canoeing.	5	•			•	•		•	•	•					
Buskin River (H-5) 196 acres 4 mi. s.e. on Base-Town Rd. in Kodiak.	50	•	•	•				•		•					
Captain Cook (D-10) 3,466 acres 24 mi. n. of Kenai on N. Kenai Rd.	6	•	•	•	•	•		•	•	•					
Chena River (A-12) 254,000 acres 27 mi. e. of Fairbanks on Chena Hot Springs Rd.	47	•	•	•				•		•		•	•	•	
Chilkat (G-10) 6,045 acres 7 mi. s. of Haines on Haines Hwy.	9	•	•	•	•	•		•		•			•		
Chilkoot Lake (G-10) 80 acres 11 mi. n. of Haines on Lutak Rd., Milepost 10.	10	•	•		•	•		•		•					
Chugach (C-11) 495,204 acres just e. of Anchorage on Glenn Hwy. Numerous access points. Horse rental. *(See Anchorage p. 285)*	11	•	•	•	•	•		•		•	•	•	•	•	
Clam Gulch (D-10) 129 acres s. of Soldotna on Sterling Hwy., Milepost 117.	12	•	•					•		•					
Clearwater (B-12) 27 acres 11 mi. s.e. of Delta Junction on Alaska Hwy., Milepost 1415, then 8 mi. n.e. on side road.	13	•			•	•		•		•					

RECREATION AREAS

	MAP LOCATION	CAMPING	PICNICKING	HIKING TRAILS	BOATING	BOAT RAMP	BOAT RENTAL	FISHING	SWIMMING	PETS ON LEASH	BICYCLE TRAILS	WINTER SPORTS	VISITOR CENTER	LODGE/CABINS	FOOD SERVICE
Deep Creek (D-10) 155 acres near Ninilchik on Sterling Hwy., Milepost 138.	15	•	•		•	•		•		•					
Denali (C-10) 324,240 acres n. of Talkeetna on Parks Hwy., Milepost 135-164.	52	•	•	•	•	•		•		•					
Donnelly Creek (B-12) 42 acres s. of Delta Junction on Richardson Hwy., Milepost 238.	16	•	•					•		•					
Dry Creek (C-12) 372 acres n. of Glennallen on Richardson Hwy., Milepost 117.5.	17	•	•	•				•		•					
Eagle Trail (C-12) 640 acres s. of Tok on Glenn Hwy., Milepost 312.3.	18	•	•	•						•					
Fielding Lake (C-12) 300 acres s. of Delta Junction on Richardson Hwy., Milepost 201.	53	•			•	•		•		•					
Finger Lake (C-11) 47 acres 4 mi. w. of Palmer on Palmer-Wasilla Rd., then 1 mi. n. and .5 mi. w.	19	•	•		•	•		•	•	•			•		
Fort Abercrombie (H-5) 183 acres 4.5 mi. s.e. of Kodiak on Miller Point. Historic. (See Kodiak p. 306)	20	•	•	•	•			•	•	•				•	
Halibut Point (H-11) 22 acres 4 mi. n.e. of Sitka on Halibut Rd.	54	•	•					•		•					
Harding Lake (B-12) 169 acres .5 mi. n.e. from Milepost 321 on the Richardson Hwy.	21	•	•		•	•		•	•	•			•		
Izaak Walton (D-10) 8 acres e. of Soldotna off Glenn Hwy.	22	•	•					•		•					
Johnson Lake (D-11) 324 acres 16 mi. s. of Soldotna on Glenn Hwy.	23	•	•					•		•					
Kachemak Bay (D-10) 368,290 acres near Seldovia, at the end of Sterling Hwy., then by boat or plane across Kachemak Bay.	25	•	•	•	•			•		•					
Kepler-Bradley Lakes (C-11) 344 acres e. of Palmer on Glenn Hwy., Milepost 36.4.	55		•	•				•	•						
Lake Louise (C-11) 90 acres n.w. of Glennallen on Glenn Hwy., Milepost 160.	26	•	•		•	•		•		•					
Little Nelchina (C-12) 22 acres s.e. of Glennallen on Glenn Hwy., Milepost 137.4.	56	•		•	•			•							
Little Tonsina (C-12) 103 acres near Copper Center on Richardson Hwy., Milepost 65.	28	•	•					•		•					
Long Lake (C-11) 480 acres 7 mi. e. of Sutton on Glenn Hwy.	29	•	•		•	•		•		•					
Lower Chatanika River (A-11) 120 acres n.w. of Fairbanks off SR 2, Milepost 9.	8	•	•		•	•		•		•					
Matanuska Glacier (C-11) 229 acres e. of Palmer on Glenn Hwy., Milepost 101.	30	•	•	•						•					
Moon Lake (B-12) 22 acres 18 mi. w. of Tok on Alaska Hwy.	32	•	•		•			•	•	•					
Moose Creek (C-11) 40 acres near Palmer on Glenn Hwy., Milepost 54.4.	57	•	•	•						•					
Mosquito Lake (G-10) 5 acres 27.5 mi. w. of Haines on Haines Hwy., then 2.5 mi. on Mosquito Lake Rd.	33	•	•		•	•		•	•	•		•		•	
Nancy Lake, South (C-11) 22,685 acres 3.5 mi. s. of Willow on Parks Hwy., then 7 mi. w. on side road.	34	•	•	•	•			•	•	•		•	•		
Ninilchik (D-10) 97 acres n. of Homer on Sterling Hwy., Milepost 135.	58	•	•					•		•					
Portage Cove (G-10) 7 acres s. of Haines at 1 Beach Rd.	59	•	•					•		•					
Quartz Lake (B-11) 600 acres 2 mi. n.w. of Delta Junction on Alaska Hwy.	36	•	•		•	•	•	•	•	•		•			•
Rocky Lake (C-10) 48 acres 28 mi. w. of Palmer via Wasilla off Parks Hwy. at Milepost 3.5 of Big Lake Rd.	37	•	•		•	•		•		•					

RECREATION AREAS

RECREATION AREAS	MAP LOCATION	CAMPING	PICNICKING	HIKING TRAILS	BOATING	BOAT RAMP	BOAT RENTAL	FISHING	SWIMMING	PETS ON LEASH	BICYCLE TRAILS	WINTER SPORTS	VISITOR CENTER	LODGE/CABINS	FOOD SERVICE
Salcha River (B-12) 61 acres s.e. of North Pole on Alaska Hwy., Milepost 323. Canoeing.	38		•		•	•		•		•					
South Rolly Lake (C-10) 200 acres just w. of Wasilla off Parks Hwy. at Milepost 6.5 of Nancy Lake Pkwy.	39	•	•		•			•	•	•		•			
Squirrel Creek (C-12) 350 acres near Copper Center on Richardson Hwy., Milepost 79.5.	40	•	•					•		•					
Tok River (B-12) 9 acres 5 mi. e. of Tok Junction on Alaska Hwy., Milepost 1309.	41	•						•	•	•					
Upper Chatanika River (A-11) 73 acres n.e. of Fairbanks off Steese Hwy.	7	•	•		•			•		•					
OTHER															
Brushkana (B-11) 15 acres 30 mi. e. of Cantwell on Denali Hwy., Milepost 104.	51	•	•					•		•					
Cripple Creek (A-12) 5 acres 50 mi. n.e. of Fairbanks on Steese Hwy., Milepost 60.	60	•	•					•		•					
Paxson Lake (C-12) 80 acres 10 mi. s. of Paxson on Richardson Hwy., Milepost 175.	43	•	•		•	•		•		•					
Salmon Lake (C-3) 20 acres 40 mi. n. of Nome.	61	•						•		•					
Sourdough (C-12) 140 acres 35 mi. n. of Glennallen on the Richardson Hwy., Milepost 148.	44	•	•		•	•		•		•					
Tangle Lakes (B-12) 100 acres 22 mi. w. of Paxson on Denali Hwy., Milepost 22.	45	•	•		•	•		•		•					
Walker Fork (E-8) 10 acres 80 mi. n.e. of Tok on Taylor Hwy., Milepost 82.	62	•	•	•				•		•					
West Fork (E-8) 10 acres 65 mi. n.e. of Tok on Taylor Hwy., Milepost 49.	63	•	•					•		•					

Alaska Temperature Averages
Maximum/Minimum
From the records of the National Weather Service

	JAN	FEB	MAR	APR	MAY	JUN	JUL	AUG	SEP	OCT	NOV	DEC
Anchorage	21/3	27/10	33/14	45/28	54/37	63/43	64/50	63/48	55/39	63/28	28/16	21/7
Barrow	-9/-24	-13/-24	-8/-22	7/-8	25/12	36/28	45/33	43/33	33/27	21/12	5/-8	-6/-17
Fairbanks	-8/-22	10/-15	59/36	43/18	59/36	72/46	72/48	64/43	54/33	36/18	12/-6	1/-17
Juneau	30/19	32/21	37/25	45/30	54/37	63/45	63/48	63/46	55/43	46/37	39/28	33/25
Kotzebue	1/-13	3/-11	7/-11	23/3	37/25	50/37	59/46	55/45	46/36	30/19	12/1	3/-11
Nome	12/-2	12/-2	16/0	28/14	41/28	52/39	55/45	54/45	48/36	36/25	23/10	12/-2

Points of Interest

ADMIRALTY ISLAND NATIONAL MONUMENT (H-11)

Admiralty Island, part of Tongass National Forest *(see place listing p. 315),* is accessible by floatplane from Juneau and Sitka or via ferries of the Alaska Marine Highway to Angoon. Between the rocky beaches and high mountain peaks lie a million acres of coastal rain forests, freshwater lakes and streams, alpine meadows and dense thickets of wild currants and other berries.

Alaskan brown bears outnumber human beings, and the greatest concentration of bald eagles in North America nests along the coast. Beavers, martens, minks, river otters, Sitka black-tailed deer and weasels share the island with Vancouver Canada geese and trumpeter and whistling swans. Offshore are harbor seals, sea lions and whales.

Motorboating and sea-kayaking are popular in protected saltwater bays, and a canoe portage trail connects nine interior lakes to bays on the east and west shores. Rustic cabins can be reserved, and campsites and open shelters are available on a first-come-first-served basis. Most of the island is a wilderness area; be prepared for rain and follow no-trace camping practices.

For more information write the U.S. Forest Service *(see Fast Facts).*

ANCHORAGE (C-10,F-6)
pop. 226,300, elev. 118'

Anchorage, on a high bluff enfolded by the two branches of Cook Inlet, lies as far west as the Hawaiian Islands and as far north as Helsinki, Finland. The tides in the inlet rise from 30 to 33 feet; the surrounding mountains loom several thousand feet overhead. The protective mountain barrier and the proximity of the ocean afford Anchorage a surprisingly moderate climate, relative to most of Alaska.

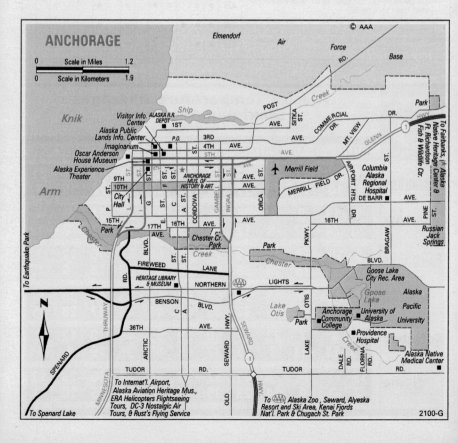

Anchorage is Alaska's largest city and is home to almost half of the state's residents. While not a dazzling metropolis, each summer the city is beautifully decorated with almost 100,000 hanging flower baskets brimming with brightly-colored blooms.

Established in 1915 as the construction headquarters for the Alaska Railroad, it is the transportation and business center of south-central Alaska and a major winter recreation area. Anchorage's heritage as a road town is recalled by a number of historic buildings, notably the Pioneer Schoolhouse in Ben Crawford Memorial Park and two nearby one-room log cabins. As well, landmarks denote both Russian and American Indian heritage.

Anchorage suffered from the effects of the 1964 Good Friday earthquake, one of the strongest in history, which destroyed much of downtown. Earthquake Park, at the west end of Northern Lights Boulevard, has a walking trail and interpretive signs that provide information about the massive temblor. The park also provides a stunning vista of Cook Inlet.

The dramatic beauty of the nearby mountains, inlets and glaciers offers an easily accessible sampling of Alaska's natural splendors. Two roads affording beautiful views link to Anchorage; scenic SR 1/9 extends south to Seward, and SR 1 extends north to Glennallen.

From Anchorage visitors also can take various sightseeing tours of the area, including the Kenai Peninsula and places of interest inaccessible by road. Trolley, flightseeing and other types of tours given by Anchorage City Trolley Tours depart daily May through September from 612 W. 4th Avenue between F and G streets; phone (907) 276-5603. Among the more novel sightseeing trips are dog sled tours, which leave from the Alyeska Resort and Ski Area *(see Girdwood p. 296)* December through March.

The Alaska Backpacker Shuttle offers daily shuttle service from Anchorage to Denali National Park and Fairbanks mid-May to mid-September; phone (907) 344-8775.

One-hour float trips on the Matanuska River depart by van from Anchorage to the launch point. Panning for gold is available an hour from downtown. For a different perspective, try flightseeing—operators can be found at the airport and Lake Hood.

Alaska Sightseeing Tours, SAVE Gray Line of Alaska *(see ad p. 283)* and Princess Tours offer a float adventure on Eagle River; tours to Barrow, Kodiak Island, Kotzebue, Matanuska Valley, Nome, Portage Glacier and Prudhoe Bay; fishing on the Kenai River; cruises on Prince William Sound to Columbia Glacier; and a tour of Anchorage.

These agencies also offer 2-, 3- and 4-day round trips between Anchorage and Denali National Park. The trips include travel in railway cars equipped with glass ceiling panels. These same three companies also offer longer excursions to the interior and cruises up the Inside Passage.

Anchorage serves as the starting line for the 1,049-mile Iditarod Trail Race, which begins the first Saturday in March. The actual mileage of the race is 1,161

The Alaska Highway

On March 9, 1942, the U.S. Army Corps of Engineers began bulldozing its way through mountains and forests to create a direct land route linking the United States to the Alaska Territory. The Alaska Highway originated as an emergency passage for American troops during World War II following the Japanese occupation of the Aleutian Islands, which extend southwestward from the Alaska Peninsula.

More than 11,000 troops worked  on the road, and American Indians, trappers and prospectors were hired to help. Canada supplied the right of way and materials in exchange for use of the road following the war. The workers built 133 log and pontoon bridges and dug more than 8,000 culverts. Despite untold hardships and the worst winter in recorded history, the highway was completed in just 8 months. In 1943 the highway became public, and for the next 7 years more than 70 companies and 16,000 civilian workers labored to turn it into a year-round, all-weather road.

The 1,523-mile Alaska Highway takes its travelers on a wilderness tour starting at Dawson Creek, British Columbia, through the Yukon Territory and on through Delta Junction to Fairbanks. The scenery is picture perfect, with an abundance of spruce forests, magnificent mountain passes, lakes, rivers and glacial ice formations. Bears, moose and other wildlife can appear at any time.

The road is maintained daily, but be aware that conditions often change depending on the weather. Take your time, drive with your headlights on and drive defensively. Always be alert for bumps and holes in the road. Gas, food and lodging are conveniently found every 20 to 50 miles.

miles; however, 1,049 is often used as a symbolic figure because the distance is always more than 1,000 miles, and 49 was added to signify Alaska's rank as the 49th state. Dogs and mushers travel over the Alaska Range and across frozen Norton Bay, arriving in Nome nearly 2 weeks later.

Anchorage Convention and Visitors Bureau: 524 W. Fourth Ave., Anchorage, AK 99501; phone (907) 276-4118 or (800) 446-5352. *See color ad.*

Self-guiding tours: A guide outlining a walking tour and driving tours north and south of the city is available at Log Cabin Visitor Information Center, Fourth Avenue and F Street; phone (907) 274-3531.

ALASKA AVIATION HERITAGE MUSEUM, 4721 Aircraft Dr., is on the s. shore of Lake Hood near Anchorage International Airport. On display are 29 vintage aircraft including a 1931 American Pilgrim. Visitors also can observe restorations in progress. Memorabilia and photographs chronicle the history of civilian and military aviation in Alaska; films are shown continuously.

Allow 30 minutes minimum. Daily 9-6; closed major holidays in winter. Admission $6; over 62 and active military with ID $4.50; ages 6-12, $2.75. Phone (907) 248-5325.

SAVE **ALASKA EXPERIENCE THEATER,** 705 W Sixth Ave., presents "Alaska the Greatland," a 40-minute documentary projected onto a domed screen. Filmed from planes, river rafts and trains, the narrated documentary dramatizes the splendors of Alaska's great outdoors. An earthquake exhibit presents information about the 1964 Alaska earthquake, which measured 9.2 on the Richter scale.

Shows daily on the hour 9-9, early June-Sept 15; noon-6, rest of year. Admission to theater $7 over 60 (in winter) and ages 5-12, $4. Earthquake exhibit $5; over 60 (in winter) and ages 5-12, $4. Combined admission $10; over 60 (in winter), and ages 5-12, $7. AE, DS, MC, VI Phone (907) 276-3730.

★**ALASKA NATIVE HERITAGE CENTER** is approx. 3 mi. e. on Glenn Hwy. to N. Muldoon Rd exit, then .5 mi. n. to 8800 Heritage Center Dr Situated on 26 wooded acres, the center presents information about the five regional, native groups that inhabit Alaska: the Aleut and Alutiiq; Athabascan; Eyak, Tlingit, Haida and Tsimshian; Inupiaq and St. Lawrence Island Yupik; and Yup'ik and Cup'ik tribes.

The main building offers a Gathering Place for storytelling, dance and musical performances as well as a theater for films. The Hall of Cultures exhibit is divided into five areas in which multimedia displays about weaving, fishing, philosophy, moose hunting and dance are presented. Artisans create and display their crafts in adjacent studios.

Outside, life-size replicas of different types of housing (built by natives) surround a pond; tribal members at each locale give insight to traditions and customs. Allow 2 hours minimum. Daily 9-9, May-Sept. Admission $19.95; ages 7-16, $14.95. MC, VI. Phone (907) 330-8000 or (800) 315-6608. *See color ad p. 287.*

ALASKA PUBLIC LANDS INFORMATION CENTER, 605 W. Fourth Ave., offers information about Alaska's state and federal public lands. Exhibits include displays about Alaska's native culture and wildlife; films and interpretive programs are offered during the summer season. Visitors can plan their own trips with assistance from the staff. State park permits also are available. Daily 8-8, June-Aug.; Mon.-Fri. 10-5:30, rest of year. Closed winter holidays. Free. Phone (907) 271-2737.

ALASKA ZOO, 7.5 mi. s. on SR 1 (Seward Hwy.), then 2 mi. e. on O'Malley Rd., embraces a 30-acre wooded area with many arctic and Alaskan native animals, including Siberian tigers. Allow 1 hour, 30 minutes minimum. Daily 9-6, May 1 to mid-Sept.; 10-5, rest of year. Closed Thanksgiving and Dec. 25. Admission $7; senior citizens $6; ages 13-18, $5; ages 3-12, $4. Phone (907) 346-3242.

ALYESKA RESORT AND SKI AREA—
see Girdwood p. 296.

★**ANCHORAGE MUSEUM OF HISTORY AND ART,** 121 W. Seventh Ave., has exhibits focusing on the art, history and cultures of Alaska. The

Alaska Gallery includes objects dating from prehistoric times through European exploration, Russian settlement, the gold rush era, World War II and statehood. Full-scale dioramas of an Athabaskan tent; Yupik Eskimo, Tlingit and Aleut houses; a gold miner's cabin; an early Anchorage house; Quonset huts (in use during World War II); and moose boats provide insight to early Alaskan life.

In addition, a display about the Alaska Pipeline features a sample of the 4-foot-tall pipe. "Art of the Far North" contains drawings and paintings by Alaska's first explorers to current artists. Other highlights include summer films, a children's gallery and traveling exhibitions.

Food is available. Allow 1 hour minimum. Sun.-Fri. 9-9, Sat. 9-6 (guided tours at 10, 11, 1 and 2), mid-May to mid-Sept.; Tues.-Sat. 10-6, Sun. 1-5, rest of year. Closed Jan. 1, Thanksgiving and Dec. 25. Admission $5; over 65, $4.50; under 18 free. Phone (907) 343-4326.

CHUGACH STATE PARK, e. on Glenn Hwy., is noted for its mountains, rivers and lakes. Eagle River Nature Center offers wildlife displays, guided nature walks and views of the Chugach Mountains. The park's headquarters is in the historic Potter Point Section House, 12 miles south of the city on Seward Highway. Activities range from berry picking and wildlife watching at Eklutna Lake to hiking and cross-country skiing. The park also is a great place from which to spot moose.

Visitor center open Tues.-Sun. 10-5. Section house open Mon.-Fri. 8-4:30. Free. Parking $3. Phone (907) 345-5014. *See Recreation Chart and the AAA Western Canada and Alaska CampBook.*

SAVE **ERA HELICOPTERS FLIGHTSEEING TOURS AND DC-3 NOSTALGIC AIR TOURS,** 6160 S. Carl Brady Dr., offers narrated 50-minute and 2-hour helicopter tours of Anchorage and the nearby Chugach Mountains. Dall sheep and mountain goats can be seen in the mountains and valleys of Chugach State Park. Other tours are offered in Denali, Juneau and Valdez.

Era Classic Airlines also offers air tours aboard refurbished DC-3 planes. Typical routes include Mt. McKinley, Prince William Sound, Knik Glacier, the Alaska Range and the Harding Icefield.

Helicopter daily 8-6. DC-3 daily May-Sept. Helicopter $171-$299. DC-3 tours $139. Flights require a minimum of 4 passengers. Free transportation from area hotels. AE, DS, MC, VI. Phone (907) 266-8351 or (800) 843-1947 for helicopter reservations, or (907) 266-8394 for DC-3 reservations.

FORT RICHARDSON FISH AND WILDLIFE CENTER is in Bldg. 600 on the Fort Richardson U.S. Army post, 9 mi. n. of downtown Anchorage on Glenn Hwy.; obtain directions at the main gate. Displays of more than 200 mounted trophies include 95 species of Alaskan wildlife and fish. Guided tours are available. Allow 30 minutes minimum. Mon.-Wed. and Fri. 9-11:30 and 1-4:30, Thurs. 1-4:30. Free. Phone (907) 384-0431.

HERITAGE LIBRARY AND MUSEUM, in the National Bank of Alaska Building at Northern Lights Blvd. and C St., displays Eskimo and other native artifacts, an extensive collection of walrus ivory carvings and paintings by Alaskan artists. Allow 30 minutes minimum. Mon.-Fri. noon-4. Free. Phone (907) 265-2834.

THE IMAGINARIUM, Fifth Ave. and G St., is a hands-on science discovery center offering exhibits that explore nature, science and technology. Highlights of the displays are a polar bear den, a bubble lab, insects, wetlands and a small planetarium. Allow 1 hour minimum. Mon.-Sat.

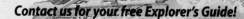

10-6, Sun. noon-5; closed major holidays. Admission $5; over 65 and ages 2-12, $4. Phone (907) 276-3179.

MAJOR MARINE TOURS—*see Whittier p. 317.*

OSCAR ANDERSON HOUSE MUSEUM, 420 M St. in Elderberry Park, was built in 1915 on one of the first townsite lots in Anchorage. The small wood-frame house has been restored and furnished in period and offers a fine view of Cook Inlet. Allow 30 minutes minimum. Guided tours are given Tues.-Sat. 11-4, June 1 to mid-Sept. Admission $3; senior citizens $2; ages 5-12, $1. Phone (907) 274-2336.

PORTAGE GLACIER RECREATION AREA— *see Chugach National Forest p. 289.*

RUST'S FLYING SERVICE departs from the south shore of Lake Hood off International Airport Rd. at Anchorage International Airport. Narrated sightseeing tours by sea plane offer views of Knik and Columbia glaciers, Mount McKinley and Denali National Park. Wildlife and marine life viewing opportunities, such as bear sightings, vary with tours. Ten-hour fishing trips, glacier landings and river float trips also are available. Flights require a minimum of two passengers. Inquire about weather policies.

Allow 1 hour, 30 minutes minimum. Daily by appointment; closed Jan. 1, Thanksgiving and Dec. 25. Fare $139-$199; under 12, $69.50-$99.50. AE, MC, VI. Phone (907) 243-1595, or (800) 544-2299 out of Alaska.

26 GLACIER CRUISE BY PHILLIPS' CRUISES— *see Whittier p. 317.*

RECREATIONAL ACTIVITIES

Fishing

- Jake's Alaska Wilderness Outfitters, 2910 W. 31st Ave. Write P.O. Box 104179, Anchorage, AK 99510. Daily June-Sept. Phone (907) 522-1133 or (800) 478-9657.

BARROW (A-5) pop. 3,500, elev. 2′

The northernmost settlement in Alaska, Barrow is 340 miles north of the Arctic Circle on the edge of the omnipresent Arctic icepack. The sun does not go below the horizon for 82 days from early May to early August or rise above the horizon for 51 days between November and January. The town is reached by daily scheduled flights from Anchorage and Fairbanks. Husky-sled dogs still are used, but snowmobiles have become more popular.

Barrow is one of the world's largest Eskimo settlements. Although to some extent the people continue to follow their old traditions, the trend is toward a more modern way of life: The North Slope oil discovery created great wealth in the area.

The Post-Rogers Memorial, at the airport, commemorates the deaths of Will Rogers and his pilot, Wiley Post, who were killed in a 1935 plane crash 12 miles down the coast.

CHUGACH NATIONAL FOREST (D-12,G-6)

Elevations in the forest range from sea level at the Pacific Ocean at Prince William Sound to 13,176 ft. at Mount Marcus Baker. Refer to AAA maps for additional elevation information.

Second in size only to the Tongass National Forest *(see place listing p. 315)*, Chugach (CHEW-gatch) National Forest covers 5,400,000 acres, roughly the size of New Hampshire. It extends along the Gulf of Alaska from Cape Suckling to Seward and includes many of the islands and much of the land bordering Prince William Sound and the northeastern portion of the Kenai Peninsula.

Within the 700,000-acre Copper River Delta Wildlife Management Area just east of Cordova is one of the largest concentrations of trumpeter swans in North America. Also in abundance are dusky Canada geese, short-billed dowitchers, red-throated loons and green-winged teal. Prince William Sound has spectacular scenic opportunities with its 3,500 miles of coastline as well as dramatic tidewater glaciers and marine life that includes many species of whales.

Both saltwater and freshwater fishing are available in abundance in the forest. Halibut, red snapper, salmon and crabs are plentiful along the more than 3,500 miles of saltwater shoreline. Popular spots are Resurrection Bay at Seward and in Prince William Sound around Valdez and Cordova. Freshwater lakes and streams provide red salmon, Dolly Varden char and rainbow trout. A sportfishing license is required for all types of fishing within the forest.

For photographers and sport hunters, the forest offers a variety of big game, including black and brown bears, moose and Dall sheep. Hunting is subject to Alaska's fish and game management laws, seasons and bag limits.

Seward Highway offers 127 miles of scenic driving along saltwater bays, ice-blue glaciers and valleys dotted with native wildlife. The highway connects the cities of Anchorage and Seward. Bordering the forest on the northwest is SR 4; its scenic portion extends from Valdez to the junction of SR 10 west of Chitina. Portions of one of the most famous trails, The Historic Iditarod Trail, can be hiked, skied, dog sledded or explored on snowmobile.

In addition to 16 road-accessible campgrounds and 200 miles of hiking trails, the Forest Service operates 42 cabins in remote areas near lakes, bays and streams. Accessible by trail, boat or floatplane, the cabins are equipped with bunks, tables, chairs, wood or oil stoves and outdoor sanitary facilities, but not electricity.

The fee is $25 per night per party. Reservations are required and can be made up to six months in advance. Further information also can be obtained from the Chugach National Forest, 3301 C St., Suite 300, Anchorage, AK 99503, phone (907) 271-2500, or the U.S. Forest Service in Juneau *(see Fast Facts)*. Also see *Recreation Chart and the AAA Western Canada and Alaska CampBook.*

BIG GAME ALASKA, Seward Hwy. Milepost 79, is a 100-acre, drive-through wild animal park. Among the animals to be seen are musk oxen, buffaloes, Sitka blacktail deer, caribous, eagles, moose, reindeer and elks. Allow 30 minutes minimum. Daily 10-dusk (weather permitting). Admission $5; ages 4-12, $3. The maximum fee is $20 per carload. Pets are permitted. AE, MC, VI. Phone (907) 783-2025.

PORTAGE GLACIER CRUISES depart 1.5 mi. s. of the Begich-Boggs Visitor Center in the Portage Glacier Recreation Area *(see attraction listing)*. A 1-hour narrated cruise aboard the MV *Ptarmigan* takes passengers to the face of Portage Glacier. Sections of the glacier "calving" or breaking away into the lake below often can be seen.

The 200-passenger ship has a climate-controlled cabin with oversized windows and an open-air observation deck. Shuttle and tour packages from Anchorage also are available. Inquire about weather policies. Cruises depart daily at 10:30, noon, 1:30, 3 and 4:30, mid-May to late Sept. Fare $25; under 12, $12.50. MC, VI. Phone (907) 277-5581.

PORTAGE GLACIER RECREATION AREA, is 5.5 mi. e. from Milepost 79 of the Seward-Anchorage Hwy. The parking area affords a clear view across Portage Lake, 3.5 miles to Portage Glacier. Large icebergs calve off the face of the glacier into the 800-foot-deep lake. An observation platform and a wayside exhibit are at the entrance to Williwaw Campground. Wayside exhibits also are available at Explorer Glacier.

Guided tours, iceworm safaris and food are available. Picnicking is permitted. The road to and within the area is open all year. Phone (907) 783-3242.

Begich-Boggs Visitor Center contains an observatory, orientation area and exhibit hall. A 20-minute film is shown 20 minutes past every hour. Daily 9-6, Memorial Day-Labor Day; otherwise varies. Film $1. Phone (907) 783-2326.

CIRCLE HOT SPRINGS (A-12)

Circle Hot Springs is 8 miles off SR 6 (Steese Hwy.) via gravel Circle Hot Springs Rd. The town was discovered when George Crowe, a prospector on Deadwood Creek, wounded and trailed a moose across an unusually warm creek. Crowe traced the heat to the hot springs, which runs 140 degrees Fahrenheit at the source. This discovery opened the way in 1897 for Circle Hot Springs Resort, which still attracts local miners in winter and out-of-town visitors all year.

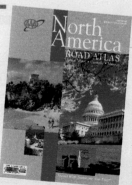

COOPER LANDING (D-11)
pop. 200

RECREATIONAL ACTIVITIES
White-water Rafting
- **Alaska Wildland Adventures** departs from the launch site on Sterling Hwy. (SR 1) Milepost 50.1. Write 16520 Sterling Hwy., Cooper Landing, AK 99572. Daily May-Sept. Other activities are offered. Phone (800) 478-4100. *See color ads.*

CORDOVA (D-12)
pop. 2,100, elev. 100′

Cordova is located on the eastern shores of Prince William Sound and is surrounded by the Chugach Mountain Range and the Chugach National Forest. The town can be reached by air from Juneau and Anchorage or via the Alaska Marine Highway from Valdez and Whittier. In the early 1900s, Cordova was the terminus of the Copper River Northwest Railroad that carried copper ore from the Kennecott Mines in McCarthy. Today the town's industry focuses on commercial fishing.

Cordova Chamber of Commerce: P.O. Box 99, Cordova, AK 99574; phone (907) 424-7260.

DELTA JUNCTION (B-11)
pop. 700

The official northern terminus of the Alaska Highway, Delta Junction is one of the state's

strongest agricultural producers. The town offers panoramic views of the Alaska Range as well as the Trans-Alaska Pipeline, the Delta Bison Range and glaciers.

BIG DELTA STATE HISTORICAL PARK AND RI-KA'S ROADHOUSE AND LANDING, at Milepost 275, Richardson Hwy., is a living-history homestead with a museum, a roadhouse, a barn, a garden and livestock and poultry pens. The roadhouse's meeting/living room and kitchen/dining room can be toured. Guided and self-guiding tours are available. Food is available. Daily 9-5, mid-May through Sept. 15; by appointment rest of year. Free. Phone (907) 895-4201 mid-May through Sept. 15, or 895-4938 rest of year. *See ad p. 290.*

★DENALI NATIONAL PARK AND PRESERVE (B-10)

Elevations in the park and preserve range from 626 ft. at the northwest corner of the park at Chilcukabena Lake to the 20,320 ft. Mount McKinley. Refer to AAA maps for additional elevation information.

Primitive and wild, Denali National Park and Preserve covers 9,375 square miles in the interior of Alaska and offers spectacular views of quiet lakes, snowcapped peaks and varicolored tundra. In addition to 20,320-foot Mount McKinley, the highest peak in North America, the park encompasses 17,400-foot Mount Foraker, 13,220-foot Silverthrone and 11,670-foot Mount Russell.

Mount McKinley, known to the early Athabascan Indians as Denali, "the great one" or "the high one," has two peaks: South Peak, the true summit, and 2 miles away, 19,470-foot North Peak. Most of the mountain is covered by ice and snow all year. Excellent views of Mount McKinley are possible along the park road (weather permitting); clouds hide the summit about 75 percent of the time in summer and 60 percent the rest of the year.

The park's many glaciers originate on the slopes of the Alaska Range. Muldrow Glacier, the largest northward-flowing glacier in Alaska, stretches from between Mount McKinley's twin peaks to within a few miles of the park road; it can be seen from several vantage points.

More than 155 species of birds and 37 kinds of mammals inhabit the park; grizzly bears, moose, Dall sheep, wolves and caribou are some of the larger mammals. Equally varied is the vegetation. The chief conifers are black and white spruce, while dwarf birch grow in thickets on the lower slopes and along the intermountain valleys. Low, boggy meadows are the habitat of stunted, twisted black spruce.

Above the river valleys, forests give way to vast stretches of wet tundra supporting shrubby plants and often underlain by permafrost. A dry alpine tundra blankets the slopes and ridges at the higher elevations.

General Information and Activities

From Anchorage and Fairbanks, the George Parks Highway (SR 3) provides access to the park all year, and SR 8 from Paxson is usually open from early June to mid-October. The park also is accessible from Anchorage or Fairbanks via the Alaska Railroad; there is daily service from late May to mid-September. Trains run northbound to Fairbanks on Saturday and southbound to Anchorage on Sunday the rest of the year. Charter flights are available from principal airports.

Denali Park Road, beginning at SR 3 at the park's eastern boundary, runs about 90 miles westward through the park, terminating at a partly abandoned mining town, Kantishna. Only the first 14.8 miles to Savage River are paved, and most of the road is narrow with many sharp curves. It is usually open from early June to mid-September. Driving conditions vary considerably with the weather and can be difficult during and after rain.

Private vehicles may be used only on the first 14.8 miles of road unless you have a registered campsite at Teklanika Campground. Transportation beyond Savage River or to Sanctuary, Igloo

and Wonder Lake campgrounds is provided by shuttle buses that operate to Eielson Visitor Center, Wonder Lake and other points in the park.

Fare for the shuttle varies with destination. The fare to Wonder Lake is $27; a ride to Eielson Visitor Center is $21. The fare to Toklat and Polychrome is $12.50. Kids age 12 and under ride for free. Kids age 13-16 ride for half price. Three- and 6-day trip passes are available with prices varying with destinations. All fares include the $4 registration fee but not the park admission fees.

More than half of the shuttle seats are available for telephone reservation. Phone (907) 272-7275 or (800) 622-7275 in advance. The rest of the spaces can be reserved only in person within 2 days of departure. Buses depart every half-hour beginning at 6 a.m. from the Visitor Center near the entrance and stop to view wildlife when conditions are safe. Shuttle buses also drop off and pick up passengers along the park road on a space-available basis.

If you want to camp outside the established campgrounds, stop at the Visitor Center for a back-country permit. Reservations for Riley Creek, Savage River, Teklanika River and Wonder Lake campgrounds may be made here.

The George Parks Highway (SR 3) runs along the eastern border of the park and offers sweeping views of the park's alpine scenery from Willow to Nenana.

Sled dog demonstrations are given by rangers at the park kennels, mile 3 on Denali Park Road. The 40-minute presentations are offered daily at 10, 2 and 4, June through August. Ranger-naturalists also present various lectures, hikes and other activities daily at Denali National Park Hotel and various campgrounds. Information about activities is available at the hotel, the Visitor Center, ranger stations and Eielson Visitor Center, or pick up a copy of the park's informational booklet, *Denali Alpenglow.*

Guided and self-guiding hikes are available along several nature trails near Denali National Park Hotel. Most hiking is cross-country.

Do not feed or disturb wildlife. Grizzly bears in particular can be dangerous; inquire at the Visitor Center about how to avoid close encounters with grizzlies. Firearms must be declared and made inoperative when you enter the park; hunting and shooting are forbidden.

Most fishing is poor in the park; only streams that are free of glacial silt are good fishing spots. No license is required within the national park; the daily creel limit is 10 fish, only two of which may be lake trout. An Alaska fishing license is required in the national preserve areas. Check at a ranger station for further information.

Temperatures during the park season can vary from 40 to 80 degrees Fahrenheit, with an average of 50 to 54 degrees June through August. Daylight generally lasts for more than 18 hours during the summer months.

A store at the park entrance contains supplies, but no gas is available. Neither food nor supplies are available within the park boundaries. The store is open approximately 7 a.m.-9 p.m. during peak season, shorter hours at other times.

Airplane tours of Mount McKinley and the Alaska Range are offered in summer; contact Denali Air, P.O. Box 82, Denali National Park, AK 99755; phone (907) 683-2261. *See Recreation Chart and the AAA Western Canada and Alaska CampBook.*

ADMISSION is $5 per person or $10 per family.

PETS are permitted in the park only if they are leashed or otherwise physically restrained; they are not allowed on trails, shuttle buses or in the back country.

ADDRESS inquiries to the Superintendent, Denali National Park and Preserve, P.O. Box 9, Denali Park, AK 99755; phone (907) 683-2294.

ALASKA CABIN NIGHT DINNER THEATRE, 1.7 mi. n. of the park entrance on George Parks Hwy. at Milepost 239, presents a 1915-era dinner show that highlights Alaska's gold-mining history. Costumed characters serve the all-you-can-eat meal. Allow 2 hours minimum. Shows daily at 5:30 and 8:30 p.m., mid-May to mid-Sept. Admission $39; under 12, $19.50. Reservations are suggested. AE, MC, VI. Phone (907) 276-7234 or 683-2215 (within 48 hours) for reservations.

DENALI WILDERNESS SAFARIS, at Milepost 215 on George Parks Hwy., offers heated airboat and jet boat rides to Alaskan "bush" country where locals share their methods of hunting, prospecting, trapping and dog mushing. Free transportation is provided from all area hotels. The 3.5-hour trip departs daily at 7 a.m. and 6 p.m. Fare, including a snack, $85; under 13, $45. Reservations are recommended. AE, MC, VI. Phone (907) 768-2660.

ERA HELICOPTERS FLIGHTSEEING TOURS, 1 mi. n. of the park entrance on George Parks Hwy. (SR 3) at Milepost 238, offers a narrated, 50-minute or 75-minute aerial tour of North America's highest mountain, Mount McKinley as well as glacier landing tours. Heli-hiking excursions also are available. Caribous, moose and Dall sheep can be seen in the valleys. Free transportation is provided from area hotels. Daily 8-6, May-Sept. Fare $171-$299. Flights require a minimum of four passengers. AE, DS, MC, VI. Phone (907) 683-2574 or (800) 843-1947. *See color ad p. 291.*

NATURAL HISTORY TOUR, departing from Denali National Park Hotel, takes visitors on a bus tour across sections of the park where they can enjoy views of the Alaska Range from Mount McKinley to Mount Deborah. Driver-guides explain the region's natural history, unusual geological formations and local flora and fauna. The 3-hour trip departs daily 7-8:30, 11-2:30 and 4-5:30, mid-May to mid-Sept. Hours may vary; phone ahead. Fare, including a snack, $35; under 12, $20. AE, DS, MC, VI. Phone (907) 276-7234 or (800) 276-7234.

TUNDRA WILDLIFE TOURS, depart from Denali National Park Hotel or will pick up visitors at local hotels. Buses travel to Toklat River, making frequent stops en route for photography. Driver-guides explain in detail the region's geology, flora and fauna on the 6- to 8-hour tours. Binoculars are recommended for spotting moose, caribou, bears and other wildlife. Inquire about weather policies. Trips depart daily 5:30-7 a.m. and 1:30-3:30 p.m. mid-May to mid-Sept. Fare, including a box lunch, $64; ages 2-11, $34.50. Reservations are recommended. AE, MC, VI. Phone (907) 276-7234 or 683-2215.

RECREATIONAL ACTIVITIES
White-water Rafting

- **Alaska Raft Adventures** departs from the McKinley Chalet at Milepost 238 on George Parks Hwy. (SR 3). Write P.O. Box 87, Denali National Park, AK 99755. Trips depart daily at 8, 1 and 6. Phone (907) 276-7234.

- [SAVE] **Denali Raft Adventures, Inc.,** 5 mi. n. of the park entrance. Write Drawer 190, Denali National Park, AK 99755. Trips depart daily mid-May to mid-Sept., check-in times at 7:30, 9, 10, 12:30, 3 and 6:30. Phone (907) 683-2234.

EAGLE (D-8) pop. 200

Eagle was settled in 1897 by 28 miners who named the town after the bald eagles that nested on the nearby bluff. In 1899, the Army established Fort Egbert and within several years, some 37 military buildings were constructed. Founded along the Yukon River near the Canadian border, Eagle is the only planned town of the gold rush.

Eagle Historical Society: P.O. Box 23, Eagle, AK 99738; phone (907) 547-2325.

EAGLE MUSEUMS are all within 1 sq. mi. of town. Tours depart from the courthouse. Visitors can partake in a walking tour that includes six restored buildings, including James Wickersham's original courthouse, the Army Mule Barn, Redman Lodge, Customs House, NCO Quarters and the Waterwagon Shed. Each building contains memorabilia portraying the small town's history. Allow 3 hours minimum. Daily 9-noon, Memorial Day-Labor Day. Admission $5, ages 1-12, free. Phone (907) 547-2297.

EKLUTNA (C-11)

More than 150 years ago Russian missionaries came to Eklutna to convert the Athabascan Indians. Devotees constructed the St. Nicholas Russian Orthodox Church; the log structure still stands in Eklutna Historical Park along Glenn Highway, Milepost 26. In the nearby cemetery gaily colored "spirit houses," built to house the souls of the deceased, adorn the grave sites. Guided tours of the historical park are available mid-May to mid-September.

FAIRBANKS (B-11,D-7)
pop. 30,800, elev. 432'
See map page 294.

Fairbanks, near the geographical center of Alaska, is a major visitor center and the northern terminus of the Alaska Railroad. The military, transportation and market nucleus of the Alaskan interior, Fairbanks is a supply point for arctic oil operations and a departure point for airlines statewide.

In 1901 Capt. E.T. Barnette founded a trading post where Fairbanks now stands—a riverboat captain refused to ferry him any farther up the Chena River due to the low water level. Gold was discovered nearby a year later, and the first wave of prospectors flooded up the river. The settlement was named for Charles Warren Fairbanks of Indiana, a U.S. senator who later became vice president to Theodore Roosevelt.

The construction of the Alaska Highway and the influx of the military into Fairbanks heralded a second boom. And in 1968 the discovery of oil in Prudhoe Bay, 390 miles north, triggered a third wave of development. Of interest is Alaskaland, a pioneer theme park at Airport and Peger roads.

Fairbanks offers a variety of winter sports, including cross-country and downhill skiing, curling, ice hockey and dog mushing. The city's geographical location allows the semiprofessional Goldpanners baseball team to play its Midnight Sun Game at 10:30 p.m. on the weekend nearest June 21 without using artificial lighting.

Local sightseeing tours to Alaska's arctic zone and other remote places throughout the state are available through [SAVE] Gray Line of Alaska *(see ad p. 283)*, the Northern Alaska Tour Co. and other tour operators. Using railway cars with skylights, Alaska Sightseeing Tours, Gray Line of Alaska and Princess Tours also offer trips between Anchorage and Fairbanks via Denali National Park. Canoes for trips on the Chena River can be rented from several outfitters.

Interesting drives include visits to Chena Hot Springs, the Trans-Alaska Pipeline and the town of Ester. Abandoned gold dredges can be seen outside of Fairbanks along the roads to Chatanika and Ester. The Alaska Public Lands Information Center, on the lower level of Courthouse Square at Third Avenue and Cushman Street, shows free movies and has information about public lands and parks; phone (907) 456-0527.

Fairbanks Visitor Information Center: 550 First Ave., Fairbanks, AK 99701; phone (907) 456-5774 or (800) 327-5774. *See color ad p. 295.*

Self-guiding tours: Information about a historical walking and driving tour is available from the Fairbanks Visitor Information Center.

ESTER GOLD CAMP, 5 mi. w. via SR 3 (George Parks Hwy.), contains buildings that date back to the Ester townsite of 1904 and Fairbanks Exploration Co., which operated a gold camp there until 1958. Food is available. Transportation is available from many local hotels. Allow 1 hour minimum. Daily 24 hours, May 28-Sept. 4. Free. Phone (907) 479-2500 or (800) 676-6925.

"Photosymphony" at Firehouse Theater presents "The Crown of Light," an audiovisual recreation of the aurora borealis, or northern lights. "The Crown of Light" is shown nightly at 6:45 and 7:45, May 28-Sept. 4 (also Wed.-Sat. at 6 in July). Admission $6; ages 3-12, $3. Reservations are suggested. The show is not recommended for infants and young children.

"Service with a Smile" in the Malemute Saloon, is a 1.5-hour performance that recounts the gold rush days in story and song; the poetry of Robert Service, author of "The Shooting of Dan McGrew," is featured. The saloon, with swinging doors and sawdust-covered floors, is filled with

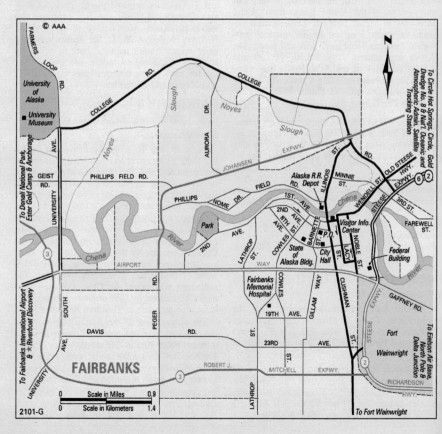

historical relics. Shows nightly at 9, May 28-Sept. 4 (also Wed.-Sat. at 7 in July). Admission $12; ages 3-12, $6. Reservations are suggested.

GOLD DREDGE NUMBER 8, n. on SR 6 to Goldstream Rd. following signs, is a five-deck ship more than 250 feet long that was built in 1928 to ply Goldstream and Engineer creeks for the precious metal. Following the 90-minute tour, visitors can pan for gold and search for bison and mammoth bones. Food is available. Daily 9-6, mid-May to mid-Sept. Admission $20, children $12.50. Phone (907) 457-6058.

NATIONAL OCEANIC AND ATMOSPHERIC ADMINISTRATION SATELLITE TRACKING STATION is 13.5 mi. n.e. on SR 6 (Steese Hwy.). The NOAA Fairbanks Command and Data Acquisition Station (FCDAS) is the northernmost civilian operated satellite tracking station on the continent. It has a long and rich history to the U.S. space program. The station's primary mission is to track, command and receive telemetry and imagery data from a suite of polar-orbiting, Earth-observing satellites used to gather data for global environmental monitoring and weather forecasting. Guided tours depart on the hour Mon.-Fri. 8-4, Sat. 9-3; otherwise by appointment. Free. Phone (907) 451-1200.

★ **RIVERBOAT DISCOVERY,** on the sternwheeler *Discovery III* docked off Airport Way on Discovery Rd., provides 3.5-hour trips on the Chena and Tanana rivers. Guides discuss area wildlife, history, anthropology, geology and customs. Views vary from wilderness to elegant houses, and the trip includes a stop at an Athabascan Indian village. Inquire about weather policies. Trips depart daily at 8:45 and 2, late May to mid-Sept. Fare $39.95; ages 3-12,

$29.95. Reservations are required. Phone (907) 479-6673. *See color ad.*

UNIVERSITY MUSEUM, on the West Ridge of the University of Alaska campus, contains natural and cultural history exhibits. Also displayed are an extensive gold collection and a steppe bison killed by

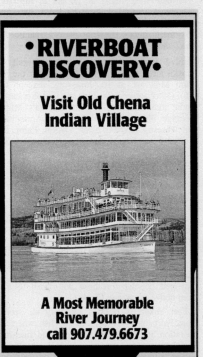

a lion 36,000 years ago and preserved in the permafrost. The "Northern Inua" and "Dynamic Aurora" shows also are presented as well as 20-minute talks about varying topics. Allow 30 minutes minimum.

Daily 9-7, June-Aug.; 9-5 in May and Sept.; Mon.-Fri. 9-5, Sat.-Sun. noon-5, rest of year. "Northern Inua" daily at 11 and 2, June-Aug. "Dynamic Aurora" daily at 10 and 3, June-Aug. Admission $5; over 59, $4.50; ages 13-18, $3. "Northern Inua" show $6.50. "Dynamic Aurora" show $3. Phone (907) 474-7505.

Guided Walking Tours of the University of Alaska last 1 to 1.5 hours. Tours depart the museum Mon.-Fri. at 10, June-Aug. (except July 5-6). Other activities include the Geophysical Institute tour (Thurs. at 2); the Alaska's Mining Heritage film (Wed. at 2:30); the Agricultural and Forestry Experimental Station Farm tour (Fri. at 2); and the Large Animal Research Station tour (Tues. and Sat. at 1:30 and 3), which features Alaskan wildlife, including musk oxen, reindeer and caribou. Phone (907) 474-7581.

FORT YUKON (C-7) pop. 600

Just north of the Arctic Circle at a point where the Yukon River is almost 3 miles wide, the Athabascan Indian village of Fort Yukon was established as a trading post by the Hudson's Bay Co. in 1847. The village was an important port during the gold rush days, and the post office has remained popular for those who wish to mail from above the Arctic Circle.

Fort Yukon is reached by daily air service from Fairbanks. Visitors can see fish wheels in operation and purchase craftwork and fine furs. Temperatures have ranged as high as 100 degrees Fahrenheit in the summer and as low as minus 78 Fahrenheit in winter.

GATES OF THE ARCTIC NATIONAL PARK AND PRESERVE (C-6)

Elevations in the park and preserve range from 300 ft. along the Kobuk River to 8,510 ft. at Mount Igikpak. Refer to AAA maps for additional elevation information.

The rocky spine of the Brooks Range forms the backbone of Gates of the Arctic National Park and Preserve's 8.5 million acres. Lying north of the Arctic Circle, this is a raw, austere landscape of sparse vegetation and jagged spires. In the heart of the Brooks Range, the boreal forest, or taiga, of spruce, birch and poplar meets the almost treeless tundra that rolls uninterrupted to the Arctic Ocean.

Despite being four times the size of Yellowstone National Park, Gates of the Arctic is a meager larder for the caribou, moose, wolves and bears that roam the park in search of food. Fortunately much of their arctic range is protected, as Gates of the Arctic is joined on either side by Noatak National Preserve and nearby Arctic National Wildlife Refuge.

It was a forester on leave, Bob Marshall, who, in exploring this uncharted region in the late 1920s, christened this land Gates of the Arctic. The term both describes and evokes the grandeur of this wilderness—the soaring immensity of sky and mountains, the burst of wildflowers in summer and the cyclical abundance of wildlife.

But as Marshall remarked, the greatest pleasure is its undeveloped and wild character, which gives the visitor the sense of being the first to visit the tundra foothills or one of the park's nameless peaks. Today a good way to enjoy the park is to follow Marshall's example and hike the park's rugged terrain, which offers challenging backpacking. A popular alternative is to canoe or raft the network of rivers and lakes.

Most visitors use various air charter services from Fairbanks and Bettles Field to reach the park's interior. The Dalton Highway skirts the park's eastern edge and is the only road that approaches the park. Because of Gates of the Arctic's fragile ecology, there are no park facilities, trails or campgrounds. For trip planning assistance and a list of outfitters, guides and air taxi operators, write Gates of the Arctic National Park and Preserve, P.O. Box 26030, Bettles, AK 99726; phone (907) 692-5494. *See Recreation Chart.*

GIRDWOOD (C-11) elev. 23'

RECREATIONAL ACTIVITIES
Skiing
• **Alyeska Ski Area**, on SR 1 (Seward Hwy.). Write Box 249, Girdwood, AK 99587. Open mid-Nov. to mid-Apr. Phone (907) 754-1111 or (800) 880-3880, or 754-7669 for ski conditions.

GLACIER BAY NATIONAL PARK AND PRESERVE (G-9)

Elevations in the park and preserve range from sea level at Glacier Bay to 15,320 ft. at Mount Fairweather. Refer to AAA maps for additional elevation information.

Blue-white glaciers flow from the snow-clad peaks of the Fairweather Range to fiordlike inlets in Glacier Bay National Park, one of the most scenic spots in Alaska. This 3,283,168-acre area stretches northward from Cross Sound to the Canadian border.

Within the park are 15,320-foot Mount Fairweather and Glacier Bay. The bay, about 65 miles long and 2.5 to 10 miles wide, was filled with ice 5,000 feet thick as recently as 200 years ago. The park contains some of the world's most impressive tidewater glaciers. Icebergs that crack off, or calve, from the nearly vertical ice cliffs dot the waters of the upper bay. Boaters are likely to encounter numerous harbor seals and an occasional whale.

This spectacular region is accessible only by plane or boat. Alaska Airlines offers flights from Juneau daily June through early September. A 10-mile road connects the park headquarters with the small community of Gustavus, where charter vessels and air and boat service to Juneau are available.

A boat tour of the bay departs from Glacier Bay Lodge each morning, late May to mid-September; phone (800) 451-5952.

Due to concern for the endangered humpback whale, permits are required from June through August for private vessels to enter Glacier Bay. An Alaska fishing license is required for fishing. Boaters should contact the National Park Service for current regulations; phone (907) 697-2627. For further information about the park contact the Superintendent, Glacier Bay National Park and Preserve, P.O. Box 140, Gustavus, AK 99826; phone (907) 697-2230. *See Recreation Chart.*

HAINES (G-10) pop. 1,200, elev. 100′

Haines lies in a spectacular setting on the Chilkat Peninsula near the northern end of Lynn Canal between the waters of the Inside Passage and the Chilkat River. The Alaska Marine Highway links Haines with Prince Rupert, British Columbia, and Bellingham, Wash., and enables visitors to connect with the Alaska Highway at Haines Junction, Milepost 1016, via SRs 7 and 4. For information about the Alaska Marine Highway phone (907) 766-2111 or (800) 642-0066, ext. 9604.

From late October through December, the 48,000-acre Chilkat Bald Eagle Preserve, between Mileposts 9 and 31 on scenic Haines Highway, harbors one of the largest congregations of bald eagles in the world. More than 3,500 of the birds gather to feed on the salmon in the Chilkat River; sometimes as many as 20 eagles roost in a tree. Use roadside pulloffs for viewing; stopping on the road is prohibited. Tour information is available at Haines Visitor Center.

Other interesting drives near Haines include Lutak Road, leading to Chilkoot Lake, and Mud Bay Road, which passes Pyramid Harbor and an old cannery with its salmon boats, before approaching Chilkat State Park *(see Recreation Chart and the AAA Canada and Alaska CampBook).* Davidson and Rainbow glaciers also are visible from this route.

Haines-Skagway Water Taxi and Scenic Cruise provides efficient transport between Haines and Skagway twice daily from May to September; phone (907) 766-3395.

Haines Visitor Center: jct. Second and Willard sts., P.O. Box 530, Haines, AK 99827; phone (907) 766-2234 or (800) 458-3579.

Self-guiding tours: A brochure featuring a walking tour is available from Haines Visitor Center.

CHILKAT BALD EAGLE PRESERVE FLOAT TRIPS, on Beach Rd., pass through the Bald Eagle Preserve on the Chilkat River and offer views of the Chilkat Mountains and bald eagles in their natural habitat. Transportation to and from the river is provided. Bring warm clothes, binoculars, camera, sunglasses and rain gear. Inquire about weather policies. Write Chilkat Guides, P.O. Box 170, Haines, AK 99827.

The 4-hour float trips depart daily, May-Sept. Departure times vary; phone ahead. Fare $80; ages 7-14, $40. Reservations are recommended. Phone (907) 766-2491.

CHILKOOT LAKE TOURS, 1183 Haines Hwy., offers sightseeing and fishing cruises of Chilkoot Lake. Brown bears, bald eagles and spawning salmon can be seen. Inquire about weather policies. Allow 3 hours minimum. Daily at 9 and 2, May 1-Sept. 15; other times by appointment.

Fare for sightseeing cruise $60; fishing cruise $70. AE, CB, MC, VI. Phone (907) 766-2891.

FORT WILLIAM H. SEWARD, s. at end of Haines Hwy., formerly Port Chilkoot, was the first permanent Army post in Alaska. The old hospital now accommodates carvers who use traditional Tlingit Indian methods for creating totems, dance masks and other items. The former parade ground contains a replica of a tribal house, a trapper's cabin, several caches and totem poles.

Walking-tour maps are available at the visitor information center and at Hotel Halsingland. Fort open daily. Free. Phone (907) 766-2234.

Chilkat Indian Dances take place at the Chilkat Center for the Arts. A multi-cultural dance group performs traditional Tlingit dances, which include elaborate ceremonial costumes, rattles, masks and woven Chilkat Dance Blankets. Performances last approximately 45 minutes. Evening shows Sun.-Tues. and Thurs. at 7:30, Wed. at 8:30, May-Sept. Admission $10, students $5. Phone (907) 766-2160.

SHELDON MUSEUM AND CULTURAL CENTER, Main St. near the boat harbor, is housed in a modern structure that displays artifacts interpreting Tlingit Indian culture and memorabilia of Haines' past. Educational videotapes about eagles and the history of Haines are presented. Allow 1 hour, 30 minutes minimum. Daily 1-5, late May to mid-Sept.; Sun.-Mon. and Wed. 1-4, Tues. and Thurs.-Fri. 3-5, rest of year. Admission $3, under 18 free. Phone (907) 766-2366.

RECREATIONAL ACTIVITIES
Fishing

- **Weeping Trout Sports Resort** is downtown at 144 2nd Ave. S. Write P.O. Box 129, Haines, AK 99827. Trips depart June-Sept. Other activities are offered. Phone (907) 766-2827.

HOMER (D-10) pop. 3,700, elev. 67′

Homer was established by Homer Pennock, who landed a party of gold and coal prospectors in the schooner *Excelsior* in 1896. Gold was not found, but the settlement remained.

Healthy fishing and tourism industries support Homer's economy. Kachemak Bay, a 30-mile arm of lower Cook Inlet, provides a usually ice-free deepwater harbor for Homer. A small boat harbor has launching facilities and charter boats. Charter planes are available in town for hunting, fishing and sightseeing expeditions. Cross-country skiing is popular in winter. The city is linked by daily air service with Anchorage, Kenai, Soldotna, Seward, Kodiak and Seldovia; the last three towns also are connected to Homer via the Alaska Marine Highway.

Skyline Drive, accessible from West and East Hill roads, follows the rim of the plateau behind the town and offers access to ski slopes and views of the bay, Homer Spit and the Kenai Mountains. Chartered bush flights afford panoramas of the bay, open coal seams and Harding Icefield to the southeast.

Homer Chamber of Commerce: P.O. Box 541, Homer, AK 99603; phone (907) 235-7740 or 235-5300.

PRATT MUSEUM is .5 blks. n. of Pioneer Ave. at 3779 Bartlett St. Highlights include a botanical garden; a marine gallery; fishing boat models; sea birds and marine mammals; a forest trail; an exhibit detailing the impact of the *Exxon Valdez* oil spill; and cultural displays, which feature Russian, Eskimo and American Indian artifacts. Alaskan art from the Kenai Peninsula is exhibited.

Allow 1 hour minimum. Sun.-Wed. 10-6, Thurs.-Sat. 10-8, June-Sept.; Tues.-Sun. noon-5, Feb.-Apr. and Oct.-Dec. Closed Thanksgiving and Dec. 25. Admission $4; over 65 and students with ID $3; ages 13-18, $2; ages 6-12, $1. Phone (907) 235-8635.

RECREATIONAL ACTIVITIES
Fishing

- **Homer Ocean Charters** is at Cannery Row boardwalk on Homer Spit Rd. Write P.O. Box 2543, Homer, AK 99603. Daily by appointment. Phone (907) 235-6212. *See ad.*

JUNEAU (G-10) pop. 26,800, elev. 12'

Juneau, Alaska's capital city, lies along the beautiful Gastineau Channel at the foot of snow-capped mounts Roberts and Juneau. The borough of Juneau covers 3,108 square miles of towering mountains, islands, saltwater bays, forested valleys and residential flatlands. Its road system extends from Thane, 6 miles southeast of downtown, northwest to Echo Cove at Milepost 40.2 on the Glacier Highway. The city is accessible by air or by sea.

When Joe Juneau and Richard Harris discovered gold in 1880, they started the first rush in American Alaska. At one time the Alaska-Juneau and Treadwell mines were producing about 20,000 tons of ore daily. Not until 1944, when the low price of gold and the high cost of extraction rendered it impractical, did mining operations cease.

The Alaska State Capitol, Fourth and Main streets, offers free 30-minute tours in summer. One block west of the capitol is the State Office Building, which contains a century-old totem pole and a Kimball Theatre pipe organ equipped with such accessories as a glockenspiel, sleigh bells and bird whistles. Free concerts are held Friday at noon in the eighth-floor atrium. Also on the eighth floor, a terrace affords panoramas of the harbor and the surrounding mountains.

Tours of one of the oldest churches in southeastern Alaska are available mid-May to mid-September. Built in 1894, St. Nicholas Russian Orthodox Church is at Fifth and Gold streets. The Shrine of St. Terese, near Milepost 23 on the Glacier Highway, is a stone chapel on an island connected to shore by a gravel causeway.

There are many ways to tour Juneau. Nearby hiking trails, which vary in length and difficulty, lead to fishing spots, scenic mountain areas, old mine ruins and points near Mendenhall Glacier. Bus tours circle points of interest in Juneau and visit Mendenhall Glacier and the log Chapel-by-the-Lake at Auke Lake. Tours depart from the cruise ship docks during the summer. Visitors also can charter boats for sightseeing or fishing.

Charter flights provide views of the icefield; among the companies that provide such service are Alaska Seaplane Service, L.A.B. Flying, Skagway Air Service, Ward Air and Wings of Alaska. Helicopter tours, float trips, gold-panning excursions and several tours of nearby

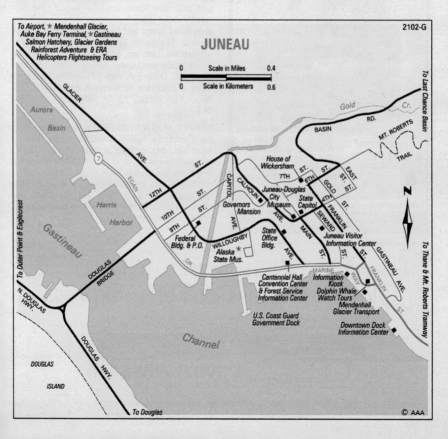

and more distant points of interest are available through Gray Line of Alaska, Northgate Tours and Cruises and other local tour companies. Northgate also offers a trolley tour of the area; phone (907) 463-5321.

Salmon bakes are held in Gold Creek Basin, Salmon Creek and at Thane Ore House daily in summer.

Juneau Convention and Visitors Bureau: 134 Third St., Juneau, AK 99801; phone (907) 586-2201 or (888) 581-2201.

Self-guiding tours: Free walking tour maps of the historical and governmental districts are available at Juneau Visitor Information Center (Davis Log Cabin), 134 Seward St. Visitor centers operate at the foot of Seward Street on Franklin Street, at the Auke Bay ferry terminal and at the airport.

★ **ALASKA STATE MUSEUM,** w. of Egan Dr. at 395 Whittier St., chronicles the state's history and preserves and exhibits Tlingit and Athabascan Indian, Eskimo and Aleut culture. Wildlife and mining displays, Russian-American historical exhibits and art of Alaska are featured. Highlights include a bald eagle nesting tree. Allow 1 hour minimum. Guided tours are available in summer. Mon.-Fri. 9-6, Sat.-Sun. 10-6, May 18-Sept. 21; Tues.-Sat. 10-4, rest of year. Admission $4, under 18 free. Phone (907) 465-2901.

DOLPHIN WHALE WATCH TOURS depart from Merchant's Wharf at 2 Marine Way. Three-hour tours on a jet boat offer the opportunity to view humpback and killer whales, porpoises, sea lions, seals and eagles. Daily 7-7, May 15-Sept. 15; Mon.-Thurs. 10-3, Apr. 15-May 14 and Sept. 16-30. Fare $95; over 64, $90; ages 2-12, $75. AE, DS, MC, VI. Phone (907) 463-3422 or (800) 770-3422. *See color ad.*

ERA HELICOPTERS FLIGHTSEEING TOURS depart from the North Douglas Airport. The narrated, 1-hour tour offers views of the capital city, abandoned mines and four glaciers in the Juneau Icefield. Highlights include a glacier landing to explore the blue ice. Free transportation is provided from downtown hotels. Allow 2 hours minimum. Daily 8-6. Fare $171-$299. Flights require a minimum of four passengers. AE, DS, MC, VI. Phone (907) 586-2030 or (800) 843-1947.

FOREST SERVICE INFORMATION CENTER, in the Centennial Hall Convention Center at 101 Egan Dr., has exhibits relating to area history and natural resources as well as films about native flora and fauna. Trail guides, maps, current conditions and recreation and cabin reservation information about Tongass National Forest and Glacier Bay National Park are available. Mon.-Fri. 8-5. Free. Phone (907) 586-8751.

★ **GASTINEAU SALMON HATCHERY,** 2697 Channel Dr., hatches more than 110 million salmon eggs annually, including chum, pink, coho and king. The hatchery features many exhibits and saltwater aquariums that contains live adult salmon and more than 100 species of southeast Alaska sea life. Guided tours are available. Allow 30 minutes minimum. Mon.-Fri. 10-6, Sat.-Sun. 10-5, mid-May to mid-Sept.; by appointment rest of year. Admission $3; ages 3-12, $1. AE, DS, MC, VI. Phone (907) 463-4810.

GLACIER GARDENS RAINFOREST ADVENTURE is at 7600 Glacier Hwy. A motorized shuttle takes passengers up Thunder Mountain through botanical gardens nestled in a lush Alaskan rainforest. Guests travel past streams, ponds, waterfalls and such flora as rhododendrons, Japanese maples and ferns. A scenic overlook at the 500-foot marker offers a spectacular view of the Mendenhall Valley and Chilkat Mountains. Allow 1 hour minimum. Daily 9-6, May-Sept. Admission $14; ages 6-12, $8. AE, MC, VI. Phone (907) 790-3377.

HOUSE OF WICKERSHAM, 213 Seventh St., was the residence of Judge James Wickersham, noted Alaskan statesman, historian and pioneer judge. Built 1898-99 on a high hill and used as a landmark by early sea captains sailing into Juneau, this large Victorian house offers panoramic views of Gastineau Channel. Featured are rare early Alaskana collections, Russian and pioneer artifacts, carvings, photographs, original furnishings and historic documents. Tues.-Sun. 10-3, May-Sept.; by appointment rest of year. Admission $15 for living history tour. Phone (907) 586-9001.

JUNEAU-DOUGLAS CITY MUSEUM, Fourth and Main sts., focuses on the city's history. Displays illustrate life in old Juneau and the city's gold mining past. A children's room provides hands-on exploring opportunities. A relief map and audiovisual presentations are other features. Mon.-Fri. 9-5, Sat.-Sun 10-5, May 10-Oct. 1; Fri.-Sat. noon-4 and by appointment rest of year. Closed winter holidays. Admission $3, students and under 18 free. Phone (907) 586-3572.

★ **MENDENHALL GLACIER,** 13 mi. n.w. via SR 7 and the Mendenhall Loop Rd., is an impressive river of blue ice, 12 miles long and 1.5 miles wide. The glacier is fed by the 1,500-square-mile Juneau Icefield, part of the Tongass National Forest *(see place listing p. 315).* Trails on either side of the glacier, which reach past the glacier face afford scenic views; the East Glacier Trail provides views of nearby Mendenhall Lake and Nugget Creek Falls. An easily traversable .5-mile nature trail explains pertinent facts about the area.

Steep Creek, near the visitor center parking lot, is a good point from which to see salmon spawning mid-July to mid-August. In early autumn visitors can view a second run in Nugget Creek; bald eagles and black bears frequent the area during this time as well. Camping and picnic facilities are available at Mendenhall Lake. Ice skating and cross-country skiing are permitted in winter.

Visitor Center offers interpretive talks, audiovisual programs and walks are offered. An observatory offers

Mountains Of Ice

Glaciers—blue-white in color, with long frozen tongues reaching into the water—cover more than 75,000 square miles in the United States, and most are found in Alaska.

If you've explored the waters of the Inside Passage or Prince William Sound, you've certainly seen them.

But how is a glacier formed? Here are the basics: Glaciers are created when more snow falls each winter than melts the following summer. As areas receive snowfall year after year, new snow layers create pressure on existing layers of snow and ice. This creates firn, small granules of compacted snow. Firn from previous years is buried and turns to ice through crystallization. The process continues, increasing the pressure on the ice field until air diminishes, and solid crystalline ice is formed.

As the layers of snow, firn and ice thicken, the lower ice can no longer support the weight of the mass, and it moves downward, smoothing surrounding mountain walls and floors and leaving grooves in a U-shaped valley.

You may be wondering why glacial ice is blue. It's actually not. Glacial ice is so concentrated that it absorbs all colors in the light spectrum except blue, which is reflected back at the viewer—making the ice *appear* blue. The lack of oxygen in the ice causes it to melt much more slowly than ice created in your freezer.

Some of the more popular glaciers to visit are Columbia, Exit, Le Conte, Mendenhall and Portage. But while you're gazing at these giant frozen wonders, keep in mind that almost 90 percent of an iceberg is below water!

spectacular views of the glacier. Daily 8:30-5, mid-May to late Sept.; Sat.-Sun. 9-4, rest of year. Phone (907) 789-0097.

MENDENHALL GLACIER TRANSPORT LTD., departing from the cruise ship dock downtown, provides sightseeing excursions of Juneau by bus. The tour offers stops at the Chapel by the Lake and Mendenhall Glacier. Allow 2 hours, 30 minutes minimum. Daily 9-3:30, May 15-Sept. 30. Ferry transfer service available Apr.-Sept. Fare $17.50, under 6 free. Phone (907) 789-5460. *See color ad p. 300.*

MOUNT ROBERTS TRAMWAY, 490 S. Franklin St. on the cruise ship dock, offers a 6-minute ride to the 2,000-foot-level of Mount Roberts. At the top, visitors can stop at the nature center, take wildlife or nature walks and view the scenery overlooking the Gastineau Channel below. "Seeing Daylight," a movie about Alaska's native Tlingit, is presented in the Chilkat Theater. Food is available. Allow 1 hour minimum. Daily 9-9, May 15-Sept. 27. Fare $17.75; ages 6-12, $10.45. AE, CB, MC, VI. Phone (907) 463-3412 or (888) 461-8726.

RECREATIONAL ACTIVITIES

Canoeing

• **Northgate Tours and Cruises**, departs from the downtown dock. Write P.O. Box 20613,

Juneau, AK 99802. Trips depart daily. Other activities are offered. Phone (907) 463-5321.

Fishing

• **Juneau Sportfishing** offers round-trip transportation from local hotels and ships. Write P.O. Box 20438, Juneau, AK 99802. Trips depart daily. Reservations are required. Phone (907) 586-1887.

• **Salmon Guaranteed Charters**, 4510 Prospect Way, Juneau, AK 99801. Daily May-Oct. Reservations are required. Phone (907) 364-3474.

Skiing

• **Eaglecrest Ski Area** is 12 mi. n.w. off the North Douglas Hwy. Write 155 S. Seward St., Juneau, AK 99801. Thurs.-Mon. 9-4, Dec.-Mar. (also Thurs. 4-9, early Jan. to mid-Mar.). Phone (907) 790-2000.

KATMAI NATIONAL PARK AND PRESERVE (G-5)

Elevations in the park and preserve range from sea level at the Shelikof Strait to 7,606 ft. at Mount Dennison. Refer to AAA maps for additional elevation information.

The 4.1-million-acre Katmai National Park and Preserve is an outstanding exhibit of volcanism. In 1912 one of the greatest volcanic explosions in recorded history turned a nameless green valley on the southern portion of the Alaska Peninsula into what became known as the Valley of Ten Thousand Smokes. For more than 45 years the eruption was attributed to Mount Katmai, but recent studies indicate that the source was a new volcanic vent called Novarupta, some 6 miles distant.

During or shortly after the eruption, the peak of Mount Katmai collapsed, forming a caldera that subsequently filled with water. Molten material released from Novarupta and surrounding vents flowed down the valley, and thousands of holes from which smoke and gases arose formed as gases and vaporized surface water percolated through the volcanic deposits. These fumaroles, which gave the valley its name, lasted only about 20 years.

Although nearly all of the "smokes" have died out, steam columns from nearby volcanoes sometimes can be seen. By air it is possible to see the jade-green lake in the crater of Mount Katmai and to circle over still-active mounts Trident, Mageik and Martin.

In addition to its superlative scenery—large lakes, rivers, glaciers and active volcanos—the

park is noted for its abundant wildlife. The most prominent mammal is the Alaskan brown bear, the world's largest carnivore, averaging 500 pounds with some reaching 1,200 pounds. It is recommended that visitors maintain at least 50 yards from individual bears and 100 yards from sows with young. Visitors also should make noises while walking or hiking.

Katmai National Park can be reached only by boat or plane. A boat ramp is at Lake Camp, 10 miles by dirt road from King Salmon. Commercial airlines serve King Salmon, 35 miles from Brooks Camp. Amphibious aircraft make daily scheduled flights between King Salmon and Brooks Camp. Bush planes can be chartered.

Daily tours to the Valley of 10,000 Smokes begin at Brooks Camp and include lunch; the fare is $67. For more information write the Superintendent, Katmai National Park and Preserve, P.O. Box 7, King Salmon, AK 99613; phone (907) 246-3305. *See Recreation Chart.*

KENAI (D-10) pop. 6,300, elev. 86′

Established as Fort St. Nicholas by Russian fur traders in 1791, Kenai (KEEN-eye) is one of the oldest permanent settlements in Alaska. Until 1953 the town grew under a squatters' rights policy. Kenai is the closest settlement to the south-central region's most promising oil-development fields and is the site of major petrochemical plants.

Kenai's Russian Orthodox Church, established in 1894, contains religious and art objects brought from Russia in 1841.

A popular and colorful pastime during the summer months in Kenai is berry picking. Such berries as Alaska blueberries (a smaller version of its common cousin), nagoonberries (reddish purple in color), cloudberries and salmonberries (both peach in color), crowberries (black in color), northern red currants, wild raspberries and cranberries grow on the peninsula.

Kenai Chamber of Commerce: 402 Overland, P.O. Box 497, Kenai, AK 99611; phone (907) 283-7989.

KENAI VISITORS & CULTURAL CENTER, 11471 Kenai Spur Hwy., offers visitor information as well as displays on Kenai's history and culture. Exhibits focus on native Alaskan artifacts, the oil industry and its impact on Kenai, nature and marine life, and Lake Clark National Park. Audio-visual presentations are available. Allow 30 minutes minimum. Mon.-Fri. 9-8, Sat.-Sun. 10-7, May 15-Sept. 15; Mon.-Fri. 8:30-5, Sat.-Sun. noon-5, rest of year. Donations. Phone (907) 283-1991.

KENAI NATIONAL WILDLIFE REFUGE— *see Soldotna p. 314.*

KENAI FJORDS NATIONAL PARK (D-11)

> Elevations in the park range from sea level at Nuka Bay to 6,400 ft. at a peak on the Harding Icefield. Refer to AAA maps for additional elevation information.

Kenai Fjords National Park covers about 600,000 acres on the southeastern side of the Kenai Peninsula. Access to the park is by private vehicle, plane or boat from Seward. Air charters also are available from other communities on the Kenai Peninsula. Scheduled bus service and commuter flights are available between Seward and Anchorage. Several tour companies offer trips to Exit Glacier and boat trips to the fjords.

The park encompasses a coastal mountain range that includes most of Harding Icefield, one of the four largest icefields in the United States. A remnant of the ice age, it blankets all but the top of the Kenai Mountains. Along the coast is the rugged shoreline of the glacier-carved Kenai Fjords. Seals, porpoises, whales and sea otters are some of the 23 marine mammal species that inhabit the coastal waters.

Stories In Cedar

The art of totem pole carving in Alaska originated with the Tlingit, Haida and Tsimshian native tribes. Abundant food supplies along the Inside Passage allowed the natives the leisure time necessary to develop their elaborate craft.

Cedar totem poles served many purposes. Each figure on the pole represented an element in a story, and together the figures recorded the legends and histories of the tribes, who have no written language.

Genealogy poles, erected in front of an owner's house, identified a clan, told a family story or conveyed the family's status. Crests (usually in the shapes of eagles or ravens) denoted the clans of the husband and wife. Mortuary poles included a compartment for the ashes of a deceased clan member or chief and were carved in honor of that individual. Shame poles were created to chastise someone who wronged the clan or village—the pole remained standing until the debt was repaid tenfold. Other totem poles conveyed mythological or legendary stories, or commemorated a notable event, such as a birth or a good deed.

Colors were limited to natural pigments made from salmon eggs or hematite. Black was the primary color; red was used for secondary elements; and blue-green was used for highlighting.

An intimate knowledge of native traditions is necessary to fully interpret the totem poles, but there are common figures that are relatively easy to identify: the raven, a symbol of the creator, who changes form at will; the eagle, representing peace and friendship; the killer whale, a symbol of strength; and the beaver, bear and wolf.

Exit Glacier is the most accessible of the glaciers that flow from Harding Icefield. Twelve miles north of Seward via the Seward Highway and the dirt Exit Glacier Road, the glacier is reached by a .7-mile trail that begins at the Exit Glacier parking area. A strenuous all-day route leads from the base of Exit Glacier to Harding Icefield. Bald eagles, moose, bears and mountain goats inhabit the area.

Picnicking and back-country camping are permitted; a 9-site walk-in tent campground is available. Hikes to the glacier and nature walks are conducted daily at Exit Glacier by park rangers on duty, Memorial Day through Labor Day. Winter activities at Exit Glacier include skiing, snowmobiling, snowshoeing and dog sledding. Boat and air charters provide access to the coast during the summer.

Park headquarters and a visitor center are in Seward on 4th Avenue next to the harbor master's office. Slide shows, exhibits and information about ranger-conducted activities are available. Headquarters and visitor center open daily 9-6, Memorial Day-Labor Day; Mon.-Fri. 8-7, rest of year. Admission to Exit Glacier is $5 per vehicle. For information write the Superintendent, Kenai Fjords National Park, P.O. Box 1727, Seward, AK 99664; phone (907) 224-3175 or 224-2132 for mailing information. *See Recreation Chart.*

KETCHIKAN (I-12) pop. 8,300

Five miles long and a half-mile wide, Alaska's southernmost city sits on stilts at the base of the Tongass National Forest *(see place listing p. 315)*. On Revillagigedo Island, separated from the mainland by Behm Canal, Ketchikan claims to be the salmon capital of the world. An average annual rainfall of 156 to 162 inches makes it the wettest community in North America. The city's economic base relies on fishing, canning, mineral exploration, tourism and logging and cold-storage operations.

The town is populated with native culture and contains the largest concentration of Tlingit (KLINK-it), Haida (HY-dah), and Tsimshian (SIMP-shee-ane) people in Alaska. This heritage can be seen in the many totem poles that populate the area. Totem poles—tall cedar logs carved with eagles, ravens, wolves, bears, whales and other figures—depict stories or designate clans or lineage, and Ketchikan is reputed to contain the most in the world.

Creek Street is a relic of Ketchikan's rough-and-tumble past. Built on stilts over Ketchikan Creek, the street was once the site of a thriving red-light district. Highlights include art galleries, shops and a museum. The creek is a spawning ground for salmon.

Alaska Sightseeing Tours, Gray Line of Alaska and Princess Tours are among the companies that offer tours of the city. Ketchikan Information Center can provide a more complete list. Charter aircraft, boats, rental cars, buses and taxis are available at the Ketchikan Visitors Bureau, the airport and the ferry terminal.

Southeast Alaska Visitor Center: 50 Main St., Ketchikan, AK 99901; phone (907) 228-6214, 228-6219 or TDD 228-6237.

Self-guiding tours: Maps of a 2-hour walking tour of downtown are available at Ketchikan Visitors Bureau, 131 Front St., Ketchikan, AK 99901; phone (907) 225-6166 or (800) 770-2200.

Shopping areas: The Creek Street boardwalk area in downtown contains a number of specialty shops and boutiques.

CLASSIC TOURS picks up passengers at the downtown cruise ship dock or local accommodation. Passengers see the sights from the back seat of a restored 1955 Chevy, chauffeured by a retired schoolteacher—clad in a poodle skirt and saddle shoes. Narrated tours can accommodate up to five passengers and include visits to Saxman Native Village, Totem Heritage Center, the Creek Street boardwalk and wildlife viewing at a remote bald eagle's nest. Custom tours also can be arranged. Allow 1 hour minimum. Daily 8-6, mid-Apr. through Sept. 30. Fare $50-$70. Reservations are recommended. Phone (907) 225-3091.

DEER MOUNTAIN TRIBAL HATCHERY AND EAGLE CENTER, .5 mi. n.e. at 1158 Salmon Rd. across the bridge from the Totem Heritage Center, raises king (chinook) and coho (silver) salmon, and steelhead and rainbow trout. A videotape presentation is offered, and visitors can taste samples of smoked salmon. Bald eagles also are featured in a landscaped enclosure. Allow 30 minutes minimum. Daily 8-4:30. Guided tour $6.95. Phone (907) 225-6760.

SAXMAN NATIVE VILLAGE, 2.5 mi. s. on S. Tongass Hwy., is a Tlingit (KLINK-it) Indian village of about 350 residents. The totem park contains 30 totem poles, and master carvers can be seen at work in the carving center. Other highlights include the Beaver Tribal House and the Old School House. The Cape Fox Dancers perform based on audience attendance. Guided tours are available.

Allow 30 minutes minimum. Daily 8-5, holidays 9-3, mid-May through Sept. 30; otherwise varies rest of year. Free. Guided tour $30; under 12, $15. MC, VI. Phone (907) 225-4846, ext. 301.

TONGASS HISTORICAL MUSEUM, in Ketchikan's Centennial Building at 629 Dock St., displays pioneer items, artwork, and artifacts of the southeast Alaskan Indian tribes. Allow 30 minutes minimum. Daily 8-5, early May-Sept.; Wed.-Fri. 1-5, Sat.-Sun. 1-4, rest of year. Also open when cruise ships are in port. Closed winter holidays. Admission $3. Phone (907) 225-5600.

TOTEM BIGHT STATE HISTORIC PARK, 10 mi. n. on N. Tongass Hwy., displays more than a dozen poles and a model of a Tlingit clan house. The site is reached by a short trail through a forest from the parking area. A brochure describes typical totem characters and gives insight to the art of totem carving. More totem poles are in Saxman Native Village, 2.5 miles south on S. Tongass Highway. Allow 30 minutes minimum. Daily 6 a.m.-10 p.m. Donations. Phone (907) 247-8574.

TOTEM HERITAGE CENTER, 601 Deermount St., displays 19th-century totem poles retrieved from abandoned villages and conducts workshops emphasizing traditional Tlingit, Haida and Tsimshian art. Tours and crafts demonstrations are given. Allow 30 minutes minimum. Mon.-Sat. 8-5, Sun. 9-5, mid-May through Sept. 30; Tues.-Fri. 1-5 and during classes, rest of year. Closed winter holidays. Admission $2, mid-May through Sept. 30; free to all Sun. afternoons and rest of year. Phone (907) 225-5900.

KLONDIKE GOLD RUSH NATIONAL HISTORICAL PARK—*see Skagway p. 313.*

KOBUK VALLEY NATIONAL PARK (C-5)

Elevations in the park range from 100 ft. at the point where the Kobuk River flows out of the southwest corner of the park to 4,700 ft. in the Brooks Range, which forms the park's northern border. Refer to AAA maps for additional elevation information.

Some 25 miles north of the Arctic Circle, where the boreal forest gives way to the frozen tundra, sits 1,710,000-acre Kobuk Valley National Park in the heart of the arctic wildlands. The broad Kobuk Valley is enclosed almost completely by the Baird Mountains to the north and the Waring Mountains to the south. Traversing the valley from east to west, the wide and placid Kobuk River offers good fishing and idyllic float trips. The swifter Salmon River, a designated Wild and Scenic River, flows south from the Baird Mountains.

Preserved within the park are the 25-square-mile Great Kobuk Sand Dunes, the largest active dunes in the Arctic. Created by the grinding action of ancient glaciers, the sand was carried by wind and water to a wide area south of the Kobuk River. The 100-foot dunes are accessible by a difficult hike from the river along Kavet Creek.

Home to seminomadic tribes for more than 12,500 years, the region still supports the native Inupiats; they are granted by law the right to continue subsistence hunting, trapping and other practices. Important to their survival is North America's largest caribou herd, numbering some 500,000. Many can be seen crossing the Kobuk River in September during their migration southward.

Other wildlife common to the region include moose, grizzly and black bears, wolves, red foxes, lynxes, wolverines and martens. Golden eagles can be seen in the northern latitudes; other birds include sandhill cranes, arctic loons, American golden plovers and arctic terns.

The park attracts experienced backpackers, campers and river travelers. Though the park is open year-round, the elements limit most visits to June through September. Fishing is good when the rivers are clear of silt; catches include salmon, pike, arctic char, whitefish and grayling. An Alaska fishing license is required. Hunting is not permitted, but it is legal to carry a firearm for protection from bears.

Access to the region is by daily commercial flights from Anchorage and Fairbanks to Kotzebue *(see place listing p. 307),* where connections to the villages of Kiana and Ambler can be made. Air taxi service into the park is available from Kotzebue, Kiana and Ambler. There are no facilities, services, trails or campgrounds in the park; a ranger station near Onion Portage is open June through September. The park headquarters in Kotzebue is open year-round Mon.-Fri. 8-5.

Due to its location, the area is subject to harsh weather and high winds. It is advisable to carry protection against hypothermia, mosquitos and biting flies.

For trip planning assistance and a list of authorized outfitters, guides and air taxi operators, write the Superintendent, Northwest Alaska Areas, P.O. Box 1029, Kotzebue, AK 99752; phone (907) 442-3760 or 442-3890. *See Recreation Chart.*

KODIAK (H-6) pop. 6,400

A Russian explorer-trader's quest for sea otter pelts led to the European settlement of Kodiak Island in 1784. The community of Kodiak was established about 1792 when Alexander Baranov moved his headquarters from the original 1784 settlement at Three Saints Bay, making Kodiak the first capital of Russian America. The blue, onionlike domes of the Holy Resurrection Russian Orthodox Church recall the days when the Russian Empire in the North Pacific was administered from Kodiak.

One of the oldest communities in Alaska, Kodiak also is a leading commercial fishing port. The town is on the northeastern tip of Kodiak Island, which is home to the Kodiak brown bear.

Kodiak was nearly destroyed twice; in June 1912, an eruption from Mount Novarupta covered the town with ash. On Good Friday in 1964 an earthquake in southcentral Alaska created tsunamis that enveloped the islands. Citizens found refuge on nearby Pillar Mountain and returned with the task of rebuilding the city.

Kodiak can be reached by air service from Anchorage or by the Alaska Marine Highway, a passenger/vehicle ferry, from Homer and Seward. Reservations are required well in advance for the ferry; write Alaska Marine Highway, P.O. Box

703, Kodiak, AK 99615, or phone (907) 486-3800 or (800) 526-6731.

Kodiak Island Convention and Visitors Bureau: 100-AAA Marine Way, Kodiak, AK 99615; phone (907) 486-4782.

BARANOV MUSEUM, in the Erskine House on the harbor front, has collections of early Russian and Alaskan artifacts as well as American household furnishings from the early 20th century. The building, which dates from 1808, was used by Alexander Baranov as a warehouse for storing furs. Original log construction methods can be examined inside. Allow 1 hour minimum. Mon.-Sat. 10-4, Sun. noon-4, May-Aug.; Mon.-Wed. and Fri.-Sat. 10-3, Sept.-Jan. and Mar.-Apr. Closed major holidays. Admission $2, under 12 free. Phone (907) 486-5920.

FORT ABERCROMBIE STATE HISTORICAL PARK, 4.5 mi. n.e. on Miller Point, is a World War II fortification. The 183-park offers a view of the rocky coastline and nearby islands. Interpretive programs are given, and hiking trails are available. World War II artifacts remain, and the visitor center offers natural-history displays and information about Alaska's participation in World War II. Tidal pools are within walking distance of the visitor center. Picnicking is permitted. Daily 24 hours. Free. Phone (907) 486-6339. *See Recreation Chart and the AAA Western Canada and Alaska CampBook.*

KODIAK ALUTIIQ DANCERS, 713 Rezanof Dr., present traditional Alutiiq dances in an authentic "barabara," or underground earthen hut. The elaborately costumed dancers express cultural and spiritual values that have survived for thousands of years. Narration is provided. Allow 30 minutes minimum. Daily at 3:30, June-Sept.; by appointment rest of year. Closed legal holidays. Admission $15. Reservations are recommended. Phone (907) 486-4449.

KODIAK NATIONAL WILDLIFE REFUGE occupies the southwestern two-thirds of Kodiak Island and 50,000 acres on Ban Island and the northwestern tip of Afognak Island. The 1,865,000 acres were set aside to preserve the habitat of the Kodiak bear, specimens of which weigh up to 1,500 pounds. Among other inhabitants are Sitka black-tailed deer, tundra voles, sea lions and bald eagles.

The refuge is accessible only by plane and boat. Guide service, required for the hunting of brown bear by nonresidents, can be obtained at Kodiak. Cabins are available for public use; write the Refuge Manager, Kodiak National Wildlife Refuge, 1390 Buskin River Rd., Kodiak, AK 99615; phone (907) 487-2600.

Visitor Center, 1 mi. n. of state airport, offers displays, videotapes, audiovisual presentations and information about the refuge. Allow 1 hour minimum. Mon.-Fri. 8-4:30, Sat. noon-4:30, Apr.-Sept.; Mon.-Fri. 8-4:30, rest of year. Closed holidays.

KODIAK TOURS, which makes pickups and dropoffs at the airport and local hotels, offers narrated tours of the island tailored to the interests of the visitor. The U.S. Coast Guard Base, Kodiak Island National Wildlife Refuge Center, Fort Abercrombie and Buskin River state parks, Pillar Mountain and Lake Iliamma are among the sites. Stops to enjoy the island's wildlife and scenery are available. Inquire about weather policies. Write Kodiak Tours, P.O. Box 8630, Kodiak, AK 99615.

Tours lasting 6 hours depart daily at 10. Evening tours also are available. Full-day fare $50; fares include all applicable admissions. Evening fare $15, senior citizens $12. Reservations are suggested. Phone (907) 486-2628.

KOTZEBUE (C-4)
pop. 2,800, elev. 20'

Kotzebue, on the Baldwin Peninsula, sits on glacial moraine on the eastern edge of Kotzebue Sound, named after the Russian sailor Otto Von Kotzebue, the first European to visit the area around 1818. Originally inhabited by the Kikiktagruk Inupiat Eskimos for many centuries, the area was used as a seasonal trading center for the various Eskimo tribes due to its position at the confluence of the Noatak and Kobuk rivers. Its establishment as a permanent city began in 1899 with a Quaker mission.

Kotzebue is situated 33 miles above the Arctic Circle in the treeless tundra; the sun rises each year in early June and remains above the horizon for only 38 days. A spectacular ice breakup takes place for 2 weeks between mid-May and mid-June.

The second-largest Eskimo village in Alaska, Kotzebue is reached only by daily air service from Anchorage, Nome and Fairbanks. Arrangements for bush plane flights over the surrounding tundra and to the Kobuk River for hunting and fishing expeditions can be made at the airport. Nana Museum of the Arctic, near the airport, offers a slide show and a tour.

City of Kotzebue Information: P.O. Box 46, Kotzebue, AK 99752; phone (907) 442-3401.

LAKE CLARK NATIONAL PARK AND PRESERVE (F-5)

Elevations in the park and preserve range from sea level along Cook Inlet to 10,197 ft. at Mount Redoubt. Refer to AAA maps for additional elevation information.

Ice and fire meet in this mountainous crossroads of almost 4 million acres. The Pacific crust grinds beneath the North American plate, creating the Chigmit Mountains, a jagged array of spires and two steaming volcanoes, Mount Redoubt and Mount Iliamna. Mount Redoubt, the more active, last erupted in December 1989; it continues to emit steam and, less frequently, ash.

Covered by massive ice fields, the seemingly impenetrable Chigmit Mountains are formed by the linkage of two great ranges, the Alaska and the Aleutian. Together the ranges divide the park into distinct areas: the eastern flank's coastal plain bordering Cook Inlet and the lake and tundra region on the western flank. Lake Clark, 50 miles long, juts in from the southwest.

Moisture abounds along the park's coastal area, which is characterized by rocky cliffs along its southern portion, giving way to tidal marshes and grasslands in the north. In contrast to the luxuriant alder thickets and Sitka spruce along Cook Inlet, the park's western landscape is distinguished by lakes, boreal forests and rolling tundra highlands.

Numerous glacier-fed rivers and creeks are channeled through Lake Clark, creating one of the richest sockeye salmon spawning grounds in the world. The park was created primarily to protect this fruitful breeding area.

Although the park is open all year, most people visit during the peak of the summer season, late June through August. Even in summer months, weather conditions vary in the interior; it is advisable to bring protection against insects as well as clothing for sunny, wet or freezing weather. Visitors should outfit themselves in Kenai, Homer or Anchorage, as the communities closer to the park have limited supplies.

For anglers the rivers and lakes on the park's western side provide a variety of trophy-size fish, including salmon, arctic grayling and trout. A 2- to 3-mile trail to Tanalian Falls and Kontrashibuna Lake is accessible from Port Alsworth, near Lake Clark. The open foothills are ideal for backpacking. River-running also is popular on the Mulchatna, Tlikakila and Chilikadrotna rivers, all federally designated wild and scenic rivers.

As there are no roads in the park, access is almost exclusively by air. Most travelers charter aircraft; the closest airport is south of the park in Iliamna. A 1- to 2-hour flight from Anchorage, Homer or Kenai will provide access to most points within the park and preserve.

The National Park Service facility is at Port Alsworth and contains a visitor center with displays regarding natural history topics. While there are minimal National Park facilities— staffed patrol cabins at Telaquana Lake, Twin Lakes, Crescent Lake and Chinitna Bay—there are a number of private lodges and cabins in the park.

For information about accommodations as well as a list of outfitters and maps, write the Superintendent, Lake Clark National Park and Preserve, 4230 University Dr., Suite 311, Anchorage, AK 99508; phone (907) 271-3751. *See Recreation Chart.*

The Last Great Race

To commemorate the 1925 event in which 20 mushers relayed serum to Nome to save children who contracted diphtheria, the first Iditarod Race took place on Mar. 3, 1973.

Beginning in Anchorage and culminating in Nome, the race trail covers some 1,000 miles of terrain, takes between 9-17 days to complete and can reach temperatures of minus 60 F.

In preparation for the great race, the trail is broken and marked with

reflector tape, and checkpoints are chosen where teams stop to eat and rest. Since it's not feasible for mushers to carry all of their provisions in their sleds, the bulk of food and supplies is shipped to the checkpoints prior to the race.

To aid in endurance, dogs ingest 5,000 calories or more each day, gobbling such delicacies as moose, caribou or even seal meat. Concern for the dogs' health is strong: Booties are worn for paw protection, and about 25 veterinarians man the checkpoints to examine each dog.

While teams may begin the race with as many as 16 dogs, some drop from the race. "Dropped dogs"—dogs that do not finish the race due to dehydration, flu or fatigue—are carried to the nearest checkpoint and flown back to Anchorage. A musher must finish the race with at least five dogs.

Teams travel at night as well as during the day, and dogs rest about 10-12 hours per 24-hour period. But mushers don't enjoy that luxury: Responsible for feeding and caring for the dogs (including changing their booties every 100 miles), they rarely sleep more than 2 hours per night.

The goal? Nome's Burled Arch on Front Street. At this finish line, teams are greeted by cheering crowds and the sounding of the city's fire siren.

MISTY FIORDS NATIONAL MONUMENT (H-12)

East of Ketchikan and within the Tongass National Forest *(see place listing p. 315)*, Misty Fiords National Monument covers about 3,580 square miles of wilderness. The area is accessible by float plane from Ketchikan and other communities near the national forest. An information center and cruises to the monument are available in Ketchikan *(see place listing p. 304)*.

Behm Canal, a deep inlet of the Pacific Ocean, leads to the interior of the monument, where Walker Cove and Rudyerd Bay are surrounded by rock walls that rise 3,000 feet. Geological features include mineral springs, 237-foot-tall New Eddystone Rock, 3,150-foot-tall Punchbowl Face, lava flows, five major rivers and hundreds of small streams. The region receives more than 120 inches of precipitation each year. Bald eagles, brown and black bears, wolves and mountain goats inhabit the area; whales, porpoises, seals and sea lions can be sighted in Behm Canal or in the ocean nearby.

Recreational activities include backpacking, picnicking, birdwatching, hunting, fishing and crabbing. Rustic cabins are available for $25-$45 per day; reservations may be made by calling Reserve America, (877) 444-6777. For further information contact the Monument Ranger, Misty Fiords National Monument, Tongass National Forest, 3031 Tongass, Ketchikan, AK 99901; phone (907) 225-2148.

NOME (D-3) pop. 3,500, elev. 13′

Gold on the beaches at Nome lured thousands to the remote shores of the Bering Sea in 1898. At the height of the gold rush, 20,000 people lived in Nome, once the largest settlement in Alaska. Nome's name is said to be a melding of the words "No Name."

On the Seward Peninsula, Nome is the judicial and commercial center of northwestern Alaska and the main supply point for nearby mining districts and Eskimo villages. The city is accessible daily by plane from Anchorage or Fairbanks. Charter flights are available to various Eskimo villages as well as Provideniya, Russia, Nome's sister city.

A diphtheria epidemic in 1925 threatened the town, and the necessary serum was delivered by dog team, thus creating the Iditarod Trail Race. The race, which begins in Anchorage *(see place listing p. 280)* in early March, encompasses treacherous climbs, river passages and bone-chilling blizzards. Mushers cross the finish line in Nome, exhausted but invigorated by cheers from supporters lining the chute on Front Street.

One of the activities during the final week of the race is the Bering Sea Ice Classic, a six-hole golf tournament that is played on the frozen Bering Sea.

The Midnight Sun Festival celebrates the summer solstice, the longest day of the year with almost a full-day of sunlight. The June 21st festival lasts several days and includes a parade, softball games, re-enactments of gold-rush era bank robberies and The Nome River Raft Race.

Nome Convention and Visitors Bureau: P.O. Box 240-AAA, Nome, AK 99762; phone (907) 443-5535.

CARRIE MCLAIN MEMORIAL MUSEUM is at 200 E. Front St. The museum displays Eskimo art, archeological artifacts and memorabilia from Nome's gold rush years. Highlighted until fall 1999 is "Alaska Gold: Life on the New Frontier 1898-1906." Daily noon-8, June-Sept.; Tues.-Sat. noon-6, rest of year. Closed holidays. Free. Phone (907) 443-6630.

PALMER (C-11) pop. 2,900, elev. 240'

The peaks of the Chugach and Talkeetna mountains rise above Palmer, a city surrounded by the lush pastures and dairy and vegetable farms of the fertile Matanuska Valley, where cabbages can grow to weigh more than 70 pounds. A drive to Wasilla *(see place listing p. 317)* provides a good view of the valley and its farms. The Matanuska Agricultural Experimental Farm, 7 miles southwest, welcomes visitors.

Palmer lies near the the intersection of the Glenn and George Parks highways (SRs 1 and 3), both of which are scenic highways. An interesting drive is along a narrow, rough, winding road that follows Willow Creek through formerly rich gold areas. The road crosses Hatcher Pass en route to Willow.

Palmer Visitor and Information Center: Valley Way between Fireweed and Elmwood, Box 115, Palmer, AK 99645; phone (907) 745-2880.

Self-guiding tours: Brochures describing a walking tour of downtown Palmer are available at the Visitor and Information Center.

INDEPENDENCE MINE STATE HISTORICAL PARK, 19 mi. n. on Hatcher Pass Rd., is a 761-acre park in the 221,000-acre Hatcher Pass region. The park preserves 15 buildings and numerous artifacts from its heyday as a gold boom town in the 1930s and 1940s. The history of the mine is chronicled in a museum and at the visitor center. Walking trails lead visitors past many of the mine camp's buildings, including bunkhouses, warehouses, the commissary and mess halls. Guided tours are available.

Park open daily. Visitor center open daily 11-7, June 15-Labor Day; Sat.-Sun. 11-7, day after Labor Day-Sept. 15. Guided tours are given Mon.-Fri. at 1:30 and 3:30, Sat.-Sun. at 1:30, 3:30 and 4:30, the second week of June-Labor Day. Admission $5 per private vehicle. Guided tours $3; senior citizens and under 10, $2. Phone (907) 745-2827 or 745-3975.

MUSK OX FARM, 2 mi. n. at Milepost 50.1 on the Glenn Hwy., is said to be the only musk ox domestication project in the world. The shaggy creatures are valued for their fine underwool called "qiviut." Eskimos knit the hair, eight times warmer by weight than wool, into hats and scarves. Guided tours offer insight into the animal's history and behavior and allow observation from fenced walkways. Daily 10-6, mid-May to late Sept. Admission $8; over 65 and ages 13-18, $6.50; ages 6-12, $5. Phone (907) 745-4151.

RECREATIONAL ACTIVITIES
White-water Rafting

- SAVE **Nova** is on Glenn Hwy. at Milepost 76.5. Write P.O. Box 1129, Chickaloon, AK 99674. Trips depart daily May-Sept.; dates and times vary. Other activities are offered. Phone (907) 745-5753 or (800) 746-5753.

PETERSBURG (H-11)
pop. 3,200, elev. 28'

Petersburg, at the north end of Mitkof Island, is an Alaska Marine Highway port. In 1897 Norwegian Peter Buschmann decided to build a cannery on Mitkof Island at the head of picturesque Wrangell Narrows, but first he had to build a sawmill to supply lumber for the cannery.

The cannery at the north end of Nordic Drive was completed in 1900; the facility packed 32,750 cases of salmon during its first production year. Now Petersburg Fisheries, the firm is a pioneer in Alaska's expanding bottom-fishing and shrimping industries.

Nicknamed "Little Norway," Petersburg boasts brightly painted wooden houses decorated with hand-painted floral designs, a traditional craft called rosemaling.

Among the nearby points of interest is Le Conte Glacier, an active tidewater glacier south of Petersburg; it can be reached via chartered plane, helicopter or boat. In nearby Frederick Sound whale-watching is popular; the area is home to orca and humpback whales as well as other sea mammals.

Petersburg Visitor Information Center: First and Fram sts., P.O. Box 810, Petersburg, AK 99833; phone (907) 772-4636.

CLAUSEN MEMORIAL MUSEUM, 203 Fram St., features exhibits about commercial fishing and canning, a dugout Tlinkit Indian canoe, tools and artifacts. A "Fisk" fountain and a 126.5-pound king salmon, said to be a world record catch, also are on display. Guided tours are available. Mon.-Sat. 10-4:30, May 1-Sept. 10; Wed. and Sat. 12:30-4, rest of year. Closed Jan. 1, Thanksgiving and Dec. 25. Admission $2, under 12 free. Phone (907) 772-3598.

SEWARD (D-11) pop. 2,700, elev. 70'

Named for William H. Seward, who negotiated the purchase of Alaska, Seward is an ice-free port in a setting of great beauty. At the northeast end of a bay named Resurrection by Russians who arrived in its waters on Easter, the city is surrounded by lush, tall mountains and ice fields.

Charter boats and planes can be hired for fishing, hunting and sightseeing trips. Seward is the southern terminus of the Seward Highway, a scenic highway that extends north to Anchorage through an alpine terrain of glaciers and lakes. Seward also is the main access point to Kenai Fjords National Park *(see place listing p. 303)*, which includes Exit Glacier, one of the few accessible glaciers.

Seward Community Library at 5th Avenue and Adams Street shows movies and slides of the havoc wreaked by the 1964 Good Friday earthquake.

Seward Chamber of Commerce: P.O. Box 749, Seward, AK 99664; phone (907) 224-8051.

Self-guiding tours: Guides containing information about a walking tour are available at the chamber of commerce office on Seward Highway or at the Information Center, 3rd Avenue and Jefferson Street.

ALASKA SEALIFE CENTER, Seward Hwy. (SR 9) at Milepost 0, is dedicated to preserving the ocean kingdom through research, rehabilitation and education. Highlights include tanks containing sea mammals and birds in their underwater habitats, including the Stellar sea lion, harbor seal and puffin. Exhibits range from the 1989 Exxon Valdez Oil Spill and Alaska Water Gallery to the interactive tidepool touch tank and salmon fish ladder. A laboratory features discovery programs. Allow 1 hour, 30 minutes minimum. Daily 8-8, holidays 9-3. Admission $12.50; ages 7-12, $10. AE, DS, MC, VI. Phone (907) 224-6300 or (800) 224-2525. *See color ad p. 311.*

IDIDARIDE SUMMER SLED DOG TOURS is off Seward Hwy. (SR 9) milepost 3.6, 1 mi. w. on Exit Glacier Rd, .2 mi. n. on Old Exit Glacier Rd. (gravel road) following signs. An experienced Iditarod racer offers a summer version of a sled dog ride aboard a wheeled sled during a 2-mile trip through Box Canyon. Visitors can tour the dog kennel to socialize with the husky puppies and witness a sled dog training demonstration. A videotape also is available. Allow 1 hour, 30 minutes minimum. Daily 8-7, May-Sept. Admission $27.50; ages 2-11, $15. MC, VI. Phone (907) 224-8607.

KENAI COASTAL TOURS, departing from the Seward small boat harbor, offers narrated sightseeing cruises of the coastline of Kenai Fjords National Park and Resurrection Bay. It is possible to see such wildlife as mountain goats, puffins, bald eagles, sea otters, sea lions and humpback and killer whales. A 6-hour National

Park tour stops at a tidewater glacier and the Chiswell Islands, and a Resurrection Bay Wildlife tour stops at a lodge on Fox Island. Inquire about weather policies. Arrive 1 hour before departure. For reservations write Kenai Coastal Tours, 513 W. 4th Ave., Dept. A3, Anchorage, AK 99501.

Trips depart daily Mar.-Nov. National Park tour departs at 11:30; wildlife tour departs at noon. National park tour fare $99; under 12, $49. Wildlife tour fare $54; under 12, $27. Transportation by air, railroad or van is available from Anchorage for an additional fee. Reservations are recommended. AE, DS, MC, VI. Phone (907) 277-2131 or (800) 770-9119.

SAVE ★ **KENAI FJORDS TOURS**, which depart from the small boat harbor, offers glacier and wildlife cruises into the waters that surround Kenai Fjords National Park (*see place listing p. 303*). A variety of marine mammals and sea birds inhabit the area. Active tidewater glaciers can be seen. Inquire about weather policies. Meals are included. For reservations write Kenai Fjords Tours, P.O. Box 1889, Seward, AK 99664.

Tours depart daily, late Mar.-Nov. Six-hour Kenai Fjords National Park tours depart at 8, 11:30 and 3. Northwestern Fjords tours last 9.5 hours and depart at 9. Three-hour Resurrection Bay wildlife tours depart at 8 and 2:30. Fox Island Salmon Bake cruises last 5 or 7.5 hours and depart at 10 and

noon. Park tour $99; under 12, $49. Fjord tour $139; under 12, $69. Bay tour $54; under 12, $27. Salmon Bake cruises $74 ($115 for longer tour); under 12, $37 ($57 for longer tour). AE, DS, MC, VI. Phone (907) 224-8068 or (800) 478-8068. *See color ad & p. 284 & p. 303.*

SAVE **MAJOR MARINE TOURS** depart 1 blk. e. of Seward Hwy. at the boat harbor, boardwalk #2. Narrated sightseeing cruises visit Kenai Fjords, Chiswell Islands and Kenai Fjords National Park. Bald eagles, otters, porpoises and sea lions can be seen. Food is available. Inquire about weather policies. Cruises depart daily, early May-late Sept. Half-day cruise departs at 1 and 6, full-day cruise departs at 11:30. Half-day fare $49; ages 3-11, $24. Full-day fare $99; ages 3-11, $49. DS, MC, VI. Phone (907) 274-7300 or (800) 764-7300. *See color ad p. 310.*

SAVE **RENOWN CHARTERS & TOURS** offers cruises departing from bldg. #5 of the small boat harbor on the boardwalk. Three tours are available: a 2.5-hour wildlife and glacier cruise in Resurrection Bay; a 4-hour whale-watching cruise to the Aialik Cape; or a 6-hour cruise into Kenai Fjords National Park. Lunch is included on all tours.

Wildlife and glacier cruise departs at noon, 3 and 6, mid-May to mid-Sept.; at noon, rest of year. Whale-watching cruise departs at 10:30 and

3, mid-May to mid-Sept. National park cruise departs at 10:30, mid-May to mid-Sept. Reservations are recommended. Check-in is 30 minutes prior to departure. Wildlife and glacier cruise fare $49; whale-watching cruise fare $59; national park cruise fare $99. AE, DS, MC, VI. Phone (907) 224-3806 or 272-1961. *See color ad p. 286.*

SCENIC MOUNTAIN AIR (FLIGHTSEEING) operates wheeled planes from Seward Airport and float planes from Trail Lake in Moose Pass. Among sights on the varied tours are Harding Icefield, Columbia Glacier and Mount McKinley. Flying/fishing and flying/hiking tours also are available. Flights depart daily 8 a.m.-10 p.m., May 1-early Oct. (weather permitting). Fares $69-$249, depending on weight, size of party and tour type. DS, MC, VI. Phone (907) 288-3646.

SEWARD HISTORICAL SOCIETY MUSEUM, 336 3rd Ave., has exhibits about the main events in Seward's history. A collection of native baskets and ivory carvings is displayed. Daily 9-5, May-Sept.; otherwise varies. Admission $2; under 18, 50c. Phone (907) 224-3902.

RECREATIONAL ACTIVITIES
Hiking
- **Glacier Quest Eco-Tours**, 205 4th St. Write P.O. Box 806, Seward, AK 99664. Daily May-Oct.; otherwise by request. Other activities are offered. Phone (907) 224-5770 or (877) 444-5770.

Summer Activities
- **Alaska Kayak Camping Co.,** depart from Lowell Point or Bear Lake. Write P.O. Box 1101, Seward, AK 99664. Trips depart daily May-Sept. Phone (907) 224-6056.

SITKA (H-10) pop. 8,600

Surrounded by high peaks and small wooded islands, historic Sitka is accessible by air or the Alaska Marine Highway.

In 1804 Russians led by Alexander Baranov established a settlement on the site of an ancient Tlingit (KLINK-it) village; that settlement became the capital of Russian America. Originally named New Archangel, it was a thriving port of nearly 3,000 when San Francisco was just a mission village. Castle Hill marks the site of Baranov's headquarters and commemorates the 1867 ceremony that transferred ownership of Alaska from Russia to the United States.

The colorfully costumed New Archangel Dancers perform Russian dances in the Harrigan Centennial Hall auditorium when large ships are in port in summer. For cruise ship and ferry passengers, Sitka Tours offers a short bus tour of Sitka, which includes guide service and round-trip transportation from the port. Boat tours to view wildlife and the surrounding area also are available.

Sitka Convention and Visitors Bureau: Dept. A, Box 1226, Sitka, AK 99835; phone (907) 747-5940.

ISABEL MILLER MUSEUM, in the Centennial Building, has exhibits about the Tlingit, Russian settlers, fishing, forestry and the Alaska Purchase. Tlingit basketry and wood carvings are exhibited. An 8-foot-square diorama depicts Sitka as it appeared in 1867, the time Alaska was transferred to the United States from Russia. Allow 30 minutes minimum. Daily 10-5, mid-May to late Sept.; Tues.-Sat. 10-noon and 1-4, rest of year. Donations. Phone (907) 747-6455.

SHELDON JACKSON MUSEUM is at 104 College Dr. on the Sheldon Jackson College campus. Housed in one of the first concrete structures built in Alaska, it is reputed to be the oldest continuing museum in Alaska. Displays of Eskimo, Aleut and Northwest Coast and Athabaskan Indian artifacts include pelts, sleds, kayaks, ceremonial masks, and tools and utensils of wood, bone and ivory. Allow 30 minutes minimum. Daily 9-5, mid-May to mid-Sept.; Tues.-Sat. 10-4, rest of year. Closed holidays. Admission $3, under 18 free. Phone (907) 747-8981.

★SITKA NATIONAL HISTORICAL PARK (H-10)

The 107-acre Sitka National Historical Park consists of two units: the fort site, 1 mile east of Sitka, and the Russian Bishop's House on Lincoln Street near Crescent Harbor. These sites commemorate the area's Tlingit (KLINK-it) Indian heritage, as well as its Russian legacy.

The fort was the site of the Battle of Sitka, fought in 1804 between the Kiksadi Tlingit Indians and the fur hunters and Aleut natives of the Russian-American Co. The battle marked the last major resistance by Alaskan natives to European domination.

The park consists of a temperate rain forest and a coastal intertidal area with 2 miles of trails. During August and September, visitors may view salmon spawning in Indian River, which flows through the park.

The park is noted for its fine collection of 28 Tlingit and Haida (HY-dah) totem poles, some of which are more than a century old. The visitor center contains exhibits and audiovisual presentations about the area's history and culture. In the Southeast Alaska Indian Cultural Center within the visitor center, skilled native artisans demonstrate traditional crafts. The center is open daily.

Visitor center open daily 8-5, mid-May through Sept. 30; Mon.-Fri. 8-5, rest of year. Free admission to park. Address inquiries to the Superintendent, Sitka National Historical Park, 106 Metlakatla St., Box 738, Sitka, AK 99835; phone (907) 747-6281.

THE RUSSIAN BISHOP'S HOUSE, on Lincoln St. across from Crescent Harbor, is a two-story log structure built in 1842. It is one of the last surviving colonial Russian buildings in North America. Restored to its 1853 appearance, the building reflects the influence of the Russian Orthodox Church and the traders of the Russian-American Co., who made Sitka the capital of colonial Russian America. The house served as a bishop's residence for some 130 years. Original furniture can be seen.

Allow 30 minutes minimum. Daily and holidays 9-1 and 2-5, May 15-Sept. 30; by appointment rest of year. Admission $3, under 12 free, family rate $6. Phone (907) 747-6281.

SKAGWAY (G-10) pop. 700, elev. 2'

During the icy winter of 1897-98 hordes of enthusiastic would-be prospectors who had heard of the Klondike gold strike swarmed ashore at Skagway. They assembled their gear and began the trek over treacherous mountains and down raging rivers to the Klondike. Within 3 months of the first gold strike, the settlement at Skagway grew from one cabin into a thriving city of more than 20,000 people. But the gold rush ended suddenly, and those who had come to Skagway moved on.

The notorious outlaw Jefferson R. "Soapy" Smith and Frank Reid, who represented the outraged citizenry, shot it out in a battle that cost both men their lives. Gold Rush Cemetery, 1.5 miles from town, contains the graves of both "Soapy" Smith and Frank Reid.

A stop on many summer cruises along the Inside Passage, Skagway is the northern terminus of the Alaska Marine Highway. Sightseeing opportunities include visits to Reid's Falls and flower gardens; tours of the city and the harbor; flightseeing tours to Glacier Bay, gold rush trails and the Juneau Ice Cap; motorcoach excursions to Dyea and Carcross, Yukon Territory; and hiking trips to AB Mountain and the Dewey Lakes.

Skagway Chamber of Commerce: P.O. Box 194, Skagway, AK 99840; phone (907) 983-1898.

THE DAYS OF '98 SHOW WITH SOAPY SMITH, presented at the Eagles' Hall at Sixth and Broadway, includes a stage show with original songs, a cancan line, a historic shoot-out and mock gambling. Mock gambling nightly at 7. Stage shows daily at 10:30, 2 and 8, mid-May to late Sept. Evening shows $14; ages 3-12, $7. Matinees $12; ages 3-12, $6. Phone (907) 983-2545.

KLONDIKE GOLD RUSH NATIONAL HISTORICAL PARK includes Chilkoot Trail and White Pass, over which each prospector was required to pack nearly a ton of food and gear on his journey to fortune. A visitor center in a restored railroad depot at Broadway and Second Avenue offers exhibits about Skagway during the gold rush era, the Mascot Saloon and the Moore prop-

erty. False-front buildings and boardwalks along Broadway in Skagway comprise a historic district. Information about Chilkoot Trail conditions is available at the Trail Center; for reservations to hike the trail, phone (800) 661-0486. A $10 fee is required for all reservations, and it's a good idea to reserve a spot during summer.

Ranger-guided tours and slide presentations are offered, and a Gold Rush orientation film is presented hourly in the visitor center. Visitor center daily 8-8, June-Aug.; 8-6, in May and Sept.; otherwise varies. Trail Center daily 8-5, mid-May to Sept. Park free. Fee to hike Chilkoot Trail $35 Canadian; under 17, $17.50. Phone (907) 983-2921 for the visitor center or 983-9234 for the trail center.

TRAIL OF '98 MUSEUM, in Arctic Brotherhood Hall on Broadway between Second and Third sts., has displays pertaining to Alaskan history and native cultures, including a Tlingit war canoe, photographs, documents, gold rush relics and native artifacts. Daily 9-5, May-Sept. Admission $2, students $1. Phone (907) 983-2420.

★ **WHITE PASS & YUKON ROUTE,** 2nd Ave. and Spring St. at Broadway, chugs across mountain rivers and chasms during full-day and half-day narrated narrow-gauge rides on a rail line built in 1898 to carry people and supplies to the Klondike gold rush. Passengers travel round trip in a period parlor car to the summit of White Pass, past granite gulches, cascading waterfalls, Lake Bennett, B.C., and spectacular scenery. A narrator tells the story of the stampede north into the gold fields and through some of the most rugged terrain in the United States and Canada.

Ticket office open daily 8-5. Trips depart daily at 8:30 and 1 (also Tue.-Wed. at 4:30), mid-May to mid-Sept. Fare $78; ages 3-12, $39. AE, DS, MC, VI. Phone (907) 983-2217 or (800) 343-7373.

DID YOU KNOW

The northernmost region of Alaska receives almost 3 months of continuous sunlight.

SOLDOTNA (D-11) pop. 3,500

Soldotna's location on the Kenai Peninsula at the junction of Sterling and Kenai Spur highways has ensured its steady growth since homesteading began in 1947. World War II veterans were among the first homesteaders; they were given a 90-day preference right in choosing and filing for land.

The area is rich with opportunities for year-round recreation—hiking, fishing, camping, canoeing and ice fishing are favored activities. Nearby Kenai River yields record catches of salmon and rainbow trout.

Soldotna Chamber of Commerce and Visitor Information Center: 44790 Sterling Hwy., Soldotna, AK 99669; phone (907) 262-9814.

KENAI NATIONAL WILDLIFE REFUGE, with its headquarters in Soldotna, covers about 1,970,000 acres. The refuge was established in 1941 by President Franklin D. Roosevelt to preserve the area's large moose population. Other wildlife include Dall sheep, coyotes, black bears and bald eagles. Fishing and hunting are subject to state and federal regulations. Boat ramps, trails and camping and picnic facilities are available. The refuge is open all year, except when its roads are impassable. Phone (907) 262-7021. *See the AAA Western Canada and Alaska CampBook.*

Visitor Center, 1 mi. s.e. of the Kenai River Bridge on Ski Hill Rd., exhibits wildlife dioramas and presents films. Mon.-Fri. 8-4:30, Sat.-Sun. 9-6, June 1-Labor Day.

STERLING (D-10)
pop. 1,800, elev. 198'

RECREATIONAL ACTIVITIES
Fishing

- **Great Alaska Fish Camp,** 33881 Sterling Hwy., Sterling, AK 99672. Trips are offered mid-May through Sept. 30. Other activities are offered. Phone (800) 544-2261. *See color ad p. 287.*

Summer Activities

- **Alaska Adventu-Res,** 33881 Sterling Hwy., Sterling, AK 99672. Various types of trips are offered mid-May through Sept. 30. Phone (800) 262-9666.

TALKEETNA (C-11)
pop. 300, elev. 355'

Situated at the confluence of the Talkeetna, Susitna and Chulitna rivers, Talkeetna takes its name from the Tanaina Indian word for "river of plenty." The village was an important supply station for gold prospectors from the late 1800s to 1940, but is now a popular staging area for outdoors enthusiasts.

Talkeetna Chamber of Commerce: P.O. Box 334, Talkeetna, AK 99676; phone (907) 733-2330.

Self-guiding tours: A map of a downtown walking tour is available at Talkeetna Historical Society Museum *(see attraction listing)* and the visitor center next to Village Park on Main Street.

SAVE **K-2 AVIATION,** on Talkeetna Spur Rd., offers flightseeing tours of sites within Denali National Park. Various combinations of tours are offered, such as flying/fishing, flying/mining and flying/rafting. Overnight trips, walking tours and customized package tours also are available. Bears, caribou, Dall sheep and moose are visible on many of the trips. Daily 7 a.m.-9 p.m., May-Sept. Admission $85-$1,800 (depending on type of tour). Reservations are required. AE, MC, VI. Phone (907) 733-2291 or (800) 764-2291.

SAVE **MUSEUM OF NORTHERN ADVENTURE,** on Main St. across from the post office, recounts the human and natural history of northern Alaska with dioramas, life-size wax figures, sound effects, photographs and newspaper articles. A trophy room contains big-game and other wildlife taxidermy. Allow 30 minutes minimum. Daily 11-7, mid-May to mid-Sept. Admission $3.50;

over 65, $3; under 13, $2.50; family rate $10. AE, MC, VI. Phone (907) 733-3999.

TALKEETNA AIR TAXI, departing from the airport on Talkeetna Spur Rd., offers flightseeing tours of the area. Scenic views from the air include Denali National Park, Mount McKinley and nearby glaciers. Other activities—such as white-water rafting, mountain climbing, hiking and camping—also are offered. Daily 8-8, May-Sept.; 9-4, rest of year. Fare $90-$175. DS, MC, VI. Phone (907) 733-2218 or (800) 533-2219. *See color ad.*

TALKEETNA HISTORICAL SOCIETY MUSEUM, in four buildings 1 blk. s. of Main St., displays a wealth of local history memorabilia within re-creations of a log cabin, a one-room schoolhouse and a railroad depot. Of interest is a large-scale model of Mount McKinley and the surrounding area. Allow 30 minutes minimum. Daily 10:30-5:30, May-Sept.; Fri.-Sun. 11-5 in Apr. and Oct.; Sat.-Sun. 11-5, rest of year. Admission $2, under 12 free. Phone (907) 733-2487.

TOK (B-12) pop. 900

On the Alaska Highway 94 miles from the Canadian border, Tok is a trade center for nearby Athabascan villages. Some claim that Tok's name derives from the native word meaning "peace crossing"; others insist that the village was originally named Tokyo and shortened to Tok during World War II.

A center for dog breeding, training and mushing, Tok claims the title "Dog Capital of Alaska."

Tok Chamber of Commerce: P.O. Box 389, Tok, AK 99780; phone (907) 883-5887 or 883-5775 in summer.

ALASKA PUBLIC LANDS INFORMATION CENTER, jct. of the Alaska and Glenn hwys., includes displays and photographs of Alaskan animals, a historical timeline, a large map of Alaska with illuminated points of interest and an information center. Daily 8-8, Memorial Day-Sept. 30; 8-4:30, rest of year. Closed holidays. Free. Phone (907) 883-5666 or 883-5667.

TETLIN NATIONAL WILDLIFE REFUGE is in e. central Alaska, directly s. of the Alaska Hwy. and n. of Wrangell-St. Elias National Park and Preserve. The gateway to Alaska, the refuge occupies 730,000 acres. More than 143 nesting birds and 47 migrants, including bald eagles, trumpeter swans and ospreys flock here. Black and grizzly bears, moose, wolves and caribous are permanent residents. The Tetlin Visitor Center is at Milepost 1229 on the Alaska Hwy.

Hunting and fishing are permitted. Two public campgrounds are operated by the refuge. Refuge open daily 24 hours. Free. Phone (907) 883-5312.

TONGASS NATIONAL FOREST (G-9)

Elevations in the forest range from sea level at the Pacific Ocean to 10,290 ft. at Mount Ratz. Refer to AAA maps for additional elevation information.

The largest of the national forests, Tongass National Forest covers about 17 million acres in southeastern Alaska. In 1907 Teddy Roosevelt created the forest, taking the name from the "Tongass" clan of Tlingit Indians that lived along the southern edge of the forest's present-day boundaries. It boasts more than 5 million acres of preserved wilderness, including Misty Fiords National Monument *(see place listing p. 308)* and Admiralty Island National Monument *(see place listing p. 280).*

Consisting mostly of islands, the forest also includes a mountainous mainland strip deeply cleft by rock-walled fiords, bays, inlets and channels with glaciers, ice fields and waterfalls. The abundant wildlife includes trumpeter swans, bald eagles and Alaskan brown (grizzly) bears. Licenses are required for hunting and fishing.

The Forest Service provides numerous cabins. Many rental cabins are near lakes and streams or high in the alpine meadows. Although a few can be reached by boat or trail, most are accessible only by charter plane from Annette Island, Craig, Juneau, Ketchikan, Petersburg, Sitka, Wrangell and Yakutat. Charter planes seating two to five people cost about $200-$250 an hour.

A $25-$45 per-party-per-night fee is charged for cabins. There is a 7-night limit May through September; a 10-night limit the rest of the year. Cabin permits are necessary and can be requested up to 180 days prior to use; full payment is required at the time the reservation is made. Forest information centers with exhibits, films and cabin reservation information are in Juneau *(see place listing p. 299)*, Ketchikan *(see place listing p. 304)* and Petersburg *(see place listing p. 309)*.

For further information write the Forest Service Information Center, 101 Egan Dr., Juneau, AK 99801 or the Southeast Alaska Visitor Center, 50 Main St., Ketchikan, AK 99901; phone (907) 586-8751 or 228-6220. *See Recreation Chart and the AAA Western Canada and Alaska CampBook.*

★ **MENDENHALL GLACIER—***see Juneau p. 301.*

VALDEZ (C-11) pop. 4,100, elev. 15′

Called the "Switzerland of Alaska," Valdez (val-DEES) is ringed by snowcapped mountains.

VISIT *Valdez* ALASKA

Whether you enjoy world class fishing, flightseeing, glacier cruises, good roads, tax-free shopping, or crossing Prince William Sound... Valdez provides the right activities for the perfect Alaska adventure.

For free information contact:
Valdez Convention & Visitors Bureau
800-770-5954 • 907-835-2984

www.alaska.net/~valdezak
Fax: 907-835-4845
P.O. Box 1603-AA • Valdez, AK 99686

As the northernmost ice-free port, the town was established in 1898 as an outfitting point for miners taking the hazardous pack trail over Valdez Glacier to the northern gold fields.

Access into Valdez is by scheduled air service, ferry or via the scenic Richardson Highway. Thompson Pass, Milepost 26 on Richardson Highway, offers a spectacular view of the Chugach Mountains, valley rivers and historic Keystone Canyon. Near Milepost 16 is scenic Bridal Veil and Horsetail falls. Also on the route is Worthington Glacier State Park at Milepost 29, which has walking trails. The foot of Valdez Glacier is accessible via Airport Road, 4 miles east.

Nearby glaciers in Prince William Sound include Blackstone, Mears, Shoup and Columbia. Cruises are available to Columbia, the second largest tidewater glacier in North America.

Because of heavy damage from the tsunami wave following the 1964 Good Friday earthquake, the town was moved 4 miles west to the stable site on Port Valdez. Valdez is the southern terminus for the TransAlaska Pipeline; crude oil is loaded on tankers at the port terminal and shipped to refineries.

Valdez Convention and Visitors Bureau: P.O. Box 1603-3A, Valdez, AK 99686; phone (907) 835-2984 or (800) 770-5954. *See color ad.*

ALYESKA PIPELINE MARINE TERMINAL TOUR departs from the downtown visitor center at 212 Titikien St. The 2-hour narrated bus tour visits the terminus of the 800-mile Alaska Pipeline. Visitors are permitted off the bus at an observation area. Tours depart daily at 10, 1 and 7:30, mid-May through Aug. 31 Admission $15; ages 6-12, $7.50. AE, CB, DS, MC, VI. Phone (907) 835-2686.

ERA HELICOPTERS FLIGHTSEEING TOURS departs from the Valdez Airport; free transportation is provided from area hotels. The narrated, 1- and 2-hour tours offer views of Prince William Sound and Columbia Glacier. Highlights include a landing beside Shoup Glacier, wildlife viewing in the sound or a landing on Growler Island. Sea otters, whales, bald eagles and seals can be seen. Heli-hiking excursions also are available.

Daily 8-6. Fare $171-$299. Flights require a minimum of four passengers. AE, DS, MC, VI. Phone (907) 835-2595, or (800) 843-1947.

[SAVE] **GRAY LINE PIPELINE TERMINAL TOUR,** departing from the Westmark-Valdez Hotel lobby, offers a 2-hour narrated bus tour of the outside facilities at the Valdez oil terminal of the Alyeska Pipeline Service Co., where Alaska's crude oil emerges from the pipeline for shipment by tanker to the "Lower 48." Sights include the oil storage tank farm, tanker berths and a monument dedicated to the 70,000 men and women who designed and built the Alaska Pipeline. Visitors are permitted to exit the bus at an observation area.

Write Gray Line of Alaska, 300 Elliott Ave. W., Dept. AAA, Seattle, WA 98119. Tours daily at 10 and 7, mid-May to mid-Sept. Fare $23; under 13, $11.50. Reservations are required. Phone (907) 277-5581 or (800) 544-2206.

STAN STEPHENS CRUISES, 3 blks. e. of jct. Richardson Hwy. and Meals St. at 100 Fidalgo Dr., offers 5.5- 8.5- and 10.5-hour narrated cruises on Prince William Sound to Columbia Glacier. The longer tour includes a stop at Growler Island Wilderness Camp for sightseeing and a buffet meal. An overnight camping trip to Growler Island and other packages also are available.

Trips depart daily, May-Sept. Fare $65-$110; ages 6-12, $46-$76. Reservations are recommended. AE, DS, MC, VI. Phone (907) 835-4731 or (800) 992-1297. *See color ad.*

VALDEZ MUSEUM, at 217 Egan Dr., has exhibits about pioneers, goldseekers, local history, glaciers and the pipeline as well as photographs of Valdez before and after the 1964 earthquake. A 1907 Ahrens firetruck and a Fresnel lighthouse lens also are featured. A model of the Valdez oil terminal is displayed, and an exhibit illustrates the effects and the clean up efforts of the *Exxon Valdez* oil spill of March 1989. A sea life exhibit features aquariums.

Each summer the museum presents a quilt exhibit. Allow 30 minutes minimum. Daily 9-6, Memorial Day-Labor Day; schedule varies rest of year. Admission $3, senior citizens $2.50, under 14 free. Phone (907) 835-2764.

WORTHINGTON GLACIER, about 30 mi. e. on the Richardson Hwy., is Alaska's most accessible glacier. Milepost 28.7 provides an excellent viewpoint; a road leads to the glacier. Camping at the foot of the glacier is permitted.

WASILLA (C-11) pop. 4,000

Founded in 1917, Wasilla is a growing community in the Matanuska-Susitna Valley named after a respected Athabascan Indian chief. Home to the Iditarod Trail Committee headquarters, the town has two warm-water lakes. Dorothy G. Page Museum on Main Street contains historical artifacts; the Old Wasilla Town Site behind the museum preserves Wasilla's first school, two log cabins, a smithy and the town's first public bath. Wasilla lies near the intersection of SRs 1 and 3, both of which are scenic highways.

Greater Wasilla Chamber of Commerce: 415 E. Railroad Ave., Wasilla, AK 99654; phone (907) 376-1299.

SAVE **MUSEUM OF ALASKA TRANSPORTATION AND INDUSTRY,** Milepost 47 on Parks Hwy., displays various items relating to Alaska's transportation and industrial history. Fifteen acres of outdoor exhibits include aircraft, boats, tractors, dog sleds, snowmobiles, farm implements, railroad cars, firetrucks, antique automobiles and memorabilia from early railroading days. Also featured are aviation photographs, vintage farm equipment and engines.

Steam train rides are given every third Saturday and holidays during summer. Picnicking is permitted. Daily 9-6, May-Sept.; Tues.-Sat. 9-5, rest of year. Admission $5; over 55 and ages 8-19, $4; family rate $12. Phone (907) 376-1211.

WHITTIER (D-11) pop. 200

MAJOR MARINE TOURS depart from the tour boat dock. A narrated sightseeing cruise tours 50 miles of the Prince William Sound, including Blackstone, Beloit and eight other glaciers. Bald eagles, otters, porpoises and sea lions can be seen. Inquire about weather policies. Allow 6 hours minimum. Departures daily at 11:45, mid-May to mid-Sept. Fare $99; under 11, $49. AE, DS, MC, VI. Phone (907) 274-7300 or (800) 764-7300.

SAVE **26 GLACIER CRUISE BY PHILLIPS' CRUISES,** which departs from the port of Whittier, offers a 5-hour narrated Catamaran cruise of Prince William Sound, particularly the College and Harriman fjords. Passengers also can view calving tidewater glaciers, mountains and wildlife, including seals, whales, sea otters and birds. For reservations write Phillips' Cruises, 519 W. Fourth Ave., Suite 100, Anchorage, AK 99501.

Allow a full day. Cruises depart daily early May-late Sept. Fare $119; ages 2-11, $49. Round-trip train fare from Portage is an additional $20. Motorcoach or rail service is offered from Anchorage at an additional cost. Reservations are recommended. AE, DS, MC, VI. Phone (907) 276-8023 or (800) 544-0529. *See color ad p. 284.*

WILLOW (C-11) pop. 300

SAVE **LUCKY HUSKY,** milepost 80 on Parks Hwy., offers an exciting ride in a 14-foot basket sled pulled by huskies and driven by an experienced musher. After the tour, visitors can view the kennels where a petting area is available. Fall tours in September last 30 minutes and mushers demonstrate how the lead dogs work on voice commands. Allow 30 minutes minimum. Daily 10-6, May-Sept.; by appointment rest of year. Fare $18. Fall tour $60. DS, MC, VI. Phone (907) 495-6470.

WRANGELL (H-11)
pop. 2,500, elev. 37′

Petroglyphs pecked into shale rock and elaborately carved totem poles, cedar monuments of the Stikine (STIK-een) and Tlingit (KLINK-it) Indians, are interesting aspects of Wrangell. Although European and American explorers visited the area in the late 1700s, Russians began trading here by 1811 and established a redoubt in Wrangell in 1834. The only Alaskan town to have existed under Russian, British and American rule, it also survived three gold rushes—In 1861, 1872 and 1898 the lure of riches brought a rush of miners and settlers.

Petroglyphs can be seen on a beach at the north end of Wrangell Island. Of undetermined age, some carvings face the water, others the shore or sky. They are best viewed at low tide. Nearby Anan Creek allows the opportunity to observe sea lions and seals and watch black bear fish for salmon.

Other attractions include the nine totem poles (some are replicas carved by the Civilian Conservation Corps in the late 1930s) on Shakes Island in Wrangell Harbor, as well as the four totem poles in Kiksadi Totem Park at Front and Episcopal streets. Artifacts are displayed in Chief Shakes Tribal House, also on the island. A large concentration of bald eagles gather in Wrangell from January to mid-April waiting for smelt to run up the Stikine River. A visitor center is in the Stikine Inn, at Front Street and Stikine Avenue.

Wrangell Chamber of Commerce: P.O. Box 49, Wrangell, AK 99929; phone (907) 874-3901 or (800) 367-9745.

WRANGELL MUSEUM, 4 blks. s. of the ferry terminal, on the ground floor of the Community

Center on Church St., contains local natural history and mineral displays, petroglyphs, original totems and a collection of basketry, beadwork, stone tools and other artifacts crafted by native peoples. Also featured are representations of other cultures that influenced the settlement of the area. Of interest are the original carved houseposts from the Bear Tribal House. An extensive photograph collection is also available.

Allow 30 minutes minimum. Mon.-Fri. 10-5, Sat. 1-5, other times when cruise ships and ferries are in port, May-Sept.; Tues.-Fri. 10-noon and 1-4, rest of year. Admission $2, under 16 free. Phone (907) 874-3770.

WRANGELL-ST. ELIAS NATIONAL PARK AND PRESERVE (C-12,F-8)

Elevations in the park and preserve range from sea level at the Gulf of Alaska to 18,008 ft. at Mount St. Elias. Refer to AAA maps for additional elevation information.

The country's largest national park, Wrangell-St. Elias National Park and Preserve is a place of overpowering dimensions, embracing an area larger than Massachusetts, Rhode Island and Connecticut combined; glaciers five times the size of Manhattan; and nine of the 16 highest peaks in North America.

In this 13-million-acre park, the collision of two continental plates has produced some of the world's highest coastal ranges. Forming a barrier along the Gulf of Alaska are the Chugach Mountains, and paralleling them to the north are the Wrangell Mountains.

Between these two ranges are the St. Elias Mountains, extending like the stem of the letter "Y" into Canada's Kluane National Park. Atop these towering peaks are ice fields so immense that they act as a natural cooling system, affecting areas as far south as Chicago and the Central Plains.

As imposing as its ice fields are, it was another commodity traded by the Ahtna Dene or "people of the Copper River" that caught the world's attention. These and other tribes forged tools of locally mined copper. The first person of European descent to verify the source of the copper trading was Lt. Henry Allen, who in 1885 explored much of Alaska's interior.

Fifteen years later two miners discovered the malachite cliffs above the Kennicott Glacier, which became one of the world's richest sources of copper. The subsequent founding of the Kennecott Mine became one of the most significant events in Alaska's history: The great wealth and development it spawned affected not only Alaska

but the entire nation. Currently the ruined mine is all that remains of this immense enterprise.

Legacies of the Kennecott Mine and the Yukon gold fields are some of the area's roads, which provide limited access to the park. One of Alaska's oldest roadways is the Richardson Highway, which was opened during the gold rush in 1899 and was the first all-Alaska route to the Yukon gold fields. Both the Richardson and Glenn highways follow the curve of the park's western boundary and offer several spectacular views of 12,010-foot Mount Drum, 14,163-foot Mount Wrangell and 16,237-foot Mount Sanford.

Two other roads penetrate the park's interior—the Chitina-McCarthy and the Nabesna. Both of these gravel roads offer good views of the mountains and are convenient jumping-off places for hiking and river-running. The 60-mile McCarthy Road follows an abandoned railroad bed. Visitors should allow a minimum of 3 hours to drive between Chitina and McCarthy. Before using either of these routes, check with the ranger stations in Slana and Chitina.

The park's visitor center, 3 miles north of Copper Center on Old Richardson Highway, provides trip-planning assistance and information about park activities. Fishing, hiking, rafting and wildlife- viewing, especially of the park's large population of Dall sheep, are just some of the activities pursued in the park.

For more information write the Superintendent, Wrangell-St. Elias National Park and Preserve, P.O. Box 439, Copper Center, AK 99573; phone (907) 822-5234. *See Recreation Chart.*

YUKON-CHARLEY RIVERS NATIONAL PRESERVE (B-12,D-8)

Elevations in the preserve range from 600 ft. on the Yukon River where it leaves the preserve near Circle to 6,435 ft. in the Cirque Lakes area on the Charley River drainage. Refer to AAA maps for additional elevation information.

More than 140 miles of the Yukon River and the entire watershed of the Charley River are encompassed within the 2.5 million acres of the Yukon-Charley Rivers National Preserve. John McPhee remarked in his book "Coming into the Country" that New Jersey could easily fit into this vast emptiness between Eagle and Circle.

Although only two year-round residents now live within the the preserve's boundaries, it was not always so sparsely populated. During the gold rush, the Yukon—a summer waterway and winter highway—was thronged with people who briefly transformed such communities as Circle into the "Paris of the North." This rough-and-tumble gold rush region was the grist of Robert Service's poetry and Jack London's stories.

Now quiet has returned, and where riverboats once departed from Eagle, river runners make the 5- to 10-day float down the river to Circle. One of the pleasures of this trip is the opportunity to see Peregrine falcons, an endangered species who make their home in the bluffs along the river. Hikers can catch a glimpse of caribou and Dall sheep in the preserve's upland regions and moose in the lowlands.

The Taylor and Steese highways are the primary summer access routes to the national preserve, terminating respectively in Eagle and Circle just outside the preserve's boundaries. The scenic portion of the Taylor Highway from Chicken to Eagle runs through mountains, rolling tundra and river valleys. Most people, however, reach the park by boat or float on the Yukon River and its tributaries.

The preserve has no roads and no established trails or maintained public airstrips. Four public-use cabins are available on a first-come, first-served basis. Food service, basic supplies, lodgings and charter boat and air service are available during the summer months in nearby Eagle and Circle. A list of authorized guides can be obtained from the preserve headquarters and visitor center in Eagle.

In addition, the Bureau of Land Management administers Fort Egbert and a campground in Eagle (*see the AAA Western Canada and Alaska CampBook*). A visitor center, open Mon.-Fri. 8-5, Memorial Day-Labor Day, can be contacted at P.O. Box 167, Eagle, AK 99738; phone (907) 547-2233. For more information write the Superintendent, Yukon-Charley Rivers National Preserve, P.O. Box 74718, Fairbanks, AK 99707-4718. *See Recreation Chart.*

Alberta

AIRDRIE —See Calgary p. 354.

ATHABASCA pop. 2,300

—— LODGING ——

BEST WESTERN ATHABASCA INN Phone: (780)675-2294
(AAA) (SAVE) All Year 1P: $89-$109 2P: $99-$119 XP: $10 F17
◆◆◆ **Location:** 1 km s on Hwy 2. 5211 41 Ave T9S 1A5. Fax: 780/675-3890. **Terms:** Small pets only, $10 fee.
Motor Inn **Facility:** 65 rooms. Split level building on sloping terrain, newly renovated guest rooms are nicely appointed
and well-equipped. 4 stories, no elevator; interior corridors; whirlpool. **Dining:** Restaurant, coffee shop; 6
am-10 pm; $6-$19; cocktails; nightclub. **Services:** winter plug-ins. **All Rooms:** extended cable TV. **Cards:** AE,
CB, DI, DS, JC, MC, VI. **Special Amenities:** Free local telephone calls and free newspaper.
(See color ad p 324 & below)

BANFF pop. 6,100

—— LODGINGS ——

BANFF CARIBOU LODGE Phone: (403)762-5887
(AAA) Property failed to provide current rates
◆◆◆ **Location:** Banff Ave at Marmot St, opposite Rotary Park. 521 Banff Ave T0L 0C0 (PO Box 279).
Motor Inn Fax: 403/762-5918. **Terms:** [AP], [BP], [CP] & [MAP] meal plans; check-in 4 pm; cancellation fee imposed;
package plans. **Facility:** 200 rooms. Impressive lobby with log beam ceiling and large fieldstone fireplace.
Moderate sized guest rooms, some feature private balcony with wonderful view. All rooms with video games.
4 stories; interior corridors; sauna, steamroom, whirlpools. **Dining:** Restaurant; 6:30 am-11 pm; $10-$22; cocktails.
Services: gift shop. Fee: area transportation, ski shuttle. **Recreation:** ski desk & ski wax room. **Cards:** AE, DI, DS, JC,
MC, VI. *(See color ad below)*

BANFF PARK LODGE RESORT HOTEL & CONFERENCE CENTRE Phone: (403)762-4433
◆◆◆ 6/1-9/30 1P: $239-$310 2P: $239-$310 XP: $15 F16
Motor Inn 10/1-12/23 1P: $139-$205 2P: $139-$205 XP: $10 F16
3/1-5/31 1P: $129-$205 2P: $129-$205 XP: $10 F16
12/24-2/28 1P: $139-$175 2P: $139-$175 XP: $15 F16
Location: Between Caribou and Wolf sts. 222 Lynx St T0L 0C0 (PO Box 2200). Fax: 403/762-3553. **Terms:** Cancellation fee
imposed; package plans. **Facility:** 212 rooms. Renovated property featuring modern public areas and very spacious guest
rooms. All rooms with private balcony and hair dryer. In the heart of downtown Banff. Heated underground parking. 3 stories;
interior corridors; heated pool. **Dining:** entertainment. **Services:** gift shop. Fee: area transportation. **Cards:** AE, DI, JC,
MC, VI. *(See color ad p 323)*

BANFF PTARMIGAN INN

CAA SAVE — ◆◆◆ — Motor Inn

Phone: (403)762-2207

6/1-10/15	1P: $178-$193	2P: $193-$208	XP: $15	F16
12/23-2/28	1P: $90-$146	2P: $100-$156	XP: $15	F16
3/1-5/31	1P: $101-$111	2P: $111-$121	XP: $15	F16
10/16-12/22	1P: $88-$98	2P: $98-$108	XP: $15	F16

Location: Sw of Moose St. 337 Banff Ave T0L 0C0 (PO Box 1840). Fax: 403/762-3577. **Terms:** [AP], [BP] & [MAP] meal plans; check-in 3:30 pm; 3 day cancellation notice; cancellation fee imposed; package plans; pets, $25 dep req. **Facility:** 134 rooms. Recently renovated property. 8 whirlpool rooms with gas fireplace, $275-$300; 2-3 stories; interior corridors; sauna, steamroom, whirlpools. **Dining:** Restaurant; 6 am-11 pm; $10-$17; cocktails. **Services:** gift shop; winter plug-ins. Fee: massage, area transportation, ski hills. **Recreation:** ski lockers. Fee: bicycles. **All Rooms:** extended cable TV. **Cards:** AE, DI, DS, JC, MC, VI. **Special Amenities:** Free local telephone calls.

BANFF ROCKY MOUNTAIN RESORT

CAA — ◆◆◆ — Complex

Phone: (403)762-5531

	1P:	2P:	XP:	
All Year	1P: $140-$290	2P: $140-$290	XP: $15	F16

Location: Banff Ave at Tunnel Mountain Rd, just s of Trans Canada Hwy 1. 1029 Banff Ave T0L 0C0 (Box 100). Fax: 403/762-5166. **Terms:** [BP] meal plan; check-in 5 pm; 3 day cancellation notice; cancellation fee imposed; package plans; pets, $15 extra charge. **Facility:** 100 rooms. Variety of accommodations from suites to condominiums. All feature living room with wood burning or gas fireplace and private balcony or patio. All rooms with hair dryer. 30 two-bedroom units. 5 whirlpool rooms; 2 stories; exterior corridors; heated pool, sauna, whirlpools; 2 tennis courts, 2 squash courts; playground. **Dining:** Restaurant; 7 am-10:30 pm; $14-$25; cocktails. **Services:** area transportation; winter plug-ins. Fee: massage. **Recreation:** barbecue, volleyball court. Fee: bicycles. **All Rooms:** extended cable TV. **Some Rooms:** 62 kitchens. **Cards:** AE, DI, DS, JC, MC, VI. *(See color ad below)*

THE BANFF VOYAGER INN

CAA SAVE — ◆◆ — Motor Inn

Phone: (403)762-3301

	1P:	2P:	XP:	
6/1-9/30	1P: $115-$145	2P: $115-$145	XP: $15	F16
12/19-2/28	1P: $55-$125	2P: $55-$125	XP: $15	F16
3/1-5/31 & 10/1-12/18	1P: $55-$75	2P: $55-$75	XP: $15	F16

Location: 1.2 km ne, corner Marmot. 555 Banff Ave T0L 0C0 (PO Box 1540). Fax: 403/762-4131. **Terms:** Cancellation fee imposed; package plans. **Facility:** 88 rooms. Economy style accommodations featuring average sized guest rooms with modern decor. All rooms have private balcony. 3 suites & 7 studios with whirlpool, $80-$95 for up to 2 persons; 6 whirlpool rooms; 2 stories; interior corridors; heated pool, sauna, whirlpool. **Dining:** Restaurant; 7 am-11 & 5:30-9:30 pm; patio dining in season noon-4 pm; $9-$18; cocktails. **Services:** winter plug-ins. **Cards:** AE, JC, MC, VI. **Special Amenities:** Free local telephone calls.

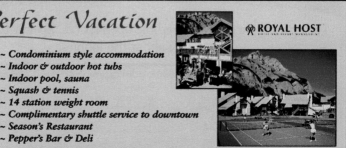

BEST WESTERN SIDING 29 LODGE

				Phone: (403)762-5575	
CAA SAVE	10/1-2/28	1P: $85-$195	2P: $85-$195	XP: $10	F12
◆◆◆	7/1-9/30	1P: $195	2P: $195		
	6/1-6/30	1P: $175	2P: $175		
Motel	3/1-5/31	1P: $85-$110	2P: $85-$110	XP: $10	F12

Location: 1.3 km ne off Banff Ave. 453 Marten St T0L 0C0 (PO Box 1387). Fax: 403/762-8866. **Terms:** Cancellation fee imposed; pets. **Facility:** 57 rooms. Contemporary room decor and attractive public areas. Located in a quiet part of town. All rooms with hair dryer. 2 two-bedroom units. Units with kitchen, $135-$185; 8 whirlpool rooms, $195-$250; 3 stories; interior corridors; small heated indoor pool, whirlpool. **Dining:** Restaurant nearby. **Services:** Fee: area transportation, ski shuttle. **All Rooms:** extended cable TV. **Cards:** AE, DI, DS, JC, MC, VI. **Special Amenities:** Early check-in/late check-out and free local telephone calls. *(See color ad below)*

BOW VIEW MOTOR LODGE

				Phone: 403/762-2261	
◆◆◆	All Year	1P: $85-$165	2P: $85-$165	XP: $10	F8

Motor Inn **Location:** Between Lynx St and Bow Ave, on Wolf St. 228 Bow Ave T0L 0C0 (PO Box 339). Fax: 403/762-8093. **Terms:** 7 day cancellation notice, in season. **Facility:** 57 rooms. Most rooms have small balcony. Slightly higher priced rooms offer a panoramic view of river. Compact to moderate sized rooms; simple, but contemporary appointments. 3 two-bedroom units. 3 stories; interior corridors; small heated pool. **Services:** winter plug-ins. **Cards:** AE, CB, DI, DS, JC, MC, VI. *(See color ad p 325)*

BREWSTER'S MOUNTAIN LODGE

				Phone: (403)762-2900	
CAA SAVE	6/9-9/30	1P: $189-$219	2P: $189-$219	XP: $15	F12
◆◆◆	5/1-6/8	1P: $159-$179	2P: $159-$179	XP: $15	F12
	10/1-2/28	1P: $119-$169	2P: $119-$169	XP: $15	F12
Motel	3/1-4/30	1P: $139-$159	2P: $139-$159	XP: $15	F12

Location: Center; just w off Banff Ave. 208 Caribou St T0L 0C0 (PO Box 2286). Fax: 403/762-2970. **Terms:** Check-in 4 pm; 3 day cancellation notice; cancellation fee imposed; package plans. **Facility:** 73 rooms. Beautifully appointed rooms featuring a contemporary lodge decor with a Southwest flavour that includes log pine furnishings and duvets. A few rooms overlook inner courtyard. All rooms with hair dryer and satellite TV. 17 whirlpool rooms, $229-$269; 3 stories; interior corridors; sauna, whirlpool. **Dining:** Restaurant; 7-10 am. **Services:** gift shop. **Cards:** AE, MC, VI. **Special Amenities:** Free room upgrade and preferred room (each subject to availability with advanced reservations).

BUFFALO MOUNTAIN LODGE

				Phone: (403)762-2400
♦♦♦	10/10-2/28	1P: $175-$325	2P: $175-$325	XP: $25 F13
Complex	6/1-10/9	1P: $212-$288	2P: $212-$288	XP: $25 F13
	3/1-5/31	1P: $158-$234	2P: $158-$234	XP: $25 F13

Location: 1.6 km ne on Tunnel Mountain Rd. (PO Box 1326, T0L 0C0). Fax: 403/762-4495. **Terms:** Check-in 4 pm; 3 day cancellation notice; cancellation fee imposed. **Facility:** 108 rooms. Spacious rooms with gas or wood burning fireplace. Main lodge features hand-hewn timber construction, cathedral ceiling and gracious seating areas. "Premier rooms" offer artistic elegance. All rooms with hair dryer. 2 stories; exterior corridors. **Services:** winter plug-ins. Fee: area transportation. **Some Rooms:** 20 efficiencies. **Cards:** AE, DI, MC, VI.

BUMPER'S INN

				Phone: 403/762-3386
♦♦	10/1-2/28	1P: $85-$132	2P: $85-$132	XP: $10 F12
Motel	6/3-9/30	1P: $132	2P: $132	XP: $10 F12
	3/1-6/2	1P: $85	2P: $85	XP: $10 F12

Location: 1.2 km ne on Banff Ave at jct of Marmot St. 603 Banff Ave T0L 0C0 (PO Box 1328). Fax: 403/762-8842. **Facility:** 39 rooms. Average sized rooms, all overlook an attractively landscaped courtyard setting. Most rooms feature a patio or balcony. All rooms with hair dryer. 1 two-bedroom unit. 2 stories; exterior corridors. **Services:** winter plug-ins. Fee: area transportation. **Cards:** AE, MC, VI.

CANADIAN PACIFIC BANFF SPRINGS HOTEL

				Phone: (403)762-2211
⊚	5/1-10/6	1P: $317-$499	2P: $317-$499	XP: $25 F17
	3/1-4/30 & 10/7-2/28	1P: $135-$245	2P: $135-$245	XP: $25 F17
♦♦♦♦ Classic Resort				

Location: Just s on Banff Ave over bridge, 0.5 km e. 405 Spray Ave T0L 0C0 (PO Box 960). Fax: 403/762-5755. **Terms:** [AP], [BP] & [MAP] meal plans; check-in 4 pm; 3 day cancellation notice; cancellation fee imposed; package plans; pets, $20 extra charge, in smoking rooms. **Facility:** 770 rooms. **Historic.** World-renowned hotel known as the "Castle in the Rockies" offers compact guest rooms to spacious 1-bedroom suites, some with upscale Scottish baronial decor. European-style spa and a cutting edge conference centre. 26 whirlpool rooms, $294-$1257; 9 stories; interior corridors; mountain view; putting green; 2 heated pools, wading pool, saunas, steamrooms, whirlpools; 5 tennis courts. Fee: 27 holes golf. **Dining:** Dining room, 10 restaurants, deli; 24 hrs; $22-$36; cocktails; afternoon tea; entertainment. **Services:** gift shop; winter plug-ins. Fee: massage, area transportation. **Recreation:** hiking trails, jogging, audio visual theatre, beauty salon. Fee: downhill & cross country skiing, tobogganing; bicycles, horseback riding. **All Rooms:** extended cable TV, honor bars. **Some Rooms:** 20 efficiencies, safes. **Cards:** AE, DI, DS, JC, MC, VI.

CASTLE MOUNTAIN VILLAGE
◆◆◆
Cottage

All Year   1P: $185-$330   Phone: 403/762-3868

Location: 32 km w on Hwy 1, at Castle jct, 1 km ne on Hwy 1A (Bow Valley Pkwy). (PO Box 1655, T0L 0C0). Fax: 403/762-8629. **Terms:** 14 day cancellation notice; cancellation fee imposed; pets, $20 extra charge. **Facility:** 19 rooms. Attractively decorated contemporary log chalets. A few offer studio-style, others feature rustic charm. All rooms with gas or wood burning fireplace. Well stocked grocery store. Occasional sounds from nearby passing trains. 4 two-bedroom units. 1 story; exterior corridors; mountain view. **Services:** winter plug-ins. **Recreation:** cross country skiing. **All Rooms:** kitchens, combo or shower baths. **Cards:** MC, VI.

CHARLTON'S CEDAR COURT
(CAA) (SAVE)
◆◆◆
Motel

Phone: (403)762-4485

6/1-9/30	1P: $180-$205	2P: $180-$205	XP: $15 F16
1/7-2/28	1P: $115-$135	2P: $115-$135	XP: $15 F16
3/1-5/31 & 10/1-1/6	1P: $110-$130	2P: $110-$130	XP: $15 F16

Location: 1 km ne. 513 Banff Ave T0L 0C0 (PO Box 1478). Fax: 403/762-2744. **Terms:** [BP], [CP] & [MAP] meal plans; check-in 4 pm; cancellation fee imposed; package plans. **Facility:** 63 rooms. 24 loft units feature a gas fireplace. Small patio deck on the 2nd floor overlooks the majestic mountains. Excellent amenities in all rooms. All rooms with hair dryer and video games. 2-3 stories; exterior corridors; small heated indoor pool, steamroom, whirlpool. **Dining:** Restaurant nearby. **Services:** winter plug-ins. Fee: area transportation, ski shuttle. **All Rooms:** extended cable TV. **Some Rooms:** 16 efficiencies. **Cards:** AE, DI, JC, MC, VI. *(See color ad below)*

DOUGLAS FIR RESORT & CHALETS
(CAA)
◆◆◆
Complex

Phone: (403)762-5591

6/9-9/16	1P: $188-$198	2P: $218-$238	XP: $10 F14
9/17-1/6	1P: $108-$198	2P: $128-$238	XP: $10 F14
3/1-6/8 & 1/7-2/28	1P: $108-$142	2P: $128-$172	XP: $10 F14

Location: 1.6 km ne on Tunnel Mountain Rd. (PO Box 1228, T0L 0C0). Fax: 403/762-8774. **Terms:** Check-in 4 pm. **Facility:** 133 rooms. Quiet location, wooded hillside with scenic mountain views. A mix of 2- and 3-bedroom rustic chalets; 1- and 2-bedroom condos with fireplace and spacious lodge suites. 2 whirlpool rooms, $225-$315; 2-3 stories; interior/exterior corridors; heated pool, saunas, waterslide, whirlpools; racquetball court, 1 tennis court, squash court. **Dining:** Dining room nearby. **Services:** winter plug-ins. Fee: area transportation, ski area & town center. **All Rooms:** kitchens, extended cable TV, safes. **Some Rooms:** Fee: VCR. **Cards:** AE, DI, MC, VI. *(See color ad p 327)*

HIDDEN RIDGE CHALETS
(CAA) (SAVE)
◆◆◆
Complex

Phone: (403)762-3544

All Year   1P: $128-$275   2P: $128-$275   XP: $15   F15

Location: 2.4 km ne. 901 Coyote Dr Tunnel Mtn T0L 0C0 (PO Box 519). Fax: 403/762-2804. **Terms:** Check-in 4 pm; cancellation fee imposed; package plans. **Facility:** 83 rooms. Fine view of Bow Valley. Units vary from large condo apartment to 4-plex. Small chalets offer older, rustic appeal, with best view of the valley. All rooms with balcony or private porch, fireplace and hair dryer. 32 two-bedroom units, 11 three-bedroom units. 2 stories; exterior corridors; mountain view; large outdoor hot tub. **Services:** winter plug-ins. Fee: area transportation, ski shuttle. **Recreation:** barbecue decks, fire wood provided. **All Rooms:** kitchens, extended cable TV. **Cards:** MC, VI. **Special Amenities:** Free local telephone calls.

HIGH COUNTRY INN

	6/2-9/30	1P: $140-$180	2P: $140-$180	XP: $10	F12
	10/1-2/28	1P: $69-$140	2P: $69-$140	XP: $10	F12
	3/1-6/1	1P: $95-$135	2P: $95-$135	XP: $10	F12

Phone: (403)762-2236

Motor Inn **Location:** N of Rabbit St. 419 Banff Ave T0L 0C0 (PO Box 700). Fax: 403/762-5084. **Terms:** Cancellation fee imposed. **Facility:** 70 rooms. Beautifully appointed rooms with warm, earthtone colours, most duvets, many with balcony. Inviting lobby features a comfortable seating area with a stone fireplace. 1 two-bedroom unit. Whirlpool room; 3 stories; interior corridors; smoke free premises; heated pool, sauna, whirlpools. **Dining:** Restaurant; 7:30 am-10:30 & 5:30-10:30 pm; $10-$26; cocktails. **Services:** winter plug-ins. Fee: area transportation, ski areas. **Recreation:** ski lockers. **All Rooms:** extended cable TV. **Cards:** AE, MC, VI. *(See color ad below)*

HOMESTEAD INN

	6/1-9/30	1P: $129-$139	2P: $139	XP: $10	F12
	10/1-2/28	1P: $60-$110	2P: $60-$110	XP: $10	F12
	5/1-5/31	1P: $68-$78	2P: $78	XP: $10	F12
	3/1-4/30	1P: $60	2P: $60	XP: $10	F12

Phone: 403/762-4471

Motel **Location:** Between Caribou and Wolf sts; downtown. 218 Lynx St T0L 0C0 (PO Box 669). Fax: 403/762-8877. **Terms:** Cancellation fee imposed. **Facility:** 27 rooms. Spacious accommodations, pleasant modern style decor. Located in the heart of downtown Banff. 3 stories, no elevator; exterior corridors. **Services:** winter plug-ins. Fee: area transportation. **Cards:** AE, MC, VI.

IRWIN'S MOUNTAIN INN

Phone: 403/762-4566

6/2-9/30	1P: $125-$145	2P: $125-$145	XP: $10 F16
3/1-6/1	1P: $75-$85	2P: $75-$85	XP: $5 F16
10/1-2/28	1P: $60-$65	2P: $60-$65	XP: $5 F16

Motor Inn **Location:** 1 km ne. 429 Banff Ave T0L 0C0 (PO Box 1198). Fax: 403/762-8220. **Terms:** Check-in 4 pm; cancellation fee imposed. **Facility:** 65 rooms. Property features a range of accommodations from standard guest rooms to spacious suites, all with contemporary decor. Within easy walking distance to downtown Banff. 11 whirlpool rooms, $65-$200; 3 stories; interior corridors; sauna, steamroom, whirlpool. **Dining:** Restaurant; 7 am-11 & 5-11 pm; $10-$25; cocktails. **Services:** winter plug-ins. Fee: massage; area transportation; ski areas. **Recreation:** ski lockers. **Cards:** AE, MC, VI. *(See color ad below)*

JOHNSTON CANYON RESORT

Phone: 403/762-2971

6/16-9/23	1P: $109-$245	2P: $109-$245	XP: $10
5/19-6/15 & 9/24-10/1	1P: $79-$195	2P: $79-$195	XP: $10

Cottage **Location:** 24 km nw on Hwy 1A (Bow Valley Pkwy) at Johnston Canyon. Hwy 1A T0L 0C0 (PO Box 875). Fax: 403/762-0868. **Terms:** Open 5/19-10/1; check-in 4 pm; pets. **Facility:** 41 rooms. Established in 1927, this mix of original older wood-framed cottages range from average sized to spacious full size units with cooking facilities. A few have compact bathrooms. Unique vintage decor, most beds with duvets. 1 story; exterior corridors; 1 tennis court. **Services:** gift shop. **All Rooms:** combo or shower baths. **Cards:** MC, VI. *(See color ad below)*

RED CARPET MOTOR INN

Phone: 403/762-4184

All Year   1P: $75-$125   2P: $85-$160   XP: $11   F18

Location: 1 km ne. 425 Banff Ave T0L 0C0 (PO Box 1800). Fax: 403/762-4894. **Terms:** Small pets only. **Facility:** 52 rooms. Units vary in size, most are spacious. Some mountain view from rooms facing Banff Ave. Contemporary appeal. 7 whirlpool rooms, $85-$185; 3 stories; interior/exterior corridors; 2 whirlpools, 11/1-4/30. **Dining:** Restaurant nearby. **Services:** winter plug-ins. Fee: area transportation, ski shuttle. **Cards:** AE, MC, VI.

THE RIMROCK RESORT HOTEL

Phone: (403)762-3356

5/20-10/6	1P: $240-$340	2P: $240-$340	XP: $20	F18
12/22-2/28	1P: $180-$220	2P: $180-$220	XP: $20	F18
3/1-5/19 & 10/7-12/21	1P: $150-$190	2P: $150-$190	XP: $20	F18

Location: 4 km s via Sulphur Mountain Rd, adjacent to Upper Hot Springs Pool. 100 Mountain Dr T0L 0C0 (PO Box 1110). Fax: 403/762-4132. **Terms:** Check-in 4 pm; 3 day cancellation notice. **Facility:** 346 rooms. Unique property built entirely on a mountain slope offering a spectacular mountain view. Large, tastefully decorated public areas. 37 suites, 11 with fireplace, $135-$1200; 53 whirlpool rooms; 9 stories; interior corridors; heated pool, sauna, steamroom, whirlpool. **Dining:** Restaurant; 6 am-10 pm; $10-$39; also, Ristorante Classico, see separate listing; entertainment. **Services:** gift shop; area transportation, downtown; winter plug-ins. Fee: massage. **Recreation:** sports court, aerobics room, squash court. Fee: scheduled ski area shuttle. **All Rooms:** extended cable TV, honor bars. **Cards:** AE, CB, DI, DS, JC, MC, VI. *(See color ad below)*

RUNDLESTONE LODGE
Phone: (403)762-2201

◆◆◆
Motor Inn

6/2-10/15 | 1P: $145-$165 | 2P: $155-$170
3/1-6/1 & 10/16-2/28 | 1P: $85-$105 | 2P: $95-$125

Location: 0.9 km ne. 537 Banff Ave T0L 0C0 (PO Box 489). Fax: 403/762-4501. **Terms:** Cancellation fee imposed. **Facility:** 96 rooms. Superior style guest rooms in the lodge. Attractive lobby with fireplace and cozy guest seating area. All rooms with hair dryer. 2 two-bedroom units. 3 stories; interior corridors; designated smoking area. **Services:** gift shop. Fee: area transportation. **Cards:** AE, CB, DI, DS, MC, VI. *(See color ad below)*

TRAVELLER'S INN
Phone: (403)762-4401

(CAA) (SAVE)
◆◆◆
Motel

6/1-9/30 | 1P: $180-$190 | 2P: $180-$190 | XP: $15 | F17
12/23-2/28 | 1P: $90-$145 | 2P: $90-$145 | XP: $15 | F17
10/1-12/22 | 1P: $100-$125 | 2P: $100-$125 | XP: $15 | F17
3/1-5/31 | 1P: $90-$125 | 2P: $90-$125 | XP: $15 | F17

Location: At Moose St. 401 Banff Ave T0L 0C0 (PO Box 1017). Fax: 403/762-5905. **Terms:** Cancellation fee imposed; package plans. **Facility:** 89 rooms. Attractive units, some with separate seating area. Most rooms with private balcony or patio. Exterior courtyard with extra large whirlpool. 20 two-bedroom units. 3 stories; interior/exterior corridors; sauna, steamroom. **Dining:** Coffee shop; 7-10 am, closed 11/1-11/30. **Services:** gift shop; winter plug-ins. Fee: area transportation, ski hills. **Recreation:** ski locker, ski rental, ski shop open in winter; video library. **Some Rooms:** Fee: VCR. **Cards:** AE, MC, VI.

RUNDLESTONE LODGE
Major Expansion in 1997 Including 45' Lap Pool and Restaurant
1-800-661-8630 • Internet: rundlestone.com

TUNNEL MOUNTAIN CHALETS

Phone: (403)762-4515

6/1-9/30	1P: $193	2P: $231	XP: $15 F14
3/1-5/31 & 10/1-2/28	1P: $153	2P: $193	XP: $15 F14

Complex

Location: 1.6 km ne on Tunnel Mountain Rd. (PO Box 1137, T0L 0C0). Fax: 403/762-5183. **Terms:** Check-in 4 pm; cancellation fee imposed. **Facility:** 75 rooms. Provides a mix of chalet and condo units; all with fireplace and pleasant mountain view. Room furnishing is basic but kitchens are very well equipped. 59 two-bedroom units. 24 whirlpool rooms; 2 stories; exterior corridors; small heated indoor pool, sauna, steamroom, whirlpools. **Dining:** Restaurant nearby. **Services:** winter plug-ins. Fee: area transportation. **Recreation:** video library. **All Rooms:** extended cable TV. **Some Rooms:** Fee: VCR. **Cards:** AE, MC, VI. *(See color ad p 330)*

The following lodging was either not inspected or did not meet AAA rating requirements but is listed for your information only.

CHARLTON'S ROYAL CANADIAN LODGE

Phone: 403/762-3307

[fyi]

Motel

Under construction, scheduled to open May 2000. **Location:** 1 km ne. 459 Banff Ave T0L 0C0 (PO Box 1478). Fax: 403/762-4094. **Planned Amenities:** 99 rooms, coffeemakers, refrigerators. *(See color ad p 326)*

--- **RESTAURANTS** ---

THE BISTRO RESTAURANT

Dinner: $12-$20

Phone: 403/762-8900

Continental

Location: Corner of Wolf and Bear sts; in Wolf and Bear Mall. **Hours:** 5 pm-11 pm. **Reservations:** suggested; for dinner. **Features:** casual dress; children's menu; cocktails; street parking; a la carte. The Bistro's comfortable atmosphere and casual dining are complemented by a contemporary cuisine that blends Continental and Asian influences. They offer unusual roesti—potato-type—pizza, a nice selection of wines by the glass and professional service. **Cards:** MC, VI.

BUFFALO MOUNTAIN LODGE DINING ROOM

Lunch: $8-$12   **Dinner:** $18-$35   **Phone:** 403/762-2400

Regional
Canadian

Location: 1.6 km ne on Tunnel Mountain Rd; in Buffalo Mountain Lodge. **Hours:** 7 am-10 pm. **Reservations:** suggested. **Features:** No A/C; casual dress; children's menu; health conscious menu; cocktails & lounge; a la carte. You'll appreciate the casual elegance in this restaurant's mountain setting. Its Rocky Mountain cuisine features wild-game meat, robust flavors and an excellent wine list. After-dinner drinks and a cigar menu are offered fireside in the lounge. Smoke free premises. **Cards:** AE, DI, MC, VI.

BUMPER'S THE BEEF HOUSE
◆
Steakhouse

Dinner: $8-$28 **Phone:** 403/762-2622
Location: Banff Ave at Marmot St. 603 Banff Ave T0L 0C0. **Hours:** 4:30 pm-10 pm; to 9:30 pm in fall. **Reservations:** suggested. **Features:** children's menu; senior's menu; salad bar; cocktails & lounge. Established in 1975, this restaurant is situated in an A-frame building, where the decor is a blend of the Old West and a mountain chalet, with the loft-lounge overlooking the dining room. The menu specializes in Alberta prime rib and barbecue pork ribs. **Cards:** AE, DI, MC, VI.

CABOOSE STEAK & LOBSTER RESTAURANT
(CAA)
◆◆
Steak and
Seafood

Dinner: $14-$28 **Phone:** 403/762-3622
Location: In railway depot at jct Elk and Lynx sts. **Hours:** 5 pm-10 pm. Closed: 12/25. **Reservations:** suggested. **Features:** children's menu; salad bar; cocktails & lounge. The Caboose features an informal, relaxed atmosphere and subtle railroad-theme decor enhanced by occasional sound effects of passing trains. The menu specializes in prime rib, steak and seafood. There's a karaoke lounge also. Friendly, attentive service. **Cards:** AE, DI, JC, MC, VI.

COYOTES DELI & GRILL
(CAA)
◆◆
Regional
American

Lunch: $7-$10 **Dinner:** $11-$18 **Phone:** 403/762-3963
Location: Town centre; just w of Banff Ave. 206 Caribou St T0L 0C0. **Hours:** 7:30 am-11 pm. Closed: 12/25. **Reservations:** suggested. **Features:** casual dress; health conscious menu items; cocktails; street parking; a la carte. Coyotes features a relaxed and lively deli-bistro setting and a contemporary Southwest cuisine with an accent on creativity and color. They have an open-kitchen concept and an attractive choice of wines by the glass. Knowledgeable server staff. Smoke free premises. **Cards:** AE, DI, MC, VI.

GIORGIO'S TRATTORIA
(CAA)
◆◆
Italian

Dinner: $12-$21 **Phone:** 403/762-5114
Location: Centre. 219 Banff Ave T0L 0C0. **Hours:** 4:30 pm-10:30 pm; to 10 pm off season. **Features:** No A/C; carryout; cocktails; street parking; a la carte. This restaurant's beautiful Southern and Mediterranean decor offers a casual and warm ambience. The cuisine features pizza cooked in a wood-burning oven and fresh pasta made in-house. All dishes have contemporary preparation and attractive presentation. **Cards:** MC, VI.

LE BEAUJOLAIS
(CAA)
◆◆◆◆
Danish

Dinner: $27-$35 **Phone:** 403/762-2712
Location: Near bridge; nw corner of Banff Ave and Buffalo St; upstairs. 212 Buffalo St T0L 0C0. **Hours:** 6 pm-11 pm. Closed: 11/1-11/30. **Reservations:** suggested. **Features:** dressy casual; cocktails; street parking; a la carte. This restaurant offers fine dining in elegant surroundings. Its cuisine is a harmony of traditional elements prepared with a contemporary flair. An excellent wine list and gourmet prix fixe menu are also featured. Smoking is permitted in the lobby only. **Cards:** MC, VI.

RISTORANTE CLASSICO
(CAA)
◆◆◆◆
Northern
Italian

Dinner: $20-$39 **Phone:** 403/762-1840
Location: 4 km s via Sulphur Mountain Rd, adjacent to Upper Hot Springs Pool; in The Rimrock Resort Hotel. 100 Mountain Dr T0L 0C0. **Hours:** 6 pm-10 pm. **Reservations:** suggested. **Features:** casual dress; health conscious menu; cocktails & lounge; fee for valet parking; a la carte, also prix fixe. This restaurant's rich, elegant decor offers a quiet, intimate dining experience with a spectacular view of the mountain valley. Its cutting-edge cuisine features unusual plate presentations of dishes such as Atlantic salmon, Arctic caribou, and venison. **Cards:** AE, DI, DS, JC, MC, VI. *(See color ad below)*

ST-JAMES'S GATE OLDE IRISH PUB
◆◆
American

Lunch: $8-$18 **Dinner:** $8-$18 **Phone:** 403/762-9355
Location: Centre; just w of Banff Ave. 205 Wolf St T0L 0C0. **Hours:** 11 am-2 am, Sat & Sun from 10 am. **Features:** carryout; cocktails & lounge; entertainment; street parking; a la carte. This modern-day version of a rustic pub serves traditional cuisine such as shepherd's pie, steak and Guinness pie, and O'Grady's Irish stew. It also offers an impressive selection of single-malt scotch, local and imported draught beer, and cigars. **Cards:** AE, MC, VI.

TICINO SWISS-ITALIAN RESTAURANT Dinner: $12-$24 Phone: 403/762-3848

◆ ◆ ◆
Continental

Location: 1 km n on Banff Ave. 415 Banff Ave T0L 0C0. **Hours:** 7:30 am-10:30 & 5:30-10:30 pm. **Reservations:** suggested. **Features:** casual dress; children's menu; cocktails. In this southern Switzerland-inspired decor, you can expect finely presented specialties from the Ticino area including the famous fondue as well as elaborate lamb, duck and veal preparation. Their morning meals feature an Alpine buffet. Charming service. **Cards:** AE, DI, JC, MC, VI. ⊠

BROOKS pop. 10,100

—— **LODGINGS** ——

THE DOUGLAS COUNTRY INN Phone: (403)362-2873
◆ ◆ ◆
Country Inn
Property failed to provide current rates
Location: On Hwy 873, 6.5 km n of jct Trans Canada Hwy 1. (PO Box 463, T1R 1B5). Fax: 403/362-2100. **Terms:** [BP] meal plan; pets, in heated kennel. **Facility:** 7 rooms. Small, beautifully appointed guest rooms offering a charming country setting. Short drive to attractions. 1 story; interior corridors; smoke free premises. **Services:** winter plug-ins. **All Rooms:** combo or shower baths. **Cards:** MC, VI.

HERITAGE INN Phone: (403)362-6666
◆ ◆
Motor Inn
All Year 1P: $78 2P: $83-$88 XP: $5 F12
Location: On Hwy 873, 0.8 km s jct Trans Canada Hwy 1. 1303 2nd St W T1R 1B8 (PO Box 907). Fax: 403/362-7319. **Terms:** Pets, $5 extra charge. **Facility:** 106 rooms. A tropical style atrium area with small waterfall, fish pond and whirlpool. Contemporary guest room decor. 2 stories; interior corridors. **Dining:** nightclub. **Services:** area transportation; winter plug-ins. **Some Rooms:** efficiency. **Cards:** AE, CB, DI, MC, VI.

SUPER 8 MOTEL-BROOKS Phone: (403)362-8000
◆ ◆
Motel
7/1-10/31 1P: $65-$67 2P: $67-$68 XP: $10 F12
3/1-6/30 & 11/1-2/28 1P: $60-$65 2P: $62-$67 XP: $10 F12
Location: From Trans Canada Hwy (Hwy 1), 0.3 km sw on SR 542 (E Brooks exit). 1240 Cassils Rd E T1R 1B6 (PO Box 1417). Fax: 403/362-8008. **Terms:** [CP] meal plan; pets, $50 dep req. **Facility:** 60 rooms. All rooms with contemporary appointments. Those on 1st floor offer 2 entrances, 1 directly on parking area. 2 stories; interior corridors. **Services:** winter plug-ins. **Cards:** AE, DI, DS, MC, VI.

Destination Calgary

A versatile city with an abundance of theaters and shopping malls, Calgary seems to have something for everyone.

You can attend a horse show, join in a rousing celebration of the Wild West or browse through unique marketplaces. Want to ride down a rushing river? Calgary won't leave you high and dry.

Calgary skyline.
Unusual buildings and the Calgary Tower make this city stand out.
(See mention page 50)

Eau Claire Market, Calgary.
This shopping complex next to the Bow River and Prince's Island Park has specialty stores, kiosks and eateries.
(See mention page 55)

The Calgary Stampede.
The Royal Canadian Mounted Police Musical Ride is a part of the lively July event.
(See mention page 46)

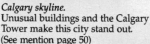

Airdrie

Cochrane

See Vicinity map page 338

Strathmore

See Downtown map page 337

Calgary

Okotoks

Canoeing in Calgary.
Parks and natural areas provide plenty of opportunities to get soaked to the skin or just get your feet wet. Also available are bicycling, camping, golfing, hiking, walking, ice skating and cross-country skiing.
(See mention page 55)

*P*laces included in this AAA Destination City:

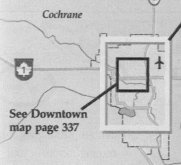

Calgary *pop. 768,100*

This index helps you "spot" where approved accommodations are located on the detailed maps that follow. Rate ranges are for comparison only and show the property's high season. Turn to the listing page for more detailed rate information and consult display ads for special promotions. Restaurant rate range is for dinner, unless only lunch (L) is served.

✈ Airport Accommodations

Spotter/Map Page Number	OA	CALGARY	Diamond Rating	Rate Range High Season	Listing Page
57 / p. 338	⊛	Best Western Airport Inn, 10 km s of airport	◆◆	$100-$145	342
51 / p. 338	⊛	Best Western Port O'Call Inn, 6 km s of Calgary International Airport	◆◆◆	$134-$169 SAVE	343
60 / p. 338	⊛	The Coast Plaza Hotel, 12 km s of airport	◆◆◆	$165-$175 SAVE	344
54 / p. 338	⊛	Comfort Inn And Suites-Airport, 8 km s of airport	◆◆◆	$99-$219 SAVE	345
65 / p. 338	⊛	Country Inn & Suites By Carlson, 5.7 km s of airport	◆◆◆	$99-$109 SAVE	345
52 / p. 338		Hampton Inn & Suites-Calgary Airport, 5.8 km s of airport	◆◆◆	$104-$124	348
59 / p. 338		Holiday Inn Calgary Airport, 10 km s of airport	◆◆◆	$114-$145	348
58 / p. 338	⊛	Radisson Hotel Calgary Airport, 10 km s of airport	◆◆◆	$99-$139 SAVE	351
56 / p. 338	⊛	Super 8 Motel Calgary Airport, 8 km s of airport	◆◆	$90-$159 SAVE	352

DOWNTOWN CALGARY

Spotter/Map Page Number	OA	DOWNTOWN CALGARY - Lodgings	Diamond Rating	Rate Range High Season	Listing Page
1 / p. 337	⊛	Sheraton Suites Calgary Eau Claire - see color ad p 402	◆◆◆◆	$165-$314 SAVE	340
4 / p. 337	⊛	The Westin Calgary	◆◆◆◆	$160-$425	340
5 / p. 337		Prince Royal Suites Hotel	◆◆	$205-$240	339
6 / p. 337		Delta Bow Valley - see color ad p 339	◆◆◆	$170	338
7 / p. 337	⊛	Ramada Hotel Downtown	◆◆◆	$119-$225 SAVE	339
8 / p. 337		The Palliser Fairmont Hotel & Resort	◆◆◆◆	$175-$269	339
9 / p. 337	⊛	Holiday Inn Calgary Downtown	◆◆◆	$179-$209 SAVE	338
		DOWNTOWN CALGARY - Restaurants			
① / p. 337		River Cafe	◆◆◆	$14-$32	341
② / p. 337		Don Quijote	◆◆	$12-$22	340
③ / p. 337		Owl's Nest Dining Room	◆◆◆◆	$24-$36	341
④ / p. 337		Indochine	◆◆	$9-$16	341
⑤ / p. 337		Silver Dragon Restaurant	◆◆	$6-$17	341
⑦ / p. 337	⊛	The Conservatory - see color ad p 339	◆◆◆◆	$21-$33	340
⑧ / p. 337		Florentine	◆◆◆	$22-$27	341
⑨ / p. 337		Celadon	◆◆◆	$7-$24	340
⑫ / p. 337		Thai Sa-On Restaurant	◆◆	$6-$13	341
⑬ / p. 337		Cannery Row	◆◆	$11-$20	340
⑭ / p. 337		McQueens Upstairs	◆◆◆	$17-$35	341
⑯ / p. 337		Divino Bistro-Winebar	◆◆	$9-$17	340
⑰ / p. 337		The Panorama Dining Room	◆◆◆	$23-$38	341
⑱ / p. 337		Mescalero	◆◆	$17-$24	341
⑳ / p. 337	⊛	La Chaumiere Restaurant	◆◆◆◆	$18-$29	341
㉑ / p. 337		Da Paolo Ristorante	◆◆◆	$11-$29	340
㉒ / p. 337		Entre Nous	◆◆◆	$18-$24	340

CALGARY

Spotter/Map Page Number	OA	CALGARY - Lodgings	Diamond Rating	Rate Range High Season	Listing Page
33 / p. 338	⊛	Ramada Crowchild Inn - see color ad p 350	◆◆◆	$130-$150 [SAVE]	351
35 / p. 338	⊛	Four Points Sheraton Hotel and Suites, Calgary West - see color ad p 402, p 347	◆◆◆	$129 [SAVE]	347
37 / p. 338	⊛	Budget Host Motor Inn - see color ad p 344	◆◆	$89-$115 [SAVE]	343
40 / p. 338	⊛	Super 8 Motel Northwest	◆◆	$70-$150 [SAVE]	352
41 / p. 338	⊛	Best Western Village Park Inn - see color ad p 342, p 339	◆◆◆	$129-$149 [SAVE]	343
42 / p. 338		Hampton Inn & Suites Northwest - see color ad p 348	◆◆◆	$109-$189	348
45 / p. 338	⊛	Calgary North Travelodge	◆◆	$90-$150 [SAVE]	344
46 / p. 338	⊛	Econo Lodge Bannff Trail	◆◆	$89-$149 [SAVE]	346
47 / p. 338	⊛	Days Inn-Calgary West - see color ad p 345	◆◆	$95-$120 [SAVE]	345
48 / p. 338	⊛	Econo Lodge Motel Village	◆◆	$89-$149 [SAVE]	346
49 / p. 338	⊛	Holiday Inn Express University	◆◆◆	$110-$180 [SAVE]	349
50 / p. 338		Rosedale House Bed & Breakfast	◆◆	$90-$120	351
51 / p. 338	⊛	Best Western Port O'Call Inn - see color ad p 339, p 342	◆◆◆	$134-$169 [SAVE]	343
52 / p. 338		Hampton Inn & Suites-Calgary Airport - see color ad p 348	◆◆◆	$104-$124	348
53 / p. 338	⊛	Greenwood Inn Hotels - see color ad p 373, p 347	◆◆◆	$129-$159 [SAVE]	347
54 / p. 338	⊛	Comfort Inn And Suites-Airport	◆◆◆	$99-$219 [SAVE]	345
55 / p. 338		Royal Inn North Calgary	◆◆◆	$95-$159	351
56 / p. 338	⊛	Super 8 Motel Calgary Airport	◆◆	$90-$159 [SAVE]	352
57 / p. 338	⊛	Best Western Airport Inn - see color ad p 339	◆◆	$100-$145	342
58 / p. 338	⊛	Radisson Hotel Calgary Airport - see color ad p 350	◆◆◆	$99-$139 [SAVE]	351
59 / p. 338		Holiday Inn Calgary Airport - see color ad p 349	◆◆◆	$114-$145	348
60 / p. 338	⊛	The Coast Plaza Hotel	◆◆◆	$165-$175 [SAVE]	344
61 / p. 338	⊛	Paradise Acres Bed & Breakfast - see color ad p 629	◆◆	$60-$75 [SAVE]	350
62 / p. 338	⊛	Calgary Westways Guest House	◆◆◆	$70-$105 [SAVE]	344
63 / p. 338	⊛	Lord Nelson Inn	◆◆	$95-$135 [SAVE]	350
64 / p. 338		Inglewood Bed & Breakfast	◆◆	$70-$125	349
65 / p. 338	⊛	Country Inn & Suites By Carlson - see color ad p 345	◆◆◆	$99-$109 [SAVE]	345
66 / p. 338	⊛	Best Western Suites Downtown - see color ad p 339, p 343	◆◆◆	$110-$145 [SAVE]	343
67 / p. 338	⊛	Elbow River Inn & Casino - see color ad p 346	◆	$59-$109	346
68 / p. 338	⊛	Quality Hotel & Conference Centre	◆◆	$89-$119 [SAVE]	350
69 / p. 338	⊛	Holiday Inn Calgary South	◆◆◆	$95-$145 [SAVE]	349
70 / p. 338	⊛	Blackfoot Inn	◆◆◆	$125-$165 [SAVE]	343
71 / p. 338	⊛	Calgary South Travelodge	◆◆	$90-$150 [SAVE]	344
72 / p. 338		Glenmore Inn and Convention Centre	◆◆◆	$119-$145	347
74 / p. 338	⊛	Carriage House Inn	◆◆◆	$129-$139 [SAVE]	344
76 / p. 338	⊛	Stetson Village Inn	◆◆	$75-$80 [SAVE]	351
77 / p. 338	⊛	Best Western Hospitality Inn - see color ad p 342, p 339	◆◆◆	$115-$190 [SAVE]	342
		CALGARY - Restaurants			
36 / p. 338		Palki	◆◆	$5-$13	353
39 / p. 338		Alberta King of Subs	◆	$2-$10	352
40 / p. 338		Lina's Italian Market & Cappuccino Bar	◆	$5	353

Spotter/Map Page Number	OA	CALGARY - Restaurants (continued)	Diamond Rating	Rate Range High Season	Listing Page
㊶ / p. 338		Rose Cafe	◆◆	$6-$17	353
㊷ / p. 338		Maurya	◆◆	$8-$15	353
㊸ / p. 338		Santorini Greek Taverna	◆◆	$10-$20	354
㊹ / p. 338		Saigon	◆◆	$5-$12	354
㊺ / p. 338		Boogie's	◆	$5-$10	352
㊻ / p. 338	CAA	**La Dolce Vita Ristorante Italiano & Enoteca Da Franco**	◆◆◆	$11-$25	353
㊼ / p. 338		La Brezza	◆◆	$12-$22	353
㊽ / p. 338		The Salmon Cove	◆◆	$9-$22	354
㊾ / p. 338		Sultan's Tent	◆◆	$10-$29	354
㊿ / p. 338		Restaurant Indonesia	◆◆	$7-$11	353
(51) / p. 338		Kyoto 17	◆◆	$5-$14	352
(53) / p. 338		Fleur de Sel	◆◆◆	$15-$19	352
(54) / p. 338		Deane House Historic Site Restaurant	◆◆	$8-$10(L)	352
(55) / p. 338		Lily's Rendezvous	◆◆	$8-$12	353
(56) / p. 338	CAA	**Pfanntastic Pannenkoek Haus**	◆◆	$5-$11	353
(57) / p. 338		Leo Fu's	◆◆	$7-$13	353
(58) / p. 338	CAA	**The Inn on Lake Bonavista**	◆◆◆	$17-$30	352

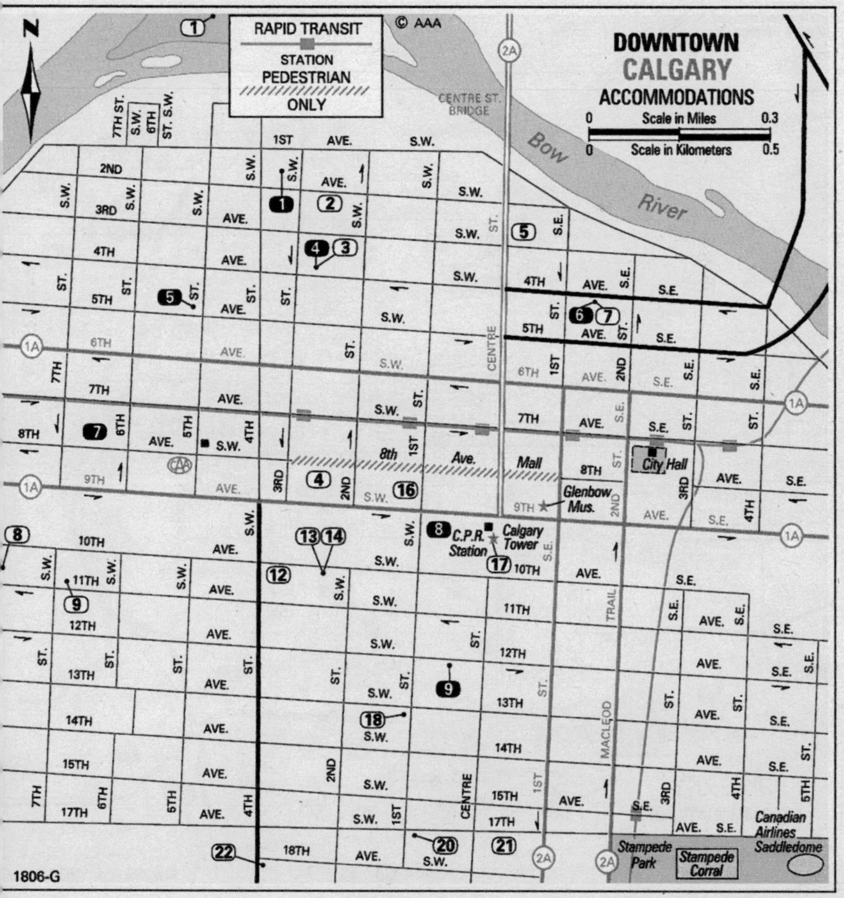

DOWNTOWN CALGARY　(See map p. 337; index p. 335)

── LODGINGS ──

DELTA BOW VALLEY　　　　　　　　　　　　　　　　　　　　**Phone:** (403)266-1980　**6**
◆◆◆　All Year　　　　　　　　1P: $170　　2P: $170　　　　　XP: $10　　F18
Hotel　　**Location:** 1st St SE and 4th Ave SE. 209 4th Ave SE T2G 0C6. Fax: 403/266-0007. **Terms:** Pets. **Facility:** 398 rooms. Comfortable large guest rooms with view of downtown or river valley. All rooms with iron and ironing board. 25 stories; interior corridors; heated pool. Fee: parking. **Services:** gift shop. **Some Rooms:** honor bars. **Cards:** AE, DI, DS, JC, MC, VI. *(See color ad p 339)*

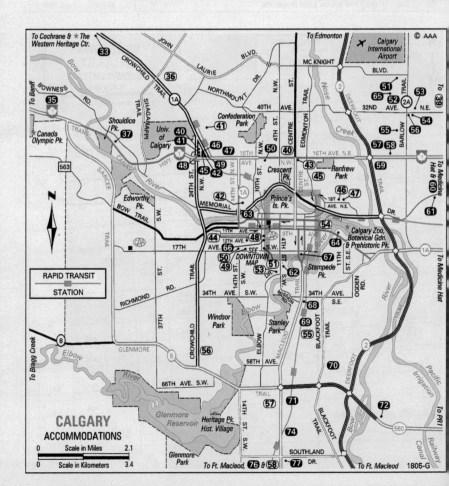

HOLIDAY INN CALGARY DOWNTOWN　　　　　　　　　　　**Phone:** (403)266-4611　**9**
ⒶⒶ ⑤ᴬⱽᴱ　7/6-7/16　　　　　　1P: $179-$209　　2P: $179-$209　　XP: $10　　F18
　　　　7/17-11/15　　　　　1P: $149-$189　　2P: $149-$189　　XP: $10　　F18
◆◆◆　3/1-7/5　　　　　　　1P: $139-$189　　2P: $139-$189　　XP: $10　　F18
Hotel　　11/16-2/28　　　　　1P: $139-$159　　　　　　　　　XP: $10　　F18
Location: Centre, at 1st St SW. 119 12th Ave SW T2R 0G8. Fax: 403/237-0978. **Terms:** Pets, $20 extra charge. **Facility:** 188 rooms. Renovated spacious rooms with patio door. Centrally located and close to Stampede Grounds. All rooms with hair dryer, iron, ironing board and voice mail. Whirlpool room; 12 stories; interior corridors; heated pool. **Dining:** Restaurant; 6 am-11 pm; $8-$19; cocktails. **Services:** winter plug-ins. **Recreation:** in-room video games. **All Rooms:** combo or shower baths, extended cable TV. **Cards:** AE, CB, DI, DS, JC, MC, VI. **Special Amenities:** Free local telephone calls and free newspaper.

(See map p. 337)

THE PALLISER FAIRMONT HOTEL & RESORT Phone: (403)262-1234 **8**
♦♦♦ All Year 1P: $175-$269 2P: $175-$269 XP: $25 F18
Classic Hotel **Location:** 9th Ave SW at 1st St SW. 133 9th Ave SW T2P 2M3. Fax: 403/260-1260. **Terms:** Check-in 4 pm; small pets only, $20 extra charge. **Facility:** 405 rooms. **Historic.** A remodeled historic turn-of-the-century hotel. Various room sizes with tasteful traditional decor and modern luxury appointments, including a few with computers and internet access. All rooms with iron and ironing board. 12 stories; interior corridors; heated pool. Fee: parking. **Services:** gift shop; winter plug-ins. Fee: massage. **All Rooms:** honor bars. **Cards:** AE, CB, DI, DS, JC, MC, VI. A Canadian Pacific Hotel.

PRINCE ROYAL SUITES HOTEL Phone: (403)263-0520 **5**
♦♦ 6/10-7/18 1P: $205 2P: $205-$240 XP: $15 F16
Suite Hotel 3/1-6/9 & 7/19-2/28 1P: $175 2P: $175-$210 XP: $15 F16
Location: 618 5th Ave SW T2P 0M7. Fax: 403/298-4888. **Terms:** Cancellation fee imposed. **Facility:** 301 rooms. Recently renovated spacious, well-equipped 1- and 2-bedroom apartments and small suites. All rooms with a hair dryer, iron and ironing board. 64 two-bedroom units. 28 stories; interior corridors. Fee: parking. **Services:** winter plug-ins. **All Rooms:** kitchens. **Cards:** AE, CB, DI, DS, JC, MC, VI.

RAMADA HOTEL DOWNTOWN Phone: (403)263-7600 **7**
AAA SAVE 6/1-7/31 1P: $119-$215 2P: $129-$225 XP: $10 F18
♦♦♦ 3/1-5/31 & 8/1-2/28 1P: $99-$215 2P: $109-$225 XP: $10 F18
Hotel **Location:** At 6th St. 708 8th Ave SW T2P 1H2. Fax: 403/237-6127. **Terms:** 3 day cancellation notice; cancellation fee imposed; small pets only, in designated rooms. **Facility:** 201 rooms. Guest room decor varies from modest accommodations to the recently renovated units that offer a more upscale and sophisticated look. All rooms with hair dryer, iron and ironing board. 7 whirlpool rooms; 9 stories; interior corridors; heated pool. Fee: parking. **Dining:** Restaurant; 6:30 am-10 pm; $7-$15; cocktails. **Services:** gift shop. **All Rooms:** extended cable TV. **Cards:** AE, CB, DI, DS, JC, MC, VI. **Special Amenities:** Free local telephone calls and free newspaper.

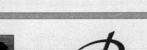

(See map p. 337)

SHERATON SUITES CALGARY EAU CLAIRE　　　　　　　　Phone: (403)266-7200　🔲
CAA SAVE　　All Year　　　　　　　1P: $165-$299　　　2P: $165-$314　　XP: $15　　　F1🔲
◆◆◆◆　　**Location:** At 3rd St SW and 2nd Ave SW. 255 Barclay Parade SW T2P 5C2. Fax: 403/266-1300. **Terms:** 3☐
Suite Hotel　day cancellation notice; cancellation fee imposed. **Facility:** 323 rooms. Nicely appointed suites with excellen☐
　　　　　amenities. Ideal accommodations for both business and leisure travellers. Eau Claire market adjacent. 44 whirl☐
　pool rooms, $185-$319; suites, $165-$314; 15 stories; interior corridors; heated pool, sauna, whirlpool☐
Fee: parking. **Dining:** Restaurant; 6 am-midnight; $8-$19; cocktails. **Services:** gift shop. **All Rooms:** extended cable TV, hono☐
bars. **Some Rooms:** safes. **Cards:** AE, DI, DS, JC, MC, VI. **Special Amenities:** Free newspaper. *(See color ad p 402)*

THE WESTIN CALGARY　　　　　　　　　　　　　　　Phone: (403)266-1611　🔲
CAA　　　All Year　　　　　　　1P: $160-$425　　　2P: $160-$425
◆◆◆◆　　**Location:** Corner of 4th Ave and 3rd St. 320 4th Ave SW T2P 2S6. Fax: 403/233-7471. **Terms:** Cancellatio☐
Hotel　　fee imposed; small pets only. **Facility:** 525 rooms. Guest rooms in Main Tower offer a slight western theme☐
　　　　Premiere Tower rooms are more upscale and luxurious. All rooms with hair dryer, iron, ironing board and voic☐
　　　　mail. 17-20 stories; interior corridors; heated pool, saunas, whirlpool. Fee: parking. **Dining:** Restaurant; 6:3☐
am-11:30 pm; $7-$36; cocktails; also, Owl's Nest Dining Room, see separate listing. **Services:** gift shop. **Recreation:** in-room☐
video games. **All Rooms:** extended cable TV, honor bars. **Cards:** AE, DI, DS, JC, MC, VI.

─── RESTAURANTS ───

CANNERY ROW　　　　　**Lunch:** $10-$16　　**Dinner:** $11-$20　　**Phone:** 403/269-8889　🔲
◆◆　　　　**Location:** Downtown at 2nd St SW. 317 10th Ave SW T2R 0A5. **Hours:** 11:30 am-4 & 5:30-10 pm☐
Seafood　　Thurs-Sat to 11 pm. **Closed:** 1/1 & 12/25. **Features:** casual dress; children's menu; carryout; cocktails ☐
　　　　　lounge; a la carte. This restaurant has a fun, exciting ambience, an open kitchen and an oyster bar. The☐
offer superb seafood, pasta, appetizers and entrees, and an attractive wine list and by-the-glass selection. Reservations are☐
required for weekday lunch. Fine service. **Cards:** AE, DI, DS, MC, VI.

CELADON　　　　　　　**Lunch:** $5-$12　　**Dinner:** $7-$24　　**Phone:** 403/261-2600　🔲
◆◆◆　　　**Location:** Corner 7th St SW. 720 11th Ave SW T2R 0E4. **Hours:** 11:30 am-2 & 5:30-10 pm. Closed majo☐
Regional　　holidays & Sun. **Reservations:** suggested. **Features:** dressy casual; carryout; cocktails & lounge; a la carte☐
Canadian　The decor is inviting and funky at this cafe lounge offering imaginative Asian-Western fusion such as baked☐
　　　　　chicken and shiitake dumplings, duck sausage, and pistachio creme brulee. Dishes have excellent flavors☐
and artistic presentations. Great service. **Cards:** AE, DI, MC, VI.

THE CONSERVATORY　　　**Lunch:** $13-$16　　**Dinner:** $21-$33　　**Phone:** 403/205-5433　🔲
CAA　　　**Location:** 1st St SE and 4th Ave SE; in Delta Bow Valley. 209 4th Ave SE T2G 0C6. **Hours:** 11:30 am-2 ☐
◆◆◆◆　　5:30-10:30 pm, Sat from 5:30 pm. Closed major holidays & Sun. **Reservations:** suggested☐
Continental　**Features:** dressy casual; health conscious menu items; cocktails & lounge; fee for parking & valet parking; ☐
　　　　　la carte, also prix fixe. The Conservatory features a very creative cuisine emphasizing a progressive☐
　　　　　approach to this region's game and fresh fish. The small intimate dining room has a semiformal atmosphere☐
A wide selection of Canadian VQA wines is offered. Knowledgeable staff. **Cards:** AE, DI, DS, JC, MC, VI.
(See color ad p 339)

DA PAOLO RISTORANTE　　**Lunch:** $8-$15　　**Dinner:** $11-$29　　**Phone:** 403/228-5556　🔲
◆◆◆　　　**Location:** Just w on 17th Ave S from MacLeod Trail S (becomes Hwy 2 S). 121 17th Ave SE T2G 1H3☐
Italian　　**Hours:** 11:30 am-2:30 & 5-11 pm, Sat from 5 pm. Closed major holidays & 7/17-7/30☐
　　　　　Reservations: suggested. **Features:** semi-formal attire; health conscious menu items; cocktails. Da Paolo's☐
is a popular restaurant serving traditional fare with a warm, welcoming attitude. Dozens of fresh pastas and seafood dishes☐
are complemented by chicken and veal entrees. The wine list includes well-chosen Italian selections. Service is formal☐
Cards: AE, DI, MC, VI.

DIVINO BISTRO-WINEBAR　　**Lunch:** $9-$17　　**Dinner:** $9-$17　　**Phone:** 403/263-5869　🔲
◆◆　　　　**Location:** At 9th Ave SW. 817 1st SW T2P 7N1. **Hours:** 11:30 am-11 pm. Closed major holidays & Sun☐
Southwest　**Reservations:** suggested. **Features:** health conscious menu; cocktails; fee for parking; a la carte. This☐
Continental　restaurant's cuisine is imaginative, colorful and creative, with some flavorful touches from California and the☐
　　　　　Mediterranean. Its casual and relaxed ambience may remind you of a European cafe. The server staff is☐
friendly, prompt and attentive. **Cards:** AE, MC, VI.

DON QUIJOTE　　　　　**Lunch:** $9-$19　　**Dinner:** $12-$22　　**Phone:** 403/205-4244　🔲
◆◆　　　　**Location:** Across from Eau Claire market. 309 2nd Ave SW T2P 0C5. **Hours:** 11 am-2:30 & 4:30-11 pm☐
Spanish　　Thurs & Fri-2 am, Sat 5 pm-2 am, Sun 5 pm-11 pm. Closed major holidays. **Reservations:** suggested☐
　　　　　Features: dressy casual; cocktails & lounge; entertainment. This restaurant is a good place to have tapas☐
and dance the salsa. Focusing on the seafood of the Spanish ports, it relies heavily on the tradition of butter, garlic an☐
lemon. Try the rich custard-filled cake soaked in Cinzano. Service is excellent. **Cards:** AE, MC, VI.

ENTRE NOUS　　　　　　**Lunch:** $8-$23　　**Dinner:** $18-$24　　**Phone:** 403/228-5525　🔲
◆◆◆　　　**Location:** E side of 4th St, corner 18th Ave SW. 1800 4th St SW T2S 2S5. **Hours:** 11 am-10 pm, Sun from☐
French　　10 am. Closed major holidays. **Reservations:** suggested. **Features:** dressy casual; Sunday brunch; health☐
　　　　　conscious menu items; cocktails; a la carte. Style AND substance are the standards at Entre Nous. This☐
restaurant has captured the elegance of a fine restaurant and the atmosphere of a casual bistro. The delicious food i☐
delicate, precise and beautifully presented. The staff is very knowledgeable. **Cards:** AE, CB, DI, MC, VI.

(See map p. 337)

FLORENTINE Lunch: $10-$20 Dinner: $22-$27 Phone: 403/232-6028 (8)
◆◆◆ **Location:** 10th Ave and 8th St SW. 1014 8th St SW T2R 1K2. **Hours:** 11:30 am-2 & 5:30-9 pm, Fri & Sat
Canadian 5:30 pm-10 pm. Closed major holidays, Sun & Mon. **Reservations:** suggested. **Features:** dressy casual;
cocktails; a la carte. Florentine's is a small, chic cafe where creativity is the operative word. Its imaginative
menu features fresh ingredients and innovations such as the Alberta lamb rubbed with cinnamon and chili. The staff is
friendly, attentive and knowledgeable. Smoke free premises. **Cards:** AE, DI, MC, VI. ✕

INDOCHINE Lunch: $7-$12 Dinner: $9-$16 Phone: 403/263-6929 (4)
◆◆ **Location:** Corner 2nd St SW; Bankers Hall, 2nd floor. 315 8th Ave SW T2P 4K1. **Hours:** 11:30 am-9:30 pm.
Vietnamese Closed: 12/25 & Sun. **Reservations:** suggested; lunch. **Features:** health conscious menu items; cocktails; a
la carte. A combination of Vietnamese and French cuisines makes for an eclectic menu with an accent on
healthy choices and colorful plate presentations that include banana leaves, yellow daisies and orchids. Its cozy setting has
an open annex. Flawless service. Smoke free premises. **Cards:** MC, VI. ✕

LA CHAUMIERE RESTAURANT Lunch: $8-$15 Dinner: $18-$29 Phone: 403/228-5690 (20)
ⓐ **Location:** Corner of 1st St and 17th Ave SW. 139 17th Ave SW T2S 0A1. **Hours:** 11:45 am-2:30 & 5:30-10
◆◆◆◆ pm, Sat from 5:30 pm. Closed major holidays & Sun. **Reservations:** required. **Features:** semi-formal attire;
Continental cocktails; a la carte. You'll appreciate this restaurant's exquisite cuisine with French influence and the elegant
semiformal setting of its open, airy dining room. The steamed seabass on a bed of lentils is excellent. The
wine list has more than 600 international selections. **Cards:** AE, DI, MC, VI. ✕

McQUEENS UPSTAIRS Lunch: $11-$15 Dinner: $17-$35 Phone: 403/269-4722 (14)
◆◆◆ **Location:** Downtown at 2nd St SW. 317 10th Ave SW T2R 0A5. **Hours:** 11:30 am-2 & 5:30-10 pm, Fri &
Seafood Sat-11 pm. Closed: 1/1, 12/24 & 12/25. **Reservations:** suggested. **Features:** dressy casual; health
conscious menu; cocktails; entertainment; a la carte. McQueens Upstairs features an inviting, elegant
ambience enlivened by music from a pianist or jazz duo. Its selection of flavorful seafood, steak and chicken is prepared
with creativity, style and color. Many wines are offered by the glass. **Cards:** AE, DI, DS, MC, VI. ✕

MESCALERO Lunch: $7-$12 Dinner: $17-$24 Phone: 403/266-3339 (18)
◆◆◆ **Location:** Corner of 1st St and 13th Ave SW. 1315 1st St SW T2R 0V5. **Hours:** 11:30 am-10 pm, Thurs-11
Southwest pm, Fri & Sat-midnight. Closed: 12/23-12/26. **Reservations:** suggested. **Features:** Sunday brunch; cocktails;
Mexican street parking; a la carte. A charming, rustic Mexican decor and warm, lively atmosphere will greet you at
Mescalero's. This restaurant has an exciting menu of lamb, beef, veal, chicken and seafood dishes grilled
over an applewood fire and creatively presented. Service is flawless. **Cards:** AE, DI, MC, VI. ✕

OWL'S NEST DINING ROOM Lunch: $10-$18 Dinner: $24-$36 Phone: 403/266-1611 (3)
◆◆◆◆ **Location:** Corner of 4th Ave and 3rd St; in The Westin Calgary. 320 4 Ave SW T2P 2S6. **Hours:** 11:30 am-2
Continental & 5:30-11 pm, Sat from 5:30 pm. Closed major holidays & Sun. **Reservations:** suggested. **Features:** dressy
casual; children's menu; health conscious menu; cocktails & lounge; fee for parking & valet parking; a la
carte, also prix fixe. The superior taste, appearance and freshness of meals will exceed your expectations at this formal,
fine-dining restaurant. The Atlantic salmon and beef tenderloin are excellent. Exclusive wines are offered by the glass.
Service is attentive and cordial. **Cards:** AE, DI, DS, JC, MC, VI. ♿ ✕

THE PANORAMA DINING ROOM Lunch: $10-$15 Dinner: $23-$38 Phone: 403/266-7171 (17)
ⓐ **Location:** At top of Calgary Tower; in Palliser Square. 101 9th Ave SW T2P 1J9. **Hours:** 7:30 am-3 & 5-9
◆◆◆ pm, 8 am-3 & 5-8:30 pm in winter. **Reservations:** suggested. **Features:** Sunday brunch; children's menu;
Continental cocktails; fee for parking; a la carte. The Panorama's cuisine features salmon, steak and chicken dishes
served by friendly, attentive servers. Its revolving room atop the city's tallest building offers a spectacular
view of the Calgary area and Rocky Mountains. An elevation fee is charged. **Cards:** AE, DI, MC, VI. ✕

RIVER CAFE Lunch: $7-$12 Dinner: $14-$32 Phone: 403/261-7670 (1)
◆◆ **Location:** On Prince's Island, on the Bow River. **Hours:** Open 3/1-12/31; 11 am-11 pm, Sat & Sun brunch
Regional 10 am-3 pm. Closed: 12/25. **Reservations:** suggested. **Features:** health conscious menu items; cocktails;
Canadian fee for parking; a la carte. Located in heart of Prince's Island Park, this enchanting restaurant features a
decor of natural wood and a large fireplace. The large outdoor deck open in season. There is no parking at
restaurant, so use one of the downtown lots. Smoke free premises. **Cards:** AE, DI, MC, VI. ✕

SILVER DRAGON RESTAURANT Lunch: $6-$17 Dinner: $6-$17 Phone: 403/264-5326 (5)
ⓐ **Location:** In Chinatown. 106 3rd Ave SE T2G 0B6. **Hours:** 10:30 am-midnight, Fri & Sat-2 am, Sun 9:30
◆◆ am-10:30 am. **Reservations:** suggested. **Features:** carryout; cocktails; a la carte. The Silver Dragon
Chinese Restaurant specializes in excellent Cantonese and Szechwan cuisine and serves a delicious dim sum
selection each day. The ginger beef is excellent, the contemporary decor features nouveau Oriental artwork,
and servers are very cordial. **Cards:** AE, DI, JC, MC, VI. ✕

THAI SA-ON RESTAURANT Lunch: $6-$13 Dinner: $6-$13 Phone: 403/264-3526 (12)
◆◆ **Location:** At 4th St SW. 351 10th Ave SW T2R 0A5. **Hours:** 11:30 am-2 & 5-10 pm, Fri & Sat-11 pm.
Thai Closed major holidays & Sun. **Reservations:** suggested. **Features:** casual dress; health conscious menu;
cocktails; street parking; a la carte. Here you'll discover a well-prepared cuisine characterized by decorative
presentation and a good use of spices and condiments. Many vegetarian items are offered. The quiet, casual ambience is
enhanced by music and artwork from Thailand. Fine service. Smoke free premises. **Cards:** AE, MC, VI. ✕

CALGARY pop. 768,100 (See map p. 338; index p. 336)

——— LODGINGS ———

BEST WESTERN AIRPORT INN   Phone: (403)250-5015

CAA	6/1-9/30	1P: $100-$125	2P: $145	XP: $10	F12
◆◆	3/1-5/31	1P: $99-$109	2P: $121	XP: $6	F12
	10/1-12/31 & 1/1-2/28	1P: $89-$99	2P: $111	XP: $6	F12

Motor Inn   **Location:** 1 km e of jct Deerfoot Tr (Hwy 2) and 16th Ave NE (Trans Canada Hwy 1). 1947 18 Ave NE T2E 7T8. Fax: 403/250-5019. **Facility:** 75 rooms. Contemporary guest rooms with a few vintage appointments. 3 stories; interior corridors; small heated pool. **Dining:** Coffee shop; 7 am-11 & 6-9 pm; $7-$14; cocktails. **Services:** winter plug-ins. **All Rooms:** extended cable TV. **Some Rooms:** 12 efficiencies, no utensils. **Cards:** AE, DI, DS, MC, VI.
(See color ad p 339)

BEST WESTERN HOSPITALITY INN   Phone: (403)278-5050

CAA SAVE	5/16-9/30	1P: $115-$185	2P: $120-$190	XP: $5	F16
◆◆◆	1/1-2/28	1P: $99-$164	2P: $104-$169	XP: $5	F16
	3/1-5/15 & 10/1-12/31	1P: $94-$159	2P: $99-$164	XP: $5	F16

Motor Inn   **Location:** On Hwy 2 (Macleod Tr), corner of Southland Dr. 135 Southland Dr SE T2J 5X5. Fax: 403/278-5050. **Terms:** Weekly & monthly rates avail; 7 day cancellation notice; small pets only, in smoking rooms. **Facility:** 261 rooms. Lush atrium and pool area. Property features 2 different styles of guest rooms, larger executive style units to slightly smaller, all with attractive contemporary appointments. All rooms with hair dryer, iron and ironing board. 11 suites $109-$299; 6 whirlpool rooms, $190-$335; 3-8 stories; interior corridors; heated pool, whirlpool. **Dining:** 2 restaurants; 6:30 am-11 pm, Sun 7 am-10 pm; $7-$20; cocktails; nightclub. **Services:** gift shop; winter plug-ins. **Recreation:** in-room video games. **All Rooms:** combo or shower baths, extended cable TV. **Cards:** AE, CB, DI, DS, MC, VI. **Special Amenities:** Free local telephone calls and free newspaper. *(See color ad below & p 339)*

(See map p. 338)

BEST WESTERN PORT O'CALL INN
Phone: (403)291-4600   **51**

AAA SAVE

	10/1-2/28	1P: $134-$169	2P: $134-$169	XP: $5	F17
	5/1-9/30	1P: $139-$159	2P: $139-$159	XP: $5	F17
	3/1-4/30	1P: $134-$149	2P: $134-$149	XP: $5	F17

Motor Inn   **Location:** 2.5 km ne of jct Hwy 2 (Deerfoot Tr); at 19th St NE. 1935 McKnight Blvd NE T2E 6V4. Fax: 403/250-6827. **Terms:** [BP] meal plan; monthly rates avail; cancellation fee imposed. **Facility:** 201 rooms. Ample sized guest rooms; all attractively decorated with contemporary colors. Modern and bright public areas. Underground heated parking. All rooms with iron, ironing board and voice mail. 9 whirlpool rooms, $239-$399; 6-7 stories; interior corridors; heated pool, steamrooms, whirlpool; racquetball court. **Dining:** Restaurant; 6 am-11 pm, Sat from 6:30 am, Sun 6:30 am-10 pm; $10-$23; cocktails. **Services:** gift shop; winter plug-ins. **Recreation:** in-room video games. **All Rooms:** extended cable TV. **Some Rooms:** honor bars. **Cards:** AE, DI, DS, JC, MC, VI. **Special Amenities: Early check-in/late check-out and free newspaper.** (See color ad p 339 & p 342)

BEST WESTERN SUITES DOWNTOWN
Phone: (403)228-6900   **66**

AAA SAVE

	7/21-9/30	1P: $110-$145	2P: $110-$145	XP: $10	F18
	6/1-7/20	1P: $145	2P: $145	XP: $10	F18
	3/1-5/31	1P: $89-$110	2P: $89-$110	XP: $10	F18
	10/1-2/99	1P: $89-$99	2P: $89-$99	XP: $10	F18

Suite Hotel   **Location:** Corner of 8th St and 13th Ave SW. 1330 8th St SW T2R 1B6. Fax: 403/228-5535. **Terms:** [CP] meal plan; weekly & monthly rates avail; 3 day cancellation notice; cancellation fee imposed; small pets only. **Facility:** 123 rooms. A mix of guest rooms from standard to separate bedroom units with cooking facilities. In the trendy 17th Ave district, just n of Mount Royal Village shopping complex. Business oriented hotel. All rooms with iron and ironing board. 25 two-bedroom units. 6 whirlpool rooms, $155-$175; 15 stories; interior corridors; sauna. **Dining:** Restaurant nearby. **Services:** winter plug-ins. **All Rooms:** extended cable TV. **Some Rooms:** 82 efficiencies. **Cards:** AE, CB, DI, DS, JC, MC, VI. **Special Amenities: Free local telephone calls and free newspaper.** (See color ad p 339 & below)

BEST WESTERN VILLAGE PARK INN
Phone: (403)289-0241   **41**

AAA SAVE

| | All Year | 1P: $129-$149 | 2P: $129-$149 | XP: $10 | F18 |

Motor Inn   **Location:** Just ne of jct Trans Canada Hwy 1 and Crowchild Tr; in Motel Village. 1804 Crowchild Tr NW T2M 3Y7. Fax: 403/289-4645. **Terms:** Package plans; small pets only, in designated rooms. **Facility:** 160 rooms. Spacious modern rooms. Gracious public area with a relaxed tropical decor. All rooms with hair dryer, iron and ironing board. 3 whirlpool rooms, 5 stories; interior corridors; heated pool, whirlpool. **Dining:** Restaurant; 6:30 am-11 pm; $7-$20; cocktails. **Services:** gift shop. **All Rooms:** extended cable TV. **Some Rooms:** safes. **Cards:** AE, CB, DI, DS, MC, VI. **Special Amenities: Early check-in/late check-out and free newspaper.** (See color ad p 342 & p 339)

BLACKFOOT INN
Phone: (403)252-2253   **70**

AAA SAVE

| | All Year | 1P: $125-$165 | 2P: $125-$165 | XP: $10 | F16 |

Motor Inn   **Location:** At 58th Ave SE; access to property from 58th Ave only. 5940 Blackfoot Tr SE T2H 2B5. Fax: 403/252-3574. **Terms:** Monthly rates avail; 3 day cancellation notice; cancellation fee imposed; package plans; pets. **Facility:** 200 rooms. Rooms offer a variety of decor; the 2 distinct sections have been renovated at different times. Overall well appointed and attractive. Good variety of entertainment outlets. 7 stories; interior corridors; heated pool, sauna, whirlpool. **Dining:** Dining room, restaurant; 6:30 am-11 pm; $8-$23; cocktails; sports bar, Yuk Yuk Comedy Club. **Services:** gift shop; winter plug-ins. **Recreation:** exercise equipment for room use. **All Rooms:** extended cable TV. **Some Rooms:** honor bars. **Cards:** AE, DI, MC, VI. **Special Amenities: Free newspaper.**

BUDGET HOST MOTOR INN
Phone: (403)288-7115   **37**

AAA SAVE

	7/7-7/16	1P: $89-$99	2P: $99-$115	XP: $5	F12
	7/17-9/30	1P: $69-$79	2P: $75-$92	XP: $5	F12
	3/1-7/6	1P: $64-$74	2P: $69-$84	XP: $5	F12
	10/1-2/28	1P: $59-$69	2P: $69-$84	XP: $5	F12

Motel   **Location:** On Trans Canada Hwy 1 (16th Ave NW) at 43rd St NW. 4420 16th Ave NW T3B 0M4. Fax: 403/286-4899. **Terms:** Weekly rates avail, off season. **Facility:** 72 rooms. Bright, modern, average sized guest rooms, some facing south feature patio doors but no patio. 30 efficiencies, $10 extra charge; 3 stories; interior corridors. **Services:** winter plug-ins. **All Rooms:** extended cable TV. **Cards:** AE, MC, VI. **Special Amenities: Free local telephone calls and free room upgrade (subject to availability with advanced reservations).** (See color ad p 344)

(See map p. 338)

CALGARY NORTH TRAVELODGE
Phone: (403)289-0211

CAA SAVE ◆◆ Motel

6/4-9/3	1P: $90-$135	2P: $110-$135	XP: $5
1/1-2/28	1P: $73-$83	2P: $83-$99	XP: $5
3/1-6/3	1P: $73-$79	2P: $83-$94	XP: $5
9/4-12/31	1P: $73-$79	2P: $83-$84	XP: $5

Location: Jct 16th Ave (Trans Canada Hwy 1) and Banff Tr NW; in Motel Village. 2304 16th Ave NW T2M 0M5. Fax: 403/282-6924. **Terms:** 3 day cancellation notice; cancellation fee imposed. **Facility:** 56 rooms. Good sized guest rooms. 2 stories; exterior corridors; heated pool. **Dining:** Restaurant nearby. **Services:** winter plug-ins. **All Rooms:** extended cable TV. **Some Rooms:** Fee: refrigerators. **Cards:** AE, DI, MC, VI. **Special Amenities:** Free local telephone calls and free newspaper.

CALGARY SOUTH TRAVELODGE
Phone: (403)253-1111

CAA SAVE ◆◆ Motel

6/4-9/3	1P: $90-$135	2P: $110-$150	XP: $5
1/1-2/28	1P: $73-$88	2P: $83-$99	XP: $5
3/1-6/3 & 9/4-12/31	1P: $73-$85	2P: $83-$99	XP: $5

Location: On Hwy 2 (Macleod Tr) at 70th Ave S. 7012 Macleod Tr S T2H 0L3. Fax: 403/253-2879. **Terms:** day cancellation notice; cancellation fee imposed. **Facility:** 62 rooms. Spacious guest rooms, ground floor rooms have outside access to parking lot. Short distance to Chinook Shopping Centre. 2 stories; interior/exterior corridors; heated pool. **Dining:** Restaurant nearby. **Services:** winter plug-ins. **All Rooms:** extended cable TV. **Cards:** AE, DI, MC, VI. **Special Amenities:** Free local telephone calls and free newspaper.

CALGARY WESTWAYS GUEST HOUSE
Phone: 403/229-1758

CAA SAVE ◆◆ Historic Bed & Breakfast

5/1-9/20	1P: $70-$90	2P: $80-$105	XP: $25
9/21-11/20	1P: $65-$85	2P: $75-$95	XP: $25
3/1-4/30	1P: $60-$79	2P: $70-$90	XP: $20
11/21-2/28	1P: $60-$75	2P: $70-$90	XP: $20

Location: 1.7 km s on MacLeod Tr S, 0.5 km w. 216 25th Ave SW T2S 0L1. Fax: 403/228-6265. **Terms:** [BP] meal plan; weekly rates avail; age restrictions may apply; 7 day cancellation notice; pets, small dogs on premises. **Facility:** 5 rooms. Unassuming B&B built in 1912. Rooms vary in style and size. Top floor rooms are very spacious, modern and include extra amenities. Whirlpool room, $75-$165; 3 stories, no elevator; interior corridors; smoke free premises; whirlpool. **Services:** winter plug-ins. **Recreation:** video library. **All Rooms:** combo or shower baths, extended cable TV. **Cards:** AE, MC, VI.

CARRIAGE HOUSE INN
Phone: (403)253-1101

CAA SAVE ◆◆◆ Motor Inn

6/1-9/15	1P: $129-$139	2P: $129-$139	XP: $10
3/1-5/31 & 9/16-2/28	1P: $115-$125	2P: $115-$125	XP: $5

Location: On Hwy 2, corner of 90th Ave SW. 9030 Macleod Tr S T2H 0M4. Fax: 403/259-2414. **Terms:** Weekly & monthly rates avail; pets, $5 extra charge. **Facility:** 157 rooms. Spacious, ornate lobby with a European ambience. 2 whirlpool rms, $175-$255; 4-10 stories; interior corridors; heated pool, saunas, whirlpool. **Dining:** Dining room, coffee shop; 6:30 am-11:30 pm, Sun 7 am-11 pm; $15-$21; cocktails; nightclub. **Services:** gift shop; winter plug-ins. **Recreation:** adult games room, in-room video games. **All Rooms:** extended cable TV. **Some Rooms:** honor bars. **Cards:** AE, CB, DI, DS, JC, MC, VI. **Special Amenities:** Free newspaper and free room upgrade (subject to availability with advanced reservations).

THE COAST PLAZA HOTEL
Phone: (403)248-8888

CAA SAVE ◆◆◆ Motor Inn

All Year	1P: $165-$175	2P: $165-$175	XP: $15

Location: Just s of jct 16th Ave (Trans Canada Hwy 1) and 36th St NE, just w on 12th Ave NE, adjacent to Franklin Mall. 1316 33rd St NE T2A 6B6. Fax: 403/248-0749. **Terms:** [CP] meal plan; package plans; pets, $25 dep req. **Facility:** 248 rooms. Convention oriented property. Comfortable guest rooms, all with pleasant modern decor. Close to shopping malls and several restaurants. All rooms with iron, ironing board and video games. whirlpool rooms, $305; 6-12 stories; interior corridors; heated pool, saunas, whirlpool. **Dining:** Restaurant; 6:30 am-11:30 pm; $8-$20; cocktails; nightclub. **Services:** gift shop; winter plug-ins. **All Rooms:** extended cable TV. **Some Rooms:** kitchen. **Cards:** AE, DI, DS, MC, VI. **Special Amenities:** Free local telephone calls and free newspaper.

See map p. 338)

OMFORT INN AND SUITES-AIRPORT   Phone: (403)735-1966   **54**

(AAA) (SAVE)
◆◆◆
Motel

| | 5/1-9/30 | 1P: $99-$199 | 2P: $109-$219 | XP: $10 | F18 |
| | 3/1-4/30 & 10/1-2/28 | 1P: $79-$129 | 2P: $89-$149 | XP: $10 | F18 |

Location: Just se of jct 32nd Ave NE and Barlow Tr NE. 3111 26th St NE T1Y 7E4. Fax: 403/735-1955. **Terms:** [CP] meal plan. **Facility:** 66 rooms. Newer property with very good sized rooms; all nicely appointed and with hair dryer. 8 whirlpool rooms; 4 stories; interior corridors; heated pool, steamroom, waterslide, whirl-pool. **Dining:** Restaurant nearby. **Services:** winter plug-ins. **All Rooms:** extended cable TV. **Some Rooms:** Fee: VCR. **Cards:** AE, DI, DS, MC, VI. **Special Amenities: Free breakfast and free local telephone calls.**

COUNTRY INN & SUITES BY CARLSON   Phone: (403)250-1800   **65**

(AAA) (SAVE)
◆◆◆
Motel

| | All Year | 1P: $99 | 2P: $109 | XP: $10 | F18 |

Location: Barlow Tr at 39th Ave NE. 2481 39th Ave NE T2E 8V8. Fax: 403/250-2121. **Terms:** [ECP] meal plan; 15 day cancellation notice. **Facility:** 106 rooms. Well appointed rooms and 1-bedroom suites. Graceful country decor throughout the property. All rooms with hair dryer, iron and ironing board. 4 whirlpool rooms, $125; 3 stories; interior corridors; heated pool, whirlpool. **Dining:** Breakfast room 6-9:30 am, Sat & Sun 7-10:30 am. **Services:** winter plug-ins. **All Rooms:** combo or shower baths, extended cable TV. **Some Rooms:** Fee: VCR. **Cards:** AE, DI, DS, MC, VI. **Special Amenities: Free breakfast and free newspaper.** *(See color ad below)*

DAYS INN-CALGARY WEST   Phone: (403)289-1961   **47**

(AAA) (SAVE)
◆◆
Motor Inn

| | 6/1-9/30 | 1P: $95-$110 | 2P: $105-$120 | XP: $15 | F12 |
| | 3/1-5/31 & 10/1-2/28 | 1P: $85-$100 | 2P: $95-$110 | XP: $15 | F12 |

Location: 5.2 km nw on Trans Canada Hwy 1. 1818 16th Ave NW T2M 0L8. Fax: 403/289-3901. **Terms:** [CP] meal plan; pets, $10 extra charge. **Facility:** 130 rooms. Average sized guests rooms. Rooms facing south feature private balcony. Close to North Hill Shopping Centre and S.A.I.T. 4 stories; interior corridors; small heated pool. **Dining:** Dining room, coffee shop; 6:30 am-11:30 pm, Sun 7 am-11 pm; $8-$25; cocktails; night club. **Services:** winter plug-ins. **All Rooms:** combo or shower baths, extended cable TV. **Some Rooms:** Fee: VCR. **Cards:** AE, CB, DI, JC, MC, VI. **Special Amenities: Free local telephone calls and free newspaper.** *(See color ad below)*

(See map p. 338)

ECONO LODGE BANFF TRAIL

Phone: (403)289-1921

CAA SAVE

◆ ◆

Motel

| 5/1-9/30 | 1P: $89-$139 | 2P: $99-$149 | XP: $10 |
| 3/1-4/30 & 10/1-2/28 | 1P: $69 | 2P: $79 | XP: $10 |

Location: In Motel Village; just n of jct Trans Canada Hwy 1 (16th Ave NW) and Banff Tr NW. 2231 Banff Tr NW T2M 4L2. Fax: 403/282-2149. **Terms:** Weekly & monthly rates avail; 3 day cancellation notice. **Facility:** 6 rooms. Offers a wide range of accommodations from average sized rooms, to newer, well appointed units with refrigerator and microwave, or spacious 1-bedroom suites with a kitchen. All rooms with hair dryer. 2 stories; exterior corridors. **Dining:** Restaurant nearby. **Services:** winter plug-ins. **All Rooms:** extended cable TV. **Some Rooms:** 26 kitchens. **Cards:** AE, DI, DS, MC, VI. **Special Amenities:** Free local telephone calls and free newspaper.

ECONO LODGE MOTEL VILLAGE

Phone: (403)289-2561

CAA SAVE

◆ ◆

Motel

| 5/1-9/30 | 1P: $89-$139 | 2P: $99-$149 | XP: $10 |
| 3/1-4/30 & 10/1-2/28 | 1P: $69 | 2P: $79 | XP: $10 |

Location: In Motel Village; jct Trans Canada Hwy 1 (16 Ave NW) and Banff Tr NW. 2440 16th Ave NW T2M 0M5. Fax: 403/282-9713. **Terms:** Weekly & monthly rates avail; 3 day cancellation notice. **Facility:** 56 rooms. Rooms vary in size, all offer most contemporary appointments. 2 stories; interior/exterior corridors; sauna. **Dining:** Restaurant nearby. **Services:** winter plug-ins. **All Rooms:** extended cable TV. **Some Rooms:** 16 efficiencies. **Cards:** AE, CB, DI, DS, MC, VI. **Special Amenities:** Free local telephone calls and preferred room (subject to availability with advanced reservations).

ELBOW RIVER INN & CASINO

Phone: (403)269-6771

CAA

◆

Motor Inn

| All Year | 1P: $59-$99 | 2P: $69-$109 |

Location: Jct Macleod Tr and 1st St SE; opposite Stampede Park. 1919 Macleod Tr SE T2G 4S1. Fax: 403/237-5181. **Terms:** 3 day cancellation notice; pets. **Facility:** 77 rooms. Set along the banks of the Elbow River. Rooms at the back overlook lush riverbank. Large casino at 1 end of property. 3 stories; interior corridors. **Dining:** Restaurant; 6:30 am-2 & 5-10 pm, Sun from 7 am; $4-$10; cocktails. **Services:** winter plug-ins. **Recreation:** jogging. **Some Rooms:** 4 efficiencies. **Cards:** AE, MC, VI. *(See color ad below)*

(See map p. 338)

FOUR POINTS SHERATON HOTEL AND SUITES, CALGARY WEST

Phone: (403)288-4441   35

(AA) (SAVE)

◆◆◆

Hotel

6/1-10/15	1P: $129	2P: $129	XP: $10 F12
3/1-5/31	1P: $119	2P: $119	XP: $10 F12
10/16-2/28	1P: $109	2P: $109	XP: $10 F12

Location: Opposite Canada Olympic Park. 8220 Bowridge Cr NW T3B 2V1. Fax: 403/288-4442. **Terms:** 3 day cancellation notice; package plans. **Facility:** 118 rooms. Nicely appointed and well equipped guest rooms ranging from standard units to 1-bedroom suites, a few with whirlpool and/or gas fireplace. All rooms with hair dryer and video games. 10 whirlpool rooms, $169-$249; 3 stories; interior corridors; heated pool, waterslide, whirlpool. **Dining:** Restaurant; 6 am-midnight; $6-$15; cocktails. **Services:** winter plug-ins. Fee: massage. **All Rooms:** extended cable TV. **Cards:** AE, DI, DS, MC, VI. **Special Amenities:** Early check-in/late check-out and free newspaper. *(See color ad p 402 & below)*

GLENMORE INN AND CONVENTION CENTRE

Phone: (403)279-8611   72

◆◆◆

Motor Inn

All Year	1P: $119-$145	2P: $119-$145	XP: $10

Location: 3 km e of Hwy 2 (Deerfoot Tr) Glenmore E exit; at Ogden Rd. 2720 Glenmore Tr SE T2C 2E6. Fax: 403/236-8035. **Terms:** Check-in 4 pm; 3 day cancellation notice; cancellation fee imposed. **Facility:** 169 rooms. Recently opened tower rooms are beautifully appointed with oak furnishing and warm earth tone colours. Rooms in the original section feature a mix of contemporary and vintage appointments. All rooms with hair dryer. 2 stories; interior corridors. **Services:** gift shop; winter plug-ins. Fee: area transportation. **Cards:** AE, DI, DS, MC, VI.

GREENWOOD INN HOTELS

Phone: (403)250-8855   53

(AA) (SAVE)

◆◆◆

Motor Inn

All Year	1P: $129-$149	2P: $139-$159	XP: $10 F18

Location: From Barlow Tr N, just e on 32nd Ave NE, then just n. 3515 26th ST NE T1Y 7E3. Fax: 403/250-8050. **Terms:** 30 day cancellation notice; package plans; pets, in designated rooms. **Facility:** 210 rooms. Modern property with beautifully appointed public areas. Guest room decor is vibrant and includes excellent furnishings. All rooms with hair dryer, iron, ironing board and voice mail. Heated underground parking avail. Luxury king room with steam shower, $149, 1-bedroom suite, $199, 1-bedroom suite with gas fireplace & whirlpool, $279; 2 whirlpool rooms, $279-$299; 6 stories; interior corridors; heated pool, steamroom, whirlpool. **Dining:** Restaurant; 6 am-11 pm, Sat & Sun from 6:30 am; $12-$18; cocktails. **Services:** gift shop; winter plug-ins. **All Rooms:** combo or shower baths, extended cable TV. **Cards:** AE, DI, MC, VI. **Special Amenities:** Free local telephone calls and free newspaper. *(See color ad p 373 & below)*

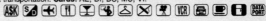

(See map p. 338)

HAMPTON INN & SUITES-CALGARY AIRPORT   **Phone:** (403)250-4667   52

◆◆◆   5/16-9/15   1P: $104-$124   2P: $104-$124

Motel   3/1-5/15   1P: $99-$124   2P: $99-$124

           9/16-2/28   1P: $99-$124   2P: $99-$124   XP: $10

Location: Barlow Tr at 37th Ave NE. 2420 37th Ave NE T2E 8S6. Fax: 403/250-5788. **Terms:** [ECP] meal plan. **Facility:** 104 rooms. Spacious units, contemporary decor. Very good amenities, including iron, ironing board, hair dryer and voice mail in each unit. Well appointed and spacious lobby with an adjoining breakfast room. 4 stories; interior corridors; small heated indoor pool. **Services:** area transportation; winter plug-ins. **Some Rooms:** 26 kitchens. **Cards:** AE, DI, DS, MC, VI.
(See color ad below)

HAMPTON INN & SUITES NORTHWEST   **Phone:** (403)289-9800   42

◆◆◆   5/1-9/30   1P: $109-$189   2P: $119-$189

Motel   3/1-4/30 & 10/1-2/28   1P: $89-$124   2P: $99-$124

           Location: In Motel Village; just n of jct Trans Canada Hwy 1 (16th Ave NW) and Banff Trl NW. 2231 Banff Trl NW T2M 4L2. Fax: 403/289-9200. **Terms:** [ECP] meal plan; check-in 4 pm; 3 day cancellation notice; package plans. **Facility:** 96 rooms. Beautifully appointed rooms and 1-bedroom suites with mini kitchen including a dishwasher. All rooms with hair dryer, iron and ironing board. Heated underground parking. 4 stories; interior corridors; small heated indoor pool. **Services:** gift shop. **Cards:** AE, DI, DS, MC, VI. *(See color ad below)*

HOLIDAY INN CALGARY AIRPORT   **Phone:** (403)230-1999   59

◆◆◆   6/1-9/30   1P: $114-$145   2P: $114-$145   XP: $10   F19

Motor Inn   3/1-5/31 & 10/1-2/28   1P: $84-$145   2P: $84-$145   XP: $10   F19

Location: 1 km e of jct Deerfoot Tr (Hwy 2) and 16th Ave NE (Trans Canada Hwy 1). 1250 McKinnon Dr NE T2E 7T7. Fax: 403/277-2623. **Terms:** Pets. **Facility:** 170 rooms. Attractive and contemporary units. 5th floor features all king beds. All rooms with hair dryer, iron, ironing board and video games. 5 stories; interior corridors; heated pool. **Services:** gift shop; winter plug-ins. **Cards:** AE, CB, DI, DS, JC, MC, VI. *(See color ad p 349)*

(See map p. 338)

HOLIDAY INN CALGARY SOUTH

Phone: (403)287-2700　[69]

CAA SAVE ◆◆◆ Motor Inn

5/1-9/30	1P: $95-$130	2P: $110-$145	XP: $10	F18
10/1-2/28	1P: $90-$130	2P: $110-$140	XP: $10	F18
3/1-4/30	1P: $90-$126	2P: $110-$140	XP: $10	F18

Location: Corner of 42nd Ave and MacLoed Tr S. 4206 MacLeod Tr S T2G 2R7. Fax: 403/243-4721. **Terms:** Weekly & monthly rates avail; small pets only, on ground floor. **Facility:** 154 rooms. All rooms attractively furnished with contemporary appointments and very good amenity packages. 3 whirlpool rooms; 4 stories; interior corridors; heated pool, whirlpool. **Dining:** Restaurant; 7 am-10:30 pm; $6-$20; cocktails. **Services:** winter plug-ins. **All Rooms:** extended cable TV. **Cards:** AE, CB, DI, DS, JC, MC, VI.

HOLIDAY INN EXPRESS UNIVERSITY

Phone: (403)289-6600　[49]

CAA SAVE ◆◆◆ Motel

6/4-9/3	1P: $110-$160	2P: $110-$180	XP: $5	F17
1/1-2/28	1P: $78-$99	2P: $78-$109	XP: $5	F17
9/4-12/31	1P: $78-$95	2P: $78-$105	XP: $5	F17
3/1-6/3	1P: $78-$95	2P: $78-$105	XP: $8	F17

Location: 16 Ave (Trans Canada Hwy 1) and Banff Tr NW; in Motel Village. 2227 Banff Tr NW T2M 4L2. Fax: 403/289-6767. **Terms:** [CP] meal plan; 3 day cancellation notice; cancellation fee imposed; small pets only, in smoking rooms. **Facility:** 64 rooms. Large guest rooms, pleasantly decorated. Close to McMahon Stadium and Calgary's light rail transit system. 3 stories; interior corridors; sauna, whirlpool, outdoor pool privileges shared with Calgary North Travelodge next door. **Dining:** Restaurant nearby. **Services:** winter plug-ins. **All Rooms:** combo or shower baths, extended cable TV. **Cards:** AE, DI, DS, MC, VI. **Special Amenities:** Free breakfast and free local telephone calls.

INGLEWOOD BED & BREAKFAST

Phone: 403/262-6570　[64]

◆◆ Bed & Breakfast

All Year　　1P: $70-$115　　2P: $80-$125

Location: Just n of 9th Ave and 9th St SE. 1006 8th Ave SE T2G 0M4. Fax: 403/262-6570. **Terms:** [BP] meal plan; check-in 4 pm; 10 day cancellation notice; cancellation fee imposed. **Facility:** 3 rooms. Located in one of Calgary's oldest neighborhoods, only minutes walk to area attractions. Modern guest rooms. 2 stories; interior corridors; smoke free premises. **Services:** winter plug-ins. **All Rooms:** shower baths. **Some Rooms:** color TV. **Cards:** MC, VI.

(See map p. 338)

LORD NELSON INN
Phone: (403)269-8262   63

	5/1-9/30	1P: $95-$135	2P: $95-$135	XP: $10	F18
	3/1-4/30 & 10/1-2/28	1P: $80-$95	2P: $80-$95	XP: $10	F18

Motor Inn   **Location:** 8th Ave at 10 St SW. 1020 8th Ave SW T2P 1J2. Fax: 403/269-4868. **Terms:** Cancellation fee imposed. **Facility:** 55 rooms. Spacious units, all with balcony. Close to downtown and the light rail transit line. 2 whirlpool rooms, $140-$195; suites, $90-$135; 9 stories; interior corridors. **Dining:** Restaurant; 7 am-9 pm, Sat & Sun 8 am-2 pm; $5-$15; cocktails. **Services:** winter plug-ins. **All Rooms:** extended cable TV. **Cards:** AE, CB, DI, DS, MC, VI. **Special Amenities:** Early check-in/late check-out.

PARADISE ACRES BED & BREAKFAST
Phone: (403)248-4748   61

	All Year	1P: $60-$65	2P: $70-$75	XP: $15	D15

Bed & Breakfast   **Location:** From Calgary City limits, 5.7 km e on Hwy 1 (Trans Canada), 0.9 km s. 243105 Paradise Rd T2M 4L5 (Box 20, Site 2, RR 6). Fax: 403/235-3916. **Terms:** [BP] meal plan; check-in 4 pm; 19 day cancellation notice; cancellation fee imposed. **Facility:** 4 rooms. Spacious, contemporary home located on prairie land just outside the city. Elegant seating areas, bedrooms featuring pleasant homelike decor, ensuite or private bathrooms. 2 stories; interior corridors; smoke free premises. **All Rooms:** combo or shower baths. **Cards:** AE, MC, VI. **Special Amenities:** Free breakfast and free local telephone calls. *(See color ad p 629)*

QUALITY HOTEL & CONFERENCE CENTRE
Phone: (403)243-5531   68

	5/16-9/30	1P: $89-$119	2P: $89-$119	XP: $10	F18
	10/1-2/28	1P: $89-$109	2P: $89-$109	XP: $10	F18
	3/1-5/15	1P: $79-$99	2P: $79-$99	XP: $10	F18

Motor Inn   **Location:** Corner of Macleod Tr and 38th Ave SE. 3828 Macleod Tr S T2G 2R2. Fax: 403/243-6962. **Terms:** Weekly & monthly rates avail; check-in 4 pm; small pets only, $10 extra charge, in smoking rooms. **Facility:** 134 rooms. Rooms vary in style and size. Executive rooms in the new building include a wet bar, refrigerator and microwave. All rooms with hair dryer and voice mail. 4 stories; interior corridors; heated pool, whirlpool. **Dining:** Restaurant; 6:30 am-10 pm; $6-$12; cocktails. **Services:** gift shop; winter plug-ins. **Recreation:** hair salon, in-room video games. **All Rooms:** extended cable TV. **Cards:** AE, DI, DS, JC, MC, VI. **Special Amenities:** Free local telephone calls and free room upgrade (subject to availability with advanced reservations).

(See map p. 338)

RADISSON HOTEL CALGARY AIRPORT Phone: (403)291-4666 58
(CAA) (SAVE) All Year 1P: $99-$139 2P: $99-$139 XP: $10 F18
◆◆◆ **Location:** 0.5 km e of jct Trans Canada Hwy 1 and 16th Ave NE and Hwy 2. 2120 16th Ave NE T2E 1L4.
Motor Inn Fax: 403/291-6498. **Terms:** Cancellation fee imposed; pets, $10 extra charge, in smoking room. **Facility:** 184 rooms. Spacious guest rooms, most with private balcony. Very attractive public areas including an inviting lobby with dome-shaped skylight. All rooms with hair dryer, iron and ironing board. A few family theme rooms. 2 whirlpool rooms, $299; 10 stories; interior corridors; heated pool, whirlpool. **Dining:** Restaurant; 24 hrs; $5-$20; cocktails; entertainment, nightclub. **Services:** gift shop; winter plug-ins. **Recreation:** in-room video games. **All Rooms:** extended cable TV. **Cards:** AE, DI, DS, JC, MC, VI. **Special Amenities:** Free newspaper and free room upgrade (subject to availability with advanced reservations). *(See color ad p 350)*

RAMADA CROWCHILD INN Phone: (403)288-5353 33
(CAA) (SAVE) 5/1-9/4 1P: $130-$140 2P: $140-$150 XP: $10 F18
  9/5-2/28 1P: $125-$135 2P: $135-$145 XP: $10 F18
◆◆◆ 3/1-4/30 1P: $115-$130 2P: $125-$140 XP: $10 F18
Motor Inn **Location:** Crowchild Tr at 53rd St NW. 5353 Crowchild Tr NW T3A 1W9. Fax: 403/286-8966. **Terms:** [CP] meal plan; 10 day cancellation notice; pets. **Facility:** 57 rooms. Excellently maintained property with some very attractive public areas. Spacious guest rooms with a mix of decor styles. A relaxed atmosphere in the pub. 3 stories; interior corridors; heated pool, whirlpool. **Dining:** Restaurant; 6 am-11 pm, Sun 7 am-9 pm, buffet 11:30 am-2 & 4:30-8 pm; $6-$20; cocktails. **Services:** winter plug-ins. **All Rooms:** extended cable TV. **Some Rooms:** Fee: VCR. **Cards:** AE, CB, DI, JC, MC, VI. **Special Amenities:** Free breakfast and free local telephone calls. *(See color ad p 350)*

ROSEDALE HOUSE BED & BREAKFAST Phone: 403/284-0010 50
◆◆ 5/19-2/28 1P: $90-$105 2P: $105-$120 XP: $15 D12
Bed & 3/1-5/18 1P: $85-$100 2P: $100-$115 XP: $15 D12
Breakfast **Location:** Sw corner of 16th Ave (Trans Canada Hwy) and 7A St NW. 1633 7A St NW T2M 3K2. Fax: 403/284-9568. **Terms:** [BP] meal plan; check-in 4 pm; 7 day cancellation notice; cancellation fee imposed; small dog on premises. **Facility:** 4 rooms. In a pleasant residential setting, nicely decorated guest rooms in a modern style decor. Reservations preferred but drop-ins welcome. E-mail service avail. 2 stories; interior corridors; smoke free premises. **Services:** winter plug-ins. **All Rooms:** combo or shower baths. **Some Rooms:** color TV. **Cards:** AE, MC, VI.

ROYAL INN NORTH CALGARY Phone: (403)291-2003 55
◆◆◆ All Year 1P: $95-$159 2P: $95-$159 XP: $10 F16
Hotel **Location:** 27th Ave NE and Barlow Tr. 2828 23rd St NE T2E 8T4. Fax: 403/291-2019. **Terms:** Check-in 4 pm. **Facility:** 201 rooms. A beautiful hotel with many upscale touches including designer Western Canadian furniture in the lobby and tastefully appointed guest rooms. All rooms with hair dryer, iron, ironing board and video games. 6 stories; interior corridors. **Services:** gift shop; winter plug-ins. **Cards:** AE, CB, DI, MC, VI.

STETSON VILLAGE INN Phone: 403/271-3210 76
(CAA) (SAVE) 6/2-9/30 1P: $75 2P: $80 XP: $5 F12
  3/1-6/1 & 10/1-2/28 1P: $63 2P: $68 XP: $5 F12
◆◆ **Location:** Macleod Tr S and 99th Ave SE. 10002 Macleod Tr S T2J 3K9. Fax: 403/271-2588. **Terms:** 7 day
Motor Inn cancellation notice. **Facility:** 34 rooms. Across from the Real Canadian Superstore. Very handsome rooms. Excellent budget accommodation. 2 stories; exterior corridors. **Dining:** Restaurant; 7 am-10 pm, Sun-3 pm; $5-$14; cocktails. **Services:** winter plug-ins. **All Rooms:** extended cable TV. **Cards:** AE, DI, MC, VI.

(See map p. 338)

SUPER 8 MOTEL CALGARY AIRPORT

Phone: (403)291-9888　56

| | 5/1-9/30 | 1P: $90-$149 | 2P: $100-$159 | XP: $10 | F12 |
| | 3/1-4/30 & 10/1-2/28 | 1P: $70-$90 | 2P: $80-$100 | XP: $10 | F12 |

CAA SAVE
◆◆
Motel

Location: Corner of 32nd Ave and Barlow Tr NE. 3030 Barlow Tr NE T1Y 1A2. Fax: 403/291-3000. **Terms:** Small pets only, $10 extra charge. **Facility:** 61 rooms. New property offering good sized rooms and contemporary furnishings. 4 stories; interior corridors. **Dining:** Restaurant nearby. **Services:** winter plug-ins. **All Rooms:** extended cable TV. **Cards:** AE, DI, DS, MC, VI. **Special Amenities:** Free breakfast and free local telephone calls.

SUPER 8 MOTEL NORTHWEST

Phone: (403)289-9211　40

| | 6/22-8/31 | 1P: $70-$130 | 2P: $80-$150 | XP: $10 | F12 |
| | 3/1-6/21 & 9/1-2/28 | 1P: $50-$90 | 2P: $60-$100 | XP: $10 | F12 |

CAA SAVE
◆◆
Motel

Location: In Motel Village; just n of jct Trans Canada Hwy 1 and Crowchild Tr. 1904 Crowchild Tr NW T2M 3Y7. Fax: 403/282-7824. **Terms:** [CP] meal plan; cancellation fee imposed. **Facility:** 59 rooms. Simple but well appointed guest rooms of various sizes. 10 two-bedroom units. 12 efficiencies, $5-$20 extra charge; 2 stories; exterior corridors; small heated pool. **Dining:** Restaurant nearby. **Services:** winter plug-ins. **All Rooms:** extended cable TV. Fee: safes. **Cards:** AE, CB, DI, DS, MC, VI. **Special Amenities:** Free breakfast and free local telephone calls.

The following lodging was either not inspected or did not meet AAA rating requirements but is listed for your information only.

HILTON GARDEN INN-CALGARY AIRPORT

Phone: 403/717-1999

| | 6/9-7/16 | 1P: $174 | 2P: $174 | XP: $20 | F16 |
| | 1/1-2/28 | 1P: $130 | 2P: $130 | XP: $20 | F16 |

fyi
Hotel

| | 3/1-6/8 & 7/17-12/31 | 1P: $125 | 2P: $125 | XP: $20 | F16 |

Too new to rate, opening scheduled for June 1999. **Location:** 2335 Pegasus Rd NE T2E 8C3. Fax: 403/717-1901. **Terms:** 60 day cancellation notice; cancellation fee imposed. **Amenities:** 135 rooms, radios, coffeemakers, microwaves, refrigerators, pool, exercise facilities. *(See color ad p 283 & opposite Introduction)*

RESTAURANTS

ALBERTA KING OF SUBS

◆
Canadian

Lunch: $2-$10　**Dinner:** $2-$10　**Phone:** 403/293-5809　39

Location: McKnight Blvd and 52nd St NE. 7196 Temple Dr NE T1Y 4E8. **Hours:** 11 am-9 pm, Fri & Sat-10 pm. Closed: 12/25. **Features:** carryout; beer only. Montreal-style smoked-meat sandwiches and hot grilled subs are the specialties at this strip-mall eatery, which has only nine tables and a counter to order from. French fries, coleslaw, sugar pies and friendly, polite service are also offered. **Cards:** VI.

BOOGIE'S

◆
American

Lunch: $5-$10　**Dinner:** $5-$10　**Phone:** 403/230-7070　45

Location: Corner 8th Ave NE. 908 Edmonton Tr NE T2E 3K1. **Hours:** 10:30 am-10 pm. Closed: 1/1, 4/23, 12/25 & Sun. **Features:** carryout. You'll be served tasty burgers filled with character at this restaurant. The burgers are grilled to order and served by the French owners, a friendly couple who also offer fresh lemonade, cappuccinos, fashion advice and updates on French politics.

DEANE HOUSE HISTORIC SITE RESTAURANT　Historical

◆◆
Canadian

Lunch: $8-$10　**Phone:** 403/269-7747　54

Location: Corner 8th St. 806 9th Ave SE T2P 2M5. **Hours:** 11 am-2 pm, Sun from 10 am; also Fri Night Mystery From History Dinner Theatre, 6:30 pm-10:30 pm, $49.75. Closed major holidays. **Reservations:** suggested. **Features:** casual dress; Sunday brunch; health conscious menu items; cocktails. The glassed-in, verandah dining room offers a lovely view of the Elbow River along with fresh scones, homemade soup, eggs Benedict, French toast, quiche, bacon and eggs and gingerbread cake. Friday evening is the Mystery from History dinner theater. Smoke free premises. **Cards:** AE, MC, VI.

FLEUR DE SEL

◆◆◆
Nouvelle
French

Dinner: $15-$19　**Phone:** 403/228-9764　53

Location: 4th St and 21st Ave SW, in the Tivoli Theatre Building. #2 2015 4th St SW T2S 1W6. **Hours:** 11 am-2 & 5-midnight, Sat & Sun from 5 pm. Closed major holidays, Mon & 8/7-8/27. **Reservations:** required. **Features:** health conscious menu items; cocktails & lounge; street parking; a la carte. Fleur de Sel is a quaint, cozy, brasserie-style restaurant where the delicious nouvelle-classic food is sophisticated and artfully presented. The funky, soft decor and live music give real French ambience, and the service is welcoming and impeccable. **Cards:** AE, DI, DS, MC, VI.

THE INN ON LAKE BONAVISTA

CAA
◆◆◆
Continental

Lunch: $7-$13　**Dinner:** $17-$30　**Phone:** 403/271-6711　58

Location: 11.2 km se via Hwy 2 (Macleod Tr), 0.8 km e on Anderson Rd to Bonaventure Dr, just s to Lake Bonavista Dr and 1.2 km e to Lake Bonavista Shopping Centre. 747 Lake Bonavista Dr SE T2J 0N2. **Hours:** 11:30 am-2 & 5-11 pm, Sun 10:30 am-2 & 5-9 pm. Closed major holidays. **Reservations:** suggested. **Features:** Sunday brunch; children's menu; health conscious menu; cocktails & lounge; a la carte. This exclusive dining room and lounge features a country elegance and a nice view of the lake. Its cuisine offers contemporary creations but honours traditions with well-known French specialties, some prepared tableside. Table appointments are very nice. **Cards:** AE, DI, MC, VI.

KYOTO 17

◆◆
Ethnic

Lunch: $5-$8　**Dinner:** $5-$14　**Phone:** 403/245-3188　51

Location: Corner 17th Ave and 8th St SW, basement level of the Devenish Bldg. 908 17th Ave SW T2T 0A3. **Hours:** 11:30 am-2 & 5-10 pm, Sat & Sun from 5 pm. Closed major holidays. **Reservations:** suggested. **Features:** carryout; cocktails & lounge; street parking; a la carte. This restaurant features a sushi bar, rice, curry, Japanese noodles and full dinners with teriyaki chicken and steak. The decor is contemporary, with the entrance on 16th Ave. There's metered parking during the day, but no charge in the evening. **Cards:** AE, DI, MC, VI.

(See map p. 338)

LA BREZZA Lunch: $9-$13 Dinner: $12-$22 Phone: 403/262-6230 47
◆◆
Italian **Location:** In Bridgeland; at 9th St NE. 990 1st Ave NE T2E 4J9. **Hours:** 11:30 am-2:30 & 5-midnight, Sat & Sun from 5 pm. **Reservations:** suggested. **Features:** casual dress; cocktails; a la carte. While La Brezza's cozy, intimate decor boasts of local sports celebrities, its cuisine features fine dishes that include pasta, seafood and veal specialties. Great swordfish. Its warm and relaxed ambience is enhanced by its setting in a former residence. **Cards:** AE, MC, VI. ✕

LA DOLCE VITA RISTORANTE ITALIANO &
ENOTECA DA FRANCO Lunch: $9-$13 Dinner: $11-$25 Phone: 403/263-3445 46
CAA **Location:** 916 1st Ave NE T2E 0C5. **Hours:** 11:30 am-2 & 5:30-10:30 pm, Sat 5:30 pm-11 pm. Closed major
◆◆◆ holidays & Sun. **Reservations:** suggested. **Features:** semi-formal attire; cocktails; street parking; a la carte.
Italian Located in "Little Italy," La Dolce Vita features casual dining upstairs and more formal dining downstairs. This restaurant offers fresh pasta, seafood and veal prepared with a balance of traditions and imaginative presentations. Service is professional. Smoke free premises. **Cards:** AE, DI, MC, VI. ✕

LEO FU'S Lunch: $7-$8 Dinner: $7-$13 Phone: 403/255-2528 57
◆◆
Chinese **Location:** Just w of MacLeod Tr, across from "Ikon" Bldg. 511 70th Ave SW T2V 2B4. **Hours:** 11:30 am-2 & 4:30-10 pm, Fri-11:30 pm, Sat 4:30 pm-11:30 pm, Sun 4:30 pm-10 pm. Closed: 12/25 & for lunch other major holidays. **Features:** dressy casual; health conscious menu items; carryout; cocktails; a la carte. You'll enjoy this out-of-the-way restaurant serving consistently adventurous Szechwan and Mandarin cuisine. Dishes include crispy chunks of beef served in a savory orange sauce, and a delicious salt-and-pepper squid. The servers are polite and attentive. **Cards:** AE, DI, MC, VI. ✕

LILY'S RENDEZVOUS Lunch: $8-$12 Dinner: $8-$12 Phone: 403/243-8779 55
◆◆
Chinese **Location:** E of MacLeod Tr, on 46th Ave S. 4714 1st St SW T2G 0A2. **Hours:** 11:30 am-2 & 4:30-10 pm, Sat from 4:30 pm, Sun 4:30 pm-9 pm. Closed major holidays & Mon. **Reservations:** suggested; weekends. **Features:** casual dress; health conscious menu items; carryout; cocktails; a la carte. Lily's features an extensive selection of Peking cuisine with several spicy dishes such as shrimp with garlic, chicken 'n' cashews, "chili" beef, barbecue ribs, pork and vegetable dumplings, and butterflied prawns. Service is genuinely friendly. **Cards:** AE, MC, VI. ✕

LINA'S ITALIAN MARKET & CAPPUCCINO BAR Lunch: $4-$9 Dinner: $5 Phone: 403/277-9166 40
◆
Italian **Location:** Corner 21st Ave NW. 2211 Centre St NW T2E 2T4. **Hours:** 9 am-9 pm, Fri-Sun to 5 pm. Closed: 4/23 & 12/25. **Features:** carryout; beer & wine only; a la carte. This family-owned, coffee-bar-style restaurant has eight tables and over-the-counter ordering. It offers homemade pizza, pasta, soups, salads and authentic Italian pastries. Check out the family-size tiramisu in the cooler. Service is casual and friendly. **Cards:** AE, MC, VI. ✕

MAURYA Lunch: $10 Dinner: $8-$15 Phone: 403/270-3133 42
◆◆
Ethnic **Location:** At 12th St NW. #100, 1204 Kensington Rd NW T2N 3P5. **Hours:** 11:30 am-2 & 5-10 pm, Fri & Sat-11 pm. **Reservations:** suggested. **Features:** dressy casual; Sunday brunch; health conscious menu; cocktails; street parking; a la carte. A finely prepared and tasty East Indian cuisine, specializing in tandoori and including many vegetarian dishes, is offered at Maurya's. The extensive lunch buffet has more than a dozen items, and the relaxing ambience is inviting, cozy and friendly. Smoke free premises. **Cards:** AE, DI, MC, VI. ✕

PALKI Lunch: $7-$8 Dinner: $5-$13 Phone: 403/282-9797 36
◆◆
Northern **Location:** From Hwy 1, 3 mi n on Shagnappi Tr, e on Northland Dr, w at first traffic light, behind Northland
Indian Mall; in the Dalbrent Centre near Northland Village. 3604 52nd Ave NW T2L 1V9. **Hours:** 11 am-9 pm, Fri & Sat-10 pm, Sun 5 pm-9 pm. **Reservations:** suggested. **Features:** carryout; cocktails; a la carte. The charming hosts here serve pure Punjabi cuisine, with 20 vegetarian dishes. They can perk it up, but mostly it's intense, well-balanced food, expertly cooked. Most evenings, dishes are made to order, so plan to take your time. This is a special place. Smoke free premises. **Cards:** AE, MC, VI. ✕

PFANNTASTIC PANNENKOEK HAUS Lunch: $5-$11 Dinner: $5-$11 Phone: 403/243-7757 56
CAA **Location:** Just ne of jcts Hwy 8 (Glenmore Tr) and Crowchild Tr; in small strip mall. 2439 54th Ave SW T3E
◆◆ 1M4. **Hours:** 11 am-8 pm, Sat & Sun from 8 am. Closed: Mon. **Reservations:** accepted. **Features:** dressy
Dutch casual; health conscious menu items; cocktails. This restaurant offers 75 varieties of meal-size Dutch crepes served with various toppings. A savory selection for dinner and a sweet choice for dessert make for a tasty meal. Soups and salads are also offered. The service is super-friendly. **Cards:** AE, MC, VI. ✕

RESTAURANT INDONESIA Lunch: $7-$8 Dinner: $7-$11 Phone: 403/244-0645 50
◆◆
Indonesian **Location:** 1604 14th St SW T3C 1E2. **Hours:** 11:30 am-2:30 & 5-11 pm, Sat 5 pm-11:30 pm, Sun 5 pm-9 pm. Closed major holidays & Mon. **Reservations:** suggested. **Features:** dressy casual; carryout; cocktails. Choices such as satay, chili-basil chicken and gado-gado are offered here. The offerings will please your palate with rich, intense flavors. The food is colorful, fresh and jumping with memories of the Spice Islands. Try the favorite aduk-aduk tempeh. **Cards:** AE, MC, VI. ✕

ROSE CAFE Lunch: $6-$10 Dinner: $6-$17 Phone: 403/220-9888 41
◆◆
West **Location:** In Brentwood shopping complex; just nw of Crowshild Tr and 32nd Ave NW. #17 3802 Brentwood
Canadian Rd NW T2L 1K8. **Hours:** 11 am-11 pm, Fri & Sat-midnight, Sun 10 am-10 pm. Closed: 12/25. **Features:** Sunday brunch; children's menu; health conscious menu; carryout; cocktails & lounge; a la carte. You'll enjoy the cheerful, upbeat atmosphere of the Rose Cafe. Its cuisine focuses on West Coast and Asian influences and offers imaginative versions of popular dishes. Specialty burgers and sandwiches are offered, and there's a children's play area. **Cards:** AE, MC, VI. ✕

(See map p. 338)

SAIGON
◆ ◆
Vietnamese

Lunch: $5-$12   **Dinner:** $5-$12   **Phone:** 403/228-4200   44

Location: 1221 12th Ave SW T3C 3R8. **Hours:** 11 am-10 pm, Fri & Sat-11 pm, Sun 4:30 pm-10 pm. Closed: 12/25. **Reservations:** accepted. **Features:** casual dress; health conscious menu; carryout; cocktails; street parking. The Saigon's very good cuisine has a French influence. The specialties of this family-owned restaurant include citronella chicken, light cha gio, large bowls of noodles and hearty servings of beef. Steamed mussels and fried calamari are also on the menu. **Cards:** AE, DI, MC, VI.

THE SALMON COVE
◆ ◆
Seafood

Lunch: $7-$14   **Dinner:** $9-$22   **Phone:** 403/244-3311   48

Location: Corner 13th Ave SW. 1238 8th St SW T2R 1A9. **Hours:** 11 am-10 pm, Fri-11 pm, Sat 5-11 pm, Sun 5-10 pm. Closed major holidays. **Reservations:** suggested. **Features:** carryout; cocktails; a la carte. You'll enjoy the Salmon Cove, a neighborhood restaurant that's the ideal place for salmon fanatics who like to have a choice of how it's prepared. Steak, chicken, lamb and several pasta dishes complete the menu. There's patio dining in season. **Cards:** AE, DI, MC, VI.

SANTORINI GREEK TAVERNA
◆ ◆
Greek

Lunch: $6-$10   **Dinner:** $10-$20   **Phone:** 403/276-8363   43

Location: Just s of 16th Ave and Centre St N. 1502 Centre St N T2E 2R9. **Hours:** 11 am-11 pm, Fri-midnight, Sat noon-midnight, Sun 4 pm-11 pm. Closed: 1/1, 12/25, 12/26 & Mon. **Reservations:** suggested; weekends. **Features:** casual dress; carryout; cocktails; a la carte. This restaurant's distinctive and very good cuisine features authentic dishes, souvlakia, seafood and lamb as well as complete dinners serving an array of delicacies. Friendly service, soothing decor. There's a small parking lot behind the restaurant. **Cards:** AE, DI, MC, VI.

SULTAN'S TENT
◆ ◆
Traditional
Moroccan

Dinner: $10-$29   **Phone:** 403/244-2333   49

Location: Just w of 8th St SW. 909 17th Ave SW T2T 0A4. **Hours:** 5:30 pm-10:30 pm, Fri & Sat-11 pm. Closed: Sun. **Reservations:** suggested. **Features:** This restaurant's cuisine features delicacies such as tagine, couscous, merguez, lamb, a five-course sultan's feast and other traditional dishes. The decor, which is inspired by the Berber culture of North Africa, offers warm and intimate seating. **Cards:** AE, DI, MC, VI.

The following restaurant has not been inspected by AAA but is listed for your information only.

OUTWEST COOKHOUSE AND CORRAL   **Phone:** 403/262-9378
fyi   Not inspected. **Location:** 200 Barclay Parade SW. **Features:** Specialties of this progressive, Western-style restaurant feature prime rib and AAA grade steak.

The Calgary Vicinity

AIRDRIE pop. 16,000

—— LODGING ——

SUPER 8 MOTEL-AIRDRIE   **Phone:** (403)948-4188

CAA SAVE   7/1-9/30   1P: $90   2P: $90   XP: $10   F12
     3/1-6/30 & 10/1-2/28   1P: $65   2P: $65
◆ ◆
Motel   **Location:** Hwy #2 Airdrie (east) exit, 0.8 km e on Hwy 587 e, then 1.8 km s. 815 E Lake Blvd T4B 2A2. Fax: 403/948-4299. **Terms:** [CP] meal plan; 10 day cancellation notice; pets, with permission. **Facility:** 49 rooms. Contemporary guest room decor. All rooms with hair dryer. 3 stories; interior corridors. **Dining:** Restaurant nearby. **Services:** winter plug-ins. **All Rooms:** extended cable TV. **Cards:** AE, CB, DI, MC, VI. **Special Amenities:** Free breakfast and free local telephone calls.

COCHRANE pop. 7,400

—— LODGING ——

BOW RIVER INN   **Phone:** 403/932-7900

◆ ◆ ◆   5/16-9/30   1P: $79-$89   2P: $89-$99   XP: $5   F5
Motel   3/1-5/15, 10/1-12/31 & 1/1-2/28   1P: $59-$79   2P: $69-$89   XP: $5   F5
   Location: Hwy 1A, 1 km sw on Hwy 22. 3 Westside Dr T0L 0W0 (Box 1270). Fax: 403/932-1880. **Terms:** Small pets only. **Facility:** 44 rooms. New property offering spacious rooms, contemporary decor and extra amenities. At-door parking. All rooms with hair dryer. Excellent housekeeping. 1 story; exterior corridors. **Services:** winter plug-ins. **Cards:** AE, MC, VI.

OKOTOKS pop. 8,500

------ **LODGING** ------

OKOTOKS COUNTRY INN
◆◆
Motel

11/1-2/28	1P: $62-$82	2P: $67-$97	XP: $5	F10
3/1-10/31	1P: $62-$72	2P: $67-$87	XP: $5	F10

Phone: 403/938-1999

Location: On Hwy 2A (Northridge Dr), ne of Sheep River. 59 River Side Gate T0L 1T0 (PO Box 741). **Fax:** 403/938-3936. **Terms:** [CP] meal plan; 3 day cancellation notice; cancellation fee imposed; package plans; pets, $5 extra charge. **Facility:** 40 rooms. A new property offering average sized units, all with contemporary furnishings. 2 stories; interior corridors. **Services:** winter plug-ins. **Cards:** AE, DI, DS, MC, VI.

------ **RESTAURANT** ------

LA P'TITE TABLE   **Lunch:** $5-$8   **Dinner:** $13-$23   **Phone:** 403/938-2224
◆◆◆
French   **Location:** Across street from information center. From Northridge Dr, 1 km e via Elizabeth Ave. 52 N Railway St T0L 1T0. **Hours:** 11 am-2 & 5:30-10 pm, Sat from 5:30 pm. Closed: 4/23, 12/25, Sun, Mon & Canada Day. **Reservations:** suggested. **Features:** dressy casual; cocktails; street parking; also prix fixe. You'll enjoy this lovely gem tucked away in the suburbs. Its historic-looking exterior is complemented by artwork inside, and its menu specializes in eye-appealing contemporary-traditional French cooking. The friendly service is cordial and welcoming. Smoke free premises. **Cards:** MC, VI.

STRATHMORE pop. 5,300

------ **LODGINGS** ------

BEST WESTERN STRATHMORE INN   **Phone:** (403)934-5777
(CAA) (SAVE)
◆◆◆
Motel

6/15-9/6	1P: $70-$140	2P: $75-$140	XP: $6	F18
3/1-6/14 & 9/7-2/28	1P: $60-$80	2P: $65-$85	XP: $6	F18

Location: Centre; on Trans Canada Hwy 1, jct SR 817. 550 Hwy 1 T1P 1M6. **Fax:** 403/934-5730. **Terms:** [CP] meal plan; monthly rates avail; check-in 4 pm; 21 day cancellation notice; package plans; pets, $50 dep req. **Facility:** 50 rooms. Contemporary guest room decor with simple touches. Average sized lobby with a cozy seating area with a gas fireplace. A few 1-bedroom suites. 2 stories; interior corridors; heated pool, whirlpool. **Dining:** Restaurant nearby. **Services:** winter plug-ins. **Recreation:** exercise equipment. **All Rooms:** extended cable TV. **Cards:** AE, CB, DI, DS, MC, VI. **Special Amenities:** Free breakfast and free local telephone calls. (See color ad p 389)

SUPER 8 MOTEL   **Phone:** 403/934-1808
◆◆
Motel   Property failed to provide current rates

Location: Just n on SR 817. 450 Westlake Rd T1P 1H8. **Fax:** 403/934-1952. **Terms:** [CP] meal plan; pets, $10 extra charge, in smoking rooms. **Facility:** 49 rooms. Contemporary guest room decor. 2 stories; interior/exterior corridors. **Services:** winter plug-ins. **Cards:** AE, DI, DS, MC, VI.

This ends listings for the Calgary Vicinity.
The following page resumes the alphabetical listings of
cities in Alberta.

CANMORE pop. 8,400

─────── LODGINGS ───────

BANFF BOUNDARY LODGE

CAA SAVE
◆◆◆
Condominium

Phone: (403)678-9555

12/21-2/28	1P: $99-$179	2P: $109-$229
6/16-9/23	1P: $179	2P: $99-$222
3/1-6/15 & 9/24-12/20	1P: $99-$119	2P: $109-$139

Location: Just e of Banff National Park east gate, parallel to Hwy 1, Harvie Heights exit. 1000 Harvie Heights Rd T1W 2W2. Fax: 403/678-2851. **Terms:** Weekly rates avail; 3 day cancellation notice; package plans; small pets only, $10 extra charge. **Facility:** 42 rooms. Contemporary 1- or 2-bedroom units with full kitchen and living room with gas fireplace. All rooms with hair dryer. Rates for up to 6 persons; 1-2 stories; exterior corridors; whirlpool. **Services:** winter plug-ins. Fee: area transportation, Banff & Canmore. **Recreation:** picnic area with gas barbecue, video library. **All Rooms:** kitchens, extended cable TV. **Special Amenities:** Early check-in/late check-out and free room upgrade **(subject to availability with advanced reservations).** *(See color ad p 324)*

BEST WESTERN GREEN GABLES INN

CAA SAVE
◆◆◆
Motor Inn

Phone: (403)678-5488

6/23-10/15	1P: $149-$159	2P: $149-$159	XP: $10	F17
5/19-6/22	1P: $119-$129	2P: $119-$129	XP: $10	F17
10/16-2/28	1P: $79-$109	2P: $79-$109	XP: $10	F17
3/1-5/18	1P: $79-$99	2P: $79-$99	XP: $10	F17

Location: 5.2 km e of Banff National Park East Gate, on Hwy 1A (Bow Valley Tr). 1602 2nd Ave T1W 1M8. Fax: 403/678-2670. **Terms:** [CP] meal plan; check-in 4 pm; cancellation fee imposed; package plans. **Facility:** 61 rooms. A good mix of accommodations from average sized guest rooms to larger suites with gas fireplace and breathtaking mountain scenery. 34 whirlpool rooms; 2 stories; interior corridors; steamroom, whirlpool. **Dining:** Dining room; 7 am-2 & 5-10 pm; $16-$25; cocktails. **Services:** winter plug-ins. Fee: area transportation, ski hills. **All Rooms:** extended cable TV. **Some Rooms:** 10 efficiencies. **Cards:** AE, DI, DS, MC, VI. **Special Amenities:** Free breakfast and free local telephone calls. *(See color ad p 330 & p 324)*

BEST WESTERN POCATERRA INN

CAA SAVE
◆◆◆
Motel

Phone: (403)678-4334

6/23-10/15	1P: $159-$179	2P: $159-$179	XP: $10	F17
5/19-6/22	1P: $129-$149	2P: $129-$149	XP: $10	F17
10/16-2/28	1P: $89-$119	2P: $89-$119	XP: $10	F17
3/1-5/18	1P: $89-$109	2P: $89-$109	XP: $10	F17

Location: 5.8 km e of Banff National Park East Gate, on Hwy 1A (Bow Valley Tr). 1725 Mountain Ave T1W 2W1. Fax: 403/678-3999. **Terms:** [CP] meal plan; check-in 4 pm; cancellation fee imposed; package plans. **Facility:** 83 rooms. Attractive cathedral ceiling lobby featuring mountain Canadiana and large stone fireplace. Contemporary elegance in all units, with luxurious amenities such as fireplace and some with whirlpool. Beautiful interior design. 4 stories; interior corridors; heated pool, sauna, steamroom, waterslide, whirlpool. **Services:** winter plug-ins. Fee: area transportation, ski areas. **Recreation:** ski storage room; game room. **All Rooms:** extended cable TV. **Cards:** AE, DI, DS, MC, VI. **Special Amenities:** Free breakfast and free local telephone calls. *(See color ad p 330 & p 324)*

BOW VALLEY MOTEL

CAA
◆◆
Motel

Phone: 403/678-5085

6/9-9/24	1P: $95-$100	2P: $95-$110	XP: $10	F12
9/25-2/28	1P: $45-$75	2P: $50-$85	XP: $5	F12
3/1-6/8	1P: $50-$75	2P: $55-$80	XP: $5	F12

Location: Central on 8th St. 610 8th St T1W 2B5. Fax: 403/678-6560. **Terms:** Weekly rates avail, off season; cancellation fee imposed; package plans. **Facility:** 25 rooms. Fine budget accommodation featuring large, well appointed rooms. Located downtown. Impressive mountain setting. 8 efficiencies, $5-$10 extra charge; outdoor whirlpool. **Dining:** Restaurant nearby. **Services:** winter plug-ins. **All Rooms:** extended cable TV. **Cards:** AE, DS, MC, VI.

ANMORE REGENCY SUITES

Phone: (403)678-3799

6/1-9/18	1P: $114-$164	2P: $154-$174	XP: $10	F6
3/1-4/3	1P: $104-$124	2P: $114-$134	XP: $10	F6
4/4-5/31 & 9/19-2/28	1P: $74-$94	2P: $84-$114	XP: $10	F6

⬛ SAVE
◆ ◆ ◆
partment **Location:** 5.8 km e of Banff National Park gates; on Hwy 1A, via Canmore exit, from Hwy 1 (Trans Canada). 1206 Bow Valley Tr T1W 1N6. Fax: 403/678-3413. **Terms:** Weekly rates avail; check-in 4 pm; 2 night min stay, season; package plans. **Facility:** 39 rooms. Large units with well-equipped contemporary kitchen. Simple overall decor, ome with gas burning fireplace. All units with small private patio or balcony and voice mail. Best suited for families. 19 two- edroom units. All rates based on family occupancy, up to 6 persons; 20 three-bedroom units, $109-$209 up to 8 persons, de- ending on season; 3 stories; interior corridors. **Services:** winter plug-ins. **Recreation:** barbecue area. **All Rooms:** kitchens, xtended cable TV. **Some Rooms:** Fee: VCR. **Cards:** AE, DI, MC, VI. **Special Amenities:** Free local telephone calls. *See color ad p 356)*

HE DRAKE INN

Phone: (403)678-5131

6/1-9/30	1P: $89	2P: $99-$109	XP: $8	F12
3/1-5/31 & 10/1-2/28	1P: $49	2P: $59-$69	XP: $8	F12

⬛ SAVE
◆ ◆ ◆
otel **Location:** Center; Main St at Railway Ave. 909 Railway Ave T1W 1P3. Fax: 403/678-4562. **Terms:** 3 day can- cellation notice; cancellation fee imposed; pets, $10 extra charge. **Facility:** 26 rooms. On edge of downtown. Canmore creek rooms overlooking a spring-fed creek, the other more modest units have mountain views. 2-3 ories, no elevator; exterior corridors; sauna, whirlpool. **Dining:** Restaurant; hrs may vary with eason; $6-$10; cocktails. **Services:** winter plug-ins. **All Rooms:** extended cable TV. **Cards:** AE, MC, VI. *See color ad below)*

OUR POINTS HOTEL SHERATON

Phone: (403)609-4422

12/16-2/28	1P: $149-$250	2P: $149-$250	XP: $15	F18
6/14-10/9	1P: $149-$240	2P: $180-$229	XP: $15	F18
3/1-6/13 & 10/10-12/15	1P: $69-$109	2P: $69-$109	XP: $15	F18

⬛ SAVE
◆ ◆ ◆
otel **Location:** Hwy 1 W, 2nd exit; Hwy 1 E, 3rd exit; located on n side of Hwy 1. #1 Silver Tip Trl T1W 2Z7. Fax: 403/609-0008. **Terms:** [AP], [BP] & [MAP] meal plans; cancellation fee imposed. **Facility:** 99 rooms. rand alpine style hotel set at the foot of a majestic mountain community just off the hwy. The guest rooms are beautifully ap- inted and include warm vivid earthtone colours. All rooms with hair dryer. 11 whirlpool rooms, $124-$325; 3 stories; interior rridors; golf course privileges; whirlpool. **Dining:** Restaurant; 6:30 am-10:30 pm; $7-$24; cocktails. **Services:** gift shop; area ansportation; ski areas; winter plug-ins. **Recreation:** hiking trails. **All Rooms:** extended cable TV. **Cards:** AE, DI, DS, MC, VI. pecial Amenities: Free newspaper and preferred room (subject to availability with advanced reservations). *See color ad p 325 & p 402)*

HE GEORGETOWN INN

Phone: (403)678-3439

6/24-9/16	1P: $109-$126	2P: $119-$136	XP: $20	
3/1-6/23 & 9/17-2/28	1P: $62-$99	2P: $72-$109	XP: $20	

◆ ◆ ◆
ountry Inn **Location:** 5.7 km e of Banff National Park East gate, on Hwy 1A (Bow Valley Tr), via Canmore exit from Trans anada Hwy 1. 1101 Bow Valley Tr T1W 1N4. Fax: 403/678-6909. **Terms:** [BP] meal plan; cancellation fee imposed. acility: 24 rooms. Traditional English-style inn offering the comforts of a bed and breakfast and the privacy of an old fash- ned inn. Newer section features spacious, individually appointed guest rooms with duvets and gas fireplace. Some antiques. stories; interior corridors; designated smoking area; mountain view. **Services:** winter plug-ins. Fee: area transportation. ards: AE, DS, MC, VI.

OWARD JOHNSON CANMORE/BANFF

Phone: (403)609-4656

5/15-10/6	1P: $159-$189	2P: $159-$189	XP: $15	F17
3/1-5/14 & 10/7-2/28	1P: $99-$109	2P: $99-$109	XP: $15	F17

⬛ SAVE
◆ ◆ ◆
otor Inn **Location:** 5.6 km e of Banff National Park East gate, on Hwy 1A, via Canmore exit, from Trans Canada Hwy 1. 1402 Bow Valley Tr T1W 1N5. Fax: 403/609-2773. **Terms:** 3 day cancellation notice; cancellation fee im- posed; small pets only. **Facility:** 202 rooms. Attractive units, contemporary design. All rooms with hair dryer d video games. Some face railroad tracks. 4 whirlpool rooms, $109-$275; 3 stories; interior corridors; small heated indoor ol, waterslide, whirlpool. **Dining:** Restaurant; 7 am-11 & 6-11 pm; $9-$18. **Services:** gift shop; winter plug-ins. Fee: area ansportation. **All Rooms:** extended cable TV. **Some Rooms:** 21 efficiencies. **Cards:** AE, CB, DI, DS, JC, MC, VI. pecial Amenities: Free local telephone calls. *(See color ad p 358)*

THE LADY MACDONALD COUNTRY INN　　　　　　　　　　**Phone:** (403)678-3665

	6/1-2/28	1P: $135-$200	2P: $135-$200	XP: $10	F12
	3/1-5/31	1P: $85-$150	2P: $85-$150	XP: $10	F12

◆◆◆　**Location:** 5.7 km e of Banff National Park East gate, on Hwy 1A, via Canmore exit from Trans Canada Hwy
Bed &　　1. 1201 Bow Valley Tr T1W 1P5. Fax: 403/678-9714. **Terms:** [BP] meal plan. **Facility:** 11 rooms. A charming
Breakfast　country inn with a variety of room sizes from average to spacious. Loft units avail. All rooms with hair dryer. 5
　　　　rooms with gas fireplace; whirlpool room; 2 stories; interior corridors; designated smoking area; mountain view.
Dining: Breakfast 8-9:30 am. **Services:** winter plug-ins. **All Rooms:** extended cable TV. **Cards:** AE, MC, VI.
Special Amenities: Free breakfast and free local telephone calls.

MCNEILL HERITAGE INN　　　　　　　　　　　　　　　**Phone:** 403/678-4884

◆◆◆　　　　　　　　Property failed to provide current rates
Historic Bed　**Location:** Just s of downtown; follow signs to Nordic Centre, cross bridge to first T intersection, turn right 0.8
& Breakfast　km. 500 Three Sisters Dr T1W 2P3. Fax: 403/678-4884. **Terms:** [BP] meal plan; age restrictions may apply;
　　　　check-in 5 pm; 7 day cancellation notice; cancellation fee imposed on premises. **Facility:** 5 rooms. Individually appointed guest rooms with contemporary appeal. In a secluded location, this beautifully restored heritage house features some antiques and artifacts preserving the historic nature of the property. 2 stories; interior corridors; smoke free
premises; mountain view. **Services:** winter plug-ins. **Recreation:** fishing; hiking trails. **All Rooms:** combo or shower baths.
Cards: MC, VI.

PAINTBOX LODGE　　　　　　　　　　　　　　　　　**Phone:** (403)678-3956

	6/1-9/30	1P: $79-$99	2P: $89-$109	XP: $10	F6
	3/1-5/31 & 10/1-2/28	1P: $50-$70	2P: $55-$75	XP: $10	F6

◆◆　**Location:** Centre, just s of Railway Ave (across bridge from fire station). 629 10th St T1W 2A2.
Lodge　Fax: 403/678-4134. **Terms:** [BP] meal plan; 7 day cancellation notice; cancellation fee imposed. **Facility:** 8
　　　rooms. Contemporary rooms with some rustic alpine touches. Dining area includes hand crafted picnic table
and log furnishings that face the stone fireplace. 1 bedroom suite with full kitchen, $99; 2 stories; interior corridors; smoke free
premises. **Dining:** Restaurant nearby. **Services:** winter plug-ins. **All Rooms:** combo or shower baths, extended cable TV.
Cards: MC, VI.

QUALITY RESORT-CHATEAU CANMORE　　　　　　　　**Phone:** (403)678-6699

	6/1-10/31	1P: $109-$165	2P: $109-$165	XP: $15	F17
	12/23-2/28	1P: $149	2P: $149	XP: $15	F17
	3/1-5/31 & 11/1-12/22	1P: $99	2P: $99	XP: $15	F17

Location: 4.8 km e of Banff National Park gate, on Hwy 1A. 1720 Bow Valley Tr T1W 1P7. Fax: 403/678-6954. **Terms:** Cancellation fee imposed; package plans; pets, $10 extra charge, in chalets only. **Facility:** 118 rooms. Modern property featuring
a wide range of accommodations from standard guest rooms to condo units with full washer/dryer. All rooms with hair dryer
and voice mail. Some rooms face railroad tracks. 23 two-bedroom units. 4 stories; interior/exterior corridors; heated pool.
Services: gift shop; area transportation; winter plug-ins. Fee: massage. **Recreation:** ice skating; sports court. Fee: bicycles.
Some Rooms: 24 kitchens. **Cards:** AE, DI, JC, MC, VI.

RADISSON HOTEL & CONFERENCE CENTRE　　　　　　**Phone:** (403)678-3625

	6/1-9/25	1P: $189	2P: $189	XP: $10	F18
	12/24-2/28	1P: $99-$169	2P: $99-$169	XP: $10	F18
	3/1-5/31 & 9/26-12/23	1P: $99-$109	2P: $99-$109	XP: $10	F18

◆◆◆　**Location:** 6 km e of Banff National Park East gate, on Hwy 1A via Canmore exit from Trans Canada Hwy 1
Motor Inn　511 Bow Valley Tr T1W 1N7. Fax: 403/678-3765. **Terms:** [AP], [BP] & [MAP] meal plans; check-in 4 pm; cancellation fee imposed; package plans; pets, $10 extra charge. **Facility:** 235 rooms. Main building offers contemporary looking
hotel style guest rooms. Newer rooms in Chalet style 2 story buildings with exterior walkways are equally well appointed. Most
rooms with mountain view. All rooms with hair dryer. 16 two-bedroom units. 1-bedroom efficiencies. 2-bedroom kitchen units
with diswasher; 2 whirlpool rooms, $159-$249; 2-3 stories; interior/exterior corridors; heated pool, steamroom, whirlpool; playground. **Dining:** Restaurant; 7 am-10 pm; $11-$17; cocktails. **Services:** gift shop; winter plug-ins. Fee: massage, area transportation, ski hills. **Recreation:** picnic area with fire pit. **All Rooms:** extended cable TV. **Some Rooms:** 16 efficiencies, 16
kitchens. **Cards:** AE, DI, DS, JC, MC, VI. **Special Amenities:** Free local telephone calls and free room upgrade (subject
to availability with advanced reservations). (See color ad p 359)

CKY MOUNTAIN SKI LODGE
Phone: 403/678-5445

6/1-9/30	1P: $85-$95	2P: $95-$110
10/1-2/28	1P: $55-$95	2P: $70-$110
3/1-5/31	1P: $55	2P: $70

Location: 4.8 km e of Banff National Park East gate, on Hwy 1A, via Canmore exit from Trans Canada Hwy 1. 1711 Bow Valley Tr T1W 2T8 (Box 8070). Fax: 403/678-6484. **Terms:** Pets, in designated rooms. **cility:** 82 rooms. Standard motel units to 1- and 2-bedroom apartments with full kitchen and fireplace, attractively furnished. rooms with hair dryer. 23 two-bedroom units. 22 loft units; 2 stories; exterior corridors; sauna, whirlpool; playground. **ing:** Restaurant nearby. **Services:** winter plug-ins. **All Rooms:** extended cable TV. **Some Rooms:** 7 efficiencies, 54 hens. **Cards:** AE, DI, MC, VI. *(See color ad p 329)*

NDLE MOUNTAIN MOTEL AND GASTHAUS
Phone: (403)678-5322

6/9-9/30	1P: $93-$115	2P: $93-$125	XP: $10	F17
12/26-2/28	1P: $55-$93	2P: $55-$103	XP: $10	F17
3/1-6/8	1P: $65-$75	2P: $65-$75	XP: $10	F17
10/1-12/25	1P: $55-$65	2P: $55-$75	XP: $10	F17

Location: 4.8 km e of Banff National Park East gate, on Hwy 1A, adjacent to Trans Canada Hwy 1. 1723 Bow ley Tr T1W 1L7. Fax: 403/678-5813. **Terms:** [CP] meal plan; weekly rates avail, off season; check-in 4 pm; cancellation fee osed; small pets only, $7 extra charge. **Facility:** 51 rooms. In scenic mountain community; attractive Bavarian-style exterior. me suites featuring a fireplace, cozy log cabin type units to larger family style cabin units. 6 suites, $150-$230 for up to 6 sons; 1-2 stories; exterior corridors; small heated indoor pool, whirlpool; playground. **Dining:** Restaurant; 7 am-10 pm; from om off season; $10-$19; cocktails. **Services:** winter plug-ins. **Recreation:** firepit. **All Rooms:** extended cable TV. me Rooms: 9 efficiencies, 18 kitchens. **Cards:** AE, DI, MC, VI. **Special Amenities:** Early check-in/late check-out and e local telephone calls. *(See color ad p 329)*

NDLE RIDGE CHALETS
Phone: (403)678-5387

6/15-9/15	1P: $99-$134	2P: $99-$144	XP: $5	F16
3/1-6/14 & 9/16-2/28	1P: $69-$99	2P: $69-$109	XP: $5	F16

Location: 1 km e of Banff National Park East gate on Trans Canada Hwy 1, Harvie Heights exit. 1100 Harvie ttage Heights Rd T1W 2W2. Fax: 403/678-2690. **Terms:** Weekly rates avail; check-in 4 pm; cancellation fee imposed; pets, $10 extra charge in smoking cabins. **Facility:** 38 rooms. Surrounded by the beautiful Rocky Moun- s. Individual cabins offer kitchen, wood burning fireplace and range in size from studio to 3-bedroom units. 7 two-bedroom ts. 1 three-bedroom unit, $144 in season; 1 story; exterior corridors. **Services:** area transportation, Canmore/Banff; winter g-ins. **Recreation:** cross country skiing; hiking trails. **All Rooms:** combo, shower or tub baths, extended cable TV. rds: AE, MC, VI. *(See color ad below & p 328)*

THE STOCKADE LOG CABINS
Phone: (403)678-521
CAA SAVE   All Year   1P: $68-$110   2P: $68-$110   XP: $15   F
◆
Cottage   **Location:** 1 km e of Banff National Park East gate on Trans Canada Hwy 1; Harvie Heights exit. 1050 Harv
Heights Rd T1W 2W2. Fax: 403/678-6463. **Terms:** Check-in 4 pm; cancellation fee imposed; pets, $10 ext
charge. **Facility:** 13 rooms. Compact or larger rustic log cabins, many with fireplace, offering country char
decor. Picturesque mountain scenery. 5 two-bedroom units. 1 story; exterior corridors. **Services:** winter plu
ins. Fee: area transportation, Banff/Canmore. **All Rooms:** combo or shower baths, extended cable TV. **Some Rooms:**
kitchens. **Cards:** MC, VI. **Special Amenities:** Preferred room (subject to availability with advanced reservations).

--------- **RESTAURANTS** ---------

PEPPERMILL RESTAURANT
Dinner: $11-$21   Phone: 403/678-229
◆◆◆   **Location:** Center. 726 9th St T1W 2V7. **Hours:** 5 pm-10 pm. Closed: 12/24, 12/25, Tues & 10/14-11/
Continental   **Reservations:** suggested. **Features:** casual dress; children's menu; cocktails. The fine European/Swi
cuisine of Peppermill's is fresh, colorful and inspired. The fresh smoked salmon and Alberta beef w
invigorate your palate, and the casual dining atmosphere has a certain home-style ambience. Locals praise this fi
restaurant. **Cards:** AE, MC, VI.

THE SHERWOOD HOUSE
Lunch: $6-$10   Dinner: $6-$25   Phone: 403/678-521
CAA   **Location:** Corner of 8th St and 8th Ave. 838 8th St T1W 2B7. **Hours:** 7 am-9:30 pm, Fri & Sat-10 p
Sun-9 pm. Closed: 12/25. **Reservations:** suggested. **Features:** No A/C; children's menu; health conscio
◆◆   menu items; carryout; cocktails & lounge; a la carte. The Sherwood House is famous for its Roc
Continental   Mountain-inspired cuisine of seafood, chicken, pasta, pizza and Angus beef. The restaurant is an authenti
log cabin with rustic stone fireplace and relaxed atmosphere. There's patio dining weather permittin
Cards: AE, DI, MC, VI.

SINCLAIRS
Lunch: $7-$12   Dinner: $12-$22   Phone: 403/678-537
◆◆   **Location:** Corner 6th Ave and 8th St. 637 8th St, Unit #1 T1W 2B1. **Hours:** 11:30 am-10 pm. Closed: 1/
Continental   12/25 & Mon 10/1-5/31. **Reservations:** suggested. **Features:** No A/C; carryout; cocktails; street parking; a
carte. The menu at Sinclairs features a nice selection of lamb, beef, salmon, and gourmet pizza and pas
This restaurant offers warm and cozy dining in the relaxed, intimate atmosphere of an old Victorian home. Couples enj
romantic nights here. **Cards:** AE, MC, VI.

--------- *The following restaurant has not been inspected by AAA* ---------
but is listed for your information only.

CHEZ FRANCOIS
Phone: 403/678-61
fyi   Not inspected. **Location:** 4.8 km e of Banff National Park gate, on Hwy 1A, exit Canmore. 1602 2nd A
T1W 1P7. **Features:** Casual fine dining features classic French cuisine, seafood and pasta.

CARDSTON pop. 3,400

--------- **LODGINGS** ---------

CARDSTON SUPER 8 MOTEL
Phone: (403)653-800
CAA SAVE   10/16-2/28   1P: $60-$80   2P: $75-$135   XP: $5   F
◆◆   5/15-10/15   1P: $80-$90   2P: $90-$105   XP: $5   F
Motel   3/1-5/14   1P: $56-$67   2P: $65-$77   XP: $5   F
Location: Centre; on Hwy 2. 404 Main St T0K 0K0 (Box 1710). Fax: 403/653-8004. **Terms:** Cancellation f
imposed. **Facility:** 45 rooms. Contemporary rooms with a bright and cheerful decor. 5 two-bedroom units.
whirlpool rooms, $90-$125; 2 stories; interior corridors; heated pool, whirlpool. **Dining:** Restaurant nearby. **Services:** wint
plug-ins. **All Rooms:** extended cable TV. **Cards:** AE, JC, MC, VI.

FLAMINGO MOTEL
Phone: (403)653-39
◆◆   6/9-9/10   1P: $57   2P: $65-$75   XP: $7   F
Motel   3/1-6/8 & 9/11-2/28   1P: $50   2P: $57-$65   XP: $5   F
Location: 1 km s on Hwy 2, just s of Remington Carriage Ctr. 848 Main St S T0K 0K0 (PO Box 9
Fax: 403/653-3863. **Terms:** Cancellation fee imposed; pets, $5 extra charge. **Facility:** 38 rooms. Hilltop location. Rooms w
2nd level offer a view of township. All rooms are well appointed with simple decor. 7 two-bedroom units. 2 stories; exterior co
ridors; heated pool; playground. **Services:** area transportation; winter plug-ins. **Some Rooms:** 6 kitchens. **Cards:** AE, CB,
DS, MC, VI.

THOMSON'S RANGEVIEW RANCH
Phone: (403)653-229
◆   6/1-9/15   1P: $150
Ranch   **Location:** 4 km s on Hwy 2, 10.7 km e on Hwy 501, from Jefferson sign 16 km n on dirt road. (PO Box 28, S
10, T0K 0K0). Fax: 403/653-1650. **Terms:** Open 6/1-9/15; [AP] meal plan; 30 day cancellation notice; canc
lation fee imposed. **Facility:** 6 rooms. Rustic accommodations for the adventure oriented traveller seeking a true western e
perience in the foothills of the Canadian Rockies. 2 two-bedroom units. 1 story; exterior corridors. **Services:** are
transportation. **Recreation:** swimming, fishing; horseback riding. **All Rooms:** combo, shower or tub baths. **Cards:** MC, VI.

--------- **RESTAURANT** ---------

COBBLESTONE MANOR Historical
Dinner: $10-$18   Phone: 403/653-15
◆◆   **Location:** 1 km s on Hwy 2, w on 7th Ave. 173 7th Ave W T0K 0K0. **Hours:** Open 4/1-12/31; 4:30
American   pm; to 8 pm off season. Closed: 12/25. **Reservations:** suggested. **Features:** children's menu; a la car
The Cobblestone offers casual, family dining in an elegant historical landmark home built in 1889. Inside ti
fieldstone building are are three original fieldstone fireplaces and elaborately designed and executed woodwork ceilings a
walls. **Cards:** MC, VI.

CLARESHOLM pop. 3,400

―――― LODGING ――――

BLUEBIRD MOTEL   Phone: 403/625-3395
◆◆   5/1-10/31   1P: $59-$79   2P: $59-$79
Motel   11/1-2/28   1P: $58-$66   2P: $58-$66
              3/1-4/30   1P: $58-$66   2P: $58-$66   XP: $6   F16
Location: 0.5 km n on Hwy 2. 5505 1st St W T0L 0T0 (PO Box 1888). Fax: 403/625-3395. **Terms:** Pets, in specified rooms.
Facility: 23 rooms. Duplex cottage units and regular motel units. Large guest rooms, offering unique charm. A few heritage
rooms featuring antique furnishings and decor. Meticulously clean rooms. All rooms with hair dryer. 8 two-bedroom units. 1
story; exterior corridors. **Services:** winter plug-ins. **All Rooms:** combo or shower baths. **Some Rooms:** 16 efficiencies.
Cards: MC, VI.

COCHRANE —See Calgary p. 354.

COLD LAKE pop. 4,100

―――― LODGING ――――

NEW FRONTIER MOTEL   Phone: (780)639-3030
[AAA] [SAVE]   All Year   1P: $38-$54   2P: $48-$80   XP: $6   F12
◆◆   **Location:** In centre of town, on Hwy 28. 1002 8th Ave T9M 1N2 (PO Box 8310). Fax: 780/639-4929.
Motel   **Terms:** [CP] meal plan; weekly & monthly rates avail; cancellation fee imposed; small pets only, $10 extra
              charge. **Facility:** 48 rooms. Some rooms with sofa bed and kitchen. 2 stories; exterior corridors. **Dining:** Res-
              taurant nearby. **Services:** winter plug-ins. **All Rooms:** extended cable TV. **Cards:** AE, MC, VI.
Special Amenities: Free breakfast and free local telephone calls.

DEAD MAN'S FLATS pop. 1,300

―――― LODGINGS ――――

GREEN ACRES MOTEL   Phone: 403/678-5344
[AAA]   6/1-9/30   1P: $75-$79   2P: $85-$119   XP: $5   F12
◆   3/1-5/31 & 10/1-2/28   1P: $50   2P: $60-$89   XP: $5   F12
Motel   **Location:** On Trans Canada Hwy 1; at Dead Man's Flats Service Centre. 200 2nd Ave T1W 2W4.
              Fax: 403/678-6691. **Terms:** Weekly & monthly rates avail, off season; 7 day cancellation notice; cancellation
              fee imposed; small pets only, $5 extra charge. **Facility:** 14 rooms. Hidden away from hwy and service centre.
Many flowers adorn the grounds in spring. Various mix of guest rooms from average size to larger family units. Most with vin-
tage appointments. 2 two-bedroom units. 6 efficiencies, $78-$99 for up to 6 persons; 1 story; exterior corridors; sauna.
Dining: Restaurant nearby. **Services:** winter plug-ins. **All Rooms:** combo or shower baths. **Cards:** AE, DI, DS, MC, VI.

PIGEON MOUNTAIN MOTEL

Phone: 403/678-575

(CAA)
Motel
◆ ◆

6/1-9/30	1P: $70-$75	2P: $75-$85	XP: $5	
3/1-5/31 & 10/1-2/28	1P: $48-$62	2P: $50-$68	XP: $5	

Location: On Trans Canada Hwy 1; at Dead Man's Flats Service Centre. 250 1st Ave T1W 2W4 (PO Bo
8038, T1W 2T8). Fax: 403/678-5761. **Terms:** 3 day cancellation notice; cancellation fee imposed; small pet
only. **Facility:** 16 rooms. Comfortable units with vintage appointments. Impressive mountain scenery. 8 two
bedroom units. 2 stories; exterior corridors. **Dining:** Restaurant nearby. **Services:** winter plug-ins. **Cards:** AE, DI, JC
MC, VI.

DIDSBURY pop. 3,600

-------- LODGINGS --------

A TOUCH OF HOME

Phone: (403)335-835

◆ ◆
Bed &
Breakfast

Property failed to provide current rates
Location: From Hwy 2, 7.3 km w on Hwy 582 which becomes 20th Ave, just s on 16th St. 1610 15th Ave T0M
0W0 (PO Box 1914). **Terms:** [BP] meal plan. **Facility:** 3 rooms. Country home with a small gazebo in th
backyard. 2 stories; interior corridors; smoke free premises.

SUPER 8 MOTEL-DIDSBURY

Phone: 403/335-808

◆ ◆
Motel

6/16-8/31	1P: $62	2P: $67	XP: $10	F1
9/1-2/28	1P: $55	2P: $60	XP: $5	F1
3/1-6/15	1P: $52	2P: $57	XP: $5	F1

Location: Just e, 7.7 km w of Hwy 2, exit Didsbury. 1714 20th Ave T0M 0W0 (PO Box 550). Fax: 403/335-8842. **Terms:** [CP
meal plan; pets. **Facility:** 32 rooms. Average sized rooms with contemporary and attractive decor. Adjacent to property, a larg
sport complex with pool and waterslides. 3 stories, no elevator; interior corridors. **Services:** winter plug-ins. **Some Rooms
Fee:** VCR. **Cards:** AE, DI, DS, JC, MC, VI.

DRUMHELLER pop. 6,600

-------- LODGINGS --------

HOO-DOO MOTEL

Phone: 403/823-566

◆
Motel

6/1-9/30	1P: $70-$75	2P: $70-$80	XP: $5	F1
5/1-5/31	1P: $45-$50	2P: $50-$55	XP: $5	F1
3/1-4/30 & 10/1-2/28	1P: $40-$45	2P: $45-$49	XP: $5	F1

Location: 1 km s on Hwy 9. T0J 0Y0 (PO Box 310). Fax: 403/823-7573. **Facility:** 32 rooms. Large guest rooms featuring a
older decor, guest rooms are clean and well maintained. 2 stories; exterior corridors. **Services:** winter plug-ins. **Some Rooms
Fee:** VCR. **Cards:** AE, MC, VI.

INN AT HEARTWOOD MANOR

Phone: (403)823-649

(CAA)
◆ ◆ ◆
Country Inn

3/1-10/1	1P: $89-$189	2P: $89-$189	XP: $10	F1
10/2-2/28	1P: $69-$150	2P: $69-$150	XP: $10	F1

Location: Just e of Hwy 9 (Downtown). 320 N Railway Ave E T0J 0Y4. Fax: 403/823-4935. **Terms:** [BP] mea
plan; 3 day cancellation notice; cancellation fee imposed; package plans. **Facility:** 10 rooms. Charming olde
residence skillfully renovated. Offers rooms varying in size, all with contemporary details. Well-harmonized t
antique furniture, many with gas burning fireplace. All rooms with hair dryer. 1 two-bedroom unit. 9 whirlpool rooms, $99-$189
2 stories; interior corridors; smoke free premises. **Dining:** Dinner served on request. **Services:** winter plug-ins. Fee: massage
Recreation: full selection of natural healing therapy, beauty salon services. **All Rooms:** combo or tub baths, extended cabl
TV. **Cards:** MC, VI.

NEWCASTLE COUNTRY INN

Phone: 403/823-835

◆ ◆
Country Inn

5/1-9/15	1P: $70-$90	2P: $80-$90	XP: $10	D1
3/1-4/30 & 9/16-11/30	1P: $50	2P: $50-$80	XP: $10	D1
12/1-2/28	1P: $40	2P: $50-$80	XP: $10	D1

Location: 1.7 km sw on 3rd Ave W turning into Newcastle Tr. 1130 Newcastle Tr T0J 0Y2. Fax: 403/823-2373. **Terms:** [BP
meal plan; cancellation fee imposed. **Facility:** 11 rooms. In quiet location. Property offering large common area, well appointe
with "country home" decor. Units vary in size. 2 stories; interior corridors; smoke free premises. **Services:** winter plug-ins
Cards: MC, VI.

TASTE THE PAST BED & BREAKFAST

Phone: 403/823-588

◆ ◆
Historic Bed
& Breakfast

All Year   1P: $60   2P: $75   XP: $20
Location: On Hwy 9 E (2nd St W), town centre; at 3rd Ave W. 281 2nd St W T0J 0Y0 (PO Box 865
Fax: 403/823-4516. **Terms:** [BP] meal plan; check-in 4 pm; 14 day cancellation notice. **Facility:** 3 rooms. I
large beautifully restored home. Rooms offer vintage country charm. Cozy common area with piano. 3 stories
interior corridors; smoke free premises. **All Rooms:** combo or shower baths. **Cards:** MC, VI.

Destination Edmonton

E dmonton, nicknamed "Gateway to the North," was once a place for gold miners to stop and gather provisions for their rough journey into the icy Klondike.

D isappointed prospectors who eventually returned to help build Edmonton indeed struck gold: Today the shining city is a mecca of culture and recreation with its lovely theaters, parks and gardens.

Edmonton Skyline.
A sparkling city, a blanket of snow and a sunny day prove all that glitters is not gold.

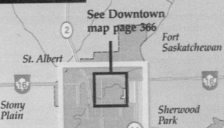

Citadel Theatre, Edmonton.
Live shows run September through May in this complex that has four theaters, an amphitheater and an atrium. (See mention page 71)

Francis Winspear Centre, Edmonton.
Are etudes and concertos music to your ears? Set aside some time to attend a performance by the Edmonton Symphony Orchestra at the center in Sir Winston Churchill Square. (See mention page 71)

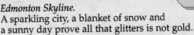

See Downtown map page 366

St. Albert

Fort Saskatchewan

Stony Plain

Sherwood Park

See Vicinity map page 367

Edmonton

Leduc

Bicycling in Edmonton.
Many city parks offer trails for bicycling. Fitness buffs also can jog, hike, golf, skate and ski. (See mention page 70)

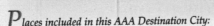

P laces included in this AAA Destination City:

Edmonton *pop. 616,300*

his index helps you "spot" where approved accommodations are located on the detailed maps that follow. Rate ranges are r comparison only and show the property's high season. Turn to the listing page for more detailed rate information and con- ult display ads for special promotions. Restaurant rate range is for dinner, unless only lunch (L) is served.

✈ Airport Accommodations

Spotter/Map Page Number	OA	EDMONTON INTERNATIONAL AIRPORT	Diamond Rating	Rate Range High Season	Listing Page
	Ⓐ	**Best Western Denham Inn and Suites, 8 km se of airport**	◆◆◆	$79-$89 SAVE	377
68 / p. 367	Ⓐ	**The International Inn, 3.7 km e of airport**	◆◆◆	$115-$125 SAVE	394
67 / p. 367		Nisku Inn and Conference Centre, 3.5 km e of airport	◆◆	$85	394

DOWNTOWN EDMONTON

Spotter/Map Page Number	OA	DOWNTOWN EDMONTON - Lodgings	Diamond Rating	Rate Range High Season	Listing Page
1 / p. 366		Delta Edmonton Centre Suite Hotel - see color ad p 368	◆◆◆	$94-$124	368
3 / p. 366		The Westin Edmonton	◆◆◆◆	$240-$270	369
6 / p. 366		Days Inn Downtown Edmonton	◆◆	$60-$90	368
7 / p. 366		Hotel Macdonald	◆◆◆◆	$129-$179	369
9 / p. 366		Alberta Place Suite Hotel	◆◆	$71-$90	368
10 / p. 366		Union Bank Inn	◆◆◆	Failed to provide	369
11 / p. 366	Ⓐ	**Crowne Plaza-Chateau Lacombe - see color ad p 368**	◆◆◆	$99-$139 SAVE	368
13 / p. 366	Ⓐ	**Edmonton House Suite Hotel - see color ad p 369**	◆◆◆	$99 SAVE	369
		DOWNTOWN EDMONTON - Restaurants			
① / p. 366		The Creperie	◆◆	$9-$22	370
② / p. 366		Bistro Praha	◆◆	$6-$16	370
③ / p. 366		Khazana	◆◆◆	$10-$20	370
④ / p. 366		Pradera Cafe	◆◆◆	$10-$27	370
⑥ / p. 366		Hardware Grill	◆◆◆	$20-$30	370
⑦ / p. 366		Madison's Grill	◆◆◆	$9-$20	370
⑨ / p. 366		Cafe Select	◆◆	$10-$20	370
⑪ / p. 366		The Harvest Room	◆◆◆	$21-$32	370
⑬ / p. 366		La Ronde Revolving Restaurant	◆◆◆	$16-$33	370

EDMONTON

Spotter/Map Page Number	OA	EDMONTON - Lodgings	Diamond Rating	Rate Range High Season	Listing Page
27 / p. 367		Edmonton Inn - see color ad p 372	◆◆	$65	372
29 / p. 367		Ramada Inn and Conference Centre - see color ad p 375	◆◆◆	$65	375
30 / p. 367	Ⓐ	**Chateau Louis Hotel & Conference Centre - see color ad p 372**	◆◆	$79-$99 SAVE	371
31 / p. 367	Ⓐ	**The Mayfield Inn & Suites, Edmonton - see color ad p 374**	◆◆◆	$99-$139 SAVE	374
32 / p. 367	Ⓐ	**Best Western Westwood Inn - see color ad p 369, p 371**	◆◆◆	$89-$99 SAVE	371
34 / p. 367	Ⓐ	**West Harvest Inn - see color ad p 375**	◆◆	$69-$89 SAVE	375
35 / p. 367	Ⓐ	**Continental Inn**	◆◆	$69-$79 SAVE	372
38 / p. 367		Glenora Bed & Breakfast Inn	◆◆◆	$60-$140	373

Spotter/Map Page Number	OA	**EDMONTON - Lodgings (continued)**	Diamond Rating	Rate Range High Season	Listing Page
39 / p. 367	⬡	Holiday Inn Express Hotel & Suites	◆◆◆	$89-$174 SAVE	374
41 / p. 367		Comfort Inn	◆◆	$83-$99	372
44 / p. 367		Fantasyland Hotel	◆◆◆	$165	373
45 / p. 367		Campus Tower Suite Hotel	◆◆	$99	371
46 / p. 367	⬡	Holiday Inn Convention Centre - see color ad p 373	◆◆◆	$89 SAVE	373
47 / p. 367		Argyll Plaza Hotel	◆◆	$65-$69	371
49 / p. 367	⬡	Best Western Cedar Park Inn - see color ad p 369	◆◆◆	$89-$109 SAVE	371
51 / p. 367	⬡	Ramada Inn and Water Park	◆◆	$79 SAVE	375
52 / p. 367	⬡	Delta Edmonton South Hotel and Conference Centre - see color ad p 372	◆◆◆	$84-$109 SAVE	372
55 / p. 367	⬡	Greenwood Inn Hotels - see color ad p 373, p 347	◆◆◆	$109-$139 SAVE	373
56 / p. 367	⬡	Holiday Inn The Palace - see color ad p 374	◆◆◆	$89 SAVE	374
59 / p. 367	⬡	Travelodge Beverly Crest	◆◆	$73-$79 SAVE	375
		EDMONTON - Restaurants			
22 / p. 367		Chianti	◆◆	$7-$16	376

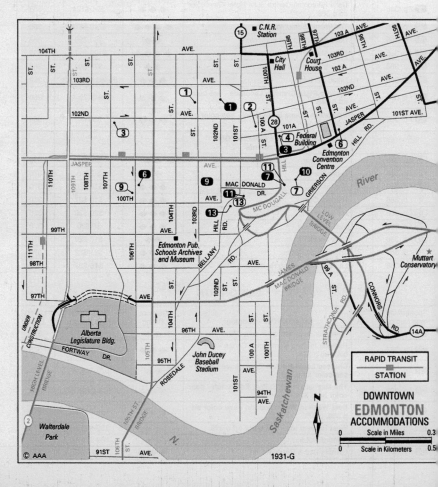

DOWNTOWN
EDMONTON
ACCOMMODATIONS

© AAA

1931-G

Spotter/Map Page Number	OA	**EDMONTON** - Restaurants (continued)	Diamond Rating	Rate Range High Season	Listing Page
㉓ / below		Mayfield Inn Dinner Theatre	◆ ◆	$21-$64	376
㉔ / below	Ⓐ	**Xian Szechuan Restaurant**	◆ ◆	$8-$16	376
㉖ / below		Royal Fork Buffet Restaurant	◆	$11	376
㉗ / below		La Spiga	◆ ◆ ◆	$13-$22	376
㉙ / below		Manor Cafe	◆ ◆	$8-$17	376
㉚ / below		Lemongrass Cafe	◆ ◆	$6-$15	376
㉛ / below		Yiannis Taverna	◆ ◆	$13-$20	377
㉞ / below		Von's Steak & Fish House	◆ ◆	$12-$40	376
㉟ / below		Jack's Grill	◆ ◆ ◆	$19-$24	376

Edmonton Vicinity

Spotter/Map Page Number	OA	**NISKU** - Lodgings	Diamond Rating	Rate Range High Season	Listing Page
㊐ / below		Nisku Inn and Conference Centre	◆ ◆	$85	394
㊑ / below	Ⓐ	**The International Inn**	◆ ◆ ◆	$115-$125 SAVE	394

DOWNTOWN EDMONTON   (See map p. 366; index p. 365)

—— LODGINGS ——

ALBERTA PLACE SUITE HOTEL   **Phone:** (780)423-1565   **9**
◆◆   All Year   1P: $71-$90   2P: $71-$90   XP: $8   F18
Apartment   **Location:** Just s of Jasper Ave. 10049 103rd St T5J 2W7. Fax: 780/426-6260. **Terms:** [CP] meal plan; 7 day cancellation notice; small pets only. **Facility:** 85 rooms. Well-equipped, all suite property. All downtown services nearby. 19 stories; interior corridors; heated pool. **Services:** winter plug-ins. Fee: massage. **All Rooms:** kitchens. **Cards:** AE, DI, MC, VI.

CROWNE PLAZA-CHATEAU LACOMBE   **Phone:** (780)428-6611   **11**
(CAA) (SAVE)   All Year   1P: $99-$139   2P: $99-$139   XP: $10   F18
◆◆◆   **Location:** At jct 101st St, MacDonald Dr and Bellamy Hill. 10111 Bellamy Hill T5J 1N7. Fax: 780/425-6564.
Hotel   **Terms:** Monthly rates avail; package plans; small pets only. **Facility:** 307 rooms. A unique round high-rise tower design with wonderful views of the city. Spacious rooms overlooking picturesque N Saskatchewan River Valley. All rooms with iron and ironing board. Whirlpool room; suites avail; 24 stories; interior corridors. Fee: parking. **Dining:** Dining room; 6:30 am-11 pm; $17-$27; cocktails; also, La Ronde Revolving Restaurant, see separate listing. **Services:** gift shop; winter plug-ins. **Recreation:** in-room video games. **All Rooms:** extended cable TV. Some Rooms: honor bars. **Cards:** AE, CB, DI, DS, JC, MC, VI. **Special Amenities:** Early check-in/late check-out and free local telephone calls. *(See color ad below)*

DAYS INN DOWNTOWN EDMONTON   **Phone:** (780)423-1925   **6**
◆◆   All Year   1P: $60-$80   2P: $60-$90
Motor Inn   **Location:** Just s of Jasper Ave, downtown. 10041 106th St T5J 1G3. Fax: 780/424-5302. **Terms:** Pets, $8 extra charge. **Facility:** 72 rooms. Good budget accommodation, family-oriented. Most rooms with contemporary furnishings. 5 stories; interior corridors. **Services:** winter plug-ins. **Some Rooms:** 5 efficiencies. **Cards:** AE, CB, DI, DS, MC, VI.

DELTA EDMONTON CENTRE SUITE HOTEL   **Phone:** (780)429-3900   **1**
◆◆◆   All Year   1P: $94-$124   2P: $94-$124   XP: $10   F18
Hotel   **Location:** 102nd St at 103rd Ave. 10222 102nd St T5J 4C5. Fax: 780/426-0562. **Terms:** Cancellation fee imposed; small pets only. **Facility:** 169 rooms. Conveniently attached to large shopping complex. Spacious accommodations and contemporary decor with upscale amenities including hair dryer, iron, ironing board, and video games. A few rooms with fax machine and printer. 7 stories; interior corridors. Fee: parking. **Services:** winter plug-ins. **All Rooms:** honor bars. **Cards:** AE, CB, DI, DS, JC, MC, VI. *(See color ad below)*

(See map p. 366)

EDMONTON HOUSE SUITE HOTEL   Phone: (780)420-4000   🔟🔢
(AA) (SAVE)   All Year   1P: $99   2P: $99   XP: $5   F18
◆◆◆   **Location:** Just se of jct 102nd St and 100th Ave. 10205 100th Ave T5J 4B5. Fax: 780/420-4008.
Suite Hotel   **Terms:** Weekly & monthly rates avail; package plans; small pets only, $200 dep req. **Facility:** 299 rooms. Spacious units with balcony overlooking the river valley or with view of downtown. Full size kitchen in every suite. All rooms with hair dryer, iron, ironing board and video games. 2 bedroom suites, $195; 34 stories; interior corridors; heated pool. **Dining:** Restaurant; 6:30 am-10 am; $7-$17; cocktails. **Services:** winter plug-ins. Fee: massage. **Recreation:** convenience store, game room, library. **All Rooms:** kitchens, extended cable TV. **Some Rooms:** Fee: VCR. **Cards:** AE, DI, MC, VI. **Special Amenities:** Free newspaper. *(See color ad below)*

🔣🔣🔣🔣🔣🔣🔣🔣🔣🔣🔣🔣🔣

HOTEL MACDONALD   Phone: 780/424-5181   🔟
◆◆◆◆   All Year   1P: $129-$179   XP: $20   F17
Classic Hotel **Location:** Just s of Jasper Ave. 10065 100th St T5J 0N6. Fax: 780/424-8017. **Terms:** Cancellation fee imposed; package plans; pets, $20 extra charge, in kennel. **Facility:** 198 rooms. **Historic.** Historic originally opened in 1915 this completely restored chateau-style hotel is situated on top of a hill with a wonderful view of the river valley. Elegant rooms with many luxury level services offered.1 two-bedroom unit. 9 stories; interior corridors; heated pool. Fee: parking. **Services:** gift shop; winter plug-ins. Fee: massage. **All Rooms:** honor bars. **Some Rooms:** Fee: VCR. **Cards:** AE, CB, DI, DS, JC, MC, VI. A Canadian Pacific Hotel.

🔣🔣🔣🔣🔣🔣🔣🔣🔣🔣🔣🔣🔣🔣

UNION BANK INN   Phone: 780/423-3600   🔟
◆◆◆   Property failed to provide current rates
Historic   **Location:** Corner 101st St. 10053 Jasper Ave T5J 1S5. Fax: 780/423-4623. **Terms:** [BP] meal plan; package
Country Inn   plans. **Facility:** 14 rooms. Exceptionally restored landmark building with boutique style accommodations featuring individually designed guest rooms, each with a gas fireplace. 3 stories; interior corridors; designated smoking area. **Services:** winter plug-ins. **Some Rooms:** Fee: VCR. **Cards:** AE, DI, DS, MC, VI.

🔣🔣🔣🔣🔣🔣🔣🔣

THE WESTIN EDMONTON   Phone: (780)426-3636   🔢
◆◆◆◆   1/1-2/28   1P: $240-$260   2P: $250-$270   XP: $10   F18
Hotel   3/1-12/31   1P: $235-$255   2P: $245-$265   XP: $10   F18
            Location: 101A Ave at 100th St. 10135 100th St T5J 0N7. Fax: 780/428-1454. **Terms:** Small pets only. **Facility:** 413 rooms. Very spacious guest rooms, contemporary public areas. Located in the heart of downtown Edmonton. All rooms with hair dryer, iron, ironing board and 2 line phones. 20 stories; interior corridors; heated pool. Fee: parking. **Services:** gift shop. **All Rooms:** honor bars. **Cards:** AE, DI, DS, JC, MC, VI.

🔣🔣🔣🔣🔣🔣🔣🔣🔣🔣🔣🔣🔣🔣

(See map p. 366)

———— **RESTAURANTS** ————

BISTRO PRAHA   Lunch: $6-$16   Dinner: $6-$16   Phone: 780/424-4218   ②
◆◆   **Location:** Downtown, just n of Jasper Ave. 10168 100A St T5J 0R6. **Hours:** 11 am-2 am, Sun 5 pm-1 am.
Continental   Closed major holidays & 1/2. **Reservations:** suggested. **Features:** carryout; cocktails; street parking; a la
          carte. Bistro Praha's features a very good European cuisine with hearty portions of steak tartare, Wiener
schnitzel, filet mignon, tenderloin and other specialties. Its warm, inviting and tasteful decor is highlighted with antique
elements. Friendly service. **Cards:** AE, DI, MC, VI.   ✕

CAFE SELECT   Lunch: $8-$13   Dinner: $10-$20   Phone: 780/423-0419   ⑨
◆◆   **Location:** Just s of Jasper Ave. 10018-106 St T5J 1G1. **Hours:** 11:30 am-2 am, Fri-11 pm, Sun from 5 pm.
Continental   Closed: 1/1, 12/24 & 12/25. **Reservations:** suggested. **Features:** cocktails; street parking; a la carte. You'll
          enjoy the comfortable, intimate atmosphere of Cafe Select, which offers a menu of traditional favorites such
as rack of lamb and beef tenderloin as well as a lighter fare of salads and other dishes. Outdoor patio dining is available in
season. **Cards:** AE, CB, DI, MC, VI.   ✕

THE CREPERIE   Lunch: $7-$12   Dinner: $9-$22   Phone: 780/420-6656   ①
◆◆   **Location:** Just n of 102nd Ave. 10220 103rd St T5J 0Y8. **Hours:** 11:30 am-10 pm, Fri-11
French   pm, Sun-9 pm. Closed: 12/25. **Reservations:** suggested. **Features:** dressy casual; children's menu; health
          conscious menu items; cocktails; fee for parking; a la carte. This charming restaurant is very good, especially
for groups. The dinner menu offers a variety of stuffed crepes, beef and seafood prepared with inspiration from the French.
The decor of dark wood is conducive to quiet and intimate conversation. **Cards:** AE, DI, MC, VI.   ✕

HARDWARE GRILL   Lunch: $9-$15   Dinner: $20-$30   Phone: 780/423-0969   ⑥
◆◆◆   **Location:** Corner of 97th St. 9698 Jasper Ave T5H 3V5. **Hours:** 11:30 am-2 & 5-9:30 pm, Fri & Sat 5
Regional   pm-10:30 pm. Closed major holidays & Sun. **Reservations:** suggested. **Features:** street parking; a la carte.
Canadian   You'll really appreciate this restaurant—it's a former hardware store converted into a trendy, upscale dining
          room. Its innovative Northwest cuisine specializes in delicious cedar-planked salmon. They have an excellent
wine list and incredible service. **Cards:** AE, DI, MC, VI.   ✕

THE HARVEST ROOM   Lunch: $11-$20   Dinner: $21-$32   Phone: 780/424-5181   ⑪
◆◆◆   **Location:** Just s of Jasper Ave; in Hotel Macdonald. 10065 100th St T5J 0N6. **Hours:** 6:30 am-10 pm, Sat
Continental   & Sun from 7 am. **Reservations:** suggested. **Features:** dressy casual; Sunday brunch; children's menu;
          health conscious menu items; cocktails & lounge; fee for parking & valet parking; a la carte. The Harvest
Room is cafe-style dining with an open kitchen and a creative, complex menu that displays freshness and health-conscious
preparation. The Nova Scotia lobster and grilled Newfoundland scallops salad and pan-seared seabass dishes are excellent.
Cards: AE, DI, DS, JC, MC, VI.   ♿ ✕

KHAZANA   Lunch: $10   Dinner: $10-$20   Phone: 780/702-0330   ③
◆◆◆   **Location:** Corner 102nd Ave. 10177 107 St T5J 1J5. **Hours:** 11:30 am-2:30 & 5-10:30 pm, Fri-11 pm, Sat 5
Indian   pm-11 pm, Sun 4:30 pm-8:30 pm. Closed: 12/25. **Reservations:** suggested. **Features:** health conscious
          menu items; carryout; cocktails; street parking; a la carte. Khazana's features an authentic, tasty tandoori
cuisine of papadams, fresh Nan bread, peshawari kebab (lamb), boti kebab (prime beef) and murgh tandoori (chicken). The
inviting, upscale decor includes original artwork from New Delhi and costumed servers. **Cards:** AE, MC, VI.   ✕

LA RONDE REVOLVING RESTAURANT   Dinner: $16-$33   Phone: 780/428-6611   ⑬
◆◆◆   **Location:** At jct 101st St, MacDonald Dr and Bellamy Hill; in Crowne Plaza-Chateau Lacombe. 10111
Continental   Bellamy Hill T5J 1N7. **Hours:** 5:30 pm-11 pm, Sun 10:30 am-2 & 5-11 pm, Mon 5 pm-11 pm.
          Reservations: suggested. **Features:** casual dress; Sunday brunch; children's menu; health conscious menu items;
cocktails & lounge; fee for parking & valet parking; a la carte, also prix fixe. This revolving rooftop restaurant offers a
panoramic view of the city. Its atmosphere is elegant, yet casual, and its cuisine features European classics with Asian
influences. Prix fixe selections cater to couples and include aperitifs and champagnes. **Cards:** AE, DI, DS, JC, MC, VI.   ✕

MADISON'S GRILL   Lunch: $8-$14   Dinner: $9-$20   Phone: 780/423-3600   ⑦
◆◆◆   **Location:** Corner 101st St; in Union Bank Inn. 10053 Jasper Ave T5J 1S5. **Hours:** 7 am-10 pm, Fri &
Continental   Sat-midnight. **Reservations:** suggested. **Features:** dressy casual; Sunday brunch; health conscious menu
          items; cocktails & lounge; a la carte. This popular restaurant features a cuisine flavored with contemporary
touches. The menu includes steamed mussels, langostinos, and lamb—all prepared and served with fresh herbs and
mashed purple potatoes. Many specialty coffees and teas are offered. Smoke free premises. **Cards:** AE, DI, DS, MC, VI.   ✕

PRADERA CAFE   Lunch: $9-$12   Dinner: $10-$27   Phone: 780/493-8994   ④
◆◆◆   **Location:** 101A Ave at 100th St; in The Westin Edmonton. 10135 100 St T5J 0N7. **Hours:** 6:30 am-11 pm,
Nouvelle   Sat & Sun from 7 am. **Reservations:** suggested. **Features:** casual dress; Sunday brunch; children's menu;
Canadian   health conscious menu; cocktails & lounge; fee for parking & valet parking; a la carte. You'll enjoy the
          excellent menu of Pradera; it has international influences and features English-cut prime rib, fresh lake trout
and chateaubriand, with superb presentations. The dining room is elegant and inviting; the service is quite sharp.
Cards: AE, DI, DS, JC, MC, VI.   ⌂ ✕

EDMONTON pop. 616,300 (See map p. 367; index p. 365)

———— LODGINGS ————

ARGYLL PLAZA HOTEL
◆◆
Motor Inn
Phone: (780)438-5876 47 F16
All Year   1P: $65-$69   2P: $65-$69   XP: $5
Location: 63rd Ave at 99th St. 9933 63rd Ave T6E 6C9. Fax: 780/436-5813. **Terms:** [CP] meal plan; check-in 4 pm; package plans; pets. **Facility:** 48 rooms. At one end of strip mall. Rooms are spacious and offer decor of mixed styles. All rooms with hair dryer. 3 stories; interior corridors. **Services:** winter plug-ins. **Some Rooms:** 25 efficiencies. **Cards:** AE, DI, MC, VI.

BEST WESTERN CEDAR PARK INN
(AAA) (SAVE)
◆◆◆
Motor Inn
Phone: (780)434-7411 49 F
All Year   1P: $89-$109   2P: $89-$109   XP: $10
Location: Calgary Tr at 51st Ave. 5116 Calgary Tr Northbound T6H 2H4. Fax: 780/437-4836. **Terms:** Small pets only, specified floors. **Facility:** 190 rooms. Special landscaping touches in the summer. Some rooms with their own private balcony, sun deck on roof. Fresh and contemporary room decor. All rooms with hair dryer, iron and ironing board. Suites, $139-$150 breakfast included; 2 whirlpool rooms; 5 stories; interior corridors; small heated indoor pool, saunas. **Dining:** Restaurant; 6:30 am-11 pm, Sun 7 am-10 pm; $7-$18; cocktails. **Services:** gift shop; area transportation, West Edmonton Mall; winter plug-ins. **All Rooms:** extended cable TV. **Cards:** AE, DI, DS, JC, MC, VI. **Special Amenities: Early check-in/late check-out and free local telephone calls.** *(See color ad p 369)*

BEST WESTERN WESTWOOD INN
◆◆◆
Motor Inn
Phone: (780)483-7770 32 F17
6/4-9/4   1P: $89   2P: $99   XP: $10   F17
3/1-6/3 & 9/5-2/28   1P: $79   2P: $89   XP: $10   F17
Location: Hwy 16A at 180th St. 18035 Stony Plain Rd T5S 1B2. Fax: 780/486-1769. **Facility:** 169 rooms. Easy driving distance to the West Edmonton Mall. Spacious rooms with very good amenities. All rooms with hair dryer and voice mail. 9 whirlpool suites, $140; 81 whirlpool rooms, $125-$140; 3-6 stories; interior corridors; small heated indoor pool, saunas, steamroom, whirlpool. **Dining:** Restaurant; 6 am-11 pm, Sun-1 pm; $6-$19; cocktails. **Services:** winter plug-ins. **Recreation:** small video game room, squash court. **All Rooms:** extended cable TV, honor bars. **Cards:** AE, DI, DS, MC, VI. **Special Amenities: Early check-in/late check-out and free local telephone calls.** *(See color ad p 369 & below)*

CAMPUS TOWER SUITE HOTEL
◆◆
Suite Hotel
Phone: (780)439-6060 45 F17
All Year   1P: $99   2P: $99   XP: $10
Location: At 111th St and 87th Ave. 11145 87th Ave T6G 0Y1. Fax: 780/433-4410. **Facility:** 90 rooms. Apartment style accommodation offering spacious units most with 1 separate bedroom. In the trendy university area, across the street from the hospital. All rooms with hair dryer, iron and ironing board. 10 two-bedroom units. 16 stories; interior corridors. **Services:** area transportation; winter plug-ins. **All Rooms:** kitchens. **Some Rooms:** Fee: VCR. **Cards:** AE, DI, MC, VI.

CHATEAU LOUIS HOTEL & CONFERENCE CENTRE
(AAA) (SAVE)
◆◆
Motor Inn
Phone: (780)452-7770 30 F12
All Year   1P: $79-$99   2P: $79-$99   XP: $10
Location: On Kingsway and 117th St. 11727 Kingsway T5G 3A1. Fax: 780/454-3436. **Terms:** Weekly & monthly rates avail; small pets only, $5 extra charge in designated rooms. **Facility:** 146 rooms. Spacious rooms offering decor with a style inspired from King Louis XIV. Overall appeal varies from elegant to a few modest units. Specialty suites & 3 whirlpool suites, $129-$279; 3 stories; interior corridors. **Dining:** Dining room; 6:30 am-midnight, Sat from 7 am, Sun 8 am-midnight; Sun brunch & Ukrainian buffet; $10-$25; cocktails; nightclub. **Services:** winter plug-ins. **Recreation:** pool tables, video games. **All Rooms:** extended cable TV. **Some Rooms:** honor bars. **Cards:** AE, DI, MC, VI. **Special Amenities: Free local telephone calls and free newspaper.** *(See color ad p 372)*

(See map p. 367)

COMFORT INN   ◆◆   Motel   **Phone:** (780)484-4415   **41**

	6/16-9/15	1P: $83-$89	2P: $89-$99	
	9/16-2/28	1P: $77-$79	2P: $85-$89	
	4/1-6/15	1P: $73-$79	2P: $83-$89	
	3/1-3/31	1P: $69-$75	2P: $77-$85	XP: $4 F18

Location: On 100th Ave at 176th St. 17610 100th Ave T5S 1S9. Fax: 780/481-4034. **Terms:** 3 day cancellation notice; package plans; pets. **Facility:** 100 rooms. Contemporary decor, convenient patio door and at-door parking on the 1st floor. All rooms with hair dryer. 2 stories; interior corridors. **Services:** winter plug-ins. Fee: area transportation. **Some Rooms:** Fee: refrigerators. **Cards:** AE, DI, DS, MC, VI.

CONTINENTAL INN   CAA SAVE   ◆◆   Motor Inn   **Phone:** (780)484-7751   **35**

All Year   1P: $69-$79   2P: $69-$79   XP: $5   F12

Location: On Stony Plain Rd (Hwy 16A) at 166th St. 16625 Stony Plain Rd T5P 4A8. Fax: 780/484-9827. **Terms:** 7 day cancellation notice. **Facility:** 100 rooms. Spacious rooms offering good, budget-style accommodations. Newly constructed rooms on upper floors. All rooms with hair dryer. 2 one-bedroom suites with wet bar, refrigerator & microwave, $175; 6 stories; interior corridors. **Dining:** Dining room, coffee shop; 6 am-11:30 pm, Sun 7 am-10 pm; $5-$15; 11 stories; interior corridors; small heated indoor pool, whirlpool. **Services:** winter plug-ins. Fee: area transportation, West Edmonton Mall. **All Rooms:** extended cable TV. **Cards:** AE, MC, VI. **Special Amenities:** Free room upgrade and preferred room (each subject to availability with advanced reservations).

DELTA EDMONTON SOUTH HOTEL AND CONFERENCE CENTRE   CAA SAVE   ◆◆◆   Hotel   **Phone:** (780)434-6415   **52**

All Year   1P: $84-$109   2P: $84-$109   XP: $10   F18

Location: At jct Calgary Tr (Hwy 2) and Whitemud Frwy. 4404 Calgary Tr T6H 5C2. Fax: 780/436-9247. **Terms:** Monthly rates avail; small pets only, $20 extra charge. **Facility:** 237 rooms. Rooms in the east tower are spacious. All rooms with progressive, contemporary decor. Excellent amenities package. 6 whirlpool rooms, $165-$275; 11 stories; interior corridors; small heated indoor pool, whirlpool. **Dining:** Dining room, coffee shop, deli; 6 am-midnight; $7-$14; cocktails. **Services:** gift shop; winter plug-ins. Fee: massage. **All Rooms:** extended cable TV. **Cards:** AE, DI, DS, JC, MC, VI. **Special Amenities:** Free local telephone calls and free newspaper. *(See color ad below)*

EDMONTON INN   ◆◆   Motor Inn   **Phone:** (780)454-9521   **27**

All Year   1P: $65   2P: $65   XP: $10   F18

Location: 4 km nw on Kingsway Ave at 119th St. 11830 Kingsway Ave T5G 0X5. Fax: 780/453-7360. **Terms:** Small pets only. **Facility:** 115 rooms. Tropical style lobby featuring large rock garden with flowing stream encircling lobby. 9 stories; interior corridors. **Dining:** nightclub. **Services:** gift shop; area transportation; winter plug-ins. **Cards:** AE, DI, DS, JC, MC, VI. *(See color ad below)*

(See map p. 367)

FANTASYLAND HOTEL
◆◆◆
Hotel

Phone: (780)444-3000   **44**   F16

All Year   1P: $165   2P: $165   XP: $10

Location: 87th Ave at 178th St; in West Edmonton Mall (sw end). 17700 87th Ave T5T 4V4. Fax: 780/444-3294. **Terms:** Check-in 4 pm; cancellation fee imposed; package plans. **Facility:** 354 rooms. Offers a variety of room styles, from standard to executive. Famous for its theme rooms such as trains, trucks or inspired locations such as Rome, Polynesia, Africa, Arabia and Hollywood. All rooms with hair dryer. 12 stories; interior corridors. Fee: miniature golf. **Services:** winter plug-ins. **Recreation:** Fee: ice skating. **Cards:** AE, DI, MC, VI.

GLENORA BED & BREAKFAST INN
◆◆◆
Bed & Breakfast

Phone: (780)488-6766   **38**   D13

All Year   1P: $60-$125   2P: $75-$140   XP: $15

Location: At 124th St. 12327 102nd Ave T5N 0L8. Fax: 780/488-5168. **Terms:** [BP] meal plan; check-in 4 pm. **Facility:** 21 rooms. Tastefully restored property offering units of various sizes and appointments. All rooms decorated with antiques. A few rooms with wet bar. Attractive common area with library and games. Located close to downtown services. 3 stories, no elevator; interior corridors; smoke free premises. **Services:** winter plug-ins. **Some Rooms:** 4 kitchens. **Cards:** AE, CB, DI, MC, VI.

GREENWOOD INN HOTELS
(CAA) [SAVE]
◆◆◆
Motor Inn

Phone: (780)431-1100   **55**   F18

All Year   1P: $109-$129   2P: $109-$139   XP: $10

Location: Calgary Tr northbound, just n of Whitemud. 4485 Calgary Tr N T6H 5C3. Fax: 780/437-3455. **Terms:** Cancellation fee imposed. **Facility:** 224 rooms. Attractive, contemporary room style; all with hair dryer, iron and ironing board. Some rooms with steam shower for 2; others with large table seating 4 persons. Heated underground parking. 3 one-bedroom suites, $225; whirlpool room; 6 stories; interior corridors; steamroom, whirlpool, small heated indoor saltwater lap pool. **Dining:** 2 restaurants; 6 am-11 pm, Sun from 6:30 am; $6-$24; cocktails. **Services:** gift shop; winter plug-ins. **All Rooms:** combo or shower baths, extended cable TV. **Cards:** AE, DI, JC, MC, VI. **Special Amenities:** Free local telephone calls and free newspaper. *(See color ad below & p 347)*

HOLIDAY INN CONVENTION CENTRE
(CAA) [SAVE]
◆◆◆
Motor Inn

Phone: (780)468-5400   **46**   F12

All Year   1P: $89   2P: $89   XP: $10

Location: From Hwy 14, just s via 50th St exit, then just e. 4520 76th Ave T6B 0A5. Fax: 780/466-0451. **Terms:** Pets. **Facility:** 93 rooms. Nicely appointed rooms with bright and cheerful decor. All rooms with hair dryer, iron and ironing board. 2 whirlpool rooms, $199-$249; 6 stories; interior corridors; heated pool, steamroom, whirlpool. **Dining:** Restaurant; 6 am-10 pm, businesss lounge with internet access & coffee bar; $6-$14; cocktails. **Services:** gift shop; area transportation, West Edmonton Mall; winter plug-ins. **Recreation:** in-room video games. **All Rooms:** extended cable TV. **Cards:** AE, DI, DS, MC, VI. **Special Amenities:** Free local telephone calls and free newspaper. *(See color ad below)*

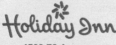

(See map p. 367)

HOLIDAY INN EXPRESS HOTEL & SUITES　　　　　　　　　　　　　　**Phone:** (780)483-4000　③

(CAA) (SAVE)　All Year　　　　　　1P: $89-$174　　　2P: $89-$174　　　XP: $10　　　　F18
◆◆◆　**Location:** On 100th Ave, just w of 178th St. 10017 179A St T5S 2L4. **Fax:** 780/481-6227. **Terms:** [CP] meal
Motel　plan; check-in 4 pm; small pets only. **Facility:** 102 rooms. Cutting edge property with a spacious, well-appointed lobby and breakfast room. Upscale rooms; suites feature wet bar, refrigerator and microwave. A few rooms with steam shower. Excellent amenities. Rates for up to 4 persons; 2 whirlpool rooms, $129-$250; suites, $109-$179; 4 stories; interior corridors; heated pool, steamroom, whirlpool. **Dining:** Restaurant nearby. **Services:** gift shop; winter plug-ins. **Recreation:** game room. **All Rooms:** extended cable TV. **Cards:** AE, CB, DI, MC, VI. **Special Amenities: Free breakfast and free local telephone calls.**

HOLIDAY INN THE PALACE　　　　　　　　　　　　　　　　　　**Phone:** (780)438-1222　⑤

(CAA) (SAVE)　All Year　　　　　　1P: $89　　　　　2P: $89　　　　　XP: $10　　　　F16
◆◆◆　**Location:** Just s of Whitemud Dr. 4235 Calgary Tr N T6J 5H2. **Fax:** 780/438-0906. **Terms:** Small pets only,
Motor Inn　$10 extra charge. **Facility:** 136 rooms. A contemporary palace-style architecture; atrium courtyard area features a waterfall and lush plants. Rooms are spacious and feature hair dryer, iron and ironing board. 8 whirlpool rooms, $189-$275; suites, $135-$250; 5 stories; interior corridors; steamroom, whirlpools. **Dining:** Restaurant; 6:30 am-10 pm; $6-$18; cocktails. **Services:** gift shop; area transportation, West Edmonton Mall; winter plug-ins. **Recreation:** hair salon, in-room video games. **All Rooms:** extended cable TV. **Cards:** AE, CB, DI, DS, JC, MC, VI. **Special Amenities: Early check-in/late check-out and free local telephone calls.** *(See color ad below)*

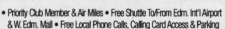

THE MAYFIELD INN & SUITES, EDMONTON　　　　　　　　　　　**Phone:** (780)484-0821　③

(CAA) (SAVE)　All Year　　　　　　1P: $99-$139　　　2P: $99-$139　　　XP: $15　　　　F18
◆◆◆　**Location:** 1.6 km n of jct Hwy 2 and 16A on Mayfield Rd. 16615 109th Ave T5P 4K8. **Fax:** 780/486-1634.
Hotel　**Terms:** [BP] meal plan; cancellation fee imposed; package plans; pets, $30 extra charge. **Facility:** 327 rooms. Provides a mix of room styles ranging from standard units to multi-room suites. Room appointments range from good to luxurious. Some luxury level services offered. All rooms with hair dryer, iron and ironing board. 96 executive suites, $139-$250. 12 efficiencies, $98-$125; 52 whirlpool rooms, $189-$299; 10 stories; interior corridors; heated pool, saunas, whirlpool; racquetball courts, squash. **Dining:** 2 dining rooms, coffee shop; 6:30 am-midnight, Sun-11 pm; $9-$30; cocktails; also, Mayfield Inn Dinner Theatre, see separate listing. **Services:** gift shop; area transportation, West Edmonton Mall; winter plug-ins. Fee: massage. **Recreation:** video game room. **All Rooms:** extended cable TV. **Some Rooms:** safes. **Cards:** AE, DI, DS, MC, VI. **Special Amenities: Free breakfast.** *(See color ad below)*

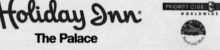

(See map p. 367)

RAMADA INN AND CONFERENCE CENTRE
◆◆◆
Motor Inn
All Year
Phone: (780)454-5454   ②⑨
F
Location: 4 km nw on Kingsway Ave at 119th St. 11834 Kingsway Ave T5G 3J5. Fax: 780/453-7360.
1P: $65   2P: $65   XP: $10
Terms: Small pets only. **Facility:** 316 rooms. Tropical style lobby featuring large rock garden with flowing stream encircling lobby. All rooms with video game. 15 stories; interior corridors. **Dining:** nightclub. **Services:** gift shop; area transportation; winter plug-ins. *(See color ad below)*

RAMADA INN AND WATER PARK
(CAA) (SAVE)
◆◆
Motor Inn
All Year
Phone: (780)434-3431 ⑤①
Location: Just n of 51st Ave. 5359 Calgary Trail N T6H 4J9. Fax: 780/437-3714. **Terms:** Cancellation fee imposed. **Facility:** 122 rooms. Good budget accommodation offering spacious rooms most with balcony. Waterpark is bonus attraction for those traveling with children. 6 two-bedroom units. 7 stories; interior corridors; heated pool, wading pool, whirlpool, 2 waterslides. **Dining:** Restaurant; 6:30-10:30 am, 11:30-1:30 & 5:30-9 pm; $8-$12; cocktails. **Services:** winter plug-ins. **All Rooms:** extended cable TV. **Cards:** AE, MC, VI.
1P: $79   2P: $79   XP: $10

TRAVELODGE BEVERLY CREST
(CAA) (SAVE)
◆◆
Motor Inn
5/2-9/1
3/1-5/1 & 9/2-2/28
Phone: (780)474-0456 ⑤⑨
1P: $73   2P: $79   XP: $6   F17
1P: $67   2P: $73   XP: $6   F17
Location: 8 km e of Capilano Dr, 1 km s from W Hwy 16 (Yellowhead Tr) on Victoria Tr exit. 3414 118th Ave T5W 0Z4. Fax: 780/479-3542. **Terms:** Small pets only. **Facility:** 86 rooms. Average sized guest rooms offering comfortable and simple decor. A good choice for the budget traveller. All rooms with hair dryer. 2 stories; interior corridors. **Dining:** Dining room, coffee shop; 6 am-11 pm, Sun-10 pm; $8-$20; cocktails; nightclub. **Services:** winter plug-ins. **All Rooms:** extended cable TV. **Some Rooms:** Fee: VCR. **Cards:** AE, DI, DS, MC, VI. **Special Amenities:** Early check-in/late check-out and free newspaper.

WEST HARVEST INN
(CAA) (SAVE)
◆◆
Motor Inn
All Year
Phone: (780)484-8000 ③④
F16
Location: Hwy 16A at 178th St. 17803 Stony Plain Rd T5S 1B4. Fax: 780/486-6060. **Facility:** 161 rooms. The executive section offers a slightly more upscale decor, very attractive restaurant and public areas. Most rooms are spacious. All rooms with hair dryer. 10 executive suites, $140; 12 whirlpool rooms; 3 stories; interior corridors. **Dining:** Restaurant; 6:30 am-11 pm, Sun-10 pm; $6-$15; cocktails; also, Xian Szechuan Restaurant, see separate listing. **Services:** winter plug-ins. Fee: area transportation. **All Rooms:** combo or shower baths, extended cable TV. **Cards:** AE, DI, MC, VI. **Special Amenities:** Free local telephone calls. *(See color ad below)*
1P: $69-$79   2P: $79-$89   XP: $5

(See map p. 367)

———— *The following lodging was either not inspected or did not* ————
meet AAA rating requirements but is listed for your information only.

THE VARSCONA HOTEL   Phone: 780/434-6111
[fyi]   Not inspected. **Location:** 8208 106 St. Facilities, services, and decor characterize a mid-range property.

———— **RESTAURANTS** ————

CHIANTI   **Lunch:** $7-$16   **Dinner:** $7-$16   **Phone:** 780/439-9829   ㉒
◆◆   **Location:** Corner 105th Street. 10501 82nd Ave NW T6E 2A3. **Hours:** 11 am-2 & 5-10 pm. Closed: 12/25.
Italian   **Features:** cocktails; street parking; a la carte. Chianti's is a long-established, lively restaurant located in a
            former post office building. Entrees include pasta, veal, seafood and chicken. Half portions of pasta are
available. All regular pastas are $5.95 Mon-Tue. Service is friendly and efficient. **Cards:** AE, DI, MC, VI.   [X]

JACK'S GRILL   **Dinner:** $19-$24   **Phone:** 780/434-1113   ㉟
◆◆◆   **Location:** Whitemud Frwy, exit 111th St, 0.8 km n on 111th St, just w on 57th Ave; in strip mall n of 57th.
Regional   5842 111th St T6H 3G1. **Hours:** 5 pm-11 pm. Closed: Christmas week. **Reservations:** suggested.
Canadian   **Features:** dressy casual; health conscious menu; cocktails; a la carte. Jack's chef is an architect who builds
            an unusual, inventive cuisine with fresh ingredients and flavors, and French and West Coast influences. The
ambience is a relaxed, casual elegance with upscale appeal. There's patio dining in season. Superb service. **Cards:** AE, DI,
MC, VI.   [X]

LA SPIGA   **Lunch:** $8-$13   **Dinner:** $13-$22   **Phone:** 780/482-3100   ㉗
◆◆◆   **Location:** Just s 102nd Ave. 10133 125th St T5N 1S7. **Hours:** 11:30 am-2 & 5-11 pm. Closed major
Italian   holidays & Sun. **Reservations:** suggested. **Features:** semi-formal attire; cocktails; a la carte. La Spiga
            features intimate, elegant, formal dining in a charming two-story mansion dating to 1913. The menu features
a northern Italian cuisine. The pollo rotolo is wonderful, and the tiramisu is out-of-this-world. Semi-casual atmosphere.
Superb service. **Cards:** AE, DI, MC, VI.   [X]

LEMONGRASS CAFE   **Lunch:** $6-$15   **Dinner:** $6-$15   **Phone:** 780/413-0088   ㉚
◆◆   **Location:** Just w of 104 St, on Allard Way in small strip mall. 10417- 51 Ave T6H 0K4. **Hours:** 11 am-2 &
Vietnamese   5-9:30 pm, Fri-10 pm, Sat 5-10 pm, Sun 5-9:30 pm. Closed: 10/11, 12/25 & Mon. **Reservations:** suggested;
            weekends. **Features:** carryout; cocktails; a la carte. This is a bright and cheerful cafe offering exciting,
colorful, fresh, healthy and well-presented creations such as spiced salmon in banana leaf and vermicelli combinations. They
also have innovative desserts and a selection of single-malt scotch. **Cards:** MC, VI.

MANOR CAFE   **Lunch:** $7-$10   **Dinner:** $8-$17   **Phone:** 780/482-7577   ㉙
◆◆   **Location:** Just s of 102nd Ave. 10109 125th St T5N 1S7. **Hours:** 11 am-11 pm, Fri & Sat-midnight, Sun 4:30
Continental   pm-10 pm. Sun brunch, 5/9-9/5. Closed major holidays. **Reservations:** suggested. **Features:** health
            conscious menu items; carryout; cocktails; a la carte. The Manor Cafe is located in the beautifully restored
home of one of Alberta's former attorneys general. The decor is charming, warm, and intimate, with a casual feel. Its
bistro-style menu includes progressive and innovative international dishes. **Cards:** AE, MC, VI.   [X]

MAYFIELD INN DINNER THEATRE   **Dinner:** $21-$64   **Phone:** 780/483-4051   ㉓
◆◆   **Location:** 1.6 km n of jct Hwy 2 and 16A on Mayfield Rd; in The Mayfield Inn & Suites, Edmonton. 16615
American   109th Ave T5P 4K8. **Hours:** 6 pm-8 pm, showtime 8 pm, Fri & Sat showtime 8:15 pm, Sun 10:30-11:45 am
            & 5:30-7:15 pm, showtime noon & 7:30 pm. Closed: 12/24, 12/25 & Mon. **Reservations:** required.
Features: semi-formal attire; Sunday brunch; cocktails; buffet. The Mayfield Inn features well-known TV stars performing on
stage, and an attractive, well-stocked buffet, with a Wednesday matinee at reduced rates for seniors, and student specials
Tues-Thurs and Sun evenings. Smoking is not allowed on Sundays. **Cards:** AE, DI, JC, MC, VI.   [X]

ROYAL FORK BUFFET RESTAURANT   **Lunch:** $7   **Dinner:** $11   **Phone:** 780/484-7025   ㉖
◆   **Location:** Stony Plain Rd at 150th St. 15061 Stony Plain Rd T5P 4W1. **Hours:** 11 am-8:30 pm, Fri & Sat-9
American   pm, Sun & major holidays 11 am-8 pm. Closed: 12/25. **Features:** children's menu. This popular buffet
            restaurant has a casual, family-oriented atmosphere and a nice selection of salads, seafood, beef and pork
dishes. Dinner prices go into effect at 4 pm, all day Sunday and major holidays. The staff is friendly and courteous.
Cards: VI.   [X]

VON'S STEAK & FISH HOUSE   **Lunch:** $6-$11   **Dinner:** $12-$40   **Phone:** 780/439-0041   ㉞
◆◆   **Location:** Just s of Whyte Ave at 103rd St. 10309 81st Ave T6E 1X3. **Hours:** 11:30 am-10 pm, Sun from 5
Steak and   pm. Closed: 12/24-12/26. **Reservations:** suggested. **Features:** casual dress; children's menu; cocktails &
Seafood   lounge; a la carte. Located in Strathcona, an old part of town, this restaurant offers casual dining in a warm,
            quiet ambience with a large riverstone fireplace and wood-beam structure. The menu displays influences
from Louisiana and the Mediterranean. Great for beef lovers. **Cards:** AE, DI, MC, VI.   [X]

XIAN SZECHUAN RESTAURANT   **Lunch:** $7   **Dinner:** $8-$16   **Phone:** 780/484-8883   ㉔
[CAA]   **Location:** Hwy 16A at 178th St; adjacent West Harvest Inn. 10080 178th St T5S 1B4. **Hours:** 11 am-2:30 &
            4:30-11 pm, Fri-midnight, Sat 4 pm-midnight, Sun 4 pm-10 pm. Closed major holidays for lunch, 10/11, 12/25
◆◆   & 12/26. **Reservations:** suggested. **Features:** casual dress; carryout; cocktails; a la carte. This restaurant
Chinese   features an extensive selection of Szechwan and other provincial dishes. The ginger beef is out-of-this-world;
            the hot and sour soup is terrific! The setting is bright, modern and airy, and the server staff is attentive and
knowledgeable. **Cards:** AE, DI, MC, VI.   [X]

(See map p. 367)

YIANNIS TAVERNA   **Lunch:** $5-$8   **Dinner:** $13-$20   **Phone:** 780/433-6768   [31]
◆◆   **Location:** Corner 104th St. 10444 82 Ave NW (Whyte Ave) T6E 2A2. **Hours:** 11:30 am-11 pm, Fri & Sat-1
Greek   am, Sun & Mon from 5 pm. **Closed:** 1/1, 4/23 & 12/25. **Reservations:** suggested; on weekends.
          Features: health conscious menu items; carryout; cocktails; street parking; a la carte. This is a lively,
traditional Greek restaurant with a quaint sidewalk patio. Weekend entertainment features the Hasapiko dance, belly dancing
at 8:30 pm, and guests may join in and try the Zorba dance later in the evening. **Cards:** AE, DI, MC, VI.   [X]

───── *The following restaurants have not been inspected by AAA* ─────
but are listed for your information only.

DOAN'S   **Phone:** 780/424-3034
[fyi]   Not inspected. **Location:** 10023 107th Ave. **Features:** Simple, neatly furnished and spacious dining room
          serves classic Vietnamese dishes such as hearty rice and noodle soup. Several meat dishes expertly spiced
by Doan's signature sauces.

RIVER CITY GRILL   **Phone:** 780/451-0096
[fyi]   Not inspected. **Location:** 14218 96 Ave. **Features:** Expect an internationally inspired menu in this intimate
          neighborhood restaurant located in the West End.

The Edmonton Vicinity

FORT SASKATCHEWAN pop. 12,400

─────── LODGING ───────

BEST WESTERN FORT INN AND SUITES   **Phone:** (780)998-7888
◆◆◆   All Year   1P: $99   2P: $109   XP: $10   F17
Motor Inn   **Location:** Just e of Hwy 15/21 and 101st St. 10115 88th Ave T8L 2T3. Fax: 780/998-2540. **Terms:** Pets, $150
          dep req. **Facility:** 70 rooms. Spacious rooms and suites. 4 stories; interior corridors. **Services:** winter plug-ins.
Cards: AE, DI, MC, VI.   [icons row]

LEDUC pop. 14,300

─────── LODGING ───────

BEST WESTERN DENHAM INN AND SUITES   **Phone:** (780)986-2241
[CAA] [SAVE]   All Year   1P: $79-$89   2P: $79-$89   XP: $10   F12
          Location: From Hwy 2, Leduc/City Centre exit, just e. 5207 50th Ave T9E 6V3. Fax: 780/986-1511.
◆◆◆   **Terms:** [BP] meal plan; check-in 4 pm. **Facility:** 97 rooms. Rooms vary in style and size. The tower section
Motor Inn   rooms are spacious, well-appointed and feature extra amenities. 2 whirlpool suites, $89-$129; 2-5 stories; in-
          terior corridors; whirlpool. **Dining:** Restaurant; 6:30 am-9 pm, Fri & Sat-10 pm, Sun 8 am-9 pm; $7-$14; health
conscious menu items; cocktails. **Services:** winter plug-ins. **All Rooms:** extended cable TV. **Some Rooms:** Fee: VCR.
Cards: AE, DI, DS, JC, MC, VI. **Special Amenities:** Free local telephone calls and free newspaper.
(See color ad p 389 & below)   [icons row]

SHERWOOD PARK pop. 39,600

—————— LODGINGS ——————

THE BERRY INN BED & BREAKFAST   **Phone:** 780/662-3313
◆   All Year   1P: $55   2P: $65   XP: $15   F6
Bed &   **Location:** From Hwy 21 jct, 26.6 km e on Hwy 14, 2 km n. 5127 Range Rd 203 T8G 1E8. **Fax:** 780/662-2595.
Breakfast   **Terms:** [BP] meal plan; check-in 4 pm; 14 day cancellation notice; cancellation fee imposed. **Facility:** 4 rooms.
In very quiet rural area in log house. All facilities are equipped for guests with reduced mobility. Large game room, attractive sunroom with fireplace, shared kitchenette and TV parlour with pool table. 2 stories; interior corridors; smoke free premises. **Services:** gift shop; winter plug-ins. **Recreation:** cross country skiing; hiking trails. **Cards:** MC, VI.

FIRST CANADA INNS   **Phone:** (780)464-1000
(AA) (SAVE)   All Year   1P: $69-$99   2P: $69-$99   XP: $10   F14
◆◆◆   **Location:** Just sw of Hwy 16, Broadmoor Blvd exit. 26 Strathmoor Dr T8H 2B6. **Fax:** 708/464-1043.
Motor Inn   **Terms:** Check-in 4 pm; small pets only. **Facility:** 88 rooms. Nicely appointed guest rooms with a warm, charming decor. Some rooms with a gas fireplace. Modern, state-of-the-art truck stop facility adjoined to the property. Features a medical centre, hair salon and game room. 2 stories; interior corridors. **Dining:** Restaurant, deli; 6 am-10 pm; $10-$15; cocktails. **Services:** gift shop. **Fee:** massage. **All Rooms:** extended cable TV. **Cards:** AE, DI, MC, VI. **Special Amenities:** Early check-in/late check-out and free local telephone calls.

FRANKLIN'S INN   **Phone:** (780)467-1234
(AA) (SAVE)   All Year   1P: $75-$85   2P: $81-$91   XP: $10   F11
◆◆   **Location:** At Granada Blvd. 2016 Sherwood Dr T8A 3X3. **Fax:** 780/467-3907. **Terms:** Pets, $5 extra charge,
Motor Inn   in smoking rooms. **Facility:** 40 rooms. Adjacent to shopping complex. Standard units offer simple yet contemporary appeal. A few suites with spacious seating area. 5 whirlpool rooms; 3 stories; interior corridors. **Dining:** Restaurant; 6 am-9 pm, Fri-11 pm, Sat 7 am-11 pm, Sun 7 am-9 pm; $5-$10; cocktails. **Services:** gift shop; winter plug-ins. **Recreation:** VLT machines & off-track racing in lounge. **All Rooms:** extended cable TV. **Cards:** AE, DI, MC, VI. **Special Amenities:** Free local telephone calls and preferred room (subject to availability with advanced reservations).

RAMADA LIMITED-EDMONTON EAST/SHERWOOD PARK   **Phone:** (780)467-6727
(AA) (SAVE)   All Year   1P: $89   2P: $99   XP: $10   F18
◆◆◆   **Location:** From Hwy 14, 1.5 km e on Baseline Rd, 0.4 km n on Broadmoor Rd; from Hwy 16, 2.5 km s via
Motel   Broadmoor Rd exit. 30 Broadway Blvd T8H 2A2. **Fax:** 780/467-5685. **Terms:** [ECP] meal plan; pets. **Facility:** 63 rooms. Nicely appointed rooms with contemporary appeal. All rooms with hair dryer. Excellent housekeeping and maintanence. 4 stories; interior corridors; whirlpool. **Services:** winter plug-ins. **All Rooms:** extended cable TV. **Cards:** AE, CB, DI, DS, JC, MC, VI. **Special Amenities:** Free breakfast and free local telephone calls.

—————— RESTAURANT ——————

CARTER'S RESTAURANT   **Lunch:** $5-$15   **Dinner:** $5-$15   **Phone:** 780/449-3765
◆   **Location:** Just e of Sherwood Dr. 100, 101 Granada Blvd T8A 4W2. **Hours:** 8 am-9 pm, Fri & Sat-10 pm.
American   **Reservations:** accepted. **Features:** children's menu; carryout; cocktails & lounge; a la carte. Carter's friendly staff serves a good variety of dishes such as sandwiches, burgers, pasta, beef, chicken, stir-fry, fajitas and the occasional Ukrainian plate. This is a casual, family-style restaurant with a bright and contemporary Southwest look. **Cards:** AE, DI, MC, VI.

SPRUCE GROVE

—————— LODGING ——————

**The following lodging was either not inspected or did not
meet AAA rating requirements but is listed for your information only.**

SUPER 8 MOTEL SPRUCE GROVE   **Phone:** 780/960-0088
[fyi]   All Year   1P: $65-$86   2P: $65-$86   XP: $7   F12
Motel   Too new to rate, opening scheduled for December 1999. **Location:** West of Edmonton 23 km on Hwy 16A. 500 St Mathews Ave T7X 3B5 (PO Box 4326). **Terms:** Cancellation fee imposed. **Amenities:** 48 rooms, pets, radios, coffeemakers, refrigerators, pool, exercise facilities. **Cards:** AE, DI, DS, MC, VI.

STONY PLAIN pop. 8,300

—————— LODGINGS ——————

THE LAKEHOUSE BED & BREAKFAST   **Phone:** (780)963-9330
◆◆   All Year   1P: $50-$70   2P: $50-$70   XP: $10   D10
Bed &   **Location:** From Hwy 16A, 6 km w of Stony Plain exit, 2 km n on Range Rd 14 (s of Hubbles Lake Resort),
Breakfast   between Hwy 16 and 16A. (Box 56, Site 8, RR2, T7Z 1X2). **Fax:** 703/963-9330. **Terms:** [BP] meal plan; age restrictions may apply; check-in 4 pm; 5 day cancellation notice; cat on premises. **Facility:** 3 rooms. Warm hospitality in a modern country home setting with view of the lake. Large outdoor deck avail during spring and summer months. 2 stories; interior corridors; smoke free premises. **Services:** winter plug-ins. **Recreation:** canoeing, paddleboats; cross country skiing; hiking trails. **Some Rooms:** color TV.

RAMADA INN & SUITES

Phone: (780)963-0222

CAA SAVE

Motor Inn

◆◆◆

All Year   1P: $61-$125   2P: $68-$125   XP: $7   F17
Location: 2 km e on Hwy 16A. 3301 43rd Ave T7Z 1L1. Fax: 780/963-6030. **Terms:** Pets, $4 extra charge. **Facility:** 88 rooms. Types of rooms range from spacious standard units to more luxurious suites and lofts. Tastefully decorated with contemporary furnishings. Rooms on main floor open on parking area as well as interior. All rooms with hair dryer. 6 two-bedroom units. 12 whirlpool rooms, $99-$125; 2 stories; interior/exterior corridors; heated pool, sauna, whirlpool. **Dining:** Restaurant; 6:30 am-10 pm, Sun-9 pm; $5-$16; cocktails. **Services:** winter plug-ins. **All Rooms:** extended cable TV. **Some Rooms:** 30 efficiencies, 13 kitchens. **Cards:** AE, MC, VI. **Special Amenities:** Early check-in/late check-out and free local telephone calls.

STONY MOTOR INN

Phone: (780)963-3444

CAA SAVE

Motor Inn

◆◆

All Year   1P: $49-$78   2P: $52-$81   XP: $7   F12
Location: From Hwy 16A, 0.8 km s on SR 779 (Stony Plain exit). 4620 48th St T7Z 1L4. Fax: 780/963-9492. **Terms:** Monthly rates avail; check-in 4 pm; small pets only, $3 extra charge. **Facility:** 48 rooms. Close to town services. Spacious units in rooms with kitchenettes. Decor is mostly contemporary, with a different style on each floor. Whirlpool room, $78-$92; 2 stories; interior corridors. **Dining:** Restaurant; 6 am-10 pm; $5-$13; cocktails. **Services:** winter plug-ins. **All Rooms:** extended cable TV. **Some Rooms:** 8 kitchens. **Cards:** AE, MC, VI. **Special Amenities:** Early check-in/late check-out and free local telephone calls.

This ends listings for the Edmonton Vicinity.
The following page resumes the alphabetical listings of
cities in Alberta.

EDSON pop. 7,400

——— LODGINGS ———

BEST WESTERN HIGH ROAD INN
◆◆◆   All Year   1P: $109-$129   2P: $114-$134   XP: $5   F16
Motor Inn   **Location:** Center; on 2nd Ave. 300 52nd St T7E 1V8 (PO Box 7770). Fax: 780/723-1868. **Terms:** Check-in 4
pm; small pets only. **Facility:** 67 rooms. Modern property with a beautifully appointed lobby. Guest rooms are
spacious and nicely furnished. All rooms with hair dryer; some business class with in-room fax, iron and ironing board. 4 stories; interior corridors; heated pool. **Services:** winter plug-ins. **Cards:** AE, DI, DS, JC, MC, VI. *(See color ad p 369)*

THE GUEST HOUSE   Phone: (780)723-4486
[CAA] [SAVE]   All Year   1P: $71-$77   2P: $77-$83   XP: $6
◆◆   **Location:** 1 km e on Hwy 16. 4411 4th Ave T7E 1B8. Fax: 780/723-2006. **Facility:** 108 rooms. 2 separate
Motel   buildings; the main building and a 2-story brick building with large rooms and simple decor. Impeccable cleanliness. 1 two-bedroom unit. 2 whirlpool rooms; 1-3 stories, no elevator; interior/exterior corridors; sauna, steamroom. **Dining:** Restaurant nearby. **Services:** winter plug-ins. **All Rooms:** extended cable TV.
Some Rooms: 34 kitchens. **Cards:** AE, DI, MC, VI. **Special Amenities:** Early check-in/late check-out and free local telephone calls.

SUPER 8 MOTEL   Phone: 780/723-2500
◆◆   All Year   1P: $64   2P: $68   XP: $4   F12
Motel   **Location:** 1.1 km e on Hwy 16. 4300 2nd Ave T7E 1B8. Fax: 780/723-2544. **Terms:** [CP] meal plan.
MC, VI.   **Facility:** 45 rooms. Newer property. 2 stories; interior corridors. **Services:** winter plug-ins. **Cards:** AE, DI, DS,

FORT MACLEOD pop. 3,000

——— LODGINGS ———

D.J. MOTEL   Phone: 403/553-4011
◆   6/1-9/30   1P: $40-$48   2P: $48-$64   XP: $5
Motel   3/1-5/31 & 10/1-2/28   1P: $38-$44   2P: $44-$54   XP: $5
    Location: Centre. 416 Main St T0L 0Z0 (PO Box 37). Fax: 403/553-4507. **Terms:** Cancellation fee imposed;
pets, $5 extra charge, in smoking rooms. **Facility:** 15 rooms. Downtown location; rooms are spacious offering a country charm.
7 two-bedroom units. 1 story; exterior corridors. **Services:** winter plug-ins. **All Rooms:** combo or shower baths. **Cards:** AE,
DS, MC, VI.

FORT MOTEL   Phone: 403/553-3606
◆   Property failed to provide current rates
Motel   **Location:** Centre. 451 Main St T0L 0Z0 (PO Box 1032). Fax: 403/553-2718. **Terms:** 4 day cancellation notice.
    Facility: 14 rooms. Duplex and quad style units. All rooms offer an older decor. 1 two-bedroom unit. 1 story;
exterior corridors. **Services:** winter plug-ins. **Some Rooms:** 3 efficiencies. **Cards:** DI, MC, VI.

SUNSET MOTEL   Phone: 403/553-4448
[CAA] [SAVE]   5/18-9/30   1P: $50-$70   2P: $50-$70   XP: $6
◆◆   3/1-5/17 & 10/1-2/28   1P: $38-$54   2P: $38-$54   XP: $4
Motel   **Location:** 1 km w on Hwy 2 and 3. 104 Hwy 3W T0L 0Z0 (PO Box 398). Fax: 403/553-2784. **Terms:** Pets.
    Facility: 22 rooms. Spacious guest rooms with a pleasant, simple decor. A unique weather protected enclosure is provided at most of the guest room doors. Excellent housekeeping. 1 three-bedroom unit, 8 twobedroom units. 3 efficiencies, $10 extra charge. Coin laundry adjacent to property; 1 story; exterior corridors. **Services:** gift
shop; winter plug-ins. **All Rooms:** combo or shower baths, extended cable TV. **Cards:** AE, DI, DS, MC, VI.

——— RESTAURANTS ———

AUNTY LYNDA'S DINING ROOM   **Lunch:** $5-$9   **Dinner:** $6-$23   Phone: 403/553-2655
◆◆   **Location:** Downtown, at 2nd Ave. 2-170 24th St T0L 0Z0. **Hours:** 8 am-8 pm, Fri-9 pm. Closed: Sun &
Canadian   12/25. **Features:** casual dress; carryout; cocktails; a la carte. This charming restaurant's menu offers a good
    selection of seafood, veal, beef and pasta dishes, creative burgers, and pies and cheesecake that are
home-baked. It also offers espresso and cappuccino. The clean, bright and homey decor has a country flair. **Cards:** MC, VI.

JOHNNY'S RESTAURANT   **Lunch:** $5-$8   **Dinner:** $5-$16   Phone: 403/553-3939
◆◆   **Location:** Next to Empress Theatre. 225 24th St (Main St) T0L 0Z0. **Hours:** 10 am-9 pm, Sun 11 am-8 pm.
Chinese   Closed: 1/1 & 12/25. **Reservations:** suggested. **Features:** children's menu; carryout; cocktails; a la carte.
    Johnny's has an extensive selection of Western and Chinese dishes prepared by the highly trained
chef/owner. Fresh ingredients, generous portions and unsurpassed friendliness make this a gem of a place! Entrees include
salmon, veal, prawns, ribs, steak. **Cards:** AE, MC, VI.

SCARLET & GOLD INN   **Lunch:** $4-$11   **Dinner:** $6-$18   Phone: 403/553-3337
[CAA]   **Location:** At jct northbound and southbound lanes of Hwy 3; at s end of town. 2323 7th Ave T0L 0Z0.
◆◆   **Hours:** 6 am-10:30 pm, Fri & Sun-11 pm. Closed: 1/1, 12/25 & 12/26. **Reservations:** suggested; in summer.
American   **Features:** Sunday brunch; children's menu; carryout; cocktails & lounge; a la carte. You'll enjoy the Scarlet &
    Gold Inn's coffee shop and dining room facilities. Its varied menu offers steak and seafood selections for
dinner, and lighter fare for lunch. Prime rib is featured in the summer. This place is good for casual, family
dining. **Cards:** AE, MC, VI.

FORT MCMURRAY

——— LODGINGS ———

SAWRIDGE HOTEL
◆◆
Motor Inn
Phone: (780)791-7900
All Year   1P: $119   2P: $129   XP: $10   F18
Location: 6 km s; just e of Hwy 63, exit MacKenzie Blvd. 530 MacKenzie Blvd T9H 4C8. **Fax:** 780/743-4654.
Terms: Check-in 4 pm; cancellation fee imposed; package plans. **Facility:** 190 rooms. Well appointed spacious units surrounding an interior courtyard with pool and lush garden. All rooms with iron and ironing board. 3 stories; interior corridors; heated pool. **Services:** winter plug-ins. Fee: massage. **Some Rooms:** honor bars. **Cards:** AE, DI, MC, VI.

The following lodging was either not inspected or did not
meet AAA rating requirements but is listed for your information only.

SUPER 8 MOTEL
[fyi]
Phone: 780/799-8450
Not inspected. **Location:** 321 Sakitawa Tr. Facilities, services, and decor characterize a basic property.

FORT SASKATCHEWAN —*See Edmonton p. 377.*

GRANDE PRAIRIE pop. 31,100

——— LODGINGS ———

SERVICE PLUS INNS AND SUITES
◆◆◆
Motel
Phone: (780)538-3900
All Year   1P: $74-$85   2P: $78-$99   XP: $10   F14
Location: 2.2 km w on Hwy 2, just n (adjacent to casino). 10810 107th A Ave T8V 7A9. **Fax:** 780/532-8558.
Terms: [ECP] meal plan; package plans; pets, $10 extra charge. **Facility:** 99 rooms. Nicely appointed rooms ranging from standard, large business class, to family suites with a bunk bed, microwave and refrigerator. All rooms with hair dryer and video games. 4 stories; interior corridors; small heated indoor pool. **Services:** winter plug-ins. **Cards:** AE, DI, MC, VI.

STANFORD INN
◆◆
Motor Inn
Phone: (780)539-5678
All Year   1P: $60-$65   2P: $64-$75   XP: $5   F14
Location: 2.8 km w on Hwy 2. 11401 100 Ave T8V 5M6. **Fax:** 780/538-3913. **Terms:** Pets, $5 extra charge.
Facility: 206 rooms. Many units with kitchen facilities. Spacious units offering a range of room decor and styles. Exterior and public areas feature mural paintings by local artist. All rooms with hair dryer. 2 stories; interior/exterior corridors. **Services:** winter plug-ins. **Some Rooms:** 60 efficiencies, 75 kitchens. **Cards:** AE, MC, VI.

TRAVELODGE TRUMPETER MOTOR INN
(CAA) (SAVE)
◆◆
Motor Inn
Phone: (780)539-5561
All Year   1P: $79-$89   2P: $89-$99   XP: $10   F17
Location: 100 St at 121 Ave. 12102 100 St T8V 5P1. **Fax:** 780/538-4636. **Terms:** Package plans. **Facility:** 120 rooms. Excellent budget accommodations. Rooms range from regular size to spacious. Rooms on 3rd floor offer more upscale furnishings and appointments. All rooms with hair dryer. 3 suites $99-$169. 10 executive suites, $79-$99; 3 whirlpool rooms, $149-$169; 3 stories; interior corridors; small heated indoor pool, whirlpool. **Dining:** Dining room, coffee shop; licensed game room; 11 am-1 am; $6-$20; cocktails. **Services:** winter plug-ins. **All Rooms:** extended cable TV. **Some Rooms:** Fee: VCR. **Cards:** AE, DI, DS, MC, VI. **Special Amenities:** Free local telephone calls and free newspaper.

——— RESTAURANT ———

THE GOLDEN STAR
◆◆
Chinese
Lunch: $4-$10   **Dinner:** $9-$13   **Phone:** 780/532-7549
Location: Centre. 10112 101st Ave T8V 0Y2. **Hours:** 11 am-11 pm, Sun-8:30 pm. **Closed:** 12/25.
Features: casual dress; carryout; cocktails & lounge; street parking; a la carte. You'll enjoy the friendly atmosphere and contemporary setting of Golden Star, which also serves a few Western specialties. The Shanghai noodles with black bean sauce is quite tasty. Dim sum is offered Sat-Sun, and the servers are prompt and cordial. **Cards:** AE, DI, MC, VI.

HINTON pop. 10,000

——— LODGINGS ———

CRESTWOOD HOTEL
(CAA) (SAVE)
◆◆
Motor Inn
Phone: (780)865-4001
6/1-9/30   1P: $89   2P: $99   XP: $5   F12
3/1-5/31 & 10/1-2/28   1P: $59   2P: $69   XP: $5   F12
Location: 1 km w on Hwy 16. 678 Carmichael Ln T7V 1S9. **Fax:** 780/865-8886. **Terms:** Monthly rates avail; small pets only, $10 extra charge, on ground floor. **Facility:** 97 rooms. A pleasant restaurant area surrounded by several lush plants. Good sized rooms, with simple but pleasant decor. 6 kitchens, $125; 2 whirlpool rooms, $175; 3 stories, no elevator; interior corridors; heated pool, sauna. **Dining:** Restaurant; 6 am-midnight, Sun-11 pm; $7-$20; cocktails. **Services:** winter plug-ins. **All Rooms:** extended cable TV. **Cards:** AE, DI, MC, VI. **Special Amenities:** Free local telephone calls and free newspaper.

HOLIDAY INN

CAA SAVE
◆◆◆
Motor Inn

			Phone: (780)865-3321
6/1-9/30	1P: $89-$99	2P: $99-$109	XP: $10 F16
3/1-5/31 & 10/1-2/28	1P: $65-$75	2P: $75-$85	XP: $10 F16

Location: 0.5 km w on Hwy 16. 393 Gregg Ave T7V 1N1. Fax: 780/865-7856. **Terms:** Pets, $50 dep req. **Facility:** 104 rooms. Nicely appointed rooms, all with hair dryer. 2 whirlpool rooms, $140-$200; 2 stories; interior corridors; heated pool. **Dining:** Restaurant; 5:30 am-11 pm; $7-$16; cocktails. **Services:** winter plug-ins. **All Rooms:** extended cable TV. **Cards:** AE, DI, DS, MC, VI. **Special Amenities: Free local telephone calls.**

OVERLANDER MOUNTAIN LODGE

CAA SAVE
◆◆
Complex

			Phone: (780)866-2330
3/1-9/30	1P: $99-$175	2P: $99-$175	XP: $20 F15
10/1-2/28	1P: $95-$100	2P: $95-$100	XP: $15 F15

Location: On Hwy 16, 24 km w of Hinton townsite. Hwy 16 T7V 1X5 (PO Box 6118). Fax: 780/866-2332. **Terms:** 14 day cancellation notice; cancellation fee imposed. **Facility:** 41 rooms. Rustic elegance in lodge units, country charm in cabins, all log construction. Spacious and attractive mountain style public areas, wood burning fireplace. Also 5 separate condo-chalets with full kitchen, and a few upscale motel rms. 3 two-bedroom units, 2 three-bedroom units. 8 whirlpool rooms; 1-2 stories; interior/exterior corridors. **Dining:** Dining room; Limited food selection from 3 pm; 7 am-10:30 & 5:30-9 pm; $21-$34; health conscious menu; cocktails. **Services:** winter plug-ins. Fee: area transportation. **All Rooms:** combo or shower baths. **Some Rooms:** 3 efficiencies, 5 kitchens. **Cards:** AE, DI, MC, VI. **Special Amenities: Free newspaper.** *(See ad below)*

ROCKY RIVER INN

CAA SAVE
◆◆
Motel

			Phone: (780)816-1960
6/1-9/30	1P: $85	2P: $95	XP: $5 F12
3/1-5/31 & 10/1-2/28	1P: $62	2P: $72	XP: $5 F12

Location: 2.3 km e on Hwy 16. 358 Smith St T7V 2A1. Fax: 780/865-4064. **Terms:** Weekly & monthly rates avail, off season. **Facility:** 40 rooms. Spacious and contemporary rooms. Rates for up to 4 persons; 2 stories; interior corridors. **Dining:** Restaurant; 6 am-11 pm; $4-$20; cocktails. **Services:** winter plug-ins. **All Rooms:** extended cable TV. **Some Rooms:** 4 efficiencies. **Cards:** AE, MC, VI. **Special Amenities: Free local telephone calls and free newspaper.**

SUPER 8 MOTEL

◆◆
Motel

			Phone: 780/817-2228
6/1-8/31	1P: $90-$100	2P: $95-$105	XP: $5
9/1-9/30	1P: $65-$75	2P: $69-$90	XP: $5
3/1-5/31 & 10/1-2/28	1P: $59-$69	2P: $62-$83	XP: $5

Location: 1.6 km e on Hwy 16. 284 Smith St T7V 2A1. Fax: 780/817-2880. **Terms:** [CP] meal plan; pets, $10 extra charge, with permission. **Facility:** 48 rooms. Newer property. 2 stories; interior corridors; small heated indoor pool. **Services:** winter plug-ins. **Cards:** AE, MC, VI.

JASPER pop. 4,300

——— LODGINGS ———

ALPINE VILLAGE

◆◆◆
Cottage

			Phone: 780/852-3285
6/9-9/23	1P: $140-$220	2P: $140-$220	XP: $10 F7
4/28-6/8 & 9/24-10/15	1P: $70-$170	2P: $70-$170	XP: $10 F7

Location: From jct of Hwy 16 and 93, 1.4 km s on Hwy 93, then just e on Hwy 93A. (PO Box 610, T0E 1E0). **Terms:** Open 4/28-10/15; 7 day cancellation notice; cancellation fee imposed. **Facility:** 41 rooms. Scenic wooded location along Athabasca River. Individual log cabins ranging from charming rustic units with forest view to very modern cabins with river view, many with woodburning fireplace and outdoor patio. 8 two-bedroom units. 1 story; exterior corridors; playground. **All Rooms:** combo or shower baths. **Some Rooms:** 3 efficiencies, 25 kitchens. **Cards:** MC, VI. *(See color ad p 383)*

BECKER'S ROARING RIVER CHALETS

Phone: 780/852-3779

6/2-9/23	1P: $110-$155	2P: $110-$155
9/24-10/9	1P: $60-$100	2P: $70-$110
5/1-6/1	1P: $60-$100	2P: $70-$110	XP: $10	F12

(CAA) ◆◆◆ Cottage

Location: 6.8 km s on Hwy 93. (PO Box 579, T0E 1E0). Fax: 780/852-7202. **Terms:** Open 5/1-10/9; 7 day cancellation notice; cancellation fee imposed. **Facility:** 118 rooms. Quiet wooded setting along the Athabasca River. Accommodations range from large, modern duplex log cabins to intimate rustic honeymoon cabins and riverview cabins. 26 two-bedroom units, 3 three-bedroom units. 2 four-bedroom loft units $310, for up to 8 persons; 2 stories; exterior corridors; playground. **Dining:** Restaurant; 8 am-11 & 5:30-10 pm; $14-$27; cocktails. **Services:** gift shop. **All Rooms:** combo or shower baths. **Some Rooms:** 22 efficiencies, 77 kitchens. **Cards:** AE, MC, VI.

THE CHARLTON'S CHATEAU JASPER

Phone: (780)852-5644

6/9-9/30	1P: $300-$325	2P: $300-$325	XP: $25	F16
5/1-6/8 & 10/1-2/28	1P: $175-$200	2P: $175-$200	XP: $25	F16
3/1-4/30	1P: $125-$150	2P: $125-$150	XP: $25	F16

(CAA) (SAVE) ◆◆◆ Motor Inn

Location: Corner of Juniper and Geikie sts. 96 Geikie St T0E 1E0 (PO Box 1418). Fax: 780/852-4860. **Terms:** [AP], [BP], [CP] & [MAP] meal plans; check-in 4 pm; 5 day cancellation notice; cancellation fee imposed. **Facility:** 119 rooms. Quiet location. Gracious public areas. Well-coordinated and spacious rooms. All rooms with hair dryer and excellent bathroom amenities. Rooftop patio. 7 whirlpool rooms; 3 stories; interior corridors; heated pool, whirlpool. **Dining:** Cocktails; also, Le Beauvallon, see separate listing. **Services:** gift shop; area transportation; winter plug-ins. **Recreation:** in-room video games. **All Rooms:** extended cable TV. **Cards:** AE, CB, DI, DS, JC, MC, VI. *(See color ad below)*

JASPER HOUSE BUNGALOWS

Phone: 780/852-4535

6/10-9/25	1P: $120-$175	2P: $120-$175	XP: $10
4/25-6/9 & 9/26-10/15	1P: $70-$140	2P: $70-$140	XP: $10

(CAA) ◆◆◆ Cottage

Location: 4 km s on Hwy 93. (PO Box 817, T0E 1E0). Fax: 780/852-5335. **Terms:** Open 4/25-10/15; 7 day cancellation notice. **Facility:** 56 rooms. Wooded area set along the Athabasca River. Many cedar log duplex units. Accommodations range from remodeled contemporary units to slightly more rustic, older units. 15 two-bedroom units. 33 kitchen suites, $120-$175; whirlpool room; 1 story; exterior corridors. **Dining:** Restaurant; 7 am-10 & 5:30-10 pm; $11-$20; cocktails. **Services:** gift shop. **Recreation:** barbecue area, horseshoe pits. Fee: bicycles. **All Rooms:** combo or shower baths. **Cards:** AE, DI, MC, VI.

JASPER INN
Phone: 780/852-4461
◆◆◆
Motor Inn
Property failed to provide current rates
Location: 1.2 km ne at Geikie and Bonhomme sts. 98 Geikie St T0E 1E0 (PO Box 879). Fax: 780/852-5916.
Terms: Check-in 4 pm; cancellation fee imposed; package plans; pets, $10 extra charge, in limited rooms.
Facility: 143 rooms. Many rooms feature a fireplace, either gas or woodburning. Some 2 story units with loft bedroom; many units with private balcony. Style of decor varies. 28 two-bedroom units, no elevator; interior/exterior corridors; heated pool. **Services:** winter plug-ins. **Some Rooms:** 94 kitchens. **Cards:** AE, CB, DI, DS, JC, MC, VI.

JASPER PARK LODGE
Phone: 780/852-3301

	1P	2P	XP	
5/22-10/7	1P: $344-$517	2P: $344-$517	XP: $25	F18
4/29-5/21	1P: $329-$502	2P: $329-$502	XP: $25	F18
10/8-2/28	1P: $112-$502	2P: $112-$502	XP: $25	F18
3/1-4/28	1P: $112-$217	2P: $112-$217	XP: $25	F18

◆◆◆◆
Classic Resort
Location: 4.8 km ne via Hwy 16; 3.2 km se off hwy 16, follow signs for lodge. Lodge Rd T0E 1E0 (PO Box 40). Fax: 780/852-5107. **Terms:** Check-in 4 pm; 3 day cancellation notice; cancellation fee imposed; pets, $30 extra charge. **Facility:** 442 rooms. **Historic.** Internationally reknown resort, picturesquely set by Lac Beauvert. Rooms vary in size and appointments in beautiful log cabin style building. The natural beauty of the environment adds to the unique concept of the resort. 4 two-bedroom units, 9 three-bedroom units. 1-2 stories; exterior corridors; heated pool; 4 tennis courts. Fee: 18 holes golf. **Dining:** entertainment. **Services:** gift shop; winter plug-ins. Fee: massage, area transportation. **Recreation:** cross country skiing, ice skating, tobogganing. Fee: fishing; bicycles, horseback riding. Rental: boats, canoes. **All Rooms:** honor bars. **Cards:** AE, CB, DI, DS, JC, MC, VI. A Canadian Pacific Hotel. *(See color ad below)*

LOBSTICK LODGE
Phone: (780)852-4431

	1P	2P	XP	
6/1-9/30	1P: $196-$220	2P: $196-$220	XP: $10	F15
11/1-2/28	1P: $80-$160	2P: $80-$160	XP: $10	F15
10/1-10/31	1P: $131-$150	2P: $131-$150	XP: $10	F15
3/1-5/31	1P: $96-$150	2P: $96-$150	XP: $10	F15

⒜⒜
◆◆◆
Motor Inn
Location: 1.2 km ne at Geikie and Juniper sts. 94 Geikie St T0E 1E0 (PO Box 1200). Fax: 780/852-4142.
Terms: [AP], [BP], [CP] & [MAP] meal plans; check-in 4 pm; package plans; pets, in smoking rooms. **Facility:** 139 rooms. Spacious units with a southwestern flair. Kitchen units feature a separate seating area. Very quiet location. All rooms with hair dryer. 3 stories; interior corridors; heated pool, wading pool, sauna, steamroom, whirlpools. **Dining:** Restaurant; 6:30 am-11 & 5-10 pm; $8-$20; cocktails. **Services:** gift shop; winter plug-ins. **Recreation:** sun deck. **All Rooms:** extended cable TV. **Some Rooms:** 43 kitchens. Fee: VCR. **Cards:** AE, DI, JC, MC, VI.

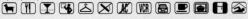

MARMOT LODGE　　　　　　　　　　　　　　　　　　　　　　　　　　　　Phone: (780)852-4471

	6/1-9/30	1P: $179-$225	2P: $179-$225	XP: $10	F15
	10/1-10/31	1P: $110-$160	2P: $110-$160	XP: $10	F15
◆◆	3/1-5/31	1P: $88-$160	2P: $88-$160	XP: $10	F15
Motor Inn	11/1-2/28	1P: $70-$140	2P: $70-$140	XP: $10	F15

Location: 1.6 km ne. 86 Connaught Dr T0E 1E0 (PO Box 1200). Fax: 780/852-3280. **Terms:** Check-in 4 pm; package plans; small pets only, in smoking rooms. **Facility:** 107 rooms. 3 distinct types of rooms, from standard to deluxe. All are spacious and offer an original decor inspired from the Hudson Bay saga and native heritage. Some rooms with gas fireplace; all with hair dryer. 1 two-bedroom unit. Whirlpool room; 2 stories; exterior corridors; heated pool, sauna, whirlpool. **Dining:** Restaurant; 7 am-11 & 5-10 pm; $8-$26; cocktails. **Services:** winter plug-ins. **All Rooms:** extended cable TV. **Some Rooms:** 33 kitchens. **Cards:** AE, DI, JC, MC, VI.

THE MOUNT ROBSON INN　　　　　　　　　　　　　　　　　　　　　　　Phone: 780/852-3327

	6/10-9/30	1P: $163-$199	2P: $163-$199	XP: $10	F12
	5/1-6/9	1P: $97-$119	2P: $97-$119	XP: $5	F12
◆◆◆	3/1-4/30	1P: $65-$104	2P: $65-$104	XP: $5	F12
Motor Inn	10/1-2/28	1P: $69-$103	2P: $69-$103	XP: $5	F12

Location: 1 km sw. 902 Connaught Dr T0E 1E0 (PO Box 88). Fax: 780/852-5004. **Terms:** Cancellation fee imposed. **Facility:** 78 rooms. Units are large and roomy with the exception of some average sized single units. All rooms with hair dryer. 5 whirlpool rooms, $135-$285; 2 stories; exterior corridors; whirlpools. **Dining:** Restaurant; 7 am-11 pm; from 4 pm off season; $12-$21; cocktails. **Services:** winter plug-ins. **Recreation:** video rentals. **All Rooms:** extended cable TV. **Some Rooms:** Fee: VCR. **Cards:** AE, DI, MC, VI. *(See color ad p 384)*

PATRICIA LAKE BUNGALOWS　　　　　　　　　　　　　　　　　　　　　Phone: 780/852-3560

◆◆◆	6/9-9/18	1P: $72-$170	2P: $72-$170	XP: $10	F12
Cottage	5/1-6/8 & 9/19-10/9	1P: $51-$125	2P: $51-$125	XP: $10	F12

Location: 4.8 km nw via Pyramid Lake Rd. Pyramid Lake Rd T0E 1E0 (PO Box 657). Fax: 780/852-4060. **Terms:** Open 5/1-10/9; age restrictions may apply; check-in 3:30 pm; 7 day cancellation notice; cancellation fee imposed; small pets only, at owners discretion. **Facility:** 37 rooms. Quiet and secluded location overlooking Patricia Lake. Most rooms recently renovated, with contemporary appointments, a few with fireplace. Cabins with mountain and lake view. All rooms with hair dryer. 3 two-bedroom units. 1 story; exterior corridors; boat dock; playground. **Recreation:** fishing. Fee: bicycles, horseback riding. Rental: boats, canoes, paddleboats. **All Rooms:** combo or shower baths. **Some Rooms:** 20 efficiencies, 8 kitchens. **Cards:** AE, MC, VI. *(See ad below)*

PYRAMID LAKE RESORT
CAA SAVE
◆◆
Complex

				Phone: (780)852-4900
	5/1-9/30	1P: $149-$299	2P: $149-$299	XP: $10 F12
	3/1-4/30 & 10/1-2/28	1P: $69-$199	2P: $69-$199	XP: $10 F12

Location: 6 km nw via Pyramid Lake Rd. (PO Box 388, T0E 1E0). Fax: 780/852-7007. **Terms:** Check-in 4 pm; 7 day cancellation notice. **Facility:** 64 rooms. Simple, newly renovated duplex units to contemporary 8-plex chalet units set on a hillside with a majestic view of the mountains and Pyramid Lake. 6 two-bedroom units. 8 efficiencies with whirlpool & gas fireplace, $125-$155, $85-$125 off season; 12 whirlpool rooms, $99-$129; 2 stories; exterior corridors; boat ramp. **Dining:** Coffee shop; 7 am-10 pm, in season; $8-$16; cocktails. **Services:** gift shop; winter plug-ins. **Recreation:** barbecue patio. Fee: fishing, 2 person kayaks; bicycles. Rental: boats, canoes, paddleboats. **Some Rooms:** 36 efficiencies. **Cards:** MC, VI. *(See color ad p 385)*

SAWRIDGE HOTEL AND CONFERENCE CENTRE
CAA SAVE
◆◆◆
Motor Inn

				Phone: (780)852-5111
	5/1-9/30	1P: $170-$233	2P: $170-$233	XP: $25 F17
	10/1-2/28	1P: $116-$170	2P: $116-$170	XP: $25 F17
	3/1-4/30	1P: $116	2P: $116	XP: $15 F17

Location: 1.7 km e. 82 Connaught Dr T0E 1E0 (PO Box 2080). Fax: 780/852-5942. **Terms:** [BP] & [MAP] meal plans; check-in 4 pm; 3 day cancellation notice; cancellation fee imposed. **Facility:** 154 rooms. Attractive cedar structure. Spacious contemporary units with a few vintage appointments; many with balcony, all with hair dryer. 3 whirlpool rooms, $200-$375; suites, $200-$375; 3 stories; interior corridors; heated pool, sauna, whirlpools. **Dining:** Dining room, restaurant; 6:30 am-11 pm; $12-$25; cocktails; nightclub. **Services:** gift shop; winter plug-ins. Fee: massage. **Recreation:** tanning salon. **All Rooms:** extended cable TV. **Cards:** AE, CB, DI, DS, JC, MC, VI. **Special Amenities: Free local telephone calls and preferred room (subject to availability with advanced reservations).**

SUNWAPTA FALLS RESORT
CAA
◆◆
Motor Inn

				Phone: (780)852-4852
	6/13-9/22	1P: $159	2P: $159	XP: $10 F12
	5/7-6/12 & 9/23-10/15	1P: $99	2P: $99	XP: $10 F12

Location: 55 km s on Hwy 93 (Icefields Pkwy). Hwy 93 T0E 1E0 (PO Box 97). Fax: 780/852-5353. **Terms:** Open 5/7-10/15; check-in 4 pm; pets, cabins. **Facility:** 52 rooms. Rustic and wooded setting located within a short walking distance of Sunwapta Falls. Rustic duplex type cabins or more contemporary lodge accommodations. 1-2 stories; exterior corridors. **Dining:** Restaurant; 7 am-11 pm, hrs vary off season; $13-$27; cocktails. **Services:** gift shop. **Recreation:** fishing. Fee: whitewater rafting; bicycles. **Some Rooms:** 20 efficiencies. **Cards:** AE, CB, DI, DS, JC, MC, VI. *(See color ad below)*

TEKARRA LODGE
(CAA) (SAVE)
◆◆
Cottage

4/28-10/9   1P: $139-$199   2P: $139-$199   XP: $10   F12
Location: From jct Hwy 93 and 16, 1.4 km s on Hwy 93, 1.2 km ne. Hwy 93 A T0E 1E0 (Box 669). Fax: 780/852-4636. **Terms:** Open 4/28-10/9; [CP] meal plan, in lodge rooms; check-in 4 pm; 7 day cancellation notice; cancellation fee imposed; 2 night min stay, 6/1-9/30; pets, $10 extra charge. **Facility:** 52 rooms. Quiet location; offers a variety of units, from charming rustic cabins to simply appointed rooms in lodge. All cabins with wood burning fireplace. 10 lodge rooms, $139 for 2 persons; 1-2 stories; interior/exterior corridors; playground. **Dining:** Restaurant; 7:30 am-10:30 & 5-10 pm; $11-$18; cocktails. **Recreation:** jogging, horseshoes, watercolour workshops 5/1-5/31 & 9/1-9/30. Fee: bicycles. **All Rooms:** combo or shower baths. **Some Rooms:** 10 efficiencies, 32 kitchens. **Cards:** AE, DI, MC, VI. *(See color ad p 386)*

───── **RESTAURANTS** ─────

EDITH CAVELL DINING ROOM
◆◆◆◆
Continental

Dinner: $61   Phone: 780/852-3301
Location: 4.8 km ne via Hwy 16; 3.2 km se off hwy via Maligne Rd, follow signs for lodge; in Jasper Park Lodge. Lodge Rd T0E 1E0. **Hours:** 6 pm-10 pm. **Reservations:** required; in summer. **Features:** dressy casual; health conscious menu items; cocktails & lounge; entertainment; valet parking; prix fixe, a la carte. Edith Cavell's features a delightful, complex nouvelle cuisine with inspiration from the Northwest. The restaurant has a formal dining room overlooking Lac Beauvert and Mount Edith Cavell, a rich decor, exquisite table appointments and excellent service. Smoke free premises. **Cards:** AE, DI, DS, JC, MC, VI.

LE BEAUVALLON
(CAA)
◆◆◆
Continental

Lunch: $9-$15   Dinner: $18-$39   Phone: 780/852-5644
Location: Corner of Juniper and Geikie sts; in The Charlton's Chateau Jasper. 96 Geikie St T0E 1E0. **Hours:** 7 am-1 & 5:30-10 pm. **Reservations:** suggested. **Features:** children's menu; cocktails & lounge; a la carte. Le Beauvallon specializes in a sophisticated, Canadian cuisine featuring Alberta game and West Coast seafood. Its rich furnishings and excellent rustic decor are attractive, comfortable and spacious. Their fine service is guest-oriented. Smoke free premises. **Cards:** AE, DI, DS, JC, MC, VI.

PAPA GEORGE'S RESTAURANT
◆◆
Continental

Lunch: $5-$9   Dinner: $9-$18   Phone: 780/852-3351
Location: Centre; in Astoria Hotel. 404 Connaught Dr T0E 1E0. **Hours:** 7 am-2 & 5-10 pm; 10/16-5/23 from 7:30 am. **Closed:** 12/25 & 11/1-11/30. **Reservations:** suggested. **Features:** children's menu; health conscious menu items; carryout; cocktails; a la carte. You'll enjoy the family dining in Papa George's bistro setting. They have a varied menu with international flavor and specialize in hearty sandwiches, freshly baked bread and pastry, duck a l'orange, lamb, fresh seafood, pork and Alberta steak. **Cards:** AE, MC, VI.

SOMETHING ELSE RESTAURANT
◆◆
Greek

Lunch: $6-$9   Dinner: $11-$17   Phone: 780/852-3850
Location: Just w of Connaught Dr. 621 Patricia St T0E 1E0. **Hours:** 11 am-11 pm. **Closed:** 12/25. **Features:** children's menu; carryout; cocktails; a la carte. The menu at Something Else features large portions of lamb, chicken and pizza dishes. The preparations here are a flavorful mix of international flavors. The staff provides friendly, cheerful and prompt service in a modest and casual atmosphere. **Cards:** AE, DI, DS, MC, VI.

KANANASKIS

───── **LODGINGS** ─────

DELTA LODGE AT KANANASKIS
◆◆◆
Resort

Phone: 403/591-7711
6/1-10/3	1P: $197-$287	2P: $197-$287	XP: $25	F18
5/1-5/31	1P: $134-$197	2P: $134-$197	XP: $25	F18
10/4-2/28	1P: $125-$189	2P: $125-$189	XP: $25	F18
3/1-4/30	1P: $116-$170	2P: $116-$170	XP: $25	F18

Location: From Trans Canada Hwy 1, 23.5 km s on Hwy 40 (Kananaskis Tr), then 3 km on Kananaskis Village access road, follow signs. Kanaskis Village T0L 2H0. Fax: 403/591-7770. **Terms:** Check-in 4 pm; 3 day cancellation notice; cancellation fee imposed; package plans; pets, $100 extra charge. **Facility:** 325 rooms. Beautiful resort nestled in a tranquil mountain village within easy reach of multiple recreational activities. Rooms vary from standard luxury rooms with country charm, to very spacious whirlpool units and loft suites, excellent amenities. 3 stories; interior corridors; heated pool; 6 lighted tennis courts. Fee: parking. **Services:** gift shop; area transportation; winter plug-ins. Fee: massage. **Recreation:** cross country skiing; sports court. Fee: horseback riding. **Cards:** AE, DI, DS, JC, MC, VI.

KANANASKIS INN & CONFERENCE CENTRE   **Phone:** 403/591-7500

◆◆   6/1-9/30   1P: $160-$200   2P: $160-$200   XP: $15   F17
Motor Inn   3/1-5/31 & 10/1-2/28   1P: $95-$135   2P: $95-$135   XP: $15   F17
            Location: From Trans Canada Hwy 1, 23.5 km s on Hwy 40 (Kananaskis Tr), then 3 km on Kananaskis Village access road following signs. (PO Box 10, T0L 2H0). Fax: 403/591-7633. **Terms:** Check-in 4 pm; 3 day cancellation notice; cancellation fee imposed; package plans. **Facility:** 95 rooms. Breathtaking mountain scenery. In the heart of major recreational area. Spacious rooms, all with duvets, a few with loft bedroom. 3 two-bedroom units. 3 stories; interior corridors; heated pool. **Services:** gift shop; winter plug-ins. **Recreation:** hiking trails. **Some Rooms:** 32 efficiencies. **Cards:** AE, DI, DS, JC, MC, VI. *(See color ad p 387)*

──── **RESTAURANT** ────

L'ESCAPADE DINING ROOM   **Dinner:** $18-$31   **Phone:** 403/591-7711

◆◆◆◆   **Location:** From Trans Canada Hwy 1, 23.5 km s on Hwy 40 (Kananaskis Tr), then 3 km on Kananaskis
Regional   Village access road, follow signs; in Delta Lodge at Kananaskis. Kananaskis Village T0L 2H0. **Hours:** Open
Canadian   5/1-10/15; 6:30 pm-10 pm. Closed: Sun, Mon, 5/1-5/31 & 10/1-10/31. **Reservations:** suggested.
            Features: dressy casual; children's menu; health conscious menu items; cocktails & lounge; fee for valet parking; a la carte. You'll love this restaurant's dynamic Canadian cuisine emphasizing fresh ingredients, wild-game selections and intriguing sauces and accompaniments. The venison chops and Pacific halibut are superb. Excellent service. Piano entertainment offered nightly. **Cards:** AE, DI, DS, JC, MC, VI.

LAKE LOUISE pop. 500

──── **LODGINGS** ────

CANADIAN PACIFIC CHATEAU LAKE LOUISE   **Phone:** (403)522-3511

◆◆◆◆   12/20-2/28   2P: $199-$489   XP: $25   F18
Classic Resort   6/1-9/30   2P: $359-$439   XP: $25   F18
            3/1-5/31 & 10/1-12/19   2P: $179-$439   XP: $25   F18
Location: 3 km up the hill from the village. 111 Lake Louise Dr T0L 1E0. Fax: 403/522-3834. **Terms:** [AP] meal plan; check-in 4 pm; 3 day cancellation notice; cancellation fee imposed; 2 night min stay, 12/1-4/30; pets, $30 extra charge in smoking rooms. **Facility:** 489 rooms. Historic majestic hotel nestled amidst glaciers, jagged peaks and Glacier Lake. Rooms vary in style and size, some with lake view. Grand lobby and European-style dining facilities make this a "jewel in the Rockies". 8 stories; interior corridors; small heated indoor pool. **Dining:** entertainment. **Services:** gift shop; area transportation; winter plug-ins. Fee: massage. **Recreation:** hiking trails. Fee: cross country skiing, ice skating; horseback riding. Rental: canoes. **All Rooms:** honor bars. **Some Rooms:** safes. **Cards:** AE, DI, DS, JC, MC, VI.

MOUNTAINEER LODGE   **Phone:** (403)522-3844

(AAA)   6/15-9/24   1P: $150-$240   2P: $160-$240   XP: $10   F10
◆◆◆   6/1-6/14   1P: $85-$140   2P: $95-$140   XP: $10   F10
Motel   9/25-10/31   1P: $70-$140   2P: $75-$140   XP: $10   F10
            5/1-5/31   1P: $70-$100   2P: $75-$100   XP: $5   F10
            Location: Just e of 4-way stop. 101 Village Rd T0L 1E0 (PO Box 150). Fax: 403/522-3902. **Terms:** Open 5/1-10/31; check-in 4 pm; 7 day cancellation notice. **Facility:** 78 rooms. 2 separate buildings, spacious contemporary rooms in the lodge, comfortable average sized rooms in motel section. Many rooms with a mountain view. All rooms with hair dryers. 4 two-bedroom units. For reservations in winter, phone (403) 522-3844. 4 family units, $110-$240 for up to 8 persons; 2 stories; interior/exterior corridors; steamroom, whirlpool. **Dining:** Restaurant nearby. **All Rooms:** combo or shower baths. **Cards:** AE, MC, VI. *(See color ad below)*

RESTAURANTS

THE BAKER CREEK BISTRO   **Lunch:** $8-$12   **Dinner:** $20-$26   **Phone:** 403/522-2182
◆◆◆   **Location:** 11 km e on Hwy 1A (Bow Valley Pkwy). Hwy 1A T0L 1E0. **Hours:** 8 am-10:30, noon-2:30 & 5-10
Regional   pm; to 9 pm in ski season. Closed: 4/15-5/15, 10/15-12/01 & Mon-Tues 12/1-4/15. **Reservations:** suggested.
Canadian   **Features:** No A/C; children's menu; cocktails & lounge; a la carte. The Baker Creek Bistro features a cozy,
log-cabin-style restaurant with a warm-spirited ambience. Their menu offers many regional dishes such as
lamb chops, baked chicken and beef tenderloin with an accent on fresh herbs and spices and hearty portions. Smoke free
premises. **Cards:** MC, VI.

LAKE LOUISE STATION   Historical   **Lunch:** $5-$8   **Dinner:** $12-$24   **Phone:** 403/522-2600
◆◆◆   **Location:** From 4 way stop, just s via underpass, 1 km w. 200 Sentinel Rd T0L 1E0. **Hours:** 11:30 am-10
Canadian   pm. Closed: 12/25. **Reservations:** suggested. **Features:** No A/C; dressy casual; cocktails & lounge; a la
carte. This restaurant is located in a beautifully restored heritage railway station that includes a 1925 dining
car. The progressive Continental cuisine offers lasagna, chicken, pork ribs, stuffed halibut, salmon, rack of lamb and even
build-your-own pizza. **Cards:** MC, VI.

POST HOTEL DINING ROOM   **Lunch:** $7-$20   **Dinner:** $25-$38   **Phone:** 403/522-3989
◆◆◆◆   **Location:** In village. Just w at main intersection. 200 Pipestone Rd T0L 1E0. **Hours:** 7-11 am, 11:30-2 &
Continental   5-10 pm. Closed: 10/20-12/10. **Reservations:** suggested; dinner, particularly in summer. **Features:** No A/C;
dressy casual; children's menu; cocktails & lounge; a la carte. The delicious food at the Post Hotel has the
reputation as the best in Western Canada. Dinner offers several European classics; each is wonderfully flavorful and
colorfully presented. A less extensive menu is offered at lunch. A cigar room is available. Smoke free premises. **Cards:** AE,
MC, VI.

LEDUC —*See Edmonton p. 377.*

LETHBRIDGE pop. 63,100

LODGINGS

BEST WESTERN HEIDELBERG INN   **Phone:** (403)329-0555
(AAA) (SAVE)   6/1-2/28   1P: $87-$94   2P: $92-$99   XP: $5   F18
◆◆◆   3/1-5/31   1P: $79-$86   2P: $84-$91   XP: $5   F18
Hotel   **Location:** 4 km se on Hwy 4 and 5. 1303 Mayor Magrath Dr T1K 2R1. Fax: 403/328-8846. **Terms:** Cancella-
tion fee imposed. **Facility:** 66 rooms. Very spacious and well appointed guest rooms. 9 stories; interior corri-
dors; sauna. **Dining:** Restaurant; 6 am-11 pm; Sun & holidays 6:30 am-10:30 pm; $6-$18; cocktails.
Services: winter plug-ins. **All Rooms:** extended cable TV. **Some Rooms:** Fee: VCR. **Cards:** AE, CB, DI, DS, JC, MC, VI.
Special Amenities: Free local telephone calls and free newspaper. *(See color ad below)*

CHELLSEA HOUSE BED & BREAKFAST   **Phone:** 403/381-1325
◆◆   All Year   1P: $50-$65   2P: $80-$100
Bed &   **Location:** From Hwy 3 near W Lethbridge, 5.7 km s on S University Dr, just w on McGill, then n. 9 Dalhousie
Breakfast   Rd W T1K 3X2. Fax: 403/381-0228. **Terms:** [BP] meal plan; 5 day cancellation notice. **Facility:** 4 rooms. Lo-
cated in a quiet residential neighbourhood, rooms vary in style and size. Beautifully landscaped backyard. 1
story; interior corridors; smoke free premises. **Some Rooms:** combo or shower baths, shared bathrooms, color TV.
Cards: MC, VI.

DAYS INN LETHBRIDGE

CAA [SAVE]
◆ ◆
Motel

Phone: (403)327-6000

6/1-2/28	1P: $55-$63	2P: $59-$68	XP: $5	F12
3/1-5/31	1P: $53-$62	2P: $57-$66	XP: $5	F12

Location: Centre; corner of 3rd Ave and Scenic Dr. 100 3rd Ave S T1J 4L2. Fax: 403/320-2070. **Terms:** [CP] meal plan; package plans; pets. **Facility:** 91 rooms. Provides a mix of room sizes from average to very good. Some rooms overlook the centre courtyard while others overlook the coulee. Kitchen suite, $73; family room, $81; 2 whirlpool rooms; 2 stories; exterior corridors; whirlpool. **Dining:** Restaurant nearby. **Services:** winter plug-ins. **All Rooms:** extended cable TV. **Cards:** AE, DI, DS, JC, MC, VI. **Special Amenities:** Free local telephone calls.

HOWARD JOHNSON EXPRESS INN

CAA [SAVE]
◆ ◆
Motel

Phone: (403)327-4576

All Year	1P: $65-$70	2P: $70-$75	XP: $5	F17

Location: 3.2 km se on Hwy 4 and 5, Mayor Magrath Dr. 1026 Mayor MaGrath Dr T1K 2P8. Fax: 403/329-0074. **Terms:** [CP] meal plan. **Facility:** 37 rooms. Spacious guest rooms all with a pleasant room decor. All rooms feature large bay windows that let in natural light. Closed 12/25-1/1. 2 whirlpool suites, $120-$130; 2 stories; exterior corridors; heated pool. **Dining:** Restaurant nearby. **Services:** winter plug-ins. **All Rooms:** extended cable TV. **Cards:** AE, CB, DI, DS, MC, VI. **Special Amenities:** Free breakfast and free local telephone calls.

LETHBRIDGE LODGE

CAA [SAVE]
◆ ◆ ◆
Motor Inn

Phone: (403)328-1123

All Year	1P: $109	2P: $119	XP: $10	F18

Location: Centre; Scenic Dr at 4th Ave S. 320 Scenic Dr T1J 4B4. Fax: 403/328-0002. **Terms:** Cancellation fee imposed; small pets only, $10 fee. **Facility:** 191 rooms. Very impressive tropical inner courtyard with brick pathways leading through. All rooms facing the courtyard feature balcony. Attractive and spacious units. All rooms with hair dryer. 4 executive suites, $169; 4 stories; interior corridors; heated pool, whirlpool. **Dining:** Dining room, restaurant; 6:30 am-11 pm; $15-$25; cocktails; also, Anton's, see separate listing; nightclub. **Services:** gift shop. **All Rooms:** extended cable TV. **Cards:** AE, DI, DS, JC, MC, VI. **Special Amenities:** Free local telephone calls and free newspaper. *(See color ad below)*

PEPPER TREE INN

CAA [SAVE]
◆ ◆
Motel

Phone: (403)328-4436

6/16-9/15	1P: $60-$70	2P: $78-$88	XP: $4	F16
3/1-6/15 & 9/16-11/15	1P: $50-$60	2P: $65-$75	XP: $4	F16
11/16-2/28	1P: $48-$52	2P: $60-$70	XP: $4	F16

Location: 3.2 km se on Hwy 4 and 5 (Mayor Magrath Dr). 1142 Mayor Magrath Dr T1K 2P8. Fax: 403/328-4436. **Terms:** Weekly rates avail; 3 day cancellation notice; pets, $5 extra charge. **Facility:** 56 rooms. Good budget oriented accommodation offering average sized rooms with a simple decor. 16 efficiencies, $49-$80; 2 stories; exterior corridors; small heated pool, whirlpool. **Dining:** Restaurant nearby. **Services:** winter plug-ins. **All Rooms:** extended cable TV. **Cards:** AE, DI, DS, MC, VI. **Special Amenities:** Free breakfast and free local telephone calls.

QUALITY INN

CAA [SAVE]
◆ ◆ ◆
Motel

Phone: (403)328-6636

All Year	1P: $67-$72	2P: $72-$75	XP: $5	F18

Location: 3.2 km se on Hwy 4 and 5 (Mayor Magrath Dr) at 10th Ave S. 1030 Mayor Magrath Dr T1K 2P8. Fax: 403/327-4037. **Terms:** [CP] meal plan; 7 day cancellation notice; pets, $5 extra charge, in specified rooms. **Facility:** 56 rooms. Average to better sized rooms, contemporary decor. 2 stories; interior/exterior corridors; small heated indoor pool, whirlpool. **Dining:** Restaurant nearby. **Services:** winter plug-ins. **All Rooms:** extended cable TV. **Cards:** AE, DI, MC, VI. **Special Amenities:** Free breakfast and free local telephone calls.

SUPER 8 LODGE

◆ ◆
Motor Inn

Phone: (403)329-0100

6/1-9/30	1P: $66-$76	2P: $66-$80
10/1-2/28	1P: $64-$72	2P: $64-$77
3/1-5/31	1P: $63-$70	2P: $63-$76

Location: 2.4 km se on Hwy 4 and 5 (Mayor Magrath Dr) at 7th Ave S. 2210 7th Ave S T1J 1M7. Fax: 403/327-3600. **Terms:** 7 day cancellation notice; small pets only. **Facility:** 91 rooms. Spacious units offering a simple yet comfortable room decor. 2 stories; exterior corridors; heated pool; playground. **Services:** winter plug-ins. **Some Rooms:** 25 efficiencies, 3 kitchens. **Cards:** AE, DI, DS, MC, VI.

TRAVELODGE LETHBRIDGE EL RANCHO HOTEL
◆◆ All Year 1P: $69 2P: $69 XP: $10 F17
Motor Inn **Location:** 2.4 km se on Hwy 4 and 5, just s of Hwy 3. 526 Mayor Magrath Dr T1J 3M2. Fax: 403/327-5075. **Phone:** (403)327-5701
Terms: 7 day cancellation notice; pets. **Facility:** 105 rooms. Guest units vary in size and style, all with contemporary decor. 5 two-bedroom units. 2-3 stories; interior corridors; heated pool. **Services:** gift shop; winter plug-ins. **All Rooms:** combo or shower baths. **Some Rooms:** efficiency. Fee: VCR. **Cards:** AE, DI, DS, MC, VI.

RESTAURANTS

ANTON'S Lunch: $9 Dinner: $17-$32 **Phone:** 403/328-1123
◆◆◆ **Location:** Centre; Scenic Dr at 4th Ave S; in Lethbridge Lodge. 320 Scenic Dr T1J 4B4. **Hours:** 11:30 am-2
Continental & 5-10 pm, Fri-11 pm, Sat 5 pm-11 pm, Sun 9:30 am-2 & 5-8 pm. **Reservations:** suggested.
Features: children's menu; cocktails & lounge; a la carte. The excellent menu at Anton's offers a Continental cuisine with French influences and some tableside preparations. The baked salmon in phyllo and rack of lamb Provencal are excellent. Noon buffet Monday-Friday. Brunch and evening buffet Sunday only. **Cards:** AE, DI, DS, JC, MC, VI.

SVEN ERICKSEN'S FAMILY RESTAURANT Lunch: $5-$8 Dinner: $10-$20 **Phone:** 403/328-7756
◆◆ **Location:** 4.4 km se on Hwy 4 and 5 (Mayor Magrath Dr). 1715 Mayor Magrath Dr T1K 2R7. **Hours:** 11
American am-midnight, Sun 10 am-9 pm. Closed: 12/25 & 12/26. **Reservations:** suggested. **Features:** casual dress; Sunday brunch; children's menu; carryout; cocktails & lounge. This restaurant has a long-standing reputation for fine food. The varied lunch and dinner menu includes Alberta beef steaks, prime rib, seafood, chicken, veal and Wiener schnitzel. Its unpretentious service enhances the casual-dining atmosphere. **Cards:** AE, DI, MC, VI.

TREATS EATERY Lunch: $5-$15 Dinner: $5-$15 **Phone:** 403/380-4880
◆◆ **Location:** 3.2 km se on Hwy 4 and 5 (Mayor Magrath Dr) at 10th Ave S. 1104 Mayor Magrath Dr T1K 2P9.
American **Hours:** 11 am-10 pm, Fri & Sat-11 pm, Sun noon-10 pm. Closed: 1/1 & 12/25. **Reservations:** suggested.
Features: children's menu; carryout; cocktails & lounge; a la carte. This is a casual, fun establishment with an unusual Western theme, although they don't offer Western-style dishes. The menu features deli-style burgers, sandwiches and quiche as well as health-conscious dishes and more elaborate dinner items. **Cards:** AE, DI, MC, VI.

LLOYDMINSTER pop. 11,300—See also LLOYDMINSTER, SK

LODGINGS

TROPICAL INN **Phone:** (780)875-7000
All Year 1P: $58-$120 2P: $58-$190 XP: $5 F18
◆◆ **Location:** Jct Hwy 17 and 16, 1 km w. 5621 44 St T9V 0B2. Fax: 780/875-7828. **Terms:** Weekly & monthly
Motor Inn rates avail; small pets only. **Facility:** 147 rooms. Mostly spacious rooms with pleasant contemporary decor. Rooms in motel section are standard size and decor is simpler. 35 whirlpool rooms, $65-$95; 2-8 stories; interior/exterior corridors; heated pool, sauna, waterslide, whirlpool. **Dining:** Dining room, restaurant; 6 am-10 pm, Fri & Sat 7 am-11 pm; $7-$15; cocktails. **Services:** winter plug-ins. **All Rooms:** extended cable TV. **Some Rooms:** kitchen. **Cards:** AE, CB, DI, DS, MC, VI. **Special Amenities:** Free local telephone calls and preferred room (subject to availability with advanced reservations).

WAYSIDE INN **Phone:** (780)875-4404
◆◆ All Year 1P: $67-$82 2P: $75-$92 XP: $8 F13
Motor Inn **Location:** 0.8 km w on Hwy 16 from jct Hwy 17. 5411 44th St T9V 0A9. Fax: 780/875-7210. **Terms:** Pets, $5
extra charge. **Facility:** 96 rooms. Spacious rooms offering various room styles and decor, large bay windows. Beautifully appointed rooms on the upper floors. 6 stories; interior corridors; small heated indoor pool. **Dining:** entertainment, nightclub. **Services:** winter plug-ins. **Cards:** AE, DI, MC, VI.

WEST HARVEST INN **Phone:** (780)875-6113
◆◆ All Year 1P: $69 2P: $74 XP: $5 F16
Motor Inn **Location:** From jct Hwy 17 and 16, 1 km w. 5620 44th St T9V 0B6. Fax: 780/875-2265. **Terms:** Small pets
only, in smoking rooms. **Facility:** 97 rooms. Spacious units offering a choice of remodeled executive style rooms to regular standard units with a simple room decor. All rooms with hair dryer and video games. 2 stories; interior/exterior corridors; small heated indoor pool. **Services:** winter plug-ins. **Cards:** AE, DI, DS, MC, VI.

MEDICINE HAT pop. 46,800

LODGINGS

BEST WESTERN INN **Phone:** (403)527-3700
◆◆◆ All Year 1P: $69-$199 2P: $75-$199
Motel **Location:** On Trans Canada Hwy 1; 0.4 km w of jct Hwy 3 access 7th St SW. 722 Redcliff Dr T1A 5E3.
Fax: 403/526-8689. **Terms:** [CP] meal plan; small pets only. **Facility:** 110 rooms. Along the tourist services access road with choice of restaurants within easy walking distance. Rooms vary in size from large and charming suites to smaller but very modern units. 6 two-bedroom units. 2 stories; interior/exterior corridors; 2 heated pools. **Services:** winter plug-ins. **Cards:** AE, DI, DS, JC, MC, VI. *(See color ad p 389)*

COMFORT INN & SUITES

◆◆◆	6/1-9/30	1P: $80-$140	2P: $83-$150	XP: $5	F17
Motel	3/1-5/31	1P: $75-$130	2P: $78-$140	XP: $5	F17
	10/1-2/28	1P: $70-$125	2P: $73-$135	XP: $5	F17

Phone: (403)504-1700

Location: 5 km se; opposite Medicine Hat Mall; just n off Trans Canada Hwy 1, corner Dunmore Rd. 2317 Trans Canada Way SE T1B 4E9. Fax: 403/527-1579. **Terms:** [CP] meal plan; package plans. **Facility:** 71 rooms. Spacious rooms with contemporary appeal, some with balcony. All rooms with hair dryer and voice mail. 3 stories; interior corridors; small heated indoor pool. **Services:** winter plug-ins. **Some Rooms:** Fee: VCR. **Cards:** AE, DI, DS, JC, MC, VI.

IMPERIAL INN

(CAA) SAVE	6/28-9/4	1P: $59-$64	2P: $63-$74	XP: $4
◆◆◆	3/1-6/27 & 9/5-2/28	1P: $54-$59	2P: $58-$69	XP: $4

Phone: (403)527-8811

Motor Inn   **Location:** 3.6 km se; opposite Southview Shopping Mall; just n off Trans Canada Hwy 1. 3282 13th Ave SE T1B 1H8. Fax: 403/526-7039. **Terms:** Weekly rates avail; pets, $5 extra charge. **Facility:** 102 rooms. Tastefully decorated and immaculately clean. 7 two-bedroom units. 6 whirlpool rooms; 2 stories; interior/exterior corridors; heated pool, sauna, steamroom, whirlpools. **Dining:** Restaurant, coffee shop; 7 am-10 & 11 am-midnight, Sat 7 am-11 & 4:30-midnight, Sun 7 am-11 & 4:30-9 pm; $4-$20; cocktails. **Services:** winter plug-ins. **All Rooms:** extended cable TV. **Cards:** AE, DI, DS, MC, VI. **Special Amenities:** Early check-in/late check-out and free local telephone calls. *(See color ad below)*

MEDICINE HAT LODGE HOTEL & CONVENTION CENTRE

◆◆◆	All Year	1P: $89-$149	2P: $99-$169	XP: $10	F18

Phone: (403)529-2222

Hotel   **Location:** E end approach to city at jct Trans Canada Hwy 1. 1051 Ross Glen Dr SE T1B 3T8. Fax: 403/529-1538. **Terms:** Pets, except 3rd floor. **Facility:** 189 rooms. Located across from large shopping mall. Rooms are spacious and offer contemporary appointments. Some rooms with balcony opening on the inner courtyard/pool area. All rooms with hair dryer. 4 stories; interior corridors; heated pool. **Services:** gift shop; winter plug-ins. Rental: bicycles. **Cards:** AE, CB, DI, DS, MC, VI.

RANCHMEN MOTEL

◆	All Year	1P: $34	2P: $38	XP: $4

Phone: 403/527-2263

Motel   **Location:** On Trans Canada Hwy 1 at 16th St SW. 1617 Bomford Crescent SW T1A 5E7. Fax: 403/529-9775. **Terms:** Small pets only. **Facility:** 44 rooms. A well maintained property with a variety of room styles and sizes. 6 two-bedroom units. 1-2 stories; exterior corridors; miniature golf. **Services:** winter plug-ins. **Some Rooms:** 2 kitchens. **Cards:** AE, DS, MC, VI.

SUPER 8 MOTEL

◆◆	6/1-9/30	1P: $61-$81	2P: $66-$91	XP: $5	F12
Motel	3/1-5/31	1P: $60-$80	2P: $65-$90	XP: $5	F12
	10/1-11/30	1P: $58-$78	2P: $63-$88	XP: $5	F12
	12/1-2/28	1P: $55-$75	2P: $60-$85	XP: $5	F12

Phone: (403)528-8888

Location: Trans Canada Way at 13 Ave SE; just n off Trans Canada Hwy 1. 1280 Trans Canada Way SE T1B 1J5. Fax: 403/526-4445. **Terms:** [CP] meal plan; small pets only, in specific rooms. **Facility:** 70 rooms. Budget accommodations featuring a mix of average to spacious guest rooms all with contemporary decor. 2-3 stories, no elevator; interior/exterior corridors; heated pool. **Services:** winter plug-ins. **Some Rooms:** 8 kitchens. **Cards:** AE, DI, DS, JC, MC, VI.

TRAVELODGE/TRAVELODGE MEDICINE HAT

(CAA) SAVE	6/1-9/30	1P: $90-$95	2P: $99-$105	XP: $10 F
◆◆◆	3/1-5/31 & 10/1-2/28	1P: $79-$85	2P: $89-$95	XP: $10 F

Phone: (403)527-2275

Motor Inn   **Location:** 2.8 km sw on Trans Canada Hwy 1 at jct Hwy 3. 1100 Redcliff Dr SW T1A 5E5. Fax: 403/526-7842. **Terms:** Weekly & monthly rates avail; pets, in designated rooms. **Facility:** 129 rooms. Main building features good sized rooms with contemporary appeal. Small motel section adjacent the property offers nicely furnished efficiencies, ideal for the budget oriented traveler. 2 executive suites, $85-$140; 2 whirlpool rooms; 2 stories; interior/exterior corridors; 2 heated pools, sauna, waterslide, whirlpool. **Dining:** Restaurant; 6 am-11 pm, Sun 7 am-9 pm; $5-$17; cocktails. **Services:** winter plug-ins. **All Rooms:** extended cable TV. **Some Rooms:** 33 efficiencies. **Cards:** AE, CB, DI, DS, MC, VI. **Special Amenities:** Free local telephone calls and free newspaper.

RESTAURANTS

BEEFEATER STEAKHOUSE   **Lunch:** $6-$13   **Dinner:** $8-$30   Phone: 403/526-6925

CAA
◆◆
Steak and
Seafood

Location: 3.6 km se; oppsite Southview Shopping Mall; just n on 13th Ave SE off Trans Canada Hwy 1. 3286 13th Ave SE T1B 1H8. **Hours:** 11 am-midnight, Sat-4:30 pm, Sun 4:30 pm-10 pm. Closed: 12/25 & 12/26. **Reservations:** suggested. **Features:** salad bar; cocktails & lounge. You'll appreciate the good value you'll receive at this restaurant, which offers relaxed dining in an attractive library-like setting. The menu specializes in prime rib and seafood, with a good selection of sandwiches at lunch. Good, efficient service. **Cards:** AE, DI, MC, VI.

BLACK ANGUS RESTAURANT   **Dinner:** $12-$26   Phone: 403/529-0777

◆◆
American

Location: 2.4 km sw; just s of Trans Canada Hwy 1, at 7th St. 925 7th St SW T1A 7H1. **Hours:** 4 pm-11 pm, Sun-10 pm. Closed: 12/25 & 12/26. **Reservations:** suggested. **Features:** children's menu; cocktails & lounge. The Black Angus features family dining in elegant surroundings, with an impressive selection of good steak and beef dishes as well as seafood, pasta and ribs. Servers are friendly and attentive. The decor is somewhat formal, yet the atmosphere is casual. **Cards:** AE, DI, MC, VI. ⊠

MAMMA'S RISTORANTE   **Dinner:** $10-$24   Phone: 403/529-2222

◆◆
Italian

Location: E end approach to city on Trans Canada Hwy 1, at jct Dunmore Rd; in Medicine Hat Lodge Hotel & Convention Centre. 1051 Ross Glen Dr SE T1B 3T8. **Hours:** 5 pm-10 pm. **Reservations:** suggested. **Features:** children's menu; cocktails & lounge; valet parking; a la carte. Mamma's features a varied menu that includes pasta, seafood, veal and Alberta beef. The restaurant is situated in an elegant garden setting with a casual and relaxed atmosphere. The service here is an ideal example of efficiency and politeness. **Cards:** AE, DI, DS, MC, VI. ⊠

MARIO'S RESTAURANT   **Lunch:** $6-$9   **Dinner:** $9-$20   Phone: 403/529-2600

◆◆
Italian

Location: At corner 5th Ave and 5th St SE. 439 5th Ave SE T1A 2P9. **Hours:** 11:30 am-2 & 5-11 pm, Sat from 5 pm. Closed: 1/1, 12/25, 12/26 & Sun. **Reservations:** suggested. **Features:** children's menu; carryout; cocktails & lounge. You'll enjoy the delicious offerings on Mario's northern Italian dinner menu; it features nicely prepared homemade pasta, breast of chicken, veal, steak and seafood. The setting is comfortable and casual in a Mediterranean decor. Fine service. **Cards:** AE, DI, MC, VI. ⊠

MORLEY pop. 2,200

LODGING

NAKODA LODGE   Phone: (403)881-3949

CAA
◆◆
Motor Inn

Property failed to provide current rates

Location: From Trans Canada Hwy 1, 4 km n on Hwy 1X (Seebe exit), then 5.5 km e. Hwy 1A T0L 1N0 (PO Box 149). Fax: 403/881-3901. **Terms:** [BP] meal plan. **Facility:** 50 rooms. On Stoney Indian Reserve toward the gateway to Banff National Park. On Chief Hector Lake. Owned and operated by Wesley Band-Stoney Tribe. Spacious rooms with magnificent view of the lake and mountains, a few with fireplace. 2 stories; interior corridors; heated pool, sauna, whirlpool. **Dining:** Restaurant; 7 am-7 pm, hrs vary off season; $9-$17. **Services:** gift shop; winter plug-ins. **Recreation:** Fee: fishing. Rental: canoes. **Cards:** AE, DI, MC, VI. ⊓⊔ ⧆ ⊠ ⟨K⟩ ⊠ ⊠

MOUNTAIN VIEW pop. 100

LODGING

ROCKY RIDGE COUNTRY RESORT   Phone: (403)653-2350

◆◆
Country Inn

6/15-9/14	1P: $80-$95	2P: $80-$95	XP: $10 F5
3/1-6/14 & 9/15-2/28	1P: $65-$75	2P: $65-$75	XP: $10 F5

Location: Hwy 5, 1 km n following signs by village church. (Box 117, T0K 1N0). Fax: 403/653-1640. **Terms:** [BP] meal plan; check-in 4 pm; cancellation fee imposed. **Facility:** 7 rooms. Attractively decorated with rustic charm. Many well-appointed common areas with wood burning fireplace. Rooms vary in size and style. 2 units with loft, all with natural wood accent. All rooms with hair dryer. 2 stories; interior corridors; smoke free premises. **Services:** winter plug-ins. **Recreation:** canoeing; cross country skiing. **Cards:** MC, VI. *(See color ad p 397)* (ASK) (S▱) ⊓⊔ ⊠ ⟨K⟩ ⊠ ⊠ ⊠

NISKU   (See map p. 367; index p. 367)

―――― LODGINGS ――――

THE INTERNATIONAL INN   Phone: (780)955-3001   [68]
(CAA) (SAVE)   All Year   1P: $115   2P: $125   XP: $5   F18
◆◆◆   **Location:** 30 km s; from Hwy 2, exit Edmonton International Airport/Nisku Business Park (10th Ave), 0.8 km
Motel   e. 501 11th Ave T9E 7N5. Fax: 780/955-3006. **Terms:** Small pets only. **Facility:** 30 rooms. Spacious rooms
           with very good quality furnishings. All rooms with hair dryer. 2 stories; interior corridors. **Dining:** Dining room;
           6:30 am-11 pm; $8-$17. **Services:** winter plug-ins. **All Rooms:** extended cable TV. **Cards:** AE, DI, MC, VI.
Special Amenities: Free local telephone calls. [icons]

NISKU INN AND CONFERENCE CENTRE   Phone: (780)955-7744   [67]
◆◆   All Year   1P: $85   2P: $85   XP: $10   F16
Motor Inn   **Location:** 30 km s; from Hwy 2, exit Edmonton International Airport/Nisku Business Park (10th Ave), 0.5 km
            e. 1103 4th St T5J 2T2 (Box 9801, Edmonton International Airport, EDMONTON). Fax: 780/955-7743.
Terms: Pets, $10 extra charge. **Facility:** 156 rooms. Rooms vary in size and type of decor, many with 2 entrances. Long term
parking avail for a fee. All rooms with hair dryer. Inviting public areas. 2 stories; interior corridors; heated pool. **Services:** gift
shop; area transportation; winter plug-ins. Fee: massage. **Cards:** AE, DI, MC, VI.
[icons]

―――― *The following lodging was either not inspected or did not* ――――
meet AAA rating requirements but is listed for your information only.

HOLIDAY INN EXPRESS-EDMONTON INTERNATIONAL AIRPORT   Phone: 780/995-1000
[fyi]   All Year   1P: $99-$109   2P: $99-$109   XP: $10   F16
Motel   Too new to rate, opening scheduled for September 1999. **Location:** 30 km s, from Hwy 2, exit Edmonton In-
           ternational Airport/Nisku Business Park (10th Ave). 1102 4th St T9E 8E2. Fax: 780/955-3009. **Terms:** [ECP]
           meal plan. **Amenities:** 83 rooms, radios, coffeemakers, microwaves, refrigerators, exercise facilities.
Cards: AE, DI, DS, JC, MC, VI. *(See ad below)*

OKOTOKS —*See Calgary p. 355.*

PEACE RIVER pop. 6,500

―――― LODGING ――――

TRAVELLER'S MOTOR HOTEL   Phone: (780)624-3621
(CAA) (SAVE)   All Year   2P: $49-$62
◆◆   **Location:** Just off Hwy 2 southbound; town center exit. 9510 100th St T8S 1S9 (PO Box 7290).
Motor Inn   Fax: 780/624-4855. **Terms:** 14 day cancellation notice; small pets only. **Facility:** 141 rooms. Rooms vary in
            style and size in the main building and 2 separate outside buildings, some are beautifully appointed and fea-
ture extra amenities. Voice mail system. 2 two-bedroom units. 14 whirlpool rooms, $84-$89; 2 stories;
interior/exterior corridors; complimentary golf pass; sauna. **Dining:** Dining room, coffee shop; 5:30 am-midnight, sports bar;
$10-$25; cocktails. **Services:** winter plug-ins. **All Rooms:** extended cable TV. **Some Rooms:** 2 efficiencies. **Cards:** AE, DI,
DS, MC, VI. **Special Amenities: Free local telephone calls and free room upgrade (subject to availability with advanced
reservations).** [icons]

PINCHER CREEK pop. 3,700

———— LODGINGS ————

HERITAGE INN
◆◆
Motor Inn
			Phone: (403)627-5000
6/1-2/28	1P: $68	2P: $78	XP: $5	F12
3/1-5/31	1P: $66	2P: $76	XP: $5	F12

Location: SR 3, 4.7 km s on SR 6. 919 Waterton Ave (Hwy 6) T0K 1W0 (PO Box 399). Fax: 403/627-3936. **Terms:** 7 day cancellation notice; small pets only. **Facility:** 42 rooms. Warm and contemporary guest room decor featuring very good quality furnishings. 2 stories; interior corridors. **Dining:** nightclub. **Services:** winter plug-ins. **Cards:** AE, DI, DS, MC, VI.

SUPER 8 MOTEL-PINCHER CREEK
◆◆
Motel
| | | | **Phone:** (403)627-5671 |
| All Year | 1P: $63 | 2P: $69 | XP: $4 | F12 |

Location: SR 3, 2.6 km s on SR 6. 1307 Freebarn Ave T0K 1W0 (Box 1628). Fax: 403/627-5408. **Terms:** [CP] meal plan; pets, $10 dep req. **Facility:** 39 rooms. Simple, attractive and contemporary decor. 3 stories, no elevator; interior corridors. **Services:** winter plug-ins. **Cards:** AE, DI, DS, MC, VI.

———— RESTAURANT ————

SWISS ALPINE RESTAURANT
◆◆
Ethnic
| **Lunch:** $5-$23 | **Dinner:** $5-$23 | **Phone:** 403/627-5079 |

Location: 1 km e, jct Hwy 6 and Main St. 988 Main St T0K 1W0. **Hours:** 7 am-10 pm, Sun-9 pm. Closed: 1/1 & 12/25. **Reservations:** suggested; in summer. **Features:** children's menu; carryout; cocktails & lounge; a la carte. This popular restaurant features Swiss croute, crepes, lamb, Alberta beef, sandwiches, pasta and stir-fry dishes, which are prepared with fresh ingredients and a Swiss flair. Sunday night has a prime rib special. The rustic decor displays art for sale. **Cards:** AE, DI, MC, VI.

RED DEER pop. 60,100

———— LODGINGS ————

BLACK KNIGHT INN
◆◆◆
Motor Inn
| | | | **Phone:** (403)343-6666 |
| All Year | 1P: $90-$120 | 2P: $90-$120 | XP: $10 | F18 |

Location: 1.8 km s on Hwy 2A (Gaetz Ave). 2929 50th Ave T4R 1H1. Fax: 403/340-8970. **Terms:** Check-in 4 pm. **Facility:** 98 rooms. Very spacious guest rooms with a mix of upscale and vintage appointments. Inviting public areas. All rooms with hair dryer. 8 stories; interior corridors; heated pool. **Services:** gift shop; winter plug-ins. **Cards:** AE, DI, MC, VI.

HOLIDAY INN EXPRESS-RED DEER
(CAA) (SAVE)
◆◆◆
Motel
| | | **Phone:** (403)343-2112 |
| All Year | 1P: $89 | 2P: $99 |

Location: 1.8 km e on Hwy 2A (Gaetz Ave). 2803 50th Ave T4R 1H1. Fax: 403/340-8540. **Terms:** Cancellation fee imposed; small pets only, $10 extra charge. **Facility:** 92 rooms. Beautifully appointed guest rooms, a few face indoor pool courtyard. All rooms with hair dryer, iron & ironing board. 2 whirlpool rooms, $140; 2 stories; interior corridors; small heated indoor pool, steamroom, whirlpool. **Dining:** Restaurant nearby. **Services:** winter plug-ins. **All Rooms:** extended cable TV. **Cards:** AE, DI, DS, JC, MC, VI. **Special Amenities:** Free breakfast and free local telephone calls.

HOLIDAY INN RED DEER
◆◆◆
Motor Inn
| | | **Phone:** (403)342-6567 |
| All Year | 1P: $89 | 2P: $89 |

Location: 3.2 km nw; 0.8 km e of Hwy 2, 67th St exit. 6500 67th St T4P 1A2. Fax: 403/343-3600. **Terms:** 24 day cancellation notice; pets. **Facility:** 77 rooms. Spacious rooms, very good appointments and amenities. Well-equipped rooms for guests with reduced mobility. All rooms with hair dryer, iron, ironing board and voice mail. 4 stories; interior corridors. **Services:** winter plug-ins. Fee: massage. **Cards:** AE, CB, DI, DS, JC, MC, VI.

REST E-Z INN
(CAA) (SAVE)
◆◆
Motel
| | | | **Phone:** 403/343-8444 |
| All Year | 1P: $55-$70 | 2P: $65-$75 | XP: $7 |

Location: From Hwy 2 exit South Red Deer. On service road. 37557 Hwy 2 T4E 1B1. Fax: 403/342-4310. **Terms:** [CP] meal plan. **Facility:** 75 rooms. Average sized guest rooms with contemporary amenities. 2 stories; exterior corridors. **Services:** winter plug-ins. **All Rooms:** extended cable TV. **Some Rooms:** 20 efficiencies. **Cards:** AE, JC, MC, VI.

SERVICE PLUS INNS AND SUITES
◆◆◆
Motel
| | | | **Phone:** (403)342-4445 |
| All Year | 1P: $89-$99 | 2P: $104 | XP: $15 | F16 |

Location: 3.6 km nw, 0.5 km e of Hwy 2, 67th St exit. 6853 66th St T4P 3T5. Fax: 403/342-4433. **Terms:** [ECP] meal plan; pets, $10 extra charge. **Facility:** 69 rooms. Nicely appointed contemporary guest rooms and suites. All rooms with hair dryer. 4 stories; interior corridors; small heated indoor pool. **Services:** winter plug-ins. **Cards:** AE, DI, MC, VI.

TRAVELODGE RED DEER
(CAA) (SAVE)
◆◆
Motor Inn
| | | **Phone:** (403)346-2011 |

Location: 1.8 km e on Hwy 2A (Gaetz Ave). 2807 50th Ave T4R 1H6. Fax: 403/346-1075. **Terms:** Monthly rates avail; small pets only, $50 deg req, in smoking rooms. **Facility:** 136 rooms. Pleasant accommodations. Rooms vary in size and offer contemporary decor. 1 section with exterior entrance with at-door parking. 3 stories; interior/exterior corridors; heated pool, whirlpool. **Dining:** Coffee shop; 6:30 am-noon & 5-9 pm; extended hrs in summer; $10-$15; cocktails. **Services:** winter plug-ins. **All Rooms:** extended cable TV. **Some Rooms:** 3 kitchens. **Cards:** AE, CB, DI, MC, VI. **Special Amenities:** Free local calls and free newspaper.

RESTAURANTS

SHAUNEY'S   **Lunch:** $6-$9   **Dinner:** $10-$20   **Phone:** 403/342-2404
◆ ◆   **Location:** Centre; 48th St just w of 51st Ave opposite Hudson Bay store. 4909 48th St T4N 1A8.
American   **Hours:** 11:30 am-11 pm. Closed major holidays & Sun. **Reservations:** suggested. **Features:** carryout; cocktails & lounge; a la carte. The locally popular Shauney's has a bright and cheerful decor with a casual atmosphere. Its menu emphasizes beef and seafood dishes prepared with a Continental flair. An extensive sandwich selection is offered at lunchtime. Validated parking. **Cards:** AE, MC, VI. ⊠

WILDFLOWER BISTRO   **Lunch:** $5-$7   **Dinner:** $9-$13   **Phone:** 403/341-5400
◆ ◆   **Location:** 1 km e on Hwy 2A (Gaetz Ave) on service road; from Hwy 2, exit Hwy 2A. 1927 Gaetz Ave T4R
Continental   1Z4. **Hours:** 11 am-10:30 pm, Sat from 4:30 pm, Sun 4:30 pm-9:30 pm. **Features:** cocktails; a la carte. The menu at the Wildflower Bistro features a variety of prime rib, chicken, steak, ribs, seafood and stir-fry dishes. Its bright, open and airy atmosphere has a cheerful feel, and its distinctive decor includes a pottery collection from Spain and Mexico. **Cards:** AE, MC, VI. ♿ ⊠

ROCKY MOUNTAIN HOUSE pop. 5,800

LODGING

CHINOOK INN   **Phone:** 403/845-2833
◆   All Year   1P: $60-$70   2P: $68-$79   XP: $7   F10
Motel   **Location:** 1.3 km w on Hwy 11, then s. 5321 59th Ave T0M 1T3. Fax: 403/845-6845. **Terms:** [CP] meal plan.
               Facility: 19 rooms. In quiet location outside town, Contemporary rooms with large weather proof windows. Attractive and well tended landscaping. All rooms with hair dryer. 1 story; interior corridors. **Services:** winter plug-ins. **Cards:** AE, CB, DI, DS, JC, MC, VI.
ASK S/D ⊠ ⊠ 🎥 🖥 💻 🛢 ⊠

SASKATCHEWAN RIVER CROSSING

LODGING

COLUMBIA ICEFIELD CHALET   **Phone:** 780/852-6552
◆ ◆ ◆   Property failed to provide current rates
Motor Inn   **Location:** 50 km n on Hwy 93 (Icefield Pkwy). Hwy 93 N T0L 0C0 (PO Box 1140, BANFF). Fax: 780/852-6568.
               Terms: Open 5/1-10/15. **Facility:** 32 rooms. Modern Rocky Mountain stone chalet perched in a glacial valley overlooking Athabasca and Dome Glaciers. Spacious rooms, a few with loft. Several stairs to busy "terminal" area. Luggage assistance avail. Enviro-friendly site. 3 stories; interior corridors; designated smoking area. **Services:** gift shop. Fee: area transportation. **Cards:** AE, MC, VI.
🍴 🐾 ⊠ 🎥 🖥 📠 DATA PORT ⊠

SHERWOOD PARK —*See Edmonton p. 378.*

SPRUCE GROVE —*See Edmonton p. 378.*

ST. ALBERT

RESTAURANT

The following restaurant has not been inspected by AAA but is listed for your information only.

PANE E VINO   **Phone:** 780/459-8090
[fyi]   Not inspected. **Location:** 512 St. Albert Tr. **Features:** Visitors from around the globe seek out this restaurant for the authentic cuisine from the many regions of Italy.

STONY PLAIN —*See Edmonton p. 378.*

STRATHMORE —*See Calgary p. 355.*

TABER pop. 7,200

LODGING

HERITAGE INN   **Phone:** (403)223-4424
◆ ◆   All Year   1P: $70   2P: $75-$79   XP: $5   F12
Motor Inn   **Location:** 1 km e of jct Hwy 3 and 36 S, on Hwy 3. 4830 46th Ave T1G 2A4. Fax: 403/223-1733. **Terms:** Small pets only. **Facility:** 74 rooms. A tropical style atrium area with small waterfall, fish pond and whirlpool. Contemporary guest room decor. 2 stories; interior corridors. **Dining:** nightclub. **Services:** winter plug-ins. **Some Rooms:** 2 efficiencies. **Cards:** AE, DI, DS, MC, VI.
ASK 🐾 🍴 🍸 🐾 🖥 ⊠ 🎥 📠 💻 🛢

TROCHU pop. 1,000

------ LODGING ------

ST. ANN RANCH BED & BREAKFAST
◆◆
Historic Bed
& Breakfast
All Year   1P: $40-$60   2P: $65-$85   XP: $10   D
Phone: 403/442-3924
Location: From Hwy 2, 55 km e on Hwy 27, 3 km n on Hwy 21, 1 km e on PR 585, then 0.5 km s on King George Ave. (St. Ann Ranch; PO Box 670, T0M 2C0). Fax: 403/442-4264. **Terms:** [BP] meal plan; 7 day cancellation notice; cancellation fee imposed. **Facility:** 7 rooms. In carefully renovated centennial farmhouse. Rooms range from compact to more spacious, all with tasteful antique appointments. Breakfast area divided in smaller seating section, allowing for intimacy. 4 stories, no elevator; interior corridors; smoke free premises. **Services:** winter plug-ins. **Recreation:** cross country skiing; hiking trails. **Some Rooms:** combo shower or tub baths, shared bathrooms. **Cards:** MC.

VALLEYVIEW pop. 1,900

------ LODGING ------

RAVEN MOTOR INN
◆
Motel
All Year   1P: $58-$70   2P: $65-$75   XP: $5   F12
Phone: (780)524-3383
Location: Jct Hwy 49 and 43. 4606 50th St T0H 3N0 (PO Box 816). Fax: 780/524-2732. **Terms:** Pets. **Facility:** 35 rooms. A well maintained property with 2 separate buildings, all rooms feature patio doors that face into the centre grassy courtyard. Large clean rooms with a slightly older style decor. 1 story; exterior corridors; miniature golf; heated pool. **Services:** winter plug-ins. **Cards:** AE, DI, MC, VI.

WAINWRIGHT pop. 5,100

------ RESTAURANT ------

THE HONEY POT
◆◆
American
           Lunch: $5-$9   **Dinner:** $6-$18   **Phone:** 780/842-4094
Location: 1 km s on Main St from jct Hwy 14, then just w at clock tower. 823 2nd Ave T9W 1C5. **Hours:** 11 am-2 & 5-11 pm, Sun 11 am-2 & 4:30-8:30 pm. Closed: 12/24-12/26. **Reservations:** suggested. **Features:** Sunday brunch; children's menu; senior's menu; cocktails & lounge; street parking; a la carte. You'll receive a good meal and excellent value at this tucked-away restaurant. Its friendly and casual ambience enhances the country charm of its Western-style barnwood exterior. The extensive menu features homemade breads, pies, soups and sandwiches. **Cards:** AE, DI, DS, MC, VI.

WATERTON PARK pop. 300

------ LODGINGS ------

ASPEN VILLAGE INN
(CAA)
◆◆◆
Motel
5/1-10/9   1P: $126-$139   2P: $126-$139   XP: $10   F16
Phone: 403/859-2255
Location: Centre. 111 Windflower Ave T0K 2M0 (PO Box 100). Fax: 403/859-2033. **Terms:** Open 5/1-10/9; cancellation fee imposed; package plans. **Facility:** 51 rooms. Attractive, well-coordinated guest rooms, all with duvet. Mix of room styles from motel to cottages, few with gas fireplace. All rooms with hair dryer. 1 two-bedroom unit. 5 cottages, $174 for up to 6 persons.; 3 whirlpool rooms; 1-2 stories; exterior corridors; mountain view; whirlpool; playground. **Dining:** Restaurant nearby. **All Rooms:** combo or shower baths. **Some Rooms:** 6 efficiencies. **Cards:** AE, DI, DS, MC, VI.

BAYSHORE INN

5/4-9/17	1P: $129-$139	2P: $129-$139	XP: $10 F12
4/14-5/3 & 9/18-10/9	1P: $89-$99	2P: $89-$99	XP: $10 F12

Phone: (403)859-2211

◆◆
Motor Inn

Location: Centre. 111 Waterton Ave T0K 2M0 (PO Box 38). Fax: 403/859-2291. **Terms:** Open 4/14-10/9; pets, in designated rooms. **Facility:** 70 rooms. Quiet mountain setting featuring large rooms. Many rooms with a private patio or balcony, some rooms offer a view of Waterton Lake or the marina, some overlook main street. 5 two-bedroom units. 3 whirlpool rooms, $149-$199; 2 stories; exterior corridors; whirlpool. **Dining:** Dining room, coffee shop; 7 am-10 pm; $7-$20; cocktails. **Services:** gift shop. **Recreation:** hiking trails, video library. **All Rooms:** combo or shower baths. **Some Rooms:** Fee: VCR. **Cards:** AE, DS, MC, VI. *(See color ad below)*

CRANDELL MOUNTAIN LODGE
◆◆◆   6/2-9/20
Motel   3/1-6/1 & 9/21-2/28
     Phone: 403/859-2288

| | 1P: $116-$154 | 2P: $119-$168 | XP: $10 | F12 |
| | 1P: $86-$134 | 2P: $96-$138 | XP: $10 | F12 |

Location: Centre. 102 Mount View Rd T0K 2M0 (PO Box 114). Fax: 403/859-2288. **Terms:** 7 day cancellation notice. **Facility:** 17 rooms. Charming country inn-like atmosphere; each room with distinct style. Some with gas fireplace, all rooms with hair dryer. 4 two-bedroom units. 2 kitchens; designated smoking area. **Recreation:** hiking trails. **All Rooms:** combo or shower baths. **Cards:** AE, DS, MC, VI. *(See color ad p 398)* 🛗✕🍴🆎📠💻📺✕

KILMOREY LODGE
(AA)   All Year
◆◆◆
Historic
Country Inn
     Phone: 403/859-2334

| | 1P: $89-$137 | 2P: $89-$137 | XP: $10 | F16 |

Location: Centre. 117 Evergreen Ave T0K 2M0 (PO Box 100). Fax: 403/859-2342. **Terms:** Cancellation fee imposed; package plans. **Facility:** 23 rooms. Landscaped, quiet location on Waterton Lake's Emerald Bay. Exquisite country inn offering a range of room sizes; most decorated with finely restored antiques. All with hair dryer. 2 two-bedroom units. 2 king suites, $171 for 2 persons; 2-two room units, $165-$171 for up to 5 persons; 2 barrier-free units, $171; 2 whirlpool rooms; 3 stories, no elevator; interior corridors. **Dining:** The Lamp Post Dining Room, see separate listing. **Services:** gift shop; winter plug-ins. **Recreation:** hiking trails, nordic ski trails. **All Rooms:** combo or shower baths. **Cards:** AE, DI, DS, MC, VI. 🍴✕🍴🆎📠💻📺✕

THE LODGE AT WATERTON LAKES
(AA) SAVE   6/9-9/15
◆◆◆   3/1-6/8 & 9/16-2/28
Resort
     Phone: (403)859-2151

| | 1P: $145-$175 | 2P: $145-$175 | XP: $12 | F15 |
| | 1P: $75-$115 | 2P: $75-$115 | XP: $12 | F15 |

Location: Centre. 101 Clematis Ave T0K 2M0 (PO Box 4). Fax: 403/859-2229. **Terms:** Check-in 4 pm; package plans; small pets only, $20 extra charge, in smoking rooms. **Facility:** 80 rooms. Well appointed environmentally themed guest rooms, a few with kitchenettes and a few deluxe suites with gas fireplace. All rooms with hair dryer and satellite television. 17 whirlpool rooms, $110-$155; 2 stories; interior/exterior corridors; heated pool, sauna, steamroom, whirlpool. **Dining:** Dining room, deli; 7 am-11 pm; $12-$25; cocktails. **Services:** gift shop; winter plug-ins. Fee: massage. **Recreation:** cross country skiing; hiking trails, aerobic room. Fee: cross country ski equip, snowshoes; bicycles. **Some Rooms:** 9 efficiencies. **Cards:** AE, DI, DS, MC, VI. **Special Amenities:** Free newspaper and free room upgrade (subject to availability with advanced reservations). *(See color ad p 398)* 🅂🏨🍴🍸🍽🏊♿🛗📺📠💻📺📺🚹✕

WATERTON GLACIER SUITES
(AA)   5/6-9/15
◆◆◆   3/1-5/5
Motel   9/16-2/28
     Phone: (403)859-2004

	1P: $159-$249	2P: $159-$249	XP: $10	F12
	1P: $115-$145	2P: $115-$145		
	1P: $115-$145	2P: $115-$145	XP: $10	F12

Location: Centre. 107 Windflower Ave T0K 2M0. Fax: 403/859-2118. **Terms:** [CP] meal plan. **Facility:** 26 rooms. Impressive hand-hewn log frame stucco building offering spacious 1-bedroom suites, junior suites and loft units. All rooms with gas fireplace, whirlpool, balcony, hair dryer and satellite TV. 26 whirlpool rooms; 2 stories; exterior corridors; designated smoking area. **Dining:** Restaurant nearby. **Some Rooms:** Fee: VCR. **Cards:** AE, DS, MC, VI. *(See color ad p 398)* ⒶⓈⓀ🍴✕📼📠💻📺📺📠

─────── **RESTAURANT** ───────

THE LAMP POST DINING ROOM   Country Inn   **Lunch:** $8-$13   **Dinner:** $14-$28   **Phone:** 403/859-2334
◆◆   **Location:** Centre; in Kilmorey Lodge. 117 Evergreen Ave T0K 2M0. **Hours:** 7:30 am-10 pm. Closed: 12/25.
Continental   **Reservations:** suggested; for dinner. **Features:** children's menu; health conscious menu items; carryout; cocktails; a la carte. This charming country-inn-style restaurant features an exciting, appealing lunch menu and more extensive dinner selections. Specialties include Alberta beef, wild game and fresh British Columbia salmon. A non-smoking policy applies evenings only. **Cards:** AE, DI, DS, MC, VI. ✕

WESTEROSE pop. 100

─────── **LODGING** ───────

VILLAGE CREEK COUNTRY INN   **Phone:** 780/586-0006
◆◆◆   Property failed to provide current rates
Motel   **Location:** From Hwy 13, just n on Norris Beach Rd; 28 km w of Hwy 2. 9 Village Dr T0C 2V0 (General Delivery). Fax: 780/586-3520. **Terms:** Check-in 4 pm; 7 day cancellation notice; package plans. **Facility:** 12 rooms. Good sized rooms with tasteful appointments, including a duvet. The inn is tucked away behind a bustling, quaint and modern resort town village with several shops. All rooms with hair dryer, iron, and ironing board. 2 stories; interior/exterior corridors. **Services:** winter plug-ins. **Cards:** MC, VI. 🍴🚪✕📼📠💻📺📺📠✕

WESTLOCK pop. 4,800

─────── **LODGING** ───────

HIGHWAY MOTOR INN   **Phone:** 780/349-3138
◆   Property failed to provide current rates
Motel   **Location:** 0.3 km n jct Hwy 44 and 18. East Service Rd, Hwy 44 T0G 2L0 (10227 - 104 Ave, T7P 1L3). Fax: 780/349-4321. **Terms:** Small pets only, $10 extra charge, downstairs rooms. **Facility:** 18 rooms. Large rooms offering excellent budget style accommodation. Some rooms with more modern appointments. 2 stories; interior/exterior corridors. **Services:** winter plug-ins. **All Rooms:** combo or shower baths. **Some Rooms:** efficiency. **Cards:** AE, MC, VI. 🍴📠✕🆎💻📺📺📠

WETASKIWIN pop. 11,000

——— LODGINGS ———

THE KARRIAGE HOUSE BED & BREAKFAST 1908
◆◆ All Year   1P: $55   2P: $65-$85   XP: $10   F8
Historic Bed   **Location:** 1.6 km e on 50th Ave, n on 47th. 5215 47th St T9A 1E1. **Terms:** [BP] meal plan; check-in 4 pm; 3
& Breakfast   day cancellation notice; cancellation fee imposed; package plans. **Facility:** 4 rooms. Turn-of-the-century prop-
erty offering rooms with charming country decor or a more secluded cottage in the garden. 2 stories; interior
corridors; smoke free premises. **Services:** winter plug-ins. **Some Rooms:** combo or shower baths, shared bathrooms.
Cards: MC, VI.

Phone: 780/352-5996

SUPER 8 MOTEL
◆◆ 6/1-9/1   1P: $69   2P: $69   XP: $5   F17
Motel   3/1-5/31 & 9/2-2/28   1P: $64   2P: $64   XP: $5   F17
Location: On Hwy 2A, just s of jct Hwy 13W. 3820 56th St T9A 2B2. Fax: 780/361-0388. **Terms:** [CP] meal
plan; pets, with permission. **Facility:** 49 rooms. Newer property. Some rooms with at-door parking. 2 stories; interior/exterior
corridors. **Services:** winter plug-ins. **Cards:** AE, MC, VI.

Phone: (780)361-3808

WAYSIDE INN
◆◆ All Year   1P: $65   2P: $65
Motor Inn   **Location:** Just n of Hwy 13W, on Hwy 2A. 4103 56 St T9A 1V2. Fax: 780/352-0459. **Terms:** Check-in 4 pm;
pets, in smoking rooms. **Facility:** 28 rooms. Conveniently located close to all services. This inn offers simple
appointments in rooms ranging from compact to more spacious. 2 stories; interior corridors. **Dining:** nightclub.
Services: winter plug-ins. **Cards:** AE, DI, MC, VI.

Phone: (780)352-6681

——— RESTAURANT ———

THE MACEACHERN TEA HOUSE   **Lunch:** $5-$8
◆◆ **Location:** 50th Ave at 47th St. 4719 50th Ave T9A 0R9. **Hours:** 9:30 am-4:30 pm. Closed major holidays &
Continental   Sun. **Reservations:** suggested; for lunch. **Features:** cocktails. This is a delightful restaurant in a charming
turn-of-the-century home, close to downtown. The menu features homemade soups, salads, fresh baked
rolls, muffins, bagels, sandwiches and desserts, as well as scones for afternoon tea. Very friendly service. Smoke free
premises. **Cards:** MC, VI.

Phone: 780/352-8308

WHITECOURT pop. 7,800

——— LODGINGS ———

GREEN GABLES INN
◆◆ All Year   1P: $68-$80   2P: $73-$85   XP: $5   F10
Motor Inn   **Location:** 2 km se on Hwy 43. 3527 Highway St T7S 1P3 (PO Box 1530). Fax: 780/778-2510. **Facility:** 49
rooms. Very spacious rooms. Outstanding housekeeping makes this property a real gem. All rooms with hair
dryer. 1 story; interior corridors. **Services:** winter plug-ins. **Some Rooms:** Fee: VCR. **Cards:** AE, DI, MC, VI.

Phone: 780/778-4537

QUALITY INN
◆◆ All Year   1P: $75-$90   2P: $79-$95   XP: $6   F18
Motor Inn   **Location:** On Hwy 43, 0.5 kn e of Hwy 32. 5420 47th Ave T7S 1P3 (PO Box 1438). Fax: 780/778-4219.
Terms: Pets, designated rooms. **Facility:** 74 rooms. Riverside location. Pulp mill nearby. 2 stories; interior cor-
ridors. **Services:** winter plug-ins. **Cards:** AE, DI, MC, VI.

Phone: (780)778-5477

British Columbia

ABBOTSFORD pop. 105,400

---------- LODGINGS ----------

ABBOTSFORD TRAVELODGE   **Phone:** 604/853-1880
◆◆◆   Property failed to provide current rates
Motor Inn   **Location:** Trans Canada Hwy 1 exit 92 Town Centre, just n on Hwy 11. 2020 Sumas Way V2S 2C7.
          Fax: 604/853-1951. **Facility:** 61 rooms. Not your typical Travelodge. Guest rooms feature a modern upscale
decor, while the top floor is set aside for business travelers with larger rooms and desks. Enjoy a unique bath experience in
the extra large soaker-style bathtub. 3 stories; interior corridors; heated pool. **Cards:** AE, DI, DS, MC, VI.

ALPINE MOTOR INN   **Phone:** (604)859-3171
◆   9/21-2/28   1P: $69-$79   2P: $75-$96   XP: $5   F16
Motel   7/1-9/20   1P: $79-$89   2P: $85-$95   XP: $5   F16
                 3/1-6/30   1P: $69-$79   2P: $75-$90   XP: $5   F16
Location: Trans Canada Hwy 1 exit 87, Clearbrook Rd. 32111 Marshall Rd V2T 1A3. Fax: 604/859-3171. **Terms:** [CP] meal
plan; pets, $10 extra charge. **Facility:** 44 rooms. Several guest rooms offer at-door parking, plus there are some inside rooms
as well. Offering good, budget style accommodations. 1-2 stories; interior/exterior corridors; heated pool. **All Rooms:** combo
or shower baths. **Some Rooms:** 5 efficiencies. **Cards:** AE, DI, DS, MC, VI.

BEST WESTERN BAKERVIEW INN   **Phone:** (604)859-1341
(CAA) (SAVE)   All Year   1P: $62-$72   2P: $79-$99   XP: $6   F12
◆◆◆   **Location:** Trans Canada Hwy 1, exit 92 Town Centre, just n on Hwy 11. 1821 Sumas Way V2S 4L5.
Motor Inn   Fax: 604/854-1385. **Terms:** 3 day cancellation notice. **Facility:** 61 rooms. A nicely maintained roadside prop-
                 erty offering large guest rooms with a pleasant, yet simple decor. 10 efficiencies, $6 extra charge; 2 stories;
                 exterior corridors; heated pool, whirlpool. **Dining:** Restaurant nearby. **All Rooms:** extended cable TV.
Cards: AE, CB, DI, MC, VI. **Special Amenities:** Free local telephone calls and free room upgrade (subject to availability
with advanced reservations).

BEST WESTERN REGENCY INN & CONFERENCE CENTRE   **Phone:** (604)853-3111
(CAA) (SAVE)   7/1-9/8   1P: $89-$109   2P: $89-$109   XP: $6   F18
                 3/1-6/30   1P: $69-$89   2P: $75-$89   XP: $6   F18
◆◆◆   9/9-2/28   1P: $69-$89   2P: $69-$89   XP: $6   F18
Motor Inn   **Location:** Trans Canada Hwy 1, exit 87 Clearbrook Rd. 32110 Marshall Rd V2T 1A1. Fax: 604/852-1750.
                 Terms: [CP] meal plan; weekly & monthly rates avail. **Facility:** 128 rooms. Just behind elementary school.
Property features 2 separate buildings with large, modern guest rooms. Executive style guest rooms featuring king beds and
large work station. 22 efficiencies, $6 extra charge. 2 full kitchen units, $150-$250; 2-3 stories; interior corridors; 2 heated
pools, whirlpools. **Dining:** Restaurant; 6 am-11 pm; $6-$10; wine/beer only. **All Rooms:** extended cable TV. **Cards:** AE, DI,
DS, MC, VI. **Special Amenities:** Free breakfast and free local telephone calls. *(See color ad below)*

HOLIDAY INN EXPRESS   **Phone:** (604)859-6211
(CAA) (SAVE)   5/1-9/15   1P: $79-$99   2P: $89-$109   XP: $10   F19
◆◆◆   3/1-4/30 & 9/16-2/28   1P: $59-$79   2P: $69-$89   XP: $10   F19
Motor Inn   **Location:** Trans Canada Hwy 1, exit 87. 2073 Clearbrook Rd V2T 2X1. Fax: 604/859-6200. **Terms:** [CP] meal
                 plan; weekly rates avail, off season; small pets only, $10 extra charge. **Facility:** 41 rooms. Located just off hwy.
                 Large, pleasant guest rooms, few feature at-door parking. Whirlpool room; 2 stories; interior/exterior corridors;
heated pool, sauna, whirlpool. **Dining:** Restaurant; 6 am-11 pm; $5-$10; wine/beer only. **All Rooms:** extended cable TV.
Some Rooms: 12 efficiencies. **Cards:** AE, DI, DS, JC, MC, VI. **Special Amenities:** Free breakfast and free local telephone
calls.

THE INN AT KING'S CROSSING   **Phone:** (604)859-2220
◆◆   Property failed to provide current rates
Motor Inn   **Location:** Trans Canada Hwy 1, exit 90, just s, then e on King Rd. 1515 College Dr V2S 8J1.
                 Fax: 604/859-2292. **Terms:** Cancellation fee imposed. **Facility:** 18 rooms. Close to Fraser Valley College. Very
large guest rooms decorated in a simple decor. Beer and wine store on property. 2 stories; interior corridors. **Cards:** AE, DI,
DS, MC, VI.

RAMADA INN-ABBOTSFORD
◆◆◆ Motor Inn
Phone: (604)870-1050

	1P: $89-$109	2P: $99-$119	XP: $15	F18
5/1-9/30				
3/1-4/30 & 10/1-2/28	1P: $79-$99	2P: $89-$109	XP: $15	F18

Location: Trans Canada Hwy 1 exit 95, Whatcom Rd. 36035 N Parallel Rd V3G 2C6. Fax: 604/870-1060. **Terms:** Cancellation fee imposed; pets, $10 extra charge. **Facility:** 119 rooms. Above average sized guest rooms catering to both the business traveler or holiday seeker. Features an indoor hockey rink along with sports equipment lockers. Sports team friendly. 4 stories; interior corridors; heated pool. **Services:** gift shop. **Cards:** AE, DI, DS, MC, VI.

WELCOME INN ABBOTSFORD
◆◆ Motel
All Year
Phone: (604)853-1141

| | 1P: $45-$66 | 2P: $50-$80 | XP: $6 | F18 |

Location: Trans Canada Hwy 1, exit 92 Town Centre, just n on Hwy 11. 1881 Sumas Way V2S 4L5. Fax: 604/853-8967. **Terms:** Cancellation fee imposed; small pets only, $5 extra charge. **Facility:** 68 rooms. Property offers 2 separate buildings, the 1 story building offers average sized guest rooms but modern decor, while the 2 story building offers larger rooms with a slightly older style decor. 1-2 stories; exterior corridors; heated pool. **Some Rooms:** 20 efficiencies. **Cards:** AE, CB, DI, DS, JC, MC, VI.

AINSWORTH HOT SPRINGS pop. 15,400

—— LODGING ——

AINSWORTH HOT SPRINGS RESORT
◆◆ Motor Inn
Phone: (250)229-4212

| | 7/1-9/4 | 1P: $111-$131 | 2P: $111-$131 | XP: $15 |
| | 3/1-6/30 & 9/5-2/28 | 1P: $106-$127 | 2P: $106-$127 | XP: $15 |

Location: 3609 Hwy 31 V0G 1A0 (PO Box 1268). Fax: 250/229-5600. **Terms:** [MAP] meal plan; 3 day cancellation notice; package plans. **Facility:** 43 rooms. Rooms are spacious and well maintained. Some offer excellent lake and mountain view. Room decor is modest. All rooms with hair dryer. Efficiencies, $10 extra charge; 4 stories; interior/exterior corridors; smoke free premises; hot springs pool, whirlpool & cave. **Dining:** Dining room; 7 am-9:30 pm; $12-$22; cocktails. **Services:** gift shop. Fee: massage. **Some Rooms:** 6 efficiencies. **Cards:** AE, DI, MC, VI. **Special Amenities:** Free local telephone calls. *(See color ad below)*

ALDERGROVE —See Vancouver p. 502.

BARRIERE pop. 1,700

—— LODGING ——

MOUNTAIN SPRINGS MOTEL
◆◆ Motel
Phone: (250)672-0090

| | 5/1-9/30 | 1P: $47-$53 | 2P: $52-$58 | XP: $5 |
| | 3/1-4/30 & 10/1-2/28 | 1P: $40-$45 | 2P: $43-$48 | XP: $5 |

Location: 1 km s on Hwy 5 (Yellowhead Hwy). 4253 Yellowhead Hwy V0E 1E0 (PO Box 1169). Fax: 250/672-2373. **Terms:** Weekly & monthly rates avail, off season; cancellation fee imposed; pets, $5 extra charge. **Facility:** 12 rooms. Very pleasant motel featuring large guest rooms with a modern style decor, set back from hwy. Very accommodating owners. 1 story; exterior corridors; putting green. **Dining:** Restaurant nearby. **Services:** winter plug-ins. **All Rooms:** extended cable TV. **Some Rooms:** 4 efficiencies. **Cards:** AE, DS, MC, VI. **Special Amenities:** Free local telephone calls and free newspaper.

BLACK CREEK pop. 2,000

—— LODGING ——

TUDOR ACRES BED & BREAKFAST
All Year   1P: $50   2P: $65-$75   XP: $15

Phone: (250)337-5764

◆
Bed &
Breakfast

Location: On Hwy 19, s end of town. 2065 Endall Rd V9J 1G8. Fax: 250/337-5764. **Terms:** [BP] meal plan. **Facility:** 3 rooms. Tudor style home on 12 acre farm. Modest room decor. 1-bedroom suite has fully equipped kitchen, private bathroom and entrance. Friendly family dog "Spud" on premises. 1 story; interior corridors; designated smoking area. **Some Rooms:** kitchen, shared bathrooms, color TV. **Cards:** VI.

BLUE RIVER

—— LODGINGS ——

GLACIER MOUNTAIN LODGE

(CAA) SAVE

5/15-9/30   1P: $70-$85   2P: $75-$95   XP: $10   F6
3/1-5/14 & 10/1-2/28   1P: $50-$65   2P: $55-$70   XP: $5   F6

Phone: (250)673-2393

◆◆
Motel

Location: On Hwy (Yellowhead Hwy) at Shell Rd, follow signs. Hwy 5 & Shell Rd V0E 1J0 (PO Box 27, VOE 1JO). Fax: 250/673-8225. **Terms:** [CP] meal plan; pets, $5 extra charge. **Facility:** 33 rooms. A very comfortable road side listing offering rather spacious guest rooms, all feature Avva spreads. Guest are welcomed in the cozy lobby area as there are several comfortable sofas and fireplace. 2 stories; interior corridors. **Dining:** Restaurant nearby. **Services:** winter plug-ins. **Cards:** AE, DI, MC, VI. **Special Amenities: Free breakfast and free local telephone calls.**

MIKE WIEGELE HELICOPTER SKIING

Phone: 250/673-8381

◆◆◆
Resort

6/10-10/15 Dly   1P: $145-$225   2P: $145-$395   XP: $30   F12
11/25-2/28 Wkly   1P: $5229-$6610

Location: On Hwy 5 (Yellowhead Hwy) at Harrwood Dr, follow signs. Harrwood Dr V0E 1J0 (Box 159). Fax: 250/673-8464. **Terms:** Open 6/10-10/15 & 11/25-2/28; [CP] meal plan; 3 day cancellation notice, in summer; package plans; pets, $25 extra charge. **Facility:** 68 rooms. World renowned heli-skiing resort features authentic log structured accommodations offering 1 room units to entire chalets for larger groups. Summer season features hiking, lake swimming and more. Winter season is heli-skiing only. 6 two-bedroom units, 9 three-bedroom units. 2 stories; exterior corridors; designated smoking area. **Services:** gift shop; winter plug-ins. Fee: massage. **Recreation:** swimming, fishing; cross country skiing, ice skating; hiking trails, jogging. Fee: bicycles, horseback riding. Rental: canoes. **Some Rooms:** 19 kitchens, color TV. **Cards:** AE, MC, VI.

BOSTON BAR pop. 500

—— RESTAURANT ——

SALMON HOUSE RESTAURANT   **Lunch:** $5-$11   **Dinner:** $11-$18   **Phone:** 604/867-9277

(CAA)
◆
Canadian

Location: 11 km s on Trans Canada Hwy 1; at Hell's Gate Airtram. **Hours:** Open 4/11-10/25; 9 am-5 pm; to 6 pm 7/1-8/31. **Features:** No A/C; children's menu; cocktails; a la carte. You travel to this restaurant on a thrilling Hell's Gate Airtram ride over the mighty Fraser River. Regular Airtram admission applies with a $1 discount to CAA/AAA members. The menu features homemade salmon chowder, salmon lasagna, sandwiches and burgers. **Cards:** DI, DS, MC, VI.

BOSWELL pop. 100

—— LODGINGS ——

DESTINY BAY RESORT
4/1-10/10   1P: $130-$180   2P: $180-$220   XP: $50

Phone: 250/223-8234

◆◆
Cottage

Location: 45 km n of Creston, 34 km s of Kootenay Lake ferry dock. 11935 Hwy 3A V0B 1A0 (PO Box 6). Fax: 250/223-8515. **Terms:** Open 4/1-10/10; [MAP] meal plan; 14 day cancellation notice; cancellation fee imposed; pets, with permission. **Facility:** 8 rooms. Scenic lakeside retreat; sod roofed cottages with porch, some with wood-burning fireplace. All rooms with hair dryer. 1 story; exterior corridors; lake view; boat dock. **Recreation:** swimming, boating, canoeing, fishing, paddleboats. **Cards:** MC, VI.

MOUNTAIN SHORES RESORT & MARINA

Phone: (250)223-8258

Property failed to provide current rates

◆◆
Motel

Location: 9 km n; 25.6 km s of Kootenay Lake ferry dock. 13485 Hwy 3A V0B 1A0 (RR 1, Box 6, Site 9). Fax: 250/223-8220. **Terms:** Open 4/1-10/15; 14 day cancellation notice; small pets only, $5 extra charge. **Facility:** 11 rooms. Scenic lakeside location. Good mountain views. 1 story; small heated pool; marina; playground. Fee: boat ramp. **Recreation:** swimming, fishing; hiking trails. **Cards:** AE, MC, VI.

BRISCO

─── LODGING ───

BRISCO BED AND BREAKFAST
Phone: 250/346-3366
(CAA) (SAVE)   5/1-10/1   1P: $55   2P: $70-$90   XP: $25
◆ ◆
Bed &   **Location:** 1 km s of general store off Hwy 95. 4930 Nelson Rd V0A 1B0 (Box 10). Fax: 250/346-3166.
Breakfast   **Terms:** Open 5/1-10/1; [BP] meal plan; age restrictions may apply; check-in 4 pm; cancellation fee imposed.
Facility: 4 rooms. Modern log frame stucco house on small acreage well back from the hwy. Good sized guest rooms with comfortable futon beds, duvet, and a few simple home-like touches. Outdoor decks offer splendid views of the Columbia Valley. 2 stories; interior corridors; smoke free premises; whirlpool. **Recreation:** rock climbing wall. **Cards:** MC, VI.

BURNABY —See Vancouver p. 502.

CACHE CREEK pop. 1,100

─── LODGINGS ───

BONAPARTE MOTEL
Phone: (250)457-9693
(CAA)   5/1-10/31   1P: $55-$65   2P: $65-$85   XP: $10   D10
◆ ◆   3/1-4/30 & 11/1-2/28   1P: $45-$55   2P: $50-$70   XP: $5   D10
Motel   **Location:** On Hwy 97; 1 km n of jct Trans Canada Hwy 1. 1395 Hwy 97 N V0K 1H0 (PO Box 487).
Fax: 250/457-9697. **Terms:** Cancellation fee imposed; small pets only, $10 extra charge; 2 rooms avail. **Facility:** 25 rooms. A pleasant property with cozy guest rooms and average in size. Some rooms feature patio door leading to outdoor pool. 4 kitchens, $15 extra charge; 4 efficiencies, $10 extra charge; 1 story; exterior corridors; heated pool, sauna, whirlpool. **Dining:** Restaurant nearby. **Services:** winter plug-ins. **All Rooms:** extended cable TV. **Cards:** AE, DS, MC, VI.

SAGE HILLS MOTEL
Phone: 250/457-6451
(CAA)   5/16-9/30   1P: $50   2P: $50   XP: $5
◆   3/1-5/15 & 10/1-2/28   1P: $45   2P: $45   XP: $5
Motel   **Location:** Just n of jct Hwy 97 and Trans Canada Hwy 1. 1390 Hwy 97 N V0K 1H0 (Box 126).
Fax: 250/457-6451. **Terms:** 3 day cancellation notice. **Facility:** 18 rooms. This is a simple, yet nicely maintained older, budget-style property offering a unique guest room decor of items you may have seen while growing up in the early 70s. The larger rooms are at the back. 5 two-bedroom units. Efficiency units, $10 extra charge; 1 story; exterior corridors; heated pool. **Dining:** Restaurant nearby. **All Rooms:** combo or shower baths, extended cable TV. **Cards:** AE, DS, MC, VI.

TUMBLEWEED MOTEL
Phone: (250)457-6522
(CAA) (SAVE)   5/1-9/30   1P: $55-$60   2P: $70-$75   XP: $5
◆   3/1-4/30 & 10/1-11/30   1P: $45-$50   2P: $55-$60   XP: $5
Motel   12/1-2/28   1P: $45   2P: $45   XP: $5
Location: On Trans Canada Hwy 1; just e of jct Hwy 97. (PO Box 287, V0K 1H0). Fax: 250/457-9233. **Terms:** Small pets only. **Facility:** 25 rooms. Cozy units offering well coordinated but modest style decor. Small stream wanders near the edge of property. 2 stories; exterior corridors. **Dining:** Restaurant nearby. **Services:** winter plug-ins. **All Rooms:** extended cable TV. **Some Rooms:** 3 efficiencies. **Cards:** AE, DI, MC, VI. **Special Amenities:** Free local telephone calls and preferred room (subject to availability with advanced reservations).

─── RESTAURANT ───

WANDER INN RESTAURANT
Lunch: $5-$10   **Dinner:** $7-$16   **Phone:** 250/457-6511
(CAA)   **Location:** Just s of jct Hwy 97. Trans Canada Hwy 1 V0K 1H0. **Hours:** 11 am-11 pm. Closed: 12/25 &
◆   12/26. **Features:** children's menu; carryout; cocktails & lounge; a la carte. The cuisine at Wander Inn
Canadian   features Cantonese dishes such as the emperor's plate with chicken, beef and stir-fry, as well as burgers, sandwiches, soup, steak and chops. Seniors and visitors like this place, which has a coffee shop and dining room section. **Cards:** AE, MC, VI.

CAMPBELL RIVER pop. 28,900

─── LODGINGS ───

ARBOUR'S GUEST HOUSE
Phone: (250)287-9873
◆   All Year   1P: $65-$75   2P: $75-$90   XP: $10
Bed &   **Location:** 2 km s on Island Hwy 19, just e on 1st Ave, then just s on Murphy St, on water side of street. 375
Breakfast   S Murphy St V9W 1Y8. Fax: 250/287-2353. **Terms:** [ECP] meal plan; age restrictions may apply; 14 day cancellation notice; cancellation fee imposed. **Facility:** 4 rooms. Located in a residential neighborhood, this private home B&B feature cozy standard type guest rooms and one larger suite with cooking facilities, although cooking is discouraged. Modern common room area. Very pleasant hosts. 2 stories; interior corridors; designated smoking area. **Some Rooms:** combo or tub baths, shared bathrooms, color TV. **Cards:** MC, VI.

BEST WESTERN AUSTRIAN CHALET

Phone: (250)923-4231

			XP: $10	F12
6/1-9/30	1P: $89-$150	2P: $99-$160	XP: $10	F12
3/1-5/31 & 10/1-2/28	1P: $79-$134	2P: $89-$144	XP: $8	F12

(AAA) (SAVE)

◆◆◆

Motel

Location: 3.2 km s on Hwy 19. 462 S Island Hwy V9W 1A5. Fax: 250/923-2840. **Terms:** Weekly & monthly rates avail, off season; package plans; small pets only, $3 extra charge. **Facility:** 55 rooms. Alpine-style village with sweeping ocean views. Contemporary guest room decor. Most units with balcony or patio. 4 two-bedroom units. 3 stories; interior/exterior corridors; putting green; heated pool, sauna, whirlpool. **Dining:** Restaurant nearby. **Recreation:** charter fishing, fishing, fish freezing. **All Rooms:** extended cable TV. **Some Rooms:** 20 efficiencies, kitchen. **Cards:** AE, DI, DS, JC, MC, VI. **Special Amenities:** Free local telephone calls and free room upgrade (subject to availability with advanced reservations). (See color ad below)

BRIGHT'S WILLOW POINT GUEST HOUSE

Phone: 250/923-1086

3/1-9/1	1P: $60-$65	2P: $75-$85	XP: $15	
9/2-2/28	1P: $55-$60	2P: $65-$75	XP: $15	

Bed & Breakfast

Location: 6 km s on Hwy 19. 2460 S Island Hwy (19) V9W 1C6. Fax: 250/923-1079. **Terms:** [BP] meal plan; age restrictions may apply. **Facility:** 3 rooms. Suburban home setting featuring comfortable, but average sized guest rooms. 1 story; interior corridors; designated smoking area. **Cards:** MC, VI.

CAMPBELL RIVER LODGE FISHING & ADVENTURE RESORT

Phone: 250/287-7446

			XP: $6	F5
7/16-8/28	1P: $69	2P: $84	XP: $6	F5
8/29-2/28	1P: $50-$60	2P: $55-$70	XP: $6	F5
4/16-7/15	1P: $60	2P: $70	XP: $6	F5
3/1-4/15	1P: $50	2P: $55	XP: $6	F5

◆

Motor Inn

Location: On Hwy 19, nw of downtown, across from Redwood St. 1760 Island Hwy V9W 2E7. Fax: 250/287-4063. **Terms:** [CP] meal plan; 3 day cancellation notice; cancellation fee imposed; package plans; small pets only, $6 extra charge. **Facility:** 28 rooms. Once past the front part of the building, you will find a rustic "lodge" type setting featuring a unique lobby filled with wooden log walls and fine wood carvings. Guest rooms are modest with strong housekeeping. 2 stories; interior/exterior corridors. **Services:** gift shop. **All Rooms:** combo or shower baths. **Cards:** AE, MC, VI.

CAMPBELL RIVER SUPER 8

Phone: (250)286-6622

6/1-9/15	1P: $78-$83	2P: $83-$91	XP: $6	F12
4/16-5/31	1P: $62	2P: $68-$70	XP: $6	F12
9/16-2/28	1P: $59-$62	2P: $65-$70	XP: $6	F12
3/1-4/15	1P: $58	2P: $64-$66	XP: $6	F12

◆◆

Motel

Location: 3 km s on Hwy 19. 340 S Island Hwy V9W 1A5. Fax: 250/286-6622. **Terms:** [CP] meal plan; cancellation fee imposed; pets. **Facility:** 39 rooms. Comfortable accommodations offering average sized guest rooms; right along the hwy on the south end of town. 2 stories; interior corridors; heated pool. **Cards:** AE, CB, DI, DS, JC, MC, VI.

ELK FALLS FISHING RESORT MOTEL

Phone: (250)286-6796

			XP: $10	D14
6/1-10/15	1P: $65-$69	2P: $79-$85	XP: $10	D14
10/16-2/28	1P: $49-$59	2P: $49-$69	XP: $10	D14
3/1-5/31	1P: $45-$59	2P: $49-$65	XP: $10	D14

(AAA) (SAVE)

◆◆

Cottage

Location: From jct of Hwy 19 and 28, 0.5 km w on Hwy 28. 2320 Campbell River Rd V9W 4N7. Fax: 250/286-6119. **Terms:** 30 day cancellation notice, 30 day for guided fishing excursions. **Facility:** 10 rooms. Charming 1 bedroom duplex cottages situated in a park-like setting along Campbell River. Enjoy 1 of 3 open fire pits or barbecue area with view of river. Something different from run of mill motels. 1 story; exterior corridors. **Recreation:** fishing, salmon guiding service, including boat & motor, fish freezing & packaging. Fee: charter fishing. **All Rooms:** combo or shower baths, extended cable TV. **Cards:** AE, MC, VI. **Special Amenities:** Free local telephone calls.

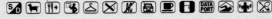

PAINTER'S LODGE

CAA	6/17-9/1	1P: $160-$205	2P: $160-$205	XP: $15 F12
◆◆◆	5/16-6/16	1P: $135-$175	2P: $135-$175	XP: $15 F12
	3/31-5/15	1P: $110-$145	2P: $110-$145	XP: $15 F12
Resort	9/2-10/15	1P: $135	2P: $135	XP: $15 F12

Phone: (250)286-1102

Location: 2 km n on Hwy 19 from jct Hwy 19 and 28, just e. 1625 MacDonald Rd V9W 4S5. Fax: 250/286-0158. **Terms:** Open 3/31-10/15; 7 day cancellation notice; cancellation fee imposed; package plans. **Facility:** 94 rooms. Several buildings situated along wonderfully manicured lawns and gardens, some guest rooms have views of the marina and water. All guest rooms are spacious with private balcony. Geared for families or the die hard fisherman. 2 two-bedroom units. Whirlpool room; 3 stories; exterior corridors; heated pool, whirlpools; 2 tennis courts; playground. **Dining:** Restaurant; 7:30 am-11 & noon-10 pm; $17-$23; cocktails. **Services:** gift shop. Fee: area transportation, golf course. **Recreation:** charter fishing, fishing; hiking trails. Fee: guided fishing tours. **All Rooms:** extended cable TV. **Some Rooms:** 3 efficiencies, 2 kitchens. **Cards:** AE, DI, MC, VI.

TOWN CENTRE INN

◆◆	6/1-9/30	1P: $64-$69	2P: $74-$84	XP: $5 F12
Motel	3/1-5/31 & 10/1-2/28	1P: $59-$64	2P: $69-$79	XP: $5 F12

Phone: (250)287-8866

Location: From Hwy 19, just e on Elm St, on the corner of 16th Ave. 1500 Elm St V9W 3A6. Fax: 250/287-3944. **Facility:** 34 rooms. A pleasant little property with strong housekeeping, close to the downtown area. 2 stories; exterior corridors. **Some Rooms:** Fee: VCR. **Cards:** AE, MC, VI.

------ **RESTAURANTS** ------

GOURMET BY THE SEA

Dinner: $17-$29　　**Phone: 250/923-5234**

◆◆ Steak and Seafood

Location: 18 km s on Hwy 19. 4378 S Island Hwy V9H 1E8. **Hours:** 5:30 pm-10 pm, Sun from 5 pm. Closed: 12/24, 12/25, Mon & Tues. **Reservations:** required; dining room. **Features:** cocktails & lounge; a la carte. You'll enjoy the food and the view here, where the setting overlooks the beautiful Strait of Georgia and the coastal mountain range. The bistro has a casual feel, and the dining room is a bit more upscale. Reservations are recommended for the dining room. **Cards:** AE, MC, VI.

HARVEST RESTAURANT

Dinner: $10-$24　　**Phone: 250/923-4202**

◆◆ Continental

Location: 3.2 km s on Hwy 19. 428 S Island Hwy V9W 1A5. **Hours:** 7 am-11 & 5-10 pm. Closed: 1/1 & 12/25. **Features:** No A/C; children's menu; carryout; cocktails & lounge; a la carte. This small restaurant is located at the rear of a large and popular pub. The dinner menu features a mix of German fare such as schnitzels, but also includes prime rib and chicken selections. Families are made to feel welcome here. It isn't open for lunch. **Cards:** AE, MC, VI. *(See color ad p 407)*

CASTLEGAR pop. 7,000

------ **LODGING** ------

BEST WESTERN FIRESIDE INN

CAA SAVE	6/1-9/30	1P: $89-$105	2P: $95-$107	XP: $5 F
◆◆◆	4/1-5/31	1P: $82-$95	2P: $89-$97	XP: $5 F
Motor Inn	3/1-3/31 & 10/1-2/28	1P: $75-$87	2P: $82-$89	XP: $5 F

Phone: (250)365-2128

Location: Jct of Hwy 3 and 22. 1810 8th Ave V1N 2Y2. Fax: 250/365-2158. **Terms:** Package plans. **Facility:** 57 rooms. 2 stories; interior/exterior corridors; sauna, whirlpool; racquetball court. **Dining:** Restaurant; 6:30 am-9 pm; $11-$19; cocktails. **Services:** winter plug-ins. **All Rooms:** combo or shower baths, extended cable TV. **Some Rooms:** 47 efficiencies. Fee: VCR. **Cards:** AE, DI, DS, MC, VI. **Special Amenities:** Free local telephone calls and free room upgrade (subject to availability with advanced reservations).

CHASE pop. 2,500

------ **LODGINGS** ------

CHASE COUNTRY INN MOTEL

◆◆	5/1-10/31	1P: $60	2P: $68-$76	XP: $10 F6
Motel	3/1-4/30 & 11/1-2/28	1P: $50	2P: $56-$62	XP: $6 F6

Phone: 250/679-3333

Location: Trans Canada Hwy 1 and Coburn St. 576 Coburn St V0E 1M0 (Box 1031). Fax: 250/679-8018. **Terms:** Cancellation fee imposed; small pets only, $5 extra charge. **Facility:** 21 rooms. A very pleasant property offering comfortable accommodations with nice-sized guest rooms and a modern decor. 2 stories; exterior corridors. **Services:** winter plug-ins. **Cards:** MC, VI.

QUAAOUT LODGE RESORT

CAA SAVE	5/1-10/31	1P: $125-$175	2P: $125-$175	XP: $10 F12
◆◆◆	3/1-4/30 & 11/1-2/28	1P: $85-$140	2P: $85-$140	XP: $10 F12
Lodge				

Phone: (250)679-3090

Location: Trans Canada Hwy 1, exit Squilax Bridge, then Little Shuswap Rd 2.5 km w. V0E 1M0 (PO Box 1215). Fax: 250/679-3039. **Terms:** Check-in 4 pm; cancellation fee imposed; package plans; pets, $10 extra charge. **Facility:** 72 rooms. A secluded lodge in forested area on Little Shuswap Lake. Unique and brightly appointed rooms. The world famous Adams River Salmon Run can be viewed nearby or experience an Indian Sweat Lodge. 6 whirlpool rms with gas fireplace, $140-$165; 3 stories; interior corridors; beach, heated pool, sauna, whirlpool; boat dock; playground. **Dining:** Restaurant; 7 am-9 pm; $15-$20; cocktails. **Services:** gift shop. Fee: massage. **Recreation:** swimming, fishing; hiking trails, jogging. Fee: bicycles, horseback riding. Rental: canoes. **Cards:** AE, MC, VI. **Special Amenities:** Free local telephone calls and preferred room (subject to availability with advanced reservations).

SCOTCH CREEK COTTAGES RESORT

(AAA) (SAVE)

◆ ◆ ◆

Cottage

	6/24-9/5	1P: $200-$295	2P: $200-$295	Phone: (250)675-5355
	5/1-6/23 & 9/6-10/20	1P: $125-$200	2P: $125-$200	XP: $25 F16
				XP: $15 F16

Location: Trans Canada Hwy 1, 18 km e on Squilax Rd to Scotch Creek, 1 km n on Scotch Creek Warf Rd, then 1 km e. 4044 Express Point Rd (3549 Eagle Bay Rd, BLIND BAY, V0E 1H1). **Fax:** 250/675-3549. **Terms:** Open 5/1-10/20; weekly rates avail; 60 day cancellation notice; cancellation fee imposed; 7 night min stay, 6/25-9/6. **Facility:** 13 rooms. Along the shores of Shuswap Lake, these fully self-contained cottages offer spacious units with a pleasant modern decor along with outside deck. Cottages able to accommodate up to 6 persons comfortably. 1 story; exterior corridors; beach; boat dock; playground. **Recreation:** swimming; barbecue area, horseshoe pit, volleyball court. **All Rooms:** kitchens, shower baths. **Cards:** MC, VI.

CHEMAINUS pop. 3,500

——— LODGING ———

FULLER LAKE MOTEL

◆ ◆

Motel

	5/1-9/30	1P: $60-$75	2P: $70-$85	Phone: 250/246-3282
	3/1-4/30 & 10/1-2/28	1P: $50-$65	2P: $50-$75	XP: $10 D12
				XP: $10 D12

Location: On Trans Canada Hwy 1 and Henry Rd. 9300 Trans Canada Hwy V0R 1K0 (PO Box 39). **Fax:** 250/246-3445. **Terms:** Cancellation fee imposed; small pets only, $5 extra charge. **Facility:** 34 rooms. Comfortable, up-to-date economy style lodging featuring a mix of average sized guest rooms to units with a separate bedroom and sitting area. Solid housekeeping. 2 stories; exterior corridors. **Some Rooms:** 12 efficiencies, 8 kitchens. **Cards:** AE, MC, VI.

CHETWYND pop. 3,000

——— RESTAURANT ———

THE SWISS INN

(AAA)

◆ ◆

Continental

Lunch: $4-$11   **Dinner:** $8-$18   **Phone:** 250/788-2566
Location: 1 km e on Hwy 97. 4812 N Access Rd V0C 1J0. **Hours:** 11 am-2 & 5-10 pm, Sat from 5 pm. Closed major holidays, 12/24 & Sun. **Features:** children's menu; carryout; cocktails. The casual and lively Swiss Inn features European and international specialties such as homemade sausage, spaetzle and schnitzel as well as its popular pizza, charbroiled steak, and prime rib dinners on Fri and Sat nights. Its atmosphere is cozy and warm. **Cards:** AE, MC, VI.

CHILLIWACK —See Vancouver p. 503.

CHRISTINA LAKE pop. 6,900

——— LODGING ———

NEW HORIZON MOTEL

(AAA) (SAVE)

Motel

	5/16-10/15	1P: $65-$85	2P: $69-$90	Phone: (250)447-9312
	10/16-2/28	1P: $55-$72	2P: $59-$77	XP: $10
	3/1-5/15	1P: $52-$70	2P: $56-$75	XP: $10
				XP: $10

Location: Just e on Hwy 3. 2037 Hwy 3 V0H 1E0 (PO Box 266). **Fax:** 250/447-9488. **Terms:** [CP] meal plan; weekly rates avail; 7 day cancellation notice; cancellation fee imposed; package plans; small pets only, $3 extra charge, with permission. **Facility:** 10 rooms. Guest rooms feature mainly contemporary furnishings with a few vintage apointments. Excellent housekeeping. 1 story; exterior corridors. **Recreation:** basketball. **All Rooms:** extended cable TV. **Some Rooms:** 6 kitchens. **Cards:** AE, DI, MC, VI. **Special Amenities:** Free breakfast and free local telephone calls.

CLEARWATER pop. 3,500

——— LODGINGS ———

DUTCH LAKE MOTEL

◆ ◆

Motel

	3/1-9/30	1P: $80	2P: $80	Phone: (250)674-3325
	10/1-2/28	1P: $50-$55	2P: $60-$65	XP: $8 F10
				XP: $5 F10

Location: Hwy 5 (Yellowhead Hwy) at Roy Rd. 333 Roy Rd V0E 1N0 (RR2 Box 5116). **Fax:** 250/674-2916. **Facility:** 27 rooms. Modern property offering large, comfortable guest rooms. Just off the main hwy, yet set back into the trees for a tranquil setting. 2 stories; exterior corridors. **Services:** winter plug-ins. **Recreation:** swimming, fishing. Rental: boats, canoes. **Some Rooms:** 12 efficiencies. **Cards:** AE, MC, VI.

JASPER WAY INN

(AAA)

◆

Motel

	5/1-9/30	1P: $45-$90	2P: $50-$90	Phone: (250)674-3345
	3/1-4/30	1P: $40-$80	2P: $45-$80	XP: $5
	10/1-2/28	1P: $40-$80	2P: $45-$80	XP: $5

Location: 1 km w on Old N Thompson Hwy just off Hwy 5 (Yellowhead Hwy). 57 E Old N Thompson Hwy V0E 1N0 (RR2 Box 2127). **Fax:** 250/674-2687. **Terms:** Cancellation fee imposed; small pets only. **Facility:** 16 rooms. An older but very well maintained property situated along Dutch Lake, adjacent to public beach area. Guest rooms range from average size to large 2-bedroom units. Quiet location, away from hwy with a wonderful view of lake. 10 kitchens, $5 extra charge; 1 story; exterior corridors; boat dock. **Dining:** Restaurant nearby. **Services:** winter plug-ins. **Recreation:** swimming, fishing. Rental: boats, canoes. **All Rooms:** combo or shower baths, extended cable TV. **Cards:** AE, DI, MC, VI.

COQUITLAM —*See Vancouver p. 505.*

COURTENAY pop. 17,300

———— LODGINGS ————

BEST WESTERN COLLINGWOOD INN
(CAA)
◆ ◆ ◆
Motor Inn

All Year   1P: $82   2P: $92   Phone: (250)338-1464   XP: $10   F12
Location: 1 km s on Island Hwy 19. 1675 Cliffe Ave V9N 2K6. Fax: 250/338-1464. **Terms:** Weekly & monthly rates avail; 3 day cancellation notice; package plans; small pets only, $8 extra charge, in smoking rooms. **Facility:** 45 rooms. A unique west coast cedar structure featuring spacious guest rooms with modern decor. 10 loft units with kitchen, $109-$159 for 6-8 persons; 2 stories; exterior corridors. **Dining:** Restaurant; 6:30 am-2 & 5-9 pm; $7-$16; cocktails. **Recreation:** fishing charters & guide. **All Rooms:** extended cable TV. **Some Rooms:** 18 efficiencies. **Cards:** AE, DI, DS, MC, VI.

THE COAST WESTERLY HOTEL
◆
Motor Inn

All Year   1P: $79-$104   2P: $89-$104   Phone: (250)338-7741   XP: $10   F18
Location: 1 km s on Island Hwy 19. 1590 Cliffe Ave V9N 2K4. Fax: 250/338-5442. **Terms:** 30 day cancellation notice; cancellation fee imposed; package plans; small pets only, $10 extra charge. **Facility:** 108 rooms. Located along Hwy 19 that leads to either Campbell River or Comox. This mature property features some fine upgraded business class rooms to comfortable standard style rooms, all with private balcony. 4 stories; interior corridors; heated pool. **Cards:** AE, DI, JC, MC, VI.

GREYSTONE MANOR BED & BREAKFAST
◆ ◆
Historic Bed
& Breakfast

All Year   1P: $60   2P: $80   Phone: 250/338-1422   XP: $20
Location: 4 km s on Island Hwy 19. 4014 Haas Rd V9N 8H9 (RR 6, Site 684 C2). **Terms:** [BP] meal plan; age restrictions may apply; check-in 4 pm. **Facility:** 3 rooms. A secluded property situated in a quiet acreage overlooking some of the water. A lovely English-style garden, really spectacular during spring/summer. Guest rooms are cozy with a pleasant, simple decor. 2 stories; interior corridors; smoke free premises. **All Rooms:** combo or shower baths. **Cards:** MC, VI.

KINGFISHER OCEANSIDE RESORT & SPA
◆ ◆
Motor Inn

5/1-9/30   1P: $104-$275   2P: $109-$275   Phone: (250)338-1323   XP: $10   F18
10/1-2/28   1P: $94-$104   2P: $104-$114
3/1-4/30   1P: $89-$99   2P: $99-$109   XP: $10   F18
Location: 8 km s on Island Hwy 19. 4330 S Island Hwy V9N 8H9 (Site 672, RR 6, C-1). Fax: 250/338-0058. **Terms:** Cancellation fee imposed; package plans; small pets only, $7 extra charge, in limited numbers. **Facility:** 45 rooms. A secluded property featuring a range of accommodations. Either a waterfront unit with efficiency or a standard motel room with large balcony and spectacular view of the water. Full fitness centre and spa treatments. 2 stories; exterior corridors; heated pool; 1 tennis court. **Recreation:** charter fishing, fishing. **Some Rooms:** 20 efficiencies. **Cards:** AE, DI, DS, JC, MC, VI.

TRAVELODGE COURTENAY
(CAA) (SAVE)
◆
Motel

5/1-2/28   1P: $70   2P: $77   Phone: (250)334-4491   XP: $7   F18
3/1-4/30   1P: $67   2P: $77   XP: $7   F18
Location: 1.8 km s of downtown, on Island Hwy 19, adjacent Driftwood mall. 2605 S Island Hwy V9N 2L8. Fax: 250/334-4694. **Terms:** [CP] meal plan; weekly & monthly rates avail; 14 day cancellation notice; small pets only, $50 dep req. **Facility:** 92 rooms. Simple budget style accommodations offering average sized guest rooms with a simple style decor. Sports teams welcome. 20 efficiencies, $5 extra charge; 2 stories; exterior corridors; heated pool, sauna. **Dining:** Restaurant nearby. **All Rooms:** extended cable TV. **Cards:** AE, DI, JC, MC, VI. **Special Amenities:** Free breakfast and free local telephone calls. *(See color ad below)*

——— RESTAURANT ———

THE OLD HOUSE RESTAURANT   **Lunch:** $7-$10   **Dinner:** $9-$18   **Phone:** 250-338-5406
◆◆   **Location:** From Island Hwy 19, jct 17th St; before the 17th St Bridge. 1760 Riverside Ln V9N 8C7.
Canadian   **Hours:** 11 am-9:30 pm, Sat-Sun from 9:30 am. Closed: 12/25. **Features:** No A/C; children's menu; cocktails;
a la carte. This locally popular dining spot is housed in a rustic 1938 home with cozy fireplaces and
tantalizing wood aromas. Sitting on two acres of beautiful gardens, the site overlooks the grounds and a working mill across
the river. Friendly, attentive service. **Cards:** AE, DI, MC, VI.   ⊠

COWICHAN BAY

——— LODGINGS ———

DREAM WEAVER BED & BREAKFAST   **Phone:** 250-748-7688
◆◆   All Year   1P: $55-$75   2P: $70-$130   XP: $15   F5
Bed &   **Location:** Cowichan Bay Rd and Botwood Ln. 1682 Botwood Ln V0R 1N0. Fax: 250-748-4519. **Terms:** [BP]
Breakfast   meal plan; 7 day cancellation notice; cat on premises. **Facility:** 4 rooms. A modern "Victorian" style home right
in the heart of Cowichan Bay, featuring private entrance, gas fireplace and whirlpool. Some delightful little
shops nearby. 3 stories, no elevator; interior/exterior corridors; designated smoking area. **Cards:** MC, VI.

🛗 ⊠ 🅰 ☎ VCR 🖨 💻 📶

WESSEX INN   **Phone:** 250-748-4214
◆   Property failed to provide current rates
Motel   **Location:** Just n on Cowichan Bay Rd. 1846 Cowichan Bay Rd V0R 1N0. Fax: 250-746-8200. **Facility:** 30
rooms. Simple, basic style accommodations. Guest rooms are average in size with the more modern rooms
near the front of the property with views of the ocean bay. 2 stories; exterior corridors. **Cards:** AE, DI, MC, VI.

🅰 ⊠ 🅰 💻 📶

CRANBROOK pop. 18,100

——— LODGINGS ———

BULL RIVER RANCH   **Phone:** (250)429-3760
CAA SAVE   3/1-12/31   1P: $90   2P: $95   XP: $10
          Location: 15 km n on Hwy 95; 21.9 km se of Ft Steele on Ft Steele-Wardner Rd, 12 km ne on gravel road
Ranch   follow signs; Hwy 3 W, 41 km e of Cranbrook, use Ft Steele Rd. V1C 4H7 (PO Box 133). Fax: 250/426-3324.
          Terms: Open 3/1-12/31; 14 day cancellation notice. **Facility:** 7 rooms. Working ranch nestled in scenic moun-
tain location. Cozy 1-bedroom log cabins with fireplace and porch. All cabins are equipped with full size kitchen.
Idyllic location well worth the drive. 1 two-bedroom cottage; 1 story; exterior corridors. **Recreation:** swimming, boating, ca-
noeing, fishing; bicycles, hiking trails, jogging. Fee: horseback riding. **All Rooms:** kitchens, shower baths. **Special Amenities:**
Free local telephone calls and preferred room (subject to availability with advanced reservations).

🛬 🅰 🅰 ☎ 📶 ⊠

HERITAGE INN OF THE SOUTH   **Phone:** (250)489-4301
◆◆   6/1-9/30   1P: $85   2P: $94   XP: $5   F12
Motor Inn   1/1-2/28   1P: $82   2P: $90   XP: $5   F12
          10/1-12/31   1P: $79   2P: $87   XP: $5   F12
          3/1-5/31   1P: $76   2P: $83   XP: $5   F12
Location: Centre; Hwy 3 and 95. 803 Cranbrook St N V1C 3S2. Fax: 250-489-5758. **Terms:** 30 day cancellation notice; cancellation fee imposed; package plans; small pets only. **Facility:** 101 rooms. Attractive public areas and restaurant. Guest room
styles vary and reflect the different stages in renovation. 1 two-bedroom unit. 3 stories, no elevator; interior corridors; heated
pool. **Services:** winter plug-ins. **Cards:** AE, DI, DS, MC, VI.

SD 🐾 🍴 🍸 🅰 🅰 ⊠ 🎿 🖨 💻 📶 DATA/PORT 🅰

MODEL A INN   **Phone:** (250)489-4600
CAA SAVE   3/1-9/30   1P: $75-$150   2P: $80-$150   XP: $5   F15
◆◆◆   10/1-9/30   1P: $65-$100   2P: $70-$100   XP: $5   F15
Motel   **Location:** 2.5 km n on Hwy 3 and 95. 1908 Cranbrook St N V1C 3T1. Fax: 250/489-0906. **Terms:** Small pets
          only, $5 extra charge. **Facility:** 46 rooms. Contemporary property offering spacious units with attractive ap-
          pointments. Whirlpool room, $100-$150; 2 stories; exterior corridors. **Services:** winter plug-ins. **All Rooms:** ex-
tended cable TV. **Cards:** AE, DI, DS, MC, VI. **Special Amenities:** Early check-in/late check-out and free room upgrade
(subject to availability with advanced reservations).   SD 🛬 🐾 🅰 ⊠ 🎿 🖨 💻 🅰 📶

PONDEROSA MOTEL   **Phone:** 250/426-6114
CAA SAVE   5/1-9/30   1P: $40-$45   2P: $50-$60   XP: $5   F12
◆   3/1-4/30 & 10/1-2/28   1P: $40-$45   2P: $45-$50   XP: $5   F12
Motel   **Location:** 2.5 km w on Hwy 3. 500 Van Horne St S V1C 4H3. Fax: 250-426-6221. **Terms:** Weekly rates avail,
          10/1-5/1; small pets only, $5 extra charge. **Facility:** 10 rooms. Rustic western country log exterior. Rooms are
          modest and homey. 1 story; exterior corridors; mini golf, 1 round free for guests. **Services:** winter plug-ins.
Recreation: country western theme. **All Rooms:** extended cable TV. **Some Rooms:** 2 efficiencies. **Cards:** MC, VI.

SD 🐾 🅰 ⊠ 🎿 💻 🅰 📶

SUPER 8 MOTEL   **Phone:** 250/489-8028
◆◆   7/1-9/30   1P: $80-$85   2P: $89-$94   XP: $10   F12
Motel   3/1-6/30 & 10/1-11/30   1P: $70-$75   2P: $79-$84   XP: $10   F12
          12/1-2/28   1P: $69-$74   2P: $78-$83   XP: $10   F12
Location: Just w of jct Hwy 93 and 95, corner of 30th Ave. 2370 Cranbrook St N V1C 3T2. Fax: 250-489-1223. **Terms:** [CP]
meal plan; package plans; pets, in designated rooms. **Facility:** 48 rooms. Good sized rooms with contemporary appeal. 2 stories; interior corridors. **Services:** winter plug-ins. **Cards:** AE, DI, MC, VI.

ASK SD 🛬 🐾 🅰 🅰 ⊠ VCR 🖨 DATA/PORT

———— RESTAURANT ————

HEIDI'S
◆◆
Continental

| | Lunch: $5-$9 | Dinner: $7-$21 | Phone: 250/426-7922 |

Location: Centre; on 9th Ave S. 821 C Baker St V1C 1A3. **Hours:** 11 am-2:30 & 5-9 pm, Fri & Sat 5 pm-10 pm. Closed major holidays & Sun. **Reservations:** suggested. **Features:** children's menu; health conscious menu items; carryout; cocktails; street parking. This cozy, comfortable European-style restaurant serves an extensive menu of international fare that includes rotisserie chicken, schnitzels, bratwurst and steak. Prime rib is offered Fridays and Saturdays. The server staff is charming and attentive. Smoke free premises. **Cards:** AE, MC, VI.

CRESTON pop. 4,800

———— LODGINGS ————

CITY CENTRE MOTEL
◆
Motel

| | All Year | 1P: $36-$40 | 2P: $40-$55 | XP: $5 | Phone: 250/428-2257 |
| | | | | | F5 |

Location: Just n of Hwy 3. 220 15th Ave N V0B 1G0 (PO Box 40). **Terms:** 3 day cancellation notice; pets. **Facility:** 23 rooms. An older property featuring home style guest rooms with a modest type room decor. Quiet location and close to downtown. 2 stories; exterior corridors. **Services:** winter plug-ins. **Cards:** AE, CB, DI, DS, MC, VI.

DOWNTOWNER MOTOR INN
◆
Motel

	4/1-10/31	1P: $40-$46	2P: $52-$58	XP: $5	Phone: (250)428-2238
					F8
	3/1-3/31 & 11/1-2/28	1P: $33-$35	2P: $42-$44	XP: $4	F8

Terms: Cancellation fee imposed; pets, $4 extra charge. **Facility:** 23 rooms. Vintage style guest rooms, ideal for the budget-oriented traveler. 2 stories; interior corridors. **Services:** winter plug-ins. **Cards:** AE, DI, DS, MC, VI.

Location: Corner of 12th Ave N. 1218 Canyon St V0B 1G0 (PO Box 490, V0B 1G0). Fax: 250/428-9974.

SUNSET MOTEL
Ⓒ
◆◆
Motel

| | 5/1-10/15 | 1P: $48-$56 | 2P: $53-$58 | XP: $5 | Phone: (250)428-2229 |
| | 3/1-4/30 & 10/16-2/28 | 1P: $42-$46 | 2P: $45-$51 | XP: $5 | |

Location: 1 km e on Hwy 3. 2705 Canyon St V0B 1G0 (PO Box 186). Fax: 250/428-2251. **Terms:** Cancellation fee imposed; small pets only, $5 extra charge. **Facility:** 24 rooms. Very well maintained property offering a variety of guest rooms from average to spacious. Short drive to downtown. 7 efficiencies, $5 extra charge.; 5 whirlpool rooms; 2 stories; exterior corridors; heated pool. **Dining:** Restaurant nearby. **Services:** winter plug-ins. **All Rooms:** extended cable TV. **Cards:** AE, CB, DI, DS, JC, MC, VI.

CUMBERLAND pop. 2,500

———— LODGING ————

WELLINGTON HOUSE BED & BREAKFAST
◆◆
Bed &
Breakfast

| | All Year | 1P: $60 | 2P: $75-$90 | XP: $25 | Phone: (250)336-8809 |
| | | | | | F |

Location: Island Hwy 19 to Cumberland exit, 10 km w on Royston Rd/Dunsmuir Ave, then just s on Sutton Rd. 2593 Derwent Ave V0R 1S0 (PO Box 689). Fax: 250/336-2321. **Terms:** [BP] meal plan; age restrictions may apply; check-in 4 pm; 5 day cancellation notice. **Facility:** 4 rooms. A modern home with modern conveniences. Lovely backyard garden featuring the remains of an "original weigh scale" used to weigh the coal wagons from the surrounding coal mines of the early part of the century. 2 stories; interior corridors; designated smoking area. **Some Rooms:** shared bathrooms, color TV. **Cards:** VI.

DAWSON CREEK pop. 11,100

———— LODGINGS ————

THE GEORGE DAWSON INN
Ⓒ SAVE
◆◆
Motor Inn

	6/1-8/31	1P: $65-$75	2P: $70-$80	XP: $10	Phone: (250)782-9151
					F18
	3/1-5/31 & 9/1-2/28	1P: $62-$72	2P: $67-$77	XP: $10	F18

Location: 2 km s on Hwy 2. 11705-8th St V1G 4N9. Fax: 250/782-1617. **Terms:** Small pets only, $5 extra charge. **Facility:** 80 rooms. Spacious rooms offering simple appointments. Whirlpool room; 3 stories; interior corridors. **Dining:** Dining room, coffee shop; 6 am-10 pm; $12-$30; cocktails. **Services:** winter plug-ins. **All Rooms:** extended cable TV. **Some Rooms:** Fee: VCR. **Cards:** AE, DI, MC, VI. **Special Amenities:** Free breakfast and free room upgrade (subject to availability with advanced reservations).

TRAIL INN
Ⓒ
◆◆◆
Motel

| | All Year | 1P: $64-$79 | 2P: $74-$87 | XP: $7 | Phone: (250)782-8595 |
| | | | | | F5 |

Location: Jct Alaska and Hart (97 N) hwys. 1748 Alaska Ave V1G 1P4. Fax: 250/782-9657. **Terms:** [CP] meal plan; small pets only, $6 extra charge in designated rooms. **Facility:** 41 rooms. Very well maintained property with spacious rooms offering a mix of room styles. Many have been recently renovated. 2 stories; exterior corridors. **Services:** winter plug-ins. **All Rooms:** extended cable TV. **Some Rooms:** Fee: microwaves. **Cards:** AE, CB, DI, DS, MC, VI.

------ **RESTAURANT** ------

ALASKA CAFE & DINING ROOM   **Lunch:** $6-$20   **Dinner:** $6-$20   **Phone:** 250/782-7040
(AA)   **Location:** Just s of Mile 'O' post, town centre. 10213 10th St V1G 4G7. **Hours:** 11 am-10 pm. Closed major
◆ ◆   holidays & 12/26. **Reservations:** suggested. **Features:** children's menu; health conscious menu items;
American   carryout; cocktails; street parking; a la carte. You'll enjoy the unusual Alaskan-style setting of this restaurant,
located in a landmark building with a hotel and public house. Its extensive menu offers international cuisine
with an emphasis on American and seafood creations. Weekend entertainment. **Cards:** AE, MC, VI.   [X]

DELTA —See Vancouver p. 506.

DUNCAN pop. 4,600

------ **LODGINGS** ------

BEST WESTERN COWICHAN VALLEY INN   **Phone:** (250)748-2722
(AA) [SAVE]   6/26-9/4   1P: $89-$99   2P: $95-$105   XP: $6   F16
          3/1-6/25 & 9/5-2/28   1P: $85-$95   2P: $91-$101   XP: $6   F16
◆ ◆ ◆   **Location:** 3 km n on Trans Canada Hwy 1. 6474 Trans Canada Hwy V9L 6C6. Fax: 250/748-2207.
Motor Inn   **Terms:** Small pets only. **Facility:** 42 rooms. Comfortable, contemporary style guest rooms. Attractive land-
scaping touches along hwy frontage. Whirlpool room; 2 stories; interior corridors; heated pool. **Dining:** Restau-
rant; 6:30 am-9 pm; $10-$20; cocktails. **All Rooms:** extended cable TV. **Some Rooms:** Fee: VCR. **Cards:** AE, DI, DS, JC,
MC, VI. **Special Amenities:** Free local telephone calls and free newspaper.
[S/D] [icons]

DAYS INN DUNCAN   **Phone:** (250)748-0661
(AA) [SAVE]   6/1-9/15   1P: $59-$94   2P: $59-$94   XP: $5   F17
          3/1-5/31 & 9/16-2/28   1P: $39-$69   2P: $39-$69   XP: $5   F17
◆ ◆   **Location:** 1.5 km s on Trans Canada Hwy 1. 5325 Trans Canada Hwy V9L 3X5 (PO Box 308).
Motor Inn   Fax: 250/748-4469. **Terms:** Small pets only, $5 extra charge. **Facility:** 35 rooms. A nice roadside listing fea-
turing a pleasant, modern decor but average sized guest rooms. Perfect for singles or couples but more than
2 people could be uncomfortable. On site 50s style diner along with a working man's pub. 3 stories, no elevator; interior corridors. **Dining:** Restaurant; 7 am-9 pm; $6-$12; cocktails. **All Rooms:** extended cable TV. **Some Rooms:** 4 kitchens.
Cards: AE, DI, JC, MC, VI.   [icons] [DATA PORT]

FAIRBURN FARM COUNTRY MANOR   **Phone:** (250)746-4637
◆ ◆   4/1-10/15   1P: $80-$125   2P: $95-$140   XP: $20
Historic Bed   **Location:** 7 km s on Trans Canada Hwy 1, 5 km w on Koksilah Rd, 3 km further w on Jackson Rd to the very
& Breakfast   end of this "no exit" road. 3310 Jackson Rd V9L 6N7. Fax: 250/746-4637. **Terms:** Open 4/1-10/15; [BP] meal
plan; 14 day cancellation notice; cancellation fee imposed; 2 night min stay. **Facility:** 6 rooms. Built in 1884,
Fairburn Farm was known as a millionaire's country estate. Today this working farm B & B invites guests to help in the daily
chores. Guest rooms are pleasantly decorated, 2 rooms with gas fireplace. 2 stories; interior corridors; designated smoking
area. **All Rooms:** combo, shower or tub baths. **Cards:** MC, VI.   [ASK] [icons]

FALCON NEST MOTEL   **Phone:** 250/748-8188
◆ ◆   5/1-9/30   1P: $54-$61   2P: $60-$67   XP: $7
Motel   3/1-4/30 & 10/1-2/28   1P: $44-$51   2P: $50-$57   XP: $7
          Location: 1.5 km n on Trans Canada Hwy 1. 5867 Trans Canada Hwy 1 V9L 3R9. Fax: 250/748-7829.
Terms: Cancellation fee imposed; small pets only, $7 extra charge. **Facility:** 24 rooms. Very fine, well kept accommodations
geared for those on a budget. 2nd floor rooms with A/C in summer. Nicely tended grounds and pool area. 2 stories; exterior
corridors; heated pool. **Cards:** AE, MC, VI.   [ASK] [icons]

SILVER BRIDGE INN & CONFERENCE CENTRE   **Phone:** (250)748-4311
◆ ◆   7/1-9/30   1P: $59-$69   2P: $64-$84   XP: $5   F16
Motor Inn   3/1-6/30 & 10/1-2/28   1P: $55-$69   2P: $59-$79   XP: $5   F16
          Location: Just n of the Silver Bridge. 140 Trans Canada Hwy V9L 3P7. Fax: 250/748-1774. **Terms:** Cancel-
lation fee imposed; pets, $10 extra charge. **Facility:** 33 rooms. Contemporary style lodging. Guest rooms are quite large and
nicely maintained. Most 1st floor rooms are suites with a separate living room area. Pleasant inner courtyard area. 2 stories;
exterior corridors. **Cards:** AE, DI, MC, VI.   [ASK] [icons]

THE WHITE HOUSE B&B   **Phone:** (250)748-4480
◆   All Year   1P: $65-$70   2P: $69-$79   XP: $15   F3
Bed &   **Location:** 10 km n on Trans Canada Hwy 1. 7905 Trans Canada Hwy V0R 3C0 (PO Box 8, WESTHOLME).
Breakfast   **Terms:** [BP] meal plan; 7 day cancellation notice. **Facility:** 3 rooms. A different style of B & B, guest rooms all
have their own private outdoor entrances. Rooms are quite spacious with simple, at home decor. Breakfast is
served upstairs in owners cozy kitchen. 2 stories; exterior corridors; designated smoking area. **All Rooms:** shower baths.
Cards: MC.   [ASK] [icons]

------ **RESTAURANT** ------

DOGHOUSE A FAMILY RESTAURANT   **Lunch:** $6-$10   **Dinner:** $7-$13   **Phone:** 250/746-4614
◆ ◆   **Location:** Corner of Truck Rd and Trans Canada Hwy 1. 271 Trans Canada Hwy 1 V9L 3P7. **Hours:** 6
Canadian   am-10 pm. Closed: 12/25. **Features:** children's menu; senior's menu; carryout; cocktails; a la carte. You'll
enjoy the quality home-style cooking, generous family servings and reasonable prices at this restaurant,
which has been in business since 1955. Known locally for their special fish 'n' chips, they also offer veal cutlets and
homemade desserts. **Cards:** AE, MC, VI.   [X]

ENDERBY pop. 2,800

—— LODGING ——

HOWARD JOHNSON FORTUNES LANDING

(CAA) (SAVE)
◆
Motor Inn

5/15-9/14	1P: $59	2P: $69	XP: $10	F18
3/1-5/14 & 9/15-2/28	1P: $49	2P: $59	XP: $10	F18

Phone: (250)838-6825

Location: 1 km n on Hwy 97A. 1510 George St V0E 1V0 (Box 168). **Fax:** 250/838-6887. **Terms:** Weekly & monthly rates avail; 4 day cancellation notice; cancellation fee imposed; small pets only, $5 extra charge. **Facility:** 33 rooms. Good budget oriented accommodations featuring comfortable guest rooms. Overlooking courtyard with grassy areas and outdoor pool. On site pub for adults along with family-style restaurant. 1 two-bedroom unit. 2 stories; exterior corridors; heated pool, whirlpool. **Dining:** Restaurant; 7 am-9 pm; $10-$15; wine/beer only. **All Rooms:** extended cable TV. **Some Rooms:** kitchen. **Cards:** AE, DI, MC, VI. **Special Amenities: Free local telephone calls and free newspaper.**

FAIRMONT HOT SPRINGS pop. 400

—— LODGING ——

FAIRMONT HOT SPRINGS RESORT

(CAA) (SAVE)
◆ ◆ ◆
Resort

5/19-10/9 & 12/16-2/28	1P: $159-$239	2P: $159-$239	XP: $6	F5
3/1-5/18 & 10/10-12/15	1P: $99-$169	2P: $99-$169	XP: $6	F5

Phone: (250)345-6311

Location: 1.6 km s off Hwy 93 and 95. 5225 Fairmont Resort Rd V0B 1L0 (PO Box 10). **Fax:** 250/345-6616. **Terms:** Check-in 4 pm; 3 day cancellation notice; package plans. **Facility:** 140 rooms. Family resort on terraced, landscaped grounds. A few bi-level and loft units in picturesque mountain valley. All rooms with hair dryer. Extensive all seasons recreational facilities. 10 two-bedroom units. 3 stories; interior/exterior corridors; saunas, 4 mineral pools, 2 indoor mineral baths, hydrotherapy; 4 tennis courts; playground. Fee: 36 holes golf, miniature golf, driving range, golf lessons. **Dining:** Dining room, coffee shop; 7 am-11 pm; $14-$25; cocktails. **Services:** gift shop; winter plug-ins. Fee: massage. **Recreation:** fishing; cross country skiing, ski instruction & equipment; jogging. Fee: downhill skiing; horseback riding, helicopter rides, esthetics. **All Rooms:** extended cable TV. **Some Rooms:** 49 efficiencies. **Cards:** AE, CB, DI, MC, VI. **Special Amenities: Free local telephone calls.**

FERNIE pop. 4,900

—— LODGINGS ——

CEDAR LODGE

(CAA) (SAVE)
◆ ◆
Motor Inn

All Year	1P: $61-$115	2P: $71-$125	XP: $10	F12

Phone: (250)423-4622

Location: On Hwy 3; 1 km e of W Bridge. 1101 7th Ave V0B 1M0 (PO Box 1477). **Fax:** 250/423-3011. **Terms:** Cancellation fee imposed; package plans; pets, $5 extra charge. **Facility:** 47 rooms. Along main hwy through town. Spacious units featuring pleasant and simple decor. 2 two-bedroom kitchen units, $10 extra charge; 6 whirlpool rooms; 2 stories; interior corridors; heated pool, sauna, whirlpool. **Dining:** Restaurant; 6:30 am-2 & 4:30-10 pm, Sat from 7 am, Sun-9 pm; $8-$23; cocktails. **Services:** winter plug-ins. **All Rooms:** extended cable TV. **Some Rooms:** 2 efficiencies. **Cards:** AE, DI, MC, VI. **Special Amenities: Free local telephone calls.**

LITTLE WITCH LOG INN

◆ ◆
Motel

12/1-2/28	1P: $75-$89	2P: $89-$99	XP: $10	F12
3/1-5/31	1P: $59-$89	2P: $69-$99	XP: $10	F12
6/1-9/4	1P: $69-$79	2P: $79-$89	XP: $10	F12
9/5-11/30	1P: $59-$69	2P: $69-$79	XP: $10	F12

Phone: (250)423-4696

Location: 1.8 km e on Hwy 3 (adjacent to informational center). 141 Commerce Rd V0B 1M0 (RR1 Site 11 Comp 1). **Fax:** 250/423-4698. **Terms:** Check-in 5 pm; 14 day cancellation notice; cancellation fee imposed. **Facility:** 6 rooms. Modern log structure featuring bright and cheerful guest rooms with pine furnishings and duvets. Restaurant showcases delectable European specialties. 2 stories; exterior corridors; smoke free premises. **Services:** winter plug-ins. **Cards:** AE, MC, VI.

PARK PLACE LODGE

(CAA) (SAVE)
◆ ◆ ◆
Motor Inn

3/1-4/30	1P: $80-$154	2P: $99-$179	XP: $10	F6
5/1-12/19	1P: $70-$134	2P: $79-$159	
12/20-2/28	1P: $80-$154	2P: $99	

Phone: (250)423-6871

Location: At 7th St. 742 Hwy 3 V0B 1M0 (PO Box 2560). **Fax:** 250/423-3773. **Terms:** Cancellation fee imposed; package plans; small pets only. **Facility:** 64 rooms. Large rooms, all with modern decor and opening on an interior courtyard with pool and whirlpool. 2 stories; interior corridors; heated pool, saunas, whirlpool. **Dining:** Restaurant; 6 am-2 & 5-9 pm; $8-$17; cocktails. **Services:** winter plug-ins. **Recreation:** bicycles, hiking trails. **All Rooms:** extended cable TV. **Some Rooms:** Fee: VCR. **Cards:** AE, DI, DS, MC, VI. **Special Amenities: Free local telephone calls and free room upgrade (subject to availability with advanced reservations).**

SUPER 8 MOTEL-FERNIE

◆ ◆
Motel

Property failed to provide current rates

Phone: 250/423-6788

Location: 1.5 km w on Hwy 3. 2021 Hwy 3 V0B 1M1. **Fax:** 250/423-6799. **Terms:** Pets, $25 dep req, in smoking rooms. **Facility:** 42 rooms. Contemporary style and simplicity of room decor. 3 stories; interior corridors. **Services:** winter plug-ins. **Cards:** AE, DI, DS, JC, MC, VI.

TIMBERLINE VILLAGE CONDOMINIUMS
Phone: 250/423-6878

CAA	11/20-2/28	1P: $190-$290	2P: $250-$380	XP: $15	F5
◆◆◆	3/1-4/23	1P: $160-$170	2P: $200-$215	XP: $15	F5
	5/15-11/19	1P: $105-$120	2P: $135-$150	XP: $15	F5

Condominium   **Location:** 6.5 km w on Hwy 3; 1.4 km n on Ski Area Rd, just w. 52 Timberline Crescent V0B 1M1. Fax: 250/423-7006. **Terms:** Open 3/1-4/23 & 5/15-2/28; weekly & monthly rates avail; check-in 4 pm; 30 day cancellation notice; cancellation fee imposed; package plans. **Facility:** 74 rooms. Resort nestled near the base of Fernie Mountain ski hill. Units vary in style and size, offer a gas fireplace. Most with balcony and spacious living area with contemporary kitchen. Recently built Aspen Lodge has an elevator. 2 two-bedroom units for up to 8 persons; 3 stories, no elevator; interior corridors; smoke free premises; whirlpools, outdoor hot tub. **Services:** area transportation, ski lift; winter plug-ins. **Recreation:** cross country skiing, snowmobiling; bicycles, hiking trails. Fee: fly fishing; downhill skiing; horseback riding. **All Rooms:** extended cable TV. **Cards:** AE, MC, VI.

FIELD

―――― LODGINGS ――――

KICKING HORSE LODGE
Phone: 250/343-6303

◆◆	7/6-8/31	1P: $118-$162	2P: $118-$162	XP: $14	F6
Lodge	6/1-7/5	1P: $76-$138	2P: $76-$138	XP: $12	F6
	9/1-2/28	1P: $58-$138	2P: $58-$138	XP: $12	F6
	3/1-5/31	1P: $58-$104	2P: $58-$104	XP: $10	F6

Location: Centre. 100 Centre St V0A 1G0 (2650 25th Ave NE, SALMON ARM, V1E 3C7). Fax: 250/343-6355. **Terms:** Check-in 4 pm; 7 day cancellation notice; cancellation fee imposed; package plans; small pets only, $10 extra charge. **Facility:** 14 rooms. In the centre of a quaint railway town surrounded by majestic Rocky Mountains. Cozy rooms in a chalet style lodge. 3 stories, no elevator; exterior corridors; designated smoking area. **Services:** winter plug-ins. **Recreation:** cross country skiing; hiking trails, jogging. **Some Rooms:** 5 efficiencies, kitchen. **Cards:** MC, VI.

―――― The following lodging was either not inspected or did not ――――
meet AAA rating requirements but is listed for your information only.

EMERALD LAKE LODGE & CONFERENCE CENTRE
Phone: 250/343-6321

[fyi]   Not inspected. **Location:** Hwy 1, exit at Emerald Rd, then 8 km. Emerald Lake Rd V0A 1G0 (Box 10). Facilities, services, and decor characterize a mid-range property. **Services:** winter plug-ins.

FORT NELSON   pop. 4,400

―――― LODGING ――――

WOODLANDS INN
Phone: 250/774-6669

◆◆◆	All Year	1P: $86-$89	2P: $96-$99	XP: $10	F16

Motor Inn   **Location:** Centre, on Hwy 97. 3995 50th Ave S V0C 1R0 (PO BOX 568, B0C 1R0). Fax: 250/774-6657. **Facility:** 91 rooms. Modern facility with nicely appointed guest rooms. 4 stories; interior corridors. **Services:** gift shop; winter plug-ins. **All Rooms:** combo or shower baths. **Some Rooms:** 3 efficiencies. Fee: microwaves, VCR. **Cards:** AE, DI, DS, MC, VI.

FORT ST. JOHN   pop. 15,000

―――― LODGINGS ――――

BEST WESTERN COACHMAN INN
Phone: (250)787-0651

CAA SAVE	All Year	1P: $84	2P: $89	XP: $10	F17

◆◆◆
Motel   **Location:** 2 km s on Hwy 97. 8540 Alaska Rd V1J 5L6. Fax: 250/787-5266. **Terms:** Small pets only, $15 extra charge, in designated rooms. **Facility:** 70 rooms. Spacious rooms. 2 stories; interior corridors; whirlpool. **Dining:** Restaurant; 6 am-11 pm; $8-$16; cocktails. **Services:** winter plug-ins. **All Rooms:** extended cable TV. **Cards:** AE, DI, DS, MC, VI. **Special Amenities:** Early check-in/late check-out and free local telephone calls.

RAMADA LIMITED
Phone: (250)787-0779

◆◆◆	1/1-2/28	1P: $89-$99	2P: $97-$107	XP: $8	F18
Motel	3/1-12/31	1P: $87-$95	2P: $95-$103	XP: $8	F18

Location: Centre, corner 100th St. 10103 98 Ave V1J 1P8. Fax: 250/787-0709. **Terms:** [CP] meal plan; check-in 4 pm; small pets only, $10 extra charge, in smoking rooms. **Facility:** 73 rooms. Newer property offering nicely appointed rooms with excellent amenities. 3 stories, no elevator. **Services:** winter plug-ins. **All Rooms:** combo or shower baths. **Some Rooms:** 16 efficiencies. **Cards:** AE, DI, DS, MC, VI.

GALIANO ISLAND —*See Gulf Islands p. 418.*

GIBSONS   pop. 3,700

―――― LODGINGS ――――

CEDARS INN
Phone: (604)886-3008

CAA SAVE	All Year	1P: $74-$79	2P: $79-$83	XP: $5	F12

◆◆◆
Motel   **Location:** Hwy 101 and Shaw Rd opposite Sunnycrest Mall; 6 km n from ferry terminal. 895 Sunshine Coast Hwy V0N 1V0 (PO Box 739). Fax: 604/886-3046. **Terms:** Weekly rates avail; small pets only, $10 extra charge. **Facility:** 45 rooms. Very large guest rooms; all with a pleasant, modern decor. Convenient hwy location. 3 executive suites, $95-$110; 2 stories; interior/exterior corridors; heated pool, sauna, whirlpool. **Dining:** Coffee shop; 7 am-3 pm; $4-$10. **All Rooms:** combo or shower baths. **Some Rooms:** 13 efficiencies. **Cards:** AE, DI, DS, MC, VI. **Special Amenities:** Free local telephone calls and free newspaper.

RITZ MOTEL LTD

Phone: (604)886-3343

CAA SAVE ◆◆ Motel

	1P: $70-$89	2P: $79-$89	XP: $8	F12
5/1-9/30				
3/1-4/30 & 10/1-2/28	1P: $65-$84	2P: $74-$84	XP: $8	F12

Location: 4 km n on Hwy 101 from ferry terminal, just w on Gower Point Rd, then just s on Douglas Rd, across from the Gibsons Marina. 505 Gower Point Rd V0N 1V0 (PO Box 1022). Fax: 604/886-8189. **Terms:** Weekly rates avail. **Facility:** 30 rooms. Scenic harbour and mountain views from some guest rooms. Some with balcony. 2-3 stories, no elevator; exterior corridors. **Dining:** Restaurant nearby. **All Rooms:** efficiencies. **Cards:** AE, MC, VI.

-------- RESTAURANT --------

CHEZ PHILIPPE Country Inn   **Dinner:** $16-$27   Phone: 604/886-2188
◆◆
French **Location:** Hwy 101, 6 km s on Veterans Rd to Fichett St, just sw to King St, 1 km sw to Chaster, 8 km sw to Gowers Pt Rd following Bonniebrook Lodge signs. 1532 Ocean Beach Esplanade RR5 V0N 1V5. **Hours:** 5:30 pm-8:30 pm. Closed: 1/1-1/31; Tues-Thurs 9/15-5/18. **Reservations:** suggested. **Features:** No A/C; cocktails; a la carte. Situated across from a public beach, this country inn setting features a cozy, intimate restaurant and a special view of the ocean to watch cruise ships pass or enjoy the sun set. Table d'hote selections are offered nightly. Good selection of wines. **Cards:** AE, DI, MC, VI.

GOLD BRIDGE

-------- LODGINGS --------

MORROW CHALETS

Phone: (250)238-2462

◆◆◆ Cottage

| 3/1-4/15 & 1/5-2/28 | 1P: $150-$260 | 2P: $150-$260 | XP: $20 | F16 |
| 4/16-1/4 | 1P: $150-$230 | 2P: $150-$230 | XP: $20 | F16 |

Location: 8 km n on the Tyaughton Lake turnoff, follow signs. (General Delivery, V0K 1P0). Fax: 250/238-2462. **Terms:** Check-in 4 pm; 30 day cancellation notice; cancellation fee imposed. **Facility:** 4 rooms. 4 log cabin units, all fully self-contained, situated on the shores of Tyaughton Lake. These chalets are very large and can accommodate as many as 6 or more persons. Enjoy both summer and winter activities. 2 stories; exterior corridors; designated smoking area. **All Rooms:** kitchens. **Cards:** MC, VI.

TYAX MOUNTAIN LAKE RESORT

Phone: (250)238-2221

◆◆◆ Resort

6/1-9/30	1P: $114	2P: $134	XP: $20	F12
3/1-4/30	1P: $109	2P: $124	XP: $20	F12
5/1-5/31 & 10/1-2/28	1P: $98	2P: $114	XP: $20	F12

Location: 20 km ne of Gold Bridge; 88 km w of Lillooet on a mix of paved and gravel road, then 8 km n. Tyaughton Lake Rd V0K 1P0. Fax: 250/238-2528. **Terms:** Check-in 4 pm; 30 day cancellation notice; cancellation fee imposed; package plans. **Facility:** 34 rooms. A family-oriented wilderness destination resort features log-style main lodge accommodation or huge log chalets. Rooms that face the lake have private balcony. Recommended hwy travel from Lillooet. 5 three-bedroom units. 2 stories; interior corridors; 1 tennis court; playground. **Services:** gift shop. **Recreation:** canoeing, fishing, paddleboats; cross country skiing, ice skating, tobogganing; hiking trails. Fee: snowmobiling; bicycles, horseback riding. Rental: boats. **Some Rooms:** 5 kitchens. **Cards:** AE, MC, VI. *(See color ad below)*

GOLDEN pop. 4,000

-------- LODGINGS --------

BEST WESTERN MOUNTAIN VIEW INN

Phone: (250)344-2333

CAA ◆◆◆ Motel

7/1-8/31	1P: $140	2P: $140-$190	XP: $15	F16
3/1-6/30 & 9/1-9/30	1P: $90-$140	2P: $90-$190	XP: $10	F16
10/1-2/28	1P: $80-$140	2P: $80-$190	XP: $5	F16

Location: On Hwy 1; s service road 0.7 km w of jct Hwy 95 and Trans Canada Hwy 1. 1024 11th St N V0A 1H0 (PO Box 2400). Fax: 250/344-2317. **Terms:** Cancellation fee imposed; package plans; small pets only, $10 extra charge, in smoking rooms. **Facility:** 72 rooms. Spacious rooms offering contemporary appeal with a touch of luxury. Gracious lobby featuring a gas burning fireplace and pleasant seating area. All rooms with hair dryer. 3 stories; interior corridors; heated pool. **Dining:** Restaurant nearby. **Services:** gift shop; winter plug-ins. **Recreation:** Fee: snowmobile tours, white water rafting. **All Rooms:** extended cable TV. **Some Rooms:** Fee: VCR. **Cards:** AE, DI, DS, MC, VI.

COLUMBIA VALLEY LODGE
◆◆

Country Inn

Phone: 250/348-2508

4/1-10/31	1P: $45-$65	2P: $55-$75	XP: $10	F6

Location: 23 km s on Hwy 95. 2304 Hwy 95 S V0A 1H0 (PO Box 2669). Fax: 250/348-2505. **Terms:** Open 4/1-10/31; [BP] meal plan; 3 day cancellation notice; cancellation fee imposed. **Facility:** 12 rooms. Alpine style chalet featuring comfortable guest rooms with large bathrooms. 2nd floor guest rooms have private balcony with panoramic view of mountain valley. European style dining room. 2 stories; interior/exterior corridors. **Services:** winter plug-ins. Rental: canoes. **All Rooms:** combo or shower baths. **Cards:** MC, VI.

(ASK) (S/D) (¶¶) (X) (K/) (☎) (🖨) (X)

GOLDEN GATE MOTEL
(CAA) (SAVE)
◆

Motel

Phone: 250/344-2252

7/1-8/31	1P: $60-$65	2P: $65-$75	XP: $8	F5
6/1-6/30 & 9/1-2/28	1P: $45-$50	2P: $55-$75	XP: $8	F5
3/1-5/31	1P: $35	2P: $40-$45	XP: $5	F5

Location: On Trans Canada Hwy 1, 1.5 km e of jct Hwy 95. 1408 Golden View Rd V0A 1H0 (PO Box 566). **Facility:** 38 rooms. Budget type accommodations offering good, clean guest rooms with an older type decor. Hilltop location. 2 stories; exterior corridors. **Dining:** Restaurant nearby. **Services:** winter plug-ins. **All Rooms:** extended cable TV. **Cards:** AE, MC, VI.

(S/D) (¶¶+) (X)

GOLDEN RIM MOTOR INN
(CAA) (SAVE)
◆◆

Motor Inn

Phone: 250/344-2216

7/1-8/31	1P: $90-$98	2P: $98-$100	XP: $10	F5
6/1-6/30	1P: $79-$84	2P: $90-$95	XP: $6	F5
9/1-2/28	1P: $48-$84	2P: $59-$95	XP: $10	F5
3/1-5/31	1P: $48-$54	2P: $59-$69	XP: $5	F5

Location: 1.5 km e on Hwy 1 from jct Hwy 95. 1416 Golden View Rd V0A 1H0 (PO Box 510). Fax: 250/344-6673. **Terms:** Weekly rates avail; 3 day cancellation notice; cancellation fee imposed; small pets only, $6 extra charge. **Facility:** 69 rooms. Off main hwy on a hilltop, some guest rooms have a great view of the valley and surrounding mountains. Most rooms with comtemporary appeal. Spacious rooms. 26 kitchens, $8 extra charge; whirlpool room, $145-$180; 2-3 stories; exterior corridors; 2 heated pools, sauna, waterslide, whirlpool. **Dining:** Restaurant; 7 am-11 pm; 10/15-1/31 5 pm-10 pm, hrs may vary; $10-$17; cocktails. **Services:** winter plug-ins. **Recreation:** recreation room. **All Rooms:** extended cable TV. **Cards:** AE, DI, MC, VI.

(🛏) (¶¶) (△) (X) (🏊) (🖨) (🗄) (△) (☂)

HILLSIDE LODGE & CHALETS
(CAA)
◆◆◆

Complex

Phone: (250)344-7281

6/16-9/20	1P: $90-$115	2P: $90-$115	XP: $25	F4
3/1-6/15 & 9/21-2/28	1P: $80-$98	2P: $80-$98	XP: $25	F4

Location: 15 km w on Hwy 1, follow signs n of hwy. 1740 Seward Frontage Rd V0A 1H0 (PO Box 2603). Fax: 250/344-7281. **Terms:** [BP] & [MAP] meal plans; weekly rates avail; 5 day cancellation notice; cancellation fee imposed; small pets only. **Facility:** 10 rooms. Charming European style property, cozy and contemporary chalets with woodstoves and a porch. Lodge rooms are gracefully decorated and spacious, all with balcony. Outdoor deck offers spectacular river/mountain views. 1-2 stories; exterior corridors; smoke free premises. **Dining:** Dinner served on request, for guests only; wine/beer only. **Services:** winter plug-ins. Fee: area transportation, shuttle to ski hills. **Recreation:** cross country skiing, snowmobiling. Fee: horseback riding. **All Rooms:** combo or shower baths. **Cards:** MC, VI.

(🛏) (X) (K/) (☎) (🖨) (🖳) (H) (🚶) (X)

KAPRISTO LODGE
(CAA) (SAVE)
◆◆◆

Bed &
Breakfast

Phone: (250)344-6048

All Year	1P: $140-$180	2P: $170-$200	XP: $25	F6

Location: From jct Hwy 1 and 95, 14 km s on Hwy 95, 1 km se on Austin Rd, then 0.7 km se, follow signs. 1297 Campbell Rd V0A 1H0 (PO Box 90). Fax: 250/344-6755. **Terms:** [AP], [BP] & [MAP] meal plans; weekly rates avail; 21 day cancellation notice; cancellation fee imposed; package plans; pets on premises. **Facility:** 6 rooms. A family-style European pension with a distinctive Canadian flavour, nestled in a secluded mountain area. All rooms tastefully decorated with natural woods, some with a great view. Large garden and patio with pergola. 1 two-bedroom unit. Whirlpool room; 2 stories; interior corridors; smoke free premises; sauna, outdoor whirlpool. **Dining:** Lunch & dinner served to guests upon request. **Services:** winter plug-ins. Fee: area transportation. **Recreation:** cross country skiing, snowshoeing; bicycles. Fee: river floating; heli-hiking; horseback riding. **Cards:** MC, VI. **Special Amenities:** Early check-in/late check-out and free breakfast.

(S/D) (✈) (X) (K/) (☎) (🖨) (🗄) (H) (X)

RONDO MOTEL
(CAA) (SAVE)
◆◆

Motel

Phone: 250/344-5295

6/25-9/10	1P: $70-$74	2P: $80-$84	XP: $8	F6
9/11-10/31	1P: $55-$65	2P: $60-$70	XP: $8	F6
3/1-6/24	1P: $45-$65	2P: $55-$70	XP: $8	F6
11/1-2/28	1P: $45-$50	2P: $55-$60	XP: $8	F6

Location: Jct Hwy 1 and 95, 2 km s on 10th Ave and just w on Park Dr downtown just past metal bridge. 904 Park Dr V0A 1H0 (Box 258). Fax: 250/344-2645. **Terms:** Cancellation fee imposed. **Facility:** 42 rooms. Wide mix of accommodations and styles, from kitchen units to average sized guest rooms. All with a pleasant, simple decor. 1-2 stories; exterior corridors; small heated indoor pool, sauna, whirlpool. **Dining:** Restaurant nearby. **Services:** winter plug-ins. **All Rooms:** extended cable TV. **Some Rooms:** 14 kitchens. **Cards:** AE, MC, VI.

(S/D) (¶¶+) (X) (🏊) (△) (☂)

RESTAURANTS

KATERINA'S RESTAURANT
◆

American

Lunch: $5-$10   **Dinner:** $9-$20   **Phone:** 250/344-5695

Location: Jct Hwy 1 and 95, 2 km s on 10th Ave, just past bridge, downtown. 827 10th Ave S V0A 1H0. **Hours:** 11 am-11 pm. Closed major holidays. **Features:** children's menu; senior's menu; health conscious menu items; carryout; cocktails. Katerina's is a delightful restaurant serving an extensive menu with traditional steak and seafood entrees, as well as Mediterranean specialties of pasta, stir-fry and pizza. They also offer a good selection of coffee from the cappuccino bar. **Cards:** MC, VI.

(X)

SISTERS & BEANS
◆◆

West
Canadian

Lunch: $6-$10   **Dinner:** $8-$19   **Phone:** 250/344-2443

Location: In town centre, just e at 12th St. 1122 10th Ave S V0A 1H0. **Hours:** 11 am-9 pm. Closed: Mon & 9/1-6/30. **Reservations:** suggested. **Features:** No A/C; casual dress; children's menu; carryout; cocktails; a la carte. The charming Sisters & Beans features an international menu of health-conscious curries, pastas, salads, hummus, tzatziki, spanikopita and burgers, plus fondue offered weekly in winter. Its warm and casual ambience is set in a restored centennial home. **Cards:** MC, VI.

(♿) (X)

GRAND FORKS pop. 4,000

—— LODGINGS ——

IMPERIAL MOTEL
◆
Motel

				Phone: (250)442-8236
3/1-10/31	1P: $55-$60	2P: $60-$65	XP: $6	F12
11/1-2/28	1P: $49-$55	2P: $55-$60	XP: $6	F12

Location: Downtown, corner of Hwy 3. 7389 Riverside Dr V0H 1H0 (PO Box 2558). Fax: 250/442-8082. **Terms:** Cancellation fee imposed; small pets only. **Facility:** 25 rooms. Beautifully maintained property with a mix of contemporary and vintage guest room appointments. 2 stories; exterior corridors. **Some Rooms:** 6 kitchens. **Cards:** AE, DI, MC, VI.

(ASK) (S🐾) 🐾 ✕ ⚑ 🖨 💻 📷 📱

WESTERN TRAVELLER
(CAA) (SAVE)
◆ ◆
Motel

				Phone: (250)442-5566
6/1-9/30	1P: $55-$63	2P: $62-$70	XP: $5	F
3/1-5/31 & 10/1-2/28	1P: $46-$53	2P: $53-$62	XP: $5	F

Location: W end of town on Hwy 3. 1591 Central Ave V0H 1H0 (PO Box 1780). Fax: 250/442-2019. **Terms:** Weekly rates avail; cancellation fee imposed; small pets only, $7 extra charge. **Facility:** 26 rooms. Good sized guest rooms offering a modest but pleasant room decor, superior housekeeping and accommodating owners. 1 kitchen, $7 extra charge; 2 stories; exterior corridors. **Dining:** Restaurant nearby. **Services:** winter plug-ins. **All Rooms:** extended cable TV. **Cards:** AE, DI, MC, VI. **Special Amenities:** Free local telephone calls.

(S🐾) 🐾 📶 (🔧) ✕ 📱

—— RESTAURANT ——

THE CHEF'S GARDEN　　**Lunch:** $6-$16　　**Dinner:** $6-$20　　**Phone:** 250/442-0257
◆ ◆
Ethnic

Location: 5.5 km w on Hwy 3. 4415 Hwy 3 V0H 1H0. **Hours:** 11 am-9 pm. Closed: Mon, 1/1-1/31 & 12/24-12/26. **Reservations:** suggested. **Features:** carryout; cocktails; a la carte. The menu at Chef's Garden offers a mix of traditional Russian (Doukhobor) fare and American dishes. The homemade borscht and the combination dinner will truly satisfy the diner looking for an authentic Russian meal. The decor features antique portraits. Smoke free premises. **Cards:** MC, VI.

✕

Gulf Islands

GALIANO ISLAND pop. 1,000

—— LODGINGS ——

THE BELLHOUSE INN
◆ ◆
Historic Bed
& Breakfast

				Phone: (250)539-5667
7/1-9/15	1P: $125-$185	2P: $135-$195	XP: $20	
3/1-6/30	1P: $85-$175	2P: $95-$195	XP: $20	
11/1-11/1	1P: $85-$175	2P: $95-$175	XP: $20	
11/2-2/28	1P: $85-$150	2P: $85-$150	XP: $20	

Location: From Sturdies Bay ferry terminal, 0.5 km nw on Main Rd, 0.5 km w on Burrill Rd, 0.5 km s on Jack Rd. 29 Farmhouse Rd V0N 1P0 (Box 16, Site 4). Fax: 250/539-5316. **Terms:** [BP] meal plan; age restrictions may apply; 7 day cancellation notice; cancellation fee imposed; 2 night min stay, weekends 7/1-8/31. **Facility:** 4 rooms. Turn-of-the century farmhouse inn with cozy, contemporary rooms, most with balcony. Waterfront location. 2 stories; interior corridors; designated smoking area. **All Rooms:** combo or shower baths. **Cards:** MC, VI.

✕ (🔧) 🆗

WOODSTONE COUNTRY INN
◆ ◆ ◆
Country Inn

			Phone: (250)539-2022
3/1-11/30 & 2/1-2/28	1P: $110-$185	2P: $110-$185	XP: $35

Location: From Sturdies Bay ferry terminal, 3.5 km nw on Strudies Bay Rd. 743 Georgeson Bay Rd V0N 1P0. Fax: 250/539-5198. **Terms:** Open 3/1-11/30 & 2/1-2/28; [BP] meal plan; age restrictions may apply; 7 day cancellation notice; cancellation fee imposed. **Facility:** 12 rooms. A modern style Country Inn featuring nicely decorated guest rooms, with the ground level rooms featuring a walk out patio. Cozy guest common area with large wood burning fireplace. Views of surrounding country side. 2 stories; interior corridors; designated smoking area. **Cards:** AE, MC, VI.

(ASK) (S🐾) 📶 ✕ 🆗 🖨

MAYNE ISLAND pop. 547

—— LODGING ——

OCEANWOOD COUNTRY INN
◆ ◆ ◆
Country Inn

				Phone: (250)539-5074
6/16-9/15	1P: $149-$319	2P: $159-$329	XP: $25	
3/1-6/15 & 9/16-10/30	1P: $109-$269	2P: $119-$279	XP: $25	

Location: From ferry terminal right on Dalton Dr to Mariners Way; right turn then immediate left onto Dinner Bay Rd, follow for 0.8 km. 630 Dinner Bay Rd V0N 2J0. Fax: 250/539-3002. **Terms:** Open 3/1-10/30; [BP] meal plan; age restrictions may apply; 10 day cancellation notice; cancellation fee imposed; 2 night min stay. **Facility:** 12 rooms. A secluded inn situated on 10 acres of forested land on a little bay overlooking Navy Channel. 8 guest rooms feature fireplace with whirlpool or soaker tub. 3 stories, no elevator; interior corridors; designated smoking area. **Recreation:** bicycles. **All Rooms:** combo or shower baths. **Cards:** MC, VI.

📶 (🔧) ✕ 🆗 🆗 🖨 ✕

QUADRA ISLAND pop. 3,600

—— LODGINGS ——

QUADRA RESORT **Phone:** 250/285-3279
◆ 6/1-9/30   1P: $80   2P: $80   XP: $10
Cottage 5/1-5/31   1P: $72   2P: $72   XP: $10
Location: From Campbell River ferry terminal, 6 km on West Rd, then just w on Raydon Rd, follow signs to Heriot Bay. (PO Box 638, QUATHIASKI COVE, V0P 1N0). Fax: 250/285-3279. **Terms:** Open 5/1-9/30; 30 day cancellation notice; cancellation fee imposed; 3 night min stay, 6/15-9/15. **Facility:** 6 rooms. A nicely maintained set of older style cottages situated on terraced hillside offering wonderful views of the ocean inlet. A secluded setting with nicely tended grounds. Take the Quadra Island ferry from Campbell River. 1 story; exterior corridors. Fee: boat dock. **Recreation:** fishing. Fee: canoeing, charter fishing. **All Rooms:** kitchens, B/W TV.

TAKU RESORT **Phone:** (250)285-3031
ⒸⒶⒶ 7/1-8/31   1P: $99-$225   2P: $99-$225   XP: $20   F14
◆◆ 9/1-10/31   1P: $75-$175   2P: $75-$175   XP: $15   F14
Complex 3/1-6/30   1P: $55-$175   2P: $55-$175   XP: $15   F14
  11/1-2/28   1P: $55-$120   2P: $55-$120   XP: $10   F14
Location: From Campbell River ferry terminal, 8 km n on West Rd, then just w on Heriot Bay Rd, follow signs to Heriot Bay. 616 Taku Rd V0P 1H0 (PO Box 1, HERIOT BAY). Fax: 250/285-3712. **Terms:** Weekly rates avail; 30 day cancellation notice; cancellation fee imposed; small pets only, $5 extra charge. **Facility:** 15 rooms. Features a selection of motel style units to individual A-framed cottages; all with wonderful views of the ocean. Nicely tended grounds. 10 min ferry trip from Campbell river. 1 story; exterior corridors; designated smoking area; beach, whirlpool; 1 tennis court; boat ramp. Fee: boat dock. **Dining:** Restaurant nearby. **Recreation:** swimming, canoeing, fishing; half court basketball, horseshoes, volleyball court. **All Rooms:** kitchens. Cards: AE, MC, VI. *(See color ad below)*

―――― *The following lodging was either not inspected or did not* ――――
meet AAA rating requirements but is listed for your information only.

APRIL POINT LODGE **Phone:** 250/285-2222
[fyi] Not inspected. **Location:** Take car ferry from Campbell River; n off Ferry Rd at Greene Rd, 1 km to Pidcock and April Point rds, then 3.2 km n. V9W 4Z9 (PO Box 1, CAMPBELL RIVER). Facilities, services, and decor characterize a mid-range property. **Terms:** Open 4/1-10/30;

SALTSPRING ISLAND pop. 9,200

—— LODGINGS ——

ANNE'S OCEANFRONT HIDEAWAY B & B **Phone:** 250/537-0851
ⒸⒶⒶ [SAVE] 5/1-9/30   1P: $185-$230   2P: $185-$230
◆◆◆ 3/1-4/30 & 10/1-2/28   1P: $155-$200   2P: $155-$200
Bed & **Location:** 11 km nw from Ganges township. 168 Simson Rd V8K 1E2. Fax: 250/537-0861. **Terms:** [BP] meal
Breakfast plan; age restrictions may apply; 7 day cancellation notice; cancellation fee imposed. **Facility:** 4 rooms. Newly constructed, adult oriented home featuring a wrap around veranda with a spectacular ocean view. All rooms have a unique hydro massage tub. 4 whirlpool rooms; 3 stories; interior corridors; designated smoking area; whirlpool. **All Rooms:** shower baths. Cards: AE, MC, VI.

THE OLD FARMHOUSE BED & BREAKFAST **Phone:** (250)537-4113
  Property failed to provide current rates
◆◆◆ **Location:** 4 km n on Lower-Ganges Northend Rd from Ganges township. 1077 Northend Rd V8K 1L9.
Historic Bed Fax: 250/537-4969. **Terms:** Open 3/1-9/30; [BP] meal plan; age restrictions may apply; 7 day cancellation no-
& Breakfast tice; cancellation fee imposed. **Facility:** 4 rooms. Beautifully restored 100 year-old farmhouse is situated among tall trees, orchards and garden. All guest rooms feature hardwood floors, private bath and balcony or patio. Close to St Mary lake and Ganges Village. 2 stories; interior corridors; designated smoking area. Cards: MC, VI.

SALTY SPRINGS SEA SPA RESORT

◆◆◆	6/15-9/15	1P: $165-$329	2P: $165-$329	XP: $25
Cottage	3/1-6/14 & 9/16-10/31	1P: $136-$329	2P: $136-$329	XP: $25
	11/1-2/28	1P: $93-$329	2P: $93-$329	XP: $25

Phone: (250)537-4111

Location: 10 km nw from Ganges. 1460 N Beach Rd V8K 1J4. Fax: 250/537-2939. **Terms:** Age restrictions may apply; check-in 4 pm; 30 day cancellation notice; cancellation fee imposed; package plans. **Facility:** 12 rooms. Very pleasant gothic arch cottages offer a tranquil setting overlooking panoramic ocean views, private deck with barbecue and soothing natural mineral bath in each cottage. Try the spa and wellness centre for extra pampering. 2 two-bedroom units. 1 story; exterior corridors; designated smoking area. **Services:** Fee: massage. **Recreation:** fishing; bicycles. **All Rooms:** kitchens, shower baths. **Cards:** AE, MC, VI.

SEABREEZE INN

◆◆	5/16-9/18	1P: $89-$99	2P: $89-$99	XP: $10	F10
Motel	9/19-2/28	1P: $69-$79	2P: $69-$79		
	3/1-5/15	1P: $69-$79	2P: $69-$79	XP: $10	F10

Phone: (250)537-4145

Location: 1 km s on Fulford-Ganges Rd, from Ganges. 101 Bittancourt Rd V8K 2K2. Fax: 250/537-4323. **Terms:** 4 day cancellation notice; cancellation fee imposed; pets, on approval. **Facility:** 27 rooms. Just outside of the Ganges township, on a hillside above the Ganges Harbour. Large, comfortable guest rooms offer a pleasant country like charm. 2 stories; exterior corridors. **Cards:** AE, MC, VI.

------ **RESTAURANTS** ------

HARBOUR HOUSE BISTRO

Lunch: $6-$10   Dinner: $9-$18   Phone: 250/537-4700

◆◆

Canadian

Location: In Ganges, at the intersection of Upper and Lower Ganges Rd. 121 Upper Ganges Rd V8K 2S2. **Hours:** 8 am-2 & 5-9 pm; from 11 am in winter. **Reservations:** suggested. **Features:** No A/C; casual dress; children's menu; carryout; cocktails; a la carte. The Harbour House features an extensive menu with daily specials, a casual and elegant decor, a friendly and attentive staff and a good view of Ganges Harbour. A pianist plays Saturday and Sunday evenings, and there's an outdoor garden patio. **Cards:** AE, MC, VI.

MOBY'S MARINE PUB

Lunch: $7-$10   Dinner: $8-$13   Phone: 250/537-5559

◆

Canadian

Location: 1 km n on Lower Ganges Rd, then just e. 124 Upper Ganges Rd V8K 2S2. **Hours:** 10 am-midnight, Fri & Sat 11 am-1 am, Sun from 11 am. Closed: 12/25 & 12/26. **Features:** Sunday brunch; carryout; cocktails; a la carte. Across from the Harbour House Hotel, this unpretentious working man's pub in the marina has great views. You won't find table cloths, but you will find hearty pub food served late into the evening seven days a week. Patrons must be at least 19 years old. **Cards:** MC, VI.

RESTAURANT HOUSE PICCOLO

Dinner: $18-$29   Phone: 250/537-1844

◆◆◆

Canadian

Location: In Ganges Township, crosstreet Lower Ganges Rd. 108 Hereford Ave V8K 2V9. **Hours:** 5 pm-10 pm. Closed: 12/25 & 12/26. **Reservations:** required. **Features:** No A/C; casual dress; cocktails; street parking; a la carte. You'll enjoy this restaurant's cozy setting, tucked away from the busy shops of Ganges. The menu offers delightful Scandinavian and European classics and seafood dishes. An impressive selection of reasonably priced wines is offered. Reservations a must. Smoke free premises. **Cards:** AE, DI, MC, VI.

The previous listings were for the Gulf Islands.
This page resumes the alphabetical listings
of cities in British Columbia.

HARRISON HOT SPRINGS pop. 900

—— LODGINGS ——

HARRISON HOT SPRINGS RESORT

(CAA)

◆◆◆
Complex

			Phone: (604)796-2244
7/1-9/30	1P: $149-$179	2P: $149-$179	XP: $10 F16
4/1-6/30	1P: $139-$169	2P: $139-$169	XP: $10 F16
3/1-3/31 & 10/1-2/28	1P: $129-$159	2P: $129-$159	XP: $10 F16

Location: Just w on lakefront. 100 Esplanade Ave V0M 1K0. Fax: 604/796-3682. **Terms:** Check-in 4 pm; 7 day cancellation notice; cancellation fee imposed; package plans; small pets only, in bungalows. **Facility:** 303 rooms. Located along the shores of Harrison Lake this resort features many recreational activities. Guest room views vary from lakeshore to courtyard to mountain views. 34 two-bedroom units. 8 stories; interior corridors; beach, 5 heated pools, saunas, indoor/outdoor hot therapeutic mineral pools; 2 tennis courts; playground. Fee: 9 holes golf. **Dining:** Dining room, restaurant, cafeteria; 7 am-3 & 5-10 pm; $13-$24; cocktails; entertainment. **Services:** gift shop. Fee: massage. **Recreation:** swimming; hiking trails, jogging. Fee: bicycles. Rental: boats, paddleboats. **All Rooms:** combo or shower baths, extended cable TV. **Some Rooms:** honor bars. **Cards:** AE, DI, DS, MC, VI.

HARRISON VILLAGE MOTEL

◆◆
Motel

			Phone: 604/796-2616
6/2-9/15	1P: $74-$89	2P: $74-$89	XP: $10 F16
5/2-6/1	1P: $65-$80	2P: $69-$84	XP: $10 F16
3/1-5/1 & 9/16-2/28	1P: $59-$74	2P: $65-$80	XP: $10 F16

Location: On the lakefront. 280 Esplanade Ave V0M 1K0 (PO Box 115). **Facility:** 18 rooms. A well looked after older property featuring a mixture of guest rooms from average sized standard rooms to larger full kitchen units. Most rooms have balcony. Located directly across from the swimming beach. 4 two-bedroom units. 2 stories; interior/exterior corridors; heated pool. **All Rooms:** combo or shower baths. **Cards:** MC, VI.

QUALITY HOTEL

(CAA) (SAVE)

◆◆◆
Motel

		Phone: (604)796-5555
All Year	1P: $89-$159 2P: $89-$159	XP: $10

Location: Corner of Hwy 9 (Hot Springs Rd) and Lillooet Ave. 190 Lillooet Ave V0M 1K0. Fax: 604/796-3731. **Terms:** Cancellation fee imposed; small pets only, $10 fee. **Facility:** 88 rooms. Nicely decorated guest rooms featuring a modern decor. Close to beach, swimming area and several restaurants. 33 whirlpool rooms, $129-$169; 4 stories; interior corridors; sauna, steamroom, whirlpool. **Dining:** 7 am-midnight coffee bar. **All Rooms:** extended cable TV. **Some Rooms:** efficiency. **Cards:** AE, DI, DS, MC, VI. **Special Amenities:** Free local telephone calls and preferred room (subject to availability with advanced reservations). *(See color ad below)*

—— RESTAURANTS ——

BLACK FOREST RESTAURANT   **Dinner:** $13-$20   Phone: 604/796-9343

◆◆
German

Location: Just w on lakefront. 180 Esplanade Ave V0M 1K0. **Hours:** 5 pm-10 pm. **Reservations:** suggested; summer. **Features:** early bird specials; cocktails; a la carte. You'll enjoy the steak and West Coast salmon at the Black Forest, which also serves German specialties of beef rouladen and schnitzel. The Alpine decor features a central European flair in its paintings and murals. Visitors like the warm, cozy atmosphere. **Cards:** AE, MC, VI.

THE COPPER ROOM   **Dinner:** $20-$30   Phone: 604/796-2244

◆◆◆
Continental

Location: Just w on lakefront; in Harrison Hot Springs Hotel. 100 Esplanade Ave V0M 1K0. **Hours:** 6 pm-10 pm. **Reservations:** required. **Features:** casual dress; children's menu; cocktails & lounge; entertainment; fee for valet parking; a la carte. You'll appreciate the Copper Room for its popular evening dining and dancing. This restaurant is also known for its delicious prime rib and Fraser Valley local produce. Nightly entertainment is featured Tue-Sat, and a dress code is imposed. Smoke free premises. **Cards:** AE, DI, DS, MC, VI.

HARRISON MILLS pop. 100

———— LODGING ————

HISTORIC FENN LODGE BED & BREAKFAST
◆◆   All Year   1P: $100-$130   2P: $100-$130   **Phone:** (604)796-9798
XP: $30
Historic Bed   **Location:** From Hwy 7, 4 kms n of the Sasquatch Inn, watch for signs. 15500 Morris Valley Rd V0M 1L0 (PO
& Breakfast   Box 67). Fax: 604/796-9274. **Terms:** [BP] meal plan; age restrictions may apply; 7 day cancellation notice.
Facility: 7 rooms. This very unique old home was originally built in 1903, many of its original guest rooms and
furniture remain today. The grounds offer a peek back to an earlier time with an old barn and shed and a hand built rock wall.
2 stories; interior corridors; designated smoking area. **Some Rooms:** shower or tub baths, shared bathrooms.
Cards: MC, VI.

HOPE pop. 3,400

———— LODGINGS ————

ALPINE MOTEL
(CAA) [SAVE]   6/16-9/30   1P: $64-$68   2P: $68-$72   XP: $10   D4
◆◆   5/15-6/15   1P: $58-$68   2P: $64-$70   XP: $10   D4
Motel   3/1-5/14 & 10/1-2/28   1P: $54-$60   2P: $56-$62   XP: $10   D4
     Location: Westbound from Hwy 5 exit 173; eastbound from Hwy 5 exit 170, just n from lights. 505 Old Hope-
Princeton Way V0X 1L0 (PO Box 708). Fax: 604/869-9932. **Terms:** Cancellation fee imposed; small pets only,
$5 extra charge. **Facility:** 14 rooms. Large, comfortable guest rooms featuring a slightly older style decor. 1 two-bedroom unit.
6 efficiencies, $7 extra charge; 1 story; exterior corridors. **Dining:** Restaurant nearby. **All Rooms:** extended cable TV.
Cards: AE, MC, VI. **Special Amenities:** Free local telephone calls and free room upgrade (subject to availability with
advanced reservations).

BEST CONTINENTAL MOTEL
(CAA)   6/1-10/15   1P: $55-$65   2P: $60-$80   XP: $5   F3
◆◆   3/1-5/31 & 10/16-2/28   1P: $50-$58   2P: $55-$65   XP: $5   F3
Motel   **Location:** From Hwy 5, exit 170 to downtown; Fraser Ave at Fort St. 860 Fraser Ave V0X 1L0 (PO Box 1396).
Fax: 604/869-3164. **Terms:** 3 day cancellation notice. **Facility:** 13 rooms. Guest rooms offer good, clean, basic
accommodations with some nice decorated touches. 2 stories; exterior corridors. **Dining:** Restaurant nearby.
Cards: AE, MC, VI.

BEST WESTERN HERITAGE INN
(CAA) [SAVE]   7/1-10/15   1P: $99-$109   2P: $109-$119   XP: $10   F12
◆◆◆   5/15-6/30   1P: $99   2P: $109   XP: $10   F12
Motel   3/1-5/14 & 10/16-2/28   1P: $69   2P: $89   XP: $10   F12
     Location: Hwy 5 westbound exit 173; eastbound exit 170, then just n from lights. 570 Old Hope-Princeton Way
V0X 1L0 (PO Box 1787). Fax: 604/869-7106. **Terms:** [CP] meal plan. **Facility:** 26 rooms. Large guest rooms,
pleasantly decorated, with at-door parking. 2 two-bedroom unit, $139-$159; 1-2 stories; exterior corridors; whirlpool.
Dining: Restaurant nearby. **Some Rooms:** 4 efficiencies. **Cards:** AE, DI, DS, MC, VI. **Special Amenities:** Free breakfast and
free local telephone calls.

COLONIAL '900' MOTEL
(CAA) [SAVE]   5/15-10/15   1P: $70-$95   2P: $75-$95   XP: $5
◆◆◆   3/1-5/14 & 10/16-2/28   1P: $52-$70   2P: $55-$75   XP: $5
Motel   **Location:** Westbound from Hwy 5 exit 173; eastbound from Hwy 5 exit 170, 1 km n from lights. 900 Old Hope-
Princeton Way V0X 1L0 (PO Box 849). Fax: 604/869-5228. **Terms:** Cancellation fee imposed. **Facility:** 16
rooms. Excellently maintained property featuring immaculate, clean and spacious guest rooms. Property features a Colonial theme throughout and attractive landscaping. 4 executive-style guest rooms avail. 1 two-bedroom unit. 2 efficiencies & 4 kitchens, $5 extra charge; 1 story; exterior corridors; smoke free premises. **Dining:** Restaurant nearby.
Services: gift shop; winter plug-ins. **All Rooms:** extended cable TV. **Cards:** AE, MC, VI. **Special Amenities:** Free local telephone calls and preferred room (subject to availability with advanced reservations).

INN-TOWNE MOTEL
(CAA) [SAVE]   6/15-9/15   1P: $54-$110   2P: $58-$110   XP: $8   F5
         3/1-6/14   1P: $50-$99   2P: $54-$99   XP: $6   F5
◆◆   9/16-10/31   1P: $50-$97   2P: $54-$99   XP: $6   F5
Motel   11/1-2/28   1P: $44-$90   2P: $52-$90   XP: $6   F5
     Location: From Hwy 5, exit 170, 1 km n to downtown; near the s end of the Fraser River Bridge. 510 Trans-
Canada Hwy V0X 1L0 (PO Box 1037). Fax: 604/869-7222. **Terms:** 7 day cancellation notice; cancellation fee imposed; pets,
$4 extra charge. **Facility:** 26 rooms. A well maintained, older property featuring average sized guest rooms with a pleasant
older style decor. Comfortable walking distance to downtown. 2 suites with whirlpool & gas fireplace; 1-2 stories; exterior corridors; heated pool, sauna, whirlpool. **Dining:** Restaurant nearby. **Recreation:** Fee: tanning bed. **All Rooms:** extended cable
TV. **Some Rooms:** 11 efficiencies, 3 kitchens. **Cards:** AE, DI, MC, VI. **Special Amenities:** Free local telephone calls and
preferred room (subject to availability with advanced reservations).

PARK MOTEL
(CAA) [SAVE]   5/1-10/31   1P: $60-$70   2P: $65-$80   XP: $5   F7
         3/1-4/30   1P: $45-$55   2P: $50-$60
◆◆   11/1-2/28   1P: $45-$55   2P: $50-$60   XP: $3   F7
Motel   **Location:** From Hwy 5, exit 170 to downtown, just n on Wallace St. 832 4th Ave V0X 1L0 (PO Box 1388).
Fax: 604/869-5819. **Facility:** 19 rooms. Located in the heart of downtown. Guest rooms range from above average in the standard rooms to average in the efficiencies. Pleasing guest room decor. 8 two-bedroom units. 3 kitchen units,
$10 extra charge; 1-2 stories; exterior corridors. **Dining:** Restaurant nearby. **Cards:** AE, MC, VI. **Special Amenities:** Early
check-in/late check-out and free room upgrade (subject to availability with advanced reservations).

QUALITY INN
Phone: (604)869-9951

CAA SAVE

◆◆◆
Motel

6/1-9/30	1P: $76	2P: $86	XP: $6	F18
3/1-5/31 & 10/1-2/28	1P: $64-$70	2P: $70-$76	XP: $6	F18

Location: Westbound from Hwy 5 exit 173; eastbound from Hwy 5 exit 170, just n from lights. 350 Old Hope Princeton Way V0X 1L0 (PO Box 353). Fax: 604/869-9421. **Terms:** [CP] meal plan; small pets only, must be attended. **Facility:** 25 rooms. Comfortable, large guest rooms with a pleasant, modern decor. 16 Efficiencies, $6 extra charge; 2 stories; interior corridors; heated pool, sauna, whirlpool. **Dining:** Restaurant nearby. **All Rooms:** extended cable TV. **Cards:** AE, DI, DS, JC, MC, VI. **Special Amenities:** Free breakfast and free local telephone calls.

ROYAL LODGE MOTEL
Phone: (604)869-5358

◆
Motel

5/1-9/30	1P: $55-$60	2P: $60-$65	XP: $5	F12
10/1-10/31	1P: $45-$50	2P: $50-$55	XP: $5	F12
3/1-4/30	1P: $40-$50	2P: $45-$55	XP: $5	F12
11/1-2/28	1P: $35-$40	2P: $40-$45	XP: $5	F12

Location: Westbound from Hwy 5 exit 173; eastbound from Hwy 5 exit 170, just n from lights. 580 Old Hope Princeton Way V0X 1L0 (Box 398). Fax: 604/869-5856. **Facility:** 21 rooms. Good, economy style accommodations featuring clean, average sized guest rooms with a simple decor. 2 stories; exterior corridors. **Some Rooms:** 5 efficiencies. **Cards:** AE, DI, DS, MC, VI.

SKAGIT MOTOR INN
Phone: (604)869-5220

CAA SAVE

◆◆◆
Motel

6/1-9/30	1P: $75-$80	2P: $85-$95	XP: $10	F10
3/1-5/31 & 10/1-2/28	1P: $65-$70	2P: $75-$80	XP: $10	F10

Location: From Hwy 5 exit 170, to downtown; just e of Water Ave. 655 3rd Ave V0X 1L0 (PO Box 908). Fax: 604/869-5856. **Terms:** [CP] meal plan; 3 day cancellation notice. **Facility:** 31 rooms. In quiet residential neighborhood, only blocks from downtown. All guest rooms are ground level with at-door parking. Pleasant guest room decor ranges from modern to slightly older in efficiency units with lots of room to move around in. 3 two-bedroom units. 11 efficiencies, $10 extra charge; 1 story; exterior corridors; whirlpool. **All Rooms:** extended cable TV. **Cards:** AE, DI, MC, VI. **Special Amenities:** Free local telephone calls and free room upgrade (subject to availability with advanced reservations).

SWISS CHALETS
Phone: (604)869-9020

CAA SAVE

◆
Cottage

4/1-10/31	1P: $55	2P: $65	XP: $10	F
3/1-3/31 & 11/1-2/28	1P: $49	2P: $59	XP: $10	F

Location: From Hwy 5, exit 170, 1 km n to downtown, near the s end of the Fraser River Bridge. 456 Trans-Canada Hwy V0X 1L0 (PO Box 997). Fax: 604/869-7588. **Terms:** 5 day cancellation notice; small pets only, $5 extra charge. **Facility:** 24 rooms. Alpine designed chalet style units offering rustic to above average units. Some units with wood or gas fireplace. 1 two-bedroom unit. 8 kitchens, $6-$10 extra charge, for up to 4 persons; 1-2 stories; exterior corridors. **Dining:** Restaurant nearby. **All Rooms:** combo or shower baths, extended cable TV. **Cards:** AE, DI, DS, MC, VI. **Special Amenities:** Free local telephone calls.

WINDSOR MOTEL
Phone: 604/869-9944

◆
Motel

Property failed to provide current rates

Location: From Hwy 5, exit 170 downtown; 3rd Ave at Wallace St. 778 3rd Ave V0X 1L0. Fax: 604/869-9975. **Terms:** Small pets only. **Facility:** 24 rooms. For the budget conscious, guest rooms offer limited decor and older furnishings. In the heart of downtown. 2 stories; interior corridors. **Cards:** AE, MC, VI.

——— RESTAURANTS ———

ALPENHAUS RESTAURANT
Dinner: $8-$17
Phone: 604/869-5714

◆◆
Continental

Location: Downtown Hope, Wallace St at Fraser Ave. 273 Wallace St V0X 1L0. **Hours:** 4 pm-10 pm in winter. Closed: 1/1, 12/25 & Mon in winter. **Reservations:** suggested; in summer. **Features:** cocktails; street parking; a la carte. This Alpine-style restaurant features a German cuisine of schnitzel as well as several Greek and Italian meals as well as a few East Indian dishes. The decor is European and is comfortable, relaxed and casual. The server staff is friendly and attentive. **Cards:** AE, DI, MC, VI.

HOME RESTAURANT
Lunch: $4-$8
Dinner: $7-$12
Phone: 604/869-5558

◆
Canadian

Location: From Hwy 5 exit 173, just n from lights. 665 Old Hope Princeton Way V0X 1L0. **Hours:** 6 am-9 pm; to 11 pm 7/1-8/31. Closed: 12/25. **Features:** children's menu; senior's menu; carryout; beer & wine only; a la carte. You'll enjoy this very popular family-style eatery, which features all your favorites—burgers, meat loaf, club-house sandwiches, mountain-men breakfasts and homemade soups, sauces and pies. Food is king here, and you'll want to come back again and again. **Cards:** MC, VI.

ROLLY'S RESTAURANT
Lunch: $6-$10
Dinner: $6-$12
Phone: 604/869-7448

◆
Canadian

Location: From Hwy 5 exit 170 to downtown; Hudson Bay St. 880 Fraser Ave V0X 1L0. **Hours:** 6 am-9 pm, to 10 pm in summer. Closed: 12/25. **Features:** children's menu; cocktails; a la carte. Rolly's is a great casual, family-dining experience with breakfast served all day. Their home-style cooking menu features chicken teriyaki, halibut, salmon, pasta, Angus beef, fish 'n' chips and more. The open and casual atmosphere is very comfortable. **Cards:** AE, MC, VI.

INVERMERE pop. 2,700

—— LODGING ——

BEST WESTERN INVERMERE INN   Phone: (250)342-9246

(CAA) (SAVE)

5/1-9/30	1P: $125	2P: $140	XP: $10 F12
3/1-4/30 & 10/1-2/28	1P: $95	2P: $110	XP: $10 F12

◆◆◆
Motor Inn
Location: Centre; 3 km w of Hwy 93 and 95 at Invermere exit. 1310 7th Ave V0A 1K0 (PO Box 2340). Fax: 250/342-6079. **Terms:** Check-in 4 pm; cancellation fee imposed. **Facility:** 46 rooms. In centre of picturesque small town. Units are spacious and offer attractive and contemporary decor, creative wrought iron and granite effect furnishings. 3 stories, no elevator; interior corridors; mountain view; exterior hot tub. **Dining:** Restaurant; 7 am-10 pm; hrs vary off season; $11-$17; cocktails. **Services:** winter plug-ins. **All Rooms:** extended cable TV. **Some Rooms:** Fee: VCR. **Cards:** AE, DI, DS, MC, VI. **Special Amenities:** Free local telephone calls.

—— RESTAURANTS ——

THE BLACK FOREST RESTAURANT   Dinner: $13-$24   Phone: 250/342-9417

(CAA)
◆◆
Continental
Location: On Hwy 93 and 95 at jct Invermere Crossroads. #492 Hwy 93 & 95 V0A 1K0. **Hours:** 5 pm-11 pm; to 10 pm off season. **Reservations:** suggested. **Features:** early bird specials; cocktails & lounge; entertainment; a la carte. The Black Forest offers a good selection of schnitzels, wurst, steak and seafood finely prepared with a respect for tradition. Table d'hotes are offered daily. The decor and relaxed ambience are inspired by Europe. This is a local favorite of birders. **Cards:** AE, DI, MC, VI.

MYRTLES ON MAIN RESTAURANT   Lunch: $5-$10   Dinner: $7-$22   Phone: 250/342-0281

◆
American
Location: Centre. 1321 7th Ave V0A 1K0. **Hours:** 11 am-9 pm. Closed: 1/1, 12/25 & 12/26. **Reservations:** suggested. **Features:** children's menu; carryout; cocktails; a la carte. Myrtles is housed in a quaint heritage home built in 1925. Lunch features a nice array of soups, salads, sandwiches and hot entrees. Dinner offers more sophisticated items with several pasta and Continental dishes. It's excellent for the family at lunch. **Cards:** AE, MC, VI.

STRAND'S OLD HOUSE RESTAURANT   Historical   Dinner: $13-$29   Phone: 250/342-6344

◆◆◆
Continental
Location: Centre. 818 12th St V0A 1K0. **Hours:** 5 pm-10 pm; to 10:30 pm in summer. Closed: 12/25. **Reservations:** suggested. **Features:** casual dress; children's menu; early bird specials; health conscious menu; cocktails; a la carte. Strand's Old House features intimate dining in a restored historical house. You'll enjoy the offerings of tuna sashimi, Indonesian seafood linguini, Vietnamese pork tenderloin, steak, lamb and wild game. Order pasta in smaller or full-dinner portions. **Cards:** AE, DI, MC, VI.

ISKUT pop. 300

—— LODGING ——

RED GOAT LODGE   Phone: 250/234-3261

(CAA)
◆◆
Bed & Breakfast

All Year	1P: $65	2P: $85-$95	XP: $10 F12

Location: 5.3 km s on Hwy 37. (Box 101, V0J 1K0). Fax: 250/234-3261. **Terms:** [ECP] meal plan; cancellation fee imposed. **Facility:** 4 rooms. In a remote wilderness area, just steps away from a lake. Property is also the site for a small RV park and separate youth hostel. Guest rooms offer a simple decor with a nice home-like feel. 2 stories; interior corridors; designated smoking area. **Recreation:** Fee: boating, canoeing. **Some Rooms:** combo or shower baths, shared bathrooms. **Cards:** MC, VI.

KAMLOOPS pop. 76,400

—— LODGINGS ——

ABERDEEN INN   Phone: (250)851-0111

(CAA) (SAVE)

5/1-9/30	1P: $75-$85	2P: $95	XP: $10 F8
3/1-4/30 & 10/1-2/28	1P: $55-$60	2P: $65	XP: $10 F8

◆◆◆
Motel
Location: Trans Canada Hwy 1, exit 368. 1860 Rogers Pl V1S 1T7. Fax: 250/851-0380. **Terms:** Cancellation fee imposed; package plans. **Facility:** 63 rooms. Modern property featuring modern style guest rooms. Close to Aberdeen Mall. 8 efficiency units with apartment sized fridge & stove, $10 extra charge; 6 whirlpool rooms, $125-$150; 2 stories; interior corridors; heated pool, sauna, whirlpool. **Dining:** Restaurant nearby. **Services:** winter plug-ins. **All Rooms:** extended cable TV. **Cards:** AE, DI, DS, MC, VI. **Special Amenities:** Early check-in/late check-out and free local telephone calls. (See color ad p 425)

A SUPER VIEW MOTEL   Phone: 250/374-8100

(CAA) (SAVE)

5/1-9/30	1P: $58-$78	2P: $85	XP: $5 F10
3/1-4/30 & 10/1-2/28	1P: $55-$60	2P: $65	XP: $5 F10

◆◆
Motel
Location: Trans Canada Hwy 1 exit 368, then just n. 1200 Rogers Way V1S 1N5. Fax: 250/374-3749. **Terms:** Weekly & monthly rates avail, off season; small pets only, $5 extra charge, in select rooms. **Facility:** 38 rooms. Hilltop location with most rooms offering panoramic views of the city. Guest rooms offer a comfortable yet simple style decor. Close to Aberdeen Mall. 4 whirlpool rooms, $89-$129; 3 stories, no elevator; exterior corridors; heated pool. **Dining:** Restaurant nearby. **All Rooms:** extended cable TV. **Some Rooms:** 16 efficiencies. **Cards:** AE, DI, DS, MC, VI.

BEST WESTERN KAMLOOPS
◆◆◆ All Year
Motor Inn
Phone: (250)828-6660
1P: $122-$250   2P: $137-$250   XP: $15   F14
Location: Trans Canada Hwy 1 exit 368, just n. 1250 Rogers Way V1S 1N5. Fax: 250/828-6698. **Terms:** 3 day cancellation notice; cancellation fee imposed; package plans. **Facility:** 162 rooms. Tropical style atrium area features fountains and small stream. Large older type guest rooms. Choose between an inside unit or outside unit with small patio deck. Close to the Aberdeen Mall. 3 stories; interior corridors; heated pool. **Services:** winter plug-ins. **Cards:** AE, DI, DS, JC, MC, VI.

CASA MARQUIS MOTOR INN
(CAA) (SAVE)
◆
Motel
Phone: (250)372-7761
5/1-9/30   1P: $49-$55   2P: $55-$65   XP: $8   F12
3/1-4/30 & 10/1-2/28   1P: $40-$45   2P: $45-$55   XP: $5   F12
Location: Just n of the corner of 5th Ave and Columbia St downtown; via City Centre. 530 Columbia St V2C 2V1. Fax: 250/374-0455. **Terms:** Weekly rates avail, off season; cancellation fee imposed; small pets only, $5 extra charge. **Facility:** 34 rooms. Good budget-oriented accommodations offering modest guest room decor. Close to downtown, hospital and courthouse. Efficiency units, $8 extra charge; 2 stories; exterior corridors. **Dining:** Restaurant nearby. **Services:** winter plug-ins. **All Rooms:** extended cable TV. **Cards:** AE, DI, MC, VI. **Special Amenities:** Free local telephone calls and free newspaper.

COMFORT INN & SUITES
(CAA) (SAVE)
◆◆◆
Motel
Phone: (250)372-0987
5/1-9/30   1P: $95-$135   2P: $105-$135   XP: $10   F18
3/1-4/30 & 10/1-2/28   1P: $80-$90   2P: $80-$90   XP: $10   F18
Location: Trans Canada Hwy 1 exit 368, Hillside Ave. 1810 Rogers Pl V1S 1T7. Fax: 250/372-0967. **Terms:** [CP] meal plan; weekly & monthly rates avail, off season; package plans. **Facility:** 128 rooms. Hilltop location with some guest rooms offering a fine view of valley. Property offers a modern decor with comfortable guest rooms. Only property with on site waterslide. 17 whirlpool rooms, $169-$180; interior corridors; 2 heated pools, whirlpools. **Dining:** Restaurant nearby. **Some Rooms:** 31 efficiencies. **Cards:** AE, DI, DS, JC, MC, VI. **Special Amenities:** Free breakfast and free local telephone calls.

COURTESY MOTEL
◆◆◆
Motel
Phone: (250)372-8533
6/1-9/30   1P: $58-$68   2P: $67-$77   XP: $10
3/1-5/31 & 10/1-2/28   1P: $52-$64   2P: $54-$74   XP: $10
Location: 2.4 km e on Trans Canada Hwy, s side of service access road. 1773 Trans Canada Hwy E V2C 3Z6. Fax: 250/374-2877. **Terms:** Cancellation fee imposed; package plans; pets, $7 extra charge. **Facility:** 45 rooms. A wonderfully maintained property offering upscale style guest rooms with a pleasant, modern decor; includes a few large family style kitchen units with a separate bedroom area. 2 stories; exterior corridors; heated pool. **Services:** winter plug-ins. **Cards:** AE, DI, DS, MC, VI.

DAYS INN
◆◆
Motor Inn
Phone: (250)374-5911
5/16-9/15   1P: $84-$94   2P: $99-$109   XP: $10   F14
9/16-10/31   1P: $79-$89   2P: $89-$99   XP: $10   F14
3/1-5/15 & 11/1-2/28   1P: $74-$84   2P: $84-$94   XP: $10   F14
Location: Trans Canada Hwy 1 exit 368, just s. 1285 Trans Canada Hwy W V2E 2J7. Fax: 250/374-6922. **Terms:** Cancellation fee imposed; package plans; pets, $10 extra charge, $40 dep req. **Facility:** 62 rooms. Hilltop location with some rooms offering views of the city. Guest rooms are good size with a comfortable decor. Located close to Aberdeen Mall. 3 stories; interior corridors; heated pool. **Cards:** AE, DI, JC, MC, VI.

DREAM LODGE
◆◆
Motel
Phone: (250)314-9889
5/16-9/15   1P: $70-$75   2P: $75-$90   XP: $10   F10
3/1-5/15 & 9/16-2/28   1P: $65-$70   2P: $75-$90   XP: $10   F10
Location: Trans Canada Hwy 1, exit 368 then just n. 1855 Rogers Pl V1S 1N5. Fax: 250/314-0599. **Terms:** Small pets only. **Facility:** 40 rooms. 1 two-bedroom unit. 3 stories; interior corridors; heated pool. **Some Rooms:** 22 efficiencies. **Cards:** AE, MC, VI.

FOUNTAIN MOTEL

Phone: (250)374-4451

6/1-9/30	1P: $52-$56	2P: $58-$68	XP: $5	F11
3/1-5/31 & 10/1-2/28	1P: $40-$46	2P: $46-$56	XP: $5	F11

CAA SAVE
◆
Motel

Location: Corner of 5th Ave and Columbia St downtown; via City Centre. 506 Columbia St V2C 2V1. **Fax:** 250/374-2469. **Terms:** Weekly rates avail, off season; 3 day cancellation notice; cancellation fee imposed; pets, $5 extra charge. **Facility:** 19 rooms. Good, budget oriented property offering clean, cozy average sized guest rooms. Close to downtown and hospital, across from court house. Efficiencies, $8 extra charge; 2 stories; exterior corridors. **Dining:** Restaurant nearby. **Services:** winter plug-ins. **All Rooms:** extended cable TV. **Some Rooms:** Fee: microwaves. **Cards:** AE, MC, VI. **Special Amenities:** Free local telephone calls and preferred room (subject to availability with advanced reservations).

FOUR POINTS HOTEL SHERATON

Phone: (250)374-4144

5/16-10/10	1P: $160-$173	2P: $160-$173	XP: $15	F15
3/1-5/15 & 10/11-2/28	1P: $152-$164	2P: $152-$164	XP: $15	F15

CAA SAVE
◆ ◆ ◆
Hotel

Location: Trans Canada Hwy 1 exit 368, then just n. 1175 Rogers Way V1S 1R5. **Fax:** 250/374-0449. **Terms:** 14 day cancellation notice. **Facility:** 78 rooms. Kamloops newest property geared for the business traveller or simply for a very comfortable overnight stop. On a hillside with many rooms offering splendid views. Efficiency units, $20 extra charge; 6 whirlpool rooms, $200-$209; 4 stories; interior corridors; heated pool, sauna, waterslide, whirlpool. **All Rooms:** extended cable TV. **Some Rooms:** 40 efficiencies. **Cards:** AE, DI, DS, MC, VI. **Special Amenities:** Early check-in/late check-out and free newspaper.

GRANDVIEW MOTEL

Phone: (250)372-1312

6/15-9/30	1P: $66	2P: $71-$81	XP: $10	F18
4/1-6/14	1P: $55	2P: $60-$70	XP: $5	F18
3/1-3/31	1P: $49	2P: $53-$60	XP: $5	F18
10/1-2/28	1P: $47	2P: $52-$57	XP: $5	F18

CAA SAVE
◆ ◆
Motel

Location: Trans Canada Hwy 1, exit 369 2 km n on Columbia St, or exit 370 Summit Dr to Columbia St, via City Centre Rt. 463 Grandview Terr V2C 3Z3. **Fax:** 250/372-0847. **Terms:** Weekly rates avail, off season; small pets only, $5 extra charge. **Facility:** 26 rooms. Family owned and operated, this established property offers a quiet, hilltop location with comfortable guest rooms. Shaded picnic area with gas barbecue. 2 stories; exterior corridors; heated pool. **Dining:** Restaurant nearby. **Services:** winter plug-ins. **All Rooms:** extended cable TV. **Some Rooms:** 6 efficiencies. **Cards:** AE, DI, MC, VI. **Special Amenities:** Free local telephone calls and free newspaper. *(See color ad below)*

HOLIDAY INN EXPRESS KAMLOOPS

Phone: (250)372-3474

7/1-9/30	1P: $114-$124	2P: $121-$131	XP: $7	F18
4/15-6/30	1P: $106-$116	2P: $113-$123	XP: $7	F18
3/1-4/14 & 10/1-2/28	1P: $95-$105	2P: $102-$112	XP: $7	F18

CAA SAVE
◆ ◆ ◆
Motel

Location: Trans Canada Hwy 1 exit 367, Pacific Way. 1550 Versatile Dr V1S 1X4. **Fax:** 250/372-1585. **Terms:** [CP] meal plan; package plans. **Facility:** 82 rooms. Very pleasant, well maintained property featuring lovely Santa Fe style decor in the public areas as well as the guest rooms. Executive level rooms avail on top floor. Whirlpool suite with gas fireplace, $155-$185 for up to 2 persons; 4 stories; interior corridors; heated pool, whirlpool. **Dining:** Restaurant nearby. **Services:** winter plug-ins. **All Rooms:** extended cable TV. **Cards:** AE, DI, DS, JC, MC, VI. **Special Amenities:** Free breakfast and free local telephone calls.

HOSPITALITY INN

Phone: (250)374-4164

7/1-9/30	1P: $72-$79	2P: $77-$84	XP: $7	F12
5/16-6/30	1P: $66-$73	2P: $72-$79	XP: $7	F12
3/1-5/15	1P: $62-$69	2P: $67-$74	XP: $7	F12
10/1-2/28	1P: $57-$64	2P: $62-$69	XP: $7	F12

CAA SAVE
◆ ◆ ◆
Motor Inn

Location: Trans Canada Hwy 1, eastbound exit 369 2 km n on Columbia St; westbound exit 370 Summit Dr to Columbia St, via City Centre Rt. 500 W Columbia St V2C 1K6. **Fax:** 250/374-6971. **Terms:** Weekly & monthly rates avail, off season; package plans; small pets only, $10 extra charge. **Facility:** 77 rooms. On hilltop with many rooms offering a fine panoramic view of the city and the valley; some rooms do have a restricted view. Close to Sahali Centre Mall. 14 efficiencies, $7 extra charge; 2 stories; exterior corridors; heated pool, sauna, whirlpool. **Dining:** Restaurant; 7 am-10 pm; $8-$17; cocktails. **Services:** winter plug-ins. **All Rooms:** extended cable TV. **Cards:** AE, DI, DS, MC, VI. **Special Amenities:** Free local telephone calls and preferred room (subject to availability with advanced reservations).

KAMLOOPS SUPER 8 MOTEL
◆◆   6/1-9/15   1P: $80   2P: $90   Phone: (250)374-8688
Motel   4/16-5/31   1P: $60   2P: $70   XP: $6   F12
         9/16-2/28   1P: $50   2P: $70   XP: $6   F12
         3/1-4/15   1P: $50   2P: $60   XP: $6   F12
Location: Trans Canada Hwy 1 exit 367 Pacific Way. 1521 Hugh Allan Dr V1S 1P4. Fax: 250/374-8688. **Terms:** [CP] meal plan; pets, with permission. **Facility:** 47 rooms. A solid, budget style accommodation. Guest rooms offer a comfortable style decor, for those looking for a nice, simple style motel. 2 stories; interior corridors. **Cards:** AE, CB, DI, DS, JC, MC, VI.

KAMLOOPS TRAVELODGE
Phone: (250)372-8202
(CAA) (SAVE)   5/1-9/30   1P: $76-$89   2P: $84-$99   XP: $3   F17
         3/1-4/30   1P: $57-$64   2P: $62-$74   XP: $5   F17
◆◆   10/1-2/28   1P: $57-$64   2P: $57-$64   XP: $5   F17
Motor Inn   **Location:** Corner of 4th Ave and Columbia St downtown; via City Centre. 430 Columbia St V2C 2T5. Fax: 250/372-1459. **Terms:** Cancellation fee imposed; package plans; small pets only. **Facility:** 68 rooms. Features 2 separate buildings with 1 section located across the street. Pleasantly decorated rooms with an inviting sauna/whirlpool area. Close to downtown, hospital and court house. 9 two-bedroom units. 2 stories; exterior corridors; heated pool. **Dining:** Restaurant; 6:30 am-9 pm; $6-$14; cocktails. **Services:** winter plug-ins. **All Rooms:** combo or shower baths, extended cable TV. **Cards:** AE, DI, JC, MC, VI. **Special Amenities: Free local telephone calls and free newspaper.**

KAMLOOPS TRAVELODGE MOUNTVIEW
Phone: 250/374-4788
(CAA) (SAVE)   5/1-9/30   1P: $85-$95   2P: $90-$100   XP: $6   F17
◆◆◆   3/1-4/30 & 10/1-2/28   1P: $65-$75   2P: $70-$80   XP: $6   F17
Motel   **Location:** Trans Canada Hwy 1 exit 368. 1225 Rogers Way V1S 1R9. Fax: 250/374-4017. **Terms:** Package plans. **Facility:** 53 rooms. An up-to-date property offering 2 styles of guest rooms; from pleasant, average style standard rooms to executive style units featuring a larger work station and more amenities. A few units feature a murphy bed. 1 two-bedroom unit. 7 family suites, $15-$30 extra charge; 20 efficiency units, $6-$10 extra charge; 2 whirlpool rooms, $130-$150; 3 stories; exterior corridors; heated pool, whirlpool. **Dining:** Restaurant nearby. **All Rooms:** extended cable TV. **Cards:** AE, CB, DI, DS, JC, MC, VI. *(See color ad below)*

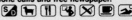

LAMPLIGHTER MOTEL
Phone: (250)372-3386
(CAA) (SAVE)   All Year   1P: $40-$62   2P: $48-$70   XP: $5
◆   **Location:** 3.2 km e on Trans Canada Hwy 1, s side of service access road. 1901 Trans Canada Hwy E V2C 3Z9. Fax: 250/372-8740. **Terms:** Cancellation fee imposed; small pets only, $5 extra charge. **Facility:** 31 rooms. Standard style motel type property offering comfortable guest rooms with at-door parking. Several restaurants within walking or driving distance. 1 story; exterior corridors; sauna, whirlpool. **Services:** winter plug-ins. **All Rooms:** extended cable TV. **Some Rooms:** efficiency, 2 kitchens. **Cards:** AE, DI, DS, JC, MC, VI. **Special Amenities: Early check-in/late check-out and free local telephone calls.**

MAVERICK MOTOR INN
Phone: (250)374-9666
◆◆   5/1-9/30   1P: $89-$99   2P: $99-$109   XP: $10   F16
Motor Inn   3/1-4/30 & 10/1-2/28   1P: $69-$79   2P: $79-$89   XP: $10   F16
         Location: Trans Canada Hwy 1, exit 368. 1250 W Trans Canada Hwy V2C 6R3. Fax: 250/374-5645. **Facility:** 42 rooms. A nice economy style lodging with rooms that face away from hwy offering some wonderful views of the valley. 2 stories; interior corridors; heated pool. **All Rooms:** honor bars. **Some Rooms:** 5 efficiencies. **Cards:** AE, DI, DS, JC, MC, VI.

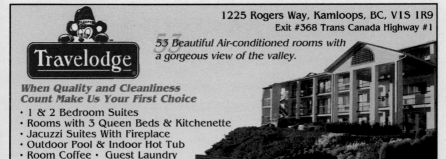

RAMADA INN-KAMLOOPS
CAA SAVE
◆◆◆
Motor Inn

6/1-9/30	1P: $99-$109	2P: $109-$129	XP: $10	F16
3/1-5/31 & 10/1-2/28	1P: $69-$99	2P: $79-$99	XP: $10	F16

Phone: (250)374-0358

Location: Trans Canada Hwy 1, exit 369 2 km n on Columbia St; or exit 370 Summit Dr to Columbia St, via City Centre Rt. 555 W Columbia St V2C 1K7. Fax: 250/374-0691. **Terms:** Weekly & monthly rates avail, off season; package plans. **Facility:** 90 rooms. Hilltop location with many guest rooms offering a fine panoramic view of the city and valley. Some rooms do have a restricted view. Close to Sahali Centre Mall. 8 efficiencies, $10 extra charge; 2-3 stories; interior/exterior corridors; heated pool, sauna, whirlpool. **Dining:** Restaurant; 6:30 am-10:30 & 5-10 pm; $9-$18; cocktails. **Services:** winter plug-ins. **All Rooms:** extended cable TV. **Some Rooms:** Fee: VCR. **Cards:** AE, DI, JC, MC, VI. **Special Amenities:** Free newspaper and free room upgrade (subject to availability with advanced reservations). *(See color ad below)*

RANCHLAND MOTEL
◆◆
Motel

5/16-2/28	1P: $38-$59	2P: $42-$63	XP: $4	F5
3/1-5/15	1P: $42-$52	2P: $46-$56	XP: $4	F5

Phone: (250)828-8787

Location: 4.5 km e on Trans Canada Hwy 1 exit River Rd, then just w along service access road. 2357 Trans-Canada Hwy E V2C 4A8. Fax: 250/828-8786. **Terms:** Pets. **Facility:** 36 rooms. A beautifully maintained property featuring very pleasant guest rooms with a bright, clean decor. 2 stories; exterior corridors. **Services:** winter plug-ins. **Cards:** AE, MC, VI.

STAY'N SAVE INNS
CAA SAVE
◆◆◆
Motel

7/1-9/30	1P: $109-$119	2P: $119-$129	XP: $10	F16
5/1-6/30	1P: $99-$109	2P: $109-$119	XP: $10	F16
3/1-4/30 & 10/1-2/28	1P: $79-$89	2P: $89-$99	XP: $10	F16

Phone: (250)374-8877

Location: Trans Canada Hwy 1, exit 369 Columbia St at Notre Dame Dr; or Summit Dr, exit 370 at Notre Dame Dr. 1325 Columbia St W V2C 6P4. Fax: 250/372-0507. **Terms:** Weekly rates avail; cancellation fee imposed; package plans; small pets only, in selected rooms. **Facility:** 83 rooms. Fine accommodations, featuring large guest rooms with a pleasant, modern decor. Some of the efficiency units feature a separate bedroom area. Efficiencies, $10 extra charge; 3 stories; exterior corridors; heated pool, sauna, whirlpool. **Dining:** Restaurant nearby. **Services:** winter plug-ins. **All Rooms:** extended cable TV. **Cards:** AE, DI, MC, VI. **Special Amenities:** Free local telephone calls and free newspaper. *(See color ad p 431 & p 540)*

THE THOMPSON HOTEL & CONFERENCE CENTRE   Phone: (250)374-1999
◆◆   5/1-9/30   1P: $82-$92   2P: $108-$118   XP: $10   F18
Motor Inn   3/1-4/30 & 10/1-2/28   1P: $67-$87   2P: $77-$97   XP: $10   F18
          Location: Downtown, at 6th Ave. 650 Victoria St V2C 2B4. Fax: 250/374-9997. **Terms:** Cancellation fee imposed; package plans; pets. **Facility:** 99 rooms. Attractive accommodations in the heart of downtown. Comfortable, guest rooms; all with pleasant, simple decor and colors. 1 blk from downtown casino. 3 stories, no elevator; interior corridors; heated pool. **Services:** winter plug-ins. **Cards:** AE, DI, DS, MC, VI.

THRIFT INN   Phone: (250)374-2488
ⒸⒶⒶ   5/20-10/8   1P: $37-$43   2P: $39-$50   XP: $2   F6
            3/1-5/19   1P: $27-$33   2P: $29-$38   XP: $2   F6
◆   10/9-2/28   1P: $28   2P: $30-$32   XP: $5   F6
Motel   **Location:** 4.8 km e on Trans Canada Hwy 1, just e of jct River Rd along service access road, follow signs. 2459 Trans Canada Hwy E V2C 4A9. Fax: 250/374-2488. **Terms:** [CP] meal plan; small pets only. **Facility:** 66 rooms. An older, no frills motel offering basic budget oriented accomodations. Guest rooms are average in size with an older, modest room decor. Located on the s side of hwy. 2 stories; exterior corridors; heated pool. **Dining:** Restaurant nearby. **All Rooms:** extended cable TV. **Cards:** MC, VI. *(See color ad p 428)*

──────── **RESTAURANTS** ────────

CHAPTERS VIEWPOINT   Lunch: $4-$15   Dinner: $11-$39   Phone: 250/374-3224
◆◆   **Location:** Trans Canada Hwy 1, exit 369 2 km n on Columbia St, or exit 370 Summit Dr to Columbia St via
Canadian   City Centre Rt; in Panorama Inn. 610 W Columbia St V2C 1L1. **Hours:** 7 am-10 pm. Closed: 12/25 & 12/26. **Reservations:** suggested. **Features:** cocktails; a la carte. This restaurant's great location offers a spectacular view of the city and surrounding hills. The well-prepared menu features New Mexican cuisine, Alberta beef and prime rib. The decor is Pacific Northwest and makes use of the Douglas fir for beams. **Cards:** AE, MC, VI.

MISTRAL GRILL & TAPA BAR   Lunch: $6-$10   Dinner: $11-$20   Phone: 250/376-1277
◆◆   **Location:** 2 km nw on Tranquille Rd via the Overlander Bridge. 227 Tranquille Rd V2B 3G2. **Hours:** 11
German   am-11 pm, Sat from 4 pm. Closed: 12/25. **Reservations:** suggested. **Features:** cocktails; a la carte. The Mistral features casual dining in pleasant surroundings with many authentic Greek dishes such as roast lamb and souvlakia as well as steak, seafood and prime rib dishes. The tapa bar is a lounge-type area, but food is served here also. **Cards:** AE, MC, VI.

ORIENTAL GARDENS RESTAURANT   Lunch: $5-$10   Dinner: $10-$20   Phone: 250/372-2344
◆◆   **Location:** Victoria St at 5th Ave, downtown. 545 Victoria St V2C 2B1. **Hours:** Noon-2:30 pm & 5 pm-11 pm,
Ethnic   Fri & Sat-midnight. **Reservations:** suggested. **Features:** cocktails; a la carte. Delicious Japanese and Chinese entrees are featured at this restaurant, where a full sushi bar and Japanese-style private dining booths are also offered. If you park in the lot to the side, ask the restaurant staff to validate your ticket stub. **Cards:** AE, MC, VI.

KELOWNA pop. 89,400

──────── **LODGINGS** ────────

BEST WESTERN INN-KELOWNA   Phone: (250)860-1212
ⒸⒶⒶ SAVE   5/1-9/30   1P: $119-$159   2P: $129-$159   XP: $10   F17
◆◆◆   3/1-4/30 & 10/1-2/28   1P: $89-$129   2P: $99-$139   XP: $10   F17
Motor Inn   **Location:** 1 km s of jct Hwy 33 and 97 N, corner of Leckie Rd. 2402 Hwy 97 N V1X 4J1. Fax: 250/860-0675. **Terms:** Weekly rates avail, off season; package plans; pets, extra charge, in smoking rooms. **Facility:** 99 rooms. Large, expansive property featuring well manicured courtyard area, next door to Central Park golf course. Large, modern and well maintained guest rooms. All rooms with balcony facing beautiful pool and courtyard. 2 whirlpool rooms, $149-$249; 2 stories; interior/exterior corridors; heated pool, heated outdoor pool & whirlpool enclosed in winter; 1 tennis court. **Dining:** Restaurant; 7 am-10 pm; $5-$15; cocktails. **Recreation:** Fee: in-room video games. **All Rooms:** combo or shower baths, extended cable TV. **Cards:** AE, CB, DI, DS, MC, VI. **Special Amenities:** Free local telephone calls and free newspaper.

BIG WHITE MOTOR LODGE   Phone: (250)860-3982
ⒸⒶⒶ SAVE   6/14-9/6   1P: $83   2P: $106   XP: $10   F12
            9/7-2/28   1P: $59-$71   2P: $76-$87   XP: $10   F12
◆◆   5/1-6/13   1P: $71   2P: $87   XP: $10   F12
Motel   3/1-4/30   1P: $59   2P: $76   XP: $10   F12
          Location: From Hwy 97 N (Harvey Ave) just w on Spall Rd, follow signs. 1891 Parkinson Way V1Y 7V6. Fax: 250/860-1095. **Terms:** Package plans; pets, $10 extra charge, must be registered. **Facility:** 50 rooms. Close to Spall Shopping Plaza and Kelowna Rec Centre. Featuring a pleasant little courtyard area with tables and barbecue. Excellently maintained guest rooms featuring a cozy decor; just like home. 8 two-bedroom units; 1 three-bedroom kitchen unit; 2 stories; exterior corridors; heated pool, sauna, whirlpool. **Dining:** Restaurant nearby. **All Rooms:** extended cable TV. **Some Rooms:** 13 efficiencies, 20 kitchens. **Cards:** AE, DI, MC, VI. **Special Amenities:** Free local telephone calls.

COMFORT INN   Phone: (250)769-2355
ⒸⒶⒶ SAVE   7/1-9/15   1P: $110-$130   2P: $115-$135   XP: $5   F18
            5/1-6/30   1P: $95-$115   2P: $100-$120   XP: $5   F18
◆◆   3/1-4/30 & 9/16-2/28   1P: $80-$100   2P: $85-$105   XP: $5   F18
Motor Inn   **Location:** Jct Hwy 97 and Bartley Rd, s to Ross Rd. 1655 Westgate Rd V1Z 3P1. Fax: 250/769-2370. **Terms:** [CP] meal plan; 3 day cancellation notice; package plans. **Facility:** 80 rooms. On the west side of Kelowna, this pleasant but simple property offers average sized guest rooms with a basic style decor. 1 two-bedroom unit. 6 whirlpool rooms; 2 stories; interior corridors; heated pool, whirlpool. **Dining:** Restaurant; 11:30 am-9 pm, Fri & Sat-10 pm; $6-$16; cocktails. **Some Rooms:** 25 efficiencies. **Cards:** AE, DI, DS, MC, VI.

DILWORTH MOTOR LODGE

Phone: 250/762-9666

6/16-9/15	1P: $89	2P: $89-$98	XP: $10	F
3/1-6/15 & 9/16-10/10	1P: $62	2P: $62-$68	XP: $10	F
10/11-2/28	1P: $55	2P: $62	XP: $10	F

(CAA)
◆ ◆
Motel

Location: Hwy 97 N (Harvey Ave), just w. 1755 Dilworth Dr V1Y 8R1. **Fax:** 250/862-8484. **Facility:** 48 rooms. Just behind the White Spot Restaurant. Wonderfully maintained and family run mature property featuring nice, large guest rooms that are meticulously clean and very well maintained. Close to Orchard Park Mall. 2 kitchens & 9 efficiencies, $6 extra charge; 3 stories, no elevator; interior corridors; heated pool, sauna, whirlpool, sundecks. **Dining:** Restaurant nearby. **All Rooms:** extended cable TV. **Cards:** AE, DI, MC, VI.

THE GRAPEVINE BED & BREAKFAST

Phone: (250)860-5580

◆ ◆ ◆
Bed &
Breakfast

5/1-10/15	1P: $85-$95	2P: $85-$95	XP: $20
3/1-4/30 & 10/16-2/28	1P: $75-$85	2P: $75-$85	XP: $20

Location: Hwy 97 N (Harvey Ave), 4 km w on Dilworth Dr, then just n. 2621 Longhill Rd V1V 2G5. **Fax:** 250/860-5586. **Terms:** [BP] meal plan; age restrictions may apply; check-in 4 pm; 7 day cancellation notice; package plans. **Facility:** 4 rooms. Country charm close to the city. Surrounded by orchard trees, this exceptional home features cozy guest rooms, lovingly decorated. Guests advised that this is a "no-shoes" home. 2 stories; interior corridors; designated smoking area. **All Rooms:** combo or shower baths. **Cards:** AE, DI, MC, VI.

HOLIDAY INN EXPRESS KELOWNA

Phone: (250)763-0500

◆ ◆ ◆
Motor Inn

6/2-9/30	1P: $129-$139	2P: $129-$139	XP: $10	F19
4/7-6/1	1P: $99-$114	2P: $99-$114	XP: $10	F19
3/1-4/6 & 10/1-2/28	1P: $89-$99	2P: $89-$99	XP: $10	F19

Location: 1 km s of jct Hwy 97 N and 33. 2429 Hwy 97 N V1X 4J2. **Fax:** 250/763-7555. **Terms:** [CP] meal plan; check-in 4 pm; package plans. **Facility:** 120 rooms. An excellently maintained property featuring large guest rooms, all with a pleasant modern style decor. Across the street from Central Park Golf Course. 4 stories; interior corridors; heated pool. **Cards:** AE, CB, DI, DS, JC, MC, VI.

KELOWNA MOTOR INN

Phone: (250)762-2533

(CAA) (SAVE)
◆ ◆
Motel

5/1-9/30	1P: $85-$95	2P: $89-$99	XP: $10	D18
3/1-4/30 & 10/1-2/28	1P: $59-$65	2P: $65-$75	XP: $10	D18

Location: Corner of Hwy 97 N (Harvey Ave) and Gordon Dr. 1070 Harvey Ave V1Y 8S4. **Fax:** 250/868-3874. **Terms:** Weekly & monthly rates avail, off season; 48 day cancellation notice; package plans. **Facility:** 50 rooms. Located close to Capri Mall. This wonderful property features cozy guest rooms ranging from standard units to larger efficiency units; some with a separate bedroom. Meticulous housekeeping, all with pleasant decor. 4 two-bedroom units. 17 efficiencies, $10 extra charge; whirlpool room, suites, $145-$165; 2 stories; exterior corridors; heated pool, steamroom, whirlpool. **Dining:** Restaurant nearby. **All Rooms:** extended cable TV. **Some Rooms:** Fee: VCR. **Cards:** AE, DI, DS, MC, VI. **Special Amenities:** Free local telephone calls.

LAKE OKANAGAN RESORT

Phone: (250)769-3511

◆ ◆
Resort

6/16-9/16	1P: $170-$199	2P: $170-$199
3/1-6/15 & 9/17-11/1	1P: $120-$140	2P: $120-$140
11/2-2/28	1P: $75-$85	2P: $75-$85

Location: 2.5 km sw on Hwy 97, 17 km nw on Westside Rd (narrow winding road), follow signs. 2751 Westside Rd V1Z 3T1. **Fax:** 250/769-6665. **Terms:** Check-in 4 pm; 14 day cancellation notice; cancellation fee imposed; package plans. **Facility:** 125 rooms. Along the shores of Okanagan Lake, this older resort complex features a mixture of room styles and sizes, many have views of lake or golf course. Quiet, peaceful setting. 3-6 stories; interior/exterior corridors; 3 heated pools; 7 tennis courts (3 lighted); marina; playground. **Services:** gift shop. **Recreation:** swimming, fishing; hiking trails, jogging. Fee: boating, waterskiing; bicycles, horseback riding. Rental: paddleboats. **Some Rooms:** 27 efficiencies, 98 kitchens. Fee: VCR. **Cards:** AE, DI, MC, VI.

OTELLA'S GUEST HOUSE

Phone: 250/763-4922

◆ ◆
Bed &
Breakfast

5/1-10/15	1P: $75-$115	2P: $85-$125	XP: $25
3/1-4/30 & 10/16-2/28	1P: $70-$105	2P: $80-$115	XP: $25

Location: From Hwy 97 (Harvey Ave), 2 km n on Spall Rd/Glenmore Rd, just w on High Rd, just n on Clifton Rd, just ne on Caramillo, then just n. 42 Altura Rd V1V 1B6. **Fax:** 250/763-4982. **Terms:** [BP] meal plan; age restrictions may apply; 10 day cancellation notice; cancellation fee imposed; package plans. **Facility:** 4 rooms. This Alpine style home is nestled in a park-like setting with lovely views of the valley and surrounding mountains. Various patios and extensive garden add to the residential home like setting. This is a no-shoes house. 2 stories; interior corridors; smoke free premises. **Some Rooms:** combo or shower baths, shared bathrooms, color TV. **Cards:** MC, VI.

PANDOSY INN

Phone: (250)762-5858

(CAA)
◆ ◆
Motel

Property failed to provide current rates

Location: From Hwy 97 N, 3 km s on Pandosy St which becomes Lakeshore Rd. 3327 Lakeshore Rd V1W 3S9. **Fax:** 250/762-6664. **Terms:** Weekly & monthly rates avail, off season; 7 day cancellation notice, 6/30-9/6; cancellation fee imposed; small pets only, $10 extra charge, with prior notice. **Facility:** 60 rooms. A nicely maintained property featuring kitchen and separate bedroom. Guest rooms are very clean with a modest style decor. Located across from Gyro Beach Park. 2 stories; exterior corridors; heated pool, whirlpool. **Dining:** Restaurant nearby. **All Rooms:** extended cable TV. **Cards:** AE, DI, MC, VI.

RAMADA LODGE HOTEL

Phone: (250)860-9711

◆ ◆
Motor Inn

Property failed to provide current rates

Location: Hwy 97 N (Harvey Ave) at Dilworth Dr. 2170 Harvey Ave V1Y 6G8. **Fax:** 250/860-3173. **Terms:** Check-in 4 pm; package plans; small pets only, $10 extra charge. **Facility:** 135 rooms. Across from Orchard Park Mall. Property features 3 different sections with all guest rooms nicely appointed and quite spacious. 3 stories; interior/exterior corridors; heated pool. **Services:** gift shop. **Cards:** AE, DI, DS, MC, VI.

Before you hit the open road, tear along the dotted line!

**Save $5.00 off the CAA/AAA room rate.
See back for participating hotels.**

Holiday Inn
HOTELS · RESORTS

1-800-HOLIDAY
www.holiday-inn.com

**Save $5.00 off the CAA/AAA room rate.
See back for participating hotels.**

Holiday Inn
HOTELS · RESORTS

1-800-HOLIDAY
www.holiday-inn.com

Save $5.00 off the CAA/AAA room rate. See back for participating hotels.

Holiday Inn
EXPRESS

Stay Smart℠

1-800-HOLIDAY
www.hiexpress.com

 **TourBookMark**

Lodging Listing Symbols

Member Values

- Official Appointment
- Offers minimum 10% discount
- SYC&S chain partners
- May offer discount
- Offers senior discount
- Informational listing only

Member Services

- Airport transportation
- Pets allowed
- Restaurant on premises
- Restaurant off premises (walking distance)
- 24-hour room service
- Cocktail lounge

Special Features

- Business services
- Valet parking
- Laundry service
- Child care
- Fully accessible
- Semi-accessible
- Roll-in showers
- Hearing impaired

In-Room Amenities

- Non-smoking rooms
- No air conditioning
- No telephones
- No cable TV
- Movies
- VCR
- Radio
- Coffee maker
- Microwave
- Refrigerator
- Data port/modem line

Sports/Recreation

- Outdoor pool
- Indoor Pool
- Indoor/outdoor pool
- Fitness center
- Recreational facilities

Call property for detailed information about fees & restrictions relating to the lodging listing symbols.

Lodging Reservation and Deposit Definitions

Reservation:

A temporary hold on lodgings, usually until 4 or 6 p.m. on the arrival date.

Reservation Confirmation:

Once the reservation process is complete, a "confirmation number" is assigned to the guest for future reference. When ample notice is given, a copy of the reservation details and confirmation number is mailed to the guest.

Credit Card Guaranteed Reservation:

When reserved lodgings have been secured with a credit card number, the room will be held for the first night regardless of arrival time, but will be billed to the credit card if the guest fails to arrive at all (is a "no show"). Credit card guarantees usually pertain to the first night only.

Reservation Deposit:

These funds are collected from the guest in advance of arrival to secure reserved lodgings. A reservation deposit can be in the form of cash, check, money order, credit card transaction or other means to transfer funds. One or more days' payment may be required depending on the length of the stay.

Prepaid Reservation:

Reserved lodgings that are fully paid in advance of arrival.

Cancellation Policy:

Published terms/conditions set by lodging by which the guest can cancel a reservation and recover all, or a portion of, the deposit/full payment. Sometimes a "service charge" or "cancellation fee" is levied regardless of how far in advance the reservation was cancelled.

Cancellation Number:

Upon receipt of a cancellation, it is customary for lodgings to assign a "cancellation number" that is given to the caller for future reference.

For reservations call
1-800-HOLIDAY
your travel professional or the hotel direct.

Holiday Inn HOTELS · RESORTS

ALBERTA	
Calgary-Airport	403-230-1999
Calgary-Downtown	403-266-4611
Calgary-Macleod Trail South	403-287-2700
Convention Centre (S.E. Edmonton)	780-468-5400
Edmonton-The Palace	780-438-1222
Red Deer	403-342-6567

BRITISH COLUMBIA	
Chilliwack - Downtown	604-795-4788
Osoyoos	250-495-7223
Vancouver-Airport	604-821-1818
Vancouver-Centre (Broadway)	604-879-0511
Vancouver-Coquitlam	604-931-4433
Vancouver-Downtown	604-684-2151
Vancouver-Metrotown (Burnaby)	604-438-1881

MANITOBA	
Winnipeg Airport/West	204-885-4478
Winnipeg-South	204-452-4747

NEW BRUNSWICK	
Fredericton	506-363-5111

NEWFOUNDLAND	
Corner Brook	709-634-5381
St. John's	709-722-0506

NOVA SCOTIA	
Halifax-Centre	902-423-1161
Halifax-Harbourview	902-463-1100

ONTARIO	
Barrie	705-728-6191
Burlington	905-639-4443
Fort Erie	905-871-8333
Guelph	519-836-0231
Kingston-Waterfront	613-549-8400
Kitchener-Waterloo	519-893-1211
Oakville-Centre	905-842-5000
Sault Ste. Marie-Waterfront	705-949-0611
St. Catharines	905-934-8000
Toronto On King (Downtown)	416-599-4000
Toronto-Airport	416-675-7611
Toronto-Airport East	416-240-7511
Toronto-Brampton	905-792-9900
Toronto-Markham	905-474-0444
Toronto-Mississauga	905-855-2000
Toronto-West	905-890-5700
Trenton	613-394-4855
Windsor (Ambassador Bridge)	519-966-1200

QUEBEC	
Hull - Ottawa Plaza La Chaudière	819-778-3880
Montreal-Airport	514-739-3391
Montreal-Centre Ville (Dwntwn/Conv. Ctr)	514-878-9888
Montreal-Longueuil	450-646-8100
Montreal-Midtown	514-842-6111
Montreal-Pointe-Claire	514-697-7110
Quebec City-Sainte-Foy	418-653-4901
Saguenay Convention Centre	418-548-3124

Holiday Inn HOTELS · RESORTS

ALBERTA	
Calgary-Airport	403-230-1999
Calgary-Downtown	403-266-4611
Calgary-Macleod Trail South	403-287-2700
Convention Centre (S.E. Edmonton)	780-468-5400
Edmonton-The Palace	780-438-1222
Red Deer	403-342-6567

BRITISH COLUMBIA	
Chilliwack - Downtown	604-795-4788
Osoyoos	250-495-7223
Vancouver-Airport	604-821-1818
Vancouver-Centre (Broadway)	604-879-0511
Vancouver-Coquitlam	604-931-4433
Vancouver-Downtown	604-684-2151
Vancouver-Metrotown (Burnaby)	604-438-1881

MANITOBA	
Winnipeg Airport/West	204-885-4478
Winnipeg-South	204-452-4747

NEW BRUNSWICK	
Fredericton	506-363-5111

NEWFOUNDLAND	
Corner Brook	709-634-5381
St. John's	709-722-0506

NOVA SCOTIA	
Halifax-Centre	902-423-1161
Halifax-Harbourview	902-463-1100

ONTARIO	
Barrie	705-728-6191
Burlington	905-639-4443
Fort Erie	905-871-8333
Guelph	519-836-0231
Kingston-Waterfront	613-549-8400
Kitchener-Waterloo	519-893-1211
Oakville-Centre	905-842-5000
Sault Ste. Marie-Waterfront	705-949-0611
St. Catharines	905-934-8000
Toronto On King (Downtown)	416-599-4000
Toronto-Airport	416-675-7611
Toronto-Airport East	416-240-7511
Toronto-Brampton	905-792-9900
Toronto-Markham	905-474-0444
Toronto-Mississauga	905-855-2000
Toronto-West	905-890-5700
Trenton	613-394-4855
Windsor (Ambassador Bridge)	519-966-1200

QUEBEC	
Hull - Ottawa Plaza La Chaudière	819-778-3880
Montreal-Airport	514-739-3391
Montreal-Centre Ville (Dwntwn/Conv. Ctr)	514-878-9888
Montreal-Longueuil	450-646-8100
Montreal-Midtown	514-842-6111
Montreal-Pointe-Claire	514-697-7110
Quebec City-Sainte-Foy	418-653-4901
Saguenay Convention Centre	418-548-3124

Holiday Inn EXPRESS

ALASKA	
Anchorage	907-248-8848

ALBERTA	
Edmonton	780-483-4000
Red Deer	403-343-2112

BRITISH COLUMBIA	
Abbotsford (Vancouver Area)	604-859-6211
Kamloops	250-372-3474
Kelowna	250-763-0500
Langley	604-882-2000
Vancouver-Airport	604-273-8080
Vancouver-Northshore	604-987-4461

NEW BRUNSWICK	
Moncton	506-384-1050

NOVA SCOTIA	
Halifax/Bedford	902-445-1100

ONTARIO	
Cornwall	613-937-0111
Hamilton-Stoney Creek	905-578-1212
Toronto-East	416-439-9666
Toronto-North York	416-665-3500

PRINCE EDWARD ISLAND	
Charlottetown	902-892-1201

SAFARI INN

◆
Motel

Phone: (250)860-8122

6/1-8/31	1P: $59	2P: $69	XP: $10	F5
9/1-11/30	1P: $49	2P: $59	XP: $10	F5
3/1-5/31 & 12/1-2/28	1P: $45	2P: $55	XP: $5	F5

Location: Just s of Hwy 97 N and jct Hwy 33, behind National/Tilden Rental car. 1651 Powick Rd V1X 4L1. Fax: 250/860-0828. **Terms:** 3 day cancellation notice; cancellation fee imposed; package plans; small pets only, $5 extra charge. **Facility:** 37 rooms. A good, basic budget-oriented property offering average sized guest rooms with pleasant, but basic decor. Large court-yard area surrounded by large trees and grass. Located away from main hwy. 12 two-bedroom units. 2 stories; exterior corridors; heated pool. **Cards:** AE, DS, JC, MC, VI.

SIESTA MOTOR INN

(CAA)
◆◆◆
Motel

Phone: (250)763-5013

6/21-9/15	1P: $89-$118	2P: $89-$118	XP: $10	D12
9/16-2/28	1P: $79-$109	2P: $79-$109	XP: $10	D12
3/1-6/20	1P: $74-$104	2P: $74-$104	XP: $10	D12

Location: Hwy 97 N, 2.8 km s on Pandosy St which becomes Lakeshore Rd. 3152 Lakeshore Rd V1W 3T1. Fax: 250/763-1265. **Terms:** Weekly & monthly rates avail, off season; 7 day cancellation notice, 6/20-9/21; small pets only, $10 fee. **Facility:** 96 rooms. Well maintained property offering a range of accommodations from standard style rooms to units with kitchen and separate bedroom. Located close to Gyro Beach Park and Kelowna General Hospital. 4 two-bedroom units. 2 stories; exterior corridors; 2 heated pools, sauna, whirlpools; playground. **Dining:** Restaurant nearby. **All Rooms:** extended cable TV. **Cards:** AE, DI, MC, VI. *(See color ad below)*

STAY'N SAVE INN

(CAA) (SAVE)
◆◆◆
Motor Inn

Phone: (250)862-8888

7/1-9/30	1P: $109-$119	2P: $119-$129	XP: $10	F16
5/1-6/30	1P: $99-$109	2P: $109-$119	XP: $10	F16
3/1-4/30 & 10/1-2/28	1P: $79-$89	2P: $89-$99	XP: $10	F16

Location: Corner of Hwy 97 N and Gordon Dr. 1140 Harvey Ave V1Y 6E7. Fax: 250/862-8884. **Terms:** Weekly rates avail, off season; cancellation fee imposed; package plans; small pets only, with prior notice. **Facility:** 101 rooms. A strong, well maintained property offering good, clean accommodations. Guest rooms are large and offer a pleasant modern decor. Located close to Capri Mall. Efficiencies, $10 extra charge; 3 stories; exterior corridors; heated pool, sauna, whirlpool. **Dining:** Restaurant; 7 am-10 pm; $6-$12; wine/beer only. **Services:** winter plug-ins. **All Rooms:** extended cable TV. **Cards:** AE, DI, MC, VI. **Special Amenities:** Free local telephone calls and free newspaper. *(See color ad below & p 540)*

SUPER 8 MOTEL

◆◆	7/1-9/30	1P: $74	2P: $84	XP: $5	F12
Motel	5/1-6/30	1P: $64	2P: $74	XP: $5	F12
	3/1-4/30 & 10/1-2/28	1P: $60	2P: $70	XP: $5	F12

Phone: 250/762-8222

Location: 0.5 km n on Hwy 97 N and jct Hwy 33. 2592 Hwy 97 N V1X 4J4. Fax: 250/762-3398. **Terms:** Package plans. **Facility:** 60 rooms. A strong, modern property offering average sized guest rooms with modern style decor. Close to area shopping and golf course. 2 stories; exterior corridors; heated pool. **Cards:** AE, DI, DS, MC, VI.

TOWN & COUNTRY MOTEL

◆	6/1-9/15	1P: $70-$80	2P: $80-$90	XP: $10	D12
Motel	3/1-5/31 & 9/16-10/31	1P: $54-$64	2P: $59-$69	XP: $5	D12
	11/1-2/28	1P: $50-$60	2P: $54-$64	XP: $5	D12

Phone: (250)860-7121

Location: 0.5 km n on Hwy 97 N and jct Hwy 33. 2629 Hwy 97 N V1X 4J6. Fax: 250/868-3376. **Terms:** Cancellation fee imposed; package plans; small pets only, $5 extra charge. **Facility:** 32 rooms. This well maintained property features modern guest rooms with a simple but pleasant decor. Guest rooms range from simple sleeping units to full size kitchen units with a separate bedroom. 2 stories; exterior corridors; heated pool. **All Rooms:** combo or shower baths. **Cards:** AE, JC, MC, VI.

TRAVELLER'S CHOICE

ⓐⓐ SAVE	5/19-9/30	1P: $89-$99	2P: $89-$109	XP: $8	F12
◆◆	3/1-5/18 & 10/1-2/28	1P: $65-$75	2P: $65-$85	XP: $8	F12

Phone: (250)762-3221

Motel **Location:** From Hwy 97 N (Harvey Ave), just e. 1780 Gordon Dr V1Y 3H2. Fax: 250/762-7261. **Terms:** Weekly & monthly rates avail, off season; package plans. **Facility:** 43 rooms. Across from Capri Mall, this property features a mixture of different guest room styles and sizes. There are larger full kitchen units to comfortable standard sized guest rooms. 2 two-bedroom units. 13 kitchens, $5-$15 extra charge; 2 stories; exterior corridors; heated pool, whirlpool. **Dining:** Restaurant nearby. **Recreation:** Fee: bicycles. **All Rooms:** extended cable TV. **Some Rooms:** Fee: VCR. **Cards:** AE, CB, DI, DS, MC, VI. **Special Amenities:** Early check-in/late check-out and free local telephone calls.

TRAVELODGE KELOWNA "ABBOTT VILLA"

ⓐⓐ SAVE	5/1-9/30	1P: $88-$140	2P: $88-$140	XP: $10	F16
◆◆	10/1-2/28	1P: $71-$86	2P: $71-$131	XP: $10	F16
Motor Inn	3/1-4/30	1P: $68-$82	2P: $68-$125	XP: $10	F16

Phone: (250)763-7771

Location: From Hwy 97 N, just W. 1627 Abbott St V1Y 1A9. Fax: 250/762-2402. **Terms:** Package plans. **Facility:** 53 rooms. Located downtown directly across the street from Kelowna City Park. Renovated guest rooms feature a pleasant, but simple decor, ranging from average sized standard rooms to slightly larger rooms. 3 whirlpool rooms, $180-$230; 2 stories; exterior corridors; heated pool, sauna, whirlpool. **Dining:** Restaurant; 7 am-10 pm; $5-$7; wine/beer only. **All Rooms:** extended cable TV. **Some Rooms:** 3 kitchens. **Cards:** AE, DI, JC, MC, VI. **Special Amenities:** Free local telephone calls and free newspaper.

──────── *The following lodging was either not inspected or did not* ────────
meet AAA rating requirements but is listed for your information only.

THE GRAND OKANAGAN LAKEFRONT RESORT & CONFERENCE CENTER   Phone: 250/763-4500

[fyi] Not inspected. **Location:** From Hwy 97, 1 km w. 1310 Water St V1Y 9P3. Facilities, services, and decor characterize a mid-range property.

──────── **RESTAURANTS** ────────

CHRISTOPHER'S   **Dinner:** $15-$30   Phone: 250/861-3464

◆◆ **Location:** Downtown. 242 Lawrence Ave V1Y 6L3. **Hours:** 4:30 pm-10 pm, Fri & Sat-11 pm. Closed: 12/25.
Steak and **Reservations:** suggested. **Features:** casual dress; salad bar; cocktails; a la carte. You'll enjoy the quaint
Seafood dining room, personalized attention and fresh seafood at Christopher's. Selections also include steak, a good salad bar and desserts. Large groups are accommodated at this local favorite, and the atmosphere may be boisterous. **Cards:** AE, DI, MC, VI.

THE FINER CHOICE IN DINING   **Lunch:** $5-$11   **Dinner:** $10-$20   Phone: 250/763-0422

ⓐⓐ **Location:** Centre. 237 Lawrence Ave V1Y 6L2. **Hours:** 11:30 am-2 & 5-10 pm; Thurs & Fri-2 pm; from 5 pm
6/1-9/30. Closed: 1/1-2/14 & Sun 9/15-5/1. **Reservations:** required; in summer. **Features:** dressy casual;
◆◆◆ early bird specials; senior's menu; health conscious menu items; cocktails; a la carte. The very extensive
Continental menu at this restaurant includes veal, chicken, seafood, beef and vegetarian dishes. Portions are generous, and the good-quality local wines are worth a try. For free parking, be sure to ask for a voucher as you enter. Friendly service. **Cards:** AE, CB, DI, MC, VI.

MEKONG RESTAURANT   **Lunch:** $6-$9   **Dinner:** $8-$14   Phone: 250/763-2238

◆◆ **Location:** Hwy 97 N and Gordon Dr; in Alpine Lodge Motor Inn. 1030 Harvey Ave V1Y 8S4. **Hours:** 11:30
Traditional am-10 pm. Closed: 12/25. **Reservations:** accepted. **Features:** casual dress; health conscious menu;
Chinese carryout; cocktails; a la carte. This restaurant features Szechwan cuisine and fresh mouth-watering food! Ask about the signature dishes, deluxe meal for 2-10 people, green curry and thick Shanghai noodles. The decor is bright, fresh and contemporary. They may be busy at peak meal times. **Cards:** AE, DI, MC, VI.

KIMBERLEY pop. 6,700

------ LODGING ------

QUALITY INN

◆◆	9/16-12/26	1P: $65-$75	2P: $85-$95	XP: $5	F
Motor Inn	12/27-2/28	1P: $65-$75	2P: $75-$85	XP: $5	F
	7/2-9/15	1P: $60-$65	2P: $65-$85	XP: $5	F
	3/1-7/1	1P: $55-$60	2P: $65-$80	XP: $5	F

Phone: (250)427-2266

Location: Centre. 300 Wallinger Ave V1A 1Z4. Fax: 250/427-7621. **Terms:** 7 day cancellation notice; cancellation fee imposed; package plans; pets, $5 extra charge, in smoking rooms. **Facility:** 42 rooms. Nicely appointed, contemporary guest room decor. 3 stories, no elevator; interior corridors. **Services:** area transportation; winter plug-ins. **Cards:** AE, DI, DS, JC, MC, VI.

LADYSMITH pop. 6,500

------ LODGING ------

SEAVIEW MARINE RESORT

◆	5/1-9/30	1P: $60	2P: $70	XP: $10	D11

Phone: 250/245-3768

Cottage   **Location:** 2.5 km s on Trans Canada Hwy 1, 3 km se. 11111 Chemainus Rd V0R 2E0 (RR 4). **Terms:** Open 5/1-9/30; 14 day cancellation notice; cancellation fee imposed; small pets only, in selected units. **Facility:** 5 rooms. Individual cottages decorated slightly differently from one another giving them a charm all their own. Operated by a very personable couple. Pleasant landscaping touches with lots of greenery. 4 two-bedroom units. 1 story; exterior corridors. **All Rooms:** kitchens. **Cards:** MC, VI.

LANGLEY —See Vancouver p. 507.

LANTZVILLE pop. 400

------ RESTAURANT ------

WINCHELSEA HOUSE RESTAURANT   **Lunch:** $8-$12   **Dinner:** $16-$23   **Phone:** 250/390-3241
◆◆   **Location:** From Island Hwy 19 just e on Ware Rd, then just n on Lantzville Rd. 7143 Caillet Rd V0R 2H0.
Continental   **Hours:** 11:30 am-2 & 5:30-9 pm. Closed: 12/24 & 12/26. **Reservations:** suggested. **Features:** No A/C; Sunday brunch; early bird specials; cocktails; a la carte. Located in a charming country home in the village of Lantzville, this restaurant's menu reflects a blend of West Coast and French cuisine with house specialties of salmon, mussels, beef, chicken, pork and pasta. A table d'hote menu is offered daily. **Cards:** AE, DI, MC, VI.

LOGAN LAKE pop. 2,500

------ LODGING ------

LOGAN LAKE LODGE

◆	All Year	1P: $55-$65	2P: $59-$69	XP: $5	F12

Phone: (250)523-9466

Motor Inn   **Location:** Centre of Meadow Creek Rd and Chartrand Cresent. 111 Chartrand Ave V0K 1W0 (PO Box 1190). Fax: 250/523-9467. **Terms:** 7 day cancellation notice; cancellation fee imposed; pets, $25 extra charge. **Facility:** 21 rooms. Geared for those who like to fish with 25 world class lakes close by or for sports enthusiasts there's the sports arena located across the street. Guest rooms are simple but very comforable for the budget minded traveler. 2 stories; interior corridors. **Cards:** AE, MC, VI.

MADEIRA PARK pop. 700

------ LODGING ------

SUNSHINE COAST RESORT

◆◆	6/1-9/15	1P: $110-$120	2P: $110-$120	XP: $10	F12
Cottage	5/2-5/31	1P: $85-$95	2P: $85-$95	XP: $10	F12
	9/16-2/28	1P: $75-$95	2P: $75-$95	XP: $10	F12
	3/1-5/1	1P: $75-$85	2P: $75-$85	XP: $10	F12

Phone: (604)883-9177

Location: Just n of Madeira Park Rd, watch for signs. 12695 Sunshine Coast Hwy 101 V0N 2H0. Fax: 604/883-8171. **Terms:** 7 day cancellation notice; cancellation fee imposed; pets, $5 extra charge. **Facility:** 4 rooms. Fully self-contained units in a lovely campground setting. All units with marvelous view of deep water marina and Pender Harbour. 1 two-bedroom unit. 2 stories; interior corridors. **Recreation:** charter fishing, fishing. Rental: boats, canoes. **All Rooms:** combo or shower baths. **Some Rooms:** 3 efficiencies, kitchen. **Cards:** AE, MC, VI.

MALAHAT —See Victoria p. 548.

MANNING PARK pop. 100

———— LODGING ————

MANNING PARK RESORT   Phone: (250)840-8822

(CAA)	12/1-2/28	1P: $109	2P: $114-$139	XP: $5	F11
◆ ◆	3/1-5/18	1P: $59-$109	2P: $64-$114	XP: $5	F11
	5/19-10/8	1P: $79-$89	2P: $84-$109	XP: $5	F11
Lodge	10/9-11/30	1P: $59	2P: $64-$74	XP: $5	F11

Location: Crowsnest Hwy 3, midway between Hope and Princeton. Hwy 3 V0X 1R0. Fax: 250/840-8848.
Terms: 14 day cancellation notice, in cabins; cancellation fee imposed; package plans; pets, $3 extra charge, in cabins.
Facility: 73 rooms. This year-round resort features both cross country and down hill skiing in the winter months and great hiking and mountain secenery in the summer. Accommodations include cottages, cabins or standard rooms. 15 two-bedroom units, 5 three-bedroom units. 20 cabins & 4 chalets for 4-12 persons, $99-$259; 2 stories; interior/exterior corridors; saunas; 2 lighted tennis courts; playground. **Dining:** Dining room, coffee shop; 7 am-9 pm, hrs vary off season; $8-$17; cocktails. **Services:** gift shop. **Recreation:** fishing; downhill & cross country skiing, ice skating, snowmobiling; jogging. Fee: ski rentals & instruction. Rental: canoes. **Some Rooms:** 24 kitchens. Fee: VCR. **Cards:** AE, MC, VI.

(ASK) (SD) (🐾) (🍴) (🖥) (🦴) (⚴) (✕) (🏋) (☎) (📹) (VCR) (🖦) (🖥) (📷) (🛏) (✕)

MAPLE RIDGE —See Vancouver p. 508.

MAYNE ISLAND —See Gulf Islands p. 418.

MCBRIDE pop. 700

———— LODGING ————

NORTH COUNTRY LODGE   Phone: (250)569-0001

(CAA)	All Year	1P: $54-$70	2P: $58-$99	XP: $7	F6

Location: Just w of village main exit, on Hwy 16, n service road. 868 N Frontage Rd V0J 2E0 (PO Box 567). Fax: 250/569-0002. **Terms:** Cancellation fee imposed; pets, in designated rooms. **Facility:** 38 rooms. Contemporary units; rooms on ground floor with at-door parking. 4 two-bedroom suites, $85-$125. 4 kitchenettes, $68-$78; 2 stories; exterior corridors; whirlpool. **Dining:** Restaurant; 6 am-11 pm; $7-$22; cocktails. **Services:** winter plug-ins. **Recreation:** exercise equipment. **Some Rooms:** 4 efficiencies, 4 kitchens. **Cards:** AE, MC, VI.

(🐾) (🍴) (🖥) (✕) (🏋) (✈) (🖥) (🛏) (DATA PORT)

MERRITT pop. 7,600

———— LODGINGS ————

BEST WESTERN NICOLA INN   Phone: (250)378-4253

(CAA) (SAVE)	6/23-9/3	1P: $95-$105	2P: $102-$112	XP: $8	F12
◆ ◆ ◆	5/15-6/22	1P: $85-$95	2P: $92-$102	XP: $8	F12
Motor Inn	9/4-2/28	1P: $75-$95	2P: $82-$102	XP: $8	F12
	3/1-5/14	1P: $75-$85	2P: $82-$92	XP: $8	F12

Location: Hwy 5 exit 290, 1 km w. 4025 Walters St V1K 1K1. Fax: 250/378-6869. **Terms:** Cancellation fee imposed. **Facility:** 54 rooms. A very attractive and well maintained property featuring large, richly decorated guest rooms. 6 whirlpool rooms; 2 stories; exterior corridors; heated pool, whirlpool. **Dining:** Restaurant; 6:30 am-9 pm; $7-$16; cocktails. **Services:** winter plug-ins. **All Rooms:** extended cable TV. **Cards:** AE, DI, DS, MC, VI. **Special Amenities:** Free local telephone calls. (See color ad below)

(SD) (🍴) (🦴) (⚴) (✕) (✈) (VCR) (🖦) (🖥) (📷) (🛏) (🏔) (♿)

MERRITT MOTOR INN

				Phone: (250)378-9422
CAA SAVE	3/1-9/28	1P: $60-$65	2P: $65-$70	XP: $5 F10
◆◆	9/29-2/28	1P: $55-$60	2P: $60-$65	XP: $5 F10

Motor Inn   **Location:** Hwy 5 exit 290, just w. 3561 Voght St V1K 1C5. Fax: 250/378-5465. **Terms:** Small pets only, $5 extra charge. **Facility:** 35 rooms. A budget oriented property offering large guest rooms, modestly decorated. Efficiencies, $5 extra charge; 2 stories; exterior corridors; heated pool, whirlpool. **Dining:** Restaurant; 7 am-9 pm; $5-$15; wine/beer only. **All Rooms:** extended cable TV. **Cards:** AE, DI, DS, MC, VI. **Special Amenities: Free breakfast and free local telephone calls.**

MERRITT TRAVELODGE

				Phone: (250)378-8830
CAA SAVE	5/15-9/30	1P: $65	2P: $69	XP: $5 F12
◆◆	3/1-5/14	1P: $55	2P: $60	
Motor Inn	10/1-2/28	1P: $55	2P: $60	XP: $5 F12

Location: Hwy 5, exit 290, then just w. 3581 Voght St V1K 1C5. Fax: 250/378-6335. **Terms:** Weekly rates avail, off season; small pets only, $5 extra charge. **Facility:** 34 rooms. A strong budget style property offering large guest rooms with a simple, modest decor. Parking avail at the rear of the property that does allow for easy access to the 2nd floor guest rooms. Whirlpool room, $95-$125; 3 stories, no elevator; interior corridors; heated pool, whirlpool. **Dining:** Restaurant; 8 am-9 pm; $9-$14; wine/beer only. **All Rooms:** extended cable TV. **Some Rooms:** 5 kitchens. **Cards:** AE, CB, DI, DS, MC, VI. **Special Amenities: Free local telephone calls and free room upgrade (subject to availability with advanced reservations).**

MISSION —*See Vancouver p. 509.*

NAKUSP pop. 1,700

—— **LODGING** ——

THE SELKIRK INN

				Phone: 250/265-3666
◆◆	5/1-10/31	1P: $50-$54	2P: $50-$62	XP: $5
Motel	3/1-4/30 & 11/1-2/28	1P: $45-$49	2P: $45-$54	XP: $5

Location: Just n. 210 W 6th Ave V0G 1R0 (PO Box 370). Fax: 250/265-4799. **Terms:** Small pets only, $20 dep req. **Facility:** 39 rooms. A few blks from the beach. Rooms are fairly modern looking and extremely well maintained. 2 stories; interior corridors. **All Rooms:** combo or shower baths. **Cards:** AE, MC, VI.

NANAIMO pop. 70,100

—— **LODGINGS** ——

BEST WESTERN DORCHESTER HOTEL

				Phone: (250)754-6835
CAA SAVE	All Year	1P: $81-$108	2P: $81-$108	XP: $10 F12

◆◆◆   **Location:** From Trans Canada Hwy 1 to Comox Rd. 70 Church St V9R 5H4. Fax: 250/754-2638. **Terms:** Cancellation fee imposed; package plans. **Facility:** 65 rooms. Downtown and opposite the Sea Plane Terminal. Historic Hotel   This fully restored heritage building was built in the 1890s. Guest rooms offer good views of the ocean or city. Parking may be limited in summer. 4 stories; interior corridors. **Dining:** Restaurant; 7 am-10 pm; $10-$20; cocktails. **Services:** gift shop. **All Rooms:** extended cable TV. **Cards:** AE, DI, JC, MC, VI. **Special Amenities: Free local telephone calls and free newspaper.** *(See color ad p 440)*

COLONIAL MOTEL

				Phone: 250/754-4415
CAA SAVE	7/1-9/4	1P: $54-$62	2P: $60-$68	XP: $6 F12
◆	3/1-6/30 & 9/5-10/9	1P: $49-$57	2P: $55-$63	XP: $6 F12
Motel	10/10-2/28	1P: $44-$52	2P: $50-$58	XP: $6 F12

Location: 1 km s on Hwy 19A (Terminal Ave) from Departure Bay ferry terminal. 950 Terminal Ave N V9S 4K4. Fax: 250/753-1611. **Terms:** Weekly rates avail, monthly rates off season; cancellation fee imposed. **Facility:** 9 rooms. An older, mature property featuring very clean, but basic style accommodations for those on a budget or quick, inexpensive stop over. Very accommodating owner. 2 stories; interior/exterior corridors. **Recreation:** kayak rentals. **All Rooms:** extended cable TV. **Some Rooms:** 4 efficiencies. **Cards:** AE, MC, VI.

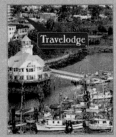

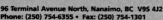

FOUR POINTS SHERATON NANAIMO

◆◆◆
Motor Inn

Phone: (250)758-3000

7/1-9/30	1P: $119	2P: $119	XP: $10	F12
3/1-6/30 & 10/1-2/28	1P: $99	2P: $99	XP: $10	F12

Location: 6 km n on Hwy 19A (Island Hwy) from departure Bay Ferry, then just e. 4900 Rutherford Rd V9T 5P1. Fax: 250/729-2808. **Terms:** Package plans. **Facility:** 75 rooms. A truly business-friendly listing. Guest rooms feature a variety of large suites with jetted tubs to pleasant standard style guest rooms with large bathrooms. Close to Rutherford Mall. 4 stories; interior corridors; heated pool. **Cards:** AE, DI, DS, JC, MC, VI. *(See color ad p 402)*

HARBOURVIEW DAYS INN

CAA SAVE

◆◆
Motor Inn

Phone: (250)754-8171

7/1-8/31	1P: $68	2P: $78	XP: $10	F14
4/1-6/30	1P: $65	2P: $75	XP: $10	F14
3/1-3/31 & 9/1-2/28	1P: $62	2P: $72	XP: $10	F14

Location: 2 km s on Island Hwy 1. 809 Island Hwy S V9R 5K1. Fax: 250/754-8557. **Terms:** Weekly & monthly rates avail, off season; small pets only, $7 extra charge. **Facility:** 79 rooms. Hilltop location on the s end of town. Some guest rooms have view of the harbour and nearby mill. Guest rooms are nice and comfortable with a simple decor. 2 stories; interior corridors; heated pool, whirlpool. **Dining:** Restaurant; 7 am-10 pm; $9-$16; cocktails. **All Rooms:** extended cable TV. **Some Rooms:** 16 efficiencies. Fee: VCR. **Cards:** AE, DI, DS, JC, MC, VI. **Special Amenities:** Free local telephone calls and free room upgrade (subject to availability with advanced reservations).

LONG LAKE INN

CAA SAVE

◆◆◆
Motel

Phone: (250)758-1144

6/1-9/30	1P: $119-$139	2P: $119-$149	XP: $15	F12
3/1-5/31 & 10/1-2/28	1P: $99-$119	2P: $109-$129	XP: $15	F12

Location: 5 km n on Hwy 19A from Departure Bay ferry terminal. 4700 Island Hwy N V9T 1W6. Fax: 250/758-5832. **Terms:** Weekly rates avail; package plans. **Facility:** 62 rooms. Wonderfully spacious guest rooms, all with balcony or patio. All rooms feature wonderful view of the lake. 4 whirlpool rooms, $179-$199; 3 stories; exterior corridors; beach, sauna, whirlpool; boat dock. **Dining:** Coffee shop. **Recreation:** swimming; barbecue grills, horseshoes, volleyball. Fee: 12-passenger motor pontoon boat. Rental: canoes, paddleboats. **All Rooms:** extended cable TV. **Some Rooms:** 18 efficiencies, 3 kitchens. **Cards:** AE, DI, DS, MC, VI. **Special Amenities:** Free local telephone calls. *(See ad p 527)*

TRAVELODGE NANAIMO

CAA SAVE

◆◆
Motel

Phone: (250)754-6355

6/1-9/30	1P: $78-$83	2P: $84-$95		F17
3/1-5/31	1P: $69-$74	2P: $75-$86	XP: $8	
10/1-2/28	1P: $73-$78	2P: $79-$85		

Location: At jct Hwy 19A and 1, access from either hwy. 96 Terminal Ave N V9S 4J2. Fax: 250/754-1301. **Terms:** Weekly & monthly rates avail; pets, on 1st floor. **Facility:** 78 rooms. Contemporary style guest rooms, all with private patio. 3 stories; interior corridors; sauna. **Dining:** Restaurant nearby. **All Rooms:** extended cable TV. **Some Rooms:** 8 efficiencies. **Cards:** AE, DI, MC, VI. **Special Amenities:** Free breakfast and free local telephone calls. *(See color ad p 435)*

—— RESTAURANTS ——

THE GROTTO

◆◆
Seafood

Dinner: $9-$18 **Phone:** 250/753-3303

Location: 1.6 km n; on Waterfront Row near BC Ferries. 1511 Stewart Ave V9S 4K3. **Hours:** 5 pm-10 pm. Closed: 12/25 & Mon. **Reservations:** suggested. **Features:** casual dress; cocktails; a la carte. This locally popular West Coast-style restaurant features steak, baby back ribs, charbroiled tuna, pasta, a sushi adventure and homemade cheesecake and creme brulee. The rustic decor displays a nautical motif and provides a comfortable, casual atmosphere. **Cards:** AE, MC, VI.

ZOUGLA

◆◆
Canadian

Lunch: $7-$11 **Dinner:** $12-$24 **Phone:** 250/716-3233

Location: Island Hwy and Brechin Rd, on the road to Departure Bay ferry terminal. 2021 Estevan Rd V9S 3Y9. **Hours:** 11 am-11 pm. Closed: 12/25 & 12/26. **Features:** casual dress; cocktails; a la carte. You'll enjoy this restaurant's offerings of steaks, seafood and Mediterranean specialties such as moussaka, spanakopita and souvlakia. Floor-to-ceiling windows offer a great view of the ocean and mountains. Couples and travelers like the relaxing ambience. **Cards:** AE, MC, VI.

NANOOSE BAY pop. 100

—— LODGING ——

FAIRWINDS SCHOONER COVE RESORT

◆◆◆
Motor Inn

Phone: (250)468-7691

5/1-10/31	1P: $109-$134	2P: $124-$149	XP: $15	F12
4/1-4/30 & 11/1-2/28	1P: $99-$109	2P: $104-$114	XP: $15	F12
3/1-3/31	1P: $89-$99	2P: $104-$114	XP: $10	F12

Location: From Island Hwy, 8.5 km se following signs, via Powderpoint Rd (becoming Fairwinds Dr). 3521 Dolphin Dr V0R 2R0 (PO Box 12 Schooner House RR 2). Fax: 250/468-5744. **Terms:** 3 day cancellation notice; cancellation fee imposed; package plans. **Facility:** 30 rooms. Very spacious modern rooms, all with queen beds, in a country club setting alongside the ocean. Choose from a harbour view or mountain view room. 2 stories; interior corridors; heated pool; 2 tennis courts. Fee: 18 holes golf; marina. **Services:** gift shop. Fee: massage. **Recreation:** charter fishing, fishing. Rental: boats. **Cards:** AE, DI, MC, VI.

NARAMATA

———— LODGING ————

THE VILLAGE MOTEL   Phone: (250)496-5535
CAA SAVE   6/15-9/15   1P: $59-$86   2P: $59-$86   XP: $5
◆◆   3/1-6/14 & 9/16-2/28   1P: $48-$68   2P: $48-$70   XP: $4
Motel   **Location:** 14 km n on Naramata Rd from Penticton. 244 Robinson Dr V0H 1N0 (PO Box 194).
Fax: 250/496-5744. **Terms:** 14 day cancellation notice; cancellation fee imposed; small pets only, $8 extra
charge. **Facility:** 9 rooms. This delightful motel features all the comforts of home in cozy, very modern guest
rooms. Excellent housekeeping and attractive landscaping make this a real gem. 6 efficiencies & 1 kitchen, $8 extra charge;
1 story; exterior corridors; designated smoking area. **Dining:** Restaurant nearby. **Recreation:** Fee: bicycles. **All Rooms:** extended cable TV. **Cards:** AE, MC, VI. **Special Amenities: Preferred room (subject to availability with advanced
reservations).**

NELSON pop. 9,600

———— LODGINGS ————

BEST WESTERN BAKER STREET INN   Phone: (250)352-3525
CAA SAVE   All Year   1P: $89-$129   XP: $10
◆◆◆   **Location:** At jct Hwy 6 and 3A, at Baker St. 153 Baker St V1L 4H1. Fax: 250/352-2995. **Terms:** [BP] & [ECP]
Motor Inn meal plans; check-in 4 pm; package plans; small pets only, $5 extra charge. **Facility:** 70 rooms. Beautifully re-
stored historic building on the w side of the downtown area. Very well appointed guest rooms and public areas
including an inviting lobby with gas fireplace. All rooms with hair dryer. 2 whirlpool rooms; 4 stories; interior corridors; whirlpool. **Dining:** Restaurant; 6 am-9 pm, Fri & Sat-10 pm; $7-$10; cocktails. **Services:** Fee: area transportation, ski
hill. **All Rooms:** extended cable TV. **Cards:** AE, CB, DI, DS, MC, VI.

NORTH SHORE INN   Phone: (250)352-6606
◆◆   5/1-9/30   1P: $59-$72   2P: $69-$85   XP: $7   F6
Motel   3/1-4/30 & 10/1-2/28   1P: $53-$67   2P: $62-$77   XP: $7   F6
Location: 3 km n on Hwy 3A via Nelson Bridge. 687 Hwy 3A V1L 5P7 (PO Box 119). Fax: 250/354-1772.
Terms: [CP] meal plan. **Facility:** 30 rooms. Guest room decor features a mix of contemporary and vintage appointments. Most
feature balcony that overlooks beautiful Kootenay Lake. 1 two-bedroom unit. 3 stories, no elevator; interior corridors; lake view.
Cards: AE, DI, MC, VI.

———— RESTAURANT ————

FIDDLERS GREEN RESTAURANT   **Dinner: $13-$22**   Phone: 250/825-4466
CAA   **Location:** 10 km n on Hwy 3A. Lower 6 Mile Rd V1L 5P4. **Hours:** 5:30 pm-9 pm, 5/1-10/15; Sun 10:30
◆◆◆   am-1 & 5:30-9 pm. Closed: Mon & Tues (off season). **Reservations:** suggested. **Features:** No A/C; casual
Continental dress; Sunday brunch; health conscious menu; cocktails; a la carte. Located in a heritage house with large
gardens and country charm, this restaurant features a progressive menu with an accent on fresh herbs and
spices, eye-appealing presentations and British Columbia wines. Charming service. Garden and fireside
dining. **Cards:** MC, VI.

NEW DENVER pop. 600

———— LODGING ————

SWEET DREAMS GUESTHOUSE   Phone: (250)358-2415
◆◆   All Year   1P: $45-$55   2P: $70-$85   XP: $20   F12
Country Inn **Location:** 0.4 km w of Hwy 6, across street from lake. 702 Eldorado St V0G 1S0 (PO Box 177).
Fax: 250/358-2556. **Terms:** [BP] meal plan; check-in 5 pm; 7 day cancellation notice; cancellation fee imposed;
package plans. **Facility:** 5 rooms. Beautifully landscaped patio area. Attractive, contemporary room decor offers finished pine
look with wicker furnishings and duvet bedspreads. Inviting dining room. 2 stories; interior corridors; smoke free premises.
Recreation: hiking trails. Rental: canoes. **Cards:** MC, VI.

NEW WESTMINSTER —See Vancouver p. 509.

NORTH VANCOUVER —See Vancouver p. 510.

OLIVER pop. 4,300

———— LODGING ————

SOUTHWIND INN   Phone: (250)498-3442
◆   5/1-2/28   1P: $79-$95   2P: $79-$95   XP: $12   F17
Motor Inn 3/1-4/30   1P: $69-$85   2P: $69-$85   XP: $12   F17
Location: 1.2 km s on Hwy 97. (PO Box 1500, V0H 1T0). Fax: 250/498-3938. **Terms:** Pets. **Facility:** 46
rooms. Featuring a western cedar decor in the public areas as well as in some guest rooms. Recommend asking for courtyard
view rooms, with its lush landscaping and view of the pool. 2 stories; interior corridors; heated pool. **Some Rooms:** 11 efficiencies. **Cards:** AE, DI, MC, VI.

──────── RESTAURANT ────────

JACQUES NEIGHBORHOOD GRILL　　　**Dinner:** $12-$20　　　**Phone:** 250/498-4418
(CAA)
◆ ◆
Continental
Location: Just s on Hwy 97 from 350th Ave. V0H 1T0. **Hours:** 5 pm-11 pm. Closed: Mon. **Reservations:** suggested. **Features:** casual dress; cocktails; a la carte. The French-born chef/owner of Jacques prepares flavorful specialties such as steak seared with peppercorns and coated with a Chardonnay cream sauce, and maple-glazed pork medallions. The distinctive wine-cellar theme creates a cozy country-inn atmosphere. **Cards:** AE, DI, MC, VI.　　　⊠

100 MILE HOUSE pop. 1,900

──────── LODGINGS ────────

108 RESORT BEST WESTERN　　　　　　　　　　　　　　　　**Phone:** (250)791-5211

(CAA) (SAVE)			
5/16-10/14	1P: $125-$135	2P: $135-$165	XP: $10　F12
12/19-2/28	1P: $125-$135	2P: $135-$145	XP: $10　F12
3/1-5/15 & 10/15-12/18	1P: $85-$125	2P: $95-$135	XP: $10　F12

◆ ◆ ◆
Resort
Location: 9.6 km n on Hwy 97; 1.6 km nw on signed access road, in 108 Recreational Ranch. 4816 Telqua Dr V0K 2Z0 (PO Box 2, 108 MILE RANCH). Fax: 250/791-6537. **Terms:** Weekly & monthly rates avail, off season; cancellation fee imposed; package plans. **Facility:** 62 rooms. Overlooking golf course and lake, in fine country setting of over 600 acres. Spacious rooms, all with balcony or patio. 2 stories; exterior corridors; putting green; beach access, heated pool, saunas, whirlpool; 4 tennis courts (2 lighted); boat dock; playground. Fee: 18 holes golf. **Dining:** Restaurant; 7 am-10 pm; $12-$19; cocktails. **Services:** gift shop; winter plug-ins. **Recreation:** swimming, fishing; ice skating, tobogganing, night cross country skiing, sleigh rides; hiking trails, jogging, 5000 ft airstrip with hangar & wagon rides. Fee: snowmobiling, ski equipment & instruction; bicycles, horseback riding. Rental: canoes. **All Rooms:** extended cable TV. **Some Rooms:** 8 efficiencies. Fee: VCR. **Cards:** AE, DI, DS, JC, MC, VI.

100 MILE HOUSE SUPER 8　　　　　　　　　　　　　　　　**Phone:** 250/395-8888

◆ ◆			
5/1-9/30	1P: $77	2P: $88	XP: $7　F12
4/1-4/30	1P: $72	2P: $79	XP: $7　F12
3/1-3/31 & 10/1-2/28	1P: $67	2P: $72	XP: $7　F12

Motel
Location: 1 km s on Hwy 97. 989 Alder Ave V0K 2E0 (Box 759). Fax: 250/395-8880. **Terms:** Small pets only, $10 extra charge. **Facility:** 28 rooms. Modern guest rooms offer very nice, comfortable accommodations on s end of town. 2 stories; exterior corridors. **Services:** winter plug-ins. **Cards:** AE, DI, MC, VI.

RED COACH INN　　　　　　　　　　　　　　　　　　　　**Phone:** (250)395-2266

(CAA) (SAVE)			
5/1-10/31	1P: $79	2P: $85	XP: $6　F16
3/1-4/30 & 11/1-2/28	1P: $71	2P: $77	XP: $6　F16

◆ ◆ ◆
Motor Inn
Location: On Hwy 97, on the n end of town. 170 Cariboo Hwy N V0K 2E0 (PO Box 760). Fax: 250/395-2446. **Terms:** Pets, $10 extra charge. **Facility:** 49 rooms. Modern property offering a range of guest rooms. Some are average in size; others are more spacious but all offer good, clean, accommodations. 2 two-bedroom units. 2 stories; interior/exterior corridors; heated pool, sauna, whirlpool. **Dining:** Restaurant; 6:30 am-9 pm; $9-$14; cocktails. **Services:** gift shop; winter plug-ins. **All Rooms:** combo or shower baths, extended cable TV. **Some Rooms:** Fee: VCR. **Cards:** AE, DI, MC, VI. **Special Amenities:** Early check-in/late check-out and free local telephone calls.

──────── RESTAURANT ────────

MARMOT RIDGE RESTAURANT & LOUNGE　　　**Lunch:** $6-$10　　**Dinner:** $6-$17　　**Phone:** 250/395-6036
◆ ◆
Canadian
Location: On Hwy 97, n end of town. **Hours:** 11 am-9 pm, Thurs-Sat to 10 pm, Sun 10:30 am-9 pm. Closed: 12/25. **Reservations:** suggested. **Features:** casual dress; children's menu; cocktails & lounge; a la carte. Located atop a hill with a nice view of a nine-hole golf course, this restaurant has a menu featuring daily specials, sandwiches, burgers and stir-fry. Downstairs there's an open lounge with pool tables. (The minimum age for the lounge is 19.). **Cards:** MC, VI.　　　⊠

OSOYOOS pop. 4,000

──────── LODGINGS ────────

BELLA VILLA RESORT MOTEL　　　　　　　　　　　　　　　**Phone:** (250)495-6751

(CAA) (SAVE)			
6/26-9/15	1P: $70-$90	2P: $85-$100	XP: $10　D18
9/16-11/1	1P: $50-$70	2P: $60-$80	XP: $5　D18
3/1-6/25	1P: $45-$65	2P: $50-$70	XP: $5　D18
11/1-2/28	1P: $30-$45	2P: $45-$55	XP: $5　D18

◆
Motel
Location: Just off Hwy 3 E, turn onto Ponderosa Dr, just e of Bridge on Hwy 3 E. 6904 Ponderosa DR V0H 1V0 (RR 1). Fax: 250/495-6753. **Terms:** Weekly & monthly rates avail; 30 day cancellation notice; cancellation fee imposed. **Facility:** 14 rooms. Beachside location. Guest rooms offer a charming decor with various sizes from average to spacious. A few units offer lake view. 2 stories; exterior corridors; smoke free premises; beach; boat dock. **Dining:** Restaurant nearby. **Recreation:** swimming, boating; bicycles. **All Rooms:** kitchens, extended cable TV. **Cards:** MC, VI. **Special Amenities:** Free room upgrade and preferred room (each subject to availability with advanced reservations).

BEST WESTERN SUNRISE INN　　　　　　　　　　　　　　　**Phone:** (250)495-4000

(CAA) (SAVE)			
All Year	1P: $80-$125	2P: $80-$125	XP: $10　F17

◆ ◆ ◆
Motor Inn
Location: Jct of Hwy 97 and 3, 3 km on Hwy 3. 5506 Main St V0H 1V0 (PO Box 305). Fax: 250/495-4001. **Terms:** [ECP] meal plan; check-in 4 pm; 7 day cancellation notice; cancellation fee imposed; package plans. **Facility:** 66 rooms. Modern property located near Osoyoos Lake. 3 whirlpool rooms, $115-$150; 3 stories; interior corridors; small heated indoor pool, whirlpool. **Dining:** Restaurant, coffee shop; 7 am-10 pm; $8-$15; cocktails. **Services:** winter plug-ins. **Recreation:** game room. **All Rooms:** extended cable TV. **Some Rooms:** 9 efficiencies, 29 kitchens. **Cards:** AE, DI, DS, JC, MC, VI. **Special Amenities:** Free breakfast and free local telephone calls.

DESERT MOTOR INN

◆
Motor Inn

6/15-9/15	1P: $65-$94	2P: $75-$129	XP: $15	F
3/1-6/14	1P: $40-$60	2P: $50-$90	XP: $15	F
9/16-2/28	1P: $35-$65	2P: $45-$90	XP: $15	F

Phone: (250)495-6525

Location: Jct Hwy 97 and 3, 2 km e on Hwy 3. 7702 Main St V0H 1V0 (PO Box 458). Fax: 250/495-6226. **Terms:** 14 day cancellation notice. **Facility:** 52 rooms. Along the lake. Rooms range from average in size to quite spacious. Some feature a balcony. Well maintained. A few rooms are contemporary looking. 2 two-bedroom units. 2 stories; interior/exterior corridors; heated pool. **Recreation:** swimming. **Some Rooms:** 19 efficiencies. **Cards:** AE, MC, VI.

HOLIDAY INN SUNSPREE RESORT

(CAA) (SAVE)
◆ ◆ ◆
Motor Inn

3/1-9/15	1P: $135-$195	2P: $145-$205	XP: $10	F19
9/16-11/1	1P: $89-$199	2P: $99-$150	XP: $10	F19
11/2-2/28	1P: $79-$99	2P: $89-$109	XP: $10	F19

Phone: (250)495-7223

Location: Jct of Hwy 97 and 3, 1.9 km e on Hwy 3. 7906 Main St V0H 1V0 (PO Box 1019). Fax: 250/495-6899. **Terms:** Check-in 4 pm; 30 day cancellation notice, in season; cancellation fee imposed; package plans. **Facility:** 85 rooms. Located along the shore of beautiful Osoyoos Lake with great mountain views. All rooms with balcony or patio, hair dryer, iron, ironing board and video games. 51 two-bedroom units. Whirlpool room; 3 stories; interior corridors; lake view; beach, heated pool, whirlpool, beach volleyball; boat dock, marina; playground. Fee: sea doos. **Dining:** Restaurant; 6:30 am-10 pm; $9-$25; cocktails. **Recreation:** swimming; arcade. Fee: boating, canoeing. Rental: paddleboats. **All Rooms:** combo or shower baths, extended cable TV. **Some Rooms:** 77 kitchens. **Cards:** AE, DI, DS, JC, MC, VI. **Special Amenities:** Free local telephone calls.

POPLARS MOTEL ON THE LAKE

◆ ◆
Motel

7/1-9/10	1P: $65-$85	2P: $75-$110
3/1-6/30 & 9/11-2/28	1P: $45-$55	2P: $50-$65

Phone: 250/495-6035

Location: 1.6 km e on Hwy 3, just s on 67th St. 6404 67th St/Cottonwood Dr V0H 1V0 (Box 212). Fax: 250/495-2736. **Terms:** 14 day cancellation notice; cancellation fee imposed. **Facility:** 34 rooms. Wide variety of pleasant guest rooms, most offer full kitchen facilities. Direct access to beach. Some units offer a nice lake view. 4 two-bedroom units. 2-3 stories, no elevator; exterior corridors. **Recreation:** swimming, boating. **Some Rooms:** 6 efficiencies, 28 kitchens. **Cards:** AE, CB, DI, DS, JC, MC, VI.

WESTRIDGE MOTOR INN

(CAA) (SAVE)
◆ ◆
Motel

6/17-9/4	1P: $75-$100	2P: $85-$110	XP: $10	F5
5/1-6/16 & 9/5-2/28	1P: $55-$75	2P: $65-$85	XP: $10	F5
3/1-4/30	1P: $45-$65	2P: $55-$75	XP: $10	F5

Phone: (250)495-7322

Location: At jct Hwy 3 and 97. 9913 Hwy 3 V0H 1V0 (PO Box 431). Fax: 250/495-5126. **Terms:** 3 day cancellation notice; package plans; small pets only, $5 extra charge. **Facility:** 26 rooms. A real gem of a property including cozy and contemporary guest rooms with attractive decor. Inviting landscaping. Various sized guest rooms range from average to large. Brew pub and restaurant adjacent. Whirlpool room, $65-$105; 1-2 stories; exterior corridors; heated pool, sauna, whirlpool. **Recreation:** game room. **All Rooms:** extended cable TV. **Some Rooms:** 14 efficiencies, kitchen. **Cards:** AE, DI, DS, MC, VI. **Special Amenities:** Free local telephone calls.

—— **RESTAURANTS** ——

THE CHALET HELVETIA

◆ ◆
Continental

Lunch: $5-$8   **Dinner:** $10-$24   **Phone:** 250/495-7552

Location: Just s off Main St at 85th St. 8312 74th Ave V0H 1V0. **Hours:** 11:30 am-2 & 5:30-10 pm, hrs vary in winter. Closed major holidays, Mon & Sun off season. **Reservations:** suggested; in summer. **Features:** children's menu; senior's menu; carryout; cocktails. This chalet has a Swiss chef/owner and specializes in steaks, seafood and schnitzel. All dressings, sauces and vegetables are fresh, and dishes are prepared from scratch. The warm, quiet atmosphere is cozy and hospitable. Service is pleasant and informal. **Cards:** AE, DI, MC, VI.

DIAMOND STEAK AND SEAFOOD HOUSE

◆ ◆
Steak and
Seafood

Dinner: $9-$24   **Phone:** 250/495-6223

Location: Centre; Hwy 3 (Main St) at 89 St. 8903 Main St V0H 1V0. **Hours:** 4 pm-10 pm. Closed: 12/25, 1/1 & Feb. **Features:** children's menu; senior's menu; carryout; cocktails; street parking; a la carte. This is an excellent family restaurant with tasty food and attentive service. A nice selection of pasta, pizza and Greek specialties is offered. The broiled chicken breast with peppercorn and a brandy demi-glaze sauce is simply delectable!. **Cards:** AE, MC, VI.

FINNY'S NEIGHBOURHOOD RESTAURANT

◆ ◆
Canadian

Lunch: $6-$10   **Dinner:** $10-$17   **Phone:** 250/495-2224

Location: Corner of 85th St and 78th Ave, across from Post Office. 8309 78th Ave V0H 1V0. **Hours:** 11 am-9 pm, to 10 pm 7/1-8/31. Closed: 9/2, 11/23, 12/24-12/29. **Reservations:** suggested; in summer. **Features:** children's menu; senior's menu; carryout; cocktails. The menu at Finny's features an extensive menu of sandwiches, salads, seafood, steaks, burgers and home-style desserts. All are served in large portions. The very pleasant decor is open and airy with lots of windows, and the service is quite friendly. **Cards:** MC, VI.

PARKSVILLE pop. 9,500

--- LODGINGS ---

BEACH ACRES RESORT   Phone: (250)248-3424

(CAA) (SAVE)   6/30-9/30 Wkly   1P: $1250-$1750   2P: $1250-$1750   XP: $12   F9
♦♦♦   6/9-6/29 Dly   1P: $125-$199   2P: $125-$199   XP: $12   F9
Cottage   10/1-2/28 Dly   1P: $105-$195   2P: $105-$195   XP: $12   F9
               3/1-6/8 Dly   1P: $105-$185   2P: $105-$185   XP: $12   F9

Location: From Island Hwy 19 Parksville exit, 1.5 km n on Hwy 19A. 25-1015 E Island Hwy V9P 2E4.
Fax: 250/248-6145. **Terms:** Weekly rates avail, monthly, 10/1-5/31; check-in 4 pm; 30 day cancellation notice, 3 day off
season; cancellation fee imposed. **Facility:** 49 rooms. A unique mix of condominiums situated on several acres. Some are set
back and secluded, some sit on a cliff overlooking the ocean and some sit right on the beach. Modern and fully equipped. Offering a true home-like feeling. 47 two-bedroom units. 1-2 stories; exterior corridors; designated smoking area; beach, heated
pool, sauna, whirlpool; 3 tennis courts; playground. **Dining:** Restaurant; 8 am-9:30 pm; hrs vary off season; $14-$20; cocktails. **Services:** gift shop. **Recreation:** swimming; basketball, game room, volleyball. **All Rooms:** kitchens, combo or shower
baths. **Some Rooms:** Fee: VCR. **Cards:** AE, DI, MC, VI. **Special Amenities: Free room upgrade and preferred room (each
subject to availability with advanced reservations).** 🍴 🛎 ⬛ ✖ 🎬 VCR 📷 💻 🖥 🛏 🏊 ✖

BEST WESTERN BAYSIDE INN   Phone: (250)248-8333

(CAA) (SAVE)   7/1-9/30   1P: $129-$169   2P: $129-$169   XP: $10   F12
♦♦♦   3/1-6/30 & 10/1-2/28   1P: $79-$109   2P: $79-$109   XP: $10   F12
Motor Inn   **Location:** Island Hwy 19 N Parksville exit, 8 km n on Hwy 19A. 240 Dogwood St V9P 2H5 (PO Box 1720).
               Fax: 250/248-4689. **Terms:** 3 day cancellation notice; package plans; small pets only, $10 extra charge.

Facility: 59 rooms. Lovely, oceanfront setting with cheerful, contemporary rooms; many rooms feature a balcony with wonderful ocean views. When the tide is out, the beach is known for building sand castles. 3 stories; interior corridors; beach, heated pool, sauna, steamroom, whirlpool. Fee: squash. **Dining:** Restaurant; patio dining avail in summer; sports
bar; 7 am-10 pm; $11-$20; cocktails. **Services:** gift shop; area transportation, train & bus station. Fee: massage.
Recreation: swimming, fishing; PADI dive shop; beach volleyball. Fee: scuba diving & equipment. **All Rooms:** extended cable
TV. **Cards:** AE, CB, DI, DS, JC, MC, VI. **Special Amenities: Free local telephone calls and free newspaper.**
(See color ad below)   🛎 🐕 🍴 🍸 🛎 ⬛ 🏋 ✖ 📷 💻 🛏 🏊 ♿ ✖

GRAY CREST SEASIDE RESORT

Phone: (250)248-6513

CAA SAVE

◆◆◆
Cottage

6/30-9/4	1P: $173-$193	2P: $173-$193	XP: $10 D17
3/1-6/29 & 9/5-2/28	1P: $115-$145	2P: $115-$145	XP: $10 D17

Location: Island Hwy 19 N Parksville exit, 1.9 km n on Hwy 19A. 1115 E Island Hwy V9P 2E2. **Fax:** 250/248-6799. **Terms:** Weekly & monthly rates avail; check-in 4 pm; 30 day cancellation notice, 7/1-8/31; cancellation fee imposed; 7 night min stay, 7/1-8/31. **Facility:** 36 rooms. Spacious modern units set back in the forest alongside the ocean. Most are 2-bedroom units with full kitchen, many including dishwasher. All with fireplace. Manicured lawn setting. Whirlpool room, $125; 3 stories; exterior corridors; beach, heated pool, sauna, whirlpool; playground. **Dining:** Restaurant nearby. **Services:** Fee: massage. **Recreation:** swimming. Fee: tanning beds. **All Rooms:** combo or shower baths, extended cable TV. **Cards:** AE, DI, JC, MC, VI. **Special Amenities:** Free local telephone calls.
(See color ad p 440)

MARINA VIEW B & B

Phone: (250)248-9308

◆
Bed & Breakfast

4/1-10/31	1P: $70-$90	2P: $85-$95	XP: $20

Location: From Hwy 19 exit Parksville, 10 km n on Hwy 19A; then just e on Wright Rd, follow B & B hwy signs. 895 Glenhale Crescent V9P 1Z7. **Fax:** 250/248-9408. **Terms:** Open 4/1-10/31; [BP] meal plan; age restrictions may apply; 7 day cancellation notice; cancellation fee imposed. **Facility:** 3 rooms. Cozy rooms filled with personal touches; pleasant location overlooking the ocean, with large sun deck and solarium for guests to enjoy the scenery. 2 stories; interior corridors; designated smoking area. **All Rooms:** combo or shower baths. **Cards:** MC, VI.

THE OCEANSIDE INN

Phone: (250)248-2232

◆◆◆
Motel

7/1-8/31	1P: $99-$149	2P: $109-$159	XP: $10 F12
9/1-10/31	1P: $89-$139	2P: $99-$149	XP: $10 F12
3/1-6/30	1P: $79-$109	2P: $89-$119	XP: $10 F12
11/1-2/28	1P: $69-$99	2P: $79-$109	XP: $10 F12

Location: Island Hwy 19 N, Parksville exit, 8 km n on Hwy 19A. 424 W Island Hwy V9P 1K8. **Fax:** 250/248-3273. **Terms:** [CP] meal plan; cancellation fee imposed; package plans; small pets only, $10 extra charge. **Facility:** 87 rooms. Comfortable, modern guest rooms, all with queen sized bed. 3 stories; interior corridors; heated pool. **Cards:** AE, CB, DI, DS, JC, MC, VI.

SANDCASTLE INN

Phone: (250)248-2334

CAA SAVE

◆◆◆
Motel

7/1-9/30	1P: $85-$125	2P: $85-$125	XP: $10 F12
6/16-6/30	1P: $69-$109	2P: $69-$109	XP: $10 F12
3/1-6/15	1P: $59-$89	2P: $59-$99	XP: $10 F12
10/1-2/28	1P: $59-$89	2P: $59-$89	XP: $10 F12

Location: Island Hwy 19 N Parksville exit, 6.5 km n on Hwy 19A. 374 W Island Hwy V9P 1K8. **Fax:** 250/248-7330. **Terms:** [CP] meal plan; weekly rates avail, monthly, off season; 48 day cancellation notice; package plans. **Facility:** 36 rooms. Backing onto a quiet residential neighborhood, this modern property offers a variety of nicely decorated guest rooms close to the beach and mini golf. 3 stories; interior corridors. **Dining:** Restaurant nearby. **All Rooms:** combo or shower baths, extended cable TV. **Some Rooms:** 16 efficiencies. **Cards:** AE, DI, MC, VI. **Special Amenities:** Free breakfast and free local telephone calls.

TIGH NA MARA RESORT HOTEL

CAA
◆◆◆
Complex

7/1-8/31	1P: $109-$209	2P: $109-$209	XP: $10	D16
3/1-6/30	1P: $94-$179	2P: $94-$179	XP: $10	D16
9/1-2/28	1P: $75-$179	2P: $75-$179	XP: $10	D16

Phone: (250)248-2072

Location: Island Hwy 19 N Parksville exit, 2 km n on Hwy 19A. 1095 E Island Hwy V9P 2E5. Fax: 250/248-4140. **Terms:** Weekly & monthly rates avail; 30 day cancellation notice; cancellation fee imposed; package plans; pets, in cottages, off season. **Facility:** 142 rooms. Unique cluster of lovely log lodges, cottages and condos set in the forest alongside a sandy beach. Some with fine ocean views; all with wood-burning fireplace. 25 two-bedroom units. 3 night min stay in lodge, 7 night for cottages & condos 7/1-8/31; 64 whirlpool rooms, $99-$209; 1-3 stories; exterior corridors; beach, heated pool, steamroom, whirlpool; 1 tennis court; playground. **Dining:** Cocktails; also, Tigh Na Mara Resort Restaurant, see separate listing. **Services:** gift shop; area transportation, bus & train station. **Recreation:** swimming. Rental: paddleboats. **All Rooms:** extended cable TV. **Some Rooms:** 12 efficiencies, 97 kitchens. Fee: VCR. **Cards:** AE, DI, MC, VI. *(See color ad p 441)*

V.I.P. MOTEL

CAA SAVE
◆◆
Motel

6/2-10/15	1P: $82-$88	2P: $87-$93	XP: $10	F12
3/1-6/1 & 10/16-2/28	1P: $54-$59	2P: $64-$69	XP: $10	F12

Phone: (250)248-3244

Location: Island Hwy 19 N Parksville exit, 6.5 km n on Hwy 19A. 414 W Island Hwy V9P 1K8. Fax: 250/248-0018. **Terms:** [CP] meal plan; cancellation fee imposed; pets. **Facility:** 21 rooms. A wonderfully maintained property offering large guest rooms that are nicely decorated. Very guest oriented offering little extras such as hair dryer and a "I forgot" service. At-door parking. 2 two-bedroom units. 13 kitchens, $10 extra charge; 1 story; exterior corridors. **Dining:** Restaurant nearby. **Recreation:** barbecue patio. **All Rooms:** extended cable TV. **Cards:** AE, CB, DI, DS, JC, MC, VI. **Special Amenities:** Free breakfast and free local telephone calls.

------- RESTAURANTS -------

KALVAS RESTAURANT

◆◆
Steak and
Seafood

Dinner: $12-$22   Phone: 250/248-6933

Location: Island Hwy 19 N, Parksville exit, 6.5 km n on Hwy 19A. 180 Molliet St V0R 2S0. **Hours:** 5 pm-10 pm, Sat-11 pm. **Reservations:** suggested. **Features:** casual dress; cocktails; a la carte. You'll surely enjoy the Alpine, log-cabin decor and high-quality, home cooking with fresh ingredients at this restaurant. It features an extensive menu of fresh seafood such as lobster, crab and oysters, as well as duck, pheasant and steak. Cozy setting. **Cards:** MC, VI.

TIGH NA MARA RESORT RESTAURANT

◆◆◆
Canadian

Lunch: $7-$9   Dinner: $14-$21   Phone: 250/248-2333

Location: Island Hwy 19 N Parksville exit, 2 km n on Hwy 19A; in Tigh Na Mara Resort Hotel. 1095 E Island Hwy V9P 2E5. **Hours:** 7 am-3 & 5-9:30 pm, appetizers only served 3 pm-5 pm. **Reservations:** suggested. **Features:** Sunday brunch; children's menu; cocktails & lounge; a la carte. Featuring a West Coast seafood cuisine, this restaurant also offers pastas, steak, a very popular Sunday brunch and more casual breakfast and lunch offerings. The country-elegant setting in a log building is informal, warm and friendly. Good service. **Cards:** AE, DI, MC, VI.

PARSON pop. 3,300

------- LODGING -------

TIMBER INN-CHALET & RESTAURANT

◆◆
Country Inn

6/1-9/20	1P: $75-$125	2P: $75-$125	XP: $15	F7
3/1-5/31 & 9/21-2/28	1P: $65-$98	2P: $65-$98	XP: $15	F7

Phone: (250)348-2228

Location: 34 km s of Golden on Hwy 95; 0.5 km s of general store/post office. Follow signs. 3483 Hwy 95 V0A 1L0 (Box 139). Fax: 250/348-2292. **Terms:** 3 day cancellation notice; cancellation fee imposed; pets, $5 extra charge. **Facility:** 6 rooms. Casual mountain retreat or wooded acreage. Welcoming public areas include country style restaurant featuring home cooked German specialties. Room decor is fresh and simple. 2 units with balcony and mountain view. 3 stories, no elevator; interior corridors; designated smoking area. **Services:** winter plug-ins. Fee: massage. **Recreation:** bicycles, hiking trails. **All Rooms:** combo or shower baths. **Cards:** MC, VI.

PEACHLAND pop. 4,500

------- LODGING -------

HATHEUME LAKE RESORT

◆◆
Cottage

All Year		2P: $110-$140	XP: $17	F12

Phone: 250/767-2642

Location: 42 km w on 97C, exit Sunset Main Rd, follow signs 26 km on Bear Creek Rd. PO Box 490 V0H 1X0. Fax: 250/767-2642. **Terms:** Pets, $17 extra charge, with prior approval. **Facility:** 10 rooms. A very remote property featuring individual cottages, fully self-contained, on the shore of Hatheume Lake. Guests should bring their own groceries for length of stay. A true fisherman's resort or simply a quiet retreat getaway. 1 story; exterior corridors; boat dock. **Recreation:** swimming, fishing; cross country skiing; hiking trails. Fee: boating; snowmobiling; bicycles. **All Rooms:** kitchens. **Cards:** AE, MC, VI.

PENTICTON pop. 31,000

——— LODGINGS ———

BEST WESTERN INN AT PENTICTON
Phone: (250)493-0311

CAA SAVE
♦♦♦
Motor Inn

5/1-9/30	1P: $109-$119	2P: $119	XP: $10	F16
3/1-4/30, 10/1-12/31 & 1/1-2/28	1P: $79-$99	2P: $89-$99	XP: $10	F16

Location: 4 km s. 3180 Skaha Lake Rd V2A 6G4. Fax: 250/493-5556. **Terms:** Cancellation fee imposed; package plans. **Facility:** 67 rooms. A modern property featuring many spacious guest rooms with most units facing into well manicured courtyard area. Half a block from large waterslide park, 2 km from Skaha Lake. 2 two-bedroom units. 4 whirlpool rooms; 2 stories; exterior corridors; 2 heated pools, whirlpool; playground. **Dining:** Restaurant; 7 am-10 pm; $6-$12; cocktails. **All Rooms:** extended cable TV. **Some Rooms:** 7 efficiencies, 15 kitchens. **Cards:** AE, DI, DS, MC, VI. **Special Amenities:** Free room upgrade (subject to availability with advanced reservations).
(See color ad below)

EMPIRE MOTEL
Phone: 250/493-2323

♦♦♦
Motel

6/25-9/8	1P: $76-$85	2P: $80-$95	XP: $5	F12
3/1-6/24 & 9/9-2/28	1P: $50-$65	2P: $58-$75	XP: $5	F12

Location: 4.5 km s. 3495 Skaha Lake Rd V2A 6G6. Fax: 250/493-4270. **Terms:** 15 day cancellation notice. **Facility:** 32 rooms. A charming and very well maintained property featuring a country inn style decor. Attractively landscaped grounds in season. Large courtyard area features pool and barbecue areas. 2 blks from Skaha Lake. 2 stories; exterior corridors; heated pool; playground. **Cards:** AE, DS, MC, VI.

GOLDEN SANDS RESORT
Phone: (250)492-4210

CAA SAVE
♦ ♦
Motel

6/26-9/7	1P: $80	2P: $90	XP: $10	F4
9/8-2/28	1P: $60-$70	2P: $70-$80	XP: $10	F4
3/1-6/25	1P: $70	2P: $80	XP: $10	F4

Location: Riverside Dr and Lakeshore Dr W. 1028 Lakeshore Dr W V2A 1C1. Fax: 250/492-0339. **Terms:** Weekly & monthly rates avail, off season; 14 day cancellation notice; small pets only, $5 extra charge, $25 max. **Facility:** 39 rooms. Directly across from Okanagan Lake, close to downtown and convention centre. Self contained units offering very good but modest guest rooms, with most units featuring a separate bedroom. 1 three-bedroom unit, 8 two-bedroom units. 2 stories; exterior corridors; beach, heated pool, sauna, whirlpool. **Dining:** Restaurant nearby. **Recreation:** swimming. **All Rooms:** extended cable TV. **Some Rooms:** 33 kitchens. **Cards:** MC, VI. **Special Amenities:** Early check-in/late check-out and preferred room (subject to availability with advanced reservations).

PENTICTON LAKESIDE RESORT & CONFERENCE CENTRE
Phone: (250)493-8221

CAA SAVE
♦♦♦
Hotel

7/1-9/5	1P: $137-$155	2P: $137-$155	XP: $15	F16
5/15-6/30	1P: $102-$125	2P: $102-$125	XP: $15	F16
9/6-2/28	1P: $92-$125	2P: $92-$125	XP: $15	F16
3/1-5/14	1P: $92-$112	2P: $92-$112	XP: $15	F16

Location: Main St at Lakeshore Dr W. 21 Lakeshore Dr W V2A 7M5. Fax: 250/493-0607. **Terms:** Check-in 4 pm; package plans; pets, $20 extra charge. **Facility:** 204 rooms. Downtown along the lake front. This resort property features large, comfortable guest rooms with a mix of city or lake views. All rooms with balcony. 3 whirlpool rooms; 6 stories; interior corridors; beach, heated pool, sauna, whirlpool; boat dock. **Dining:** Restaurant; 7 am-10 pm; $10-$18; cocktails; patio dining in summer only. **Services:** gift shop. Fee: massage. **Recreation:** swimming, fishing. Rental: boats, canoes, paddleboats. **All Rooms:** extended cable TV. **Cards:** AE, CB, DI, DS, JC, MC, VI. **Special Amenities:** Early check-in/late check-out and free room upgrade (subject to availability with advanced reservations).

PENTICTON SLUMBER LODGE
Phone: 250/492-4008

♦ ♦
Motor Inn

7/1-8/31	1P: $88-$97	2P: $88-$106	XP: $10	F12
9/1-10/31	1P: $70-$79	2P: $70-$88	XP: $10	F12
3/1-6/30	1P: $60-$79	2P: $60-$88	XP: $10	F12
11/1-2/28	1P: $52-$61	2P: $52-$70	XP: $10	F12

Location: From Hwy 97, n on Riverside Dr, 1.5 km e. 274 Lakeshore Dr W V2A 1B8. Fax: 250/492-7528. **Terms:** 14 day cancellation notice; cancellation fee imposed; pets, in smoking rooms. **Facility:** 40 rooms. Directly across the street from Okanagan Lake and the public beach area. This renovated property features many separate bedroom units; all with a pleasant, modern decor. 3 two-bedroom units. 2 stories; exterior corridors; heated pool. **Some Rooms:** 20 kitchens. **Cards:** AE, MC, VI.

PENTICTON TRAVELODGE

CAA SAVE
♦ ♦
Motel

	1P: $90-$110	2P: $90-$110	XP: $10	F17
6/16-8/31				
3/1-6/15 & 9/1-2/28	1P: $55-$95	2P: $55-$95	XP: $10	F17

Phone: (250)492-0225

Location: From Eckhart Ave (Hwy 97), just ne. 950 Westminster Ave W V2A 1L2. Fax: 250/493-8340. **Terms:** Weekly rates avail; 7 day cancellation notice; cancellation fee imposed. **Facility:** 34 rooms. Some large guest rooms, most with enclosed balcony. Meticulous housekeeping. Located close to the Peach Bowl Convention Centre. 2 kitchens, $10 extra charge; 3 stories; interior/exterior corridors; 2 heated pools, sauna, waterslide, whirlpool. **Dining:** Coffee shop; 7 am-1:30 pm. **Services:** winter plug-ins. **All Rooms:** extended cable TV. **Cards:** AE, CB, DI, MC, VI.

RAMADA COURTYARD INN & SUITES

CAA
♦ ♦ ♦
Motel

Property failed to provide current rates

Phone: (250)492-8926

Location: 1.2 km w on Hwy 97. 1050 Eckhart Ave W V2A 2C3. Fax: 250/492-2778. **Terms:** Weekly & monthly rates avail, off season; package plans; small pets only, $10 fee, in designated rooms. **Facility:** 90 rooms. Located along main hwy. Guest rooms feature a pleasant, country type charm decor and all rooms have patio deck that overlooks mature landscaped courtyard. Newer rooms in tower. 1 two-bedroom unit. 1 story; exterior corridors; heated pool, whirlpool; playground. **Dining:** Restaurant; 11:30 am-midnight; $7-$12; cocktails. **All Rooms:** extended cable TV. **Cards:** AE, DI, DS, MC, VI.

RIORDAN HOUSE BED & BREAKFAST

♦ ♦ ♦
Bed &
Breakfast

| All Year | 1P: $60-$85 | 2P: $45-$75 | XP: $20 |

Phone: 250/493-5997

Location: Corner of Winnipeg St and Eckhardt Ave. 689 Winnipeg St V2A 5N1. Fax: 250/493-5997. **Terms:** [CP] meal plan; age restrictions may apply; cancellation fee imposed. **Facility:** 3 rooms. This 1920 heritage home is situated in a quiet residential neighborhood. The entire home is lovingly decorated in antiques. A short leisurely walk to downtown or area restaurants. 2 stories; interior corridors; designated smoking area. **Services:** gift shop. **Cards:** AE, DI, MC, VI.

SPANISH VILLA RESORT

CAA SAVE
♦ ♦
Motel

| All Year | 1P: $58-$98 | 2P: $68-$120 | XP: $15 |

Phone: (250)492-2922

Location: Corner Power St and Lakeshore Dr W. 890 Lakeshore Dr W V2A 1C1. Fax: 250/492-2922. **Terms:** Weekly rates avail, monthly off season; 7 day cancellation notice; cancellation fee imposed; package plans; pets. **Facility:** 60 rooms. Directly across the street from Okanagan Lake; this well maintained property features a range of accommodations from large kitchen units to standard style guest rooms. 1 three-bedroom unit, 5 two-bedroom units. 2 stories; exterior corridors; beach, heated pool. **Recreation:** swimming. **All Rooms:** extended cable TV. **Cards:** AE, CB, DI, DS, JC, MC, VI. **Special Amenities:** Free local telephone calls and free room upgrade (subject to availability with advanced reservations).

SWISS SUNSET INN

♦ ♦
Motel

| 7/1-9/2 | 1P: $60-$80 | 2P: $70-$100 | XP: $10 | D12 |
| 3/1-6/30 & 9/3-2/28 | 1P: $45-$75 | 2P: $50-$75 | XP: $10 | D12 |

Phone: 250/492-8209

Location: 3.4 km s. 2604 Skaha Lake Rd V2A 6G1. Fax: 250/492-5170. **Terms:** 10 day cancellation notice; cancellation fee imposed. **Facility:** 25 rooms. Well maintained property offering a variety of guest room sizes from average to large in the kitchen units. All guest rooms overlook landscaped courtyard area. 2 stories; exterior corridors; heated pool. **Cards:** MC, VI.

WATERFRONT INN

♦ ♦
Motel

| 7/1-9/10 | 1P: $58-$95 | 2P: $58-$95 | XP: $10 | D10 |
| 5/1-6/30 & 9/11-10/15 | 1P: $48-$75 | 2P: $48-$75 | XP: $10 | D10 |

Phone: (250)492-8228

Location: Hwy 97 to Channel Pkwy and Skaha Lake Rd, then just ne to Lee Ave; adjacent to Skaha Park. 3688 Parkview St V2A 6H1. Fax: 250/492-8228. **Terms:** Open 5/1-10/15; 30 day cancellation notice; small pets only, $5 extra charge. **Facility:** 21 rooms. Located 1 blk from Skaha Lake. Guest rooms range from average size in the standard rooms to larger size in the kitchen units. Simple style decor, close to beaches, lake and park. 1 two-bedroom unit. 2 stories; exterior corridors. **Cards:** AE, MC, VI.

—— RESTAURANTS ——

GRANNY BOGNER'S

♦ ♦ ♦
Continental

Dinner: $18-$23   **Phone:** 250/493-2711

Location: 2 blks w of Main St, on corner of Argyle St. 302 Eckhardt Ave W V2A 2A9. **Hours:** 5:30 pm-9:30 pm. Closed: Mon. **Reservations:** suggested. **Features:** cocktails. You'll enjoy this unusual, rustic, 100-year-old heritage mansion on a quiet residential street. Granny Bogner's menu features a fine selection of seafood and steak, with some house specials like duckling, veal and ostrich. Business people like this place. **Cards:** AE, MC, VI.

THEO'S RESTAURANT

♦ ♦
Greek

Lunch: $6-$12   **Dinner:** $11-$37   **Phone:** 250/492-4019

Location: Just s on Main St. 687 Main St V2A 5C9. **Hours:** 11 am-midnight, Sun 4 pm-11 pm. Closed: 12/25. **Reservations:** suggested. **Features:** cocktails; a la carte. Located downtown, this is an established restaurant specializing in traditional Greek salad, souvlakia, moussaka and roast lamb as well as steak and seafood. The Mediterranean decor is warm and family-oriented. Park on the street or behind restaurant. **Cards:** AE, DI, MC, VI.

PITT MEADOWS —*See Vancouver p. 511.*

PORT ALBERNI pop. 18,500

——— **LODGINGS** ———

BEST WESTERN BARCLAY HOTEL　　　　　　　　　　　　　　　**Phone:** (250)724-7171

(CAA) (SAVE)

	5/1-9/30	1P: $89-$119	2P: $99-$119	XP: $10	F17
	3/1-4/30 & 10/1-2/28	1P: $69-$99	2P: $79-$99	XP: $10	F17

♦♦♦
Motor Inn
Location: Just s on Gertrude St from Johnson Rd (Hwy 4). 4277 Stamp Ave V9Y 7X8. Fax: 250/724-9691. **Facility:** 86 rooms. Nicely renovated listing featuring very pleasant and comfortable guest rooms. Known as Port Alberni's largest full facility property with on site beer and wine store, sports bar, pub and ample parking. Whirlpool room, $159; 5 stories; interior corridors; heated pool, sauna, whirlpool. **Dining:** Restaurant; 6 am-9 pm; $9-$15; cocktails. **All Rooms:** extended cable TV. **Cards:** AE, DI, DS, MC, VI. **Special Amenities:** Free local telephone calls.

CEDAR WOOD LODGE　　　　　　　　　　　　　　　　　　**Phone:** 250/724-6800

♦♦

	6/23-9/30	1P: $115	2P: $125	XP: $15	D13
	3/1-6/22 & 10/1-2/28	1P: $80	2P: $90	XP: $15	D13

Bed & Breakfast
Location: 3 km w on River Rd (Hwy 4) from Johnston Rd. 5895 River Rd V9Y 6Z5. Fax: 250/724-6887. **Terms:** [ECP] meal plan; cancellation fee imposed. **Facility:** 8 rooms. This thoroughly modern lodge type home features very comfortable guest rooms designed with both business and vacation traveller in mind. All rooms have air massage tub and gas fireplace. 2 stories; interior corridors; designated smoking area. **Cards:** AE, MC, VI.

COAST HOSPITALITY INN　　　　　　　　　　　　　　　　**Phone:** (250)723-8111

♦♦　　　All Year　　　　　　　1P: $125　　　　　2P: $140　　　　　XP: $10　　　　F18
Motor Inn
Location: 3.2 km sw of jct Hwy 4 via City Centre/Port Alberni South Rt. 3835 Redford St V9Y 3S2. Fax: 250/723-0088. **Terms:** 3 day cancellation notice; package plans; small pets only. **Facility:** 50 rooms. Very comfortable guest rooms and nicely maintained property, geared for both the business or holiday traveler. 2 stories; interior corridors. **Cards:** AE, DI, JC, MC, VI.

TIMBERLODGE & RV CAMPGROUND　　　　　　　　　　　**Phone:** (250)723-9415

♦　　　　　　　　　　　Property failed to provide current rates
Motor Inn
Location: 5 km e on Hwy 4; at jct City Centre/Port Alberni South Rt. (Site 210, C 12, RR 2, V9Y 7L6). Fax: 250/723-0311. **Terms:** Pets, $10 extra charge. **Facility:** 22 rooms. Located on main hwy just before entering the township. This basic, budget oriented property offers decent guest rooms, perfect for those on a budget and looking for a place for the night. Rooms overlook campground. 2 stories; exterior corridors; heated pool. **Some Rooms:** Fee: VCR. **Cards:** AE, MC, VI.

——— **RESTAURANT** ———

LITTLE BAVARIA RESTAURANT　　　**Lunch:** $6-$9　　　**Dinner:** $11-$18　　　**Phone:** 250/724-4242
♦♦　　　**Location:** Corner of 4th Ave and Argyle. 3035 4th Ave V9Y 2B8. **Hours:** 11 am-2:30 & 5-10 pm, Sat & Sun
German　　from 5 pm. Closed: lunch on holidays. **Reservations:** required. **Features:** casual dress; cocktails; street parking; a la carte. This quaint restaurant features a pleasant Bavarian decor with an accent on good old-fashioned German food. Schnitzel, Hungarian goulash, cabbage rolls, steak, seafood, and fondue for two are on the menu. Couples and business people like this place. **Cards:** AE, MC, VI.

PORT COQUITLAM —*See Vancouver p. 512.*

PORT HARDY pop. 5,300

——— **LODGINGS** ———

HAMILTON'S BED & BREAKFAST　　　　　　　　　　　　　**Phone:** (250)949-6638
♦　　　All Year　　　　　　　1P: $48　　　　　2P: $60-$65　　　　XP: $15
Bed & Breakfast
Location: From Hwy 19, 1 km nw on Granville St which becomes Park Dr, then just w. 9415 Mayor's Way V0N 2P0 (PO Box 1926). **Terms:** [ECP] meal plan; age restrictions may apply. **Facility:** 3 rooms. A Suburban home-stay featuring comfortable but modest guest room decor. Owner specializes in an expanded continental breakfast with homemade preserves, breads and fresh fruit plate. 1 story; interior corridors; designated smoking area.

PIONEER INN

Phone: (250)949-7271

(CAA) (SAVE)	5/15-10/15	1P: $82-$94	2P: $92-$104	XP: $10	F11
	3/1-5/14 & 10/16-2/28	1P: $46-$66	2P: $54-$74	XP: $8	F11

◆
Motor Inn

Location: 1 km w off Island Hwy 19 on Byng Rd. 4965 Byng Rd V0N 2P0 (PO Box 699). Fax: 250/949-7334.
Terms: Weekly & monthly rates avail; 7 day cancellation notice; cancellation fee imposed; small pets only.
Facility: 36 rooms. Located on the bank of the Quatse River, offering a quiet off hwy location. The accommodations are modest, with an older style decor but it's still a comfortable overnight stay for those who don't mind a few rough spots. 1 two-bedroom unit. 2 stories; exterior corridors; playground. **Dining:** Restaurant, coffee shop; 6:30 am-10 pm; $5-$10; cocktails. **All Rooms:** combo or shower baths, extended cable TV. **Some Rooms:** 21 efficiencies. **Cards:** AE, DI, MC, VI.
Special Amenities: Free local telephone calls.

---

*The following lodging was either not inspected or did not
meet AAA rating requirements but is listed for your information only.*

QUARTERDECK INN

Phone: 250/902-0455

(fyi)	3/1-9/30	1P: $90-$110	2P: $100-$140	XP: $10	F12
	10/1-2/28	1P: $80-$95	2P: $90-$115	XP: $10	F12

Motor Inn

Too new to rate, opening scheduled for June 1999. **Location:** Hwy 19, then 1.5 km n. 6555 Hardy Bay Rd V0N 2P0 (Box 910). Fax: 250/902-0454. **Terms:** [CP] meal plan; 3 day cancellation notice. **Amenities:** 40 rooms, pets, restaurant, radios, coffeemakers, microwaves, refrigerators. **Cards:** AE, MC, VI.

--- **RESTAURANTS** ---

SNUGGLES DINING ROOM

Dinner: $12-$25

Phone: 250/949-7575

◆ ◆
Northern
Italian

Location: In Pioneer Inn. V0N 2P0. **Hours:** 6 pm-10 pm. Closed: 12/25. **Reservations:** suggested.
Features: No A/C; cocktails; a la carte. Delicious fresh seafood choices such as mussels and salmon from North Vancouver Island are the specialties at this restaurant, but steak, prime rib and chicken are also good selections. Its cozy, intimate dining room is quite romantic. Homemade desserts. **Cards:** MC, VI.

SPORTSMAN'S STEAK HOUSE

Dinner: $14-$22

Phone: 250/949-7811

◆ ◆
Steak and
Seafood

Location: Centre; across from information centre. 6400 Market St V0N 2P0. **Hours:** 5 pm-9 pm, Fri & Sat-10 pm. Closed: 12/25. **Features:** No A/C; carryout; cocktails. Families appreciate this restaurant's warm, friendly atmosphere and good value—it's ideal for the budget-minded. The menu offers steak, prime rib, fresh local seafood, barbecue, pasta, pizza and cheesecake. The service is prompt and attentive.
Cards: AE, MC, VI.

STINK CREEK CAFE

Lunch: $3-$8

Phone: 250/949-8117

◆
American

Location: From Hwy 19, 1 km nw (towards water) on Granville St, then just ne. 7030 Market St V0N 2P0.
Hours: 5 am-6 pm. Closed major holidays & 12/26. **Features:** No A/C; street parking. Don't let the name fool you, the food is excellent! Homemade soup and sandwiches along with mouth-watering pastry, pie and muffins. Try the specialty "rhubarb muffins." Located downtown. **Cards:** AE, MC, VI.

PORT RENFREW

--- **LODGING** ---

ARBUTUS BEACH LODGE

Phone: (250)647-5458

◆	5/16-9/15	1P: $55-$85	2P: $65-$95	XP: $15
Bed &	3/1-5/15 & 9/16-11/15	1P: $45-$85	2P: $55-$95	XP: $15
Breakfast	11/16-2/28	1P: $35-$65	2P: $45-$75	XP: $15

Location: Klannanith St at Queesto Dr, follow signs to waterfront. 5 Queesto Dr V0S 1K0. Fax: 250/647-5552.
Terms: [BP] meal plan; age restrictions may apply; 7 day cancellation notice; cancellation fee imposed. **Facility:** 5 rooms. A simple property featuring average sized guest rooms with average style decor. Located along waterfront and beach. 2 stories; interior corridors; designated smoking area. **All Rooms:** combo or shower baths. **Cards:** MC, VI.

POWELL RIVER pop. 13,100

--- **RESTAURANT** ---

THE SHINGLEMILL BISTRO

Lunch: $6-$15

Dinner: $8-$20

Phone: 604/483-2001

◆ ◆
Continental

Location: 6.4 km n of Ferry Terminal via Hwy 101 N, first right after bridge. 6233 Powell Pl V8A 4S6.
Hours: 11 am-3 & 5-9 pm, Fri-10 pm, Sat 11 am-10 pm, Sun 9 am-9 pm. Closed: 12/25.
Reservations: required. **Features:** casual dress; children's menu; senior's menu; carryout; cocktails & lounge; a la carte. You can watch from this bistro's patio as floatplanes take off and land on Powell Lake. The menu offers Alaskan king crab legs, chicken in phyllo pastry, steak and pasta—all prepared with West Coast flair. Families and seniors like the friendly service. **Cards:** AE, DI, DS, MC, VI.

PRINCE GEORGE pop. 75,200

——— LODGINGS ———

BEST WESTERN CITY CENTRE
Phone: (250)563-1267

🅰️ SAVE

	1P: $105-$110	2P: $115-$125	XP: $10	F18
3/1-9/30				
10/1-2/28	1P: $95-$105	2P: $105-$115	XP: $10	F18

◆ ◆ ◆
Motor Inn
Location: Just n of Victoria (Hwy 16) and Patricia Blvd. 910 Victoria St V2L 2K8. Fax: 250/563-9904. **Terms:** Check-in 4 pm; cancellation fee imposed. **Facility:** 53 rooms. In the downtown area. Guest rooms offer a modern, upbeat style decor. 4 larger suites for up to 4 persons, $110-$140; 2 stories; exterior corridors; heated pool, saunas. **Dining:** Restaurant; 7 am-3 pm, Sat & Sun from 8 am; $5-$10. **Services:** winter plug-ins. **All Rooms:** extended cable TV. **Cards:** AE, DI, DS, MC, VI. **Special Amenities:** Free local telephone calls and free room upgrade (subject to availability with advanced reservations).

CARMEL MOTOR INN
Phone: 250/564-6339

◆ ◆

| All Year | 1P: $50-$60 | 2P: $65-$75 | XP: $10 | F12 |

Motor Inn
Location: 1 km s on Hwy 97 from jct Hwy 16 (Yellowhead Hwy). 1502 Hwy 97S V2L 5L9. Fax: 250/562-0597. **Facility:** 90 rooms. Good, moderate style accommodations featuring average sized guest rooms with a pleasant, simple style decor. Rooms in the separate building are slightly more modern. 2 stories; exterior corridors. **Services:** gift shop; winter plug-ins. **All Rooms:** combo or shower baths. **Cards:** AE, DI, MC, VI.

CONNAUGHT MOTOR INN
Phone: (250)562-4441

🅰️ SAVE

| All Year | 1P: $63-$72 | 2P: $68-$77 | XP: $10 | F11 |

◆
Motor Inn
Location: Corner of Victoria (Hwy 16) and Patricia Blvd. 1550 Victoria St V2L 2L3. Fax: 250/562-4441. **Terms:** Weekly & monthly rates avail; pets, $5 extra charge. **Facility:** 97 rooms. A "no frills" older property that offers a wide range of room styles starting with smaller, older style decor rooms to rooms that have been somewhat renovated with a more modern decor. Strong housekeeping a plus. 19 efficiencies, $10 extra charge; 3 stories, no elevator; exterior corridors; heated pool, sauna, whirlpool. **Dining:** Restaurant; 6 am-11 pm; $9-$15; wine/beer only. **Services:** winter plug-ins. **All Rooms:** combo or shower baths, extended cable TV. **Some Rooms:** Fee: VCR. **Cards:** AE, DI, MC, VI. **Special Amenities:** Free local telephone calls and preferred room (subject to availability with advanced reservations). *(See color ad below)*

ECONO LODGE
Phone: (250)563-7106

🅰️ SAVE

	1P: $75	2P: $85	XP: $5	F18
5/1-10/31				
3/1-4/30 & 11/1-2/28	1P: $65	2P: $75	XP: $5	F18

◆ ◆
Motel
Location: From Victoria St, just w on 3rd Ave. 1915 3rd Ave V2M 1G6. Fax: 250/561-7216. **Facility:** 30 rooms. A simple but pleasant listing located just off the main drag (Victoria St). Guest rooms offer a modern decor, some rooms with at-door parking. Whirlpool room; 2 stories; interior/exterior corridors; whirlpool. **All Rooms:** extended cable TV. **Cards:** AE, DI, MC, VI. **Special Amenities:** Free local telephone calls.

——— RESTAURANTS ———

CHINA SAIL RESTAURANT
Lunch: $9-$15   **Dinner:** $9-$15   Phone: 250/564-2828

◆ ◆
Chinese
Location: 1.7 km w on 5th Ave from Hwy 97, corner of 5th and Tabor. 4288 5th Ave V2N 7A2. **Hours:** 11:30 am-11 pm, Fri & Sat-midnight, Sun 2 pm-9 pm. Closed: 12/25 & 12/26. **Reservations:** accepted. **Features:** carryout; cocktails; a la carte. A local favorite for more than 20 years, this restaurant continues to serve delicious Chinese and Canadian dishes. You may select an individual meal, family dinner or combination plate; all are reasonably priced. Good food and good service. **Cards:** AE, MC, VI.

RIC'S GRILL, STEAK SEAFOOD & CHOP HOUSE
Lunch: $7-$13   **Dinner:** $11-$19   Phone: 250/614-9096

◆ ◆
Steak and Seafood
Location: George St & 5th Ave. 547 George St V2L 1R7. **Hours:** 11:30 am-10 pm, Fri-11 pm, Sat 4:30 pm-11 pm, Sun 4:30 pm-10 pm. Closed major holidays & 12/24. **Reservations:** suggested. **Features:** cocktails; street parking; a la carte. Ric's is located downtown and close to the city's casino. Specializing in steak, this restaurant features Western Canadian beef known as "sterling silver," which is cooked any way you like it. Bustling atmosphere. Try a cozy booth for two. **Cards:** AE, MC, VI.

PRINCE RUPERT pop. 16,700

———— LODGINGS ————

ALEEDA MOTEL

Phone: (250)627-1367

	5/16-9/30	1P: $58	2P: $76	XP: $6	D11
	3/1-5/15 & 10/1-2/28	1P: $40	2P: $48	XP: $5	D11

Motel

Location: Corner of 3rd Ave W and 8th St. 900 3rd Ave W V8J 1M8. Fax: 250/624-3132. **Terms:** Weekly & monthly rates avail, off season; cancellation fee imposed; pets, $5 extra charge. **Facility:** 31 rooms. A very well maintained older property featuring simple, clean guest rooms. Close to the downtown area. 18 efficiencies, $6 extra charge; 2 stories; interior corridors. **Dining:** Restaurant nearby. **All Rooms:** extended cable TV. **Cards:** AE, MC, VI.

HIGHLINER INN

Phone: (250)624-9060

	5/1-9/30	1P: $120	2P: $130-$150	XP: $10	F12
	10/1-2/28	1P: $100	2P: $120-$140	XP: $10	F12
	3/1-4/30	1P: $100	2P: $120	XP: $10	F12

Motor Inn

Location: Corner of 1st Ave W and 7th St. 815 1st Ave W V8J 1B3. Fax: 250/627-7759. **Terms:** Weekly & monthly rates avail, off season. **Facility:** 94 rooms. Downtown location. Guest rooms are fairly spacious with a pleasant yet modest style room decor. All rooms have balcony and views vary from ocean to city scape. 17 stories; interior corridors. **Dining:** Restaurant; 6:30 am-9 pm; $8-$18; cocktails. **All Rooms:** extended cable TV. **Cards:** AE, DI, DS, MC, VI. **Special Amenities:** Free local telephone calls and preferred room (subject to availability with advanced reservations).

TOTEM LODGE MOTEL

Phone: (250)624-6761

	All Year	1P: $59-$75	2P: $65-$79	XP: $8	F12

Motel

Location: 1.6 km w on Hwy 16 (2nd Ave W) from downtown. 1335 Park Ave V8J 1K3. Fax: 250/624-3831. **Terms:** [CP] meal plan; weekly & monthly rates avail. **Facility:** 31 rooms. Closest listed property to B.C. and Alaska ferry terminal. Comfortable accommodations with a modest style decor. Solid housekeeping. Car parking for walk on ferry passengers avail. 29 kitchens, $7 extra charge. Car storage for ferry, $3; 3 stories; interior corridors. **Dining:** Restaurant nearby. **All Rooms:** extended cable TV. **Cards:** AE, MC, VI. **Special Amenities:** Early check-in/late check-out and free local telephone calls.

———— *The following lodging was either not inspected or did not meet AAA rating requirements but is listed for your information only.* ————

CREST MOTOR HOTEL

Phone: 250/624-6771

[fyi]

Not inspected. **Location:** From Hwy 16 just nw on 2nd Ave W, downtown. 222 1st Ave W V8J 3P6 (PO Box 277). Facilities, services, and decor characterize a mid-range property.

———— RESTAURANTS ————

GALAXY GARDENS

Lunch: $6-$19   **Dinner:** $6-$19   Phone: 250/624-3122

Chinese

Location: 3rd Ave W at 8th St, downtown. 844 3rd Ave W V8J 1M6. **Hours:** 11:30 am-10 pm. Closed major holidays. **Features:** carryout; cocktails; street parking; a la carte. You'll enjoy the salt-and-pepper prawns at this restaurant featuring a Cantonese cuisine. They also serve Western dishes like burgers and sandwiches. The Oriental artwork makes for a friendly and homey atmosphere, and the server staff is attentive. **Cards:** AE, DI, MC, VI.

THE WATERFRONT CAFE

Lunch: $8-$15   **Dinner:** $12-$24   Phone: 250/624-6771

Canadian

Location: In Crest Motor Hotel. 222 1st Ave W V8J 3P6. **Hours:** 6:30 am-2 & 5-9 pm. **Features:** children's menu; cocktails & lounge; a la carte. The Waterfront Cafe offers absolutely the best, most incredible view of the harbor and mountains as the hotel sits atop a cliff overlooking the strait. This all-day restaurant serves traditional dishes such as pasta, burgers, steak and seafood. **Cards:** AE, DI, DS, MC, VI.

PRINCETON pop. 2,800

—— LODGING ——

BEST WESTERN PRINCETON INN **Phone:** (250)295-3537

CAA SAVE   3/1-11/1   1P: $89-$109   2P: $99-$139   XP: $10   F12
◆◆◆   11/2-2/28   1P: $79-$89   2P: $89-$129   XP: $10   F12
Motel   **Location:** On Hwy 3, town centre. 169 Hwy 3 V0X 1W0 (PO Box 1555). Fax: 250/295-3547. **Terms:** [CP] meal plan; weekly rates avail, off season; small pets only, $10 fee, in smoking rooms. **Facility:** 43 rooms. Along the main hwy in the centre of town. The guest rooms are pleasantly decorated in modern colors and furniture. Very large, fully equipped kitchen units. 2 stories; exterior corridors; heated pool, sauna, whirlpool. **Dining:** Restaurant nearby. **Services:** winter plug-ins. **All Rooms:** extended cable TV. **Cards:** AE, CB, DI, DS, JC, MC, VI. **Special Amenities:** Free breakfast and free local telephone calls. *(See color ad below)*

QUADRA ISLAND —*See Gulf Islands p. 419.*

QUALICUM BAY pop. 19,900

—— RESTAURANT ——

SANDBAR CAFE   **Lunch:** $6-$10   **Dinner:** $7-$11   **Phone:** 250/757-9995
◆   **Location:** On Island Hwy 19A. 6087 W Island Hwy V0R 1G0. **Hours:** 8 am-8 pm. Closed: 12/25.
Canadian   **Features:** No A/C; beer & wine only; a la carte. The Sandbar Cafe is a roadside-style diner and features a very nice view of the water. The traditional fare of very good food includes a daily selection of tasty sandwiches and homemade soups. The coffee is always fresh! Friendly and prompt service. **Cards:** MC, VI.

QUALICUM BEACH pop. 6,700

—— LODGINGS ——

BAHARI BED & BREAKFAST **Phone:** 250/752-9278
◆◆   6/16-9/30   1P: $105-$175   2P: $125-$185
Bed &   3/1-6/15, 10/1-11/30 & 2/1-2/28 1P: $65-$125   2P: $85-$125
Breakfast   **Location:** Hwy 19, exit Qualicum Beach/Port Alberni, 4 km e on Memorial Ave, then 11 km n on Hwy 19A. 5101 Island Hwy W V9K1Z1. Fax: 250/752-9038. **Terms:** Open 3/1-11/30 & 2/1-2/28; [BP] meal plan; age restrictions may apply; 7 day cancellation notice; cancellation fee imposed. **Facility:** 4 rooms. A unique Japanese theme greets the visitor to this B&B, from the comfortable guest rooms, 3 of which offer spectacular hilltop views overlooking Georgia Strait, to the pathway leading to a secluded hot tub. 2 stories; interior corridors; designated smoking area. **All Rooms:** combo or shower baths. **Some Rooms:** color TV. **Cards:** AE, MC, VI.

OCEAN CREST MOTEL **Phone:** (250)752-5518
CAA SAVE   6/16-9/15   1P: $75-$85   2P: $75-$85   XP: $10   D12
◆◆   3/1-6/15 & 9/16-2/28   1P: $55-$65   2P: $55-$65   XP: $10   D12
Motel   **Location:** Hwy 19, exit Qualicum Beach/Port Alberni, 4 km e on Memorial Ave, then 3 km n on Hwy 19A. 3292 W Island Hwy V9K 2C6. Fax: 250/752-5798. **Terms:** Weekly & monthly rates avail, off season. **Facility:** 18 rooms. A wonderful up-to-date economy style property featuring very pleasant, clean and comfortable guest rooms. Across the hwy from the public beach with direct access where birds and wildlife abound. 8 efficencies, $8 extra charge; 2 stories; exterior corridors; smoke free premises. **Dining:** Restaurant nearby. **All Rooms:** extended cable TV. **Cards:** AE, DI, DS, MC, VI. **Special Amenities:** Free local telephone calls and preferred room (subject to availability with advanced reservations).

OLD DUTCH INN (BY THE SEA)   Phone: 250/752-6914
◆◆   6/1-9/30   1P: $79-$109   2P: $89-$109   XP: $10
Motor Inn   3/1-5/31 & 10/1-2/28   1P: $64-$99   2P: $69-$99   XP: $10
Location: From Hwy 19, exit Qualicum Beach/Port Alberni, 4 km e on Memorial Ave at jct Hwy 19A. 2690 Island
Hwy W V9K 1G8. Fax: 250/752-6910. Terms: Cancellation fee imposed; package plans; small pets only, $10 extra charge.
Facility: 35 rooms. A charming Dutch theme throughout. Several guest rooms have views of the ocean bay located across the
street. Guest rooms are large offering a comfortable guest room decor. Excellent housekeeping. 2 stories; interior corridors;
heated pool. Services: gift shop. All Rooms: combo or shower baths. Cards: AE, DI, MC, VI.

THE SHOREWATER CONDOMINIUM RESORT   Phone: 250/752-6901
◆◆   6/16-9/15   1P: $125-$175   2P: $125-$175   XP: $10
Condominium   9/16-2/28   1P: $79-$110   2P: $79-$110   XP: $10
                3/1-6/15   1P: $79-$99   2P: $79-$99   XP: $10
Location: From Hwy 19, exit Qualicum Beach/Port Alberni, 4 km e on Memorial Ave then 3 km n Hwy 19A. 3295 Island Hwy
W V9K 2C6. Fax: 250/752-2731. Terms: 30 day cancellation notice; cancellation fee imposed. Facility: 24 rooms. Pleasantly
decorated condo unit with the individual owners special touches. All of the units sit directly on the beach and feature wonderful
ocean views. Half the units feature a separate sleeping loft and a few feature gas fireplace. 2 stories; exterior corridors; oceanfront. All Rooms: kitchens. Cards: MC, VI.

--------- RESTAURANTS ---------

MONTE CHRISTO QUALICUM BEACH   Dinner: $10-$22   Phone: 250/752-1468
◆◆   Location: From Hwy 19, exit Qualicum Beach/Port Alberni, 4 km e on Memorial Ave, 4 km e on Memorial Ave on Hwy
Steak and   19 A. 3353 W Island Hwy V9K 2N2. Hours: 4 pm-9 pm, Fri & Sat-10 pm. Closed: 1/1 & 12/25.
Seafood   Reservations: suggested; in season. Features: No A/C; children's menu; senior's menu; cocktails & lounge;
            a la carte. This fun and popular restaurant features a wide array of menu items such as steak, tiger prawns,
a Greek platter, lamb chops, chicken teriyaki, pasta and barbecue dishes. There's also a menu for those with smaller
appetites. Several lodgings are nearby. Cards: AE, MC, VI.

OLD DUTCH INN DINING ROOM   Lunch: $5-$10   Dinner: $11-$25   Phone: 250/752-6914
◆◆◆   Location: From Hwy 19, exit Qualicum Beach/Port Alberni, 4 km on Memorial Ave at jct Hwy 19A; in Old
Ethnic   Dutch Inn (By The Sea). 2690 Island Hwy W V9K 1G8. Hours: 7 am-9 pm. Reservations: suggested.
            Features: children's menu; early bird specials; cocktails & lounge; a la carte. You'll enjoy the wonderful
ocean view at this restaurant, which offers creatively prepared, world-famous pastries as well as early bird specials and
Dutch specialties. The servers dressed in Dutch costumes complete the Old Dutch atmosphere and decor. Cards: AE, DI,
MC, VI.

QUESNEL pop. 8,500

--------- LODGINGS ---------

TALISMAN INN   Phone: (250)992-7247
(CAA)   All Year   1P: $55-$65   2P: $65-$81   XP: $5   F12
◆◆   Location: 1 km n of Carson Ave, on Hwy 97. 753 Front St V2J 2L2. Fax: 250/992-3126. Terms: Cancellation
Motel   fee imposed; small pets only, on ground floor. Facility: 87 rooms. Property features 3 different sections and
                styles of room decor, from a modest type guest room in main building to large efficiency units in 2nd bldg.
                Wonderfully clean and well maintained. Close to hospital and river walk area. Efficiency & kitchen units, $6
extra charge; 28 whirlpool rooms, $81-$105; 2 stories; interior corridors; whirlpool. Dining: Restaurant nearby.
Services: winter plug-ins. All Rooms: extended cable TV. Cards: AE, DI, DS, JC, MC, VI.

TOWER INN SUITES AND HOTELS   Phone: (250)992-2201
◆◆   5/1-9/30   1P: $70   2P: $75   XP: $5   F12
Motor Inn   3/1-4/30 & 10/1-2/28   1P: $65   1P: $70   XP: $5   F12
                Location: From Hwy 97, just e on Shepherd Ave. 500 Reid St V2J 2M9. Fax: 250/992-5201. Facility: 64
rooms. Located downtown, close to local hospital. Large, clean guest rooms with modern decor. 1 two-bedroom unit. 4 stories;
interior corridors. Cards: AE, DI, DS, MC, VI.

RADIUM HOT SPRINGS pop. 500

--------- LODGINGS ---------

BIG HORN MOTEL   Phone: (250)347-9522
◆   5/1-9/15   1P: $45-$58   2P: $45-$63   XP: $5   D5
Motel   9/16-12/31   1P: $40-$48   2P: $45-$59   XP: $5   D5
                1/1-2/28   1P: $40-$50   2P: $45-$55   XP: $5   D5
                3/1-4/30   1P: $40-$43   2P: $43-$48   XP: $5   D5
Location: From Hwy 93/95 (4-way stop), just s, then just w. 4881 St Marys St V0A 1M0 (PO BOX 176). Terms: Package plans.
Facility: 20 rooms. A mix of old and new in various sizes and styles, resulting in cozy although modest room ambiance. Gazebo and barbecue in courtyard. 8 two-bedroom units. 1 story; exterior corridors. Fee: miniature golf. Services: winter plug-
ins. Some Rooms: 8 efficiencies. Cards: MC, VI.

CEDAR MOTEL

CAA SAVE

◆◆

Motel

6/1-9/20	1P: $52-$72	2P: $52-$72	XP: $10	F6
3/1-5/31 & 9/21-2/28	1P: $41-$51	2P: $41-$51	XP: $6	F6

Phone: (250)347-9463

Location: Off Hwy 93 and 95, 0.3 km s of jct Hwy 93, on service road (Main St). 7593 Main St W V0A 1M0 (PO Box 157). Fax: 250/347-9303. **Terms:** Cancellation fee imposed; package plans; pets, $4 extra charge with permission. **Facility:** 17 rooms. Spacious units offering a homelike ambiance. Decor enhanced with natural wood and alpine accents. 2 two-bedroom units. 8 kitchens, $7-$10 extra charge; 2 stories; exterior corridors. **Dining:** Restaurant nearby. **Services:** winter plug-ins. **All Rooms:** extended cable TV. **Cards:** AE, CB, DI, DS, MC, VI. **Special Amenities:** Free local telephone calls. *(See ad below)*

THE CHALET EUROPE

◆◆

Motel

5/15-10/1	1P: $95-$125	2P: $95-$125	XP: $10	F6
3/1-5/14	1P: $65-$95	2P: $65-$95	XP: $2	F6
10/2-2/28	1P: $65-$95	2P: $65-$95	XP: $10	F6

Phone: 250/347-9305

Location: Just e of jct Hwy 93 and 95, 1 km off Hwy 93 up the hill. 5063 Madsen Rd V0A 1M0 (PO Box 456). Fax: 250/347-9306. **Terms:** [CP] meal plan; 7 day cancellation notice; cancellation fee imposed; pets, $10 extra charge. **Facility:** 17 rooms. Hilltop location with panoramic mountain valley view. Alpine styled; balconies. All units offer a seating area separate from bedroom. Homelike ambiance. All rooms with hair dryer. 3 stories, no elevator; exterior corridors. **Services:** gift shop; winter plug-ins. **Recreation:** hiking trails, jogging. **All Rooms:** efficiencies. **Cards:** AE, DI, DS, MC, VI. *(See ad below)*

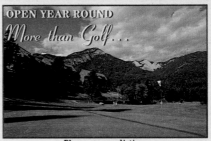

LIDO MOTEL
Phone: 250/347-9533

◆◆
Motel

| | 6/16-9/15 | 1P: $44-$54 | 2P: $50-$68 | XP: $10 |
| | 3/15-6/15 & 9/16-10/31 | 1P: $36-$44 | 2P: $38-$56 | XP: $6 |

Location: Hwy 93 and 95 S, Stanley St w to Main St W, then s. 4876 McKay St V0A 1M0 (PO Box 36). **Terms:** Open 3/15-10/31; cancellation fee imposed; pets. **Facility:** 11 rooms. Charming cabin style accommodation offering well appointed units with country home decor. 8 two-bedroom units. 1 story; exterior corridors. **Services:** winter plug-ins. **All Rooms:** combo or shower baths. **Some Rooms:** 9 efficiencies. **Cards:** DS, MC, VI.

MOTEL BAVARIA
Phone: 250/347-9915

(CAA) (SAVE)
◆◆
Motel

	7/1-9/30	1P: $60-$65	2P: $65-$70	XP: $8	F6
	5/16-6/30	1P: $50-$55	2P: $55-$60	XP: $8	F6
	3/1-5/15 & 10/1-2/28	1P: $40-$45	2P: $45-$52	XP: $6	F6

Location: Just w off Hwy 95; on Pioneer Ave. 4872 McKay St V0A 1M0 (PO Box 148). Fax: 250/347-9218. **Terms:** 3 day cancellation notice. **Facility:** 24 rooms. Spacious rooms offering pleasant, simple decor. Very well maintained property. A few units offer upgraded decor, 1 with a wood burning fireplace. 11 efficiencies, $8 extra charge. Deluxe whirlpool rm with microwave, refrigerator & vcr, $100; 2 stories; exterior corridors; mountain view. **Services:** winter plug-ins. **Recreation:** gazebo barbecue area. **All Rooms:** extended cable TV. **Cards:** AE, MC, VI.

SPRINGS AT RADIUM GOLF RESORT
Phone: (250)347-9311

(CAA) (SAVE)
◆◆◆
Resort

	6/1-9/30	1P: $129-$280	2P: $129-$280		
	4/1-5/31 & 10/1-10/31	1P: $109-$190	2P: $109-$190	XP: $10	F16
	3/1-3/31	1P: $79	2P: $140	XP: $10	F16

Location: 3 km s on Hwy 93 and 95, 1 km e. 8100 Radium Golf Course Rd V0A 1M0 (PO Box 310). Fax: 250/347-6299. **Terms:** Open 3/1-10/31; [BP] meal plan; check-in 4 pm; 3 day cancellation notice; cancellation fee imposed; package plans. **Facility:** 120 rooms. Set in a scenic, quiet mountain valley; most rooms have private balcony overlooking golf course. All rooms with hair dryer and voice mail. Some luxury level services offered. 24 two-bedroom units, 6 three-bedroom units. No extra person charge in condo; 12 whirlpool rooms, $109-$189; 2-3 stories, no elevator; exterior corridors; golf equipment & instruction, pro shop; heated pool, sauna, whirlpools; racquetball court, 2 lighted tennis courts, squash-1 court. Fee: 36 holes golf. **Dining:** Restaurant; 7 am-10 pm; $14-$18; cocktails. **Services:** winter plug-ins. Fee: massage. **Recreation:** cross country skiing. **All Rooms:** extended cable TV. **Some Rooms:** 30 kitchens. **Cards:** AE, DI, MC, VI. **Special Amenities:** Free room upgrade and preferred room (each subject to availability with advanced reservations). *(See color ad p 451)*

SUNRISE SUITE MOTEL
Phone: (250)347-0008

◆◆◆
Apartment

| | 6/1-10/1 | 1P: $75-$85 | 2P: $85-$135 | XP: $10 | F9 |
| | 3/1-5/31 & 10/2-2/28 | 1P: $55-$95 | 2P: $65-$110 | XP: $10 | F9 |

Location: From jct Hwy 93/95, 0.7 km n on Hwy 95, just sw. 7371 Prospector Ave V0A 1M0 (PO Box 581). Fax: 250/347-0028. **Terms:** Check-in 4 pm; 4 day cancellation notice; package plans; small pets only, with permission. **Facility:** 8 rooms. Modern property well back from hwy. 1-3 bedroom apts are beautifully appointed and include a full-size kitchen; some with dishwasher, dining area and living room. Ceiling fans. 1-2 stories; exterior corridors; designated smoking area; miniature golf. **Services:** gift shop; winter plug-ins. **All Rooms:** kitchens. **Cards:** MC, VI.

SUNSET MOTEL
Phone: (250)347-9863

(CAA) (SAVE)
◆◆
Motel

| | 3/1-6/14 & 10/1-2/28 | 1P: $42-$50 | 2P: $46-$80 | XP: $8 | F12 |
| | 6/15-9/30 | 1P: $54-$60 | 2P: $58-$70 | XP: $8 | F12 |

Location: Hwy 93 and 95 S, w to service road (Main St) and just s. 4883 McKay St V0A 1M0 (PO Box 86). Fax: 250/347-9862. **Terms:** Pets, with permission. **Facility:** 20 rooms. Charmingly decorated units offering a well harmonized mix of older and newer elements with a European flair. 5 two-bedroom units. 3-bedroom unit, $95-$110; 1 story; exterior corridors. **Services:** winter plug-ins. **Recreation:** barbecues & picnic tables. **All Rooms:** combo or shower baths, extended cable TV. **Cards:** MC, VI. **Special Amenities:** Preferred room (subject to availability with advanced reservations).

VILLAGE COUNTRY INN AND TEA ROOM
Phone: (250)347-9392

(CAA)
◆◆◆
Country Inn

	7/1-9/3	1P: $94-$115	2P: $94-$115	XP: $15
	5/19-6/30	1P: $84-$115	2P: $84-$115	XP: $15
	9/4-2/28	1P: $69-$115	2P: $69-$115	XP: $15
	3/1-5/18	1P: $69-$105	2P: $69-$105	XP: $15

Location: Just s from jct Hwy 93 and 95, w on St Joseph St (across from playground). 7557 Canyon Ave V0A 1M0 (PO Box 15). Fax: 250/347-9375. **Terms:** [BP] meal plan; age restrictions may apply; 3 day cancellation notice; cancellation fee imposed. **Facility:** 13 rooms. Modern Victorian inn with European enhancements and hospitality. Average sized rooms with duvets and hand-crafted furniture. Stone fireplace centered in the tea room with piano. Suites, $115; 2 stories; interior corridors; smoke free premises; mountain view. **Dining:** Dining room; 7:30 am-10 & 5-10:30 pm, dinner upon req only. Open to general public; afternoon tea. **Services:** winter plug-ins. **Recreation:** games in tea room. **All Rooms:** combo or shower baths, extended cable TV. **Cards:** AE, MC, VI.

—— RESTAURANT ——

THE OLD SALZBURG RESTAURANT
Lunch: $7-$10　　Dinner: $12-$25　　Phone: 250/347-6553

(CAA)
◆◆
Continental

Location: Just w of jct SR 93 and 95, in town centre. 4943 Hwy 93 V0A 1M0. **Hours:** 11:30 am-4 & 5-11 pm, to 10 pm off season. Closed: 11/1-11/30, 1/2-1/31, Mon & Tues in winter, off season for lunch. **Reservations:** suggested; in summer. **Features:** casual dress; children's menu; carryout; cocktails; a la carte. This restaurant offers traditional Austrian and Continental dishes such as schnitzel, hearty spatzle, pasta, chicken and steak. Its atmosphere is warm, with a mountain village ambience. It provides friendly service, and outdoor patio dining in season. **Cards:** MC, VI.

REVELSTOKE pop. 8,000

——— LODGINGS ———

BEST WESTERN WAYSIDE INN

Phone: (250)837-6161

	5/15-9/30	1P: $99-$129	2P: $109-$139	XP: $6	F12
	3/1-5/14 & 10/1-2/28	1P: $79-$109	2P: $89-$119	XP: $6	F12

(AAA) (SAVE)
◆◆◆
Motor Inn

Location: N side of Trans Canada Hwy 1, at intersection nearest east end of Columbia River Bridge. 1901 LaForme Blvd V0E 2S0 (PO Box 59). Fax: 250/837-5460. **Terms:** Pets, in designated rooms. **Facility:** 88 rooms. Quiet location just off the main hwy, surrounded by the majestic Monashee and Selkirk Mountains. Spacious and well appointed rooms, all rooms with hair dryer. 2 stories; interior/exterior corridors; mountain view; heated pool, saunas, whirlpool. **Dining:** Restaurant; 6:30 am-9 pm; to 10 pm in season; $8-$18; cocktails. **Services:** winter plug-ins. **Recreation:** Fee: helicopter skiing. **All Rooms:** extended cable TV. **Cards:** AE, CB, DI, DS, JC, MC, VI. **Special Amenities:** Free local telephone calls.

THE REGENT INN

Phone: (250)837-2107

	3/1-4/30 & 7/1-9/30	1P: $99-$129	2P: $99-$179	XP: $15	F15
	5/1-6/30 & 10/1-2/28	1P: $89-$119	2P: $99-$129	XP: $15	F15

(AAA) (SAVE)
◆◆◆
Motor Inn

Location: 2 km s from Trans Canada Hwy 1; in historic downtown adjacent to Grizzly Plaza. 112 1st St E V0E 2S0 (PO BOX 582). Fax: 250/837-9669. **Terms:** [CP] meal plan; cancellation fee imposed; package plans; small pets only. **Facility:** 52 rooms. A fully restored historic structure located in the heart of downtown. Rooms range from average size to spacious, all well appointed and include a duvet. Inviting breakfast room. Majestic mountain setting. 4 two-bedroom units. Deluxe whirlpool rm, $179; 3 stories, no elevator; interior corridors; sauna, whirlpools. **Dining:** The One Twelve Restaurant, see separate listing. **Services:** winter plug-ins. **Recreation:** Fee: helicopter skiing, mountain guides. **All Rooms:** extended cable TV. **Some Rooms:** Fee: VCR. **Cards:** AE, MC, VI. **Special Amenities:** Free breakfast and free room upgrade (subject to availability with advanced reservations).

SUPER 8 MOTEL REVELSTOKE

Phone: (250)837-0888

	6/21-9/8	1P: $95-$100	2P: $100-$110	XP: $5	F12
	9/9-9/30	1P: $80-$85	2P: $85-$90	XP: $5	F12
	3/1-6/20	1P: $85-$85	2P: $70-$90	XP: $5	F12
	10/1-2/28	1P: $55-$65	2P: $60-$70	XP: $5	F12

(AAA) (SAVE)
◆◆
Motel

Location: S side of Trans Canada Hwy 1, just e of Columbia River Bridge at Victoria Rd (town centre exit). 1700 W Victoria Rd V0E 2S0 (Box 2964). Fax: 250/837-0880. **Facility:** 44 rooms. Contemporary decor in standard size units or suites offering a separate living area. Spacious lobby, with pleasant seating by fireplace. 1 two-bedroom unit. 2 stories; interior corridors; whirlpool, small heated salt water indoor pool. **Dining:** Restaurant nearby. **Services:** winter plug-ins. **All Rooms:** extended cable TV. **Cards:** AE, MC, VI. **Special Amenities:** Free local telephone calls.

SWISS CHALET MOTEL

Phone: (250)837-4650

	7/1-9/5	1P: $49-$59	2P: $59-$75	XP: $7	D6
	5/1-6/30	1P: $45-$55	2P: $49-$65	XP: $5	D6
	9/6-2/28	1P: $35-$55	2P: $39-$65	XP: $5	D6
	3/1-4/30	1P: $35-$45	2P: $39-$49	XP: $5	D6

(AAA)
◆
Motel

Location: 0.9 km s from Hwy 1. 1101 Victoria Rd V0E 2S0 (PO Box 359). Fax: 250/837-2485. **Terms:** [CP] meal plan; weekly rates avail, off season; small pets only, $5 extra charge, in designated rooms. **Facility:** 22 rooms. An older but well-maintained property offering rooms of various sizes. Located close to town centre. 2 two-bedroom units. 1-2 stories; interior/exterior corridors. **Dining:** Coffee shop. **Services:** winter plug-ins. **All Rooms:** combo or shower baths, extended cable TV. **Some Rooms:** 4 efficiencies. **Cards:** AE, MC, VI.

——— RESTAURANTS ———

BLACK FOREST RESTAURANT

Dinner: $12-$25   Phone: 250/837-3495

(AAA)
◆◆
Continental

Location: 5 km w on Hwy 1. V0E 2S0. **Hours:** 5 pm-9 pm. Closed: 12/25, Tues & 11/1-11/30. **Reservations:** suggested. **Features:** casual dress; children's menu; cocktails. The Black Forest is a gem of a restaurant. It features flavorful food, excellent service and a family-style, Alpine atmosphere. The baked Cajun shrimp are out of this world, and the turkey forestiere is excellent also. Say hello to the friendly owners. **Cards:** AE, DI, MC, VI.

THE ONE TWELVE RESTAURANT

Lunch: $9-$14   Dinner: $15-$28   Phone: 250/837-2107

◆◆◆
American

Location: 2 km s from Trans Canada Hwy 1; at Victoria Rd in historic downtown adjacent to Grizzly Plaza; in The Regent Inn. 112 1st St E V0E 2S0. **Hours:** 11:45 am-2 & 5:30-9 pm. Closed major holidays. **Reservations:** suggested. **Features:** health conscious menu items; cocktails & lounge; a la carte. The One Twelve features an elegant, comfortable heritage decor and a menu specializing in excellent salads, steaks, lamb, veal and British Columbia salmon. Dishes are prepared exquisitely by a fine European chef who uses only the freshest ingredients. **Cards:** AE, DI, MC, VI.

THREE VALLEY GAP DINING ROOM

Lunch: $6-$15   Dinner: $7-$17   Phone: 250/837-2109

◆
Canadian

Location: 19.2 km w on Trans Canada 1 on Three Valley Lake; in Three Valley Gap Resort Motor Inn. **Hours:** Open 4/2-10/12; 7 am-9 pm. **Features:** children's menu; cocktails; a la carte. The menu at Three Valley Gap offers fish 'n' chips, burgers, sandwiches, quite a few salads, and chicken and beef entrees. The pleasant dining room overlooks the lake and spectacular mountain scenery, and the servers are friendly and attentive. Smoke free premises. **Cards:** AE, DI, DS, MC, VI.

TONY'S ROMA

Lunch: $5-$12   Dinner: $9-$16   Phone: 250/837-4106

◆◆
Italian

Location: Downtown. 306 Mackenzie Ave V0E 2S0. **Hours:** 11 am-11 pm; to 10 pm off season. Closed: Sun in winter. **Features:** casual dress; children's menu; carryout; cocktails; a la carte. Tony's Italian fare is prepared with North American influences and includes popular versions of pasta, pizza, veal and poultry dishes. Local microbrewery products are featured also. The rustic decor is comfortable, appealing and welcoming to families. **Cards:** AE, MC, VI.

RICHMOND —*See Vancouver p. 512.*

ROBERTS CREEK pop. 13,100

——— LODGING ———

WELCOME INN BED & BREAKFAST
◆◆
Bed & Breakfast

	5/1-9/30	1P: $65-$100	2P: $75-$100	XP: $20	D12
	3/1-4/30 & 10/1-2/28	1P: $55-$100	2P: $65-$100	XP: $20	D12

Phone: (604)270-0318

Location: Hwy 101 and Flume Rd, 16 km n from the Langdale Ferry terminal. 1176 Flume Rd V0N 2W0 (General Delivery). Fax: 604/740-0318. **Terms:** [BP] meal plan; check-in 4 pm; 7 day cancellation notice. **Facility:** 4 rooms. Comfortable guest rooms inside the house or a self contained garden cottage with separate bedrooms and living room. Just a short drive to Gibsons for restaurants and sightseeing. 2 stories; interior corridors; designated smoking area. **Cards:** MC, VI.

ROGERS PASS pop. 3,300

——— LODGING ———

BEST WESTERN GLACIER PARK LODGE
(CAA) (SAVE)
◆◆◆
Motor Inn

	7/1-9/30	1P: $115-$140	2P: $125-$150	XP: $10	F12
	5/1-6/30	1P: $95-$105	2P: $105-$115	XP: $10	F12
	10/1-2/28	1P: $75-$85	2P: $85-$95	XP: $10	F12
	3/1-4/30	1P: $65-$75	2P: $75-$85	XP: $10	F12

Phone: (250)837-2126

Location: On Trans Canada Hwy 1; in Glacier National Park, near Summit Pass. (The Summit, V0E 2S0). Fax: 250/837-2130. **Terms:** [MAP] meal plan; check-in 4 pm; 3 day cancellation notice; cancellation fee imposed; package plans. **Facility:** 50 rooms. Spectacular mountain scenery. Alpine structure on mountain slope in secluded, remote area. Busy tour bus stopover in summer. Guest rooms are large and have all the modern conveniences. Satellite TV. 2 stories; interior corridors; mountain view; sauna, whirlpool, covered heated pool open all year. **Dining:** Dining room, cafeteria; 24 hrs; $17-$24; cocktails. **Services:** gift shop. **Cards:** AE, CB, DI, DS, MC, VI. **Special Amenities:** Free local telephone calls and free room upgrade (subject to availability with advanced reservations). *(See color ad below)*

TAKE A HIKE!

Three Diamond luxury in a rustic wilderness setting. Stay awhile & explore 140 kilometres of safe, groomed trails. Take a leisurely stroll or conquer a glacier. Guides available. Spectacular scenery, historical museum, full amenities including heated pool, hot tub & sauna.

Best Western
Glacier Park Lodge

ROGERS PASS, BC CANADA
Telephone: (250) 837-2126
Toll Free: 1-888-567-4477
www.glacierparklodgecanada.com

The heart of Glacier National Park

ROSSLAND pop. 3,800

──── LODGINGS ────

SWISS ALPS INN   **Phone: (250)362-7364**

CAA SAVE   3/1-3/31 & 12/21-2/28   1P: $49-$59   2P: $59-$69
◆   4/1-12/20   1P: $38-$49   2P: $44-$59
Motor Inn   **Location:** 1 km w on Hwy 3B, at jct of Hwy 22. 1199 Nancy Green Hwy V0G 1Y0 (PO Box 1071).
Fax: 250/362-7315. **Terms:** [BP] meal plan; 60 day cancellation notice; cancellation fee imposed; package
plans; pets, $5 extra charge. **Facility:** 40 rooms. Average to compact units, most feature newer decor while a
few remain modest in appeal. Easy access to local ski area. 2 stories; exterior corridors; whirlpool. **Dining:** Restaurant; 7
am-11 & 4-8 pm; $8-$15; cocktails. **Services:** area transportation; ski hills; winter plug-ins. **Recreation:** Fee: bicycles.
All Rooms: extended cable TV. **Some Rooms:** 5 efficiencies. **Cards:** AE, MC, VI. **Special Amenities:** Early check-in/late
check-out and free local telephone calls.

UPLANDER HOTEL   **Phone: (250)362-7375**

CAA SAVE   12/20-2/28   1P: $86-$128   2P: $96-$135   XP: $6   F11
◆◆◆   3/1-12/19   1P: $79-$128   2P: $86-$135   XP: $6   F11
Motor Inn   **Location:** Centre; on Hwy 3B. 1919 Columbia Ave V0G 1Y0 (PO Box 1510). Fax: 250/362-7375.
Terms: Monthly rates avail; 30 day cancellation notice; cancellation fee imposed; package plans. **Facility:** 67
rooms. Traditional cedar structure in downtown mountain village with good views. Rooms may offer a slightly
older decor but are very well appointed. 14 efficiencies, $10 extra charge; 3 stories; interior corridors; sauna, whirlpool.
Dining: Dining room, coffee shop; 6:30 am-9 pm; $13-$23; cocktails. **Services:** gift shop; winter plug-ins. **All Rooms:** extended cable TV. **Cards:** AE, DI, MC, VI. **Special Amenities:** Free local telephone calls.

SAANICHTON —See Victoria p. 548.

SALMO pop. 1,200

──── RESTAURANTS ────

CHARLIE'S PIZZA & SPAGHETTI HOUSE   **Lunch:** $5-$18   **Dinner:** $5-$18   **Phone:** 250/357-9335
CAA   **Location:** Centre; just e of Hwy 6. 205 4th St V0G 1Z0. **Hours:** 6:30 am-9 pm; to 8 pm 11/1-5/1. Closed:
◆   12/25. **Features:** children's menu; senior's menu; health conscious menu; carryout; beer & wine only. This
Italian   charming diner-style restaurant is located at the heart of a small village in the Kootenays. It opens early for
breakfast and serves snacks and meals throughout the day. North American and Italian dishes and friendly
service are featured here. **Cards:** MC, VI.

TRAPPER JOHN'S RESTAURANT   **Lunch:** $6-$9   **Dinner:** $10-$20   **Phone:** 250/357-2296
◆   **Location:** Jct of Hwy 3 and 6, 0.4 km w on Hwy 3. **Hours:** 9 am-9 pm. Closed: 12/25 & 12/26.
Canadian   **Reservations:** accepted. **Features:** casual dress; carryout; salad bar; cocktails; a la carte. You'll enjoy the
unusual log structure of Trapper John's, where the menu offers home-cooked family fare of burgers,
sandwiches and pita pockets for lunch and steaks and pastas for dinner. The service is quite friendly and attentive; the
decor is pleasant. **Cards:** MC, VI.

SALMON ARM pop. 14,700

──── LODGINGS ────

THE COAST SHUSWAP LODGE   **Phone: (250)832-7081**

CAA SAVE   5/1-9/30   1P: $130   2P: $140   XP: $10   F18
◆◆◆   3/1-4/30 & 10/1-2/28   1P: $99   2P: $109   XP: $10   F18
Motor Inn   **Location:** 1 km w on Trans Canada Hwy 1. 200 Trans Canada Hwy W V1E 4P6 (PO Box 1540).
Fax: 250/832-6753. **Terms:** Package plans; small pets only. **Facility:** 40 rooms. Property features attractive
guest rooms and public areas. Ground floor guest rooms that face courtyard area have a small patio leading
to pool area. 5 superior rooms, $115-$150; whirlpool room; 2 stories; interior corridors; heated pool, whirlpool. **Dining:** Restaurant; 6 am-11 pm; $8-$14; wine/beer only. **All Rooms:** extended cable TV. **Some Rooms:** honor bars. **Cards:** AE, DI, DS,
JC, MC, VI. **Special Amenities:** Free local telephone calls.

SUPER 8 MOTEL   **Phone:** 250/832-8812

◆◆   Property failed to provide current rates
Motel   **Location:** 1 km e on Trans Canada Hwy 1. 2901 10th Ave NE V1E 4N1. Fax: 250/832-2217. **Terms:** [CP] meal
plan; pets, with permission. **Facility:** 39 rooms. Good budget oriented accommodations. Guest rooms are average in size but all offer a pleasant simple decor. On the top of hill on the east end of town. 2 stories; interior corridors.
Cards: AE, CB, DI, DS, JC, MC, VI.

TRAVELODGE-SALMON ARM   **Phone:** (250)832-9721

CAA SAVE   6/16-9/15   1P: $75   2P: $82-$92   XP: $7   F17
◆◆   9/16-2/28   1P: $62   2P: $67-$72   F17
Motel   3/1-6/15   1P: $62   2P: $67-$72   XP: $7   F17
             Location: 3 km w on Trans Canada Hwy 1. 2401 Trans Canada Hwy W V1E 4P7 (PO Box 1575).
Fax: 250/832-3557. **Terms:** Cancellation fee imposed; pets, $5 extra charge. **Facility:** 38 rooms. On the w end
of town and situated next to an open pasture. Average sized guest rooms with modern decor. 2 stories; exterior corridors;
heated pool, whirlpool. **Dining:** Restaurant nearby. **All Rooms:** extended cable TV. **Some Rooms:** Fee: VCR. **Cards:** AE, DI,
DS, MC, VI.

SALTSPRING ISLAND —See Gulf Islands p. 419.

SAVONA

——— LODGING ———

LAKESIDE COUNTRY INN   Phone: (250)373-2528

◆◆◆   6/15-9/15   1P: $89-$139   2P: $89-$139   XP: $10
Motel   5/1-6/14 & 9/16-11/30   1P: $79-$109   2P: $79-$109   XP: $10
             3/1-4/30   1P: $59-$89   2P: $59-$89   XP: $10

Location: Trans Canada Hwy 1, exit Savona, along the Business Frontage Rd. 7001 Savona Access Rd V0K 2J0 (Box 260). **Fax:** 250/373-2432. **Terms:** Open 3/1-11/30; small pets only, with approval. **Facility:** 9 rooms. This delightful property features a country inn style decor and small patio decks overlooking Kamloops Lake. The units range from average size to slightly larger kitchen units. Quiet country setting. 1 two-bedroom unit. 2 stories; exterior corridors; designated smoking area; boat dock. **Services:** winter plug-ins. **Recreation:** swimming, fishing; bicycles, hiking trails. Rental: boats, canoes, paddleboats. **All Rooms:** combo or shower baths. **Some Rooms:** efficiency, 3 kitchens. **Cards:** AE, DI, MC, VI.

SECHELT pop. 7,300

——— LODGING ———

BELLA BEACH MOTOR INN   Phone: 604/885-7191

◆   Property failed to provide current rates
Motor Inn   **Location:** 5 km s on Hwy 101. 4748 Hwy 101 V0N 3A0 (RR 1, C-21). **Fax:** 604/885-3794. **Terms:** Small pets only, $10-$20 extra charge. **Facility:** 30 rooms. Directly across the street from the beach with all of the guest rooms featuring their own private balcony with wonderful view of the ocean. Guest units are simple but nicely decorated, a few units offer a separate bedroom area. 6 two-bedroom units. 2 stories; exterior corridors; ocean view. **Some Rooms:** 11 efficiencies. **Cards:** AE, MC, VI.

SICAMOUS pop. 2,800

——— LODGINGS ———

MARA LAKE INN   Phone: (250)836-2126

CAA SAVE   7/1-8/31   1P: $65-$90   2P: $70-$95   XP: $5   F16
◆◆   3/1-6/30 & 9/1-11/1   1P: $50-$80   2P: $55-$85   XP: $5   F16
Motor Inn   11/2-2/28   1P: $45-$55   2P: $50-$60   XP: $5   F16

Location: Jct Hwy 1 and 97A, 2.5 km s on Hwy 97A. (PO Box 218, V0E 2V0). **Fax:** 250/836-2975. **Terms:** Weekly rates avail; check-in 4 pm; 7 day cancellation notice. **Facility:** 32 rooms. Lake front property with all rooms overlooking Mara Lake. 7 rustic cabin-type units avail. Guest rooms offer basic, yet cozy accommodations. Small private sandy beach area with dock. Limited number of room open in winter. 1 two-bedroom family room with efficiency, $79-$119. Large family suite with refrigerator,$89-$139; 2 stories; exterior corridors; beach; boat dock. **Dining:** Restaurant; 8 am-10 pm, in season, closed for winter; $9-$15; cocktails. **Recreation:** swimming; game room. Rental: canoes. **All Rooms:** combo or shower baths, extended cable TV. **Some Rooms:** 13 efficiencies. **Cards:** MC, VI.

RAINBOW VALLEY BED & BREAKFAST   Phone: (250)836-3268

CAA SAVE   3/1-10/15   1P: $65-$90   2P: $75-$105   XP: $20
◆◆◆   10/16-2/28   1P: $55-$80   2P: $65-$95   XP: $20
Bed &   **Location:** Jct Hwy 97A and 1, 0.6 km n on Hwy 1, just n. 1409 Rauma Rd V0E 2V0. **Fax:** 250/836-3008.
Breakfast   **Terms:** [BP] meal plan; check-in 5 pm; 21 day cancellation notice. **Facility:** 4 rooms. Modern stucco house features very spacious guest rooms. Adjacent common area with some kitchen amenities. 1 three-bedroom unit with full kitchen, washer, dryer and private entrance. 2 stories; interior/exterior corridors; smoke free premises. **Services:** winter plug-ins. **All Rooms:** extended cable TV. **Cards:** MC, VI. **Special Amenities:** Free breakfast and free local telephone calls.

SICAMOUS SUPER 8 MOTEL   Phone: 250/836-4988

◆◆   6/26-9/15   1P: $87-$108   2P: $97-$118   XP: $10   F12
Motel   3/1-6/25 & 9/16-2/28   1P: $55-$77   2P: $66-$88   XP: $10   F12

Location: Trans Canada Hwy 1, s on Hwy 97A, then just w on Main St to traffic circle, then just s. 1122 Riverside Ave V0E 2V0 (PO Box 490). **Fax:** 250/836-2466. **Terms:** [CP] meal plan; pets. **Facility:** 22 rooms. Good budget accommodations featuring average sized guest rooms with a pleasant, simple style decor. Near the water. 2 stories; exterior corridors. **Cards:** AE, MC, VI.

SIDNEY —See Victoria p. 549.

SILVERTON pop. 200

——— LODGINGS ———

BLUE SKY RESORT
◆◆   **Phone:** (250)358-2362
Cottage
6/15-9/14	1P: $135	2P: $135	XP: $15 F6
3/1-6/14	1P: $95-$115	2P: $95-$115	XP: $15 F6
9/15-10/14	1P: $115	2P: $115	XP: $15 F6
10/15-2/28	1P: $95	2P: $95	XP: $15 F6

Location: 1 km s on Hwy 6, 1.9 km via Red Mountain Rd. 8021 Lower Galena Farm Rd V0G 2B0 (Box 179). **Fax:** 250/358-7270. **Terms:** 10 day cancellation notice; cancellation fee imposed. **Facility:** 4 rooms. Modern log cabins nestled on small, open acreage in a wooded area. Well equipped kitchens and living area with 2 separate bedrooms upstairs, all with top quality futon beds and duvets. 2 stories; exterior corridors; smoke free premises; mountain view. **Recreation:** hiking trails. **All Rooms:** kitchens, shower baths. **Cards:** MC, VI. ⊗ ⊗ ⊗ ⊡ ⊟ ⊗

WILLIAM HUNTER CABINS
◆◆   **Phone:** (250)358-2844
Cottage   All Year   2P: $75-$98   XP: $10 F6
           Location: Centre. 303 Lake Ave V0G 2B0 (PO Box 180). **Fax:** 250/358-2841. **Terms:** 10 day cancellation notice; package plans; small pets only. **Facility:** 6 rooms. Spacious hand crafted log cabin suites with contemporary deco including pine furnishings. 1 story; exterior corridors; smoke free premises. **Services:** winter plug-ins.
All Rooms: efficiencies. **Some Rooms:** color TV. **Cards:** MC, VI. (ASK) (S⊘) ⊟ ⊟ ⊗ ⊗ ⊡ ⊟ ⊟

SMITHERS pop. 5,600

——— LODGING ———

ASPEN MOTOR INN
(CAA) (SAVE)   **Phone:** (250)847-4551
◆◆   5/1-9/30   1P: $71   2P: $77   XP: $10 F12
Motor Inn 3/1-4/30 & 10/1-2/28   1P: $66   2P: $72   XP: $10 F12
           Location: 1.5 km w on Hwy 16. 4628 Yellowhead Hwy V0J 2N0 (PO Box 756). **Fax:** 250/847-4492.
           Terms: Package plans; small pets only, $5 extra charge, in smoking rooms. **Facility:** 60 rooms. Large and modern guest rooms in a cedar constructed building. Right along the hwy on the w end of town. 10 efficiencies, $5 extra charge; 5 larger suites with efficiencies, $109; 2 stories; exterior corridors; heated pool, saunas, whirlpool. **Dining:** Restaurant; 6:30 am-10 pm; $10-$16; cocktails. **Services:** winter plug-ins. **All Rooms:** extended cable TV. **Cards:** AE, DI, DS, MC, VI. **Special Amenities:** Free local telephone calls. (S⊘) ⊟ ⊟ ⊟ ⊗ ⊗ ⊡ ⊟ ⊟ ⊟

SOOKE —See Victoria p. 550.

SORRENTO

——— RESTAURANT ———

HOME RESTAURANT   **Lunch:** $6-$8   **Dinner:** $8-$12   **Phone:** 250/675-3552
◆   **Location:** Trans Canada Hwy 1, in the Petro Canada Gas Station. 1235C Trans Canada Hwy V0E 2W0.
Canadian   **Hours:** 7 am-10 pm. **Features:** children's menu; senior's menu; carryout; beer & wine only; a la carte.
           Looking for delicious home-style cooking and large portions? Then this is the place. This basic diner features good food at a decent price. Homemade desserts are their specialty and they are scrumptious! The service here is very friendly too. **Cards:** MC, VI. ⊗

SQUAMISH pop. 14,000

——— LODGINGS ———

BEST WESTERN SEA TO SKY HOTEL   **Phone:** (604)898-4874
◆◆   All Year   1P: $79-$119   2P: $79-$119   XP: $10 F12
Motor Inn **Location:** 4.5 km n on Hwy 99 at Garibaldi Way. 40330 Tantalus Way V0N 1T0 (PO Box 310, GARIBALDI HIGHLANDS). **Fax:** 604/898-3692. **Terms:** 24 day cancellation notice; package plans. **Facility:** 52 rooms. Adjacent to the Highland Mall, offering extra large guest rooms with modern decor. 3 stories; interior corridors. **Cards:** AE, DS, MC, VI. (ASK) (S⊘) ⊟ ⊟ ⊟ ⊗ ⊟ ⊡ ⊟ ⊟ ⊟

SUPER 8 MOTEL OF SQUAMISH   **Phone:** (604)815-0883
◆◆   All Year   1P: $89-$109   2P: $89-$109   XP: $10 F12
Motel   **Location:** 1.5 km n on Hwy 99 at Industrial Way. 38922 Progress Way V0N 3G0. **Fax:** 604/815-0884.
           Terms: Check-in 4 pm; cancellation fee imposed; package plans. **Facility:** 87 rooms. Offering very large guest rooms whether it's a standard room or suite. Local Squamish Nations artwork adorn the lobby area, the slate flooring in the public areas comes from a local quarry. 4 stories; interior corridors; heated pool. **Cards:** AE, DI, DS, JC, MC, VI. (ASK) (S⊘) ⊟ ⊟ ⊟ ⊟ ⊟ ⊗ ⊟ ⊟ ⊟ (DATA PORT) ⊟ ⊟

SUMMERLAND pop. 10,600

———— LODGING ————

SUMMERLAND MOTEL
◆◆
Motel

	1P: $89-$99	2P: $89-$99	XP: $8
6/1-9/7	1P: $89-$99	2P: $89-$99	XP: $8
9/8-11/30	1P: $71-$81	2P: $71-$81	XP: $8
4/1-5/31	1P: $65-$75	2P: $65-$75	XP: $8

Phone: (250)494-4444

Location: 5 km s on Hwy 97. 2107 Tait St V0H 1Z0 (RR 4 Hwy 97S). Fax: 250/494-4448. **Terms:** Open 4/1-11/30; [CP] meal plan; 10-day cancellation notice; cancellation fee imposed; small pets only, $10 extra charge. **Facility:** 17 rooms. This charming roadside motel features a lovely "country theme" in its guest rooms. Each unit features its own patio deck that overlooks an attractively landscaped courtyard and swimming pool. 1 story; exterior corridors; designated smoking area; heated pool. **Cards:** MC, VI.

SUN PEAKS

———— LODGINGS ————

NANCY GREENE'S CAHILTY LODGE
CAA SAVE
◆◆◆
Lodge

| | 1P: $119-$369 | 2P: $119-$369 | XP: $20 | F |
| All Year | 1P: $119-$369 | 2P: $119-$369 | XP: $20 | F |

Phone: (250)578-7454

Location: Hwy 5, 31 km ne on Todd Mountain Rd, follow signs into village. 3220 Village Way V0E 1Z1. Fax: 250/578-7451. **Terms:** Check-in 4 pm; 14 day cancellation notice; cancellation fee imposed; package plans. **Facility:** 190 rooms. Built and owned by one of Canada's well known olympic ski champion, Nancy Greene, this lodge features year-round activities along with true ski-in, ski out access to the slopes. Lobby has Nancy's gold and silver olympic metals. 1 three-bedroom unit, 5 two-bedroom units, 2 & 3 bedroom units, for up to 4 persons; 4 stories; interior corridors; whirlpool. **Dining:** Restaurant; 7 am-10 pm; $10-$25; cocktails. **Services:** gift shop. **Some Rooms:** 36 efficiencies, 40 kitchens. **Cards:** AE, DI, DS, JC, MC, VI.

SUNDANCE LODGE
◆◆◆
Lodge

	1P: $140-$230	2P: $160-$355	XP: $20	F15
3/1-3/26 & 1/3-2/28	1P: $140-$230	2P: $160-$355	XP: $20	F15
11/25-1/2	1P: $115-$190	2P: $135-$230	XP: $20	F15
3/27-11/24	1P: $85-$130	2P: $85-$155	XP: $20	F15

Phone: (250)578-0200

Location: Hwy 5, 31 km ne on Tood Mountain Rd, follow signs into village. 3160 Creekside Way V0E 1Z1. Fax: 250/578-0222. **Terms:** 30 day cancellation notice; cancellation fee imposed; package plans. **Facility:** 84 rooms. A year-round resort featuring summer activities like hiking, golfing and mountain biking to winter skiing. The lodge is located at the base of chair lift. Only 45 minutes drive north of Kamloops. Modern accommodations. 5 two-bedroom units. 4 stories; interior corridors; designated smoking area. **Services:** gift shop. **Some Rooms:** 50 efficiencies, 23 kitchens. Fee: VCR. **Cards:** AE, DI, DS, MC, VI.

SURREY —See Vancouver p. 517.

TERRACE pop. 12,800

———— LODGINGS ————

BEST WESTERN TERRACE INN AND CONFERENCE CENTRE
◆◆◆
Motor Inn

	1P: $69-$99	2P: $79-$109	XP: $5	F12
3/1-11/30	1P: $69-$99	2P: $79-$109	XP: $5	F12
12/1-2/28	1P: $69-$89	2P: $79-$99	XP: $5	F12

Phone: 250/635-0083

Location: Hwy 16 just e on Greig Ave, follow City Centre signs. 4553 Greig Ave V8G 1M7. Fax: 250/635-0092. **Terms:** Package plans; small pets only, $10 extra charge. **Facility:** 62 rooms. A pleasant high-rise building featuring large and nicely decorated guest rooms. Catering to the business traveler, as there are large work stations and internet access avail. 5 stories; interior corridors. **Cards:** AE, DI, DS, JC, MC, VI.

COAST INN OF THE WEST
CAA SAVE
◆◆◆
Motor Inn

| | 1P: $75-$105 | 2P: $85-$115 | XP: $10 | F17 |
| All Year | 1P: $75-$105 | 2P: $85-$115 | XP: $10 | F17 |

Phone: (250)638-8141

Location: Hwy 16 to City Centre, 0.5 km e to Emerson, just n. 4620 Lakelse Ave V8G 1R1. Fax: 250/638-8999. **Terms:** Small pets only. **Facility:** 60 rooms. Downtown and close to shopping centre. Guest rooms offer an upscale decor along with some nice public areas and pub. 3 stories, no elevator; interior corridors. **Dining:** Restaurant; 6:30 am-10 pm; $7-$14; cocktails. **All Rooms:** extended cable TV. **Cards:** AE, DI, DS, JC, MC, VI. **Special Amenities:** Free local telephone calls and free room upgrade (subject to availability with advanced reservations).

TOFINO pop. 1,200

———— LODGINGS ————

BEST WESTERN TIN WIS RESORT
CAA SAVE
◆◆◆
Motor Inn

	1P: $175-$225	2P: $175-$225	XP: $15	F12
7/1-9/30	1P: $175-$225	2P: $175-$225	XP: $15	F12
3/1-6/30	1P: $110-$180	2P: $110-$180	XP: $15	F12
10/1-2/28	1P: $90-$160	2P: $90-$160	XP: $15	F12

Phone: (250)725-4445

Location: 3.5 km s on Hwy 4. 1119 Pacific Rim Hwy V0R 2Z0 (Box 389). Fax: 250/725-4447. **Facility:** 86 rooms. Contemporary rooms in a distinctively West Coast-style property; scenic beach. All rooms with spectacular ocean view and balcony or patio; some with fireplace. 3 whirlpool rooms, $220-$280; 2 stories; exterior corridors; beach, whirlpool. **Dining:** Restaurant; 7 am-11 & 5-9 pm; $11-$24; cocktails. **Services:** gift shop. **Recreation:** swimming. **All Rooms:** extended cable TV. **Cards:** AE, DI, DS, MC, VI. **Special Amenities:** Free local telephone calls and preferred room (subject to availability with advanced reservations).

CABLE COVE INN
Phone: 250/725-4236

CAA

◆◆◆

Bed & Breakfast

7/1-10/15	2P: $160-$210
4/1-6/30	2P: $140-$190
3/1-3/31 & 10/16-2/28	2P: $125-$175

Location: From centre, just n to Main St via First St, then just w. 201 Main St V0R 2Z0 (PO Box 339). **Fax:** 250/725-2857. **Terms:** [CP] meal plan; age restrictions may apply; 7 day cancellation notice; cancellation fee imposed; 2 night min stay, 7/1-8/31. **Facility:** 6 rooms. Upscale inn with fine views over the harbour; all rooms with fireplace and private deck and whirlpool. Tasteful contemporary decor, including a nice sampling of First Nations art. Breakfast trays delivered to the rooms. 6 whirlpool rooms, $160-$210; 2 stories; interior corridors; designated smoking area. **Cards:** AE, MC, VI.

CRYSTAL COVE BEACH RESORT
Phone: 250/725-4213

◆◆◆

Cottage

5/19-10/9	2P: $180-$230	XP: $15	D16
3/1-5/18	2P: $130-$180	XP: $15	D16
10/10-2/28	2P: $110-$160	XP: $15	D16

Location: 4.5 km s on Hwy 4. 1165 Cedarwood Pl V0R 2Z0 (Box 559). **Fax:** 250/725-4219. **Terms:** 14 day cancellation notice; cancellation fee imposed; pets, off season. **Facility:** 23 rooms. Individual log cottages featuring all the conveniences of home, fridge, stove and fireplace in all units except for 2 studio type units. A few units have view of the ocean and beach area. Located in listed campground. 14 two-bedroom units. 1 story; exterior corridors; playground. **Recreation:** swimming. **All Rooms:** combo or shower baths. **Some Rooms:** 21 kitchens. **Cards:** AE, MC, VI.

HIMWITSA LODGE
Phone: (250)725-2017

◆◆◆

Motor Inn

6/1-9/30	1P: $160	2P: $225	XP: $20
10/1-2/28	1P: $165	2P: $185	XP: $20
3/1-5/31	1P: $160	2P: $185	

Location: Just n of centre via First St. 300 Main St V0R 2Z0 (PO Box 176). **Fax:** 250/725-2361. **Terms:** 7 day cancellation notice; cancellation fee imposed. **Facility:** 4 rooms. Spacious contemporary rooms upstairs from a popular gallery and gift shop; all with private deck and a fine harbour view, most with hot tub on deck. Nicely appointed rooms accented by quality First Nations artwork. Check-in at gallery. 2 stories; interior corridors; designated smoking area. **Services:** gift shop. **Some Rooms:** 3 efficiencies, kitchen. **Cards:** AE, MC, VI.

MIDDLE BEACH LODGE
Phone: (250)725-2900

CAA

◆◆◆

Complex

3/1-6/15 & 6/16-9/30	2P: $105-$370	XP: $25	F3
10/1-2/28	2P: $75-$225	XP: $25	F3

Location: 3 km s on Hwy 4. 400 McKenzie Beach Rd V0R 2Z0 (Box 100). **Fax:** 250/725-2901. **Terms:** [CP] meal plan; 7 day cancellation notice; cancellation fee imposed; 2 night min stay, 4/1-9/30; package plans. **Facility:** 58 rooms. This unique complex features a mix of accommodations from self-contained oceanfront cabins to a completely separate lodge for "adults only" featuring cozy but compact rooms with duvet spreads and small private decks. 2 stories; interior/exterior corridors; designated smoking area; beach. **Recreation:** swimming; game room. **All Rooms:** extended cable TV. **Some Rooms:** 24 efficiencies, color TV. **Cards:** AE, MC, VI.

PACIFIC SANDS BEACH RESORT
Phone: (250)725-3322

CAA

◆◆◆

Suite Complex

6/30-9/30	1P: $155-$210	2P: $155-$210	XP: $20	D11
3/1-6/29 & 10/1-10/28	1P: $120-$165	2P: $120-$165	XP: $20	D11
10/29-2/28	1P: $85-$125	2P: $85-$125	XP: $20	D11

Location: 7 km s on Hwy 4. 1421 Pacific Rim Hwy V0R 2Z0 (PO Box 237). **Fax:** 250/725-3155. **Terms:** 7 day cancellation notice; cancellation fee imposed. **Facility:** 65 rooms. On Cox Bay and bordering Pacific Rim National Park. Accommodations range from studio, 1- and 2-bedroom suites and 2-bedroom cottages, most with fireplace. Overlooking mile long expanse of sandy beach and endless waves. 15 two-bedroom units. 3 whirlpool rooms; 1-3 stories, no elevator; exterior corridors; beach. **Recreation:** hiking trails, barbecue & fire pit. **All Rooms:** extended cable TV. **Some Rooms:** 18 efficiencies, 46 kitchens, color TV. **Cards:** AE, MC, VI.

SCHOONER MOTEL
Phone: 250/725-3478

CAA

◆◆

Motel

Property failed to provide current rates

Location: Campbell St and 2nd St, downtown. 311 Campbell St V0R 2Z0 (PO Box 202). **Fax:** 250/725-3499. **Terms:** 14 day cancellation notice; cancellation fee imposed. **Facility:** 16 rooms. A good downtown location with mountain and inlet views. Westcoast cedar with comfortable modern rooms. 2 stories; exterior corridors. **Dining:** Restaurant nearby. **All Rooms:** combo or shower baths, extended cable TV. **Cards:** MC, VI.

WEIGH WEST MARINE RESORT
Phone: 250/725-3277

CAA SAVE

◆◆

Motor Inn

All Year	1P: $104-$185	2P: $104-$185	XP: $10	F12

Location: 2 km e on Hwy 4. 634 Campbell St V0R 2Z0 (PO Box 69). **Fax:** 250/725-3922. **Terms:** 7 day cancellation notice; cancellation fee imposed. **Facility:** 63 rooms. On inner harbour with ocean and mountain views featuring comfortable, but modest guest rooms on hillside with various sets of stairs and some climbing needed to get to rooms. Geared toward boaters and fishermen. 2-3 stories, no elevator; exterior corridors. **Fee:** marina. **Dining:** Restaurant; 7 am-10 pm; $9-$20; cocktails. **Recreation:** charter fishing, fishing. **All Rooms:** combo or shower baths, extended cable TV. **Some Rooms:** 23 efficiencies. **Cards:** AE, DI, DS, MC, VI.

WICKANINNISH INN

CAA SAVE

◆◆◆◆

Lodge

	6/1-9/30	1P: $300-$400	2P: $320-$400	XP: $20	F18
	10/1-10/31	1P: $210-$310	2P: $230-$310	XP: $20	F18
	3/1-5/31	1P: $180-$280	2P: $200-$280	XP: $20	F18
	11/1-2/28	1P: $160-$260	2P: $180-$260	XP: $20	F18

Phone: (250)725-3100

Location: 4.3 km e on Hwy 4. Osprey Ln at Chesterman Bch V0R 2Z0 (PO Box 250). Fax: 250/725-3110. **Terms:** 7 day cancellation notice; cancellation fee imposed; package plans; pets, $20 extra charge, 6 rooms only. **Facility:** 46 rooms. Wonderfully large guest rooms, all with gas fireplace, private balcony and soaker tub. The area is known for its wild winter storms or calm sandy beaches in the summer. 6 whirlpool rooms, $160-$400; 3 stories; interior corridors; designated smoking area; beach, steamroom. **Dining:** Restaurant; 8 am-11, noon-2:30 & 5-9 pm; $15-$25; cocktails. **Services:** Fee: massage. **Recreation:** swimming; full spa & treatment rooms. **All Rooms:** extended cable TV, honor bars. **Some Rooms:** Fee: VCR. **Cards:** AE, DI, JC, MC, VI. **Special Amenities: Free local telephone calls and free newspaper.**

---- **RESTAURANTS** ----

LOFT RESTAURANT

◆◆

Canadian

Lunch: $5-$9   **Dinner:** $10-$19   Phone: 250/725-4241

Location: Campbell St and 2nd Ave, downtown. 346 Campbell St V0R 2Z0. **Hours:** 7 am-10 pm; to 9 pm 10/1-5/31. Closed: 12/25. **Features:** No A/C; casual dress; cocktails; a la carte. The Loft features West Coast-style casual dining and offers a good selection of fresh seafood, including Dungeness crab, salmon, halibut and Vancouver Island oysters. Cozy cedar-paneled dining rooms provide a nice display of regional art and photos. **Cards:** AE, MC, VI.

POINTE RESTAURANT

◆◆◆◆

Regional
Canadian

Lunch: $8-$14   **Dinner:** $24-$37   Phone: 250/725-3100

Location: 4.3 km e on Hwy 4: in Wickaninnish Inn. Osprey Ln/Chesterman Bch V0R 2Z0. **Hours:** 8 am-11, noon-2:30 & 5-9 pm. **Reservations:** required; at dinner. **Features:** casual dress; children's menu; cocktails & lounge; fee for valet parking; a la carte. Built above the rocks and jutting out into the ocean, this restaurant offers breathtaking scenery of wild waves in the winter. The Canadian West Coast cuisine features fresh seafood and a good selection of wines. Walk-ins welcome for breakfast and lunch. Smoke free premises. **Cards:** AE, DI, JC, MC, VI.

RAINCOAST CAFE

◆◆

Regional
Canadian

Lunch: $7-$12   **Dinner:** $12-$20   Phone: 250/725-2215

Location: Downtown, Fourth and Campbell sts. 101-120 Fourth St V0R 2Z0. **Hours:** 11:30 am-3 & 5:30-10 pm, to 8:30 pm in winter. **Reservations:** required; dinner. **Features:** No A/C; casual dress; beer & wine only; a la carte. Located in a shopping complex, this small, intimate bistro features a distinctive Pacific Rim cuisine, fresh ingredients, local seafood, pasta and vegetarian dishes, but no red meat. The decor displays an open kitchen, patio dining and artwork. Smoke free premises. **Cards:** VI.

TRAIL pop. 7,700

---- **LODGINGS** ----

BEST WESTERN TERRA NOVA HOTEL

CAA SAVE

◆◆◆

Motor Inn

All Year   1P: $85-$99   2P: $95-$109   XP: $10   F12

Phone: (250)368-3355

Location: Centre; on Hwy 3B. 1001 Rossland Ave V1R 3N7. Fax: 250/368-3930. **Terms:** Weekly & monthly rates avail; 24 day cancellation notice; cancellation fee imposed; package plans. **Facility:** 58 rooms. Central location hotel offering many services. Newly renovated guest rooms are beautifully appointed with light maplewood furnishings that blend with bright and warm decor. 2 junior suites with whirlpool, $175-$225; 4 stories; interior corridors; whirlpool. **Dining:** Dining room, coffee shop; 6 am-9 pm, Fri & Sat-10 pm; $13-$23; cocktails. **Services:** winter plug-ins. **Recreation:** exercise equipment. **All Rooms:** extended cable TV. **Cards:** AE, CB, DI, DS, JC, MC, VI. **Special Amenities: Early check-in/late check-out and free room upgrade (subject to availability with advanced reservations).**

RAY LYN MOTEL

CAA SAVE

◆◆

Motel

All Year   1P: $55-$70   2P: $55-$70   XP: $10   F6

Phone: (250)368-5541

Location: 1.6 km w on Hwy 3B. 118 Wellington Ave V1R 2K2. Fax: 250/368-6788. **Terms:** Weekly rates avail; cancellation fee imposed; package plans. **Facility:** 29 rooms. Spacious units offering a decor of mixed styles, but conveniently appointed. At-door parking. 1 section at the back offers the most quiet units. Attractive front yard with tall trees and greenery. 1 story; exterior corridors; heated pool. **Dining:** Restaurant nearby. **Services:** winter plug-ins. **All Rooms:** extended cable TV. **Some Rooms:** 6 efficiencies, 5 kitchens. **Cards:** MC, VI. **Special Amenities: Early check-in/late check-out and free local telephone calls.**

---- **RESTAURANT** ----

COLANDER RESTAURANT

CAA

◆

Italian

Lunch: $5-$9   **Dinner:** $8-$15   Phone: 250/364-1816

Location: Centre. 1475 Cedar Ave V1R 4C5. **Hours:** 11:30 am-2 & 4:30-8:30 pm, Sat & Sun from 4:30 pm. Closed: 12/25. **Reservations:** suggested. **Features:** casual dress; children's menu; carryout; cocktails & lounge; street parking. The Colander offers a nice selection of items at a self-service buffet. Lunch includes items such as pasta, chicken, burgers, subs and sandwiches; dinner is more extensive. Regional beers are served also. Pleasant atmosphere. Fee for to-go container. **Cards:** MC, VI.

UCLUELET pop. 1,700

—— LODGING ——

CANADIAN PRINCESS RESORT   **Phone:** 250/726-7771
[fyi]   Not inspected. **Location:** 1 km e on Peninsula Rd. 1948 Peninsula Rd V0R 3A0 (PO Box 939). Facilities, serv-
         ices, and decor characterize a mid-range property. **Terms:** Open 3/1-9/30;

VALEMOUNT pop. 1,300

—— LODGINGS ——

BEST WESTERN CANADIAN LODGE   **Phone:** 250/566-8222
◆◆   Property failed to provide current rates
Motel   **Location:** Just e of Hwy 5 (Yellowhead). 1501 5th Ave V0E 2Z0 (PO Box 1118). Fax: 250/566-4260.
         Terms: Package plans; pets, $5 extra charge. **Facility:** 36 rooms. Contemporary guest room. 2 stories; exterior
corridors. **Services:** winter plug-ins. **Some Rooms:** 6 efficiencies. **Cards:** AE, DI, DS, MC, VI.

CANOE MOUNTAIN LODGE   **Phone:** (250)566-9171
(CAA) [SAVE]   6/15-9/15   1P: $114   2P: $123   XP: $7   F13
◆◆◆   3/1-6/14 & 9/16-2/28   1P: $70   2P: $75   XP: $7   F13
Motel   **Location:** Just e of Hwy 5 (Yellowhead). 1465 5th Ave V0E 2Z0 (BOX 1029). Fax: 250/566-4198. **Facility:** 47
         rooms. Well-appointed guest rooms with European charm. Inviting lobby with stone fireplace. Kitchens, $10
         extra charge; 2 stories; interior corridors; sauna, steamroom, whirlpool. **Dining:** Restaurant nearby.
Services: gift shop; winter plug-ins. **All Rooms:** combo or shower baths. **Cards:** AE, DI, MC, VI. **Special Amenities:** Early
check-in/late check-out and free local telephone calls.

DREAM CATCHER INN LODGE AND LOG CHALETS   **Phone:** (250)566-4226
◆◆   6/1-9/30   1P: $65-$98   2P: $75-$108   XP: $15   F6
Complex   3/1-5/31   1P: $65-$88   2P: $70-$88   XP: $10   F6
         10/1-2/28   1P: $65-$88   2P: $70-$88   XP: $15   F6
Location: 0.6 km n off Hwy 5. 310 Hwy 5 N V0E 2Z0 (PO Box 1012). Fax: 250/566-9128. **Terms:** Cancellation fee imposed.
Facility: 8 rooms. Guest rooms vary in style and size; all with contemporary appointments. 3 one-bedroom log cabins with
separate living room with an efficiency. Nicely landscaped grounds, secluded from hwy. 1-2 stories; interior/exterior corridors;
smoke free premises. **Services:** winter plug-ins. **Recreation:** bicycles. **Some Rooms:** color TV. **Cards:** AE, MC, VI.

Destination Vancouver

*L*ose yourself in Vancouver. There's much to do, and getting there is half the fun.

*Y*ou can walk to downtown attractions, parks and shops; let SkyTrain whisk you to suburban destinations; or ride a ferry to the outer limits for recreation.

Vancouver skyline.
Mountains hovering in the background soften the city's jagged silhouette.

Granville Island.
This reclaimed warehouse district sports a relaxed atmosphere and promises exceptional dining experiences.
(See mention page 153)

See Downtown map page 470

West Vancouver

North Vancouver

Burnaby

Vancouver

Coquitlam

New Westminster

Port Coquitlam

Richmond

Pitt Meadows

Delta

Maple Ridge

Surrey

Mission

Chilliwack

White Rock

Langley

See Vicinity map page 468

Aldergrove

UNITED STATES

CANADA

BRITISH COUMBIA

WASHINGTON

Shopping around.
Shopping is high-end on Vancouver's Robson Street, but don't miss trendy Yaletown, historic Gastown and exotic Chinatown.
(See mention page 153)

*P*laces included in this AAA Destination City:

Beaches on the bay.
English Bay is embraced by beaches that are just minutes from downtown Vancouver.
(See mention page 152)

Vancouver pop. 514,000

This index helps you "spot" where approved accommodations are located on the detailed maps that follow. Rate ranges are for comparison only and show the property's high season. Turn to the listing page for more detailed rate information and consult display ads for special promotions. Restaurant rate range is for dinner, unless only lunch (L) is served.

✈ Airport Accommodations

Spotter/Map Page Number	OA	VANCOUVER	Diamond Rating	Rate Range High Season	Listing Page
137 / p. 468	⊕	**Best Western Abercorn Inn, 4 km e of airport**	◆◆◆	$129-$139 ⊠	512
149 / p. 468	⊕	**Best Western Richmond Inn Hotel & Convention Cente, 5 km se of airport**	◆◆	$139-$265 ⊠	512
141 / p. 468	⊕	**Comfort Inn-Airport, 2.6 km e**	◆◆◆	$110-$130 ⊠	512
143 / p. 468		Delta Pacific Resort and Conference Centre, 5 km e of airport	◆◆◆	$155	513
136 / p. 468		Delta Vancouver Airport, 2.4 km e of airport	◆◆◆	$155	513
148 / p. 468	⊕	**Executive Airport Plaza & Conference Centre, 5 km se of airport**	◆◆◆	$119-$199 ⊠	513
147 / p. 468		Four Points Hotel Vancouver Airport, 5 km se of Airport/Richmond	◆◆◆	$140-$180	513
152 / p. 468		Hilton Vancouver Airport, 5 km se of airport	◆◆◆	$159-$169	513
142 / p. 468		Holiday Inn Express Vancouver Airport, 4 km e of airport	◆◆◆	Failed to provide	514
139 / p. 468	⊕	**Radisson President Hotel & Suites, 4 km se of airport**	◆◆◆◆	$260-$290	515
150 / p. 468	⊕	**Ramada Inn Vancouver Airport, 5 km se of airport/Richmond**	◆◆	$132-$152 ⊠	515
145 / p. 468	⊕	**Stay'n Save Inns, 5 km e of airport**	◆◆◆	$114-$134 ⊠	515
140 / p. 468	⊕	**Travelodge Hotel Vancouver Airport, 5 km e of airport**	◆◆	$129-$139 ⊠	516
151 / p. 468		Vancouver Airport Marriott, 5 km se of airport/Richmond	◆◆◆	$149-$165	516
54 / p. 468	⊕	**Hampton Inn Vancouver Airport, 3 km e of airport**	◆◆◆	$109-$139 ⊠	494
67 / p. 468	⊕	**Quality Inn Airport, 9 km ne of airport**	◆◆	$99-$139 ⊠	496

DOWNTOWN VANCOUVER

Spotter/Map Page Number	OA	DOWNTOWN VANCOUVER - Lodgings	Diamond Rating	Rate Range High Season	Listing Page
1 / p. 470	⊕	**The Westin Bayshore**	fyi	$307-$382 ⊠	486
2 / p. 470		Lord Stanley Suites on the Park	◆◆◆	$175-$210	479
3 / p. 470		Renaissance Vancouver Hotel Harbourside - see color ad p 482	◆◆◆	$266	482
4 / p. 470		Sylvia Hotel	◆◆	$85-$125	484
5 / p. 470	⊕	**Empire Landmark Hotel & Conference Centre**	◆◆	$210-$250 ⊠	475
6 / p. 470	⊕	**Best Western Sands**	◆◆◆	$159-$199 ⊠	473
7 / p. 470	⊕	**Listel Vancouver - see color ad p 479**	◆◆◆	$240-$320 ⊠	479
8 / p. 470	⊕	**Pacific Palisades Hotel**	◆◆◆	$350-$450 ⊠	480
9 / p. 470		Blue Horizon Hotel - see color ad p 473	◆◆◆	$179-$199	473
10 / p. 470		Canadian Pacific Waterfront Centre Hotel	◆◆◆◆	$299	474
11 / p. 470	⊕	**The Pan Pacific Hotel Vancouver - see color ad p 480**	◆◆◆◆◆	$445-$525 ⊠	480
12 / p. 470	⊕	**Hyatt Regency Vancouver - see ad p 477**	◆◆◆◆	$230-$265 ⊠	478
13 / p. 470	⊕	**Days Inn Downtown - see color ad p 475**	◆◆◆	$149-$199 ⊠	474
14 / p. 470	⊕	**"O" Canada House**	◆◆◆	$158-$225 ⊠	480

Spotter/Map Page Number	OA	DOWNTOWN VANCOUVER - Lodgings (continued)	Diamond Rating	Rate Range High Season	Listing Page
15 / p. 470	⊛	The Sutton Place Hotel - see color ad p 484	◆◆◆◆◆	$269-$429 ⅏	484
16 / p. 470	⊛	Metropolitan Hotel - see color ad p 479	◆◆◆◆	$335-$395 ⅏	480
17 / p. 470		Delta Vancouver Suites - see color ad p 476	◆◆◆	$215	474
18 / p. 470		Canadian Pacific Hotel Vancouver	◆◆◆◆	$299	474
19 / p. 470	⊛	West End Guest House - see color ad p 485	◆◆◆	$105-$225	485
20 / p. 470	⊛	Four Seasons Hotel Vancouver	◆◆◆◆◆	$420-$480 ⅏	475
21 / p. 470		Terminal City Club Tower Hotel	◆◆◆	Failed to provide	484
22 / p. 470		Ramada Limited Downtown Vancouver	◆◆◆	$175-$195	481
23 / p. 470	⊛	Wedgewood Hotel - see color ad p 485	◆◆◆◆	$200-$680 ⅏	485
24 / p. 470	⊛	Sunset Inn Travel Apartments - see color ad p 483	◆◆◆	$128-$168	484
25 / p. 470	⊛	Sheraton Wall Centre Hotel - see color ad p 482, p 402	◆◆◆◆	$399 ⅏	483
26 / p. 470	⊛	Holiday Inn Hotel & Suites Vancouver Downtown	◆◆◆	$169-$199 ⅏	477
27 / p. 470		Bosman's Motor Hotel	◆◆	$109-$125 ⅏	473
28 / p. 470	⊛	Howard Johnson Inn - see color ad p 477	◆◆	$129-$169 ⅏	478
30 / p. 470	⊛	Hampton Inn & Suites Downtown Vancouver - see color ad p 472	◆◆◆	$195-$250 ⅏	477
31 / p. 470	⊛	Best Western Chateau Granville	◆◆◆	$199-$219 ⅏	470
32 / p. 470	⊛	Landis Hotel & Suites - see color ad p 478	◆◆	$275-$500 ⅏	478
33 / p. 470	⊛	Residence Inn by Marriott, Vancouver	◆◆◆	$199-$235 ⅏	482
34 / p. 470	⊛	Ramada Inn & Suites Downtown Vancouver - see color ad p 481	◆◆◆	$149-$199 ⅏	481
35 / p. 470		The Georgian Court Hotel	◆◆◆	$185-$260	476
36 / p. 470		Quality Hotel-Inn at False Creek - see color ad p 471	◆◆	$149-$229	481
37 / p. 470	⊛	Best Western Downtown Vancouver - see color ad p 472	◆◆◆	$144-$209 ⅏	470
38 / p. 470		Executive Plaza Hotel - see color ad p 471	◆◆◆	$129-$360	475
39 / p. 470	⊛	Granville Island Hotel - see color ad p 471	◆◆◆	$209-$219 ⅏	476
40 / p. 470		Crowne Plaza Hotel Georgia	◆◆◆	$299-$349	474
		DOWNTOWN VANCOUVER - Restaurants			
1 / p. 470		CINCIN	◆◆◆	$10-$22	487
4 / p. 470		Chartwell	◆◆◆◆	$19-$37	486
5 / p. 470		Cloud 9	◆◆	$25-$45	487
6 / p. 470		Bacchus Restaurant	◆◆◆◆	$14-$30	486
7 / p. 470		Diva at the Met - see color ad p 479	◆◆◆	$18-$30	487
8 / p. 470		Five Sails Restaurant	◆◆◆◆◆	$22-$42	487
9 / p. 470		Kobe Japanese Steak House	◆◆	$15-$43	487
14 / p. 470	⊛	The William Tell	◆◆◆	$18-$30	488
18 / p. 470		Joe Fortes Seafood & Chop House	◆◆◆	$12-$25	487
22 / p. 470	⊛	A Kettle Of Fish	◆◆	$14-$25	486
24 / p. 470		Anderson's Fine Dining On False Creek	◆◆	$17-$24	486
25 / p. 470		Bandi's	◆◆	$15-$25	486
28 / p. 470		The Chili Club	◆◆	$10-$20	486
29 / p. 470		Da Pasta Bar on Robson	◆◆	$10-$16	487
30 / p. 470		The Hermitage	◆◆◆	$18-$26	487
31 / p. 470		Il Giardino	◆◆◆	$15-$35	487
32 / p. 470		Indigo Bistro	◆◆◆	$14-$29	487
33 / p. 470		Le Crocodile	◆◆◆◆	$25-$30	488
36 / p. 470		Mescalero	◆◆	$15-$25	488
37 / p. 470		Rex Rotisserie & Grill	◆◆	$13-$30	488

Spotter/Map Page Number	OA	DOWNTOWN VANCOUVER - Restaurants (continued)	Diamond Rating	Rate Range High Season	Listing Page
㊴ / p. 470		Rain City Grill	◆◆◆	$9-$23	488
㊵ / p. 470		900 West	◆◆◆	$18-$25	488
㊶ / p. 470		Settebello Restaurant	◆◆◆	$15-$19	488
㊷ / p. 470		Uforia Restaurant	◆◆◆	$19-$29	488
㊸ / p. 470		Borgo Antico	◆◆◆	$13-$28	486
㊺ / p. 470		Water Street Cafe	◆◆	$10-$18	488
㊼ / p. 470		Villa de Lupo	◆◆◆	$16-$27	488

VANCOUVER

Spotter/Map Page Number	OA	VANCOUVER - Lodgings	Diamond Rating	Rate Range High Season	Listing Page
(54) / p. 468	CAA	**Hampton Inn Vancouver Airport**	◆◆◆	$109-$139 SAVE	494
(55) / p. 468	CAA	**The Atrium Inn Vancouver - see color ad p 490**	◆◆◆	$135-$165 SAVE	490
(56) / p. 468	CAA	**Best Western Exhibition Park - see color ad p 490**	◆◆◆	$125-$180 SAVE	491
(57) / p. 468	CAA	**Holiday Inn-Vancouver Centre**	◆◆	$169-$209	494
(59) / p. 468		Arbutus House B & B	◆◆	$95-$165	490
(60) / p. 468		Camilla House Bed & Breakfast - see color ad p 629	◆◆	$85-$145	492
(61) / p. 468		Johnson Heritage House Bed & Breakfast	◆◆◆	$105-$185	495
(62) / p. 468		Cherub Inn	◆◆◆	$124-$175	492
(63) / p. 468	CAA	**Biltmore Hotel - see color ad p 492**	◆◆	$89-$119 SAVE	491
(64) / p. 468		Windsor Guest House B & B	◆◆	$55-$115	497
(65) / p. 468		The London Guard Motel - see color ad p 496	◆	$60-$70	495
(66) / p. 468	CAA	**Days Inn-Vancouver Metro**	◆◆	$89-$129 SAVE	494
(67) / p. 468	CAA	**Quality Inn Airport**	◆◆	$99-$139 SAVE	496
(68) / p. 468		Chelsea Cottage B & B	◆◆	$85-$120	492
(69) / p. 468	CAA	**Quality Inn & Suites Metrotown**	◆◆	$109 SAVE	497
(70) / p. 468	CAA	**Albion Guest House**	◆◆	$110-$155	489
(71) / p. 468	CAA	**Plaza 500 Hotel - see color ad p 478**	◆◆◆	$160-$185 SAVE	495
(72) / p. 468	CAA	**2400 Motel - see color ad p 496**	◆◆	$71-$105	497
(73) / p. 468	CAA	**Best Western Motor Inn - see ad p 491**	◆◆	$100-$140	491
(74) / p. 468		Columbia Cottage	◆◆	$115-$135	493
		VANCOUVER - Restaurants			
(56) / p. 468		Bo-Jik Vegetarian Restaurant	◆	$9-$14	497
(58) / p. 468		Monk McQueen's	◆◆◆	$16-$26	498
(60) / p. 468		Calhoun's	◆	$7-$8	497
(61) / p. 468		Da Pasta Bar on Yew	◆◆	$11-$17	497
(65) / p. 468	CAA	**The Fish House at Stanley Park**	◆◆◆	$16-$25	498
(67) / p. 468		Las Margaritas Restaurante y Cantina	◆◆	$9-$13	498
(68) / p. 468		The Living Room Bistro	◆◆	$11-$20	498
(69) / p. 468		Lombardo's Ristorante Pizzeria	◆	$6-$15	498
(71) / p. 468		Portobello Ristorante	◆◆◆	$14-$18	498
(73) / p. 468		Pink Pearl Chinese Restaurant	◆◆	$10-$19	498
(74) / p. 468		Quattro on Fourth	◆◆◆	$13-$28	498
(76) / p. 468		The Ouisi Bistro	◆◆	$6-$17	498
(77) / p. 468		Rossini's Pasta Palazzo	◆◆	$10-$18	498
(80) / p. 468		Spumante's Cafe Restaurante	◆◆	$10-$19	499
(81) / p. 468		Star Anise	◆◆◆	$20-$32	499
(84) / p. 468		Tomato Fresh Food Cafe	◆	$7-$14	499
(86) / p. 468		Won More Szechuan Restaurant	◆	$6-$11	499
(87) / p. 468	CAA	**The Cannery**	◆◆◆	$18-$27	497
(89) / p. 468	CAA	**Teahouse Restaurant**	◆◆◆	$17-$28	499
(90) / p. 468		Capers Courtyard Cafe	◆	$5-$8	497
(91) / p. 468		Le Grec	◆◆	$9-$15	498

Vancouver Vicinity

Spotter/Map Page Number	OA	PORT COQUITLAM - Lodgings	Diamond Rating	Rate Range High Season	Listing Page
45 / p. 468	ⒶⒶ	Best Western Poco Inn & Suites - see color ad p 512	◆◆◆	$99-$169	512
		WEST VANCOUVER - Lodgings			
83 / p. 468	ⒶⒶ	Beachside Bed & Breakfast	◆	$150-$250	518
		WEST VANCOUVER - Restaurant			
99 / p. 468		Salmon House on the Hill	◆◆	$14-$22	518
		NORTH VANCOUVER - Lodgings			
91 / p. 468	ⒶⒶ	Holiday Inn Express Vancouver North Shore - see color ad p 495	◆◆	$139 ⓢ	511
92 / p. 468	ⒶⒶ	Canyon Court Motel - see color ad p 474	◆◆	$79-$109 ⓢ	511
94 / p. 468	ⒶⒶ	Best Western Capilano Inn & Suites - see color ad p 473	◆◆◆	$109-$149 ⓢ	510
95 / p. 468		A Gazebo in the Garden B & B	◆◆	$95-$150	510
98 / p. 468	ⒶⒶ	Grouse Inn - see color ad p 495	◆◆	$118-$148 ⓢ	511
		NORTH VANCOUVER - Restaurants			
105 / p. 468		Kilby's Restaurant	◆◆	$10-$21	511
106 / p. 468		Moustache Cafe North	◆◆	$25-$30	511
		BURNABY - Lodgings			
103 / p. 468	ⒶⒶ	Holiday Inn Metrotown - see ad p 502	◆◆◆	$134-$169 ⓢ	502
106 / p. 468	ⒶⒶ	Stay'n Save Inn Vancouver Burnaby - see color ad p 431, p 540	◆◆◆	$114-$134 ⓢ	503
107 / p. 468		Executive Inn Hotels - see color ad p 471	◆◆◆	$99-$179	502
108 / p. 468		Lake City Motor Inn - see color ad p 494	◆◆◆	$87-$102	503
110 / p. 468	ⒶⒶ	Radisson Hotel Burnaby	◆◆◆	$160 ⓢ	503
111 / p. 468	ⒶⒶ	Best Western Kings Inn and Conference Centre - see color ad p 493	◆◆◆	$129-$169 ⓢ	502
		BURNABY - Restaurants			
110 / p. 468		The Hart House on Deer Lake	◆◆	$16-$27	503
111 / p. 468		HORIZON'S	◆◆◆	$17-$24	503
		COQUITLAM - Lodgings			
116 / p. 468	ⒶⒶ	Best Western Coquitlam Inn Convention Centre - see color ad p 471	◆◆◆	$129-$139 ⓢ	505
118 / p. 468		Holiday Inn Coquitlam/Vancouver - see color ad p 496	◆◆◆	$119-$169	505
119 / p. 468	ⒶⒶ	Best Western Chelsea Inn - see color ad p 505	◆◆	$94-$125 ⓢ	505
		COQUITLAM - Restaurant			
115 / p. 468		The Barrel Steakhouse	◆◆◆	$13-$28	506
		PITT MEADOWS - Lodgings			
128 / p. 468		Ramada Inn & Suites Hotel Royale	◆◆◆	$112	511
		RICHMOND - Lodgings			
136 / p. 468		Delta Vancouver Airport - see color ad p 514	◆◆◆	$155	513
137 / p. 468	ⒶⒶ	Best Western Abercorn Inn	◆◆◆	$129-$139 ⓢ	512
139 / p. 468	ⒶⒶ	Radisson President Hotel & Suites - see ad p 489	◆◆◆◆	$260-$290	515
140 / p. 468	ⒶⒶ	Travelodge Hotel Vancouver Airport	◆◆	$129-$139 ⓢ	516
141 / p. 468	ⒶⒶ	Comfort Inn-Airport - see color ad p 513	◆◆◆	$110-$130 ⓢ	512
142 / p. 468		Holiday Inn Express Vancouver Airport	◆◆◆	Failed to provide	514
143 / p. 468		Delta Pacific Resort and Conference Centre - see color ad p 514	◆◆◆	$155	513
145 / p. 468	ⒶⒶ	Stay'n Save Inns - see color ad p 431, p 540	◆◆◆	$114-$134 ⓢ	515
146 / p. 468		Holiday Inn Vancouver Airport	◆◆◆	$139	514

Spotter/Map Page Number	OA	RICHMOND - Lodgings (continued)	Diamond Rating	Rate Range High Season	Listing Page
147 / p. 468		Four Points Hotel Vancouver Airport - see color ad p 402	◆◆◆	$140-$180	513
148 / p. 468	ⓐ	**Executive Airport Plaza & Conference Centre - see color ad p 471**	◆◆◆	$119-$199 🆂	513
149 / p. 468	ⓐ	**Best Western Richmond Inn Hotel & Convention Center - see color ad p 491**	◆◆	$139-$265 🆂	512
150 / p. 468	ⓐ	**Ramada Inn Vancouver Airport**	◆◆	$132-$152 🆂	515
151 / p. 468		Vancouver Airport Marriott - see color ad p 515	◆◆◆	$149-$165	516
152 / p. 468		Hilton Vancouver Airport - see color ad p 283, opposite Introduction	◆◆◆	$159-$169	513
		RICHMOND - Restaurants			
120 / p. 468		Papi's Ristorante Italiano	◆◆◆	$15-$24	516
121 / p. 468	ⓐ	**Steveston Seafood House**	◆◆◆	$13-$22	516
122 / p. 468		The Pier	◆◆◆	$16-$29	516
123 / p. 468		Suehiro Japanese Steakhouse	◆◆	$25-$45	516
		DELTA - Lodgings			
157 / p. 468	ⓐ	**Delta Town & Country Inn - see color ad p 489**	◆◆	$95-$125 🆂	506
158 / p. 468		River Run Cottages	◆◆◆	$120-$210	506
160 / p. 468	ⓐ	**Primrose Hill Guest House**	◆◆	$75-$145	506
161 / p. 468	ⓐ	**Best Western Tsawwassen Inn**	◆◆◆	$119-$129 🆂	506
163 / p. 468	ⓐ	**Southlands House "By The Sea"**	◆◆◆	$135-$175	506
164 / p. 468		Ingrid's on Twelfth European Bed & Breakfast	◆◆	$65-$120	506
		DELTA - Restaurant			
128 / p. 468	ⓐ	**La Belle Auberge**	◆◆◆	$22-$25	507
		NEW WESTMINSTER - Lodgings			
170 / p. 468	ⓐ	**Inn at Westminster Quay - see color ad p 494**	◆◆◆	$170-$215 🆂	509
		NEW WESTMINSTER - Restaurants			
133 / p. 468		Burger Heaven	◆	$5-$10	509
134 / p. 468		Viet-Thai Oriental	◆	$10-$14	510
137 / p. 468		La Rustica Ristorante	◆◆	$11-$20	509
139 / p. 468		Restaurant des Gitans	◆◆◆	$17-$26	509
		SURREY - Lodgings			
175 / p. 468	ⓐ	**Sheraton Guildford Hotel Surrey - see color ad p 402 & ad p 517**	◆◆◆	$119-$179	517
176 / p. 468	ⓐ	**Days Hotel-Surrey Centre - see color ad p 493**	◆◆◆	$110-$116 🆂	517
177 / p. 468	ⓐ	**Motel Hollywood**	◆	$55-$69 🆂	517
179 / p. 468	ⓐ	**Ramada Limited Surrey-Langley**	◆◆◆	$113 🆂	517
		SURREY - Restaurant			
142 / p. 468		Yokohama Japanese Restaurant	◆◆	$10-$21	517
		WHITE ROCK - Lodgings			
184 / p. 468	ⓐ	**Best Western Pacific Inn Resort & Conference Ctr - see color ad p 519**	◆◆◆	$109-$129 🆂	519
185 / p. 468	ⓐ	**Seacrest Motel & RV Park**	◆◆	$60-$80	519
		WHITE ROCK - Restaurant			
145 / p. 468		La Baia Italian Restaurant	◆◆	$10-$20	519

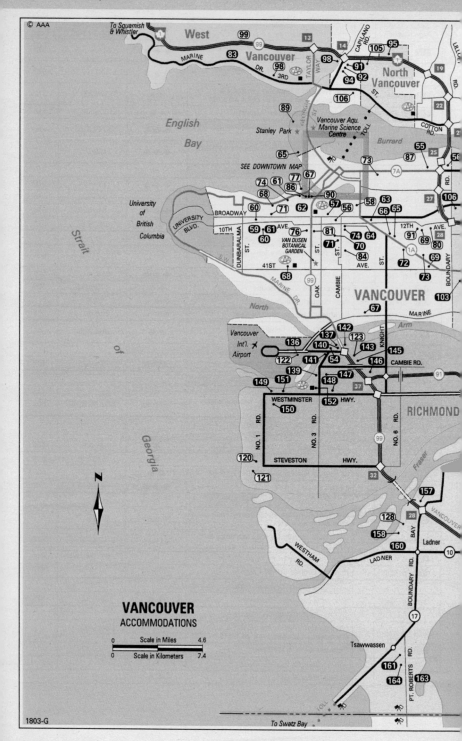

© AAA

To Squamish & Whistler

West Vancouver

North Vancouver

English Bay

Stanley Park

Vancouver Aqu. Marine Science Centre

Burrard

SEE DOWNTOWN MAP

University of British Columbia

Strait

of

Georgia

VANCOUVER

North

Vancouver Int'l. Airport

RICHMOND

WESTMINSTER HWY.

STEVESTON HWY.

WESTHAM RD.

Tsawwassen

To Swatz Bay

VANCOUVER
ACCOMMODATIONS

Scale in Miles   0 — 4.6
Scale in Kilometers   0 — 7.4

1803-G

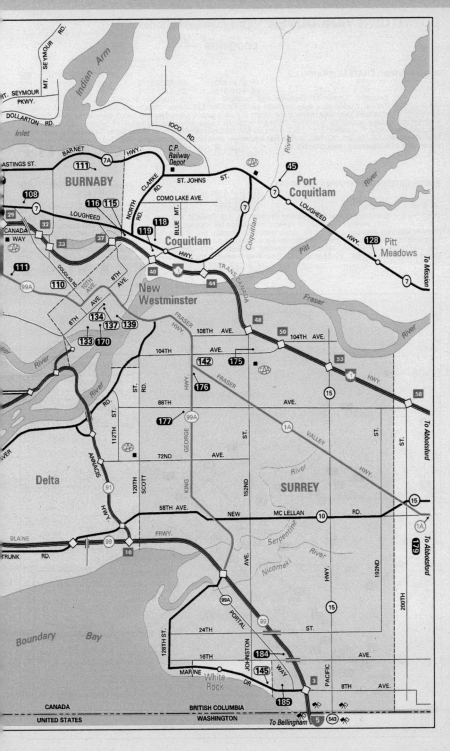

DOWNTOWN VANCOUVER   (See map below; index p. 463)

———— LODGINGS ————

BEST WESTERN CHATEAU GRANVILLE   Phone: (604)669-7070   **31**

(CAA) (SAVE)
◆◆◆
Hotel

| | 5/1-10/15 | 1P: $199-$209 | 2P: $209-$219 | XP: $20 | F16 |
| | 3/1-4/30 & 10/16-2/28 | 1P: $119-$199 | 2P: $139-$209 | XP: $20 | F16 |

Location: Corner of Granville and Helmckln sts. 1100 Granville St V6Z 2B6. Fax: 604/669-4928. **Terms:** Weekly rates avail; package plans. **Facility:** 148 rooms. Close to the end of Granville St Bridge in downtown core area. Many guest rooms feature a separate bedroom and sitting room with a more moderate wing section located across the lane from the main hotel. All rooms are nicely decorated. 15 stories; interior corridors. Fee: parking. **Dining:** Restaurant; 7 am-1 & 5-9 pm; $8-$14; cocktails. **All Rooms:** extended cable TV. **Some Rooms:** honor bars. **Cards:** AE, CB, DI, DS, JC, MC, VI. **Special Amenities:** Free room upgrade and preferred room (each subject to availability with advanced reservations).

BEST WESTERN DOWNTOWN VANCOUVER   Phone: (604)669-9888   **37**

(CAA) (SAVE)
◆◆◆
Motor Inn

	5/1-10/15	1P: $144-$199	2P: $149-$209	XP: $20	F12
	10/16-2/28	1P: $89-$139	2P: $99-$159	XP: $10	F12
	3/1-4/30	1P: $89-$129	2P: $99-$159	XP: $10	F12

Location: Corner of Drake and Granville sts. 718 Drake St V6Z 2W6. Fax: 604/669-3440. **Terms:** [CP] meal plan; weekly rates avail, off season; cancellation fee imposed; package plans. **Facility:** 143 rooms. Downtown property featuring spacious guest rooms, nicely decorated. Rooftop exercise room. Close to several downtown restaurants. Easy walking distance to GM Place and Stanley Park. 3 penthouse units, $200-$350; 3 whirlpool rooms, $109-$219; 12 stories; interior corridors; saunas, whirlpool. Fee: parking. **All Rooms:** extended cable TV, safes. **Some Rooms:** 30 efficiencies. **Cards:** AE, DI, DS, JC, MC, VI. **Special Amenities:** Free breakfast and free newspaper. (See color ad p 472)

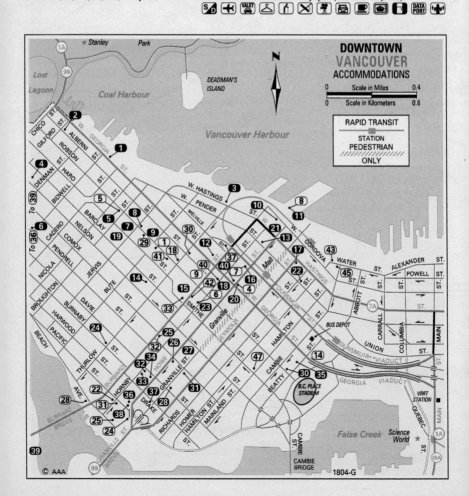

1804-G

(See map p. 470)

BEST WESTERN SANDS   Phone: (604)682-1831   6

6/15-10/9	1P: $159-$199	2P: $159-$199	XP: $15 F12
5/1-6/14	1P: $139-$179	2P: $139-$179	XP: $15 F12
3/1-4/30 & 10/10-2/28	1P: $99-$139	2P: $99-$139	XP: $15 F12

Motor Inn   **Location:** Davie at Denman St. 1755 Davie St V6G 1W5. Fax: 604/682-3546. **Terms:** Small pets only. **Facility:** 121 rooms. Close to English Bay and short walk to Stanley Park. Stylish guest rooms with modern decor and furnishings. Quieter guest rooms face the back. 6 stories; interior corridors; designated smoking area; sauna. Fee: parking. **Dining:** Restaurant; 7 am-11 pm; $8-$15; cocktails. **All Rooms:** extended cable TV. **Cards:** AE, CB, DI, DS, JC, MC, VI. **Special Amenities: Free newspaper and free room upgrade (subject to availability with advanced reservations).**

BLUE HORIZON HOTEL   Phone: (604)688-1411   9

5/13-10/20	1P: $179-$199	2P: $179-$199	XP: $15 F16
3/1-5/12 & 10/21-2/28	1P: $109-$129	2P: $109-$149	XP: $15 F16

Hotel   **Location:** Robson at Bute St. 1225 Robson St V6E 1C3. Fax: 604/688-4461. **Terms:** Cancellation fee imposed. **Facility:** 214 rooms. Along trendy Robson St. Very spacious guest rooms offering nice, comfortable accommodations. All rooms feature private balcony with incredible views of the city and mountains. 31 stories; interior corridors; heated pool. Fee: parking. **All Rooms:** safes. **Some Rooms:** honor bars. **Cards:** AE, DI, MC, VI. *(See color ad below)*

BOSMAN'S MOTOR HOTEL   Phone: (604)682-3171   27

5/16-9/30	1P: $109-$119	2P: $119-$125	XP: $10 F12
3/1-5/15 & 10/1-2/28	1P: $69-$79	2P: $79-$89	XP: $10 F12

Motel   **Location:** Just s of Nelson St. 1060 Howe St V6Z 1P5. Fax: 604/684-4010. **Terms:** Small pets only. **Facility:** 102 rooms. An upgraded older downtown property featuring comfortable, moderate guest rooms. Quieter rooms face the back parking lot. Shopping and dining nearby. 4 stories; interior corridors; designated smoking area; heated pool. **Dining:** Coffee shop; 7 am-10 pm, Sat & Sun-1 pm; $4-$10. **All Rooms:** extended cable TV. **Cards:** AE, DI, MC, VI. **Special Amenities: Early check-in/late check-out and free newspaper.**

(See map p. 470)

CANADIAN PACIFIC HOTEL VANCOUVER

Phone: (604)684-3131 [18]

◆◆◆◆

	6/1-10/31	1P: $299	2P: $299	XP: $30	F18
Classic Hotel	4/1-5/31	1P: $209	2P: $209	XP: $30	F18
	3/1-3/31 & 11/1-2/28	1P: $199	2P: $199	XP: $30	F18

Location: Corner of Burrard at W Georgia St, enter from Hornby St. 900 W Georgia St V6C 2W6. Fax: 604/662-1924. **Terms:** Cancellation fee imposed; package plans; pets, $20 extra charge. **Facility:** 556 rooms. **Historic.** This downtown historic city landmark hotel features gracious public areas with boutiques, shops and other services. Guest rooms reflect an old fashioned charm and elegance that range from above average to spacious. 21 stories; interior corridors; heated pool. Fee: parking. **Dining:** entertainment. **Services:** gift shop. Fee: massage. **All Rooms:** honor bars. **Some Rooms:** 7 efficiencies. **Cards:** AE, DI, JC, MC, VI.

CANADIAN PACIFIC WATERFRONT CENTRE HOTEL

Phone: (604)691-1991 [10]

◆◆◆◆

	6/1-10/31	1P: $299	2P: $299	XP: $30	F18
Hotel	4/1-5/31	1P: $209	2P: $209	XP: $30	F18
	3/1-3/31 & 11/1-2/28	1P: $199	2P: $199	XP: $30	F18

Location: Opposite Canada Pl at Waterfront; motor entrance use Howe St. 900 Canada Place Way V6C 3L5. Fax: 604/691-1838. **Terms:** Cancellation fee imposed; package plans; small pets only, $25 extra charge. **Facility:** 489 rooms. Across from the Convention Centre and cruise ship terminal. Guest oriented property featuring attractive guest rooms offering either a city or harbour view. Walking distance to downtown shopping. 23 stories; interior corridors; heated pool. Fee: parking. **Dining:** entertainment. **Services:** Fee: massage. **All Rooms:** honor bars. **Some Rooms:** Fee: VCR. **Cards:** AE, DI, DS, JC, MC, VI.

CROWNE PLAZA HOTEL GEORGIA

Phone: (604)682-5566 [40]

◆◆◆

| | 5/1-10/14 | 1P: $299-$329 | 2P: $319-$349 | XP: $20 | F16 |
| Classic Hotel | 3/1-4/30 & 10/15-2/28 | 1P: $219-$249 | 2P: $239-$269 | XP: $20 | F16 |

Location: Corner W Georgia and Howe sts. 801 W Georgia St V6C 1P7. Fax: 604/642-5579. **Terms:** Cancellation fee imposed; package plans; small pets only, designated rooms. **Facility:** 313 rooms. **Historic.** 1927 historic hotel completely renovated back to its original splendor. Walk back into time with the amazingly restored public areas. Guest rooms offer up-to-date and modern conveniences for business travellers. 12 stories; interior corridors. Fee: parking. **Services:** gift shop. **All Rooms:** combo or shower baths. **Cards:** AE, DI, DS, JC, MC, VI.

DAYS INN DOWNTOWN

Phone: (604)681-4335 [13]

(AAA) SAVE

| | 5/1-10/14 | 1P: $149-$179 | 2P: $169-$199 | XP: $10 | F13 |
| | 3/1-4/30 & 10/15-2/28 | 1P: $105-$155 | 2P: $105-$155 | XP: $10 | F13 |

◆◆◆

Motor Inn **Location:** At W Pender and Hornby sts. 921 W Pender St V6C 1M2. Fax: 604/681-7808. **Terms:** Cancellation fee imposed. **Facility:** 85 rooms. A 1914 English style heritage building in the heart of downtown. Various sized guest rooms with modern decor. Restricted views due to nearby buildings. All rooms with ceiling fan. Close to cruise ship terminal and Convention. 5 two-bedroom units. 6 stories; interior corridors; designated smoking area. **Dining:** Restaurant; 7 am-2 pm, Sat & Sun-11 am; $5-$9; cocktails. **All Rooms:** combo or shower baths, extended cable TV. Fee: safes. **Cards:** AE, DI, DS, JC, MC, VI. *(See color ad p 475)*

DELTA VANCOUVER SUITES

Phone: (604)689-8188 [17]

◆◆◆

| | 5/1-9/30 | 1P: $215 | 2P: $215 | XP: $20 | F17 |
| Hotel | 3/1-4/30 & 10/1-2/28 | 1P: $159 | 2P: $159 | XP: $20 | F17 |

Location: Corner of Seymour and W Hastings. 550 W Hastings St V6B 1L6. Fax: 604/605-8881. **Terms:** Check-in 4 pm; cancellation fee imposed; small pets only. **Facility:** 226 rooms. This downtown hotel is geared for business travelers, all rooms feature a pleasant, modern decor with a separate bedroom. There is a huge work desk with all plug ins and modems conveniently placed. 23 stories; interior corridors; heated pool. Fee: parking. **All Rooms:** honor bars. **Cards:** AE, DI, DS, JC, MC, VI. *(See color ad p 476)*

(See map p. 470)

EMPIRE LANDMARK HOTEL & CONFERENCE CENTRE   Phone: (604)687-0511   5

	7/1-9/30	1P: $210-$230	2P: $230-$250	XP: $20	F
	5/1-6/30	1P: $195-$215	2P: $215-$235	XP: $20	F
	3/1-4/30 & 10/1-2/28	1P: $120-$140	2P: $140-$160	XP: $20	F

Hotel   **Location:** Robson at Broughton St. 1400 Robson St V6G 1B9. Fax: 604/687-2801. **Terms:** Cancellation fee imposed; package plans. **Facility:** 358 rooms. This property features average sized guest rooms with a pleasant but simple decor, all rooms feature balcony with great views of the harbour, city and mountains. The revolving rooftop restaurant is a must see. All rooms with hair dryer. 42 stories; interior corridors; sauna, whirlpool. Fee: parking. **Dining:** Dining room, restaurant; 6:30 am-10:30 & 5-11 pm; $14-$28; cocktails; also, Cloud 9, see separate listing. **Services:** gift shop. **All Rooms:** extended cable TV. **Some Rooms:** honor bars. **Cards:** AE, DI, JC, MC, VI. **Special Amenities: Early check-in/late check-out and free room upgrade (subject to availability with advanced reservations).**

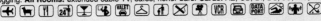

EXECUTIVE PLAZA HOTEL   Phone: (604)688-7678   38

	5/1-10/15	1P: $129-$350	2P: $139-$360	XP: $20	F12
	3/1-4/30 & 10/16-2/28	1P: $89-$139	2P: $99-$149	XP: $10	F12

Hotel   **Location:** Howe and Pacific sts, at the foot of Granville St Bridge. 1379 Howe St V6Z 2R5. Fax: 604/688-7679. **Terms:** Cancellation fee imposed. **Facility:** 131 rooms. A boutique-style property. Guest rooms in the hotel are average in size but nicely decorated in a pleasant, modern decor. Condo units avail for extended stays. Unobstructive views of the city and parts of the harbour. 23 two-bedroom units. 18 stories; interior corridors. Fee: parking. **All Rooms:** safes. **Some Rooms:** 30 kitchens. **Cards:** AE, DI, MC, VI. *(See color ad p 471)*

FOUR SEASONS HOTEL VANCOUVER   Phone: (604)689-9333   20

	5/1-10/31	1P: $420-$450	2P: $450-$480	XP: $30	F18
	11/1-2/28	1P: $295-$325	2P: $315-$355	XP: $30	F18
	3/1-4/30	1P: $285-$315	2P: $315-$345	XP: $30	F18

Hotel   **Location:** Howe at W Georgia St. 791 W Georgia St V6C 2T4. Fax: 604/684-4555. **Terms:** Package plans; pets. **Facility:** 385 rooms. Located in the heart of downtown and connected to large indoor shopping complex. 28 stories; interior corridors; designated smoking area; heated pool, saunas, whirlpool. Fee: parking. **Dining:** Dining room; 6:30 am-11 pm; $19-$37; cocktails; also, Chartwell, see separate listing. **Services:** gift shop; area transportation, downtown. Fee: massage. **Recreation:** jogging. **All Rooms:** extended cable TV, safes, honor bars. **Cards:** AE, CB, DI, DS, JC, MC, VI.

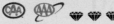

(See map p. 470)

THE GEORGIAN COURT HOTEL
◆◆◆
Hotel

5/1-10/15	1P: $185-$240	2P: $205-$260	XP: $20
3/1-4/30 & 10/16-2/28	1P: $115-$135	2P: $115-$150	XP: $20

Phone: (604)682-5555   35
F17
F17

Location: Robson at Beatty St. 773 Beatty St V6B 2M4. Fax: 604/682-8830. **Terms:** Package plans; small pets only, $20 extra charge. **Facility:** 180 rooms. Opposite BC Place stadium, close to General Motors Place Stadium and within easy walking distance to Vancouver's theatre district. Guest rooms are quite spacious and nicely decorated. 1 two-bedroom unit. 12 stories; interior corridors; designated smoking area. Fee: parking. **Services:** gift shop. **All Rooms:** honor bars. **Cards:** AE, DI, JC, MC, VI.

GRANVILLE ISLAND HOTEL
(AA) SAVE
◆◆◆
Hotel

5/1-9/30	1P: $209	2P: $219	XP: $10
3/1-4/30 & 10/1-2/28	1P: $129	2P: $139	XP: $10

Phone: (604)683-7373   39
F16
F16

Location: Granville Island below bridge, follow well marked signs. 1253 Johnston St V6H 3R9. Fax: 604/683-3061. **Terms:** Cancellation fee imposed; package plans; pets. **Facility:** 54 rooms. A converted warehouse has been turned into unique waterfront hotel situated on bustling Granville Island. Attractive guest rooms with various views of the harbour. An on site micro brewery serves the upscale restaurant. 3 stories; interior corridors; sauna, whirlpool. Fee: parking. **Dining:** Restaurant; 7 am-10 pm; $12-$18; cocktails. **All Rooms:** extended cable TV, honor bars. **Cards:** AE, DI, JC, MC, VI. **Special Amenities:** Free newspaper and free room upgrade (subject to availability with advanced reservations). (See color ad p 471)

(See map p. 470)

HAMPTON INN & SUITES DOWNTOWN VANCOUVER   Phone: (604)602-1008   30
(CAA) (SAVE)
◆◆◆
Motor Inn

5/1-10/14	1P: $195-$250	2P: $195-$250
10/15-2/28	1P: $119-$139	2P: $119-$139
3/1-4/30	1P: $109-$129	2P: $109-$129

Location: Corner of Robson and Beatty sts. 111 Robson St V6B 2M4. Fax: 604/602-1007. **Terms:** [ECP] meal plan; cancellation fee imposed. **Facility:** 132 rooms. Across the street from BC Place, featuring a very modern property with extra large suites and upgraded amenities. 11 whirlpool rooms, $129-$260; 16 stories; interior corridors; sauna, whirlpool. Fee: parking. **Dining:** Restaurant nearby. **Services:** gift shop. **All Rooms:** extended cable TV, safes. **Some Rooms:** 22 efficiencies. **Cards:** AE, DI, DS, JC, MC, VI. **Special Amenities:** Free breakfast and free local telephone calls. *(See color ad p 472)*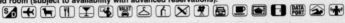

HOLIDAY INN HOTEL & SUITES VANCOUVER DOWNTOWN   Phone: (604)684-2151   26
(CAA) (SAVE)
◆◆◆
Hotel

5/1-10/15	1P: $169-$179	2P: $189-$199	XP: $20 F19
3/1-4/30, 10/16-2/28	1P: $129-$139	2P: $149-$159	XP: $20 F19

Location: Corner of Helmcken and Howe sts. 1110 Howe St V6Z 1R2. Fax: 604/684-4736. **Terms:** Weekly & monthly rates avail; small pets only. **Facility:** 245 rooms. A mix of average to large, but well equipped guest rooms decorated in traditional Holiday Inn style. An unsupervised Kids Playcentre features video games and jungle gym. 18 efficiencies, $259-$299; whirlpool room; 7 stories; interior corridors; heated pool, saunas. Fee: parking. **Dining:** Restaurant; 6:30 am-11 pm; $8-$15; cocktails. **Services:** gift shop. **All Rooms:** combo or shower baths, extended cable TV. **Some Rooms:** color TV, honor bars. **Cards:** AE, CB, DI, JC, MC, VI. **Special Amenities:** Early check-in/late check-out and preferred room (subject to availability with advanced reservations).

(See map p. 470)

HOWARD JOHNSON INN   Phone: (604)688-8701 [28]

(CAA) [SAVE]
	6/1-9/30	1P: $129-$159	2P: $139-$169	XP: $15	F17
	3/1-5/31	1P: $79-$99	2P: $89-$109	XP: $15	F17
♦♦	10/1-2/28	1P: $69-$89	2P: $79-$99	XP: $15	F17

Motor Inn   **Location:** Granville and Davie sts. 1176 Granville St V6Z 1L8. Fax: 604/688-8335. **Terms:** [CP] meal plan; weekly & monthly rates avail; cancellation fee imposed; package plans. **Facility:** 110 rooms. Located on very unusual Granville St. Renovated guest rooms range from average sized standard units to larger one bedrooms. On premise "swing bar" features various jazz type bands. 5 stories; interior corridors. Fee: parking. **All Rooms:** extended cable TV. **Cards:** AE, DI, MC, VI. **Special Amenities:** Free newspaper and free room upgrade (subject to availability with advanced reservations). *(See color ad p 477)*

HYATT REGENCY VANCOUVER   Phone: (604)683-1234 [12]

(CAA) [SAVE]
| | All Year | 1P: $230 | 2P: $265 | XP: $35 | F18 |

♦♦♦♦
Hotel   **Location:** Burrard at W Georgia St; in Royal Centre shopping plaza. 655 Burrard St V6C 2R7. Fax: 604/689-3707. **Terms:** Check-in 4 pm; cancellation fee imposed. **Facility:** 645 rooms. In the heart of downtown connected to the Royal Centre Shopping Plaza. Large guest rooms, pleasant public areas. 34 stories; interior corridors; heated pool, sauna. Fee: parking. **Dining:** Restaurant, cafeteria; 6:30 am-11 pm; $10-$20; cocktails. **Services:** gift shop. Fee: massage. **All Rooms:** extended cable TV, honor bars. **Cards:** AE, CB, DI, DS, JC, MC, VI. *(See ad p 477)*

LANDIS HOTEL & SUITES   Phone: (604)681-3555 [32]

(CAA) [SAVE]
	5/1-10/31	1P: $275-$500	2P: $275-$500	XP: $10	F12
	11/1-2/28	1P: $160-$220	2P: $160-$220	XP: $10	F12
♦♦	3/1-4/30	1P: $160-$190	2P: $160-$190	XP: $10	F12

Apartment   **Location:** Between Drake & Davie sts. 1200 Hornby St V6Z 1W2. Fax: 604/681-9222. **Terms:** [CP] meal plan; weekly & monthly rates avail; cancellation fee imposed. **Facility:** 51 rooms. In the heart of downtown these fully equipped apartments have 2-bedrooms with either 800 or 1000 sq feet all with great views of downtown or the mountains. Perfect for families on long term stays. 18 stories; interior corridors; heated pool. Fee: parking. **Dining:** Restaurant nearby. **All Rooms:** kitchens, extended cable TV. **Cards:** AE, DI, DS, JC, MC, VI. **Special Amenities:** Early check-in/late check-out and free breakfast. *(See color ad below)*

(See map p. 470)

LISTEL VANCOUVER

Phone: (604)684-8461   **7**

5/1-10/14	1P: $240-$300	2P: $260-$320	XP: $20	F18
3/1-4/30 & 10/15-2/28	1P: $150-$190	2P: $170-$210	XP: $20	F18

Motor Inn

Location: Robson at Jervis St. 1300 Robson St V6E 1C5. Fax: 604/684-7092. **Terms:** Cancellation fee imposed. **Facility:** 130 rooms. Art and elegance on Robson St, 2 floors have on display original and limited edition art works curated by local gallery. The suites are wonderfully decorated, while the standard guest rooms are comfortable but a bit plain. 10 suites $400-$600, $200-$300 off season; 6 stories; interior corridors; heated pool, whirlpool. Fee: parking. **Dining:** Restaurant; 7 am-11 pm; $15-$22; cocktails. **All Rooms:** extended cable TV, honor bars. **Cards:** AE, DI, DS, JC, MC, VI. **Special Amenities:** Free newspaper. (See color ad below)

LORD STANLEY SUITES ON THE PARK

Phone: (604)688-9299   **2**

◆◆◆

5/1-10/15	1P: $175-$210	2P: $175-$210	XP: $20	F12
10/16-1/2	1P: $135-$210	2P: $135-$210	XP: $20	F12
1/3-2/28	1P: $145	2P: $145	XP: $20	F12
3/1-4/30	1P: $135	2P: $135	XP: $20	F12

Apartment

Location: Alberni and Gilford sts. 1889 Alberni St V6G 3G7. Fax: 604/688-9297. **Terms:** Cancellation fee imposed. **Facility:** 100 rooms. Near the entrance to renowned Stanley Park. Guest rooms feature unobstructed views of the water, mountains or city; private workroom with desk; enclosed balcony, washer/dryer. Secured entrance and underground parking. 14 stories; interior corridors. Fee: parking. **All Rooms:** kitchens. **Cards:** AE, DI, MC, VI.

(See map p. 470)

METROPOLITAN HOTEL

CAA SAVE   ◆◆◆◆   Hotel

Phone: (604)687-1122   **16**

5/1-10/31	1P: $335-$365	2P: $365-$395	XP: $30 F18
11/1-2/28	1P: $265-$295	2P: $295-$315	XP: $30 F18
3/1-4/30	1P: $225-$285	2P: $285-$305	XP: $30 F18

Location: Between Georgia and Dunsmuir sts. 645 Howe St V6C 2Y9. Fax: 604/643-7267. **Terms:** Cancellation fee imposed; package plans; small pets only. **Facility:** 197 rooms. Understated decor in oak furnishings. Guest rooms range from average sized to spacious suites. Across the street from the Pacific Mall. 3 whirlpool rooms; 18 stories; interior corridors; heated pool, saunas, steamroom, whirlpool. Fee: parking. **Dining:** Restaurant; 6:30 am-11 pm; $18-$34; cocktails. **Services:** area transportation, downtown. Fee: massage. **Recreation:** sports court. **All Rooms:** extended cable TV, honor bars. **Some Rooms:** Fee: VCR. **Cards:** AE, DI, DS, JC, MC, VI. **Special Amenities:** Free local telephone calls and free newspaper. *(See color ad p 479)*

"O" CANADA HOUSE

CAA SAVE   ◆◆◆   Historic Bed & Breakfast

Phone: 604/688-0555   **14**

5/1-10/31	1P: $158-$203	2P: $175-$225	XP: $20
11/1-2/28	1P: $113-$144	2P: $125-$160	
3/1-4/30	1P: $113-$144	2P: $125-$160	XP: $20

Location: Barclay St at Thurlow St. 1114 Barclay St V6E 1H1. Fax: 604/488-0556. **Terms:** [BP] meal plan; weekly rates avail; age restrictions may apply; 7 day cancellation notice; cancellation fee imposed. **Facility:** 5 rooms. A beautifully restored 1897 home just steps away from several restaurants and shops. Quiet neighborhood, attractive landscaping. National anthem "O Canada" was written in this home in 1909. All rooms with fans. 3 stories, no elevator; interior corridors; designated smoking area. **Recreation:** video library. **All Rooms:** combo or shower baths, extended cable TV. **Cards:** MC, VI.

PACIFIC PALISADES HOTEL

CAA SAVE   ◆◆◆   Suite Hotel

Phone: (604)688-0461   **8**

5/1-10/15	1P: $350-$425	2P: $375-$450	XP: $25 F18
3/1-4/30 & 10/16-2/28	1P: $250-$325	2P: $275-$350	XP: $25 F18

Location: Robson at Jarvis St. 1277 Robson St V6E 1C4. Fax: 604/688-4374. **Terms:** Weekly rates avail; cancellation fee imposed; package plans; small pets only, $25 extra charge. **Facility:** 233 rooms. On trendy Robson St, all of the guest rooms are quite spacious, with a mix of standard rooms to 1-bedroom units. Superb view of either downtown or the mountains and harbour. Upscale extended stay suites avail. Whirlpool room; 20-23 stories; interior corridors; heated pool, sauna, whirlpool. Fee: parking. **Dining:** Restaurant; 6:30 am-11 pm, Sat & Sun from 7 am; $8-$20; cocktails; entertainment. **Services:** gift shop. Fee: massage. **Recreation:** Fee: bicycles, tanning bed. **All Rooms:** extended cable TV, honor bars. **Some Rooms:** 17 kitchens. Fee: VCR. **Cards:** AE, DI, JC, MC, VI. **Special Amenities:** Free newspaper and free room upgrade (subject to availability with advanced reservations).

THE PAN PACIFIC HOTEL VANCOUVER

CAA SAVE   ◆◆◆◆   Hotel

Phone: (604)662-8111   **11**

5/1-10/31	1P: $445-$525	2P: $445-$525	XP: $30 F18
11/1-2/28	1P: $380-$430	2P: $380-$430	XP: $30 F18
3/1-4/30	1P: $370-$420	2P: $370-$420	XP: $30 F18

Location: At Canada Pl, motor entrance off Howe St. 999 Canada Pl V6C 3B5. Fax: 604/685-8690. **Terms:** Package plans; small pets only. **Facility:** 504 rooms. Cruise ship terminal and Convention Centre location right along the waterfront. Rooms range from average size to suites, all with fine harbour views. Close to downtown shopping and the famous Gastown area. 27 whirlpool rooms; 23 stories; interior corridors; designated smoking area; heated pool, saunas, steamrooms, whirlpools. Fee: parking; racquetball court. **Dining:** 2 dining rooms, restaurant; 6:30 am-11 pm; $18-$40; cocktails; also, Five Sails Restaurant, see separate listing; entertainment. **Services:** gift shop. Fee: massage. **All Rooms:** extended cable TV, safes, honor bars. **Cards:** AE, CB, DI, JC, MC, VI. **Special Amenities:** Free local telephone calls and free newspaper. *(See color ad below)*

(See map p. 470)

QUALITY HOTEL-INN AT FALSE CREEK Phone: (604)682-0229   **36**

Hotel	6/1-10/7	1P: $149-$209	2P: $169-$229	XP: $20	F18
	5/1-5/31	1P: $129-$169	2P: $149-$189	XP: $20	F18
	3/1-4/30 & 10/8-2/28	1P: $89-$129	2P: $99-$149	XP: $20	F18

Location: N end of Granville St Bridge, Drake at Howe St. 1335 Howe St V6Z 1R7. Fax: 604/662-7566. **Terms:** Cancellation fee imposed; package plans; small pets only, $10. **Facility:** 157 rooms. Top 3 floors feature very nice executive style guest rooms. Upper most floor has full family suites with full cooking facilities. Lower 3 floors feature a mature decor with pine furniture. 7 stories; interior corridors; heated pool. Fee: parking. **Some Rooms:** 15 kitchens, color TV. **Cards:** AE, DI, DS, JC, MC, VI. *(See color ad p 471)*

RAMADA INN & SUITES DOWNTOWN VANCOUVER Phone: (604)685-1111   **34**

Motor Inn	7/1-9/30	1P: $149-$189	2P: $159-$199	XP: $10	F18
	5/1-6/30	1P: $99-$149	2P: $109-$159	XP: $10	F18
	3/1-4/30	1P: $79-$109	2P: $89-$119		F18
	10/1-2/28	1P: $79-$109	2P: $89-$119	XP: $10	F18

Location: Davie and Granville sts. 1221 Granville St V6Z 1M6. Fax: 604/685-0707. **Terms:** Weekly rates avail; check-in 4 pm; cancellation fee imposed. **Facility:** 116 rooms. Downtown, this renovated property offers very comfortable guest rooms with up-to-date guest room amenities for both the holiday and business traveller. Various sized guest rooms from average to large. 4 whirlpool rooms; 6 stories; interior corridors. Fee: parking. **All Rooms:** combo or shower baths, extended cable TV. **Some Rooms:** 5 efficiencies. **Cards:** AE, DI, DS, JC, MC, VI. **Special Amenities:** Free local telephone calls and free newspaper. *(See color ad below)*

RAMADA LIMITED DOWNTOWN VANCOUVER Phone: (604)488-1088   **22**

| Historic Motor Inn | 5/1-10/15 | 1P: $175 | 2P: $195 | XP: $15 | F18 |
| | 3/1-4/30 & 10/16-2/28 | 1P: $110 | 2P: $125 | XP: $15 | F18 |

Location: W Pender at Richards St. 435 W Pender St V6B 1V2. Fax: 604/488-1090. **Terms:** [CP] meal plan; package plans. **Facility:** 80 rooms. Downtown location offering some very pleasant boutique style guest rooms geared for both the business traveler and the sightseer. Double paned windows virtually eliminate street noise making for a quiet night sleep. 6 stories; interior corridors. Fee: parking. **Cards:** AE, DI, DS, JC, MC, VI.

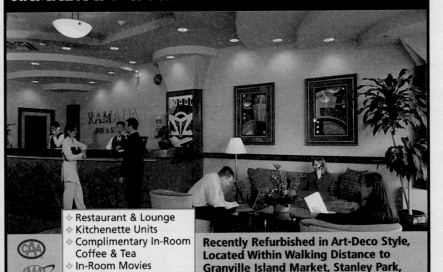

(See map p. 470)

RENAISSANCE VANCOUVER HOTEL HARBOURSIDE
◆◆◆   5/1-10/31   1P: $266   2P: $266   **Phone: (604)689-9211**   ❸
Hotel   11/1-2/28   1P: $179   2P: $179   XP: $30   F18
     3/1-4/30   1P: $176   2P: $176   XP: $25   F18
     XP: $25   F18
Location: W Hastings at Thurlow. 1133 W Hastings St V6E 3T3. Fax: 604/691-2731. **Terms:** Cancellation fee imposed; package plans; small pets only. **Facility:** 439 rooms. Choose between a spectacular view of the harbour and distant North Shore or a city view. All rooms are very nicely decorated and designed with the business traveller in mind. Close to downtown shopping and Stanley Park. 23 stories; interior corridors; heated pool. Fee: parking. **Services:** gift shop. **All Rooms:** honor bars. **Cards:** AE, CB, DI, DS, JC, MC, VI. *(See color ad below)*

[icons]

RESIDENCE INN BY MARRIOTT, VANCOUVER
(CAA) (SAVE)   6/16-9/30   1P: $199-$235   2P: $199-$235   **Phone: (604)688-1234**   ㉝
     5/1-6/15   1P: $180   2P: $180   XP: $20   F16
◆◆◆   3/1-4/30 & 10/1-2/28   1P: $130-$150   2P: $130-$150   XP: $20   F16
Suite Hotel   XP: $20   F16
Location: Corner of Hornby and Davie sts. 1234 Hornby St V6Z 1W2. Fax: 604/689-1762. **Terms:** [ECP] meal plan; weekly & monthly rates avail; check-in 4 pm; pets, $75 fee, $15 extra charge. **Facility:** 200 rooms. Downtown high-rise hotel features a range of guest rooms from full kitchen units to efficiency units, many with balcony offering views of the city skyline. 22 stories; interior corridors; heated pool, sauna, whirlpool. Fee: parking. **Dining:** Restaurant; 6:30 am-10 pm, hrs vary in winter; $12-$16; cocktails. **Services:** area transportation, downtown. **All Rooms:** extended cable TV. **Some Rooms:** 127 efficiencies, 68 kitchens. **Cards:** AE, DI, DS, JC, MC, VI. **Special Amenities:** Free breakfast and free newspaper.

[icons]

(See map p. 470)

SHERATON WALL CENTRE HOTEL

Phone: (604)331-1000 **25**

	1P: $399	2P: $399	XP: $30	F16
5/15-10/22	1P: $269	2P: $269	XP: $30	F16
3/1-5/14	1P: $239	2P: $239	XP: $30	F16
10/23-2/28				

Hotel

Location: At Burrard and Helmken sts. 1088 Burrard St V6Z 2R9. Fax: 604/331-1001. **Terms:** Monthly rates avail; check-in 4 pm; cancellation fee imposed; package plans. **Facility:** 455 rooms. Guest rooms range from compact size in the standard units to spacious suites. Across from St. Paul's Hospital. 15 two-bedroom units. 12 whirlpool rooms; 35 stories; interior corridors; heated pool, sauna, steamroom, whirlpools. Fee: parking. **Dining:** Restaurant; 6:30 am-10 pm; $15-$25; cocktails. **Services:** gift shop. Fee: massage. **All Rooms:** extended cable TV, safes. **Some Rooms:** 35 efficiencies, 54 kitchens, honor bars. **Cards:** AE, DI, JC, MC, VI. **Special Amenities:** Free newspaper and free room upgrade **(subject to availability with advanced reservations).** *(See color ad p 482 & p 402)*

OUR TRAVEL APARTMENTS PUT VANCOUVER AT YOUR FEET

Our downtown location provides you with easy walking distance to Stanley Park or Robson Street. Deluxe accommodation comes fully equipped with full kitchen and separate bedroom.

- All suites with balconies & Cable T.V. Some suites with air-conditioning
- Minutes from the beach, shopping and attractions

- Free Parking
- For Reservations Call:
  604-688-2474
  In Canada & USA Call
  Toll Free: 1-800-786-1997

Approved

S U N S E T   I N N

TRAVEL APARTMENTS

1111 Burnaby Street, Vancouver, B.C. V6E 1P4 • Fax (604) 669-3340

Visit our website: www.sunsetinn.com • email: sunset_inn@msn.com

(See map p. 470)

SUNSET INN TRAVEL APARTMENTS
Phone: (604)688-2474 **24**

(CAA)

Apartment

6/1-9/30	1P: $128-$168	2P: $128-$168	XP: $10
10/1-10/31	1P: $88-$98	2P: $108-$128	XP: $10
3/1-5/31	1P: $88-$118	2P: $98-$128	XP: $10
11/1-2/28	1P: $68-$88	2P: $88-$98	XP: $10

Location: Thurlow and Burnaby sts. 1111 Burnaby St V6E 1P4. Fax: 604/669-3340. **Terms:** Weekly & monthly rates avail, off season; 3 day cancellation notice. **Facility:** 50 rooms. Along a pleasant residential street. 1 blk from well known Davie St with its trendy bars and restaurants. Very large separate bedroom units featuring all the comforts of home and great views. 11 stories; interior corridors. **All Rooms:** extended cable TV. **Cards:** AE, DI, MC, VI. *(See color ad p 483)*

THE SUTTON PLACE HOTEL
Phone: (604)682-5511 **15**

(CAA) (SAVE)

Hotel

5/1-10/31	1P: $269-$429	2P: $269-$429	XP: $30	F17
1/1-2/28	1P: $189-$289	2P: $189-$289	XP: $30	F17
11/1-12/31	1P: $185-$285	2P: $185-$285	XP: $30	F17
3/1-4/30	1P: $179-$279	2P: $179-$279	XP: $30	F17

Location: Between Smythe and Robson. 845 Burrard St V6Z 2K6. Fax: 604/682-5513. **Terms:** Weekly & monthly rates avail; cancellation fee imposed; package plans. **Facility:** 397 rooms. Attractive, yet understated guest rooms with superior residential style furnishings. Attentive and very guest oriented staff. Monthly residential style suites avail. 21 stories; interior corridors; designated smoking area; heated pool, whirlpool, sauna for women; steam room for men. Fee: parking. **Dining:** Restaurant; 6:30 am-11 pm; $18-$30; cocktails; entertainment. **Services:** gift shop; area transportation, downtown. Fee: massage. **Recreation:** Fee: esthetics services. **All Rooms:** extended cable TV, honor bars. **Cards:** AE, CB, DI, DS, JC, MC, VI. **Special Amenities:** Free newspaper. *(See color ad below)*

SYLVIA HOTEL
Phone: (604)681-9321 **4**

Historic Motor Inn

3/1-10/31	1P: $85-$125	2P: $85-$125	XP: $10	F18
11/1-2/28	1P: $65-$115	2P: $65-$116		

Location: Beach Ave at Guilford St, across from English Bay. 1154 Gilford St V6G 2P6. Fax: 604/682-3551. **Terms:** Pets. **Facility:** 119 rooms. An ivy covered heritage building built in 1912 features several different styles and sizes of guest rooms, ranging from compact to average with an older, modest room decor. Quiet residential area close to Stanley Park and English Ba. 8 stories; interior corridors. Fee: parking. **Some Rooms:** 5 efficiencies, 15 kitchens, color TV. **Cards:** AE, DI, MC, VI.

TERMINAL CITY CLUB TOWER HOTEL
Phone: 604/681-4121 **21**

Hotel

Property failed to provide current rates

Location: W Hastings and Hornby sts. 837 W Hastings St V6C 1B6. Fax: 604/488-8604. **Facility:** 60 rooms. This property is a private members club with a full service hotel that is open to the public and as a privileged guest extends its welcome to enjoy their reading library and fitness centre. 30 stories; interior corridors; heated pool. Fee: parking. **Cards:** AE, DI, JC, MC, VI.

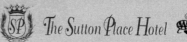

(See map p. 470)

WEDGEWOOD HOTEL   Phone: (604)689-7777   **23**

5/1-2/28   1P: $200-$660   2P: $220-$680   XP: $20   F14
3/1-4/30   1P: $200-$640   2P: $220-$660   XP: $20   F14

Hotel   **Location:** Between Smythe and Robson sts. 845 Hornby St V6Z 1V1. Fax: 604/608-5348. **Terms:** Cancellation fee imposed; package plans. **Facility:** 89 rooms. A wonderfully intimate and very stylish boutique style hotel featuring elegantly appointed rooms and suites. Very attentive staff. Penthouse suites, $660-$680; 13 stories; interior corridors; designated smoking area; sauna. Fee: parking. **Dining:** Dining room; 6:30 am-11 pm; $10-$24; cocktails; afternoon tea; also, Bacchus Restaurant, see separate listing. **Services:** Fee: massage. **All Rooms:** extended cable TV, safes, honor bars. **Cards:** AE, CB, DI, DS, JC, MC, VI. **Special Amenities:** Free newspaper and free room upgrade (subject to availability with advanced reservations). *(See color ad below)*

WEST END GUEST HOUSE   Phone: (604)681-2889   **19**

5/5-10/19   1P: $105-$205   2P: $160-$225   XP: $20   F12
12/15-2/28   1P: $100-$185   2P: $125-$205
3/1-4/30   1P: $100-$130   2P: $160-$200   XP: $15   F12
10/20-12/14   1P: $95-$175   2P: $120-$190   XP: $15   F12

Bed & Breakfast   **Location:** Corner of Haro and Broughton sts. 1362 Haro St V6E 1G2. Fax: 604/688-8812. **Terms:** [BP] meal plan; 3 day cancellation notice; cancellation fee imposed. **Facility:** 8 rooms. Historical pink home preserving the original Victorian era. Located in a quiet residental area. Cozy, intimate period rooms. Most rooms with ceiling fan. All with bathrobes. Inquire about the "resident ghost". 2 stories; interior corridors; designated smoking area. **Dining:** Restaurant nearby. **Recreation:** bicycles. **All Rooms:** combo or shower baths, extended cable TV. **Cards:** AE, DS, MC, VI. *(See color ad below)*

(See map p. 470)

──────── *The following lodgings were either not inspected or did not* ────────
meet AAA rating requirements but are listed for your information only.

THE WESTIN BAYSHORE **Phone: (604)682-3377** ➊
(CAA) (SAVE)

	6/1-10/13	1P: $307-$357	2P: $332-$382
(fyi)	1/1-2/28	1P: $179-$199	2P: $204-$224
	3/1-5/31	1P: $175-$195	2P: $200-$215
Hotel	10/14-12/31	1P: $175-$185	2P: $200-$210

Under major renovation, scheduled to be completed June 2000. **Last rated:** ◆ ◆ ◆ ◆ **Location:** W Georgia at Cardero St, near the entrance to Stanley Park. 1601 W Georgia St V6G 2V4. Fax: 604/687-3102. **Terms:** Package plans; small pets only. **Facility:** 517 rooms. Excellent harbour, city and mountain view from many rooms. Direct access by land, sea or air. 4 acres of beautifully landscaped gardens. Some environ-friendly rooms. 9-16 stories; interior corridors; 2 heated pools, saunas, steamroom, whirlpool. Fee: parking; marina. **Dining:** Restaurant; 6:30 am-2:30 & 5-10 pm; $14-$24; cocktails. **Services:** gift shop; area transportation, downtown. Fee: massage. **Recreation:** charter fishing; jogging. Fee: boating, sail-boating; bicycles. **All Rooms:** extended cable TV, honor bars. **Some Rooms:** safes. **Cards:** AE, DI, DS, JC, MC, VI. **Special Amenities: Free newspaper.**

[icons]

THE WESTIN GRAND, VANCOUVER **Phone: 604/602-1999**
(fyi)

| | 5/16-10/15 | 1P: $349-$389 | 2P: $349-$389 | XP: $25 |
| Hotel | 3/1-5/15 & 10/16-2/28 | 1P: $299-$339 | 2P: $299-$339 | XP: $25 |

Too new to rate, opening scheduled for June 1999. **Location:** Between Homer and Richards sts. 433 Robson St V6B 6L9. Fax: 604/647-2502. **Amenities:** 207 rooms, restaurant, radios, coffeemakers, microwaves, refrigerators, pool, exercise facilities. **Cards:** AE, DI, DS, JC, MC, VI.

──────── **RESTAURANTS** ────────

A KETTLE OF FISH **Lunch:** $9-$13 **Dinner:** $14-$25 **Phone:** 604/682-6661 ㉒
(CAA)
◆ ◆
Seafood
Location: Corner of Hornby and Pacific sts. 900 Pacific St V6Z 2E3. **Hours:** 11:30 am-2 & 5:30-9:30 pm, Sat & Sun from 5:30 pm. Closed: 1/1, 10/11, 11/11 & 12/24-12/26. **Reservations:** suggested. **Features:** health conscious menu items; cocktails; fee for parking; a la carte. You'll enjoy this restaurant's enchanting, casually elegant atmosphere and lush garden setting. They are known for their commitment to fresh seafood, and the "kettle" fish soup is their specialty. Visitors and locals alike dine here. Fun, friendly staff. Smoke free premises. **Cards:** AE, DI, JC, MC, VI.

ANDERSON'S FINE DINING ON FALSE CREEK **Lunch:** $9-$11 **Dinner:** $17-$24 **Phone:** 604/684-3777 ㉔
◆ ◆
Continental
Location: Pacific Blvd and Granville St. 1661 Granville St V6Z 1N3. **Hours:** 11:30 am-1:30 & 5:30-9:30 pm, Sat from 5:30 pm. Closed major holidays & Sun. **Reservations:** suggested. **Features:** casual dress; cocktails & lounge; a la carte. You'll enjoy the wonderful view of the ocean, harbor and Barrard St. Bridge available from this restaurant, which offers a Continental French cuisine that includes seafood, chicken and beef. The upscale decor and atmosphere are quite attractive. Smoke free premises. **Cards:** AE, DI, JC, MC, VI.

BACCHUS RESTAURANT **Lunch:** $9-$14 **Dinner:** $14-$30 **Phone:** 604/608-5319 ➏
◆ ◆ ◆ ◆
Northern
Continental
Location: Between Smythe and Robson sts; in Wedgewood Hotel. 845 Hornby St V6Z 1V1. **Hours:** 6:30 am-11 pm. **Reservations:** suggested. **Features:** dressy casual; Sunday brunch; cocktails & lounge; entertainment; fee for parking; valet parking; a la carte. The Bacchus Restaurant features elegant dining with a caring, attentive staff. The creative menu reflects a Mediterranean influence, and meals display expert preparation and presentation. The fresh oven-baked seabass is delicious. Extensive wine list. **Cards:** AE, DI, DS, JC, MC, VI.

BANDI'S **Lunch:** $9-$12 **Dinner:** $15-$25 **Phone:** 604/685-3391 ㉕
◆ ◆
Ethnic
Location: Between Beach Ave and Pacific Blvd. 1427 Howe St V6Z 1R9. **Hours:** 11:30 am-2 & 6-11 pm, Sat from 5:30 pm, Sun 5:30 pm-10 pm. Closed: 12/25. **Reservations:** required. **Features:** casual dress; cocktails; street parking; a la carte. Bandi's features Hungarian cuisine at its best. Good choices: roast crisp duck, lamb cutlets, chicken paprikas and pork tenderloin. The setting is an intimate, century-old house with a cozy fireplace. The owner runs the restaurant with a personal touch. **Cards:** AE, MC, VI.

BORGO ANTICO **Lunch:** $8-$14 **Dinner:** $13-$28 **Phone:** 604/683-8376 ㊸
◆ ◆ ◆
Northern
Italian
Location: Water at Cambie St, in Gastown. 321 Water St V6B 1B8. **Hours:** 11:30 am-11 pm, Sat from 5:30 pm. Closed major holidays & Sun. **Reservations:** suggested. **Features:** cocktails; fee for parking; a la carte. Located in the heart of Old Gastown, this restaurant is housed in a century-old Hudson Bay Trading Company warehouse. Tables upstairs offer a great harbor view; the downstairs area is like dining in a Tuscan villa. The prosciutto di parma is excellent. Smoke free premises. **Cards:** AE, DI, JC, MC, VI.

CHARTWELL **Lunch:** $17-$21 **Dinner:** $19-$37 **Phone:** 604/689-9333 ➍
◆ ◆ ◆ ◆
Continental
Location: Howe at W Georgia St; in Four Seasons Hotel Vancouver. 791 W Georgia St V6C 2T4. **Hours:** 6:30 am-11, noon-2:30 & 5:30-11 pm. **Reservations:** suggested. **Features:** dressy casual; children's menu; health conscious menu items; cocktails & lounge; fee for valet parking; a la carte. You'll enjoy this restaurant's understated elegance warmed by the glow of a fireplace. The highest-quality ingredients are used, and meals such as rack of lamb, salmon and lobster are expertly presented. Friendly, attentive service. Validated parking. Smoke free premises. **Cards:** AE, CB, DI, DS, JC, MC, VI.

THE CHILI CLUB **Lunch:** $6-$10 **Dinner:** $10-$20 **Phone:** 604/681-6000 ㉘
◆ ◆
Thai
Location: Between Thurlow and Hornby, under the Burrard bridge, next to the Aquatic Center. 1018 Beach Ave V6E 1T7. **Hours:** 11:30 am-2 & 5-10 pm, Sat-11 pm. Closed: 12/25. **Reservations:** suggested. **Features:** cocktails; a la carte. If you are looking for authentic Thai cuisine made as hot as you like it, this is the place to try. Spices, such as lemon grass and ginger, as well as other ingredients are flown in direct from Thailand for consistency. There is ample free parking. **Cards:** AE, DI, MC, VI.

(See map p. 470)

CINCIN
◆◆◆
Italian

Lunch: $8-$16   Dinner: $10-$22   Phone: 250/688-7338   ①
Location: Downtown, Robson St at Thurlow St. 1154 Robson St V6E 1B5. **Hours:** 11:30 am-2:30 & 5:30-11 pm, Sat & Sun from 5 pm. **Closed:** 1/1 & 12/25. **Reservations:** suggested. **Features:** casual dress; cocktails; fee for parking; a la carte. The menu at this restaurant features homemade sausage, pasta and thin-crust, wood-oven pizza. The bustling atmosphere is known as a trendy place—sometimes film stars dine here. The service is prompt and attentive. **Cards:** AE, DI, JC, MC, VI.

CLOUD 9
◆◆◆
Continental

Dinner: $25-$45   Phone: 604/687-0511   ⑤
Location: Robson at Broughton St; in Empire Landmark Hotel and Conference Centre. 1400 Robson St V6G 1B9. **Hours:** 6:30 am-10:30 & 5-11:30 pm, Sun 6:30 am-11 pm. **Reservations:** suggested. **Features:** Sunday brunch; cocktails; fee for parking; a la carte. Cloud 9, a revolving restaurant on the 42nd floor, offers the most spectacular views of downtown, the mountains and inlet. The menu's longtime specialty is "Swan's Lake," a delicate puff pastry filled with ice cream and swimming on a raspberry lake. Smoke free premises. **Cards:** AE, DI, JC, MC, VI.

DA PASTA BAR ON ROBSON
◆◆
Italian

Lunch: $6-$13   Dinner: $10-$16   Phone: 604/688-1288   ㉙
Location: Robson St and Bute. 1232 Robson St V6E 1C1. **Hours:** 11:30 am-10 pm. **Closed:** 1/1, 12/25 & 12/26. **Features:** cocktails; fee for parking; a la carte. You'll certainly enjoy this restaurant's fresh pasta with a Canadian West Coast flair. Combine your favorite pasta with one of their 15 creative sauces. Or try a delicious pizza. The decor is close and cozy, but seating may be limited. Smoke free premises. **Cards:** AE, DI, MC, VI.

DIVA AT THE MET
◆◆◆
Regional
Canadian

Lunch: $13-$18   Dinner: $18-$30   Phone: 604/602-7788   ⑦
Location: Between Georgia and Dunsmuir sts; in Metropolitan Hotel. 645 Howe St V6C 2Y9. **Hours:** 6:30-11 am, 11:30-2:30 & 5:30-10 pm, Thurs-Sat to 11 pm; Sat & Sun 7 am-2:30 pm. **Reservations:** suggested. **Features:** casual dress; children's menu; cocktails & lounge; fee for parking; valet parking; a la carte. Diva at the Met has a casual, elegant-bistro ambience and a delightful cuisine combining European and Oriental knowledge. Meals are presented with a nice display of colors and reflect the health-conscious concern of the chef. Good service. **Cards:** AE, DI, DS, JC, MC, VI. *(See color ad p 479)*

FIVE SAILS RESTAURANT
◆◆◆◆
Continental

Dinner: $22-$42   Phone: 604/662-8111   ⑧
Location: At Canada Place. Motor entrance off Howe St; in The Pan Pacific Hotel Vancouver. 300-999 Canada Pl V6C 3B5. **Hours:** 6 pm-10 pm. **Closed:** 1/1, 1/11, 11/11, 12/25 & 12/26. **Reservations:** required. **Features:** semi-formal attire; health conscious menu items; cocktails & lounge; valet parking; a la carte. Five Sails features extraordinary meals, excellent flavors, artful presentations, and breathtaking views of the harbor. The sophisticated menu includes roasted lobster, pan-seared halibut and a diverse wine list. Professional service. Validated parking. Smoke free premises. **Cards:** AE, DI, JC, MC, VI.

THE HERMITAGE
◆◆◆
Traditional
French

Lunch: $10-$16   Dinner: $18-$26   Phone: 604/689-3237   ㉚
Location: Blk 1000 on Robson near Burrard, off street in a courtyard. 115 1025 Robson St V6E 4A9. **Hours:** 11:30 am-2:30 & 5:30-10:30 pm, Sat from 5:30 pm, Sun 6 pm-10 pm. **Closed:** 1/1, 1/2, 12/25 & 12/26. **Reservations:** suggested. **Features:** cocktails; fee for parking; a la carte. This restaurant's chef/owner, a former chef to King Leopold of Belgium, offers a menu that includes delicious rack of lamb, crepes suzette and many French specialties. The servers are trained to be proper and exact. Patio dining available in fair weather. **Cards:** AE, DI, JC, MC, VI.

IL GIARDINO
◆◆◆
Italian

Lunch: $12-$16   Dinner: $15-$35   Phone: 604/669-2422   ㉛
Location: Corner of Pacific and Hornby sts. 1382 Hornby St V6Z 1W5. **Hours:** noon-2:30 & 5:30-11 pm, Sat & Sun from 6 pm. **Closed** major holidays. **Reservations:** required. **Features:** casual dress; cocktails & lounge; fee for valet parking; a la carte. This very nice restaurant, which specializes in game, fowl and pasta, is designed to look like the Tuscan farmhouse of the owner, Umberto Menghi. The very charming decor has bright colors, open beams and exquisite furniture. Wonderful wines, good service. **Cards:** AE, DI, MC, VI.

INDIGO BISTRO
◆◆◆
Continental

Lunch: $9-$15   Dinner: $14-$29   Phone: 604/893-7150   ㉜
Location: Burrard and Helmken sts; in Sheraton Wall Center Hotel. 1088 Burrard St V6Z 2R9. **Hours:** 6:30 am-10 pm. **Reservations:** suggested. **Features:** dressy casual; children's menu; cocktails; fee for parking & valet parking; a la carte. A contemporary all-day eatery, the Indigo Bistro features a nice blend of French and Italian cuisines. Entrees include fresh seafood, chicken, beef and veal. Distinctive pieces created by local artisans highlight the decor. Servers are knowledgeable. **Cards:** AE, DI, JC, MC, VI.

JOE FORTES SEAFOOD & CHOP HOUSE
◆◆◆
Seafood

Lunch: $7-$12   Dinner: $12-$25   Phone: 604/669-1940   ⑱
Location: Thurlow at Robson St. 777 Thurlow St V6E 3V5. **Hours:** 11:30 am-11 pm, Fri & Sat-midnight. **Closed:** 12/25 & 12/26. **Reservations:** suggested. **Features:** Sunday brunch; cocktails & lounge; fee for valet parking; a la carte. A San Francisco-style seafood grill along trendy Robson St., this restaurant features delightful rooftop garden dining in season. They also have a popular oyster bar and fireplace lounge. Be sure to ask about turn-of-the-century legend Joe Fortes. **Cards:** AE, DS, MC, VI.

KOBE JAPANESE STEAK HOUSE
◆◆
Steak and
Seafood

Dinner: $15-$43   Phone: 604/684-2451   ⑨
Location: Corner of Alberni and Burrard sts. 1042 Alberni St V6E 1A3. **Hours:** 5 pm-10 pm. **Closed** major holidays. **Reservations:** required. **Features:** cocktails & lounge; fee for parking & valet parking; a la carte. Visitors and locals alike enjoy this restaurant's style of dinner, which seats several guests at a teppan table where the chef prepares your meal of steak, chicken, shrimp or lobster on the grill in front of you. Valet parking is available Thu-Sat. **Cards:** AE, DI, DS, JC, MC, VI.

(See map p. 470)

LE CROCODILE
Lunch: $15-$19   **Dinner:** $25-$30   **Phone:** 604/669-4298   ③③
◆◆◆◆
French
Location: Smithe and Burrard sts. 100-909 Burrard St V6Z 2N2. **Hours:** 11:30 am-2 & 5:30-10 pm, Sat 5:30 pm-10:30 pm. Closed major holidays & Sun. **Reservations:** required. **Features:** casual dress; cocktails; fee for parking & valet parking; a la carte. Le Crocodile is a true French restaurant with an emphasis on beef and seafood. The signature dish is Alsatian onion pie, and offerings include pan-fried Dover sole filleted tableside and grilled lamb chops. You'll like the bustling atmosphere and servers. **Cards:** AE, DI, MC, VI.

MESCALERO
Lunch: $6-$10   **Dinner:** $15-$25   **Phone:** 604/669-2399   ③⑥
◆◆
Regional
American
Location: Jct Davie St. 1215 Bidwell St V6G 2K7. **Hours:** 11 am-3 & 5:30-10 pm, winter hrs vary. **Reservations:** suggested. **Features:** cocktails & lounge; a la carte. The Mescalero features a delightfully unusual Santa Fe, New Mexico, decor and atmosphere. The tapas menu offers wild combinations and unusual spices to make this an intriguing dining experience. The juicy chicken sandwich on focaccio flatbread is superb. **Cards:** AE, MC, VI.

900 WEST
Lunch: $13-$20   **Dinner:** $18-$25   **Phone:** 604/669-9378   ④⓪
◆◆◆
Regional
Canadian
Location: Corner of Burrard at W Georgia St, enter from Hornby St; in Canadian Pacific Hotel Vancouver. 900 W Georgia St V6C 2W6. **Hours:** 11:30 am-3 & 5-11 pm, Sat & Sun from 5 pm. **Reservations:** suggested. **Features:** casual dress; cocktails & lounge; entertainment; fee for parking; valet parking; a la carte. This restaurant presents an impressive dining room featuring the "Grand Era" in keeping with the historical nature of the hotel. The Pacific Rim menu highlights many local vegetables, meat and a large selection of wines. Prompt, attentive service. **Cards:** AE, DI, DS, JC, MC, VI.

RAIN CITY GRILL
Lunch: $9-$15   **Dinner:** $9-$23   **Phone:** 604/685-7337   ③⑨
◆◆◆
Continental
Location: Just n of jct Denman and Davie sts. 1193 Denman St V6G2NI. **Hours:** 11:30 am-2:30 & 5-11 pm, Sat & Sun from 10:30 am. Closed: 12/24 & 12/25. **Reservations:** required. **Features:** casual dress; Sunday brunch; cocktails; street parking & fee for valet parking; a la carte. You'll enjoy the Rain City's Pacific Northwest cuisine with a menu that includes fresh ingredients and weekly changes. The atmosphere is simple yet stately, the server staff is attentive and nicely attired, and the wine list is extensive. Limited seating. Smoke free premises. **Cards:** AE, DI, MC, VI.

REX ROTISSERIE & GRILL
Lunch: $8-$16   **Dinner:** $13-$30   **Phone:** 604/683-7390   ③⑦
◆◆
Spanish
Location: Dunsmuir and Burrard, plaza level of Bentall Centre. 1055 Dunsmuir St V7X 1G4. **Hours:** 11:30 am-10 pm, Thurs & Fri-11 pm, Sat 5 pm-11 pm. Closed: 1/1, 12/25 & Sun. **Reservations:** suggested. **Features:** casual dress; carryout; cocktails; fee for parking; a la carte. Featuring hot rotisserie chicken and prime rib, also fresh made sandwiches and some pasta. Patio dining in season. Validated parking after 5 pm. **Cards:** AE, DI, MC, VI.

SETTEBELLO RESTAURANT
Lunch: $11-$19   **Dinner:** $15-$19   **Phone:** 604/681-7377   ④①
◆◆◆
Northern
Italian
Location: Thurlow and Robson sts. 1133 Robson St V6E 1B5. **Hours:** 11:30 am-10 pm, Fri & Sat-11 pm. Closed: 12/25. **Reservations:** suggested. **Features:** cocktails; fee for parking; a la carte. Settebello's offers authentic Mediterranean dining and an excellent selection of grilled meats, special pizzas from a wood-burning oven, and pastas such as fettuccini Bombay and piccata parmigiana. The warm, friendly atmosphere also has an outdoor patio. Smoke free premises. **Cards:** AE, JC, MC, VI.

UFORIA RESTAURANT
Lunch: $11-$15   **Dinner:** $19-$29   **Phone:** 604/685-7770   ④②
◆◆◆
Seafood
Location: Robson and Burrard sts. 860 Burrard St V6Z 1X9. **Hours:** 11:30 am-10:30 pm, Fri-11 pm, Sat & Sun 5:30 pm-11 pm. Closed: 12/25. **Reservations:** suggested. **Features:** casual dress; cocktails & lounge; entertainment; fee for parking; a la carte. The delicious food is the real star of this restaurant, which features wonderful seafood and game dishes prepared with fresh ingredients and cooked to perfection. A variety of live music is offered Thursday-Saturday. Wines by the glass are terrific. **Cards:** AE, DI, MC, VI.

VILLA DE LUPO
Dinner: $16-$27   **Phone:** 604/688-7436   ④⑦
◆◆◆
Italian
Location: Between Robson and Smithe. 869 Hamilton St V6B 2R7. **Hours:** 5:30 pm-11 pm. Closed: 1/1, 11/25 & 12/25. **Reservations:** required. **Features:** casual dress; cocktails; fee for parking & valet parking; a la carte. You'll enjoy the fine cuisine at this restaurant; all meals—such as homemade pasta and the lamb osso bucco—are prepared with fresh, local ingredients. The menu also features a wide range of fine wines, and the lovely atmosphere has a romantic feel. Smoke free premises. **Cards:** AE, DI, MC, VI.

WATER STREET CAFE
Lunch: $10-$15   **Dinner:** $10-$18   **Phone:** 604/689-2832   ④⑤
◆◆
Italian
Location: Cambie and Water sts; in Gastown. 300 Water St V6B 1B6. **Hours:** 11:30 am-10 pm, Fri & Sat-11 pm. Closed: 12/24 & 12/25. **Reservations:** suggested. **Features:** casual dress; cocktails; a la carte. Located in a Victorian building across the street from Old Gastown's steam clock landmark, the Water Street Cafe features elegant yet casual dining with a Continental and Italian cuisine inspired with British Columbia and Canadian West Coast touches. **Cards:** AE, MC, VI.

THE WILLIAM TELL
Lunch: $8-$12   **Dinner:** $18-$30   **Phone:** 604/688-3504   ①④
ⒶⒶ
◆◆◆
Swiss
Location: Robson at Beatty St; in The Georgian Court Hotel. 765 Beatty St V6B 2M4. **Hours:** 7 am-2 & 6-9:30 pm, Sat 7 am-11 & 6-10 pm, Sun 7-11 am & 5:30-8 pm. Closed major holidays. **Reservations:** suggested. **Features:** casual dress; cocktails & lounge; fee for parking; valet parking; a la carte. Tiger prawns, rainbow trout, rack of lamb and steak tartare are the favorites at the established, popular William Tell's. The restaurant displays an attractive, European-style elegance. Sunday night features a Swiss-style buffet. Smoking in lounge only. Smoke free premises. **Cards:** AE, DI, JC, MC, VI.

VANCOUVER pop. 514,000   (See map p. 468; index p. 465)

——— LODGINGS ———

ALBION GUEST HOUSE
All Year
(AA)
◆ ◆
Bed &
Breakfast
MC, VI.

Phone: (604)873-2287 **70**
1P: $110-$145   2P: $125-$155   XP: $25   D12
Location: 2.5 km s on Cambie St and just w. 592 W 19th Ave V5Z 1W6. Fax: 604/879-5682. **Terms:** [BP] meal plan; age restrictions may apply; 7 day cancellation notice; cancellation fee imposed. **Facility:** 4 rooms. Located on quiet residential street. Renovated older home with average sized guest rooms, landscaped lawn and garden areas with an outdoor hot tub. Several neighborhood restaurants nearby. 2 stories; interior corridors; smoke free premises; street parking only; whirlpool. **Recreation:** bicycles. **Some Rooms:** color TV. **Cards:** AE,

(See map p. 468)

ARBUTUS HOUSE B & B   **Phone:** (604)738-6432   59
◆◆   5/1-10/31   1P: $95-$155   2P: $105-$165   XP: $25
Bed &   3/1-4/30   1P: $75-$105   2P: $85-$120   XP: $25
Breakfast   **Location:** Just w on 29th Ave from Granville St, corner of 29th Ave and Maple Cr. 4470 Maple Crescent V6J 4B3. Fax: 604/738-6433. **Terms:** Open 3/1-10/31; [BP] meal plan; age restrictions may apply; 7 day cancellation notice; cancellation fee imposed. **Facility:** 5 rooms. Located in quiet residential neighborhood, this modern 2 story home features spacious guest rooms, top floor guest room has gas fireplace. All have ceiling fan, modern bathroom and attractive landscaping touches. 2 stories; interior corridors; smoke free premises. **Some Rooms:** color TV.

THE ATRIUM INN VANCOUVER   **Phone:** (604)254-1000   55
CAA SAVE   4/16-10/15   1P: $135   2P: $165   XP: $15   F18
◆◆◆   3/1-4/15 & 10/16-2/28   1P: $110   2P: $125   XP: $15   F18
Motor Inn   **Location:** Corner of Renfrew and E Hasting sts. 2889 E Hastings St V5K 2A1. Fax: 604/253-1234. **Terms:** [CP] meal plan; check-in 4 pm. **Facility:** 105 rooms. Atrium type public areas, guest rooms are large and comfortable with a pleasant decor. Close to the PNE grounds, racetrack and coliseum. 4 stories; interior corridors. **Dining:** Restaurant; 7 am-11 pm; $11-$14; cocktails. **Services:** gift shop; area transportation, downtown. **All Rooms:** extended cable TV. **Some Rooms:** 4 efficiencies. **Cards:** AE, CB, DI, DS, JC, MC, VI. **Special Amenities:** Free breakfast and preferred room (subject to availability with advanced reservations). *(See color ad below)*

(See map p. 468)

BEST WESTERN EXHIBITION PARK   Phone: (604)294-4751 **56**

7/1-9/30	1P: $125-$160	2P: $135-$180	XP: $10 F12
5/1-6/30	1P: $90-$125	2P: $99-$140	XP: $10 F12
3/1-4/30 & 10/1-2/28	1P: $69-$90	2P: $79-$110	XP: $10 F12

Motel

Location: Exit 26 from Trans Canada Hwy 1; jct Hwy 1 and 7A. 3475 E Hastings St V5K 2A5. Fax: 604/294-1269. **Terms:** [CP] meal plan. **Facility:** 58 rooms. Exceptionally clean and well coordinated with very large standard guest rooms and very large two-room family suites, which are not your typical two bedroom units. Close to the PNE grounds, racetrack and coliseum. 22 two-bedroom units. 3 stories; interior corridors; saunas, whirlpool. **Dining:** Restaurant nearby. **All Rooms:** extended cable TV. **Cards:** AE, CB, DI, DS, JC, MC, VI. **Special Amenities:** Free breakfast and free newspaper. (See color ad p 490)

BEST WESTERN MOTOR INN   Phone: (604)430-3441 **73**

5/1-9/30	1P: $100-$130	2P: $110-$140	XP: $10 F17
3/1-4/30 & 10/1-2/28	1P: $80-$110	2P: $90-$120	XP: $10 F17

Motor Inn

Location: 8 km se on Hwy 1A and 99A (Kingsway). 3075 Kingsway V5R 5J8. Fax: 604/430-8594. **Terms:** Cancellation fee imposed. **Facility:** 60 rooms. Featuring large guest rooms with pleasant style decor. Rooms on top floors offer wonderful views of downtown and mountains. 2 two-bedroom units. 3 stories; interior corridors; sauna, whirlpool. **Dining:** Restaurant; 8 am-2 & 5-10 pm; $10-$16; wine/beer only. **All Rooms:** extended cable TV. **Cards:** AE, DI, DS, MC, VI. (See ad below)

BILTMORE HOTEL   Phone: (604)872-5252 **63**

6/1-9/30	1P: $89-$109	2P: $99-$119	XP: $10 F12
3/1-5/31 & 10/1-2/28	1P: $69-$89	2P: $79-$99	XP: $10 F12

Motor Inn

Location: Corner of W 12th Ave and Kingsway (1A/99A). 395 Kingsway V5T 3J7. Fax: 604/874-3003. **Terms:** Weekly rates avail; cancellation fee imposed. **Facility:** 96 rooms. A very well-maintained property. Public areas offer a pleasant decor. Guest rooms are only average in size but strong housekeeping and a pleasant, contemporary decor make this a very good economy style property. 7 stories; interior corridors; seasonal smoking area; small pool, seasonal. **Dining:** Restaurant, coffee shop; 6:30 am-9 pm, Sat & Sun 7 am-2 pm; $7-$14; cocktails. **All Rooms:** extended cable TV, safes. **Cards:** AE, DI, DS, MC, VI. **Special Amenities:** Free room upgrade (subject to availability with advanced reservations). (See color ad p 492)

(See map p. 468)

CAMILLA HOUSE BED & BREAKFAST   **Phone:** (604)737-2687   60

◆◆   5/1-10/15   1P: $85-$135   2P: $95-$145   XP: $20

Bed &   3/1-4/30 & 10/16-2/28   1P: $60-$100   2P: $70-$110   XP: $10

Breakfast   **Location:** From Hwy 99 (Oak St), 3 km w on W 16th Ave, just n on Trafalgar St. 2538 W 13th Ave V6X 2T1. Fax: 604/737-2586. **Terms:** [BP] meal plan; age restrictions may apply; 14 day cancellation notice; cancellation fee imposed. **Facility:** 5 rooms. Located in tree-lined Kitsilano area, close to shopping, restaurants and public transit. This private home features attractively decorated guest rooms with just a touch of the "Orient" in their public areas. 2 stories; interior corridors; designated smoking area. (See color ad p 629)

CHELSEA COTTAGE B & B   **Phone:** (604)266-2681   63

◆◆   5/1-10/15   1P: $85-$110   2P: $95-$120   XP: $25

Bed &   3/1-4/30 & 10/16-10/31   1P: $75-$100   2P: $85-$110   XP: $25

Breakfast   11/1-2/28   1P: $65-$85   2P: $75-$95   XP: $25

Location: From Hwy 99 (Granville St) 1 km w on W 49th Ave, just n on W Boulevard, then just w. 2143 W 46th Ave V6M 2L2. Fax: 604/266-7540. **Terms:** [BP] meal plan; age restrictions may apply; check-in 4 pm; 7 day cancellation notice. **Facility:** 4 rooms. Located in wonderfully lush and well-treed residential neighborhood, within easy walking distance to area restaurants, shopping and transit. Guest rooms are lovingly decorated with many little "extras" for a pleasant stay. 2 stories; interior corridors; designated smoking area. **Some Rooms:** combo or shower baths, shared bathrooms. **Cards:** MC, VI.

CHERUB INN   **Phone:** (604)733-3166   62

◆◆◆   5/2-10/31   1P: $124-$160   2P: $139-$175   XP: $15   F10

Historic Bed   3/1-5/1 & 11/1-2/28   1P: $109-$139   2P: $119-$149   XP: $15   F10

& Breakfast   **Location:** From Hwy 99 (Granville St) 2.5 km w on W Broadway, then just n on Trafalgar St. 2546 W 6th Ave V6K 1W5. Fax: 604/733-3106. **Terms:** [BP] meal plan; age restrictions may apply; 7 day cancellation notice; cancellation fee imposed. **Facility:** 4 rooms. Built in 1913, this grand and lovingly restored home features an assortment of stained glass windows and large, comfortable guest rooms decorated in rich wood accents. In quiet neighborhood with easy access to downtown area. 2 stories; interior corridors; designated smoking area. **All Rooms:** combo or shower baths. **Some Rooms:** color TV. **Cards:** MC, VI.

(See map p. 468)

COLUMBIA COTTAGE
◆◆   6/1-9/30   1P: $115   2P: $135   **Phone:** (604)874-5327
Bed &   3/1-5/31 & 10/1-2/28   1P: $95   2P: $110   XP: $20
Breakfast   **Location:** Just e on W 14th Ave from Cambie St. 205 W 14th Ave V5Y 1X2. Fax: 604/879-4547. **Terms:** [BP]
          meal plan; 14 day cancellation notice; cancellation fee imposed. **Facility:** 5 rooms. In residential neighborhood
just blks from City Hall and Vancouver General Hospital and only minutes to downtown via the Cambie St Bridge. Pleasant
guest rooms, nicely decorated. 2 stories; interior corridors; smoke free premises; street parking only. **All Rooms:** combo or
shower baths. **Some Rooms:** color TV. **Cards:** MC, VI.

(See map p. 468)

DAYS INN-VANCOUVER METRO

				Phone: (604)876-5531	66
(AAA) SAVE	7/1-9/30	1P: $89-$129	2P: $89-$129	XP: $10	F13
◆◆	5/1-6/30	1P: $79-$99	2P: $79-$99	XP: $10	F13
Motel	10/1-2/28	1P: $49-$79	2P: $49-$79	XP: $10	F13
	3/1-4/30	1P: $49-$69	2P: $49-$69	XP: $10	F13

Location: 6 km se on Hwy 1A and 99A (Kingsway). 2075 Kingsway V5N 2T2. Fax: 604/872-2676. **Terms:** [CP] meal plan; weekly & monthly rates avail. off season. **Facility:** 66 rooms. Featuring a pleasant, landscaped interior courtyard which all of the guest rooms overlook. Modern look and decor throughout. 2 stories; exterior corridors. **Dining:** Restaurant nearby. **All Rooms:** combo or shower baths, extended cable TV. **Cards:** AE, DI, DS, JC, MC, VI. **Special Amenities:** Free breakfast and free newspaper.

🆓 🛅 ✕ 🎤 🖨 📺 🖐

HAMPTON INN VANCOUVER AIRPORT

				Phone: (604)232-5505	54
(AAA) SAVE	5/16-9/30	1P: $109-$129	2P: $119-$139	XP: $10	F17
◆◆◆	10/1-2/28	1P: $90-$100	2P: $90-$100	XP: $10	F17
Motel	3/1-5/15	1P: $85-$95	2P: $85-$95	XP: $10	F17

Location: Hwy 99 N exit 39 (Bridgeport/airport), Hwy 99 S exit 39 A (airport). 8811 Bridgeport Rd V6X 1R9. Fax: 604/232-5508. **Terms:** [CP] meal plan; cancellation fee imposed. **Facility:** 112 rooms. A modern property offering very comfortable guest rooms, the king bedded rooms offer larger working desks and data port phones. Restaurants within easy walking distance. Elaborate breakfast setup. 5 stories; interior corridors. **Services:** area transportation, within 10 km. **All Rooms:** extended cable TV. **Cards:** AE, DI, DS, JC, MC, VI. **Special Amenities:** Free breakfast and free local telephone calls.

🆓 ✈ 🐾 🖎 🛖 ✕ 🎤 🖨 📺 🖐

HOLIDAY INN-VANCOUVER CENTRE

				Phone: (604)879-0511	57
(AAA)	4/30-5/27	1P: $169-$179	2P: $199-$209	XP: $10	F18
◆◆	5/28-9/30	1P: $189	2P: $209	XP: $10	F18
Hotel	10/1-2/28	1P: $169	2P: $189	XP: $10	F18
	3/1-4/29	1P: $169	2P: $169	XP: $10	F18

Location: Between Heather and Willow sts. 711 W Broadway V5Z 3Y2. Fax: 604/872-7520. **Terms:** Cancellation fee imposed; package plans; small pets only, in smoking rooms. **Facility:** 200 rooms. A high-rise property offering some very nice views of the city or mountains. A few guest rooms with balcony. 16 stories; interior corridors; designated smoking area; heated pool, sauna. Fee: parking. **Dining:** Restaurant; 7 am-10 pm; $7-$18; cocktails. **Services:** gift shop. **All Rooms:** extended cable TV. **Cards:** AE, DI, DS, JC, MC, VI.

ASK 🆓 🐾 🍴 🖵 🐾 🖎 ✕ 🎤 🖨 📺 🖐 DATA PORT 🏊 🖐

(See map p. 468)

JOHNSON HERITAGE HOUSE BED & BREAKFAST   Phone: (604)266-4175   [61]

Bed &   ◆◆◆   5/5-10/31   1P: $105-$165   2P: $125-$185
Breakfast   4/1-5/4   1P: $85-$120   2P: $95-$130
Location: 1.5 km w on W 33rd Ave from Granville St, just s on Vine St and just e. 2278 W 34th Ave V6M 1G6. Fax: 604/266-4175. **Terms:** Open 4/1-10/31; [BP] meal plan; age restrictions may apply; 14 day cancellation notice; cancellation fee imposed. **Facility:** 4 rooms. A 1920s restored Craftsman style home featuring an eclectic array of Canadiana collectibles, carousel horses, coffee grinders, clocks, toys, a gas pump and wooden propeller. Charming guest rooms and lush landscaping. 2 stories; interior corridors; smoke free premises; street parking only. **All Rooms:** combo or shower baths. **Some Rooms:** color TV.

THE LONDON GUARD MOTEL   Phone: 604/430-4646   [65]

Motel   ◆   7/1-9/30   1P: $60-$70   2P: $60-$70   XP: $10
3/1-6/30 & 10/1-2/28   1P: $50-$65   2P: $50-$65   XP: $10
Location: 6.8 km se on Hwy 1A and 99A (Kingsway). 2227 Kingsway. Fax: 604/430-8951. **Terms:** Pets, $2 extra charge. **Facility:** 46 rooms. This older but well maintained property offers a range of comfortable guest rooms, from compact to larger units with a separate bedroom. This property prides itself on its spring flowers and landscaping touches. 16 two-bedroom units. 1 story; exterior corridors. **All Rooms:** combo or shower baths. **Cards:** MC, VI. (See color ad p 496)

PLAZA 500 HOTEL   Phone: (604)873-1811   [71]

[AAA] [SAVE]   5/1-9/30   1P: $160-$185   2P: $160-$185   XP: $25   F14
◆◆◆   3/1-4/30 & 10/1-2/28   1P: $120-$145   2P: $120-$145   XP: $25   F14
Hotel   **Location:** Corner of W 12th Ave at Cambie St. 500 W 12th Ave St V5Z 1M2. Fax: 604/873-5103. **Terms:** Check-in 4 pm; 14 day cancellation notice; cancellation fee imposed; package plans. **Facility:** 153 rooms. Beautifully decorated guest rooms located in 2 types of buildings. The tower features slightly larger rooms with private balcony and wonderful views. Slightly restricted views in lower tower. Close to General Hospital and City Hall. 17 stories; interior corridors. Fee: parking. **Dining:** Restaurant; 6:30 am-10:30 pm; $8-$20; cocktails. **All Rooms:** extended cable TV. **Cards:** AE, DI, JC, MC, VI. **Special Amenities:** Early check-in/late check-out and free newspaper. (See color ad p 478)

(See map p. 468)

QUALITY INN AIRPORT

5/16-9/30	1P: $99-$139	2P: $99-$139
3/1-5/15 & 10/1-2/28	1P: $63-$90	2P: $63-$90

Phone: (604)321-6611
XP: $10
XP: $10

Motor Inn

Location: Corner of SE Marine Dr and Fraser St. 725 SE Marine Dr V5X 2T9. Fax: 604/327-3570. **Terms:** [CP] meal plan; weekly & monthly rates avail. in winter. **Facility:** 100 rooms. A mature property with some very comfortable and nicely coordinated guest rooms. 2nd floor features a casino but no slot machines. Lower level features a bowling center. On-site liquor store. 6 stories; interior corridors. **Dining:** Coffee shop; 6:30 am-9 pm, sports bar; $6-$15; wine/beer only. **Services:** gift shop; area transportation, within 8 km. **All Rooms:** extended cable TV. **Cards:** AE, DI, DS, JC, MC, VI. **Special Amenities:** Free breakfast and free local telephone calls.

(See map p. 468)

QUALITY INN & SUITES METROTOWN

Phone: (604)433-8255   69

5/1-9/30	1P: $109	2P: $109	XP: $10 F16
3/1-4/30 & 10/1-2/28	1P: $69		2P: $69 XP: $10 F16

Location: 11 km se on Hwy 1A and 99A (Kingsway). 3484 Kingsway V5R 5L6. Fax: 604/433-8359. **Terms:** [CP] meal plan; weekly rates avail, off season; cancellation fee imposed; package plans. **Facility:** 123 rooms. Offering 2 different styles of guest rooms, from comfortable but average sized rooms to large spacious suites with a separate bedroom area. A short drive to Metro Town Centre Mall. 3-4 stories; interior corridors; heated pool. **Dining:** Restaurant; 6 am-9 pm; $8-$15; cocktails. **All Rooms:** extended cable TV. **Cards:** AE, DI, DS, JC, MC, VI. **Special Amenities:** Free breakfast and free local telephone calls.

2400 MOTEL

Phone: 604/434-2464   72

5/1-9/30	1P: $71-$105	2P: $71-$105	XP: $10 F14
3/1-4/30 & 10/1-11/30	1P: $55-$89	2P: $55-$89	XP: $10 F14
12/1-2/28	1P: $51-$85	2P: $51-$85	XP: $10 F14

Location: 7.2 km se on Hwy 1A and 99A (Kingsway). 2400 Kingsway V5R 5G9. Fax: 604/430-1045. **Terms:** Cancellation fee imposed; small pets only, $4 extra charge. **Facility:** 65 rooms. A very well maintained and super clean set of older style bungalows featuring a variety of room sizes from large family units with full kitchen to cozy, smaller units for up to 2 persons. A real shinning gem of a property. 26 two-bedroom units. 1 story; exterior corridors. **Dining:** Restaurant nearby. **All Rooms:** combo or shower baths, extended cable TV. **Some Rooms:** 36 kitchens. **Cards:** AE, MC, VI. *(See color ad p 496)*

WINDSOR GUEST HOUSE B & B

Phone: (604)872-3060   64

5/15-10/15	1P: $55-$95	2P: $75-$115	XP: $15 F8
3/1-5/14 & 10/16-2/28	1P: $45-$85	2P: $65-$105	XP: $10 F8

Location: Yukon St and W 11th Ave. 325 W 11th Ave V5Y 1T3. Fax: 604/873-1147. **Terms:** [BP] meal plan; 3 day cancellation notice. **Facility:** 10 rooms. Close to City Hall and Vancouver General Hospital. Many restaurants nearby. Guest rooms offer average sized rooms with simple style decor. 4 stories, no elevator; interior corridors; designated smoking area. **Cards:** AE, JC, MC, VI.

The following lodging was either not inspected or did not meet AAA rating requirements but is listed for your information only.

DELTA PINNACLE

Phone: 604/684-1128

5/1-10/31	1P: $249-$400	2P: $249-$400	XP: $20 F20
3/1-4/30 & 11/1-2/28	1P: $179-$350	2P: $179-$370	XP: $20 F20

Too new to rate, opening scheduled for January 2000. **Location:** Hwy 1, exit Hastings St. 1128 Hastings St V6E 4R5. Fax: 604/298-1128. **Amenities:** 438 rooms, pets, radios, coffeemakers, pool, exercise facilities. *(See color ad p 476)*

--- **RESTAURANTS** ---

O-JIK VEGETARIAN RESTAURANT

Lunch: $9-$14   Dinner: $9-$14   Phone: 604/872-5556   56

Location: From Granville St, 1 km e. 820 W Broadway V5Z 1J8. **Hours:** 11 am-3 & 5-9 pm. **Reservations:** suggested; weekends. **Features:** health conscious menu items; carryout; street parking; a la carte. 100% Chinese vegetarian dishes utilizing exotic vegetables, tofu, rice and noodles to create a unique taste sensation. Daily lunch specials. Smoke free premises. **Cards:** MC, VI.

CALHOUN'S

Lunch: $4-$7   Dinner: $7-$8   Phone: 604/737-7062   60

Location: W Broadway at Carnarvon St; just w of MacDonald St. 3035 W Broadway V6K 2G9. **Hours:** Open 24 hrs. Closed: 12/25 & 12/26. **Features:** carryout; beer & wine only; a la carte. In the shopping district along West Broadway, this self-serve eatery features a nice selection of fresh food and desserts. The Tandoori chicken, vegetarian cannelloni and chocolate turtle cake are good choices. Sandwiches and coffees too. Limited seating. Smoke free premises. **Cards:** AE, MC, VI.

THE CANNERY

Lunch: $10-$15   Dinner: $18-$27   Phone: 604/254-9606   87

Location: 4 km e on Hastings St E to Victoria Dr, 1 km n across railroad tracks following signs; at foot of Victoria Dr. 2205 Commissioner St V5L 1A4. **Hours:** 11:30 am-2:30 & 5:30-10 pm, Sat & Sun from 5 pm. Closed: 12/25 & 12/26. **Reservations:** suggested. **Features:** casual dress; cocktails & lounge; a la carte. The Cannery is a charming country-style restaurant in quiet Stanley Park. The setting offers a breathtaking view of the harbor, sea lions at play, and mountains. Their many fresh seafood dishes such as the salmon Wellington and local wines are excellent. Smoke free premises. **Cards:** AE, DI, DS, MC, VI.

CAPERS COURTYARD CAFE

Lunch: $5-$8   Dinner: $5-$8   Phone: 604/739-6676   90

Location: W 4th Ave and Vine St. 2285 W 4th Ave V6K 4S2. **Hours:** 8 am-9 pm. **Features:** health conscious menu items; street parking; a la carte. This restaurant overlooking the ocean offers cafeteria-style counter service and many vegetarian options as well as fish, chicken and beef. Sandwiches, salads and soups are made with fresh, organic ingredients. Warm and cozy, with limited seating. Smoke free premises. **Cards:** AE, MC, VI.

DA PASTA BAR ON YEW

Lunch: $8-$15   Dinner: $11-$17   Phone: 604/738-6515   61

Location: W 1st Ave and Yew St; in Kitsilano District. 2201 W 1st Ave V6K 1E9. **Hours:** 11:30 am-10:30 pm, Sat & Sun from 9 am. Closed: 12/25. **Reservations:** accepted. **Features:** casual dress; carryout; cocktails; a la carte. The Da Pasta Bar cuisine has a West Coast Canadian flair, and you can combine your favorite pasta with one of their many creative sauces. The cool-jazz ambience is cozy and close, the decor features artwork by local artists, and the service is friendly. Smoke free premises. **Cards:** AE, DI, MC, VI.

(See map p. 468)

THE FISH HOUSE AT STANLEY PARK   Lunch: $10-$16   Dinner: $16-$25   Phone: 604/681-7275   65
Location: Beach Ave entrance to Stanley Park, (next to tennis courts). 8901 Stanley Park Dr V6G 3E2
Hours: 11:30 am-10 pm, Sun from 11 am. Closed: 12/24-12/26. Reservations: suggested. Features: N
A/C; Sunday brunch; early bird specials; cocktails; fee for parking; a la carte. Located in the lush and quie
Seafood   surroundings of Stanley Park, this restaurant features a wide variety of fresh seafood wonderfully prepare
with a Canadian West Coast influence. Its casual atmosphere offers patio dining in season. Pay parking lo
Smoke free premises. Cards: AE, DI, DS, JC, MC, VI.

LAS MARGARITAS RESTAURANTE Y CANTINA   Lunch: $7-$10   Dinner: $9-$13   Phone: 604/734-7117   67
Location: Maple and W 4th aves. 1999 W 4th Ave V6J 1M7. Hours: 11:30 am-10 pm, Sat-11 pm. Closed
Mexican   1/1 & 12/25. Reservations: suggested. Features: casual dress; Sunday brunch; children's menu; healt
conscious menu items; carryout; cocktails; a la carte. Las Margaritas features a bright, festive atmospher
accented with Mexican artifacts. The menu includes healthy choices and offers fajitas, grilled salmon burritos and chipotl
chicken. The server staff is prompt and attentive. Reservations are required. Cards: AE, DI, MC, VI.

LE GREC   Lunch: $8-$10   Dinner: $9-$15   Phone: 604/733-7399   91
Location: Between Maple & Arbutus sts. 2041 W 4th Ave N6J 1N3. Hours: 11:30 am-10:30 pm, Sat & Su
Greek   9:30 am-11 pm. Closed: 1/1, 12/25 & 12/26. Reservations: accepted. Features: No A/C; casual dress
carryout; cocktails & lounge; street parking; a la carte. This restaurant is open for lunch and dinner daily, fo
breakfast on weekends. Lunch features "demophagos," meaning "people's food at midday done simply and inexpensively."
Each dish is just $2.95 till 5:30 pm, all day Wednesdays. Colorful surroundings. Smoke free premises. Cards: AE, MC, VI.

THE LIVING ROOM BISTRO   Dinner: $11-$20   Phone: 604/737-7529   68
Location: W 4th Ave at Bayswater St. 2958 W 4th Ave V6K 1R4. Hours: 5 pm-1 am, Sun-midnight. Closed
Continental   12/25. Reservations: suggested. Features: casual dress; cocktails; street parking; a la carte. Thi
restaurant lives up to its name. It has an old Victorian-style living room setting with a neighborhood feel an
a candlelit, cozy atmosphere with tables that are placed close together. The casual-style service is friendly and attentive
Smoke free premises. Cards: AE, MC, VI.

LOMBARDO'S RISTORANTE PIZZERIA   Lunch: $6-$11   Dinner: $6-$15   Phone: 604/251-2240   69
Location: 1st St and Commercial Dr. 120,1641 Commercial Dr V5L 3A4. Hours: 11 am-11 pm, Sun 4 pm-1
Italian   pm. Closed: 12/25. Features: carryout; beer & wine only; street parking; a la carte. Located in the Mercat
Mall, Lombardo's is known as one of the oldest brick-oven pizza houses in town, and it offers 15 types c
pizza. The lasagna is very good also. Locals and visitors alike enjoy the family-style atmosphere. Seating is a bit limited
Cards: AE, MC, VI.

MONK MCQUEEN'S   Lunch: $10-$15   Dinner: $16-$26   Phone: 604/877-1351   58
Location: 6 Ave at Moberly Rd, just w of Cambie St Bridge. 601 Stamps Landing V5Z 3Z1. Hours: 11:3
Seafood   am-10:30 pm, Sat & Sun from 11 am. Closed: 12/25. Reservations: suggested. Features: casual dress
Sunday brunch; children's menu; cocktails & lounge; a la carte. You'll enjoy this restaurant's great view of th
mountains and south shore of False Creek with all its sailboats. Casual dining is downstairs. A more upscale experience i
upstairs, with live jazz played Wed-Sun evenings. Paid parking or valet service. Cards: AE, DI, MC, VI.

THE OUISI BISTRO   Lunch: $6-$11   Dinner: $6-$17   Phone: 604/732-7550   76
Location: Granville St and W 14th Ave. 3014 Granville St V6H 3J8. Hours: 11 am-11 pm. Closed: 12/25
Cajun   Reservations: suggested. Features: Sunday brunch; cocktails; street parking; a la carte. Located alon
trendy Granville St. with its mix of high-end shops and restaurants, this low-key restaurant serves Louisian
Creole and Cajun dishes from its open-style kitchen. They also have live jazz Sunday and Tuesday nights. Metered stree
parking. Cards: AE, MC, VI.

PINK PEARL CHINESE RESTAURANT   Lunch: $4-$10   Dinner: $10-$19   Phone: 604/253-4316   73
Location: Just w of Clark Dr. 1123 E Hastings St V6A 1S2. Hours: 9 am-3 & 5-10 pm, Fri & Sat-11 pm
Chinese   Reservations: accepted. Features: cocktails; a la carte. Pink Pearl's focus is on fresh ingredients, loca
produce and West Coast seafood. An excellent and varied array of dim sum items is offered 9 am-3 pm Thi
restaurant has received numerous write-ups in newspapers, magazines and travel guides. Cards: AE, DI, MC, VI.

PORTOBELLO RISTORANTE   Dinner: $14-$18   Phone: 604/734-0697   71
Location: W Broadway at Trafalgar. 2585 W Broadway V6K 2E9. Hours: 5:30 pm-10:30 pm, Fri & Sat-1
Italian   pm. Closed: Mon. Reservations: suggested. Features: casual dress; cocktails; street parking; a la carte
This is a family-owned restaurant that's quite popular with the locals and well-known for its outstanding foo
and Sicilian flat bread. The restaurant features a cuisine representing Italy's north and south regions. Its decor is fun, funk
and colorful. Smoke free premises. Cards: AE, MC, VI.

QUATTRO ON FOURTH   Dinner: $13-$28   Phone: 604/734-4444   74
Location: W 4th Ave and Trafalgar St. 2611 W Fourth Ave V6K 1P8. Hours: 5 pm-midnight, Sun-11 pm
Italian   Closed: 12/24-12/27. Reservations: suggested. Features: casual dress; health conscious menu items
cocktails; street parking; a la carte. Quattro on Fourth features an airy, fun and lively decor; it makes you fee
like you're in Tuscany. This place has a great local reputation, as its pasta and other dishes are heartful, full-flavored an
created with healthy ingredients. Good service too. Smoke free premises. Cards: AE, DI, MC, VI.

ROSSINI'S PASTA PALAZZO   Lunch: $10-$18   Dinner: $10-$18   Phone: 604/737-8080   77
Location: Cornwall and Yew sts. 1525 Yew St V6J 3E5. Hours: 8 am-1 am, Sat from 9 am, Sun
Italian   am-midnight. Reservations: suggested. Features: casual dress; Sunday brunch; carryout; cocktails &
lounge; entertainment; street parking; a la carte. Located in the trendy Kits Beach area, this family-run
locally popular restaurant offers inexpensive pasta meals, which are accompanied by jazz sessions every evening. You ca
choose from 20 different pasta sauces and several veal dishes. Cards: AE, DI, MC, VI.

(See map p. 468)

SPUMANTE'S CAFE RESTAURANTE   **Lunch:** $9-$15   **Dinner:** $10-$19   **Phone:** 604/253-8899   ⑧⓪
◆◆   **Location:** Between 1st St and 2nd Ave. 1736 Commercial Dr V5N 4A3. **Hours:** 11:30 am-2:30 & 5-10 pm,
Northern   Sat from 5 pm. Closed: 12/25 & Mon. **Reservations:** suggested. **Features:** cocktails; street parking; a la
Italian   carte. Spumante's provides a romantic atmosphere for diners to enjoy their many traditional dishes as well
as more than 30 combination dishes. Meals are prepared fresh each day. The server staff is friendly and fun,
and the decor is comfortable and cozy. **Cards:** MC, VI.   ✕

STAR ANISE   **Dinner:** $20-$32   **Phone:** 604/737-1485   ⑧①
◆◆◆   **Location:** Jct W 12th Ave and Granville St. 1485 W 12th Ave V6H 1M6. **Hours:** 5:30 pm-11 pm. Closed:
Regional   12/25. **Reservations:** required. **Features:** casual dress; cocktails; a la carte. You'll appreciate the superb
Canadian   Pacific Rim cuisine—with West Coast Canadian touches—at this restaurant. The menu features local
seafood, meat dishes such as Alberta pork chops, and excellent local wines. Seating is limited; reservations
are recommended. Smoke free premises. **Cards:** AE, DI, MC, VI.   ✕

TEAHOUSE RESTAURANT   **Lunch:** $12-$18   **Dinner:** $17-$28   **Phone:** 604/669-3281   ⑧⑨
ⓐⓐ   **Location:** Ferguson Point in Stanley Park. 7501 Stanley Park Dr V6G 3E2. **Hours:** 11:30 am-2:30 & 5:30-10
◆◆◆   pm, Sat & Sun brunch. Closed: 12/25. **Reservations:** suggested. **Features:** No A/C; casual dress; cocktails;
Continental   fee for parking; a la carte. The Teahouse has a charming country-garden setting in Stanley Park, with a
spectacular view of the harbor and mountains. Entrees include salmon torndos and roasted rack of lamb.
Couples and visitors especially enjoy the atmosphere of casual elegance. Smoke free premises. **Cards:** AE,
MC, VI.   ✕

TOMATO FRESH FOOD CAFE   **Lunch:** $5-$8   **Dinner:** $7-$14   **Phone:** 604/874-6020   ⑧④
◆   **Location:** Corner of Cambie and 17th sts. 3305 Cambie St V5Z 2W6. **Hours:** 9 am-10 pm. Closed: 1/1 &
Canadian   12/25. **Features:** Sunday brunch; children's menu; health conscious menu items; carryout; beer & wine only;
street parking; a la carte. This unusual converted soda-shop cafe features lively colors in an eclectic decor.
The menu includes fresh ingredients for salads, pasta, sourdough and multigrain sandwiches. Table spacing is close and
seating can be limited in peak periods. Smoke free premises. **Cards:** AE, MC, VI.   ✕

WON MORE SZECHUAN RESTAURANT   **Lunch:** $6-$11   **Dinner:** $6-$11   **Phone:** 604/737-2889   ⑧⑥
◆   **Location:** W 4th Ave and Cypress. 1944 W 4th Ave V6J 1M5. **Hours:** 11:30 am-2:30 & 5-10 pm, Sat & Sun
Chinese   from 5 pm. Closed: 1/1 & 12/25. **Features:** carryout; beer & wine only; street parking; a la carte. If you
appreciate hot, spicy and full-flavored cooking, you'll certainly enjoy Won More. Their Szechwan dishes
utilize plenty of ginger and garlic spices. The honey garlic boneless pork dish is superb! And the server staff is friendly and
attentive. **Cards:** MC, VI.   ✕

The following restaurants have not been inspected by AAA but are listed for your information only.

AQUA RIVER   **Phone:** 604/683-5599
[fyi]   Not inspected. **Location:** 200 Granville St. **Features:** By the waterfront, you'll get views of Canada Place,
cruise ships, helicopters leaving a nearby pad, and possibly a celebrity or two checking in at two of
Vancouver's hotels. Try the house-smoked salmon carpaccio or one of 24 amazing martinis.

AVENUE GRILL   **Phone:** 604/266-8183
[fyi]   Not inspected. **Location:** 2114 W 41st Ave. **Features:** This is a long-established hangout for locals in
Kerrisdale, a Vancouver suburb, that does a solid job of providing straightforward contemporary fare.

BISHOP'S   **Phone:** 604/738-2025
[fyi]   Not inspected. **Location:** 2183 W Fourth Ave. **Features:** Regulars are treated like family and newcomers
like welcomed guests at this favorite haunt of locals and visiting celebrities. Preparation is impeccable, but
simple, e.g., baked fillet of while salmon, grilled veal chop, apple creme brulee in cored apple.

CARDERO'S   **Phone:** 604/669-7666
[fyi]   Not inspected. **Location:** 1583 Coal Harbour Quay. **Features:** This casual waterfront bar and dining room
opens out to spectacular Coal Harbour marina and mountain views. A reasonably priced menu is offered
along with their value-oriented wine list. The patio is one of the city's prime porches for evening gatherings.

CENTURY GRILL   **Phone:** 604/688-8088
[fyi]   Not inspected. **Location:** 1095 Hamilton St. **Features:** The food looks as good as the crowd. Try their
signature dish of ahi-tuna fillet, champion steaks and well-made pastas. Also, take a look at their
ever-changing "fresh sheet" to really test this restaurant.

THE CREEK   **Phone:** 604/685-7070
[fyi]   Not inspected. **Location:** 1253 Johnston St. **Features:** In the Granville Island Hotel under the Granville St.
Bridge, this large and often boisterous room represents the arrival of San Francisco style big-box dining. The
cooking is generally strong, with dishes like braised lamb served with a cassoulet.

C RESTAURANT   **Phone:** 604/681-1164
[fyi]   Not inspected. **Location:** One blk below Beach Ave. 1600 Howe St. **Features:** Located on the Falsecreek
waterfront, this eatery is very well known for superior seafood served with sun pouring through huge
windows onto white linen and tile. It's like a little piece of the French Riviera.

DELILAH'S   **Phone:** 604/687-3424
[fyi]   Not inspected. **Location:** 1739 Comox St. **Features:** This infamous restaurant is known for its martinis and
over-the-top atmosphere.

(See map p. 468)

EZOGIKU NOODLE CAFE
Phone: 604/685-8606

[fyi]   Not inspected. **Location:** 1329 Robson St. **Features:** If it weren't for the word "noodle" in the name, it could easily be mistaken for yet another espresso bar. However, inside you'll find that the Chinese egg noodle is the mainstay, deftly cooked and chewy, in a rich, steaming broth.

FARRAGO
Phone: 604/684-4044

[fyi]   Not inspected. **Location:** 1138 Homer St. **Features:** This is Mediterranean, sun-belt cooking in a Yaletown room with one of the most charming courtyards in town. Try the roasted garlic and caramelized-onion flan, salt-cod and potato pizza, topped with caviar. The signature dish is slow-roasted duck.

GRAND KING
Phone: 604/876-7855

[fyi]   Not inspected. **Location:** 705 W Broadway. **Features:** For all around quality, value and service, this Chinese restaurant is hard to beat. Local ingredients are used to enhance each dish and the dim sum is exceptional. This is one of the few Chinese restaurants with real choices on the wine list.

GRAND PATTAYA
Phone: 604/876-0676

[fyi]   Not inspected. **Location:** 656 Leg-In-Boot Sq. **Features:** Worldlier-than-usual decor and superb False Creek views make this a good candidate for everyday Thai dining. Try the charcoal-grilled beef, marinated in lime juice and chilies, pineapple-fried rice with bits of squid, or steamed, yellow-curry crab.

IMPERIAL
Phone: 604/688-8191

[fyi]   Not inspected. **Location:** 355 Burrard St. **Features:** This restaurant wows visitors with its dramatic room looking out onto Burrard Inlet, and its impressive food. Lobster in black-bean sauce, pan-fried scallops garnished with coconut laced deep-fried milk and Dim Sum are especially savory.

LA TERRAZZA
Phone: 604/899-4449

[fyi]   Not inspected. **Location:** 1088 Cambie St & Pacific Blvd. **Features:** Experience the art of fresh, Italian cuisine served in the ambience of a classical villa. Imagination and flair typify the menu. Try the grilled eggplant stuffed with goat cheese, arugula and sun-dried tomatoes served on a tomato coulis.

LE GAVROCHE
Phone: 604/685-3924

[fyi]   Not inspected. **Location:** 1616 Alberni St. **Features:** For two decades, Le Gavroche has been home to Vancouver lovers of fine, French wine and cuisine. This Victorian house on quiet street features an astonishing wine cellar of over 12,000 bottles, with a French focus.

LORENZO'S
Phone: 604/731-2712

[fyi]   Not inspected. **Location:** 3605 W 4th at Dunbar. **Features:** Visiting Lorenzo's is like visiting friends in the old country—friends who cook fantastic pasta, served al dente and cooked to order. Signature dishes like scampi, osso bucco and grilled halibut with a citrus basil sauce making dining here memorable.

LUMIERE
Phone: 604/739-8185

[fyi]   Not inspected. **Location:** 2551 W Broadway. **Features:** Lumiere truly is a French restaurant, the kind you'll find in France. For a fixed price, diners are offered seven or eight courses meant to be experienced over several glorious hours.

MOUSTACHE CAFE
Phone: 604/739-1990

[fyi]   Not inspected. **Location:** 2118 Burrard St. **Features:** This colorful dining room at 5th and Burrard has reinvented the idea of the Mediterranean restaurant with its open kitchen and bright murals. Daily specials are a large part of their fare, along with a few regular, signature dishes.

PHNOM PENH RESTAURANT
Phone: 604/734-8898

[fyi]   Not inspected. **Location:** 955 W Broadway. **Features:** Experience award-winning Cambodian fare, exemplary hot and sour soups, unbeatable garlic-pepper squid, prawns or crab, steamed rice cakes dressed with pork, shrimp, coconut and scallions. The menu is extensive.

PICCOLO MONDO
Phone: 604/688-1633

[fyi]   Not inspected. **Location:** 850 Thurlow St. **Features:** The regular menu favorites include the ravioline in brodo ricco soup and squid-ink risotto. Summer brings lighter fare like fresh halibut and an ever-changing array of menu specials.

PROVENCE
Phone: 604/222-1980

[fyi]   Not inspected. **Location:** 4473 W 10th Ave. **Features:** This is a popular West Point Grey bistro. Try their signature dish, a spiced roast of lingcod served with sauteed spinach, roasted cherry tomatoes and a lemon tart. Desserts are this bistro's specialty.

RASPUTIN
Phone: 604/879-6675

[fyi]   Not inspected. **Location:** 457 W Broadway. **Features:** This Russian restaurant features a large list of iced vodkas. A heart-rending chicken Kiev is reasonably priced, but you may want to dive into mounds of shining, sevruga caviar.

SAWASDEE
Phone: 604/876-4030

[fyi]   Not inspected. **Location:** 4250 Main St. **Features:** A comfortable interior and courteous service make Vancouver's oldest Thai restaurant an excellent choice. The rich, coconut-perfumed, barbecued duck curry is a must-try, as are goong phad med-manuang and the stir-fried prawns.

SEASONS IN THE PARK
Phone: 604/874-8008

[fyi]   Not inspected. **Location:** Queen Elizabeth Park. **Features:** A window seat in this expansive room yields one of the best views possible of Queen Elizabeth Park, the neighborhood and the skyline. The emphasis is on West Coast fish, poultry and veggies. End with "sunburned" lemon pie.

(See map p. 468)

SINGAPORE RESTAURANT   **Phone:** 604/874-6161
fyi   Not inspected. **Location:** 546 W Broadway. **Features:** This cozy eatery is still great for the rustic, nonya cooking from Singapore. Dishes range from scorching sambal bunchies, a chili-tossed dish of green beans and prawns, to a wonderful, spiced satay arriving with an intense peanut sauce.

SOPHIE'S COSMIC CAFE   **Phone:** 604/732-6810
fyi   Not inspected. **Location:** Between Arbutus & Maple. 2095 W 4th Ave. **Features:** This funky, diner-cum-garage sale is a must-see. The diner is filled with stuff from your childhood. Try the huge, spicy burgers and chocolate shakes, or the stick-to-your-ribs-style breakfast.

STEPHO'S   **Phone:** 604/683-2555
fyi   Not inspected. **Location:** 1124 Davie St. **Features:** This very popular, west end, Greek restaurant almost always has a line waiting, but it's worth the wait to try very generous plates of rice, roast potatoes, souvlaki or lamb and great Greek salads.

TOJO'S   **Phone:** 604/872-8050
fyi   Not inspected. **Location:** 202-777 W Broadway. **Features:** Tojo's has served a distinct brand of Japanese seafood haiku for almost 30 years. Dishes include Tojo tuna, pine-mushroom soup, shrimp dumplings with hot mustard sauce, lightly steamed monkfish and sauteed halibut cheeks. A known celebrity hangout!.

TRAFALGARS AT SWEET OBSESSION   **Phone:** 604/739-0555
fyi   Not inspected. **Location:** 2603 W 16th Ave. **Features:** Locals drop in to this cake and pastry shop for morning or afternoon treats, a delicious lunch or a weekend brunch. Take-out cake and pastries are available. The small, bright room with wrap-around windows offers a pleasant view.

WILD GARLIC   **Phone:** 604/730-0880
fyi   Not inspected. **Location:** 2120 W Broadway. **Features:** Don't let the name worry you. This is a professional restaurant, melding Asian and European influences to yield dishes like jasmine-smoked sea bass with red pepper coulis and steamed, sticky-rice or seared, garlic halibut and vegetarian spring rolls.

YALETOWN BREWING   **Phone:** 604/688-0039
fyi   Not inspected. **Location:** 1111 Mainland St. **Features:** Located in the heart of Vancouver's chic Yaletown area, this brew-pub has a charming, warehouse look. The California-style menu goes well with the six superior home brews, like Frank's Nut Brown Ale or Red Brick Bitter.

The Vancouver Vicinity

ALDERGROVE pop. 11,500

——— LODGING ———

BEST WESTERN COUNTRY MEADOWS
(CAA) (SAVE)
♦♦♦
Motor Inn

	6/16-8/31	1P: $80-$85	2P: $85-$95	XP: $10	F12
	5/1-6/15	1P: $70-$80	2P: $75-$80	XP: $10	F12
	3/1-4/30 & 9/1-2/28	1P: $65-$70	2P: $70-$75	XP: $10	F12

Phone: (604)856-9880

Location: Trans Canada Hwy 1, exit 73 264th St/Aldergove, 5 km s on 264th St (Hwy 13). 3070 264th St V4W 3E1. Fax: 604/856-0086. **Terms:** [CP] meal plan; weekly & monthly rates avail, off season; cancellation fee imposed; package plans. **Facility:** 78 rooms. Modern property with large, comfortable guest rooms all with a pleasant, modern style decor. 1 two-bedroom unit. 2 whirlpool rooms, $129-$149; 2 stories; interior corridors; heated pool, whirlpool. **Dining:** Restaurant; 7 am-10 pm; $6-$11; wine/beer only. **All Rooms:** extended cable TV. **Some Rooms:** 23 efficiencies, kitchen. **Cards:** AE, DI, DS, MC, VI. **Special Amenities:** Free breakfast and free room upgrade (subject to availability with advanced reservations). *(See color ad p 507)*

BURNABY pop. 179,200 (See map p. 468; index p. 466)

——— LODGINGS ———

BEST WESTERN KINGS INN AND CONFERENCE CENTRE
(CAA) (SAVE)
♦♦♦
Motor Inn

| | 5/1-2/28 | 1P: $129-$169 | 2P: $139-$169 | XP: $10 | F17 |
| | 3/1-4/30 | 1P: $125-$164 | 2P: $135-$164 | XP: $10 | F17 |

Phone: (604)438-1383 [111]

Location: Just e of Metrotown Centre. 5411 Kingsway V5H 2G1. Fax: 604/438.2954. **Facility:** 141 rooms. A fine property featuring attractive landscaping touches, guest rooms offer modern decor, many at-door parking. Kitchen & efficiency units, $10-$15 extra charge; 3 whirlpool rooms; 2 stories; exterior corridors; heated pool. **Dining:** Restaurant; 7 am-2 & 5 - 9 pm, Sat & Sun 7 am-11:30 & 5-10 pm; $7-$15; cocktails. **All Rooms:** extended cable TV. **Cards:** AE, DI, DS, MC, VI. **Special Amenities:** Free local telephone calls and free newspaper. *(See color ad p 493)*

EXECUTIVE INN HOTELS
♦♦♦
Suite Hotel

| | 5/1-10/15 | 1P: $99-$169 | 2P: $109-$179 | XP: $20 | F12 |
| | 3/1-4/30 & 10/16-2/28 | 1P: $89-$139 | 2P: $99-$149 | XP: $20 | F12 |

Phone: (604)298-2010 [107]

Location: Trans Canada Hwy 1, exit Willingdon Ave N to Lougheed Hwy, then 1 km w. 4201 Lougheed Hwy V5C 3Y6. Fax: 604/298-1123. **Terms:** Cancellation fee imposed. **Facility:** 125 rooms. Large and spacious suite style guest rooms, all with separate seating area. Convention oriented listing. 4 stories; interior corridors; heated pool. **Services:** gift shop; area transportation. **All Rooms:** safes. **Cards:** AE, DI, MC, VI. *(See color ad p 471)*

HOLIDAY INN METROTOWN
(CAA) (SAVE)
♦♦♦
Motor Inn

	6/16-9/30	1P: $134-$159	2P: $135-$169	XP: $10	F19
	10/1-2/28	1P: $89-$154	2P: $89-$164	XP: $10	F19
	3/1-6/15	1P: $89-$154	2P: $89-$154	XP: $10	F19

Phone: (604)438-1881 [103]

Location: In Metrotown Centre Shopping Mall across from Eton Centre. 4405 Central Blvd V5H 4M3. Fax: 604/438-1883. **Facility:** 100 rooms. Attached to large shopping complex, this upgraded property features very attractive guest rooms all done in a unique "art decor" style. Top floor set aside as an "executive floor". Close to skytrain station. 6 stories; interior corridors; heated pool. **Dining:** Restaurant; 6:30 am-9 pm, Sat & Sun 7 am-10 pm; $10-$17; cocktails. **All Rooms:** extended cable TV. **Cards:** AE, DI, DS, MC, VI. **Special Amenities:** Free local telephone calls and free newspaper. *(See ad below)*

(See map p. 468)

LAKE CITY MOTOR INN
◆◆◆   Phone: 604/294-5331   108
Motel
| | 5/1-10/15 | 1P: $87-$92 | 2P: $92-$102 | XP: $5 | F12 |
| | 3/1-4/30 & 10/16-2/28 | 1P: $72 | 2P: $77-$87 | XP: $5 | F12 |

Location: Boundary Rd, 3 km e on Lougheed Hwy at Holdom Ave, entrance on n side of hwy. 5415 Lougheed Hwy V5B 2Z7. Fax: 604/294-5629. **Terms:** [CP] meal plan; small pets only, $5 extra charge. **Facility:** 48 rooms. A family run property features several separate cedar buildings; all with light cooking facilities. Guest rooms are large and pleasantly decorated. Lush landscaping and quiet residential surroundings. 2 stories; exterior corridors; heated pool. **All Rooms:** efficiencies. **Cards:** AE, DI, DS, MC, VI. *(See color ad p 494)*

RADISSON HOTEL BURNABY
(CAA) (SAVE)   Phone: (604)430-2828   110
◆◆◆
Hotel
| | All Year | 1P: $160 | 2P: $160 | XP: $10 | F18 |

Location: Trans Canada Hwy 1, exit 29 Willingdon Ave S, just w on Canada Way and n on Sumner St. 4331 Dominion St V5G 1C7. Fax: 604/430-9230. **Terms:** Cancellation fee imposed. **Facility:** 275 rooms. 2 separate sections; rooms overlooking the courtyard are smaller in size, the tower rooms are larger with their own private balcony. Nicely decorated guest rooms. 4-21 stories; interior corridors; 2 heated pools. **Dining:** Restaurant; 6:30 am-10:30 pm; $11-$24; cocktails. **Services:** gift shop. **All Rooms:** extended cable TV. **Cards:** AE, MC, VI. **Special Amenities:** Free breakfast and free newspaper.

STAY'N SAVE INN VANCOUVER BURNABY
(CAA) (SAVE)   Phone: (604)473-5000   106
◆◆◆
Motor Inn
| | 5/1-6/30 & 7/1-9/30 | 1P: $114-$124 | 2P: $124-$134 | XP: $10 | F16 |
| | 3/1-4/30 & 10/1-2/28 | 1P: $99-$109 | 2P: $109-$119 | XP: $10 | F16 |

Location: Trans Canada Hwy 1 exit 28 Grandview Hwy, just n on Boundary Rd. 3777 Henning Dr V5C 6N5. Fax: 604/473-5095. **Terms:** Weekly rates avail, off season; cancellation fee imposed; small pets only. **Facility:** 128 rooms. A well maintained, new property featuring large, attractively decorated guest rooms with the business or corporate traveller in mind. Across the street from large movie studio complex. 3 stories; interior corridors; sauna, whirlpool. **Dining:** Restaurant; 6 am-10 pm; $8-$15; wine/beer only. **All Rooms:** extended cable TV. **Some Rooms:** 40 efficiencies. **Cards:** AE, DI, MC, VI. **Special Amenities:** Free local telephone calls and free newspaper. *(See color ad p 431 & p 540)*

The following lodging was either not inspected or did not meet AAA rating requirements but is listed for your information only.

HILTON VANCOUVER METROTOWN
(fyi)   Phone: 604/438-1200
Hotel
| | 5/1-9/30 | 1P: $219-$284 | 2P: $219-$284 | XP: $20 | F12 |
| | 3/1-4/30 & 10/1-2/28 | 1P: $179-$244 | 2P: $179-$244 | XP: $20 | F12 |

Too new to rate, opening scheduled for October 1999. **Location:** Trans Canada Hwy 1, exit 29. 6083 McKay Ave V5H 4L9. **Terms:** Cancellation fee imposed. **Amenities:** 283 rooms, radios, coffeemakers, refrigerators, pool, exercise facilities. *(See color ad p 283)*

--- RESTAURANTS ---

THE HART HOUSE ON DEER LAKE
◆◆   Lunch: $10-$16   Dinner: $16-$27   Phone: 604/298-4278   110
Continental
Location: Trans Canada Hwy 1 exit 33, Kensington South, 1 km e on Canada Way to Sperling Ave, follow signs. 6664 Deer Lake Ave V5E 4H3. **Hours:** 11:30 am-2 & 5:30-10 pm, Sun 10 am-2 pm. **Reservations:** suggested. **Features:** casual dress; Sunday brunch; cocktails; a la carte. This restaurant is a turn-of-the century Tudor-style country home that has been turned into a lovely setting overlooking Deer Lake and two acres of lush lawn. The menu features wild game, prime rib and rack of lamb along with lighter fare for lunch. **Cards:** AE, DI, MC, VI.

HORIZON'S
◆◆◆   Lunch: $8-$13   Dinner: $17-$24   Phone: 604/299-1155   111
Regional
Steak and
Seafood
Location: From Lougheed Hwy, 5 km n on Gaglardi Way, 1 km w on University Dr, then just n, watch for signs. 100 Centennial Way V5A 2X9. **Hours:** 11:30 am-2 & 5-9 pm, Sun from 11 am. Closed: 12/24 & 12/25. **Reservations:** suggested. **Features:** casual dress; Sunday brunch; cocktails; a la carte. Horizon's hilltop location in Burnaby Mountain Park gives you a spectacular view of the city and mountains. Its menu specializes in alderwood-fired fresh seafood and steak as well as rack of lamb and roasted duck. This is a casual, fine-dining experience. **Cards:** AE, DI, MC, VI.

CHILLIWACK pop. 60,200

--- LODGINGS ---

BEST WESTERN RAINBOW COUNTRY INN
(CAA) (SAVE)   Phone: (604)795-3828
◆◆
Motor Inn
| | 5/1-9/30 | 1P: $99 | 2P: $109 | XP: $10 | F12 |
| | 3/1-4/30 & 10/1-2/28 | 1P: $79 | 2P: $89 | XP: $10 | F12 |

Location: Trans Canada Hwy 1 exit 116, Lickman Rd. 43971 Industrial Way V2R 3A4. Fax: 604/795-5039. **Terms:** Cancellation fee imposed; small pets only, $5 extra charge. **Facility:** 74 rooms. Located just off the hwy. Guest rooms are quite spacious. Several rooms have a balcony or patio that overlook lush courtyard setting with numerous plants and a flowing stream. 8 whirlpool rooms, $85-$119; 2 stories; interior corridors; heated pool, sauna, whirlpool. **Dining:** Restaurant, coffee shop; 5:30 am-midnight; $6-$19; cocktails. **Services:** gift shop. **Cards:** AE, DI, DS, MC, VI. **Special Amenities:** Early check-in/late check-out and preferred room (subject to availability with advanced reservations).

CHILLIWACK TRAVELODGE

CAA SAVE

◆ ◆
Motor Inn

6/1-9/30	1P: $69	2P: $75	XP: $6 F18
3/1-5/31 & 10/1-2/28	1P: $59	2P: $64	XP: $6 F18

Phone: (604)792-4240

Location: Trans Canada Hwy 1, eastbound exit 119B; westbound exit 119A, then just n. 45466 Yale Rd W V2R 1A9. Fax: 604/792-2325. **Terms:** [CP] meal plan; weekly & monthly rates avail, off season; 3 day cancellation notice; small pets only, $5 extra charge. **Facility:** 82 rooms. Just off the main hwy. Offering large, comfortable guest rooms with a simple decor. 18 efficiencies, $5 extra charge; 2 stories; interior corridors; heated pool, whirlpool. **Dining:** Restaurant; 6 am-11 pm; $6-$10; wine/beer only. **All Rooms:** extended cable TV. **Some Rooms:** Fee: VCR. **Cards:** AE, DI, DS, MC, VI. **Special Amenities: Free breakfast and free local telephone calls.** (See color ad below)

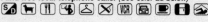

COMFORT INN

◆ ◆
Motel

7/1-9/15	1P: $69-$97	2P: $77-$105	XP: $8 F18
5/1-6/30	1P: $66-$94	2P: $74-$102	XP: $8 F18
9/16-2/28	1P: $64-$92	2P: $72-$100	XP: $4 F18
3/1-4/30	1P: $62-$90	2P: $70-$98	XP: $4 F18

Phone: (604)858-0636

Location: Trans Canada Hwy 1 eastbound exit 119A; westbound exit 119B, s on Vedder Rd, then 1 km w. 45405 Luckakuck Way V2R 3C7. Fax: 604/858-0116. **Terms:** Pets. **Facility:** 83 rooms. Located just off main hwy and close to 2 shopping malls. Good clean comfortable and basic accommodations offering average sized guest rooms. Ground floor rooms have patio door leading out to parking lot. 2 stories; interior corridors. **Cards:** AE, CB, DI, DS, JC, MC, VI.

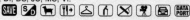

HOLIDAY INN CHILLIWACK-DOWNTOWN

CAA SAVE

◆ ◆ ◆
Motor Inn

5/1-9/30	1P: $85-$109	2P: $85-$119	XP: $10 F18
10/1-2/28	1P: $80-$99	2P: $80-$109	XP: $10 F18
3/1-4/30	1P: $75-$98	2P: $75-$98	XP: $10 F18

Phone: (604)795-4788

Location: Trans Canada Hwy 1 eastbound exit 119B; westbound exit 119A, 3 km n, then just w. 45920 1st Ave V2P 7K1. Fax: 604/795-4680. **Terms:** Check-in 4 pm; package plans; small pets only, $10 extra charge. **Facility:** 110 rooms. Located in the heart of downtown. This high-rise building features large, comfortable guest rooms with some very nice views of the surrounding mountains and city. 3 whirlpool rooms; 9 stories; interior corridors; heated pool, sauna, whirlpool. **Dining:** Restaurant; 7 am-10 pm; $8-$18; cocktails. **All Rooms:** extended cable TV. **Cards:** AE, DI, DS, MC, VI. **Special Amenities: Free room upgrade (subject to availability with advanced reservations).**

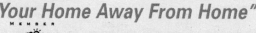

RAINBOW MOTOR INN

CAA SAVE
◆
Motel

All Year   1P: $59   2P: $69   XP: $5   F12
Location: Trans Canada Hwy 1, eastbound exit 119B; westbound exit 119A, then 1 km n. 45620 Yale Rd W V2P 2N2. Fax: 604/792-6475. **Terms:** Weekly & monthly rates avail; small pets only, $2 extra charge. **Facility:** 40 rooms. Comfortable guest rooms geared for those on a budget. About half the motel offers a modest room decor and the other half offers a more modern decor. At-door parking. Well manicured landscaping touches. Efficiency units, $5 extra charge; 1 story; exterior corridors. **Dining:** Restaurant nearby. **All Rooms:** extended cable TV. **Some Rooms:** 19 efficiencies. **Cards:** AE, DI, MC, VI. **Special Amenities:** Free local telephone calls and preferred room (subject to availability with advanced reservations). *(See color ad p 504)*

─── **RESTAURANT** ───

LA MANSIONE RISTORANTE

◆◆◆
Italian

Dinner: $13-$24   **Phone:** 604/792-8910
Location: Trans Canada Hwy 1, exit 119 to downtown, 3.6 km n. 46290 Yale Rd E V2P 2P6. **Hours:** 5:30 pm-10 pm, Sat & Sun from 5 pm. Closed: 12/25. **Reservations:** suggested. **Features:** early bird specials; cocktails; a la carte. La Mansione's beautiful downtown site was built in 1911 and has long been one of the area's most important historical buildings. The restaurant's menu features steak, seafood, lamb, veal and pasta specialties, and its setting is cozy and informal. **Cards:** AE, DI, MC, VI.

COQUITLAM pop. 101,800   (See map p. 468; index p. 466)

─── **LODGINGS** ───

BEST WESTERN CHELSEA INN

CAA SAVE
◆◆
Motor Inn

Phone: (604)525-7777   119
6/1-9/30   1P: $94-$99   2P: $104-$125   XP: $2   F12
3/1-5/31 & 10/1-2/28   1P: $68-$74   2P: $74-$89   XP: $2   F12
Location: Trans Canada Hwy 1, exit 40B. 725 Brunette Ave V3K 1C3. Fax: 604/525-7777. **Facility:** 61 rooms. Property offers large, very modern guest rooms. 10 efficiencies, $10 extra charge; 3 stories; interior corridors; heated pool, sauna, whirlpool. **Dining:** Restaurant; 7 am-11 pm; $9-$16; cocktails. **All Rooms:** extended cable TV. **Cards:** AE, DI, DS, JC, MC, VI. **Special Amenities:** Early check-in/late check-out and free newspaper. *(See color ad below)*

BEST WESTERN COQUITLAM INN CONVENTION CENTRE

CAA SAVE
◆◆◆
Motor Inn

Phone: (604)931-9011   116
All Year   1P: $129   2P: $139   XP: $10   F12
Location: Trans Canada Hwy 1, exit 37 Cariboo Rd/Gaglardi Way, 2 km e on Lougheed Hwy (Hwy 7), just s. 319 North Rd V3K 3V8. Fax: 604/931-7298. **Terms:** Cancellation fee imposed. **Facility:** 106 rooms. Some theme suites and executive type rooms avail. Lush courtyard area. All rooms with hair dryer, iron and ironing board. 16 two-bedroom kitchen units, $189-$209; 5 whirlpool rooms, $199-$279; 2 stories; interior/exterior corridors; designated smoking area; heated pool, sauna, whirlpool. **Dining:** Restaurant, coffee shop; 6 am-10 pm; $9-$19; cocktails; also, The Barrel Steakhouse, see separate listing; entertainment. **All Rooms:** extended cable TV. **Some Rooms:** Fee: VCR. **Cards:** AE, CB, DI, DS, JC, MC, VI. **Special Amenities:** Early check-in/late check-out and free newspaper. *(See color ad p 471)*

HOLIDAY INN COQUITLAM/VANCOUVER

◆◆◆
Motor Inn

Phone: (604)931-4433   118
6/16-9/15   1P: $119-$159   2P: $129-$169   XP: $10   F19
3/1-6/15   1P: $99-$119   2P: $109-$129   XP: $10   F19
9/16-2/28   1P: $89-$109   2P: $99-$119   XP: $10   F19
Location: Trans Canada Hwy 1, exit 37 Cariboo Rd/Gaglardi Way, 3.5 km e on Lougheed Hwy (Hwy 7). 631 Lougheed Hwy V3K 3S5. Fax: 604/931-4250. **Facility:** 84 rooms. A fine property featuring attractive modern guest rooms in various sizes, including spacious executive suites. Some units with at-door parking. All rooms with hair dryer, iron and ironing board. 4 two-bedroom units. 2 stories; interior/exterior corridors; heated pool. **Cards:** AE, DI, DS, JC, MC, VI. *(See color ad p 496)*

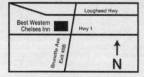

(See map p. 468)

—————— RESTAURANT ——————

THE BARREL STEAKHOUSE   **Lunch:** $6-$13   **Dinner:** $13-$28   **Phone:** 604/931-9122   (115)
◆◆◆   **Location:** Trans Canada Hwy 1, exit 37 Cariboo Rd/Gaglardi Way, 2 km e on Lougheed Hwy (Hwy 7), just
Steak and   s; in Best Western Coquitlam Inn Convention Centre. 319 North Rd V3K 3V8. **Hours:** 11:30 am-2 & 5-9 pm,
Seafood   Fri & Sat-10 pm. **Reservations:** suggested. **Features:** casual dress; Sunday brunch; children's menu;
cocktails & lounge; a la carte. Prime rib is featured at this restaurant, but it also offers lamb, veal, chicken,
barbecue ribs, certified Angus beef and daily specials. The decor is casual with a splash of neon color, and there's a tropical
courtyard behind the restaurant. **Cards:** AE, DI, DS, JC, MC, VI.   ⊠

DELTA pop. 95,400   (See map p. 468; index p. 467)

—————— LODGINGS ——————

BEST WESTERN TSAWWASSEN INN   **Phone:** (604)943-8221   161
(CAA) (SAVE)   5/1-9/30   1P: $119   2P: $129   XP: $10   F16
          3/1-4/30 & 10/1-2/28   1P: $89   2P: $99   XP: $10   F16
◆◆◆   **Location:** Hwy 99, exit 28 Tsawwassen Ferries, then 8 km w on Hwy 17; only 5 km from the Island Ferry Ter-
Motor Inn   minal. 1665 56th St V4L 2B2. Fax: 604/943-8299. **Terms:** Weekly & monthly rates avail; package plans; small
pets only, in courtyard rooms. **Facility:** 149 rooms. In the centre of Tsawwassen. Features 3 separate buildings with various rooms and sizes, from standard motel rooms to spacious suites with full kitchen. 6 whirlpool rooms, $149-
$285; 3 stories; interior corridors; 2 heated pools, sauna, whirlpool. **Dining:** Restaurant; 6 am-10:30 pm; $8-$18; cocktails.
Services: gift shop; area transportation, ferry terminal. **All Rooms:** extended cable TV. **Some Rooms:** 36 efficiencies, 19
kitchens. **Cards:** AE, DI, DS, JC, MC, VI. **Special Amenities:** Free breakfast and free room upgrade (subject to availability
with advanced reservations).

DELTA TOWN & COUNTRY INN   **Phone:** (604)946-4404   157
(CAA) (SAVE)   5/15-10/14   1P: $95-$125   2P: $95-$125   XP: $10   F16
          3/1-5/14 & 10/15-2/28   1P: $80-$110   2P: $80-$110   XP: $10   F16
◆◆   **Location:** Hwy 99 at jct Hwy 17, exit 28 Ladner/Tsawwassen Ferries; 12 km ne on Hwy 17 of Tsawwassen-
Motor Inn   Victoria Ferry terminal. 6005 Hwy 17 at Hwy 99 V4K 5B2. Fax: 604/946-5916. **Terms:** [CP] meal plan; weekly
          & monthly rates avail; 14 day cancellation notice; cancellation fee imposed; small pets only. **Facility:** 49 rooms.
This pleasant property sits in a rural farming area, rooms at the back feature a small private patio overlooking the fields, pool
area and domed tennis courts. Inquire about their upgraded business class rooms. Short drive to Ferry. Whirlpool room; suites,
$129-$169; 2 stories; interior corridors; heated pool; 5 tennis courts (4 indoor, 4 lighted). **Dining:** Restaurant; 6 am-9:30 pm,
Sun from 7 am; $8-$16; cocktails. **Services:** gift shop. **All Rooms:** extended cable TV. **Cards:** AE, DI, MC, VI.
Special Amenities: Free breakfast and free local telephone calls. (See color ad p 489)

INGRID'S ON TWELFTH EUROPEAN BED & BREAKFAST   **Phone:** 604/943-4378   164
◆◆   All Year   1P: $65-$110   2P: $75-$120   XP: $10   F
Bed &   **Location:** Hwy 99 exit 28 Tsawwassen Ferries, 8 km w on Hwy 17; 2 km s on 52nd St, then just w. 5447 12th
Breakfast   Ave V4M 2B2. Fax: 604/943-4378. **Terms:** [BP] meal plan; age restrictions may apply; 7 day cancellation no-
          tice. **Facility:** 3 rooms. In the centre of Tsawwassen. Warmly decorated guest rooms with an assortment of an-
tique style furniture offering an at-home feel. Outside patio deck in summer. Beauty salon on site. 2 stories; interior corridors;
designated smoking area. **All Rooms:** combo or shower baths. **Cards:** VI.

PRIMROSE HILL GUEST HOUSE   **Phone:** (604)940-8867   160
(CAA)   4/1-12/31   1P: $75-$125   2P: $85-$145   XP: $10
          1/1-2/28   1P: $65-$100   2P: $75-$125
◆◆   3/1-3/31   1P: $65-$100   2P: $75-$125   XP: $10
Historic Bed   **Location:** From Hwy 17, 1.8 km w on Ladner Trunk Rd to Elliott St, just n on 48th Ave, in downtown Ladner
& Breakfast   Village. 4919 48th Ave V4K 1V4. Fax: 604/940-0234. **Terms:** [BP] meal plan; weekly rates avail; age restric-
          tions may apply; check-in 4 pm; 3 day cancellation notice. **Facility:** 6 rooms. Built during the Edwardian era in
the year 1913. This fully restored residence features a quaint Victorian style motif with high ceilings and rich wood paneling.
Whirlpool room; 2 stories; interior corridors; designated smoking area. **Dining:** Restaurant nearby. **All Rooms:** combo, shower
or tub baths. **Cards:** AE, MC, VI.

RIVER RUN COTTAGES   **Phone:** (604)946-7778   158
◆◆◆   5/1-9/30   1P: $120-$200   2P: $130-$210   XP: $20
Bed &   3/1-4/30 & 10/1-2/28   1P: $119-$165   2P: $119-$175   XP: $20
Breakfast   **Location:** From Hwy 17, 2.5 km n on Ladner Trunk Rd which becomes 47A St and then becomes River Rd W;
          in Ladner Village. 4551 River Rd W V4K 1R9. Fax: 604/940-1970. **Terms:** [BP] meal plan; age restrictions may
apply; check-in 4 pm; 21 day cancellation notice, x; cancellation fee imposed; small pets only. **Facility:** 4 rooms. Individual cottages on the mighty Fraser River delta. Choose from an exquisitely crafted floating cottage, or 2 cottages on the riverbank with
private boardwalk deck with view of the river. 1 story; exterior corridors; designated smoking area. **Recreation:** bicycles.
All Rooms: efficiencies, combo or shower baths. **Cards:** MC, VI.

SOUTHLANDS HOUSE "BY THE SEA"   **Phone:** 604/943-1846   163
(CAA)   All Year   1P: $135-$175   2P: $135-$175
◆◆◆   **Location:** Hwy 99 exit 28 Tsawwassen Ferries, 8 km w on Hwy 17, 2 km s on 52nd St, 1 km e on 12th Ave.
Bed &   1160 Boundary Bay Rd V4L 2P6. Fax: 604/943-2481. **Terms:** [BP] meal plan; age restrictions may apply; 7 day
Breakfast   cancellation notice; cancellation fee imposed. **Facility:** 6 rooms. Right next to the Boundary Regional Park, a
          bird watchers paradise as this park is home to several species of birds. This expansive home overlooks the
park and ocean, guest rooms are beautifully decorated. 2 stories; interior/exterior corridors; designated
smoking area; whirlpool. **All Rooms:** extended cable TV. **Cards:** AE, MC, VI.

(See map p. 468)

──────── RESTAURANT ────────

LA BELLE AUBERGE   **Dinner: $22-$25**   **Phone: 604/946-7717**   128
Ⓐ   **Location:** From Hwy 17, 1.8 km w on Ladner Trunk Rd to Elliott St, then just n, in downtown Historic Ladner
◆◆◆   Village. 4856 48th Ave V4K 1V2. **Hours:** 6 pm-midnight. Closed: Mon. **Reservations:** suggested.
French   **Features:** No A/C; casual dress; health conscious menu items; cocktails; a la carte. This charming Ladner
                      home has been transformed into a comfortable inn serving fine French cuisine. The restaurant is owned and
                      operated by a chef and Olympic gold medalist on the Canadian culinary team. A six-course meal for $40-$50
per person is offered. **Cards:** AE, DI, MC, VI.   ⊠

LANGLEY pop. 22,500

──────── LODGINGS ────────

BEST WESTERN LANGLEY INN   **Phone: (604)530-9311**
Ⓐ SAVE   7/1-9/10   1P: $109-$115   2P: $109-$115   XP: $6   F6
◆◆◆   3/1-6/30 & 9/11-2/28   1P: $95-$99   2P: $95-$99   XP: $6   F6
Motor Inn   **Location:** Trans Canada Hwy 1, exit 58 200th St/Langley City, 5 km s on 200th St, 1 km e on Hwy 10, corner
                of Glover Rd and Hwy 10. 5978 Glover Rd V3A 4H9. Fax: 604/530-2438. **Terms:** [CP] meal plan; weekly rates
avail, off season; cancellation fee imposed. **Facility:** 78 rooms. A pleasant, upscale property featuring fine,
modern guest rooms. Executive style guest rooms with king bed avail. 21 efficiencies, $6 extra charge. Executive suite with full
kitchen & 2 bedrooms $110-$130; 2 stories; interior corridors; heated pool, whirlpool. **Dining:** Restaurant; 6:30 am-11 pm; $6-
$11; wine/beer only. **All Rooms:** extended cable TV. **Some Rooms:** kitchen. **Cards:** AE, DI, DS, MC, VI. **Special Amenities:**
Free breakfast. *(See color ad below)*   🛱 🍴 ♿ 🛋 ⊠ 📷 🖨 💻 🖥 🔌 DATA PORT 🛥 🛗

EAGLE'S REACH ON THE BLUFF AT FORT LANGLEY BED & BREAKFAST   **Phone: (604)888-4470**
◆◆◆   All Year   1P: $70-$95   2P: $90-$115
Bed &   **Location:** From Trans Canada Hwy 1, exit 66 (232 St), 3 mi nw on 232 St, 2 km n on Glover Rd, e on Mavis
Breakfast   St, then 2 km e on River Rd, just s on Armstrong Rd to 87th Ave. 24658 87th Ave V1M 2R3.
                Fax: 604/888-4773. **Terms:** [BP] meal plan; age restrictions may apply; 7 day cancellation notice; cancellation
fee imposed. **Facility:** 4 rooms. A magnificent home situated atop a hillside with wonderful views of the river and mountains.
On-site entertainment facilities like pinball machines, pool table and in-home theatre with giant screen. 2 stories; interior corridors; designated smoking area; putting green; heated pool. **All Rooms:** combo or shower baths. **Cards:** MC, VI.
                                          🛱 🛋 ⊠ 🖨 💻 🛥 🛗 ⊠

HOLIDAY INN EXPRESS HOTEL & SUITES   **Phone: (604)882-2000**
Ⓐ SAVE   All Year   1P: $89-$107   2P: $89-$107
◆◆◆   **Location:** Trans Canada Hwy 1, exit 58 (Langey City/200th St), 1 km e on 200th St. 8750 204th St V1M 2Y5.
Motel   Fax: 604/882-2008. **Terms:** [CP] meal plan; check-in 4 pm; package plans; small pets only, $10 extra charge.
                Facility: 86 rooms. An excellent roadside listing featuring attractive guest rooms with many modern amenities.
Impressive indoor pool area. 5 whirlpool rooms; 4 stories; interior corridors; heated pool, sauna, steamroom,
whirlpool. **Dining:** Restaurant nearby. **All Rooms:** extended cable TV. **Cards:** AE, DI, DS, JC, MC, VI. **Special Amenities:**
Free breakfast and free local telephone calls.
                  🛱 🐾 🍴 ♿ 🛗 🛋 ⊠ 📷 🖨 💻 🖥 🔌 DATA PORT 🛥 🛗

TRAVELODGE-LANGLEY MOTOR INN   **Phone: (604)533-4431**
Ⓐ SAVE   5/15-9/15   1P: $59-$74   2P: $64-$84   XP: $5   F8
◆   3/1-5/14 & 9/16-2/28   1P: $54-$69   2P: $59-$79   XP: $5   F8
Motel   **Location:** Trans Canada Hwy 1 exit 58, (200th St/Langley City), 5 km s, 2.5 km w on Hwy 10, then 1.5 km e.
                21653 Fraser Hwy V3A 4H1. Fax: 604/514-7620. **Terms:** Weekly & monthly rates avail, off season; small pets
                only, $5 extra charge. **Facility:** 65 rooms. On the e end of the Langley Airport. This standard style motel fea-
tures good, comfortable accommodations. 2 stories; exterior corridors. **Dining:** Restaurant nearby. **All Rooms:** extended cable
TV. **Some Rooms:** 18 efficiencies. **Cards:** AE, MC, VI. **Special Amenities:** Free local telephone calls.
                                          🛱 🐾 🍴 🛋 ⊠ 💻 🔌

WESTWARD INN   Phone: (604)534-9238

CAA SAVE   5/16-9/10   1P: $62-$66   2P: $66-$72

◆◆   3/1-5/15 & 9/11-2/28   1P: $50-$58   2P: $54-$60

Motel   **Location:** Trans Canada Hwy 1, exit 58 (200th St/Langley City), 5 km s on 200th St, 1 km w on Hwy 10, then just w. 19650 Fraser Hwy V3A 4C7. Fax: 604/534-0629. **Terms:** Weekly & monthly rates avail, off season; pets, $4 extra charge. **Facility:** 55 rooms. An older property featuring 2 separate buildings all with parking in front of guest rooms. Rooms are average in size and decor. Close to Willow Brook Shopping Centre. 19 two-bedroom units. 21 kitchens, $15 extra charge; 1 story; exterior corridors. **Dining:** Restaurant nearby. **All Rooms:** extended cable TV. **Some Rooms:** Fee: VCR. **Cards:** AE, MC, VI. **Special Amenities: Free local telephone calls and preferred room (subject to availability with advanced reservations).**

---------- **RESTAURANT** ----------

OLD COUNTRY INN   **Dinner:** $14-$24   **Phone:** 604/534-8696

◆◆◆   **Location:** Corner of 206th St, downtown. 20598 Fraser Hwy V3A 4G2. **Hours:** 5 pm-10:30 pm, Sat-11 pm,

Continental   Sun-10 pm. **Reservations:** suggested. **Features:** cocktails; a la carte. Old Country Inn is a distinctive European specialty house with a wide selection of schnitzel, chicken, steak, seafood, specialty desserts and some items prepared tableside. The intimate atmosphere has a cozy, casual elegance and fine service. **Cards:** AE, MC, VI.

MAPLE RIDGE pop. 56,200

---------- **LODGINGS** ----------

MAPLE RIDGE INN AND SUITES   Phone: (604)463-5111

CAA SAVE   6/1-9/30   1P: $109-$129   2P: $119-$139   XP: $5   F16

◆◆   3/1-5/31 & 10/1-2/28   1P: $99-$119   2P: $109-$129   XP: $5   F16

Motor Inn   **Location:** 2 km w on Lougheed Hwy (Hwy 7) from downtown Maple Ridge. 21735 Lougheed Hwy V2X 2S2. Fax: 604/463-3113. **Terms:** Weekly rates avail, off season; check-in 4 pm; 7 day cancellation notice. **Facility:** 61 rooms. Large guest rooms with a modern style decor offering above average accommodations. 6 efficiencies, $10 extra charge; whirlpool room, $169-$199; 2 stories; exterior corridors. **Dining:** Restaurant; 6:30 am-10 pm; $6-$12; wine/beer only. **Some Rooms:** kitchen. **Cards:** AE, CB, DI, DS, JC, MC, VI. **Special Amenities: Early check-in/late check-out and free room upgrade (subject to availability with advanced reservations).**

TRAVELODGE MAPLE RIDGE   Phone: (604)467-1511

◆   All Year   1P: $69-$99   2P: $89-$129   XP: $10

Motel   **Location:** 2 km w on Lougheed Hwy (Hwy 7) from downtown Maple Ridge. 21650 Lougheed Hwy V2X 2S1. Fax: 604/467-1532. **Terms:** Small pets only, $50 dep req. **Facility:** 58 rooms. Budget oriented property offering average-sized guest rooms. 2 stories; interior corridors. **Some Rooms:** 26 efficiencies. Fee: VCR. **Cards:** AE, DI, JC, MC, VI.

---------- **RESTAURANTS** ----------

THE GOURMET HIDEAWAY   **Dinner:** $15-$25   **Phone:** 604/463-7122

◆◆   **Location:** Lougheed Hwy (Hwy 7) just s on 224th St. 11598 224th St V2X 7E9. **Hours:** 5:30 pm-10:30 pm,

French   Sun from 5 pm. Closed: Mon. **Reservations:** required. **Features:** casual dress; cocktails; a la carte. Set in a Tudor mansion overlooking the Fraser River, this restaurant offers house specialties of chicken cordon bleu, roasted duck, rack of lamb, filet mignon, vegetarian dishes, seafood and pasta. Also offered: a nice selection of appetizers and wines. **Cards:** AE, DI, DS, MC, VI.

ROOSTER'S QUARTERS   **Lunch:** $5-$13   **Dinner:** $8-$13   **Phone:** 604/463-9691

◆◆   **Location:** Lougheed Hwy (Hwy 7), 3 blks n on 226th St. 22590 Dewdney Trunk Rd V2X 3J9. **Hours:** 11:30

Canadian   am-9:30 pm, Sat & Sun-10:30 pm. Closed: 12/25 & 12/26. **Reservations:** suggested. **Features:** carryout; cocktails; a la carte. You'll like this restaurant decorated in a chicken motif with ceramic hens and pictures of roosters. What do they specialize in? Chicken, of course. The cordon bleu is excellent. Park behind the building; the entrance is near Canada Safeway on 226th St. Smoke free premises. **Cards:** AE, MC, VI.

MISSION pop. 30,500

—— LODGING ——

BEST WESTERN MISSION CITY LODGE   Phone: (604)820-5500

(CAA) [SAVE]
5/1-9/30	1P: $85-$95	2P: $85-$95	XP: $7 F12
10/1-2/28	1P: $78-$90	2P: $78-$90	XP: $7 F12
3/1-4/30	1P: $75-$85	2P: $75-$85	XP: $7 F12

◆◆◆
Motor Inn   **Location:** Just w of Hwy 11, corner of Lougheed Hwy (7) and Hurd St. 32281 Lougheed Hwy V2V 3J8. Fax: 604/820-5510. **Terms:** Small pets only, $10 extra charge. **Facility:** 80 rooms. A hilltop location gives most of the guest rooms a wonderful view of the valley and distant mountains. All guest rooms are fairly spacious and nicely decorated. Whirlpool room, $175-$200; 4 stories; interior corridors; heated pool, sauna, whirlpool. **Dining:** Restaurant; 6:30 am-11 pm; $8-$15; cocktails. **All Rooms:** extended cable TV. **Some Rooms:** 5 efficiencies. **Cards:** AE, CB, DI, DS, MC, VI. **Special Amenities: Free local telephone calls and preferred room (subject to availability with advanced reservations).** *(See color ad below)*

NEW WESTMINSTER pop. 49,400   (See map p. 468; index p. 467)

—— LODGING ——

INN AT WESTMINSTER QUAY   Phone: (604)520-1776   **170**

(CAA) [SAVE]
5/2-10/1	1P: $170-$215	2P: $180-$215	XP: $10 F16
10/2-2/28	1P: $160-$195	2P: $170-$205	XP: $10 F16
3/1-5/1	1P: $150-$195	2P: $160-$195	XP: $10 F16

◆◆◆
Hotel   **Location:** Adjacent to public market along the waterfront, follow signs to Westminster Quay. 900 Quayside Dr V3M 6G1. Fax: 604/520-5645. **Terms:** Package plans. **Facility:** 126 rooms. Along the Fraser River. Large guest rooms, updated decor. Many rooms feature private balcony with great view of the river; all rooms with iron and ironing board. 10 whirlpool rooms, $195-$205; 9 stories; interior corridors; sauna, whirlpool. Fee: parking. **Dining:** Restaurant; 6:30-9:30 am, 11:30-2 & 5-11 pm; $12-$20; cocktails. **All Rooms:** extended cable TV, honor bars. **Cards:** AE, DI, DS, JC, MC, VI. **Special Amenities: Free newspaper.** *(See color ad p 494)*

—— RESTAURANTS ——

BURGER HEAVEN   **Lunch:** $5-$10   **Dinner:** $5-$10   **Phone:** 604/522-8339   **133**
◆
American   **Location:** Just s of Royal Ave. 77 Tenth St V3M 3X4. **Hours:** 11:30 am-9 pm, Fri & Sat-10 pm. Closed major holidays & 12/24-1/4. **Features:** children's menu; beer & wine only; fee for parking; a la carte. This locally popular dining spot features all kinds of burgers—chicken, veggie, beef—cooked to order and served with many different fresh toppings. They also have a wide variety of sandwiches, a living-room atmosphere, beer, wine and coolers. **Cards:** AE, MC, VI.   [X]

LA RUSTICA RISTORANTE   **Lunch:** $6-$9   **Dinner:** $11-$20   **Phone:** 604/525-6355   **137**
◆◆
Italian   **Location:** 3rd Ave and 6th St, just nw of City Hall. 228 6th St V3L 3A4. **Hours:** 11:30 am-2 & 5-10 pm, Fri-11 pm, Sat 5-11 pm, Sun 5-10 pm. Closed: 12/25 & 12/26. **Reservations:** suggested; weekends. **Features:** No A/C; cocktails; street parking; a la carte. This restaurant's traditional homemade cuisine is complemented by French and Continental dishes. The veal piccata and pepper steak are good choices. The setting was converted from two older side-by-side houses. The servers are pleasant and friendly. **Cards:** AE, DI, MC, VI.   [X]

RESTAURANT DES GITANS   **Lunch:** $12-$18   **Dinner:** $17-$26   **Phone:** 604/524-6122   **139**
◆◆◆
French   **Location:** Corner of Columbia at 4th St. 389 Columbia V3L 1A7. **Hours:** 11:30 am-2 & 5:30-10 pm, Sat from 5:30 pm. Closed: 1/1, Sun & 12/24-12/26. **Reservations:** required. **Features:** casual dress; cocktails; entertainment; a la carte. This restaurant features an elegant atmosphere, a cuisine that blends French and Swiss influences and in-house pastries. A lovely decor and attentive service complement the menu. There's metered street parking or across the street at Front St. Parkade. **Cards:** AE, MC, VI.   [X]

(See map p. 468)

VIET-THAI ORIENTAL   **Lunch:** $6-$8   **Dinner:** $10-$14   **Phone:** 604/525-5055   `134`
◆   **Location:** 3rd Ave and 6th St. 258 Sixth St V3L 3A4. **Hours:** 11:30 am-2:30 & 5-10 pm, Sat & Sun from 5
Ethnic   pm. Closed major holidays. **Features:** carryout; cocktails; a la carte. Bamboo and rattan create a casual and
Oriental dining atmosphere. Featured items on the menu are Tiger prawns, hot and sour soup, vegetarian
dishes and curry. Remember that Thai and Vietnamese food can be spicy. There is free parking at rear. **Cards:** AE, MC, VI.

NORTH VANCOUVER pop. 41,500   (See map p. 468; index p. 466)

——— LODGINGS ———

A GAZEBO IN THE GARDEN B & B   **Phone:** (604)983-3331   `95`
◆ ◆   All Year   1P: $95-$110   2P: $110-$150   XP: $25
Historic Bed   **Location:** Trans Canada Hwy 1, exit 18 (Lonsdale Ave), 1 km n, then just e. 310 St James Rd V7N 1L2.
& Breakfast   Fax: 604/980-3215. **Terms:** [CP] meal plan; age restrictions may apply; check-in 5 pm; 10 day cancellation notice; cancellation fee imposed. **Facility:** 4 rooms. Located in a wonderfully quiet residential neighborhood. Built
in 1910, this home is a fine example of Frank Lloyd Wright's prairie style architecture. The gardens are a sight to behold along
with a "gazebo" in the centre. 2 stories; interior corridors; designated smoking area. **Some Rooms:** combo or shower baths,
shared bathrooms, color TV. **Cards:** MC, VI.

BEST WESTERN CAPILANO INN & SUITES   **Phone:** (604)987-8185   `94`
(CAA) (SAVE)   6/1-9/30   1P: $109-$129   2P: $149
◆ ◆ ◆   5/1-5/31   1P: $90-$99   2P: $109
Motor Inn   10/1-2/28   1P: $70-$80   2P: $99
3/1-4/30   1P: $70-$80   2P: $90
Location: Trans Canada Hwy 1, exit 14 Capilano Rd, 1.5 km s; from n end of Lions Gate Bridge, 1 km e on
Marine Dr, then just n. 1634 Capilano Rd V7P 3B4. Fax: 604/987-5153. **Terms:** Weekly & monthly rates avail, off season.
Facility: 74 rooms. Modern property featuring a mix of accommodations from average sized guest rooms to large efficiency
units. Pleasant guest room decor. 1 two-bedroom unit. 1 kitchen unit $129-$195, for up to 6 persons; Whirlpool suite, $100-
$160; 2 stories; exterior corridors; heated pool, sauna. **Dining:** Coffee shop; 7 am-2:30 pm; $5-$11. **All Rooms:** extended
cable TV. **Cards:** AE, CB, DI, DS, MC, VI. **Special Amenities:** Free local telephone calls and free newspaper.
(See color ad p 473)

(See map p. 468)

CANYON COURT MOTEL

Phone: (604)988-3181   92

6/1-9/30	1P: $79-$109	2P: $79-$109 XP: $10 F12
3/1-5/31 & 10/1-2/28	1P: $59-$69	2P: $59-$69 XP: $10 F12

Location: Trans Canada Hwy 1 exit 14 Capilano Rd, 1.5 km s; from n end of Lions Gate Bridge 1 km e on Marine Dr, then just n. 1748 Capilano Rd V7P 3B4. Fax: 604/990-1554. **Terms:** Weekly & monthly rates avail, off season. **Facility:** 88 rooms. Wide range of accommodations, from average sized standard rooms to larger guest rooms with small kitchen to some units with 2 bedrooms. Modest style decor and furnishings. 15 two-bedroom units. 42 kitchens, $10 extra charge; 2 stories; exterior corridors; heated pool. **Dining:** Restaurant nearby. **All Rooms:** extended cable TV. **Cards:** AE, DI, DS, MC. **Special Amenities:** Free local telephone calls and free newspaper. (See color ad p 474)

GROUSE INN

Phone: (604)988-7101   98

6/1-10/10	1P: $118-$148	2P: $128-$148
5/1-5/31	1P: $79-$99	2P: $79-$109
10/11-2/28	1P: $79-$99	2P: $79-$99
3/1-4/30	1P: $69-$89	2P: $69-$99

Location: Trans Canada Hwy 1, exit 14 Capilano Rd, 1.5 km s; from n end of Lion's Gate Bridge 1 km e on Marine Dr. 1633 Capilano Rd V7P 3B3. Fax: 604/988-7102. **Terms:** Weekly & monthly rates avail, 11/1-4/30; cancellation fee imposed. **Facility:** 80 rooms. Very good economy style accommodations offering large, comfortable guest rooms. Mix of room types and styles from regular standard rooms to full kitchen units. 9 two-bedroom units. 3 whirlpool rooms, $109-$235; 2 stories; exterior corridors; heated pool. **Dining:** Coffee shop; 7 am-3 pm; $3-$8. **All Rooms:** extended cable TV. **Some Rooms:** 17 efficiencies, 6 kitchens. Fee: VCR. **Cards:** AE, CB, DI, DS, JC, MC, VI. **Special Amenities: Free local telephone calls and free newspaper.** (See color ad p 495)

HOLIDAY INN EXPRESS VANCOUVER NORTH SHORE

Phone: (604)987-4461   91

5/1-10/15	1P: $139	2P: $139 XP: $10 F
3/1-4/30 & 10/16-2/28	1P: $89	2P: $89 XP: $10 F

Location: Trans Canada Hwy 1, exit 14 Capilano Rd, then 1.5 km s; from n end of Lions Gate Bridge, 1 km e on Marine Dr, then just n. 1800 Capilano Rd V7P 3B6. Fax: 604/984-4244. **Terms:** [CP] meal plan. **Facility:** 73 rooms. Large guest rooms featuring an upscale style decor. At-door parking on ground level. Short drive to several North Shore attractions, Capilano Suspension Bridge and Grouse Mountain. 2 stories; exterior corridors; heated pool; playground. **Dining:** Restaurant nearby. **All Rooms:** extended cable TV. **Some Rooms:** 4 kitchens. **Cards:** AE, CB, DI, DS, JC, MC, VI. **Special Amenities: Free breakfast and free local telephone calls.** (See color ad p 495)

The following lodging was either not inspected or did not meet AAA rating requirements but is listed for your information only.

HOLIDAY INN NORTH VANCOUVER

Phone: 604/985-3111

[fyi]   Under construction, scheduled to open March 2000. **Location:** From Trans Canada Hwy 1, exit 22 (Mt Seymoor Pkwy) then just n. 700 Lillooet Rd V7I 2M5. Fax: 604/985-0857. **Planned Amenities:** 162 rooms, restaurant, radios, coffeemakers, pool, exercise facilities. (See color ad p 510)

Motor Inn

RESTAURANTS

KILBY'S RESTAURANT

Lunch: $9-$14   **Dinner:** $10-$21   Phone: 604/990-4334   105

Location: 1.8 km n on Capilano Rd, 1 km e on Ridgewood Dr, just s. 3108 Edgemont Blvd V7R 2N6.
Continental   **Hours:** 11:30 am-2:30 & 5-9:30 pm, Sun from 5 pm. Closed major holidays. **Reservations:** accepted. **Features:** cocktails; street parking; a la carte. Smoke free premises. **Cards:** AE, MC, VI.

MOUSTACHE CAFE NORTH

Lunch: $15-$18   **Dinner:** $25-$30   Phone: 604/987-8461   106

Location: Pemberton and Marine Dr. 1265 Marine Dr V7P 1T3. **Hours:** 11:30 am-2:30 & 5:30-10:30 pm, Sat
Italian   from 5:30 pm. Closed major holidays & Sun. **Reservations:** suggested. **Features:** casual dress; beer & wine only; a la carte. You'll like this restaurant's cozy setting in a 1918 home—it's comfortable and colorful. Regular menu items include spice-crusted beef carpaccio, mustard aioli, asiago and capers, homemade potato gnocci with tomato cream and fresh sage. Parking at rear. **Cards:** AE, MC, VI.

PITT MEADOWS pop. 13,600   (See map p. 468; index p. 466)

LODGING

RAMADA INN & SUITES HOTEL ROYALE

Phone: (604)460-9859   128

5/1-9/30	1P: $112	2P: $112 XP: $10 F16
3/1-4/30 & 10/1-2/28	1P: $89	2P: $89 XP: $10 F16

Motor Inn   **Location:** Lougheed Hwy (Hwy 7) and Harris Rd. 19267 Lougheed Hwy V3Y 2J5. Fax: 604/460-9857. **Terms:** Package plans. **Facility:** 80 rooms. Pitt Meadows newest property featuring very modern guest rooms and public areas. 3 stories; interior corridors; heated pool. **Some Rooms:** 5 efficiencies. **Cards:** AE, DI, DS, JC, MC, VI.

PORT COQUITLAM pop. 46,700 (See map p. 468; index p. 466)

──── LODGING ────

BEST WESTERN POCO INN & SUITES   **Phone:** (604)941-6216   **45**
5/1-9/30	1P: $99-$155	2P: $99-$169	XP: $10 F12
3/1-4/30 & 10/1-2/28	1P: $89-$125	2P: $89-$135	XP: $10 F12

Motor Inn   **Location:** 3.5 km e of Coquitlam on Lougheed Hwy (Hwy 7). 1545 Lougheed Hwy V3B 1A5. Fax: 604/941-6212. **Terms:** Small pets only, $10 extra charge. **Facility:** 99 rooms. Close to Coquitlam Shopping Centre. A very well maintained property featuring a wide range of accommodations. From at-door parking to 3 unique theme suites. 10 kitchens & 12 efficiencies, $10 extra charge; 4 whirlpool rooms, $250-$300; 2 stories; interior/exterior corridors; sauna, whirlpool. **Dining:** Restaurant; 6:30 am-10 pm; $7-$12; wine/beer only. **All Rooms:** extended cable TV. **Cards:** AE, DI, DS, MC, VI. *(See color ad below)*

(ASK) (S/D) 🛏 🍴 ▽ 🐾 ⌂ ❌ 🎥 📠 💻 📺 🔌 (DATA PORT) 📶

RICHMOND pop. 148,900 (See map p. 468; index p. 466)

──── LODGINGS ────

BEST WESTERN ABERCORN INN   **Phone:** (604)270-7576   **137**
7/1-9/30	1P: $129-$139	2P: $129-$139	XP: $15 F16
5/1-6/30	1P: $99-$109	2P: $99-$109	XP: $15 F16
3/1-4/30 & 10/1-2/28	1P: $89-$99	2P: $89-$99	XP: $15 F16

Motor Inn   **Location:** Hwy 99 N exit 39 (Bridgeport/Airport); Hwy 99 S exit 39A (Airport). 9260 Bridgeport Rd V6X 1S1. Fax: 604/270-0001. **Facility:** 97 rooms. Distinctively styled as Scottish country inn featuring spacious, carefully kept rooms. 16 whirlpool rooms, $159-$189; 3 stories; interior corridors. **Dining:** Restaurant; 6:30 am-10 pm; $10-$18; cocktails. **All Rooms:** extended cable TV, honor bars. **Cards:** AE, CB, DI, DS, JC, MC, VI. **Special Amenities:** Free newspaper and preferred room (subject to availability with advanced reservations).

(S/D) ✈ 🍴 ▽ 🐾 ⌂ ❌ 🎥 📠 💻 (DATA PORT) 📶

BEST WESTERN RICHMOND INN HOTEL & CONVENTION CENTER   **Phone:** (604)273-7878   **149**
7/1-9/30	1P: $139-$265	2P: $139-$265	XP: $15 F17
5/1-6/30	1P: $125-$265	2P: $125-$265	XP: $15 F17
10/1-2/28	1P: $99-$250	2P: $99-$250	XP: $15 F17
3/1-4/30	1P: $99-$240	2P: $99-$240	XP: $15 F17

Motor Inn   **Location:** Corner of Minoru Rd and Westminster Hwy. 7551 Westminster Hwy V6X 1A3. Fax: 604/278-0188. **Terms:** Cancellation fee imposed; package plans; small pets only, $10 extra charge. **Facility:** 390 rooms. A mature listing that's convention oriented. A featured highlight are the very spacious guest rooms; all with private balcony. Looking for something different, try a room overlooking the lush courtyard. 3 whirlpool rooms; 6-7 stories; interior corridors; heated pool, saunas, whirlpool. **Dining:** Restaurant; 6 am-midnight; $9-$20; cocktails. **Services:** gift shop. **Recreation:** Fee: bicycles. **All Rooms:** extended cable TV. **Cards:** AE, CB, DI, DS, MC, VI. **Special Amenities:** Early check-in/late check-out and preferred room (subject to availability with advanced reservations). *(See color ad p 491)*

(S/D) ✈ 🛏 🍴 24 ▽ 🐾 ⌂ ❌ 🎥 📠 💻 🔌 (DATA PORT) ⟲ 📶 ❌

COMFORT INN-AIRPORT   **Phone:** (604)278-5161   **141**
5/15-9/30	1P: $110-$130	2P: $110-$130
3/1-5/14 & 10/1-2/28	1P: $79-$89	2P: $79-$89

Motor Inn   **Location:** From Hwy 99 N exit 39 to Airport; from Hwy 99 S, Bridgeport Rd exit to Airport. 3031 #3 Rd & Sea Island Way V6X 2B6. Fax: 604/207-2380. **Terms:** Weekly rates avail; pets, $40 dep req. **Facility:** 129 rooms. Touch down into comfort with a choice of standard guest rooms or large suites with separate sitting area. Across the street from a full casino, walking trails along the mighty Fraser River or Richmond's largest mall. 3 stories; interior corridors; heated pool. **Dining:** Restaurant; 6 am-11 pm; $8-$12; cocktails. **Services:** area transportation. **All Rooms:** extended cable TV. **Cards:** AE, DI, DS, JC, MC, VI. *(See color ad p 513)*

(S/D) ✈ 🛏 🍴 🐾 ⌂ ❌ 🎥 📠 💻 (DATA PORT) ⟲

(See map p. 468)

DELTA PACIFIC RESORT AND CONFERENCE CENTRE   Phone: (604)278-9611   **143**
◆◆◆   5/1-9/30   1P: $155   2P: $155   XP: $30   F18
Hotel   3/1-4/30 & 10/1-2/28   1P: $139   2P: $139   XP: $20   F18
    Location: From Vancouver, southbound via Hwy 99 exit 39 Richmond; northbound via Hwy 99 exit 39 Bridge-port. 10251 St. Edwards Dr V6X 2M9. Fax: 604/276-1121. **Terms:** Package plans; pets, $25 dep req. **Facility:** 436 rooms. 3 different guest towers featuring large, guest rooms all with unique room decor and furnishings. Situated on beautifully land-scaped courtyard. Property geared for families with an excellent children's program. 2-21 stories; interior corridors; designated smoking area; 3 heated pools; 4 tennis courts (4 indoor, 4 lighted); playground. Fee: parking. **Services:** gift shop; area trans-portation. Fee: massage. **Recreation:** Fee: bicycles. **Some Rooms:** honor bars. **Cards:** AE, DI, DS, JC, MC, VI.
(See color ad p 514)

DELTA VANCOUVER AIRPORT   Phone: (604)278-1241   **136**
◆◆◆   5/1-9/30   1P: $155   2P: $155   XP: $20   F18
Hotel   3/1-4/30 & 10/1-2/28   1P: $139   2P: $139   XP: $20   F18
    Location: Corner of Russ Baker Way and Cessna Rd, near the Moray Bridge. 3500 Cessna Dr V7B 1C7. Fax: 604/276-1975. **Terms:** Small pets only, $25 extra charge. **Facility:** 415 rooms. On 9 acres of landscaped grounds over-looking the Fraser River and marina. An older hotel with average sized guest rooms but pleasant decor. All rooms with iron and ironing board. 10 stories; interior corridors; heated pool. Fee: parking; boat dock, marina. **Services:** gift shop; area trans-portation. Fee: massage. **Recreation:** Fee: charter fishing. **Some Rooms:** honor bars. **Cards:** AE, DI, DS, JC, MC, VI.
(See color ad p 514)

EXECUTIVE AIRPORT PLAZA & CONFERENCE CENTRE   Phone: (604)278-5555   **148**
(CAA) (SAVE)   5/1-10/15   1P: $119-$179   2P: $139-$199   XP: $10   F16
    3/1-4/30 & 10/16-2/28   1P: $89-$169   2P: $109-$189   XP: $10   F16
◆◆◆   **Location:** Corner of Gilbert Rd and Westminster Hwy. 7311 Westminster Hwy V6X 1A3. Fax: 604/278-0255.
Motor Inn   **Terms:** Weekly & monthly rates avail; cancellation fee imposed. **Facility:** 235 rooms. Large guest rooms with choice of standard type guest rooms to suites with a separate sitting area. Convention oriented. 30 efficiency units, $10 extra charge; 34 whirlpool rooms, $129-$159; 3 stories; interior corridors; heated pool, whirlpool. **Dining:** 2 restau-rants; 6:30 am-midnight; $10-$20; cocktails. **All Rooms:** extended cable TV, safes. **Cards:** AE, DI, MC, VI. **Special Amenities:** Free room upgrade (subject to availability with advanced reservations).** *(See color ad p 471)*

FOUR POINTS HOTEL VANCOUVER AIRPORT   Phone: (604)214-0888   **147**
◆◆◆   5/1-9/30   1P: $140-$180   2P: $140-$180   XP: $10   F18
Hotel   3/1-4/30 & 10/1-2/28   1P: $120-$150   2P: $120-$150   XP: $10   F18
    Location: From #3 Rd, just e on Alder Bridge Way, then just n on Hazelbridge Way. 8368 Alexandra Rd V6X 4A6. Fax: 604/214-0887. **Terms:** Cancellation fee imposed; package plans. **Facility:** 139 rooms. Superior accommodations and modern facilities are the features of this new property, with emphasis towards the business traveler. In the heart of Rich-mond's shopping and entertainment district with the Lansdowne Mall nearby. 6 stories; interior corridors; heated pool. **Cards:** AE, DI, DS, JC, MC, VI. *(See color ad p 402)*

HILTON VANCOUVER AIRPORT   Phone: (604)273-6336   **152**
◆◆◆   5/1-9/30   1P: $159-$169   2P: $159-$169   XP: $10   F18
Hotel   10/1-2/28   1P: $149-$159   2P: $149-$159   XP: $10   F18
    3/1-4/30   1P: $139-$149   2P: $139-$149   XP: $10   F18
Location: Corner of Minoru Rd & Westminster Hwy. 5911 Minoru Blvd V6X 4C7. Fax: 604/273-6337. **Terms:** Cancellation fee imposed; package plans. **Facility:** 237 rooms. New airport accommodations offering a beautiful spacious lobby, restaurant anbd lounge area. A large portion of the guest rooms are suites with separate sitting area, geared for business traveler with latest in internet access. 2 two-bedroom units. 15 stories; interior corridors; heated pool; 1 lighted tennis court. **Services:** gift shop. **Cards:** AE, DI, DS, JC, MC, VI. *(See color ad p 283 & opposite Introduction)*

(See map p. 468)

HOLIDAY INN EXPRESS VANCOUVER AIRPORT   **Phone:** 604/273-8080   [142]
◆◆◆   Property failed to provide current rates
Motel   **Location:** Hwy 99 N exit 39 (Bridgeport/Airport); Hwy 99 S exit 39A (Airport). 9351 Bridgeport Rd V6X 1S3.
         Fax: 604/214-8488. **Terms:** [CP] meal plan; check-in 4 pm. **Facility:** 107 rooms. Large, comfortable and very
modern guest rooms. Theme kid suites with bunk bed, separate TV with video games and room to romp. 8 stories; interior
corridors. **Some Rooms:** 30 efficiencies. **Cards:** AE, DI, JC, MC, VI.

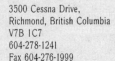

HOLIDAY INN VANCOUVER AIRPORT   **Phone:** (604)821-1818   [146]
◆◆◆   5/1-9/30   1P: $139   2P: $139   XP: $10   F18
Motor Inn 3/1-4/30 & 10/1-2/28   1P: $119   2P: $119   XP: $10   F18
         Location: Hwy 99 N exit 39 (Bridgeport/Airport) to St Edwards Dr; Hwy 99 S exit 39A (Richmond/airport), then
e. 10720 Cambie Rd V6X 1K8. Fax: 604/821-1819. **Terms:** Check-in 4 pm. **Facility:** 165 rooms. Large, comfortable guest
rooms with modern decor. For families, there are themed kids suites with bunk beds and plenty of room to romp. All rooms
with iron and ironing board. 6 stories; interior corridors. **Some Rooms:** 20 efficiencies. **Cards:** AE, DI, DS, JC, MC, VI.

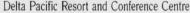

(See map p. 468)

RADISSON PRESIDENT HOTEL & SUITES

Phone: (604)276-8181 **139**

5/1-10/15	1P: $260-$290	2P: $260-$290	XP: $15	F17
3/1-4/30 & 10/16-2/28	1P: $215-$245	2P: $215-$245	XP: $15	F17

Location: Corner of #3 and Cambie rds. 8181 Cambie Rd V6X 3X9. Fax: 604/276-8136. **Terms:** Cancellation fee imposed; small pets only. **Facility:** 184 rooms. Well appointed guest rooms feature a mix of 1-bedroom suites with sitting room or standard guest rooms. Guest oriented staff. 12 stories; interior corridors; heated pool, whirlpool. **Dining:** Restaurant; 6:30 am-10 pm; $14-$22; cocktails. **Services:** gift shop. **All Rooms:** extended cable TV. Fee: safes. **Cards:** AE, DI, DS, JC, MC, VI. (See ad p 489)

RAMADA INN VANCOUVER AIRPORT

Phone: (604)207-9000 **150**

5/1-9/30	1P: $132-$152	2P: $132-$152	XP: $10	F17
1/1-2/28	1P: $99-$119	2P: $99-$119	XP: $10	F17
3/1-4/30 & 10/1-12/31	1P: $95-$115	2P: $95-$115	XP: $10	F17

Location: Corner of Alderbridge Way and Westminster Hwy. 7188 Westminster Hwy V6X 1A1. Fax: 604/207-9466. **Terms:** Small pets only. **Facility:** 77 rooms. New listing featuring a variety of guest room sizes from standard type to larger business type with added amenities. 4 whirlpool rooms; 4 stories; interior corridors; designated smoking area. **Dining:** Restaurant nearby. **All Rooms:** extended cable TV. **Cards:** AE, DI, DS, JC, MC, VI. **Special Amenities:** Free breakfast and free local telephone calls.

STAY'N SAVE INNS

Phone: (604)273-3311 **145**

7/1-9/30	1P: $114-$124	2P: $124-$134	XP: $10	F16
5/1-6/30	1P: $94-$104	2P: $104-$114	XP: $10	F16
3/1-4/30 & 10/1-2/28	1P: $84-$94	2P: $94-$104	XP: $10	F16

Location: Hwy 99 N, exit 39 (Bridgeport/Airport) to St Edwards Dr; Hwy 99 S, exit 39A (Richmond/Airport). 10551 St Edwards Dr V6X 3L8. Fax: 604/273-9522. **Terms:** Weekly rates avail. off season; cancellation fee imposed; small pets only, limited rooms. **Facility:** 206 rooms. A wonderfully kept airport property offering very comfortable guest rooms. For larger rooms inquire about units with separate bedrooms. Efficiency units, $10 extra charge; suites, $104-$154; 3 stories; exterior corridors; whirlpool. **Dining:** Restaurant; 6:30 am-10 pm; $5-$9; wine/beer only. **All Rooms:** extended cable TV. **Cards:** AE, DI, MC, VI. **Special Amenities:** Free local telephone calls and free newspaper. (See color ad p 431 & p 540)

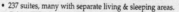

(See map p. 468)

TRAVELODGE HOTEL VANCOUVER AIRPORT   Phone: (604)278-5155   **140**

CAA SAVE	7/1-9/30	1P: $129-$139	2P: $129-$139	XP: $10	F17
	5/1-6/30	1P: $119-$129	2P: $119-$129	XP: $10	F17
◆◆	3/1-4/30 & 10/1-2/28	1P: $99-$119	2P: $99-$119	XP: $10	F17

Motor Inn   **Location:** Hwy 99 N, exit 39 (Bridgeport/Airport) to St Edwards Dr; Hwy 99 S, exit 39A, (Richmond/Airport). 3071 St Edwards Dr V6X 3K4. Fax: 604/278-5125. **Facility:** 160 rooms. Average sized guest rooms offering good, comfortable accommodations. 10 stories; interior corridors; heated pool, whirlpool. **Dining:** Restaurant; 7 am-10 pm; $8-$18; cocktails. **All Rooms:** extended cable TV. **Cards:** AE, DI, DS, JC, MC, VI. **Special Amenities:** Free breakfast and free local telephone calls.

VANCOUVER AIRPORT MARRIOTT   Phone: (604)276-2112   **151**

◆◆◆	5/1-9/30	1P: $149-$165	2P: $149-$165	XP: $10	F18
Hotel	3/1-4/30 & 10/1-2/28	1P: $129-$145	2P: $129-$145	XP: $10	F18

Location: Corner of Minoru Rd and Westminster Hwy. 7571 Westminster Hwy V6X 1A3. Fax: 604/276-0112. **Terms:** Check-in 4 pm; cancellation fee imposed; package plans; small pets only. **Facility:** 237 rooms. A new listing catering to the corporate traveller. Very comfortable rooms; all with large, spacious work desk. Many with a separate sleeping area. Many modern conveniences. 2 two-bedroom units. 18 stories; interior corridors; heated pool. Fee: parking. **Cards:** AE, DI, DS, JC, MC, VI. *(See color ad p 515)*

The following lodging was either not inspected or did not
meet AAA rating requirements but is listed for your information only.

THE FAIRMONT VANCOUVER AIRPORT   Phone: 604/207-5200

fyi	All Year	1P: $149-$269	2P: $149-$269	XP: $20	F18

Hotel   Too new to rate, opening scheduled for October 1999. **Location:** In Vancouver International Airport. 3111 Grant McCamanhie Way V7B 1X9 (PO Box 23798). **Terms:** Cancellation fee imposed. **Amenities:** 392 rooms, pets, restaurant, radios, coffeemakers, pool, exercise facilities. **Cards:** AE, DI, DS, JC, MC, VI.

(See color ad p 515)

—— RESTAURANTS ——

PAPI'S RISTORANTE ITALIANO   Lunch: $8-$15   Dinner: $15-$24   Phone: 604/275-8355   **120**

◆◆◆   **Location:** Jct Moncton St and No 1 Rd, in Steveston Village. 12251 No 1 Rd V7E 1T6. **Hours:** 11:30 Northern   am-2:30 & 5-11 pm, Sat & Sun from 5 pm. Closed: 12/25. **Reservations:** suggested. **Features:** No A/C; Italian   casual dress; early bird specials; cocktails; street parking; a la carte. The menu at Papi's is changed monthly in order to emphasize seasonal specialties. This restaurant provides an ongoing variety of new and delicious creations in a traditional cuisine. The service is prompt, friendly and attentive. **Cards:** AE, DI, MC, VI.

THE PIER   Lunch: $7-$13   Dinner: $16-$29   Phone: 604/276-1962   **122**

◆◆◆   **Location:** Corner of Russ Baker Way and Cessna Rd, near the Moray Bridge; in Delta Vancouver Airport. Continental   3500 Cessna Dr V7B 1C7. **Hours:** 11:30 am-2:30 & 6-11 pm, Sat 6 pm-midnight, Sun 10 am-2:30 & 6-10 pm. Closed: lunch 10/1-6/1. **Reservations:** suggested. **Features:** Sunday brunch; children's menu; health conscious menu; cocktails; fee for parking; a la carte. The Pier features delicious sterling silver beef—the highest grade of Canadian beef—and top-quality seafood in its meals. Couples on a romantic evening out will enjoy the quiet setting with its very nice view of the water. Validated parking. **Cards:** AE, DI, DS, JC, MC, VI.

STEVESTON SEAFOOD HOUSE   Dinner: $13-$22   Phone: 604/271-5252   **121**

CAA   **Location:** Jct Moncton St and No 1 Rd, in Steveston Village. 3951 Moncton St V7E 3A2. **Hours:** 5:30-10 pm, Fri & Sat-10:30 pm. Closed: 12/24-12/26. **Reservations:** suggested. **Features:** casual dress; cocktails; ◆◆◆   street parking; a la carte. You'll enjoy your fine-dining experience at this restaurant located in the historic Seafood   village of Steveston. The menu offers ocean-fresh seafood based on availability. The prawns and scallops are delicious, and the warm and friendly decor is quite pleasant. **Cards:** AE, DI, MC, VI.

SUEHIRO JAPANESE STEAKHOUSE   Lunch: $8-$16   Dinner: $25-$45   Phone: 604/278-9611   **123**

◆◆   **Location:** From Vancouver, southbound via Hwy 99 exit 39 Richmond; northbound via Hwy 99 exit 39 Japanese   Bridgeport; in Delta Pacific Resort and Conference Centre. 10251 St. Edwards Dr V6X 2M9. **Hours:** 11:30 am-2:30 & 5:30-9 pm. Closed major holidays. **Reservations:** suggested. **Features:** cocktails & lounge; fee for parking; a la carte. When you dine here, you may choose to sit at a teppan table close to the grill to watch the chef prepare your meal of seafood, beef or chicken. This restaurant looks like an authentic samurai home surrounded by beautiful gardens. Pay parking lot. **Cards:** AE, DI, DS, JC, MC, VI.

The following restaurant has not been inspected by AAA
but is listed for your information only.

FLOATA SEAFOOD RESTAURANT   Phone: 604/270-8889

fyi   Not inspected. **Location:** 4380 No. 3 Rd. **Features:** This is an immense, 1,000 seat restaurant, where the menu is Cantonese seafood.

SURREY pop. 304,500 (See map p. 468; index p. 467)

——— LODGINGS ———

DAYS HOTEL-SURREY CENTRE

CAA (SAVE) ◆◆◆ Motor Inn

			Phone: (604)588-9511	176
8/1-9/30	1P: $110	2P: $116	XP: $6	F18
5/1-7/31	1P: $96	2P: $102	XP: $6	F18
10/1-2/28	1P: $90	2P: $96	XP: $6	F18
3/1-4/30	1P: $88	2P: $94	XP: $6	F18

Location: Jct Fraser Hwy (1A) and Hwy 99A (King George Hwy). 9850 King George Hwy V3T 4Y3. Fax: 604/588-7949. **Terms:** Small pets only, $5 extra charge, in smoking rooms. **Facility:** 85 rooms. Older property with wood trim highlights in the public areas. Guest rooms are well coordinated and large. Close to skytrain station and Surrey Place Mall. 6 stories; interior corridors; heated pool, sauna, whirlpool. **Dining:** Dining room, coffee shop; 6 am-10 pm, Sun-9 pm; $9-$16; cocktails. **All Rooms:** extended cable TV. **Cards:** AE, DI, DS, JC, MC, VI. **Special Amenities:** Early check-in/late check-out and free local telephone calls. *(See color ad p 493)*

MOTEL HOLLYWOOD

CAA (SAVE) ◆ Motel

			Phone: (604)591-1900	177
All Year	1P: $55	2P: $69	XP: $5	

Location: 1.5 km s on King George Hwy (99A) from Fraser Hwy (1A). 9155 King George Hwy V3V 5W1. Fax: 604/591-1577. **Terms:** 3 day cancellation notice; cancellation fee imposed. **Facility:** 23 rooms. Located close to Skytrain and shopping, this property offers comfortable average sized guest rooms with a simple style decor. Perfect for those on a budget. Whirlpool room, $65; 2 stories; interior corridors. **All Rooms:** extended cable TV. **Some Rooms:** 5 efficiencies. **Cards:** AE, DS, MC, VI. **Special Amenities:** Free local telephone calls and preferred room (subject to availability with advanced reservations).

RAMADA LIMITED SURREY-LANGLEY

CAA (SAVE) ◆◆◆ Motor Inn

			Phone: (604)576-8388	179
6/16-9/15	1P: $113	2P: $113	XP: $10	F17
4/1-6/15 & 9/16-2/28	1P: $93	2P: $93	XP: $10	F17
3/1-3/31	1P: $88	2P: $88	XP: $10	F17

Location: Trans Canada Hwy 1 exit 58, 5 km s on 200th St, then 2 km w on Hwy 10, corner of 192nd St and Hwy 10. 19225 Hwy 10 V3S 8V9. Fax: 604/576.8332. **Terms:** [CP] meal plan; weekly rates avail, off season; small pets only, $10 extra charge. **Facility:** 85 rooms. A modern property featuring large, comfortable guest rooms with a pleasant upscale decor. 3 stories; interior corridors; heated pool, whirlpool. **Dining:** Restaurant; 6 am-11 pm; $7-$15; wine/beer only. **All Rooms:** extended cable TV. **Cards:** AE, DI, DS, MC, VI. **Special Amenities:** Free breakfast and free local telephone calls.

SHERATON GUILDFORD HOTEL SURREY

CAA ◆◆◆ Hotel

			Phone: (604)582-9288	175
6/1-9/30	1P: $119-$179	2P: $119-$179	XP: $20	F18
3/1-5/31 & 10/1-2/28	1P: $89-$119	2P: $89-$119	XP: $20	F18

Location: Trans Canada Hwy 1 E, exit 48, 1 km s on 152 St, then just e; Trans Canada Hwy 1 W, exit 50, then just w. 15269 104th Ave V3R 1N5. Fax: 604/582-9712. **Terms:** Monthly rates avail; check-in 4 pm; cancellation fee imposed; package plans; small pets only, $50 extra charge. **Facility:** 278 rooms. Situated in the greater Vancouver area with easy access to the frwy, transit and the large Guilford shopping mall. Business friendly, but families most welcome. Exceptionally large guest rooms with views of mts and city. 6 whirlpool rooms; 20 stories; interior corridors; heated pool, whirlpool. Fee: parking. **Dining:** Restaurant; 6:30 am-10 pm; $16-$31; cocktails. **Services:** gift shop. **All Rooms:** extended cable TV. **Some Rooms:** Fee: VCR. **Cards:** AE, DI, JC, MC, VI. *(See color ad p 402 & ad below)*

——— RESTAURANT ———

YOKOHAMA JAPANESE RESTAURANT

◆◆ Japanese

Lunch: $7-$10   **Dinner:** $10-$21   **Phone:** 604/584-4555   142

Location: Just e off King George Hwy at 104 Ave, on Whalley Ring Rd. 10356 137th St V3T 4H4. **Hours:** 11:30 am-2:30 & 5-10 pm, Fri & Sat-11 pm, Sun 5-10 pm. **Reservations:** suggested; weekends. **Features:** cocktails; a la carte. You'll appreciate the decor and food at this restaurant, which offers tatami rooms and a full sushi bar. The combination dinner includes beef teriyaki, tempura, noodles, rice and dessert. The service is pleasant, and the atmosphere is happy and cozy. **Cards:** AE, MC, VI.

WEST VANCOUVER pop. 40,900   (See map p. 468; index p. 466)

——— LODGING ———

BEACHSIDE BED & BREAKFAST

				Phone: (604)922-7773	[83]
	5/1-10/31	1P: $150-$250	2P: $150-$250	XP: $30	D12
	3/1-4/30 & 11/1-2/28	1P: $120-$200	2P: $120-$200	XP: $30	D12

Bed & Breakfast

Location: From Trans Canada Hwy 1, exit 10 21 St, 6 km w on Marine Dr to Ferndale Ave, then just s. 4208 Evergreen Ave V7V 1H1. Fax: 604/926-8073. **Terms:** [BP] meal plan; age restrictions may apply; check-in 5 pm; 14 day cancellation notice; cancellation fee imposed; 2 night min stay. **Facility:** 4 rooms. Located on a quiet cul de sac with the home right along a beachfront. Variety of guest room sizes and style, with the guest common room overlooking the sea. 2 whirlpool rooms, $200-$250; 1 story; interior/exterior corridors; smoke free premises; whirlpool. **Dining:** Restaurant nearby. **Cards:** MC, VI.

——— RESTAURANTS ———

SALMON HOUSE ON THE HILL   **Lunch:** $8-$13   **Dinner:** $14-$22   **Phone:** 604/926-3212 [99]

◆◆
Seafood

Location: Trans Canada Hwy 1, exit 10, follow signs. 2229 Folkestone Way V7S 2Y6. **Hours:** 11:30 am-2:30 & 5-10 pm, Fri & Sat 5 pm-11 pm. Closed: 12/24 & 12/25. **Reservations:** suggested; evenings. **Features:** Sunday brunch; senior's menu; cocktails & lounge; a la carte. You'll certainly appreciate the incredible panoramic view of the city and harbor from the Salmon House's hilltop location. The restaurant's cuisine specializes in Pacific Rim influences, with fresh British Columbia salmon as the house specialty. **Cards:** AE, DI, MC, VI.

——— *The following restaurants have not been inspected by AAA* ———
but are listed for your information only.

AMBLESIDE BISTRO   Phone: 604/922-1117

[fyi]   Not inspected. **Location:** Marine Dr and 15th St. 235 W 15th St V7T 2X1. **Features:** The charming bar, fireplace and accessible prices are what this restaurant has going for it. Try the off-menu seafood appetizers or their long list of evening specials.

BEACH HOUSE ON DUNDARAVE PIER   Phone: 604/922-1414

[fyi]   Not inspected. **Location:** 150 25th St. **Features:** The menu at this dramatic West Vancouver waterfront setting leans towards seafood, Italian and local favorites. The wine list is exceptional.

WHITE ROCK pop. 17,200   (See map p. 468; index p. 467)

——— LODGINGS ———

BEST WESTERN PACIFIC INN RESORT & CONFERENCE CTR   Phone: (604)535-1432   [184]

CAA (SAVE)   5/1-9/30   1P: $109-$119   2P: $119-$129   XP: $10   F12
◆◆◆   3/1-4/30 & 10/1-2/28   1P: $99-$109   2P: $109-$119   XP: $10   F12
Motor Inn   **Location:** 1 km n on Hwy 99 from Canada/US border, exit 2 White Rock/8th Ave, then just n. 1160 King George Hwy V4A 4Z2. Fax: 604/531-6979. **Terms:** Weekly rates avail; 30 day cancellation notice; package plans. **Facility:** 150 rooms. A unique property featuring a Central American theme accented with folk art from Mexico. Huge atrium with a tropical style setting. Spacious guest rooms, attractively decorated. Short drive to the beaches of White Rock. 5 whirlpool rooms, $199-$219; 4 stories; interior corridors; heated pool, sauna, whirlpool. **Dining:** Dining room, restaurant; 6:30 am-10 pm; $9-$20; cocktails; nightclub. **Services:** area transportation, golf & beaches. **All Rooms:** extended cable TV. **Cards:** AE, CB, DI, DS, MC, VI. **Special Amenities:** Early check-in/late check-out and free room upgrade (subject to availability with advanced reservations). *(See color ad below)*

SEACREST MOTEL & RV PARK   Phone: (604)531-4720   [185]
CAA   All Year   1P: $60-$80   2P: $60-$80   XP: $10   F13
◆◆   **Location:** Hwy 99 exit 2 (White Rock), 1 km w on 8th Ave, follow signs. 864 160th St V4A 4W4.
Motel   Fax: 604/531-4735. **Terms:** Weekly & monthly rates avail, off season. **Facility:** 12 rooms. Cozy motel featuring comfortable guest rooms within easy walking distance to the White Rock pier, restaurants and shopping district. Nicely landscaped grounds. 1 story; exterior corridors. **All Rooms:** combo or shower baths, extended cable TV. **Some Rooms:** 8 efficiencies. **Cards:** MC, VI.

——— RESTAURANTS ———

LA BAIA ITALIAN RESTAURANT   Dinner: $10-$20   Phone: 604/531-6261   [145]
◆◆   **Location:** Hwy 99, exit 2 White Rock/8th Ave, 1.5 km w. 15791 Marine Dr V4B 1E5. **Hours:** 5 pm-10 pm, Fri
Italian   & Sat-11 pm. Closed: 1/1, 12/25 & 12/26. **Reservations:** suggested. **Features:** cocktails; a la carte. The varied cuisine at this restaurant offers delicious rack of lamb and veal marsala. The bright and airy decor displays antiques and a nice view of the park. The atmosphere is cozy and the service is friendly and attentive. Visitors like this place. **Cards:** AE, MC, VI.

——— The following restaurant has not been inspected by AAA ———
but is listed for your information only.

GIRAFFE   Phone: 604/538-6878
[fyi]   Not inspected. **Location:** 15053 Marine Dr. **Features:** This waterfront charmer boasts some innovative cooking, from sourdough-crusted halibut, roasted tomato coulis to rack of lamb served with apricot-mint chutney. The view is marvelous.

The previous listings were for the Vancouver Vicinity.
This page resumes the alphabetical listings
of cities in British Columbia.

VERNON pop. 31,800

—— LODGINGS ——

BEST WESTERN VERNON LODGE & CONFERENCE CENTRE   Phone: (250)545-3385

(CAA) (SAVE)   6/1-9/30   1P: $99-$119   2P: $109-$129   XP: $10   F13
♦♦♦   3/1-5/31 & 10/1-2/28 1P: $79-$99   2P: $89-$109   XP: $10   F13
Motor Inn   **Location:** 1.5 km n on Hwy 97. 3914 32nd St V1T 5P1. Fax: 250/545-7156. **Terms:** Cancellation fee imposed;
package plans; pets, $10 extra charge, no cats. **Facility:** 127 rooms. Attractive guest rooms all meticulously
kept. A natural flowing creek winds directly through the lush tropical courtyard. All rooms with hair dryer and
video games. 6 whirlpool rooms, $160-$180; 3 stories, no elevator; interior corridors; heated pool, whirlpool. **Dining:** Restaurant; 6:30 am-11 pm; $11-$20; cocktails. **Services:** gift shop. **Recreation:** hair salon. **All Rooms:** extended cable TV.
Cards: AE, DI, DS, JC, MC, VI.

BEST WESTERN VILLAGER MOTOR INN   Phone: (250)549-2224

(CAA)   5/16-9/15   1P: $73-$81   2P: $79-$109   XP: $6   F12
♦♦   3/1-5/15 & 9/16-12/31 1P: $63-$71   2P: $89-$89   XP: $6   F12
Motel   1/1-2/28   1P: $69   2P: $75   XP: $6   F12
              Location: 2.5 km n; across Village Green Mall. 5121 26th St V1T 8G4. Fax: 250/549-2224. **Terms:** [CP] meal
plan; cancellation fee imposed; package plans; small pets only, with permission. **Facility:** 53 rooms. All units
are spacious, well maintained and offer a pleasant decor. Attractive courtyard and pool area. 10 efficiencies, $8 extra charge;
2 stories; interior/exterior corridors; heated pool, whirlpool. **Dining:** Restaurant nearby. **Services:** winter plug-ins.
All Rooms: extended cable TV. **Some Rooms:** Fee: VCR. **Cards:** AE, DI, DS, MC, VI. *(See color ad below)*

COMFORT INN   Phone: (250)542-4434

(CAA) (SAVE)   6/1-10/31   1P: $84-$89   2P: $94-$99   XP: $5   F16
♦♦   3/1-5/31 & 11/1-2/28   1P: $74-$89   2P: $84-$89   XP: $5   F16
Motel   **Location:** 1 km n on Hwy 97 (32nd St) at corner of 43rd Ave. 4204 32nd St N V1T 5P4. Fax: 250/542-3479.
Terms: Weekly rates avail, off season; cancellation fee imposed; pets, with permission. **Facility:** 62 rooms.
Many units with balcony. 3 stories; interior corridors; heated pool, whirlpool. **Dining:** Restaurant nearby.
All Rooms: extended cable TV. **Some Rooms:** 14 efficiencies. **Cards:** AE, CB, DI, MC, VI. **Special Amenities:** Free local
telephone calls and free room upgrade (subject to availability with advanced reservations).

LAKESIDE ILLAHEE INN   Phone: (250)260-7896

(CAA)   6/1-9/15   1P: $119-$159   2P: $129-$169   XP: $25   F3
♦♦♦   3/1-5/31 & 9/16-11/1   1P: $109-$139   2P: $119-$149   XP: $25   F3
Bed &   11/2-2/28   1P: $89-$129   2P: $99-$139   XP: $25   F3
Breakfast   **Location:** From Hwy 97, s of Vernon, 2 km sw on College Way, then 2 km to Jade and Juniper Bay sign, 3 km
s on Kidston Rd; then turn right. 15010 Tamarack Dr V1B 2E1. Fax: 250/260-7826. **Terms:** [BP] meal plan;
weekly rates avail; 7 day cancellation notice; cancellation fee imposed. **Facility:** 4 rooms. Contemporary, exquisite inn located on beautiful Kalamalka Lake offering a sandy beach with excellent swimming. All guest rooms with access
to large semi-private balcony with lake view. 1 two-bedroom unit $159-$226 for up to 4 persons; 3 stories; interior/exterior corridors; smoke free premises; lake view; beach, whirlpool. **Services:** Fee: massage. **Recreation:** swimming; hiking trails.
Fee: canoeing, power boat; pre-arranged tour includes kayaking, horseback trail rides, wine tour, jetboat wild river ride.
All Rooms: combo or shower baths. **Some Rooms:** kitchen. **Cards:** AE, MC, VI.

THE MARIA ROSE BED & BREAKFAST

◆◆

Bed & Breakfast

All Year

Phone: (250)549-4773

| 1P: $45-$65 | 2P: $65-$80 | XP: $20 |

Location: 9.5 km e on Silver Star Rd, follow the Silver Star Resort signs. 8083 Aspen Rd V1B 3M9. **Fax:** 250/549-4789. **Terms:** [BP] meal plan; check-in 4 pm; 10 day cancellation notice; cancellation fee imposed; small pets only, $10 extra charge, with permission. **Facility:** 4 rooms. Between the city of Vernon and Silver Star Mountain Resort. Charming rooms each individually decorated in a royal theme. Common room with fireplace located in main house. Very pleasant hosts. 2 stories; exterior corridors; smoke free premises. **Services:** winter plug-ins. **Some Rooms:** combo or shower baths, shared bathrooms, color TV. **Cards:** MC, VI.

SCHELL MOTEL

Ⓐ
◆
Motel

5/1-9/30
3/1-4/30 & 10/1-2/28

Phone: 250/545-1351

| 1P: $50-$65 | 2P: $56-$77 | XP: $6 | F10 |
| 1P: $38-$65 | 2P: $42-$77 | XP: $6 | F10 |

Location: Centre; corner 35th St and 30th Ave. 2810 35th St V1T 6B5. **Fax:** 250/545-2287. **Terms:** Weekly & monthly rates avail, off season; 4 day cancellation notice; cancellation fee imposed; package plans; pets, $5 extra charge. **Facility:** 32 rooms. Good, comfortable accommodations featuring average sized guest rooms in standard units. Mixed style furnishings and decor in the kitchen units. Suite with kitchen. 16 one-& two-bedroom efficiencies, $8 extra charge; 2 stories; exterior corridors; heated pool, sauna, whirlpool. **All Rooms:** extended cable TV. **Cards:** AE, MC, VI.

THE TUCK INN BED & BREAKFAST

◆◆◆

Bed & Breakfast

All Year

Phone: (250)545-3252

| 1P: $45-$55 | 2P: $65-$75 | XP: $20 | F10 |

Location: On 30 Ave (turning into Pleasant Valley Rd), at 24 St. 3101 Pleasant Valley Rd V1T 4L2. **Fax:** 250/549-3254. **Terms:** [BP] meal plan; 7 day cancellation notice, 14 day in summer; cancellation fee imposed; package plans. **Facility:** 4 rooms. Charmingly restored property decorated with Victorian style. Units vary in size and appointments. Intimate seating areas on main floor, carefully landscaped yard. Phone for guest use on upstairs landing. 2 stories; interior corridors; smoke free premises. **Cards:** AE, MC, VI.

VERNON TRAVELODGE

◆◆

Motel

5/15-9/15
3/1-5/14 & 9/16-2/28

Phone: (250)545-2161

| 1P: $59-$69 | 2P: $64-$84 | XP: $5 | F18 |
| 1P: $49-$59 | 2P: $53-$68 | XP: $5 | F18 |

Location: Hwy 97 (32nd St), just e on 28th Ave, near Polson Park. 3000 28th Ave V1T 1W1. **Fax:** 250/545-5536. **Terms:** Package plans; small pets only, $5 extra charge. **Facility:** 39 rooms. Comfortable simple motel in the heart of downtown. 2 stories; exterior corridors; heated pool. **All Rooms:** combo or shower baths. **Some Rooms:** 2 efficiencies. **Cards:** AE, DI, MC, VI.

WILDWOOD BED & BREAKFAST

◆◆

Bed & Breakfast

5/1-10/31 & 12/16-2/28
3/1-4/30 & 11/1-12/15

Phone: (250)545-2747

| 1P: $75-$95 | 2P: $95-$125 | XP: $60 |
| 1P: $65-$85 | 2P: $85-$105 | XP: $45 |

Location: 2 km n on Hwy 97, 8 km ne on 48th Ave which becomes Silver Star Rd, just nw. 7454 Wildwood Rd V1B 3N8. **Fax:** 250/545-0518. **Terms:** [BP] meal plan; age restrictions may apply; 7 day cancellation notice; cancellation fee imposed; package plans. **Facility:** 3 rooms. Suburban home close to Silver Star provincial recreation area. Units are simple but attractively furnished, 1 has a private access to the patio. Beautiful view of surrounding hills. All rooms with hair dryer. 1 story; interior corridors; smoke free premises. **Services:** winter plug-ins. **Fee:** area transportation. **Recreation:** Fee: bicycles. **Cards:** VI.

--------- **RESTAURANTS** ---------

AMARIN THAI RESTAURANT

◆◆

Thai

Lunch: $8-$14   **Dinner:** $9-$14   **Phone:** 250/542-9300

Location: Centre; just s of 30th Ave. 2903 31st St V1T 5H6. **Hours:** 11:30 am-2:30 & 5-10 pm, Sat & Sun from 5 pm. **Reservations:** suggested. **Features:** health conscious menu items; carryout; cocktails; a la carte. The menu is extensive at Amarin's. It offers many salads, some with meat, and includes beef, seafood, chicken and pork dishes. The stylish decor is warm and appealing and includes Thai artifacts and artwork. Fine service. Parking is limited. Smoke free premises. **Cards:** AE, MC, VI.

AVONLEA RESTAURANT

◆◆◆

Continental

Lunch: $7-$12   **Dinner:** $11-$30   **Phone:** 250/558-3900

Location: 1.5 km n on Hwy 97 (32nd St), across from Vernon Square Mall; in Prestige Inn Vernon. 4411 32nd St V1T 9G8. **Hours:** 7 am-10 pm. **Reservations:** suggested. **Features:** casual dress; Sunday brunch; children's menu; early bird specials; health conscious menu items; carryout; cocktails & lounge; entertainment; a la carte. The Avonlea Restaurant features local favorites and several versions of well-known Continental specialties. The grilled halibut is good. The relaxed and comfortable ambience presents a pianist for entertainment on weekends. Friendly service. **Cards:** AE, DI, MC, VI.

INTERMEZZO RESTAURANT

◆◆

Italian

Dinner: $10-$17   **Phone:** 250/542-3853

Location: Hwy 97 (32nd St), just w. 3206 34th Ave V1T 6M1. **Hours:** 5 pm-10 pm, Sun-9 pm. Closed: 12/24 & 12/25. **Features:** carryout; cocktails & lounge; street parking; a la carte. You'll enjoy the wide variety of pasta, chicken, seafood, barbecue ribs and the specialty veal, prepared in six classic ways, at the Intermezzo, which is located downtown behind a small shopping complex. Meals are delicious and attractively presented. **Cards:** AE, MC, VI.

--------- *The following restaurant has not been inspected by AAA* ---------
but is listed for your information only.

MACGREGORS COURTYARD RESTAURANT

[fyi]

Phone: 250/549-4199

Not inspected. **Location:** Just s on Hwy 97, just w on 25th Ave; in Tiki Village Motor Inn. 2408 34th St V1T 5W8. **Features:** Patio dining and daily Continental specials. Featuring local fare and wines.

Destination Victoria

*T*he Trans-Canada Highway ends in Victoria, but your journey isn't complete until you've seen the city and its surroundings.

*W*ander down cobblestone streets lined with Victorian lampposts. Tour one glorious English garden after another. Do the town in a double-decker bus. Or cruise to neighboring islands.

A piece of the skyline.
Overlooking the Inner Harbour are the Parliament Buildings, perhaps the most impressive elements of the Victoria skyline—especially at night.
(See listing page 169)

Whale watching.
Don't miss one of the area's most exciting natural attractions; you'll find several excursion boats in Victoria.
(See mention page 170)

BRITISH COLUMBIA
WASHINGTON

Ferry boats.
Victoria's passenger and automobile ferries serve as "commuter buses" to and from the island city.
(See mention page 163)

✈ *Sidney*

Saanichton

Malahat

Victoria ⑰

See Vicinity map page 525

Sooke

CANADA
UNITED STATES

Tallyho!
Horse-drawn carriages make for romantic sightseeing in Victoria.
(See mention page 162)

*P*laces included in this AAA Destination City:

Victoria *pop. 73,500*

This index helps you "spot" where approved accommodations are located on the detailed maps that follow. Rate ranges are for comparison only and show the property's high season. Turn to the listing page for more detailed rate information and consult display ads for special promotions. Restaurant rate range is for dinner, unless only lunch (L) is served.

Spotter/Map Page Number	OA	VICTORIA - Lodgings	Diamond Rating	Rate Range High Season	Listing Page
1 / p. 525	ⒶⒶ	Quality Resort at Mount Douglas Park - see color ad p 538	◆◆◆	$119-$299 SAVE	537
2 / p. 525	ⒶⒶ	Days Inn Victoria Waterway - see color ad p 532	◆◆◆	$125-$156 SAVE	531
3 / p. 525	ⒶⒶ	Mayfair Motel	◆	$55-$79 SAVE	536
4 / p. 525	ⒶⒶ	Blue Ridge Inns	◆◆	$84-$94 SAVE	528
5 / p. 525	ⒶⒶ	Ingraham Hotel	◆◆	$69-$79 SAVE	535
6 / p. 525	ⒶⒶ	Tally Ho Motor Inn	◆	$89-$99 SAVE	541
7 / p. 525	ⒶⒶ	Holiday Inn Victoria	◆◆	$155 SAVE	534
8 / p. 525	ⒶⒶ	Chateau Victoria	◆◆◆	$147-$260 SAVE	530
9 / p. 525		Sunnymeade House Inn	◆◆	$79-$169	541
10 / p. 525	ⒶⒶ	Best Western Inner Harbour - see color ad p 529	◆◆◆	$155-$385 SAVE	528
11 / p. 525	ⒶⒶ	Robin Hood Motel - see color ad p 538	◆◆	$57-$81 SAVE	538
12 / p. 525		Prior House B&B Inn	◆◆◆	$145-$275	537
13 / p. 525	ⒶⒶ	Cheltenham Court Motel	◆	$80-$99 SAVE	530
14 / p. 525		City Garden Hotel	◆◆	Failed to provide	530
15 / p. 525	ⒶⒶ	Oxford Castle Inn - see color ad p 537	◆◆	$88-$138 SAVE	537
16 / p. 525		Comfort Inn Waterside	◆◆	$89-$185	530
17 / p. 525		King's House Bed & Breakfast	◆◆	$110-$150	535
18 / p. 525		Humboldt House Bed & Breakfast	◆◆	$275-$315	535
19 / p. 525	ⒶⒶ	Stay'n Save Inn - see color ad p 431, p 540	◆◆◆	$114-$134 SAVE	540
20 / p. 525		Swans Hotel - see color ad p 540	◆◆◆	$169-$249	541
21 / p. 525		Bedford Regency Hotel	◆◆	$165-$250	527
22 / p. 525	ⒶⒶ	Traveller's Inn-Central - see color ad p 542	◆	$80-$120	542
23 / p. 525		Villa Blanca Bed & Breakfast	◆◆	$85-$150	544
24 / p. 525	ⒶⒶ	The Victoria Regent Hotel - see color ad p 543	◆◆◆	$179-$359 SAVE	544
25 / p. 525		The Empress	◆◆◆◆	$89-$314	533
26 / p. 525	ⒶⒶ	Traveller's Inn-Downtown - see color ad p 542	◆	$70-$90	542
27 / p. 525	ⒶⒶ	Days Inn on the Harbour - see color ad p 532	◆◆◆	$163-$203 SAVE	531
28 / p. 525	ⒶⒶ	Admiral Motel - see color ad p 526	◆◆◆	$169-$195 SAVE	526
29 / p. 525	ⒶⒶ	Ramada Huntingdon Manor	◆◆◆	$153-$233 SAVE	538
30 / p. 525	ⒶⒶ	Harbour Towers Hotel	◆◆◆	$139-$239 SAVE	533
31 / p. 525	ⒶⒶ	Royal Scot Suite Hotel - see color ad p 539	◆◆◆	$145-$325 SAVE	539
32 / p. 525		Holland House Inn	◆◆◆	Failed to provide	534
33 / p. 525	ⒶⒶ	Embassy Inn	◆◆◆	$119-$179	533
34 / p. 525	ⒶⒶ	Helm's Inn - see color ad p 534	◆◆	$110-$145 SAVE	534
35 / p. 525	ⒶⒶ	Shamrock Motel	◆	$89-$119 SAVE	540
36 / p. 525	ⒶⒶ	Crystal Court Motel	◆	$60-$95	530
37 / p. 525	ⒶⒶ	Executive House Hotel - see color ad p 524	◆◆	$145-$175 SAVE	533
38 / p. 525		The Beaconsfield Inn	◆◆◆	$200-$395	527
39 / p. 525		Abigail's Hotel - see color ad p 526	◆◆◆	$119-$329	526
40 / p. 525	ⒶⒶ	Green Gables Inn - see color ad p 529	◆◆◆	$119-$169 SAVE	533
41 / p. 525	ⒶⒶ	Traveller's Inn-In Town - see color ad p 542	◆	$70-$90 SAVE	543
42 / p. 525		Oak Bay Beach Hotel - see color ad p 536	◆◆◆	$189-$199	536
43 / p. 525	ⒶⒶ	Ocean Pointe Resort Hotel & Spa	◆◆◆	$159-$409 SAVE	537
46 / p. 525	ⒶⒶ	Best Western Carlton Plaza Hotel - see color ad p 528	◆◆◆	$149-$189 SAVE	528
48 / p. 525		Dashwood Seaside Manor - see color ad p 531	◆◆	$185-$385 SAVE	530
49 / p. 525	ⒶⒶ	Queen Victoria Inn	◆◆◆	$85-$325 SAVE	538
50 / p. 525		A Haterleigh Heritage Inn	◆◆◆	$225-$323	527
52 / p. 525	ⒶⒶ	Howard Johnson Canterbury Inn - see color ad p 535	◆◆	$99-$140 SAVE	535

Spotter/Map Page Number	OA	VICTORIA - Lodgings (continued)	Diamond Rating	Rate Range High Season	Listing Page
53 / p. 525	⊕	Casa Linda Motel	◆	$55-$75 SAVE	530
55 / p. 525	⊕	Travelodge Victoria - see color ad p 543	◆ ◆ ◆	$110-$180 SAVE	544
59 / p. 525		Andersen House Bed & Breakfast	◆ ◆ ◆	$175-$250	527
61 / p. 525		Heathergate House Bed & Breakfast	◆ ◆	$100-$160	533
62 / p. 525		Oak Bay Guest House - see color ad p 536	◆ ◆	$125-$160	537
63 / p. 525		Ryan's Bed & Breakfast	◆ ◆ ◆	$135-$185	540
64 / p. 525	⊕	Union Club of British Columbia	◆ ◆ ◆	$169-$249 SAVE	544
65 / p. 525		An Ocean View Bed & Breakfast	◆	$105-$165	527
66 / p. 525	⊕	The Magnolia Hotel & Suites	◆ ◆ ◆ ◆	$239-$399 SAVE	536
67 / p. 525		Iris Garden Country Manor Bed & Breakfast	◆ ◆	$105-$160	535
68 / p. 525	⊕	Dutchman Inn - see color ad p 531	◆	$75-$105 SAVE	531
		VICTORIA - Restaurants			
1 / p. 525		Hunan Village	◆ ◆	$8-$15	545
2 / p. 525		Barkley's Steak & Seafood	◆ ◆	$15-$25	544
4 / p. 525	⊕	The Blethering Place Tea Room & Restaurant - see color ad p 544	◆ ◆	$8-$15	545
5 / p. 525		Spinnakers Brew Pub & Restaurant - see ad p 546	◆ ◆	$6-$16	546
6 / p. 525	⊕	Taj Mahal	◆ ◆	$12-$22	547
7 / p. 525		Periklis Restaurant	◆ ◆	$10-$18	546
9 / p. 525		Millos Restaurant	◆ ◆ ◆	$9-$18	546
10 / p. 525		Shakespeare Dining Room	◆ ◆	$12-$25	546
11 / p. 525		Herald Street Cafe	◆ ◆ ◆	$12-$23	545
13 / p. 525		The Empress Room	◆ ◆ ◆ ◆	$30-$40	545
14 / p. 525	⊕	Victoria Harbour House Restaurant	◆ ◆ ◆	$12-$25	547
15 / p. 525	⊕	James Bay Tea Room & Restaurant	◆	$12-$15	545
16 / p. 525		Topo's Ristorante	◆ ◆	$8-$23	547
17 / p. 525		The Marina Restaurant	◆ ◆ ◆	$14-$26	545
22 / p. 525		Cecconi's Trattoria	◆ ◆	$8-$14	545
25 / p. 525		The George & Dragon	◆	$6-$13	545
27 / p. 525		Haultain's Fish & Chips	◆	$6-$10	545
28 / p. 525		Il Terrazzo	◆ ◆	$13-$25	545
31 / p. 525		Pagliacci's	◆ ◆	$16-$20	546
32 / p. 525		Pescatore's Fish House & Piano Bar	◆ ◆	$18-$25	546
34 / p. 525		Pluto's	◆	$7-$11	546
36 / p. 525		Six Mile Pub	◆	$4-$11	546

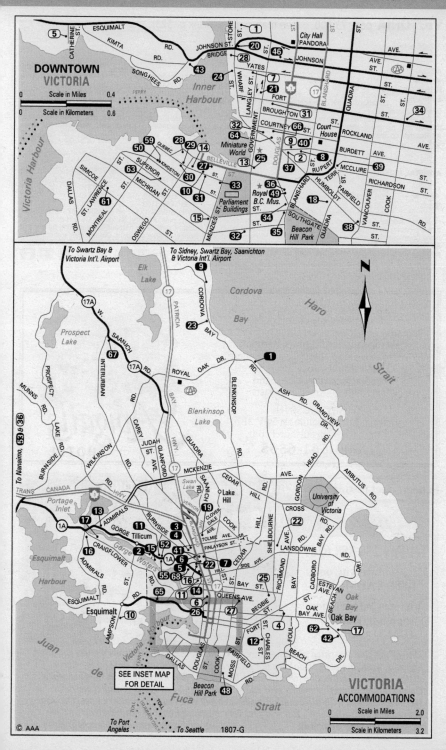

DOWNTOWN VICTORIA

City Hall
PANDORA

Inner Harbour

Scale in Miles   0   0.4
Scale in Kilometers   0   0.6

Victoria Harbour

FERRY

Miniature World

Parliament Buildings

Royal B.C. Mus.

Beacon Hill Park

To Swartz Bay & Victoria Int'l. Airport

To Sidney, Swartz Bay, Saanichton & Victoria Int'l. Airport

Elk Lake

Cordova Bay

Haro

Prospect Lake

Blenkinsop Lake

Strait

To Nanaimo,

Royal

Swan Lake

Portage Inlet

Lake Hill

University of Victoria

Esquimalt

Tillicum

Gorge Waters

Craigflower

Esquimalt Harbour

Admirals

Esquimalt

Oak Bay

Juan de Fuca Strait

To Port Angeles   To Seattle   1807-G

SEE INSET MAP FOR DETAIL

Beacon Hill Park

VICTORIA ACCOMMODATIONS

Scale in Miles   0   2.0
Scale in Kilometers   0   3.2

© AAA

VICTORIA pop. 73,500 (See map p. 525; index p. 523)

———— LODGINGS ————

ABIGAIL'S HOTEL
◆◆◆
Historic Bed
& Breakfast

Phone: (250)388-5363 39

5/1-10/15	1P: $119-$329	2P: $199-$329	XP: $30	D18
3/1-4/30 & 10/16-1/1	1P: $159-$263	2P: $159-$263	XP: $30	D18
1/2-2/28	1P: $119-$197	2P: $119-$197	XP: $30	D18

Location: Just w of Vancouver St. 906 McClure St V8V 3E7. Fax: 250/388-7787. **Terms:** [BP] meal plan; age restrictions may apply; 7 day cancellation notice; package plans. **Facility:** 24 rooms. Distinctive tudor-style residence circa 1930s; elegantly appointed rooms with an old-fashioned appeal. Some rooms with wood-burning fireplace. Some rooms with bathtub and handheld shower. 4 stories, no elevator; interior corridors; designated smoking area. **Services:** gift shop. **All Rooms:** combo or shower baths. **Cards:** AE, MC, VI. *(See color ad below)*

ADMIRAL MOTEL
CAA SAVE
◆◆◆
Motel

Phone: (250)388-6267 28

7/1-9/30	1P: $169-$185	2P: $179-$195	XP: $10	F11
3/1-6/30	1P: $89-$129	2P: $89-$139	XP: $10	F11
10/1-12/22	1P: $79-$109	2P: $89-$119	XP: $10	F11
12/23-2/28	1P: $79-$99	2P: $89-$109	XP: $10	F11

Location: Corner of Belleville and Quebec sts. 257 Belleville St V8V 1X1. Fax: 250/388-6267. **Terms:** [CP] meal plan; weekly & monthly rates avail, off season; cancellation fee imposed; pets. **Facility:** 32 rooms. Cozy rooms that feature a pleasing guest room decor. All rooms with balcony or patio and pleasant view of the harbour. Easy walking distance to many downtown attractions and restaurants. Near US Ferry Terminal. 3 stories; exterior corridors. **Dining:** Restaurant nearby. **All Rooms:** extended cable TV. **Some Rooms:** 27 efficiencies. **Cards:** AE, DS, MC, VI. **Special Amenities: Free breakfast and free local telephone calls.** *(See color ad below)*

(See map p. 525)

A HATERLEIGH HERITAGE INN
Phone: (250)384-9995   [50]

◆◆◆

Historic Bed & Breakfast

6/1-10/31	1P: $225-$323	2P: $225-$323
4/1-5/31 & 11/1-2/28	1P: $195-$263	2P: $195-$263
3/1-3/31	1P: $155-$232	2P: $155-$232

Location: Corner of Pendray and Kingston sts, just s of US Ferry Terminal. 243 Kingston St V8V 1V5. Fax: 250/384-1935. **Terms:** [BP] meal plan; age restrictions may apply; check-in 4 pm; 14 day cancellation notice; cancellation fee imposed. **Facility:** 6 rooms. A 1901 Victorian home designated a Heritage home, lovingly restored with a mix of modern and antique style decor. Within easy walking distance to downtown, Parliament buildings and inner harbour. 1 two-bedroom unit. 2 stories; interior corridors; designated smoking area. **Cards:** MC, VI.

ANDERSEN HOUSE BED & BREAKFAST
Phone: 250-388-4565   [59]

◆◆◆

Historic Bed & Breakfast

6/1-9/30	1P: $175-$250	2P: $175-$250	XP: $45
5/1-5/31	1P: $135-$195	2P: $145-$215	XP: $45
10/1-2/28	1P: $105-$185	2P: $145-$185	XP: $45
3/1-4/30	1P: $95-$165	2P: $145-$185	XP: $45

Location: Pendray and Kingston sts. 301 Kingston St V8V 1V5. Fax: 250/388-4563. **Terms:** [BP] meal plan; age restrictions may apply; 10 day cancellation notice; cancellation fee imposed. **Facility:** 4 rooms. Charming 1891 home successfully blending rich historic detail with comfortable, contemporary furnishings and art. Most rooms are quite spacious; each has its own designated balcony and private entrance. Close to US ferry terminal. 1 two-bedroom unit. 3 stories, no elevator; interior/exterior corridors; designated smoking area; street parking only. **All Rooms:** combo or shower baths. **Cards:** MC, VI.

AN OCEAN VIEW BED & BREAKFAST
Phone: 250/386-7330   [65]

◆

Bed & Breakfast

5/1-10/1	1P: $105-$145	2P: $115-$165	XP: $30

Location: From Douglas St, 1.5 km w on Pandora St which becomes Esquimalt Rd, just n on Dalton St to Suffolk St. 715 Suffolk St V9A 3J5. Fax: 250/389-0280. **Terms:** Open 5/1-10/1; [BP] meal plan; age restrictions may apply; check-in 4 pm; 7 day cancellation notice; cancellation fee imposed. **Facility:** 6 rooms. This residential home is situated on the west side of downtown and in a quiet neighborhood. Guest rooms are a bit on the average size, but quite cozy with a bright, whimsical decor. Enjoy sweeping views of the Strait of Juan deFuca and Mts. 2 stories; interior corridors. **All Rooms:** combo or shower baths. **Cards:** MC, VI.

THE BEACONSFIELD INN
Phone: (250)384-4044   [38]

◆◆◆

Historic Bed & Breakfast

6/15-9/15	1P: $200-$395	2P: $200-$395	XP: $65
9/16-10/15	1P: $150-$295	2P: $150-$295	XP: $65
3/1-6/14	1P: $125-$295	2P: $125-$295	XP: $65
10/16-2/28	1P: $125-$225	2P: $125-$225	XP: $65

Location: At Vancouver St. 998 Humboldt St V8V 2Z8. Fax: 250/384-4052. **Terms:** [BP] meal plan; age restrictions may apply; 7 day cancellation notice; cancellation fee imposed; 2 night min stay, some weekends. **Facility:** 9 rooms. 1905 mansion luxuriously restored. Rooms reflect authentic Edwardian atmosphere, with leaded glass windows, mahogany wood floors and fine antiques. Gourmet breakfast; attentive, professional staff. 4 stories, no elevator; interior corridors; designated smoking area. **All Rooms:** combo or shower baths. **Cards:** MC, VI.

BEDFORD REGENCY HOTEL
Phone: (250)384-6835   [21]

◆◆

Hotel

5/1-10/18	1P: $165-$250	2P: $165-$250	XP: $20	F16
3/1-4/30 & 10/19-2/28	1P: $110-$150	2P: $110-$150	XP: $20	F16

Location: Between Fort and Yates sts. 1140 Government St V8W 1Y2. Fax: 250/386-8930. **Terms:** [CP] meal plan. **Facility:** 40 rooms. Located in the heart of the shopping district. Rooms vary in size, with many unique historic architectural details reflecting the 1800s construction. Some rooms with wood burning fireplace. 5 stories; interior corridors; off site parking only. **All Rooms:** combo or shower baths. **Cards:** AE, DI, MC, VI.

(See map p. 525)

BEST WESTERN CARLTON PLAZA HOTEL Phone: (250)388-5513 **46**

5/1-9/30	1P: $149-$189	2P: $149-$189	XP: $20 F18
3/1-4/30 & 10/1-2/28	1P: $79-$109	2P: $79-$109	XP: $20 F18

Location: Between Douglas and Broad sts. 642 Johnson St V8W 1M6. Fax: 250/388-5343. **Terms:** Weekly & monthly rates avail. off season; 14 day cancellation notice; package plans. **Facility:** 103 rooms. In the heart of downtown. Behind this 1912 exterior are thoroughly modern guest rooms offering spacious kitchen units to comfortable standard size guest rooms. 7 two-bedroom units. 7 stories; interior corridors. Fee: parking. **Dining:** Restaurant; 7 am-10 pm; $8-$15; cocktails. **Services:** gift shop. **All Rooms:** extended cable TV. **Some Rooms:** 5 efficiencies, 42 kitchens. **Cards:** AE, DI, DS, JC, MC, VI. **Special Amenities:** Free local telephone calls and free newspaper. *(See color ad below)*

Hotel

BEST WESTERN INNER HARBOUR Phone: (250)384-5122 **10**

6/1-9/30	1P: $155-$385	2P: $155-$385	XP: $15 F12
3/1-5/31 & 10/1-2/28	1P: $105-$275	2P: $105-$275	XP: $15 F12

Location: Corner of Oswego and Quebec sts, just s of the US Ferry Terminal. 412 Quebec St V8V 1W5. Fax: 250/384-5122. **Terms:** [CP] meal plan; weekly & monthly rates avail, off season. **Facility:** 74 rooms. Spacious guest rooms, all nicely decorated with private balcony. Close to Parliament buildings and downtown area. Limited view of harbour due to tall trees. 1 two-bedroom unit. 8 stories; interior corridors; heated pool, sauna, whirlpool. **Dining:** Restaurant nearby. **All Rooms:** extended cable TV. **Some Rooms:** 72 kitchens, utensils extra charge. Fee: VCR. **Cards:** AE, DI, DS, MC, VI. **Special Amenities:** Free breakfast and free room upgrade **(subject to availability with advanced reservations).** *(See color ad p 529)*

Motel

BLUE RIDGE INNS Phone: (250)388-4345 **4**

7/1-9/30	1P: $84	2P: $94	XP: $10 F16
5/1-6/30	1P: $69	2P: $79	XP: $10 F16
3/1-4/30 & 10/1-2/28	1P: $59	2P: $69	XP: $10 F16

Location: 3.5 km n. 3110 Douglas St V8Z 3K4. Fax: 250/388-7613. **Terms:** Weekly rates avail; cancellation fee imposed; small pets only. **Facility:** 61 rooms. Excellent budget style accommodations featuring a range of guest rooms from 12 junior rooms with shower only to larger efficiency units with separate bedroom. All rooms with fan. 2 stories; exterior corridors; heated pool, sauna. **Dining:** Coffee shop; 6:30 am-3:30 pm; $5-$9. **All Rooms:** combo or shower baths, extended cable TV. **Some Rooms:** 11 efficiencies. **Cards:** AE, DI, MC, VI. **Special Amenities:** Free local telephone calls.

Motel

(See map p. 525)

CASA LINDA MOTEL
Phone: (250)474-2141　53

CAA SAVE ◆ Motel

	7/1-9/5	1P: $55	2P: $60-$75	XP: $6	F12
	5/1-6/30	1P: $47	2P: $56-$66	XP: $6	F12
	3/1-4/30 & 9/6-2/28	1P: $44	2P: $49-$55	XP: $6	F12

Location: 12 km n on Hwy 1, exit Colwood, 2.8 km s to jct 14 and 1A (Goldstream Ave); just w of intersection. 364 Goldstream Ave V9B 2W3. Fax: 250/474-6470. **Terms:** Weekly & monthly rates avail, off season; cancellation fee imposed. **Facility:** 27 rooms. Opposite the Royal Colwood Golf Course. Pleasant grounds and exterior. Guest rooms feature a modest decor but well maintained. 3 two-bedroom units. 2 stories; exterior corridors. **All Rooms:** extended cable TV. **Some Rooms:** 10 kitchens. **Cards:** AE, MC, VI. **Special Amenities:** Early check-in/late check-out and free local telephone calls.

CHATEAU VICTORIA
Phone: (250)382-4221　8

CAA SAVE ◆◆◆ Hotel

	7/1-10/14	1P: $147-$230	2P: $177-$260	XP: $15	F18
	5/1-6/30	1P: $127-$210	2P: $157-$250	XP: $15	F18
	3/1-4/30 & 10/15-2/28	1P: $99-$180	2P: $126-$180	XP: $15	F18

Location: Downtown; Douglas St at Burdett. 740 Burdett Ave V8W 1B2. Fax: 250/380-1950. **Terms:** Weekly & monthly rates avail, off season; package plans. **Facility:** 178 rooms. Many large guest rooms featuring separate sitting area, balcony or regular standard rooms on lower floors. Rooftop restaurant with spectacular views. Close to downtown and inner harbour area. 7 two-bedroom units. 2 whirlpool rooms; 19 stories; interior corridors; designated smoking area; heated pool, whirlpool. **Dining:** Restaurant; 6:30 am-10:30 pm; $12-$19; cocktails. **Services:** area transportation, downtown. **All Rooms:** extended cable TV. **Some Rooms:** 36 kitchens. Fee: VCR. **Cards:** AE, DI, DS, JC, MC, VI.

CHELTENHAM COURT MOTEL
Phone: (250)385-9559　13

CAA SAVE ◆ Motel

| | 3/1-9/15 | 1P: $80-$95 | 2P: $90-$99 |
| | 9/16-2/28 | 1P: $45-$55 | 2P: $55-$60 |

Location: From Douglas St, 4.5 km w. 994 Gorge Rd W V9A 1P2. Fax: 250/383-2394. **Terms:** Weekly & monthly rates avail, off season; 4 day cancellation notice. **Facility:** 19 rooms. Across the street from Gorge Waterway Park with a lovely walkway along waterfront. Property offers a variety of room styles and sizes from large duplex units to single motel style units. 12 one-& two-bedroom housekeeping units, $125-225 for 4-8 persons; 1 story; exterior corridors. **All Rooms:** extended cable TV. **Cards:** AE, MC, VI. **Special Amenities:** Free local telephone calls.

CITY GARDEN HOTEL
Phone: (250)388-0788　14

◆◆ Motor Inn

Property failed to provide current rates

Location: 2 km n on Douglas St, corner of Gorge Rd and Hillside St. 2852 Douglas St V8T 4M5. Fax: 250/388-0787. **Facility:** 100 rooms. Just outside of the downtown area but close to all area attractions. Guest rooms are nicely decorated with various sizes from standard size to large family units with cooking facilities. 4 stories; interior corridors; heated pool. **Some Rooms:** 58 efficiencies. **Cards:** AE, MC, VI.

COMFORT INN WATERSIDE
Phone: (250)388-7861　16

◆◆ Motor Inn

	7/1-9/30	1P: $89-$175	2P: $99-$185	XP: $10	F18
	5/1-6/30	1P: $69-$135	2P: $79-$145	XP: $10	F18
	10/1-2/28	1P: $59-$125	2P: $69-$135	XP: $10	F18
	3/1-4/30	1P: $59-$89	2P: $69-$99	XP: $10	F18

Location: From Douglas St, 5 km w on Gorge Rd, then just s on Admirals Rd. 101 Island Hwy V9B 1E8. Fax: 250/388-7862. **Facility:** 96 rooms. Along the Gorge Waterway. Large guest rooms with a pleasant, modern decor. Many connecting rooms. 2 stories; interior/exterior corridors; heated pool. **Some Rooms:** 30 efficiencies, 16 kitchens. **Cards:** AE, DI, DS, MC, VI.

CRYSTAL COURT MOTEL
Phone: 250/384-0551　36

CAA ◆ Motel

	10/1-2/28	1P: $60-$62	2P: $83-$95	XP: $5
	6/1-9/30	1P: $75-$77	2P: $78-$90	XP: $5
	3/1-5/31	1P: $55-$57	2P: $58-$70	XP: $5

Location: At Douglas St, adjacent the Royal BC Museum. 701 Belleville St V8W 1A2. Fax: 250/384-5125. **Terms:** Weekly rates avail, off season. **Facility:** 57 rooms. Well-kept older property for the budget traveller. Mix of room sizes and styles, from compact studios to larger suites with full kitchen. 29 kitchens, $2 extra charge; 2 stories; exterior corridors. **Dining:** Restaurant nearby. **All Rooms:** extended cable TV. **Cards:** DS, MC, VI.

DASHWOOD SEASIDE MANOR
Phone: (250)385-5517　48

CAA SAVE ◆◆ Historic Complex

	6/1-9/30	1P: $185-$375	2P: $195-$385	XP: $45	F
	10/1-10/31	1P: $125-$215	2P: $135-$225	XP: $35	F
	3/1-5/31	1P: $75-$215	2P: $85-$225	XP: $25	F
	11/1-2/28	1P: $75-$165	2P: $85-$175	XP: $25	F

Location: 1 km e of Douglas St on Dallas Rd. 1 Cook St V8V 3W6. Fax: 250/383-1760. **Terms:** [BP] meal plan; weekly & monthly rates avail, off season; 14 day cancellation notice; cancellation fee imposed; small pets only, $25 extra charge, 1 floor. **Facility:** 14 rooms. Built in 1912, this tudor style manor sits on the corner of a residential neighborhood and offers a fine view of the ocean and distant mountains. All units have fully stocked fridge for self cater breakfast. 3 whirlpool rooms; 3 stories, no elevator; interior corridors; designated smoking area. **All Rooms:** efficiencies. **Cards:** AE, DI, MC, VI. **Special Amenities:** Free breakfast and preferred room (subject to availability with advanced reservations).
(See color ad p 531)

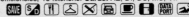

(See map p. 525)

DAYS INN ON THE HARBOUR
Phone: (250)386-3451 ㉗

7/1-9/30	1P: $163-$203	2P: $163-$203	XP: $10	F12
5/1-6/30	1P: $135-$165	2P: $135-$165	XP: $10	F12
3/1-4/30 & 10/1-2/28	1P: $79-$135	2P: $79-$135	XP: $10	F12

CAA SAVE ◆◆◆ Motor Inn **Location:** Entrance on Oswego at Quebec St. 427 Belleville St V8V 1X3. Fax: 250/386-6999. **Terms:** Weekly & monthly rates avail, off season; cancellation fee imposed. **Facility:** 71 rooms. Nicely decorated, average sized guest rooms. Compact corner rooms. Located in heart of the harbour, close to Parliment Buildings, shops and across from US Ferry Terminal. 20 efficiencies, $10 extra charge; 4 stories; interior corridors; heated pool, whirlpool. **Dining:** Restaurant; 7 am-10 pm; $7-$16; cocktails. **All Rooms:** combo or shower baths, extended cable TV. Fee: safes. **Some Rooms:** Fee: VCR. **Cards:** AE, DI, DS, JC, MC, VI. **Special Amenities:** Early check-in/late check-out and free room upgrade (subject to availability with advanced reservations). *(See color ad p 532)*

DAYS INN VICTORIA WATERWAY
Phone: (250)386-1422 ❷

5/1-10/1	1P: $125-$156	2P: $125-$156	XP: $10
3/1-4/30 & 10/2-2/28	1P: $95-$115	2P: $95-$115	XP: $10

CAA SAVE ◆◆◆ Motor Inn **Location:** From Douglas St, 1.4 km w. 123 Gorge Rd E V9A 1L1. Fax: 250/386-1254. **Terms:** Weekly & monthly rates avail, off season. **Facility:** 94 rooms. Renovated property offering a wide range of nicely decorated guest rooms, from larger rooms with a separate bedroom to a few full size kitchen units and many standard sized guest rooms. An English style pub located on site. 4 stories; interior corridors; heated pool. **Dining:** Restaurant; 7 am-1 & 5-10 pm; $7-$11; cocktails. **All Rooms:** extended cable TV. **Some Rooms:** 3 efficiencies, 9 kitchens. **Cards:** AE, DI, DS, MC, VI. **Special Amenities:** Free local telephone calls. *(See color ad p 532)*

DUTCHMAN INN
Phone: (250)386-7557 ㊸

6/1-9/30	1P: $75-$85	2P: $95-$105	
3/1-5/31	1P: $55-$65	2P: $68-$75	XP: $10	F12
10/1-2/28	1P: $45-$55	2P: $60-$70	

CAA SAVE ◆ Motel **Location:** From Douglas St, just w, Gorge Rd & Rock Bay Ave. 2828 Rock Bay Ave V8T 4S1. Fax: 250/383-8337. **Terms:** Weekly & monthly rates avail, off season; small pets only, $5 extra charge. **Facility:** 39 rooms. Outside the downtown area, but just a short drive away. Budget oriented listing offering comfortable standard sized guest rooms to larger kitchen units with sitting area. Ask for north facing second floor rooms for better view. 2 stories; exterior corridors; whirlpool. **Dining:** Restaurant nearby. **All Rooms:** extended cable TV. **Some Rooms:** 14 kitchens. **Cards:** AE, MC, VI. *(See color ad below)*

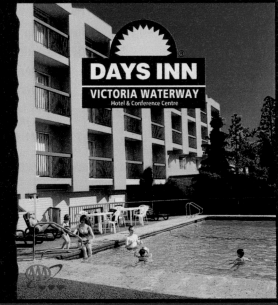

(See map p. 525)

EMBASSY INN   **Phone:** (250)382-8161   🔟
(CAA)   7/1-10/15   1P: $119-$179   2P: $139-$179   XP: $15   F14
                   5/1-6/30   1P: $89-$145   2P: $99-$145   XP: $15   F14
◆◆◆   3/1-4/30 & 10/16-2/28   1P: $65-$89   2P: $69-$99   XP: $15   F14
Motor Inn   **Location:** Adjacent to Parliament buildings, at Quebec St. 520 Menzies St V8V 2H4. Fax: 250/382-4224.
                   Terms: Weekly & monthly rates avail, off season; cancellation fee imposed. **Facility:** 103 rooms. Well main-
tained property featuring 2 distinct sections. The more contemporary tower section offers large guest rooms with private balcony. The harbour section features older guest rooms and decor very clean and neat. 3-4 stories; interior/exterior corridors;
heated pool, sauna. **Dining:** Restaurant; 7 am-9:30 pm; $8-$14; cocktails. **All Rooms:** extended cable TV. **Some Rooms:** 15
efficiencies, 36 kitchens. **Cards:** AE, DI, MC, VI.

THE EMPRESS   **Phone:** (250)384-8111   🔟
◆◆◆◆   All Year   1P: $89-$314   2P: $89-$314   XP: $30   F18
Classic Hotel   **Location:** Government at Wharf St, just n of the Parliament buildings. 721 Government St V8W 1W5.
                   Fax: 250/385-1323. **Terms:** Check-in 4 pm; package plans; small pets only, $50 fee, in smoking rooms.
Facility: 460 rooms. **Historic.** Landmark property reigning over the Inner Harbour. Outstanding example of Victorian-era ar-
chitecture originally designed in 1908. Rooms vary in size and style but all carefully decorated to compliment the property. 7
stories; interior corridors; heated pool. Fee: parking. **Dining:** entertainment. **Services:** gift shop. Fee: massage. **Cards:** AE,
DI, DS, JC, MC, VI. A Canadian Pacific Hotel.

EXECUTIVE HOUSE HOTEL   **Phone:** (250)388-5111   🔟
(CAA) (SAVE)   6/15-9/30   1P: $145-$175   2P: $145-$175   XP: $15   F16
                   5/1-6/14   1P: $99-$175   2P: $99-$175   XP: $15   F16
◆◆   3/1-4/30 & 10/1-2/28   1P: $79-$175   2P: $79-$175   XP: $15   F16
Hotel   **Location:** At Burdett St. 777 Douglas St V8W 2B5. Fax: 250/385-1323. **Terms:** Weekly & monthly rates avail,
                   off season; package plans; small pets only, $15 extra charge. **Facility:** 179 rooms. An older style high-rise fea-
turing a range of guest room styles and types from average sized standard guest rooms on floors 1 and 2 to larger 1 bedroom
suites. Close to the heart of downtown Victoria. 3 two-bedroom units. 81 kitchens & 21 efficiencies, $15 extra charge. 2 large
executive style suites with fireplace & whirlpool, $395-$695; 17 stories; interior corridors; sauna, steamroom, whirlpool.
Fee: parking. **Dining:** Dining room, restaurant; 7 am-11 pm; $6-$14; cocktails; also, Barkley's Steak & Seafood, see separate
listing. **Services:** area transportation, Inner Harbour/downtown. Fee: massage. **All Rooms:** extended cable TV. **Cards:** AE,
DI, DS, JC, MC, VI. **Special Amenities: Free newspaper and free room upgrade (subject to availability with advanced
reservations).** (See color ad p 524)

GREEN GABLES INN   **Phone:** (250)385-6787   🔟
(CAA) (SAVE)   6/16-9/30   1P: $119-$159   2P: $129-$169   XP: $10   F12
                   3/1-6/15 & 10/1-2/28   1P: $89-$99   2P: $89-$109   XP: $10   F12
◆◆◆   **Location:** At Courtney and Blanshard sts. 850 Blanshard St V8W 2H2. Fax: 250/385-5800. **Terms:** Weekly &
Motor Inn   monthly rates avail, off season. **Facility:** 56 rooms. In the heart of downtown, offering very comfortable and
                   large guest rooms with a cheerful, modern guest room decor. English style pub on premises, 11 am-1 am. Ef-
ficiency units, $10 extra charge; 2 whirlpool rooms, $109-$169; 3 stories; interior corridors. **Dining:** Restaurant; 7 am-9 pm;
$8-$15; cocktails. **All Rooms:** utensils extra charge, extended cable TV. **Cards:** AE, DI, MC, VI. **Special Amenities: Free
local telephone calls and free room upgrade (subject to availability with advanced reservations).** (See color ad p 529)

HARBOUR TOWERS HOTEL   **Phone:** (250)385-2405   🔟
(CAA) (SAVE)   6/1-10/9   1P: $139-$239   2P: $139-$239   XP: $15   F16
                   4/16-5/31   1P: $109-$199   2P: $109-$199   XP: $15   F16
◆◆◆   10/10-2/28   1P: $109-$159   2P: $109-$159   XP: $15   F16
Hotel   3/1-4/15   1P: $84-$135   2P: $84-$135   XP: $15   F16
                   Location: Between Osweyo and Pendray Sts. 345 Quebec St V8V 1W4. Fax: 250/385-4453. **Terms:** Weekly
& monthly rates avail, off season; cancellation fee imposed; package plans; small pets only. **Facility:** 186 rooms. A well maintained property offering large guest rooms with a pleasant decor; executive style room on the top 2 floors. Choice between
efficiency or standard-style guest rooms. Close to US Ferry Terminal and Parliment buildings. 1 three-bedroom unit, 21 two-
bedroom units. 8 whirlpool rooms, $375-$660; 12 stories; interior corridors; heated pool, sauna, whirlpool. Fee: parking.
Dining: Restaurant; 7 am-10 pm; $11-$20; cocktails. **Services:** gift shop; area transportation, downtown. Fee: massage.
Recreation: hair salon. **All Rooms:** extended cable TV, honor bars. **Some Rooms:** 110 efficiencies. **Cards:** AE, DI, JC,
MC, VI. **Special Amenities: Free newspaper.**

HEATHERGATE HOUSE BED & BREAKFAST   **Phone:** (250)383-0068   🔟
◆◆   4/16-10/22   1P: $100-$160   2P: $100-$160   XP: $30
Bed &   10/23-2/28   1P: $85-$135   2P: $85-$135   XP: $25
Breakfast   3/1-4/15   1P: $75-$125   2P: $75-$125   XP: $25
                   Location: Between St. Lawrence and Montreal sts. 122 Simcoe St V8V 1K4. Fax: 250/383-4320. **Terms:** [BP]
meal plan; age restrictions may apply; 7 day cancellation notice; cancellation fee imposed. **Facility:** 4 rooms. Features 3 rooms
in the house along with 1 cottage that has a full kitchen, washer/dryer and 2 separate bedrooms. Nicely decorated in an English decor. Quiet residential neighborhood. 1 two-bedroom unit. 2 stories; interior/exterior corridors; designated smoking area.
All Rooms: combo or shower baths. **Some Rooms:** color TV. **Cards:** MC, VI.

(See map p. 525)

HELM'S INN   Phone: (250)385-5767   **34**
CAA SAVE   7/1-9/30   1P: $110-$145   2P: $110-$145   XP: $15   F12
                5/19-6/30   1P: $90-$110   2P: $90-$110   XP: $15   F12
◆ ◆   3/1-5/18 & 10/1-2/28   1P: $65-$85   2P: $65-$85   XP: $15   F12
Apartment   **Location:** Corner of Douglas and Superior sts. 600 Douglas St V8V 2P8. Fax: 250/385-2221. **Terms:** Weekly & monthly rates avail; check-in 4 pm. **Facility:** 42 rooms. Opposite Beacon Hill Park. Accommodations provided in 3 detached buildings featuring standard units without kitchen, studio units with kitchen and large 1-bedroom units with kitchen that sleeps 6. 3 stories, no elevator; interior corridors. **Dining:** Restaurant nearby. **All Rooms:** extended cable TV. **Some Rooms:** 36 kitchens. **Cards:** AE, DI, MC, VI. **Special Amenities:** Free local telephone calls. *(See color ad below)*

HOLIDAY INN VICTORIA   Phone: (250)382-4400   **7**
CAA SAVE   6/1-9/30   1P: $155   2P: $155   XP: $20   F18
                3/1-5/31 & 10/1-2/28   1P: $115-$129   2P: $115-$129   XP: $10   F18
◆ ◆   **Location:** 2.6 km n on Blanshard St (Hwy 17), just s of Finlayson St. 3020 Blanshard St V8T 5B5.
Motor Inn   Fax: 250/382-4053. **Terms:** Weekly & monthly rates avail. **Facility:** 126 rooms. Very comfortable and super clean guest rooms. Choose between the main building or the annex building with a few outside entrances to guest rooms. Close to shopping mall. Efficiencies, $10 extra charge; 3 stories; interior/exterior corridors; sauna, whirlpool. **Dining:** Restaurant; 6:30 am-10 pm; $9-$21; cocktails. **Services:** gift shop. **All Rooms:** utensils extra charge, extended cable TV. **Cards:** AE, DI, DS, JC, MC, VI. **Special Amenities:** Early check-in/late check-out.

HOLLAND HOUSE INN   Phone: (250)384-6644   **32**
◆ ◆ ◆   Property failed to provide current rates
Historic Bed   **Location:** At Government St, just s of the Parliament Buildings. 595 Michigan St V8V 1S7. Fax: 250/384-6117.
& Breakfast   **Terms:** [BP] meal plan; age restrictions may apply; 7 day cancellation notice; cancellation fee imposed. **Facility:** 14 rooms. Elegant but relaxed ambiance at this 1930s residence. Large rooms tastefully decorated with country antiques and some rooms with gas fireplace. Charming library/lounge with open-log fire on chilly nights. 3 stories, no elevator; interior corridors; designated smoking area. **Cards:** AE, MC, VI.

(See map p. 525)

HOWARD JOHNSON CANTERBURY INN   Phone: (250)382-2151   52

(CAA) (SAVE)

	7/1-9/15	1P: $99-$109	2P: $109-$140	XP: $10	F12
	5/1-6/30	1P: $65-$85	2P: $75-$95	XP: $10	F12
	3/1-4/30 & 9/16-2/28	1P: $59-$69	2P: $69-$89	XP: $10	F12

Motor Inn   **Location:** From Douglas St, 1.5 km w. 310 Gorge Rd E V8T 2W2. Fax: 250/382-3856. **Terms:** Weekly & monthly rates avail, off season. **Facility:** 80 rooms. Located in a residential area and along motel strip road. Property features a range of room styles and sizes from large standard rooms to spacious full kitchen suites, offering budget style accommodations. 45 kitchens, $10 extra charge; 3 stories, no elevator; interior corridors; heated pool, sauna. **Dining:** Restaurant; 7:30 am-1:30 & 5-9:30 pm; $8-$15; cocktails. **All Rooms:** extended cable TV. **Cards:** AE, DI, DS, MC, VI. **Special Amenities:** Early check-in/late check-out and free breakfast. *(See color ad below)*

HUMBOLDT HOUSE BED & BREAKFAST   Phone: 250/383-0152   18

| | 5/1-10/15 | 1P: $275-$315 | 2P: $275-$315 |
| | 3/1-5/14 & 10/16-2/28 | 1P: $145-$315 | 2P: $145-$315 |

Historic Bed & Breakfast   **Location:** Humboldt and Quadra sts. 867 Humboldt St V8V 2Z6. Fax: 250/383-6402. **Terms:** [BP] meal plan; age restrictions may apply; 7 day cancellation notice; cancellation fee imposed; 2 night min stay, weekends 7/1-8/31. **Facility:** 5 rooms. Pleasant guest rooms with large whirlpool and wood burning fireplaces. Built in 1895, the home has been authentically renovated to reflect the Victorian era. Just steps away from the downtown area. 2 stories; interior corridors; designated smoking area. **Cards:** MC, VI.

INGRAHAM HOTEL   Phone: (250)385-6731   5

(CAA) (SAVE)

| | 5/2-2/28 | 1P: $69 | 2P: $79 | XP: $10 | F12 |
| | 3/1-5/1 | 1P: $59 | 2P: $65 | XP: $10 | F12 |

Motor Inn   **Location:** 2.2 km n on Douglas St (Hwy 1), just s of Finlayson St. 2915 Douglas St V8T 4M8. Fax: 250/385-6912. **Facility:** 50 rooms. A comfortable, mature property featuring large guest rooms with pleasant decor. 3 stories; interior corridors. **Dining:** Restaurant; 6 am-8 pm, Sun 8 am-3 pm; $6-$12; cocktails. **All Rooms:** extended cable TV. **Cards:** AE, MC, VI. **Special Amenities:** Free local telephone calls and preferred room (subject to availability with advanced reservations).

IRIS GARDEN COUNTRY MANOR BED & BREAKFAST   Phone: (250)744-2253   67

| | 6/1-9/30 | 1P: $105-$155 | 2P: $110-$160 |
| | 3/1-5/31 & 10/1-2/28 | 1P: $90-$120 | 2P: $95-$125 |

Bed & Breakfast   **Location:** From Hwy 17 exit Royal Oak Dr, then just n, 4.5 km w on W Saanich Rd, watch for sign. 5360 W Saanich Rd V9E 1J8. Fax: 250/744-5690. **Terms:** [BP] meal plan; age restrictions may apply; check-in 4 pm; 7 day cancellation notice; cancellation fee imposed. **Facility:** 4 rooms. Named for the over 3,000 Iris's growing on 3 acres, truly a sight to behold in the spring. This charming character home features down duvets and large guest rooms. Indoor pool open just in the spring/summer. 2 stories; interior corridors; designated smoking area. **All Rooms:** combo or shower baths. **Cards:** MC, VI.

KING'S HOUSE BED & BREAKFAST   Phone: (250)382-2460   17

| | 5/1-10/15 | 1P: $110-$150 | 2P: $110-$150 | XP: $20 |
| | 3/1-4/30 & 10/16-2/28 | 1P: $75-$110 | 2P: $75-$110 | XP: $20 |

Bed & Breakfast   **Location:** From Blanshard (Hwy 17), 1 km w on Bay St, right turn on Tyee St which becomes Craigflower Rd, follow for 3.2 km. 945 Dellwood Rd V9A 6P2. Fax: 250/388-9774. **Terms:** [ECP] meal plan; age restrictions may apply; 7 day cancellation notice. **Facility:** 4 rooms. Created with a real sense of "Old English" style. The bold, earthy colors and hardwood floors speak of an era long since passed. An exceptional home in quiet, residential area, close to the Gorge Vale Golf Course. 2 stories; interior corridors; designated smoking area. **Some Rooms:** color TV. **Cards:** MC, VI.

(See map p. 525)

THE MAGNOLIA HOTEL & SUITES   Phone: (250)381-0999   [66]

6/1-10/15	1P: $239-$399	2P: $239-$399	XP: $20 F16
4/16-5/31	1P: $209-$289	2P: $209-$289	XP: $20 F16
3/1-4/15 & 10/16-2/28	1P: $169-$249	2P: $169-$249	XP: $20 F16

Hotel   **Location:** Courtney and Gordon sts. 623 Courtney St V8W 1B8. Fax: 250/381-0988. **Terms:** [CP] meal plan; package plans. **Facility:** 66 rooms. Victoria's newest European boutique style hotel located in the heart of downtown. Elegant guest rooms with lavish bathroom. 6 large family suites for up to 4 persons, $269-$419; 7 stories; interior corridors. Fee: parking. **Dining:** 2 restaurants; noon-10 pm; $10-$20; cocktails. **All Rooms:** extended cable TV, honor bars. **Cards:** AE, DI, DS, JC, MC, VI. **Special Amenities:** Free local telephone calls and free room upgrade (subject to availability with advanced reservations).

MAYFAIR MOTEL   Phone: (250)388-7337   [3]

7/1-9/30	1P: $55-$65	2P: $65-$79	XP: $10 F12
5/1-6/30	1P: $45-$55	2P: $55-$69	XP: $10 F12
3/1-4/30 & 10/1-2/28	1P: $29-$39	2P: $39-$55	XP: $10 F12

Motel   **Location:** 3.5 km n on Douglas St. 650 Speed Ave V8Z 1A4. Fax: 250/388-7398. **Terms:** Weekly & monthly rates avail, off season. **Facility:** 22 rooms. A mature property with all guest rooms featuring a separate kitchen area. Guest rooms offer various sizes and configurations but all are quite spacious and nicely maintained. Owner assures a good night sleep. 3 stories; interior corridors. **All Rooms:** kitchens, utensils extra charge, extended cable TV. **Cards:** AE, MC, VI. **Special Amenities:** Free local telephone calls and preferred room (subject to availability with advanced reservations).

OAK BAY BEACH HOTEL   Phone: (250)598-4556   [42]

6/16-9/15	1P: $189-$199	2P: $189-$199	XP: $25 F12
4/16-6/15 & 9/16-2/28	1P: $149-$179	2P: $149-$179	XP: $25 F12
3/1-4/15	1P: $119-$179	2P: $119-$179	XP: $25 F12

Historic Motor Inn   **Location:** 6.8 km e via Oak Bay Ave, just s. 1175 Beach Dr V8S 2N2. Fax: 250/598-6180. **Terms:** [CP] meal plan; cancellation fee imposed; package plans. **Facility:** 50 rooms. Tudor-style mansion, quiet residential setting featuring fine landscaping and view of bay. Various styles and sizes of guest rooms, some with ocean view. Individual room decor; cozy public areas. 4 suites with fireplace. 3 stories; interior corridors. **Services:** gift shop; area transportation. **Cards:** AE, DI, JC, MC, VI. *(See color ad below)*

(See map p. 525)

OAK BAY GUEST HOUSE
◆ ◆
Historic Bed & Breakfast

Phone: (250)598-3812   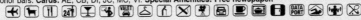 62

6/1-9/15	1P: $125-$160	2P: $125-$160	XP: $20
10/16-2/28	1P: $55-$120	2P: $65-$120	XP: $15
9/16-10/15	1P: $85-$115	2P: $95-$115	XP: $20
3/1-5/31	1P: $55-$115	2P: $65-$115	

Location: 4.8 km e on Oak Bay Ave which becomes Newport Ave. 1052 Newport Ave V8S 5E3. Fax: 250/598-0369. **Terms:** [BP] meal plan; age restrictions may apply; 7 day cancellation notice; cancellation fee imposed. **Facility:** 11 rooms. Restored manor featuring attractive public areas with wood paneled walls and open wood beams. Due to age of this historic type building the guest rooms are average size with some compact bathrooms. Charming decor. Lush land. 2 stories; interior corridors; designated smoking area. **All Rooms:** combo or shower baths. **Cards:** AE, MC, VI. *(See color ad p 536)*

OCEAN POINTE RESORT HOTEL & SPA
(CAA) (SAVE)
◆ ◆ ◆
Hotel

Phone: (250)360-2999   43

6/1-10/9	1P: $159-$409	2P: $159-$409	XP: $30	F16
4/16-5/31	1P: $134-$319	2P: $134-$319	XP: $25	F16
10/10-2/28	1P: $144-$249	2P: $144-$249	XP: $25	F16
3/1-4/15	1P: $119-$224	2P: $119-$224	XP: $25	F16

Location: Just w of Johnson St Bridge, Esquimalt at Tyee rds. 45 Songhees Rd V9A 6T3. Fax: 250/360-1041. **Terms:** Weekly & monthly rates avail; check-in 4 pm; cancellation fee imposed; package plans; small pets only. **Facility:** 250 rooms. Fine location on Inner Harbor with wonderful views of city or mountain. Large guest rooms, nicely decorated. Short walk to downtown area or paved walkway around harbour. 9 stories; interior corridors; heated pool, sauna, whirlpool; racquetball court, 2 lighted tennis courts. Fee: parking. **Dining:** Dining room, restaurant; 6:30 am-10 pm; $15-$40; cocktails; entertainment. **Services:** gift shop; area transportation; downtown/inner harbour. Fee: massage. **Recreation:** full European spa. **Some Rooms:** honor bars. **Cards:** AE, CB, DI, JC, MC, VI. **Special Amenities:** Free newspaper.

OXFORD CASTLE INN
(CAA) (SAVE)
◆ ◆
Motel

Phone: (250)388-6431   15

5/16-9/28	1P: $88-$118	2P: $118-$138	XP: $10	F8
3/1-5/15	1P: $64-$68	2P: $88	XP: $10	F8
9/29-2/28	1P: $62-$64	2P: $68	XP: $10	F8

Location: From Douglas St, 2 km w. 133 Gorge Rd E V9A 1L1. Fax: 250/388-6437. **Terms:** Weekly & monthly rates avail, off season; cancellation fee imposed; small pets only, $15 extra charge. **Facility:** 58 rooms. In a residential area and along a motel strip road. Designed somewhat as a castle; this property offers large units with fully equipped kitchen and separate living room. All units feature balcony. Nicely landscaped grounds. 55 kitchens, $15 extra charge; 4 stories; interior corridors; heated pool, sauna, whirlpool. **Dining:** Restaurant nearby. **All Rooms:** extended cable TV. **Cards:** AE, DI, MC, VI. **Special Amenities:** Early check-in/late check-out and free local telephone calls. *(See color ad below)*

PRIOR HOUSE B&B INN
◆ ◆ ◆
Historic Bed & Breakfast

Phone: 250/592-8847   12

6/16-9/30	2P: $145-$275	XP: $45
4/1-6/15 & 10/1-2/28	2P: $135-$235	XP: $45
3/1-3/31	2P: $110-$205	XP: $45

Location: From Blanshard St, 2 km e on Fort St, then just s. 620 St. Charles St V8S 3N7. Fax: 250/592-8223. **Terms:** [BP] meal plan; age restrictions may apply; check-in 4 pm; 14 day cancellation notice; cancellation fee imposed. **Facility:** 6 rooms. A wonderfully restored 1912 manor home featuring lush landscaped grounds. Antique furniture decorate all guest rooms, along with wood burning fireplace. Quiet, tree lined neighborhood. 1 two-bedroom unit. 3 stories, no elevator; interior corridors; designated smoking area. **All Rooms:** combo or shower baths. **Cards:** MC, VI.

QUALITY RESORT AT MOUNT DOUGLAS PARK
(CAA) (SAVE)
◆ ◆ ◆
Motel

Phone: (250)658-2171   1

7/1-9/30	1P: $119-$299	2P: $119-$299	XP: $20	F12
5/1-6/30	1P: $99-$249	2P: $99-$249	XP: $20	F12
3/1-4/30 & 10/1-2/28	1P: $79-$239	2P: $79-$239	XP: $20	F12

Location: 10 km n on Hwy 17, exit Royal Oak Dr, 2 km e to Cordova Bay Rd follow to Mount Douglas Park. 4550 Cordova Bay Rd V8X 3V5. Fax: 250/658-4596. **Terms:** [CP] meal plan; weekly rates avail, off season; cancellation fee imposed; package plans. **Facility:** 36 rooms. Quiet, hillside setting with ocean or park view. Most with private balcony; some with gas fireplace. Rooms in the tower are very spacious with modern decor; rooms in the lodge are smaller but feature efficiencies. 2 penthouse suites with whirlpool & gas fireplace, $189-$229; 7 whirlpool rooms, $189-$299; 4 stories; interior/exterior corridors; sauna, steamroom. **Recreation:** Fee: European skin care studio. **All Rooms:** extended cable TV. **Cards:** AE, DI, DS, JC, MC, VI. **Special Amenities:** Free breakfast and free room upgrade (subject to availability with advanced reservations). *(See color ad p 538)*

(See map p. 525)

QUEEN VICTORIA INN

(CAA) (SAVE)	3/1-5/15	1P: $85-$325	2P: $85-$325	XP: $20	F15
◆◆◆	5/16-9/30	1P: $135-$205	2P: $135-$205	XP: $20	F15
Hotel	10/1-2/28	1P: $85-$125	2P: $85-$125	XP: $20	F15

Phone: (250)386-1312   **49**

Location: Douglas and Superior sts. 655 Douglas St V8V 2P9. Fax: 250/381-4312. **Terms:** Weekly & monthly rates avail, off season. **Facility:** 146 rooms. Close to the Parliament Building, museum and inner harbour. Comfortable guest rooms, all with balcony. Several rooms offer sweeping views of the city. 7 two-bedroom units. Efficiency, $10 extra charge; 3 whirlpool rooms, $125-$435; 9 stories; interior corridors; heated pool, sauna, whirlpool. Fee: parking. **Dining:** Restaurant; 7 am-9 pm; $15-$20; cocktails. **Services:** area transportation, within Inner Harbour. **All Rooms:** extended cable TV. **Some Rooms:** 108 efficiencies. **Cards:** AE, DI, DS, JC, MC, VI. **Special Amenities:** Free room upgrade and preferred room (each subject to availability with advanced reservations).

RAMADA HUNTINGDON MANOR

(CAA) (SAVE)	6/16-10/15	1P: $153-$233	2P: $153-$233	XP: $15	F18
◆◆◆	5/12-6/15	1P: $133-$213	2P: $133-$213	XP: $15	F18
Motor Inn	3/1-5/11 & 10/16-2/28	1P: $83-$163	2P: $83-$163	XP: $15	F18

Phone: (250)381-3456   **29**

Location: Between Oswego and Pendray sts. 330 Quebec St V8V 1W3. Fax: 250/382-7666. **Terms:** Weekly & monthly rates avail, off season; cancellation fee imposed; package plans. **Facility:** 116 rooms. Up-to-date property with English-style interior design. 40 bi-level suites with air conditioning, the rest of the room have fans. All rooms with iron and ironing board. Close to US Ferry Terminal. 58 efficiencies, $10 extra charge; 3 stories; interior corridors; sauna, whirlpool. Fee: parking. **Dining:** Restaurant; 7 am-9:30 pm; $10-$16; cocktails. **All Rooms:** utensils extra charge, extended cable TV. **Cards:** AE, DI, DS, JC, MC, VI. **Special Amenities:** Free newspaper.

ROBIN HOOD MOTEL

(CAA) (SAVE)	5/19-9/30	1P: $57-$66	2P: $63-$81	XP: $5
◆◆	10/1-2/28	1P: $46-$56	2P: $51-$61	XP: $5
Motel	3/1-5/18	1P: $46-$51	2P: $51-$57	XP: $5

Phone: (250)388-4302   **11**

Location: From Douglas St, 2.4 km w. 136 Gorge Rd E V9A 1L4. Fax: 250/383-4399. **Terms:** Weekly & monthly rates avail, off season; small pets only, $5 extra charge. **Facility:** 55 rooms. Landscaped grounds which include a few giant cedar trees. Suburban location along motel strip offering very large comfortable but, moderate style guest rooms. Just outside the downtown core area. 32 kitchen units, $10-$15 extra charge; 2 stories; exterior corridors. **Dining:** Restaurant nearby. **All Rooms:** extended cable TV. **Cards:** AE, DI, MC, VI. **Special Amenities:** Early check-in/late check-out and free local telephone calls. (See color ad below)

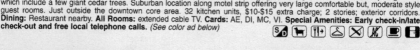

(See map p. 525)

ROYAL SCOT SUITE HOTEL

				Phone: (250)388-5463	**31**
CAA SAVE	6/1-9/30	1P: $145-$325	2P: $145-$325	XP: $20	F16
◆◆◆	3/1-5/31 & 10/1-2/28	1P: $99-$245	2P: $99-$245	XP: $20	F16

Apartment   **Location:** Between Menzies and Oswego sts, just w of Parliament buildings, s of US Ferry Terminal. 425 Quebec St V8V 1W7. Fax: 250/388-5452. **Terms:** Weekly & monthly rates avail, off season; cancellation fee imposed. **Facility:** 176 rooms. A wonderfully maintained property offering lush landscaping touches along with some very nice contemporary studio or 1-bedroom suites. All are decorated with an at-home feel. Some nice luxury touches plus friendly staff. 3 royal suites, $259-$339. 2 two-bedroom suites, $249-$319 for 4-6 persons; 4 stories; interior corridors; heated pool, saunas, whirlpool. **Dining:** Restaurant; 7 am-9 pm; $7-$15; cocktails. **Services:** gift shop; area transportation, downtown. **Recreation:** billiards table, video game room. **All Rooms:** extended cable TV. **Some Rooms:** 150 kitchens. Fee: VCR. **Cards:** AE, DI, MC, VI. *(See color ad below)*

(See map p. 525)

RYAN'S BED & BREAKFAST
Phone: 250/389-0012   63

♦♦♦

Historic Bed
& Breakfast

6/5-10/15	1P: $135-$185	2P: $135-$185	XP: $30
3/1-6/4	1P: $95-$145	2P: $95-$145	XP: $25
10/16-12/31	1P: $75-$135	2P: $75-$135	XP: $25
1/1-2/28	1P: $65-$120	2P: $65-$120	XP: $20

Location: Between Montreal and Oswego sts. 224 Superior St V8V 1T3. Fax: 250/389-2857. **Terms:** [BP] meal plan; age restrictions may apply; 7 day cancellation notice; small pets only. **Facility:** 6 rooms. 1892 home with an atmosphere of a bygone era; public areas are particularly nice, trimmed with lacey curtains, cabinets with fine china and oil paintings in heavy gilded frames. 2 stories; interior corridors; designated smoking area. **All Rooms:** combo or shower baths. **Cards:** MC, VI.

(ASK) 🛏 ✕ 🅺 📶

SHAMROCK MOTEL
Phone: (250)385-8768   35

(CAA) (SAVE)

♦

Apartment

6/1-9/30	1P: $89-$119	2P: $89-$119	XP: $10	F5
10/1-2/28	1P: $64-$94	2P: $64-$94	XP: $10	F5
3/1-5/31	1P: $59-$89	2P: $59-$89	XP: $10	F5

Location: Douglas and Superior Sts. 675 Superior St V8V 1V1. Fax: 250/385-1837. **Terms:** Weekly & monthly rates avail, off season; small pets only, $5 extra charge. **Facility:** 15 rooms. A nicely maintained, older property offering comfortable accommodations for those on a budget. Located across the street from Becon Hill Park, short walk to downtown and museums. 3 stories, no elevator; exterior corridors. **All Rooms:** kitchens, extended cable TV. **Cards:** AE, DI, MC, VI. **Special Amenities:** Free local telephone calls and preferred room (subject to availability with advanced reservations).

(SD) 🛏 ✕ 🅺 📺 📶

STAY'N SAVE INN
Phone: (250)475-7500   19

(CAA) (SAVE)

♦♦♦

Motel

7/1-9/30	1P: $114-$124	2P: $124-$134	XP: $10	F16
5/1-6/30	1P: $99-$109	2P: $109-$119	XP: $10	F16
3/1-4/30 & 10/1-2/28	1P: $79-$89	2P: $89-$99	XP: $10	F16

Location: 3 km n on Blanshard (Hwy 17); corner of Blanchard and Cloverdale Ave. 3233 Maple St V8X 4Y9. Fax: 250/475-7599. **Terms:** Weekly rates avail, off season; cancellation fee imposed; small pets only, certain rooms. **Facility:** 117 rooms. Modern structure offers spacious comfortable rooms. Suburban area. 48 efficiencies, $10 extra charge; suites, $99-$144; 3 stories; exterior corridors. **Dining:** Restaurant nearby. **All Rooms:** extended cable TV. **Cards:** AE, DI, MC, VI. **Special Amenities:** Free local telephone calls and free newspaper. *(See color ad p 431 & below)*

(SD) 🛏 🍴 🐾 △ 🏋 ✕ 📹 📟 📺 📶 (DATA PORT) 📶

(See map p. 525)

SUNNYMEADE HOUSE INN
◆◆
Bed &
Breakfast

Phone: (250)658-1414   9

5/16-9/15	1P: $79-$169	2P: $79-$169	XP: $30
3/1-5/15 & 9/16-2/28	1P: $69-$135	2P: $69-$135	XP: $20

Location: 12 km n on Hwy 17, exit Cordova Bay, 3 km e on Sayward/Cordova Bay Rd, across from service station. 1002 Fenn Ave V8Y 1P3. Fax: 250/658-1414. **Terms:** [BP] meal plan; age restrictions may apply; 7 day cancellation notice; cancellation fee imposed. **Facility:** 6 rooms. Residential setting within easy walking distance to beach, restaurants and shops. Charming guest rooms with an at-home feel. 2 stories; interior corridors; designated smoking area. **All Rooms:** combo or shower baths.

SWANS HOTEL
◆◆◆
Apartment

Phone: (250)361-3310   20

7/1-9/30	1P: $169-$249	2P: $169-$249	XP: $20	F12
5/1-6/30	1P: $135-$205	2P: $135-$205	XP: $20	F12
10/1-2/28	1P: $115-$189	2P: $115-$189	XP: $20	F12
3/1-4/30	1P: $109-$179	2P: $109-$179	XP: $20	F12

Location: Pandora Ave and Store St. 506 Pandora Ave V8W 1N6. Fax: 250/361-3491. **Terms:** Check-in 4 pm; cancellation fee imposed. **Facility:** 29 rooms. Excellent blend of old and new, with cheerful contemporary furnishings in a restored 1913 building. Many bi-level suites, with bedrooms upstairs. The owners original artwork collection is displayed in each room. 13 two-bedroom units. 2 stories; interior corridors. Fee: parking. **All Rooms:** kitchens. **Some Rooms:** Fee: VCR. **Cards:** AE, DI, JC, MC, VI. (See color ad p 540)

TALLY HO MOTOR INN
(CAA) (SAVE)
◆
Motor Inn

Phone: (250)386-6141   6

7/1-8/31	1P: $89	2P: $89-$99	XP: $5	F19
3/1-6/30	1P: $52-$59	2P: $59-$69	XP: $5	F19
9/1-9/30	1P: $59	2P: $69	XP: $5	F19
10/1-2/28	1P: $52-$55	2P: $54-$59	XP: $5	F19

Location: 2.4 km n on Douglas St (Hwy 1), just s of Finlayson St. 3020 Douglas St V8T 4N4. Fax: 250/380-9990. **Terms:** Pets. **Facility:** 50 rooms. A mature property featuring basic, budget-oriented rooms with a simple, but functional guest room decor. 2 stories; interior corridors; heated pool. **Dining:** Restaurant; 7 am-8 pm; $7-$12; cocktails. **All Rooms:** extended cable TV. **Cards:** AE, DI, DS, JC, MC, VI. **Special Amenities:** Free local telephone calls and free newspaper.

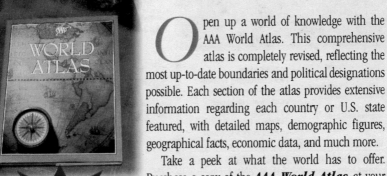

(See map p. 525)

TRAVELLER'S INN-CENTRAL

				Phone: (250)386-1000	22
7/1-10/15	1P: $80-$110	2P: $90-$120	XP: $10		F14
5/1-6/30	1P: $60-$90	2P: $70-$100	XP: $10		F14
3/1-4/30 & 10/16-2/28	1P: $40-$70	2P: $50-$80	XP: $10		F14

Motel **Location:** 2.2 km n on Doulgas St (Hwy 1) at Burnside Rd. 2898 Douglas St V8T 4M9. Fax: 250/386-1001. **Terms:** [CP] meal plan; weekly & monthly rates avail, off season; 3 day cancellation notice. **Facility:** 58 rooms. For those who like large king beds then this is the place. The rooms offer very nice, comfortable accommodations. 2 whirlpool rooms; suites avail; 3 stories; interior corridors. **Dining:** Restaurant nearby. **All Rooms:** extended cable TV. **Some Rooms:** 15 efficiencies. **Cards:** AE, MC, VI. (See color ad below)

TRAVELLER'S INN-DOWNTOWN

				Phone: (250)381-1000	26
7/1-10/15	1P: $70-$80	2P: $80-$90	XP: $10		F14
5/1-6/30	1P: $50-$60	2P: $60-$70	XP: $10		F14
3/1-4/30 & 10/16-2/28	1P: $30-$40	2P: $40-$50	XP: $10		F14

Motel **Location:** Corner of Douglas and Chatham sts. 1850 Douglas St V8T 4K6. Fax: 250/381-1001. **Terms:** [CP] meal plan. **Facility:** 78 rooms. Just outside the downtown core. This budget oriented property offers some surprisingly spacious guest rooms with a large number of king beds. Top floor rooms have small patio deck with nice views. 2 whirlpool rooms; 3 stories; interior corridors. **All Rooms:** extended cable TV. **Some Rooms:** kitchen. **Cards:** AE, MC, VI. (See color ad below)

(See map p. 525)

TRAVELLER'S INN-IN TOWN

Phone: (250)978-1000   **41**

7/1-10/15	1P: $70-$80	2P: $80-$90	XP: $10 F14
5/1-6/30	1P: $50-$60	2P: $60-$70	XP: $10 F14
3/1-4/30 & 10/16-2/28	1P: $30-$40	2P: $40-$50	XP: $10 F14

(AAA) (SAVE)

Motel

◆

Location: 2.4 km n on Douglas St (Hwy 1), just s of Finlayson St. 3025 Douglas St V8T 4N2. Fax: 250/978-1001. **Terms:** Weekly rates avail, off season; small pets only, $10 extra charge. **Facility:** 46 rooms. An older but well-maintained budget property. Guest rooms range from average to above average in size and feature an eclectic array of furnishings. All rooms with fan. Affiliated with the Stay'n Save Motor Inns. 15 efficiencies, $6.50 extra charge; 2 stories; exterior corridors. **Dining:** Restaurant nearby. **All Rooms:** combo or shower baths, extended cable TV. **Cards:** AE, DI, MC, VI. **Special Amenities:** Free local telephone calls. *(See color ad p 542)*

(See map p. 525)

TRAVELODGE VICTORIA
Phone: (250)388-6611   **55**

CAA SAVE

	6/1-9/30	1P: $110-$160	2P: $130-$180	XP: $10	F12
♦♦♦	3/1-5/31	1P: $70-$120	2P: $85-$150	XP: $5	F12
Motor Inn	10/1-2/28	1P: $57-$90	2P: $62-$110	XP: $5	F12

Location: From Douglas St, 2 km w. 229 Gorge Rd E V9A 1L1. Fax: 250/388-4153. **Terms:** Weekly & monthly rates avail, off season; 3 day cancellation notice; cancellation fee imposed. **Facility:** 73 rooms. A very nice property offering a variety of room types from average sized to larger units; all with a fresh, contemporary decor. Nicely landscaped grounds. 3 stories, no elevator; exterior corridors; heated pool, saunas. **Dining:** Restaurant; 7 am-2 & 5-9 pm; $10-$16; cocktails. **All Rooms:** extended cable TV. **Some Rooms:** 35 kitchens. **Cards:** AE, DI, DS, JC, MC, VI. **Special Amenities:** Free local telephone calls and free newspaper. *(See color ad p 543)*

UNION CLUB OF BRITISH COLUMBIA
Phone: (250)384-1151   **64**

CAA SAVE

	5/1-9/30	1P: $169-$249	2P: $169-$249	XP: $10	F18
♦♦♦	10/1-2/28	1P: $129-$189	2P: $129-$189	XP: $10	F18
Classic Hotel	3/1-4/30	1P: $109-$189	2P: $109-$189	XP: $10	F18

Location: Humboldt and Gordon sts. 805 Gordon St V8W 1Z6. Fax: 250/384-0538. **Terms:** [CP] meal plan; age restrictions may apply. **Facility:** 25 rooms. **Historic.** Unique, adult oriented accommodations in a private club featuring superior historic detail of Victorian refinement. Parking lot blk away. Dress code in effect in all public areas due to private club affiliation. 8 larger suites avail; 4 suites with harbor views; 3 stories; interior corridors. **Dining:** Dining room; room guests & club members only; Wed-Sat 5 pm-10 pm; $17-$25. **Recreation:** billiards room. **All Rooms:** extended cable TV. **Cards:** AE, DI, MC, VI. **Special Amenities:** Free breakfast and free newspaper.

THE VICTORIA REGENT HOTEL
Phone: (250)386-2211   **24**

CAA SAVE

	6/16-10/16	1P: $179-$299	2P: $179-$359	XP: $20	F16
♦♦♦	4/28-6/15	1P: $149-$259	2P: $149-$259	XP: $20	F16
Condominium	3/1-4/27 & 10/17-2/28	1P: $119-$239	2P: $119-$239	XP: $20	F16

Location: Whaft and Yates Sts. 1234 Wharf St V8W 3H9. Fax: 250/386-2622. **Terms:** [CP] meal plan; weekly & monthly rates avail, off season; cancellation fee imposed. **Facility:** 45 rooms. On the Inner harbour, these spacious modern units provide simple elegance. Most with superb inner harbour views and balcony. 11 standard style hotel rooms without kitchens avail. 27 two-bedroom units. 5 whirlpool rooms, $299-$409; 8 stories; interior corridors. **Dining:** Coffee shop; 7-11 am. **All Rooms:** extended cable TV, honor bars. **Some Rooms:** 35 kitchens. **Cards:** AE, DI, DS, JC, MC, VI. **Special Amenities:** Free breakfast and free local telephone calls. *(See color ad p 543)*

VILLA BLANCA BED & BREAKFAST
Phone: (250)658-4190   **23**

♦♦

	5/16-9/30	1P: $85-$115	2P: $115-$150	XP: $25
Bed &	3/1-5/15 & 10/1-2/28	1P: $65-$95	2P: $85-$110	XP: $25
Breakfast				

Location: 12 km n on Hwy 17, exit Cordova Bay, 5 km e on Sayward/Cordova Bay Rd. 4918 Cordova Bay Rd V8Y 2J5. Fax: 250/658-4120. **Terms:** [BP] meal plan; 7 day cancellation notice; cancellation fee imposed. **Facility:** 4 rooms. Lovingly decorated private home with pleasant guest rooms. Attractive landscaped yard with a reflecting pond in the backyard. Restaurants short drive on Cordova Bay Rd. 2 stories; interior corridors; designated smoking area. **All Rooms:** combo or shower baths. **Cards:** MC, VI.

------ **RESTAURANTS** ------

BARKLEY'S STEAK & SEAFOOD
Dinner: $15-$25   Phone: 250/382-7111   **2**

♦♦

Steak and
Seafood

Location: Centre; in Executive House Hotel. 777 Douglas St V8W 2B5. **Hours:** 5 pm-11 pm. **Reservations:** suggested. **Features:** casual dress; cocktails; fee for parking & valet parking; a la carte. Barkley's has a casually elegant, Victorian atmosphere and an attentive, professional server staff. This restaurant's very good dishes include steak and seafood, of course, but the menu also offers pasta selections and a choice of Continental dishes. **Cards:** AE, DI, DS, JC, MC, VI.

(See map p. 525)

THE BLETHERING PLACE TEA ROOM & RESTAURANT
Lunch: $6-$10   **Dinner:** $8-$15   **Phone:** 250/598-1413   (4)

Canadian
◆◆

Location: Corner of Monterey and Oak Bay aves; in Oak Bay Village. 2250 Oak Bay Ave V8R 1G5. **Hours:** 8 am-9 pm. **Reservations:** accepted. **Features:** No A/C; casual dress; carryout; beer & wine only; a la carte. Built in 1912, this building is the oldest in the "village." Its English-style decor matches its English-style fare featuring prime rib and Yorkshire pudding and Welsh rarebit. Afternoon tea is served 11 am-7:30 pm. Families are welcomed here. Smoke free premises. **Cards:** AE, DI, DS, JC, MC, VI.

(See color ad p 544)   ✕

CECCONI'S TRATTORIA
Lunch: $8-$14   **Dinner:** $8-$14   **Phone:** 250/592-0454   (22)

Italian
◆◆

Location: Corner of N Dairy and Shelbourne sts. 3201 Shelbourne St V8P 5G9. **Hours:** 11 am-10 pm, Sun from 5 pm. **Closed:** 12/25. **Features:** cocktails; a la carte. This casual, Italian-style, family-dining restaurant features wonderful wood-oven pizza, fresh pasta and a nice selection of dessert. The fettuccine Marco Polo and salmon al forno are very good. It's located just north of the Hillside Shopping Centre. **Cards:** AE, MC, VI.   ✕

THE EMPRESS ROOM   Historical
Dinner: $30-$40   **Phone:** 250/384-8111   (13)

Regional Canadian
◆◆◆◆

Location: Government at Wharf St, just n of the Parliament buildings; in The Empress. 721 Government St V8W 1W5. **Hours:** 6 pm-10 pm. **Reservations:** suggested. **Features:** semi-formal attire; cocktails; entertainment; fee for parking & valet parking; a la carte. The Empress Room offers superior dining in an atmosphere of elegance and refinement. Its sophisticated cuisine is enhanced by outstanding Victorian architecture. The distinguished wine list and polished, excellent service complete the experience. Smoke free premises. **Cards:** AE, DI, DS, JC, MC, VI.   ✕

THE GEORGE & DRAGON
Lunch: $6-$11   **Dinner:** $6-$13   **Phone:** 250/388-4458   (25)

Canadian
◆

Location: Corner of Fernwood and Gladstone. 1302 Gladstone V8R 1S1. **Hours:** 10 am-midnight, Sun 11 am-11 pm. **Closed:** 12/25. **Features:** carryout; cocktails & lounge; street parking; a la carte. You're sure to enjoy this distinctive English-style pub featuring lots of "pub grub" such as Philly cheese steaks, burgers, steamed mussels, sandwiches, tortellinis and more. They offer live jazz or blues Wed-Sat nights. Locals love this place. **Cards:** MC, VI.   ✕

HAULTAIN'S FISH & CHIPS
Lunch: $6-$10   **Dinner:** $6-$10   **Phone:** 250/383-8332   (27)

Seafood
◆

Location: Just e of Cook St. 1127 Haultain St V8T 1V4. **Hours:** 11:30 am-7:30 pm, Sun 3:30 pm-7 pm. **Closed:** Mon in winter. **Features:** casual dress; carryout; beer & wine only; a la carte. You can dine in or take out an order from this small, neighborhood-favorite restaurant located in a quiet residential area. Fish 'n' chips is their specialty, but they also serve burgers and specialty dinners. Seating can be limited at times. **Cards:** MC, VI.   ✕

HERALD STREET CAFE
Lunch: $9-$12   **Dinner:** $12-$23   **Phone:** 250/381-1441   (11)

Regional Canadian
◆◆◆

Location: Government & Herald sts. 546 Herald St V8W 1S6. **Hours:** 11:30 am-3 & 5:30-10 pm, Thurs-11 pm, Fri & Sat-midnight, Sun from 11 am, Mon & Tues from 5:30 pm. **Reservations:** suggested. **Features:** No A/C; casual dress; Sunday brunch; cocktails; street parking; a la carte. The Herald Street Cafe features an eclectic offering of West Coast favorites, and the menu displays the chef's skill and imagination. The lamb sandwich, crab cakes and roasted tomato and garlic bisque are well-known. More than 350 international wines. Smoke free premises. **Cards:** AE, DI, MC, VI.   ✕

HUNAN VILLAGE
Lunch: $8-$15   **Dinner:** $8-$15   **Phone:** 250/382-0661   (1)

Chinese
◆◆

Location: Fisgard and Government sts. 546 Fisgard St V8W 1R4. **Hours:** 11 am-11 pm, Sun 5 pm-10 pm. **Closed:** 12/25. **Features:** casual dress; carryout; cocktails & lounge; a la carte. Located in Victoria's Chinatown district, this restaurant specializes in Hunan and Cantonese meals. Hot and spicy beef, smoked duck or ham dishes are the local favorites. There's metered street parking or spaces nearby in pay parking lots. **Cards:** AE, DI, MC, VI.   ✕

IL TERRAZZO
Lunch: $7-$11   **Dinner:** $13-$25   **Phone:** 250/361-0028   (28)

Italian
◆◆

Location: Jct Warf St near Market Square main entrance off Waddington Alley. 555 Johnson St V8W 1M2. **Hours:** 11:30 am-3 & 5-10:30 pm, Fri & Sat-11 pm, Sun 5 pm-10:30 pm. **Closed:** 1/1 & 12/25. **Reservations:** suggested. **Features:** No A/C; casual dress; cocktails; street parking; a la carte. Situated in an old courtyard, Il Terrazzo offers excellent meals such as Australian lamb, ostrich, pasta and seafood, with emphasis on wood-burning-oven specialties. Wine choices are extensive, with a nice by-the-glass selection. Fast, friendly service. **Cards:** AE, MC, VI.   ✕

JAMES BAY TEA ROOM & RESTAURANT
Lunch: $7-$8   **Dinner:** $12-$15   **Phone:** 250/382-8282   (15)

Canadian
◆

Location: Corner of Superior and Menzies, just s of the Parliament buildings. 332 Menzies St V8V 2G9. **Hours:** 7 am-8 pm, Sun from 8 am. **Closed:** 12/24-12/26. **Reservations:** suggested. **Features:** carryout; beer & wine only; minimum charge-$3; a la carte. This popular place in a 1907 home has an intimate atmosphere featuring memorabilia and photos of Britain's Royal Family. The menu offers omelets, pot pies, Yorkshire pudding, bangers and kidney pie. Afternoon tea is $6.75; high tea $10, served all day. Smoke free premises. **Cards:** AE, MC, VI.   ✕

THE MARINA RESTAURANT
Lunch: $9-$16   **Dinner:** $14-$26   **Phone:** 250/598-8555   (17)

Continental
◆◆◆

Location: 6 km e via Oak Bay Ave, just s. 1327 Beach Dr V8S 2N4. **Hours:** 11:30 am-2:30 & 5-10 pm, Fri & Sat-11 pm, Sun from 10 am. **Closed:** 12/25. **Reservations:** required; in summer. **Features:** Sunday brunch; children's menu; early bird specials; cocktails; a la carte. Located in the Oak Bay Marina, this restaurant provides beautiful sweeping views of the ocean, harbor and mountains. Its menu features a Pacific Northwest cuisine with a twist, showcasing fresh local and exotic seafood as well as burgers and sandwiches. **Cards:** AE, DI, JC, MC, VI.   ✕

(See map p. 525)

MILLOS RESTAURANT **Lunch:** $7-$9 **Dinner:** $9-$18 **Phone:** 250/382-4422 ⑨
◆◆◆ **Location:** Just e of Douglas St. 716 Burdett Ave V8W 3G2. **Hours:** 11 am-11 pm, Sun from 4 pm. Closed:
Greek 12/25. **Reservations:** suggested. **Features:** No A/C; casual dress; children's menu; early bird specials;
carryout; cocktails & lounge; entertainment; street parking; a la carte. You'll enjoy the tasty specialties at this
established restaurant, which offers rack of lamb, pita sandwiches, salads, pasta, baklava and cheesecake. Belly dancing is
performed nightly in season, weekends in the off-season. Look for the windmill outside. **Cards:** AE, DI, MC, VI. ✖

PAGLIACCI'S **Lunch:** $8-$10 **Dinner:** $16-$20 **Phone:** 250/386-1662 ㉛
◆◆ **Location:** Jct Fort St. 1011 Broad St V8W 2A1. **Hours:** 11:30 am-11 pm, Sat & Sun-midnight. Closed: 12/25.
Italian **Features:** No A/C; Sunday brunch; health conscious menu items; carryout; cocktails. This popular New
York-style restaurant has an extensive and entertaining menu. Pasta is the specialty here; they also serve a
cheese-and-meat tortellini and a New York steak marinated in Kentucky bourbon. Walls are adorned with celebrity photos.
Cards: AE, MC, VI. ✖

PERIKLIS RESTAURANT **Lunch:** $8-$9 **Dinner:** $10-$18 **Phone:** 250/386-3313 ⑦
◆◆ **Location:** Just e of Wharf St. 531 Yates St V8W 1K7. **Hours:** 11:30 am-3 & 5-11:30 pm, Sat & Sun 5 pm-11
Greek pm. Closed: 1/1, 12/25 & lunch on holidays. **Reservations:** suggested. **Features:** No A/C; casual dress;
carryout; cocktails; fee for parking; a la carte. The Periklis features tasty authentic favorites—from tzatziki to
baklava—as well as steak, seafood and chicken. The cheerful, authentic ambience presents belly dancing performances at
dinner every night in season, weekends in the off-season. **Cards:** AE, MC, VI. ✖

PESCATORE'S FISH HOUSE & PIANO BAR **Dinner:** $18-$25 **Phone:** 250/385-4512 ㉜
◆◆ **Location:** Just e of the Inner Harbour; at Government St. 614 Humboldt St V8W 1A4. **Hours:** 4:30 pm-10
Seafood pm; to 11 pm 6/1-10/31. Closed: 1/1 & 12/25. **Reservations:** suggested. **Features:** casual dress; cocktails; a
la carte. Pescatore's is a chic bistro with excellent fresh seafood such as salmon Wellington and trout stuffed
with crab and brie, and great beverage choices such as espresso, cappuccino and martinis. This is hip and funky fine
dining, with live jazz on weekends. **Cards:** AE, DI, MC, VI. ✖

PLUTO'S **Lunch:** $7-$11 **Dinner:** $7-$11 **Phone:** 250/385-4747 ㉞
◆ **Location:** Corner of Cook and View sts. 1150 Cook St V8V 3Z9. **Hours:** 8 am-10 pm, Sun-11 pm. Closed:
Southwest 12/25. **Features:** No A/C; Sunday brunch; children's menu; health conscious menu; carryout; cocktails; a la
Mexican carte. You'll enjoy this funky-looking turquoise-and-pink art-deco structure that used to be a gas station. Their
menu features Southwest-style mesquite-grilled chicken, beef and fish burgers as well as a selection of
pastas, wraps and Mexican food. **Cards:** AE, MC, VI. ✖

SHAKESPEARE DINING ROOM **Lunch:** $7-$12 **Dinner:** $12-$25 **Phone:** 250/388-4353 ⑩
◆◆ **Location:** 4 km w via Esquimalt Rd (over the Johnson St Bridge), just s; in Olde England Inn. 429 Lampson
English St V9A 5Y9. **Hours:** 8 am-8:30 pm, Fri & Sat-9 pm. **Reservations:** suggested. **Features:** No A/C; Sunday
brunch; children's menu; cocktails; a la carte. Traditional English fare specializing in roasted prime rib with
Yorkshire pudding is offered at Shakespeare's. The distinctive atmosphere recreates a bygone era, with Olde English
antiques, and servers in period costumes. Visitors enjoy this restaurant. **Cards:** AE, DI, DS, MC, VI. ✖

SIX MILE PUB **Lunch:** $4-$10 **Dinner:** $4-$11 **Phone:** 250/478-3121 ㊱
◆ **Location:** Trans Canada Hwy 1, exit 10 (Colwood/Sook), 1 km s. 494 Island Hwy V9B 1H5. **Hours:** 11
Canadian am-11 pm, Sun-10 pm. Closed: 12/25. **Features:** casual dress; carryout; cocktails & lounge; a la carte. Built
in 1855, this restaurant is known as "BC's oldest working man's pub." They serve burgers, oysters, pot pies,
soups, sandwiches, and beer on tap. Pool tables and dartboards are part of the entertainment package. The minimum age
to enter pub is 19. **Cards:** DI, MC, VI.

SPINNAKERS BREW PUB & RESTAURANT **Lunch:** $6-$10 **Dinner:** $6-$16 **Phone:** 250/386-2739 ⑤
◆◆ **Location:** 2 km nw over Johnson St Bridge, just s. 308 Catherine St V9A 3S8. **Hours:** 7 am-11 pm. Closed:
Canadian 12/25. **Reservations:** suggested. **Features:** No A/C; children's menu; carryout; cocktails & lounge; a la
carte. Spinnakers is a fun, lively pub/restaurant/bakery featuring terrific breads, a wonderful mile-high apple
pie, good Cajun halibut burgers, homemade soups and a stand-up bar area. This is Canada's first in-house brewery, and
you can tour the brew house. **Cards:** AE, DI, MC, VI. *(See ad below)* ✖

(See map p. 525)

TAJ MAHAL   Lunch: $6-$10   Dinner: $12-$22   Phone: 250/383-4662   ⑥
(AA)   Location: Between Douglas and Government sts. 679 Herald St V8W 1S8. Hours: 11:30 am-2 & 5-10 pm,
◆◆   Sat noon-2:30 & 5:30-11 pm, Sun 5 pm-10 pm. Closed: 12/25. Reservations: suggested. Features: casual
East Indian   dress; carryout; cocktails; street parking; a la carte. The menu at Taj Mahal features a nice selection of
traditional favorites such as peach chutney and lamb over saffron rice. Dishes are spiced to order from mild
to fiery hot. The ambience is informal and friendly, and the service is prompt and attentive. Cards: AE, DI,
DS, MC, VI.   ⊠

TOPO'S RISTORANTE   Lunch: $6-$12   Dinner: $8-$23   Phone: 250/383-1212   ⑯
◆◆   Location: 2.3 km n on Douglas St (Hwy 1), just s of Finlayson St. 2950 Douglas St V8T 4N4. Hours: 11:30
Italian   am-2:30 & 5-10 pm, Fri-11 pm, Sat 5 pm-11 pm, Sun 5 pm-9 pm. Closed: 1/1 & 12/25. Features: No A/C;
casual dress; senior's menu; cocktails; a la carte. Topo's features excellent homemade pasta and freshly
prepared specialties. The menu offers a wide variety of half-portions for lighter appetites and many vegetarian dishes. The
restaurant has a cheerful, informal atmosphere. Smoking on outdoor deck only. Smoke free premises. Cards: AE, DI,
MC, VI.   ⊠

VICTORIA HARBOUR HOUSE RESTAURANT   Lunch: $8-$13   Dinner: $12-$25   Phone: 250/386-1244   ⑭
(AA)   Location: Corner of Oswego and Quebec sts. 607 Oswego St V8V 4W9. Hours: 11:30 am-11:30 pm,
◆◆◆   11/1-3/31 from 5 pm. Reservations: suggested. Features: No A/C; early bird specials; cocktails; a la carte.
Steak and   Victoria Harbour House is a popular and long-established restaurant located in the Inner Harbour area. The
Seafood   menu specializes in nicely prepared steak, seafood and chicken dishes. This informal dining experience is
complemented by the friendly server staff. Cards: AE, MC, VI.   ⊠

───────── *The following restaurants have not been inspected by AAA* ─────────
but are listed for your information only.

BOWMAN'S RIB HOUSE   Phone: 250/385-5380
[fyi]   Not inspected. Location: 825 Burdett Ave. Features: Located in a landmark hotel, built in 1897, this
family-owned rib house has been in business since 1953. Mouth watering king/queen size spare ribs are
served with a salad or potato, veggies and garlic bread. Families are always welcome.

CAPITAL STEAKHOUSE   Phone: 250/920-4846
[fyi]   Not inspected. Location: 619 Courtney St. Features: Created in the tradition of quality steakhouses, only
the very best steak is served here. One of Victoria's most extensive wine lists complements your dining
experience. Reservations are recommended.

CHEZ DANIEL RESTAURANT   Phone: 250/592-7424
[fyi]   Not inspected. Location: In Oak Bay, just w of Beach Dr. 2524 Estevan at Beach Ave V8R 2S7.
Features: One of Victoria's finest French restaurants and tucked away in Oak Bay. The expansive menu is
rich and wide, ranging from salmon in vermouth and cream sauce to duck in a fine chestnut sauce. The bisque is wonderful!
Plan to make an evening of it.

HARBOUR CANOE CLUB   Phone: 250/361-1940
[fyi]   Not inspected. Location: 450 Swift St. Features: This is a full service marine brew pub with over 150 seats
and sun-drenched patio overlooking the working harbor and marina. The Canoe Club offers traditional pub
fare, ales and lagers.

KOTO JAPANESE RESTAURANT   Phone: 250/382-1514
[fyi]   Not inspected. Location: 510 Fort St. Features: This authentic Japanese restaurant is noted for its grace
and charm. You can dine in private tatami rooms or the open dining room. The menu is composed of
tempura, teriyaki steak, sukiyaki or ginger pork, with an extensive sushi bar.

PABLO'S   Phone: 250/388-4255
[fyi]   Not inspected. Location: 225 Quebec St. Features: In a magnificent Victorian home, the entrees have had
the locals praising this French restaurant for over 20 years. Start the evening with a wide range of hors
d'oeuvres. Candlelight are dinners prepared at your table.

RESTAURANT MATISSE   Phone: 250/480-0883
[fyi]   Not inspected. Location: Corner Yates and Wharf sts. 512 Yates St V8W 1K8. Features: Relax and enjoy
authentic French cuisine at its best. Savor the fresh bread, rack of lamb, duck, rabbit, seafood and possibly
the best creme brulee in the world. A profusion of fresh flowers and soft lighting provide a perfect Parisian ambience.

THAI SIAM RESTAURANT   Phone: 250/383-9911
[fyi]   Not inspected. Location: Between Government & Wharf. 512 Fort St. Features: Located along the beautiful
Inner Harbour, this eatery has some of the finest Thai cuisine in the city. Try the ample portions of melt in
your mouth satay with special peanut sauce, Tom Yum Koong, a Thai national favorite, red and green curry dishes.

YUEN'S CHINESE   Phone: 250/382-8812
[fyi]   Not inspected. Location: 866 Yates St. Features: The MSG-free family recipes are featured in this eatery's
15-item, high-quality lunch buffet and in the 184-item dinner buffet.

The Victoria Vicinity

MALAHAT pop. 3,200

—— LODGINGS ——

THE AERIE RESORT

(CAA)	6/2-10/1	1P: $250-$325	2P: $250-$325	XP: $35
◆◆◆◆	4/14-6/1 & 10/2-2/28	1P: $195-$255	2P: $195-$255	XP: $35
Country Inn	3/1-4/13	1P: $145-$195	2P: $145-$195	XP: $35

Phone: (250)743-7115

Location: 32 km n of Victoria off Trans Canada 1, use Spectacle Lake turn off, then follow signs. 600 Ebadora Ln V0R 2L0 (PO Box 108). Fax: 250/743-4766. **Terms:** [BP] meal plan; age restrictions may apply; 7 day cancellation notice; cancellation fee imposed; package plans. **Facility:** 23 rooms. Luxury retreat perched in the mountains for spectacular views over the ocean. Decor is elegant and rather fanciful, with rococo furnishings and soft pastel colors. Helicopter pad for high-flying travellers. 16 suites with fireplace & whirlpool; 2 stories; interior corridors; designated smoking area; mountain view; heated pool, sauna, whirlpools; 1 tennis court. **Dining:** Dining room; 5:30 pm-9:30 pm; open breakfast & lunch for inn guests only; $25-$29; restaurant, see separate listing; entertainment. **Services:** Fee: massage. **Recreation:** spa services. **All Rooms:** extended cable TV, honor bars. **Cards:** AE, DI, MC, VI.

MALAHAT BUNGALOWS MOTEL

(CAA) (SAVE)	6/1-9/30	1P: $62-$100	2P: $125	XP: $10	D12
◆◆	3/1-5/31 & 10/1-2/28	1P: $50-$80	2P: $100	XP: $10	D12
Cottage				

Phone: (250)478-3011

Location: On Trans Canada Hwy 1 (Malahat Dr), 26 km n of Victoria. V0R 2L0 (PO Box 48). Fax: 250/478-3011. **Terms:** Weekly & monthly rates avail, off season; 3 day cancellation notice; cancellation fee imposed; pets, $6 extra charge. **Facility:** 18 rooms. Located about 1/2 hour drive from Victoria. Individual style bungalows featuring an older, but quaint, style decor. 8 units feature wood burning fireplace. Some bungalows are located close to the hwy. 5 two-bedroom units. 1 story; exterior corridors; whirlpool, small above ground pool; playground. **Dining:** Restaurant nearby. **All Rooms:** combo or shower baths, extended cable TV. **Some Rooms:** 11 kitchens. **Cards:** MC, VI. **Special Amenities:** Free room upgrade (subject to availability with advanced reservations).** (See color ad p 534)

—— RESTAURANTS ——

THE AERIE DINING ROOM

Dinner: $29-$35

(CAA)	
◆◆◆◆	
Nouvelle French	

Phone: 250/743-7115

Location: 32 km n of Victoria off Trans Canada 1, use Spectacle Lake turn off, then follow signs; in The Aerie Resort. 600 Ebadora Ln V0R 2L0. **Hours:** 5:30 pm-9:30 pm. **Reservations:** suggested. **Features:** dressy casual; cocktails; a la carte. This restaurant features formal dining and a Northwest-influenced cuisine with fresh local ingredients. A seven-course meal at $65 per person is available. The unusual location in a mountain resort offers outstanding views from a comfortable setting. Smoke free premises. **Cards:** AE, DI, MC, VI.

MALAHAT MOUNTAIN INN

Lunch: $6-$13   **Dinner:** $8-$20

◆◆	
Regional Canadian	

Phone: 250/478-1944

Location: On Trans Canada Hwy 1, 26 km n of Victoria. 265 Trans Canada Hwy V0R 2L0. **Hours:** 11 am-9:30 pm. Closed: 12/25. **Reservations:** suggested. **Features:** No A/C; children's menu; senior's menu; cocktails; a la carte. This restaurant offers gourmet dining in a relaxed setting. It's perched on a hill with a stunning view of the mountains and ocean. The menu displays a Pacific Northwest influence on seafood such as the coconut-crusted prawns. Presentation is exceptional. **Cards:** AE, MC, VI.

SAANICHTON pop. 14,600

—— LODGINGS ——

QUALITY INN WADDLING DOG

◆◆	7/1-9/30	1P: $99-$129	2P: $109-$129	XP: $10	F18
Motor Inn	5/1-6/30 & 10/1-2/28	1P: $79-$89	2P: $79-$89	XP: $10	F18
	3/1-4/30	1P: $69-$79	2P: $69-$79	XP: $10	F18

Phone: (250)652-1146

Location: Corner of Hwy 17 and Mt Newton Crossroad. 2476 Mt Newton Crossroad V8M 2B8. Fax: 250/652-4946. **Terms:** [CP] meal plan; cancellation fee imposed; pets, $5 extra charge. **Facility:** 30 rooms. Named after "John" the resident basset hound, the waddling dog features a unique design replicating an "Old English Tudor Manor". Beer and wine shoppe has wide selection of local BC beverages. Close to airport and both ferry's. 3 stories; interior corridors. **Cards:** AE, CB, MC, VI.

SUPER 8 VICTORIA/SAANICHTON

◆◆	6/1-9/15	1P: $90	2P: $100	XP: $6	F12
Motel	9/16-2/28	1P: $50-$70	2P: $50-$70	XP: $6	F12
	4/16-5/31	1P: $70	2P: $70	XP: $6	F12
	3/1-4/15	1P: $50	2P: $60	XP: $6	F12

Phone: (250)652-6888

Location: Just e of Hwy 17. 2477 Mt Newton Crossroad V8M 2B7. Fax: 250/652-6800. **Terms:** [CP] meal plan; pets. **Facility:** 51 rooms. Modern economy style lodging. Pleasant decor with the single bed rooms featuring a comfy reclining chair. Close to airport and both BC and Washington state ferry's. 2 stories; interior corridors. **Some Rooms:** Fee: refrigerators, microwaves. **Cards:** AE, DI, DS, JC, MC, VI.

SIDNEY pop. 10,700

─── LODGINGS ───

BEST WESTERN EMERALD ISLE MOTOR INN

Phone: (250)656-4441

7/1-9/15	1P: $119-$149	2P: $129-$169	XP: $10	F12
5/1-6/30	1P: $99-$109	2P: $109-$129	XP: $10	F12
9/16-2/28	1P: $85-$99	2P: $89-$109	XP: $10	F12
3/1-4/30	1P: $79-$99	2P: $89-$99	XP: $10	F12

Motor Inn
Location: Just e of Hwy 17 on Beacon Ave, exit Sidney; 5 km s of Swartz Bay Ferry. 2306 Beacon Ave V8L 1X2. Fax: 250/655-1351. **Terms:** Weekly & monthly rates avail, off season; cancellation fee imposed; pets, $20 extra charge. **Facility:** 65 rooms. Super large guest rooms that gives that comfortable spacious feel, all are nicely decorated. Conveniently located to the airport, BC ferry and Washington state ferry. 6 suites with kitchen $115-$260 for up to 4 persons; 8 whirlpool rooms, $149-$275; 2 stories; interior corridors; sauna, whirlpool. **Dining:** Restaurant; 7 am-9 pm; $5-$10; cocktails. **All Rooms:** extended cable TV. **Cards:** AE, DI, DS, MC, VI. **Special Amenities:** Early check-in/late check-out and free room upgrade (subject to availability with advanced reservations). (See ad p 527)

CEDARWOOD INN & SUITES

Phone: (250)656-5551

6/15-9/30	1P: $99-$190	2P: $99-$190	XP: $15
3/1-6/14	1P: $79-$150	2P: $79-$150	XP: $15
10/1-2/28	1P: $69-$135	2P: $69-$135	XP: $15

Motel
Location: From Hwy 17, just e on McTavish Rd, then 1.4 km s on Lochside Dr. 9522 Lochside Dr V8L 1N8. Fax: 250/656-1551. **Terms:** Weekly & monthly rates avail, off season; cancellation fee imposed; small pets only, $10 extra charge. **Facility:** 42 rooms. Along a quiet residential neighborhood that's directly across the street from the ocean waterfront and close to the Washington state ferry. A wonderfully maintained listing featuring cedar wood decor, large rooms and a few cozy cottages. 1 two-bedroom unit with full kitchen, $160 for up to 2 persons; 4 whirlpool rooms; 2 stories; exterior corridors. **All Rooms:** extended cable TV. **Some Rooms:** 6 efficiencies, 34 kitchens. **Cards:** AE, DI, MC, VI.

THE LATCH COUNTRY INN

Phone: (250)656-6622

3/1-3/31	1P: $99-$269	2P: $99-$269	XP: $25
6/16-9/30	1P: $140-$250	2P: $140-$250	XP: $30
4/1-6/15 & 10/1-2/28	1P: $120-$180	2P: $120-$180	XP: $30

Classic Country Inn
Location: From Beacon Ave, 2 km n on Resthaven Dr, then 1 km e. 2328 Harbour Rd V8L 2P8. Fax: 250/656-6212. **Terms:** Age restrictions may apply; 14 day cancellation notice; cancellation fee imposed; 2 night min stay, weekends 6/1-9/15; package plans. **Facility:** 7 rooms. **Historic.** In 1926, famous architect Samual MacLure designed this remarkable inn. The exterior features fir slags with the bark still left on. Porches and balconies built with tree trunks of various sizes. Wonderfully appointed guest rooms. 2 stories; interior corridors; designated smoking area. **Dining:** Dining room; 5 pm-8:30 pm; closed Tues; $15-$20; breakfast for inn guests only, 8:30-10 am. **All Rooms:** combo or shower baths, extended cable TV. **Cards:** AE, MC, VI.

VICTORIA AIRPORT TRAVELODGE SIDNEY

Phone: (250)656-1176

6/1-9/30	1P: $115-$125	2P: $145-$165	XP: $10	F15
10/1-2/28	1P: $69-$79	2P: $79-$99		
3/1-5/31	1P: $62-$69	2P: $69-$99	XP: $10	F15

Motel
Location: Just e of Hwy 17; 5 km s of Swartz Bay Ferry. 2280 Beacon Ave V8L 1X1. Fax: 250/656-7344. **Terms:** Weekly & monthly rates avail, off season; 14 day cancellation notice; small pets only. **Facility:** 52 rooms. An older property featuring nice sized guest rooms with a remodeled decor. Many ground floor rooms open out to pool/courtyard area. Conveniently located to the airport, BC ferry and Washington state ferry. 2 stories; interior corridors; heated pool. **All Rooms:** extended cable TV. **Cards:** AE, CB, DI, DS, MC, VI. **Special Amenities:** Free breakfast and free newspaper.

─── RESTAURANTS ───

BLUE PETER PUB

Lunch: $6-$15   **Dinner:** $6-$15   **Phone:** 250/656-4551

Canadian
Location: From Beacon Ave, 2 km n on Resthaven Dr to Harbour Rd, then just e. 2270 Harbour Rd V8L 2P6. **Hours:** 11:30 am-11 pm, Fri & Sat-midnight. Closed: 12/25. **Features:** No A/C; casual dress; cocktails; a la carte. This pub located along the wharf has a great view of the harbor. Fresh seafood, steak and pasta are featured, and the laid-back environment offers sections: one for families with kids, one with a fireplace, and one with pool tables. Outdoor patio too. **Cards:** MC, VI.

DEEP COVE CHALET

Lunch: $15-$22   **Dinner:** $25-$45   **Phone:** 250/656-3541

French
Location: From Hwy 17, Wain Rd/Deep Cove exit, 1 km w on Wain Rd, 3 km nw on Tatlow Rd. 11190 Chalet Rd V8L 4R4. **Hours:** Noon-2:30 & 5:30-10 pm, Sunday brunch 11:30 am-2 pm. Closed: Mon & 12/24. **Reservations:** suggested. **Features:** No A/C; casual dress; cocktails; a la carte. Visitors and locals alike enjoy this delightful restaurant hidden away in a setting that offers a spectacular view of the inlet. The menu features country French cuisine plus fresh seafood, lamb, ostrich, caribou, wild boar, and a nice variety of wines. **Cards:** AE, MC, VI.

SOOKE

——— LODGINGS ———

MARKHAM HOUSE BED & BREAKFAST
Phone: (250)642-7542

(CAA) SAVE

◆◆◆

Bed & Breakfast

7/1-9/30	1P: $105-$195	2P: $115-$195	XP: $25
12/16-2/28	1P: $95-$179	2P: $105-$179	XP: $25
3/1-6/30 & 10/1-12/15	1P: $85-$169	2P: $95-$169	XP: $25

Location: 10 km e on Hwy 14. (1853 Connie Rd, VICTORIA, V9C 4C2). Fax: 250/642-7538. **Terms:** [BP] meal plan; age restrictions may apply. **Facility:** 4 rooms. Extensive landscaped grounds with trails and ponds. Afternoon tea at arrival. Feather beds and duvets. 3 rooms in the house and 1 private cottage with kitchenette, deck and whirlpool. 2 whirlpool rooms; 2 stories; interior corridors; smoke free premises. **All Rooms:** combo or shower baths. **Some Rooms:** color TV. **Cards:** AE, CB, DI, DS, JC, MC, VI. **Special Amenities: Early check-in/late check-out and free breakfast.**

OCEAN WILDERNESS COUNTRY INN
Phone: (250)646-2116

(CAA) SAVE

◆◆

Bed & Breakfast

5/16-10/15	1P: $90-$175	2P: $95-$180	XP: $15 F
3/1-5/15 & 10/16-2/28	1P: $75-$120	2P: $85-$145	XP: $15 F

Location: 14 km w on Hwy 14. 109 W Coast Rd V0S 1N0. Fax: 250/646-2317. **Terms:** [BP] meal plan; cancellation fee imposed; package plans; pets, $10 extra charge. **Facility:** 9 rooms. Quiet location overlooking ocean, pleasant rooms varied size and decor. A few with ocean view. Private trail to secluded stone beach. 2 stories; interior/exterior corridors; designated smoking area; whirlpool. **Services:** Fee: massage. **Cards:** AE, MC, VI. **Special Amenities: Free room upgrade (subject to availability with advanced reservations).**

SOOKE HARBOUR HOUSE
Phone: (250)642-3421

(CAA) SAVE

◆◆◆

Country Inn

5/1-10/31		2P: $280-$512	XP: $35 F12
3/1-4/30 & 11/1-2/28		2P: $175-$420	XP: $35 F12

Location: 2 km w on Hwy 14. 1528 Whiffen Spit Rd V0S 1N0. Fax: 250/642-6988. **Terms:** [BP] & [CP] meal plans; cancellation fee imposed; package plans; pets, $20 extra charge. **Facility:** 28 rooms. A splendid little "inn" overlooking the ocean and the mist shrouded mountains of Washington State in the distance. Each room has wood burning fireplace, terrace or balcony. A colorful edible flower garden adds to view. 10 whirlpool rooms; 4 stories; interior/exterior corridors; designated smoking area; beach. **Dining:** Restaurant; open for dinner 5:30-9:30 pm; $24-$35; cocktails. **Services:** gift shop. Fee: massage. **All Rooms:** combo or shower baths. **Cards:** AE, DI, JC, MC, VI. **Special Amenities: Free breakfast and free newspaper.**

This ends listings for the Victoria Vicinity.
The following page resumes the alphabetical listings of cities in British Columbia.

WASA pop. 100

—— LODGING ——

WASA LAKESIDE B & B
◆◆
Bed & Breakfast
4/1-10/31   1P: $125   2P: $150
Phone: (250)422-3688
XP: $25
Location: Hwy 93 and 95, e at Wasa Lake Provincial Park, just s on Poplar Rd, then just e following signs. Spruce Rd V0B 2K0 (Box 122). Fax: 250/422-3551. **Terms:** Open 4/1-10/31; [BP] meal plan; check-in 4 pm; 30 day cancellation notice. **Facility:** 4 rooms. Casual, fun-loving, young family ambiance. 2 units in main home, 2 others in separate cabin by the lake with yet another cabin with private, detached bathrooms. Beach access, water activities. 1-3 stories; interior corridors; smoke free premises; boat dock. **Services:** winter plug-ins. **Recreation:** swimming, canoeing, paddleboats, windsurfing; bicycles. Fee: sailboating, waterskiing. **All Rooms:** combo, shower or tub baths. **Some Rooms:** color TV. **Cards:** MC, VI.

WESTBANK

—— LODGINGS ——

CHATEAU CHRISTIAN LAURENN BED & BREAKFAST
◆◆◆
Bed & Breakfast
All Year   1P: $119   2P: $119
Phone: (250)768-9695
XP: $25
Location: 1.5 km s on Hwy 97, 2.3 km w on Glenrosa. 3542 Ranch Rd V4T 1A1. Fax: 250/768-9695. **Terms:** [BP] meal plan; age restrictions may apply; 3 day cancellation notice. **Facility:** 2 rooms. Located along a hillside in a quiet residential neighborhood, offering panoramic views of Okanagan Lake, city and surrounding mountains. Private guest entrance. Just a short drive to downtown Kelowna. 2 stories; interior corridors; smoke free premises. **Cards:** VI.

HOLIDAY INN
◆◆◆
Motel
6/1-9/30   1P: $109
10/1-11/30   1P: $86
3/1-5/31   1P: $75-$82
12/1-2/28   1P: $75
Phone: (250)768-8879
XP: $10   F18
XP: $10   F18
XP: $10   F18
Location: 4 km n of Coquihalla connector on Hwy 97. 2569 Dobbin Rd V4T 2J6. Fax: 250/768-8891. **Terms:** 7 day cancellation notice; package plans; pets, $10 fee. **Facility:** 78 rooms. Management can arrange vineyard tours. All rooms with iron and ironing board. 2 two-bedroom units. 3 stories; interior corridors; heated pool. **Services:** winter plug-ins. **Some Rooms:** 2 kitchens. **Cards:** AE, CB, DI, DS, JC, MC, VI.

WICKLOW BED & BREAKFAST
◆◆◆
Bed & Breakfast
7/1-8/31   1P: $80   2P: $90
3/1-6/30 & 9/1-10/31   1P: $70   2P: $80
11/1-2/28   1P: $60   2P: $70
Phone: (250)768-1330
XP: $20
XP: $20
XP: $20
Location: From Hwy 97, 6 km s on Boucherie Rd, then just e. 1454 Green Bay Rd V4T 2B8. Fax: 250/768-1335. **Terms:** [BP] meal plan; 21 day cancellation notice; cancellation fee imposed. **Facility:** 4 rooms. A charming waterfront home on Okanagan Lake offering fine views of the lake, vineyards and mountains. English landscaped garden extends to private sandy beach and boat dock. 2 stories; interior/exterior corridors; smoke free premises; boat dock. **Recreation:** swimming. **Cards:** MC, VI.

—— RESTAURANT ——

AGAPI'S GREEK TAVERNA
◆◆
Greek
Lunch: $6-$10   **Dinner:** $9-$31   **Phone:** 250/768-1231
Location: Centre. 180-2300 Carrington Rd V4T 2N6. **Hours:** 11:30 am-2 & 5-9 pm, Sat 11 am-11 pm, Sun 10 am-9 pm. Closed: 12/25. **Reservations:** suggested. **Features:** casual dress; Sunday brunch; cocktails; a la carte. Agapi's menu offers a good selection of dishes, a cheery decor, wicker chairs and an outdoor terrace in season. The fresh baked Greek flat bread dipped in tzatziki is a treat! Try the fine-grind Greek coffee, but don't stir the grounds on the bottom. **Cards:** AE, DI, MC, VI.

WEST VANCOUVER —See Vancouver p. 518.

WHISTLER pop. 7,200

—— LODGINGS ——

ALTA VISTA CHALET INN
◆◆
Bed & Breakfast
3/1-4/15   1P: $140-$150   2P: $150-$160
11/25-2/28   1P: $115-$140   2P: $125-$160
4/16-11/24   1P: $90-$110   2P: $100-$130
Phone: (604)932-4900
XP: $30   F10
XP: $30   F10
XP: $25   F10
Location: From Hwy 99, w on Hillcrest Dr (Alta Vista), n on Alpine Crest, then w. 3229 Archibald Way V0N 1B3. Fax: 604/932-4933. **Terms:** [BP] meal plan; cancellation fee imposed. **Facility:** 8 rooms. Alpine style chalet situated in a wooded and quiet residential neighborhood close to Alta Lake. Guest rooms feature that "at home" feeling. 3 stories; no elevator; interior corridors; designated smoking area. **Some Rooms:** color TV. **Cards:** AE, DS, JC, MC, VI.

THE BLACKCOMB LODGE

CAA SAVE	12/26-2/28	1P: $240-$600	2P: $240-$600	XP: $35	F12
◆ ◆	11/23-12/25	1P: $175-$510	2P: $175-$510	XP: $35	F12
Motor Inn	3/1-4/26	1P: $145-$320	2P: $145-$320	XP: $15	F12
	4/27-11/22	1P: $119-$199	2P: $119-$199	XP: $15	F12

Location: From Hwy 99, just e on Village Gate Blvd (Whistler Village), then just s. 4220 Gateway Dr V0N 1B4. Fax: 604/932-6826. **Terms:** Check-in 4 pm; 45 day cancellation notice, 30 day in winter; cancellation fee imposed; package plans. **Facility:** 72 rooms. Located in the heart of Whistler Village. These studio-type apartments combine the sleeping and cooking facilities into 1 room. Some of the studios feature a loft with sleeping area. 3 stories; interior corridors; designated smoking area; heated pool, sauna, whirlpool. Fee: parking. **Dining:** Restaurant nearby. **All Rooms:** extended cable TV. **Some Rooms:** 66 kitchens. **Cards:** AE, MC, VI. **Special Amenities: Free room upgrade and preferred room (each subject to availability with advanced reservations).**

CANADIAN PACIFIC CHATEAU WHISTLER RESORT

◆ ◆ ◆ ◆	3/1-4/15 & 12/16-2/28	1P: $349-$449	2P: $349-$449	XP: $30	F18
Hotel	4/16-12/15	1P: $249-$399	2P: $249-$399	XP: $30	F18

Location: From Hwy 99, 1 km e on Lorimer Rd, then just w on Blackcomb Way. 4599 Chateau Blvd V0N 1B4. Fax: 604/938-2055. **Terms:** Check-in 4 pm; 45 day cancellation notice; cancellation fee imposed; package plans; small pets only, $20 extra charge. **Facility:** 558 rooms. An inspiring chateau structure, just steps from the base of Blackcomb Mountain. Gracious public areas. Rooms range from standard rooms to larger suites. 12 stories; interior corridors; 18 holes golf; 2 heated pools; 3 tennis courts. Fee: parking. **Dining:** entertainment. **Services:** gift shop. Fee: massage. **Recreation:** hiking trails, jogging. Fee: bicycles. **All Rooms:** safes, honor bars. **Cards:** AE, DI, DS, JC, MC, VI.

CHALET LUISE

◆ ◆ ◆	12/20-1/6		2P: $220-$280	XP: $25	F11
Bed &	3/1-4/8		2P: $170-$210	XP: $25	F11
Breakfast	1/7-2/28		2P: $130-$210	XP: $25	F11
	4/9-12/19		2P: $100-$155	XP: $25	F11

Location: From Hwy 99, exit Nancy Green Dr, follow to Ambassador Crescent. 7461 Ambassador Crescent V0N 1B0 (PO Box 352). Fax: 604/938-1531. **Terms:** [BP] meal plan; age restrictions may apply; 14 day cancellation notice, in winter, 14 day in summer; cancellation fee imposed; package plans. **Facility:** 8 rooms. A charming alpine chalet situated in a quiet residential area and featuring friendly Swiss hospitality. Guest rooms feature pine furniture and down comforters. 2 honeymoon suites with gas fireplace. 2 stories; interior corridors; designated smoking area. **All Rooms:** combo or shower baths. **Cards:** MC, VI.

DELTA WHISTLER RESORT

CAA SAVE	12/22-2/28		2P: $229	XP: $30	F18
◆ ◆ ◆	3/1-4/24		2P: $219	XP: $30	F18
Hotel	4/25-12/21		2P: $139	XP: $30	F18

Location: From Hwy 99, follow Whistler Way. 4050 Whistler Way V0N 1B4. Fax: 604/932-7332. **Terms:** Check-in 4 pm; 30 day cancellation notice, in winter, 7 day in summer; cancellation fee imposed; package plans; pets, $30 extra charge. **Facility:** 292 rooms. Property offers very large guest rooms, many with balcony. In the heart of Whistler Village and opposite driving range. 86 whirlpool rooms; 8 stories; interior corridors; heated pool, steamroom, whirlpools; 2 lighted tennis courts. Fee: parking. **Dining:** Restaurant; 6:30 am-10 pm; $14-$20; cocktails. **Services:** gift shop. Fee: massage. **Recreation:** Fee: ski; bicycles. **All Rooms:** extended cable TV, honor bars. **Some Rooms:** 98 kitchens. **Cards:** AE, DI, JC, MC, VI.

DELTA WHISTLER VILLAGE SUITES

CAA SAVE	12/15-1/7	1P: $315-$469	2P: $315-$469	XP: $30	F18
◆ ◆ ◆	1/8-2/28	1P: $299-$439	2P: $299-$439	XP: $30	F18
Suite Hotel	3/1-4/23	1P: $220-$310	2P: $220-$310	XP: $30	F18
	4/24-12/14	1P: $160-$237	2P: $160-$237	XP: $30	F18

Location: From Hwy 99, just e on Village Gate Blvd, then just n on Northlands Blvd, just e. 4308 Main St V0N 1B4. Fax: 604/938-6335. **Terms:** Check-in 4 pm; 14 day cancellation notice, in summer, 45 day in winter; cancellation fee imposed; package plans; small pets only, $15 extra charge. **Facility:** 210 rooms. This full service, suite hotel, features a range of accommodations from standard type rooms with microwave and fridge to larger 2-bedroom units with full stove and fridge. In the heart of Whistler Village. 75 two-bedroom units. 6 stories; interior corridors; heated pool, sauna, steamrooms, whirlpool. Fee: parking. **Dining:** Restaurant; 8 am-11 pm; $12-$20; cocktails. **Recreation:** Fee: ski avail; bicycles. **All Rooms:** extended cable TV. **Some Rooms:** 184 kitchens, color TV. **Cards:** AE, DI, JC, MC, VI.

THE DURLACHER HOF ALPINE INN

CAA SAVE	12/18-2/28	1P: $129-$159	2P: $179-$259		
◆ ◆ ◆	3/1-3/31	1P: $129-$159	2P: $179-$259	XP: $30	D12
Bed &	4/1-12/17	1P: $99-$129	2P: $139-$199		

Location: 1.5 km n on Hwy 99. 7055 Nesters Rd V0N 1B0 (PO Box 1125). Fax: 604/938-1980. **Terms:** [BP] meal plan; age restrictions may apply; 30 day cancellation notice; 2 night min stay, weekends; package plans. **Facility:** 8 rooms. Traditional Austrian hospitality in authentic alpine pension. Guest rooms feature hand carved pine furniture and goose down duvets. Most rooms with open balcony. Meticulous housekeeping. 4 whirlpool rooms, $199-$259; 3 stories, no elevator; interior corridors; smoke free premises; sauna, whirlpool. **All Rooms:** combo or shower baths. **Cards:** MC, VI. **Special Amenities: Free breakfast and free room upgrade (subject to availability with advanced reservations).**

EDELWEISS PENSION

Phone: 604/932-3641

Bed & Breakfast

10/1-2/28	1P: $79-$135	2P: $99-$145	XP: $20	F6
3/1-4/30	1P: $125	2P: $145	XP: $20	F6
6/1-9/30	1P: $89	2P: $99-$129	XP: $20	F6
5/1-5/31	1P: $75	2P: $89-$119	XP: $20	F6

Location: 1.5 km n on Hwy 99, 1 km e. 7162 Nancy Green Dr V0N 1B0 (PO Box 850). Fax: 604/938-1746. **Terms:** [BP] meal plan; 30 day cancellation notice; cancellation fee imposed; package plans. **Facility:** 8 rooms. Alpine style building modeled after the European pensions (country inn type accommodations found in Europe). Guest rooms are average in size and decor, but do offer a cozy nights sleep. Short drive to village and restaurants. 2 stories; interior corridors; designated smoking area. **Services:** area transportation; winter plug-ins. **All Rooms:** combo or shower baths. **Cards:** AE, MC, VI.

EDGEWATER LODGE

Phone: (604)932-0688

Lodge

All Year   1P: $105-$199   2P: $105-$199   XP: $25   F8

Location: 4 km n of Whistler Village via Hwy 99, e on Alpine Way. 8841 Hwy 99 V0N 1B0 (PO Box 369). Fax: 604/932-0686. **Terms:** [ECP] meal plan; age restrictions may apply; 14 day cancellation notice; cancellation fee imposed; package plans; small pets only, $20 extra charge. **Facility:** 12 rooms. A contemporary style lodge located on the shores of Green Lake. Guest rooms offer average sized accommodations. All rooms have a view of the lake with some rooms offering adjoining rooms with queen sofa beds and private patio. 1 story; exterior corridors; designated smoking area; whirlpool. **Dining:** Dining room; dinner for guests & public 6 pm-9 pm, reservations recommended; $15-$25; cocktails. **Services:** Fee: area transportation; ski hills & village. **Recreation:** fishing. Fee: kayaking; horseback riding. Rental: boats, canoes, paddleboats. **All Rooms:** combo or shower baths, extended cable TV. **Cards:** AE, MC, VI. **Special Amenities: Free breakfast.**

GLACIER LODGE

Phone: (604)938-3455

Condominium

12/16-1/3	1P: $149-$259	2P: $149-$259	XP: $20	F12
1/4-2/28	1P: $179-$209	2P: $179-$209	XP: $20	F12
3/1-4/30	1P: $139-$209	2P: $139-$209	XP: $20	F12
5/1-12/15	1P: $119-$149	2P: $119-$149	XP: $20	F12

Location: From Hwy 99, 1 km e on Lorimer Rd, then just w on Blackcomb Way. 4573 Chateau Blvd V0N 1B0 (Box 1044). Fax: 604/932-2176. **Terms:** Check-in 4 pm; package plans. **Facility:** 105 rooms. Located in Whistler's upper village at the base of Blackcomb mountain. Featuring standard hotel rooms with no cooking facilities to studio units. 1- and 2-bedroom suites with cooking facilities. 8 two-bedroom units. 3 stories; interior corridors; heated pool. Fee: parking. **Some Rooms:** 85 kitchens. **Cards:** AE, DI, DS, JC, MC, VI. *(See ad below)*

THE HEARTHSTONE LODGE

Phone: (604)932-4161

Condominium

12/23-2/28	1P: $269-$655	2P: $269-$935	XP: $20	F12
3/1-4/6	1P: $259-$340	2P: $259-$475	XP: $20	F12
11/19-12/22	1P: $219-$290	2P: $219-$405	XP: $20	F12
4/7-11/18	1P: $110-$220	2P: $110-$310	XP: $20	F12

Location: Hwy 99, just e on Village Gate Blvd to Whistler Way. 4211 Sunshine Pl V0N 1B4. Fax: 604/932-6622. **Terms:** Check-in 4 pm; 45 day cancellation notice, in summer, 45 day in winter; cancellation fee imposed. **Facility:** 19 rooms. In the heart of Whistler Village. All units are very spacious, a few have in-room sauna, several have fireplace. 7 two-bedroom units. 3 stories, no elevator; interior corridors. **All Rooms:** kitchens. **Cards:** AE, MC, VI.

HOLIDAY INN SUNSPREE RESORT WHISTLER

Phone: (604)938-0878

Condominium

12/22-2/28	1P: $209-$550	2P: $209-$550	XP: $20	F18
3/1-4/2	1P: $239-$399	2P: $239-$399	XP: $20	F18
11/17-12/21	1P: $149-$299	2P: $149-$299	XP: $20	F18
4/3-11/16	1P: $109-$279	2P: $109-$279	XP: $20	F18

Location: From Hwy 99, just e on Village Gate Blvd. 4295 Blackcomb Way V0N 1B4. Fax: 604/938-9943. **Terms:** Check-in 4 pm; 30 day cancellation notice; cancellation fee imposed. **Facility:** 115 rooms. In the heart of Whistler Village. New concept in condo-style accommodations. Studio-style units feature murphy beds and queen-sized sofa bed, gas fireplace, with many featuring ensuite washer/dryer. 8 two-bedroom units. 2 one-bedroom & loft & 3 two-bedroom & loft, $195-$485. 5 two-bedroom units $230-$555; 115 whirlpool rooms; 6 stories; interior corridors; whirlpool. Fee: parking. **Dining:** Restaurant nearby. **All Rooms:** extended cable TV. **Some Rooms:** 25 efficiencies, 90 kitchens. **Cards:** AE, DI, DS, JC, MC, VI. **Special Amenities: Free local telephone calls and free newspaper.**

LE CHAMOIS
◆◆◆
Hotel

			Phone: (604)932-8700
12/16-1/3	1P: $199-$489	2P: $199-$489	XP: $20	F12
1/4-2/28	1P: $369-$429	2P: $369-$429	XP: $20	F12
3/1-4/30	1P: $299-$419	2P: $299-$419	XP: $20	F12
5/1-12/15	1P: $159-$199	2P: $159-$199	XP: $20	F12

Location: From Hwy 99, 1 km e on Lorimer Rd, then just w. 4557 Blackcomb Way V0N 1B0 (Box 1044). Fax: 604/905-2576. **Terms:** Check-in 4 pm; cancellation fee imposed; package plans. **Facility:** 54 rooms. Located right next to the Blackcomb mountain chair lifts, in Whistler's upper village. These very spacious guest rooms will surprise you; many feature a 2-bedroom, perfect for large families or groups. 1 two-bedroom unit, 6 three-bedroom units. 6 stories; interior corridors; heated pool. Fee: parking. **Cards:** AE, DI, DS, JC, MC, VI.

LORIMER RIDGE PENSION
◆◆◆
Bed &
Breakfast

			Phone: (604)938-9722
12/20-2/28	1P: $155-$175	2P: $175-$205	
3/1-4/1	1P: $130-$150	2P: $155-$175	
4/2-12/19	1P: $109-$139	2P: $129-$155	

Location: From Hwy 99, just ne on Lorimer Rd, (Whistler Cay). 6231 Piccolo Dr V0N1B6. Fax: 604/938-9155. **Terms:** [BP] meal plan; age restrictions may apply; 30 day cancellation notice, in winter, 14 day in summer; package plans. **Facility:** 8 rooms. A cozy mountain lodge modeled after the European pensions (similar to a country inn but they don't serve dinner). Situated in a quiet residential neighborhood. Pine wood furniture throughout. 2 stories; interior corridors; designated smoking area. **All Rooms:** shower baths. **Cards:** MC, VI.

THE PAN PACIFIC LODGE
CAA SAVE
◆◆◆
Hotel

			Phone: (604)905-2999
3/1-4/15	1P: $275-$325	2P: $275-$325	XP: $30	F18
11/23-2/28	1P: $190-$240	2P: $190-$240	XP: $30	F18
4/16-11/22	1P: $140-$170	2P: $140-$170	XP: $30	F18

Location: From Hwy 99, just e on Village Gate Blvd, then just s on Blackcomb Way. 4320 Sundial Cresent V0N 1B4. Fax: 604/905-2995. **Terms:** 7 day cancellation notice; cancellation fee imposed; package plans. **Facility:** 121 rooms. In Whistler Village and close to Whistler mountain. A luxurious property featuring lovely wood accents throughout the public area and guest rooms. Some rooms feature murphy bed, all have fireplace. Irish pub on site. 25 two-bedroom units. 8 stories; interior corridors; designated smoking area; steamroom, whirlpools. Fee: parking. **Dining:** 2 restaurants; 7 am-11 pm; $10-$13; cocktails. **Services:** area transportation, within Whistler Village. **All Rooms:** kitchens, extended cable TV, safes. **Some Rooms:** Fee: VCR. **Cards:** AE, DI, JC, MC, VI. **Special Amenities:** Free room upgrade (subject to availability with advanced reservations).

RADISSON BLACKCOMB SUITES
◆◆◆
Condominium

			Phone: (604)932-7222
12/16-1/3	1P: $149-$259	2P: $149-$259	XP: $20	F12
1/4-2/28	1P: $179-$209	2P: $179-$209	XP: $20	F12
3/1-4/30	1P: $139-$209	2P: $139-$209	XP: $20	F12
5/1-12/15	1P: $119-$149	2P: $119-$149	XP: $20	F12

Location: From Hwy 99, 1 km e on Lorimer Rd, then se on Blackcomb Way, then just w. 4800 Spearhead Dr V0N 1B0. Fax: 604/932-7100. **Terms:** Check-in 4 pm; cancellation fee imposed; package plans. **Facility:** 191 rooms. On Blackcomb mountain, these fully self-contained units feature loads of space to freely move around. Geared for families or small groups. 77 two-bedroom units. 5 stories; interior corridors; heated pool. Fee: parking. **All Rooms:** kitchens. **Cards:** AE, DI, JC, MC, VI.

RESIDENCE INN BY MARRIOTT
◆◆◆
Condominium

			Phone: (604)905-3400
12/16-1/3	1P: $199-$450	2P: $199-$450		
1/4-2/28	1P: $299-$349	2P: $299-$349	XP: $20	F12
3/1-4/30	1P: $249-$339	2P: $249-$339	XP: $20	F12
5/1-12/15	1P: $159-$199	2P: $159-$199	XP: $20	F12

Location: From Hwy 99, 1 km e on Lorimer Rd (Upper Village), just se on Blackcomb Way, then just w. 4899 Painted Cliff Rd V0N 1B4. Fax: 604/905-3432. **Terms:** [CP] meal plan; check-in 4 pm; cancellation fee imposed; package plans; pets, $20 extra charge. **Facility:** 186 rooms. Fully self-contained units with the ability to ski in and out of slopes. Choose from studio units, 1- or 2-bedroom units; all with gas fireplace. 6 stories; interior corridors; designated smoking area; heated pool. Fee: parking. **All Rooms:** kitchens. **Cards:** AE, DI, DS, JC, MC, VI. (See ad p 555)

SUMMIT LODGE

CAA SAVE ◆◆◆ Hotel

Phone: (604)932-2778

3/1-4/23	1P: $315-$435	2P: $315-$435	XP: $30	F18
11/23-2/28	1P: $170-$435	2P: $170-$435	XP: $30	F18
4/24-9/5	1P: $129-$259	2P: $129-$259	XP: $20	F18
9/6-11/22	1P: $129-$229	2P: $129-$229	XP: $20	F18

Location: From Hwy 99, just n on Village Gate Rd, then just w on Northland Blvd. 4359 Main St V0N 1B4. Fax: 604/932-2716. **Terms:** [CP] meal plan; check-in 4 pm; 30 day cancellation notice, in summer, 30 day in winter; cancellation fee imposed; package plans; small pets only, $30 extra charge. **Facility:** 81 rooms. Located in Whistler Village, featuring very modern and upscale style guest rooms. Rich wood accents throughout guest rooms and in public areas. Service oriented staff. 6 one-bedroom units with efficiency & gas fireplace; $225-$465; 5 stories; interior corridors; heated pool, sauna, whirlpool. Fee: parking. **Dining:** Restaurant; 7 am-11 pm; $9-$15; cocktails. **All Rooms:** efficiencies, extended cable TV. **Cards:** AE, DI, JC, MC, VI. **Special Amenities: Free breakfast.**

TANTALUS RESORT CONDOMINIUM LODGE

CAA SAVE ◆◆ Condominium

Phone: (604)932-4146

All Year   1P: $165-$310   2P: $165-$310

Location: Jct Hwy 99 & Whistler Way. 4200 Whistler Way V0N 1B4. Fax: 604/932-2405. **Terms:** Check-in 4 pm; 30 day cancellation notice; cancellation fee imposed; pets. **Facility:** 76 rooms. A family-oriented property with all units being 2-bedroom suites with living room, kitchen and bath. Located just outside Whistler Village but easy walking distance to shops and restaurants. 5 stories; interior corridors; heated pool, sauna, whirlpool; 2 tennis courts. Fee: parking. **Services:** area transportation, village in winter. **All Rooms:** extended cable TV. **Cards:** AE, DI, JC, MC, VI. **Special Amenities: Free local telephone calls and preferred room (subject to availability with advanced reservations).**

WHISTLER VILLAGE INN & SUITES

CAA SAVE ◆◆◆ Apartment

Phone: (604)932-4004

11/16-2/28	1P: $279	XP: $20	F12
3/1-3/25	1P: $269	XP: $20	F12
3/26-4/29	1P: $229	XP: $20	F12
4/30-11/15	1P: $159	XP: $20	F12

Location: From Hwy 99, just e on Village Gate Blvd (Whistler Village), then just s on Blackcomb Way to Sundial Pl. 4429 Sundial Pl V0N 1B4. Fax: 604/932-3487. **Terms:** [CP] meal plan; check-in 4 pm; 30 day cancellation notice, in winter, 14 day in summer; cancellation fee imposed. **Facility:** 87 rooms. Located in the heart of Whistler Village. These studio-type apartments combine the sleeping and cooking facilities into 1 room. Some rooms feature murphy beds, others have lofts with day beds in the living area. 3 stories; interior corridors; heated pool, saunas, whirlpools. **Dining:** Restaurant nearby. **All Rooms:** extended cable TV. **Some Rooms:** 65 kitchens. **Cards:** AE, MC, VI. **Special Amenities: Free breakfast and free newspaper.** *(See color ad below)*

WOODRUN LODGE
◆◆◆
Condominium

Phone: (604)905-0500

3/1-3/31	1P: $295-$445	2P: $295-$445	XP: $20	F6
4/1-4/30 & 11/19-2/28	1P: $240-$350	2P: $240-$350	XP: $20	F6
5/1-11/18	1P: $145-$185	2P: $145-$185	XP: $20	F6

Location: From Hwy 99, 1 km e on Lorimer Rd (Upper Village), just se on Blackcomb Way, then just w on Spearhead Dr to Spearhead Pl. 4910 Spearhead Pl V0N 1B0 (PO Box 1383). Fax: 604/905-0520. **Terms:** Check-in 4 pm; 45 day cancellation notice, 30 day in summer; cancellation fee imposed. **Facility:** 85 rooms. Fully self-contained units situated on Blackcomb mountain with the ability to ski in and out to the slopes. All rooms have washer/dryer. Some of the 2-bedroom units feature an extra den. 56 two-bedroom units. 6 stories; interior corridors; heated pool. **All Rooms:** kitchens. **Cards:** AE, MC, VI.

---

*The following lodging was either not inspected or did not
meet AAA rating requirements but is listed for your information only.*

CRYSTAL LODGE

Phone: (604)932-2221

12/23-2/28	1P: $225-$275	2P: $225-$275	XP: $25	F12
4/1-4/28	1P: $107-$220	2P: $107-$220	XP: $25	F12
4/29-9/15	1P: $140-$170	2P: $140-$170	XP: $25	F12
9/16-12/22	1P: $125-$148	2P: $125-$148	XP: $25	F12

Motor Inn Under major renovation, scheduled to be completed August 2000. **Last rated:** ◆◆◆ **Location:** Hwy 99, just e on Village Gate Blvd, then follow Whistler Way. 4154 Village Green V0N 1B0 (PO Box 280). Fax: 604/932-2635. **Terms:** Check-in 4 pm; 30 day cancellation notice, in winter; cancellation fee imposed; package plans. **Facility:** 137 rooms. In the heart of Whistler Village. Most of the guest rooms offer average sized rooms in the south wing. The north wing offers larger motel style rooms to loft units with full kitchen and fireplaces. 5 suites with 2- or 3-bedrooms, fireplace, balcony & full kitchen, $267-$645; 3 whirlpool rooms; 5 stories; interior corridors; heated pool, sauna, whirlpools. Fee: parking. **Dining:** 2 restaurants; 7 am-10 pm; $10-$20; cocktails. **All Rooms:** extended cable TV. **Some Rooms:** 40 kitchens. **Cards:** AE, DI, DS, JC, MC, VI. **Special Amenities:** Early check-in/late check-out and free newspaper.

RESTAURANTS

ARAXI
◆◆◆
Italian

Lunch: $10-$15   **Dinner:** $20-$35   **Phone:** 604/932-4540
Location: In Whistler Village Square. 4222 Village Square V0N 1B4. **Hours:** 10:30 am-11 pm; from 3 pm, 11/1-5/1. **Reservations:** suggested. **Features:** No A/C; cocktails; fee for parking; a la carte. You'll enjoy Araxi's exceptionally diverse and creative menu that includes tuna tartare, tofino salmon filet and smoked pork loin. They also have an impressive wine list and enticing desserts. The vibrant and theatrical atmosphere has summer patio dining. **Cards:** AE, DI, JC, MC, VI.

LABOCCA RESTAURANT & BAR
◆◆
Continental

Lunch: $7-$11   **Dinner:** $12-$22   **Phone:** 604/932-2112
Location: In Whistler Village Square. Whistler Village Square V0N 1B0. **Hours:** 11 am-11 pm. **Reservations:** suggested; ski season. **Features:** carryout; cocktails & lounge; a la carte. This restaurant is busy and popular with both the young and mature. The menu features fondue, rack of lamb, pizza, pasta and wok cooking—a real mix of different items to suit almost every taste. The huge outdoor patio is open during the summer. Smoke free premises. **Cards:** AE, MC, VI.

SUSHI VILLAGE JAPANESE CUISINE
◆◆
Japanese

Lunch: $7-$15   **Dinner:** $12-$32   **Phone:** 604/932-3330
Location: In Westbrook Whistler Hotel, Whistler Village. 4272 Mountain Sq V0N 1B0. **Hours:** 5:30 pm-10 pm, Thurs-Sun also noon-2:30 pm. **Reservations:** suggested; weekends/winter. **Features:** cocktails; a la carte. Located opposite the Blackcomb Gondola, this restaurant specializes in fresh, tasty sushi and sashimi. They also have tatami rooms for small or large groups. The relaxed and friendly setting was one of the original six restaurants in Whistler. **Cards:** AE, DI, JC, MC, VI.

VAL D'ISERE
◆◆◆
French

Lunch: $9-$16   **Dinner:** $15-$32   **Phone:** 604/932-4666
Location: Located in Whistler Village North, Bear Lodge, Town Plaza. #8-4314 Main St V0N 1B0. **Hours:** 11:30 am-10 pm; from 5:30 pm 11/11-5/1. **Closed:** 10/15-11/5. **Reservations:** suggested. **Features:** No A/C; a la carte. This restaurant is a must-stop in Whistler. It features a wonderfully creative European menu with West Coast touches. You'll enjoy the fresh seabass, venison, lamb and beef dishes as well as the remarkable wine list and great patio dining in summer. Smoke free premises. **Cards:** AE, DI, JC, MC, VI.

THE WILDFLOWER
◆◆◆
Canadian

Lunch: $12-$17   **Dinner:** $26-$34   **Phone:** 604/938-2033
Location: From Hwy 99, 1 km e on Lorimer Rd, then just w on Blackcomb Way; in Canadian Pacific Chateau Whistler Resort. 4599 Chateau Blvd V0N 1B4. **Hours:** 7 am-10 pm. **Reservations:** suggested. **Features:** casual dress; Sunday brunch; children's menu; health conscious menu items; cocktails & lounge; fee for parking & valet parking; a la carte. The Wildflower is an attractive, all-day dining room with wonderful views of Blackcomb ski hill. The menu features sandwiches and burgers for lunch and more upscale offerings of seafood, steak and chicken for dinner. Daily buffet. Validated parking. Smoke free premises. **Cards:** AE, DI, DS, JC, MC, VI.

ZEUSKI'S TAVERNA
◆◆
Greek

Lunch: $7-$15   **Dinner:** $10-$20   **Phone:** 604/932-6009
Location: In Whistler Village North, just n of Village Gate Blvd. 40-4314 Main St V0N 1B0. **Hours:** 11 am-11 pm, Fri & Sat-midnight. **Closed:** 12/25. **Reservations:** suggested. **Features:** No A/C; children's menu; cocktails & lounge; fee for parking; a la carte. This cozy, fun restaurant offers an extensive selection of Mediterranean dishes including roasted breast of chicken, salmon exhohiko and baklava, plus good cheesecake. There's free parking after 6 pm in the nearby library lot, otherwise you'll pay. **Cards:** AE, DI, MC, VI.

———— *The following restaurants have not been inspected by AAA* ————
but are listed for your information only.

BEAR FOOT BISTRO   **Phone:** 604/932-3433
[fyi]   Not inspected. **Location:** 4121 Village Green. **Features:** They create everything from scratch, and shop the
            world for the most exquisite ingredients. Meals are prepared with flair and skill to bring out the nature of
great food. The wine cellar has over 1,100 wines. Top jazz acts weekends, summer, nights.

QUATTRO AT WHISTLER   **Phone:** 604/905-4844
[fyi]   Not inspected. **Location:** Whistler's Pinnacle Hotel. Village North. **Features:** Located in the Whistler's
            Pinnacle Hotel, the carefree atmosphere of BC's famous resort sets the tone for Quattro at Whistler. This is
a modern style of Italian cooking emphasizing lean and healthy cuisine full of flavor served.

WHITE ROCK —*See Vancouver p. 519.*

WILLIAMS LAKE pop. 10,500

———— LODGINGS ————

DRUMMOND LODGE MOTEL   **Phone:** 250/392-5334
(AA)   5/1-10/31   1P: $65-$72   2P: $75-$82   XP: $6
◆◆   3/1-4/30   1P: $59-$65   2P: $70-$78   XP: $6
Motel   11/1-2/28   1P: $53-$61   2P: $63-$70   XP: $6
        Location: 1 km s on Hwy 97. 1405 Cariboo Hwy V2G 2W3. Fax: 250/392-1117. **Terms:** [CP] meal plan; weekly
        & monthly rates avail, off season; small pets only, $5 extra charge. **Facility:** 24 rooms. A quaint roadside prop-
erty offering good, comfortable individual cottage units that are fully self contained. The standard motel units are quite large
offering, good, clean accommodations, many have views of lake or landscape. 7 kitchen units, $10 extra charge; 1-2 stories;
exterior corridors. **Dining:** Restaurant nearby. **Services:** winter plug-ins. **All Rooms:** combo or shower baths, extended cable
TV. **Cards:** AE, CB, DI, DS, MC, VI.   🐄 🛗 🛆 ✕ 🎦 📅

WILLIAMS LAKE SUPER 8 MOTEL   **Phone:** (250)398-8884
◆◆   All Year   1P: $65-$75   2P: $72-$89   XP: $10   F14
Motel   **Location:** 2 km s on Hwy 97. 1712 Broadway Ave S V2G 2W4. Fax: 250/398-8884. **Terms:** [CP] meal plan;
        small pets only. **Facility:** 52 rooms. Very good budget style accommodations offering comfortable guest rooms
with a modern style decor. On the s end of town on the main hwy. 3 stories, no elevator; interior corridors. **Services:** winter
plug-ins. **Cards:** AE, DI, DS, MC, VI.   [ASK] [S] 🐄 🛗 🛆 🏋 ✕ 🎦 [VCR] 📅

—— RESTAURANT ——

RENDEZVOUS RESTAURANT   **Lunch:** $5-$10   **Dinner:** $9-$18   **Phone:** 250/398-8312
◆◆   **Location:** From jct Hwy 97 and 20, 1 km n. 240 B Oliver St V2G 1M1. **Hours:** 11 am-7 pm, Fri & Sat-10
Canadian   pm. Closed major holidays, Sun & 7/4-7/19. **Features:** children's menu; carryout; salad bar; cocktails; a la
carte. The Rendezvous is a pleasant, downtown restaurant featuring steak, stir-fry, burgers, barbecue
chicken, ribs, sandwiches and delicious cheesecake made in-house. The large salad bar has several different offerings.
Servers are friendly and attentive. **Cards:** AE, MC, VI.   ⊠

WINDERMERE

—— LODGINGS ——

EMERALD GROVE ESTATE BED AND BREAKFAST INN   **Phone:** (250)342-4431
(CAA)   3/1-9/8 & 9/10-11/4   1P: $149-$159   2P: $169-$179   XP: $10   F17
◆◆◆   9/9-9/9 & 11/5-2/28   1P: $129-$139   2P: $149-$159   XP: $10   F17
Bed &   **Location:** On Hwy 93/95, just e. 1265 Sunridge Rd V0B 2L0 (PO Box 627). Fax: 250/342-7220. **Terms:** [BP]
Breakfast meal plan. **Facility:** 5 rooms. Spacious rooms elegantly decorated with the romantic appeal of Neo-Victorian
style. Pleasant verandah and seating area affording a great view of the valley and surrounding mountains.
Adult oriented. 2 whirlpool rooms; 2 stories; interior corridors; smoke free premises. **Services:** complimentary
evening beverages; winter plug-ins. **Recreation:** hot tub, gazebo & barbecue with picnic tables. **All Rooms:** combo or shower
baths, extended cable TV. **Some Rooms:** Fee: VCR. **Cards:** AE, DI, MC, VI.   (A$K) (S&) (⋔) (⊠) (VCR) (📦)

WINDERMERE CREEK BED AND BREAKFAST CABINS   **Phone:** (250)342-0356
◆◆◆   All Year   1P: $65-$105   2P: $65-$105   XP: $20
Bed &   **Location:** From golf course sign on Hwy 95, 3.2 km ne on Kootenay 3 Rd, then keep left on fork to Winder-
Breakfast mere Loop Rd. 1658 Windermere Loop Rd V0B 2L0 (PO Box 409). Fax: 250/342-0356. **Terms:** [CP] meal
plan; age restrictions may apply; 14 day cancellation notice; 2 night min stay, in season, cabins; package plans.
Facility: 6 rooms. On a large acreage in a beautiful mountain valley, this charming bed & breakfast also offers 2 modern loft-
style cabins with a kitchenette, or relax in the well-appointed, rustic heritage cabin built in 1887. 1-2 stories; interior/exterior
corridors; smoke free premises. **Services:** winter plug-ins. **Recreation:** cross country skiing. **Some Rooms:** 2 efficiencies,
color TV. **Cards:** MC, VI.   (⊠) (📺) (🌀) (VCR) (🖥) (📦) (📺) (📦) (⊠)

YALE pop. 1,500

—— LODGING ——

FORT YALE MOTEL   **Phone:** 604/863-2216
◆   5/15-10/15   1P: $44   2P: $49-$54   XP: $3
Motel   3/1-5/14 & 10/16-2/28   1P: $34   2P: $39-$44   XP: $3
Location: On Trans Canada Hwy 1, just n of main set of lights. 31265 Trans Canada Hwy V0K 2S0 (PO Box
44). Fax: 604/863-2436. **Terms:** Cancellation fee imposed; small pets only, $3 extra charge. **Facility:** 12 rooms. Very well
maintained, older property featuring well coordinated 70's style furniture. Guest rooms are quite large, some feature a separate bedroom with sitting room. 1 story; exterior corridors. **Cards:** AE, MC, VI.   (🛏) (📶) (⊠) (🌀) (🐾) (📦) (📦)

Manitoba

BRANDON pop. 39,200

------ LODGINGS ------

COMFORT INN
◆◆◆   5/1-9/30   1P: $64-$83   2P: $74-$93   XP: $10   F18
Motel   3/1-4/30 & 1/1-2/28   1P: $62-$82   2P: $70-$89   XP: $8   F18
            10/1-12/31   1P: $59-$75   2P: $65-$83   XP: $8   F18
Location: Northside Trans Canada service road, between Hwy 10 N and 10 S, just e of MacDonalds Restaurant. 925 Middleton Ave R7C 1A8. Fax: 204/727-2246. **Terms:** Pets, in smoking rooms. **Facility:** 81 rooms. Inviting guest rooms and cozy lobby. Ground floor rooms feature patio doors leading to parking lot. 2 stories; interior corridors; designated smoking area. **Services:** winter plug-ins. **Cards:** AE, CB, DI, DS, JC, MC, VI.

Phone: (204)727-6232

RODEWAY INN MOTEL
(CAA) (SAVE)   All Year   1P: $49-$56   2P: $56-$63   XP: $4   F6
◆   **Location:** 3.2 km s of Trans Canada Hwy 1, on Hwy 10 S. 300 18th St N R7A 6Z2. Fax: 204/725-4465.
Motel   **Terms:** Pets, $3 extra charge. **Facility:** 26 rooms. Well maintained property featuring extra large guest rooms all with 2nd entry from parking lot. Excellent housekeeping. 6 efficiencies, $6 extra charge; 1 story; interior/exterior corridors; whirlpool. **Dining:** Coffee room 7-10 am, Sun 8-11 am; restaurant nearby. **Services:** winter plug-ins. **All Rooms:** extended cable TV. **Cards:** AE, DI, DS, MC, VI. **Special Amenities:** Free breakfast and free local telephone calls.

Phone: (204)728-7230

ROYAL OAK INN
◆◆   All Year   1P: $86-$96   2P: $96-$106
Motor Inn   **Location:** 5 km s of Trans Canada Hwy 1; 1.4 km w of jct Hwy 10 (18th St) and Hwy 1A (Victoria Ave). 3130 Victoria Ave R7B ON2. Fax: 204/726-5828. **Terms:** Pets, $10 extra charge. **Facility:** 156 rooms. New section features luxury 1-bedroom suites with refrigerator and microwave. A few rooms with whirlpool and gas fireplace. All rooms with hair dryer, iron and ironing board. 2-3 stories; interior corridors; heated pool. **Dining:** entertainment, nightclub. **Services:** winter plug-ins. **Cards:** AE, DI, DS, MC, VI.

Phone: (204)728-5775

SUPER 8 MOTEL BRANDON
◆◆   Property failed to provide current rates
Motel   **Location:** On Hwy 1, s service road, just e of Hwy 10. 1570 Highland Ave R7C 1A7. Fax: 204/728-3024. **Terms:** [ECP] meal plan; pets, smoking rooms. **Facility:** 80 rooms. Contemporary decor. All rooms with hair dryer. Many services in the property's vicinity. 2 stories; interior corridors; small heated indoor pool. **Services:** winter plug-ins. **Cards:** AE, DI, DS, MC, VI.

Phone: 204/729-8024

VICTORIA INN
(CAA) (SAVE)   All Year   1P: $75-$96   2P: $82-$106   XP: $7   F18
◆◆◆   **Location:** 5 km s of Trans Canada Hwy 1; 1.8 km w of jct Hwy 10 (18th St) and Hwy 1A (Victoria Ave). 3550
Motor Inn   Victoria Ave R7B 2R4. Fax: 204/727-8282. **Terms:** Pets, $5 extra charge. **Facility:** 131 rooms. Nicely appointed rooms with hair dryer, video games, iron and ironing board. Executive rms, $150; 2 whirlpool rooms, $102-$154; 2 stories; interior corridors; heated pool, sauna, whirlpool. **Dining:** Restaurant; 7 am-11 pm, Sun 8 am-8 pm; $6-$16; cocktails. **Services:** winter plug-ins. **Recreation:** enclosed children's play area. **All Rooms:** extended cable TV. **Cards:** AE, DI, MC, VI. **Special Amenities:** Free local telephone calls and free newspaper.

Phone: (204)725-1532

------ RESTAURANT ------

KOKONAS RESTAURANT   **Lunch:** $5-$10   **Dinner:** $12-$28   **Phone:** 204/727-4395
◆◆   **Location:** On Rosser Ave between 10th and 11th sts. 1011 Rosser Ave R7A 0L5. **Hours:** 11:30 am-11:30
Steakhouse pm, Sun 5 pm-9 pm. Closed major holidays. **Reservations:** suggested. **Features:** children's menu; senior's menu; cocktails & lounge. The Kokonas Restaurant features a varied menu with lasagna, pizza, sandwiches and a nice buffet and salad bar at lunch. A few Greek selections are also offered. The atmosphere is informal yet elegant. The server staff is cordial, friendly and attentive. **Cards:** AE, DI, MC, VI.

CHURCHILL pop. 1,100

------ LODGING ------

POLAR INN
◆◆   10/1-11/30   1P: $90   2P: $110   XP: $12   F10
Motel   3/1-9/30 & 12/1-2/28   1P: $84   2P: $95   XP: $10   F10
Location: Centre. 15 Franklin St R0B 0E0 (PO Box 1031). Fax: 204/675-2647. **Terms:** 14 day cancellation notice; pets. **Facility:** 25 rooms. Conveniently located, rooms offer pleasant rustic decor and some extra amenities. 1 story; exterior corridors. **Services:** winter plug-ins. **Cards:** DI, MC, VI.

Phone: (204)675-8878

------ RESTAURANT ------

GYPSY BAKERY & COFFEE SHOP   **Lunch:** $4-$8   **Dinner:** $5-$19   **Phone:** 204/675-2322
◆   **Location:** Centre. 253 Kelsey Blvd R0B 0E0. **Hours:** 7 am-midnight, to 9 pm 11/1-5/31. Closed major
American   holidays. **Features:** No A/C; children's menu; carryout; cocktails. This incredibly popular eatery features an extensive selection of fresh baked goods, steaks, shrimp, fish, chicken, sandwiches, soups, salads, pizza and pirogies. It is THE place for to-go lunches. Fine wines and cigars are also available. Polite service. **Cards:** AE, DI, MC, VI.

DAUPHIN pop. 8,300

—————— LODGING ——————

RODEWAY INN MOTEL
◆◆
Motor Inn
All Year   1P: $56-$95   2P: $62-$105   XP: $10   D14
Location: 2.4 km s on Hwy 5A and 10A (Main St). Hwy 5 & 10 S R7N 2V4 (PO Box 602). Fax: 204/638-7475. **Terms:** Small pets only. **Facility:** 67 rooms. Rooms vary in style and size, most with contemporary appeal. New section includes 12 rooms, most are one-bedroom suites, a few feature a whirlpool. 2 stories; interior/exterior corridors; heated pool. **Services:** winter plug-ins. **Cards:** AE, DI, MC, VI.
Phone: 204/638-5102

FLIN FLON pop. 6,600

—————— LODGING ——————

VICTORIA INN NORTH
(CAA) (SAVE)
◆◆
Motor Inn
All Year   1P: $66-$74   2P: $69-$82
Location: 6 km s, from jct Hwy 10 and 10A, just w. 10 Hwy N (Box 220, R8A 1M9). Fax: 204/687-5233. **Terms:** Pets, $5 extra charge. **Facility:** 93 rooms. 3 stories, no elevator; interior corridors; heated pool, saunas, whirlpool. **Dining:** Restaurant; 6:30 am-10 pm, Sat-10 pm, Sun 8 am-9 pm; $8-$18; cocktails; nightclub. **Services:** winter plug-ins. **All Rooms:** extended cable TV. **Cards:** AE, MC, VI.
Phone: 204/687-7555

GIMLI pop. 3,100

—————— LODGING ——————

LAKEVIEW RESORT
(CAA) (SAVE)
◆◆◆
Motor Inn
12/31-2/28	1P: $67-$105	2P: $67-$105	XP: $10	F17
5/2-9/5	1P: $78-$102	2P: $78-$102	XP: $10	F17
3/1-5/1 & 9/6-12/30	1P: $64-$77	2P: $64-$77	XP: $10	F17

Location: 0.8 km e of jct Hwy 9. 10 Centre St R0C 1B0 (PO Box 1860). Fax: 204/642-4400. **Terms:** Weekly & monthly rates avail; cancellation fee imposed; small pets only, $50 dep req. **Facility:** 77 rooms. Lakefront property offers mix of standard motel units and 2-room suites. All units with balcony; some with beach and lake views. All rooms with iron and ironing board. 3 stories; interior corridors; beach, 2 heated pools, sauna, whirlpool. **Dining:** Restaurant; 7 am-10 pm, Fri & Sat-11 pm in summer; 7 am-2 & 5-10 pm in winter; $10-$17; cocktails. **Services:** gift shop; winter plug-ins. **Recreation:** swimming, fishing. **All Rooms:** extended cable TV, honor bars. **Cards:** AE, DI, DS, MC, VI. **Special Amenities:** Free breakfast and free newspaper.
Phone: (204)642-8565

GULL HARBOUR

—————— LODGING ——————

GULL HARBOUR RESORT & CONFERENCE CENTRE
◆◆
Resort
Property failed to provide current rates
Location: On Hwy 8 at top of Hecla Island in Hecla Provincial Park. (Box 1000, RIVERTON, R0C 2R0). Fax: 204/279-2000. **Terms:** Check-in 4 pm; 14 day cancellation notice; package plans. **Facility:** 93 rooms. In beautiful provincial park, the resort offers very good recreational facilities. Contemporary looking rooms vary in size. 1 two-bedroom unit. 2 stories; interior corridors; heated pool; 2 tennis courts; playground. Fee: 18 holes golf, miniature golf. **Services:** gift shop; winter plug-ins. **Recreation:** swimming, charter fishing, fishing; ice skating; hiking trails, jogging. Fee: boating; cross country skiing, tobogganing; bicycles. **Cards:** AE, DI, MC, VI.
Phone: (204)279-2041

HECLA VILLAGE

—————— LODGING ——————

SOLMUNDSON GESTA HUS
◆◆
Bed & Breakfast
5/11-1/2	1P: $55-$70	2P: $60-$75	XP: $10	F6
3/1-5/10 & 1/3-2/28	1P: $45-$55	2P: $50-$60	XP: $10	F6

Location: On Hwy 8 in Hecla Village, in Hecla Provincial Park. (Box 76, RIVERTON, R0C 2R0). Fax: 204/279-2088. **Terms:** [BP] meal plan; cancellation fee imposed; small pets only. **Facility:** 4 rooms. In the remnants of an original Icelandic settlement on Hecla Island. Rooms are compact but pleasantly decorated with brass bed and walls with natural wood. 2 stories; interior corridors; smoke free premises. **Services:** gift shop; winter plug-ins. **Recreation:** bicycles, hiking trails. **Some Rooms:** combo or shower baths, shared bathrooms, color TV. **Cards:** MC, VI.
Phone: (204)279-2088

NEEPAWA pop. 3,300

—————— LODGING ——————

NEEPAWA SUPER 8 MOTEL
◆◆
Motel
Property failed to provide current rates
Location: Hwy 16, just w of jct Rt 5. 160 Main St W R0J 1H0. Fax: 204/476-8889. **Terms:** [ECP] meal plan; pets, in smoking rooms. **Facility:** 34 rooms. Newer property with bright and cheerful rooms. 2-one bedroom suites with refrigerator, 1 with whirlpool. 2 stories; interior corridors; heated pool. **Services:** winter plug-ins. **Cards:** AE, DI, DS, MC, VI.
Phone: 204/476-8888

PORTAGE LA PRAIRIE pop. 13,100

—— LODGINGS ——

MANITOBAH INN
◆
Motor Inn

Property failed to provide current rates

Phone: 204/857-9791

Location: S side service road on Trans Canada Hwy 1 by-pass. (Box 867, R1N 3C3). **Fax:** 204/239-1025. **Terms:** Small pets only, in smoking rooms. **Facility:** 61 rooms. Outside the city, this property offers rooms opening on pool/courtyard or on the exterior. Some rooms with more contemporary appointments. 2 stories; interior corridors; heated pool; 1 tennis court. **Services:** winter plug-ins. Fee: area transportation. **Recreation:** snowmobiling. **Some Rooms:** Fee: VCR. **Cards:** AE, DI, MC, VI.

WESTGATE INN MOTEL
◆ ◆
Motel

All Year   1P: $39-$44   2P: $43-$49   XP: $2

Phone: (204)239-5200

Location: 1 km e on Trans Canada Hwy 1A. 1010 Saskatchewan Ave E R1N 3C3. **Fax:** 204/239-0588. **Terms:** Small pets only. **Facility:** 25 rooms. Good budget accommodation with spacious rooms and convenient at-door parking. 2 stories; exterior corridors. **Services:** winter plug-ins. **Cards:** AE, DI, MC, VI.

—— RESTAURANT ——

BILL'S STICKY FINGERS
◆
Canadian

Lunch: $3-$19   **Dinner:** $7-$19   **Phone:** 204/857-9999

Location: Saskatchewan Ave E at 2 St. 210 Saskatchewan Ave E R1N 0K9. **Hours:** 11 am-midnight, Sat-Sun from 4 pm. Closed: 1/1 & 12/25. **Features:** children's menu; carryout; cocktails; buffet. This comfortable, casual, older restaurant offers a wide-ranging menu that focuses on ribs, chicken, steak, lasagna, gyros and pizza, with specials offered daily. A lunch buffet that includes soup is served Mon-Fri. The service is friendly and prompt. **Cards:** AE, DI, MC, VI.

RUSSELL pop. 1,600

—— LODGING ——

THE RUSSELL INN HOTEL & CONFERENCE CENTER
CAA SAVE
◆ ◆
Motor Inn

3/17-4/2 & 12/9-2/28   1P: $80   2P: $80   XP: $3   F17
3/1-3/16 & 4/3-12/8   1P: $69   2P: $75   XP: $3   F17

Phone: (204)773-2186

Location: 1.2 km se on Hwy 16 and 83. (PO Box 578, R0J 1W0). **Fax:** 204/773-2175. **Terms:** Pets. **Facility:** 70 rooms. An excellent property. Some rooms have a contemporary decor, others slightly older. 4 theme suites, $135-$150; 4 whirlpool rooms, $135-$175; 1 story; interior/exterior corridors; sauna, whirlpools. **Dining:** Restaurant; 6 am-10 pm; $6-$20; cocktails. **Services:** winter plug-ins. **Recreation:** tanning bed. **All Rooms:** extended cable TV. **Cards:** AE, DI, MC, VI. **Special Amenities:** Free local telephone calls and free newspaper.

THE PAS pop. 5,900

—— LODGINGS ——

KIKIWAK INN
CAA SAVE
◆ ◆ ◆
Motor Inn

1/1-2/28   1P: $93   2P: $93   XP: $10   F17
3/1-12/31   1P: $90   2P: $90   XP: $10   F17

Phone: (204)623-1800

Location: 0.6 km n on Hwy 10. Hwy 10 N R9A 1K8 (PO Box 780). **Fax:** 204/623-1812. **Terms:** Package plans; small pets only, in smoking rooms. **Facility:** 60 rooms. A modern uniquely designed property with aboriginal themes throughout. Good sized guest rooms. Whirlpool room, $125-$194; 3 stories; interior corridors; small heated indoor pool, whirlpool. **Dining:** Restaurant; 6:30 am-10 pm, Sun 7 am-8:30 pm; $9-$20; cocktails. **Services:** winter plug-ins. **All Rooms:** extended cable TV. **Some Rooms:** Fee: VCR. **Cards:** AE, DI, MC, VI.

WESCANA INN
CAA SAVE
◆ ◆
Motor Inn

All Year   1P: $75   2P: $79

Phone: (204)623-5446

Location: Just s on Hwy 10. 439 Fischer Ave R9A 1M3 (PO Box 2519). **Fax:** 204/623-3383. **Terms:** Small pets only. **Facility:** 76 rooms. Well maintained property with comfortable, contemporary guest rooms. Ground floor rooms feature a drive up exterior entrance. 2 stories; interior/exterior corridors; sauna. **Dining:** Dining room, see separate listing. **Services:** winter plug-ins. **Recreation:** video library. **All Rooms:** extended cable TV. **Cards:** AE, DI, MC, VI. **Special Amenities:** Early check-in/late check-out and free room upgrade (subject to availability with advanced reservations).

---------- RESTAURANT ----------

WESCANA DINING ROOM   **Lunch:** $5-$10   **Dinner:** $8-$18   **Phone:** 204/623-5446
◆◆   **Location:** Just s on Hwy 10; in Wescana Inn. 439 Fischer Ave R9A 1M3. **Hours:** 7 am-10 pm, Sun 7 am-2
American   & 5-8 pm. Closed: 12/25. **Features:** casual dress; children's menu; carryout; cocktails & lounge. You'll enjoy
the unpretentious dining in a casual setting at this restaurant, which features an extensive menu with an
excellent selection of prime rib, steak, chicken, fish and pasta combinations. The lunch menu includes sandwiches, burgers
and salad. **Cards:** AE, DI, MC, VI.

THOMPSON pop. 14,400

---------- LODGING ----------

COUNTRY INN & SUITES BY CARLSON   **Phone:** (204)778-8879
(AAA) (SAVE)   All Year   1P: $84-$94   2P: $94-$104   XP: $10   F18
◆◆◆   **Location:** Just w of Hwy 6 on Thompson Dr N at Quartz St. 70 Thompson Dr N R8N 0Y8. **Fax:** 204/677-3225.
Motor Inn   **Terms:** [CP] meal plan; weekly & monthly rates avail; small pets only, $10 extra charge. **Facility:** 61 rooms. An
attractive country inn style property. The guest rooms are spacious with a mix of standard rooms and 2-room
suites. All rooms with iron and ironing board. 2 stories; interior corridors; heated pool, sauna, whirlpool.
Dining: Restaurant nearby. **Services:** winter plug-ins. **All Rooms:** extended cable TV, honor bars. **Cards:** AE, DI, DS, MC, VI.
Special Amenities: Free breakfast and free newspaper. *(See color ad p 566)*

WINKLER pop. 7,200

---------- LODGING ----------

WINKLER INN   **Phone:** 204/325-4381
◆◆   All Year   1P: $65-$89   2P: $65-$89   XP: $5
Motor Inn   **Location:** Center, Main St and Hwy 14. 851 Main St N R6W 4B1 (Box 968). **Fax:** 204/325-9656. **Terms:** Can-
cellation fee imposed; small pets only, $5 extra charge. **Facility:** 38 rooms. Comfortable, modern guest rooms.
Many open only on the pool side, giving a somewhat enclosed impression, with reduced daylight. 1 story; interior corridors;
heated pool. **Services:** winter plug-ins. **Some Rooms:** kitchen. **Cards:** AE, MC, VI.

Winnipeg pop. 618,500

This index helps you "spot" where approved accommodations are located on the detailed maps that follow. Rate ranges are for comparison only and show the property's high season. Turn to the listing page for more detailed rate information and consult display ads for special promotions. Restaurant rate range is for dinnner, unless only lunch (L) is served.

✈ Airport Accommodations

Spotter/Map Page Number	OA	WINNIPEG	Diamond Rating	Rate Range High Season	Listing Page
31 / p. 566		Comfort Inn, 2.3 km e of Winnipeg International Airport	◆◆◆	$75-$100	571
29 / p. 566	Ⓐ	**Country Inn & Suites By Carlson, 1.9 km e of Winnipeg International Airport**	◆◆◆	$85-$95 SAVE	571
34 / p. 566	Ⓐ	**International Inn-Best Western, 1.4 km e of Winnipeg International Airport**	◆◆	$92-$150 SAVE	572
35 / p. 566		Radisson Suite Hotel-Winnipeg Airport, 1.6 km e of Winnipeg International Airport	◆◆◆	$169-$195	572
32 / p. 566		Viscount Gort Hotel, 5 km s of Winnipeg International Airport	◆◆	$82-$150	572

DOWNTOWN WINNIPEG

Spotter/Map Page Number	OA	DOWNTOWN WINNIPEG - Lodgings	Diamond Rating	Rate Range High Season	Listing Page
3 / p. 565		Canadian Pacific The Lombard - see color ad p 567	◆◆◆◆	$99-$149	567
4 / p. 565		Ramada Marlborough Hotel	◆◆◆	$62	569
5 / p. 565	Ⓐ	**Gordon Downtowner Motor Hotel**	◆	$60-$73 SAVE	567
6 / p. 565		Radisson Hotel Winnipeg Downtown - see ad p 568	◆◆◆	$179-$194	569
9 / p. 565	Ⓐ	**Best Western Carlton Inn**	◆◆	$65-$80 SAVE	567
11 / p. 565	Ⓐ	**Crowne Plaza Winnipeg Downtown**	◆◆◆	$89-$169 SAVE	567
12 / p. 565	Ⓐ	**Place Louis Riel All-Suite Hotel - see color ad p 568**	◆◆◆	$90-$110 SAVE	569
13 / p. 565	Ⓐ	**Norwood Hotel - see color ad p 568**	◆◆◆	$82 SAVE	569
		DOWNTOWN WINNIPEG - Restaurants			
④ / p. 565		Ichiban Japanese Steak House & Sushi Bar	◆◆	$15-$29	570
⑤ / p. 565		Chef's Table	◆◆◆	$14-$29	569
⑥ / p. 565		Hy's Steak Loft	◆◆	$17-$31	570
⑦ / p. 565		Amici	◆◆◆	$15-$36	569
⑧ / p. 565		Restaurant Dubrovnik	◆◆◆	$18-$30	570
⑨ / p. 565		Branigan's	◆◆	$9-$15	569
⑩ / p. 565		Bridgeport At The Gallery	◆◆	$5-$10(L)	569
⑪ / p. 565		Bridgeport Restaurant And Cafe	◆◆	$9-$16	569
⑫ / p. 565		Mondetta World Cafe	◆◆	$7-$17	570

WINNIPEG

Spotter/Map Page Number	OA	WINNIPEG - Lodgings	Diamond Rating	Rate Range High Season	Listing Page
24 / p. 566	Ⓐ	**Holiday Inn Winnipeg South**	◆◆◆	$95 SAVE	572
25 / p. 566	Ⓐ	**Quality Inn**	◆◆◆	$60-$90 SAVE	572
26 / p. 566		Twin Pillars Bed & Breakfast	◆	$40-$52	572
28 / p. 566	Ⓐ	**Canad Inns Transcona**	◆◆	$67-$77 SAVE	571
29 / p. 566	Ⓐ	**Country Inn & Suites By Carlson - see color ad p 566**	◆◆◆	$85-$95 SAVE	571
30 / p. 566	Ⓐ	**Canad Inns Garden City**	◆◆	$67-$77 SAVE	570
31 / p. 566		Comfort Inn	◆◆◆	$75-$100	571
32 / p. 566		Viscount Gort Hotel	◆◆	$82-$150	572
33 / p. 566	Ⓐ	**Assiniboine Gordon Inn on the Park**	◆	$55-$65 SAVE	570
34 / p. 566	Ⓐ	**International Inn-Best Western**	◆◆	$92-$150 SAVE	572

Spotter/Map Page Number	OA	WINNIPEG - Lodgings (continued)	Diamond Rating	Rate Range High Season	Listing Page
35 / p. 566		Radisson Suite Hotel-Winnipeg Airport	◆◆◆	$169-$195	572
36 / p. 566	Ⓐ	Days Inn	◆◆	$99-$109 SAVE	571
37 / p. 566	Ⓐ	Canad Inns Windsor Park	◆◆	$67-$77 SAVE	571
38 / p. 566	Ⓐ	Holiday Inn Airport/West	◆◆◆	$100-$115 SAVE	571
39 / p. 566		Niakwa Inn	◆◆	$68-$77	572
40 / p. 566	Ⓐ	Dakota Village Motor Hotel	◆◆	$57-$73	571
41 / p. 566		Comfort Inn	◆◆◆	$70-$103	571
42 / p. 566	Ⓐ	Lincoln Motor Hotel	◆◆	$45-$51 SAVE	572
44 / p. 566	Ⓐ	Canad Inns Express Fort Garry	◆◆	$60-$80 SAVE	570
45 / p. 566	Ⓐ	Canad Inns Fort Garry	◆◆◆	$89-$105 SAVE	570
		WINNIPEG - Restaurants			
18 / p. 566		Tavern In The Park	◆◆◆	$14-$24	573
19 / p. 566		Yamato	◆	$6-$17	574
20 / p. 566		Mona Lisa Ristorante	◆◆	$8-$18	573
21 / p. 566		Dionysos Restaurant	◆	$10-$16	573
22 / p. 566		The Round Table Steak House & Pub	◆◆	$14-$26	573
23 / p. 566		Branigan's	◆◆	$9-$15	573
24 / p. 566		India Palace	◆◆	$8-$20	573
25 / p. 566		Maxime	◆◆	$8-$25	573

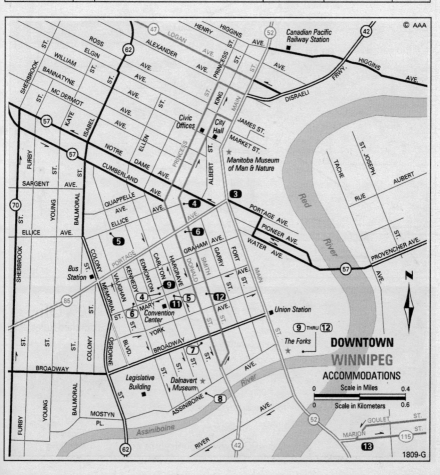

DOWNTOWN
WINNIPEG
ACCOMMODATIONS

© AAA

1809-G

Spotter/Map Page Number	OA	WINNIPEG - Restaurants (continued)	Diamond Rating	Rate Range High Season	Listing Page
26 / below		Royal Fork Buffet Restaurant	◆	$10	573
27 / below		Tiffani's Restaurant	◆ ◆	$17-$27	574
28 / below		Nibbler's Nosh	◆ ◆	$13-$17	573
30 / below	CAA	**Medicine Rock Cafe**	◆ ◆	$14-$25	573

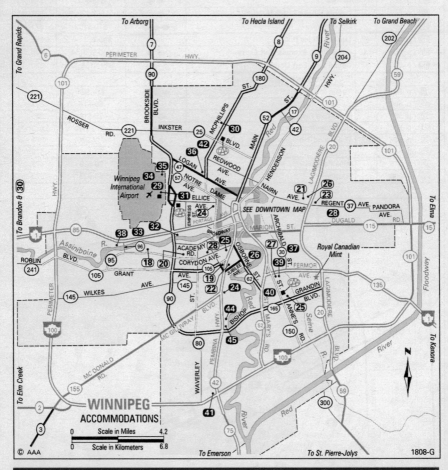

DOWNTOWN WINNIPEG   (See map p. 565; index p. 564)

——— LODGINGS ———

BEST WESTERN CARLTON INN   Phone: (204)942-0881   **9**
(CAA) (SAVE)   All Year   1P: $65-$75   2P: $70-$80   XP: $5   F17
♦ ♦   **Location:** Just s off Metro Rt 85 (Portage Ave); opposite Convention Centre. 220 Carlton St R3C 1P5.
Motor Inn   Fax: 204/943-9312. **Terms:** Weekly rates avail; pets. **Facility:** 108 rooms. Older property with compact rooms
              offering a simple decor. Budget accommodation conveniently located. 3 stories; interior corridors; heated pool,
              sauna, whirlpool. **Dining:** Restaurant; 7:30 am-1 am, Fri & Sat-2 am, Sun 8 am-midnight; $6-$25; cocktails.
Services: winter plug-ins. **Recreation:** hair salon, game room. **All Rooms:** extended cable TV. **Some Rooms:** Fee: VCR.
Cards: AE, CB, DI, DS, JC, MC, VI. **Special Amenities: Early check-in/late check-out.**

CANADIAN PACIFIC THE LOMBARD   Phone: (204)957-1350   **3**
♦ ♦ ♦ ♦   4/16-10/31   1P: $99-$139   2P: $109-$149
Hotel   11/1-2/28   1P: $89-$129   2P: $99-$139
             3/1-4/15   1P: $89-$129   2P: $99-$139   XP: $20   F18
Location: Just e of corner Portage Ave and Main St. 2 Lombard Pl R3B 0Y3. Fax: 204/949-1486. **Terms:** Cancellation fee im-
posed; package plans; pets. **Facility:** 350 rooms. On the well-known downtown corner of Portage and Main. Many luxury level
services offered. All rooms with hair dryer, iron, ironing board and video games. 21 stories; interior corridors; heated pool.
Fee: parking. **Services:** gift shop; winter plug-ins. Fee: massage. **All Rooms:** honor bars. **Some Rooms:** Fee: VCR.
Cards: AE, DI, DS, JC, MC, VI. *(See color ad below)*

CROWNE PLAZA WINNIPEG DOWNTOWN   Phone: (204)942-0551   **11**
(CAA) (SAVE)   All Year   1P: $89-$169   2P: $89-$169   XP: $15   F18
♦ ♦ ♦   **Location:** St Mary Ave at Hargrave St; adjacent to Convention Centre. 350 St Mary Ave R3C 3J2.
Hotel   Fax: 204/943-8702. **Terms:** Package plans; small pets only. **Facility:** 402 rooms. Attractive room appointments
               and luxury services. Most rooms with balcony, all with extra amenities, hair dryer, iron, ironing board and voice
               mail. 4 whirlpool rooms; 18 stories; interior corridors; 2 heated pools, wading pool, sauna, whirlpool.
Fee: parking. **Dining:** Dining room, restaurant; 6:30 am-1:30 am, Sun 7 am-midnight; billiard lounge; $18-$29; cocktails; also,
Chef's Table, see separate listing. **Services:** gift shop. **Recreation:** fitness testing. Fee: aerobic instruction. **All Rooms:** ex-
tended cable TV, honor bars. **Cards:** AE, DI, JC, MC, VI.

GORDON DOWNTOWNER MOTOR HOTEL   Phone: (204)943-5581   **5**
(CAA) (SAVE)   All Year   1P: $60-$68   2P: $63-$73   XP: $5   F16
♦   **Location:** Kennedy St at Ellice Ave. 330 Kennedy St R3B 2M6. Fax: 204/947-3041. **Terms:** Cancellation fee
Motor Inn   imposed; small pets only. **Facility:** 40 rooms. A somewhat older property with spacious rooms, all in pink tones
              and many with mirrored walls. 2 one-bedroom suites, attractively organized. 3 stories; interior corridors.
              Dining: Restaurant; 7 am-8 pm, Sun from 8 am; $3-$17; cocktails. **Services:** winter plug-ins. **All Rooms:** ex-
tended cable TV. **Cards:** AE, DI, MC, VI. **Special Amenities: Free room upgrade and preferred room (each subject to
availability with advanced reservations).**

(See map p. 565)

NORWOOD HOTEL
CAA SAVE
◆◆◆
Motor Inn

			Phone: (204)233-4475	13
All Year	1P: $82	2P: $82	XP: $10	F16

Location: On Metro Rt 115, just e of St. Mary's Rd. 112 Marion St R2H 0T1. Fax: 204/231-1910. **Facility:** 52 rooms. Located in Winnipeg's French Quarter (St. Boniface). Attractive furnishings in contemporary style. 4 stories; interior corridors. **Dining:** Restaurant; 7 am-9 pm; $8-$15; cocktails; entertainment. **Services:** winter plug-ins. **All Rooms:** extended cable TV. **Some Rooms:** Fee: VCR. **Cards:** AE, MC, VI. **Special Amenities:** Early check-in/late check-out and free local telephone calls. (See color ad p 568)

PLACE LOUIS RIEL ALL-SUITE HOTEL
CAA SAVE
◆◆◆
Suite Hotel

			Phone: (204)947-6961	12
3/23-5/1	1P: $90-$110	2P: $90-$110	XP: $10	F17
1/1-2/28	1P: $85-$105	2P: $85-$105	XP: $10	F17
3/1-3/22 & 5/2-12/31	1P: $80-$100	2P: $80-$100	XP: $10	F17

Location: Smith St at St Mary Ave. 190 Smith St R3C 1J8. Fax: 204/947-3029. **Terms:** Monthly rates avail; cancellation fee imposed; small pets only, pet release form. **Facility:** 285 rooms. Suites offering variety in sizes and furnishings, spacious living rooms, large closet space. Contemporary kitchen with full size appliances. 17 two-bedroom suites, $150; 24 stories; interior corridors. Fee: parking. **Dining:** Restaurant; 6:30 am-11 pm, Sat & Sun 7:30 am-9 pm; $5-$17; cocktails. **Services:** gift shop; winter plug-ins. **All Rooms:** kitchens, extended cable TV. **Cards:** AE, DI, MC, VI. **Special Amenities:** Free newspaper. (See color ad p 568)

RADISSON HOTEL WINNIPEG DOWNTOWN
◆◆◆
Hotel

			Phone: (204)956-0410	6
5/1-9/30	1P: $179	2P: $194	XP: $15	F18
10/1-2/28	1P: $175	2P: $190	XP: $15	F18
3/1-4/30	1P: $169	2P: $184	XP: $15	F18

Location: Portage Ave at Smith St. 288 Portage Ave R3C 0B8. Fax: 204/947-1129. **Terms:** Package plans; small pets only. **Facility:** 272 rooms. Many renovated guest rooms. All rooms with iron and ironing board. 29 stories; interior corridors; heated pool. Fee: parking. **Services:** gift shop; winter plug-ins. **All Rooms:** honor bars. **Cards:** AE, DI, MC, VI. (See ad p 568)

RAMADA MARLBOROUGH HOTEL
◆◆◆
Hotel

			Phone: (204)942-6411	4
All Year	1P: $62	2P: $62	XP: $10	F18

Location: Just n off Metro Rt 85 (Portage Ave). 331 Smith St R3B 2G9. Fax: 204/947-3724. **Terms:** Small pets only, in kennels. **Facility:** 148 rooms. Spacious rooms with attractive decor. Dining room is worth a visit, with vaulted ceilings, gothic style. Many details of original hotel architecture have been maintained in the classic taste of the 1910s. 1 two-bedroom unit. 9 stories; interior corridors. **Dining:** nightclub. **Services:** gift shop; winter plug-ins. **Cards:** AE, DI, MC, VI.

------- **RESTAURANTS** -------

AMICI
◆◆◆
Italian

Lunch: $9-$18	Dinner: $15-$36	Phone: 204/943-4997	7

Location: Broadway at Hargrave St. 326 Broadway R3C 0S5. **Hours:** 11:30 am-2 & 5-11 pm, Sat from 5 pm. Closed major holidays & Sun. **Reservations:** suggested. **Features:** cocktails & lounge; a la carte. You'll find this restaurant offers fine dining in contemporary surroundings upstairs, and casual dining and more moderate pricing at the Bombolini Wine Bar downstairs. The innovative menu features dishes with complex preparation and creative presentation. **Cards:** AE, DI, MC, VI.

BRANIGAN'S
◆◆
Canadian

Lunch: $5-$9	Dinner: $9-$15	Phone: 204/949-1734	9

Location: Behind Union Station. 162-1 Forks Market R3C 4L8. **Hours:** 11 am-2 am. Closed: 12/25. **Reservations:** accepted. **Features:** casual dress; Sunday brunch; children's menu; senior's menu; carryout; cocktails & lounge; a la carte. You'll enjoy the very good menu at this restaurant; it offers Boston clam chowder, calamari, escargot, grilled chicken, tortilla burgers, veggie sandwich melt, pastas, salmon and beef entrees. Located in a bustling market, it also has outdoor seating. **Cards:** AE, DI, MC, VI.

BRIDGEPORT AT THE GALLERY
◆◆
Canadian

Lunch: $5-$10		Phone: 204/786-2287	10

Location: Just s of Portage Ave; top floor in the Winnipeg Art Gallery. 300 Memorial Blvd R3C 1V1. **Hours:** 11:30 am-4 pm. Closed: 12/25, Sat in summer & Sun off season. **Reservations:** suggested. **Features:** casual dress; health conscious menu items; carryout; cocktails. This restaurant features a progressive menu with some Pacific Rim influences. The caesar salad and barbecue chicken wrap with salsa are delightful choices, with attractive presentations. The decor is funky, with an open kitchen and outdoor patio. **Cards:** AE, DI, MC, VI.

BRIDGEPORT RESTAURANT AND CAFE
◆◆
Canadian

Lunch: $5-$10	Dinner: $9-$16	Phone: 204/943-5529	11

Location: Behind Union Station. 109-1 Forks Market Rd R3C 4L8. **Hours:** 8:30 am-1 am; hrs may vary in off season. Closed: 12/25. **Reservations:** suggested. **Features:** casual dress; health conscious menu items; carryout; cocktails; a la carte. Located in the heart of the market, this funky restaurant has a quaint, casual cafe side and a comfortable atrium side. Its progressive menu has Pacific Rim influences and includes Greek salad, classic sandwiches and pasta specials. Friendly service. **Cards:** AE, DI, MC, VI.

CHEF'S TABLE
◆◆◆
Regional American

Lunch: $9-$15	Dinner: $14-$29	Phone: 204/946-5200	5

Location: St Mary Ave at Hargrave St; adjacent to Convention Centre; in Crowne Plaza Winnipeg Downtown. 350 St. Mary Ave R3C 3J2. **Hours:** 11:30 am-2 & 5:30-10 pm. Closed: Sun. **Reservations:** suggested. **Features:** dressy casual; health conscious menu; cocktails & lounge; fee for parking & valet parking; a la carte. The Chef's Table features a cuisine of local fare with international influences. The excellent creations display fine presentation and flavorful combinations. The smoked salmon with roasted capers is superb. You'll enjoy the small, intimate setting. **Cards:** AE, DI, DS, JC, MC, VI.

(See map p. 565)

HY'S STEAK LOFT   **Dinner:** $17-$31   **Phone:** 204/942-1000   ⑥
◆◆   **Location:** 2 blks s of Metro Rt 85 (Portage Ave). 216 Kennedy St R3C 1T1. **Hours:** 4 pm-11 pm, Fri &
Steakhouse   Sat-midnight, Sun 5 pm-9 pm. Closed major holidays. **Reservations:** suggested. **Features:** cocktail lounge;
fee for valet parking. Hy's Steak Loft is a popular and established restaurant. In addition to a nice selection
of steaks, they offer rack of lamb, veal and barbecue chicken. The atmosphere is friendly and warm. Locals and visitors
alike enjoy the private, romantic setting. **Cards:** AE, DI, DS, MC, VI.   ✕

ICHIBAN JAPANESE STEAK HOUSE & SUSHI BAR   **Dinner:** $15-$29   **Phone:** 204/925-7400   ④
◆◆   **Location:** At corner of St Mary and Carlton sts. 189 Carlton St R3C 3F1. **Hours:** 4:30 pm-11 pm, Fri &
Steakhouse   Sat-10:30 pm. Closed major holidays. **Reservations:** suggested. **Features:** casual dress; children's menu;
early bird specials; health conscious menu; carryout; cocktails; minimum charge-$9. Ichiban's features a
sushi bar and teppan-style cooking, where your meal is prepared in an entertaining manner at your table. Offerings also
include North American dishes of steak, chicken and seafood. The server staff is pleasant, cordial and attentive. **Cards:** AE,
DI, MC, VI.   ✕

MONDETTA WORLD CAFE   **Lunch:** $7-$12   **Dinner:** $7-$17   **Phone:** 204/942-7745   ⑫
◆◆   **Location:** Behind Union Station. 110-25 Forks Market R3E 4S8. **Hours:** 11 am-midnight, Thurs-Sat to 2 am,
Ethnic   Sun 10:30 am-2 am. Closed: 12/25. **Reservations:** accepted. **Features:** casual dress; children's menu;
senior's menu; carryout; cocktails & lounge; a la carte. Here's your passport to diverse dining! Mondetta
World Cafe offers international selections, a lively atmosphere, very polished service and dancing at night. Entrees include
Maui pineapple chicken, Manitoba pickerel and Thai grilled porloin steak. **Cards:** AE, DI, MC, VI.   ✕

RESTAURANT DUBROVNIK   Historical   **Lunch:** $8-$15   **Dinner:** $18-$30   **Phone:** 204/944-0594   ⑧
◆◆◆   **Location:** Between Carlton and Hargrave sts. 390 Assiniboine Ave R3C 0Y1. **Hours:** 11:30 am-3 &
Continental   5-midnight. Closed: 12/25. **Reservations:** suggested. **Features:** dressy casual; children's menu; health
conscious menu; cocktails; a la carte. Located in a beautifully restored mansion near the Assiniboine River,
this restaurant provides a warm and inviting dining room and an excellent menu with 20 artfully presented entrees such as
pork tenderloin, chicken goyko with shrimp, beef and seafood. **Cards:** AE, DI, MC, VI.   ✕

WINNIPEG   pop. 618,500   (See map p. 566; index p. 564)

——— LODGINGS ———

ASSINIBOINE GORDON INN ON THE PARK   **Phone:** (204)888-4806   ㉝
CAA [SAVE]   5/1-2/28   1P: $55-$65   2P: $55-$65   XP: $8   F16
◆   3/1-4/30   1P: $42-$52   2P: $42-$52   XP: $8   F16
Motor Inn   **Location:** Portage Ave at Lyle St. 1975 Portage Ave R3J 0J9. Fax: 204/897-9870. **Terms:** Cancellation imposed. **Facility:** 48 rooms. Most rooms with pleasant decor well-suited to the budget traveler. 2 stories;
interior/exterior corridors. **Dining:** Dining room; 7 am-11 pm, Sun 8 am-2 & 4-9 pm; $7-$17; cocktails; entertainment, nightclub. **Services:** winter plug-ins. **All Rooms:** extended cable TV. **Cards:** AE, DI, MC, VI. **Special Amenities:**
Free room upgrade and preferred room (each subject to availability with advanced reservations).
                                                        [S𝖣] [🍴] [Y] [🐾] [🖥]

CANAD INNS EXPRESS FORT GARRY   **Phone:** (204)269-6955   ㊹
CAA [SAVE]   All Year   1P: $60-$70   2P: $70-$80   XP: $10   F12
◆◆   **Location:** Pembina Hwy at Adamar Rd. 1792 Pembina Hwy R3T 2G2. Fax: 204/261-4543. **Terms:** Pets.
Motor Inn   **Facility:** 36 rooms. Good sized rooms. 2 stories; interior/exterior corridors. **Dining:** Restaurant; 11 am-11 pm,
Sat & Sun-midnight; $8-$15; cocktails; nightclub. **Services:** winter plug-ins. **All Rooms:** extended cable TV.
Cards: AE, DI, MC, VI. **Special Amenities:** Early check-in/late check-out and preferred room (subject to
availability with advanced reservations).   [S𝖣] [🛏] [🍴] [Y] [🐾] [🏊] [✕] [🖨] [💻] [📞]

CANAD INNS FORT GARRY   **Phone:** (204)261-7450   ㊺
CAA [SAVE]   All Year   1P: $89-$95   2P: $99-$105   XP: $10   F17
◆◆◆   **Location:** Pembina Hwy at Adamar Rd. 1824 Pembina Hwy R3T 2G2. Fax: 204/275-2187. **Terms:** Check-in
Motor Inn   4 pm; package plans. **Facility:** 107 rooms. Destination style city property featuring both adult and children
theme rooms, as well as nicely appointed units and 1-bedroom suites. 5 theme rooms with whirlpool, $189; 2
stories; interior corridors; heated pool, wading pool, waterslide, whirlpool. **Dining:** Restaurant; 7 am-1 am,
dinner theatre & piano bar; $8-$15; cocktails. **Services:** winter plug-ins. **All Rooms:** extended cable TV. **Cards:** AE, DI, DS,
MC, VI. **Special Amenities:** Free newspaper.
              [🍴] [Y] [🐾] [🏊] [♨] [ℹ] [📶] [✕] [🐕] [🖨] [💻] [🛎] [📞] [DATA PORT] [🌐] [🔧]

CANAD INNS GARDEN CITY   **Phone:** (204)633-0024   ㉚
CAA [SAVE]   All Year   1P: $67   2P: $77   XP: $10   F12
◆◆   **Location:** McPhillips St at Jefferson Ave. 2100 McPhillips St R2V 3T9. Fax: 204/697-3377. **Terms:** Weekly
Motor Inn   rates avail. **Facility:** 55 rooms. 2 two-bedroom units. 2 stories; interior corridors; heated pool, wading pool, wa-
terslide, whirlpool. **Dining:** Restaurant; 5 am-11 pm; $5-$11; cocktails; entertainment, nightclub.
Services: winter plug-ins. **All Rooms:** extended cable TV. **Cards:** AE, CB, DI, DS, MC, VI.
**Special Amenities: Early check-in/late check-out and preferred room (subject to availability with advanced
reservations).**   [S𝖣] [🍴] [Y] [🐾] [✕] [🖨] [💻] [📞] [🔧]

(See map p. 566)

CANAD INNS TRANSCONA
(CAA) (SAVE)
◆◆
Motor Inn
All Year   1P: $67   2P: $77   XP: $10   Phone: (204)224-1681   28 F12
Location: Regent Ave at Plessis Rd. 826 Regent Ave W R2C 3A8. Fax: 204/222-3216. **Terms:** Pets.
Facility: 50 rooms. Rooms recently renovated with pleasant decor. Property also offers various evening entertainment and recreational facilities suited to families. 3 two-bedroom units. Suite, $112; 2 stories; interior corridors; heated pool, wading pool, waterslide, whirlpool. **Dining:** Restaurant; 6 am-10 pm, Sun from 7 am; $5-$12; cocktails; entertainment, nightclub. **Services:** winter plug-ins. **All Rooms:** extended cable TV. **Cards:** AE, DI, MC, VI.
Special Amenities: Early check-in/late check-out and preferred room (subject to availability with advanced reservations).

CANAD INNS WINDSOR PARK
(CAA) (SAVE)
◆◆
Motor Inn
All Year   1P: $67   2P: $77   XP: $10   Phone: (204)253-2641   37 F12
Location: Elizabeth Rd at Lagimodiere Blvd. 1034 Elizabeth Rd R2J 1B3. Fax: 204/255-5767. **Terms:** Small pets only. **Facility:** 54 rooms. Average sized rooms with contemporary appeal. Games bar. 2 two-bedroom units. 2 stories; interior corridors; heated pool, wading pool, waterslide, whirlpool. **Dining:** Restaurant; 6:30 am-10 pm, Sat from 7 am, Sun 8 am-9 pm; $6-$11; cocktails; entertainment. **Services:** winter plug-ins.
All Rooms: extended cable TV. **Cards:** AE, CB, DI, MC, VI. **Special Amenities: Early check-in/late check-out and preferred room (subject to availability with advanced reservations).**

COMFORT INN
◆◆◆
Motel
All Year   1P: $70-$95   2P: $78-$103   XP: $6   Phone: (204)269-7390   41 F18
Location: Just n of jct Perimeter Hwy 100 and 75. 3109 Pembina Hwy R3T 4R6. Fax: 204/261-7565. **Terms:** Pets, 1st floor smoking rooms. **Facility:** 79 rooms. Well appointed rooms. Main floor offers patio doors and parking area leading directly to room. 2 stories; interior corridors. **Services:** winter plug-ins. **Some Rooms:** Fee: refrigerators. **Cards:** AE, DI, DS, JC, MC, VI.

COMFORT INN
◆◆◆
Motel
All Year   1P: $75-$90   2P: $85-$100   XP: $10   Phone: (204)783-5627   31 F18
Location: At Sargent Ave and King Edward St. 1770 Sargent Ave R3H 0C8. Fax: 204/783-5661. **Terms:** Pets, in smoking rooms. **Facility:** 81 rooms. Ground floor rooms feature patio doors that lead to parking lot. A few rooms offer upgraded amenities and superior decor. 2 stories; interior corridors. **Services:** winter plug-ins. **Some Rooms:** Fee: refrigerators. **Cards:** AE, DI, DS, JC, MC, VI.

COUNTRY INN & SUITES BY CARLSON
(CAA) (SAVE)
◆◆◆
Motel
All Year   1P: $85   2P: $95   XP: $10   Phone: (204)783-6900   29 F18
Location: Just s of jct Wellington Ave. 730 King Edward St R3H 1B4. Fax: 204/775-7197. **Terms:** [CP] meal plan; 7 day cancellation notice; small pets only, $20 dep req. **Facility:** 77 rooms. Spacious accommodations with choice of 2 room suites or standard 1 room units. Country Inn style decor. All rooms with iron and ironing board. 3 stories; interior corridors. **Dining:** Restaurant nearby. **Services:** winter plug-ins. **Recreation:** video library. **All Rooms:** extended cable TV. **Cards:** AE, DI, DS, MC, VI. **Special Amenities: Free breakfast and free newspaper.** (See color ad p 566)

DAKOTA VILLAGE MOTOR HOTEL
(CAA)
◆◆
Motor Inn
All Year   1P: $57-$67   2P: $63-$73   XP: $10   Phone: 204/256-4315   40 F12
Location: St. Marys Rd at Dunkirk Dr, jct Metro Rts 52 and 62. 1105 St. Mary's Rd R2M 3T6. Fax: 204/255-1851. **Terms:** Weekly rates avail; 4 day cancellation notice. **Facility:** 24 rooms. Pleasant smaller property, rooms offer contemporary decor, harmonized to older details. 2 stories; interior corridors. **Dining:** Restaurant; 7 am-9 pm, Sun 8 am-8 pm; $9-$16; cocktails; nightclub. **Services:** winter plug-ins. **All Rooms:** extended cable TV. **Cards:** AE, DI, DS, MC, VI.

DAYS INN
(CAA) (SAVE)
◆◆
Motor Inn
All Year   1P: $99   2P: $109   XP: $10   Phone: (204)586-8525   36 F12
Location: Just n of Logan Ave. 550 McPhillips St R2X 2H2. Fax: 204/582-5035. **Facility:** 66 rooms. Nicely appointed rooms with contemporary flair. All rooms with hair dryer, iron and ironing board. 2 stories; interior corridors; heated pool, sauna, waterslide, whirlpool. **Dining:** Restaurant; 7 am-10 pm; $6-$10; cocktails; entertainment, nightclub. **Services:** winter plug-ins. **All Rooms:** extended cable TV. **Cards:** AE, DI, DS, MC, VI. **Special Amenities: Free newspaper and free room upgrade (subject to availability with advanced reservations).**

HOLIDAY INN AIRPORT/WEST
(CAA) (SAVE)
◆◆◆
Hotel
All Year   1P: $100-$115   2P: $100-$115   XP: $20   Phone: (204)885-4478   38 F19
Location: Just e of Moray St. 2520 Portage Ave W R3J 3T6. Fax: 204/832-7424. **Terms:** Weekly & monthly rates avail; 7 day cancellation notice; package plans. **Facility:** 227 rooms. Some rooms with balcony. Offers a supervised kid's activity centre during the summer and weekends during the winter. Large guest rooms on upper floor. Recently refurbished, offering attractive decor and increased quality of amenities. 15 stories; interior corridors; heated pool, wading pool, saunas, whirlpool. **Dining:** Restaurant; 6:30 am-11 pm, Sat & Sun from 7:30 am; $13-$18; cocktails. **Services:** gift shop; area transportation, Polo Park; winter plug-ins. **All Rooms:** combo or shower baths, extended cable TV. **Some Rooms:** 10 kitchens, honor bars. **Cards:** AE, CB, DI, DS, MC, VI. **Special Amenities: Free local telephone calls and free room upgrade (subject to availability with advanced reservations).**

(See map p. 566)

HOLIDAY INN WINNIPEG SOUTH
Phone: (204)452-4747 **24**

CAA SAVE

◆◆◆

Hotel

5/1-8/31	1P: $95	2P: $95	XP: $10	F19
3/1-4/30 & 9/1-2/28	1P: $85	2P: $85	XP: $10	F19

Location: At McGillivray Blvd. 1330 Pembina Hwy R3T 2B4. Fax: 204/284-2751. **Terms:** [BP] meal plan; cancellation fee imposed; package plans; pets, in smoking rooms. **Facility:** 170 rooms. Well appointed spacious units, contemporary decor. In the vicinity of the University, along major route. All rooms with hair dryer, iron and ironing board. 11 stories; interior corridors; small heated indoor pool, wading pool, whirlpool. **Dining:** Restaurant; 6:30 am-11 pm, Sat from 7 am, Sun 7 am-10 pm; $7-$17; cocktails. **Services:** winter plug-ins. **All Rooms:** extended cable TV. **Cards:** AE, CB, DI, DS, JC, MC, VI. **Special Amenities:** Early check-in/late check-out and free local telephone calls.

INTERNATIONAL INN-BEST WESTERN
Phone: (204)786-4801 **34**

CAA SAVE

◆◆

Motor Inn

All Year	1P: $92-$140	2P: $97-$150	XP: $5	F16

Location: Wellington Ave at Berry St. 1808 Wellington Ave R3H 0G3. Fax: 204/786-1329. **Terms:** Pets, $5 extra charge. **Facility:** 288 rooms. Pleasant, basic style accommodations. Average to spacious guest rooms. Security sections also avail. 5 stories; interior corridors; 2 heated pools, sauna, waterslide, whirlpool. **Dining:** Dining room; 6:30 am-midnight, Sun from 7 am; $5-$28; cocktails. **Services:** gift shop; winter plug-ins. **Some Rooms:** honor bars. **Cards:** AE, CB, DI, DS, JC, MC, VI. **Special Amenities:** Free local telephone calls and free room upgrade (subject to availability with advanced reservations).

LINCOLN MOTOR HOTEL
Phone: (204)589-7314 **42**

CAA SAVE

◆◆

Motor Inn

All Year	1P: $45-$47	2P: $49-$51	XP: $6

Location: McPhillips St at Troy Ave. 1030 McPhillips St R2X 2K7. Fax: 204/589-8241. **Terms:** 14 day cancellation notice. **Facility:** 24 rooms. Good, basic budget style accommodations; average sized guest rooms with older style decor mixed with newer details. 2 stories; interior corridors. **Dining:** Restaurant; 7 am-11 pm, closed Sun; $5-$13; cocktails; nightclub. **Services:** winter plug-ins. **All Rooms:** extended cable TV. **Cards:** MC, VI.

NIAKWA INN
Phone: (204)255-6000 **39**

◆◆

Motor Inn

All Year	1P: $68-$72	2P: $72-$77	XP: $6

F17

Location: Just e of jct Fermor Ave and St Anne's Rd. 20 Alpine Ave R2M 0Y5. Fax: 204/253-1563. **Facility:** 75 rooms. Rooms range from average to spacious; all with attractive contemporary decor. Excellent budget accommodations. 2 stories; interior corridors; heated pool. **Services:** winter plug-ins. **Some Rooms:** Fee: VCR. **Cards:** AE, DI, MC, VI.

QUALITY INN
Phone: (204)453-8247 **25**

CAA SAVE

◆◆◆

Motor Inn

All Year	1P: $60-$80	2P: $70-$90	XP: $10

F10

Location: Pembina Hwy at Grand Ave. 635 Pembina Hwy R3M 2L4. Fax: 204/287-2365. **Terms:** 14 day cancellation notice, x; small pets only, on smoking floor. **Facility:** 69 rooms. Rooms may be compact but offer attractive decor. Many well-decorated theme rooms, all with unique features. All rooms with hair dryer, iron and ironing board. 6 whirlpool rooms, $175-$230; 4 stories; interior corridors. **Dining:** Restaurant; 7 am-10 pm, Sun 8 am-2 pm; $5-$13; cocktails. **Services:** winter plug-ins. **Recreation:** sports lounge, simulated indoor golf game. **Cards:** AE, DI, MC, VI.

RADISSON SUITE HOTEL-WINNIPEG AIRPORT
Phone: (204)783-1700 **35**

◆◆◆

Suite Hotel

1/1-2/28	1P: $169-$195	2P: $169-$195	XP: $15	F17
3/1-12/31	1P: $159-$195	2P: $159-$195	XP: $15	F17

Location: Wellington Ave at Berry St. 1800 Wellington Ave R3H 1B2. Fax: 204/786-6588. **Facility:** 160 rooms. Spacious accommodations in 2 room units, few smaller 1 room units poolside, all with very attractive furnishings. All rooms with iron and ironing board. 6 stories; interior corridors; 2 heated pools. **Services:** gift shop; winter plug-ins. **Cards:** AE, CB, DI, DS, JC, MC, VI.

TWIN PILLARS BED & BREAKFAST
Phone: 204/284-7590 **26**

◆◆

Historic Bed
& Breakfast

All Year	1P: $40-$42	2P: $50-$52	XP: $10

F8

Location: 0.6 km e of Osborne St. 235 Oakwood Ave R3L 1E5. Fax: 204/452-4925. **Terms:** [CP] meal plan; cancellation fee imposed; pets, pet on premises. **Facility:** 4 rooms. Lovely brick home built in 1901. Rooms are well appointed and offer a mix of antique and contemporary furnishings. In a residential neighborhood, across from park. 3 stories, no elevator; interior corridors. **Services:** winter plug-ins. **Some Rooms:** B/W TV, color TV.

VISCOUNT GORT HOTEL
Phone: (204)775-0451 **32**

◆◆

Motor Inn

All Year	1P: $82-$140	2P: $89-$150	XP: $10

F18

Location: Portage Ave at Rt 90. 1670 Portage Ave R3J 0C9. Fax: 204/772-2161. **Terms:** [BP] meal plan; pets, in designated rooms. **Facility:** 139 rooms. Very spacious rooms. 4-6 stories; interior corridors; heated pool. **Services:** area transportation; winter plug-ins. **Cards:** AE, DI, DS, MC, VI.

(See map p. 566)

-------- RESTAURANTS --------

BRANIGAN'S   Lunch: $5-$9   Dinner: $9-$15   Phone: 204/667-4700   ㉓
◆◆   **Location:** Just e of Lagimodiere Blvd (Rt 20), in Kildonan Place Mall. 1500 Regent Ave R2C 4J2. **Hours:** 11
Canadian   am-2 am. Closed: 12/25. **Reservations:** accepted. **Features:** casual dress; Sunday brunch; children's menu;
senior's menu; carryout; cocktails & lounge; a la carte. **Cards:** AE, DI, MC, VI.   ✖

DIONYSOS RESTAURANT   Lunch: $4-$12   Dinner: $10-$16   Phone: 204/667-3110   ㉑
◆   **Location:** Just w of Lagimodiere Blvd (Metro Rt 20). 1185 Nairn Ave R2L 0Y6. **Hours:** 11 am-11 pm, Sun 4
Greek   pm-9 pm. Closed: 12/25. **Reservations:** suggested. **Features:** casual dress; children's menu; carryout;
cocktails & lounge. This popular restaurant offers family dining and an extensive and authentic menu. Greek
salad, gyros, sandwiches, pizza, steaks and fish are included in the offerings. Large portions, good service and Gothic-style
decor complement the menu. **Cards:** AE, DI, MC, VI.   ✖

INDIA PALACE   Lunch: $6   Dinner: $8-$20   Phone: 204/774-6061   ㉔
◆◆   **Location:** Corner Simcoe St. 770 Ellice Ave G0B8. **Hours:** 11 am-11 pm. Closed: 12/25.
Indian   **Reservations:** suggested. **Features:** casual dress; carryout; cocktails; street parking; a la carte. You'll enjoy
the fresh, flavorful cuisine at this restaurant, where the tandoori chicken is exceptional. The menu is so
extensive that it will satisfy the most discerning tastes. It has a softly lit decor, and warm, caring and friendly service.
Cards: AE, DI, MC, VI.   ✖

MAXIME   Lunch: $5-$8   Dinner: $8-$25   Phone: 204/257-1521   ㉕
◆◆   **Location:** At corner of St Marys Rd and Bishop Grandin Blvd. 1131 St. Mary's Rd R2M 3T9. **Hours:** 11
Continental   am-midnight, Sun-10 pm. Closed: 1/1, 12/25 & 12/26. **Features:** dressy casual; carryout; cocktails; a la
carte. This restaurant is a favorite with locals. Its menu features pasta, pizza, Greek specialties, steak,
chicken and seafood entrees, which are served in large portions. The service is polite, professional and efficient, and the
decor is upscale. **Cards:** AE, MC, VI.   ✖

MEDICINE ROCK CAFE   Lunch: $6-$12   Dinner: $14-$25   Phone: 204/864-2451   ㉚
(AA)   **Location:** 13 km w on Hwy 1 from city limits, 4 km n on Hwy 26. 990 Hwy 26 R0H 1J0. **Hours:** 11 am-10
◆◆   pm. Closed: 12/25 & 12/26. **Reservations:** suggested. **Features:** dressy casual; Sunday brunch; children's
Canadian   menu; carryout; cocktails & lounge; a la carte. The Medicine Rock Cafe offers a beautiful, rustic ambience in
a charming log home in a rural area outside Winnipeg. Entrees include chicken piccata, fresh walleye, baked
salmon and steak. Old rifles, sabers and a stone fireplace add to the decor. **Cards:** AE, DI, MC, VI.   ✖

MONA LISA RISTORANTE   Lunch: $6-$10   Dinner: $8-$18   Phone: 204/488-3687   ⑳
◆◆   **Location:** Corner Renfrew St. 1697 Corydon R3N 0J9. **Hours:** 11:30 am-midnight, Sat from 4 pm, Sun 4
Italian   pm-9:30 pm. Closed: 12/25. **Reservations:** suggested. **Features:** casual dress; carryout; cocktails; street
parking; a la carte. This popular neighborhood restaurant features an extensive cuisine of Northern Italian
fare, including mezza lune, melengane alla parmigiana, veal and jumbo prawns. Local hockey hero memorabilia adorn the
walls in the lounge, and there's a sidewalk patio. **Cards:** AE, DI, MC, VI.   ✖

NIBBLER'S NOSH   Lunch: $5-$10   Dinner: $13-$17   Phone: 204/284-0310   ㉘
◆◆   **Location:** Corner Strafford St (Rt 70). 973 Corydon Ave R3M 0X1. **Hours:** 11:30 am-midnight, Fri-1 am, Sat
American   11 am-1 am, Sun 11 am-11 pm. Closed: 12/25. **Reservations:** suggested; weekends. **Features:** children's
menu; carryout; cocktails & lounge; a la carte. Visitors especially like this restaurant, which is noted for its
extensive menu including well-known items such as Ben's Montreal smoked-meat sandwich, corned beef sandwich and an
excellent array of desserts. Casual atmosphere. Good service. **Cards:** AE, DI, MC, VI.   ✖

THE ROUND TABLE STEAK HOUSE & PUB   Lunch: $7-$13   Dinner: $14-$26   Phone: 204/453-3631   ㉒
◆◆   **Location:** Just s of Taylor St. 800 Pembina Hwy R3M 2M7. **Hours:** 11 am-2 am. Closed: 12/25.
Steakhouse   **Reservations:** suggested. **Features:** casual dress; Sunday brunch; senior's menu; cocktails & lounge. You'll
enjoy the casual atmosphere at this restaurant, which has an English-manor decor that includes glowing
fireplaces. The house specialty is prime rib, and the menu also offers a very good variety of steak, seafood, chicken and
pasta dishes. **Cards:** AE, DI, MC, VI.   ✖

ROYAL FORK BUFFET RESTAURANT   Lunch: $7   Dinner: $10   Phone: 204/668-1960   ㉖
◆   **Location:** At jct Lagimodiere Blvd and Regent Ave W; in Kildonan Crossing Shopping Centre. 900-1615
American   Regent Ave W R2C 5C6. **Hours:** 11 am-8:30 pm, Fri & Sat-9 pm, Sun-8 pm. Closed: 12/25.
Features: casual dress; children's menu; salad bar; buffet. This restaurant features family-oriented dining
and a menu with excellent variety. Dinner prices are in effect at 4 pm and all day on Sunday. If you have a big appetite and
a limited budget, you'll do well here. Service is friendly and efficient. **Cards:** MC, VI.   ✖

TAVERN IN THE PARK   Lunch: $8-$13   Dinner: $14-$24   Phone: 204/896-7275   ⑱
◆◆◆   **Location:** In Tudor Style Pavillion. Assiniboine Park R3M 2B1. **Hours:** 11:30 am-2:30 & 5-10 pm, Sun 10
Continental   am-2 & 5-9 pm. Closed: Mon. **Reservations:** required. **Features:** dressy casual; Sunday brunch; cocktails &
lounge; a la carte. Set in the city's most famous park, this restaurant's dining room is bright, airy and
upscale. Be ready to savor its meals, which are delectable, progressive Continental fare. Its server staff is charming and
knowledgeable. One of the city's better spots. Smoke free premises. **Cards:** AE, DI, MC, VI.   ♿ ✖

(See map p. 566)

TIFFANI'S RESTAURANT   **Lunch:** $6-$11   **Dinner:** $17-$27   **Phone:** 204/256-7324   ㉗
◆ ◆   **Location:** Just e of jct Fermor Ave and St Annes Rd; in Appleton Estates Apt Bldg. 133 Niakwa Rd R2M
Continental   5J5. **Hours:** 11:30 am-2 & 5-10 pm, Fri & Sat-11 pm. Closed major holidays. **Reservations:** suggested.
                             Features: dressy casual; children's menu; cocktails; a la carte. You'll enjoy Tiffani's, an elegant dining room
offering a breathtaking view of the city from the 17th floor. The restaurant specializes in veal preparations, but the menu also
includes beef, pasta and fish entrees. The server staff is friendly and polite. **Cards:** AE, DI, MC, VI.   ⊠

YAMATO   **Lunch:** $4-$10   **Dinner:** $6-$17   **Phone:** 204/452-1166   ⑲
◆   **Location:** Near the jct of Pembina Hwy; in the Stafford Square Center. 667 B Stafford R3M 2M7. **Hours:** 11
Steak and   am-2 & 5-9 pm, Sat & Sun 5 pm-10 pm. **Reservations:** suggested. **Features:** casual dress; children's menu;
Seafood   carryout; cocktails; a la carte. A traditional Japanese cuisine that includes teppanyaki tableside cooking,
                            sushi and sashimi is offered at this restaurant. The menu also has steak and seafood dishes. Servers are
attired in Oriental costumes. Karaoke entertainment begins after 10 pm. **Cards:** AE, DI, MC, VI.   ⊠

──────── *The following restaurants have not been inspected by AAA* ────────
but are listed for your information only.

ALYCIA'S   **Phone:** 204/582-8789
[fyi]   Not inspected. **Location:** Corner McGregor St. 559 Cathedral Ave. **Features:** Eat at one of the late actor
               John Candy's favorite Ukrainian restaurants. Alycia makes her own kielbasa and pierogies stuffed with potato
and cheddar cheese.

GREEN GATES   **Phone:** 204/897-0990
[fyi]   Not inspected. **Location:** 6945 Roblin Blvd. **Features:** Eatery is located on a former estate just outside the
               city limits. Creative Manitoba regional cuisine changes every three months.

This ends listings for the Winnipeg.
The following page resumes the alphabetical listings of
cities in Manitoba.

Northwest Territories and Nunavut

YELLOWKNIFE pop. 17,300

―――― LODGING ――――

THE EXPLORER HOTEL
CAA SAVE
◆◆
Hotel

All Year   1P: $169
Location: Downtown. 48th St & 49th Ave X1A 2R3 (Postal Service 7000). Fax: 867/873-2789. **Terms:** Month
rates avail. **Facility:** 128 rooms. Spacious units, pleasant decor. Dining room with large, circular fireplace.
stories; interior corridors. **Dining:** 2 restaurants; 6 am-midnight; $17-$29; cocktails. **Services:** gift shop; wint
plug-ins. **All Rooms:** extended cable TV. **Cards:** AE, DI, JC, MC, VI.

Phone: (867)873-353
XP: $15   F1

AAA Accessibility Criteria for Travelers With Disabilities

*A*ccessibility is an important issue for travelers with disabilities In an effort to provide this imperative information to our members with disabilities, AAA/CAA has created *AAA Accessibility Criteria for Travelers With Disabilities*, brochure that outlines the criteria used by our inspectors to determine if AAA/CAA Rated® property is considered accessible.

Once all applicable criteria have been met, the appropriate icons indicating property's level of accessibility can be found in the lodging listings of the TourBook® guides.

For more information or to receive copy of this brochure, call or stop by your local AAA/CAA Club.

Saskatchewan

ANNAHEIM pop. 200

——— RESTAURANT ———

TREASURES & KEEPSAKES TEA ROOM   **Lunch: $6-$8**   **Phone: 306/598-217**
◆◆   **Location:** From Hwy 5, 15 km n on Annaheim Rd, then 0.5 km e following signs. Main St S0K 0G
German   **Hours:** Open 5/1-12/20; 10 am-6 pm, Sun from noon. **Reservations:** suggested. **Features:** No A/C; casu
dress; health conscious menu; carryout. In a restored Victorian home with a decor of dried flower bouquet
pink and lace, this restaurant has a menu offering German and East European specialties along with home-baked bread ar
pastry. Smoke free premises. **Cards:** MC, VI.

CARONPORT pop. 1,100

——— LODGING ———

THE PILGRIM INN   **Phone: (306)756-500**
(CAA) (SAVE)   All Year   1P: $65   2P: $65
◆◆◆   **Location:** Jct Main Access; on Trans Canada Hwy 1. 310 College Dr S0H 0S0. Fax: 306/756-500
Motel   **Terms:** [CP] meal plan; pets, with permission. **Facility:** 42 rooms. Newer property adjacent to a small true
stop. Well appointed lobby with a gas fireplace. Good sized rooms with bright and cheerful decor. 1-bedroo
suite with efficiency, $95; 2 stories; interior corridors; smoke free premises; 4 tennis courts. Fee: golf rang
Dining: Pilgrim Restaurant, see separate listing. **Services:** winter plug-ins. **All Rooms:** extended cable TV. **Cards:** AE, L
DS, MC, VI. **Special Amenities:** Free breakfast and free local telephone calls. *(See color ad below)*

——— RESTAURANT ———

PILGRIM RESTAURANT   **Lunch: $5-$10**   **Dinner: $5-$10**   **Phone: 306/756-333**
(CAA)   **Location:** Jct Main Access; on Trans Canada Hwy 1; in The Pilgrim Inn. Trans Canada Hwy 1 W S0H 0S
◆   **Hours:** 7 am-11 pm; from 6 am 5/1-8/31, to 10 pm in winter. Closed: 4/2, 12/25 & Sun. **Features:** children
American   menu; senior's menu; carryout; salad bar. You'll enjoy this restaurant's excellent home-style cooking featurir
freshly baked bread and pastries, pleasant country ambience, prompt, cordial service, hearty servings ar
large gift shop. Daily lunch buffet is 11 am-2 pm; supper smorgasbord 5-8 pm. **Cards:** AE, MC, VI.
(See color ad below)

ELBOW pop. 300

——— LODGING ———

LAKEVIEW LODGE MOTEL   **Phone: 306/854-444**
◆   All Year   1P: $48   2P: $53   XP: $5   F1
Motel   **Location:** Off Hwy 19, 1 km w. 447 Saskatchewan St S0H 1J0 (PO Box 269). **Terms:** Pets, $10 extra charg
Facility: 9 rooms. Quiet rural area, contemporary furnished rooms. 1 story; exterior corridors. **Services:** wint
plug-ins. **Cards:** MC, VI.

FOAM LAKE pop. 1,300

——— LODGING ———

LA VISTA MOTEL   **Phone: (306)272-334**
◆   All Year   1P: $45   2P: $50   XP: $5
Motel   **Location:** On Hwy 16. Jct Hwy 16 & 310 S0A 1A0 (PO Box 458). Fax: 306/272-4448. **Terms:** Pet
Facility: 16 rooms. Good size rooms with contemporary touches. 1 story; interior corridors. **Services:** wint
plug-ins. **Cards:** AE, MC, VI.

KINDERSLEY pop. 4,700

—— LODGING ——

BEST WESTERN WESTRIDGE MOTOR INN
◆ All Year   1P: $54-$61   2P: $65-$72   **Phone:** (306)463-4687
Motor Inn   **Location:** Jct of Hwy 7 and 21. 100 12 Ave NW S0L 1S0 (PO Box 1657). Fax: 306/463-3030. **Terms:** Small pets only. **Facility:** 43 rooms. Spacious units offering contemporary decor and convenient in room amenities. stories; interior/exterior corridors. **Services:** winter plug-ins. **Some Rooms:** 2 efficiencies. **Cards:** AE, DI, DS, MC, VI.

LANGENBURG pop. 1,100

—— LODGING ——

LANGENBURG COUNTRY INN
All Year   1P: $39-$42   2P: $45-$48   **Phone:** 306/743-2638
Motel   **Location:** On Hwy 16, 1 km e. 1041 Kaiser William Ave E S0A 2A0 (PO Box 279). Fax: 306/743-5506.   F4
Terms: Cancellation fee imposed. **Facility:** 14 rooms. Small motel with average size, modestly decorated rooms. Rural setting. 1 story; exterior corridors. **Services:** winter plug-ins. **Cards:** MC, VI.

LLOYDMINSTER pop. 19,000—See also LLOYDMINSTER, AB

—— LODGING ——

IMPERIAL 400 LLOYDMINSTER
SAVE   All Year   1P: $66-$74   2P: $74-$79   **Phone:** (306)825-4400
Motor Inn   **Location:** From jct Hwy 17 and 16, 1.2 km e on Hwy 16. 4320 44 St S9V 1R5. Fax: 306/825-6026.   F16
Terms: Cancellation fee imposed; pets. **Facility:** 100 rooms. Large rooms offering good budget accommodation. Rooms on ground floor with at-door parking. In-room video games. 2 stories; interior/exterior corridors; heated pool, waterslide, whirlpool. **Dining:** Restaurant; 6:30 am-9 pm, Sat from 7 am, Sun 7 am-2 pm; $5-$11; cocktails. **Services:** winter plug-ins. **Recreation:** in-room video games. **All Rooms:** extended cable TV. **Cards:** AE, DI, DS, MC, VI. *(See color ad p 582)*

MELVILLE pop. 4,600

—— LODGING ——

CLASSIC INN
   Phone: 306/728-4571
Property failed to provide current rates
Motor Inn   **Location:** 1.5 km e of Hwy 10, via Hwy 15 and 3rd Ave. 203 3rd Ave E S0A 2P0 (PO Box 2068).
Fax: 306/728-4857. **Facility:** 30 rooms. An older property close to downtown. Average sized guest rooms with modest furnishings. 1 story; interior corridors. **Services:** winter plug-ins. **Cards:** AE, MC, VI.

MOOSE JAW pop. 33,000

—— LODGINGS ——

HERITAGE INN
◆ 12/1-2/28   1P: $77-$150   2P: $87-$150   XP: $5   F12
Motor Inn   5/1-11/30   1P: $75-$140   2P: $85-$140   XP: $5   F12
   3/1-4/30   1P: $74-$140   2P: $84-$140   XP: $5   F12   **Phone:** (306)693-7550
Location: 1.5 km s of jct Trans Canada Hwy 1 and 2; access from Hwy 2 via Thatcher Dr. 1590 Main St N S6H 7N7 (PO Box 20). Fax: 306/692-5660. **Terms:** Pets, $25 dep req. **Facility:** 90 rooms. Attractive atrium pool area. Rooms well furnished with contemporary appointments. 2 stories; interior corridors; heated pool. **Dining:** nightclub. **Services:** winter plug-ins. **Cards:** AE, DI, DS, MC, VI.

PRAIRIE OASIS MOTEL
All Year   1P: $48-$50   2P: $56-$60   **Phone:** 306/693-8888
Motel   **Location:** Just s of jct Hwy 1 (Trans Canada Hwy) and Thatcher Dr. 955 Thatcher Dr E S6H 4N9 (PO Box 250). Fax: 306/692-0041. **Terms:** Weekly rates avail; pets, in smoking rooms. **Facility:** 40 rooms. Most rooms have kitchen area with utensils. This property is an excellent destination for families. 1 story; exterior corridors; heated pool, wading pool, waterslide, whirlpool; playground. **Dining:** Restaurant nearby. **Services:** winter plug-ins. **All Rooms:** extended cable TV. **Cards:** AE, DI, MC, VI.

SUPER 8 MOTEL-MOOSE JAW
◆   **Phone:** 306/692-8888
Property failed to provide current rates
Motel   **Location:** 1.5 km s of jct Trans Canada Hwy 1 and 2; access from Hwy 2 via Thatcher Dr. 1706 Main St N S6H 4P1 (PO Box 452, S6A 4P1). Fax: 306/693-7255. **Terms:** [CP] meal plan; pets. **Facility:** 60 rooms. Large guest rooms, pleasant decor, good budget accommodation. A few newer rooms. 3 stories; interior corridors. **Services:** winter plug-ins. **Cards:** AE, DI, DS, MC, VI.

TEMPLE GARDENS MINERAL SPA & RESORT HOTEL
Phone: (306)694-505

CAA SAVE   All Year   1P: $97-$227   2P: $97-$227   XP: $10   F1
◆◆◆   **Location:** Off Main St, next to Crescent Park; 3.2 km s of Trans Canada Hwy. 24 Fairford St E S6H 0C
Hotel   Fax: 306/694-8310. **Terms:** Package plans. **Facility:** 96 rooms. Spacious rooms nicely decorated and fu
nished. Attractive public areas with state of the art spa facilities. 24 suites with mineral water fed spa, $15
$180; 24 whirlpool rooms, $152-$227; 4 stories; interior corridors; heated pool, steamroom, whirlpool, miner
spa pool. **Dining:** Restaurant; 7 am-11 pm; $6-$19; health conscious menu; cocktails. **Services:** gift shop; winter plug-in
Fee: massage. **Recreation:** Fee: bicycles, spa treatment salon. **All Rooms:** extended cable TV. **Cards:** AE, DI, MC, VI.

〔icons〕

——— RESTAURANTS ———

HOUSTON PIZZA & STEAK HOUSE   **Lunch:** $6-$8   **Dinner:** $8-$19   Phone: 306/693-393
◆   **Location:** Just s of High St; 3.5 km s of Hwy #1. 117 Main St N S6H 0C7. **Hours:** 11 am-midnight, Fri
American   Sat-1 am, Sun 4 pm-10 pm. Closed: 12/25 & 12/26. **Features:** children's menu; senior's menu; carryou
cocktails; street parking. Touted by locals as possibly the best restaurant in town, Houston's is an ideal sp
for couples or families. The menu offers a full range of meals such as steak, spaghetti, lasagna, ribs, barbecue chicke
seafood, stir-fry and salads. Prompt service. **Cards:** AE, DI, MC, VI.   〔⟩〕

WAYNE & LAVERNE'S PIZZA & STEAK HOUSE   **Lunch:** $4-$7   **Dinner:** $5-$19   Phone: 306/694-177
◆   **Location:** Centre; just s of Hochelaga St. 622 Main St N S6H 3K4. **Hours:** 11 am-10 pm, Fri & Sat-11 pr
American   Closed: 12/25. **Features:** children's menu; health conscious menu items; carryout; cocktails; street parking;
la carte. This casual, family-oriented eatery features an Italian buffet, buffalo steaks and heart-smart entree
Its large menu includes dishes for small appetites and a children's menu. Its decor is inviting and the server staff is cordi
and prompt. **Cards:** AE, MC, VI.   〔⟩〕

NORTH BATTLEFORD pop. 14,100

——— LODGINGS ———

SUPER 8 MOTEL
Phone: (306)446-888
◆   All Year   1P: $59-$69   2P: $65-$75   XP: $3   F1
Motel   **Location:** 0.5 km nw of jct Hwy 16. 1006 Hwy 16 Bypass S9A 3W2 (PO Box 1690). Fax: 306/445-419
Terms: [CP] meal plan; pets, in smoking rooms. **Facility:** 39 rooms. Simple decor and basic budget accom
modation, in spacious units. Some rooms with extra large TV. 2 stories; interior corridors. **Services:** winter plug-ins. **Cards:** A
DI, DS, MC, VI.   〔icons〕

TROPICAL INN
Phone: (306)446-470
◆◆   3/1-5/31 & All Year   1P: $59-$69   2P: $64-$69   XP: $5   F1
Motor Inn   **Location:** Corner of Battleford Rd and Hwy 16 bypass. 1001 Hwy 16 bypass S9A 2W3. Fax: 306/446-229
Terms: Package plans; small pets only. **Facility:** 119 rooms. Spacious guest rooms, some with balcony ove
looking the pool. 2 stories; interior corridors; heated pool. **Services:** winter plug-ins. **Cards:** AE, DI, MC, VI.

〔icons〕

——— RESTAURANT ———

DA VINCI'S, RISTORANTE ITALIANO   **Dinner:** $8-$19   Phone: 306/446-470
◆◆   **Location:** Corner of Battleford Rd and Hwy 16 bypass; in Tropical Inn. 1001 Hwy 16 Bypass S9A 3W
Italian   **Hours:** 5 pm-10 pm, Fri & Sat-11 pm, Sun-9 pm. Closed major holidays. **Reservations:** suggeste
Features: casual dress; children's menu; cocktails; a la carte. Although the name suggests Italian cuisin
this quiet restaurant offers Continental dishes as well as specialties from Louisiana. In addition to pasta, the menu featur
jambalaya, blackened pickerel, steaks, chicken and veal entrees. Friendly service. **Cards:** AE, DI, DS, MC, VI.   〔⟩〕

PRINCE ALBERT pop. 34,800

——— LODGINGS ———

COMFORT INN
Phone: (306)763-446
◆◆   1/1-2/28   1P: $72-$76   2P: $84-$88   XP: $5   F1
Motel   6/1-9/30   1P: $72-$74   2P: $80-$88   XP: $5   F1
10/1-12/31   1P: $70-$72   2P: $78-$82   XP: $5   F1
3/1-5/31   1P: $68-$72   2P: $66-$80   XP: $5   F1
Location: 2.3 km s at jct Hwy 2 and Marquis Rd. 3863 2nd Ave W S6W 1A1. Fax: 306/764-2210. **Terms:** Small pets on
Facility: 62 rooms. Very good budget accommodation. Ground floor units offer convenient patio doors that lead out to parki
lot. 2 stories; interior corridors. **Services:** winter plug-ins. **Cards:** AE, DI, DS, JC, MC, VI.
〔icons〕

IMPERIAL 400 PRINCE ALBERT
Phone: (306)764-68
CAA SAVE   All Year   1P: $66-$74   2P: $74-$79   XP: $5   F
◆   **Location:** 2.1 km s at jct Hwy 2 and Marquis Rd. 3580 2nd Ave W S6V 5G2. Fax: 306/763-653
Motor Inn   **Terms:** Weekly rates avail; cancellation fee imposed; pets. **Facility:** 137 rooms. Ideal accommodations for t
budget oriented traveller. 1-2 stories; interior/exterior corridors; heated pool, waterslide, whirlpool. **Dining:** Re
taurant; 6:30 am-10 pm, Sun-2 pm; $5-$10; cocktails. **Services:** winter plug-ins. **All Rooms:** extended cab
TV. **Cards:** AE, DI, DS, JC, MC, VI. *(See color ad p 582)*
〔icons〕

TRAVELODGE PRINCE ALBERT
Phone: 306/764-6441

◆◆	7/1-8/31 & 1/1-2/28	1P: $77	2P: $87	XP: $10	F16
Motor Inn	3/1-6/30 & 9/1-12/31	1P: $72	2P: $82	XP: $10	F16

Location: 2.2 km s at jct Hwy 2 and Marquis Rd. 3551 2nd Ave W S6V 5G1. Fax: 306/763-8250.
Terms: Check-in 4 pm; pets, in designated rooms. **Facility:** 80 rooms. Recently renovated rooms and 1-bedroom suites offering a bright and contemporary decor. 2 stories; interior/exterior corridors; heated pool. **Services:** winter plug-ins. **Cards:** AE, DI, DS, MC, VI.

(ASK) (S/D) 🛏 🍴 🍽 🐾 🛋 ✕ 📷 🖨 💻 📞 (DATA PORT) 🌐

——— RESTAURANTS ———

AMY'S ON SECOND RESTAURANT **Lunch:** $5-$12 **Dinner:** $9-$20 **Phone:** 306/763-1515
◆◆ **Location:** 1.5 km s on 2nd Ave W, at 30 St W. 2990 2nd Ave W S6V 7E9. **Hours:** 11:30 am-10 pm,
Continental Thurs-Sat to 11 pm. Closed major holidays & Sun. **Reservations:** suggested. **Features:** casual dress; children's menu; health conscious menu items; carryout; cocktails; a la carte. You'll discover a warm and intimate setting here. Amy's menu specializes in the freshest ingredients for the homemade food and many regional specialties including wild rice soup, rack of lamb, excellent Saskatchewan pickerel, and cheesecakes. Smoke free premises. **Cards:** AE, DI, MC, VI.

✕

VENICE HOUSE **Lunch:** $5-$7 **Dinner:** $6-$30 **Phone:** 306/764-6555
◆◆ **Location:** 15th St and Central Ave. 1498 Central Ave S6V 4W5. **Hours:** 11 am-midnight, Fri & Sat-1:30 am.
Greek Closed: 12/25. **Reservations:** suggested. **Features:** children's menu; senior's menu; carryout; cocktails; minimum charge-$4. A casual, family-dining experience awaits you at the Venice House. The menu offers steak, pizza, spaghetti, veal and seafood dishes, but their house specialty is Greek-style ribs. The very relaxed atmosphere is quite comfortable and appealing. **Cards:** AE, DI, MC, VI.

REGINA pop. 180,400

——— LODGINGS ———

CHELTON SUITES HOTEL
Phone: (306)569-4600
◆◆ Property failed to provide current rates
Hotel **Location:** Centre, corner Rose St. 1907 11th Ave S4P 0J2. Fax: 306/569-3531. **Terms:** Pets. **Facility:** 56 rooms. Spacious and comtemporary guest rooms, all rooms with wet bar and hair dryer. Room types include studios, junior suites and large 1-bedroom suites. 5 stories; interior corridors. **Services:** winter plug-ins. **Cards:** AE, DI, MC, VI.

🛏 🍴 🍽 🐾 🛋 ✕ 📷 🖨 💻 📞 (DATA PORT)

COMFORT INN
Phone: (306)789-5522

◆◆◆	6/18-9/30	1P: $77	2P: $85	XP: $8	F18
Motel	4/1-6/17	1P: $75	2P: $83	XP: $8	F18
	10/1-2/28	1P: $74	2P: $82	XP: $8	F18
	3/1-3/31	1P: $71	2P: $79	XP: $8	F18

Location: Off Trans Canada Hwy 1, 2 km e of Ring Rd at eastern approach to Regina. 3221 East Eastgate Dr S4Z 1A4. Fax: 306/789-9964. **Terms:** Pets, in smoking rooms. **Facility:** 99 rooms. Average sized but well appointed rooms. Ground floor units have a patio door for convenient access to parking lot. A few more luxurious executive units. 2 stories; interior corridors. **Services:** winter plug-ins. **Cards:** AE, DI, DS, JC, MC, VI.

(SAVE) (S/D) 🛏 🍴 🛋 ✕ 📷 🖨 💻 (DATA PORT)

COUNTRY INN & SUITES BY CARLSON
Phone: (306)789-9117
(AAA) (SAVE) All Year 1P: $63-$99 2P: $71-$99 XP: $8 F18
◆◆◆ **Location:** Off Trans Canada Hwy 1, 2 km e of Ring Rd at eastern approach to city. 3321 E Eastgate Bay S4Z
Hotel 1A4. Fax: 306/789-3010. **Terms:** [CP] meal plan; weekly & monthly rates avail; 3 day cancellation notice; small pets only, in smoking rooms. **Facility:** 77 rooms. A charming country style decor in both the lobby and guest rooms. Choose from large standard rooms or 1-bedroom suites. Complimentary video movies. All rooms with iron and ironing board. Executive rooms, $82-$89; 3 stories; interior corridors. **Dining:** Restaurant nearby. **Services:** winter plug-ins. **All Rooms:** extended cable TV. **Cards:** AE, DI, DS, MC, VI. **Special Amenities:** Free breakfast and free newspaper. (See color ad below)

(S/D) 🛏 🍴 🛋 🏠 ✕ (VCR) 🖨 💻 📞 📞 (DATA PORT)

DELTA REGINA
◆◆◆
Hotel
All Year   1P: $109   2P: $109   **Phone:** (306)525-525█
XP: $10   F█
Location: Centre; Saskatchewan Dr at Rose St. 1919 Saskatchewan Dr S4P 4H2. Fax: 306/781-718█
Facility: 255 rooms. Elegant guest rooms, very well appointed. All rooms with hair dryer, iron, ironing boar█
video games and voice mail. 25 stories; interior corridors; heated pool. **Services:** gift shop; winter plug-ins. **Cards:** AE, D█
MC, VI.

(ASK) (S/D) (▮) (Y) (⌘) (▦) (△) (✕) (✦) (📠) (▯) (🖥) (H) (DATA PORT) (△) (H)

HOTEL SASKATCHEWAN RADISSON PLAZA
(CAA) (SAVE)
◆◆◆◆
Classic Hotel
All Year   1P: $99-$185   2P: $99-$185   **Phone:** (306)522-76█
XP: $15   F█
Location: Centre; Victoria Ave at Scarth St. 2125 Victoria Ave S4P 0S3. Fax: 306/757-5521. **Terms:** [CP] me█
plan. **Facility:** 217 rooms. **Historic.** Elegantly restored, 1927 hotel with an impressive lobby and public are█
all richly decorated down to the smallest detail. Guest rooms are traditionally furnished in a Victorian sty█
charm. 14 suites, $185-$995.; 3 whirlpool rooms; suites, $161-$799; 10 stories; interior corridors; steamroo█
whirlpool. **Dining:** Dining room; cocktails; afternoon tea; also, Cortland Hall Dining Room, see separate listing. **Services:** g█
shop; area transportation; winter plug-ins. Fee: massage. **All Rooms:** extended cable TV, honor bars. **Some Rooms:** kitche█
Cards: AE, CB, DI, DS, JC, MC, VI.

(✠) (▮) (Y) (⌘) (△) (⋔) (✕) (✦) (📠) (▯) (🖥) (H) (DATA PORT) (H)

RAMADA HOTEL & CONVENTION CENTRE
◆◆
Hotel
All Year   1P: $87-$126   2P: $87-$126   **Phone:** (306)569-16█
XP: $10   F█
Location: Centre, at Victoria Ave and Broad St. 1818 Victoria Ave S4P 0R1. Fax: 306/352-633█
Terms: Package plans; small pets only. **Facility:** 233 rooms. Rather spacious rooms with older decor. T█
floors with better appointments and extra amenities. All rooms with voice mail. 15 stories; interior corridors; heated po█
Fee: parking. **Services:** gift shop. **Cards:** AE, DI, MC, VI.

(ASK) (S/D) (🛏) (▮) (Y) (⌘) (▦) (△) (✕) (✦) (📠) (🖥) (H) (DATA PORT) (△) (H)

REGINA SUPER 8
◆◆
Motel
All Year   1P: $60   2P: $68   **Phone:** (306)789-88█
Location: Off Trans Canada Hwy 1, 1.6 km e of Ring Rd at eastern approach to Regina. 2730 Victoria Ave█
S4N 6M5. Fax: 306/789-9711. **Terms:** [CP] meal plan; 15 day cancellation notice; pets, $10 dep re█
Facility: 60 rooms. Average sized but very cozy and exceptionally clean accommodations. 3 stories, no elevator; interior co█
ridors. **Services:** winter plug-ins. **Cards:** AE, DI, DS, MC, VI.

(ASK) (S/D) (🛏) (⋔) (✕) (✦) (H) (PO█)

REGINA TRAVELODGE HOTEL
(CAA) (SAVE)
◆◆◆
Motor Inn
All Year   1P: $87   2P: $97   **Phone:** (306)586-34█
XP: $10   F█
Location: 1.5 km n of jct Trans Canada Hwy 1 and Albert St (Hwy 6). 4177 Albert St S S4S 3R█
Fax: 306/586-9311. **Terms:** 7 day cancellation notice. **Facility:** 200 rooms. An outstanding property, sor█
rooms with balcony overlooking the pool. Tastefully decorated rooms with an Irish style pub just off the lob█
All rooms with hair dryer and video games. 6 whirlpool rooms; 4 stories; interior corridors; small heated indo█
pool, waterslide, whirlpool. **Dining:** Restaurant; 6:30 am-11 pm, Sat from 7 am, Sun 7:30 am-10:30 pm; $9-$17; cocktai█
Services: gift shop; winter plug-ins. **Recreation:** children's play cave. **All Rooms:** extended cable TV. **Some Rooms:** Fee: █
frigerators. **Cards:** AE, DI, DS, MC, VI. **Special Amenities:** Free local telephone calls and free room upgrade (subject█
availability with advanced reservations).

(S/D) (▮) (Y) (⌘) (△) (⋔) (✕) (✦) (📠) (▯) (🖥) (H) (DATA PORT) (🚶) (△) (H)

WEST HARVEST INN

Phone: 306/586-6755

◆◆◆
Motor Inn

Property failed to provide current rates

Location: 1.6 km n of jct Trans Canada Hwy 1. 4025 Albert St S S4S 3R6. Fax: 306/584-1345. **Facility:** 105 rooms. Public areas with a southern flair; rooms have a mixed decor with an overall tasteful result. All rooms with hair dryer. 5 stories; interior corridors. **Services:** winter plug-ins. **Some Rooms:** Fee: refrigerators. **Cards:** AE, DI, DS, MC, VI.

⊟⊟⊟⊟⊟⊟⊟⊟⊟⊟

──────── RESTAURANTS ────────

ALFREDO'S ON SCARTH

Lunch: $5-$12   **Dinner:** $9-$18   **Phone:** 306/522-3366

◆◆
Italian

Location: Centre; corner 11th Ave. 1801 Scarth St S4P 2G9. **Hours:** 11 am-midnight. Closed major holidays & Sun. **Reservations:** suggested. **Features:** carryout; cocktails & lounge; street parking; a la carte. The extremely popular Alfredo's features a trendy-looking dining room and a separate wine bar. The restaurant's extensive menu offers an endless number of fresh pasta dishes. Good service. The downtown location is close to theatres and boutiques. **Cards:** AE, DI, MC, VI.

⊠

CORTLANDT HALL DINING ROOM

Lunch: $7-$15   **Dinner:** $12-$29   **Phone:** 306/522-7691

◆◆◆
Continental

Location: Centre; Victoria Ave at Scarth St; in Hotel Saskatchewan Radisson Plaza. 2125 Victoria Ave S4P 0S3. **Hours:** 6 am-10 pm, Sun 6:30 am-9 pm, buffet avail. **Reservations:** suggested. **Features:** casual dress; Sunday brunch; health conscious menu items; cocktails & lounge; fee for parking; a la carte. The award-winning chefs at this restaurant prepare a wide-ranging menu of delicious meals served with superb presentation and imaginative in-house desserts and pastries, and the attractive Victorian decor provides for intimate dining and exceptional view. **Cards:** AE, DI, DS, MC, VI.

♿ ⊠

THE DIPLOMAT

Lunch: $6-$13   **Dinner:** $14-$34   **Phone:** 306/359-3366

◆◆◆
Steak and
Seafood

Location: Just s of jct Broad St and Victoria Ave. 2032 Broad St S4P 1Y3. **Hours:** 11 am-2 & 4-midnight, Sat from 4 pm. Closed: Sun & 12/25. **Reservations:** suggested; weekends. **Features:** children's menu; health conscious menu; cocktails & lounge. You're sure to appreciate the excellent treatment you'll receive at this restaurant, which offers wonderful steaks, filet mignon, coq au vin and seafood, as well as an impressive choice of wines and cognacs. Elegant surroundings and knowledgeable servers. **Cards:** AE, DI, MC, VI.

⊠

GOLF'S STEAK HOUSE

Lunch: $6-$17   **Dinner:** $12-$36   **Phone:** 306/525-5808

◆◆
Steak and
Seafood

Location: Corner Victoria Ave and Hamilton St. 1945 Victoria Ave S4P 0R3. **Hours:** 11 am-midnight, Sat from 4:30 pm, Sun 4:30 pm-10 pm. Closed: 12/25. **Reservations:** suggested. **Features:** children's menu; cocktails & lounge. Golf's Steak House features hearty portions of very good steak, seafood and rack of lamb dishes that are quite tasty and served in large portions. There's a good variety to the menu. The restaurant has traditional formal decor and professional service. **Cards:** AE, DI, MC, VI.

⊠

THE HARVEST EATING HOUSE

Lunch: $5-$10   **Dinner:** $10-$25   **Phone:** 306/545-3777

◆◆
American

Location: 3 km n; corner Albert St and 2nd Ave N. 379 Albert St S4R 2N6. **Hours:** 11:30 am-11:30 pm, Sat from 4 pm, Sun 4 pm-10 pm. Closed: 12/25 & 12/26. **Features:** children's menu; salad bar; cocktails & lounge. Families, seniors and couples enjoy this restaurant, with its bright, country-style decor of barnwood walls and wagon wheels. Steak, prime rib, seafood and chicken are the specialties. Wines are offered by the glass or carafe, and servers are efficient. **Cards:** AE, DI, MC, VI.

⊠

ORLEANS

Lunch: $7-$10   **Dinner:** $8-$16   **Phone:** 306/525-3636

◆◆
Regional
American

Location: Downtown, at 11th Ave. 1822 Broad St S4P 1X6. **Hours:** 5 pm-10 pm. Closed major holidays, Sun & Mon. **Reservations:** suggested. **Features:** casual dress; children's menu; health conscious menu; cocktails; street parking; a la carte. Orleans has a warm ambience and a Louisiana-influenced cuisine with an emphasis on large portions, fresh ingredients, flavorful tastes and good presentations. The nice atmosphere has a well-protected non-smoking area. Service is warm and welcoming. **Cards:** AE, DI, MC, VI.

⊠

SASKATOON pop. 193,600

──────── LODGINGS ────────

BEST WESTERN INN & SUITES

Phone: (306)244-5552

	All Year	1P: $68-$94	2P: $73-$94	XP: $5	F15

Ⓐ SAVE

Motor Inn

Location: 2.6 km n on Hwy 16 and 11 (Idylwyld Dr). 1715 Idylwyld Dr N S7L 1B4. Fax: 306/934-5171. **Terms:** 30 day cancellation notice; cancellation fee imposed; pets. **Facility:** 91 rooms. Located in a small strip mall. Rooms on the 1st floor were more recently renovated and a few of them have a guest entrance from the parking lot. All rooms with hair dryer, iron and ironing board. 3 mini suites, $77.50, 4 full sized suites for up to 6 persons, $90; 2 stories; interior/exterior corridors; whirlpool. **Dining:** Restaurant; 6:30 am-11 pm, Sun 7 am-10 pm; $5-$20; cocktails. **Services:** winter plug-ins. Fee: massage. **All Rooms:** extended cable TV. **Cards:** AE, DI, DS, MC, VI. **Special Amenities:** Early check-in/late check-out and free local telephone calls.

⊟⊟⊟⊟⊟⊟⊟⊟⊟⊟⊟⊟

COMFORT INN

Phone: (306)934-1122

◆◆◆
Motel

6/18-10/16 & 1/1-2/28	1P: $75	2P: $83	
10/17-12/31	1P: $72	2P: $80	
3/1-6/17	1P: $72	2P: $80	XP: $4 F18

Location: 3 km n; just ne of jct Hwy 11 (Idylwyld Dr) and Circle Dr. 2155 Northridge Dr S7L 6X6. Fax: 306/934-6539. **Terms:** Small pets only. **Facility:** 80 rooms. Contemporary and spacious rooms; ground level rooms feature large patio doors to parking lot. A few rooms with more upscale appeal and additional amenities. 2 stories; interior corridors. **Services:** winter plug-ins. **Cards:** AE, CB, DI, DS, JC, MC, VI.

SAVE ⊟⊟⊟⊟⊟⊟⊟⊟⊟⊟

COUNTRY INN & SUITES BY CARLSON
CAA SAVE
◆◆◆
Motel

All Year   1P: $70   2P: $78   XP: $8   **Phone:** (306)934-3900
         F18

Location: Just w of jct Hwy 16 (Idylwyld Dr) and Circle Dr. 617 Cynthia St S7L 6B7. Fax: 306/652-3100. **Terms:** [CP] meal plan; monthly rates avail; small pets only. **Facility:** 77 rooms. Delightful country charm. Mix of spacious suites to large standard units. All rooms with iron and ironing board. 2-room suites, $80-$92 for up to 2 persons, $8 extra person; 3 stories; interior corridors. **Services:** winter plug-ins. **All Rooms:** extended cable TV, honor bars. **Cards:** AE, DI, DS, JC, MC, VI. **Special Amenities:** Free breakfast and free newspaper. *(See color ad p 581)*

DELTA BESSBOROUGH
◆◆◆
Classic Hotel

                                                  2P: $109   **Phone:** (306)244-5521
         F18

Location: Centre; at 21st St E. 601 Spadina Crescent E S7K 3G8. Fax: 306/665-7262. **Terms:** Pets. **Facility:** 225 rooms. **Historic.** Very impressive chateau on the bank of the South Saskatchewan River, meticulously landscaped grounds. Large, elegant rooms. All rooms with iron, ironing board, and video games. 6 stories; interior corridors; heated pool. Fee: parking. **Services:** gift shop; winter plug-ins. Fee: massage. **Recreation:** jogging. Fee: bicycles. **Some Rooms:** honor bars. **Cards:** AE, DI, DS, JC, MC, VI. *(See color ad below)*

RADISSON SASKATOON
CAA SAVE
◆◆◆
Hotel

3/1-6/30 & 9/1-2/28   1P: $129-$174   2P: $129-$174   XP: $10   **Phone:** (306)665-3322
7/1-8/31   1P: $109-$174   2P: $109-$174   XP: $10   F18
         F18

Location: Centre; at 4th Ave S. 405 20th St E S7K 6X6. Fax: 306/665-5531. **Terms:** [BP] meal plan; cancellation fee imposed. **Facility:** 291 rooms. Exceptional view of the South Saskatchewan River or bustling downtown area. All rooms with hair dryer, iron, ironing board and video games. 8 whirlpool rooms; 19 stories; interior corridors; heated pool, sauna, waterslide, whirlpool. Fee: parking. **Dining:** Restaurant; 6:30 am-9 pm, Sat & Sun from 7 am; $7-$17; cocktails. **Services:** gift shop. **Rental:** bicycles. **All Rooms:** extended cable TV. **Cards:** AE, CB, DI, DS, JC, MC, VI. **Special Amenities:** Free local telephone calls and free newspaper. *(See color ad below)*

RAMADA HOTEL SASKATOON
◆◆
Hotel

10/1-12/31 & 1/1-2/28   1P: $85-$95   2P: $90-$100   XP: $10   **Phone:** (306)244-2311
3/1-9/30   1P: $82-$92   2P: $87-$97   XP: $10   F18
         F18

Location: Just e of jct Hwy 11, 5 and 22nd St; adjacent to Eaton's Shopping Complex. 90 22nd St E S7K 3X6. Fax: 306/664-2234. **Terms:** Package plans; pets. **Facility:** 185 rooms. Centrally located downtown. The standard rooms are quite spacious and include a mix of old and new appointments. Wonderful view of the city. 15 stories; interior corridors; heated pool. Fee: parking. **Services:** gift shop. **Some Rooms:** honor bars. **Cards:** AE, CB, DI, DS, JC, MC, VI.

SASKATOON TRAVELODGE HOTEL
Phone: (306)242-8881

AA SAVE	3/1-3/13	1P: $82-$120	2P: $88-$130	XP: $10	F17
◆◆◆	1/1-2/28	1P: $85-$103	2P: $88-$105	XP: $10	F17
Motor Inn	3/14-12/31	1P: $82-$99	2P: $88-$99	XP: $10	F17

Facility: 269 rooms. **Location:** 3 km n; just w of jct Hwy 16 (Idylwyld Dr). 106 Circle Dr W S7L 4L6. Fax: 306/665-7378. Large units with a choice of standard, pool side, pool view with balcony and executive suites. All rooms with hair dryer, video games and voice mail. Specialty room rates.; 10 whirlpool rooms; 2-6 stories; interior corridors; 2 heated pools, wading pool, sauna, waterslide, whirlpools. **Dining:** Restaurant; 6:30 am-11:30 pm; $5-$18; cocktails; nightclub. **Services:** gift shop; winter plug-ins. **Recreation:** game room. **All Rooms:** extended cable TV. **Cards:** AE, CB, DI, DS, JC, MC, VI. **Special Amenities: Free local telephone calls and free room upgrade (subject to availability with advanced reservations).**

RESTAURANTS

CHIANTI
Lunch: $5-$16   Dinner: $6-$16   Phone: 306/665-8466
◆◆
Italian
Location: Center; corner 22nd St E. 102 Idylwyld Dr N S7L 0Y7. **Hours:** 11 am-11 pm, Sun-10 pm. Closed: 12/24 & 12/25. **Reservations:** suggested. **Features:** casual dress; children's menu; carryout; cocktails; a la carte. Chianti's features a good selection of fresh pasta creations, veal, seafood, chicken and half-portions. A pasta special for $5.75 is offered Sunday-Tuesday. The server staff is friendly and personable, and the decor suits families and couples. **Cards:** AE, DI, MC, VI. ✕

GENESIS FAMILY RESTAURANT
Lunch: $4-$8   Dinner: $7-$12   Phone: 306/244-5516
◆◆
Chinese
Location: 1 km w of Idylwyld Dr. 901D 22nd St W S7M 0R9. **Hours:** 11 am-10 pm. Closed major holidays. **Reservations:** suggested. **Features:** health conscious menu items; carryout; cocktails. The Genesis features a progressive Chinese menu offering many healthy choices—all made with fresh ingredients. Portions are large, and the diverse and creative menu includes Western dishes. Dim sum is served 11 am-2:30 pm each day. Friendly service. **Cards:** AE, MC, VI. ✕

PASTA LA VISTA
Lunch: $5-$19   Dinner: $5-$19   Phone: 306/668-2229
◆◆
West
Canadian
Location: 1.2 km e of jct Hwy 16 (Idylwyld Dr) and Circle Dr. 109-810 Circle Dr E S7K 3T8. **Hours:** 11 am-11 pm, Sun-10 pm. Closed: 12/24 & 12/25. **Reservations:** suggested. **Features:** casual dress; children's menu; carryout; cocktails & lounge; a la carte. You'll enjoy the open-kitchen concept featuring an oak-fired oven cooking up favorites such as barbecue chicken, ribs, pizza, pasta and their signature item, smoked prime rib. This restaurant's lively atmosphere offers a fun and exciting experience. **Cards:** AE, DI, MC, VI. ✕

POVERINO'S PASTA GRILL
Lunch: $6-$12   Dinner: $6-$12   Phone: 306/955-7319
◆◆
Italian
Location: 3 km n of Hwy 16, corner Louise Ave. 1625 8th St E S7H 0Z2. **Hours:** 11 am-11 pm, Sun noon-10 pm. Closed major holidays. **Reservations:** suggested. **Features:** casual dress; children's menu; carryout; cocktails; a la carte. Poverino's offers a great selection of fresh pasta and pizza baked in a wood-burning oven. Veal, chicken, steak and burgers complement the menu. This is a friendly and fun place with a bright and airy decor. All pasta is $5.95 Mon-Tue. Impressive service. **Cards:** AE, DI, MC, VI. ✕

R.J. WILLOUGHBY'S
Lunch: $6-$13   Dinner: $10-$20   Phone: 306/665-7576
◆◆
Continental
Location: Just e of jct Hwy 11, 5 and 22nd St; adjacent to Eaton's Shopping Complex; in Ramada Hotel Saskatoon. 90 22nd St E S7K 3X6. **Hours:** 7 am-11 pm. **Reservations:** suggested. **Features:** Sunday brunch; children's menu; cocktails & lounge; fee for parking; a la carte. You'll enjoy a fine-dining experience here on Friday and Saturday nights. An excellent lunch buffet is offered Monday-Friday, and a seafood buffet is Sunday night. The atmosphere is semi-casual and colorful, and servers are prompt and attentive. **Cards:** AE, CB, DI, DS, JC, MC, VI. ✕

SASKATOON STATION PLACE
Lunch: $5-$9   Dinner: $9-$19   Phone: 306/244-7777
◆◆
Continental
Location: At jct of 23rd St. 221 S Idylwyld Dr S7L 6V6. **Hours:** 10:30 am-midnight, Sun from 10 am. **Reservations:** suggested. **Features:** casual dress; Sunday brunch; senior's menu; carryout; cocktails & lounge. You'll appreciate this restaurant's exterior, which is a train station and two Pullman cars. The interior's nostalgic decor displays many train-related antiques, and the menu offers pasta, salads, chicken, burgers, sandwiches and combo platters. **Cards:** AE, DI, MC, VI. ✕

SHAUNAVON pop. 1,900

LODGING

HIDDEN HILTEN MOTEL
Phone: (306)297-4166
◆◆
Motel
All Year   1P: $45-$49   2P: $50-$52
Location: 0.5 km e from jct Hwy 13 and 37, just n. 352 5th St W S0N 2M0 (PO Box 1002). Fax: 306/297-6220. **Facility:** 13 rooms. Clean, comfortable and quiet rooms. Offers very nice budget-style accommodations. 1 story; exterior corridors. **Services:** winter plug-ins. **Cards:** AE, DI, MC, VI.

SWIFT CURRENT pop. 14,900

LODGINGS

CARAVEL MOTEL
Phone: (306)773-8385
AA SAVE
Motel
All Year   1P: $42-$47   2P: $45-$50   XP: $3   F9
Location: Just e of Central Ave. 705 N Service Rd NE S9H 3X6. Fax: 306/773-5060. **Terms:** Small pets only, $5 extra charge. **Facility:** 28 rooms. Budget style accommodation, older decor with charming and comfortable detail in furnishings. Very good room amenities. Small picnic area with barbecue. 6 kitchenettes, $5 extra charge; 1 story; exterior corridors. **Dining:** Restaurant nearby. **Services:** winter plug-ins. **All Rooms:** extended cable TV. **Cards:** AE, DI, MC, VI. **Special Amenities: Free local telephone calls and preferred room (subject to availability with advanced reservations).**

COMFORT INN

◆ ◆
Motel

5/16-9/30	1P: $72	2P: $80	XP: $4	F18
3/1-5/15 & 10/1-2/28	1P: $69	2P: $77	XP: $4	F18

Phone: (306)778-3994

Location: S Service Rd Trans Canada Hwy 1; just w of 22nd Ave NE. 1510 S Service Rd E S9H 3X6. Fax: 306/773-9312. **Terms:** Pets, in smoking rooms. **Facility:** 74 rooms. Contemporary and spacious guest rooms; ground floor rooms have a sliding patio door that leads out to the parking lot. A few executive rooms with hair dryer, iron and ironing board. 2 stories; interior corridors. **Services:** winter plug-ins. **Cards:** AE, DI, DS, JC, MC, VI.

IMPERIAL 400 SWIFT CURRENT

(CAA) (SAVE)
◆ ◆
Motor Inn

All Year	1P: $66-$74	2P: $74-$79	XP: $5	F16

Phone: (306)773-2033

Location: S Service Rd, Trans Canada Hwy 1. 1150 Begg St E S9H 3X6. Fax: 306/773-4911. **Terms:** Cancellation fee imposed; small pets only. **Facility:** 142 rooms. Family oriented. Mix of room styles and decor, some rooms are very spacious. All rooms with video games. Older but tasteful decor. 2 stories; interior/exterior corridors; heated pool, waterslide, whirlpool. **Dining:** Restaurant; 6:30 am-10 pm, Sun-8 pm; to 9 pm off season, Sun-2 pm; $6-$11; cocktails. **Services:** winter plug-ins. **All Rooms:** extended cable TV. **Cards:** AE, DI, DS, JC, MC, VI. *(See color ad p 582)*

RODEWAY INN MOTEL

(CAA) (SAVE)
◆ ◆
Motor Inn

All Year	1P: $42-$54	2P: $48-$66	XP: $5	D12

Phone: (306)773-4664

Location: Trans Canada Hwy 1, just w of 22nd Ave NE. 1200 S Service Rd E S9H 3X6. Fax: 306/773-8117. **Terms:** Small pets only, in smoking rooms. **Facility:** 28 rooms. An older property offering spacious units with 2 entrances to all guest rooms. Older but tasteful decor. 1 story; interior corridors. **Dining:** Restaurant; 6 am-10 pm, Sun 7 am-8 pm; $5-$15; cocktails. **Services:** winter plug-ins. **All Rooms:** extended cable TV. **Cards:** AE, MC, VI. **Special Amenities:** Early check-in/late check-out and free local telephone calls.

SAFARI MOTEL

(CAA) (SAVE)
◆
Motel

All Year	1P: $42-$44	2P: $46-$54	XP: $5	F10

Phone: (306)773-4608

Location: 1 km e of jct Hwy 1 and 4, along Hwy 1 (Trans Canada Hwy). 810 S Service Rd E S9H 3T9. Fax: 306/773-0835. **Terms:** Weekly & monthly rates avail; 3 day cancellation notice; pets, $5 extra charge. **Facility:** 18 rooms. Older property offering average sized rooms with an older style decor. 4 two-bedroom units. 1 story; exterior corridors. **Dining:** Restaurant nearby. **Services:** winter plug-ins. **All Rooms:** extended cable TV. **Some Rooms:** 2 efficiencies. **Cards:** AE, DI, MC, VI. **Special Amenities:** Free local telephone calls.

SUPER 8 MOTEL

◆ ◆
Motel

6/1-9/30	1P: $72-$82	2P: $77-$82	XP: $5	F12
3/1-5/31	1P: $60-$65	2P: $65-$75	XP: $5	F12
10/1-12/31 & 1/1-2/28	1P: $62-$72	2P: $67-$72	XP: $5	F12

Phone: 306/778-6088

Location: Just e of Central Ave. 405 N Service Rd E S9H 3X6. Fax: 306/778-0603. **Terms:** [CP] meal plan; 14 day cancellation notice; pets, $5 extra charge, in smoking rooms. **Facility:** 63 rooms. Newer property. 2 stories; interior corridors; small heated indoor pool. **Services:** winter plug-ins. **Cards:** AE, CB, DI, DS, MC, VI.

SWIFT CURRENT TRAVELODGE

(CAA) (SAVE)
◆ ◆
Motel

DI, MC, VI.

All Year	1P: $60	2P: $70	XP: $10	F16

Phone: (306)773-3101

Location: Just e of Central Ave, on N Service Rd. Trans Canada Hwy 1 E S9H 3X6 (N Service Rd, Hwy 1). Fax: 306/773-7399. **Terms:** Small pets only. **Facility:** 49 rooms. Spacious guest rooms. Most units feature 2 entrances. Excellent housekeeping and maintenance. 1-2 stories; exterior corridors; 2 heated pools, saunas, whirlpool. **Dining:** Restaurant nearby. **Services:** winter plug-ins. **All Rooms:** extended cable TV. **Cards:** AE, DI, MC, VI.

WESTWIND MOTEL

(CAA) (SAVE)
◆
Motel

All Year	1P: $42-$44	2P: $44-$49

Phone: (306)773-1441

Location: Off Trans Canada Hwy 1; 0.5 km w of Central Ave on N Service Rd W. 155 Begg St W S9H 3S8. Fax: 306/778-4085. **Terms:** Weekly rates avail; pets, with permission. **Facility:** 20 rooms. Good budget-style accommodations; rooms are average in size with a modest, older style. Satellite TV. 1 story; exterior corridors; heated pool. **Dining:** Restaurant; 8 am-11 pm, Sun 9 am-9 pm; $5-$10; cocktails. **Services:** winter plug-ins. **Some Rooms:** 4 efficiencies. **Cards:** AE, MC, VI. **Special Amenities:** Early check-in/late check-out and free local telephone calls.

——— RESTAURANTS ———

NANA'S RESTAURANT & LOUNGE

◆
Ethnic

Lunch: $5-$7   Dinner: $8-$18   Phone: 306/773-3365

Location: Exit 6th Ave ne, from Trans Canada Hwy 1 E. At eastern end of S Service Rd. 1520 S Service Hwy 1 Rd E S9H 3X6. **Hours:** 11 am-11 pm. Closed major holidays. **Reservations:** suggested **Features:** casual dress; children's menu; carryout; cocktails & lounge. Nana's features specialties from Mexico and Latin America served in a festive and colorful ambience. The menu also offers pork chops, chicken fingers, sirloin steak, burgers and seafood combination dishes. The service is friendly and attentive. **Cards:** AE, DI, MC, VI.

SPRINGS GARDEN RESTAURANT

◆ ◆
American

Lunch: $5-$16   Dinner: $5-$16   Phone: 306/773-2021

Location: Off Trans Canada Hwy 1, n service road; in Swift Current shopping mall. 323 1 Springsdrive S9H 3X6. **Hours:** 8:30 am-9 pm, Fri & Sat-10 pm, Sun from 9 am. Closed major holidays. **Reservations:** suggested; Thurs-Sat. **Features:** children's menu; carryout; cocktails & lounge; a la carte. The Springs Garden's decor is casual, contemporary, bright and cheerful. The menu includes a variety of popular dishes, soups, steak, chicken, seafood, pizza, ribs and Greek specialties. The server staff is friendly, efficient and prompt. **Cards:** AE, DI, MC, VI.

WONG'S KITCHEN **Lunch:** $6-$20 **Dinner:** $6-$20 **Phone:** 306/773-4636
◆ **Location:** On S Service Rd. 320 S Service Rd E S9H 3X8. **Hours:** noon-midnight, Sun-9 pm. Closed: 12/25.
Chinese **Reservations:** suggested. **Features:** carryout; cocktails; entertainment; a la carte, buffet. Wong's Kitchen is
one of the best spots in town to visit. The locally popular restaurant features Cantonese-style preparation of
s dishes. The menu also offers steak and seafood selections. A smorgasbord is served noon-2 pm each day. Helpful staff.
Cards: AE, DI, MC, VI. ⊠

WEYBURN pop. 9,700

——— LODGINGS ———

PERFECT INNS **Phone:** (306)842-2691
ⒶⒶ (SAVE) All Year 1P: $49-$72 2P: $51-$74 XP: $3 F18
◆◆ **Location:** 0.5 km w of jct Hwy 35 and 39; beside McDonald's restaurant. 238 Sims Ave S4H 2J8 (PO Box 69).
Motel Fax: 306/842-2121. **Terms:** Weekly & monthly rates avail; pets. **Facility:** 60 rooms. Good, clean budget-
oriented accommodations with modern decor. New section offers spacious, modern and well-equipped rooms.
2 two-bedroom units. 2 efficiencies, $60-$85; 1 story; interior/exterior corridors. **Dining:** Restaurant nearby.
Services: winter plug-ins. **All Rooms:** extended cable TV. **Cards:** AE, DI, DS, MC, VI. **Special Amenities:** Free local telephone calls and preferred room (subject to availability with advanced reservations). 🐾 👫 ⊠ 🎦 🖥 🍽 🔒 📋

WEYBURN INN **Phone:** (306)842-6543
ⒶⒶ (SAVE) All Year 1P: $55-$80 2P: $55-$65 XP: $6 F18
◆◆ **Location:** Centre. 5 Government Rd S4H 0N8. Fax: 306/842-2210. **Terms:** 30 day cancellation notice; cancel-
Motor Inn lation fee imposed; pets. **Facility:** 69 rooms. Spacious guest rooms. 2 stories; interior corridors; heated pool,
sauna, whirlpool. **Dining:** Dining room; 6 am-midnight; $7-$18; cocktails. **Services:** winter plug-ins.
All Rooms: extended cable TV. **Cards:** AE, DI, MC, VI. 🆔 🐾 👫 ⅋ 🎦 ⛰ ⊠ 🎦 🖨 🖥 🔒 📋 🏊

——— RESTAURANT ———

L & C FAMILY RESTAURANT/DALLAS PIZZA **Lunch:** $4-$9 **Dinner:** $5-$29 **Phone:** 306/842-2933
◆◆ **Location:** Center; just n of Hwy 39. 72 3rd St NE S4H 0V9. **Hours:** 10 am-midnight. Closed: 12/25.
American **Features:** children's menu; senior's menu; carryout; cocktails; street parking. This restaurant offers family
dining in contemporary and friendly surroundings. The menu features a wide variety of sandwiches, stir-fry,
steak, seafood, pizza, souvlakia and Greek ribs. Families, couples and business people alike enjoy this eatery. **Cards:** AE,
DI, MC, VI. ⊠

YORKTON pop. 15,200

—— LODGINGS ——

HOLIDAY INN LTD
Phone: (306)783-9781

CAA SAVE · All Year · 1P: $66 · 2P: $73 · XP: $7 · F18
◆◆
Motor Inn
Location: On Hwy 10 and 16, downtown. 100 Broadway St E S3N 0K9. Fax: 306/782-2121. **Terms:** [BP] mea plan, Mon-Fri; pets. **Facility:** 83 rooms. Spacious rooms, offering basic modest decor with some vintage ap pointments. All rooms with voice mail. Whirlpool room, $129; 2 stories; interior corridors; heated pool, sauna waterslide, whirlpool. **Dining:** Coffee shop; 7 am-9 pm; $5-$15; cocktails; nightclub. **Services:** winter plug-ins
All Rooms: extended cable TV. **Cards:** AE, DI, DS, MC, VI. **Special Amenities: Free breakfast and free local telephone calls.**

IMPERIAL 400 YORKTON
Phone: (306)783-6581

CAA SAVE · All Year · 1P: $66-$74 · 2P: $74-$79 · XP: $5 · F16
◆◆
Motor Inn
Location: At jct Hwy 9, 10 and 16 (Yellowhead Hwy). 207 Broadway Ave E S3N 3K7. Fax: 306/786-6399
Terms: Monthly rates avail; cancellation fee imposed; pets. **Facility:** 153 rooms. A family-oriented property with average sized guest rooms. All rooms with video games. 2 stories; interior/exterior corridors; heated pool, wa terslide, whirlpool. **Dining:** Restaurant; 6 am-9 pm, Sat from 7 am, Sun 7 am-8 pm; $5-$10; cocktails.
Services: winter plug-ins. **All Rooms:** extended cable TV. **Some Rooms:** Fee: refrigerators. **Cards:** AE, DI, DS, MC, VI.
(See color ad p 582)

TRAVELODGE YORKTON
Phone: (306)783-6571

◆◆ · 1/1-2/28 · 1P: $75-$140 · 2P: $89-$140
Motor Inn · 3/1-12/31 · 1P: $69-$140 · 2P: $84-$140 · XP: $10 · F17
Location: W end of town, just e of Agriplex (Hwy 10A). 345 Broadway W S3N 0N8. Fax: 306/786-3311
Terms: Check-in 4 pm; pets, $30 dep req. **Facility:** 71 rooms. Renovated property with mostly standard size rooms and a few spacious 1-bedroom suites. 2 stories; interior/exterior corridors; heated pool. **Services:** winter plug-ins. **Cards:** AE, DI, DS MC, VI.

—— RESTAURANT ——

THE GLADSTONE INN DINING ROOM · **Lunch:** $5-$14 · **Dinner:** $10-$28 · **Phone:** 306/783-4827
◆◆
Continental
Location: 0.7 km w on Hwy 10 and 16. 185 Broadway St W S3N 0M8. **Hours:** 11 am-1:45 & 5-10 pm, Sat from 5 pm. Closed major holidays & Sun. **Reservations:** suggested. **Features:** senior's menu; cocktails. The Gladstone Inn features informal dining in a pleasant ambience that highlights a rare collection of landscape paintings. The menu offers Continental specialties, which are prepared home-style, as well as North American choices like steak and seafood. **Cards:** AE, MC, VI.

Yukon Territory

BEAVER CREEK pop. 100

—— LODGING ——

WESTMARK INN BEAVER CREEK
(CAA) (SAVE) 5/15-9/15   1P: $99   2P: $99   Phone: (867)862-750
◆◆   **Location:** Alaska Hwy, 3 km s of Canadian customs post, Milepost 1202. Alaska Hwy, Milepost 1202 Y0B 1A
Motor Inn   Fax: 867/862-7902. **Terms:** Open 5/15-9/15; [CP] meal plan; check-in 4 pm; cancellation fee imposed; pet
      designated rooms. **Facility:** 161 rooms. Compact units offering fresh and attractive country decor. Co
      seating area for common use, in some wings. 1 with large screen TV. Some rooms with 3 beds; 2 stories; in
terior corridors; miniature golf. **Dining:** Restaurant; dinner theatre nightly; 6 am-9 & 6-9 pm; $8-$16; cocktails. **Services:** g
shop. **Recreation:** wildlife displays. **Cards:** AE, CB, DI, DS, JC, MC, VI. *(See color ad p 594)*

DAWSON CITY pop. 1,300

—— LODGINGS ——

BONANZA GOLD MOTEL
◆◆   All Year   1P: $119   2P: $129   Phone: (867)993-678
Motel   **Location:** 2.4 km s on Hwy 2. (Bag 5000, Y0B 1G0). Fax: 867/993-6777. **Terms:** Pets. **Facility:** 15 room
      Rooms with streamlined decor, bright and contemporary touches including pine furnishings. All rooms with fa
Shared space with busy RV park. 2 stories; exterior corridors. **All Rooms:** combo or shower baths. **Some Rooms:** efficienc
kitchen. **Cards:** MC, VI.

DAWSON CITY BED & BREAKFAST
(CAA) (SAVE) 5/1-9/30   1P: $79-$89   2P: $89-$99   XP: $20   Phone: 867/993-564
◆◆   3/1-4/30 & 10/1-2/28   1P: $69-$79   2P: $79-$89   XP: $20
Bed &   **Location:** Just off Seventh Ave. 451 Craig St Y0B 1G0 (Box 954). Fax: 867/993-5648. **Terms:** [BP] meal pla
Breakfast   **Facility:** 7 rooms. Close to Museum. Units are simply decorated and offer a true village home style. All room
      with hair dryer. 2 stories; interior corridors; smoke free premises. **Services:** area transportation; winter plu
ins. **Cards:** DI, MC, VI.

THE ELDORADO HOTEL
◆◆   5/19-9/16   1P: $119   2P: $129   XP: $10   Phone: (867)993-545
Motor Inn   3/1-5/18 & 9/17-2/28   1P: $88   2P: $93   XP: $5
      Location: Downtown. 3rd Ave & Princess St Y0B 1G0 (PO Box 338). Fax: 867/993-5256. **Terms:** Cancellatio
fee imposed. **Facility:** 52 rooms. Exterior with turn-of-the-century motif. Rooms in the main building or in the motel section.
stories; interior/exterior corridors. **Services:** winter plug-ins. **Some Rooms:** 6 efficiencies, honor bars. **Cards:** AE, DI, DS, J
MC, VI.

WESTMARK INN DAWSON CITY
(CAA) (SAVE) 5/15-9/15   1P: $169   2P: $169   XP: $30   Phone: (867)993-554
◆◆   **Location:** At 5th and Harper sts. (PO Box 420, Y0B 1G0). Fax: 867/993-5623. **Terms:** Open 5/15-9/15; ca
Motor Inn   cellation fee imposed; pets. **Facility:** 131 rooms. Well appointed units in 3 adjacent buildings, a few with room
      opening on a gracious courtyard. Elegant lounge above lobby. 2 stories; interior/exterior corridors. **Dining:** Re
      taurant; patio dining weather permitting; 6 am-9 pm; $8-$20. **Services:** gift shop. **Cards:** AE, CB, DI, DS, J
MC, VI. *(See color ad p 594)*

WHITE RAM MANOR BED & BREAKFAST

Phone: (867)993-5772

ed &
Breakfast

5/1-9/30	1P: $80	2P: $90	XP: $10	F5
3/1-4/30 & 10/1-2/28	1P: $45	2P: $50	XP: $10	F5

Location: 7th Ave & Harper St Y0B 1G0 (Box 1491). Fax: 867/993-6509. **Terms:** [BP] meal plan; age restrictions may apply; cancellation fee imposed; small pets only. **Facility:** 10 rooms. Northwestern version of a European pension. Rooms feature simple appointment while common areas offer a large and well-equipped kitchen for guest use, large porch with seating space overlooking the town. 2 stories; interior corridors; smoke free premises. **Services:** winter plug-ins. **Cards:** MC, VI.

HAINES JUNCTION pop. 600

----- LODGING -----

GATEWAY MOTEL

Phone: (867)634-2371

Motel

4/1-10/31	1P: $86	2P: $91	XP: $5	
3/1-3/31 & 11/1-2/28	1P: $60	2P: $65	XP: $5	

Location: At jct of Alaska and Haines hwys (1 and 3). Box 5460 Y0B 1L0. Fax: 867/634-2833. **Terms:** Weekly & monthly rates avail, off season; pets, $10 dep req. **Facility:** 12 rooms. Simple yet contemporary decor. Standard units as well as a separate duplex unit, with kitchen and separate bedroom. Duplex units with kitchenettes, $91-$101; 1 story; exterior corridors. **Services:** winter plug-ins. **Some Rooms:** 2 kitchens. **Cards:** AE, DS, MC, VI. **Special Amenities:** Early check-in/late check-out and free local telephone calls.

WHITEHORSE pop. 19,200

----- LODGINGS -----

EDGEWATER HOTEL

Phone: (867)667-2572

Hotel

5/1-9/30	1P: $119-$139	2P: $119-$139	XP: $10	
3/1-4/30 & 10/1-2/28	1P: $99-$119	2P: $99-$119	XP: $10	

Location: Opposite White Pass Rail Depot. 101 Main St Y1A 2A7. Fax: 867/668-3014. **Terms:** 3 day cancellation notice. **Facility:** 30 rooms. Contemporary and fresh decor in all rooms, many with upgraded amenities such as iron and ironing board. All rooms with 2-line phones. 3 stories, no elevator; interior corridors. **Dining:** Dining room; 6 am-10 pm; $15-$30; cocktails; also, The Cellar Dining Room, see separate listing. **Services:** winter plug-ins. **All Rooms:** extended cable TV. **Some Rooms:** efficiency, 2 kitchens. Fee: VCR. **Cards:** AE, DI, MC, VI. **Special Amenities:** Free local telephone calls.

HAWKINS HOUSE BED & BREAKFAST

Phone: 867/668-7638

ed &
Breakfast

6/15-8/31	1P: $136	2P: $163	XP: $15	D12
9/1-2/28	1P: $96-$116	2P: $113-$133	XP: $15	D12
5/1-6/14	1P: $116	2P: $133	XP: $15	D12
3/1-4/30	1P: $96-$99	2P: $113-$119	XP: $15	D12

Location: At 3rd Ave, downtown. 303 Hawkins St Y1A 1X5. Fax: 867/668-7632. **Terms:** [BP] meal plan; age restrictions may apply; check-in 4 pm; 3 day cancellation notice. **Facility:** 4 rooms. Exquisitely decorated units, each with its distinct style. Superior in-room amenities, include private phone line, message service and free refreshments. 2 stories; interior corridors; smoke free premises. **Services:** winter plug-ins. **Cards:** AE, DI, JC, MC, VI.

HIGH COUNTRY INN

CAA SAVE
◆ ◆
Motor Inn

	1P: $119-$199	2P: $149-$229	**Phone:** (867)667-447
5/15-9/14	1P: $119-$199	2P: $149-$229	XP: $15	F1
9/15-2/28	1P: $99-$179	2P: $119-$199	XP: $10	F1
3/1-5/14	1P: $89-$169	2P: $109-$189	XP: $10	F1

Location: 0.6 km e of Main St. 4051 4th Ave Y1A 1H1. Fax: 867/667-6457. **Terms:** Weekly & monthly rate avail; 30 day cancellation notice; pets, $10 extra charge. **Facility:** 85 rooms. Rooms vary greatly in size an style, from luxurious whirlpool units to compact bedrooms with limited furnishings. Gracious public areas. Attractive and bus tling patio lounge featuring games meat and local beer. 17 family suites; 20 whirlpool rooms, $159-$229; 4 stories; interior co ridors. **Dining:** Restaurant; 6:30 am-10 pm; $8-$25; cocktails. **Services:** area transportation, limited; winter plug-ins **All Rooms:** combo or shower baths, extended cable TV. **Some Rooms:** 20 efficiencies, 15 kitchens. Fee: VCR. **Cards:** AE CB, DI, MC, VI. **Special Amenities:** Early check-in/late check-out and free room upgrade (subject to availability wit advanced reservations). *(See color ad p 591)*

THE TOWN AND MOUNTAIN HOTEL

CAA SAVE
◆ ◆
Motor Inn

			Phone: (867)668-764
3/1-9/30	1P: $89-$109	2P: $99-$109	XP: $10	F1
10/1-2/28	1P: $59-$79	2P: $64-$89	XP: $10	F1

Location: Downtown. 401 Main St Y1A 2B6. Fax: 867/668-5822. **Terms:** Weekly & monthly rates avail, o season; pets, $10 extra charge. **Facility:** 30 rooms. Rooms vary in style from renovated executive style room with refrigerator, microwave, iron and ironing board to some that offer vintage appointments. Located right i the heart of downtown. 3 stories, no elevator; interior corridors. **Dining:** Restaurant; 7 am-9 pm; $9-$16; cocktails. **Services:** winter plug-ins. **All Rooms:** extended cable TV. **Cards:** AE, DI, DS, MC, VI. **Special Amenities:** Free local tele phone calls and free room upgrade (subject to availability with advanced reservations).

WESTMARK KLONDIKE INN WHITEHORSE

CAA SAVE
◆ ◆ ◆
Motor Inn

			Phone: (867)668-474
5/15-9/15	1P: $129	2P: $129	XP: $30	F1

Location: Between Quartz Rd and 4th Ave. 2288 2nd Ave Y1A 1C8. Fax: 867/667-7639. **Terms:** Open 5/15 9/15; cancellation fee imposed; pets. **Facility:** 99 rooms. Knotty pine furnishings, spacious units. 3 stories; in terior corridors; saunas. **Dining:** Coffee shop; 6 am-9 pm; $9-$17; cocktails. **Services:** gift shop. **Cards:** AE CB, DI, DS, JC, MC, VI. *(See color ad p 594)*

WESTMARK WHITEHORSE HOTEL & CONFERENCE CENTRE

CAA SAVE
◆ ◆ ◆
Motor Inn

			Phone: (867)393-470
5/16-9/15	1P: $159	2P: $159	XP: $30	F1
3/1-5/15 & 9/16-2/28	1P: $129	2P: $129	XP: $30	F1

Location: Centre, 2nd Ave. 201 Wood St Y1A 3T3 (PO Box 4250). Fax: 867/668-2789. **Terms:** Cancellatio fee imposed; pets. **Facility:** 181 rooms. Cedar sided structure in downtown area. Home of the "frantic follies and many bus groups during summer months. Limited parking. Style of units vary, most with contemporary ap pointments. 3 stories; interior/exterior corridors. **Dining:** Restaurant; 6 am-9 pm; from 7 am 9/16-5/15; $12-$21; cocktails. **Services:** gift shop; winter plug-ins. Fee: massage. **Recreation:** exercise equipment avail for room use, hair salon/barbe shop. **All Rooms:** extended cable TV. **Some Rooms:** Fee: VCR. **Cards:** AE, CB, DI, DS, JC, MC, VI. *(See color ad p 594)*

RESTAURANT

THE CELLAR DINING ROOM
◆ ◆
Seafood

Lunch: $3-$14   **Dinner:** $19-$40   **Phone:** 867/667-257

Location: Opposite the White Pass Rail Depot; in Edgewater Hotel. 101 Main St Y1A 2A7. **Hours:** 11:3 am-1:30 & 5-10 pm. Closed: 1/1, 12/25 & 12/26. **Reservations:** suggested. **Features:** cocktails & lounge You'll enjoy the Cellar Dining Room's offerings of prime rib, halibut, Alaskan king crab, steaks, salmon, bab back ribs, chicken, as well as a good selection of wines by the glass. Its well-appointed dining room is one of the hot spot in town. **Cards:** AE, DI, MC, VI.

Alaska

ANCHORAGE pop. 226,300

OA	✈ Airport Accommodations			
	ANCHORAGE	Diamond Rating	Rate Range High Season	Listing Page
	Anchorage Airport Courtyard by Marriott, 1.7 mi e of airport	◆◆◆	Failed to provide	594
	A to Zzzz.... B & B, 4 mi se of airport	◆◆	$75-$95	595
ⒶⒶⒶ	**Best Western Barratt Inn, 1.8 mi e of airport**	◆◆◆	$139-$167 [SAVE]	595
	Holiday Inn Express Anchorage Airport, 1.9 mi ne of airport	◆◆◆	$129	598
ⒶⒶⒶ	**Longhouse Alaskan Hotel, 2 mi e of airport**	◆◆	$139-$159 [SAVE]	598
	Microtel Inn & Suites, 2.5 mi e of airport	◆◆	$129-$149	599
ⒶⒶⒶ	**Regal Alaskan Hotel, 1.8 mi e of airport**	◆◆◆	$260-$300 [SAVE]	599

——— LODGINGS ———

ANCHORAGE AIRPORT COURTYARD BY MARRIOTT
Phone: (907)245-0322
◆◆◆
Property failed to provide current rates
Motor Inn   **Location:** Just ne of Jewell Lake and International Airport rds. 4901 Spenard Rd 99517. Fax: 907/248-1886. **Facility:** 154 rooms. Spacious, well-appointed units. Extra amenities include hair dryer, iron, ironing board and voice mail. Gracious public areas, including courtyard with sun deck and gazebo. 3 stories; interior corridors; small heated indoor pool. **Cards:** AE, DI, DS, MC, VI.

🔁 🏧 🍽 🛎 🛋 🛗 ♿ 🐾 ✕ 🎬 📠 💻 📺 🔌 DATA PORT 🏊 🛋 ✚

ANCHORAGE CLARION SUITES
Phone: (907)274-1000

ⒶⒶⒶ [SAVE]	5/16-9/20	1P: $249-$289	2P: $259-$299	XP: $10	F18
◆◆◆	5/1-5/15	1P: $149-$189	2P: $159-$199	XP: $10	F18
Motor Inn	3/1-4/30 & 9/21-2/28	1P: $119-$139	2P: $129-$149	XP: $10	F18

Location: Center; corner C St. 325 W 8th Ave 99501. Fax: 907/274-3016. **Terms:** 48 day cancellation notice; cancellation fee imposed. **Facility:** 111 rooms. Boutique style all suites property with a distinguishing lobby. Beautifully furnished and equipped guest rooms, all with iron and ironing board. 3 stories; interior corridors; small heated indoor pool, whirlpool. **Dining:** Restaurant; 5:30 am-11 pm; 6:30 am-10 pm in winter; $8-$13; cocktails. **Services:** area transportation, train depot. **Recreation:** in-room video games. Fee: bicycles. **All Rooms:** combo or shower baths, extended cable TV. **Cards:** AE, CB, DI, DS, JC, MC, VI.

🆓 🔁 🏧 🛎 🛋 🛗 🐾 ✕ 🎬 📠 💻 📺 🔌 DATA PORT 🏊 🛋 ✚ ✕

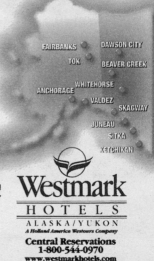

A TO ZZZZ.... B & B
◆◆
Bed &
Breakfast

5/1-9/30	1P: $75-$85	2P: $85-$95
3/1-4/30 & 10/1-2/28	1P: $60-$65	2P: $65-$75

Phone: (907)248-3436
XP: $20   F6
XP: $20   F6

Location: International Airport Rd, 1.9 mi s on Jewel Lake Rd, 0.8 mi e on Strawberry Rd, just s on Arlene St. 2701 W 80th Ave 99502. Fax: 907/248-3436. **Terms:** [BP] meal plan; 10 day cancellation notice. **Facility:** 4 rooms. Beautiful modern house with a showcase living room affording intriguing mountain views. Cozy rooms with excellent appointments, you'll feel you've never left home. Hospitable hosts. 2 stories; interior corridors. **Cards:** AE, DS, MC, VI.

AURORA WINDS RESORT
Ⓐ SAVE
◆◆◆
Bed &
Breakfast

5/15-9/30	1P: $105-$150	2P: $150-$250
3/1-4/30 & 10/1-2/28	1P: $75-$125	2P: $95-$150

Phone: (907)346-2533
XP: $25
XP: $20

Location: 6.5 mi s on US 1 (New Seward Hwy), 4 mi e on O'Malley Rd, just n on Hillside Dr, just e. 7501 Upper O'Malley Rd 99516. Fax: 907/346-3192. **Terms:** [BP] & [CP] meal plans; 3 day cancellation notice; cancellation fee imposed; package plans; pets, pet on premises. **Facility:** 5 rooms. In a quiet residential neighborhood. Over 2 acres of beautifully landscaped grounds enhance the gracious public areas and spacious guest rooms with upscale appointments. 3 whirlpool rooms; 2 stories; interior corridors; smoke free premises; whirlpool, heated indoor lap pool. **Recreation:** library room with videos, pool table. **All Rooms:** combo or shower baths. **Cards:** AE, DS, MC, VI. **Special Amenities: Free breakfast and preferred room (subject to availability with advanced reservations).**

BEST WESTERN BARRATT INN
Ⓐ SAVE
◆◆◆
Motor Inn

5/15-9/15	1P: $139-$157	2P: $149-$167
3/1-5/14 & 9/16-2/28	1P: $66-$79	2P: $66-$79

Phone: (907)243-3131
XP: $10   F12

Location: 4 mi sw, 0.4 mi n on Jewel Lake Rd. 4616 Spenard Rd 99517-3299. Fax: 907/249-4917. **Terms:** [BP] meal plan; cancellation fee imposed; small pets only, $5 extra charge, $50 dep req. **Facility:** 217 rooms. On 2 sides of hwy connected by tunnel. Wide variety of room styles with different decor in each of the 4 sections, all contemporary. Suites, $199; 2-5 stories, no elevator; interior/exterior corridors. **Dining:** Restaurant; 6 am-12:30 am; may vary in winter; $7-$18; cocktails. **Services:** area transportation; train station; winter plug-ins. **Recreation:** in-room video games. **All Rooms:** extended cable TV. **Some Rooms:** 12 kitchens, utensil deposit. Fee: VCR. **Cards:** AE, CB, DI, DS, JC, MC, VI.

CAMAI BED & BREAKFAST
◆◆
Bed &
Breakfast

5/16-9/15	1P: $75-$85	2P: $85-$95
3/1-5/15 & 9/16-2/28	1P: $50-$70	2P: $55-$75

Phone: (907)333-2219
XP: $20
XP: $10

Location: From New Seward Hwy; 3 mi e on Benson/Northern Lights Blvd, 0.6 mi s on Wesleyn Ave to Queen Ct, just e. 3838 Westminster Way 99508-4834. Fax: 907/337-3959. **Terms:** [BP] meal plan; 7 day cancellation notice. **Facility:** 2 rooms. Located in quiet residential area, both units are spacious with their own private entrance and seating area. 2 stories; interior/exterior corridors; smoke free premises. **Some Rooms:** kitchen.

COMFORT INN SHIP CREEK
◆◆
Motel

6/1-8/31	1P: $179-$219	2P: $179-$219
3/1-5/31 & 9/1-2/28	1P: $89-$119	2P: $89-$119

Phone: (907)277-6887

Location: From downtown, 3rd and E sts, 0.3 mi n on E St, across the railway, just e on Ship Creek Ave (formerly Warehouse Ave). 111 W Ship Creek Ave 99501. Fax: 907/274-9830. **Terms:** [CP] meal plan; check-in 4 pm; cancellation fee imposed; pets, in smoking rooms. **Facility:** 100 rooms. Attractive public areas and spacious rooms. Adjacent to Ship Creek in open area close to the train station. 3 stories; interior corridors; small heated indoor pool. **Services:** area transportation. **Recreation:** Fee: bicycles. **All Rooms:** combo or shower baths. **Some Rooms:** 13 efficiencies, 2 kitchens. **Cards:** AE, CB, DI, DS, JC, MC, VI. *(See color ad below)*

DAYS INN

				Phone: (907)276-7226
AAA SAVE	5/15-9/15	1P: $155-$250	2P: $155-$250	XP: $10	F17
◆◆	9/16-9/30	1P: $75-$125	2P: $75-$125	XP: $10	F17
Motor Inn	3/1-5/14	1P: $65-$125	2P: $65-$125	XP: $10	F17
	10/1-2/28	1P: $65-$100	2P: $65-$100	XP: $10	F17

Location: Downtown at Cordova. 321 E 5th Ave 99501. Fax: 907/265-5164. **Terms:** Weekly & monthly rates avail; cancellation fee imposed; pets, $25 dep req. **Facility:** 130 rooms. No elevator in one 3-story wing. Average, well kept rooms. Better amenities in 4th floor units. 4 stories; interior/exterior corridors. **Dining:** Coffee shop; 6 am-midnight; 7 am-9 pm in winter; $10-$16; cocktails. **Recreation:** tour desk. **All Rooms:** combo or shower baths, extended cable TV, safes. **Cards:** AE, CB, DI, DS, JC, MC, VI. **Special Amenities:** Free local telephone calls.

HAMPTON INN-ANCHORAGE

				Phone: (907)550-7000
◆◆◆	6/1-8/27	1P: $149-$189	2P: $159-$199	
Motel	8/28-2/28	1P: $91	2P: $101	XP: $10	F18
	3/1-5/31	1P: $89	2P: $99	

Location: Corner of Tudor Rd and C St. 4301 Credit Union Dr 99503. Fax: 907/561-7330. **Terms:** [ECP] meal plan; package plans. **Facility:** 101 rooms. Well appointed lobby with a warm, inviting decor including a fireplace, Alaskan trophies and artifacts. Spacious guest rooms. All rooms with hair dryer, iron, ironing board, 2-line phones and voice mail. 3 stories; interior corridors; small heated indoor pool. **Services:** gift shop; area transportation. **Cards:** AE, CB, DI, DS, JC, MC, VI.

HAWTHORN SUITES LTD

				Phone: (907)222-5005
◆◆◆	5/16-9/20	1P: $249-$289	2P: $259-$299	XP: $10	F16
Motor Inn	5/1-5/15	1P: $149-$189	2P: $159-$199	XP: $10	F16
	3/1-4/30 & 9/21-2/28	1P: $119-$139	2P: $129-$149	XP: $10	F16

Location: Corner L St. 1110 W 8th Ave 99501. Fax: 907/222-5215. **Terms:** [BP] meal plan; 48 day cancellation notice; cancellation fee imposed. **Facility:** 112 rooms. Boutique style all suites property with a grandiose lobby. Excellent in-room amenites include fax, iron, ironing board, 2-line phone and wet bar. 3 stories; interior corridors; small heated indoor pool. **Services:** area transportation. **Recreation:** Fee: bicycles. **Cards:** AE, DI, DS, JC, MC, VI.

HILTON ANCHORAGE

				Phone: (907)272-7411
◆◆◆	5/29-9/14	1P: $209	2P: $229	XP: $20	F18
Hotel	9/15-10/13	1P: $95	2P: $115	XP: $20	F18
	3/1-5/28 & 10/14-2/28	1P: $75	2P: $95	XP: $20	F18

Location: Downtown at E St. 500 W 3rd Ave 99501. Fax: 907/265-7042. **Terms:** Cancellation fee imposed; package plans; small pets only. **Facility:** 591 rooms. Upscale and extensive public areas with mounted polar and grizzly bears adding a touch of Alaska. Registration desk showcases glossy Alaskan jade. Elegant room decor although units vary in size and view; all with iron and ironing boar. 22 stories; interior corridors; heated pool. Fee: parking. **Services:** gift shop; area transportation. **Cards:** AE, CB, DI, DS, JC, MC, VI. *(See color ad p 283 & p 597)*

HISTORIC ANCHORAGE HOTEL

				Phone: (907)272-4553
◆◆◆	5/16-9/15	1P: $209-$249	2P: $219-$249	XP: $10	F12
Classic Hotel	3/1-5/15 & 9/16-2/28	1P: $129-$189	2P: $139-$189	XP: $10	F12

Location: Downtown at 4th and E sts. 330 E St 99501. Fax: 907/277-4483. **Terms:** [CP] meal plan; package plans, weekends off season. **Facility:** 26 rooms. **Historic.** Built in 1915, the city's oldest hotel. Units have been charmingly restored in soft tones and contemporary appointments, some luxury amenities. All rooms with hair dryer, iron and ironing board. 3 stories; interior corridors. Fee: parking. **Services:** gift shop. **All Rooms:** honor bars. **Cards:** AE, DI, DS, MC, VI.

HOLIDAY INN DOWNTOWN

Property failed to provide current rates

Phone: (907)279-8671

 Motor Inn

Location: Downtown at 3rd Ave and C St. 239 W 4th Ave 99501. Fax: 907/258-4733. **Terms:** [BP] meal plan; 3 day cancellation notice, in summer; package plans. **Facility:** 251 rooms. Sprawling property with large, comfortable lobby. Convenient access to downtown activities. All rooms with hair dryer, iron and ironing board. 3 stories; interior corridors; heated pool. **Dining:** Restaurant; 6:30 am-2 & 5-10 pm; 5 am-11 pm in summer; $7-$18; cocktails. **Cards:** AE, DI, DS, JC, MC, VI.

- Indoor Pool, Spa & Fitness Facility
- Complimentary Deluxe Continental Breakfast
- Premiere Business Center
- 24 Hour Airport Shuttle
- Free In-Room Coffee & Local Calls

Holiday Inn EXPRESS

Anchorage Airport

"21st CENTURY CONVENIENCE IN THE LAST FRONTIER"

4411 Spenard Rd.
Anchorage, AK 99517
Phone (907) 248-8848
Toll Free (800) HOLIDAY

HOLIDAY INN EXPRESS ANCHORAGE AIRPORT
◆◆◆
Motel

5/16-9/15   1P: $129   2P: $129
3/1-5/15 & 9/16-2/28   1P: $69   2P: $69

Phone: (907)248-8848

Location: 4 mi sw, 0.5 mi n on Jewell Lake Rd. 4411 Spenard Rd 99517. Fax: 907/248-8847. **Terms:** [ECP] meal plan; 3 day cancellation notice; pets, $10 extra charge, in smoking rooms. **Facility:** 78 rooms. Beautiful property with a good sized lobby featuring a gas fireplace and unique pacific northwest furnishings. Well appointed guest rooms all with 2-line phones, hair dryer, iron, ironing board and video games. 2 stories; interior corridors; small heated indoor pool. **Services:** gift shop. **Some Rooms:** Fee: VCR. **Cards:** AE, DI, DS, JC, MC, VI. *(See color ad p 597)*

LONGHOUSE ALASKAN HOTEL
AAA SAVE
◆◆
Motel

5/15-9/14   1P: $139   2P: $159
3/1-5/14 & 9/15-2/28   1P: $69   2P: $79-$89

Phone: (907)243-2133

Location: From Minnesota Dr, 1.5 mi sw on Spenard Rd, n on Wisconsin St and at 43rd Ave level, just e. 4335 Wisconsin St 99517. Fax: 907/243-6060. **Terms:** [CP] meal plan; check-in 4 pm; cancellation fee imposed. **Facility:** 54 rooms. Distinctive long log-sided buildings, located in the vicinity of Lake Spenard and the float-plane docks. Rooms vary in size and offer contemporary decor. All rooms with hair dryer and voice mail. 2 stories; interior corridors. **Dining:** Restaurant nearby. **Services:** area transportation, train station. **All Rooms:** combo or shower baths, extended cable TV. **Cards:** AE, DI, DS, MC, VI. **Special Amenities:** Free breakfast and free local telephone calls.

LYNN'S PINE POINT BED & BREAKFAST
AAA
◆◆◆
Bed &
Breakfast

4/1-9/30   1P: $85-$105   2P: $95-$115   XP: $35   D12
3/1-3/31   1P: $75-$86   2P: $85-$95   XP: $35   D12
10/1-2/28   1P: $75-$80   2P: $85-$95   XP: $35   D12

Phone: (907)333-2244

Location: From Lake Otis Pkwy; 3.8 mi e on Tudor Rd, follow n as Tudor becomes Muldoon; just w on E 36th St. 3333 Creekside Dr 99504. Fax: 907/333-1043. **Terms:** [BP] & [CP] meal plans; monthly rates avail; check-in 5 pm, check-out 9:30 am; 7 day cancellation notice; cat on premises. **Facility:** 3 rooms. Located in quiet residential area. Cozy accommodations. Extensive video library and in-room amenities. Whirlpool room; 3 stories; interior corridors; smoke free premises; whirlpool; barbecue & deck, public tennis court nearby. **Services:** complimentary evening beverages. **Recreation:** cross country skiing. **All Rooms:** combo or shower baths, extended cable TV. **Cards:** AE, DS, MC, VI.

MERRILL FIELD INN

Phone: (907)276-4547

| | 5/16-9/15 | 1P: $100-$125 | 2P: $100-$125 |
| | 3/1-5/15 & 9/16-2/28 | 1P: $55-$70 | 2P: $55-$70 |

Motel   **Location:** 1 mi e via US 1 (Glenn Hwy). Directly opposite Merrill Field Airstrip. 420 Sitka St 99501. **Fax:** 907/276-5064. **Terms:** [CP] meal plan; pets, $7 extra charge. **Facility:** 39 rooms. Compact to spacious, pleasantly decorated rooms. 2 stories; exterior corridors. **Dining:** Restaurant nearby. **Services:** winter plug-ins. **Recreation:** video library. **All Rooms:** extended cable TV. **Some Rooms:** 8 efficiencies. Fee: VCR. **Cards:** AE, CB, DI, DS, JC, MC, VI. *(See color ad p 598)*

MICROTEL INN & SUITES

Phone: (907)245-5002

| | 5/16-9/15 | 1P: $129-$149 | 2P: $129-$149 | XP: $5 | F16 |
| | 3/1-5/15 & 9/16-2/28 | 1P: $69-$79 | 2P: $69-$79 | XP: $5 | F16 |

Motel   **Location:** From jct International Airport Rd and Spenard Rd, 0.5 mi e on Frontage Rd, just n. 5205 Northwood Dr 99517. **Fax:** 907/245-5030. **Terms:** [CP] meal plan; check-in 4 pm; pets, in smoking rooms. **Facility:** 77 rooms. Newer property with a mix of standard rooms offering simple appointments and junior suites with wet bar, refrigerator and microwave. 3 stories; interior corridors. **Cards:** AE, CB, DI, DS, MC, VI. *(See color ad p 598)*

PARKWOOD INN

Phone: (907)563-3590

	6/1-9/6	1P: $115	2P: $115	XP: $10	F12
	5/16-5/31	1P: $89	2P: $89	XP: $10	F12
	3/1-5/15 & 9/7-2/28	1P: $69	2P: $69	XP: $10	F12

Motel   **Location:** From International Airport Rd, 0.4 mi n on Old Seward Hwy, just e on 45th St. 4455 Juneau St 99503. **Fax:** 907/563-5560. **Terms:** Weekly & monthly rates avail, off season; cancellation fee imposed; pets, $5 extra charge, $50 dep req. **Facility:** 50 rooms. Studio apartments featuring comfortable yet modest decor. 2 two-bedroom units. 2-bedroom suite with full kitchen, $120-$190; 3 stories, no elevator; exterior corridors. **Services:** winter plug-ins. **All Rooms:** kitchens, utensil deposit, extended cable TV. **Cards:** AE, CB, DI, DS, MC, VI. **Special Amenities:** Free local telephone calls.

RAMADA LIMITED HOTEL OF ANCHORAGE

Phone: (907)929-7000

| | 6/1-8/31 | 1P: $160-$170 | 2P: $160-$170 | XP: $10 | F18 |
| | 3/1-5/31 & 9/1-2/28 | 1P: $70-$80 | 2P: $70-$80 | XP: $10 | F18 |

Motel   **Location:** 5 mi ne on US 1 (Glenn Hwy), just s of Muldoon Rd exit. 207 Muldoon Rd 99504. **Fax:** 907/929-7070. **Terms:** [BP] meal plan. **Facility:** 50 rooms. In a commercial area. Newer property adjoined to a well-established chinese restaurant. Spacious and contemporary guest rooms. 3 stories; interior corridors. **Services:** area transportation. **Cards:** AE, CB, DI, DS, JC, MC, VI.

REGAL ALASKAN HOTEL

Phone: (907)243-2300

	5/15-9/28	1P: $260-$280	2P: $280-$300	XP: $20	F17
	9/29-2/28	1P: $150-$170	2P: $170-$190	XP: $20	F17
	3/1-5/14	1P: $145-$160	2P: $160-$180	XP: $20	F17

Hotel   **Location:** 4 mi sw, just n on Jewel Lake Rd. 4800 Spenard Rd 99517. Fax: 907/243-8815. **Terms:** Cancellation fee imposed; pets, $50 dep req. **Facility:** 248 rooms. Very attractive lobby featuring hunting trophies and photographs of local history. Guest rooms are stylish, well appointed and offer excellent in-room amenities. Small lake and attractive acreage behind property. 2 whirlpool suites with bath & steam enclosure shower; 4 stories; interior corridors; sauna, steamroom, whirlpool. **Dining:** Restaurant; 6 am-2 am; $10-$21; health conscious menu items; cocktails. **Services:** gift shop; area transportation. **Recreation:** seaplane dock on adjacent Lake Spenard. **Cards:** AE, DI, DS, JC, MC, VI. **Special Amenities:** Early check-in/late check-out and free room upgrade (subject to availability with advanced reservations).

SHERATON ANCHORAGE HOTEL

Phone: 907/276-8700

Property failed to provide current rates

Hotel   **Location:** Downtown at 6th Ave and Denali. 401 E 6th Ave 99501. Fax: 907/276-7561. **Terms:** Package plans. **Facility:** 375 rooms. Extensive collection of native artwork in public areas. All rooms with hair dryer, iron and ironing board. 16 stories; interior corridors. **Services:** gift shop. Fee: massage. **Some Rooms:** Fee: VCR. **Cards:** AE, DI, DS, JC, MC, VI.

SPRINGHILL SUITES BY MARRIOTT

Phone: (907)562-3247

◆◆◆	6/1-9/15	1P: $169	2P: $169
Motel	3/1-5/31 & 9/16-2/28	1P: $89	2P: $89

Location: Corner 36th Ave. 3401 A St 99503. Fax: 907/562-3250. **Terms:** [ECP] meal plan. **Facility:** 102 rooms. Tastefully appointed guest rooms, each with a seating area and wet bar. All rooms with hair dryer, iron and ironing board. 3 stories; interior corridors; small heated indoor pool. **Cards:** AE, CB, DI, DS, MC, VI.

SUPER 8 MOTEL-ANCHORAGE

Phone: (907)276-8884

◆	6/9-9/3	1P: $169-$1889	2P: $179-$199	XP: $10	F12
Motel	5/16-6/8	1P: $99-$119	2P: $109-$129	XP: $10	F12
	9/4-2/28	1P: $69-$89	2P: $79-$89	XP: $10	F12
	3/1-5/15	1P: $59-$79	2P: $69-$89	XP: $10	F12

Location: At 36th Ave, just n of Spenard Rd. 3501 Minnesota Dr 99503. Fax: 907/279-8194. **Terms:** Pets, $25 dep req. **Facility:** 84 rooms. Good budget accommodation, simple decor. Some renovated rooms. 4 stories; interior corridors. **Services:** area transportation; winter plug-ins. **Cards:** AE, DI, DS, JC, MC, VI.

THE VOYAGER HOTEL

Phone: (907)277-9501

AAA SAVE

◆◆◆	6/2-9/1	1P: $169	2P: $169	XP: $10
	9/2-2/28	1P: $89-$129	2P: $89-$129	XP: $10
	5/17-6/1	1P: $129	2P: $129	XP: $10
Motor Inn	3/1-5/16	1P: $89	2P: $89	XP: $10

Location: Downtown at K St and 5th Ave. 501 K St 99501. Fax: 907/274-0333. **Terms:** [CP] meal plan; weekly rates avail, except 6/1-9/15. **Facility:** 38 rooms. Tastefully decorated lobby with European charm. Large, comfortable guest rooms; all rooms with hair dryer, iron and ironing board. 4 stories; interior corridors; designated smoking area. **Dining:** Corsair Restaurant, see separate listing. **All Rooms:** efficiencies, extended cable TV. **Cards:** AE, DI, DS, JC, MC, VI. **Special Amenities:** Free local telephone calls. *(See color ad p 599)*

WESTMARK ANCHORAGE

Phone: (907)276-7676

AAA SAVE

◆◆◆	6/1-9/15	1P: $219	2P: $219	XP: $30	F12
	5/16-5/31	1P: $129	2P: $129	XP: $30	F12
	9/16-2/28	1P: $119	2P: $119	XP: $30	F12
Hotel	3/1-5/15	1P: $109	2P: $109	XP: $30	F12

Location: Downtown at G St. 720 W 5th Ave 99501. Fax: 907/276-3615. **Terms:** Cancellation fee imposed; package plans. **Facility:** 200 rooms. Spacious units, some with vintage appointments. All rooms with iron and ironing board. 14 stories; interior corridors. **Dining:** Restaurant, coffee shop; 6 am-10 pm, 6:30 am-9 pm off season; $8-$19; cocktails. **Services:** gift shop. **Recreation:** exercise equipment avail for in-room use. **All Rooms:** extended cable TV. **Cards:** AE, CB, DI, DS, JC, MC, VI. *(See color ad p 594)*

WESTMARK INN ANCHORAGE

Phone: (907)272-7561

AAA SAVE

◆◆	5/15-9/15	1P: $109	2P: $109	XP: $30	F12

Location: Downtown e, at Barrow St. 115 E Third Ave 99501. Fax: 907/272-3879. **Terms:** Open 5/15-9/15; [BP] & [CP] meal plans; cancellation fee imposed; pets, with prior approval. **Facility:** 91 rooms. Some units with balcony, simple yet contemporary decor. 3 stories; interior/exterior corridors. **Dining:** Restaurant; 6-9 am & 5-9 pm; wine/beer only. **Recreation:** tour desk. **All Rooms:** combo or shower baths. **Cards:** AE, CB, DI, DS, JC, MC, VI. *(See color ad p 594)*

------- **RESTAURANTS** -------

CORSAIR RESTAURANT

Dinner: $21-$31 **Phone:** 907-278-4502

◆◆◆ Continental

Location: Downtown at K St and 5th Ave; in The Voyager Hotel. 944 W 5th Ave 99501. **Hours:** 5 pm-10 pm, Fri & Sat-11 pm. Closed major holidays & Sun. **Reservations:** suggested. **Features:** casual dress; cocktails & lounge; fee for parking; a la carte. If you are looking for well-prepared entrees featuring fresh Alaskan seafood, veal and rack of lamb, stop here. In keeping with its name, the decor is nautical but romantic. The wine list is excellent. Open for lunch the last Fri of the month. **Cards:** AE, DI, DS, MC, VI.

CROW'S NEST RESTAURANT

Dinner: $26-$30 **Phone:** 907/276-6000

◆◆◆◆ Continental

Location: Downtown at 5th Ave and K St; in The Hotel Captain Cook. 99501. **Hours:** 6 pm-10 pm, Sun 10 am-2 pm. **Reservations:** suggested. **Features:** casual dress; Sunday brunch; health conscious menu items; cocktails & lounge; fee for valet parking; a la carte. Panoramic rooftop dining with city, mountain and Cook Inlet views. Relaxed formal style service. Beautifully presented cuisine, accent on seafood, wild game and exotic foods such as Beluga caviar, truffles, foie gras and sea beans. **Cards:** AE, DI, DS, JC, MC, VI.

FU DO CHINESE RESTAURANT

Lunch: $5-$7 **Dinner:** $8-$15 **Phone:** 907/561-6611

◆◆ Chinese

Location: From jct, Old Seward Hwy, 1 mi e. 2600 E Tudor Rd 99507. **Hours:** 11 am-10 pm, Fri & Sat-11 pm. **Reservations:** suggested. **Features:** casual dress; carryout; beer & wine only; a la carte. A good mix of Mandarin, Cantonese and Szechwan selections is offered at this restaurant. The crispy duck, orange beef and sesame chicken are good choices. The attractive dining room is situated in a brightly decorated building in a commercial area. **Cards:** AE, DI, DS, MC, VI.

GLACIER BREWHOUSE
◆◆
West
American

Lunch: $6-$13 **Dinner:** $8-$20 **Phone:** 907/274-2739

Location: Downtown at H St. 737 W 5th Ave 99501. **Hours:** 11 am-11 pm, Sun from 4 pm. Closed: 1/1, 7/4 & 12/25. **Features:** casual dress; children's menu; health conscious menu; cocktails & lounge; street parking; a la carte. The casual and cheerful ambience of this large open room is enhanced by a central fireplace and a bustling kitchen area. The menu offers Alaskan seafood, wood-fire cooked pizza and meat, served with a young and upbeat style. Handcrafted beer, of course. **Cards:** AE, VI. ⊠

HARRY'S
◆◆
American

Lunch: $6-$9 **Dinner:** $7-$19 **Phone:** 907/561-5317

Location: 1.5 mi s at C St and Benson Blvd; in Key Bank Building. 101 W Benson Blvd 99503. **Hours:** 11 am-10 pm, Sun 10 am-9 pm, to 11 pm in summer, Sun-10 pm. Closed: 12/25. **Reservations:** suggested; evenings. **Features:** casual dress; Sunday brunch; children's menu; carryout; cocktails & lounge. The cheerful and casual ambience at Harry's makes it a very popular restaurant for both lunch and dinner. Its cuisine offers a great variety of dishes prepared in a contemporary and fresh way. Weekly specials. Excellent selection of microbrewed beer. **Cards:** AE, DI, DS, MC, VI. ⊠

LAS MARGARITAS
◆◆
Mexican

Lunch: $5-$8 **Dinner:** $7-$15 **Phone:** 907/349-4922

Location: Between Artic Blvd and C St. 541 W Dimond 99515. **Hours:** 11:30 am-10 pm, Sat & Sun from 4 pm. Closed: 11/23 & 12/25. **Reservations:** suggested; weekends. **Features:** casual dress; children's menu; cocktails; a la carte. Las Margaritas is a little out of the way, but it's worth the drive. The restaurant has a charming and casual country-style ambience, and its cuisine features popular Mexican and Italian specialties including burritos, spaghetti, pizza, steak and shrimp. **Cards:** AE, DS, MC, VI. ♿ ⊠

MARX BROS. CAFE Historical
◆◆◆
Continental

Dinner: $17-$29 **Phone:** 907/278-2133

Location: Downtown at F St. 627 3rd Ave W 99501. **Hours:** 5:30 pm-9:30 pm. Closed major holidays & Sun 9/21-5/21. **Reservations:** suggested. **Features:** No A/C; casual dress; beer & wine only; street parking; a la carte. This restaurant features relaxed dining in a renovated 1916 home, and innovative preparation of Alaskan seafood, wild game, market-sensitive selections, and caesar salad prepared tableside. They also have homemade ice cream and an extensive wine list. Smoke free premises. **Cards:** AE, DI, MC, VI. ⊠

SIMON & SEAFORTS
◆◆◆
Regional
American

Lunch: $7-$14 **Dinner:** $16-$36 **Phone:** 907/274-3502

Location: Downtown between 4th and 5th aves, overlooking Cook Inlet. 420 L St 99501. **Hours:** 11:15 am-2:30 & 4:30-11 pm. Closed: 11/23 & 12/25. **Reservations:** suggested. **Features:** casual dress; children's menu; carryout; cocktails & lounge; a la carte. This local favorite specializes in fresh, creatively prepared seafood flown in daily from Homer. Angus beef from Nebraska, pasta and chicken are also good. The dining room has a scenic inlet view. Try their world-famous sipping dessert, brandy ice!. Smoke free premises. **Cards:** AE, DI, MC, VI. ⊠

THE TOP OF THE WORLD
◆◆◆
Northern
American

Dinner: $21-$29 **Phone:** 907/265-7111

Location: Downtown at E St; in Hilton Anchorage. 500 W 3rd Ave 99501. **Hours:** 6 pm-10 pm; Sunday Brunch 10:30 am-2 pm. Closed: 1/1 & 12/25. **Reservations:** suggested. **Features:** semi-formal attire; children's menu; cocktails & lounge; fee for parking & valet parking; a la carte. This is an elegant yet relaxed dining ambience with an excellent view of Anchorage. The menu features regional delicacies well-prepared with an International flair. Fall through spring, Wednesdays are special with the chef's gourmet dinners. **Cards:** AE, DI, DS, JC, MC, VI. ⊠

VILLA NOVA
◆◆
Italian

Dinner: $11-$29 **Phone:** 907/561-1660

Location: Corner International Airport Rd. 5121 Artic Blvd 99503. **Hours:** 5 pm-10 pm. Closed: 1/1, 12/25, Sun & Mon. **Reservations:** suggested. **Features:** No A/C; carryout; beer & wine only. A well-kept secret, this cozy strip mall front European style restaurant will tempt the most discerning diner with a variety of local seafood and Mediterranean dishes. The Cocciucco, veal and fillets should not be overlooked. **Cards:** AE, DS, MC, VI. ⊠

The following restaurant has not been inspected by AAA but is listed for your information only.

SULLIVAN'S STEAKHOUSE
[fyi]

Phone: 907/258-2882

Not inspected. **Location:** 320 W 5th Ave. **Features:** Experience a casual, upscale ambience with a "swing" atmosphere. This is a meat lover's paradise, balanced with a few regional seafood entrees.

CANTWELL pop. 100—*See also DENALI NATIONAL PARK AND PRESERVE.*

—— LODGING ——

BACKWOODS LODGE
				Phone: 907/768-2232
(AAA)	6/6-8/31	1P: $110-$120	2P: $110-$120	XP: $10
◆◆	9/1-9/30	1P: $90-$100	2P: $90-$110	XP: $10
Motel	3/1-6/5	1P: $90-$100	2P: $90-$100	XP: $10
	10/1-2/28	1P: $80-$90	2P: $80-$90	XP: $10

Location: From George Parks Hwy, milepost 210, just e on Denali Hwy. (Box 32, 99729). Fax: 907/768-2232. **Terms:** 7 day cancellation notice; cancellation fee imposed; pets, $25 dep req. **Facility:** 10 rooms. Spacious units with homey appeal. Secluded location in quiet wooded area. Phones in units all share 1 line. All rooms with hair dryer. 1 story; exterior corridors; smoke free premises. **Services:** winter plug-ins. **Recreation:** canoeing; hiking trails, pond with campfire area, horse-shoe pits, shared barbecue on exterior walkway. **All Rooms:** efficiencies, shower baths, extended cable TV. **Cards:** AE, DS, MC, VI. *(See color ad below)*

COOPER LANDING pop. 200

—— LODGING ——

KENAI PRINCESS WILDERNESS LODGE
				Phone: (907)595-1425
◆◆◆	6/2-9/10		2P: $229-$249	XP: $10
Lodge	5/16-6/1		2P: $129-$169	XP: $10
	3/1-5/15 & 9/11-2/28		2P: $79-$119	XP: $10

Location: From SR 1, Sterling Hwy, Milepost 47.8, just n of bridge, 2.1 mi w on gravel road. Mile 2.1 Bean Creek Rd 99572 (PO Box 676). Fax: 907/595-1424. **Terms:** 8 day cancellation notice; cancellation fee imposed. **Facility:** 86 rooms. On bluff overlooking the Kenai River and mountains. Cozy, well furnished cabin-style units in quadruplexes with screened porch and woodburning stove. All rooms with hair dryer. 1 story; exterior corridors. **Services:** gift shop. **Recreation:** charter fishing, fishing; hiking trails. Fee: cross country skiing; bicycles. **All Rooms:** combo or shower baths. **Cards:** AE, DI, MC, VI.

Take a Trip

*B*efore you head out on the open road for your next vacation, make sure you visit your local AAA/CAA Travel Agency. From TripTik® routings and TourBook® guides to cruise bookings and international tour packages, AAA/CAA's staff of knowledgeable professionals can make your next trip a dream vacation. To find out more ways AAA/CAA can help you "get away from it all," call your local AAA/CAA Travel Agency.

Travel With Someone You Trust®

DENALI NATIONAL PARK AND PRESERVE pop. 200—
See also CANTWELL & HEALY.

------ LODGINGS ------

DENALI BACKCOUNTRY LODGE   **Phone:** (907)783-2928
◆◆   6/16-8/31   1P: $630   2P: $630
Lodge   6/4-6/15 & 9/1-9/11   1P: $536   2P: $536
Location: End of the 90 mi Denali National Park Rd. (PO Box 389, GIRDWOOD, 99587). Fax: 907/783-2130.
Terms: Open 6/4-9/11; [AP] meal plan; check-out 6:30 am; 60 day cancellation notice; cancellation fee imposed; 2 night min stay; package plans. **Facility:** 30 rooms. All inclusive backcountry lodge nestled in a remote mountain valley beyond Mt McKinley. Adventure includes 2-half day bus trips through Denali National Park. Well appointed cedar cabins and hospitable staff make for a unique experience. 1 story; exterior corridors; smoke free premises. **Services:** area transportation. **Recreation:** bicycles. **All Rooms:** shower baths. **Cards:** MC, VI. *(See color ad p 292 & below)*

DENALI BLUFFS HOTEL   **Phone:** (907)683-7000
(AAA) (SAVE)   6/8-9/7   1P: $169-$184   2P: $179-$194   XP: $10   F12
             5/15-6/7 & 9/8-9/15   1P: $116-$131   2P: $126-$141   XP: $10   F12
◆◆◆   **Location:** On George Parks Hwy, milepost 238.4, 1 mi n of park entrance. (PO Box 72460, DENALI, 99707).
Motor Inn   Fax: 907/683-7500. **Terms:** Open 5/15-9/15; 30 day cancellation notice; cancellation fee imposed.
Facility: 112 rooms. Attractive public areas, lobby with high open beam ceiling and fireplace. Rooms are compact but offer fresh, contemporary appeal. Some rooms with view of mountain and valley, many with balcony. 2 stories; exterior corridors; smoke free premises. **Dining:** Coffee shop; 5 am-8 pm; $7-$10. **Services:** gift shop; area transportation. **Recreation:** tour desk. **Cards:** AE, DS, JC, MC, VI. **Special Amenities:** Free local telephone calls.

DENALI PRINCESS LODGE   **Phone:** 907/683-2282
◆◆◆   Property failed to provide current rates
Motor Inn   **Location:** On SR 3 (George Parks Hwy); 1.5 mi n of park entrance at s milepost 238.5. SR 3 99755 (PO Box 110). Fax: 907/683-1307. **Terms:** Open 5/18-9/23. **Facility:** 353 rooms. Scenic view of mountains and Nenana River. Rooms vary in decor and style, most are compact. Large and attractive public areas with dining room affording a beautiful view. 2 stories; exterior corridors; smoke free premises. **Dining:** entertainment. **Services:** gift shop; area transportation. Fee: massage. **Cards:** AE, DI, MC, VI.

DENALI RIVER CABINS   Phone: (907)683-2500

Property failed to provide current rates

⚫◆
Complex
Location: On George Parks Hwy, milepost 231.1 just s of park boundaries. (PO Box 210, DENALI NATIONAL PARK, 99755). Fax: 907/683-3504. **Terms:** Open 5/15-9/20; 30 day cancellation notice; cancellation fee imposed; package plans. **Facility:** 104 rooms. Cozy log cabins offering simple decor, some with view of the river. Newer section features good sized motel rooms with a streamlined look. 1 story; exterior corridors; smoke free premises; sauna, whirlpool. **Dining:** Restaurant; 5 am-9:30 pm; $8-$16; cocktails. **Services:** area transportation, train station. **Recreation:** hiking trails, riverside sun deck with barbecue. Fee: kayak, white water rafting; horseback riding. **All Rooms:** combo or shower baths. **Some Rooms:** color TV. **Cards:** DS, MC, VI.

⚫◆

DENALI RIVERVIEW INN   Phone: (907)683-2663

6/8-8/31	1P: $134	2P: $134	XP: $5	F5
5/15-6/7 & 9/1-9/15	1P: $89	2P: $89	XP: $5	F5

Motel
Location: On SR 3 (George Parks Hwy) milepost 238.4; 1 mi n of park entrance. (PO Box 49, 99755). Fax: 907/683-7433. **Terms:** Open 5/15-9/15; 7 day cancellation notice; cancellation fee imposed. **Facility:** 12 rooms. Good views of park, overlooking Nenana River. The rooms are well sheltered in tall trees. 2 stories; exterior corridors; smoke free premises; mountain view. **Services:** gift shop; area transportation. **Cards:** DS, MC, VI.

DENALI STATE PARK

———— LODGING ————

MT. MCKINLEY PRINCESS LODGE   Phone: 907/733-2900

Property failed to provide current rates

◆◆◆
Motor Inn
Location: From George Parks Hwy, milepost 133.1, 1 mi e on Mt McKinley View Rd. (PO Box 13550, TRAPPER CREEK, 99683-0550). Fax: 907/733-2922. **Terms:** Open 5/15-9/25. **Facility:** 238 rooms. Gracious public areas, restaurant and patio affording breathtaking view on Mt McKinley and Alaska range. Decor in units features a contemporary mountain/wilderness motif. Secluded and quiet location. All rooms with hair dryer. 2 stories; interior/exterior corridors. **Dining:** entertainment. **Services:** gift shop. Fee: area transportation. **Recreation:** hiking trails. **All Rooms:** combo or shower baths. **Cards:** AE, DI, MC, VI.

EAGLE RIVER

———— LODGING ————

EAGLE RIVER MOTEL   Phone: 907/694-5000

5/16-9/30	1P: $75-$80	2P: $84-$89	XP: $6
3/1-5/15 & 10/1-2/28	1P: $60	2P: $65	XP: $6

⚫
Motel
Location: From Glenn Hwy, Eagle River exit, just e; in town centre. 11111 Old Eagle River Rd 99577. **Terms:** Pets. **Facility:** 13 rooms. Spacious units offering simple decor. 3 stories, no elevator; exterior corridors. **Dining:** Restaurant nearby. **Services:** winter plug-ins. **All Rooms:** extended cable TV. **Some Rooms:** 8 efficiencies. **Cards:** AE, DI, DS, MC, VI. *(See color ad p 596)*

FAIRBANKS pop. 30,800

———— LODGINGS ————

A BED & BREAKFAST INN ON MINNIE STREET   Phone: (907)456-1802

5/1-9/30	1P: $100-$195	2P: $100-$195	XP: $20	F5
3/1-4/30 & 10/1-2/28	1P: $60-$125	2P: $65-$135	XP: $20	F5

◆◆◆
Bed &
Breakfast
Location: Just n of downtown, follow Cushman St over Bridge to Illinois St, just e. 345 Minnie St 99701. Fax: 907/451-1751. **Terms:** [BP] meal plan; 14 day cancellation notice; cancellation fee imposed. **Facility:** 10 rooms. 2 fully detached houses interconnected by a deck walkway facing beautifully landscaped courtyard. Rooms vary in style and size; most with contemporary appointments. All rooms with hair dryer. 1 two-bedroom unit. 1 two-bedroom suite with full kitchen, $150; whirlpool room, $130-$155; 2 stories; interior corridors; smoke free premises. **Dining:** Breakfast served 7:15 and 8 am. **Services:** winter plug-ins. **All Rooms:** extended cable TV. **Some Rooms:** 2 kitchens. **Cards:** AE, MC, VI. *(See color ad below)*

ALL SEASONS INN
Phone: (907)451-6649
◆◆◆ 5/15-9/15   1P: $115-$135   2P: $125-$150   XP: $25   D5
Bed & 3/1-5/14 & 9/16-2/28   1P: $70   2P: $75-$85   XP: $15   D5
Breakfast **Location:** Downtown; just w of Barnette St. 763 7th Ave 99701. Fax: 907/474-8448. **Terms:** [BP] meal plan; check-in 4 pm; 14 day cancellation notice; cancellation fee imposed. **Facility:** 8 rooms. Located close to all services. Some rooms are compact. All offer a crisp, contemporary decor. Operates in the style of a European pension and allows guest independence. Gracious seating areas. 2 stories; interior corridors; smoke free premises. **Services:** winter plug-ins. **Cards:** CB, DI, DS, JC, MC, VI. *(See color ad p 604)*

A TASTE OF ALASKA LODGE
Phone: (907)488-7855
◆◆◆ All Year   1P: $150   2P: $150-$200   F5
Bed & **Location:** 4.5 mi ne on US 2 (Steese Hwy), 5.3 mi e on Chena Hot Springs Rd, 0.5 mi s, follow signs. 551
Breakfast Eberhardt Rd 99712. Fax: 907/488-3772. **Terms:** [BP] meal plan. **Facility:** 10 rooms. Secluded location. 2 log cabins fully equipped with kitchen and living room or spacious units with atrium doors, in the main lodge. All units offer an attractive blend of contemporary comfort and rusticity, many antiques. 1 two-bedroom unit. Interior/exterior corridors; smoke free premises; mountain view. **Services:** winter plug-ins. **Recreation:** cross country skiing. **All Rooms:** combo or shower baths. **Cards:** AE, MC, VI.

COMFORT INN-CHENA RIVER
Phone: (907)479-8080
◆◆◆ 5/14-9/14   1P: $139-$209   2P: $139-$209
Motel 3/1-5/13 & 9/15-2/28   1P: $79-$129   2P: $79-$129
   Location: From Airport Way, just n on Pegger Rd, just e on Phillips Field Rd, follow signs in wooded area s of road. 1908 Chena Landings Loop 99701. Fax: 907/479-8063. **Terms:** [CP] meal plan; check-in 4 pm; cancellation fee imposed; pets, cats in kennel, in smoking rooms. **Facility:** 74 rooms. Spacious units offering contemporary appeal. In quiet wooded area, new development. 3 stories; interior corridors; small heated indoor pool. **Services:** area transportation; winter plug-ins. **Some Rooms:** Fee: VCR. **Cards:** AE, CB, DI, DS, JC, MC, VI. *(See color ad below)*

CRESTMONT MANOR BED & BREAKFAST
Phone: (907)456-3831
◆◆◆ 5/15-9/15   1P: $75-$120   2P: $75-$120   XP: $15   F12
Bed & 3/1-5/14 & 9/16-2/28   1P: $75   2P: $75   XP: $15   F12
Breakfast **Location:** From US 3 (Parks Hwy), Chena Pump Rd exit, just w to Chena Ridge Rd, 0.7 mi n, then just e. 510 Crestmont Dr 99708 (PO Box 82372). Fax: 907/456-3841. **Terms:** [BP] meal plan; check-in 5 pm; 30 day cancellation notice. **Facility:** 5 rooms. Newer property. Most rooms are spacious and include an ensuite bathroom. Streamlined guest room decor enhanced by the owner's hand made quilts. Large deck with inspiring views of mountain valley. 2 stories; interior corridors; smoke free premises. **All Rooms:** combo or shower baths. **Some Rooms:** color TV. **Cards:** MC, VI.

FAIRBANKS DOWNTOWN BED & BREAKFAST
Phone: (907)452-7700
◆◆ 5/15-8/31   1P: $100-$110   2P: $100-$110
Bed & **Location:** From jct Airport Way and Gillam Way, just s. 1461 Gillam Way 99701. Fax: 907/456-1116.
Breakfast **Terms:** Open 5/15-8/31; [CP] meal plan; age restrictions may apply; 14 day cancellation notice; cancellation fee imposed. **Facility:** 5 rooms. Residential location. Pleasant guest rooms with shared sitting room and full kitchen avail for guest only use. Some antiques. 2 stories; interior corridors; smoke free premises. **Services:** winter plug-ins. **All Rooms:** combo or shower baths. **Cards:** AE, DS, MC, VI.

FAIRBANKS PRINCESS HOTEL
Phone: (907)455-4477
◆◆◆ 5/16-9/15   1P: $199-$499   2P: $199-$499   XP: $10   F
Motor Inn 3/1-5/15 & 9/16-2/28   1P: $129-$349   2P: $129-$349   XP: $10   F
   Location: From jct Airport and Pikes Landing rds, just nw. 4477 Pikes Landing Rd 99709. Fax: 907/455-4476. **Terms:** Package plans. **Facility:** 200 rooms. On the Chena River. Rooms are spacious and graciously decorated. All rooms with hair dryer. 1 two-bedroom unit. 3 stories; interior corridors. **Services:** gift shop; area transportation; winter plug-ins. **Some Rooms:** kitchen. Fee: VCR. **Cards:** AE, DI, MC, VI.

FORGET-ME-NOT LODGE

◆◆◆ All Year   **Phone:** (907)474-0949

Lodge   **Location:** From US 3, Chena Pump exit, 6.5 mi nw on Chena Pump Rd (5.2 mi nw of the Pump House). 1540 Chena Ridge 99707 (PO Box 80128, 99708). Fax: 907/474-8173. **Terms:** [BP] meal plan; age restrictions may apply; 4 day cancellation notice; pets on premises. **Facility:** 10 rooms. Spectacular view of Fairbanks. Some rooms in renovated pullman railroad cars, all with artistic decor. 2 two-bedroom units. 2 stories; interior corridors; smoke free premises. **Services:** winter plug-ins. **Some Rooms:** color TV. **Cards:** MC, VI.

| | 1P: $75-$150 | 2P: $85-$150 | XP: $25 |

MIDGE'S BIRCH LANE BED & BREAKFAST

(AAA)   5/15-9/15   **Phone:** (907)388-8084

◆◆   3/1-5/14 & 9/16-2/28

Bed & Breakfast   **Location:** From Airport Rd W, 0.6 mi n on George Parks Way, 1 mi e on Geist Road, 0.4 mi s on Fairbanks Street, then 0.3 mi w. 4335 Birch Lane 99708 (PO Box 81013). Fax: 907/479-4894. **Terms:** [BP] & [CP] meal plans; weekly rates avail; check-in 4 pm; 7 day cancellation notice; cancellation fee imposed; 2 night min stay; pet on premises. **Facility:** 4 rooms. In a quiet residential neighborhood. Quaint rooms with charming country theme decor. 2 stories; interior corridors; smoke free premises. **Services:** winter plug-ins. **Recreation:** bicycles, barbecue deck. Fee: kayaks. **All Rooms:** extended cable TV. **Some Rooms:** color TV. **Cards:** MC, VI.

| | 1P: $75-$90 | 2P: $75-$90 | XP: $15 |
| | 1P: $55-$70 | 2P: $55-$70 | XP: $15 |

REGENCY FAIRBANKS HOTEL

◆◆   5/15-9/14   **Phone:** 907-452-3200

Motor Inn   3/1-5/14 & 9/15-2/28

Location: Center; just w of US 2 (Steese Expwy). 95 Tenth Ave 99701. Fax: 907/452-6505. **Terms:** Package plans; pets, with approval. **Facility:** 129 rooms. Spacious, well-equipped guest rooms with vintage appeal. 3 two-bedroom units. 3 stories; interior corridors. **Services:** gift shop; area transportation; winter plug-ins. **All Rooms:** efficiencies. **Cards:** AE, CB, DI, MC, VI.

| | 1P: $165 | 2P: $175 | XP: $10 | F12 |
| | 1P: $90 | 2P: $100 | XP: $10 | F12 |

RIVER'S EDGE RESORT

◆◆◆   **Phone:** (907)474-0286

Complex   Property failed to provide current rates

Location: From Airport Way, just n on Sportsman Way, 0.5 mi w. 4200 Boat St 99709. Fax: 907/474-3665. **Facility:** 94 rooms. Newer property with a collection of cottages located near or along the Chena River, all with patio. Nicely appointed rooms ranging from compact to spacious. Main building features a gold rush era lobby. All rooms with hair dryer. 2 stories; interior/exterior corridors; boat dock. **Services:** gift shop; area transportation; winter plug-ins. **Cards:** AE, MC, VI.

7 GABLES INN

(AAA)   5/22-9/15   **Phone:** (907)479-0751

◆◆◆   5/1-5/21

  9/16-2/28

Complex   3/1-4/30

Location: From Parks Hwy, 0.5 mi e on Geist Rd to Loftus Rd, just s to Birch Ln, just e. 4312 Birch Ln 99709 (PO Box 80488, 99708). Fax: 907/479-2229. **Terms:** [BP] meal plan; weekly rates avail; in winter; 3 day cancellation notice; cancellation fee imposed. **Facility:** 12 rooms. Located in residential area in vicinity of University. Extensive, hearty home cooked breakfast. 3 rooms have private bath outside the room. New addition adjacent to the property features two 1-bedroom suites with full kitchen. 2-bedroom unit $180, $110 off season, for up to 4 persons.; 11 whirlpool rooms; 2 stories; interior corridors; designated smoking area. **Services:** winter plug-ins. **Recreation:** canoeing; bicycles, video library. **All Rooms:** combo or shower baths, extended cable TV. **Some Rooms:** 2 efficiencies, kitchen. **Cards:** AE, CB, DI, DS, MC, VI.

	1P: $85-$130	2P: $90-$130	XP: $15
	1P: $65-$95	2P: $65-$95	XP: $10
	1P: $50-$95	2P: $50-$95	XP: $10
	1P: $50-$85	2P: $50-$85	XP: $10

WESTMARK FAIRBANKS HOTEL & CONFERENCE CENTER

(AAA) SAVE   5/16-9/15   **Phone:** (907)456-7722

◆◆◆   3/1-5/15 & 9/16-2/28

Motor Inn   **Location:** Just n of Airport Way at 10th Ave, just w of SR 2, downtown. 813 Noble St 99701. Fax: 907/451-7478. **Terms:** Cancellation fee imposed; package plans. **Facility:** 244 rooms. Courtyard and tower rooms vary in style and size, most with vintage appointments. Newly renovated public areas including grand lobby with inviting seating areas. All rooms with iron, ironing board and voice mail. 2-4 stories; interior/exterior corridors. **Dining:** Restaurant; 6 am-11 pm, espresso bar; $18-$28; cocktails. **Services:** gift shop; area transportation, train depot; winter plug-ins. **Cards:** AE, CB, DI, DS, JC, MC, VI. *(See color ad p 594)*

| | 1P: $159 | 2P: $159 | XP: $30 | F12 |
| | 1P: $129 | 2P: $129 | XP: $30 | F12 |

WESTMARK INN FAIRBANKS

(AAA) SAVE   6/1-9/15   **Phone:** (907)456-6602

◆◆   5/16-5/31

Motor Inn   **Location:** Just s of Airport Way. 1521 S Cushman St 99701. Fax: 907/452-2724. **Terms:** Open 5/15-9/15; package plans. **Facility:** 170 rooms. Average sized rooms with a mix of vintage and contemporary appointments. Whirlpool room; 2-4 stories; interior corridors. **Dining:** Restaurant; 6 am-10 & 5:30-10 pm, espresso bar; $13-$23; entertainment. **Services:** gift shop; area transportation, train station. **All Rooms:** extended cable TV. **Cards:** AE, CB, DI, DS, JC, MC, VI. *(See color ad p 594)*

| | 1P: $139 | 2P: $139 | XP: $30 | F12 |
| | 1P: $89 | 2P: $89 | XP: $30 | F12 |

--- **RESTAURANTS** ---

GAMBARDELLA'S PASTA BELLA

(AAA)   **Lunch:** $7-$9   **Dinner:** $10-$17   **Phone:** 907/456-3417

◆◆   **Location:** Downtown. 706 2nd Ave 99701. **Hours:** 11 am-10 pm, Sun 4 pm-9:30 pm. Closed: 11/23 & 12/25.

Italian   **Reservations:** suggested; dinner. **Features:** casual dress; children's menu; carryout; beer & wine only. Business travelers and couples enjoy the excellent lasagna and tiramisu at Gambardella's. And the homemade pizza, bread, pies, cheesecake, espresso and cappuccino are very good too. The warm, comfortable ambience offers a covered patio in season. **Cards:** AE, MC, VI.

THE PUMP HOUSE RESTAURANT & SALOON   Historical   **Lunch:** $5-$11   **Dinner:** $14-$30   **Phone:** 907/479-8452
Location: From jct Parks Hwy and Geist Rd (Chena Rd), just e to Chena Pump Rd, 1.3 mi s. 796 Chena Pump Rd 99709. **Hours:** 11 am-10 pm, Sun from 10 am. **Reservations:** suggested; dinner.
American   **Features:** casual dress; Sunday brunch; children's menu; carryout; cocktails & lounge. You'll enjoy this authentic experience in a tin pumphouse used in gold-mining operations; it's listed in the National Register of Historic Places. The deck has a great view of the Chena River, and the decor has a warm Victorian charm.
Daily lunch buffet. **Cards:** AE, DS, MC, VI.   ☒

THAI HOUSE RESTAURANT   **Lunch:** $6-$8   **Dinner:** $7-$15   **Phone:** 907/452-6123
◆◆   **Location:** Downtown. 526 5th Ave 99701. **Hours:** Open 3/1-12/31; 11 am-4 & 5-10 pm. Closed: Sun & 12/20-1/15. **Features:** No A/C; casual dress; carryout; beer & wine only; street parking; a la carte. This locally popular restaurant is a cozy, unassuming spot offering food to challenge your taste buds. Yellow curry powder, onion, egg, fresh ginger, chili and garlic are a few of the ingredients that bring the authentic cuisine to life. Friendly service. Smoke free premises. **Cards:** MC, VI.   ☒

GIRDWOOD

—— LODGING ——

THE WESTIN ALYESKA PRINCE HOTEL   **Phone:** (907)754-1111
◆◆◆◆   6/1-8/31   1P: $170-$220   2P: $170-$220   XP: $25   F18
Hotel   3/1-3/31, 4/1-5/31 & 9/1-2/28   1P: $125-$175   2P: $125-$175   XP: $25   F18
Location: 2 mi n on Alyeska Blvd from SR 1 (Seward Hwy), 0.9 mi w. 1000 Arlberg Ave 99587 (PO Box 249).
Fax: 907/754-2200. **Terms:** Cancellation fee imposed; package plans. **Facility:** 307 rooms. Beautiful view from most rooms. Very attractive public areas, dark woods and fireplace. Serene room decor, large windows. All rooms with hair dryer, iron and ironing board. 32 two-bedroom units. 8 stories; interior corridors; mountain view; heated pool. **Services:** gift shop; winter plug-ins. Fee: massage. **Recreation:** ice skating; hiking trails. Fee: downhill & cross country skiing; bicycles. **All Rooms:** combo or shower baths, safes. **Some Rooms:** efficiency. **Cards:** AE, CB, DI, DS, JC, MC, VI.

🍴 🍸 🐾 ⊿ ♿ ♿ ♿ ☒ 🎿 📷 📠 💻 📥 🛢 DATA PORT 📶 ♿ ☒

—— RESTAURANT ——

SEVEN GLACIERS RESTAURANT   **Dinner:** $24-$42   **Phone:** 907/754-2249
◆◆◆◆   **Location:** 2 mi n on Alyeska Blvd from SR 1 (Seward Hwy), 0.9 mi w; in The Westin Alyeska Prince Hotel.
Regional   1000 Arlberg 99587. **Hours:** 5:30 pm-9:30 pm. Closed: 4/15-5/5, 10/1-11/15, Tues-Wed 5/1-5/31 & 9/1-9/30.
American   **Reservations:** required. **Features:** No A/C; casual dress; Sunday brunch; health conscious menu; cocktails & lounge; valet parking; a la carte, also prix fixe. Seven Glaciers' unusual mountaintop location offers a spectacular setting accessible by cable car from the hotel. A creative Alaskan and West Coast cuisine specializes in wonderful seafood and wild game. Excellent American and French wines. Elegant decor. Smoke free premises. **Cards:** AE, DI, DS, JC, MC, VI.   ♿ ☒

GLENNALLEN pop. 500

—— LODGING ——

LAKE LOUISE LODGE   **Phone:** (907)822-3311
◆◆   All Year   1P: $65-$95   2P: $75-$95   XP: $15   D12
Lodge   **Location:** 27.7 mi w on US 1, 16.1 mi n on dirt road. Mile 16.1 Lake Louise Rd 99588 (HC01 Box 1716).
Fax: 907/822-3311. **Terms:** Check-in 4 pm; 14 day cancellation notice; cancellation fee imposed. **Facility:** 6 rooms. Ideal fishing destination. Rustic log structure on the shores of Lake Louise. Guest room with simple decor and contemporary appeal. Fairly busy grounds with some RV traffic and a few sleeping cabins. 2 stories; interior/exterior corridors; smoke free premises; boat dock. **Services:** winter plug-ins. **Recreation:** swimming, canoeing, charter fishing, fishing, paddleboats; snowmobiling. Rental: boats. **All Rooms:** shower baths. **Cards:** MC, VI.   ASK 📶 🍴 🍸 ☒ 🎿 📶 💻 ☒

GUSTAVUS pop. 300

—— LODGINGS ——

ANNIE MAE LODGE   **Phone:** (907)697-2346
◆◆◆   All Year   1P: $130-$155   2P: $215-$250   XP: $90   F3
Country Inn   **Location:** From airport, 3 mi w to Good River Rd, 0.5 mi to Grandpa's Farm Rd. #2 Grandpa's Farm Rd 99826
(PO BX 80). Fax: 907/697-2211. **Terms:** [AP] meal plan; 30 day cancellation notice; cancellation fee imposed.
Facility: 11 rooms. Charming homelike common seating room, patio with view on expansive marshland. Rooms in the wing section offer elegant and understated decor, contemporary appeal, most with view. 2 stories; interior/exterior corridors; smoke free premises. **Services:** area transportation. **Recreation:** fishing; bicycles. **Cards:** AE, DI, DS, MC, VI.

ASK 📶 ➕ 🍴 ⊿ ♿ ☒ 🎿 📶 ☒

MEADOW'S GLACIER BAY GUEST HOUSE   **Phone:** (907)697-2348
◆◆   All Year   1P: $187-$224   2P: $187-$224   XP: $65
Bed &   **Location:** 0.5 mi n of Gustavus dock, 1.5 mi se of airport. 12 Meadow Brook Ln 99826 (PO Box 93).
Breakfast   Fax: 907/697-2454. **Terms:** [BP] meal plan; 30 day cancellation notice; cancellation fee imposed. **Facility:** 4 rooms. Close to golf course. Interesting collection of contemporary Alaskan art on display. On banks of Salmon River overlooking Point Adolphus. 2 stories; interior corridors; designated smoking area. **Services:** area transportation. **Recreation:** fishing; bicycles. Fee: boating. **Cards:** MC, VI.   ASK ➕ ⊿ ♿ ☒ 🎿 ☒

HAINES pop. 1,200

------ LODGING ------

CAPTAIN'S CHOICE INC MOTEL
Phone: (907)766-3111

(AAA) (SAVE)
◆ ◆
Motel

3/1-10/14	1P: $94-$145	2P: $109-$145	XP: $5	F12
10/15-2/28	1P: $71-$145	2P: $81-$145	XP: $5	F12

Location: 2nd and Dalton sts. 108 2nd Ave N 99827 (PO Box 392). Fax: 907/766-3332. **Terms:** Weekly rates avail; pets, $10 extra charge. **Facility:** 39 rooms. Pine and hemlock paneled rooms overlooking Portage Cove. Whirlpool room, $145-$175; 2 stories; exterior corridors. **Services:** area transportation, ferry. **Recreation:** sundeck. **All Rooms:** extended cable TV. **Some Rooms:** Fee: VCR. **Cards:** AE, CB, DI, DS, MC, VI. **Special Amenities:** Free local telephone calls and preferred room (subject to availability with advanced reservations).

------ RESTAURANT ------

CHILKAT RESTAURANT & BAKERY
Lunch: $5-$13   **Dinner:** $10-$20   **Phone:** 907/766-2920

(AAA)
◆ ◆
American

Location: Just off Main. 5th Ave 99827. **Hours:** Open 3/1-11/30; 7 am-3 pm; hrs may vary in winter. Closed: Sun 9/1-5/31. **Features:** No A/C; casual dress; carryout; salad bar. The Chilkat features a classic menu and daily chef specials. Tasty soups and a delectable array of bakery goods are all made in-house. A terrific salad bar is offered in summer. Its bright atmosphere is homey and decorated in early 19th century style. Smoke free premises. **Cards:** AE, MC, VI.

HEALY pop. 500—See also DENALI NATIONAL PARK AND PRESERVE.

------ LODGINGS ------

DENALI DOME HOME BED & BREAKFAST
Phone: (907)683-1239

(AAA) (SAVE)
◆ ◆ ◆
Bed &
Breakfast

5/28-9/8		2P: $110	XP: $20	F5
5/11-5/27		2P: $85	XP: $20	F5
9/9-2/28	1P: $60	2P: $80	XP: $20	F5
3/1-5/10	1P: $60	2P: $75	XP: $20	F5

Location: From jct Hwy 3 and Healy Spur Rd, 0.5 mi e. 137 Healy Spur Rd 99743 (PO Box 262). Fax: 907/683-2322. **Terms:** [BP] meal plan; weekly rates avail, monthly rates in winter; check-in 4 pm; 14 day cancellation notice, x; cancellation fee imposed; pets on premises. **Facility:** 7 rooms. Comfortably furnished rooms located in unique dome-style home. Quiet, peaceful, scenic location. 1 guest room with sauna. All rooms with hair dryer. Whirlpool room; 3 stories, no elevator; interior/exterior corridors; smoke free premises. **Services:** winter plug-ins. **Recreation:** video library. **All Rooms:** combo or shower baths. **Cards:** AE, DS, MC, VI.

DENALI LAKEVIEW INN
Phone: 907/683-4035

(AAA) (SAVE)
◆ ◆ ◆
Bed &
Breakfast

6/11-9/30	1P: $90-$150	2P: $90-$150	XP: $10	F16
5/15-6/10	1P: $90-$120	2P: $90-$120	XP: $10	F16
3/1-5/14 & 10/1-2/28	1P: $55-$75	2P: $55-$75	XP: $10	F16

Location: From US 3, milepost 247, 1.2 mi w. Mile 1.2 Otto Lake Rd 99743 (PO Box 14). Fax: 907/683-2932. **Terms:** [ECP] meal plan; 7 day cancellation notice; cancellation fee imposed. **Facility:** 4 rooms. Newer inn nestled on tranquil Otto Lake. Well equipped, bright and cheerful guest room decor. Each with a deck. 2 whirlpool rooms; 2 stories; interior/exterior corridors; smoke free premises; mountain view. **All Rooms:** extended cable TV. **Cards:** MC, VI.

HEALY HEIGHTS FAMILY CABINS
Phone: (907)683-2639

(AAA)
◆ ◆ ◆
Cottage

6/1-8/31	1P: $105-$180	2P: $105-$180	XP: $10	F6
5/1-5/31 & 9/1-9/17	1P: $85-$160	2P: $85-$160	XP: $10	F6

Location: From US 3, milepost 247; 0.9 mi w on Otto Lake Rd, 1.5 mi n, following signs. Hill Top Rd 99743 (PO Box 277). Fax: 907/683-2640. **Terms:** Open 5/1-9/17; check-in 4 pm; 15 day cancellation notice; cancellation fee imposed. **Facility:** 6 rooms. Individual cabins overlooking Taiga and Tundra Valleys of the Alaska Range. Cozy and quaint. All rooms with cassette player and gas barbecue on front deck. 1 two-bedroom unit. 1 two-bedroom cabin, $180; $160 off season; 2 stories; exterior corridors; smoke free premises. **Services:** winter plug-ins. **Recreation:** 12 acres of land to explore. **All Rooms:** combo or shower baths, extended cable TV. **Some Rooms:** 4 efficiencies, 2 kitchens, color TV. **Cards:** DS, MC, VI.

TOUCH OF WILDERNESS BED & BREAKFAST
Phone: 907/683-2459

(AAA) (SAVE)
◆ ◆
Country Inn

5/26-9/6	1P: $95-$130	2P: $95-$130	XP: $15
3/1-5/25 & 9/7-10/20	1P: $70-$95	2P: $70-$95	XP: $15
10/21-2/28	1P: $60-$85	2P: $60-$85	XP: $14

Location: 2.3 mi n on US 3, 2.9 mi w on dirt road. 2.9 Stampede Rd 99743. Fax: 907/683-2455. **Terms:** [BP], [CP] & [MAP] meal plans; weekly rates avail; check-in 4 pm; 7 day cancellation notice; cancellation fee imposed. **Facility:** 9 rooms. Well appointed, spacious guest rooms with contemporary appeal. Some antiques. Inviting dining room with majestic view of Alaskan range. Gracious public areas with plenty of room to relax and unwind. 2 stories; interior/exterior corridors; smoke free premises; whirlpool. **Dining:** Dining room; 6 pm-8:30 pm, deck dining weather permitting; $16-$25. **Recreation:** video library. **Cards:** AE, DS, MC, VI.

HOMER pop. 3,700

—— LODGINGS ——

BEST WESTERN BIDARKA INN
Phone: (907)235-8148

(AAA) [SAVE]

◆◆

Motor Inn

5/16-9/15	1P: $125-$146	2P: $125-$146
3/1-5/15 & 9/16-2/28	1P: $89-$129	2P: $89-$129

Location: 0.3 mi n on SR 1. 575 Sterling Hwy 99603. **Fax:** 907/235-8140. **Terms:** [CP] meal plan; cancellation fee imposed; pets, $10 extra charge. **Facility:** 74 rooms. Variety of room sizes and furnishings from average to more comtemporary. 2 whirlpool rooms, $135-$160; 2 stories; interior/exterior corridors. **Dining:** 2 restaurants; 5 am-11 & 4-10 pm; from 4 pm off season; $11-$23; cocktails; sportsbar. **Recreation:** charter fishing; sight-seeing tours. **All Rooms:** extended cable TV. **Cards:** AE, CB, DI, DS, MC, VI. **Special Amenities:** Early check-in/late check-out and free local telephone calls.

PIONEER INN
Phone: (907)235-5670

◆◆

Motel

5/15-9/15	1P: $69-$99	2P: $69-$99	XP: $13	D10
3/1-5/14 & 9/16-2/28	1P: $45-$55	2P: $45-$55	XP: $13	D10

Location: Just e off Sterling Hwy (SR 1), at entrance of town. 244 W Pioneer Ave 99603 (PO Box 1430, 99603-1430). **Fax:** 907/235-7596. **Terms:** [CP] meal plan; 7 day cancellation notice; cancellation fee imposed. **Facility:** 7 rooms. Simple and homelike decor in units organized like small apartments. Also 2 smaller, regular units. Most rooms with bay/mountain view. 2 stories; exterior corridors; smoke free premises. **Some Rooms:** 5 kitchens. **Cards:** AE, MC, VI.

VICTORIAN HEIGHTS BED & BREAKFAST
Phone: (907)235-6357

◆◆◆

Bed & Breakfast

5/15-9/15	1P: $90-$100	2P: $90-$100	XP: $25	F6

Location: From Sterling Hwy (SR 1), 1.8 mi ne on Pioneer Ave (turns into East Rd), 2.1 mi nw on East Hill Rd, e on Cottonwood, following signs for 0.3 mi. 61495 Race Ct 99603 (PO Box 2363). **Fax:** 907/235-6357. **Terms:** Open 5/15-9/15; [BP] meal plan; 7 day cancellation notice; cancellation fee imposed; 2 night min stay, in season. **Facility:** 6 rooms. Spacious units offering fresh and tasteful decor. 2 units with private balcony and gorgeous view of the bay and mountains. 2 stories; interior corridors; smoke free premises. **Services:** winter plug-ins. **Recreation:** charter fishing. **Some Rooms:** combo or shower baths, shared bathrooms. **Cards:** MC, VI.

—— RESTAURANTS ——

CHART ROOM AT LAND'S END
Lunch: $6-$13   **Dinner:** $13-$20   Phone: 907/235-0406

◆◆

Seafood

Location: At the end of the Homer Spit. 4786 Homer Spit Rd 99603. **Hours:** 5 am-10:30 & 11-10 pm; winter hrs may vary, lounge-11 pm. **Reservations:** accepted. **Features:** No A/C; casual dress; children's menu; health conscious menu; cocktails & lounge. The Chart Room at Land's End provides a panoramic view of the mountains and bay. The menu features steak, prime rib, fresh seafood, chicken, burgers, sandwiches and pasta, as well as freshly made desserts. The service is friendly and attentive. Smoke free premises. **Cards:** AE, DI, DS, MC, VI.

—— *The following restaurants have not been inspected by AAA but are listed for your information only.* ——

CAFE CUPS
Phone: (907)235-8330

[fyi]

Not inspected. **Location:** 162 W Pioneer Ave. **Features:** This is a fresh and inviting cafe serving eclectic fare with southeast Asian, Alaskan, and West Coast influences.

THE HOMESTEAD
Phone: (907)235-8723

[fyi]

Not inspected. **Location:** 8.2 Mile Rd E. **Features:** Highly-touted by locals, this is a classic Alaskan dinner venue for fresh seafood and steak.

JUNEAU pop. 26,800

—— LODGINGS ——

ALASKA WOLF HOUSE
Phone: (907)586-2422

(AAA)

◆◆

Bed & Breakfast

4/1-10/1	1P: $85-$145	2P: $85-$145	XP: $35
3/1-3/31 & 10/2-2/28	1P: $65-$100	2P: $75-$100	XP: $15

Location: 2 mi n of downtown, from Highland Ave, 0.9 mi n on Glacier Ave, just e. 1900 Wickersham Dr 99801 (PO Box 21321, 99802). **Fax:** 907/586-9053. **Terms:** [BP] meal plan; 10 day cancellation notice; cancellation fee imposed. **Facility:** 6 rooms. Impressive cedar log home perched on a hillside in a quiet residential neighborhood. All rooms offer excellent views of Gastineau Channel. Rooms vary in style and size, some are spacious and feature contemporary appointments. 2-bedroom suite with full kitchen, $100-$145; whirlpool room, $100-$135; 2 stories; interior corridors; smoke free premises. **Recreation:** bicycles, barbecue. Fee: charter fishing. **All Rooms:** extended cable TV. **Some Rooms:** efficiency, combo or shower baths, shared bathrooms, color TV. **Cards:** AE, DS, MC, VI.

BLUEBERRY LODGE BED & BREAKFAST
Phone: 907/463-5886

◆◆

Bed & Breakfast

5/15-9/15	1P: $85	2P: $95	XP: $15
9/16-2/28	1P: $75	2P: $85	XP: $15
3/1-5/14	1P: $65	2P: $75	XP: $15

Location: On Douglas Island; 6 mi nw. 9436 N Douglas Hwy 99801. **Fax:** 907/463-5886. **Terms:** [BP] meal plan; 10 day cancellation notice; cancellation fee imposed; package plans; dogs on premises. **Facility:** 5 rooms. Charming log structure; well forested. Views of inland waterway and tideland estuary; active eagles nest. 6 mi to nordic and alpine skiing. 2 stories; interior corridors; smoke free premises. **Services:** Fee: massage. **Recreation:** bicycles. **Cards:** AE, DS, MC, VI.

FIREWEED HOUSE BED & BREAKFAST

Phone: (907)586-3885

5/1-9/30	1P: $95-$225	2P: $105-$275	XP: $30 F4
3/1-4/30 & 10/1-2/28	1P: $79-$150	2P: $89-$175	XP: $30 F4

Bed & Breakfast

Location: From airport, 12 mi s on Egan Dr to Juneau/Douglas bridge; across bridge, 5.1 mi n. 8530 N Douglas Hwy 99801. Fax: 907/586-3385. **Terms:** [BP] meal plan; 30 day cancellation notice, 30 for guest house 6/1-8/31; cancellation fee imposed; 3 night min stay, in guest house; dogs on premises. **Facility:** 6 rooms. Variety of room styles all beautifully appointed. Among the 3 in-house units, 1 offers a large bay window and spotting scope for glacier observation. Also, 1 detached studio apartment and 2 units in separate and luxurious guest house. 3 whirlpool rooms, $125-$275; 2 stories; interior/exterior corridors; smoke free premises. **Recreation:** bicycles, bird viewing. **All Rooms:** extended cable TV. **Some Rooms:** efficiency, kitchen, color TV. **Cards:** AE, MC, VI.

GOLDBELT HOTEL JUNEAU

Phone: (907)586-6900

5/16-9/15	1P: $169	2P: $169	XP: $15 F12
3/1-5/15 & 9/16-2/28	1P: $139	2P: $139	XP: $15 F12

Motor Inn

Location: Just n of Main St. 51 Egan Dr 99801. Fax: 907/463-3567. **Facility:** 105 rooms. Overlooking Gastineau Channel. Public areas with impressive native wood carvings. Spacious units offering attractive decor. All rooms with hair dryer, iron and ironing board. 7 stories; interior corridors. **Dining:** Restaurant; 6:30 am-2 & 5-10 pm, 5:30-9 pm off season. Weekend hrs may vary; $11-$20; health conscious menu items; cocktails. **Recreation:** 18 rooms with exercise bike or stair stepper. **Cards:** AE, CB, DI, DS, JC, MC, VI. **Special Amenities:** Free local telephone calls and free newspaper. *(See color ad below)*

JUNEAU AIRPORT TRAVELODGE

Phone: 907/789-9700

Property failed to provide current rates

Motor Inn

Location: At Juneau International Airport. 9200 Glacier Hwy 99801. Fax: 907/789-1969. **Facility:** 86 rooms. Spacious units, contemporary appointments. All rooms with hair dryer. 4 stories; interior corridors; small heated indoor pool. **Services:** gift shop; area transportation. **All Rooms:** combo or shower baths. **Cards:** AE, DS, MC, VI.

PEARSON'S POND LUXURY INN & GARDEN SPA

Phone: (907)789-3772

5/15-9/15	1P: $169-$229	2P: $199-$299	XP: $30
9/16-2/28	1P: $99-$139	2P: $129-$169	XP: $30
3/1-5/14	1P: $89-$129	2P: $119-$149	XP: $30

Bed & Breakfast

Location: From Egan Dr, 2.2 mi n on Mendenhall Loop Rd, 1.2 mi w on Mendenhall Loop Rd, 0.3 mi s on River Rd, just w on Kelly Ct, then just s. 4541 Sawa Cir 99801-8723. Fax: 907/789-6722. **Terms:** [CP] & [ECP] meal plans; weekly & monthly rates avail, off season; age restrictions may apply; 21 day cancellation notice; 2 night min stay, 5/15-9/15; package plans. **Facility:** 3 rooms. Modern home in forested setting overlooking pond with beautiful gardens. In vicinity of Mendenhall Glacier. Rooms offer a superb amenity package and private patio in quiet surroundings. 2 room suite avail. Advanced reservations recommended; whirlpool room, $89-$299; 3 stories, no elevator; interior/exterior corridors; smoke free premises; whirlpools; boat dock. **Services:** complimentary evening beverages. Fee: massage. **Recreation:** boating, fishing, paddleboats, fishing equipment; cross country skiing, ice skating; bicycles, barbecue facility, media library including compact disks, tapes, movies and books, yoga instruction. **All Rooms:** efficiencies, combo or shower baths, extended cable TV. **Cards:** AE, CB, DI, DS, MC, VI.

THE SILVERBOW INN BAKERY & RESTAURANT

Phone: (907)586-4146

5/16-9/15	1P: $115	2P: $125	XP: $15 F6
3/1-5/15 & 9/16-2/28	1P: $75	2P: $85	XP: $15 F6

Historic Motor Inn

Location: Downtown. 120 2nd St 99801. Fax: 907/586-4242. **Terms:** [CP] meal plan; 21 day cancellation notice, 5/15-9/15. **Facility:** 6 rooms. Restored 1914 building. On site bakery. Quaint guest rooms with cheerful, bright decor. 3 stories, no elevator; interior corridors; smoke free premises. **Cards:** AE, MC, VI.

WESTMARK BARANOF
(AAA) (SAVE)

5/16-9/15	1P: $159	2P: $159	XP: $30 F12
3/1-5/15 & 9/16-2/28	1P: $149	2P: $149	XP: $30 F12

Hotel **Location:** Downtown at 2nd and Franklin sts. 127 N Franklin St 99801. Fax: 907/586-8315. **Terms:** Cancellation fee imposed; package plans. **Facility:** 196 rooms. Attractive 1939 structure, spacious well appointed lobby. Rooms vary in size offering more contemporary decor in rooms on upper floors. 9 stories; interior corridors.
Dining: Dining room, coffee shop; 5 am-10 pm; $18-$25; cocktails. **Services:** gift shop. **Recreation:** Fee: stairsteppers or stationary bicycles. **All Rooms:** combo or shower baths, extended cable TV. **Some Rooms:** 20 kitchens. **Cards:** AE, CB, DI, DS, MC, VI. *(See color ad p 594)*

RESTAURANTS

FIDDLEHEAD RESTAURANT & BAKERY   **Lunch:** $7-$11   **Dinner:** $7-$22   **Phone:** 907/586-3150
◆◆
American **Location:** Downtown; at Whittier St. 429 W Willoughby Ave 99801. **Hours:** 7 am-9 pm, Sat & Sun from 8 am. **Closed:** 1/1, 11/23 & 12/25. **Reservations:** suggested. **Features:** casual dress; health conscious menu; carryout; cocktails & lounge; a la carte. You'll enjoy this restaurant's cafe-style dining, with more formal dining upstairs. The well-rounded menu features a good selection of seafood, pasta and vegetarian dishes as well as fresh baked desserts. Attentive service. Upstairs dining times vary. Smoke free premises. **Cards:** AE, DI, DS, MC, VI.

SILVERBOW BAKERY & BACK ROOM RESTAURANT Historical **Lunch:** $5-$10**Dinner:** $7-$15**Phone:** 907/586-4146
◆◆
Continental **Location:** Downtown; in The Silverbow Inn Bakery & Restaurant. 120 2nd St 99801. **Hours:** 6:30 am-11 pm. Closed major holidays. **Reservations:** suggested. **Features:** No A/C; casual dress; health conscious menu items; carryout; beer & wine only; a la carte. You'll have fun at the Silverbow, a restored historical structure, with its funky decor and classic and golden oldies films shown two nights a week. Kids can color on the table covers too. A New York-style bakery is adjacent and offers sinful desserts. Smoke free premises. **Cards:** AE, MC, VI.

KENAI pop. 6,300

LODGING

HARBORSIDE COTTAGES   **Phone:** (907)283-6162
◆◆
Cottage

6/1-8/31	1P: $125	2P: $125
5/1-5/31 & 9/1-10/1	1P: $100	2P: $100

Location: From town centre, at visitors information office, just s on Main St, just e. 813 Riverview Dr 99611 (PO Box 942). Fax: 907/283-0906. **Terms:** Open 5/1-10/1; [CP] meal plan; check-in 4 pm; 30 day cancellation notice. **Facility:** 5 rooms. Gracious, quaint white cottages, affording a memorable view of Cook Inlet and Kenai River Delta. Each cottage with private porch. Contemporary country decor. 1 story; exterior corridors; smoke free premises. **All Rooms:** efficiencies, shower baths. **Cards:** AE, MC, VI.

RESTAURANT

PARADISOS RESTAURANT   **Lunch:** $5-$15   **Dinner:** $9-$21   **Phone:** 907/283-2222
◆◆
Italian **Location:** Downtown. Main St & Frontage Rd 99611. **Hours:** 11 am-11 pm, Fri & Sat-midnight. Closed: 11/23 & 12/25. **Reservations:** suggested. **Features:** No A/C; casual dress; Sunday brunch; children's menu; carryout; salad bar; cocktails & lounge. Greek, Mexican and Italian selections round out this restaurant's extensive menu, which also offers steak and fresh local seafood such as halibut and Alaskan king crab legs. Expect to be served good-size portions in a bustling, welcoming ambience. **Cards:** MC, VI.

KETCHIKAN pop. 8,300

LODGINGS

BEST WESTERN LANDING   **Phone:** (907)225-5166
(AAA) (SAVE)

5/1-9/30	1P: $120-$155	2P: $130-$155	XP: $10 F12
10/1-2/28	1P: $95-$125	2P: $95-$125	XP: $10 F12
3/1-4/30	1P: $90-$120	2P: $90-$120	XP: $10 F12

Motor Inn **Location:** Across from the Alaska Marine Hwy Ferry Terminal. 3434 Tongass Ave 99901. Fax: 907/225-6900. **Terms:** Cancellation fee imposed; pets, $10 extra charge, $50 dep req. **Facility:** 76 rooms. Attractively decorated units, some spacious suites. Contemporary public areas, gas fireplace in popular upstairs pub/restaurant. 1 two-bedroom unit. Suites, $120-$150; 2-3 stories; interior/exterior corridors. **Dining:** Restaurant; 6 am-11 pm; to 10 pm 11/4-4/30; $11-$23; cocktails. **Services:** area transportation, within city limits. **Recreation:** charter fishing. **All Rooms:** extended cable TV. **Some Rooms:** kitchen. **Cards:** AE, CB, DI, DS, JC, MC, VI. **Special Amenities:** Free local telephone calls and free room upgrade (subject to availability with advanced reservations).

WESTMARK CAPE FOX LODGE   **Phone:** (907)225-8001
(AAA) (SAVE)

5/16-9/15	1P: $159-$169	2P: $159-$169	XP: $30 F12
3/1-5/15 & 9/16-2/28	1P: $129-$139	2P: $129-$139	XP: $30 F12

◆◆◆
Motor Inn **Location:** Above Creek St (Tramway from Creek St). 800 Venetia Way 99901. Fax: 907/225-8286. **Terms:** Cancellation fee imposed. **Facility:** 72 rooms. Excellent hilltop location. Good views. Spacious and attractive units, very good amenities, including hair dryer, iron and ironing board. 3 stories; interior/exterior corridors. **Dining:** Restaurant; 7 am-10 pm; $16-$28; cocktails. **All Rooms:** combo or shower baths, extended cable TV. **Cards:** AE, CB, DI, DS, MC, VI. *(See color ad p 594)*

KODIAK pop. 6,400

―――― LODGINGS ――――

BEST WESTERN KODIAK INN

(AAA) (SAVE)	5/16-9/15	1P: $139-$149	2P: $139-$149	Phone: (907)486-5712
◆◆	9/16-2/28	1P: $89-$99	2P: $99-$109	XP: $15 F12
Motor Inn	3/1-5/15	1P: $89-$99	2P: $99-$109	XP: $15 F12

Location: Center; 0.3 mi w of ferry terminal. 236 W Rezanof Dr 99615. Fax: 907/486-3430. **Terms:** Pets, $50 dep req. **Facility:** 80 rooms. Overlooking harbor. Some rooms with a view. Standard size units offering simple yet contemporary decor, a few with seating room. 3 stories; interior/exterior corridors; whirlpool. **Dining:** Restaurant; 6:30 am-11 pm; $12-$25; cocktails. **Services:** area transportation, ferry. **Recreation:** fish freezer, tour desk. **All Rooms:** extended cable TV. **Cards:** AE, DI, DS, JC, MC, VI. **Special Amenities:** Free local telephone calls and free newspaper.

BUSKIN RIVER INN   **Phone:** (907)487-2700
◆◆   Property failed to provide current rates
Motor Inn   **Location:** Opposite to Kodiak Airport. 1395 Airport Way 99615. Fax: 907/487-4447. **Terms:** Cancellation fee imposed; package plans; pets, $15 extra charge. **Facility:** 50 rooms. Pleasant and contemporary units featuring extra amenities. Tour desk in lobby, summer only. Within walking distance of airport. All rooms with hair dryer. 2 stories; interior corridors. **Services:** area transportation. **Cards:** AE, DI, DS, MC, VI.

PETERSBURG pop. 3,200

―――― LODGING ――――

TIDES INN   **Phone:** 907/772-4288
◆◆   Property failed to provide current rates
Motel   **Location:** 1 mi w of ferry terminal, then just n. 307 N First St 99833. Fax: 907/772-4286. **Terms:** [CP] meal plan. **Facility:** 48 rooms. Harbor view from a few rooms, most rooms have dated decor. 3 stories, no elevator; interior/exterior corridors. **Services:** area transportation. **Some Rooms:** 5 kitchens. **Cards:** AE, DI, DS, MC, VI.

SELDOVIA pop. 300

―――― LODGING ――――

SWAN HOUSE SOUTH B & B   **Phone:** (907)234-8888
◆◆   5/22-9/10   1P: $129-$179   2P: $139-$249   XP: $59
Bed &   **Location:** From town centre, e on Main St, ne on Airport Rd and just s on North Rd after the Seldovia Slough
Breakfast bridge; look for double swans sign. 175 Augustine Ave N 99663 (6840 Crooked Tree Dr, ANCHORAGE, 99516). Fax: 907/346-3535. **Terms:** Open 5/22-9/10; [BP] meal plan; age restrictions may apply; 14 day cancellation notice; cancellation fee imposed; pet on premises. **Facility:** 5 rooms. On hillside with large patios and view on the slough famous for high tides. Rooms are compact but cozy and all with large windows. All rooms with hair dryer. 2 stories; interior corridors; smoke free premises. **Services:** area transportation. **Some Rooms:** color TV. **Cards:** AE, DS, MC, VI.

SEWARD pop. 2,700

―――― LODGINGS ――――

BELL-IN-THE-WOODS B & B   **Phone:** (907)224-7271
◆◆	5/1-9/15	1P: $99-$170	2P: $99-$170	XP: $20
Bed &	3/1-4/30	1P: $89-$130	2P: $89-$130	XP: $15
Breakfast	9/16-2/28	1P: $79-$120	2P: $79-$120	XP: $10

Location: 6 mi n on US 9, just e on Stoney Creek Ave, just s. 13881 Bruno Rd 99664 (PO Box 345). Fax: 907/224-7271. **Terms:** [BP] meal plan; check-in 5 pm; 7 day cancellation notice; cancellation fee imposed. **Facility:** 7 rooms. 2 stories; interior corridors; smoke free premises. **All Rooms:** combo or shower baths. **Cards:** AE, DS, MC, VI.

BEST WESTERN HOTEL SEWARD

Phone: (907)224-2378

	5/1-9/15	1P: $115-$125	2P: $202-$212	XP: $10	F5
	3/1-4/30 & 9/16-2/28	1P: $59-$89	2P: $89-$109	XP: $10	F5

🅰🅰🅰 SAVE
◆◆
Motel

Location: Downtown, just n of Sea Life Center. 221 5th Ave 99664 (PO Box 670). Fax: 907/224-3112. **Terms:** 3 day cancellation notice; package plans. **Facility:** 38 rooms. Attractive lobby decorated with wildlife photos and exhibits. Rooms vary in style and sizes. Great decor in units with bay view. All rooms with hair dryer. 3 stories; interior corridors. **Dining:** Restaurant nearby. **Services:** area transportation, train; winter plug-ins. **Recreation:** video library. **All Rooms:** extended cable TV. **Cards:** AE, CB, DI, DS, JC, MC, VI. **Special Amenities:** Free local telephone calls and free newspaper.

BOX CANYON CABINS

Phone: (907)224-5046

◆◆
Cottage

	6/1-8/31	1P: $115-$175	2P: $115-$175	XP: $15	F5
	3/1-5/31	1P: $79-$175	2P: $79-$175	XP: $10	F5
	9/1-9/30	1P: $95-$165	2P: $95-$165	XP: $10	F5
	10/1-2/28	1P: $85-$125	2P: $85-$125	XP: $10	F5

Location: 3.5 mi n on SR 9, just w on exit Glacier Rd, 1 mi n. Mile 1 Old Exit Glacier Rd 99664 (HCR 64 Boc 3509). Fax: 907/224-7651. **Terms:** Check-in 4 pm; 30 day cancellation notice; cancellation fee imposed; pet on premises. **Facility:** 4 rooms. 3 modern 2-bedroom log cabins and 1 older, cozy log cabin in a secluded wooded area; most with view of the pond. Cabin decor is contemporary and all offer modern appliances. 3 two-bedroom units. 1 story; exterior corridors; smoke free premises. **Services:** winter plug-ins. **All Rooms:** kitchens, shower baths. **Cards:** MC, VI.

HARBORVIEW INN

Phone: (907)224-3217

◆◆
Motel

	6/1-9/30	1P: $119	2P: $119	XP: $10	F3
	5/2-5/31	1P: $99	2P: $99	XP: $10	F3
	3/1-5/1 & 10/1-2/28	1P: $59	2P: $59	XP: $10	F3

Location: Just n of the Alaska Sealife Center. 804 Third Ave 99664 (PO Box 1305). Fax: 907/224-3218. **Terms:** Check-in 4 pm; 3 day cancellation notice. **Facility:** 13 rooms. Newer motel with alpine flair including finished log siding and a stone chimney. Pleasant rooms with Alaskan charm. All rooms with hair dryer. 2 stories; exterior corridors; smoke free premises. **All Rooms:** combo or shower baths. **Cards:** AE, MC, VI.

HOTEL EDGEWATER

Phone: (907)224-2700

◆◆
Motor Inn

	5/27-9/3	1P: $165-$245	2P: $165-$245	XP: $10	F18
	9/4-10/15	1P: $105-$215	2P: $105-$215	XP: $10	F18
	3/1-5/26	1P: $55-$215	2P: $55-$215	XP: $10	F18
	10/16-2/28	1P: $55-$175	2P: $55-$175	XP: $10	F18

Location: Just n of Sea Life Center. 200 5th Ave 99664 (PO Box 1570). Fax: 907/244-2701. **Terms:** 3 day cancellation notice; cancellation fee imposed; package plans. **Facility:** 78 rooms. Newer property with good sized atrium lobby courtyard. Some rooms with balcony, a few with view of Resurrection Bay. All rooms with hiar dryer. 3 stories; interior corridors; smoke free premises. **Services:** gift shop; area transportation. **Cards:** DS, MC, VI.

RIVER VALLEY CABINS

Phone: (907)224-5740

◆◆
Cottage

	3/1-4/30 & 10/1-2/28	1P: $90-$180	2P: $90-$180	XP: $15	D16
	5/1-9/30	1P: $99-$120	2P: $99-$120	XP: $15	D16

Location: 3.5 mi n on SR 9, just w on exit Glacier Rd and just n on Gravel Rd, following signs 1 mi. 12672 Old Exit Glacier Rd 99664 (PO Box 1910). Fax: 907/224-2333. **Terms:** Check-in 4 pm; 14 day cancellation notice. **Facility:** 7 rooms. Attractive small cabins nestled in wooded surroundings. Cozy atmosphere. All rooms with hair dryer. 1 two-bedroom unit. 1 story; exterior corridors; smoke free premises. **Services:** area transportation. **All Rooms:** combo or shower baths. **Some Rooms:** kitchen. **Cards:** MC, VI.

SEWARD WINDSONG LODGE

Phone: (907)224-7116

◆◆
Motel

Property failed to provide current rates

Location: 3.5 mi n on SR 9, 0.5 mi w on Exit Glacier Rd. Mile 0.5 Exit Glacier Rd 99664 (PO BOX 2301). Fax: 907/224-7118. **Terms:** Open 4/15-10/31; 7 day cancellation notice. **Facility:** 72 rooms. Secluded mountain location. Attractive and contemporary guest rooms, offering a touch of Alaskan wilderness including some hand finished wood furnishings. All rooms with kettle. 2 stories; exterior corridors; smoke free premises. **Services:** gift shop; area transportation. **Cards:** AE, DS, MC, VI. *(See color ad p 603 & p 612)*

RESTAURANT

RAY'S WATERFRONT

Lunch: $7-$15 **Dinner:** $15-$23 **Phone:** 907/224-5606

◆◆
Seafood

Location: Center. **Hours:** 11 am-10:30 pm. **Reservations:** suggested. **Features:** No A/C; casual dress; cocktails & lounge; a la carte. The chef/owner at Ray's Waterfront prepares a creative Northwest cuisine with eye-catching appeal and delectable, flavorful qualities. This lively place offers a good view of the boat harbor, a nautical decor, and service that's prompt and attentive. **Cards:** MC, VI.

SITKA pop. 8,600

LODGINGS

ALASKA OCEAN VIEW B&B

Phone: (907)747-8310

◆◆◆
Bed & Breakfast

	5/15-9/30	1P: $89-$139	2P: $99-$159	XP: $25	F3
	3/1-3/15 & 10/1-2/28	1P: $79-$109	2P: $89-$139	XP: $10	F3
	3/16-5/14	1P: $84-$114	2P: $94-$129	XP: $20	F3

Location: 1 mi n on Halibut Point Rd, just e on Kashevarof St, just s. 1101 Edgecumbe Dr 99835. Fax: 907/747-3440. **Terms:** [BP] meal plan; 30 day cancellation notice; cancellation fee imposed. **Facility:** 3 rooms. Modern house in residential area. Attractive and spacious rooms, offering excellent amenities. All rooms with disk/cassette player. Check-in upon arrival in Sitka or pre-arranged time. 2 stories; interior corridors; smoke free premises. **Cards:** AE, MC, VI.

HELGA'S BED & BREAKFAST

◆◆

Bed & Breakfast

All Year   1P: $70-$78   2P: $80-$88   XP: $20   **Phone:** (907)747-5497

Location: 3 mi n on Halibut Point Rd. 2827 Halibut Point Rd 99835 (PO Box 1885). **Terms:** [CP] meal plan; age restrictions may apply; 30 day cancellation notice; cancellation fee imposed. **Facility:** 5 rooms. Located in residential area. Some rooms with a beautiful ocean view. All rooms are spacious and are stocked for in-room continental breakfast. 2 stories; interior corridors. **Recreation:** charter fishing. **All Rooms:** combo or shower baths. **Cards:** AE, MC, VI.

MOUNTAIN VIEW BED & BREAKFAST

◆◆

Bed & Breakfast

5/1-10/1   1P: $80-$90   2P: $90-$100   XP: $10   **Phone:** (907)747-8966

Location: 1.5 mi nw on Halibut Point Rd. 201 Cascade Creek Rd 99835 (Box 119). Fax: 907/747-5942. **Terms:** Open 5/1-10/1; [CP] meal plan; 7 day cancellation notice. **Facility:** 5 rooms. Hillside location, some ocean views. Some rooms in-house, others in adjacent building. All feature large working desk. 2 stories; interior/exterior corridors; smoke free premises. **Some Rooms:** color TV. **Cards:** AE, MC, VI.

WESTMARK SHEE ATIKA

(AAA) (SAVE)

◆◆

Motor Inn

5/16-2/28   1P: $129-$139   2P: $129-$139   XP: $30   F12   **Phone:** (907)747-6241
3/1-5/15   1P: $119-$129   2P: $119-$129   XP: $30   F12

Location: Center. 330 Seward St 99835. Fax: 907/747-5486. **Terms:** Cancellation fee imposed. **Facility:** 101 rooms. Most rooms have pleasant harbor or mountain view. 4 stories; interior corridors. **Dining:** Dining room; 6:30 am-2 & 5-10 pm, Sun & off season-9 pm; $11-$23; health conscious menu items; cocktails. **Recreation:** Fee: video library. **All Rooms:** combo or shower baths, extended cable TV. **Some Rooms:** kitchen. Fee: refrigerators, VCR. **Cards:** AE, CB, DI, DS, JC, MC, VI. *(See color ad p 594)*

——— RESTAURANT ———

CHANNEL CLUB

◆

Steak and Seafood

informal decor

Dinner: $15-$37   **Phone:** 907/747-9916

Location: 3.5 mi n. 2906 Halibut Point Rd 99835. **Hours:** 5 pm-10 pm, Fri & Sat-11 pm. Closed: 11/23, 12/25 & 1/1-1/27. **Reservations:** suggested; required-summer. **Features:** No A/C; casual dress; children's menu; senior's menu; carryout; salad bar; cocktails & lounge; area transportation. Locals and visitors alike enjoy this restaurant's fresh local seafood in season and quality steaks—all served in hearty portions. The features seafaring memorabilia and window seats with a good view of the water in the distance. **Cards:** AE, DI, MC, VI.

SKAGWAY pop. 700

——— LODGINGS ———

WESTMARK INN SKAGWAY

(AAA) (SAVE)

◆◆

Motor Inn

5/15-9/15   1P: $119   2P: $119   XP: $30   F12   **Phone:** (907)983-6000

Location: Just off center; at 3rd and Spring sts. 99840 (PO Box 515). Fax: 907/983-6100. **Terms:** Open 5/15-9/15; check-out 9 am; cancellation fee imposed; small pets only. **Facility:** 195 rooms. Small units with contemporary decor. A few rooms in the main building have been renovated. Located in the heart of town. 2 stories; interior/exterior corridors. **Dining:** Dining room, restaurant; 5:30 am-11 pm; $14-$20; health conscious menu; cocktails. **Services:** gift shop; area transportation, ferry. **All Rooms:** extended cable TV. **Cards:** AE, CB, DI, DS, JC, MC, VI. *(See color ad p 594)*

WIND VALLEY LODGE

(AAA)

◆◆

Motel

All Year   1P: $62-$69   2P: $75-$82   XP: $10   F12   **Phone:** (907)983-2236

Location: 1 mi n. 2199 State St 99840 (PO Box 354). Fax: 907/983-2957. **Terms:** Check-in 4 pm. **Facility:** 29 rooms. A few large units. Rooms with vintage appointments. 1 story; exterior corridors. **Dining:** Restaurant nearby. **Services:** gift shop; area transportation. **Recreation:** courtesy car from ferry & train terminal. **Cards:** AE, DS, MC, VI.

The One For All

*Y*ou know how AAA/CAA can simplify your life. Now make the lives of those you love the most a little easier–give them AAA/CAA associate memberships.

Associate members are eligible for the same security, services, and savings as primary members–emergency road service, valuable savings, access to travel services, and more. And all this protection is available for a reduced enrollment fee.

Help your family members simplify their lives with AAA/CAA associate memberships. Call or stop by your nearest AAA/CAA office today. And make AAA/CAA the one for you.

SOLDOTNA pop. 3,500

—— LODGINGS ——

AALASKA TREE TOP BED & BREAKFAST   **Phone:** (907)262-6648
◆◆   6/16-8/15   1P: $99-$125   2P: $99-$125
Bed &   5/16-6/15 & 8/16-11/1   1P: $89-$125   2P: $89-$125
Breakfast   3/1-5/15   1P: $59-$69   2P: $59-$69
Location: On SR 1 (Sterling Hwy) 1.5 mi e, 1.6 mi n on Mackey Lake Rd, 0.5 mi e. 41601 Denise Lake Rd
99669 (HC1 Box 8330). Fax: 907/260-6609. **Terms:** Open 3/1-11/1; [BP] meal plan; check-in 4 pm; 14 day cancellation notice;
cancellation fee imposed; 2 night min stay, 7/1-7/31; pets on premises. **Facility:** 6 rooms. Delightful log home with view of Denise Lake. Units are not very spacious but attractively decorated. 2 contemporary cabins each with an efficency. Hospitable
hosts who like to entertain. 2 stories; interior corridors; smoke free premises. **Services:** winter plug-ins. **Some Rooms:** safes.
Cards: MC, VI.

KENAI JIM'S LODGE   **Phone:** (907)262-1324
◆◆   6/1-7/31   1P: $85-$165   2P: $135-$185   XP: $20   F5
Apartment   5/1-5/31 & 8/1-9/30   1P: $85-$135   2P: $110-$155   XP: $20   F5
Location: From Sterling Hwy, 1.2 mi w on Kalifornsky Beach Rd, s on Polar St Register at Johnson Brothers
Guide and Charters on Sterling Hwy in downtown center. Polar St, Bldg A 99669 (PO Box 3675). **Terms:** Open 5/1-9/30; 60
day cancellation notice; package plans. **Facility:** 3 rooms. Well equipped spacious units. Quiet location near Kenai River,
pleasant mountain view. Limited housekeeping services provided. 2 stories; interior corridors; smoke free premises.
Services: winter plug-ins. **Recreation:** charter fishing. **All Rooms:** kitchens. **Cards:** DS, MC, VI.

KENAI RIVER RAVEN BED & BREAKFAST LODGE   **Phone:** (907)262-5818
◆◆◆   All Year   1P: $165   2P: $165   XP: $50   F5
Bed &   **Location:** From Sterling Hwy (SR 1), milepost 96.5, just e. Mile 0.2 Funny River Rd 99669 (PO Box 1670).
Breakfast   Fax: 907/260-3972. **Terms:** [BP] meal plan; check-in 4 pm; cancellation fee imposed; package plans.
            Facility: 8 rooms. Modern log home in secluded wooded area just steps away from the Kenai River. Charming,
bright and cheerful guest rooms offer a touch of elegance. Inviting breakfast room with stone fireplace. 3 stories; interior corridors; smoke free premises. **Services:** winter plug-ins. **Recreation:** fishing. **Some Rooms:** 4 efficiencies. **Cards:** MC, VI.

LONGMERE LAKE LODGE B & B   **Phone:** (907)262-9799
(AAA) (SAVE)   All Year   1P: $59-$125   2P: $65-$125   XP: $25   D10
         Location: 5 mi e of town, MP 88, on Sterling Hwy; 1 mi s on St Theresa Rd, just w. 35955 Ryan Ln 99669 (PO
◆◆   Box 1707). Fax: 907/262-5937. **Terms:** [BP] meal plan; check-in 4 pm; 14 day cancellation notice; cancellation
Bed &   fee imposed; pet on premises. **Facility:** 6 rooms. Secluded location on the shore of Longmere Lake. 1 spa-
Breakfast   cious apartment unit or regular bedrooms on main floor. Home-like ambiance and decor. Large seating area,
bay windows and deck, affording great views. 1 two-bedroom unit. 1 apartment for up to 6 persons.; whirlpool
room, $125; 2 stories; interior corridors; smoke free premises; boat dock. **Services:** winter plug-ins. **Recreation:** swimming,
canoeing, fishing, paddleboats; barbecue, croquet, horseshoes, volleyball. **All Rooms:** combo or shower baths.
Some Rooms: kitchen. **Cards:** MC, VI. **Special Amenities:** Free breakfast and free local telephone calls.

ORCA LODGE   **Phone:** (907)262-5649
◆◆   5/1-9/30   1P: $125   2P: $150   XP: $20   F13
Cottage   **Location:** From Sterling Hwy (SR 1), Milepost 96.5, 0.8 mi e on Funny River Rd, just n. Oehler Dr 99669 (PO
         Box 4653). Fax: 907/262-9516. **Terms:** Open 5/1-9/30; 30 day cancellation notice; package plans. **Facility:** 6
rooms. Charming log cabins located on the shore of the famous Kenai River. Best suited to fishing parties. 1 story; exterior
corridors; smoke free premises. **Recreation:** charter fishing. **All Rooms:** efficiencies. **Cards:** AE, MC, VI.
(See color ad below)

SALMON HAUS BED & BREAKFAST   **Phone:** (907)262-2400
◆◆   All Year   1P: $60-$130   2P: $60-$130   XP: $25   F5
Bed &   **Location:** From Sterling Hwy (SR 1), Milepost 96.5, 0.5 mi e. 44510 Funny River Rd 99669 (PO Box 3004 A).
Breakfast   Fax: 907/262-1888. **Terms:** [BP] meal plan; age restrictions may apply; 14 day cancellation notice; cancella-
tion fee imposed; cat on premises. **Facility:** 5 rooms. Check-ins before 10 pm. Casual, homelike ambiance.
Guest units offer simple decor. Common areas feature coffee bar, covered patio with view of Kenai River. 2 stories; interior
corridors; smoke free premises. **Services:** winter plug-ins. **Cards:** MC, VI.

TALKEETNA pop. 300

—— LODGING ——

TALKEETNA ALASKAN LODGE
◆◆◆
Motor Inn

6/9-8/27	1P: $169-$189	2P: $169-$189	XP: $10 F12
5/19-6/8	1P: $129-$149	2P: $129-$149	XP: $10 F12
3/1-5/18 & 8/28-2/28	1P: $89-$109	2P: $89-$109	XP: $10 F12

Phone: (907)733-9500

Location: Mile 12.5 Talkeetna Spur Rd 99676 (PO Box 727, 99503). **Fax:** 907/733-9545. **Terms:** Cancellation fee imposed. **Facility:** 98 rooms. Impressive lobby featuring a high-rise vaulted ceiling with a sequoia size riverstone fireplace. Guest rooms are beautifully appointed. Main lodge units are more spacious and some have a view of the Alaskan Range. 2 stories; interior/exterior corridors; smoke free premises. **Services:** gift shop; area transportation. **Cards:** AE, DI, DS, MC, VI. *(See color ad inside front cover & below)*

TOK pop. 900

—— LODGINGS ——

CLEFT OF THE ROCK BED & BREAKFAST
(AAA) (SAVE)
◆◆
Complex

5/2-10/1	1P: $80-$120	2P: $90-$125	XP: $15 F12
3/1-5/1 & 10/2-2/28	1P: $50-$60	2P: $55-$65	XP: $15 F12

Phone: (907)883-4219

Location: From jct SR 1 and 2, 3 mi w on SR 2 to Sundog Tr, 0.5 mi n. Mile .5 Sundog Tr 99780 (PO Box 122). **Fax:** 907/883-5963. **Terms:** [BP] & [CP] meal plans; weekly & monthly rates avail; check-in 5 pm; 3 day cancellation notice; pets, pet on premises, $5 extra charge, $25 dep req. **Facility:** 8 rooms. Inviting, home-like atmosphere. Nestled in tall black spruce outside of town. 3 guest rooms in main house, 5 individual cabins. Complimentary beverages and snacks in each room. Whirlpool room; 2 stories; interior/exterior corridors; smoke free premises. **Services:** winter plug-ins. **Recreation:** cross country skiing; hiking trails, basketball, video library. Fee: bicycles. Rental: canoes. **Some Rooms:** 2 efficiencies. **Cards:** AE, DS, MC, VI. **Special Amenities:** Free breakfast and free local telephone calls. *(See color ad p 629)*

WESTMARK TOK
(AAA) (SAVE)
◆◆
Motor Inn

5/15-9/15	1P: $129	2P: $129 XP: $30 F12

Phone: (907)883-5174

Location: On SR 1 at jct SR 2. 99780 (PO Box 130). **Fax:** 907/883-5178. **Terms:** 5/15-9/15; cancellation fee imposed; pets. **Facility:** 92 rooms. Many interconnected cedar structures. Comfortable, yet simply appointed units. 2 stories; exterior corridors. **Dining:** Restaurant; 5 am-9, noon-2 & 5-10 pm; $9-$20; cocktails. **Services:** gift shop. **Cards:** AE, CB, DI, DS, JC, MC, VI. *(See color ad p 594)*

—— RESTAURANTS ——

FAST EDDY'S RESTAURANT   **Lunch:** $5-$16   **Dinner:** $5-$28   **Phone:** 907/883-4411
◆◆
American   **Location:** From jct SR 1 and 2, 1 mi e on SR 2 (Alaskan Hwy). 1313 Alaskan Hwy 99780. **Hours:** 6 am-midnight. Closed: 1/1, 11/23 & 12/25. **Features:** casual dress; children's menu; carryout; salad bar; beer & wine only. Fast Eddy's is a jewel of a restaurant—an excellent family place specializing in hoagies, steaks, halibut and handmade pizzas. The diverse menu also includes gourmet burgers, sandwiches and pasta—all served in a comfortable and contemporary decor. **Cards:** AE, DS, MC, VI.

GATEWAY SALMON BAKE   **Lunch:** $7-$10   **Dinner:** $12-$18   **Phone:** 907/883-5555
◆
American   **Location:** From jct SR 1 and 2, 1 mi e on SR 2. Mile 1313.1 Alaskan Hwy 99780. **Hours:** Open 5/15-9/15; 11 am-9 pm, Sun from 4 pm. **Features:** No A/C; salad bar; area transportation. The Gateway Salmon Bake specializes in Alaskan-style cooking over a wood-flame grill. Featured foods are savory buffalo burgers, reindeer sausage, BBQ chicken and beef. Dine picnic-style in the beautiful courtyard or indoors by the potbellied stove. **Cards:** MC, VI.

VALDEZ pop. 4,100

---- LODGING ----

WESTMARK VALDEZ
Phone: (907)835-4391
AAA SAVE
5/16-9/15   1P: $99   2P: $99   XP: $30   F12
3/1-5/15 & 9/16-2/28   1P: $89   2P: $89   XP: $30   F12
◆ ◆
Motor Inn   **Location:** At small boat harbor. 100 Fidalgo Dr 99686 (PO Box 468). Fax: 907/835-2308. **Terms:** Cancellation fee imposed; pets. **Facility:** 96 rooms. Room size varies, some are compact. Some rooms feature an attractive pinewood decor, others with slightly older appointments. Restaurant with beautiful harbor view. 2 stories; interior corridors; boat dock. **Dining:** Restaurant; 5:30 am-11 pm; 7 am-10 pm 9/16-5/15; $12-$20; cocktails. **Cards:** AE, CB, DI, DS, JC, MC, VI. *(See color ad p 594)*

WASILLA pop. 4,000

---- LODGINGS ----

AGATE INN
Phone: (907)373-2290
AAA SAVE
All Year   1P: $85-$115   2P: $95-$125   XP: $10
◆ ◆ ◆
Bed &   **Location:** 2.7 mi e of Parks Hwy (SR 3) on Palmer-Wasilla High, just s on Begich, then just e. 4725 Begich
Breakfast   Cir 99654. Fax: 907/376-2294. **Terms:** [CP] meal plan; weekly rates avail; check-in 5 pm. **Facility:** 8 rooms. Large family type apartments or bedrooms in house adjacent. "Make-your-own" breakfast in the apartments. 2 domestic reindeer on property. 1 three-bedroom unit, 4 two-bedroom units. One 2-bedroom cottage with full kitchen, $205; 2 stories; interior corridors; smoke free premises. **Services:** winter plug-ins. **All Rooms:** combo or shower baths. **Some Rooms:** 6 kitchens, color TV. **Cards:** AE, DS, MC, VI. **Special Amenities:** Free breakfast and free local telephone calls.

BEST WESTERN LAKE LUCILLE INN
Phone: (907)373-1776
AAA SAVE
5/16-9/15   1P: $105-$135   2P: $105-$135   XP: $10   F12
9/16-2/28   1P: $85-$95   2P: $85-$95   XP: $10   F12
◆ ◆ ◆
3/1-5/15   1P: $75-$85   2P: $75-$85   XP: $10   F12
Motor Inn   **Location:** Just sw of George Parks Hwy on Hallea Ln. 1300 W Lake Lucille Dr 99654. Fax: 907/376-6199. **Terms:** Cancellation fee imposed; package plans. **Facility:** 54 rooms. On the shore of scenic Lake Lucille, some rooms with lake view, patio door and balcony. All rooms are spacious. 4 whirlpool rooms; 2 stories; interior corridors; beach, sauna, whirlpool. Fee: boat dock, boat ramp. **Dining:** Restaurant; patio dining; lakeshore; 7 am-10 pm; hrs vary in season; $13-$24. **Services:** gift shop. **Recreation:** swimming; ice skating, snowmobiling. Fee: boating, canoeing, sailboating, waterskiing, bumper boats, evening boat rental or evening lake cruise, ski boat, wave runner. Rental: paddleboats. **All Rooms:** extended cable TV. **Some Rooms:** Fee: VCR. **Cards:** AE, CB, DI, DS, JC, MC, VI. **Special Amenities:** Free local telephone calls.

KOZEY CABINS
Phone: (907)376-3190
◆ ◆
5/15-9/14   1P: $85-$100   2P: $95-$100   XP: $30   F5
Cottage   3/1-5/14 & 9/15-2/28   1P: $65-$70   2P: $70-$75   XP: $30   F5
Location: 1.4 mi n on Parks Hwy, 1.4 mi e on Lucille St, just s. 351 E Spruce Ave 99654. Fax: 907/376-3298. **Terms:** 7 day cancellation notice; pets, $10 extra charge, $50 dep req, no cats. **Facility:** 5 rooms. Quaint little cabins in secluded wooded area. 1 story; exterior corridors; smoke free premises. **All Rooms:** kitchens, shower baths. **Cards:** MC, VI.

YUKON DON'S B&B INN
Phone: (907)376-7472
AAA SAVE
All Year   1P: $75-$135   2P: $85-$145   XP: $10   F5
◆ ◆ ◆
Bed &   **Location:** Jct Parks Hwy, 1.5 mi s on Fairview Loop Rd. Follow signs onto Lin-Lu Rd and onto Yukon. 2221
Breakfast   Yukon Circle 99654 (1830 E Parks Hwy, Suite A-113-PM386). Fax: 907/376-7470. **Terms:** Monthly rates avail, off season; check-in 4:30 pm; 7 day cancellation notice; cancellation fee imposed. **Facility:** 8 rooms. Filled with Alaska memorabilia, each room with its own theme. Majestic mountain view. 1 cabin avail for a rustic Alaskan experience, $65-$75; 1 story; interior corridors; smoke free premises; sauna. **Services:** winter plug-ins. **All Rooms:** extended cable TV. **Some Rooms:** kitchen, color TV. **Cards:** AE, DS, MC, VI. **Special Amenities:** Free breakfast and free local telephone calls.

Where can you find

no-fee Travelers Cheques?

We drew a map for you.

For AAA members, it's easy to find no-fee American Express® Travelers Cheques. Just visit your nearest AAA office. American Express Travelers Cheques are the most recognized worldwide, and if lost or stolen can usually be replaced in a day. So whether your travels take you across the state or across the world, first come in for your American Express Travelers Cheques. It's one more way your AAA membership brings you added value and peace of mind. For no fee.

Travelers Cheques

 **Offices**

Cities with main offices are listed in **BOLD TYPE** and toll-free member service numbers in *ITALIC TYPE*.
All are closed Saturdays, Sundays and holidays unless otherwise indicated.

The type of service provided is designated below the name of the city where the office is located:
Auto travel services, including books/maps, marked maps and on-demand Triptik maps ✦
Auto travel services, including books/maps, marked maps, but no on-demand Triptik maps ●
Provides books/maps only. No marked maps or on-demand Triptik maps available ■
Travel agency services ▲

ALASKA

ANCHORAGE—AAA MOUNTAINWEST, 9191 OLD SEWARD HWY #20, 99515. SATURDAY BY APPOINTMENT MON-FRI 8-5:30. (907) 344-4310, *(888) 460-4222.*✦▲

ANCHORAGE—AAA MOUNTAINWEST, 1100 E NORTHERN LIGHTS BL, 99508. MON-FRI 8-5:30. (907) 278-4222.▲

PROVINCE OF ALBERTA

BANFF—ALBERTA MOTOR ASSOCIATION, 215 BEAR ST, T0L 0C0. MON-FRI 9-5, SAT 9-12:30. (403) 762-2266, *(800) 642-3810.*●▲

CALGARY—ALBERTA MOTOR ASSOCIATION, #100 530 8TH AVE SW, T2P 3S8. MON-FRI 8-5. (403) 262-2345, *(800) 642-3810.*●▲

CALGARY—ALBERTA MOTOR ASSOCIATION, 3650 20 AVE NE, T1Y 6E8. MON-FRI 9:30-5:30, SAT 9:30-3. (403) 590-0001, *(800) 642-3810.*●▲

CALGARY—ALBERTA MOTOR ASSOCIATION, 10816 MACLEOD TRAIL SE, T2J 5N8. MON-FRI 9:30-5, SAT 9-5. (403) 278-3530, *(800) 642-3810.*●▲

CALGARY—ALBERTA MOTOR ASSOCIATION, 220 CROWFOOT CRES NW, T3G 3N5. MON-FRI 9-5, SAT 9-5. (403) 239-6644, *(800) 642-3810.*●▲

CALGARY—ALBERTA MOTOR ASSOCIATION, 4700 17TH AVE SW, T3E 0E3. MON-FRI 8:30-5, SAT 9-3. (403) 240-5300, *(800) 642-3810.*●▲

CAMROSE—ALBERTA MOTOR ASSOCIATION, 4807 50TH ST, T4V 1P4. MON-FRI 9-5, SAT 9-12:30. (780) 672-3391, *(800) 642-3810.*●▲

EDMONTON—ALBERTA MOTOR ASSOCIATION, 10310 39A AVE, T6J 6R7. MON-FRI 8:30-5:30, SAT 9-1. (780) 430-5555, *(800) 642-3810.*●▲

EDMONTON—ALBERTA MOTOR ASSOCIATION, 9780 170 ST, T5T 5L9. MON-FRI 9:30-5:30, THU 9:30-8, SAT 9:30-1:30. (780) 484-1221, *(800) 642-3810.*●▲

EDMONTON—ALBERTA MOTOR ASSOCIATION, 5040 MANNING DR NW, T5A 5B4. MON-FRI 9-5, SAT 9-5. (780) 473-3112, *(800) 642-3810.*●▲

EDMONTON—ALBERTA MOTOR ASSOCIATION, 11220 109 ST, T5G 2T6. MON-FRI 9-5, SAT 9-5. (780) 474-8601, *(800) 642-3810.*✦▲

FORT MCMURRAY—ALBERTA MOTOR ASSOCIATION, 9816 HARDIN ST, T9H 4K3. MON-FRI 9-5, THU & FRI 9-6, SAT 9:30-2. (780) 743-2433, *(800) 642-3810.*●▲

GRANDE PRAIRIE—ALBERTA MOTOR ASSOCIATION, 11401 99 ST, T8V 2H6. MON-FRI 9-5, SAT 9-12:30. (780) 532-4421, *(800) 642-3810.*●▲

LETHBRIDGE—ALBERTA MOTOR ASSOCIATION, 120 SCENIC DR S, T1J 4R4. MON-FRI 8:30-5, THU 8:30-7, SAT 9-12:30. (403) 328-1181, *(800) 642-3810.*●▲

MEDICINE HAT—ALBERTA MOTOR ASSOCIATION, 2710 13 AVE SE, T1A 3P8. MON-FRI 9-5, SAT 9-12:30. (403) 527-1166, *(800) 642-3810.*●▲

RED DEER—ALBERTA MOTOR ASSOCIATION, 2965 BREMNER AVE, T4R 1S2. MON-FRI 9-5, SAT 9-12:30. (403) 342-6633, *(800) 642-3810.*●▲

PROVINCE OF BRITISH COLUMBIA

ABBOTSFORD—CAA BRITISH COLUMBIA, 33310 S FRASER WAY, V2S 2B4. MON-FRI 9-5:30, SAT 9-5:30. (604) 855-0530, *(800) 663-1956.*●▲

BURNABY—CAA BRITISH COLUMBIA, 4567 CANADA WAY, V5G 4T1. MON-FRI 9-5. (604) 268-5500, *(800) 663-1956.*✦▲

CHILLIWACK—CAA BRITISH COLUMBIA, #190-45428 LUCKAKUCK WAY, V2R 3S9. MON-FRI 9-5:30, SAT 9-5. (604) 858-2222, *(800) 663-1956.*●▲

COQUITLAM—CAA BRITISH COLUMBIA, 2991 LOUGHEED HWY #56, V3B 6J6. MON-FRI 9-5:30, THU 9-8, SAT 9-5. (604) 268-5750, *(800) 663-1956.*●▲

COURTENAY—CAA BRITISH COLUMBIA, 750 COMOX RD #111, V9N 3P6. MON-FRI 9-5, SAT 9-4. (250) 338-5313.●▲

DELTA—CAA BRITISH COLUMBIA, SCOTT 72 CTR 7325-120 ST, V4C 6P5. MON-FRI 9-6, THU 9-8, SAT 9-5. (604) 268-5900, *(800) 663-1956.*●▲

KAMLOOPS—CAA BRITISH COLUMBIA, 400-500 NOTRE DAME DR, V2C 6T6. MON-FRI 9-6, FRI 9-8, SAT 9-5. (250) 372-9577, *(800) 663-1956.*●▲

KELOWNA—CAA BRITISH COLUMBIA, #18-1470 HARVEY AVE, V1Y 9K8. MON-FRI 9-6, SAT 9-5. (250) 861-4554, *(800) 663-1956.*●▲

LANGLEY—CAA BRITISH COLUMBIA, 308-6339 200TH ST, V2Y 1A2. MON-FRI 9-5:30, THU 9-8, SAT 9-5. (250) 268-5950, *(800) 663-1956.*●▲

NANAIMO—CAA BRITISH COLUMBIA, METRAL PL 6581 AULDS RD, V9T 6J6. MON-FRI 9-5, THU & FRI 9-7, SAT 9-5. (250) 390-3533, *(800) 663-1956.*●▲

NELSON—CAA BRITISH COLUMBIA, 596 BAKER ST, V1L 4H9. MON-FRI 8:30-5:30, SAT 9-5. (250) 352-3535, *(800) 663-1956.*●▲

NEW WESTMINSTER—CAA BRITISH COLUMBIA, 501 SIXTH ST, V3L 3B9. MON-FRI 9-5:30, SAT 9-5. (604) 268-5700, *(800) 663-1956.*●▲

NORTH VANCOUVER—CAA BRITISH COLUMBIA, 333 BROOKSBANK AVE, V7J 3S8. MON-FRI 9-6, THU & FRI 9-8, SAT 9-5, SUN 10-5. (604) 990-1546, *(800) 663-1956.*●▲

PENTICTON—CAA BRITISH COLUMBIA, 100-2100 MAIN ST, V2A 5H7. MON-FRI 8:30-5:30, SAT 9-5. (250) 492-7016, *(800) 663-1956.*●▲

PRINCE GEORGE—CAA BRITISH COLUMBIA, 492 VICTORIA ST, V2L 2J7. MON-FRI 9-5, SAT 9-5. (250) 563-0417, *(800) 663-1956.*●▲

RICHMOND—CAA BRITISH COLUMBIA, 180-5951 NO 3 RD, V6X 2E3. MON-FRI 9-5:30, SAT 9-5. (604) 268-5850, *(800) 663-1956.*●▲

SURREY—CAA BRITISH COLUMBIA, #2 15285 101 AVE, V3R 9V8. MON-FRI 9-6, THU 9-8, SAT 9-5. (604) 205-1000, *(800) 663-1956.*●▲

VANCOUVER—CAA BRITISH COLUMBIA, 2347 W 41ST AVE, V6M 2A3. MON-FRI 9-5:30, SAT 9-5. (604) 268-5800, *(800) 663-1956.* ● ▲

VANCOUVER—CAA BRITISH COLUMBIA, 999 W BROADWAY, V5Z 1K5. MON-FRI 9-5:30, SAT 9-5. (604) 268-5600, *(800) 663-1956.* ● ▲

VERNON—CAA BRITISH COLUMBIA, 4400 32ND ST #520, V1T 9H2. MON-FRI 9-6, SAT 9-5. (250) 542-1022, *(800) 663-1956.* ● ▲

VICTORIA—CAA BRITISH COLUMBIA, 1075 PANDORA AVE, V8V 3P7. MON-FRI 9-6, THU 9-8, SAT 9-5. (250) 389-6700, *(800) 663-1956.* ● ▲

VICTORIA—CAA BRITISH COLUMBIA, #120-777 ROYAL OAK DR, V8X 4V1. MON-FRI 8:30-5:30, FRI 8:30-6:30, SAT 9-5. (250) 744-2202, *(800) 663-1956.* ● ▲

WEST VANCOUVER—CAA BRITISH COLUMBIA, 608 PARK ROYAL N, V7T 1H9. MON-FRI 9-6, THU & FRI 9-8, SAT 9-5. (604) 268-5650, *(800) 663-1956.* ● ▲

PROVINCE OF MANITOBA

ALTONA—CAA MANITOBA, 61 2ND AVE NE, R0G 0B0. MON-FRI 9-5, SAT 9-1. (204) 324-8474. ● ▲

BRANDON—CAA MANITOBA, 20 - 1300 18TH ST, R7A 6X7. MON-FRI 9-5, MAY-SEPTEMBER ONLY THU 9-8, SAT 10-2. (204) 727-1394, *(877) 222-1321.* ✛ ▲

WINNIPEG—CAA MANITOBA, 870 EMPRESS ST, R3C 2Z3. MON-FRI 9-6, SAT 10-4. (204) 987-6161. ✛ ▲

WINNIPEG—CAA MANITOBA, 1353 MCPHILLIPS ST, R2X 3A6. MON-FRI 9-6, SAT 10-4. (204) 987-6223. ● ▲

WINNIPEG—CAA MANITOBA, 501 ST ANNES RD, R2M 3E5. MON-FRI 9-6, SAT 10-4. (204) 987-6201. ● ▲

PROVINCE OF SASKATCHEWAN

ESTEVAN—CAA SASKATCHEWAN, 1340-400 KING ST, S4A 2B4. MON-FRI 9-5:30, SAT 9-5:30. (306) 637-2185. ✛ ▲

MOOSE JAW—CAA SASKATCHEWAN, 80 CARIBOU ST W, S6H 2J6. MON-FRI 9-5:30, SAT 9-5:30. (306) 693-5195. ✛ ▲

NORTH BATTLEFORD—CAA SASKATCHEWAN, 2002-100TH ST, S9A 0X5. MON-FRI 9-5:30, SAT 9-5:30. (306) 445-9451. ✛ ▲

PRINCE ALBERT—CAA SASKATCHEWAN, #29 2995 2ND AVE W, S6V 5V5. MON-FRI 9-5:30, SAT 9-5:30. (306) 764-6818. ✛ ▲

REGINA—CAA SASKATCHEWAN, 200 ALBERT ST N, S4R 5E2. MON-FRI 8:30-5. (306) 791-4321, *(800) 564-6222.* ✛ ▲

REGINA—CAA SASKATCHEWAN, 2510 E QUANCE ST, S4V 2X5. MON-FRI 9-5:30, SAT 9-5:30. (306) 791-4323. ● ▲

REGINA—CAA SASKATCHEWAN, 3806 ALBERT ST, S4S 3R2. MON-FRI 9-5:30, SAT 9-5:30. (306) 791-4322. ● ▲

SASKATOON—CAA SASKATCHEWAN, 321 4TH AVE N, S7K 2L9. MON-FRI 8:30-5:30, SAT 8:30-5:30. (306) 668-3737. ✛ ▲

SASKATOON—CAA SASKATCHEWAN, 3929 8TH ST E #204, S7H 5M2. MON-FRI 9-5:30, SAT 9-5:30. (306) 668-3770. ● ▲

SWIFT CURRENT—CAA SASKATCHEWAN, 15 DUFFERIN ST W, S9H 5A1. MON-FRI 9-5:30, SAT 9-5:30. (306) 773-3193. ✛ ▲

WEYBURN—CAA SASKATCHEWAN, 110 SOURIS AVE, S4H 2Z8. MON-FRI 9-6, SAT 9-6. (306) 842-6651. ✛ ▲

YORKTON—CAA SASKATCHEWAN, 159 BROADWAY ST E, S3N 3K6. MON-FRI 9-5:30, SAT 9-5:30. (306) 783-6536. ✛ ▲

Metric Equivalents Chart

TEMPERATURE

To convert Fahrenheit to Celsius, subtract 32 from the Fahrenheit temperature, multiply by 5 and divide by 9.
To convert Celsius to Fahrenheit, multipy by 9, divide by 5 and add 32.

ACRES

1 acre = 0.4 hectare (ha)   1 hectare = 2.47 acres

MILES AND KILOMETRES

Note: A kilometre is approximately 5/8 or 0.6 of a mile.
To convert kilometres to miles multiply by 0.6.

Miles/Kilometres		Kilometres/Miles	
15	24.1	30	18.6
20	32.2	35	21.7
25	40.2	40	24.8
30	48.3	45	27.9
35	56.3	50	31.0
40	64.4	55	34.1
45	72.4	60	37.2
50	80.5	65	40.3
55	88.5	70	43.4
60	96.6	75	46.6
65	104.6	80	49.7
70	112.7	85	52.8
75	120.7	90	55.9
80	128.7	95	59.0
85	136.8	100	62.1
90	144.8	105	65.2
95	152.9	110	68.3
100	160.9	115	71.4

LINEAR MEASURE

Customary	Metric
1 inch = 2.54 centimetres	1 centimetre = 0.4 inches
1 foot = 30 centimetres	1 metre = 3.3 feet
1 yard = 0.91 metres	1 metre = 1.09 yards
1 mile = 1.6 kilometres	1 kilometre = .62 miles

LIQUID MEASURE

Customary	Metric
1 fluid ounce = 30 millilitres	1 millilitre = .03 fluid ounces
1 cup = .24 litres	1 litre = 2.1 pints
1 pint = .47 litres	1 litre = 1.06 quarts
1 quart = .95 litres	1 litre = .26 gallons
1 gallon = 3.8 litres	

Celsius ° / Fahrenheit °

Celsius °		Fahrenheit °
100	BOILING	212
37		100
35		95
32		90
29		85
27		80
24		75
21		70
18		65
16		60
13		55
10		50
7		45
4		40
2		35
0	FREEZING	32
-4		25
-7		20
-9		15
-12		10
-15		5
-18		0
-21		-5
-24		-10
-27		-15

WEIGHT

If You Know:	Multiply By:	To Find:
Ounces	28.000	Grams
Pounds	0.450	Kilograms
Grams	0.035	Ounces
Kilograms	2.200	Pounds

PRESSURE

Air pressure in automobile tires is expressed in kilopascals. Multiply pound-force per square inch (psi) by 6.89 to find kilopascals (kPa).

24 psi = 165 kPa   28 psi = 193 kPa
26 psi = 179 kPa   30 psi = 207 kPa

GALLON AND LITRES

Gallons/Litres				Litres/Gallons			
5	19.0	12	45.6	10	2.6	40	10.4
6	22.8	14	53.2	15	3.9	50	13.0
7	26.6	16	60.8	20	5.2	60	15.6
8	30.4	18	68.4	25	6.5	70	18.2
9	34.2	20	76.0	30	7.8	80	20.8
10	38.0	25	95.0	35	9.1	90	23.4

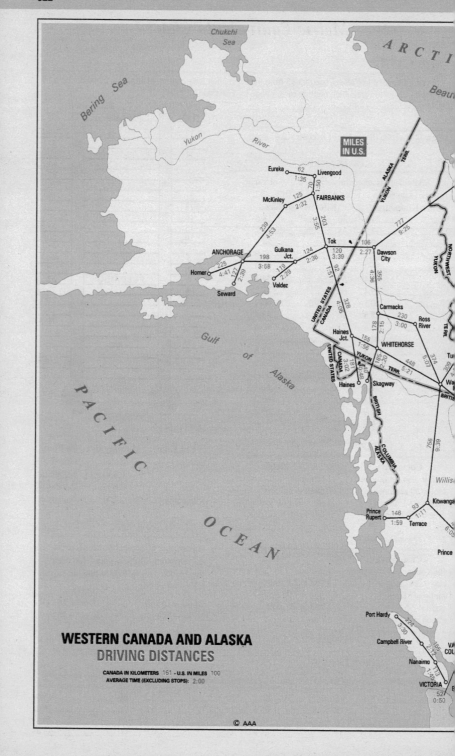

WESTERN CANADA AND ALASKA
DRIVING DISTANCES

CANADA IN KILOMETERS 161 - U.S. IN MILES 100
AVERAGE TIME (EXCLUDING STOPS): 2:00

© AAA

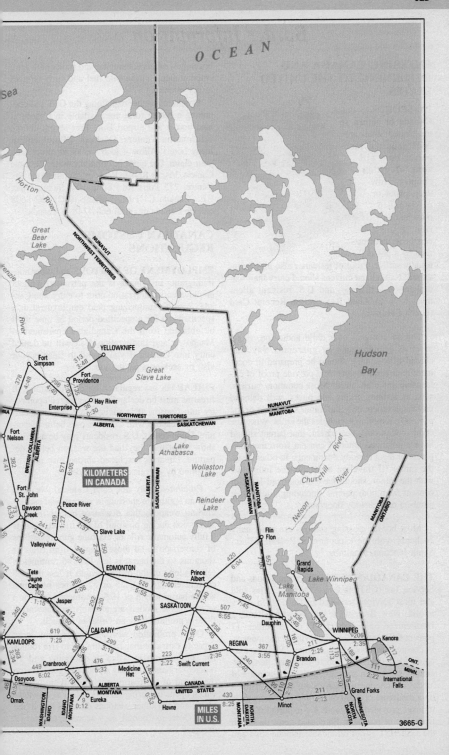

OCEAN

Sea

Horton River

Great Bear Lake

Mackenzie River

NUNAVUT

NORTHWEST TERRITORIES

Hudson Bay

YELLOWKNIFE
313
3:48

Fort Simpson
378
4:48

Fort Providence
398
4:40
203
2:05
36
1:36

Great Slave Lake

Hay River

Enterprise
36
0:30

BRITISH COLUMBIA

NORTHWEST TERRITORIES

NUNAVUT

ALBERTA   SASKATCHEWAN   MANITOBA

Fort Nelson
341
4:41

BRITISH COLUMBIA
ALBERTA

571
6:09

Lake Athabasca

Wollaston Lake

Churchill River

KILOMETERS IN CANADA

ALBERTA
SASKATCHEWAN

Fort St. John
0:53

Dawson Creek
241
2:37
139
1:27
250
2:37

Peace River
250

Slave Lake

Reindeer Lake

MANITOBA
SASKATCHEWAN

Flin Flon

Nelson River

Valleyview
346
3:50
346
2:48

MANITOBA
ONTARIO

Tete Jaune Cache
366
4:06
172

430
6:04

EDMONTON
526
5:55

600
7:00

Prince Albert

Grand Rapids

Lake Winnipeg

557

Jasper
103
1:16
412
4:30
292
3:20

123
1:40

560
7:45

Lake Manitoba

KAMLOOPS
263
3:34

CALGARY
621
6:35

SASKATOON
507
8:55

Dauphin
336
3:45

WINNIPEG

Kenora
206
2:35

449
6:02

Cranbrook
476
5:32

299
3:10

277
3:55

288

243
2:35

REGINA
367
3:55

161
2:05

211

Brandon
88

110
1:13

188

247

OSOYOOS
5:50

Medicine Hat
1:41

223
2:22

Swift Current

240
2:40

211

75
1:30

ONT.
MINN.
2:22

International Falls

Omak

WASHINGTON
IDAHO

IDAHO
MONTANA

Eureka
9
0:12

ALBERTA
MONTANA

CANADA
UNITED STATES

430
8:25

Havre
430
0:52

NORTH DAKOTA
MONTANA

Minot
211
4:13

Grand Forks

NORTH DAKOTA
MINNESOTA

MILES IN U.S.

3665-G

Border Information

ENTERING CANADA AND RETURNING TO THE UNITED STATES

PASSPORTS to enter Canada or return to the United States are NOT required for native-born citizens of either country. However, proof of citizenship must be carried; a birth certificate accompanied by a photo ID will usually suffice. Proof of residence also may be required. Naturalized citizens should carry their naturalization certificate, and U.S. resident aliens must have an Alien Registration Receipt Card (Green Card).

Due to concerns over child abduction, single parents, grandparents or guardians traveling abroad with a minor should be prepared to document their legal custody and provide proof of citizenship for each child. Most common carriers, such as airlines, trains and buses, will demand proof and accept only the minor's passport or the parents' passport that includes the child. When the child is with only one parent, that parent should have a notarized letter of consent from the other parent or legal custody documents. In other cases, the minor (if traveling alone) or the individual with the minor, should have a notarized letter of consent from both parents (including a telephone number) or a custody document.

Most border crossing stations are open daily 24 hours with the exception of Roseau, Minn.-South Junction, Manitoba.

THE CANADIAN GST: A 7 percent Goods and Service Tax (GST) is levied on most items sold and most services rendered in Canada. In Nova Scotia, New Brunswick and Newfoundland, a Harmonized Sales Tax (HST) of 15 percent (7 percent GST and 8 percent provincial component) is charged on goods and services. Visitors may apply for a GST/HST rebate on many items, including short-term accommodations (maximum of 30 days in one location). A rebate may be claimed on a minimum of $200 of eligible purchases prior to taxes provided the goods are exported 60 days from date of purchase. Purchased items on which the GST/HST is not refundable include food and beverages, tobacco, camping and trailer park fees, entertainment, automobile fuel and such services as dry cleaning.

Brochures further explaining the GST and containing a rebate form are available in Canada at land border and airport Duty Free shops, Tourist Information Centers, Customs Offices and at many hotels. Allow 4 to 6 weeks for processing your claim. For more information write: Revenue Canada, Visitor Rebate Program, Summerside Tax Centre, 275 Pope Rd., Suite 104, Summerside, P.E., Canada C1N 6C6; phone (902) 432-5608 outside Canada or (800) 668-4748 in Canada.

CANADIAN CUSTOMS REGULATIONS

EMPLOYMENT OF VISITORS and other non-immigrants in Canada is not permitted without employment authorization prior to entry into Canada. Permits authorizing paid employment at a specified job for a specified period of time must be obtained from the Canadian Department of Manpower and Immigration. You will be denied entry into Canada if you intend to finance your visit by seeking a paying job.

FIREARMS are regulated by classification. All firearms must be declared and registered upon entry into Canada. It is advised that U.S. residents register weapons with U.S. Customs before departure. Upon return, U.S. residents may be asked to show proof that they had the weapon before departure. Firearms purchased abroad may only be imported by a licensed firearms dealer.

Prohibited (may **not** enter Canada): weapons with no legitimate sporting or recreational use, including weapons that discharge bullets in rapid succession during one pull of the trigger, such as a fully automatic rifle or machine gun (regardless of conversion); and those adapted from rifles or shotguns so the barrel is less than 46 centimeters (18 in.) long or the overall length is less than 66 centimeters (26 in.); 25 or 32 caliber handguns with a barrel length of 10.5 centimeters (4.14 in.) or less (some models are exempt); and any other firearm prohibited by an Order in Council.

Other prohibited weapons include any large capacity cartridge magazine limited to five rounds for semiautomatic rifles or shotguns and 10 rounds for handguns; any device designed to stop the sound of a firearm; any knife with a blade which opens by spring pressure, such as a switchblade; and any other weapons declared prohibited by an Order in Council, such as mace, tear gas (if designed for use against humans), throwing stars,

Nunchaku sticks, belt-buckle knives, spiked wristbands, blowguns, stun guns, finger rings with blades, brass knuckles, armor-piercing handgun cartridges, explosive projectiles for small arms cartridges, shotgun cartridges containing "flechettes," a "bull pup" stock for rifles and carbines and trigger enhancement devices.

Restricted (admitted only for approved shooting competitions at which time an Authorization to Transport is required from the provincial chief firearms officer: semiautomatic firearms that have a barrel less than 47 centimeters (18.5 in.) and that discharge center-fire ammunition; and those that can be fired when reduced to less than 66 centimeters (26 in.) in length. Other restricted weapons include any firearm designed, altered or intended to be aimed and fired by the action of one hand, such as pistols and revolvers; and any firearm that is declared to be a restricted firearm by an Order in Council.

Long guns (admissible by declaration only, provided you are at least 18 years old and the gun is to be used in a recognized marksmanship competition or such other legitimate purpose as a historical re-enactment or gun show): guns described by the manufacturer as regular hunting rifles or shotguns.

Hunters may bring in, duty-free, 200 rounds of ammunition; participants in a competition, 1,500 rounds. Firearms may not be carried into Canada's national parks unless they are dismantled (barrel separated from stock) or encased so that no part of the gun is exposed. Persons intending to hunt in Canada must obtain a license from the province or territory.

In addition to these federal stipulations, most provinces and territories have their own laws regulating the transportation of firearms through their area, usually in connection with their hunting regulations. Check the Fast Facts box for special regulations and the address of the agency to query. For further information on the entry of firearms, contact Revenue Canada, Customs and Excise, Commercial Verification and Enforcement, Connaught Building, Mackenzie Avenue, Ottawa, Ontario, Canada K1A 0L5; phone (613) 954-7129.

GIFTS, excluding tobacco, alcoholic beverages and advertising matter, taken into or mailed to Canada are allowed free entry if the value of the gift does not exceed $60 (Canadian currency). Gifts valued at more than $60 are subject to the regular duty and taxes on the excess amount.

PERSONAL BAGGAGE is admissible into Canada on a temporary basis without payment of duty and taxes; *however,* a refundable security deposit may be required by Customs at the time of entry. Deposits are not normally required when visits are made for health or pleasure, provided all items are exported at the end of your trip.

When You Travel In Canada

AAA-affiliated motor clubs form the Canadian Automobile Association, with its national office at 1145 Hunt Club Rd., Suite 200, Ottawa, ON, Canada K1V 0Y3. CAA clubs provide the same services for AAA members as do the AAA clubs in the United States. Establishments displaying the Official Appointment sign have met the rigid inspection requirements of the two associations.

SEAT BELTS: The use of seat belts by vehicle drivers and all passengers is required in Canada.

RADAR DETECTORS: The possession of radar detection devices is illegal in Manitoba, New Brunswick and Yukon Territory. The use of radar detectors is illegal in Newfoundland, Northwest Territories and Nunavut, Nova Scotia, Ontario, Prince Edward Island and Québec.

INSURANCE: Obtain a yellow Non-Resident Inter-Province Motor Vehicle Liability Insurance Card from your U.S. automobile insurance agent. The card certifies that you carry statutory minimum liability requirements while driving in Canada. If renting a vehicle, check with the rental car company.

CURRENCY: All prices and admission fees quoted are in Canadian dollars. Private establishments are under no obligation to accept, convert or pay a premium on currency of other countries. It is to your financial advantage to use Canadian currency when traveling in Canada. The only means of obtaining the official exchange rate is to change U.S. funds at a bank or purchase travelers checks in Canadian currency. If you plan on carrying cash instead of travelers checks, be aware that some Canadian banks will not accept U.S. bills in large denominations for exchange.

PROVINCIAL REGULATIONS: Check the Fast Facts box for any additional regulations imposed by individual provinces or territories.

LEGAL ISSUES: Persons with felony convictions, driving while intoxicated records or other offenses may be denied admittance into Canada. Contact the Canadian embassy or nearest Canadian Consulate before travel.

Personal baggage that may be taken into Canada on a duty- and tax-free basis includes clothing and personal effects, sporting goods, automobiles, vessels, aircraft, snowmobiles, cameras, food products and other items appropriate for the purpose and duration of your visit. Tobacco products are limited per person to 50 cigars, 200 cigarettes, 400 grams (14 oz.) of tobacco, and 400 tobacco sticks. Alcoholic beverages are limited to 1.14 liters (40 oz.) of liquor, 1.5 liters (1.6 qts.) of wine or 8.5 liters (9 qts.) of beer or ale (equivalent to 24 bottles/cans). Generally, a minimum stay of 24 hours is required to transport any liquor or tobacco into Canada.

All articles above allowable quantities are subject to federal duty and taxes, as well as provincial liquor fees. Provincial fees can be paid at Customs at the time of entry in all provinces and the Yukon Territory. In the Northwest Territories and Nunavut, it is illegal to bring in more alcohol than specified above. The minimum legal age for the importation of alcoholic beverages or tobacco products is 18 or 19 years, depending on the province or territory.

Articles purchased at Canadian duty-free shops are subject to U.S. Customs exemptions and restrictions; those purchased at U.S. duty-free shops before entering Canada are subject to duty if brought back into the United States.

Persons who may require prescription drugs while visiting Canada are permitted to bring medication for their own use. Prescription drugs should be clearly identified and should be carried in the original packaging with the label listing the drug and its intended use. It also is good to bring a copy of the prescription and contact number of the doctor.

PETS AND PLANTS: Dogs and cats must be accompanied by a certificate signed by a licensed veterinarian that clearly describes the animal and declares that the animal has been vaccinated against rabies within the past 36 months; collar tags are not sufficient proof of immunization. This certificate also is needed to bring a dog back into the United States; be sure the vaccination does not expire while traveling in Canada. "Seeing Eye" dogs are exempt from these rules, as well as up to two healthy puppies and kittens under 3 months old; it is recommended that the owner obtain a certificate of health from a veterinarian indicating that an animal is too young to vaccinate.

Plants or plant material, except houseplants, must be declared. For additional information on pets and plants, contact one of the following Canadian Food Inspection Agency (CFIA) Import Service Centres: eastern Canada (514) 246-3889 or (888) 246-3889; central Canada (905) 612-6282; or western Canada (604) 541-3370 or (888) 732-6222.

RADIO COMMUNICATION EQUIPMENT: You may bring your cellular phone or citizens band radio into Canada without any prior registration. If you have an American operator's license, you may use your aircraft, marine or amateur radio without a Canadian license. All other types of radio transmitting stations may only be used in Canada if accompanied by a letter of authorization from Industry Canada's Radio and Broadcasting Branch; phone (613) 998-3372.

SPECIAL PERMITS: A CITIES (Convention on International Trade in Endangered Species) permit is required for any endangered species

brought into Canada, including those kept as pets and for any items made from them, such as coats, handbags or shoes. For further information contact the Convention on International Trade in Endangered Species, Canadian Wildlife Service; phone (819) 997-1840.

Canada has restrictions to keep objects that are of historical, cultural or scientific signification inside Canada. If you wish to take objects more than 50 years old, such as fossils, archeological artifacts, fine and decorative art, technological objects or books and archival material, out of the country, contact the Canadian Moveable Cultural Property Program, Canadian Heritage, 15 Eddy St., 3rd floor, Hull, Québec, Canada K1A 0M5; phone (819) 997-7761.

Importation of clothing, textiles, steel and certain agricultural products in excess of minimum quantities may be subject to import permit quirements under the Export and Import Permits Act. For further information, write the Department of Foreign Affairs and International Trade, Export and Import Control Bureau, P.O. Box 481, Station A, Ottawa, ON Canada K1N 9K6. Goods originating in Iraq are not admissible.

VEHICLES, including trailers not exceeding 2.6 metres (8 ft., 6 in.) in width, entering Canada for touring are generally subject to quick and routine entry procedures. You may not leave or store a car, trailer or other goods in Canada while you leave the country without either paying import duty and taxes or presenting the necessary permit to leave the items in Canada. This and any other required permits are issued by Canadian customs officials at the point of entry. Vacation trailers may not be stored in Canada during the off-season.

Vehicle registration cards are necessary for Canadian travel. If you are driving a car other than your own, you must get written permission from the owner for use of the car in Canada. A copy of the contract is required for rented cars. A valid U.S. driver's license is valid in Canada for varying periods of time as ruled by the individual provinces and territories.

Some provinces and territories have made it a statutory requirement that motorists drive with vehicle headlights on for extended periods after dawn and before dusk. In Alberta, British Columbia, New Brunswick and Prince Edward Island lights must be turned on when light conditions restrict visibility to 150 metres (500 ft.); in Manitoba, the restriction is 60 metres (200 ft.). Headlights must remain on at all times in the Yukon Territory and Northwest Territories and Nunavut. Elsewhere in Canada driving with headlights on during all hours of the day is advised.

In cases of accident involving death, injury or property damage, the Canadian provinces and territories require evidence of financial responsibility. In some provinces, you may be asked to show this evidence at any time. The penalties for not producing such evidence vary by province and territory and can result in costly and time-consuming problems if you are unprepared.

The minimum liability insurance requirement is $200,000 in all provinces and territories except Québec, which requires $50,000, and Northwest Territories and Nunavut, which requires $100,000. Should the courts' judgments exceed these figures, motorists held accountable are responsible for paying the full amount.

U.S. CUSTOMS REGULATIONS

EXEMPTIONS granted to returning U.S. residents include a $400 exemption, if not used within the prior 30 days, for residents who have have been in Canada *no less than 48 hours.* Any

National Park Entrance Fees

At Canada's national parks, the basic per person or per family entry fee gives visitors access to the park, scenic outlooks, picnic areas and a variety of facilities. Additional fees are charged for visitors who choose to use other recreational services such as campgrounds, special interpretation programs and golf courses.

Detailed information on the services, benefits, entry fees and discounts at all national parks and historic sites is available by calling the following numbers:

(800) 213-7275 for the Atlantic provinces (Newfoundland and Labrador, New Brunswick, Nova Scotia and Prince Edward Island);

(800) 463-6769 for Québec;

(800) 748-7275 for Alberta;

(604) 666-0176 for British Columbia;

(800) 661-0486 for Yukon Territory;

(800) 839-8221 for Ontario;

(888) 748-2928 for Manitoba;

(800) 748-7275 for Saskatchewan; and

(800) 661-0788 for Northwest Territories and Nunavut.

amount over the $400 exemption is subject to duty. The exemptions are based on fair retail value and apply to articles acquired for personal or household use or as gifts but *not intended for sale.* Exemptions for a family (related persons living in the same house) may be combined; thus, a family of six would be entitled to a duty-free $2,400 exemption on one declaration, even if the articles declared by one member of the family exceeded that individual's $400 exemption. Sales slips should be kept; they are proof of fair retail value. All articles for which the $400 exemption is claimed must accompany you at the time of return.

You may send bona fide gifts to friends and relatives in the United States free of duty and taxes provided the retail value of any one gift is no more than $100 and no more than one gift per day is received by any one recipient. Tobacco products, alcoholic beverages and perfume containing alcohol valued at more than $5 retail are excluded from this provision. The package containing the gift must be marked "Unsolicited Gift," with the contents and retail value indicated on the outside. These gifts are not included in your $400 exemption and are not to be declared upon your return.

If you are entitled to the $400 exemption, you may include 100 cigars and 200 cigarettes duty free. Cigarettes may be subject to state or local tax. Persons 21 years of age or over may include liquor to the amount of 1 litre per person in their $400 residents' exemption from duty and tax. In all cases, state liquor laws are enforced by Customs.

If you have been in Canada for *less than 48 hours,* you may bring back merchandise valued at $200 or less, duty and tax free. Such an exemption must not include more than 10 cigars, 50 cigarettes, 150 milliliters (4 fl. oz.) of alcoholic beverage *or* 150 milliliters (4 fl. oz.) of perfume containing alcohol. If any article brought back is subject to duty or tax or if the total value of all articles exceeds $200, no article may be exempted from duty or tax. Members of a family unit may not combine the value of their purchases under this exemption. All goods must be declared.

CERTAIN ARTICLES considered injurious or detrimental to the general welfare of the United States are *prohibited* entry by law. Among these are such items as narcotics and dangerous drugs; drug paraphernalia; hazardous articles (e.g., fire-

works, dangerous toys and toxic or poisonou substances), obscene articles and publications lottery tickets; switchblade knives; seditious o treasonable matter; and merchandise originating in Afghanistan, Cuba, Federal Republic of Yugo slavia (Serbia), Iran, Iraq, Libya, North Korea an Sudan.

Endangered species of plants and wildlife, o products made of any part of such species, are pro hibited. If you are considering the purchase o import of fur, animal skin other than leather or any product manufactured wholly or in part from wildlife, write to the U.S. Fish and Wildlife Service, Department of the Interior, Washington, DC 20240 for additiona information.

RESTRICTED ITEMS often require special licenses or controls. While some agricultural products of Canadian origin (fruit, plants with phytosanitary certificates meats, etc.) may be brought into the United States, many are restricted to prevent the introduction of plant and animal pests and diseases into this country. All must be declared to customs officials at the U.S. border. For specific information, write for the free booklet "Traveler's Tips," available in English, Spanish, Italian or Japanese from APHIS, Department of Agriculture, 6505 Belcrest Rd., Hyattsville, MD 20782.

If you require medicines containing narcotics or habit-forming drugs, including cough and headache remedies, you should have them *properly* identified and carry only such quantities as might normally be needed for a health problem. You should carry proof, either in prescriptionform or as a written statement from your physician, that the medicines are being used under a doctor's direction and are necessary for your well-being.

Other restricted items include imported automobiles; biological materials (disease organisms and vectors for research); ceramic tableware; cultural treasures; firearms and ammunition; articles bearing marks or names copying or simulating trademarked articles or trade name (e.g., watches, cameras, perfumes); pirated copies of copyrighted articles (e.g., books, records, computer programs); and pets, wildlife and fish. Additional helpful leaflets, "Visiting the U.S.: Requirements for Non-Residents," "Importing a Car," "Know Before You Go" and "Pets, Wildlife and U.S. Customs," are available by writing U.S. Customs, P.O. Box 7407, Washington, DC 20044.

Alberta

CALGARY

Paradise Acres
BED & BREAKFAST

◆ A luxurious setting with country quiet and city access
◆ Discover our city and mountain views
◆ Close to Calgary International Airport

(403) 248-4748   **http://www.paradiseacres.com**

British Columbia

VANCOUVER

Camilla House
Bed & Breakfast

Vancouver, B. C., Canada
Warm, friendly hospitality
greets you in this lovely
home. Near beaches, UBC,
downtown, transit.
Email **camillaw@lynx.bc.ca**
fax **1-604-737-2586**

phone **1-604-737-2687**
www.vancouver-bc.com/camillahouse/

Alaska

TOK

Cleft of the Rock
Bed & Breakfast

Our peaceful setting in the
black spruce forest offers
weary travelers a peaceful stay.

800-478-5646   cleftrck@polarnet.com

or fax (907) 883-5963 • (907) 883-4219
1/2 Mile Sundog Trail, Tok, Alaska 99780-0122
www.tokalaska.com/cleftroc.shtml

Discover Romance

V isit a bygone era
of romance and
elegance by spending a
romantic evening or
weekend getaway at one
of these bed & breakfasts.

Bed & Breakfast Lodgings Index

Some bed and breakfasts listed below might have historical significance. Those properties are also referenced in the Histo cal index. The indication that continental [CP] or full breakfast [BP] is included in the room rate reflects whether a property a Bed-and-Breakfast facility.

Country Inns Index

Some of the following country inns can also be considered as bed-and-breakfast operations. The indication that continent [CP] or full breakfast [BP] is included in the room rate reflects whether a property is a Bed-and-Breakfast facility.

Historical Lodgings & Restaurants Index

...me of the following historical lodgings can also be considered as bed-and-breakfast operations. The indication that conti-
...ntal [CP] or full breakfast [BP] is included in the room rate reflects whether a property is a Bed-and-Breakfast facility.

Resorts Index

...any establishments are located in resort areas; however, the following places have extensive on-premises recreational
.cilities:

Points of Interest Index

INDEX ABBREVIATIONS

SAVE *Attraction Admission Discount Index*

Comprehensive City Index

Here is an alphabetical list of all cities appearing in this TourBook® guide. Cities are presented by state/province. Page numbers under the POI column indicate where points of interest text begins. Page numbers under the L&R column indicate where lodging and restaurant listings begin.

COMPREHENSIVE CITY INDEX (CONT'D)

COMPREHENSIVE CITY INDEX (CONT'D)

Precautions Can Save A Vacation!

*T*ravelers are faced with the task of protecting themselves while in a strange environment. Although there is no way to guarantee absolute protection from crime, the experts—law enforcement officials—advise travelers to take a proactive approach to securing their property and ensuring their safety.

- Make sure the hotel desk clerk does not announce your room number; if he does, quietly request a new room assignment.

- Ask front desk personnel which areas of town to avoid and what, if any, special precautions should be taken when driving a rental car (some criminals target tourists driving rental cars).

- Never open the door to a stranger; use the peephole and request identification. If you are still unsure, call the front desk to verify the identity of the person and the purpose of his/her visit.

- Carry money separately from credit cards or use a "fanny pack." Carry your purse close to your body and your wallet in an inside coat or front trouser pocket. Never leave luggage unattended, and use your business address, if possible, on luggage tags.

- Beware of distractions staged by would-be scam artists, especially groups of children that surround you, or a stranger who accidentally spills something on you. They may be lifting your wallet.

- If using an automatic teller machine (ATM), choose one in a well-lit area with plenty of foot traffic, such as one at a grocery store. Law enforcement officials suggest that machines inside establishments are generally safer to use.

- Use room safes or safety deposit boxes provided by the hotel. Store all valuables out of sight, even when you are in the room.

- Law enforcement agencies consider card-key (electronic) door locks the most secure.

Photo Credit Index

*A special thank you to the following
organizations for their photo contributions
throughout the TourBook:*

*Archive Photos™
PhotoDisc
Tourism Vancouver
Calgary Convention and Visitors Bureau
Edmonton Tourism
Tourism Victoria
Butchart Gardens
Lee Foster
Laura Breen*